Lecture Notes in Computer Science 10104

Commenced Publication in 1973
Founding and Former Series Editors:
Gerhard Goos, Juris Hartmanis, and Jan van Leeuwen

More information about this series at http://www.springer.com/series/7407

Frédéric Desprez · Pierre-François Dutot et al. (Eds.)

Euro-Par 2016: Parallel Processing Workshops

Euro-Par 2016 International Workshops
Grenoble, France, August 24–26, 2016
Revised Selected Papers

Editors
Frédéric Desprez
Inria
Université Grenoble Alpes
Grenoble
France

Pierre-François Dutot
LIG
Université Grenoble Alpes
Grenoble
France

Workshop Editors *see next page*

ISSN 0302-9743   ISSN 1611-3349   (electronic)
Lecture Notes in Computer Science
ISBN 978-3-319-58942-8   ISBN 978-3-319-58943-5   (eBook)
DOI 10.1007/978-3-319-58943-5

Library of Congress Control Number: 2017940837

LNCS Sublibrary: SL1 – Theoretical Computer Science and General Issues

Printed on acid-free paper

This Springer imprint is published by Springer Nature
The registered company is Springer International Publishing AG
The registered company address is: Gewerbestrasse 11, 6330 Cham, Switzerland

Workshop Editors

Euro-EDUPAR
Christos Kaklamanis
CTI and University of Patras
Greece
kakl@ceid.upatras.gr

PELGA
Ana Lucia Varbanescu
University of Amsterdam
The Netherlands
a.l.varbanescu@uva.nl

HeteroPar
Loris Marchal
CNRS and University of Lyon
France
loris.marchal@ens-lyon.fr

REPPAR
Sascha Hunold
TU Wien
Austria
hunold@par.tuwien.ac.at

Resilience
Stephen L. Scott
Tennessee Tech University and Oak
Ridge National Laboratory, USA
SScott@tntech.edu

IWMSE
Korbinian Molitorisz
Agilent Technologies
USA
korbinian.molitorisz@agilent.com

ROME
Stefan Lankes
RWTH Aachen University
Germany
slankes@eonerc.rwth-aachen.de

LSDVE
Laura Ricci
University of Pisa
Italy
laura.ricci@unipi.it

UCHPC
Josef Weidendorfer
Technische Universität München
Germany
Josef.Weidendorfer@in.tum.de

PADABS
Vittorio Scarano
Università di Salerno
Italy
vitsca@dia.unisa.it

PBio
Miguel A. Vega-Rodríguez
University of Extremadura
Spain
mavega@unex.es

Preface

Euro-Par is an annual, international conference on European ground, covering all aspects of parallel and distributed processing, ranging from theory to practice, from small to the largest parallel and distributed systems and infrastructures, from fundamental computational problems to full-fledged applications, from architecture, compiler, language and interface design and implementation to tools, support infrastructures, and application performance aspects. The Euro-Par conference itself is complemented by a workshop program, where workshops dedicated to more specialized themes, to cross-cutting issues, and to upcoming trends and paradigms can be easily and conveniently organized with little administrative overhead.

This year, 14 workshop proposals were submitted, and after a careful revision process, which was led by the workshop co-chairs, 12 workshops were accepted. One workshop had to be canceled later due to a low number of submissions.

The workshops took place on the two days before the Euro-Par conference and the program included the following 11 workshops:

1. Parallel and Distributed Computing Education for Undergraduate Students (EURO-EDUPAR)
2. Algorithms, Models, and Tools for Parallel Computing on Heterogeneous Platforms (HETEROPAR)
3. Multicore Software Engineering (IWMSE)
4. Large-Scale Distributed Virtual Environments (LSDVE)
5. Parallel and Distributed Agent-Based Simulations (PADABS)
6. Parallelism in Bioinformatics (PBIO)
7. Performance Engineering for Large-scale Graph Analytics (PELGA)
8. Reproducibility in Parallel Computing (REPPAR)
9. Resiliency in High-Performance Computing in Clusters, Clouds, and Grids (RESILIENCE)
10. Runtime and Operating Systems for the Many-Core Era (ROME)
11. UnConventional High-Performance Computing (UCHPC)

All workshops together received a total of 95 submissions from 20 different countries. Each workshop had an independent Program Committee, which was in charge of selecting the papers. The workshop papers received more than three reviews per paper on average (320 reviews in total). Out of the 95 submissions, 66 papers were selected to be presented at the workshops.

The success of the Euro-Par workshops depends on the work of many individuals and organizations. We therefore thank all workshop organizers and reviewers for the time and effort that they invested. The Euro-Par vice-chair, Luc Bougé, provided guidance and support throughout the whole organizational process of the workshops. We would also like to express our sincere thanks to Springer for their help in publishing the proceedings.

Lastly, we thank all participants, panelists, and keynote speakers of the Euro-Par workshops for contributing to a productive meeting. It was a pleasure to organize and host the Euro-Par workshops 2016 in Grenoble.

October 2016   Frédéric Desprez

Organization

Euro-Par Steering Committee

Chair

Christian Lengauer   University of Passau, Germany

Vice-Chair

Luc Bougé   ENS Rennes, France

European Representatives

Emmanuel Jeannot	LaBRI-Inria, Bordeaux, France
Christos Kaklamanis	Computer Technology Institute, Greece
Paul Kelly	Imperial College, UK
Thomas Ludwig	University of Hamburg, Germany
Emilio Luque	Autonomous University of Barcelona, Spain
Tomàs Margalef	Autonomous University of Barcelona, Spain
Wolfgang Nagel	Dresden University of Technology, Germany
Rizos Sakellariou	University of Manchester, UK
Fernando Silva	University of Porto, Portugal
Henk Sips	Delft University of Technology, The Netherlands
Domenico Talia	University of Calabria, Italy
Jesper Larsson Träff	Vienna University of Technology, Austria
Denis Trystram	Grenoble Institute of Technology, France
Felix Wolf	Technische Universität Darmstadt, Germany

Honorary Members

Ron Perrott	Oxford e-Research Centre, UK
Karl Dieter Reinartz	University of Erlangen-Nuremberg, Germany

Observers

Marco Aldinucci	University of Turin, Italy
Francisco Rivera	CiTIUS, Santiago de Compostela, Spain

Euro-Par 2016 Organization

Co-chairs

Frédéric Desprez	Inria, France
Pierre-François Dutot	Université Grenoble Alpes, France
Denis Trystram	Grenoble Institute of Technology, France

Workshops

| Frédéric Desprez | Inria, France |

Local Organization

Annie Simon	Inria, France
Sophie Azzaro	Inria, France
Grégory Mounié	Grenoble Institute of Technology, France
Frédéric Wagner	Grenoble Institute of Technology, France

Second European Workshop on Parallel and Distributed Computing Education for Undergraduate Students (Euro-EDUPAR)

Today, Parallel and Distributed Computing (PDC) is omnipresent. It is encountered in all computational environments, from mobile devices, laptops, and desktops, to clusters of multicore nodes and supercomputers, usually comprising one or several coprocessors of different types (GPU, MIC, FPGA). This explains why it is vital to educate new generations of scientists and engineers about a range of PDC-related topics as we prepare them to effectively use modern computational systems. In a word, PDC-related topics must appear early and often in modern courses in Computational Science, Computer Science, and Computer Engineering.

In 2010, the IEEE Computer Society Technical Committee on Parallel Processing (TCPP) launched the Curriculum Initiative on Parallel and Distributed Computing, with Core Topics for Undergraduates. This led in 2011 to the EduPar workshop, which is dedicated to Parallel and Distributed Computing Education. Given the differences in educational environments in different parts of the world, the Euro-EDUPAR workshop starts with the aim of analyzing PDC education in a European context, i.e., within the structure and organization of European education.

Thus, the second Euro-EDUPAR was dedicated to analyzing where and how to include topics related to both PDC and HPC (high-performance computing) within the curricula of programs in Computer Science and Engineering and Computational Science, while emphasizing European undergraduate teaching. The workshop especially sought papers that report on experiences with incorporating PDC-related topics into undergraduate core courses taken by the majority of students on a degree course. Methods, pedagogical approaches, tools, and techniques that have potential for adoption across the European teaching community are of particular interest.

Topics of interest include: Parallel and Distributed Computing teaching in the European space; pedagogical issues in PDC, educational methods and learning mechanisms; novel ways of teaching PDC topics, including informal learning environments; curriculum design, models for incorporating PDC topics in core CS/CE curriculum; experience with incorporating PDC topics into core CS/CE courses; experience with incorporating PDC topics in the context of other applications learning; pedagogical tools, programming environments, and languages for PDC; e-learning, e-laboratory, Massive Open Online Courses (MOOC), Small Private Online Courses (SPOC); PDC experiences at non-university levels, secondary school, postgraduate, industry, diffusion of PDC.

Program Chairs

Christos Kaklamanis   CTI and University of Patras, Greece
Yves Robert   École normale supérieure de Lyon, France
Arnold L. Rosenberg   Northeastern University, Boston, USA

Program Committee

Marco Aldinucci	University of Turin, Italy
Rosa M. Badia	Barcelona Supercomputing Center, Spain
Olivier Beaumont	Inria Bordeaux, Sud-Ouest, France
Marco Danelutto	Università di Pisa, Italy
Alex Delis	University of Athens, Greece
Efstratios Gallopoulos	University of Patras, Greece
Chryssis Georgiou	University of Cyprus, Cyprus
Domingo Giménez	University of Murcia, Spain
Emmanuel Jeannot	Inria Bordeaux Sud-Ouest, France
Helen Karatza	Aristotle University of Thessaloniki, Greece
Thilo Kielmann	Vrije Universiteit Amsterdam, The Netherlands
Danny Krizanc	Wesleyan University, USA
Milan Mihajlovic	University of Manchester, UK
Dana Petcu	West University of Timisoara, Romania
Andrea Pietracaprina	Università di Padova, Italy
Christian Scheideler	Universität Paderborn, Germany
Fernando Silva	University of Porto, Portugal
Jesper Larsson Träff	TU Wien, Austria
Frédéric Vivien	Inria Grenoble Rhône-Alpes, France

Workshop on Algorithms, Models and Tools for Parallel Computing on Heterogeneous Platforms (HeteroPar)

HeteroPar is a forum for researchers working on algorithms, programming languages, tools, and theoretical models aimed at efficiently solving problems on heterogeneous platforms. Heterogeneity is emerging as one of the most profound and challenging characteristics of today's parallel environments. From the macro level, where networks of distributed computers, composed by diverse node architectures, are interconnected with potentially heterogeneous networks, to the micro level, where deeper memory hierarchies and various accelerator architectures are increasingly common, the impact of heterogeneity on all computing tasks is increasing rapidly. Traditional parallel algorithms, programming environments and tools, designed for legacy homogeneous multiprocessors, will at best achieve a small fraction of the efficiency and the potential performance that we should expect from parallel computing in tomorrow's highly diversified and mixed environments. New ideas, innovative algorithms, and specialized programming environments and tools are needed to efficiently use these new and multifarious parallel architectures.

The 14th International Workshop on Algorithms, Models and Tools for Parallel Computing on Heterogeneous Platforms (HeteroPar'2016) was held in Grenoble, France. For the eighth time, this workshop was organized in conjunction with the Euro-Par annual series of international conferences. The format of the workshop includes a keynote, followed by technical presentations. The workshop was well-attended (around 30 attendees).

This year, we received 17 articles for review, from 12 countries. After a thorough peer-reviewing process, we selected eight articles for presentation at the workshop. The review process focused on the quality of the papers, their innovative ideas, and their applicability to heterogeneous settings. The papers were accepted after discussion and agreement by the reviewers. As a consequence, the quality and the relevance of the selected articles were high, despite a rather high acceptance ratio (47%). The accepted articles represent an interesting mix of topics, techniques, applications, and scales, exhibiting nicely the diversity and growth of the heterogeneous computing field.

Last, but certainly not least, I would like to thank the HeteroPar Steering Committee and the HeteroPar 2016 Program Committee, who made the workshop possible. I would also like to thank Euro-Par for hosting our community, and the Euro-Par workshop chairs, Frédéric Desprez and Luc Bougé, for their help and support.

Steering Committee

Domingo Giménez   University of Murcia, Spain
Alexey Kalinov   Cadence Design Systems, Russia
Alexey Lastovetsky   University College Dublin, Ireland
Yves Robert   École normale supérieure de Lyon, France

Leonel Sousa   INESC-ID/IST, TU Lisbon, Portugal
Denis Trystronel Sousa   INESC-ID/IST, TU Lisbon, Portugal
Denis Trystram   LIG, Grenoble, France

Program Chair

Loris Marchal   CNRS and University of Lyon, France

Program Committee

Rosa M. Badia   Barcelona Supercomputing Center, Spain
Jorge Barbosa   Faculdade de Engenharia do Porto, Portugal
Olivier Beaumont   Inria Bordeaux Sud-Ouest, France
Cristina Boeres   Universidade Federal Fluminense, Brazil
Aurélien Bouteillier   University of Tennessee Knoxville, USA
Louis-Claude Canon   University of Franche-Comté, France
Edgar Gabriel   University of Houston, USA
Shuichi Ichikawa   Toyohashi University of Technology, Japan
Emmanuel Jeannot   Inria Bordeaux Sud-Ouest, France
Helen Karatza   Aristotle University of Thessaloniki, Greece
Hatem Ltaief   KAUST, Saudi Arabia
Giorgio Lucarelli   LIG, University of Grenoble-Alpes, France
Pierre Manneback   University of Mons, Belgium
Satoshi Matsuoka   Tokyo Institute of Technology, Japan
Rafael Mayo   Universidad Jaume I, Spain
Masahiro Nakao   RIKEN Advanced Institute of Computational Science,
                          Japan
Dana Petcu   West University of Timisoara, Romania
Enrique S. Quintana-Ortí Universidad Jaume I, Spain
Thomas Rauber   University of Bayreuth, Germany
Matei Ripeanu   University of British Columbia, Canada
Erik Saule   University of North Carolina at Charlotte, USA
Tom Scogland   Lawrence Livermore National Laboratory, USA
Antonio M. Vidal   Universidad Politecnica de Valencia, Spain
Frédéric Vivien   Inria Grenoble Rhône-Alpes and University of Lyon,
                          France
Jon Weissman   University of Minnesota, USA

International Workshop on Multicore Software Engineering (IWMSE)

With the general availability of multicore processors, software engineers face the challenge of developing parallel software that exploits the computing power in an optimal way. This is highly relevant for performance-critical applications of all types, but with degrading clock frequencies this is also relevant for any other application. Compared with sequential applications, our repertoire of tools and methods for cost-effectively developing reliable and performant parallel software is still quite limited.

The IWMSE workshop brings together researchers and practitioners with diverse backgrounds in order to advance the state of the art in software engineering for the various kinds of modern multicore architectures. It aims at making parallelism available to a wide range of applications using systematic software engineering methodology. We cover a broad variety of work that extends the knowledge and understanding of the software engineering and the parallel systems community as a whole. We want to establish and persist in a significant research dialogue and push the architectural boundaries of multicore engineering.

The Fifth International Workshop on Multicore Software Engineering (IWMSE 2016) was held in Grenoble, France. For the first time it was held in conjunction with the Euro-Par conference series. Previous editions were hosted by the International Conference on Software Engineering (ICSE) and the ACM SIGSOFT Symposium on the Foundations of Software Engineering (FSE). The format of IWMSE includes a keynote followed by unpublished scientific results or technical presentations. Although this year was the first time it was co-located with Euro-Par, the workshop was well-attended. During our sessions we had around 40 attendees.

In 2016, we specifically invited both researchers and practitioners to submit early research work, technical sessions, or general discussions. Besides traditional papers we accepted technical tutorials that familiarize workshop participants with languages, environments, tools, or concepts from parallel software engineering.

From the number of submitted articles we see the low awareness of this workshop. We only received six submissions from eight different countries, of which five were selected by the Program Committee for presentation at the workshop. We hope to increase the awareness for IWMSE and the number of submissions in the future.

Our review process focused on the paper quality and the level of innovation and potential for further research result, and the acceptance decision was based on the reviewers' consensus. For this first edition, we had a large acceptance ratio of 80%. Our accepted articles were well-balanced in current research trends in multicore software engineering: from multicore programming to performance optimization and defect fixing, from general-purpose techniques to specific applications, and from research to industry.

This year's keynote was held by Michael Chang, vice-president of Research and Development at Codeplay Inc., who talked about massive parallelism in C++.

I would like to thank all the authors who submitted to IWMSE and made this workshop essential. My special thank goes to the IWMSE Program Committee, who made the workshop possible. And finally, thank you for the support of the Euro-Par workshop chairs, Frédéric Desprez and Luc Bougé, for making the workshop worthwhile.

Workshop Chairs

Korbinian Molitorisz   Agilent Technologies, USA
Walter F. Tichy   Karlsruhe Institute of Technology (KIT), Germany

Program Committee

Michael Gerndt   Technical University Munich (TUM), Germany
Urs Gleim   Siemens AG, Germany
Ali Jannesari   University of California, Berkeley, USA
Wolfgang Karl   Karlsruhe Institute of Technology (KIT), Germany
Tim Mattson   Intel Corporation, USA
Korbinian Molitorisz   Agilent Technologies, USA
David Padua   University of Illinois, USA
Michael Phillipsen   University of Erlangen, Germany
Walter F. Tichy   Karlsruhe Institute of Technology (KIT), Germany
Hans Vandierendonck   Queen's University Belfast, Northern Ireland
Michael Wong   Codeplay Software, Scotland

4th Workshop on Large-Scale Distributed
Virtual Environments (LSDVE 2016)

The 4th Workshop on Large-Scale Distributed Virtual Environments (LSDVE 2016) was held in Grenoble, France. For the fourth time, this workshop was organized in conjunction with the Euro-Par annual series of international conferences. The main aim of the fourth edition of the workshop was to provide a venue for researchers to present and discuss important aspects of large-scale networked collaborative applications and of the platforms supporting them.

Recent advances in networking have led to an increasing use of information technology to support interactive networked cooperative applications. Several novel applications have emerged in this area: social networks, distributed gamification applications like Nike+ or MyStarbucksRewards, collaborative learning systems, large-scale, crowd-based applications, and collaborative work platforms. This kind of applications can be generally referred to as Large-Scale Distributed Virtual Environments (LSDVE). The definition of these applications poses several challenges, like the design of user interfaces, coordination protocols, and proper middle-ware and architectures supporting distributed cooperation. Collaborative applications may greatly benefit from the support of different kinds of platforms, both cloud and peer-to-peer, and also platforms recently proposed for the Internet of Things (IoT), like fog computing. Integration of different platforms, for instance, mobile and cloud environments, is currently a challenge. Furthermore, the analysis and validation of the huge amount of content generated by these applications require big data analysis and processing techniques.

The main aim of the workshop was to investigate open challenges for LSDVE applications, related to both the design of applications and to the definition of proper architectures. Some important challenges are, for instance, collaborative protocols design, latency reduction/hiding techniques for guaranteeing real-time constraints, large-scale processing of user information, privacy and security issues, and state consistency/persistence.

LSDVE 2016 opened with the invited talk "Use of Bio-Inspired Algorithms for the Efficient Management of Geo-distributed Data Centers," given by Carlo Mastroianni, ICAR, Institute of High-Performance Computing of the Italian National Council, Cosenza, Italy. The papers presented in the first session concerned smart cities, edges and opportunistic computing, while the second session was devoted to the European ENTICE Project. The last session includes papers related to P2P networks.

We wish to thank all who helped to make this fourth edition of the workshop a success: Carlo Mastroianni, who accepted our invitation to give a talk, the authors submitting papers, colleagues who reviewed the submitted papers and attended the sessions, and finally the Euro-Par 2016 organizers whose invaluable support greatly helped in the organization of the workshop.

Program Chairs

Laura Ricci   Department of Computer Science, University of Pisa, Italy
Alexandru Iosup   TU Delft, The Netherlands
Radu Prodan   Institute of Computer Science, Innsbruck, Austria

Program Committee

Michele Amoretti   University of Parma, Italy
Emanuele Carlini   ISTI CNR, Pisa, Italy
Patrizio Dazzi   ISTI CNR, Pisa, Italy
Kalman Graffi   University of Dusseldorf, Germany
Barbara Guidi   University of Pisa, Italy
Alexandru Iosup   TU Delft, The Netherlands
Jose A.F. de Macedo   Federal University of Cearà, Brazil
Pedro Garcia Lopez   Rovira i Virgili University, Spain
Pietro Michiardi   EURECOM, France
Alberto Montresor   University of Trento, Italy
Dana Petcu   West University of Timisoara, Romania
Florin Pop   University Politehnica of Bucarest, Romania
Radu Prodan   Institute of Computer Science, Innsbruck, Austria
Laura Ricci   University of Pisa, Italy
Alexey Vinel   Tampere University of Technology, Finland

4th Workshop on Parallel and Distributed Agent-Based Simulations (PADABS)

Agent-Based Simulation Models are an increasingly popular tool for research and management in many fields such as ecology, economics, sociology, etc. In some fields, such as social sciences, these models are seen as a key instrument in the generative approach, essential for understanding complex social phenomena. But also in policy-making, biology, military simulations, control of mobile robots and economics, the relevance and effectiveness of Agent-Based Simulation Models are recently recognized.

The need for complex and massive Agent-Based Simulation Models is a recent trend. It engages computer scientists in the field of Parallel and Distributed Computing, whose objective is to make the (possibly repeated) simulations of large Agent-Based Models efficient and tractable. In fact, while the community has developed several platforms, libraries, and tools that make the design, implementation, and testing of Agent-Based Models easy, less attention has been devoted to the theme of the performance of large models.

In this workshop, we want to bring together researchers who are interested in getting more performance from their simulations, by using synchronized, many-core simulations (e.g., GPUs), strongly coupled, parallel simulations (e.g., MPI), and loosely coupled, distributed simulations (distributed heterogeneous setting). It is a crucial objective, since having efficient and scalable simulations of large models makes it possible to use, in some cases, the simulation itself in research (the execution time being limited), and, in other cases, it allows for repeated executions of simulations of the same models with different input parameters, thereby allowing for an effective exploration of the parameter space that can lead to insights into the structure of the model.

Several frameworks have been recently developed and are active in this field. They range from the GPU-Manycore approach, to parallel and distributed simulation environments. In the first category, you can find FLAME GPU, that allows also non-GPU specialists to harness the GPU performance for real-time simulation and visualization. For tightly coupled, large computing clusters and supercomputers, a very popular framework is Repast for High-Performance Computing (REPAST-HPC), a C++-based modeling system. On the distributed side, recent work on Distributed Mason, allows non-specialists to use heterogeneous hardware and software in local-area networks to enlarge the size and speed up the simulation of complex Agent-Based models.

Our workshop is dedicated to this area: framework, tools, libraries, use cases of large, massive parallel/distributed agent-based simulations.

Therefore, our focus and positioning is on the applied side of parallel computing, with a particular emphasis on performance, but also on the expressivity of the frameworks, since the field that is the target of our research is multidisciplinary and does not include only "hard-science" scientists.

Program Chairs

Vittorio Scarano (Chair)	Università di Salerno, Italy
Gennaro Cordasco	Seconda Università di Napoli, Italy
Paul Richmond	University of Sheffield, UK
Carmine Spagnuolo	Università di Salerno, Italy (Publicity Chair)

Program Committee

Maria Chli	Aston University, UK
Claudio Cioffi-Revilla	George Mason University, USA
Biagio Cosenza	University of Innsbruck, Austria
Nick Collier	Argonne National Laboratory, USA
Rosaria Conte	CNR, Italy
Andrew Evans	University of Leeds, UK
Bernardino Frola	The MathWorks, Cambridge, UK
Joanna Kolodziej	Cracow University of Technology and AGH University of Science and Technology, Cracow, Poland
Nicola Lettieri	Università del Sannio and ISFOL, Italy
Sean Luke	George Mason University, USA
Michael North	Argonne National Laboratory, USA
Mario Paolucci	CNR, Italy
Paul Richmond	The University of Sheffield, UK
Arnold Rosenberg	Northeastern University, USA
Flaminio Squazzoni	Università di Brescia, Italy
Michela Taufer	University of Delaware, USA

4th International Workshop on Parallelism in Bioinformatics (PBio 2016)

Welcome to the proceedings of the 4th International Workshop on Parallelism in Bioinformatics (PBio 2016), which was held in conjunction with the 22nd International European Conference on Parallel and Distributed Computing (Euro-Par 2016) during August 22–26, 2016.

In Bioinformatics, we find a variety of problems that are affected by huge processing times and memory/storage consumption, due to the large size of biological data sets and the inherent complexity of biological problems. In fact, bioinformatics is one of the most exciting research areas in which Parallelism finds application. Successful examples are mpiBLAST, RAxML-HPC, or ClustalW-MPI, among many others. In conclusion, bioinformatics allows for and encourages the application of many different parallelism-based technologies. In this sense, PBio 2016 offered a set of original, high-quality research presentations, clearly focused on the application of parallelism to different bioinformatics problems.

The workshop received 18 high-quality submissions from different countries (USA, Spain, Iran, Taiwan and Germany). All 18 papers were reviewed by at least three expert reviewers. Out of them, 13 papers of high quality in emerging research areas were accepted for publication in the proceedings and presentation at the conference (acceptance rate: 72%).

The papers presented at PBio 2016 cover diverse hot topics: multithreaded computing in bioinformatics, cluster computing in bioinformatics, heterogeneous computing in bioinformatics, multi-level parallelism in bioinformatics, as well as parallel tools and applications in bioinformatics. The topics covered in the papers are timely and important, and the authors did an excellent job of presenting the material. In fact, this workshop would not have been possible without the assistance of both the authors and the Program Committee members, to whom we give many thanks.

Finally, it is important to highlight that PBio 2016 was held in the modern and lovely city of Grenoble (France), and we trust that everyone enjoyed their stay.

Program Chairs

Miguel A. Vega-Rodríguez — University of Extremadura, Spain

Sergio Santander-Jiménez — University of Extremadura, Spain

Álvaro Rubio-Largo — University Nova of Lisbon, Portugal

Program Committee

Antonio Gómez-Iglesias	Texas Advanced Computing Center, USA
César Gómez-Martín	University of Extremadura, Spain
David L. González-Álvarez	University of Extremadura, Spain
Francisco Prieto-Castrillo	MIT (Massachusetts Institute of Technology), USA
José M. Granado-Criado	University of Extremadura, Spain
María Arsuaga-Ríos	CERN, Switzerland
María Botón-Fernández	CETA-CIEMAT, Spain
Marisa da Silva Maximiano	Polytechnic Institute of Leiria, Portugal
Miguel Cárdenas-Montes	CIEMAT, Spain
Sónia M. Almeida-Luz	Polytechnic Institute of Leiria, Portugal
Víctor Berrocal-Plaza	University of Extremadura, Spain

Performance Engineering for Large-Scale Graph Analytics (PELGA)

Knowledge economy is based on data, of which graphs represent an increasing part, in advanced marketing, in social networking, in life sciences, in health and bioinformatics services, in academic networks, in hiring of professionals, etc. As a consequence, graph analytics is fast becoming a significant consumer of computing resources, due to ever larger graphs of hundreds of millions up to hundreds of billions of edges, and to the increased complexity of analysis tasks. To enable existing algorithms to fit modern architectures and scale with these new requirements, there is a growing need for performance engineering.

PELGA is a venue that aims to address this need. Its goal is to bring together specialists from both industry and academia to discuss the state of the art of graph-processing systems, with a special focus on performance. Hosting PELGA with Euro-Par allows the largest community of parallel and distributed systems in Europe and elsewhere to participate in the discussion and acknowledge the new research opportunities that large-scale graph processing presents.

PELGA is a venue that welcomes contributions focusing on graph-centric performance engineering tools and methods, workload characterization, new algorithms and graph-processing systems, and performance modeling. Less conventional workshop topics such as surveys, performance studies, comparative analyses are also encouraged, given the young age of the large-scale graph processing community. We strive to cover the specifics of three large classes of topics.

1. Systems invites contributions focusing on new graph processing systems focused on high-performance analytics, performance studies of existing systems to be used for graph processing, and comparative and/or in-depth analysis of graph processing systems.
2. Algorithms, Applications, and Architectures is the largest topic cluster, including work focusing on new high-performance graph-processing algorithms, new performance-aware applications for graph-processing algorithms, platform-specific algorithms and their performance optimization (e.g., GPUs, Xeon Phi, heterogeneous platforms) for graph analytics, algorithms and/or architectures for large-scale graph analytics, and partitioning methods for large-scale or otherwise challenging graphs.
3. Characterization, modeling, and engineering is the core of the workshop. We encourage novel contributions focusing on graph models for performance tuning and/or prediction of analytics workloads, performance models for prediction or ranking of graph-processing platforms, performance analysis and engineering of existing graph-processing algorithms, and tools and benchmarks for graph-centric performance engineering.

In summary, graph processing is a high-impact field in full development, driven by both the data owners and the analytics world. As we recognize the need to adapt traditional performance evaluation, analysis, and modeling to the needs of this dynamic new topic, PELGA is a workshop with a strong community focus, aiming to bring the challenges of large-scale graph processing to the attention of the Euro-Par community as an unconventional, yet very relevant topic for parallel and distributed computing.

We would like to thank the authors who sent us their manuscripts: Without you, this workshop could not exist. We would also like to thank the members of our Program Committee for their hard work in reviewing the submitted papers and giving constructive feedback to all authors. We would also like to extend our thanks to Dr. Frédéric Desprez, who helped us greatly in many organizational aspects. Finally, Grenoble was a wonderful host for all of us. Thank you.

Program Chairs

Ana Lucia Varbanescu   University of Amsterdam, The Netherlands
Alexandru Iosup   Delft University of Technology, The Netherlands

Program Committee

Alexandru Iosup   Delft University of Technology, The Netherlands
Arnau Prat-Perez   UPC, Spain
Holger Fröning   University of Heidelberg, Germany
Hannes Muhleisen   CWI Amsterdam, The Netherlands
Jan Hidders   Vrije Universiteit Brussel, Belgium
Josep Lluis Larriba Pey   UPC, Spain
Mihai Capota   Intel Labs, USA
Ted Willke   Intel Labs, USA
Taro Takaguchi   NII Tokyo, Japan
George Fletcher   Eindhoven University of Technology, The Netherlands
Yuechao Pan   UC Davis, USA

Third International Workshop on Reproducibility in Parallel Computing (REPPAR)

Conducting sound and reproducible experiments in parallel computing is not easy, as the hardware and software architectures of current parallel computers are most often very complex. This high complexity makes it difficult—and often impossible—for computer scientists to model such systems mathematically. Therefore, scientists rely on experiments to study new parallel algorithms, different software solutions (e.g., operating systems), or novel hardware architectures. The situation in parallel computing is made even more difficult than it would otherwise be, as parallel systems are in a constant state of flux, e.g., the total core count is rapidly growing and many programming paradigms for parallel machines have emerged and are actively being used in a hybrid fashion, e.g., MPI, OpenMP, or PGAS.

For these reasons, the workshop is concerned with experimental practices in parallel computing research. We solicit research papers and experience reports on a number of relevant topics, particularly: methods for analysis and visualization of experimental data, best practice recommendations, results of attempts to replicate previously published experiments, and tools for experimental computational sciences. Some examples of the latter include workflow management systems, experimental testbeds, and systems for archiving and querying large data files.

Program Chairs

Sascha Hunold	TU Wien, Austria
Arnaud Legrand	CNRS, LIG, Grenoble, France
Lucas Nussbaum	Université de Lorraine, LORIA, France
Mark Stillwell	Imperial College London, UK

Program Committee

Sascha Hunold	TU Wien, Austria
Arnaud Legrand	CNRS, LIG, Grenoble, France
James McClure	Virginia Tech, USA
Lucas Nussbaum	Université de Lorraine, LORIA, France
Swann Perarnau	Argonne National Lab, USA
Robert Ricci	University of Utah, USA
Luka Stanisic	Inria Bordeaux Sud-Ouest, France
Mark Stillwell	Imperial College London, UK

9th Workshop on Resiliency in High-Performance Computing in Clusters, Clouds, and Grids (Resilience 2016)

Resilience is a critical challenge as high-performance computing (HPC) systems continue to increase component counts, individual component reliability decreases [e.g., due to shrinking process technology and near-threshold voltage (NTV) operation], and software complexity increases. Application correctness and execution efficiency, in spite of frequent faults, errors, and failures, are essential to ensure the success of the extreme-scale HPC systems, cluster computing environments, Grid computing infrastructures, and Cloud computing services.

While a fault (e.g., a bug or stuck bit) is the cause of an error, its manifestation as a state change is considered an error (e.g., a bad value or incorrect execution), and the transition to an incorrect service is observed as a failure (e.g., an application abort or system crash). A failure in a computing system is typically observed through an application abort or a full/partial service or system outage. A detectable correctable error is often transparently handled by hardware, such as a single bit flip in memory that is protected with single-error correction double-error detection (SECDED) error correcting code (ECC). A detectable uncorrectable error (DUE) typically results in a failure, such as multiple bit flips in the same addressable word that escape SECDED ECC correction, but not detection, and ultimately causes an application abort. An undetectable error (UE) may result in silent data corruption (SDC), e.g., an incorrect application output. There are many other types of hardware and software faults, errors, and failures in computing systems.

Resilience for HPC systems encompasses a wide spectrum of fundamental and applied research and development, including theoretical foundations, fault detection and prediction, monitoring and control, end-to-end data integrity, enabling infrastructure, and resilient solvers and algorithm-based fault tolerance. This workshop brings together experts in the community to further research and development in HPC resilience and to facilitate exchanges across the computational paradigms of extreme-scale HPC, cluster computing, Grid computing, and Cloud computing.

The goal of this workshop is to bring together experts in the area of fault tolerance and resilience for HPC to present the latest achievements and to discuss the challenges ahead. The program of the Resilience 2016 workshop included five high-quality papers.

Workshop Chairs

Stephen L. Scott   Tennessee Tech University and Oak Ridge National Laboratory, USA

Chokchai   Louisiana Tech University, USA
(Box) Leangsuksun

Program Chairs

Patrick G. Bridges   University of New Mexico, USA
Christian Engelmann   Oak Ridge National Laboratory, USA

Program Committee

Ferrol Aderholdt	Tennessee Tech University, USA
Vassil Alexandrov	Barcelona Supercomputer Center, Spain
Dorian Arnold	University of New Mexico, USA
Wesley Bland	Intel Corporation, USA
Hans-Joachim Bungartz	Technical University of Munich, Germany
Franck Cappello	Argonne National Laboratory and University of Illinois at Urbana-Champaign, USA
Zizhong Chen	University of California at Riverside, USA
Robert Clay	Sandia National Laboratories, USA
Miguel Correia	Universidade de Lisboa, Portugal
Nathan DeBardeleben	Los Alamos National Laboratory, USA
James Elliott	North Carolina State University, USA
Kurt Ferreira	Sandia National Laboratory, USA
Michael Heroux	Sandia National Laboratories, USA
Larry Kaplan	Cray Inc., USA
Dieter Kranzlmueller	Ludwig Maximilians University of Munich, Germany
Sriram Krishnamoorthy	Pacific Northwest National Laboratory, USA
Ignacio Laguna	Lawrence Livermore National Laboratory, USA
Scott Levy	University of New Mexico, USA
Kathryn Mohror	Lawrence Livermore National Laboratory, USA
Christine Morin	Inria Rennes Bretagne-Atlantique, France
Dirk Pflueger	University of Stuttgart, Germany
Nageswara Rao	Oak Ridge National Laboratory, USA
Alexander Reinefeld	Zuse Institute Berlin, Germany
Rolf Riesen	Intel Corporation, USA
Yves Robert	ENS Lyon, France
Thomas Ropars	Université Grenoble Alpes, France
Martin Schulz	Lawrence Livermore National Laboratory, USA
Keita Teranishi	Sandia National Laboratories, USA

4th Workshop on Runtime and Operating Systems for the Many-Core Era (ROME 2016)

Since the beginning of the multicore era, parallel processing has become prevalent across the board. However, in order to continue a performance increase according to Moore's law, a new step needs to be taken: away from common multicores toward innovative many-core architectures. Such systems, equipped with a significantly higher number of cores per chip than multicores, raise challenges in both hardware and software design. On the hardware side, complex on-chip networks, scratchpads, hybrid memory cubes, non-volatile memory and stacked memory, as well as deep cache-hierarchies and novel cache-coherence strategies will enrich the current research areas in the future.

However, the ROME workshop (*R*untime and *O*perating Systems for the *M*any-Core *E*ra) focuses on the software side because without complying system software as well as runtime and operating system support, all these new hardware facilities cannot be exploited. Hence, the new challenges in hardware/software co-design are to step beyond traditional approaches and to create new programming models and operating system designs in order to exploit the theoretically available performance of future hardware as effectively and as power-aware as possible.

This focus of the ROME workshop stands in the tradition of a successful series of events originally hosted by the many-core applications research community (MARC). Prior MARC Symposia took place at the ONERA Research Center in Toulouse, at the Hasso Plattner Institute in Potsdam, and at the RWTH Aachen University. Starting in 2013, the organizers continued this series by establishing ROME as one of the co-located workshops of Euro-Par, the prime European conference for parallel and distributed computing.

While the first ROME workshop, which was hosted at Euro-Par 2013 in Aachen, was still a MARC-related, follow-up event but for a broader audience, the second ROME workshop, held in conjunction with Euro-Par 2014 in Porto, already expanded its focus to research questions arising from the upcoming generation of heterogeneous and/or massive parallel systems stepping toward a many-core dominated exascale era. In 2015, this broader focus was essentially retained for the third ROME workshop, which was held in conjunction with Euro-Par 2015 in Vienna, but the relevance of runtime and operating system aspects was stressed once again as being the primary scope of the ROME workshop series.

In this spirit, this years's ROME workshop at Euro-Par 2016 in Grenoble was once again held as a half-day workshop with many seminal and technical discussions and highly interesting presentations. The organizers were particularly happy that Rolf Riesen from Intel volunteered to deliver the invited keynote talk about "Extreme-Scale Operating Systems."

Program Chairs

Stefan Lankes   RWTH Aachen University, Germany
Carsten Clauss   ParTec Cluster Competence Center GmbH, Germany

Program Committee

Jens Breitbart   TU München, Germany
André Brinkmann   Johannes Gutenberg Universität, Mainz, Germany
Carsten Clauss   ParTec Cluster Competence Center GmbH, Germany
Christos Kartsaklis   Oak Ridge National Laboratory, USA
Florian Kluge   Universität Augsburg, Germany
Stefan Lankes   RWTH Aachen University, Germany
Timothy G. Mattson   Intel Labs, USA
Jörg Nolte   Brandenburg University of Technology (BTU), Cottbus,
                           Germany
Lena Oden   Argonne National Laboratory, USA
Antonio J. Peña   Barcelona Supercomputing Center, Spain
Andreas Polze   Hasso Plattner Institute, Postdam, Germany
Pablo Reble   RWTH Aachen University, Germany
Bettina Schnor   University of Potsdam, Germany
Oliver Sinnen   University of Auckland, New Zealand
Christian Terboven   RWTH Aachen University, Germany
Josef Weidendorfer   TU München, Germany
Carsten Weinhold   TU Dresden, Germany

Additional Reviewers

Steffen Christgau   University of Potsdam, Germany
Tim Suess   Johannes Gutenberg-Universität, Mainz, Germany

Unconventional High-Performance Computing 2016 (UCHPC16)

Recent issues with the power consumption of conventional HPC hardware have resulted in both new interest in accelerator hardware and in usage of mass-market hardware not originally designed for HPC. The most prominent examples are GPUs, but FPGAs, DSPs, and embedded designs are also possible candidates to provide higher-power efficiency, as they are used in energy-restricted environments, such as smartphones or tablets. The so-called dark silicon forecast, i.e., not all transistors may be active at the same time, may lead to even more specialized hardware in future mass-market products. Exploiting this hardware for HPC can be a worthwhile challenge.

As the word "Unconventional" in the title suggests, the workshop focuses on usage of hardware or platforms for HPC that are not (yet) conventionally used today, and may not be designed for HPC in the first place. Reasons for its use can be raw computing power, good performance per watt, or low cost in general. To address this unconventional hardware, often, new programming approaches and paradigms are required to make best use of it. Another focus of the workshop is on innovative, (yet) unconventional new programming models, and algorithms (e.g., Big Data) exploiting unconventional HPC hardware or software. To this end, UCHPC tries to capture solutions for HPC that are unconventional today but could become conventional and significant tomorrow, and thus provide a glimpse into the future of HPC.

This year was the ninth time the UCHPC workshop took place, and was the seventh time in a row that it was co-located with Euro-Par (every year since 2010). Before that, it was held in conjunction with the International Conference on Computational Science and Its Applications 2008 and with the ACM International Conference on Computing Frontiers 2009. However, UCHPC is a perfect addition to the scientific fields of Euro-Par, and this is confirmed by the continuous interest we see among Euro-Par attendees for this workshop.

While the general focus of the workshop is fixed, the topic is actually a moving target. GPUs were quite unconventional for HPC a few years ago, but today a notable portion of the machines in the Top500 list are making use of them. Due to raising costs for energy consumption, mobile processors for HPC – including on-chip GPU and DSPs – are a hot topic. FPGAs are traditionally used for architecture design exploration. However, using them directly within HPC systems allows for (reconfigurable) hardware tailored to specific application requirements and thus may result in higher energy efficiency. We invited Michaela Blott from Xilinx to give a keynote about recent trends in FPGA usage. Programmer productivity is always an issue when talking about highly efficient hardware. For a second keynote (at the end of the workshop) we invited Martin Vorbach to talk about his recent idea on a new processor architecture (Hyperion), which tries to dynamically map regular instruction streams to an array of processing elements, promising high instruction-level parallelism.

These proceedings include the final versions of the papers presented at UCHPC and accepted for publication. They take the feedback from the reviewers and workshop audience into account.

The workshop organizers/program chairs want to thank the authors of the papers for joining us in Grenoble, the Program Committee for doing the hard work of reviewing all submissions, the conference organizers for providing such a nice venue, and last but not least the large number of attendees again this year.

Program Chairs

Jens Breitbart	Technische Universität München, Germany
Josef Weidendorfer	Technische Universität München, Germany

Program Committee

Michael Bader	Technische Universität München, Germany
Denis Barthou	University of Bordeaux, France
Alex Bartzas	National Technical University of Athens, Greece
Lars Bengtsson	Chalmers University of Technology, Sweden
James Beyer	Cray Inc., USA
Michaela Blott	Xilinx, Ireland
Jens Breitbart	Technische Universität München, Germany
Georgios Dimitrakopoulos	Democritus University of Thrace, Greece
Karl Fürlinger	Ludwig-Maximilians-Universität München, Germany
Frank Hannig	University of Erlangen-Nuremberg, Germany
Anders Hast	Uppsala University, Sweden
Paul Keir	University of the West of Scotland, UK
Rainer Keller	Hochschule für Technik Stuttgart, Germany
Gaurav Khanna	University of Massachusetts Dartmouth, USA
Harald Köstler	University of Erlangen-Nuremberg, Germany
Stefan Lankes	RWTH Aachen, Germany
Dimitar Lukarski	Paralution Labs, Germany
Manfred Mücke	Materials Center Leoben, Austria
Yannis Papaefstathiou	Technical University of Crete, Greece
Bertil Schmidt	University of Mainz, Germany
Carsten Trinitis	Technische Universität München, Germany
Josef Weidendorfer	Technische Universität München, Germany
Jan-Philipp Weiss	COMSOL, Sweden
Ren Wu	HP Labs, Palo Alto, USA
Peter Zinterhof Jr.	University of Salzburg, Austria

Contents

PADABS -Workshop on Parallel and Distributed Agent-Based Simulations

PBIO - International Workshop on Parallelism in Bioinformatics

PELGA - Performance Engineering for Large-Scale Graph Analytics

REPPAR - International Workshop on Reproducibility in Parallel Computing

RESILIENCE - Workshop on Resiliency in High Performance Computing in Clusters, Clouds, and Grids

ROME - Workshop on Runtime and Operating Systems for the Many-Core Era

UCHPC - UnConventional High-Performance Computing

EUROEDUPAR - European Workshop on Parallel and Distributed Computing Education for Undergraduate Students

Lattice Boltzmann Flow Simulation on Android Devices for Interactive Mobile-Based Learning

Philipp Neumann$^{(\boxtimes)}$ and Michael Zellner

Department of Informatics, Technical University of Munich,
Boltzmannstr. 3, 85748 Garching, Germany
philipp.neumann@tum.de

Abstract. Interactive tools and learning environments have a high potential to facilitate learning. We developed the app *LB2M* for two-dimensional Lattice Boltzmann-based flow simulation on Android devices. The software enables interactive simulation and visualization of various flow scenarios. We detail the software with regard to design, simulation kernel, and visualization. In particular, we demonstrate how the app can be used to teach basics of fluid dynamics in beginner's courses at the example of cavity flow.

Keywords: Lattice Boltzmann · Smartphone · Computational fluid dynamics · Interactive · Simulation-based learning

1 Introduction

Smartphones have become our daily companion. A great variety of applications (apps) yields flexible and *highly interactive* usage of these powerful devices ranging from communication over information and education to entertainment, gaming and business.

Interactive, computer-based methods such as interactive simulations can have a very positive effect in education. Interactive simulations allow students to experiment and "play around" within a given framework. Feedback with regard to observations and success is immediate and—in case of interactive simulation on mobile devices—the students are free to conduct their studies where- and whenever they wish.

Various works, amongst others [1,2] (and references therein) and [3], point at the effectiveness of simulations in the context of discovery learning. De Jong and Van Joolingen [2] discuss that instructional measures such as provision of domain information, provision of assignments, and inclusion of model progression are essential in this context. Similarly, Bodemer and Plötzner [1] argue in the context of learning with interactive simulations that for "instance, learners can be encouraged to (1) identify parameters of the underlying model, (2) generate hypotheses about relationships between parameters, (3) test the hypotheses by designing experiments, predicting the outcomes, performing the experiments, and interpreting the results and (4) evaluate the results in the light of

© Springer International Publishing AG 2017
F. Desprez et al. (Eds.): Euro-Par 2016 Workshops, LNCS 10104, pp. 3–15, 2017.
DOI: 10.1007/978-3-319-58943-5_1

the hypotheses formulated. However, it has been demonstrated that successful learning with interactive simulations requires further support. Particularly, generating and testing hypotheses seem to be very demanding tasks."

It is also the preparation of material in form of interactive simulations and software for courses on engineering and science that has been reported in literature. For example, more than 400 simulations based on Mathematica have been developed and provided online for chemical engineering education [4]. The PhET Interactive Simulations project has been launched in 2002 at the university of Colorado and comprises a great variety of interactive math and science simulations to "engage students through an intuitive, game-like environment where students learn through exploration and discovery"[1] [5].

The use of mobile devices in form of tablet PCs and its impact on student learning is investigated in [6], focussing on a rather supportive and accompanying usage of these devices (taking notes, drawing graphs, etc.). It is found that computer science and engineering "students' motivation to learn and engage with engineering course content increases in learning environments where students make use of Tablet PCs" [6], and it is expected that a more regular use of the handheld computers "could potentially increase if faculty employed Tablet features more readily in their engineering courses". Wilson and Gramoll [7] describe a fluid dynamics app to be used in class rooms for interactive learning. Due to the high computational cost of their simulations, computations are carried out on a cluster; up to 140 users can simultaneously—and interactively—connect via the app to the cluster, compute, and afterwards visualize the results on their mobile devices.

In this contribution we take one further step and show that (and how) mobile devices can be used for *on-device* fluid dynamics simulations, and so allow for mobile computer-based learning. We incorporate the comment drawn by Bodemer and Plötzner [1] and point out how further support for interactive computer-based learning can be established.

We revise the underlying Lattice Boltzmann-based simulation methodology in Sect. 2 and present the design and usage of the fluid dynamics app *LB2M* in Sect. 3. To guarantee interactivity and related performance, we show results from performance studies and provide a comparison with related software in Sect. 4. Section 5 demonstrates the applicability of the software for interactive computer-based learning at the example of dimensional analysis in fluid dynamics. We summarize our work and give an outlook to future developments in Sect. 6.

2   Lattice Boltzmann Method

Algorithm. Fluid dynamics is governed by the Navier-Stokes equations. Various solvers are available to compute approximate solutions to these nonlinear partial differential equations. We decided to use the Lattice Boltzmann method (LBM) [8,9] as method of choice. The method is "non-traditional" in the sense

---

[1] https://phet.colorado.edu.

that it solves Navier-Stokes indirectly via discrete Boltzmann equation approximations. However, it is simple to implement, it requires less computations per time step than direct Navier-Stokes solvers, and the method in a nutshell can be explained in ten minutes[2]. The latter aspect is considered essential in the scope of mobile-based learning since basic understanding on the underlying simulation can thus be gathered by students autonomously. The Lattice Boltzmann method uses distribution functions $f_i(\mathbf{x}, t) \in \mathbb{R}_{>0}$, $i = 1, ..., Q$, to simulate the motion of a fluid on a Cartesian grid [8,9]. In each time step fluid particles collide locally in each grid cell (*collide step*). They subsequently move along directions $\mathbf{c}_i$ into neighboring grid cells, or rest inside the current one (*Streaming step*). Since complex, fully three-dimensional fluid flow simulations exhibit very high computational loads and may even require parallel or supercomputing [10], we restrict our considerations to the two-dimensional D2Q9 model (two dimensions, nine velocity directions $\mathbf{c}_i \in \mathbb{R}^2$). This is sufficient to consider fluid dynamics principles, e.g. by studying convective and diffusive flow behavior in cavity flows, or pressure drops and shear rates in channel flows. We consider the BGK collision operator for local interactions [11]. The corresponding time step rule reads

$$f_i(\mathbf{x} + \mathbf{c}_i \Delta t, t + \Delta t) = f_i(\mathbf{x}, t) - \tfrac{1}{\tau}\left(f_i(\mathbf{x}, t) - f_i^{eq}(\rho(\mathbf{x}, t), \mathbf{u}(\mathbf{x}, t))\right) \text{ with}$$

$$\rho(\mathbf{x}, t) = \sum_i f_i(\mathbf{x}, t),$$

$$\rho\mathbf{u}(\mathbf{x}, t) = \sum_i f_i(\mathbf{x}, t)\mathbf{c}_i, \tag{1}$$

$$f_i^{eq}(\rho(\mathbf{x}, t), \mathbf{u}(\mathbf{x}, t)) = w_i \rho\left(1 + \tfrac{\mathbf{c}_i \mathbf{u}}{c_s^2} + \tfrac{(\mathbf{c}_i \mathbf{u})^2}{2c_s^4} - \tfrac{\mathbf{u}^2}{2c_s^2}\right),$$

lattice-specific weights w_i and speed of sound $c_s := \tfrac{1}{\sqrt{3}}$. Density and fluid velocity are denoted by ρ and $\mathbf{u}$. The relaxation time τ is related to the kinematic viscosity ν of the fluid, $\nu := c_s^2(\tau - \tfrac{1}{2})$.

Boundary Conditions. Wall, velocity inlet and outflow conditions are realized in our app *LD2M*.

Walls are simulated via the half-way bounce back rule. Assume that a distribution function f_i would enter the fluid domain from "outside" due to streaming. Distributions $f_{inv(i)}$ that move from a fluid cell "into" a solid boundary during streaming are bounced back and stored in the current fluid cell as f_i, with the inverse defined as $\mathbf{c}_{inv(i)} := -\mathbf{c}_i$.

If the solid boundary is moving at velocity $\mathbf{u}_{boundary}$, or if we want to model a *velocity inlet* with inlet velocity $\mathbf{u}_{boundary}$, we also employ the bounce back rule, but include an additional term $\tfrac{2}{c_s^2} w_i \rho \mathbf{c}_i \mathbf{u}_{boundary}$ to account for momentum transfer at the wall.

Outflow conditions are set according to the descriptions in [12]. A distribution function is set accordingly to $f_i := f_i^{eq}(\rho_A, \mathbf{u}) + f_{inv(i)}^{eq}(\rho_A, \mathbf{u}) - f_{inv(i)}$, with $\rho_A := 1.0$.

---

[2] cf. YouTube teaching video *Of Foxes, Attackers,... and the Lattice Boltzmann Method*, https://youtu.be/trvSBGyK74g, by P. Neumann.

3 LB2M

3.1 Software Design

The app *LB2M* consists of three major parts that are executed in individual threads, cf. Fig. 1. The first part is represented by the main thread which is responsible for displaying the GUI Elements and controlling all other threads. It is further used to integrate user interactions. The second part of *LB2M* is the Lattice Boltzmann kernel which calculates the results for the next time step and computes data that are required for visualization. At the current stage, the velocity field $\mathbf{u}(\mathbf{x}, t)$ is visualized via cellwise coloring using an array of shorts with one color entry per grid cell. The third part uses OpenGL ES 2.0 to visualize the generated cell colors. *LB2M* is designed for Android devices. This has been decided due to the fact that Android clearly dominates the worldwide smartphone OS market, with a market share of 69.3%–82.8% in 2012–2015 [13].

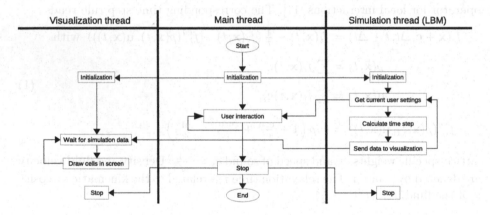

Fig. 1. Flow chart of *LB2M*.

3.2 Simulation Engine

We provide both a Java- and C++-based implementation of the LBM. Although the whole app is written in Java to guarantee portability between different Android devices, see Table 1, the C++-version yields significantly higher performance and thus allows for a more sophisticated use in interactive simulations.

Both Java- and C++-implementation are based on the standard two-field approach [14] in which two fields of distributions are used to avoid read-write conflicts during the streaming step. Due to the variety in smartphone architectures, cf. Table 1, device-specific optimization of the C++-based simulation to achieve optimal performance is difficult to establish and—with regard to upcoming architectures—hardly possible. We therefore rather focus on straight-line code and algorithmic optimization (in both implementations) to, e.g., minimize computations in the compute-intensive collide kernel, and employ shared-memory parallelization using OpenMP. This is not sufficient to reach up to the memory bandwidth roofline [15] which typically limits Lattice Boltzmann perfor mance. Yet, it yields sufficient performance for interactive two-dimensional flow simulations. The C++ simulation engine is incorporated into the Java-based framework of *LB2M* via the Java Native Interface (JNI).

Table 1. Supported Android-based devices. **Device (Android version)** shows the tested smartphone including its Android version. **Java LBM** and **C++ LBM** correspond to the Java- and C++-based Lattice Boltzmann simulation kernels. **OpenGL** denotes the visualization model of *LB2M*.

Device (Android version)	Processor	Java LBM	C++ LBM	OpenGL
HTC One (5.1.1)	Qualcomm Snapdragon 600, quad-core Krait 300 1.9 GHz	x	x	x
LG Nexus 5 (6.0)	Qualcomm Snapdragon 800, quad-core Krait 400 2.3 GHz	x	x	x
Samsung Galaxy A5 (5.0)	Qualcomm Snapdragon 410, quad-core ARM Cortex A53 1.2 GHz	x	x	x
Samsung Galaxy S3 (4.3)	Qualcomm Samsung Exynos 4412, quad-core ARM Cortex A9 1.4 GHz	x	x	x
Motorola Razr i (4.1.2)	Intel Medfield, single-core Atom Z2460 1.6 GHz	x		
Motorola Moto G (5.1.1)	Qualcomm Snapdragon 400, quad-core ARM Cortex A7 1.6 GHz	x	x	x
Huawei Ascend G7 (4.4.4)	Qualcomm Snapdragon 410, quad-core ARM Cortex A53 1.2 GHz	x	x	x
Huawei Y330-U01 (4.2.2)	MediaTek MTK6572, dual-core ARM Cortex A7 1.3 GHz	x		x

3.3 Visualization

There are various APIs available in the scope of data visualization on Android devices, with Canvas and OpenGL ES representing two of the most prominent ones. Since interactivity is essential for our app, we conducted performance benchmarks for both Canvas and OpenGL ES 2.0 in which we measured the time to visualize given numbers of rectangular grid cells. The visualization based on OpenGL ES 2.0 was clearly superior in our tests. Since OpenGL ES 2.0 is the most distributed version among OpenGL ES—50.9% as of April 4 2016 [16]—and since it also allows for backward compatibility with regard to OpenGL ES 3.0 and other (upcoming) versions, we based the visualization in *LB2M* on this approach. Per time step, the velocity field data is extracted and visualized as colored grid cells according to the velocity magnitude, see Fig. 2(a) for a visualization of a lid-driven cavity. The coloring—red/green/blue for high/medium/low velocities—can be adjusted by the user.

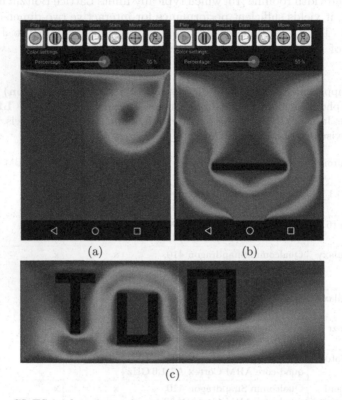

(a)   (b)

(c)

Fig. 2. OpenGL ES 2.0-based visualization of predefined scenarios of *LB2M*. (a) Evolving lid-driven cavity flow using 1000 × 1000 cells. (b) T-flow scenario with 100 × 100 cells. An additional rectangular obstacle has been added to the simulation by the user. (c) Wind tunnel scenario with 300 × 100 cells. The writing "TUM" was added by the user via several rectangular obstacles. (Color figure online)

3.4   Interactive Simulation Workflow and Usage

Specification of General Simulation Parameters. Starting *LB2M*, the user is asked to specify general simulation settings, comprising the grid size in x- and y-direction, the relaxation time τ, and the choice whether to use the Java- or the C++-based simulation kernel. If the C++ kernel is not supported by the device, *LB2M* automatically switches to the (single-threaded) Java kernel.

Boundary Setup. In the second step, the user configures the boundary conditions of the computational domain. The cells along left/right/top/bottom boundary are enumerated; any subset of boundary cells can be configured by the user to resemble inlet, outflow, or wall conditions. Alternatively, the user can choose one out of three pre-configured scenarios, cf. Fig. 2:

Cavity: the top boundary wall constantly moves from left to right at a prescribed speed. The other boundaries (left, right, bottom) are non-moving walls. This induces vortex formation inside the quadratic box.
– *Wind Tunnel*: the left boundary is configured as velocity inlet with a constant inlet velocity, the right boundary is chosen as outflow region. Top and bottom boundary resemble non-moving walls.
– *T-Flow*: the middle region of the bottom boundary is configured as velocity inlet and upper parts of the left and right boundary are chosen as outflow regions. All other boundaries are non-moving walls.

Interactive Simulation. After specifying the boundary conditions, the simulation starts in interactive mode. Besides start/stop and zoom/rotate functionality, the user can draw (rectangular) obstacles and place them at arbitrary points in the flow field. Moreover, a statistics button *Stats* shows the performance of the simulation in MLUPS (*M*ega *L*attice *U*pdates *P*er *S*econd), a common performance measure of Lattice Boltzmann codes [14].

4   Benchmarking

4.1   Related Work and Performance

In the context of mesh-based mobile computational fluid dynamics, several other apps have been recently developed.

Various simple LBM-based simulation apps for single scenarios are provided at [17]. For example *Lid-driven cavity flow* simulates a cavity; the user can only modify the kinematic viscosity via the dimenionless Reynolds number, cf. Sect. 5. The grid size is fixed (51 × 51 cells) and cannot be changed.

Albm [18] allows to interactively draw walls, or to modify the grid size (with a max. grid size of 150 × 75 cells), the number of threads, the frame rate or the visualization technique. Modification of the outer boundary conditions—and thus configuring different kinds of fluid flow scenarios—is not supported.

Besides, other apps based on solving the Navier-Stokes equations exist. Wind-Tunnel/WindTunnelFree [19] is a flexible Navier-Stokes based app which is developed for both iOS and Android devices and exploits the SIMD Neon technology to achieve high performance. On most devices, however, the resolution of the computational domain is set to 120 × 180 which "requires a lot of computational power, especially to sustain a high 30 fps frame rate" [19]. The Navier-Stokes app discussed in [20] also embeds efficient C/C++ kernels in Java code, supports obstacle placement and even free surfaces. To compute the pressure field, however, an SOR scheme is used to solve a Poisson equation in every time step which may significantly limit the overall performance.

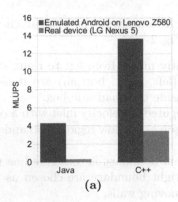 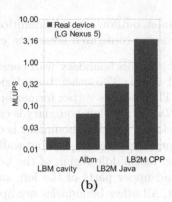

(a)   (b)

Fig. 3. Performance in MLUPS of *LB2M*. (a) Java- and C++-kernel evaluation on emulated Android system and LG Nexus 5. (b) Comparison of different apps with *LB2M*'s Java- and C++-based simulation kernels (log-scale). The C++-kernel uses a single thread; multi-threading yields a speedup of up to two (not shown).

We evaluated the performance of *LB2M* and compared it with the other LBM-based apps. For this purpose, we measured the MLUPS for each app, cf. Fig. 3. The C++-based simulation kernel of *LB2M* is significantly faster, cf. Fig. 3(a). On all investigated devices, cf. Table 1, the C++-based kernel performed at least twice as fast as the Java kernel. Due to the restricted domain size settings of *Albm* and *Lid-driven cavity flow*, a detailed quantitative comparison of the apps in terms of performance could not be achieved. Still, Fig. 3(b) clearly demonstrates the superiority of the performance of *LB2M*.

4.2 Interactivity

Interactive simulations are only possible if an acceptable frame rate—and thus a respective number of simulated time steps per second—can be retained. Currently, *LB2M* renders data of each time step which allows for very detailed visual analysis of the simulation progress and cellwise flow evolution; note that each time step invokes only interactions between neighbored cells and thus information inside the flow field is propagated at most at a rate of one cell per time step.

We measured the frames per second (fps) on our test device (Nexus 5), cf. Fig. 4. Assuming a frame rate of 15–25 fps to be still acceptable for interactive simulations, we observe that domain sizes up to 512×512 cells can be handled by *LB2M*. These domains are big enough to consider different test scenarios in fluid dynamics under various flow conditions, cf. Sect. 5.

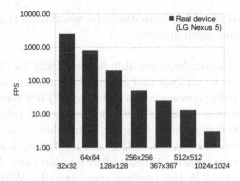

Fig. 4. Frame rate of *LB2M*, evaluated on a Nexus 5.

5 *LB2M* for Teaching

Various aspects of fluid dynamics can be investigated by different classes of users with *LB2M*. At high-school or university entry level, *LB2M* can be used to explore the phenomenological behavior of fluid flow. Examples comprise vortex formation in cavity flow or observation of laminar channel flow splitting up in front of a user-defined obstacle and merging together further downstream. In courses dedicated to basics of fluid dynamics, the concept of shear stresses in laminar flow can be considered in channel flow simulations, (weak) compressibility can be considered by channel flow initialization and respective shock front propagation, laminar flow around obstacles can be studied, etc.

In the following, we discuss how to use *LB2M* in the context of interactive computer-based learning in two exercises on *dimensional analysis* in fluid dynamics. Dimensional analysis allows to map results of numerical simulations to experimental setups by appropriate parameter scaling. A characteristic number, at which (incompressible) flows behave similar, is the *Reynolds number* $\mathrm{Re} := \frac{u_{boundary}L}{\nu}$. For a cavity scenario, $u_{boundary} = \|\mathbf{u}_{boundary}\|$ stands for the tangential velocity of the lid, L for the number of cells in each, x- and y-, direction, and ν for the kinematic viscosity.

The exercises are meant for undergraduate students—typically beginners in the field of fluid dynamics—who have just installed *LB2M* and have read Sect. 3 to become acquainted with its usage. We describe each exercise and its learning outcomes and analyze them with regard to (1)–(4) of Bodemer's and Plötzner's encouragements, cf. Sect. 1.

5.1 Exercise 1: Cavity Flow

Description. Use *LB2M* to run the following cavity configurations:

1. 100×100 cells, $u_{boundary} = 0.004$, $\tau = 1.7$
2. 100×100 cells, $u_{boundary} = 0.04$, $\tau = 1.7$
3. 100×100 cells, $u_{boundary} = 0.04$, $\tau = 0.62$
4. 200×200 cells, $u_{boundary} = 0.08$, $\tau = 0.596$

Compare the patterns of vortex formation and simulation runtime until steady-state is reached for each configuration.

Learning Outcomes. The students are able to use *LB2M* for different cavity simulations. They are able to analyze and extract information on the flow patterns from the visual flow field representation of the app. They have further observed that the given parameters—domain size, lid velocity and relaxation time—have a major impact on the flow physics: a bigger, "ring-like" vortex structure with its center located rather in the middle of the computational domain forms out for higher velocities/lower relaxation times/bigger domain sizes. Another important observation is constituted in the runtime requirements. While simulations 1–3 can be handled by a mobile device within seconds to minutes, the simulation 4 at higher velocity/lower relaxation time/bigger domain size, requires up to 20–30 min until steady state is reached. Having gathered this information, students are able to deduce appropriate parametrization, for example in terms of acceptable domain sizes and available computational power, in future simulations on their individual devices. Figure 5 shows the resulting velocity profiles and the Reynolds number for each of the four scenarios.

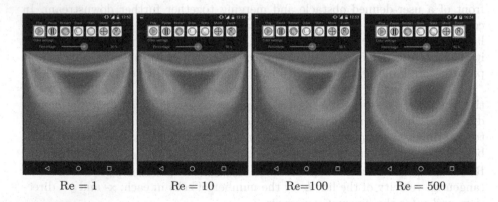

Re = 1   Re = 10   Re=100   Re = 500

Fig. 5. Cavity configurations 1–4 (from left to right) from exercise 1 at steady state.

5.2 Exercise 2: The Reynolds Number

Description. An important characteristic quantity in incompressible fluid dynamics is the Reynolds number which—in case of a cavity scenario—is given by $Re := u_{boundary}L/\nu$.

Similar to exercise 1, investigate the formation of the primary vortex as well as its final form and the location of its center at steady state for different configurations. This time,

1. fix the viscosity ν and vary $u_{boundary}$, L such that $u_{boundary} \cdot L = const$,
2. fix the velocity $u_{boundary}$ and vary ν, L such that $\frac{L}{\nu} = const$,

3. fix the domain size L and vary $u_{boundary}$, ν such that $\frac{u_{boundary}}{\nu} = const$,
4. vary all three parameters, such that Re $= const$.

Consider the four cavity parametrizations from exercise 1 and modify them, respectively. What do you observe? Which Reynolds numbers do these scenarios correspond to?

Learning Outcomes. The students are able to compute the Reynolds number for different parametrizations. In the experiments 1–4 from exercise 1, the Reynolds number is given by Re $\in \{1, 10, 100, 500\}$. By considering special cases (exercise 2, 1–3) and the general case (exercise 2, 4) of Reynolds number tuning, the students have experienced the similarity of flows at equal Reynolds numbers from their simulations. They are further able to construct parametrizations for a given Reynolds number to be used in a numerical simulation or in an experimental fluid dynamics investigation.

5.3 Supporting Students at Interactive Computer-Based Learning

According to the points (1)–(4) by Bodemer and Plötzner, exercises 1, 2 provide sufficient support for discovery learning, cf. Sect. 1: three of the most important parameters in (computational) fluid dynamics have been considered in exercise 1 to analyze flow patterns and to understand their influence on the evolving velocity field, cf. (1). The guided parameter study in exercise 2 allows students to formulate the hypothesis "Flows exhibit similar behavior under conditions 1–4", cf. (2). In this context, *LB2M* is a simple-to-use tool to interactively set up, run and evaluate numerical experiments to confirm the hypothesis, cf. (3),(4).

6 Summary

We introduced the app *LB2M* for two-dimensional fluid flow simulations on Android devices. We briefly discussed the software design of *LB2M* and demonstrated that interactive fluid flow simulations on smartphones are indeed reasonable. This allows for interactive mobile-based teaching, e.g., of basics in fluid dynamics by exploring pre- or user-defined flow scenarios on a smartphone. We showcased the use of *LB2M* for dimensional analysis in cavity flows.

We just incorporated multi-threading in *LB2M*, resulting in speedups of up to two. We currently evaluate respective applications of the app with regard to parallel computing education. Furthermore, we work towards the integration of remote computing: computationally expensive simulations can be outsourced to a server, and *LB2M* can be used to analyze and visualize the simulation results as well as (parallel) simulation performance. This will not only yield an even wider range of applicability for fluid dynamics simulations in teaching, but it will also allow for interactive exploration of parallel computing aspects and data management.

The app *LB2M* has already been used for educational purposes at the Technical University of Munich in the scope of an open day for school children. Its deployment in university courses and respective further evaluation of the app as well as its release are planned.

Acknowledgements. P. Neumann acknowledges the financial support by the priority program *1648 Software for Exascale Computing*, funded by the German Research Foundation (DFG).

References

1. Bodemer, D., Plötzner, R.: Encouraging the active integration of information during learning with multiple and interactive representations. In: Instructional Design for Multimedia Learning. Proceedings of the 5th International Workshop of SIG 6 Instructional Design of the European Association for Research on Learning and Instruction (EARLI), pp. 127–138. Waxmann, Münster (2004)
2. de Jong, T., van Joolingen, W.R.: Scientific discovery learning with computer simulations of conceptual domains. Rev. Educ. Res. **68**(2), 179–201 (1998)
3. Rieber, L.P., Tzeng, S.C., Tribble, K.: Discovery learning, representation, and explanation within a computer-based simulation: finding the right mix. Learn. Instr. **14**, 307–323 (2004)
4. Falconer, J., Nicodemus, G.: Interactive mathematica simulations in chemical engineering courses. Chem. Eng. Educ. **48**(3), 165–174 (2014)
5. Wieman, C.E., Adams, W.K., Perkins, K.K.: PhET: simulations that enhance learning. Science **322**, 682–683 (2008)
6. Amelink, C.T., Scales, G., Tront, J.G.: Student use of the Tablet PC: impact on student learning behaviors. Adv. Eng. Educ. **3**(1), 1–17 (2012)
7. Wilson, J.R., Gramoll, K.C.: Viscous fluid dynamics app for mobile devices using a remote high performance cluster. In: 122nd ASEE Annual Conference and Exposition, Paper ID 11877 (2015)
8. Succi, S.: The Lattice Boltzmann Equation for Fluid Dynamics and Beyond. Oxford University Press, Oxford (2001)
9. Wolf-Gladrow, D.: Lattice-Gas Cellular Automata and Lattice Boltzmann Models - An Introduction. Springer, Berlin (2000)
10. Schornbaum, F., Rüde, U.: Massively parallel algorithms for the lattice Boltzmann method on nonuniform grids. SIAM J. Sci. Comput. **38**(2), C96–C126 (2016)
11. Bhatnagar, P.L., Gross, E.P., Krook, M.: A model for collision processes in gases. I. Small amplitude processes in charged and neutral one-component systems. Phys. Rev. **94**(3), 511–525 (1954)
12. Körner, C., Thies, M., Hofmann, T., Thürey, N., Rüde, U.: Lattice Boltzmann model for free surface flow for modeling foaming. J. Stat. Phys. **121**(1/2), 179–196 (2005)
13. IDC: Smartphone OS Market Share, 2015 Q2 (2016). http://www.idc.com/prod serv/smartphone-os-market-share.jsp
14. Wittmann, M., Zeiser, T., Hager, G., Wellein, G.: Comparison of different propagation steps for lattice Boltzmann methods. Comput. Math. Appl. **65**(6), 924–935 (2013)
15. Williams, S., Waterman, A., Patterson, D.: Roofline: an insightful visual performance model for multicore architectures. Commun. ACM **52**, 65–76 (2009)

16. Google Android Dashboard: OpenGL Version (2016). http://developer.android. com/about/dashboards/index.html
17. Seta, T.: Open Source Lattice Boltzmann Code (2016). http://www3.u-toyama. ac.jp/seta/software/software.html
18. Brebion, M.: Albm (2016). https://www.androidpit.de/app/com.bmsofts.mbrebion. albm
19. Rizk, A., Rizk, G.: WindTunnel (2016). https://www.windtunnelapp.com
20. Mehlbeer, F., Scheufele, K., Soell, D.: Numerical Simulation in Fluid Dynamics on Android Operating System (2013). https://www.informatik.uni-stuttgart. de/studium/interessierte/bsc-studiengaenge/informatik/projekt-inf/2013-05-17/ Gruppe_1.pdf

Using Everest Platform for Teaching Parallel and Distributed Computing

Oleg Sukhoroslov[1,2(✉)]

[1] Institute for Information Transmission Problems of the Russian
Academy of Sciences (Kharkevich Institute), Moscow, Russia
sukhoroslov@iitp.ru
[2] Higher School of Economics, Moscow, Russia

Abstract. The paper presents a practical approach for building high-level services for teaching parallel and distributed computing based on Everest platform. Originally designed for publication of computing applications, the platform is suitable for rapid development of services for running different types of parallel programs on high-performance resources, as well as services for evaluation of practical assignments. As was demonstrated by using Everest for teaching two introductory PDC courses, the proposed approach helps to enhance students' practical experience while avoiding low-level interfaces and providing a level of automation necessary for scaling the course to a large number of students. In contrast to other solutions, the exploited Platform as a Service model provides the ability to quickly reuse this approach by other PDC educators without installation of the platform.

Keywords: Parallel programming · Distributed computing · Web-based interfaces · Web services · Platform as a Service

1 Introduction

The teaching of parallel and distributed computing (PDC) has increasingly gained importance during the last decade due to the ubiquity of multi-core architectures, graphical processors, cloud computing services and the need to process wast amounts of data. Aside from the theoretical foundations, practical programming exercises form an integral part of any PDC course aimed at mastering domain knowledge and developing relevant skills by working with different classes of computational systems and programming technologies.

However, providing a practical experience to the students of PDC course is challenging due to the inherent complexity of involved systems, user interfaces and technologies. A typical example is arranging practical exercises and homework assignments on a compute cluster. A common approach is to provide remote logins for each student, and then train students to use cluster command line environment to compile and submit their programs. This approach suffers from several problems. First, it introduces additional administration, teaching

F. Desprez et al. (Eds.): Euro-Par 2016 Workshops, LNCS 10104, pp. 16–27, 2017.
DOI: 10.1007/978-3-319-58943-5_2

and support overheads for the course staff. Second, it requires a considerable effort for running programs by students who are often unfamiliar with Unix environment, etc. As a result, the additional time and effort are spent by both instructors and students instead of focusing on the essential parts of the course. Due to the limited human resources the traditional approaches to teaching also do not scale well to a large number of students. Therefore new approaches are needed to make teaching PDC more efficient and reach a wider audience.

Web-based environments provide a convenient alternative for accessing parallel computing systems and supporting practical assignments on such systems. While being successfully used in teaching some PDC courses, the development of such environments represents a substantial cost to many educators. While some of existing solutions can be reused, the additional costs related to deployment, customization and administration of such systems in-house can also be significant. Therefore there is a need in generic platforms that can be reused with a minimal effort, possibly without installation as modern cloud platforms, while being flexible and supporting all common use cases.

In this paper we present an approach to automation of practical programming exercises in PDC based on using Everest platform [1,9]. While originally designed for building computational web services, the platform proved to be extremely useful for supporting educational activities as well. Everest has a number of unique features in comparison to related solutions. It implements the Platform as a Service (PaaS) model by supporting multiple users and providing all its functionality via remote interfaces. The platform is not tied to a predefined computing infrastructure by enabling users to attach external resources and bind them to applications. This makes it possible to immediately start using Everest without installation.

In order to simplify access to computing resources a number of generic services have been developed on Everest for running various types of concurrent, parallel and distributed programs. Also a number of problem-specific services has been created for each homework assignment in order to automate evaluation and provide immediate feedback to a student. The presented approach has been successfully used since 2014 for teaching two introductory PDC courses.

The paper is organized as follows: Sect. 2 discusses related work and compares the presented approach and available solutions. Section 3 provides technical details on the Everest platform and describes it's use for development of services supporting teaching activities on HPC resources. Section 4 presents several use cases from different PDC topics and describes the experience gained from using Everest in two PDC courses. Section 5 concludes and discusses future work.

2   Related Work

The use of web technologies for building convenient interfaces for accessing high-performance resources has been exploited since the emergence of the World Wide Web. In [3] authors describe several prototypes of web-based parallel programming environments, including the Virtual Programming Laboratory (VPL) used for teaching parallel programming. The emergence of grid computing and the web portal technology enabled development of grid portals facilitating access to distributed computing facilities. [10] describes an experience of building a grid portal to support an undergraduate parallel programming course.

Web-based interfaces have also been exploited to support submission and automated evaluation of programming assignments in PDC courses. In [5] authors describe a framework enabling implementation of web portals for automated testing of student programming assignments in distributed programming courses. Among the recent works, [8] describes a web-based application for automated assessment and evaluation of source code in the field of parallel programming. In [6] authors present a similar web-based system for running and validating parallel programs written in different programming paradigms.

Finally, a few web-based environments emerged to support recent PDC topics such as big data processing and general-purpose computing on GPU. WebMapReduce [4] is a web interface for Hadoop designed for teaching MapReduce programming. WebGPU is a web-based system developed to support GPU programming assignments in the Heterogeneous Parallel Programming course [2].

In comparison to existing solutions built from scratch for teaching purposes, the presented approach is based on reusing a general-purpose web platform for building computational web services. The ability to quickly build custom services and connect them to computing resources helps to significantly reduce development time. The flexibility of service-oriented approach enables development of different types of services targeting various use cases and application areas. Finally, the exploited PaaS model provides the ability to reuse this approach by other educators without installation of the platform. To our best knowledge, there are no similar attempts were previously made. These features make Everest to stand out in cases where educators need an easy to use yet flexible solution, but lack the resources needed to deploy and maintain such system in-house.

3   Technical Aspects

3.1   Everest Overview

Everest [1, 9] is a web-based platform enabling publication, sharing and execution of scientific applications across distributed computing resources. In this section we provide a brief overview of this platform.

Figure 1 shows the high-level architecture and some of the key concepts of Everest. In contrast to traditional distributed computing platforms, Everest implements the Platform as a Service model by providing its functionality via remote web and programming interfaces. A single instance of the platform can be accessed by many users in order to create, run and share applications with each other. An application added to Everest is automatically published as a web form and a web service. The latter enables programmatic access to applications, integration with third-party tools and composition of applications into

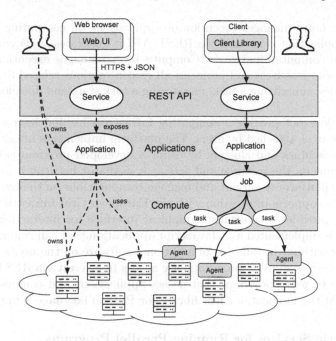

Fig. 1. High-level architecture of Everest

workflows. Another distinct feature of Everest is that it allows users to attach their computing resources and flexibly bind them to applications.

The server-side part of the platform is composed of three main layers: REST API, Applications layer and Compute layer. The client-side part includes the web user interface (Web UI) and client libraries.

REST API implements the remote programming interface providing access to all platform's capabilities. It serves as a single entry point for all clients, including Web UI and client libraries, and is implemented as a set of web services following the Representational State Transfer (REST) architectural style [7]. The API specification is open and allows implementation of third-party clients.

Applications layer implements a hosting environment for applications created by users. Applications are the core entities in Everest that represent reusable computational units that follow a well-defined model. An application has a number of *inputs* that constitute a valid request to the application and a number of *outputs* that constitute a result of computation corresponding to some request. Each application is automatically exposed as a web service via the REST API. This enables remote access to the application via Web UI and client libraries.

To simplify creation of applications Everest provides a generic skeleton for command-line applications that makes it possible to avoid programming while adding an application. In addition to description of application inputs and outputs, the user should specify the command pattern parametrized by input values and describe the mappings between inputs/outputs and files read/produced by the application.

Compute layer manages execution of applications on computing resources. When an application is invoked via REST API it generates a *job* consisting of one or more computational *tasks*. Compute layer manages execution of these tasks on remote resources and performs all routine actions related to staging of task input files, submitting a task, monitoring a task state and downloading task results.

Everest does not provide a computing infrastructure and instead relies on external resources attached by users. The platform implements integration with standalone machines and clusters by using a developed program called *agent*. The agent runs on the resource and acts as a mediator between it and Everest enabling the platform to submit and manage computations on the resource. The platform also supports integration with the European Grid Infrastructure.

Web UI provides a convenient graphical interface for interaction with the platform. It is implemented as a JavaScript application that can run in a modern web browser without installation of additional software on the user's machine.

Client libraries simplify programmatic access to Everest via REST API and enable users to write programs that access applications and compose them in workflows. At the moment, a client library for Python language is implemented.

3.2   Generic Services for Running Parallel Programs

A common challenge for students learning PDC is working on computing resources in order to run their programs on scale. The command line environment and queuing systems used on such resources are unfamiliar and too low-level for many students. Everest can be used to remove these technical barriers by creating web-based services for running parallel programs on a compute cluster. Such services are implemented as Everest applications linked to the provided resource. Since different programming models and technologies use different languages and runtime parameters it is convenient to create multiple generic applications with relevant parameters. In this section we outline steps required in order to create such applications. The complete description of these steps along with technical details can be found in user tutorial on the Everest website [1].

In order to create an application an instructor should specify via Everest Web UI application's metadata, input and output parameters, mapping of parameters to the executed command and files, etc. The core part of the application is a wrapper that takes input parameters and manages execution of a parallel program on the cluster. The wrapper can be written in any programming language since Everest runs it via command line. It usually performs program compilation, preparing of execution environment, submitting the program via queuing system, etc. The development of such wrapper is currently the most difficult part of the process, however once implemented its parts can be reused for other applications.

In order to link the application to a compute cluster used in the course the instructor should attach the cluster to Everest by installing and starting the agent. This step usually does not require much effort since the agent is easy to install under non-root user, provides integration with common batch systems and does not need inbound connectivity. It is convenient to create a dedicated account on the cluster for running the agent and student submissions from Everest. This approach also avoids creation of personal accounts for each student and associated management overheads.

Once the application is tested and ready to be used by the students, the instructor configures access to the application by specifying users and groups allowed to run it. Everest supports creation of arbitrary user groups. For teaching activities it is convenient to create two groups for students and instructors respectively and configure application to allow submissions from both groups. The students' group can be configured to allow self-registration by providing a secret code to avoid manually adding students to the group. After all is set up it is sufficient to ask students to sign up in Everest, add themselves to the required group and check the applications list.

An example of generic application for running MPI programs created on Everest is presented in Fig. 2. The submit form shown on the figure includes input parameters that should be specified by a student for submitting a job. It is also possible to specify custom job name and enable email notification when the job completes which is convenient for long-running jobs or jobs waiting in a queue. Note that this example allows only a single source file to be submitted by a user, which is often adequate for teaching purposes. However it can be easily modified to support cases that require submitting multiple source files.

Upon the job submission the student is redirected to the job page that displays dynamically updated information about the job state. Figure 3 contains a screenshot of completed job for the MPI application. The opened Outputs section provides access to output parameters produced by the job. The job page also includes sections containing general information about the job and all input parameters specified by the student. By default Everest job is accessible only by its owner. For teaching purposes it is possible to automatically share all jobs submitted by the students with the instructors group, so that in case of a problem a student can just send a link to a failed job to the instructor.

The described approach have been used to implement a number of generic services for running different types of programs described in Sect. 4.

3.3 Problem-Specific Services for Programming Assignments

The evaluation of programming assignments in PDC requires a significant effort and is one of the key scalability bottlenecks in terms of a number of students. The generic applications described above can be used for quick demonstrations, practical exercises and projects. However, they usually do not provide a feedback needed to validate solutions to programming assignments. For example, whether the program produced a correct result or has a good performance. Such immediate feedback is crucial for students since it helps to avoid manual validation and to focus on the solution. This feedback can also help instructors to reduce the time and effort needed to grade the solution.

The automated evaluation of assignments requires development of problem-specific services that run the program against the custom test suite. Such services can be implemented on Everest using the same approach as the previously

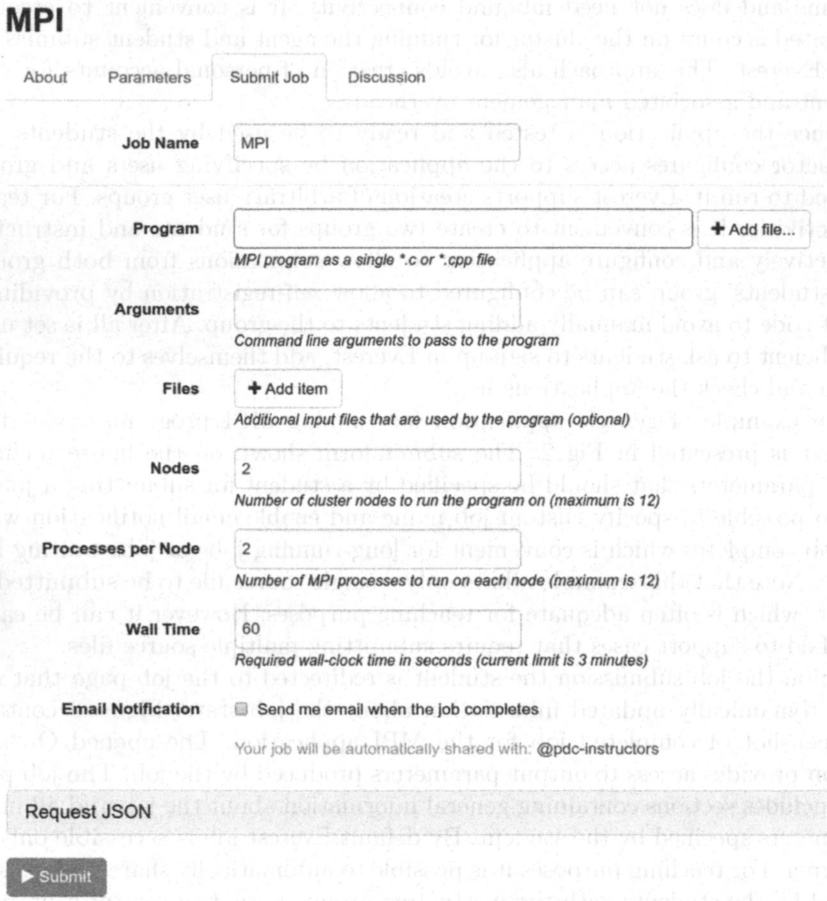

MPI

| About | Parameters | Submit Job | Discussion |

Job Name   MPI

Program   [   ] **+ Add file...**
MPI program as a single *.c or *.cpp file

Arguments   [   ]
Command line arguments to pass to the program

Files   **+ Add item**
Additional input files that are used by the program (optional)

Nodes   2
Number of cluster nodes to run the program on (maximum is 12)

Processes per Node   2
Number of MPI processes to run on each node (maximum is 12)

Wall Time   60
Required wall-clock time in seconds (current limit is 3 minutes)

Email Notification   ☐ Send me email when the job completes
Your job will be automatically shared with: @pdc-instructors

Request JSON

▶ Submit

Fig. 2. Submit form of generic application for running MPI programs

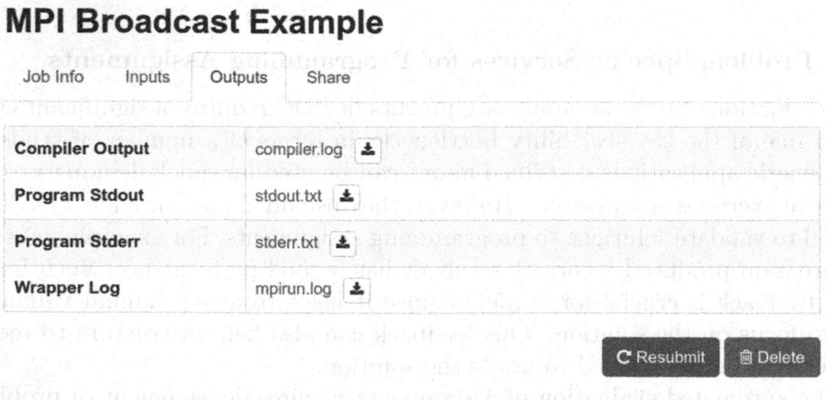

MPI Broadcast Example

| Job Info | Inputs | Outputs | Share |

Compiler Output	compiler.log ⬇
Program Stdout	stdout.txt ⬇
Program Stderr	stderr.txt ⬇
Wrapper Log	mpirun.log ⬇

C Resubmit   **🗑 Delete**

Fig. 3. Results of completed MPI job

discussed generic services. However, in this case the wrapper is replaced by a test suite for the given assignment that can execute a program multiple times with different runtime parameters and performs additional actions such as result validation and performance measurements. The outputs of problem-specific applications can include validation results, performance metrics and scores, etc.

4   Use Cases

The described approach and Everest have been successfully used since 2014 to support two PDC courses for students of various levels.

The Parallel and Distributed Computing course at The Yandex School of Data Analysis (YSDA, Moscow, Russia) is an introductory PDC course for MSc students that features the following topics: concurrency, parallel programming and distributed data processing. The course grade is based on the results of homework assignments implying writing parallel and distributed programs that are executed on a dedicated compute cluster.

The use of Everest in the YSDA course started in 2014 by development of services for evaluation of homework assignments. These services have been improved and are actively used in this course since that time. Until 2016 no generic services for running parallel programs were used, and students had direct access to the YSDA cluster via personal SSH accounts.

In 2015 a similar approach has been applied for teaching High Performance Computing course for BSc students from the Faculty of Computer Science at the Higher School of Economics (HSE, Moscow, Russia). In order to simplify working with the cluster, in addition to problem-specific services, new generic services for running different types of parallel programs have been introduced. Such services also helped to arrange more practical exercises and demos in the class. The students had no problem with accessing Everest via a web browser and were able to quickly learn and successfully use the provided services for submitting their programs both in class and while working on homework assignments.

In 2016 the complete approach using both generic and problem-specific services was used during teaching YSDA course. This time the students were able to perform all practical activities via Everest without directly accessing the cluster. As an option, it was possible to request a cluster account as in previous years to get an additional practical experience. However, only a few students used this option during the course and none of them has completely switched from using Everest to the cluster command line. The decreased support overhead and increased level of automation helped to scale the course to a larger number of students (118 enrolled students in comparison to 80 in 2015 and 48 in 2014).

According to existing experience the development of a service takes from an hour to several days depending on case. The majority of the time is consumed by implementing and debugging a wrapper or a test suite written in Python or Bash. The development of test suites and corresponding services is usually more time consuming than generic services where some previous code can be reused.

In the rest of this section we provide an overview of various services used in the mentioned courses grouped by the core subjects.

4.1   Multi-threaded Programming

Both courses include introduction to concurrency and multi-threaded programming. The C++ programming language and the standard thread support library are used for writing concurrent programs. During this part students examine various pitfalls of concurrent programming, learn how to avoid them and perform coordination between threads.

Since the students usually have no problem with compiling and running multi-threaded programs on their machines, there were no need in development of generic services for running such programs on a cluster. However, the development of problem-specific services for testing homework assignments proved to be extremely useful.

For example, in the Dining Philosophers task the students should solve the well-known problem by meeting the basic safely and liveness guarantees while also ensuring fairness, performance and scalability of their solution. The students are provided with an initial implementation that is not safe and serves as a template for a student's solution. A test suite for evaluation of solutions has been developed that performs checking of all requirements by running a program under various conditions. Besides checking safety and liveness, the test suite also measures fairness, performance and scalability of the solution. The key metrics used are min-max ratio of eat counts and mean wait time in hungry state. The scalability is evaluated by increasing the number of philosophers up to 5000. The test suite prints results of each test and overall summary including scores for all requirements and the total grade.

The developed test suite was provided to the students as a service that takes a program and runs the tests against it on a cluster. To ensure the reliable and reproducible evaluation each test run was configured to use a whole cluster node.

4.2   Parallel Programming

The parallel programming part considers OpenMP and MPI, the two most popular technologies used for shared and distributed memory systems respectively. The generic services are developed for running both kinds of parallel programs on the cluster.

While it is quite easy to compile and run OpenMP programs on students' machines, the OpenMP service provided the students with the ability to run a program on a high-end server with 12 processor cores. The input parameters include the program, command arguments, additional files and number of threads to use, while the output parameters include compiler and program outputs.

The generic MPI service enabled students to compile and run MPI programs with different runtime configurations on the cluster. The interface of this service was already presented in Sect. 3.

The YSDA course includes a programming assignment with two tasks covering both technologies. In the first task the students should implement a parallel version of the K-means method using OpenMP. A sequential implementation of the method in C++ is provided as a starting point along with a generator of input data. The solution is required to produce the same result as the initial program on the same dataset. The second task considers a parallel implementation of the Game of Life using MPI. Similarly the students are provided with a reference sequential program in C and an input data generator.

A test suite and an Everest application is developed for each task. Both test suites have a similar structure. They compile a solution and perform multiple runs with different runtime configuration (number of threads or processes), input files and other parameters. The execution time, speedup and efficiency are measured for each run. The results of a run are compared with the reference values. This enables a complete evaluation of a solution including its' correctness, performance, scalability, and dependence on input parameters. Figure 4 contains a screenshot of completed submission for the MPI assignment.

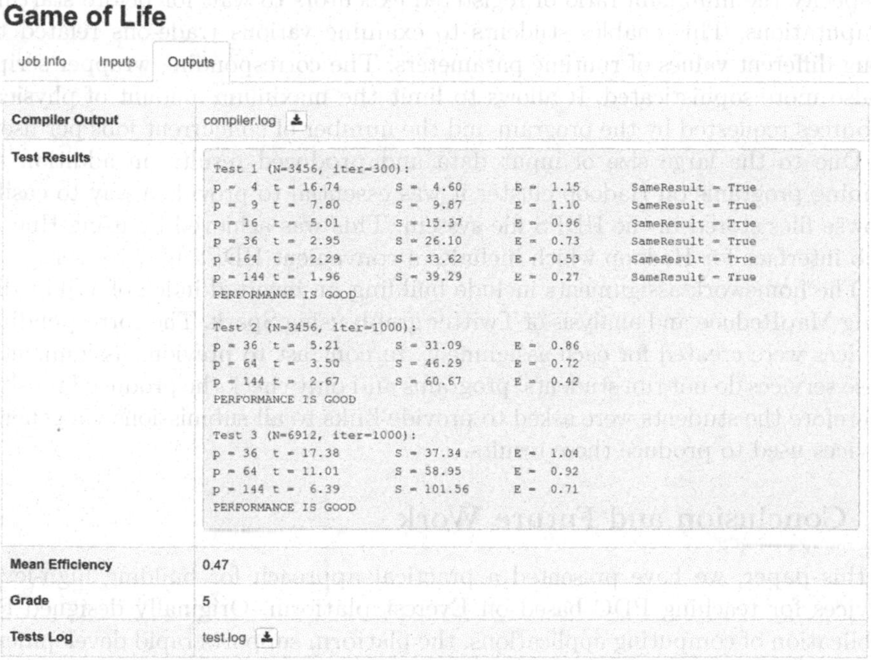

Fig. 4. Results of testing Game of Life assignment

4.3 Distributed Data Processing

This part considers distributed computing models and platforms for processing of large data sets, which are being actively developed during the last decade. Students learn the MapReduce programming model and its implementation in the Apache Hadoop platform. Another popular framework for distributed data processing considered in both courses is Apache Spark.

Two generic services were implemented for running MapReduce programs written in Python and Java respectively on the Hadoop cluster. Both services allow specifying program files, command line arguments, input and output paths in HDFS, number of reduce tasks and additional Hadoop options. The wrapper script performs submission of MapReduce job, monitors the job's state and updates status information displayed in Everest. When the job is running, a student is provided with a link to the job status page in the Hadoop web interface. After the job is completed the total resource usage in core-seconds is displayed along with a link to the job history interface with task logs. This provides enough information to troubleshoot failed programs or evaluate the program's efficiency.

Two similar services were implemented for running Spark programs written in Python or Scala/Java on the same cluster. In comparison to MapReduce services, the Spark services have more sophisticated runtime parameters such as the number of executors, cores and memory per executor. It is also possible to specify the minimum ratio of registered executors to wait for before starting computations. This enables students to examine various trade-offs related to using different values of runtime parameters. The corresponding wrapper script is also more sophisticated. It allows to limit the maximum amount of physical resources requested by the program and the number of concurrent jobs per user.

Due to the large size of input data and produced results, in addition to running programs on Hadoop cluster it was essential to provide a way to easily browse files stored in the HDFS file system. This was achieved by using Hue, a Web interface for Hadoop which includes a convenient HDFS file browser.

The homework assignments include building an inverted index of Wikipedia using MapReduce and analysis of Twitter graph using Spark. The corresponding services were created for each assignment. In contrast to previous assignments, these services do not run students' programs and only check the produced results. Therefore the students were asked to provide links to all submissions via generic services used to produce these results.

5   Conclusion and Future Work

In this paper, we have presented a practical approach for building high-level services for teaching PDC based on Everest platform. Originally designed for publication of computing applications, the platform supports rapid development of various types of computational web services. In particular, as was demonstrated by using Everest for teaching introductory PDC courses, the platform is suitable for building services for running different types of parallel programs on HPC resources, as well as services for evaluation of practical assignments.

The use of discussed services helped to provide easy-to-use interfaces to students and to reduce administration overheads. The problem-specific services ensured reliable and reproducible execution of test suites against students' solutions while providing immediate feedback to students and assisting grading by instructors.

Everest has a number of unique features in comparison to related solutions. It implements the PaaS model by supporting multiple users and providing all its functionality via remote web and programming interfaces. The latter enable integration of the platform and applications with external systems. Everest is not tied to a predefined computing infrastructure by enabling users to attach arbitrary resources and bind them to applications. This makes it possible to immediately start using Everest without installation. The platform is publicly available online to all interested users [1].

Being a general-purpose platform, Everest lacks a number of high-level features in comparison to specialized solutions. For example, in order to create a service an instructor should write a wrapper script or test suite implementing all necessary actions. While providing maximum flexibility, this approach often requires writing a boilerplate code dealing with cluster job submission or results checking. We plan to address these issues in future by implementing additional features in Everest and publishing ready-to-use blueprints to quickly reproduce the discussed services by other PDC educators.

Acknowledgements. This work is supported by the Russian Science Foundation (project No. 16-11-10352).

References

1. Everest. http://everest.distcomp.org/
2. Heterogeneous Parallel Programming. https://www.coursera.org/course/hetero
3. Dincer, K., Fox, G.C.: Design issues in building web-based parallel programming environments. In: 1997 Proceedings of the Sixth IEEE International Symposium on High Performance Distributed Computing, pp. 283–292. IEEE (1997)
4. Garrity, P., Yates, T., Brown, R., Shoop, E.: Webmapreduce: an accessible and adaptable tool for teaching map-reduce computing. In: Proceedings of the 42nd ACM Technical Symposium on Computer Science Education, pp. 183–188. ACM (2011)
5. Maggi, P., Sisto, R.: A grid-powered framework to support courses on distributed programming. IEEE Trans. Educ. **50**(1), 27–33 (2007)
6. Nowicki, M., Marchwiany, M., Szpindler, M., Bała, P.: On-line service for teaching parallel programming. In: Hunold, S., et al. (eds.) Euro-Par 2015. LNCS, vol. 9523, pp. 78–89. Springer, Cham (2015). doi:10.1007/978-3-319-27308-2_7
7. Richardson, L., Ruby, S.: RESTful web services. O'Reilly Media Inc., Sebastopol (2008)
8. Schlarb, M., Hundt, C., Schmidt, B.: SAUCE: a web-based automated assessment tool for teaching parallel programming. In: Hunold, S., et al. (eds.) Euro-Par 2015. LNCS, vol. 9523, pp. 54–65. Springer, Cham (2015). doi:10.1007/978-3-319-27308-2_5
9. Sukhoroslov, O., Volkov, S., Afanasiev, A.: A web-based platform for publication and distributed execution of computing applications. In: 2015 14th International Symposium on Parallel and Distributed Computing (ISPDC), pp. 175–184, June 2015
10. Touriño, J., Martín, M.J., Tarrío, J., Arenaz, M.: A grid portal for an undergraduate parallel programming course. IEEE Trans. Educ. **48**(3), 391–399 (2005)

Experiences with Teaching a Second Year Distributed Computing Course

Rizos Sakellariou[✉]

School of Computer Science, University of Manchester, Manchester, UK
rizos@manchester.ac.uk

Abstract. The proliferation of parallel and distributed computing in the last years has led to calls for the early introduction of parallel and distributed computing in the undergraduate curriculum arguing that the topic should and can be offered at different levels but some basic knowledge must be acquired by every computer science graduate. However, there is no widespread agreement on how this can be achieved. This paper contributes to the debate by presenting the approach and experiences from designing and teaching a second year undergraduate distributed computing course that has been running for a decade in the School of Computer Science of the University of Manchester. The course evolved to follow an approach which presents material in a way that attempts to emphasize the importance of four key pillars of abstraction, which underpin the design and management of modern distributed systems, namely: trade-offs, failures, concurrency and synchronization, performance. The paper presents the details of this approach arguing that the use of suitable abstractions allows for a rewarding learning experience that helps students familiarize with and appreciate the challenges of distributed computing at an early stage.

1 Introduction

The so-called "triumph of parallel computing" [9] is indisputable. Whether in the presence of multiple CPUs in everyday computing devices or as part of large-scale infrastructures such as Google, parallel and distributed computing manifests itself nowadays as a mainstream Computer Science topic. However, there are several indications that this trend has not fully found its way into the Computer Science curriculum, especially to the degree that would be desirable in order to train successfully future computer scientists. Motivated by such observations, a report [7], produced by a working group aiming to develop curricular guidelines for Computer Science and Engineering undergraduates, tried to identify essential topics and concepts and where in the curriculum they could be incorporated to ensure that *"all students graduating with a bachelor's degree in computer science/computer engineering receive an education that prepares them in the area of parallel and distributed computing, preparation which is increasingly important in the light of emerging technology"* [7]. Despite the elaborate discussion of how and where different concepts need to be introduced, the report did not really

© Springer International Publishing AG 2017
F. Desprez et al. (Eds.): Euro-Par 2016 Workshops, LNCS 10104, pp. 28–37, 2017.
DOI: 10.1007/978-3-319-58943-5_3

make concrete suggestions for specific new courses tailored towards an early introduction of parallel and distributed computing in the curriculum.

Traditionally, parallel and distributed computing courses have been considered as advanced courses taught at advanced undergraduate or postgraduate level. To a large extent, this reflects the historical development of parallel and distributed computing and the long track record of specialized research in the area[1]. As a result of the need to prepare graduates better in terms of parallel and distributed computing background, one may be tempted, as in [7], to identify the key concepts that need to be introduced early in the curriculum. However, as some of these concepts have been developed as part of previous specialized research, especially at a time when parallel and distributed computing was not a mainstream topic, the question is whether they carry the stamp of their time and origins, which makes them not easily amenable to early undergraduates. In other words, the question is whether educators need to think about some extra level of abstraction to introduce early undergraduates to parallel and distributed computing without risking losing them through early exposure to low-level 'heavyweight' details. Such a level of abstraction can also address the requirement to teach students principles that *"will remain relevant and abiding for the unforeseeable technologies of the next decade"*, a need that was eloquently identified in [3].

As part of a curriculum redesign more than ten years ago, it has been decided to introduce Distributed Computing to the second year programme of the primarily 3-year degree of the School of Computer Science of the University of Manchester, starting Spring 2007. The author (along with a team of two colleagues) has been responsible for the initial design of the course and since then he has delivered it (jointly or as the sole instructor since 2012) every spring with the exception of 2009 when he was on sabbatical leave. In total, over 1100 students have taken the course during these ten years. Following this experience, this paper will present:

- a detailed view on how the course has been organized and delivered;
- the approach followed/developed, which tried to emphasize four main pillars at a high level of abstraction, namely: trade-offs, failures, concurrency and synchronization, performance; and,
- some observations and suggestions stemming from the 10-year experience.

The rest of the paper is structured as follows. Section 2 presents the syllabus including lecture topics and laboratory assignments. Section 3 presents the main abstraction pillars used to introduce the course. Section 4 discusses observations from the 10-year experience. Finally, Sect. 5 concludes the paper.

---

[1] Parallel and Distributed Computing is treated here as a single field, same as in [7] and in line with most modern views and classifications. However, it should not be forgotten that parallel (primarily aiming towards high-performance) computing on one hand and distributed computing on the other have been kept apart for many years, each with its own history and research; it is only in recent years that common aspects and principles have (re)gained importance leading to some sort of convergence.

2 Syllabus

2.1 Background

The course is offered as part of the 2nd year program of the School of Computer Science of the University of Manchester during the Spring semester, which runs for twelve weeks (interrupted by the Easter break), typically from late January to the beginning of May. The method of study consists of twenty-two 50-minute lecture slots and five 2-hour laboratory sessions, where students work on specific assignments. Assessment is based on a 2-hour closed book examination, which counts for 80% of the overall mark, and marking of the laboratory assignments counting for the remaining 20%. In recent years about 150 students register for the course each year, reflecting the rather large size of the Computer Science intake of the University of Manchester. The majority of these students study towards a 3-year BSc degree in Computer Science.

2.2 Lecture Topics

Fourteen of the lecture slots are used to introduce and discuss the course topics. These topics broadly cover issues related to: (i) motivation for parallel and distributed systems; (ii) communication; (iii) naming; (iv) synchronization (including logical timing and coordination); (v) failure management; (vi) advanced topics. The remaining slots are used for guest lectures, introducing and motivating laboratory work and revision. Lectures are supported by handouts and references to two core textbooks [4,10].

Most specifically, the fourteen slots are dedicated to the following topics:

1. *Introduction to Distributed Computing:* In addition to providing the rubric for the course, the lecture is used to motivate the challenges of distributed systems using for this the so-called "eight fallacies of distributed systems" [2]. Although more than twenty years old by now, these fallacies have an important educational value as they provide a wealth of opportunities to introduce and motivate the challenges of developing distributed systems.

2. *Introduction to Parallel Computing:* The lecture is used to introduce the need for performance and the concept of scalability. Application examples are presented and Amdahl's law (despite criticism [9]) is used as a way to highlight the impact of inherently sequential parts of an application. At the same time, alternative approaches to get an upper bound on parallelism using the work of the critical path are discussed and illustrated with scientific workflow applications that appear to gain momentum as an important class of applications that benefit from parallelism and large-scale distributed computing [11].

3. *Models and Architectures:* The focus of the lecture is on different architectures and models to build distributed systems. The trade-offs of different solutions, such as client-server versus P2P, are discussed and used to highlight the observation that there is not a single architectural solution that fits everything.

4. *RPC and RMI:* The lecture introduces Remote Procedure Calls (RPCs) as a way to provide a high-level alternative to low-level send and receive constructs. The context in which the first practical implementations of RPC were developed as well as the criticism often made are mentioned and used to understand how current solutions and problems may inherit the legacy of the past. In addition, as the Computer Science syllabus in Manchester is using Java as the introductory programming language in the first year, RMI is described as the Java approach to RPC.

5. *Exercises on RPC and RMI:* These exercises attempt to consolidate understanding but also to introduce more specialized topics such as 'call by copy/restore', at-least-once and at-most-once semantics and contrast between RPC and messaging.

6. *Name and Directory Servers:* This lecture discusses naming issues following the Internet Domain Name System as a running example.

7. *Time and Logical Clocks:* This lecture discusses approaches to deal with the lack of global clock in distributed systems. Lamport clocks and Vector clocks are introduced and their properties are explained and discussed.

8. *Coordination and Agreement:* This lecture is used to motivate and describe two classical algorithms for election of a coordinator such as ring-based election and the Bully algorithm.

9. *Transactions:* This lecture is used to introduce the problems that arise from unexpected failures and the importance of treating some operations as atomic operations using as a motivating example the problems that may occur during a bank transfer if a crash occurs half way through the transfer. The four key properties of transactions, known with the acronym ACID, are introduced, and there is a discussion of how transactions can be implemented.

10. *Distributed Transactions:* This lecture describes in more detail the issues with respect to the implementation of transactions and highlights the need to strike a balance between enforcement of transaction constraints and concurrency. Furthermore, the lecture motivates distributed transactions, describes protocols such as one-phase and two-phase commit and discusses problems that may arise in this context such as distributed deadlocks and how they can be detected.

11. *Byzantine Fault Tolerance:* This lecture is used to introduce students to some key results on arbitrary (byzantine) failures. The impossibility of making an agreement when there are three generals (one of whom is a traitor) as well as a protocol for an agreement when there are four generals, three of whom are loyal, are illustrated using examples from the original 1982 paper [5]. Occasionally, the issues with Byzantine failures are illustrated in the class by assigning the role of loyal or traitor general to groups of students and let them emulate the process of trying to make an agreement.

12. *Replication:* This lecture discusses the benefits as well as the cost of replication and describes some fundamental consistency models, such as sequential consistency, causal consistency and eventual consistency. Algorithms for placing replicas are also discussed.

13. *The Integration Game:* This lecture focuses on interoperability and standardization as mechanisms that enable the development of large systems primarily focusing on a service-based model.
14. *Cloud Computing and advanced topics:* This lecture traces back the historical development of Grid computing and the move to the Cloud. It highlights problems stemming from the sheer size of data that a number of applications produce as well as the distributed collaborative nature of such applications.

Two guest lectures are typically offered every year (subject to availability). One of the guest lecturers typically comes from the banking sector and helps students understand how some of the concepts discussed in the course are present in the problems faced by a demanding, large-scale, real-world environment. Another guest lecturer with expert knowledge has often been invited to discuss more advanced topics: in early years in relation to grid computing and e-Science, in recent years in relation to Cloud Computing and virtualization.

2.3 Laboratory Assignments

There are three laboratory assignments, each one serving a different purpose and addressing different aspects of the course, exposing students to different concepts. The assignments have been repeated every year with only minor changes or adjustments.

The first assignment is a simple exercise whose only purpose is to introduce students to three different mechanisms for implementing a client-server interaction. The three mechanisms are sockets, Java RMI and Java servlets. The choice has partly been driven by the particular study programme which uses Java as an introductory programming language. This is a simple exercise but it helps introduce concepts that are not taught at an earlier stage.

The second assignment is the main laboratory exercise, counting for 60% of the laboratory mark. In this exercise students are asked to write a client to interact with a server through HTTP and XML and make a booking. Each student's client competes with other students' clients for the booking. The idea is that a server advertises 200 slots for a band and 200 slots for a hotel and a client is asked to find the earliest common slot to arrange both a band and a hotel for a wedding as soon as possible. The server introduces random failures and delays, which requires students to build robust clients capable of dealing with such problems if they arise. Bookings are made and changed all the time, which suggests that any information on availability of slots may be quickly out-of-date and a slot that appears to be free may already be taken before a request to book it is issued. To avoid having a number of clients monopolize the server, students are asked to include a deliberate delay of one second between successive requests and they are limited to two bookings for each of band and hotel. The use of a controlled environment for the server facilitates the introduction of delays and random failures (e.g., server unavailable) that help students realize the importance of building robust code.

The third assignment asks students to build a simple discrete-event simulator that simulates a queue-based system where: (i) requests arrive at a given rate; (ii) each request requires a certain amount of server time; (iii) a number of servers can serve requests from a queue that initially stores requests; and, (iv) the size of the queue is limited. For given values of each of these four parameters, students are asked to calculate over a period of time: (i) average queue size; (ii) average response time for requests; and, (iii) percentage of requests rejected. This exercise helps students appreciate the value of performance modelling and simulation as a mechanism for capacity planning when building a distributed system.

3   Objectives and Key Abstraction Pillars

The main intended learning outcome of the course, as advertised to students, is to make them aware of the principles, techniques and methods involved when dealing with distributed systems. There are four key abstractions along with a number of lesser ones that summarize the key principles emphasized through-out the course. Following the experience over the years it has emerged that an emphasis on these abstractions would create the right mindset to help students from an early level to acquire a good understanding of the issues in distributed systems.

Trade-Offs in the Design of Distributed Systems: An important message for an early course on parallel and distributed computing is to infuse the concept of trade-off between different objectives that need to be considered when designing, building and using distributed systems. Especially for distributed computing in the early years of the curriculum it is important to make clear that such trade-offs exist and emphasize their main direct implication: there is not a single solution that fits everything. Although some of the trade-offs may be relatively obvious or, in their general form, they may have been around for long enough (e.g., the interplay between cost and performance), it appears that less obvious trade-offs emerge. Taking into account the increasing heterogeneity of modern platforms, the different options made available to users and the scales envisaged for tackling new problems, one could argue that even more interesting trade-offs will emerge in parallel and distributed computing. One needs only consider frequency scaling, a technique commonly used nowadays, and ponder about how it affects the interplay between energy, cost, and performance, in not easy to predict ways [6,8]. This suggests that creating a mindset directed towards the detection and appreciation of such trade-offs is particularly important as an essential parallel and distributed computing skill for future computer scientists. The first example of a trade-off that is used early enough in the module to motivate students is a consequence of one of the eight fallacies, "latency is not zero", and relates to the interplay between latency and bandwidth. It can be easily realized that over a low-latency network the time to send several remote requests will primarily be affected by bandwidth; in this case, many small-sized requests will result in a good execution time. However, over a high-latency network, latency will dominate and many remote requests may result in long execution times because of the high latency; in this case, it can be faster to send one large-sized request to avoid the cost of high-latency. Interestingly enough, such an issue received high-profile attention as recently as 2006 in the context of a popular browser, leading to the suggestion that "computing over a high-latency network means you have to bulk up" [1].

Dealing with Failures: There is an old quote by Leslie Lamport that suggests that "a distributed system is one in which the failure of a computer you didn't even know existed can render your own computer unusable". The message that effective distributed systems need to address failures and the primary approach to do this is some sort of redundancy is repeatedly made during the course. The second laboratory assignment helps reinforce this message by getting students realize that client code that may work once is not necessarily robust enough to deal with everything that may go wrong. It is often the case that several students realize the importance of managing unpredictable situations during this laboratory exercise, something that suggests that appreciating the importance to deal with failures requires exposure to failure handling both from a theoretical and from a practical point of view.

Implications of Concurrency: Concurrency is introduced very early in the course, primarily focusing on embarrassingly parallel applications as they provide an easy way to demonstrate the benefits of parallelism and some of them are easily recognizable by students (e.g., online games). The implications of concurrent execution are discussed as a means to motivate transactions following a classical example of concurrent accesses to the same banking accounts. This allows for a good discussion of the trade-off between synchronization and the amount of parallelism available, something which is also discussed in the context of the second laboratory exercise where excessive locking would help with individual implementations but at the same time it would reduce the overall degree of parallelism in the system. It is argued that such a simple example-driven approach helps illustrate parallelism/concurrency step-by-step without overloading students with the complexity of specialized application examples often seen in the delivery of traditional high-performance computing courses. If anything, the argument is that, in the early curriculum, the illustration of concurrency and its implications or trade-offs (especially the trade-offs and interplay between concurrency and computation versus communication or synchronization) requires even more simple examples that what are currently offered by standard textbooks.

The Quest for Performance: Performance has been a key objective in the traditional parallel computing curriculum, however, it has been often downgraded in distributed computing. Nevertheless, performance objectives are always present in reality[2] and they are emphasized in different parts of the course, also in terms of capacity planning as part of the third laboratory assignment.

4 Discussion

The approach that was described above in organizing the course seems to work well. The overall student assessment of the course has been positive, consistently among the best of the year. Performance during the final examination, based on a mix of bookwork and small problem solving exercises, seems to indicate that a number of students get a good understanding of some key concepts related to distributed computing. Judging from the experience over the last decade, it appears that, in recent years, students come with an already improved understanding of distributed systems, which could be partly a result of the everyday use of many widespread distributed applications or smartphones. As a matter of fact, in early years the average mark (grade) of the students attending the course was significantly lower than their overall average mark for the year. In recent years, marks have improved (without any significant changes in the style or difficulty of the examination paper) and the average mark of the students attending the course has been broadly in line with their overall average mark for the year. This observation raises the bar with respect to the new topics and angles that have to be adopted to keep the course interesting and relevant on one hand but also to prepare students for future challenges in relation to parallel and distributed computing.

The generation of an ever increasing amount of data and the suggestion that many future distributed applications may need to handle large volumes of data raises a question on what is the best approach to introduce students to the challenges involved. During the course, there are only passing references to the volumes of data that may have to be handled in the future. This may have to followed-up by more advanced courses, especially as anecdotal evidence seems to suggest that addressing large-scale software requirements seems to be a skill much desired by industry. An additional issue that is also mentioned in passing is the issue of economy. The ever increasing availability of resources (memory, storage, etc.) often tempts programmers to write code without consideration of the amount of resources consumed. Even though earlier generations were used to face limited resources this skill seems to have gone away with the dramatic increase in the amount of resources. Yet, the increasing importance on issues such as energy minimization may suggest that resource-efficient programming will become more important in the future than it is now. This may have to be introduced in an early parallel and distributed computing course as an additional dimension whose trade-offs need to be considered.

---

[2] A guest lecturer from industry once mentioned how important and time-consuming it had been to find quick solutions in his company to ship large files between the UK and USA. Eventually the answer relied on tailored versions of TCP/IP but the solution was found through third-party products after a significant amount of time had been spent internally.

During the course, an attempt is made to give an historical perspective wherever possible. This is useful to understand the limitations of some approaches, which may have been excellent solutions at the time they were devised but may be holding understanding back in today's settings. Some examples were already given. It can be argued that giving a good historical perspective and associating different algorithms and techniques with problems and context at the time they were developed enables students to see beyond earlier limitations. In one particular case, however, when discussing consistency models, it appears that the common notation used to illustrate examples of different protocols (also adopted by [4,10]) carries lots of weight from distributed shared memory days and, every year it becomes one of the most puzzling topics for students. The question is to what extent a different notation that presents examples at a coarse-grain level (as opposed to the standard fine-grain, variable level currently used) could make things easier to understand.

An issue that clearly merits some discussion in a distributed computing course is security although one would expect that security issues are primarily addressed by specialized courses. In early versions of the course there was one lecture on security, which was dropped due to time limitations and because it was not necessarily good value for the time spent. However, one pertinent issue that has been discussed as part of the second laboratory exercise was denial of service attacks, as many students inadvertently did not add the requested one second delay in their code between successive requests to the server; such cases were monitored and, when detected, were used to discuss the problem of denial of service attack as well as the importance of capacity planning, that is planning server resources in line with the number of expected requests over a period of time.

Finally, it is interesting to trace how the course has evolved over the years to reflect experience gained, and student background in addition to changes in the field (most notably the transition from grid computing to cloud computing). The early design of the course tried to come up with a set of mostly self-contained lectures that described selected algorithms from the mainstream distributed computing literature (as an initial reference point the fourth edition of [4,10] were used). Over the years, a connecting link was developed, which crystallized in the key abstraction pillars described in Sect. 3, but most of the initial lectures remained largely unchanged. However, students in recent years started raising more often questions that added extra dimensions of complexity to some of the classical algorithms (e.g., byzantine problems with communication uncertainty, ring-based election in the presence of failures and so on). At the same time, it is the author's impression that many concepts or algorithms (such as logical clocks or election algorithms) were more easily understood and digested by students in recent years than they were in early years. This observation raises the question of whether there is scope for educators to enhance the description of some of the problems addressed by the relevant algorithms (some of which, even though classical, are a few decades old) to improve the student learning experience and possibly match some of today's problems more closely.

5   Conclusion

This paper has presented the structure of a second year distributed computing course offered by the School of Computer Science of the University of Manchester for the last decade. The approach tried to build on four main pillars at a high-level of abstraction, which allowed the introduction of a number of distributed computing topics at an early level in the curriculum. This suggests that in order to appreciate the growing challenges of the field and prepare future computer scientists well, early introduction of parallel and distributed computing in the curriculum may benefit from the introduction of and emphasis on suitable abstractions as part of appropriately (and holistically) designed courses more than simply moving some advanced (and possibly difficult to understand without suitable context) concepts to different parts of the early curriculum.

Acknowledgements. The author would like to thank Chris Kirkham and Dean Kuo who were members of the team that designed the original course. Chris, in particular, who jointly delivered the course until 2011 when he retired, and his long experience in computing contributed enormously in the early years of the course. Special thanks are also due to a number of Teaching Assistants who assisted with laboratories, the guest lecturers, and, above all, the over 1100 students who attended the course during the last ten years and helped shape it and evolve. Finally, detailed course information is available from: http://studentnet.cs.manchester.ac.uk/ugt/COMP28112/.

References

1. https://blogs.msdn.microsoft.com/oldnewthing/20060407-25/?p=31613/
2. https://en.wikipedia.org/wiki/Fallacies_of_distributed_computing
3. Adams, J., Brown, R., Shoop, E., Patterns, E.: Compelling strategies for teaching parallel and distributed computing to CS undergraduates. In: 27th IEEE International Parallel and Distributed Processing Symposium Workshops (IPDPSW), EduPar 2013 (2013)
4. Coulouris, G., Dollimore, J., Kindberg, T., Blair, G., Systems, D.: Concepts and Design, 5th edn. Addison-Wesley, Boston (2011)
5. Lamport, L., Shostak, R., Pease, M.: The Byzantine generals problem. ACM Trans. Program. Lang. Syst. (TOPLAS) **4**(3), 382–401 (1982)
6. Pietri, I., Sakellariou, R.: Cost-efficient CPU provisioning for scientific workflows on clouds. In: Altmann, J., Silaghi, G.C., Rana, O.F. (eds.) GECON 2015. LNCS, vol. 9512, pp. 49–64. Springer, Cham (2016). doi:10.1007/978-3-319-43177-2_4
7. Prasad, S.K., Gupta, A., Kant, K., Lumsdaine, A., Padua, D., Robert, Y., Rosenberg, A., Sussman, A., Weems, C.: Literacy for all in parallel and distributed computing: guidelines for an undergraduate core curriculum. CSI J. Comput. **1**(2), 81–95 (2012)
8. Rauber, T., Rünger, G.: Modeling and analyzing the energy consumption of fork-join-based task parallel programs. Concurr. Comput.: Pract. Exp. **27**(1), 211–236 (2015)
9. Schreiber, R.: A few bad ideas on the way to the triumph of parallel computing. J. Parallel Distrib. Comput. **74**(7), 2544–2547 (2014)
10. Tanenbaum, A.S., Van Steen, M.: Distributed Systems: Principles and Paradigms, 2nd edn. Prentice-Hall, Upper Saddle River (2006)
11. Taylor, I.J., Deelman, E., Gannon, D.B., Shields, M.: Workflows for e-Science: Scientific Workflows for Grids. Springer, Heidelberg (2014)

HETEROPAR - Workshop on Algorithms, Models and Tools for Parallel Computing on Heterogeneous Platforms

Distributed In-GPU Data Cache
for Document-Oriented Data Store via PCIe
over 10 Gbit Ethernet

Shin Morishima[1]([✉]) and Hiroki Matsutani[1,2,3]

[1] Keio University, 3-14-1 Hiyoshi, Kohoku-ku, Yokohama 223-8522, Japan
{morisima,matutani}@arc.ics.keio.ac.jp
[2] National Institute of Informatics, Tokyo, Japan
[3] Japan Science and Technology Agency PRESTO, Kawaguchi, Japan

Abstract. As one of NOSQL data stores, a document-oriented data store manages data as documents in a scheme-less manner. Various string match queries, such as a perfect match, begins-with (prefix) match, partial match, and regular expression based match, are performed for the documents. To accelerate such string match queries, we propose DistGPU Cache (Distributed In-GPU Data Cache), in which data store server and GPU devices are connected via a PCI-Express (PCIe) over 10 Gbit Ethernet (10 GbE), so that GPU devices that store and search documents can be added and removed dynamically. We also propose a partitioning method that distributes ranges of cached documents to GPU devices based on a hash function. The distributed cache over GPU devices can be dynamically divided and merged when the GPU devices are added and removed, respectively. We evaluate the proposed DistGPU Cache in terms of regular expression match query throughput with up to three NVIDIA GeForce GTX 980 devices connected to a host via PCIe over 10 GbE. We demonstrate that the communication overhead of remote GPU devices is small and can be compensated by a great flexibility to add more GPU devices via a network. We also show that DistGPU Cache with the remote GPU devices significantly outperforms the original data store.

1 Introduction

Recent advances on Social Networking Services, Internet of Things technologies, mobile devices, and sensing technologies are continuously generating large data sets, and a simple, scalable, and high-throughput data store is a key component for managing such big data. Structured storage or NOSQL is an attractive option for storing large data sets in addition to traditional RDBMS. NOSQL data stores typically employ a simple data structure optimized for high horizontal scalability on some selected application domains via sharding and replication over number of machines. Due to these features, NOSQL data stores are increasing their presence in Web applications and cloud-based systems that store and manage big data.

F. Desprez et al. (Eds.): Euro-Par 2016 Workshops, LNCS 10104, pp. 41–55, 2017.
DOI: 10.1007/978-3-319-58943-5_4

Document-oriented data store [1,2] is one of major classes of NOSQL. In a document-oriented data store, data are typically stored as documents in a JSON-like binary format without any predefined data structure or schema; thus it is referred to as a scheme-less data store. In the document-oriented data store, a search query retrieves documents whose values are matched to a search condition given by the search query. Especially, string search queries, such as perfect, begins-with (prefix), and regular expression based string match queries, are used in document-oriented data stores. Since the computation cost for string search increases as the number of documents increases, it becomes quite high when dealing with large data sets. To mitigate the computation cost increase, database indexes are typically employed in document-oriented data stores [7], in order to reduce the cost from $O(n)$ to $O(\log n)$, where n is the number of documents. Database indexing is a powerful technique especially for perfect and prefix string match queries. However, it cannot be directly applied to some important string search queries, such as partial and regular expression based string match queries, although database indexes for regular expression based search have been studied. A motivation of this paper is to accelerate search queries of the document-oriented data store without relying on database indexes.

To accelerate all the string search queries including the regular expression based search in document-oriented data stores, an array-based cache suitable for GPU processing of string search queries was proposed in [5]. The cache is extracted from the original document-oriented data store. When the document-oriented data store receives a string search query, the query is performed by a GPU device using the cache and the search result is returned to the original document-oriented data store. However, a serious problem of the cache is that, since it targets only a single GPU device, it is inefficient for data larger than a device memory capacity of a single GPU device. Thus, a horizontal scalability to add more GPU devices and increase the device memory capacity is required to manage a larger data set. In addition, since the number of documents in the data store increases and decreases dynamically, a flexibility to add and remove GPU devices dynamically is required.

To address these requirements, in this paper we propose DistGPU Cache (Distributed In-GPU Data Cache), in which a data store server (i.e., host) and GPU devices are connected via a PCI-Express (PCIe) over 10 Gbit Ethernet (10 GbE) technology [9], so that GPU devices that store and search data can be added and removed dynamically. We also propose a documents partitioning method that distributes ranges of cached data to GPU devices based on a hash function. DistGPU Caches can be dynamically divided and merged when the GPU devices are added and removed, respectively. An inherent concern on Dist-GPU Cache may be communication latency between the host and remote GPU devices connected via 10 GbE. However, since in our proposal, DistGPU Caches reside in GPUs' device memory, they are not transferred to the GPU devices for every search query. Thus, communication overhead can be mitigated even with remote GPU devices. The contributions of this paper are summarized as follows.

- We propose DistGPU Cache that distributes database cache over GPU devices connected via a PCIe over 10 GbE technology.
- We propose a documents partitioning method so that GPU devices that form DistGPU Cache can be added and removed dynamically.
- We evaluate document-oriented data store performance when varying the number of remote GPU devices.

The rest of paper is organized follows. Section 2 surveys related work. Section 3 proposes DistGPU Cache and the cache partitioning method for multiple remote GPU devices. Section 4 evaluates DistGPU Cache and compares it with that with local GPU devices and the original document-oriented data store using database indexes. Section 5 concludes this paper.

2   Background and Related Work

2.1   GPU-Based Regular Expression Matching

There are two approaches to implement regular expression matching: NFA (Nondeterministic Finite Automaton) based approach and DFA (Deterministic Finite Automaton) based approach. To accelerate the regular expression matching, GPU devices are used for DFA-based approach in [10] and NFA-based approach in [11]. Both the approaches have pros and cons. NFA-based approach is advantageous in terms of memory efficiency, while DFA-based approach is faster than NFA-based one. For a small rule-set regular expression matching, a DFA-based approach can be accelerated by using tokens of words in [6]. In addition, a text matching based on KMP algorithm is studied for database applications in [8]. In this paper, we implemented a DFA-based regular expression matching for GPU devices based on the design of [10].

2.2   GPU-Based Document-Oriented Data Store

To accelerate search queries of document-oriented data store, DDB Cache suitable for GPU processing was proposed in [5]. A similar idea was applied for a graph database in [4]. DDB Cache is an array-based data cache extracted from the document-oriented data store, and GPU-based string processing (e.g., regular expression based string matching) is performed for DDB Cached. Figure 1 shows a creation of DDB Cache from document-oriented data store. The upper half illustrates a simplified data structure of the document-oriented data store that includes multiple documents. The lower half illustrates its DDB Cache structure. DDB Cache is created for each field of documents. The same field name and value type are used for every document. Thus, only values are extracted from documents for each field and cached in a one-dimensional array structure as DDB Cache. Since the length of each value (e.g., string data) differs, an auxiliary array (PTR) is additionally used in DDB Cache to point the start address of field value of a specified document.

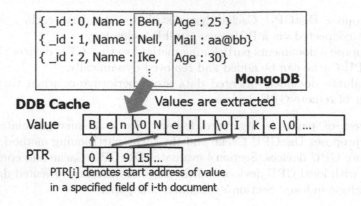

Fig. 1. DDB Cache creation.

In DDB Cache, value and auxiliary arrays are created for each field. Although Fig. 1 illustrates DDB Cache of only a single field, we can add DDB Cache for the other fields. When a search query is performed, one or more pairs of value and auxiliary arrays, which are corresponding to the field(s) specified in the query, are transferred to GPU device memory and then a string search is performed by the GPU device. Although a regular expression based string match query was accelerated by a single GPU device with DDB Cache in [5], a horizontal scalability to add or remove GPU devices dynamically was not considered though the horizontal scalability is one of the most important properties of NOSQL.

To address the horizontal scalability issue, in this paper we propose Dist-GPU Cache, in which a host and GPU devices are connected via a PCIe over 10 GbE. We employ NEC ExpEther [9] as a PCIe over 10 GbE technology. Using ExpEther, PCIe packets for hardware resources (e.g., GPU devices) are transported in 10 GbE by encapsulating the packets into an Ethernet frame. Please note that there are software services based on client-server model that provides GPU computation to clients [3], while we employ a PCIe over 10 GbE technology for connecting many GPU devices directly. In our case, pooled GPU devices can be connected to the data store server machine via 10 GbE when necessary. Thus, our proposed DistGPU Cache is well suited to recent trends on rack-scale architecture and software-defined infrastructure.

3   DistGPU Cache and Its Partition Method

3.1   System Overview

DistGPU Cache is a distributed database cache stored in many remote GPU devices. DistGPU Cache consists of certain-sized buckets, each of which is processed by a GPU device. The detail about the buckets is described in the following subsections.

Figure 2 shows an overview of the proposed system. It consists of two components: (1) document-oriented data store and (2) DistGPU Cache distributed over

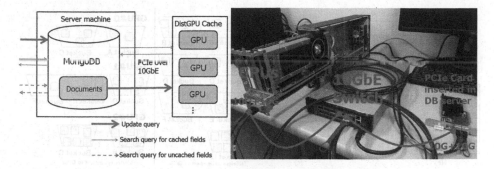

Fig. 2. Overview of DistGPU Cache.   **Fig. 3.** Photo of remote GPU devices connected via 10 GbE.

remote GPU devices accessed via 10 GbE. We use MongoDB [2] as a document-oriented data store in this paper and value fields of documents are cached in remote GPU devices as DistGPU Cache. Figure 3 shows remote GPU devices connected via a 10 GbE switch for DistGPU Cache. Remote GPU device is connected to PCIe card via two 10 GbE cables (i.e., 20 Gbps) and the PCIe card is mounted in the host machine where MongoDB and DistGPU Cache are working.

The following steps are performed for each query in the proposed system.

- For UPDATE query, new data are written to the original document-oriented data store. Cached data in GPU device memory (i.e., DistGPU Cache) are updated if necessary.
- For SEARCH query, if the target fields have been cached in DistGPU Cache, the query is transferred to a corresponding GPU device to perform the document search. The search result is returned to the client via the document-oriented store.
- For SEARCH query, if the target fields have not been cached, the query is performed by the document-oriented store and the result is returned to the client.

3.2   Partitioning of Documents Values with Hash Function

Since DistGPU Cache is built by extracting values of a specific field of the documents, values in the DistGPU Cache are independent of each other. Thus, the set of values in DistGPU Cache can be partitioned and stored into GPUs in response to the number of GPU devices and their device memory capacity, in order to perform a search query in parallel. For example, assuming two GPU devices, the first half of the documents is stored in a GPU and the latter half is stored in another GPU. However, such a simple document partitioning is inefficient, e.g., write operations are concentrated on a single partition that contains the latest documents.

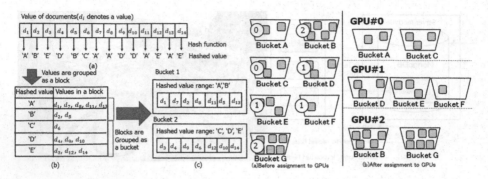

Fig. 4. Relationship between blocks and buckets using the hash function.

Fig. 5. Assignment of buckets to GPU devices.

In this paper, we propose an efficient partitioning method that distributes document values to multiple GPU devices by using a hash function. More specifically, by the hash function, document values are distributed into small blocks and they are distributed to GPU devices evenly so as to equalize their workload and reduce the reconstruction overhead.

Using the proposed partitioning method, we can utilize the hash value as an index to narrow down a search space and reduce the computation cost.

Typically, a collision resistance is required for hash functions. On the other hand, we introduce a coarse-grain hash function that generates the same hashed value for a range of consecutive values. Here we define "block" as a group of values with the same hashed value. All the values in the same block are stored into the same GPU device for search. Thus we can use such a hashed value instead of a database index for search in order to narrow down the search range.

However, a block is not suitable to be used as a bucket directly, because the number of values in each block (partitioned by the coarse-grain hash function) may differ and the number of values stored in each bucket should be balanced in order to distribute the workload of each bucket and thus improve the performance. Instead of a single block, multiple blocks (with different sizes) are grouped as a "bucket" so that sizes of buckets should be balanced. We also define "hashed value range" as a set of hashed values of blocks grouped in the same bucket. One or more buckets are assigned to a GPU device (the assignment is discussed in Sect. 3.4). This approach tolerates collisions of hashed values. It also tolerates unbalanced sizes of blocks (and thus non-uniform distribution of hashed values). Thus, a simple hash function with a low computation overhead can be used. For example, in our implementation, the first n characters of value strings are used as hashed values. By varying n, the sizes of blocks can be controlled.

Figure 4 shows relationship between blocks and buckets using the hash function. We assume that values d_1 to d_{14} are hashed and then hashed values 'A' to 'E' are generated for simplicity. Figure 4(a) shows the values in documents and their corresponding hashed values. As shown, multiple values that have the same hashed value are grouped as a block. Figure 4(b) shows the hashed values and their corresponding blocks. Since sizes of blocks differ, these blocks are packed into buckets so that the number of values in each bucket should be balanced, as shown in Fig. 4(c). In this example, blocks that have hashed values A or B are grouped as bucket 1 and those have hashed values C, D, or E are grouped as bucket 2. The sizes of buckets 1 and 2 are balanced. Blocks in a bucket are independent with each other (i.e., blocks with different hashed values coexist in a bucket). When we add a new value to DistGPU Cache, a hashed value of the new value is computed and then the new value is stored into a bucket that covers this hashed value. Although the sizes of buckets are currently balanced in Fig. 4, the number of values in each bucket will change dynamically due to write queries and thus their sizes will be unbalanced as time goes on. To handle such dynamic growth of buckets, we need to update the hashed value range of each bucket dynamically. In our design, the maximum number of values (or the maximum total sizes of values) in each bucket is predefined and if the number of values in a bucket exceeds the maximum number, the bucket is divided into two buckets.

Algorithm 1 shows a pseudo code of the proposed bucket partitioning method, assuming bucket A is divided into buckets A and B. If a bucket covers only a single hashed value, the bucket cannot be partitioned (Line 6–8). In this case, a finer hash function should be used instead. For example, when the hash function uses the first n characters as a hashed value, we can increase n. The hash function should be selected so that the number of values in each bucket does not exceed the maximum number. In Line 9–11, a half of hashed value range of bucket A is moved to bucket B. In Line 12–13, the number of values in each bucket is recomputed based on the new hashed value range. Then values in bucket A are moved to bucket B based on the new hashed value range.

Building a new DistGPU Cache or reconstructing an existing DistGPU Cache is equivalent to newly-adding whole documents to an empty bucket. In other words, first, H_A is set to all the hashed values and x_A is set to 0, then Algorithm 1 is repeated until buckets are partitioned so that their number of values does not exceed the maximum value.

3.3   Toward Schema-Less Data Structure

In a document-oriented data store, each document may have different fields. For example, a document has fields A and B, while another document may have only field C. DistGPU Cache is required to support such a scheme-less data structure.

In MongoDB, all the documents must have _id field as a primary key. Dist-GPU Cache of _id field is used as a primary key to refer to those of the other fields. To do this, DistGPU Cache of _id field needs two additional data for each field: (1) bucket ID and (2) address inside the bucket where the field value is stored. Thus, DistGPU Cache of _id field has $2 \times N$ additional arrays, where N is the number of fields, to record the bucket ID and address inside the bucket where a corresponding field value is stored.

Algorithm 1. Bucket partitioning

1: $A \leftarrow$ Original bucket to be partitioned
2: $B \leftarrow$ New bucket to be diverged
3: $H_A, H_B \leftarrow$ Hashed value ranges for A and B
4: $h_A \leftarrow$ Actual hashed values included in A ($h_A \in H_A$)
5: $x_A, x_B \leftarrow$ Numbers of hashed values in A and B
6: **if** $x_A = 1$ **then**
7:     Terminate //Bucket A cannot be partitioned any more
8: **end if**
9: **for** $i = 1$ to $\lfloor x_A/2 \rfloor$ **do**
10:     Move largest hashed value in h_A to H_B and delete it from H_A
11: **end for**
12: $x_A \leftarrow \lceil x_A/2 \rceil$ //Number of hashed values of H_A after partitioning
13: $x_B \leftarrow \lfloor x_A/2 \rfloor$ //Number of hashed values of H_B after partitioning
14: Values are moved from A to B based on new H_A

DistGPU Cache of the other fields has an additional array, in order to record the bucket ID and address in the bucket where a corresponding _id is stored. In other words, these additional arrays record the relationship between _id field and the other fields in the same document. When a field value in a document is accessed, another field value of the same document can be accessed by using these additional arrays. Please note that DistGPU Cache may not cache all the fields used in the documents. When a field value not cached in DistGPU Cache is accessed, MongoDB is invoked by specifying _id in order to retrieve all the field values.

3.4 Assignment of Buckets to GPU Devices

To store buckets in GPU device memory as DistGPU Cache, we need to take into account which buckets are stored to which GPU devices. In our design, each bucket has a random integer number which is less than the number of GPU devices (e.g., each bucket has 0, 1, or 2 as a random integer number when the number of GPU devices is three). The buckets are assigned to GPU devices based on their random integer numbers. If the number of buckets is huge, such a random assignment of buckets to GPU devices can balance the workload of GPU devices. When a new bucket is added, assignments of the other buckets to GPU devices are not changed and only the new bucket is newly assigned to a GPU device; thus the overhead to add new buckets is low.

Figure 5 shows an assignment of buckets to GPU devices. Seven buckets (Fig. 5(a)) are assigned to three GPU devices, as shown in Fig. 5(b). Once a bucket is assigned to GPU device, it resides in the same GPU device until Dist-GPU Cache is reconstructed.

In DistGPU Cache, the number of GPU devices changes dynamically and the bucket assignment also takes into account the number of GPU devices available. When a new GPU device is added, b/G buckets in existing GPU devices are randomly selected and moved to the new GPU device, where b is the number of total buckets and G is the number of total GPU devices. When an existing GPU device is removed, a new random integer number (not the current number) is generated for each bucket in the GPU device. Then buckets in the GPU device to be removed are moved to the other GPU devices based on their random integer number. When a GPU device is added or removed, a range of random integer numbers for new buckets is updated.

3.5   GPU Processing for DistGPU Cache

We use NVIDIA GPU devices and CUDA (Compute Unified Device Architecture) C development environment to implement GPU kernels.

Since in DistGPU Cache, documents are grouped as buckets and stored into GPU devices, document search is performed in bucket basis. In our design, values that generate the same hashed value are grouped as a block in a bucket; thus some search queries may scan only a limited bucket or GPU device memory. For example, a perfect or prefix search query for string values scans only a bucket or GPU device memory. On the other hand, regular expression search without any prefix cannot limit the search space and thus scans all the DistGPU Cache.

We implemented a DFA-based regular expression search kernel similar to [10] using CUDA. When a search space is limited to a single block, the CUDA kernel is executed only once. Otherwise, the CUDA kernel is executed for each bucket in the search space. In this case, since buckets are independent with each other, the CUDA kernels for different buckets are executed in asynchronous manner. We can thus hide the CPU-GPU data transfer overhead since the data transfer to/from GPU devices and computation in GPU devices can be overlapped.

4   Evaluations

4.1   Evaluation Environment

MongoDB and our DistGPU Cache are operated in the same machine. CPU of the host machine is Intel Xeon E5-2637v3 running at 3.5 GHz and memory capacity is 128 GB. Up to three NVIDIA GeForce GTX980 GPUs, each of which has a 4 GB device memory, are used for DistGPU Cache. We use MongoDB version 2.6.6 and CUDA version 6.0. For DistGPU Cache, the experiment system shown in Fig. 3 except that remote GPU devices are directly connected to the host without L2 switch for simplicity. For comparison, we evaluate the performance when the GPU devices are directly attached to the host machine via PCIe Gen3 x16.

4.2   Performance with Different Bucket Sizes

Here we evaluate the performance of DistGPU Cache when the bucket size varies. We measured the throughputs of a perfect string match query that scans only a single bucket and a regular expression based string match query that scans all

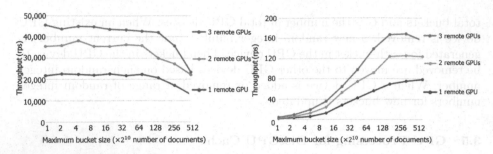

Fig. 6. Perfect string match query performance vs. bucket sizes.

Fig. 7. Regular expression based string match query performance vs. bucket sizes.

the buckets in DistGPU Cache. In addition, we measured the query execution time when the number of GPU devices varies in order to evaluate the dynamic join/leave of GPU devices vs. the bucket sizes. The number of documents in our experiments is ten million.

For the perfect string match query, ten million documents each of which has two fields, _id field and a randomly-generated 8-character string field, are generated and the perfect string match query is performed for the string field. The regular expression based string match query is also performed for the above-mentioned ten million documents.

Figure 6 shows the perfect string match query performance of DistGPU Cache when the number of GPU devices is varied from one to three and the maximum bucket size is varied from 1×2^{10} to 512×2^{10}. The throughput is represented as rps (request per second). Since a perfect string match query scans only a single bucket, the size of search space is proportional to the bucket size. Please note that when the bucket size is smaller than a certain threshold, the GPU parallelism cannot be fully utilized and thus the throughput becomes constant. As shown, when the maximum bucket size is larger than 128×2^{10} or 256×2^{10}, the throughput decreases.

Figure 7 shows the regular expression based string match query performance of DistGPU Cache. Since a regular expression based string match query scans all the buckets, the search space is constant regardless of bucket size. When the bucket size is small, since more CUDA kernels for smaller buckets are executed, the number of CUDA kernel invocations and the data transfer overhead between host and GPU devices are increased, resulting in a lower throughput. As shown, the throughput is increased until the maximum bucket size is enlarged to 128×2^{10}. The throughput is significantly decreased when the maximum bucket size is 512×2^{10} especially when the number of GPU devices is three. This is because, as the maximum bucket size is enlarged, the number of buckets is decreased, the workload cannot be divided into the three GPU devices evenly.

Figure 8 shows the execution times when the GPU devices are dynamically added or removed. The number of GPU devices are increased from one to two and decreased from two to one. In both the cases, as the maximum bucket

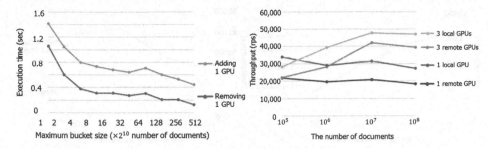

Fig. 8. Execution time when GPU devices are added or removed dynamically.

Fig. 9. Perfect string match performance when GPU devices are local and remote.

size is enlarged, the execution time is decreased. This is because, as the bucket size is enlarged, the number of buckets is decreased and the number of memory allocations and data transfer between host and GPU devices are decreased. When we compare both the cases (i.e., adding and removing GPU), the execution time of the latter case is shorter than that of the first case. This is because, when the GPU device is added, a device memory is allocated in the new GPU device and then a part of existing data are transferred to the new GPU device.

In summary, the performance is not degraded in both the perfect and regular expression based string match queries when the maximum bucket size is 128×2^{10}. Since this bucket size is proper in this evaluation environment, we use this parameter in the following experiments.

4.3   Performance with Local and Remote GPUs

In DistGPU Cache, we assume that GPU devices are connected to the host machine via 10 GbE (in our design, two STP+ cables are used for each GPU device, resulting in 20 Gbps). Of course it is possible to directly mount the GPU devices to the host machine via PCIe Gen3 x16, but the number of such local GPU devices mounted will be limited by the motherboard or chassis. Here we measured the performance when the GPU devices are directly attached to the host machine via PCIe Gen3 x16, in order to show the performance overhead due to the "remote" GPU devices.

The perfect string match and regular expression based string match queries are performed for local and remote GPU devices. Although these queries and documents are the same as those in Sect. 4.2, the number of documents are varied from one hundred thousand to one hundred million.

Figure 9 shows the perfect string match query throughputs for local and remote GPU devices when the number of GPU devices is one and three. When the number of documents is quite small, the number of buckets is also small and buckets cannot be distributed to GPU devices evenly; thus the throughput of 3GPU case is decreased when the number of documents is small. The throughput of the local GPU case is always better than that of remote GPU case. However, in the remote GPU case, the throughput increases in a higher rate compared to the

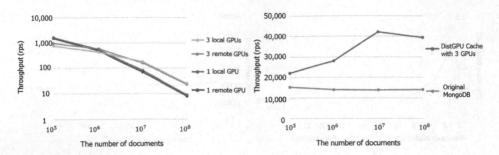

Fig. 10. Regular expression based string match performance when GPU devices are local and remote.

Fig. 11. Perfect string match performance of DistGPU Cache and original MongoDB.

local GPU case. Actually, when the number of documents is one hundred million, the throughput improvement from 1GPU to 3GPU is 2.14x for the remote GPU case, while it is only 1.73x for the local GPU case. The local GPU performance is better than the remote GPU case by 1.20x when the number of documents is one hundred million and the number of GPU devices is three; thus performance degradation of remote GPU case is not significant by taking into account the scalability benefits.

Figure 10 shows the regular expression based string match query throughputs for local and remote GPU devices. In the graph, the throughput (Y-axis) is represented as a logarithmic scale. As the number of documents is increased, the computation cost is proportionally increased and thus the throughput is degraded. However, the performance degradation is relatively slow, since the CUDA kernels are executed in parallel. The local GPU performance is better than the remote GPU case by only 1.08x when the number of documents is one hundred million and the number of GPU devices is three; thus the performance degradation of the remote GPU case is quite small.

Regarding the latency, the execution times to deal with the perfect matching query are 0.30 ms and 0.22 ms for local and remote GPU cases respectively, when the numbers of documents and GPU devices are one hundred million and three respectively. Their latencies are almost constant regardless of the number of GPU devices because we can narrow down the search space only to a single bucket stored in a single GPU device. Those of the regular expression matching query are 44.0 ms and 40.9 ms for local and remote GPU cases respectively, and the latencies are decreased as the number of GPU devices increases.

4.4 Performance Comparison with MongoDB

Here we compare the proposed DistGPU Cache using three remote GPU devices with the original MongoDB in terms of throughput using the same queries and documents as in Sect. 4.3. For MongoDB, B+tree index is used to improve the search performance of the perfect string match query, while any index is not used for the regular expression based search query since a simple indexing cannot be used for the regular expression based search query. In addition to the search

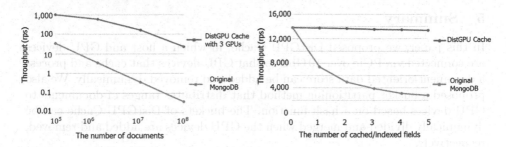

Fig. 12. Regular expression based string match performance of DistGPU Cache and original MongoDB.

Fig. 13. Write query performance of DistGPU Cache and original MongoDB.

query performance, the write throughput is measured in both the cases: DistGPU Cache and MongoDB with indexes. MongoDB is operated on a memory file system (i.e., tmpfs) for fair comparisons.

Figure 11 shows the perfect string match query throughputs of DistGPU Cache and the original MongoDB. Comparison between DistGPU Cache and MongoDB shows that the DistGPU Cache outperforms MongoDB even if the number of documents is small. When the number of documents is one hundred million, DistGPU Cache outperforms MongoDB by 2.79x.

Figure 12 shows the regular expression based string match query throughputs of DistGPU Cache and the original MongoDB. In the case of DistGPU Cache, the throughput degradation is suppressed especially when the number of documents is large. As a result, when the number of documents is one hundred million, DistGPU Cache outperforms the original MongoDB by 640.8x.

Regarding the latency, the execution times to deal with the perfect matching query are 0.30 ms and 0.071 ms for the DistGPU Cache and the original MongoDB cases respectively. On the other hand, those of the regular expression matching query are 44.0 ms and 28198.8 ms for the DistGPU Cache and the original MongoDB cases respectively as the regular expression matching query is quite compute intensive.

Figure 13 shows write query throughputs of DistGPU Cache and the original MongoDB. B+tree database indexes are used in the original MongoDB case. In this experiment, write queries that add new documents are performed on both the data stores (i.e., DistGPU Cache and the original MongoDB) where ten million documents have been already stored. Here, each document has _id field and five string fields filled with randomly-generated eight characters. As shown in Fig. 13, the write throughput of the original MongoDB is degraded as the number of indexed fields increases, while the write throughput of DistGPU Cache is almost constant even when the number of cached fields in DistGPU Cache increases.

5   Summary

In this paper, we proposed DistGPU Cache, in which a host and GPU devices are connected via PCIe over 10 GbE so that GPU devices that cache and process a document-oriented data store can be added and removed dynamically. We also proposed a bucket partitioning method that distributes ranges of documents to GPU devices based on a hash function. The buckets of DistGPU Cache can be dynamically divided and merged when the GPU devices are added and removed, respectively.

In the evaluations, we compared local and remote GPU devices on DistGPU Cache in terms of regular expression match query throughput. We also compared the DistGPU Cache with remote GPU devices and the original document-oriented data store in terms of performance. We showed that although the local GPUs case outperforms the remote GPUs case by 1.08x, the remote overhead is quite small and can be compensated by a high horizontal scalability to add more GPU devices via a network. We also showed that DistGPU Cache with GPU devices significantly outperforms the original data store.

Acknowledgements. This work was partially supported by Grant-in-Aid for JSPS Research Fellow. H. Matsutani was supported in part by JST PRESTO.

References

1. Apache Couch DB. http://couchdb.apache.org
2. MongoDB. http://www.mongodb.org
3. Duato, J., Pena, A., Silla, F., Mayo, R., Quintana-Orti, E.: rCUDA: reducing the number of GPU-based accelerators in high performance clusters. In: Proceedings of the International Conference on High Performance Computing and Simulation (HPCS 2010), pp. 224–231, June 2010
4. Morishima, S., Matsutani, H.: Performance evaluations of graph database using CUDA and OpenMP-compatible libraries. ACM SIGARCH Comput. Archit. News **42**(4), 75–80 (2014)
5. Morishima, S., Matsutani, H.: Performance evaluations of document-oriented databases using GPU and cache structure. In: Proceedings of International Symposium on Parallel and Distributed Processing with Applications, pp. 108–115, August 2015
6. Naghmouchi, J., Scarpazza, D.P., BereKovic, M.: Small-ruleset regular expression matching on GPGPUs: quantitative performance analysis and optimization. In: Proceedings of the International Conference on Supercomputing (ICS 2010), pp. 337–348, June 2010
7. Shukla, D., et al.: Schema-agnostic indexing with Azure DocumentDB. In: Proceedings of the International Conference on Very Large Data Bases (VLDB 2015), pp. 1668–1679, August 2015
8. Sitaridi, E.A., Ross, K.A.: GPU-accelerated string matching for database applications. VLDB J. 1–22 (2015)
9. Suzuki, J., Hidaka, Y., Higuchi, J., Yoshikawa, T., Iwata, A.: ExpressEther - Ethernet-based virtualization technology for reconfigurable hardware platform. In: Proceedings of International Symposium on High-Performance Interconnects, pp. 45–51, August 2006

10. Vasiliadis, G., Polychronakis, M., Ioannidis, S.: Parallelization and characterization of pattern matching using GPUs. In: Proceedings of the International Symposium on Workload Characterization (IISWC 2011), pp. 216–225, November 2011
11. Zu, Y., Yang, M., Xu, Z., Wang, L., Tian, X., Peng, K., Dong, Q.: GPU-based NFA implementation for memory efficient high speed regular expression matching. In: Proceedings of the ACM SIGPLAN Symposium on Principles and Practice of Parallel Programming (PPoPP 2012), pp. 129–140, February 2012

Resource Aggregation for Task-Based Cholesky Factorization on Top of Heterogeneous Machines

T. Cojean[1]($\boxtimes$), A. Guermouche[1], A. Hugo[2], R. Namyst[1], and P.A. Wacrenier[1]

[1] INRIA, LaBRI, University of Bordeaux, Talence, France
{terry.cojean,abdou.guermouche,raymond.namyst,pierre-andre.wacrenier}@inria.fr
[2] University of Uppsala, Uppsala, Sweden
andra.hugo@it.uu.se

Abstract. Hybrid computing platforms are now commonplace, featuring a large number of CPU cores and accelerators. This trend makes balancing computations between these heterogeneous resources performance critical. In this paper we propose *aggregating several CPU cores* in order to execute larger parallel tasks and thus improve the load balance between CPUs and accelerators. Additionally, we present our approach to exploit internal parallelism within tasks. This is done by combining two runtime systems: one runtime system to handle the task graph and another one to manage the internal parallelism. We demonstrate the relevance of our approach in the context of the dense Cholesky factorization kernel implemented on top of the StarPU task-based runtime system. We present experimental results showing that our solution outperforms state of the art implementations.

Keywords: Multicore · Accelerator · GPU · Heterogeneous computing · Task DAG · Runtime system · Dense linear algebra · Cholesky

1 Introduction

Due to recent evolution of High Performance Computing architectures toward massively parallel heterogeneous multicore machines, many research efforts have been devoted to the design of runtime systems able to provide programmers with portable techniques and tools to exploit such hardware complexity. The availability of mature implementations of task based runtime systems (*e.g.* OpenMP or Intel TBB for multicore machines, PaRSEC [6], Charm++ [12], KAAPI [9], StarPU [4] or StarSs [5] for heterogeneous configurations) has allowed programmers to rely on dynamic schedulers and develop powerful implementations of parallel libraries (*e.g.* Intel MKL[1], DPLASMA [7]).

However one of the main issues encountered when trying to exploit both CPUs and accelerators is that these devices have very different characteristics

---

This work is supported by the French National Research Agency (ANR), under the grant ANR-13-MONU-0007.

[1] https://software.intel.com/en-us/intel-mkl.

© Springer International Publishing AG 2017
F. Desprez et al. (Eds.): Euro-Par 2016 Workshops, LNCS 10104, pp. 56–68, 2017.
DOI: 10.1007/978-3-319-58943-5_5

and requirements. Indeed, GPUs typically exhibit better performance when executing kernels applied to large data sets, which we call *coarse grain kernels* (or tasks) in the remainder of the paper. On the contrary, regular CPU cores typically reach their peak performance with fine grain kernels working on a reduced memory footprint.

To work around this granularity problem, task-based applications running on such heterogeneous platforms typically adopt a medium granularity, chosen as a trade-off between coarse-grain and fine-grain kernels. A small granularity would indeed lead to poor performance on the GPU side, whereas large kernel sizes may lead to an under-utilization of CPU cores because (1) the amount of parallelism (*i.e.* task graph width) decreases when kernel size increases and (2) the efficiency of GPU increases while a large memory footprint may penalize CPU cache hit ratio. This trade-off technique is typically used by dense linear algebra hybrid libraries [2,7,14]. The main reason for using a unique task granularity in the application lies in the complexity of the algorithms dealing with heterogeneous task granularities even for very regular applications like dense linear libraries. However some recent approaches relax this constraint and are able to split coarse-grain tasks at run time to generate fine-grain tasks for CPUs [17].

The approach we propose in this paper to tackle the granularity problem is based on resource aggregation: instead of dynamically splitting tasks, we rather aggregate resources to process coarse grain tasks in a parallel manner on the critical resource, the CPU. To deal with Direct Acyclic Graphs (DAGs) of parallel tasks, we have enhanced the StarPU [4,10] runtime system to cope with parallel tasks, the implementation of which relies on another parallel runtime system (*e.g.* OpenMP). This approach allows us to delegate the division of the kernel between resources to a specialized library. We illustrate how state of the art scheduling heuristics are upgraded to deal with parallel tasks. Although our scheme is able to handle arbitrary clusters, we evaluate our solution with fixed-size ones. We show that using our solution for a dense Cholesky factorization kernel outperforms state of the art implementations to reach a peak performance of 4.6 Tflop/s on a platform equipped with 24 CPU cores and 4 GPU devices.

2 Related Work

A number of research efforts have recently been focusing on redesigning HPC applications to use dynamic runtime systems. The dense linear algebra community has massively adopted this modular approach over the past few years [2,7,14] and delivered production-quality software relying on it. For example, the MAGMA library [2], provides Linear Algebra algorithms over heterogeneous hardware and can optionally use the StarPU runtime system to perform dynamic scheduling between CPUs and GPUs, illustrating the trend toward delegating scheduling to the underlying runtime system. Moreover, such libraries often exhibit state-of-the-art performance, resulting from heavy tuning and strong optimization efforts. However, these approaches require that accelerators process a large share of the total workload to ensure a fair load balancing between resources. Additionally, all these approaches rely on an uniform tile size, consequently, all tasks have the same granularity independently from where they are executed leading to a loss of efficiency of both the CPUs and the accelerators.

Recent attempts have been made to resolve the granularity issue between regular CPUs and accelerators in the specific context of dense linear algebra. Most of these efforts rely on heterogeneous tile sizes [15] which may involve extra memory copies when split data need to be coalesced again [11]. However the decision to split a task is mainly made statically at submission time. More recently, a more dynamic approach has been proposed in [17] where coarse grain tasks are hierarchically split at runtime when they are executed on CPUs. Although this paper successes at tackling the granularity problem, the proposed solution is specific to linear algebra kernels. In the context of this paper, we tackle the granularity problem with the opposite point of view and a more general approach: rather than splitting coarse grained tasks, we aggregate computing units which cooperate to process the task in parallel. By doing so, our runtime system does not only support sequential tasks but also parallel ones.

However, calling simultaneously several parallel procedures is difficult because usually they are not aware of the resource utilization of one another and may oversubscribe threads to the processing units. This issue has been first tackled within the Lithe framework [13] a resource sharing management interface that defines how threads are transferred between parallel libraries within an application. This contribution suffered from the fact that it does not allow to dynamically change the number of resources associated with a parallel kernel. Our contribution in this study is a generalization of a previous work [10], where we introduced the so-called scheduling contexts which aim at structuring the parallelism for complex applications. Actually, our runtime system is able to cope with several flavors of inner parallelism (OpenMP, Pthreads, StarPU) simultaneously. In this paper, we showcase the use of OpenMP to manage internal task parallelism.

3 Background

We integrate our solution to the StarPU runtime system as it provides a flexible platform to deal with heterogeneous architectures. StarPU [4] is a C library providing a portable interface for scheduling dynamic graphs of tasks onto a heterogeneous set of processing units called workers in StarPU (*i.e.* CPUs and GPUs). The two basic principles of StarPU are firstly that tasks can have several implementations, for some or each of the various heterogeneous processing units available in the machine, and secondly that necessary data transfers to these processing units are handled transparently by the runtime system. StarPU tasks are defined as multi-version kernels, gathering the different implementations available for CPUs and GPUs, associated to a set of input/output data. To avoid unnecessary data transfers, StarPU allows multiple copies of the same registered data to reside at the same time in different memory locations as long as it is not modified. Asynchronous data prefetching is also used to hide memory latencies allowing to overlap memory transfers with computations when possible.

StarPU is a platform for developing, tuning and experimenting with various task scheduling policies in a portable way. Several built-in schedulers are available, ranging from greedy and work-stealing based policies to more elaborated schedulers implementing variants of the Minimum Completion Time (MCT) policy [16]. This latter family of schedulers is based on auto-tuned history-based performance models that provide estimations of the expected lengths of tasks and data transfers. The performance model of StarPU also supports the use of regressions to cope with dynamic granularities.

4   A Runtime Solution to Deal with Nested Parallelism

We introduce a set of mechanisms which aim at managing nested parallelism (i.e. task inner parallelism) within the StarPU runtime system. We consider the general case where a parallel task may be implemented on top of any runtime system. We present in Fig. 1a the standard architecture of a task-based runtime system where the task-graph is provided to the runtime and the ready tasks (in purple) are dynamically scheduled on queues associated with the underlying computing resources. We propose a more flexible scheme where tasks may feature *internal parallelism* implemented using any other runtime system. This idea is represented in Fig. 1b where multiple CPU devices are grouped to form *virtual resources* which will be referred to as *clusters*: in this example, each cluster contains 3 CPU cores. We will refer to the main runtime system as the *external runtime system* while the runtime system used to implement parallel tasks will be denoted as the *inner runtime system*. The main challenges regarding this architecture are: (1) how to constrain the inner runtime system's execution to the selected set of resources, (2) how to extend the existing scheduling strategies to this new type of computing resources, and (3) how to define the number of *clusters* and their corresponding resources. In this paper, we focus on the first two problems since the latter is strongly related to online moldable/malleable task scheduling problems which are out of the scope of this paper.

Firstly, we need to aggregate cores into a cluster. This is done thanks to a simple programming interface which allows to group cores in a compact way with respect to memory hierarchy. In practice, we rely on the hwloc framework [8], which provides the hardware topology, to build clusters containing every computing resource under a given level of the memory hierarchy (*e.g.* Socket, NUMA node, L2 cache, . . .). Secondly, forcing a parallel task to run on the set of resources corresponding to a cluster depends on whether or not the inner runtime system has its own pool of threads. On the one hand, if the inner runtime system offers a multithreaded interface, that is to say the execution of the parallel task requires a call that has to be done by each thread, the inner runtime system can directly use the StarPU workers assigned to the cluster. We show in Fig. 2a how we manage internal SPMD runtime systems. In this case, the parallel task is inserted in the local queue of each StarPU worker. On the other hand, if the inner runtime system features its own pool of threads (*e.g.* as most OpenMP implementations), StarPU workers corresponding to the cluster need to be paused until the end of the parallel task. This is done to avoid over-subscribing threads over the underlying resources. We describe in Fig. 2b how the interaction is managed. We allow only one StarPU worker to keep running. This latter called the *master worker* of the cluster, is in charge of popping the tasks assigned to the cluster by the scheduler. When tasks have to be executed, the master worker takes the role of a regular application thread with respect to the inner runtime system. In Fig. 2b, the black threads represent the StarPU workers and the pink ones the inner runtime system (*e.g.* OpenMP) threads. The master worker joins the team of inner threads while the other StarPU threads are paused.

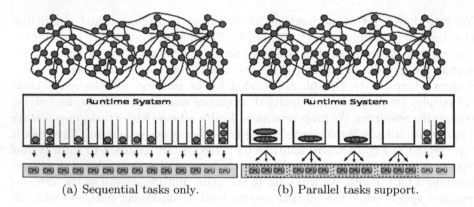

(a) Sequential tasks only.   (b) Parallel tasks support.

Fig. 1. Managing internal parallelism within StarPU.

Depending on the inner scheduling engine, the set of computing resources assigned to a cluster may be dynamically adjusted during the execution of a parallel task. This obviously requires the inner scheduler (resp. runtime system) to be able to support such an operation. For instance, parallel kernels implemented on top of runtime systems like OpenMP will not allow removing a computing resource during the execution of the parallel task. In this case we refer to the corresponding parallel task as a *moldable* one and we consider resizing the corresponding cluster only at the end of the task or before starting a new one.

From a practical point of view, we integrate in a *callback* function the specific code required to force the inner runtime to run on the selected set of resources. This prologue is transparently triggered before starting executing any sequence of parallel tasks. We call this callback the *prologue callback*. This approach can be used for most inner runtime systems as the programmer can provide the implementation of the prologue callback and thus use the necessary functions in order to provide the resource allocation required for the corresponding cluster. Such a runtime should however respect certain properties: be able to be executed on a restricted set of resources and allow the privatization of its global and static variables. From the user point of view, provided that he has parallel implementation of his kernels, using clusters in his application is straightforward: he needs to implement the callback and create clusters. In the experimental section, we use this approach to force the MKL library, which relies on OpenMP, to run on the set of resources corresponding to the clusters.

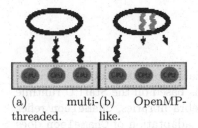

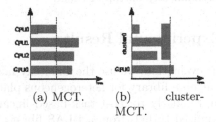

(a)   multi-(b)   OpenMP-   (a) MCT.   (b)   cluster-
threaded.   like.   MCT.

Fig. 2. Management of the pool of   **Fig. 3.** Adaptation of the MCT schedul-
threads within a cluster.   ing strategy.

4.1   Adapting MCT and Performance Models for Parallel Tasks

As presented in Sect. 3, MCT is a scheduling policy implemented in StarPU. The task's estimated length and transfer time used for MCT decisions is computed using performance prediction models. These models are based on performance history tables dynamically built during the application execution. It is then possible for the runtime system to predict for each task the worker which completes it at the earliest. Therefore, even without the programmer's involvement, the runtime can provide a relatively accurate performance estimation of the expected requirements of the tasks allowing the scheduler to take appropriate decisions when assigning tasks to computing resources.

As an illustration, we provide in Fig. 3a an example showing the behavior of the MCT strategy. In this example, the blue task represents the one the scheduler is trying to assign. This task has different length on CPU and GPU devices. The choice is then made to schedule it on the CPU0 which completes it first. We have adapted the MCT strategy and the underlying performance models to be able to select a pool of CPUs when looking for a computing resource to execute a task. We have thus introduced a new type of resource: the cluster of CPUs. The associated performance model is parametrized not only by the size and type of the task together with the candidate resource but also by the number of CPUs forming the cluster. Thus, tasks can be assigned to a cluster either explicitly by the user or by the policy depending on where it would finish first. This is illustrated in Fig. 3b, where the three CPUs composing our platform are grouped in a cluster. We can see that the expected length of the parallel task on the cluster is used to choose the resource having the minimum completion time for the task. Note that in this scenario, we chose to illustrate a cluster with an OpenMP-like internal runtime system.

This approach permits to deal with a heterogeneous architecture made of different types of processing units as well as clusters grouping different sets of processing units. Therefore, our approach is able to deal with multiple clusters sizes simultaneously with clusters of one CPU core and take appropriate decisions. Actually, it is helpful to think of the clusters as mini-accelerators. In this work, we let the user define sets of such clusters (mini-accelerators) and schedule tasks dynamically on top of them.

5   Experimental Results

For our evaluation, we use the Cholesky factorization of Chameleon [1], a dense linear algebra library for heterogeneous platforms based on the StarPU runtime system. Similarly to most task-based linear algebra libraries, Chameleon relies on optimized kernels from a BLAS library. Our adaptation of Chameleon does not change the high level task-based algorithms and subsequent DAG. We simply extend the prologue of each task to allow the use of an OpenMP implementation of MKL inside the clusters and manage the creation of clusters. We call pt-Chameleon this adapted version of Chameleon that handles parallel tasks. The machine we use is heterogeneous and composed of two 12-cores Intel Xeon CPU E5-2680 v3 (@2.5 GHz equipped with 30 MB of cache each) and enhanced with four NVidia K40m GPUs. In StarPU one core is dedicated to each GPU, consequently we report on all figures performance with 20 cores for the Chameleon and pt-Chameleon versions. We used a configuration for pt-Chameleon composed of 2 clusters aggregating 10 cores each (noted 2 × 10), so that the 10 cores of a CPU belong to a single cluster. In comparison, Chameleon uses 20 sequential CPU cores on this platform. Finally, we show on all figures the average performance and observed variation over 5 runs on square matrices.

Table 1. Acceleration factor of Cholesky factorization kernels on a GPU and 10 cores compared to one core with tile size 960 and 1920.

	DPOTRF		DTRSM		DSYRK		DGEMM	
	960	1920	960	1920	960	1920	960	1920
1 core (Gflop/s)	27.78	31.11	34.42	34.96	31.52	32.93	36.46	37.27
GPU/1 core	1.72	5.95	8.72	18.59	26.96	31.73	28.80	30.86
10 cores/1 core	5.55	7.48	6.75	8.48	6.90	8.63	7.77	8.56

We report in Table 1 the acceleration factors of using 10 cores or one GPU compared to the single core performance for each kernel of the Cholesky factorization. We conduct our evaluation using MKL for the CPUs and CuBLAS (resp. MAGMA) for the GPUs. This table highlights a sublinear scalability of using 10 cores compared to using 1 core. For example on our best kernel DGEMM we accelerate the execution by a factor of 7.77 when using 10 cores and this increases to 8.56 with a tile size of 1920. Despite this, we can see that relying on sequential kernels worsens the performance gap between the CPUs and GPUs while relying on clusters makes the set of computing resources more homogeneous. We can obtain an acceleration factor of GPU against CPUs by dividing the second line by the third one. For example, the performance gap for the DGEMM kernel with a tile size of 960 is $\simeq 29$ when using 1 core compared to a GPU whereas it is $28.80/7.77 \simeq 3.7$ when using 10 cores compared to a GPU. As a consequence, if 28 independent DGEMM of size 960 are submitted on computer of 10 cores and a GPU, the Chameleon scheduler assigns all the tasks to the GPU whereas pt-Chameleon assigns 6 tasks to the 10 core cluster and 22 tasks to GPUs. Another important aspect which can compensate some loss in efficiency is the pt-Chameleon ability to accelerate the critical path. Indeed, a cluster of 10 cores can execute the DPOTRF kernel on a tile size of 960 three times faster than on a GPU. The performance is also almost the same for the DTRSM task.

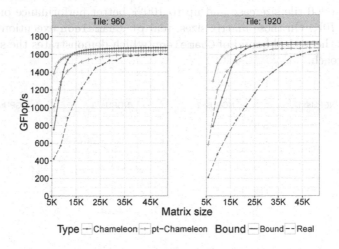

Fig. 4. Comparison of the pt-Chameleon and Chameleon Cholesky factorization with computed bounds. 20 CPUs and 1 GPU are used.

We show in Fig. 4 the performance of the Cholesky factorization for both Chameleon and pt-Chameleon with multiple tile sizes and their computed make-span theoretical lower bounds. These bounds are computed thanks to the iterative bound technique introduced in [3] which iteratively adds new critical paths until all are taken into account. As these bounds do not take communications with GPU devices into account, they are clearly unreachable in practice. These bounds show that pt-Chameleon can theoretically obtain better performance than Chameleon on small to medium sized matrices. Indeed, the CPUs are under-utilized in the sequential tasks case due to a lack of parallelism whereas using clusters lowers the amount of tasks required to feed the CPU cores. The 5 K matrix order point shows a difference of performance of 600 Gflop/s, this is close to the obtainable performance on these CPUs. For both tile sizes on large matrices (e.g. 40K), the Chameleon bound is over the pt-Chameleon one. This is due to the better efficiency of the sequential kernels since the parallel kernels do not exhibit perfect scalability, allowing the CPUs to achieve better performance per core in the sequential case. We observe that for a coarser kernel grain of 1920, the maximum achievable performance is higher, mainly thanks to a better kernel efficiency on GPUs with this size. For DGEMM kernel we can gain close to 100 Gflop/s (or 10%). We can also note that the gap between Chameleon and pt-Chameleon bound decreases slightly as we increase the tile size to 1920 thanks to a relatively better gain in efficiency per core compared to the sequential one. Additionally, the real executions are underneath the theoretical bounds. This is due to the fact that transfer time is not taken into account in the bounds. Moreover, the online MCT scheduler can exaggeratedly favor GPUs because of their huge performance bonus in the Chameleon case as was shown in [3]. Finally, this figure highlights a constantly superior performance of pt-Chameleon over Chameleon which achieves up to 65% better performance on a matrix size of 11 K for the 960 tile size case and up to 100% better performance on matrices lower than 10K. On those matrix sizes, real pt-Chameleon execution is able to go over the theoretical bound of Chameleon which demonstrates the superiority of our approach.

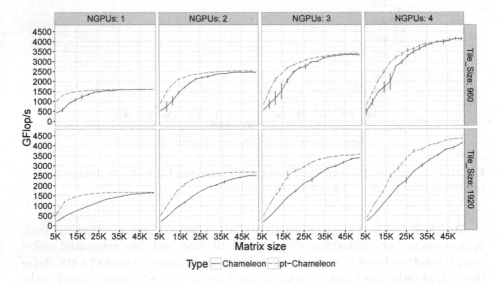

Fig. 5. Performance of the Cholesky factorization with pt-Chameleon and Chameleon with varying number of GPUs and task granularity.

We report in Fig. 5 the performance behavior of our implementation of the Cholesky factorization using the pt-Chameleon framework, compared to the existing Chameleon library. When looking at medium sized matrices we observe that pt-Chameleon is able to achieve significantly higher performance than Chameleon across all test cases. On those matrices, the Chameleon library has some performance variability. This is mainly due to bad scheduling decisions regarding tasks on the critical path in Chameleon. Indeed, if an important task is wrongly scheduled on a CPU such as a DPOTRF, we may lack parallelism for a significant period of time. Whereas in the pt-Chameleon case using parallel tasks even accelerates the critical path due to a better kernel performance, which makes the approach less sensitive to bad scheduling decisions, lowering pt-Chameleon's variance. Both Chameleon and pt-Chameleon showcase a good scalability when increasing the number of GPUs. For example the peak for 1 GPU with a tile size of 960 is at 1.6 Tflop/s and for 2 GPUs it goes up to 2.6 Tflop/s. This improvement is as expected since 1 Tflop/s is the performance of a GPU on this platform with the DGEMM kernel. Chameleon scales slightly less than pt-Chameleon with a coarse task grain size of 1920. The gap between the two versions increases when increasing the number of GPUs. As shown previously, the scheduler can schedule too many tasks on the GPUs leading to a CPU under-utilization with such a high factor of heterogeneity.

Another factor is the cache behavior of both implementations. Indeed, each processor benefits of 30MB cache and by using one cluster per processor instead of 10 independent processing units we lower by 10 the working set size. Since a tile of 960 weights 7MB whereas a tile of 1920 weights 28MB we are even able to fit entirely a 1920 tile in the LLC. This highlights another constraint: the memory contention bottleneck. We had to explicitly use the *numactl* tool to allocate pages in a round robin fashion on all 4 NUMA nodes, otherwise the behavior of Chameleon was very irregular. In fact, even with the interleave setting, we observed that some compute intensive kernels such as DGEMM could become more memory bound for the Chameleon case with a matrix size of 43K. To investigate this issue we conducted an experiment using Intel VTune where we allocated the complete matrix on one NUMA node thanks to the numactl tool. We saw that for Chameleon 59% of the DGEMM kernels were bounded by memory, whereas for pt-Chameleon only 13% were bounded by memory. We also observed over two times less cache misses on our pt-Chameleon version.

Finally, in Fig. 6 we compare pt-Chameleon to multiple dense linear algebra reference libraries: MAGMA, Chameleon and DPLASMA using the hierarchical granularity scheme presented in [17]. We make use of a constrained version ($2 \times 10c$) where the DPOTRF and DTRSM tasks are restricted to CPU workers. On this figure, the MAGMA and DPLASMA versions use the 24 CPU cores. This strategy is comparable to what is done in [17] where only DGEMM kernels are executed on GPU devices. We observe that using the regular MCT scheduler for small matrices leads to better performance since in the constrained version the amount of work done by CPUs is too large. However, when we increase the matrix size, the constrained version starts to be efficient and leads to a 5% increase in performance on average, achieving a peak of 4.6 Tflop/s on our test platform. the MAGMA performance with the We see that the absolute peak is obtained by pt-Chameleon and outperforms all the other implementations.

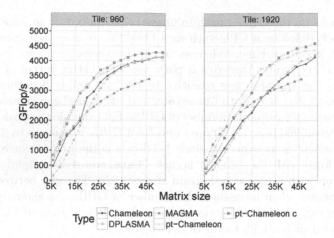

Fig. 6. Comparison of the constrained `pt-Chameleon` with baseline `Chameleon`, `MAGMA` (default parameters and multithreaded MKL) and hierarchical `DPLASMA` (internal blocking of 192 (left) and 320 (right)).

6   Conclusion

One of the biggest challenge raised by the development of high performance task-based applications on top of heterogeneous hardware lies in coping with the increasing performance gap between accelerators and individual cores. One way to address this issue is to use multiple tasks' granularities, but it requires in-depth modifications to the data layout used by existing implementations.

We propose a less intrusive and more generic approach that consists in reducing the performance gap between processing units by forming clusters of CPUs on top of which we exploit tasks' inner parallelism. Performance of these clusters of CPUs can better compete with the one of powerful accelerators such as GPUs. Our implementation extends the StarPU runtime system so that the scheduler only sees virtual computing resources on which it can schedule parallel tasks (*e.g.* BLAS kernels). The implementation of tasks inside such clusters can virtually rely on any thread-based runtime system, and runs under the supervision of the main StarPU scheduler. We demonstrate the relevance of our approach using task-based implementations of the dense linear algebra Cholesky factorization. Our implementation is able to outperform the `MAGMA`, `DPLASMA` and `Chameleon` state-of-the-art dense linear algebra libraries while using the same task granularity on accelerators and clusters.

In the near future, we intend to further extend this work by investigating how to automatically determine the optimal size of clusters. Preliminary experiments show that using clusters of different sizes sometimes leads to significant performance gains. Thus, we plan to design heuristics that could dynamically adapt the number and the size of clusters on the fly, based on statistical information regarding ready tasks.

Acknowledgment. We are grateful to Mathieu Faverge for his help for the comparison of DPLASMA and pt-Chameleon. Experiments presented in this paper were carried out using the PLAFRIM experimental testbed.

References

1. Agullo, E., Augonnet, C., Dongarra, J., Ltaief, H., Namyst, R., Thibault, S., Tomov, S.: A hybridization methodology for high-performance linear algebra software for GPUs. In: GPU Computing Gems, Jade Edition, vol. 2, pp. 473–484 (2011)
2. Agullo, E., Demmel, J., Dongarra, J., Hadri, B., Kurzak, J., Langou, J., Ltaief, H., Luszczek, P., Tomov, S.: Numerical linear algebra on emerging architectures: the PLASMA and MAGMA projects. J. Phys.: Conf. Ser. **180**(1), 012037 (2009). http://iopscience.iop.org/article/10.1088/1742-6596/180/1/012037
3. Agullo, E., Beaumont, O., Eyraud-Dubois, L., Kumar, S.: Are static schedules so bad? A case study on Cholesky factorization. In: Proceedings of IPDPS 2016 (2016)
4. Augonnet, C., Thibault, S., Namyst, R., Wacrenier, P.A.: StarPU: a unified platform for task scheduling on heterogeneous multicore architectures. Concurrency Comput.: Pract. Experience **23**, 187–198 (2011)
5. Ayguadé, E., Badia, R.M., Igual, F.D., Labarta, J., Mayo, R., Quintana-Ortí, E.S.: An extension of the starss programming model for platforms with multiple GPUs. In: Sips, H., Epema, D., Lin, H.-X. (eds.) Euro-Par 2009. LNCS, vol. 5704, pp. 851–862. Springer, Heidelberg (2009). doi:10.1007/978-3-642-03869-3_79
6. Bosilca, G., Bouteiller, A., Danalis, A., Herault, T., Lemarinier, P., Dongarra, J.: DAGuE: a generic distributed DAG engine for high performance computing. Parallel Comput. **38**(1), 37–51 (2012)
7. Bosilca, G., Bouteiller, A., Danalis, A., Herault, T., Luszczek, P., Dongarra, J.: Dense linear algebra on distributed heterogeneous hardware with a symbolic DAG approach. Theory Pract. Scalable Comput. Commun. (2013)
8. Broquedis, F., Clet-Ortega, J., Moreaud, S., Furmento, N., Goglin, B., Mercier, G., Thibault, S., Namyst, R.: hwloc: a generic framework for managing hardware affinities in HPC applications. In: Proceedings of the 2010 18th Euromicro Conference on Parallel, Distributed and Network-based Processing, PDP 2010, pp. 180–186 (2010). http://dx.doi.org/10.1109/PDP.2010.67
9. Hermann, E., Raffin, B., Faure, F., Gautier, T., Allard, J.: Multi-GPU and multi-CPU parallelization for interactive physics simulations. In: D'Ambra, P., Guarracino, M., Talia, D. (eds.) Euro-Par 2010. LNCS, vol. 6272, pp. 235–246. Springer, Heidelberg (2010). doi:10.1007/978-3-642-15291-7_23
10. Hugo, A., Guermouche, A., Wacrenier, P., Namyst, R.: Composing multiple starpu applications over heterogeneous machines: a supervised approach. IJHPCA **28**(3), 285–300 (2014)
11. Kim, K., Eijkhout, V., van de Geijn, R.A.: Dense matrix computation on a heterogenous architecture: a block synchronous approach. Technical report TR-12-04, Texas Advanced Computing Center, The University of Texas at Austin (2012)
12. Kunzman, D.M., Kalé, L.V.: Programming heterogeneous clusters with accelerators using object-based programming. Sci. Program. **19**(1), 47–62 (2011)
13. Pan, H., Hindman, B., Asanović, K.: Composing parallel software efficiently with lithe. SIGPLAN Not. **45**, 376–387. http://doi.acm.org/10.1145/1809028.1806639

68   T. Cojean et al.

14. Quintana-Ortí, G., Quintana-Ortí, E.S., van de Geijn, R.A., Zee, F.G.V., Chan, E.: Programming matrix algorithms-by-blocks for thread-level parallelism. ACM Trans. Math. Softw. **36**(3), 14:1–14:26 (2009). https://dl.acm.org/citation.cfm?id=1527288

15. Song, F., Tomov, S., Dongarra, J.: Enabling and scaling matrix computations on heterogeneous multi-core and multi-GPU systems. In: Proceedings of ICS 2012, pp. 365–376 (2012)

16. Topcuoglu, H., Hariri, S., Wu, M.Y.: Performance-effective and low-complexity task scheduling for heterogeneous computing. IEEE Trans. Parallel Distrib. Syst. **13**(3), 260–274 (2002)

17. Wu, W., Bouteiller, A., Bosilca, G., Faverge, M., Dongarra, J.: Hierarchical DAG scheduling for hybrid distributed systems. In: 29th IEEE International Parallel & Distributed Processing Symposium (IPDPS), Hyderabad, India, May 2015

Task-Based Conjugate Gradient: From Multi-GPU Towards Heterogeneous Architectures

E. Agullo[1], L. Giraud[1(✉)], A. Guermouche[2], S. Nakov[1], and J. Roman[1]

[1] Inria, Bordeaux, France
luc.giraud@inria.fr
[2] University of Bordeaux, Bordeaux, France

Abstract. Whereas most parallel High Performance Computing (HPC) numerical libaries have been written as highly tuned and mostly monolithic codes, the increased complexity of modern architectures led the computational science and engineering community to consider more modular programming paradigms such as task-based paradigms to design new generation of parallel simulation code; this enables to delegate part of the work to a third party software such as a runtime system. That latter approach has been shown to be very productive and efficient with compute-intensive algorithms, such as dense linear algebra and sparse direct solvers. In this study, we consider a much more irregular, and synchronizing algorithm, namely the Conjugate Gradient (CG) algorithm. We propose a task-based formulation of the algorithm together with a very fine instrumentation of the runtime system. We show that almost optimum speed up may be reached on a multi-GPU platform (relatively to the mono-GPU case) and, as a very preliminary but promising result, that the approach can be effectively used to handle heterogenous architectures composed of a multicore chip and multiple GPUs. We expect that these results will pave the way for investigating the design of new advanced, irregular numerical algorithms on top of runtime systems.

Keywords: High Performance Computing (HPC) · Multi-GPUs · Heterogeneous architectures · Task-based model · Runtime system · Sparse linear systems · Conjugate Gradient

1 Introduction

In the last decade, the architectural complexity of High Performance Computing (HPC) platforms has strongly increased. To cope with this complexity, programming paradigms are being revisited. Among others, one major trend consists of writing the algorithms in terms of task graphs and delegating to a runtime system both the management of the data consistency and the orchestration of the actual execution. This paradigm has been first intensively studied in the context of dense linear algebra [1–3,6–8,11,12] and is now a common utility for related

© Springer International Publishing AG 2017
F. Desprez et al. (Eds.): Euro-Par 2016 Workshops, LNCS 10104, pp. 69–82, 2017.
DOI: 10.1007/978-3-319-58943-5_6

state-of-the-art libraries such as PLASMA, MAGMA, FLAME, DPLASMA and Chameleon. Dense linear algebra algorithms were indeed excellent candidates for pioneering in this direction. First, their regular computational pattern allows one to design very wide task graphs so that many computational units can execute tasks concurrently. Second, the building block operations they rely on, essentially level-three Basic Linear Algebra Subroutines (BLAS), are compute intensive, which makes it possible to split the work in relatively fine grain tasks while fully benefiting from GPU acceleration. As a result, these algorithms are particularly easy to schedule in the sense that state-of-the-art greedy scheduling algorithms may lead to a performance close to the optimum, including on platforms accelerated with multiple Graphics Processing Units (GPUs). Because sparse direct methods rely on dense linear algebra kernels, a large effort has been made to turn them into task-based algorithms [4,9].

In this paper, we tackle another class of algorithms, the Krylov subspace methods, which aim at solving large sparse linear systems of equations of the form $\mathcal{A}x = b$, where $\mathcal{A}$ is a sparse matrix. Those methods are based on the calculation of approximated solutions in a sequence of embedded spaces, that is intrinsically a sequential numerical scheme. Second, their unpreconditioned versions are exclusively based on non compute intensive kernels with irregular memory access pattern, Sparse Matrix Vector products (SpMV) and level-one BLAS, which need very large grain tasks to benefit from GPU acceleration. For these reasons, designing and scheduling Krylov subspace methods on a multi-GPUs platform is extremely challenging, especially when relying on a task-based abstraction which requires to delegate part of the control to a runtime system. We discuss this methodological approach in the context of the Conjugate Gradient (CG) algorithm on a shared-memory machine accelerated with multiple GPUs using the StarPU runtime system [5] to process the designed task graph. The CG solver is a widely used Krylov subspace method, which is the numerical algorithm of choice for the solution of large linear systems with symmetric positive definite matrices [13].

The objective of this study is *not* to optimize the performance of CG on an individual GPU, which essentially consists of optimizing the matrix layout in order to speed up SpMV. We do *not* either consider the opportunity of reordering the matrix in order to improve the SpMV. Finally, we do *not* consider numerical variants of CG which may exhibit different parallel patterns. These three techniques are extremely important but complementary and orthogonal to our work. Instead, we rely on routines from vendor libraries (NVIDIA cuSPARSE and cuBLAS) to implement individual GPU tasks, we assume that the ordering is prescribed (we do not apply permutation) and we consider the standard formulation of the CG algorithm [13]. On the contrary, the objective is to study the opportunity to accelerate CG on multiple GPUs by designing an appropriate task flow where each individual task is processed on one GPU and all available GPUs are exploited to execute these tasks concurrently. We first propose a natural task-based expression of CG. We show that such an expression fails to efficiently accelerate CG. We then propose successive improvements on the task flow design to alleviate the synchronizations, exhibit more parallelism (wider graph) and reduce the volume of exchanges between GPUs.

The rest of the paper is organized as follows. We first propose a natural task-based expression of CG in Sect. 2. We then present the experimental set up in Sect. 3. We then show how the baseline task-based expression can be enhanced for efficiently pipelining the execution of the tasks in Sect. 4. We present a performance analysis of a multi-GPU execution in Sect. 5. Section 6 presents concluding remarks together with preliminary experiments in the fully heterogeneous case.

2   Baseline Sequential Task Flow (STF) Conjugate Gradient Algorithm

In this section, we present a first task-based expression of the CG algorithm whose pseudo-code is given in Algorithm in Fig. 1a. This algorithm can be divided in two phases, the initialization phase (lines 1–5) and the main iterative loop (lines 6–16). Since the initialization phase is executed only once, we only focus on an iteration occurring in the main loop in this study.

Three types of operations are used in an iteration of the algorithm: $SpMV$ (the sparse matrix-vector product, line 7), scalar operations (lines 9, 13, 14) and level-one BLAS operations (lines 8, 10, 11, 12, 15). In particular three different level-one BLAS operations are used: scalar product (dot, lines 8 and 12), linear combination of vectors ($axpy$, lines 10, 11 and 15) and scaling of a vector by a scalar ($scal$, line 15). The $scal$ kernel at line 15 is used in combination with an $axpy$. Indeed, in terms of BLAS, the operation $p \leftarrow r + \beta p$ consists of two successive operations: $p \leftarrow \beta p$ ($scal$) and then $p \leftarrow r + p$ ($axpy$). In our implementation, the combination of these level-one BLAS operations represents a single task called $scale\text{-}axpy$. The key operation in an iteration is the $SpMV$ (line 7) and its efficiency is thus critical for the performance of the whole algorithm.

According to our STF programming paradigm, data need to be decomposed in order to provide opportunities for executing concurrent tasks. We consider a 1D decomposition of the sparse matrix, dividing the matrix in multiple block-rows. The number of non-zero values per block-rows is balanced and the rest of the vectors follows the same decomposition.

After decomposing the data, tasks that operate on those data can be defined. The tasks derived from the main loop of Algorithm in Fig. 1a are shown in Fig. 1b, when the matrix is divided in six block-rows. Each task is represented by a box, named after the operation executed in that task, and edges represent the dependencies between tasks.

The first instruction executed in the main loop of Algorithm in Fig. 1a is the $SpMV$. When a 1D decomposition is applied to the matrix, dividing it in six parts implies that six tasks are submitted for this operation (the green tasks in Fig. 1b): $q_i \leftarrow A_i p, i \in [1, 6]$. For these tasks, a copy of the whole vector p is needed (vector p is unpartitioned). But in order to extract parallelism of other level-one BLAS operations where vector p is used (lines 8 and 15 in Algorithm in Fig. 1a), in respect with our programming, the vector p needs to be

1: $r \leftarrow b$
2: $r \leftarrow r - Ax$
3: $p \leftarrow r$
4: $\delta_{new} \leftarrow dot(r, r)$
5: $\delta_{old} \leftarrow \delta_{new}$
6: **for** $j = 0, 1, ...,$ until $\frac{\|b - Ax\|}{\|b\|} \leq$
    eps **do**
7:     $q \leftarrow Ap$ /* $SpMV$ */
8:     $\alpha \leftarrow dot(p, q)$ /* dot */
9:     $\alpha \leftarrow \delta_{new}/\alpha$ /* scalar op-
       eration */
10:    $x \leftarrow x + \alpha p$ /* $axpy$ */
11:    $r \leftarrow r - \alpha q$ /* $axpy$ */
12:    $\delta_{new} \leftarrow dot(r, r)$ /* dot */
13:    $\beta \leftarrow \delta_{new}/\delta_{old}$ /* scalar op-
       eration */
14:    $\delta_{old} \leftarrow \delta_{new}$ /* scalar
       operation */
15:    $p \leftarrow r + \beta p$ /* scale-axpy
       */
16: **end for**

(a) Algorithm.

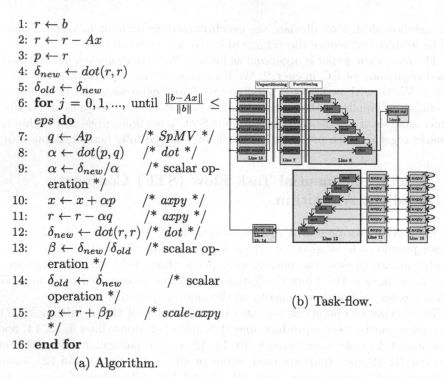

(b) Task-flow.

Fig. 1. Conjugate Gradient (CG) linear solver. (Color figure online)

partitioned. The partitioning operation is a blocking call; it thus represents a synchronization point in this task flow. Once vector p is partitioned, both vectors p and q are divided in six parts. Thus six *dot* tasks are submitted. Each *dot* operation accesses α in read-write mode, which induces a serialization of the operation. This sequence thus introduces new synchronizations in the task flow each time we need to perform a *dot* operation. The twelve *axpy* tasks (six at line 10 and six at line 11) can then all be executed in parallel. Another *dot* operation is then performed (line 12) and induces another serialization point. After the scalar operations at lines 13 and 14 in Algorithm in Fig. 1a, the last *scale-axpy* operation of the loop is executed, which updates the vector p. At this stage, the vector is partitioned in six pieces. In order to perform the *SpMV* tasks for the next iteration, an unpartitioned version of the vector p is needed. This is done with the unpartition operation, similar to the partition operation, which is a blocking call.

All in all, this task flow contains four synchronization points per iteration, two for the partition/unpartition operation and two issued from the *dot* operations. The task flow is also very thin. Section 4.1 exhibits the induced limitation in terms of pipelining, while Sects. 4.2, 4.3 and 4.4 propose successive improvements allowing us to alleviate the synchronizations and design a wider task flow, thus increasing the concurrency and the performance.

3   Experimental Setup

All the tests presented in Sect. 5 have been run on a cache coherent Non Uniform Memory Access (ccNUMA) machine with two hexa-core processors Intel Westmere Xeon X5650, each one having 18 GB of RAM, for a total of 36 GB. It is equipped with three NVIDIA Tesla M2070 GPUs, each one equipped with 6 GB of RAM memory. The task-based CG algorithm proposed in Sect. 2 is implemented on top of the StarPU v1.2. We use the opportunity offered by StarPU to control each GPU with a dedicated CPU core. To illustrate our discussion we consider the matrices presented in Table 1. All needed data is prefetched to the target GPU before the execution and assessment of all the results presented in this paper.

Table 1. Overview of sparse matrices used in this study. The `11pts-256` and `11pts-128` matrices are obtained from a 3D regular grid with 11pt discretization stencil. The `Audi_kw` and `af_0_k101` matrices come from structural mechanics simulations on irregular finite element 3D meshes.

Matrix name	nnz	$\mathcal{N}$	$nnz/\mathcal{N}$	Flop/iteration
`11pts-256`	183 M	17 M	11	2 G
`11pts-128`	23 M	2 M	11	224 M
`Audi_kw`	154 M	943 K	163	317 M
`af_0_k101`	18 M	503 K	34	38 M

Scheduling and Mapping Strategy. As discussed in Sect. 2, the task flow derived from Algorithm in Fig. 1a contains four synchronization points per iteration and is very thin, ensuring only a very limited concurrency. Pipelining this task flow efficiently is thus very challenging. In particular, dynamic strategies that led to close to optimum scheduling in dense linear algebra [2] are not well suited here. We have indeed experimented such a strategy (Minimum Completion Time (MCT) policy), but all studied variants failed to achieve a very high performance. We have thus implemented a static scheduling strategy. We perform a cyclic mapping of the block-rows on the available GPUs in order to ensure load balancing.

Building Block Operations. In order to explore the potential parallelism of the CG algorithm, we first study the performance of its building block operations, level-one BLAS and *SpMV*. The granularity does not penalize drastically the performance for *SpMV* operation. Additionally when three GPUs are used, a speed-up of 2.93 is obtained. On the other hand, in order to efficiently exploit multiple GPUs, vector with sizes of at least few millions are needed.

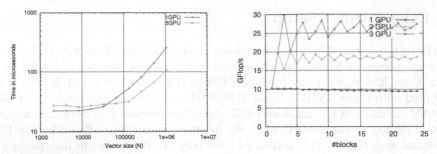

(a) Performance of the *axpy* kernel. The(b) Performance of the *SpMV* kernel on
rest of the BLAS-1 kernels follow thethe Audi_kw matrix.
same behavior.

Fig. 2. Performance of the building block operations used in the CG algorithm. All
data is prefetched before execution and performance assessment.

4   Achieving Efficient Software Pipelining

In accordance with the example discussed in Sect. 2, the matrix is split in six
block-rows and three GPUs are used. We pursue our illustration with matrix
11pts-128.

4.1   Assessment of the Proposed Task-Based CG Algorithm

Figure 3 shows the execution trace of one iteration of the task flow (Fig. 1b)
derived from Algorithm in Fig. 1a with respect to the mapping proposed in
Sect. 3. Figure 3 can be interpreted as follows. The top black bar represents the
state of the CPU RAM memory during the execution. Each GPU is represented
by a pair of bars, one for the state of the GPU and the black bar which depicts
the memory state of the GPU. When data movement occurs between different
memory nodes, they are highlighted by an arrow from the source to the destination. The top bar for each GPU represents its activity. The activity of a GPU
may have one of the three following states: active computation (green), idle (red)
or active waiting for the completion of a data transfer (purple).

An iteration starts with the execution of a *SpMV* operation (line 7 in Algorithm in Fig. 1a) which corresponds time interval $[t_0, t_1]$ in Fig. 3. Following the
cyclic mapping strategy presented in Sect. 3, each GPU is thus in charge of two
SpMV tasks. At time t_1, the vector p is unpartitioned. The vector p is partitioned
into six p_i pieces, $i \in [1, 6]$, with respect to the block-row decomposition of the
matrix. However, this data partitioning operation is a blocking call (see Sect. 2)
which means that no other task can be submitted until it is completed at time
t_1 (the red vertical bar after the *SpMV* tasks in Fig. 1b). Once vector p is partitioned, tasks for all remaining operations (lines 8–15) are submitted. The *dot*
tasks are executed sequentially with respect to the cyclic mapping strategy. The
reason for this, as explained in Sect. 2, is that the scalar α is accessed in read-
write mode. In addition, α needs to be moved to GPUs between each execution

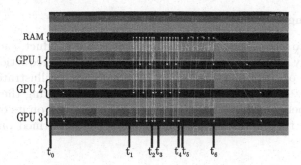

Fig. 3. Execution trace of an iteration with the CG task flow of Fig. 1b using three GPUs. (Color figure online)

of a *dot* task (time interval $[t_1, t_2]$ in Fig. 3). Once the scalar product at line 8 is computed, the scalar division follows (line 9) executed on GPU 1 (respecting the task flow in Fig. 1b). The execution of the next two instructions follows (lines 10 and 11). But before the beginning of the execution of the *axpy* tasks on GPU 2 and GPU 3, the new value of α is sent (the purple period at t_2 in Fig. 3). The *axpy* tasks (yellow tasks in Fig. 1b) are then executed during the period $[t_2, t_3]$ in parallel. The scalar product at line 12 is then executed during the time interval $[t_3, t_4]$, following the same sequence as explained above for line 8. Next, β and δ_{old} are computed on GPU 1 at time t_4 in Fig. 3, representing the scalar operations from lines 13 and 14 of Algorithm in Fig. 1a. Tasks related to the last operation of the iteration (*scale-axpy* tasks in Fig. 1b) are then processed during the time interval $[t_4, t_5]$. When all the new vector blocks p_i are calculated, the vector p is unpartitioned (red vertical bar after the *scale-axpy* tasks in Fig. 1b). As explained in Sect. 2, this data unpartition is another synchronization point and may only be executed in the RAM. All blocks p_i of vector p are thus moved by the runtime system from the GPUs to the RAM during the time interval $[t_5, t_6]$ for building the unpartitioned vector p. This vector is then used to perform the $q_i \leftarrow A_i \times p$ tasks related to the first instruction of the next iteration (*SpMV* at line 7). We now understand why the iteration starts with an active waiting of the GPUs (purple parts before time t_0): vector p is only valid in the RAM and thus needs to be copied on the GPUs.

During the execution of the task flow derived from Algorithm in Fig. 1a (Fig. 1b), the GPUs are idle during a large portion of the time (red and purple parts in Fig. 3). In order to achieve more efficient pipelining of the algorithm, we present successive improvements on the design of the task flow: relieving synchronization points (Sect. 4.2), reducing volume of communication that is achieved using a packing data mechanism (Sect. 4.3) and relying on a 2D decomposition (Sect. 4.4).

4.2 Relieving Synchronization Points

Alternatively to the sequential execution of the scalar product, each GPU j can compute locally a partial sum (α^j) and perform a StarPU reduction to compute the final value of the scalar $(\alpha = \sum_{j=1}^{n\text{-}gpus} \alpha^j)$. Figure 4a illustrates the benefit of this strategy. The calculation of the scalar product, during the time interval $[t_0, t_1]$ is now performed in parallel. Every GPU is working on its own local copy of α and once they have finished, the reduction is performed on GPU 1 just after t_1.

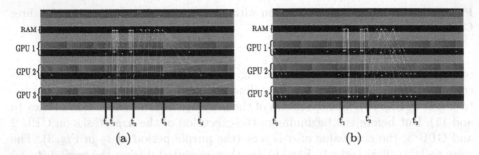

(a)   (b)

Fig. 4. Execution trace of one iteration when the *dot* is performed in reduction mode (left) and after furthermore avoiding data partitioning and unpartitioning (right). (Color figure online)

The partition (after instruction 7 of Algorithm in Fig. 1a) and unpartition (after instruction 15) of vector p, that are special features of StarPU, represent two of the four synchronization points within each iteration. They furthermore induce extra management and data movement costs. Indeed, after instruction 15, each GPU owns a valid part of vector p. For instance, once GPU 1 has computed p_1, StarPU moves p_1 to the RAM and then receives it back. Second, vector p has to be fully assembled in the main memory (during the unpartition operation) before prefetching a copy of the fully assembled vector p back to the GPUs (after time t_3 in Fig. 4a). We have designed another scheme where vector p is kept by StarPU in a partitioned form all along the execution (it is thus no longer needed to perform partitioning and unpartitioning operations at each iteration). Instead of building and broadcasting the whole unpartitioned vector p, each GPU gathers only the missing pieces. This enables us to "remove" the two synchronization points related to the partition and unpartition operations, since they are not called anymore, and decrease the overall traffic. Figure 4b illustrates the benefits of this policy. Avoiding the unpartitioning operation allows us to decrease the time required between two successive iterations from 8.8 ms to 6.6 ms. Furthermore, since the partitioning operation is no longer needed, the corresponding synchronization in the task flow control is removed. The corresponding idle time (red part at time t_0 in Fig. 4a) is removed and instructions 7 and 8 are now pipelined (period $[t_0, t_1]$ in Fig. 4b).

Coming back to Fig. 4a, one may notice that GPUs are idle for a while just before time t_1 and again just before time t_2. This is due to the reduction that finalizes each *dot* operation ($dot(p, q)$ at instruction 8 and $dot(r, r)$ at instruction 12, respectively). In Algorithm in Fig. 1a, vector x is only used at lines 10 (in read-write mode) and 6 (in read-only mode). The execution of instruction 10 can thus be moved anywhere within the iteration as long as the other input data of instruction 9, i.e. p and α have been updated to the correct values. In particular, instruction 10 can be moved after instruction 12. This delay enables StarPU to overlap the final reduction of the *dot* occurring at instruction 12 with the computation of vector x. The red part before t_2 in Fig. 4a becomes (partially) green in Fig. 4b. The considered CG formulation does not provide a similar opportunity to overlap reduction finalizing the *dot* operation at instruction 8.

4.3 Reducing Communication Volume by Packing Data

By avoiding data partition and data unpartition operations, the broadcast of vector p has been improved (from period $[t_2, t_4]$ in Fig. 4a to period $[t_3, t_4]$ in Fig. 4b), but still the communication time remains the large performance bottleneck (time interval $[t_3, t_4]$ in Fig. 4b). This volume of communication can be decreased. Indeed, if a column within the block-row A_i is zero, then the corresponding entry of p is not involved in the computation of the task $q_i \leftarrow A_i p$. Therefore, p can be pruned.

We now explain how we can achieve a similar behavior with a task flow model. Instead of letting StarPU broadcast the whole vector p on every GPU, we can define tasks that only transfer the required subset. Before executing the CG iterations, this subset is identified with a symbolic preprocessing step. Based on the structure of the block $A_{i,j}$, we determine which part of p_j is needed to build q_i. If p_j is not fully required, we do not transfer it directly. Instead, it can be packed into an intermediate data, $p_{i,j}$. StarPU provides an elegant support for implemented all these advanced techniques through the definition of new data types. We rely on that mechanism for implementing this packing scheme. Furthermore, the packing operation may have a non negligible cost whereas sometimes the values of $p_{i,j}$ that needs to be sent are almost contiguous. In those cases, it may thus be worth sending an extra amount of data in order to directly send the contiguous superset of $p_{i,j}$ ranging from the first to the last index that needs to be transferred. We have implemented such a scheme. A preliminary tuning is performed for each matrix and for each $p_{i,j}$ block to choose whether $p_{i,j}$ is packed or transferred in a contiguous way. Although StarPU can perform automatic prefetching, the prefetching operation is performed once all the dependencies are satisfied. In the present context, with the static mapping, this may be too late and further anticipation may be worthy. Therefore, we help the runtime system in performing data prefetching as soon as possible performing explicit prefetching within the callback of the *scale-axpy* task. We also do so after the computation of the α and β scalar values (lines 9 and 13 in Algorithm in Fig. 1a) for broadcasting them on all GPUs.

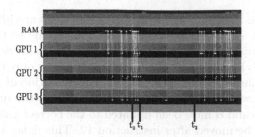

Fig. 5. Execution trace when furthermore the vector p is packed.

Figure 5 depicts the execution trace. The time interval $[t_3, t_4]$ in Fig. 4b needed for the broadcasting of the vector p has been reduced to the interval $[t_0, t_1]$ in Fig. 5. In the rest of the paper we refer to as the *full* algorithm when all the blocks are transferred, or to as the *packed* algorithm if this packing mechanism is used.

4.4   2D Decomposition

The 1D decomposition scheme requires that for each *SpMV* task, all blocks of vector p (packed or not packed) are in place before starting the execution of the task. In order to be able to overlap the time needed for broadcasting the vector p (time interval $[t_0, t_1]$ in Fig. 5), a 2D decomposition must be applied to the matrix. The matrix is first divided in block-rows, and then the same decomposition is applied to the other dimension of the matrix. Similarly as for a 1D decomposition, all the tasks *SpMV* associated with the entire block-row will be mapped on the same GPU. Contrary to the 1D decomposition, where we had to wait for the transfer of all missing blocks of the vector p, with the 2D decomposition, time needed for the transfer of the vector p can be overlapped with the execution of the *SpMV* tasks for which the blocks of the vector p are already available on that GPU. On the other hand, the 2D *SpMV* tasks yield lower performance then 1D (see Fig. 6b and 2b), since they are executed on lower granularity.

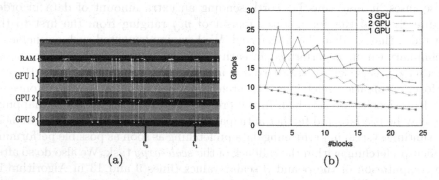

Fig. 6. Execution trace when relying of a 2D decomposition of the matrix (left) and the performance of *SpMV* kernel when 2D decomposition is applied to the matrix (right).

The result of the impact of a 2D decomposition is shown in Fig. 6a. During the time interval $[t_1, t_2]$ in Fig. 5 there is no communication, while in Fig. 6a communications are overlapped with the execution of the $SpMV$ tasks. In the rest of the paper we refer to either 1D or 2D depending on the data decomposition used. The trade-off between large task granularity (1D) and increased pipeline (2D) will be discussed in Sect. 5.

5 Performance Analysis

We now perform a detailed performance analysis of the task-based CG algorithm designed above. We propose to analyze the behavior of our algorithms in terms of *speed-up* (S) and parallel efficiency (e) with respect to the execution occurring on one single GPU. In order to understand in more details the behavior of the proposed algorithms, we decompose the parallel efficiency into three effects, following the methodology proposed in [10]: the impact on efficiency due to operating at a lower granularity $(e_{granularity})$, the impact of concurrency on the performance of individual tasks (e_{tasks}) and the impact of a suboptimum task pipelining $(e_{pipeline})$ due to a lack of concurrency. As shown in [10], the following equality holds:

$$e = e_{granularity} \times e_{tasks} \times e_{pipeline}.$$

We observed that the efficiency of the task is maximum $(e_{tasks} = 1)$. Indeed, in a multi-GPU context, the different workers do not interfere with each other (they do not share memory or caches) and hence do not deteriorate the performance of one another. In the sequel, we thus only report on $e_{granularity}$ and $e_{pipeline}$.

Table 2 presents the performance achieved for all matrices in our multi-GPU context. The optimal performance is represented for each scheme in bold value. The first thing to be observed is that for all the matrices, the pack version of our algorithm where only just the needed part of the vector p is broadcasted,

Table 2. Performance (in GHop/s) of our CG algorithm for the matrix collection presented in Table 1.

# GPUs	1D		2D		1D		2D	
	full	pack.	full	pack.	full	pack.	full	pack.
	11pts-256				11pts-128			
1	**9.74**				**9.58**			
2	12.33	19.10	16.66	17.24	11.5	17.6	14.3	16.1
3	11.70	**28.39**	13.26	23.17	9.01	**24.2**	9.22	20.6
	Audi_kw				af_0_k101			
1	**10.0**				**9.84**			
2	15.6	15.6	16.3	16.7	12.1	16.3	13.6	15.0
3	17.7	20.0	22.0	**23.6**	11.1	**19.4**	12.5	18.2

yields the optimal performance. Broadcasting entire sub-blocks is too expensive and thus considerably slows down the execution of the CG algorithm. For the matrices that have a regular distribution of the non zeros, *i.e.* the 11pts-256, 11pts-128 and the af_0_k101 matrices, the 1D algorithm outperforms the 2D algorithm. On the other hand, in the case of the Audi_kw matrix that has an unstructured pattern, the 2D algorithm which exhibits more parallelism, yields the best performance.

Table 3. Obtained speed-up (S), overall efficiency (e), effects of granularity on efficiency $e_{granularity}$ and effects of pipeline on efficiency $e_{pipeline}$ for matrices presented in Table 1 on 3 GPUs.

Matrix	11pts-256	11pts-128	Audi_kw	af_0_k101
S	2.91	2.52	2.36	1.97
e	0.97	0.84	0.79	0.65
$e_{granularity}$	0.99	0.98	0.87	0.96
$e_{pipeline}$	0.97	0.86	0.91	0.68

Table 3 allows for analyzing how the overall efficiency is decomposed according to the metrics proposed above. Dividing the 11pts-256 matrix in several block-rows does not induce a penalty on the task granularity $(e_{granularity} = 0.99 \approx 1)$. Furthermore, thanks to all the improvements of the task flow proposed in Sect. 4, a very high pipeline efficiency is achieved $(e_{pipeline} = 0.97)$, leading to an overall efficiency of the same (very high) magnitude. For the 11pts-128 matrix, the matrix decomposition induces a similar granularity penalty $e_{granularity} = 0.98$. The slightly lower granularity efficiency is a direct consequence of the matrix order. For smaller matrices, the tasks are performed on smaller sizes, thus the execution time per task is decreased. This makes our algorithm more sensitive to the overhead created by the communications induced by the dot-products and the broadcasting of the vector p, ending up with a less optimal (but still high) pipeline efficiency $(e_{pipeline} = 0.86)$. The overall efficiency for this matrix is $e = 0.84$. This phenomenon is amplified when the matrix order is getting lower, such as in the case of the af_0_k101 matrix, resulting in a global efficiency of $e = 0.65$. The Audi_kw matrix yields optimal performance with the 2D algorithm (see Sect. 4.4). Although the 2D algorithm requires to split the matrix in many more blocks inducing a higher penalty on granularity $(e_{granularity} = 0.87)$, it allows for a better overlap of communication with computation ensuring that a higher pipeline $(e_{pipeline} = 0.91)$ is achieved. With this trade-off, an overall efficiency equal to $e = 0.79$ is obtained.

6   Towards a Fully Heterogeneous CG Solver

One advantage of relying on task-based programming is that the architecture is fully abstracted. We prove here that we can benefit from this design to run on an

(a) nnz-based load balancing.   (b) Performance model-based load balancing.

Fig. 7. Traces of an execution of one iteration of the CG algorithm in the heterogeneous case (9 CPU and 3 GPU workers) with different partitioning strategies for the Audi_kw matrix. In (a), the nnz is balanced per block-row (33 μs). In (b) a feed-back from a history based performance model is used for the partitioning of the matrix (16 μs).

heterogeneous node composed of all available computational resources. Because the considered platform has 12 CPU cores and three GPUs, but that each GPU has a CPU core dedicated to handle it, we can only rely on 9 CPU workers and 3 GPU workers in total.

Figure 7 presents execution traces of preliminary experiments that rely on two different strategies for balancing the load between CPU cores and GPU. These traces show the ability of task-based programming in exploiting heterogeneous platforms. However, they also show that more advanced load balancing strategies need to be designed in order to achieve a better occupancy. This question has not been fully investigated yet and will be further investigated in a future work.

Acknowledgement. The authors acknowledge the support by the INRIA-TOTAL strategic action DIP (http://dip.inria.fr) and especially Henri Calandra who closely followed this work.

References

1. Agullo, E., Augonnet, C., Dongarra, J., Faverge, M., Langou, J., Ltaief, H., Tomov, S.: LU factorization for accelerator-based systems. In: Siegel, H.J., El-Kadi, A. (eds.) The 9th IEEE/ACS International Conference on Computer Systems and Applications, AICCSA 2011, Sharm El-Sheikh, Egypt, 27–30 December 2011, pp. 217–224. IEEE (2011)
2. Agullo, E., Augonnet, C., Dongarra, J., Faverge, M., Ltaief, H., Thibault, S., Tomov, S.: QR factorization on a multicore node enhanced with multiple GPU accelerators. In: IPDPS, pp. 932–943. IEEE (2011)
3. Agullo, E., Augonnet, C., Dongarra, J., Ltaief, H., Namyst, R., Thibault, S., Tomov, S.: Faster, cheaper, better - a hybridization methodology to develop linear algebra software for GPUs. In: Hwu, W.W. (ed.) GPU Computing Gems, vol. 2. Morgan Kaufmann, September 2010
4. Agullo, E., Buttari, A., Guermouche, A., Lopez, F.: Implementing multifrontal sparse solvers for multicore architectures with sequential task flow runtime systems. ACM Trans. Math. Softw. **43**, 13 (2016)

5. Augonnet, C., Thibault, S., Namyst, R., Wacrenier, P.-A.: STARPU: a unified platform for task scheduling on heterogeneous multicore architectures. In: Sips, H., Epema, D., Lin, H.-X. (eds.) Euro-Par 2009. LNCS, vol. 5704, pp. 863–874. Springer, Heidelberg (2009). doi:10.1007/978-3-642-03869-3_80

6. Bosilca, G., Bouteiller, A., Danalis, A., Faverge, M., Haidar, A., Hérault, T., Kurzak, J., Langou, J., Lemarinier, P., Ltaief, H., Luszczek, P., YarKhan, A., Dongarra, J.: Flexible development of dense linear algebra algorithms on massively parallel architectures with DPLASMA. In: IPDPS Workshops, pp. 1432–1441. IEEE (2011)

7. Buttari, A., Langou, J., Kurzak, J., Dongarra, J.: Parallel tiled QR factorization for multicore architectures. Concurr. Comput. Pract. Exp. 20(13), 1573–1590 (2008)

8. Kurzak, J., Ltaief, H., Dongarra, J., Badia, R.M.: Scheduling dense linear algebra operations on multicore processors. Concurr. Comput. Pract. Exp. 22(1), 15–44 (2010)

9. Lacoste, X., Faverge, M., Ramet, P., Thibault, S., Bosilca, G.: Taking advantage of hybrid systems for sparse direct solvers via task-based runtimes, May 2014

10. Nakov, S.: On the design of sparse hybrid linear solvers for modern parallel architectures. Theses, Université de Bordeaux, December 2015

11. Quintana-Ortí, G., Quintana-Ortí, E.S., Chan, E., Van Zee, F.G., van de Geijn, R.A.: Scheduling of QR factorization algorithms on SMP and multi-core architectures. In: Proceedings of PDP 2008, FLAME Working Note #24 (2008)

12. Quintana-Ortí, G., Igual, F.D., Quintana-Ortí, E.S., van de Geijn, R.A.: Solving dense linear systems on platforms with multiple hardware accelerators. ACM SIGPLAN Not. 44(4), 121–130 (2009)

13. Saad, Y.: Iterative Methods for Sparse Linear Systems, 2nd edn. Society for Industrial and Applied Mathematics, Philadelphia (2003)

Task-Based Sparse Hybrid Linear Solver for Distributed Memory Heterogeneous Architectures

Emmanuel Agullo, Luc Giraud$^{(\boxtimes)}$, and Stojce Nakov

Inria, HiePACS Project-Team, Bordeaux, France
luc.giraud@inria.fr

Abstract. Heterogeneity is emerging as one of the most challenging characteristics of today's parallel environments. However, not many fully-featured advanced numerical, scientific libraries have been ported on such architectures. In this paper, we propose to extend a sparse hybrid solver for handling distributed memory heterogeneous platforms. As in the original solver, we perform a domain decomposition and associate one subdomain with one MPI process. However, while each subdomain was processed sequentially (binded onto a single CPU core) in the original solver, the new solver instead relies on task-based local solvers, delegating tasks to available computing units. We show that this "MPI+task" design conveniently allows for exploiting distributed memory heterogeneous machines. Indeed, a subdomain can now be processed on multiple CPU cores (such as a whole multicore processor or a subset of the available cores) possibly enhanced with GPUs. We illustrate our discussion with the MAPHYS sparse hybrid solver relying on the PASTIX and CHAMELEON dense and sparse direct libraries, respectively. Interestingly, this two-level MPI+task design furthermore provides extra flexibility for controlling the number of subdomains, enhancing the numerical stability of the considered hybrid method. While the rise of heterogeneous computing has been strongly carried out by the theoretical community, this study aims at showing that it is now also possible to build complex software layers on top of runtime systems to exploit heterogeneous architectures.

Keywords: High Performance Computing (HPC) · Heterogeneous architectures · MPI · Task-based programming · Runtime system · Sparse hybrid solver · Multicore · GPU

1 Introduction

Parallel sparse linear algebra solvers are often the innermost numerical kernels in scientific and engineering applications; consequently, they are one of the most time consuming parts. In order to cope with the hierarchical hardware design of modern large-scale supercomputers, the HPC solver community has proposed

© Springer International Publishing AG 2017
F. Desprez et al. (Eds.): Euro-Par 2016 Workshops, LNCS 10104, pp. 83–95, 2017.
DOI: 10.1007/978-3-319-58943-5_7

new sparse methods. One promising approach to high-performance, scalable solution of large sparse linear systems in parallel scientific computing is to combine direct and iterative methods. To achieve a high scalability, algebraic domain decomposition methods are commonly employed to split a large size linear system into smaller size linear systems that can be efficiently and concurrently handled by a sparse direct solver while the solution along the interfaces is computed iteratively [20, 22, 37, 40]. Such an hybrid approach exploits the advantages of both direct and iterative methods. The iterative component allows us to use a small amount of memory and provides a natural way for parallelization. The direct part provides its favorable numerical properties; furthermore, this combination provides opportunities to exploit several levels of parallelism as we do in this paper. In this study we consider an actual fully-featured parallel sparse hybrid (direct/iterative) linear solver, MAPHYS[1] [3].

Starting from a baseline MPI version of the considered hybrid solver, the objective of this study is to propose a prototype extension for which each MPI process can handle heterogeneous processing units with a task-based approach, delegating the task management to a runtime system. A preliminary experimental study asseses the potential of the approach.

This paper is organized as follows. Section 2 presents the solver considered in this study and its baseline parallel design. Section 3 presents background on task-based linear algebra and sparse hybrid solvers. Section 4 presents the design of the task-based extension proposed for our sparse hybrid solver. Preliminary results are discussed in Sect. 5 while concluding remarks on this work and perspectives are discussed in Sect. 6.

2   Baseline MPI Hybrid (Direct/Iterative) Solver

We now present the sparse hybrid (direct/iterative) method (Sect. 2.1) considered in this study and its baseline parallel design (Sect. 2.2).

2.1   Method

Let $\mathcal{A}x = b$ be the linear problem and $\mathcal{G} = \{V, E\}$ the adjacency graph associated with $\mathcal{A}$. In this graph, each vertex is associated with a row or column of the matrix $\mathcal{A}$ and it exists an edge between the vertices i and j if the entry $a_{i,j}$ is non zero. In the sequel, to facilitate the exposure and limit the notation we voluntarily mix a vertex of $\mathcal{G}$ with its index depending on the context of the description. The governing idea behind substructuring or Schur complement methods is to split the unknowns in two categories: interior and interface vertices. We assume that the vertices of the graph $\mathcal{G}$ are partitioned into $\mathcal{N}$ disconnected subgraphs $\mathcal{I}_1, ...,$ $\mathcal{I}_\mathcal{N}$ separated by the global vertex separator Γ. We also decompose the vertex separator Γ into non-disjoint subsets Γ_i, where Γ_i is the set of vertices in Γ that are connected to at least one vertex of $\mathcal{I}_i$. Notice that this decomposition is not

---

[1] https://project.inria.fr/maphys/.

a partition as $\Gamma_i \cap \Gamma_j \neq \emptyset$ when the set of vertices in this intersection defines the separator of $\mathcal{I}_i$ and $\mathcal{I}_j$. By analogy with classical domain decomposition in a finite element framework, $\Omega_i = \mathcal{I}_i \cup \Gamma_i$ will be referred to as a subdomain with internal unknowns $\mathcal{I}_i$ and interface unknowns Γ_i. If we denote $\mathcal{I} = \cup \mathcal{I}_i$ and order vertices in $\mathcal{I}$ first, we obtain the following block reordered linear system

$$\begin{pmatrix} \mathcal{A}_{\mathcal{II}} & \mathcal{A}_{\mathcal{I}\Gamma} \\ \mathcal{A}_{\Gamma\mathcal{I}} & \mathcal{A}_{\Gamma\Gamma} \end{pmatrix} \begin{pmatrix} x_{\mathcal{I}} \\ x_{\Gamma} \end{pmatrix} = \begin{pmatrix} b_{\mathcal{I}} \\ b_{\Gamma} \end{pmatrix} \tag{1}$$

where x_Γ contains all unknowns associated with the separator and $x_{\mathcal{I}}$ contains the unknowns associated with the interiors. Because the interior vertices are only connected to either interior vertices in the same subgraph or with vertices in the interface, the matrix $\mathcal{A}_{\mathcal{II}}$ has a block diagonal structure, where each diagonal block corresponds to one subgraph $\mathcal{I}_i$. Eliminating $x_{\mathcal{I}}$ from the second block row of Eq. (1) leads to the reduced system

$$\mathcal{S} x_\Gamma = f \tag{2}$$

where

$$\mathcal{S} = \mathcal{A}_{\Gamma\Gamma} - \mathcal{A}_{\Gamma\mathcal{I}} \mathcal{A}_{\mathcal{II}}^{-1} \mathcal{A}_{\mathcal{I}\Gamma} \text{ and } f = b_\Gamma - \mathcal{A}_{\Gamma\mathcal{I}} \mathcal{A}_{\mathcal{II}}^{-1} b_{\mathcal{I}}. \tag{3}$$

The matrix $\mathcal{S}$ is referred to as the *Schur complement matrix*. This reformulation leads to a general strategy for solving (1). Specifically, an iterative method can be applied to solve (2). Once x_Γ is known, $x_{\mathcal{I}}$ can be computed with one additional solve for the interior unknowns via

$$x_{\mathcal{I}} = \mathcal{A}_{\mathcal{II}}^{-1} (b_{\mathcal{I}} - \mathcal{A}_{\mathcal{I}\Gamma} x_\Gamma).$$

We illustrate in Fig. 1a all these notations for a decomposition into 4 subdomains. The local interiors are disjoint and form a partition of the interior $\mathcal{I} = \sqcup \mathcal{I}_i$ (blue vertices in Fig. 1b). It is not necessarily the case for the boundaries. Indeed, two subdomains Ω_i and Ω_j may share part of their interface ($\Gamma_i \cap \Gamma_j \neq \emptyset$), such as Ω_1 and Ω_2 in Fig. 1b which share eleven vertices. Altogether, the local boundaries form the overall interface $\Gamma = \cup \Gamma_i$ (red vertices in Fig. 1b), which is not a disjoint union. Because interior vertices are only connected to vertices of their subset (either on the interior or on the boundary), matrix $\mathcal{A}_{\mathcal{II}}$ associated to the interior has a block diagonal structure, as shown in Fig. 1a. Each diagonal block $\mathcal{A}_{\mathcal{I}_i\mathcal{I}_i}$ corresponds to a local interior.

While the Schur complement system is significantly smaller and better conditioned than the original matrix $\mathcal{A}$ [34, Lemma 3.11], it is important to consider further preconditioning when employing a Krylov method. We introduce the general form of the preconditioner considered in MAPHYS. The preconditioner presented below was originally proposed in [17] and successfully applied to large problems in real life applications in [21, 24, 35]. To describe the main preconditioner in MAPHYS, considering the restriction operator $\mathcal{R}_{\Gamma_i}$ from Γ to Γ_i, we define $\bar{\mathcal{S}}_i = \mathcal{R}_{\Gamma_i} \mathcal{S} \mathcal{R}_{\Gamma_i}^T$, that corresponds to the restriction of the Schur complement to the interface Γ_i. If $\mathcal{I}_i$ is a fully connected subgraph of $\mathcal{G}$, the matrix $\bar{\mathcal{S}}_i$ is dense.

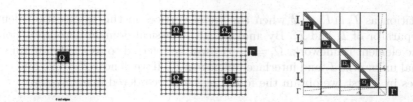

(a) Initial global graph. (b) Graph subdomains. (c) Block reordered matrix.

Fig. 1. Domain decomposition into four subdomains $\Omega_1, \ldots, \Omega_4$. The initial domain Ω may be algebraically represented with the graph $\mathcal{G}$ associated to the sparsity pattern of matrix $\mathcal{A}$ (a). The local interiors $\mathcal{I}_1, \ldots, \mathcal{I}_N$ form a partition of the interior $\mathcal{I} = \sqcup \mathcal{I}_i$ (blue vertices in (b)). They interact with each others through the interface Γ (red vertices in (b)). The block reordered matrix (c) has a block diagonal structure for the variables associated with the interior $\mathcal{A}_{\mathcal{I}\mathcal{I}}$. (Color figure online)

With these notations the Additive Schwarz preconditioner reads

$$\mathcal{M}_{AS} = \sum_{i=1}^{N} \mathcal{R}_{\Gamma_i}^T \bar{\mathcal{S}}_i^{-1} \mathcal{R}_{\Gamma_i}. \qquad (4)$$

2.2 Baseline MPI Parallelization

With all these components, the classical parallel implementation of MAPHYS can be decomposed into four main phases:

- *the partitioning step* consists of partitioning the adjacency graph $\mathcal{G}$ of $\mathcal{A}$ into several subdomains and distribute the $\mathcal{A}_i$ to different processes. For this we are able to use two state-of-the-art partitioners, SCOTCH [36] and METIS [28];
- *the factorization of the interiors* and the computation of the local Schur complement factorizes $\mathcal{A}_i$ with the PASTIX [25] or the MUMPS [9] sparse direct solver and furthermore provides the associated local Schur Complement $\mathcal{S}_i$ thanks to recent progress from the development teams of those sparse direct solvers;
- *the setup of the preconditioner* by assembling diagonal blocks of $\mathcal{S}_i$ via a few neighbour to neighbour communications and factorization of the dense local $\mathcal{S}_i$ using MKL;
- *the solve step* consists of two steps: a parallel preconditioned Krylov method performed on the reduced system (Eq. 2) to compute x_{Γ_i} where all BLAS operations are provided by MKL, followed by the back solve on the interior to compute $x_{\mathcal{I}_i}$, done by the sparse direct solver.

3 Related Work

To cope with the complexity of modern architectures, programming paradigms are being revisited. Among others, one major trend consists in writing the algorithms in terms of task graphs and delegating to a runtime system both the management of the data consistency and the orchestration of the actual execution. This paradigm has been intensively studied in the context of dense linear algebra and is now a common utility for related state-of-the-art libraries such as PLASMA [2], MAGMA [1], DPLASMA [14], CHAMELEON [4] and FLAME [39]. Dense linear algebra algorithms were indeed excellent candidates for pioneering in this direction. First, their computational pattern allows one to design very wide task graphs so that many computational units can execute tasks concurrently. Second, the building block operations they rely on, essentially level-three Basic Linear Algebra Subroutines (BLAS), are compute intensive, which makes it possible to split the work in relatively fine grain tasks while fully benefiting from GPU acceleration. As a result, these algorithms are particularly easy to schedule in the sense that state-of-the-art greedy scheduling algorithms may lead to high performance, including on platforms accelerated with multiple GPUs [4].

This trend has then been followed for designing sparse direct methods. The extra challenge in designing task-based sparse direct method is due to indirection and variable granularities of the tasks. The PASTIX team has proposed such an extension of the solver capable of running on the StarPU [11] and PaRSEC [15] runtime systems on cluster of heterogeneous nodes in the context of X. Lacoste PhD thesis [29,30]. In the meanwhile, the qr_mumps library developed by A. Buttari [16] aims at solving sparse linear least square problems and has been ported on top of those runtime systems in the context of F. Lopez PhD thesis [6,33].

With the need of solving ever larger sparse linear systems while maintaining numerical robustness, multiple sparse hybrid variants have been proposed for computing the preconditioner for the Schur complement. PDSLIN [31], SHYLU [37] and HIPS [19] first perform an exact[2] factorization of the interior of each subdomain concurrently. PDSLIN and SHYLU then compute the preconditioner with a two-fold approach. First, an approximation $\widetilde{S}$ of the (global) Schur complement S is computed. Second, this approximate Schur complement $\widetilde{S}$ is factorized to form the preconditioner for the Schur Complement system, which does not need to be formed explicitly. While PDSLIN has multiple options for discarding values lower than some user-defined thresholds at different steps of the computation of $\widetilde{S}$, SHYLU [37] also implements a structure-based approach for discarding values named *probing* and that was first proposed to approximate interfaces in DDM [18]. Instead of following such a two-fold approach, HIPS [19] forms the preconditioner by computing a global ILU factorization based on the multi-level scheme formulation from [26].

These sparse hybrid solvers have also been extended to cope with hierarchical supercomputers. Indeed, to ensure numerical robustness while exploiting all the processors of a platform, an important effort has been devoted to propose two levels of parallelism for these solvers. Designed on top of the SUPERLU_DIST [32] distributed memory sparse direct solver, PDSLIN implements a 2-level MPI (MPI+MPI) approach with finely tuned intra- and inter-subdomain load balancing [40]. A similar MPI+MPI approach has been assessed for additive

---

[2] There are also options for computing Incomplete LU (ILU) factorizations of the interiors but the related descriptions are out the scope of this paper.

Schwarz preconditioning in a prototype version of MAPHYS [23], relying on the MUMPS [9,10] and ScaLAPACK [13] sparse direct and dense distributed memory solvers, respectively. On the contrary, expecting a higher numerical robustness thanks to multi-level preconditioning, HIPS associates multiple subdomains to a single process and distributes the subdomains to the processes in order to maintain load balancing [19]. Finally, especially tuned for modern multicore platforms, SHYLU implements a 2-level MPI+thread approach [37]. A similar 2-level MPI+thread design has been investigated for MAPHYS in [35]. However, none of these extensions were tailored to exploit heterogeneous architectures.

4   Design of Task-Based Sparse Hybrid Linear Solver for Distributed Memory Heterogeneous Architectures

Although very efficient for exploiting multiple modern multicore nodes, the relatively low-level design of the 2-level parallelism sparse hybrid solvers discussed above cannot exploit heterogeneous architectures.

One solution for relieving this bottleneck would consist in fully abstracting the MPI scheme of the solver in terms of a DAG of tasks where vertices represent fine grain tasks and edges represent dependencies between them. Once the solver has been designed at such a high-level of abstraction, advanced fine-grain mapping strategies can be implemented as the burden of moving data in the system and ensuring their consistency is delegated to a runtime system. However, such a design prevents from relying on SPMD paradigms. As a consequence, it requires to fully rewrite the solver in terms of a DAG of tasks as illustrated in Fig. 2a: the DAG representing the whole numerical algorithm implemented in MAPHYS is written independently from the hardware architecture (we represent it on top of the runtime system and of the MPI processes). While there has been a lot of progress in that direction as discussed in Sect. 3 for dense (such as the DPLASMA [14] and CHAMELEON [4] task-based libraries, derived from

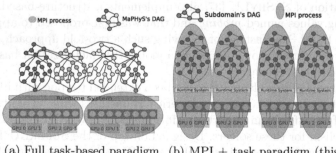

(a) Full task-based paradigm. (b) MPI + task paradigm (this study).

Fig. 2. Illustration of the execution of MAPHYS on four subdomains with two different task-based paradigms on a platform composed of two nodes of eight cores and four GPUs per node

PLASMA [2] and MAGMA [1]) and sparse direct methods (such as the task-based version of PASTIX [29] and qrm_StarPU [5]), only limited work we are aware of has been devoted to study task-based Krylov methods, the third numerical pillar on top of which hybrid solvers are built on. Indeed, a task-based version of the CG algorithm for platforms equipped with several GPUs was proposed in [7] and a fault-tolerant task-based version of this algorithm was proposed in [27], but none of them could exploit distributed memory platforms.

A second solution would consist in relying on the modular design of the hybrid solver to use appropriate libraries depending on the target architecture leading to a collection of MPI+X, MPI+Y, ... solutions to support X, Y, ... architectures respectively.

In this paper, we propose to combine both solutions with a MPI+task approach in order to benefit from the high-level modular design of the hybrid solver and abstract the architecture with task-based local sparse and direct solvers which delegate the orchestration of the execution of the tasks within computational nodes to a runtime system. With such MPI+task approach, it is not only elegant to support X, Y, ... architectures in a consistent fashion, but also possible to exploit heterogeneous $\{X + Y\}$ distributed memory architectures. Figure 2b illustrates the proposed design.

4.1 Overall Design of the MPI+task Extension of MAPHYS

In this section we explain how to create an MPI+task design of the MAPHYS solver. As illustrated in Fig. 2b, this latter approach aims at abstracting the hardware architecture relying on task-based programming and delegating the orchestration of the task within computational nodes to a runtime system. However, contrary to the full task-based abstraction depicted in Fig. 2a, each MPI process explicitly handles a DAG representing the numerical algorithm implemented in one MAPHYS subdomain. The MPI communications between subdomains are furthermore handled explicitly by MAPHYS (and not delegated to the task-based runtime system).

The goal of this preliminary study is to show the feasibility of the approach. To do so, we considered the baseline MPI version of MAPHYS and exploited the modular software architecture to substitute the multithreaded kernels with task-based versions of these kernels. We restricted our scope to the Symmetric Positive Definite (SPD) case.

In this paper we focus on the compute intensive numerical steps occurring after the *partitioning step*. Indeed, this stage is a symbolic pre-processing step; furthermore, to the best of our knowledge, none of the partitioners have yet been implemented on top of a runtime system:

– For the *factorization of the interiors*, we are relying on the task-based version of PASTIX proposed in X. Lacoste thesis [29] for which we further designed a task-based Schur complement functionality thanks to the support of the PASTIX development team.

- For the *setup of the preconditioner*, we use the task-based dense Cholesky solver from the CHAMELEON [4] library[3].
- For the *solve step*, the application of the preconditioner is performed by the CHAMELEON library and other operations involved in the iterative solution step such as level-one BLAS and matrix-vector product are executed with the multithreaded MKL library.

All in all, we use task-based sparse (PASTIX) and dense (CHAMELEON) direct solvers, both of them expressed through the StarPU task-based runtime system that we now present.

4.2   The StarPU Task-Based Runtime System

In the last decade, a large variety of task-based runtime systems have been developed. The most common strategy for the parallelization of task-based algorithms consists in traversing the DAG sequentially and submitting the tasks, as discovered, to the runtime system using a non blocking function call. The dependencies between tasks are automatically inferred by the runtime system through a data dependency analysis [8] and the actual execution of the task is then postponed to the moment when all its dependencies are satisfied. This programming model is known as a *Sequential Task Flow* (STF) model as it fully relies on `sequential consistency` for the dependency detection. This paradigm is also sometimes referred to as *superscalar* since it mimics the functioning of superscalar processors where instructions are issued sequentially from a single stream but can actually be executed in a different order and, possibly, in parallel depending on their mutual dependencies. The popularity of this model encouraged the OpenMP board to include it in the standard 4.0: the `task` construct was extended with the `depend` clause which enables the OpenMP runtime to automatically detect dependencies among tasks and consequently schedule them. Note that the abstract model that support this mechanism has been widely used before the inclusion in the standard. Among other, the StarSs [12] and StarPU [11] runtime systems have certainly strongly contributed to that progress. StarPU (read *PU) has been specifically designed for abstracting the underlying architecture so that in can execute task on any type of hardware (CPU core, GPU, ...). As a consequence, it is convenient for exploiting heterogeneous architecture. For this reason, we decided to use it for implementing the proposed task-based extension of MAPHYS.

StarPU provides a convenient interface for implementing and parallelizing applications or algorithms that can be described as a graph of tasks. Tasks have to be explicitly submitted to the runtime system along with the data they work on and the corresponding data access mode. Through data analysis, StarPU can automatically detect the dependencies among tasks and build the corresponding DAG. Once a task is submitted, the runtime tracks its dependencies and schedules its execution as soon as these are satisfied, taking care of gathering the data on the unit where the task is actually executed.

---

[3] https://project.inria.fr/chameleon/.

5   Experimental Results

In this section we present preliminary results of our task-based prototype of MAPHYS. The tests presented in this section were performed on the PlaFRIM 2 platform situated installed at Inria Bordeaux-Sud-Ouest, more precisely on the *sirocco* nodes. These nodes are composed of two Dodeca-core Haswell Intel Xeon E5-2680, for a total of 24 cores per node, and 128 GB of RAM memory. Each node is equipped with 4 Nvidia K40-M GPUs, each one having 12 GB of RAM. We consider the SPD Audi_kw matrix (size $n = 900K$ and non-zeros $nnz = 392M$) to illustrate the behavior of the proposed prototype solver. Both CHAMELEON and PASTIX use the version 1.1 of the StarPU runtime system described in Sect. 4.2. All tests were performed in double precision.

Figures 3a and b depict the traces obtained on one node, using only CPU cores or both GPUs and CPU cores, respectively. In both cases, the matrix has been decomposed in four subdomains. Each subdomain is associated with one MPI process in charge of a subset of six CPU cores (left trace Fig. 3a), or six CPU cores and one GPU (right trace Fig. 3b), respectively. The runtime system orchestrates the execution of the tasks on the different processing units. The traces represent the execution on one particular subdomain. In the heterogeneous case, each GPU has a CPU core dedicated to handle it (see Sect. 4.2).

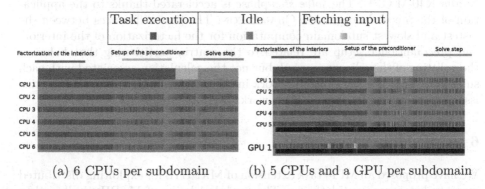

(a) 6 CPUs per subdomain   (b) 5 CPUs and a GPU per subdomain

Fig. 3. Multicore execution trace associated with one subdomain of the MPI+task MAPHYS prototype processing the Audi_kw matrix. Four subdomains (hence four processes) are used in total.

The resulting traces show the versatility of the approach that composed multi-threaded and task-based numerical kernels. The processing units are abstracted and the same code may be executed indistinguishably on the homogeneous or on the heterogeneous cases. Although the implementation is still preliminary and not optimized, Table 1 shows that the resulting timings allow for accelerating all three numerical steps with the use of one GPU per subdomain in spite of the preliminary design. The *setup of the preconditioner* benefits from the highest acceleration as it mostly consists of a dense factorization accelerated

Table 1. Minimum, average and maximum time per subdomain for the MPI+task MAPHYS prototype for the multicore case (Fig. 3a) and the heterogeneous case (Fig. 3b) processing the Audi_kw matrix. Four subdomains (hence four processes) are used in total and a dense preconditioner is applied.

		Multicore case	Heterogeneous case
Factorization of the interiors	min	19.6	23.3
	avg	37.2	31.7
	max	50.8	38.2
Setup of the preconditioner	min	4.80	1.10
	avg	7.02	3.63
	max	9.81	7.37
Solve step	min	13.1	11.8
	avg	13.2	11.8
	max	13.2	11.8

with CHAMELEON. The *factorization of the interiors* has a limited (but not negligible) acceleration because PASTIX internal kernel has not been tuned for the Nvidia K40-M GPU. The *solve step* phase is accelerated thanks to the application of the preconditioner with CHAMELEON. The time differences between the fastest and slowest subdomain computation for the factorization of the interiors and preconditioner setup are related to the matrix partitioning that balances the splitting of the adjacency graph but not the calculation associated with each subgraph. They are some ongoing work in the graph community to address this issue that is out of the scope of this work.

6   Concluding Remarks

We have proposed an MPI+task extension of MAPHYS for exploiting distributed memory heterogeneous platforms. The modular design of MAPHYS allowed to use the task-based PASTIX and CHAMELEON sparse and dense direct libraries, respectively, in order to benefit from their ability to efficiently exploit the underlying heterogeneous architecture.

Although this prototype extension of MAPHYS is working properly and showed the feasibility of the proposed approach, designing a solid MPI+task version of MAPHYS would require further work. First of all, the proposed approach still follows a bulk-synchronous parallelism [38] (also sometimes designated as fork-join approach) pattern. Indeed, the calls to PASTIX and CHAMELEON, yet local to each subdomain, induce costly pre-processing. On the one hand, PASTIX need to perform a reordering of the variables to limit fill-in and a symbolic factorization. These steps are sequential in the present prototype. Although there exist parallel implementations of these steps, they are known to have a very limited parallel efficiency. To overcome the subsequent synchronizations, it would therefore be necessary to overlap these symbolic pre-processing steps with other numerical operations. On the other hand, following PLASMA design, CHAMELEON first decomposes the dense matrix in tiles, which is also a synchronizing operation. As for PLASMA, there exists an advanced interface allowing for tackling matrices already decomposed into tiles. Using this interface would certainly alleviate the bottleneck occurring within the *setup of the preconditioner* when calling the dense solver.

Other operations involved in the iterative solution step such as level-one BLAS and matrix-vector product could be implemented with a task-based approach. In the case of a dense preconditioner, these operations could also be implemented by calling BLAS operations implemented in CHAMELEON. However, in the present state, without using the advanced interface discussed above, the synchronizations would occur multiple times per iteration. A full task-based CG solver is presented in [7] and discuss in details how synchronization points can be alleviated.

To completely alleviate the synchronizations between the different sequences into which MAPHYS is decomposed, it would be necessary to further overlap communications with computations. This could be performed with a clever usage of asynchronous MPI calls. This approach is relatively difficult to implement and has been applied to overlap main stages in MAPHYS, both in the MPI+thread version and in the MPI+task prototype discussed in this section. However, relying on this paradigm for performing fine-grain overlapping would be challenging and certainly result in a code very complex to maintain. Alternatively, the MPI calls can be appended to the task flow. Doing so, the task-based runtime system can dynamically decide when to perform the actual MPI call to the MPI layer and interleave them with fine-grain computational tasks. Modern runtime systems such as StarPU and PaRSEC provide such an opportunity. However, even in that case, the task-flow would still have to be designed accordingly to the mapping between tasks and processes. On the contrary, the full task approach (see Fig. 2a) would allows for fully abstracting the hardware architecture and makes the mapping issues practically orthogonal to the design of the task flow.

References

1. MAGMA Users' Guide, version 0.2, November 2009. http://icl.cs.utk.edu/magma
2. PLASMA Users' Guide: Parallel Linear Algebra Software for Multicore Architectures, Version 2.0, November 2009. http://icl.cs.utk.edu/plasma
3. Agullo, E., Giraud, L., Guermouche, A., Roman, J.: Parallel hierarchical hybrid linear solvers for emerging computing platforms. C. R. Acad. Sci. Mec. **339**(2–3), 96–105 (2011)
4. Agullo, E., Augonnet, C., Dongarra, J., Ltaief, H., Namyst, R., Thibault, S., Tomov, S.: Faster, cheaper, better - a hybridization methodology to develop linear algebra software for GPUs. In: Hwu, W.W. (ed.) GPU Computing Gems, vol. 2. Morgan Kaufmann, September 2010

5. Agullo, E., Buttari, A., Guermouche, A., Lopez, F.: Multifrontal QR factorization for multicore architectures over runtime systems. In: Wolf, F., Mohr, B., Mey, D. (eds.) Euro-Par 2013. LNCS, vol. 8097, pp. 521–532. Springer, Heidelberg (2013). doi:10.1007/978-3-642-40047-6_53

6. Agullo, E., Buttari, A., Guermouche, A., Lopez, F.: Implementing multifrontal sparse solvers for multicore architectures with Sequential Task Flow runtime systems. ACM Trans. Math. Softw. **43**, 13 (2016)

7. Agullo, E., Giraud, L., Guermouche, A., Nakov, S., Roman, J.: Task-based conjugate-gradient for multi-GPUs platforms. Research report RR-8192, INRIA (2012)

8. Allen, R., Kennedy, K.: Optimizing Compilers for Modern Architectures: A Dependence-Based Approach. Morgan Kaufmann, San Francisco (2002)

9. Amestoy, P.R., Duff, I.S., Koster, J., L'Excellent, J.-Y.: A fully asynchronous multifrontal solver using distributed dynamic scheduling. SIAM J. Matrix Anal. Appl. **23**(1), 15–41 (2001)

10. Amestoy, P.R., Guermouche, A., L'Excellent, J.-Y., Pralet, S.: Hybrid scheduling for the parallel solution of linear systems. Parallel Comput. **32**(2), 136–156 (2006)

11. Augonnet, C., Thibault, S., Namyst, R., Wacrenier, P.-A.: STARPU: a unified platform for task scheduling on heterogeneous multicore architectures. In: Sips, H., Epema, D., Lin, H.-X. (eds.) Euro-Par 2009. LNCS, vol. 5704, pp. 863–874. Springer, Heidelberg (2009). doi:10.1007/978-3-642-03869-3_80

12. Ayguadé, E., Badia, R.M., Igual, F.D., Labarta, J., Mayo, R., Quintana-Ortí, E.S.: An extension of the StarSs programming model for platforms with multiple GPUs. In: Sips, H., Epema, D., Lin, H.-X. (eds.) Euro-Par 2009. LNCS, vol. 5704, pp. 851–862. Springer, Heidelberg (2009). doi:10.1007/978-3-642-03869-3_79

13. Blackford, L.S., Choi, J., Cleary, A., D'Azevedo, E., Demmel, J., Dhillon, I., Dongarra, J., Hammarling, S., Henry, G., Petitet, A., Stanley, K., Walker, D., Whaley, R.C.: ScaLAPACK Users' Guide. SIAM Press, Philadelphia (1997)

14. Bosilca, G., Bouteiller, A., Danalis, A., Faverge, M., Haidar, H., Herault, T., Kurzak, J., Langou, J., Lemarinier, P., Ltaief, H., Luszczek, P., YarKhan, A., Dongarra, J.: Distributed-memory task execution and dependence tracking within DAGuE and the DPLASMA project. Innovative Computing Laboratory Technical report (2010)

15. Bosilca, G., Bouteiller, A., Danalis, A., Faverge, M., Hérault, T., Dongarra, J.J.: PaRSEC: exploiting heterogeneity to enhance scalability. Comput. Sci. Eng. **15**(6), 36–45 (2013)

16. Buttari, A.: Fine-grained multithreading for the multifrontal QR factorization of sparse matrices. SIAM J. Sci. Comput. **35**(4), C323–C345 (2013)

17. Carvalho, L.M., Giraud, L., Meurant, G.: Local preconditioners for two-level non-overlapping domain decomposition methods. Numer. Linear Algebra Appl. **8**(4), 207–227 (2001)

18. Chan, T.F.C., Mathew, T.P.: The interface probing technique in domain decomposition. SIAM J. Matrix Anal. Appl. **13**(1), 212–238 (1992)

19. Gaidamour, J., Hénon, P.: A parallel direct/iterative solver based on a Schur complement approach. In: 2013 IEEE 16th International Conference on Computational Science and Engineering, pp. 98–105 (2008)

20. Gaidamour, J., Hénon, P.: HIPS: a parallel hybrid direct/iterative solver based on a Schur complement approach. In: Proceedings of PMAA (2008)

21. Giraud, L., Haidar, A., Watson, L.T.: Parallel scalability study of hybrid preconditioners in three dimensions. Parallel Comput. **34**, 363–379 (2008)

22. Giraud, L., Haidar, A.: Parallel algebraic hybrid solvers for large 3D convection-diffusion problems. Numer. Algorithms **51**(2), 151–177 (2009)
23. Giraud, L., Haidar, A., Pralet, S.: Using multiple levels of parallelism to enhance the performance of domain decomposition solvers. Parallel Comput. **36**(5–6), 285–296 (2010)
24. Haidar, A.: On the parallel scalability of hybrid linear solvers for large 3D problems. Ph.D. thesis, Institut National Polytechnique de Toulouse, 17 December 2008
25. Hénon, P., Ramet, P., Roman, J.: PaStiX: a high-performance parallel direct solver for sparse symmetric definite systems. Parallel Comput. **28**(2), 301–321 (2002)
26. Hénon, P., Saad, Y.: A parallel multistage ILU factorization based on a hierarchical graph decomposition. SIAM J. Sci. Comput. **28**(6), 2266–2293 (2006)
27. Jaulmes, L., Casas, M., Moretó, M., Ayguadé, E., Labarta, J., Valero, M.: Exploiting asynchrony from exact forward recovery for due in iterative solvers. In: Proceedings of the International Conference for High Performance Computing, Networking, Storage and Analysis, SC 2015, pp. 53:1–53:12. ACM, New York (2015)
28. Karypis, G., Kumar, V.: MéliS - Unstructured Graph Partitioning and Sparse Matrix Ordering System - Version 2.0. University of Minnesota, June 1995
29. Lacoste, X.: Scheduling and memory optimizations for sparse direct solver on multi-core/multi-GPU cluster systems. Ph.D. thesis, LaBRI, Université Bordeaux, Talence, France, February 2015
30. Lacoste, X., Faverge, M., Ramet, P., Thibault, S., Bosilca, G.: Taking advantage of hybrid systems for sparse direct solvers via task-based runtimes, May 2014
31. Li, X.S., Shao, M., Yamazaki, I., Ng, E.G.: Factorization-based sparse solvers and preconditioners. J. Phys. Conf. Ser. **180**(1), 012015 (2009)
32. Li, X.S., Demmel, J.W.: SuperLU_DIST: a scalable distributed-memory sparse direct solver for unsymmetric linear systems. ACM Trans. Math. Softw. **29**(2), 110–140 (2003)
33. Lopez, F.: Task-based multifrontal QR solver for heterogeneous architectures. Ph.D. thesis, University Paul Sabatier, Toulouse, France (2015, submitted)
34. Mathew, T.P.A.: Domain Decomposition Methods for the Numerical Solution of Partial Differential Equations. Lecture Notes in Computational Science and Engineering, vol. 61. Springer, Heidelberg (2008). doi:10.1007/978-3-540-77209-5
35. Nakov, S.: On the design of sparse hybrid linear solvers for modern parallel architectures. Theses, Université de Bordeaux, December 2015
36. Pellegrini, F., Roman, J.: Sparse matrix ordering with Scotch. In: Hertzberger, B., Sloot, P. (eds.) HPCN-Europe 1997. LNCS, vol. 1225, pp. 370–378. Springer, Heidelberg (1997). doi:10.1007/BFb0031609
37. Rajamanickam, S., Boman, E.G., Heroux, M.A.: ShyLU: a hybrid-hybrid solver for multicore platforms. In: International Parallel and Distributed Processing Symposium, pp. 631–643 (2012)
38. Valiant, L.G.: A bridging model for parallel computation. Commun. ACM **33**(8), 103–111 (1990)
39. Van Zee, F.G., Chan, E., van de Geijn, R.A., Quintana-Orti, E.S., Quintana-Orti, G.: The libflame library for dense matrix computations. Comput. Sci. Eng. **11**(6), 56–63 (2009)
40. Yamazaki, I., Li, X.S.: On techniques to improve robustness and scalability of a parallel hybrid linear solver. In: Palma, J.M.L.M., Daydé, M., Marques, O., Lopes, J.C. (eds.) VECPAR 2010. LNCS, vol. 6449, pp. 421–434. Springer, Heidelberg (2011). doi:10.1007/978-3-642-19328-6_38

Automatic Generation of OpenCL Code for ARM Architectures

Sergio Afonso[✉], Alejandro Acosta, and Francisco Almeida

Universidad de La Laguna, San Cristóbal de La Laguna, Spain
{safonsof,aacostad,falmeida}@ull.es

Abstract. The efficient exploitation of the increasing computational capabilities of mobile devices is still a challenge. The heterogeneity of Systems on Chip (SoC) makes necessary a very specific knowledge of their hardware in order to harness their full potential. OpenCL is a well known standard for cross-platform usage of accelerator devices. We follow an annotation-based approach for solving the problem of high development cost of OpenCL programming for mobile devices. With our approach, the programmer can select from different programming models the one that offers the best performance for each section of the application. Computational results show that our automatically-generated OpenCL code can outperform Renderscript when running on the GPU of Android devices, making it the best choice for a range of parallel algorithms.

Keywords: Parallelizing compiler · Source-to-source translation · Annotation based · OpenCL · Android · ARM

1 Introduction

Technologies previously only available in desktop computers are now implemented in embedded and mobile devices. In this scenario, we can find that new processors integrating multicore architectures, GPUs and DSPs are being developed for this market. The Nvidia Tegra [15], the Qualcomm Snapdragon [16] and the Samsung Exynos [17] are some examples of platforms that go in this direction. Conceptually, the architectural model can be viewed as a traditional heterogeneous CPU/GPU system where memory is shared between processing units and acts as a high-bandwidth communication channel.

In non-unified memory architectures, it is common to have a subset of system memory addressable by the GPU. Technologies like Algorithmic Memory [12], GPUDirect [14] and Unified Virtual Addressing from Nvidia and HSA from AMD [5] are working towards a unified memory system for CPUs and GPUs on top of traditional memory architectures. At the same time, memory performance continues to be outpaced by the ever increasing demand of faster processors.

Many frameworks have been created to support the development of software for these devices. The main companies competing in this market have their own platforms: Android from Google [9], iOS from Apple [7] and Windows Phone

© Springer International Publishing AG 2017
F. Desprez et al. (Eds.): Euro-Par 2016 Workshops, LNCS 10104, pp. 96–107, 2017.
DOI: 10.1007/978-3-319-58943-5_8

from Microsoft [13]. Each of these platforms provide a high-level development framework that makes easier the creation of applications. However, they are more geared towards fast development of interactive applications than to reduce the difficulty of efficiently exploiting the underlying parallel architecture. Given the high heterogeneity existent among these devices, the creation of tools is needed to improve the development productivity while exploiting the computational capabilities of their different architectures.

Android provides three development models with distinct features that have to be used in different parts of the application in order to get the best overall performance. In [20] a detailed comparative of these models was presented and the necessity of a unified programming model for Android is highlighted.

- **Java:** A very comprehensive API is provided, so it is the easiest model to program. Most Android applications are written in Java, so Android developers should be familiar with this language.
- **Renderscript:** It is designed for computationally intensive tasks, mainly SPMD. It requires to learn a new language based on C.
- **Native C:** It provides access to native libraries, suffering from less runtime overhead than Java, which sometimes compensates the extra development cost that it supposes.

Paralldroid [1,2,4] is a development framework that allows the automatic creation of Native C and Renderscript applications—sequential and parallel— for mobile devices. Under Paralldroid, the developer annotates the main components of each Java class that has to be optimized. It uses the information provided by the annotations to generate a new program that incorporates the code sections to run on the CPU or GPU, using a specified target language. Therefore, Paralldroid unifies the different programming models of Android.

Paralldroid is an evolution of other annotation-based approaches to automatic parallelization, such as OpenMP or OpenACC, because it is higher level. OpenMP and OpenACC annotations still require the developer to annotate blocks of code inside the algorithm's implementation, whilst Paralldroid separates more clearly the implementation from the parallel semantics by applying annotations to classes, fields and methods. Our goal is to obtain comparable performance to these approaches while making it easier for the developer.

In this paper we present a new backend system for Paralldroid to support the generation of OpenCL code. OpenCL is a native library and programming language for writing high performance applications for heterogeneous systems, supporting many kinds of accelerators [10]. It provides a mechanism for parallel programming and a low-level API for communicating data and handling the different computing devices present in the hardware platform. Currently, OpenCL is not supported by the Android implementations provided by Google. However, given the heterogeneity of the mobile ecosystem, some manufacturers offer OpenCL in their devices, so it is still interesting to generate OpenCL for those.

The main contributions of this paper are:

- The importance of OpenCL in desktop systems is well known. Now, this programming model is extended to mobile devices. The code generation methodology proposed allows OpenCL code to be transparently executed from Android applications written in Java.

- The support of OpenCL opens the possibility to extend Paralldroid to platforms other than Android. The only requirements that this platform needs to meet are support for Java and an OpenCL driver.
- We analyze the performance of the different programming models supported to prove the benefits of our tool. Computational results show that this new backend improves the performance of Paralldroid-generated programs when ran in GPUs.
- Our new approach lets high-level Java application developers take advantage of more efficient GPU executions without modifying the annotated Java source code. The improvements in performance come from the use of a lower-level library for heterogeneous computing and, as a result, the increase in complexity of the code generation process.

Some tools that generate parallel code from an extension to Java have been presented in [8,18,19]. In all those cases, the Java syntax is modified to introduce new syntactic elements into the language. The main disadvantage of this approach is that those new elements are not compatible with the definition of Java, so a standard Java compiler cannot compile the source code with these extensions. Paralldroid definitions are compatible with Java, because they are a set of new annotations that a standard Java compiler can just ignore. However, the semantics of parallel methods are not preserved in that case. In [11], authors present a Domain Specific Language for generating Renderscript code. It is specific for image processing languages, and it has the downside of requiring the user to learn a new programming language. Our proposal, in contrast, is based on the main language for Android, and our target users know this language.

This paper is structured as follows: Sect. 2 introduces the development models in Android and the different alternatives it offers for exploiting mobile devices, and some of the difficulties associated to each development model are shown. Section 3 gives an overview of the methodologies proposed by Paralldroid. Section 4 presents our new backend to Paralldroid to support the generation of OpenCL code. The performance of our automatically generated OpenCL code is validated in Sect. 5 using four different image-processing applications. We measure execution times of a sequential Java implementation and of Renderscript and OpenCL implementations automatically generated by Paralldroid. We finish with some conclusions and future work in Sect. 6.

2   The Development Model in Android

Android is a Linux based operating system mainly designed for mobile devices such as smartphones and tablets. Android applications are written in Java, and the Android Software Development Kit (SDK) provides the libraries and tools needed to build, test, and debug applications. Starting in version 5.0 applications run in the Android Run Time (ART), which manages system resources allocated to each application.

Besides the development of Java applications, Android provides packages of development tools and libraries to develop native applications: The Native Development Kit (NDK). The NDK enables to implement parts of the application running in ART using native programming languages such as C and C++. Native code communicates with the main class written in Java by using the Java Native Interface (JNI). Files of native source code are compiled using the GNU compiler (GCC). Note that using native code does not result in an automatic performance increase, but it always increases application complexity. Hence, its use is only recommended in CPU-intensive operations that don't allocate much memory, such as signal processing and physics simulations. Native code is also useful for porting an existing native library to Android. We can access OpenCL from the native context if the OpenCL runtime libraries are present in the device.

In order to exploit the high computational capabilities on current devices, Android provides Renderscript, which is a high performance computation API and a programming language based on the C language (C99 standard). Renderscript allows the execution of parallel applications under several types of processors such as the CPU, GPU or DSP, selecting one of them at runtime depending on the hardware's features. Renderscript (.rs files) codes are compiled using an LLVM compiler based on Clang. Moreover, it generates a set of Java wrapper classes around the Renderscript code. Again, the use of Renderscript code does not result in an automatic performance increase, but it is useful for applications that do image processing, mathematical modelling, or any operations that require lots of parallel computation.

3   Paralldroid

Paralldroid is designed to ease the development of parallel applications on the Android platform. We assume that mobile platforms feature a classical CPU and other kind of *co-processor*, like a GPU, that can be exploited through OpenCL or Renderscript. The way Paralldroid does this is by transforming the original Java source code into another code that, preserving the same semantics, is executed in a more efficient way. The generation of code on other languages is also required in order to take advantage of all the programming models in Android, but in each algorithm the best programming model to use can be a different one due to their different features. This is why the target language is something the user explicitly indicates when using Paralldroid.

Directive based parallelism has been successfully used in applications for High Performance Computing (HPC) systems for years, and Paralldroid takes the same approach in the mobile application development world.

The methodologies proposed by Paralldroid can be defined in two points:

– **Annotation methodology:** The Target annotation creates a data environment that allows the memory management and the execution of code in the target context. Elements inside a class (fields and methods) can be used to define the data and execution models in the target context. Paralldroid

Table 1. Paralldroid annotations

Annotation	Applied to	Parameters	Scope
@Target	Classes	Value	—
@Map	Fields, method parameters	Value	@Target
@Declare	Fields, methods	—	@Target
@Parallel	Methods	—	@Target
@Input	Method parameters	—	@Parallel
@Output	Method parameters	—	@Parallel
@NumThreads	Methods, method parameters	Field	@Parallel
@Index	Method parameters	—	@Parallel

defines a set of annotations that are applied to the class fields and method definitions. These annotations allow the creation of a device data environment, specify how a variable is mapped in the device data environment (data model) and also specify how a section of code is executed in the device environment (execution model), see Table 1.
- **Generation methodology:** The Paralldroid code generation process is integrated in the OpenJDK Java compiling process. It adds a set of stages in which the Paralldroid annotations are detected and new ASTs are generated according to these annotations. For each implementation to generate from a single annotated Java source, a translator class has to be created, which takes the original AST as input and outputs another AST. To add support for a new language, only is needed a new translator for the modified Java code and the target language. This makes Paralldroid easily extensible.

4   OpenCL Code Generation

The OpenCL standard represents the most important effort to create a common high performance programming interface for heterogeneous devices. The main issue of OpenCL is the complexity of its programming model, which makes it difficult to use and to keep the maintainability of the application.

The annotation methodology proposed by Paralldroid simplifies the complexity associated to OpenCL. Based on a Java class definition, the programmer can add a set of annotations to generate OpenCL code that can be executed transparently, because it is integrated into the Java workflow. This simplifies the development of OpenCL powered Android applications and helps this standard to have a major adoption on the Android development community.

Figure 1 shows the different sets of translations classes of Paralldroid. As with any of the other target languages of Paralldroid, the way to generate new ASTs from the original source code is to create a translation class for each output AST. The Java AST translator generates the modified Java code that manages

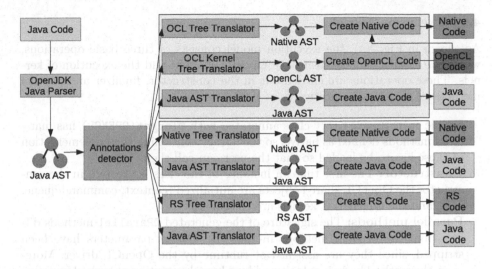

Fig. 1. Paralldroid translator classes. Our contribution is highlighted.

the data and execution models of OpenCL and forwards the implementation
of methods to the target context, according to the methodology explained in
Fig. 2. However, there is a noticeable difference between the set of translators
for OpenCL and the others. That difference is the fact that there is one extra
translator class. The OpenCL context is not directly accessible from the Java
context so, in addition to generating Java and OpenCL code, native code has
also to be created to work as a bridge between the two contexts. The OpenCL
Kernel Translator, is also unlike all other translators in that it can only generate
code for annotated methods, so it is not an "standalone" translator. This means
that it has to be called from other translator when a parallel method is found.
The OpenCL Kernel Translator outputs OpenCL C code that is inserted into the
native code as a string literal. This complex model is hidden by Paralldroid; the
programmer must only create a Java class and use the Paralldroid annotations.

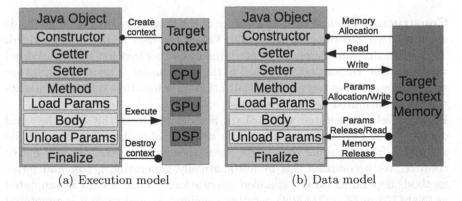

Fig. 2. Execution and data models.

4.1   Execution Model

As shown in Fig. 2(a), the execution model consists of three basic operations, which are creating and releasing the OpenCL context and the execution of kernels. These operations are carried out in the constructor, finalizer and parallel methods of the class, respectively.

- **Static initializer:** Every class annotated with `@Target(OPENCL)` has many of its methods defined as native, so the library containing the implementation of those has to be loaded so that the user can call them.
- **Constructor:** The first time an instance of the class is created, in the constructor the OpenCL shared objects are initialized (context, command queue, ...), and the OpenCL C kernels are compiled.
- **Parallel methods:** The signature of the generated `@Parallel` methods differs from the original methods in that the `@Index` parameters have been stripped, since they are assigned at runtime by the OpenCL driver. Moreover, the method body is substituted by a kernel execution enqueued in native code. The actual code of the method is translated to an OpenCL C kernel that is embedded in the native code as a string constant.
- **Methods:** All `@Declare` methods are removed from the Java class and only accessible from the target context. Every other method can also be called from Java. For methods to be callable from the target context, they have to be defined in native code and in OpenCL C code as support functions. This makes it possible to call them from sequential and parallel methods.
- **Finalizer:** All the shared OpenCL objects that were created in the first instantiation of the class have to be released when the last instance of the class is garbage-collected.

4.2   Data Model

The data model of our approach to automatically offloading computation to accelerators is shown in Fig. 2(b). The user annotates fields and method parameters in order to specify the data movements between the different contexts.

- **Constructor:** The first time an instance of the class is created, all static fields are initialized according to the default values the user might have provided. Then, each time an instance is created, the native context has to be initialized with the same values that were used in the constructor. These two things are achieved by creating two native initialization functions that take as arguments the set of initialized fields in each case.
- **Fields:** Fields annotated as `@Declare` are deleted from the Java class and only exist in the native context. The rest of fields, however, need to be accessible from external Java code, even though they exist in the native context. We accomplish this by automatically generating getter and setter methods depending on the specified annotations. When a field is annotated as `@Map(TO)` or `@Map(TOFROM)`, a setter is generated, and when it is annotated

as @Map(TOFROM) or @Map(FROM), a getter is generated. As arrays are represented in OpenCL as memory objects, these methods enqueue the required memory operations into the OpenCL command queue and transform the data format from Java to OpenCL and vice versa.

- **Methods:** When a native method that receives arrays as arguments is called, a conversion is needed between the Java and native formats and between the native and OpenCL formats. Data transfers are performed according to the @Map annotation applied to each array before and after running the body of the method. The semantic in this case is the same as that of fields.

- **Finalizer:** All memory allocated when initializing the instance is released when the garbage collector deletes it. When the last instance of the class is being deleted, then also global objects and native static fields are released.

```
1  @Target(OPENCL)
2  public class GrayScale {
3    @Declare
4    private float gMonoMult[] =
5    {0.299f, 0.587f, 0.114f};
6    @Map(TO)
7    private int width;
8    @Map(TO)
9    private int height;
10
11   public GrayScale(int width, int height){
12     this.width = width;
13     this.height = height;
14   }
15   @Parallel
16   public void test(@Map(TO) int[] srcPxs,
17     @NumThreads @Map(FROM) int[] outPxs,
18     @Index int x){
19     int acc;
20
21     acc =  (int)(((srcPxs[x]    ) & 0xff)
22          * gMonoMult[0]);
23     acc += (int)(((srcPxs[x]>> 8) & 0xff)
24          * gMonoMult[1]);
25     acc += (int)(((srcPxs[x]>>16) & 0xff)
26          * gMonoMult[2]);
27
28     outPxs[x] = (acc) + (acc << 8)
29               + (acc << 16)
30               + (srcPxs[x] << 24);
31   }
32 }
```

```
public class GrayScale {
  static {
    System.loadLibrary("grayscale");
  }
  private static int instanceCount = 0;
  private long instanceDataPtr;
  private float[] gMonoMult =
  {0.299F, 0.587F, 0.114F};
  private int width;
  private int height;
  public GrayScale(int width, int height){
    this.width = width;
    this.height = height;
    if (instanceCount == 0) initJNI();
    ++instanceCount;
    initGrayScale(gMonoMult, width, height);
  }
  public native void test(int[] srcPxstest,
    int[] outPxstest);
  public native void setWidth(int width);
  public native void setHeight(int height);
  protected void finalize(){
    destroyGrayScale();
    --instanceCount;
    if (instanceCount == 0) releaseJNI();
  }
  private native void initGrayScale(
    float[] gMonoMult, int width, int height);
  private native void destroyGrayScale();
  private static native void initJNI();
  private static native void releaseJNI();
}
```

Listing 1.1. GrayScale in Paralldroid   **Listing 1.2.** Generated Java code

4.3 Paralldroid Example

Listing 1.1 shows a Java implementation for the algorithm of conversion of an image to gray scale using Paralldroid. The @Target directive (line 1) specifies that the class has to create an OpenCL context definition and that the elements of the class have to be defined in that context. Lines 3 to 9 define its fields. The constructor is defined in lines 11 to 14. The method test (lines 16 to 31) defines the algorithm to transform an image to gray scale. The @Parallel directive specifies that this method will be executed in parallel. srcPxs and outPxs are the vectors which contain the input image and output buffer, respectively. Note the usage of the appropriate @Map directive parameter in each of them. The @NumThreads directive applied to an array means that the parallel method will be executed with as many threads as elements there are in the array, but it is also possible to specify an integer variable. The @Index directive defines the index used in the parallel execution, which is used to access the elements of the input and output vectors. The value of this variable is assigned at runtime, and its values range from zero to the number of threads minus one.

Listing 1.2 shows the code generated by our Java translator, as described in Sects. 4.1 and 4.2. The library that it loads is obtained from compiling the native code that we also generate. A set of fields have been added. instanceCount lets us initialize and release native global variables before the first instance is created and after the last one is deleted, respectively. instanceDataPtr is a field only accessed from the native code that keeps a reference to a dynamically allocated struct holding the native instance data. The constructor (lines 11 to 17) is modified to call the native global and instance initializer function.

4.4   Error Handling

A new methodology for error handling has been developed as part of this new backend for Paralldroid. This methodology was designed to ease the detection and handling of errors that could occur in the target context to make the application fail gracefully, notify or solve these problems at runtime. This methodology could be adapted to other target languages of Paralldroid providing the user with a seamless and unified way of handling errors that occur in the target contexts.

An OpenCLException class was created, which is a RuntimeException that holds specific data of the OpenCL error. This exception contains an OpenCL error code that could be used to troubleshoot the reason of the problem, and a message with either the name of the file and line number where the error was detected or the compilation log in case the error occured when compiling the OpenCL C code at runtime.

After every call to a function of the OpenCL API in the generated native code, the error code returned by the function is checked and an OpenCLException is raised if there was an error. These exceptions can be handled from the calling Java code, without any need of knowing what the native code is actually doing.

5   Computational Results

Leaving aside to future researches other relevant metrics for smartphones and tablets (e.g., power management, network management, ...), we validate the performance of the generated code using four different applications. These are based on the Renderscript image processing benchmark [6] (transforming an image to gray scale, changing contrast and saturation levels of an image and convolutions with window sizes 3×3 and 5×5). In all cases, we implemented two versions of the code: a Java sequential version and a Java version with Paralldroid annotations. From the same annotated Java code two versions were automatically generated by Paralldroid: Renderscript and OpenCL. As it was shown in [3], automatically generated Renderscript code performance was comparable to its handwritten counterpart, so we compare our generated OpenCL code to that generated Renderscript code. Our implementations were tested over a Sony Xperia Z (labelled SXZ) and an Odroid-XU3 (labelled XU3). Sony Xperia Z is based on a Qualcomm APQ8064 Snapdragon S4 Pro SoC with a Quad-core Krait CPU @ 1.5 GHz and an Adreno 320 GPU, whilst Odroid-XU3 is based on a Samsung Exynos 5422 Octa SoC with dual ARM CPUs (Cortex-A15 @ 2GHz and Cortex-A7 @ 1.3 GHz) and an 8-core ARM Mali-T628 MP6 GPU. Both devices have 2GB of RAM shared by CPU and GPU, and support OpenCL execution in their GPU.

In Fig. 3 we observe the speed-ups obtained relative to the sequential Java implementation. We depicted results for our smallest and biggest image sizes and for the finest and coarsest grain algorithms benchmarked. All OpenCL executions are done in the GPU of the device, whilst the operating system can decide at runtime where Renderscript is executed. In all our tests on the XU3, Renderscript executions were carried out on the CPU of the device, which turns out to be faster than the GPU. This may be due to the fact that XU3's GPU is not fully cache coherent, so the OpenCL driver reports that the system contains

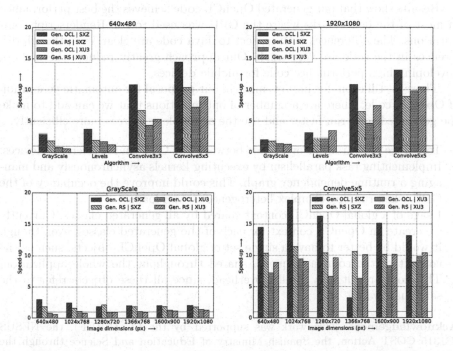

Fig. 3. Speed-up obtained with respect to the sequential Java version

two GPU devices and our generated OpenCL host code only uses one of these partitions of GPU cores. However, in almost every other case where both codes were run in a GPU our generated OpenCL code was faster.

We noticed that the input size was not as relevant as the problem's granularity regarding the performance. Coarser grain problems always experienced higher speed-ups. It is also clear from the graphs that the performance of our generated OpenCL code is more unstable than Renderscript. This could be in part due to the fact that one of the main design goals of Renderscript is to provide stable speed-ups at the expense of peak performance.

6   Conclusion

In this paper we have presented a new methodology for automatically generating OpenCL code for mobile devices. Our approach lets the developer write the whole application in a high-level programming language and, through a simple set of annotations, let the compiler take care of offloading to GPUs. Calling the offloaded code is transparent from the developer's point of view.

The Paralldroid framework has proven to ease the development of such automatic code generation tool due to its extensible design based on translator classes. It also provides us with the added value of letting the programmer choose a different target language for each class in the application, or testing and deciding the one that gives the best performance for a particular problem.

Results show that our generated OpenCL code achieves the best performance in most of the benchmarks where the GPU was used to run Renderscript computations. The differences with respect to Java code are clear, even though differences in the code are very small. Our approach greatly reduces the costs of developing high performance code for mobile devices.

There is still room for improvement in our proposal for automatic generation of OpenCL code. There are a number of optimizations that we can add to make the generated code run faster and use the available resources more efficiently:

- To reduce data transfer overheads between the CPU and accelerator devices.
- Implementing task parallelism by executing kernels asynchronously and managing a runtime dependency graph. This could improve the occupancy of the GPU when running complex heterogeneous workloads.
- Usage of a global OpenCL context shared by all generated classes. Currently we create an OpenCL context for each of the generated classes, even though it would be better to have a single set of global OpenCL objects, such as the context or the command queue, shared throughout the whole application. This could result in a smaller overhead, since all these objects refer to the same hardware.

Acknowledgement. This work was supported by the EC (ERDF), the NESUS IC1315 COST Action, the Spanish Ministry of Education and Science through the TIN2011-24598 project, and the Spanish CAPAP-H network.

References

1. Acosta, A., Afonso, S., Almeida, F.: Extending paralldroid with object oriented annotations. Parallel Comput. **57**, 25–36 (2016). http://www.sciencedirect.com/science/article/pii/S0167819116300126
2. Acosta, A., Almeida, F.: Towards a unified heterogeneous development model in android. In: 11th International Workshop HeteroPar 2013: Algorithms, Models and Tools for Parallel Computing on Heterogeneous Platforms (2013)
3. Acosta, A., Almeida, F.: Paralldroid: performance analysis of GPU executions. In: Lopes, L., et al. (eds.) Euro-Par 2014. LNCS, vol. 8806, pp. 387–399. Springer, Cham (2014). doi:10.1007/978-3-319-14313-2_33
4. Acosta, A., Almeida, F.: Performance analysis of paralldroid generated programs. In: 2014 22nd Euromicro International Conference on Parallel, Distributed, and Network-Based Processing, pp. 60–67 (2014)
5. Anandtech: AMD Outlines HSA Roadmap: Unified Memory for CPU/GPU in 2013, HSA GPUs in 2014. http://www.anandtech.com/show/5493/
6. AOSP: Android Open Source Project. http://source.android.com/
7. Apple: iOS: Apple mobile operating system. http://www.apple.com/ios
8. Dubach, C., Cheng, P., Rabbah, R., Bacon, D.F., Fink, S.J.: Compiling a high-level language for GPUs: (via language support for architectures and compilers). SIGPLAN Not. **47**(6), 1–12 (2012)
9. Google: Android mobile platform. http://www.android.com
10. Khronos Group: The open standard for parallel programming of heterogeneous systems. https://www.khronos.org/opencl/
11. Membarth, R., Reiche, O., Hannig, F., Teich, J.: Code generation for embedded heterogeneous architectures on android. In: DATE, pp. 1–6 (2014)
12. Systems, M.: Algorithmic Memory ^{TM}Technology. http://www.memoir-systems.com/
13. Microsoft: Windows Phone: Microsoft mobile operating system. http://www.microsoft.com/windowsphone
14. NVIDIA: GPUDirect Technology. http://developer.nvidia.com/gpudirect
15. NVIDIA: Tegra mobile processors: Tegra 2, Tegra 3 and Tegra 4. http://www.nvidia.com/object/tegra-superchip.html
16. Qualcomm: Snapdragon mobile processors. http://www.qualcomm.com/snapdragon
17. Samsung: Exynos mobile processors. http://www.samsung.com/global/business/semiconductor/minisite/Exynos/
18. Valentin, C., Christian, S., Pierre, K., François, K.P., Jean-François, R.: Parallel object programming with Java. http://gridgroup.hefr.ch/popj/doku.php
19. Viry, P.: Ateji PX for Java-parallel programming made simple. Ateji White Paper (2010)
20. Qian, X., Guangyu Zhu, X.F.L.: Comparison and analysis of the three programming models in Google android. In: 1st Asia-Pacific Programming Languages and Compilers Workshop (APPLC), June 2012

Workflow Performance Profiles: Development and Analysis

Dariusz Król[1,2(✉)], Rafael Ferreira da Silva[2], Ewa Deelman[2], and Vickie E. Lynch[3]

[1] Department of Computer Science and Academic Computer Center Cyfronet,
Faculty of Computer Science, Electronics and Telecommunications,
AGH University of Science and Technology, Krakow, Poland
dkrol@agh.edu.pl
[2] USC Information Sciences Institute, Marina Del Rey, CA, USA
[3] Oak Ridge National Laboratory, Oak Ridge TN, USA

Abstract. This paper presents a method for performance profiles development of scientific workflow. It addresses issues related to: workflows execution in a parameter sweep manner, collecting performance information about each workflow task, and analysis of the collected data with statistical learning methods. The main goal of this work is to increase the understanding about the performance of studied workflows in a systematic and predictable way. The evaluation of the presented approach is based on a real scientific workflow developed by the Spallation Neutron Source - a DOE research facility at the Oak Ridge National Laboratory. The workflow executes an ensemble of molecular dynamics and neutron scattering intensity calculations to optimize a model parameter value.

1 Introduction

Scientific workflows are a popular way of conducting extreme-scale scientific research, which may require composing thousands of computational jobs. Workflows have been widely used in different science domains, including astronomy and gravitational wave, seismology, and others [21]. In a workflow, each job may have different requirements for CPU, I/O, and memory. An accurate specification of these requirements (along with job's runtime) is crucial to optimize the performance and accuracy of resource provisioning and job scheduling algorithms, reduce the overall runtime, decrease resource utilization, etc.

Due to the high complexity of scientific workflows, users often do not have detailed knowledge about workflow jobs requirements. Typically, users overestimate job requirements, since an underestimation may lead to job termination (e.g., due to exceeding the maximum job runtime). Resource requirements specification can also affect job's execution, e.g. setting too few resources may lead to extreme execution time in case of large jobs. When considering running several instances of the same workflow with different input parameter values, it is fundamental that job requirements estimation have good accuracy. A common method to address this issue is to derive predictions from the analysis of past

© Springer International Publishing AG 2017
F. Desprez et al. (Eds.): Euro-Par 2016 Workshops, LNCS 10104, pp. 108–120, 2017.
DOI: 10.1007/978-3-319-58943-5_9

workflow executions. Therefore, we see the need for fine-grained monitoring tools to automatically collect such information, and to build workflow profiles.

Most of the work in workflow profiling target the peak data of job requirements [7,12]. Although this information allows the estimation of peak requirements (e.g., disk space, memory, etc.), it does not provide any insight into how resources are consumed by jobs over time within a workflow. This knowledge not only improves the overall understanding of workflow executions, but it increases the efficiency of job scheduling and resource utilization, in particular when planning large-scale workflows. Over the years, several application monitoring systems have been developed, however their practical application to produce performance profiles is often constrained by the inability to compare measurements from multiple executions.

The contributions of this paper include: (1) a holistic process for the development and analysis of workflow performance profiles; (2) description of different phases of the proposed process along with existing software, which can facilitate its practical application; (3) evaluation of the presented approach using a large high performance computing (HPC) system available at the NERSC facility [13]; and (4) the profiling of a real workflow application.

2   Performance Profiles of Scientific Workflows

Scientific workflows are often executed multiple times with different input parameter values to study distinct conditions, e.g. climate modeling with different mesh resolutions. Variations of the input parameters may lead to significant differences in resource requirements for the jobs. Understanding the relationships between the workflow's input and job performance metrics is crucial to accurately estimate these requirements. Also, it is important to understand how a variation in an input parameter may affect job performance. Discovery of these relationships is often referred to as *sensitivity analysis* [19], i.e. the assessment of how output variables are affected based on variations in the input variables. This type of analysis is mostly performed on the final values of responses, and it does not include variability of performance during job runtime. We propose an approach to conduct such analysis, which includes the temporal aspect of the workflow performance behavior, i.e. performance is measured not only at job completion, but also at different time instants during the job execution.

In this context, *a performance profile for a given job and a metric can be described as a time series with values of the metric measured in equidistant points in time during the job execution.* By collecting data from multiple executions of the same workflow configuration, we can compute statistically significant performance profiles for each job in a workflow.

2.1   End-to-End Approach to Performance Profiles Generation

The process of generating workflow performance profiles takes as input a workflow and a set of distinct input parameters. For each possible combination of

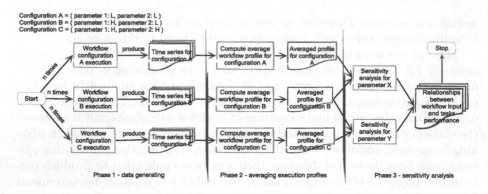

Fig. 1. Overview of the process for generating workflow performance profiles.

these parameters, a workflow execution is performed. The workflow performance data gathered using monitoring tools is then used to build average profiles, and to derive the sensitivity analysis. The ultimate goal of this process is to provide quantitative information about relationships between the input parameters and jobs' performance over time. An overview of the proposed approached is shown in Fig. 1. Below, we describe each of the process' phases in detail:

Phase 1 (Data Gathering). In this phase, a workflow execution is performed for each set of different input parameters (referred to as workflow configurations). To increase statistical significance, each configuration runs multiple times. Each workflow execution produces a set of time series for various performance metrics including CPU and memory usage, I/O load, among others. Note that for tightly-coupled parallel programs, time series performance values are collected for each individual process executed within the program.

Phase 2 (Averaging Execution Profiles). Time series of performance measurements are then used to compute *averaged execution profiles*—a time series describing a performance metric for a given job. Averaged performance profiles are computed based on multiple workflow executions of the same configuration (same set of input parameter values). The outcomes of this phase are execution profiles for each collected performance metric and for each job in a workflow.

Phase 3 (Sensitivity Analysis). The goal of this phase is to assess the impact on jobs performance by varying input parameters values. In this paper, we address this analysis with well-known statistical methods.

2.2 Generating Performance Profiles in Practice with HPC

The presented approach may pose difficulty in practice, specially when manually implementing it in HPC environments. We identify two detached aspects of our approach, which can be done in an automatic way with existing software: (1) executing and monitoring workflow executions, and (2) conducting data collection.

We use the Pegasus [4] workflow management system to run scientific workflows on different computational infrastructures. It includes *in-situ online* monitoring [8] that collects detailed information about jobs performance and the compute resources, including: system and process CPU utilization and memory usage, and process I/O. Each process in a job is monitored separately using information from the proc virtual filesystem and with system calls interception. This detailed monitoring information constitutes the basis of the workflow performance profiles.

We use Scalarm [9, 10] as a platform for parameter studies on heterogeneous computational infrastructures, i.e. to execute the same application (a scientific workflow in our case), with different input parameters. Scalarm supports different steps of this process including: input parameter space specification, application execution, and data collection. It is currently used within the EU FP7 PaaSage project [14] that aims at creating a solution for modelling and optimized deployment of cloud-oriented applications.

By combining Pegasus and Scalarm, we enable the data gathering phase of the process for generating and analyzing workflow performance profiles (Fig. 1). Both tools are generic, and support a vast number of different high performance and high throughput systems, which significantly increases the probability of successful practical application of the proposed approach.

3   Experimental Evaluation

In this section, we present an application of our method for generating and analyzing workflow performance profiles. We focus on phases 2 and 3 from the process described in Fig. 1, i.e. calculating averaged performance profiles, and conducting a sensitivity analysis of the workflow performance for different input parameters. The data gathering process (phase 1) is not discussed in this paper, since the data generation process is automatically performed by Scalarm and Pegasus. Due to limited space and a large amount of data collected, we focus our analysis to a subset of the data, which provides the most relevant information.

3.1   Scientific Workflow Application

To evaluate our approach, we use a material science-related workflow developed at the Spallation Neutron Source (SNS) facility. The workflow executes an ensemble of molecular dynamics and neutron scattering intensity calculations to optimize a model parameter value, e.g. to investigate temperature and hydrogen charge parameters for models of water molecules. The results are compared with experimental data from experiments such as QENS [2].

The SNS workflow takes as input a set of temperature values and 4 additional parameters: type of material, the number of required CPU cores, the number of timesteps in simulation, and the frequency the output data is written. Figure 2 shows a branch of the workflow to analyze one temperature value. First, each set of parameters is fed into a series of parallel molecular dynamics simulations using

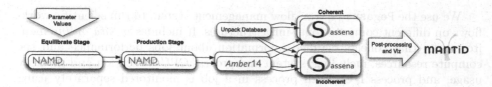

Fig. 2. A diagram of a branch of the SNS workflow.

NAMD [16]. The first simulation computes an equilibrium (namd_ID0000002), which is used by the second (namd_ID0000003) to compute the production dynamics. The output from the MD simulations has the global translation and rotation removed using AMBER's [18] *cpptraj* utility (ptraj_ID0000004), which is passed into Sassena [11] to compute coherent (sassena_ID0000005) and incoherent (sassena_ID0000006) neutron scattering intensities from the trajectories. The final outputs of the workflow are transferred to the user's desktop and loaded into Mantid [1] for analysis and visualization.

3.2   Experiment Configuration and Execution Environment

The data gathering was prepared to run 16 different configurations of the workflow created as combinations of the input parameter values. We define a two-level analysis: *low* (L) representing small values, and *high* (H) representing large values of each parameter. There are many sampling methods available in the literature (especially in case of sensitivity analysis popular techniques include Morris and Sobol' samplings) however the use of the proposed 2^k method is justified by:

- time-consuming calculations - running a production workflow hundreds of time to calculate input sensitivity would be infeasible,
- interpretation simplicity during the analysis phase,
- exploratory approach where we first use a coarse-grain sampling to develop initial understanding and then we move to a fine-grain sampling in a subspace of the input parameter space to improve initial findings.

Table 1 summarizes the values used for the analyzes. Atoms represent the material used for simulation. Cores represent the number of cores used by NAMD and Sassena jobs, respectively. Each configuration was executed 3 to 5 times to confirm performance homogeneity of task executions and to eliminate any outliers created by using shared resources, e.g. storage systems. To assess the performance impact of each parameter value on the workflow execution, we limit our analysis to pairs of configurations, where only one parameter value is varied. We focus on two specific configurations where the material used is varied: atoms_L_cores_L_timesteps_H_outfreq_L and atoms_H_cores_L_timesteps_H_outfreq_L. In this case, we can evaluate the impact of different material types on the workflow performance for small number of cores and output data frequency (L), and large timesteps (H). Sequential jobs (e.g., ptraj_ID0000004) have a very short runtime (below 1 min), thus we do not consider them in our analysis.

Table 1. Input parameter values for the SNS workflow in the experimental evaluation.

Factor level	Atoms	Cores	Timesteps	Data write freq.
L	3,692	144/72	50,000 = 0.005 ns	1,000 = 0.0001 ns
H	7,496	288/144	500,000 = 0.5 ns	5,000 = 0.0005 ns

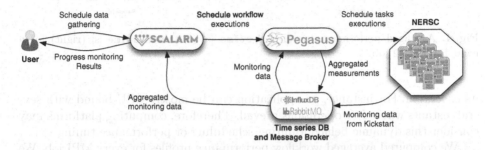

Fig. 3. Overview of the testbed used during the experimental evaluation.

Figure 3 shows an overview of the testbed used in the experiments. Workflows ran on the Hopper Supercomputer at NERSC [13], a Cray XE6 system with a peak performance of 1.28 Petaflops, while Scalarm and Pegasus were deployed on external hosts. A Pegasus workflow was launched for each configuration obtained from the set of parameters. A message broker and a time series database server were also deployed to collect online monitoring data during the workflow execution. Performance metrics were collected every 5 s, and include CPU utilization (`stime` and `utime`), I/O (`read` and `write_bytes`, `iowait`, `syscr`, and `syscw`), memory (`vmRSS` and `vmSize`), and number of threads.

3.3 Experimental Results and Discussion

We focus our analysis on the four MPI jobs for performing molecular simulation (NAMD and Sassena), since they represent most of the total CPU hours of the workflow. Although several analyzes could be derived from this data, we focus in: (1) determining whether a job is CPU- or I/O-bound; (2) studying job behavior as a function of I/O- and CPU-related metrics; and (3) studying the job performance behavior with averaged profiles.

Resource-Boundedness. Determining whether an application is CPU- or I/O-bound may aid the resolution of poor performance issues, in particular for large-scale applications. Typically, applications are classified into one of these categories based on the ratio between the time spent in the user (`utime`) and kernel (`stime`) spaces—handling I/O-related interruptions, etc. However, for long running jobs (several hours or days), an application may behave differently along

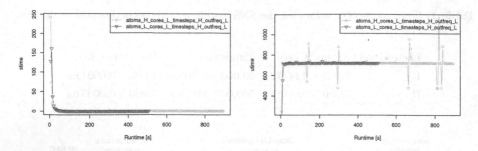

Fig. 4. Averaged performance profiles of stime [s] (left) and utime [s] (right) for a namd_ID0000002 job.

its execution. For instance, an application can be mostly CPU-bound with several instants where I/O operations prevail. Therefore, computing platforms may consider this dynamic behavior during scheduling or performance tuning.

We computed averaged workflow performance profiles for every MPI job. We combined time series from runs of the same workflow input configuration for each monitored performance metric, and then computed the average value of the metric at each monitoring interval (5 s). Averaged performance profiles show how resources are consumed by a job over time.

Overall, jobs present similar profiles for stime and utime, with larger configurations (atoms_H) having longer runtimes. Figure 4 shows an example of averaged profiles for namd_ID0000002. Most of the execution time is spent on the user space. I/O operations are mostly executed in the beginning of the execution, and then few (nearly negligible) write operations are performed along the job execution. In the utime analysis (Fig. 4-*right*), occasional spikes disrupt the linear behavior once the heaviest I/O operations have completed. These spikes are due to the short timespan of the monitoring interval. Note that peaks are often followed by troughs of similar magnitude, or vice-versa.

Jobs Behavior Analysis. Understanding jobs behavior is fundamental to the design and optimization of computing systems (e.g., job scheduling, resource provisioning, etc.). Therefore, we assess how different workflow input parameters impact jobs performance. We analyze relative cumulative value (RCV) of a performance metric as a function of normalized job runtime, which describes how many resources where consumed from the beginning of execution till the specified time moment. Since runtime varies among executions (mostly influenced by the machine's performance or external load), the scaled runtime values allow the analysis of (1) overall resource consumption over time, and of (2) infrastructure-related anomalies between different executions of the same workflow configuration. Anomalies can be inferred from abnormal behaviors of the RCV. The analysis and handling of these behaviors is out of the scope of this work.

Figure 5 shows RCVs for stime and utime from the NAMD jobs previously analyzed. Notice: for each configuration, a RCV graph was plotted for each run. There is a visible difference between both configurations for stime (Fig. 5-*left*).

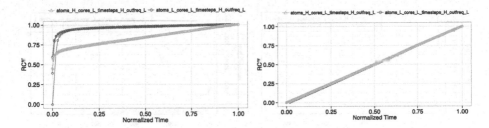

Fig. 5. RCVs of `stime` (left) and `utime` (right) for a `namd_ID0000002` job.

The configuration with the lower number of atoms (`atoms_L`) performs most of the I/O operations within the first 15% of its runtime, while `atoms_H` spreads I/O operations over time. This difference is due to: (1) the lower percentage number of I/O operations performed by `atoms_H` in the beginning of the execution; or (2) a significant increase on the number of I/O operations by `atoms_H` along the execution. In the subsequent analysis, we investigate this difference in detail. The `utime` behavior is similar and linearly correlated to the job runtime in both cases. This result indicates that computations in both configurations follow nearly the same pattern, and have a consistent number of operations throughout the job execution. This analysis confirms similarity between different runs of the workflow.

Performance Profiles. Although RCVs are useful for modeling job behaviors, they cannot characterize and quantify the differences obtained using different input parameters. The difference in `stime` between both configurations can be explained by analyzing performance profiles for I/O-related metrics. Figure 6 shows the performance profile of `write_bytes` and `read_bytes` for `namd_ID0000002` jobs with different number of atoms. The amount of data written per time interval (Fig. 6-*left*) is nearly identical for both configurations, except that `atoms_H` takes longer. Note that for the larger configuration, the magnitude of peaks and troughs on average is similar to `atoms_L`. In contrast, a significant difference on the amount of bytes read is observed in the first stage of the execution for `atoms_H` (Fig. 6-*right*). Furthermore, there is a significant amount of data that is continuously read during the job execution, while almost no read operations are performed for `atoms_L` (notice the scale difference between Fig. 6-*right* and Fig. 6-*left*). This result indicates that most of the time spent in the kernel space (Fig. 5-*left*) is due to read operations.

Figure 7 shows the I/O profile for `sasenna_ID0000005` jobs. Write operations (Fig. 7-*left*) present a particular behavior of writing significant amounts of data in a regular time interval. Moreover, `atoms_H` writes about twice as much data as `atoms_L`. In contrast to the previous analysis for the NAMD jobs, here the increase in the number of atoms seems to enable an iteration process (e.g., a loop condition). Read operations (Fig. 7-*right*) present a similar behavior, but scaled up to the configuration with the higher number of atoms.

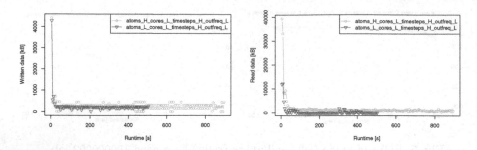

Fig. 6. Performance profile of write (left) and read (right) operations for namd_ID0000002.

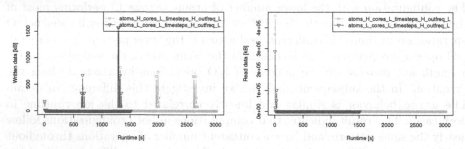

Fig. 7. Performance profile of write (left) and read (right) operations for sassena_ID0000005.

Sensitivity Analysis. The main effect of an input parameter on a response is calculated with Eq. 1 as a difference between the average response for high and low values of the input.

$$E_k = |R_{k,H} - R_{k,L}| \tag{1}$$

where $R_{k,H}$ denotes averaged simulation output (in our case resource consumption) when input parameter k is set to high values H. This difference should be interpreted as a change in the response due to a change in the input. We use main effects to describe how input parameters influence workflow performance. Figure 8 shows the normalized sensitivity for workflow jobs calculated as:

$$S_k = \frac{E_k}{\sum_i E_i} \tag{2}$$

where k denotes an input parameter, E_k is the effect of the input parameter on the model output measure at the end of job's execution. It doesn't have a unit since it is a ratio between the effect of a single parameter to summarised effect of all parameters. NAMD jobs (Fig. 8a and b) are mostly influenced by the number of simulation steps and the type of material used in the simulation.

In order to provide enhanced sensitivity analysis of workflow performance profiles, we compute sensitivity over time, i.e. the impact of each input parameter on the application response during task runtime. It is still calculated with Eq. 2

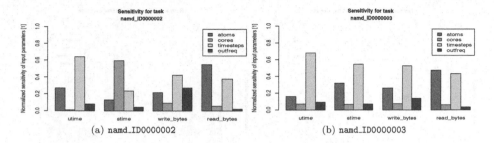

Fig. 8. Cumulative normalized sensitivity of the NAMD jobs in the SNS workflow.

however this time we calculate sensitivity for each monitoring period. Due to limited space, we only include results for the namd_ID0000002 job (Fig. 9). For utime (Fig. 9a), the number of cores has significant impact at the beginning of the execution. However, the number of timesteps becomes more influential along the execution. For runs above 500 s, there is not much variation. This behavior is due to the small number of jobs with longer runtime. In Fig. 9b, stime is mostly influenced by the material type (atoms), however cores has important impact at the beginning of the execution. Note that the output writing frequency has no significant impact for time-related metrics. Not surprisingly, write_bytes is substantially influenced by outfreq (Fig. 9c) and the number of timesteps. The material type (atoms) becomes irrelevant after the initial phase, and the number of cores does not drive any influence. In contrast, read_bytes (Fig. 9d) is heavily influenced by atoms—as it is related to the amount of data read from input files. The influence of timesteps and cores increases along the execution.

In summary, the main behaviors identified in this analysis include: (1) linear correlations between the amount of computations and job runtime in the namd jobs; (2) accumulation of I/O operations in the first stage of the execution in the namd jobs; and (3) periodic data dumps in the sassena jobs.

4   Related Work

Workflow profiling analysis is often used to drive advancements on workflow optimization studies, including job scheduling and resource provisioning. For instance, in [5,17] workflow profiles are used to model and predict execution time of workflow activities on distributed resources. In [3,6], heuristics and models are developed from workflow profiles to estimate the number of resources required to execute a workflow. We recently used profiling data from Pegasus workflows to estimate job resource consumption on distributed platforms [20]. Although our techniques yield satisfactory estimates, our studies were limited to the aggregated performance information, i.e. no time series analysis was considered. Several papers have profiled scientific workflow executions on real platforms [7,12], however none of them have collected time series data from workflow executions at the job level. Workload archives [15] are used for research on distributed

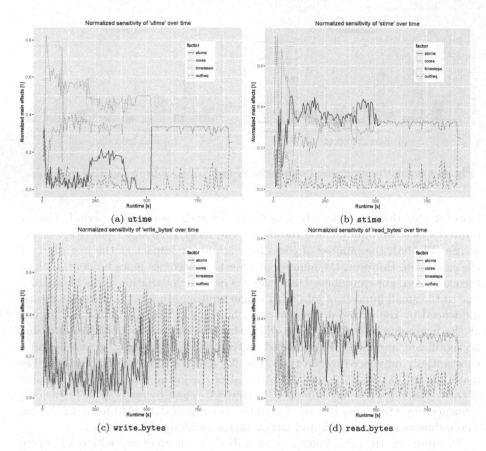

Fig. 9. Normalized sensitivity over time for `namd_ID0000002` (calculated with Eq. 2 for each monitoring period).

systems, e.g. to evaluate methods in simulation or in experimental conditions. Although the data is collected at the infrastructure and application level, the gathered data is also limited to aggregated performance information. To the best of our knowledge, this is the first work that builds and analyzes workflow profiles based on time series data collected from real workflow executions.

5   Conclusions and Future Work

In this paper, we described a generic approach for the development and analysis of workflow performance profiles, which describes application resource consumption over time. Such profiles provide much more information than the aggregated information given at the end of the execution. The presented approach is comprehensive, i.e. it takes into account the processes of generating, preparing, and analysis of data. It is independent of the analyzed workflow and can be used with existing, large-scale HPC infrastructures. The proposed approach was validated with a real-life workflow from material science running on a TOP500 machine. The analysis conducted unveiled useful insights about the workflow regarding the effect of input parameters on task performance.

As part of future we will integrate the proposed solution with Scalarm and Pegasus to minimize workflow runtime by improving job scheduling onto distributed resources based on information extracted from performance profiles, e.g. to identify which tasks can be executed in parallel on the same resource without performance disruption. We will also use the PaaSage framework to deploy and manage both tools and to run scientific workflows on cloud resources in a cost-effective way.

Acknowledgments. This research was supported by DOE under contract #DE-SC0012636, "Panorama–Predictive Modeling and Diagnostic Monitoring of Extreme Science Workflows". D. Król thanks to the EU FP7-ICT project PaaSage (317715) and Polish grant 3033/7PR/2014/2.

References

1. Arnold, O., et al.: Mantid - data analysis and visualization package for neutron scattering and SR experiments. Nucl. Instrum. Methods Phys. Res. Sect. A **764**, 156–166 (2014)
2. Borreguero, J.M., Lynch, V.E.: Molecular dynamics force-field refinement against quasi-elastic neutron scattering data. J. Chem. Theory Comput. **12**(1), 9–17 (2016)
3. Byun, E., Kee, Y., et al.: Estimating resource needs for time-constrained workflows. In: IEEE 4th International Conference on eScience (2008)
4. Deelman, E., Vahi, K., et al.: Pegasus, a workflow management system for science automation. Future Gener. Comput. Syst. **46**, 17–35 (2015)
5. Duan, R., Nadeem, F., et al.: A hybrid intelligent method for performance modeling and prediction of workflow activities in grids. In: 9th IEEE/ACM International Symposium on Cluster Computing and the Grid (2009)
6. Huang, R., Casanova, H., et al.: Automatic resource specification generation for resource selection. In: 2007 ACM/IEEE Conference on Supercomputing, SC 2007 (2007)
7. Juve, G., Chervenak, A., et al.: Characterizing and profiling scientific workflows. Future Gener. Comput. Syst. **29**(3), 682–692 (2013)
8. Juve, G., Tovar, B., et al.: Practical resource monitoring for robust high throughput computing. In: 2nd Workshop on Monitoring and Analysis for High Performance Computing Systems Plus Applications (2015)
9. Król, D., Kitowski, J.: Self-scalable services in service oriented software for cost-effective data farming. Future Gener. Comput. Syst. **54**, 1–15 (2016)
10. Kvassay, M., et al.: A novel way of using simulations to support urban security operations. Comput. Inform. **34**(6), 1201–1233 (2015)
11. Lindner, B., Smith, J.C.: Sassena—x-ray and neutron scattering calculated from molecular dynamics trajectories using massively parallel computers. Comput. Phys. Commun. **183**(7), 1491–1501 (2012)
12. Mayer, B., Worley, P., et al.: Climate science performance, data and productivity on titan. In: Cray User Group Conference (2015)
13. NERSC: Hopper. https://www.nersc.gov/users/computational-systems/hopper

14. FP7 PaaSage project website. http://www.paasage.eu/. Accessed 10 May 2016
15. Parallel workloads archive. http://www.cs.huji.ac.il/labs/parallel/workload
16. Phillips, J.C., Braun, R., et al.: Scalable molecular dynamics with NAMD on the IBM Blue Gene/l system. IBM J. Res. Dev. **26**(1.2), 177–188 (2008)
17. Pietri, I., Juve, G., et al.: A performance model to estimate execution time of scientific workflows on the cloud. In: Proceedings of 9th Workshop on Workflows in Support of Large-Scale Science (2014)
18. Salomon-Ferrer, R., et al.: An overview of the amber biomolecular simulation package. Wiley Interdiscip. Rev.: Comput. Mol. Sci. **3**(2), 198–210 (2013)
19. Saltelli, A., Ratto, M., et al.: Global Sensitivity Analysis: The Primer. Wiley, Hoboken (2008)
20. da Silva, F.R., Juve, G., et al.: Online task resource consumption prediction for scientific workflows. Parallel Process. Lett. **25**(3), 1541003 (2015)
21. Taylor, I.J., et al.: Workflows for e-Science: Scientific Workflows for Grids. Springer, London (2007)

A Data-Parallel ILUPACK for Sparse General and Symmetric Indefinite Linear Systems

José I. Aliaga[1], Matthias Bollhöfer[2], Ernesto Dufrechou[3(✉)], Pablo Ezzatti[3],
and Enrique S. Quintana-Ortí[1]

[1] Dep. de Ingeniería y Ciencia de la Computación,
Universidad Jaime I, Castellón, Spain
{aliaga,quintana}@icc.uji.es

[2] Institute of Computational Mathematics, TU Braunschweig,
Braunschweig, Germany
m.bollhoefer@tu-bs.de

[3] Instituto de Computación, Universidad de la República, Montevideo, Uruguay
{edufrechou,pezzatti}@fing.edu.uy

Abstract. The solution of sparse linear systems of large dimension is a
critical step in problems that span a diverse range of applications. For
this reason, a number of iterative solvers have been developed, among
which ILUPACK integrates an inverse-based multilevel ILU preconditioner with appealing numerical properties. In this paper, we enhance the
computational performance of ILUPACK by off-loading the execution of
several key computational kernels to a Graphics Processing Unit (GPU).
In particular, we target the preconditioned GMRES and BiCG methods
for sparse general systems and the preconditioned SQMR method for
sparse symmetric indefinite problems in ILUPACK. The evaluation on a
NVIDIA Kepler GPU shows a sensible reduction of the execution time,
while maintaining the convergence rate and numerical properties of the
original ILUPACK solver.

Keywords: Iterative solvers · Preconditioning · Incomplete LU (ILU)
factorization · Sparse triangular linear systems · Graphics processing
unit (GPU)

1 Introduction

Sparse linear systems arise in a vast number of scientific and engineering applications that range from the discretization of partial differential equations (PDEs)
to quantum physics or circuit simulation. In many of these cases, the solution of
the linear system is often the most computationally-demanding task, asking for
fast and accurate numerical solvers when the problem dimension is large [5].

An appealing approach for a wide range of applications consists in using
Krylov subspace methods, combined with preconditioning techniques, among
which those based in approximate matrix factorizations stand out [11]. A relevant
example is ILUPACK (http://ilupack.tu-bs.de), a package for the solution of

© Springer International Publishing AG 2017
F. Desprez et al. (Eds.): Euro-Par 2016 Workshops, LNCS 10104, pp. 121–133, 2017.
DOI: 10.1007/978-3-319-58943-5_10

sparse linear systems via Krylov subspace methods that relies on an inverse-based multilevel ILU (incomplete LU) preconditioning technique for general as well as Hermitian positive definite/indefinite linear systems [6].

The computation of ILUPACK's preconditioner and its application in the context of an iterative Krylov solver are computationally demanding, especially for linear systems of large dimension. This motivated the development of parallel variants of ILUPACK's CG method [11] on shared memory [2,3] and distributed memory platforms [4]. In order to expose task-parallelism, these variants calculate a preconditioner which differs from that computed by the original (sequential) ILUPACK, yielding distinct convergence rates, and usually requiring more floating point operations, with the overhead cost rapidly growing with the degree of task-parallelism being exposed [3].

In [2] we also introduced a version of ILUPACK's CG method that exploits the data-parallelism intrinsic to the main kernels in ILUPACK, off-loading them to a graphics processing unit (GPU). In contrast with the task-parallel solvers, the data-parallel version preserves the computational cost, semantics and convergence rate of the sequential implementation. In this work, we follow the same approach to accelerate ILUPACK's solvers for general (unsymmetric) and symmetric indefinite linear systems on GPUs, making the following contributions:

- We introduce data-parallel GPU versions of three relevant sparse solvers in ILUPACK: GMRES and BiCG for general systems [10], and SQMR for symmetric indefinite systems [11]. Following our work on ILUPACK's implementation of CG for symmetric positive definite systems, our new solvers maintain the computational cost, numerical properties, and convergence rate of the original routines, exposing the conventional interface to the user.
- Our experimental analysis compares the performance advantages of the different methods using a number of real problems, in particular, from the University of Florida Matrix Collection (UFMC) [7].
- Our results show that the novel GPU-enabled solvers can efficiently exploit the hardware resources of state-of-the-art GPU platforms, especially for moderate and large problems, with speed-ups of up to 3×.

We point out that there exist no parallel version of ILUPACK for the class of problems addressed in our work (not even a task-parallel one). The acceleration factors we report are those that a user of ILUPACK can presently expect.

The rest of the paper is structured as follows. In Sect. 2 we review the iterative solver integrated into ILUPACK. This is followed by a description of our proposal to accelerate the solver on GPUs in Sect. 3. Section 4 presents the experimental results, and a few remarks close the paper in Sect. 5.

2   Solution of Sparse Linear Systems with ILUPACK

Given a linear system $Ax = b$, where $A \in \mathbb{R}^{n \times n}$ is sparse and $b \in \mathbb{R}^n$, ILUPACK obtains an inverse-based multilevel ILU preconditioner $M \in \mathbb{R}^{n \times n}$ that can be leveraged in combination with a number of iterative methods to solve the system for the unknown $x \in \mathbb{R}^n$. ILUPACK offers solvers for different matrix types, precisions, and arithmetic, covering Hermitian positive definite/indefinite and general real and complex matrices. In all these cases, the most challenging task is the computation and application of the preconditioner, which respectively occur before and during the iterative solution.

2.1   Computation of the Preconditioner

The computation of ILUPACK's preconditioner is organized as follows:

1. A preprocessing that scales A by a diagonal matrix $\tilde{D} \in \mathbb{R}^{n \times n}$ and reorders the result by a permutation $\tilde{P} \in \mathbb{R}^{n \times n}$: $\hat{A} = \tilde{P}^T \tilde{D} A \tilde{D} \tilde{P}$.
2. An incomplete factorization next computes $\hat{A} \approx LDU$, where $L, U^T \in \mathbb{R}^{n \times n}$ are unit lower triangular factors and $D \in \mathbb{R}^{n \times n}$ is (block) diagonal. In some detail, $\hat{A}$ is processed in this stage yielding a partial ILU factorization:

$$\hat{P}^T \hat{A} \hat{P} \equiv \begin{pmatrix} B\ F \\ G\ C \end{pmatrix} = LDU + E = \begin{pmatrix} L_B\ 0 \\ L_G\ I \end{pmatrix} \begin{pmatrix} D_B\ 0 \\ 0\ S_c \end{pmatrix} \begin{pmatrix} U_B\ U_F \\ 0\ I \end{pmatrix} + E. \quad (1)$$

Here, $\hat{P} \in \mathbb{R}^{n \times n}$ is a permutation matrix, $\|L_B^{-1}\|, \|U_B^{-1}\| \lesssim \kappa$, with κ a user-predefined threshold, E contains the elements "dropped" during the ILU factorization, and S_C represents the approximate Schur complement assembled from the "rejected" rows and columns.
3. The process is then restarted with $A = S_c$, (until S_c is void or "dense enough" to be handled by a dense solver,) yielding a multilevel approach.

At level l, the multilevel preconditioner can be recursively expressed as

$$M_l \approx \tilde{D}^{-1} \tilde{P} \hat{P} \begin{pmatrix} L_B\ 0 \\ L_G\ I \end{pmatrix} \begin{pmatrix} D_B\ 0 \\ 0\ M_{l+1} \end{pmatrix} \begin{pmatrix} U_B\ U_F \\ 0\ I \end{pmatrix} \hat{P}^T \tilde{P}^T \tilde{D}^{-1}, \quad (2)$$

where L_B, D_B and L_F are blocks of the factors of the multilevel LDU preconditioner (with L_B, U_B^T unit lower triangular and D_B diagonal); and M_{l+1} stands for the preconditioner computed at level $l + 1$.

A detailed explanation of each stage of the process can be found in [6].

2.2   Iterative Solution and Application of the Preconditioner

In the analysis of this operation, we consider its application at level l, e.g. to compute $z := M_l^{-1} r$. This requires solving the system of linear equations:

$$\begin{pmatrix} L_B\ 0 \\ L_G\ I \end{pmatrix} \begin{pmatrix} D_B\ 0 \\ 0\ M_{l+1} \end{pmatrix} \begin{pmatrix} U_B\ U_F \\ 0\ I \end{pmatrix} \hat{P}^T \tilde{P}^T \tilde{D}^{-1} z = \hat{P}^T \tilde{P}^T \tilde{D} r. \quad (3)$$

Breaking down (3), we first recognize two transforms to the residual vector, $\hat{r} := \hat{P}^T \tilde{P}^T (\tilde{D} r)$, before the following block system is defined:

$$\begin{pmatrix} L_B\ 0 \\ L_G\ I \end{pmatrix} \begin{pmatrix} D_B\ 0 \\ 0\ M_{l+1} \end{pmatrix} \begin{pmatrix} U_B\ U_F \\ 0\ I \end{pmatrix} w = \hat{r}. \quad (4)$$

This is then solved for $w(=\hat{P}^T\tilde{P}^T\tilde{D}^{-1}z)$ in three steps,

$$\begin{pmatrix} L_B & 0 \\ L_G & I \end{pmatrix} y = \hat{r}, \quad \begin{pmatrix} D_B & 0 \\ 0 & M_{l+1} \end{pmatrix} x = y, \quad \begin{pmatrix} U_B & U_F \\ 0 & I \end{pmatrix} w = x. \tag{5}$$

where the recursion is defined in the middle step.

In turn, the expressions in (5) also need to be solved in two steps. Assuming y and $\hat{r}$ are split conformally with the factors, for the left expression we have

$$\begin{pmatrix} L_B & 0 \\ L_G & I \end{pmatrix} \begin{pmatrix} y_B \\ y_C \end{pmatrix} = \begin{pmatrix} \hat{r}_B \\ \hat{r}_C \end{pmatrix} \Rightarrow L_B y_B = \hat{r}_B, \; y_C := \hat{r}_C - L_G y_B. \tag{6}$$

Splitting the vectors as earlier, the middle step involves the diagonal-matrix multiplication and the effective recursion:

$$\begin{pmatrix} D_B & 0 \\ 0 & M_{l+1} \end{pmatrix} \begin{pmatrix} x_B \\ x_C \end{pmatrix} = \begin{pmatrix} y_B \\ y_C \end{pmatrix} \Rightarrow x_B := D_B^{-1} y_B, \; x_C := M_{l+1}^{-1} y_C. \tag{7}$$

In the recursion base step, M_{l+1} is void and only x_B has to be computed. Finally, after an analogous partitioning, the right step can be reformulated as

$$\begin{pmatrix} U_B & U_F \\ 0 & I \end{pmatrix} \begin{pmatrix} w_B \\ w_C \end{pmatrix} = \begin{pmatrix} x_B \\ x_C \end{pmatrix} \Rightarrow w_C := x_C, \; U_B w_B = x_B - U_F w_C, \tag{8}$$

where z is simply obtained from $z := \tilde{D}(\tilde{P}(\hat{P}w))$.

To save memory, ILUPACK discards the off-diagonal blocks L_G and U_F once the level of the preconditioner is calculated, keeping only the rectangular matrices G and F, frequently much sparser. Thus, (6) is changed as follows:

$$\begin{aligned} L_G = GU_B - 1D_B^{-1} \\ \Rightarrow \; y_C := \hat{r}_C - GU_B^{-1}D_B^{-1}y_B = \hat{r}_C - GU_B^{-1}D_B^{-1}L_B^{-1}\hat{r}_B, \end{aligned} \tag{9}$$

while the expressions related to (8) are modified as

$$U_F = D_B^{-1}L_B^{-1}F \quad \Rightarrow \quad U_B w_B = D_B^{-1}y_B - D_B^{-1}L_B^{-1}F w_C. \tag{10}$$

Operating with care, the final expressions are obtained,

$$\begin{aligned} L_B D_B U_B s_B = \hat{r}_B, \; L_B D_B U_B \hat{s}_B = F w_C \\ \Rightarrow \; y_C := \hat{r}_C - G s_B, \; w_B := s_B - \hat{s}_B \end{aligned} \tag{11}$$

In summary, the application of the preconditioner requires, at each level, two SpMV, solving two linear systems with coefficient matrix of the form LDU, and a few vector kernels.

3   Data-Parallel Variants of ILUPACK

In this section we describe our general strategy to obtain GPU-accelerated versions of ILUPACK's general and symmetric indefinite solvers. Our enhanced solvers can off-load the entire application of the preconditioner to the GPU, though there are problems where, for the higher levels of the preconditioner, it is more efficient to solve the sparse triangular systems in the CPU. The reason is that these kernels then become small in dimension (and, therefore, cannot achieve an acceptable occupancy in the GPU); and/or involve much denser matrix blocks, (implying a strong amount of data dependencies), and thus exhibit a modest amount of data-parallelism.

3.1 Unsymmetric Linear Systems

We targeted the acceleration of GMRES and BiCG for general linear systems. Note that the parallelization of the preconditioner application is essentially analogous for both methods, with the only major difference being that BiCG involves the application of the transposed preconditioner while GMRES does not.

Let us consider GMRES first. ILUPACK's multilevel preconditioner is stored as a linked list of structures that contain the information computed at each level. Concretely, a level contains pointers to the submatrices that form the ILU factorization: the B submatrix that comprises the LDU factored upper left block and the G and F rectangular matrices, along with the diagonal scaling and permutation vectors that correspond to $\tilde{D}$, $\tilde{P}$, and $\hat{P}$; see Subsect. 2.1.

The computational cost required to apply the preconditioner is dominated by the sparse triangular system solves (SpTrSV) and SpMV. NVIDIA's CUS-PARSE [1] provides efficient GPU implementations of these two kernels that support several common sparse matrix formats. Therefore, it is convenient for us to rely on this library. The rest of the operations are mainly vector scalings and reorderings, which gain certain importance only for highly sparse matrices of large dimension, and are accelerated in our codes via *ad-hoc* CUDA kernels.

For its unsymmetric preconditioner, ILUPACK stores B in a modified CSR format [8], with the L and U factors kept, by columns, in an interlaced manner. Concretely, only the strictly lower triangular part of L is stored as its is unit diagonal; furthermore, the diagonal entries contain the inverses of the diagonal elements of U. In order to use CUSPARSE, we thus need to split each B submatrix into separate L and U factors, stored by rows in the conventional CSR format. This transform is done only once, during the calculation of each level of the preconditioner, and occurs entirely in the CPU. After that, the L and U factors, in CSR format, are transferred to the GPU, where the triangular systems involved in the preconditioner application are solved via two consecutive calls to `cusparseDcsrsv_solve`. The analysis phase required by the CUSPARSE solver, which gathers information about the data dependencies and aggregates the rows of the triangular matrix into levels, is executed only once for each level of the preconditioner, and it runs asynchronously with respect to the host CPU.

In order to compute the SpMV on the GPU, G and F are also transferred to the device during the computation of the preconditioner. As these matrices are stored by ILUPACK in CSR format, no reorganization is needed prior to the invocation of the CUSPARSE kernel for SpMV.

The BiCG solver involves both G and F as well as their respective transposes in the calculations. Our initial approach only kept G and F in the GPU, and operated with the transposed/non-transposed matrices by setting the appropriate value for the transpose switch. Unfortunately, the implementation of SpMV in CUSPARSE delivers considerable low performance when operating with the transposed matrix. In order to overcome this, our implementation of BiCG stores both G, F and G^T, F^T in GPU memory. If the amount of GPU memory is limited, these matrices can be asynchronously transferred from CPU to GPU, with this process overlapped with computations, before they are needed.

3.2 Symmetric Indefinite Linear Systems

We addressed the parallelization of the SQMR method [11] in ILUPACK for symmetric indefinite problems. As in the general case, we need to transform the representation employed by ILUPACK for the $LDU (= LDL^T)$ leading block of each preconditioner level, in order to be able to invoke the CUSPARSE library to solve the corresponding triangular linear systems. Instead of maintaining L and D separately, ILUPACK relies on a MCSR representation, where the symmetric block-diagonal matrix D is stored inverted using $2nB$ floating point numbers, (with nB denoting the size of the leading block,) while the rest of the structure contains $\hat{L} \in \mathbb{R}^{nB \times nB}$, i.e., the strictly lower triangle of L. This matrix is kept in CSR format. ILUPACK then solves a system of the form $(\hat{L}D^{-1} + I_{nB})D(\hat{L}D^{-1} + I_{nB})^T$. Those columns that correspond to 2×2 pivots are stored interleaved, since in $\hat{L}D^{-1}$ they have the same nonzero pattern and this is exploited by the serial CPU solver.

To solve these systems with CUSPARSE, we split their structure into a symmetric tridiagonal matrix D^{-1}, which we store as two vectors of size nB, and then form matrix $\tilde{L} = (\hat{L}D^{-1} + I_{nB})$ explicitly. After this transform, at each level, we solve linear systems with coefficient matrix of the form $\tilde{L}D^{-1}\tilde{L}^T$. Here, as the inverse of D is available, this involves a tridiagonal matrix-vector product, which is performed in the GPU by means of a simple *ad-hoc* CUDA kernel.

3.3 Parallelization of SpMV and Other Kernels

In addition to the parallelization of the preconditioner, we further enhanced the solvers in ILUPACK by off-loading the SpMV to the GPU. For this purpose, it is necessary to store A in the GPU. In our implementation this matrix is transferred to the GPU memory before the iterative solve commences, and resides there until completion. The matrix is stored in CSR format and the SpMV is performed via the implementation of this kernel in CUSPARSE.

In general, the vector operations contribute little to the computational cost of the solver. Therefore, these operations are performed in the CPU. Parallelizing more complex operations, like the Gram-Schmidt orthogonalization involved in the GMRES, is considered as part of future work.

4   Experimental Evaluation

We next evaluate our GPU-enabled solvers for general/symmetric indefinite linear systems, and compare their performance to that of the corresponding routines in ILUPACK's current sequential (CPU) implementation (release 2.4).

The experiments were carried out an Intel i7-4770 processor (3.40 GHz) and 16 GB of DDR3 RAM (26 GB/s of bandwidth), connected to an NVIDIA Tesla K40 GPU, with 2,880 cuda cores (0.75 GHz), and 12 GB of DDR5 RAM (288 GB/s bw). NVIDIA CUBLAS/CUSPARSE 6.5 was employed in the experimentation. For the CPU codes we used GNU gcc (v4.9.2) with -O4 as an optimization flag. All results were obtained using IEEE double-precision arithmetic. In all cases, the total runtime includes the cost of transferring the matrix to the GPU.

4.1   Test Cases

UFMC Test Cases. We selected a range of large-scale unsymmetric matrices with dimension $n > 1,000,000$, and several symmetric indefinite ones with $n > 100,000$, all from the UFMC benchmark collection; see Table 1.

Table 1. Matrices from the UFMC used in the experiments.

Unsymmetric				Symmetric indefinite			
Matrix	n	nnz	nnz/n	Matrix	n	nnz	nnz/n
cage14	1,505,785	27,130,349	18.02	darcy003	389,874	2,097,566	5.38
memchip	2,707,524	13,343,948	4.93	F1	343,791	26,837,113	78.06
Freescale1	3,428,755	17,052,626	4.97	mario002	389,874	2,097,566	5.38
rajat31	4,690,002	20,316,253	4.33	cbig	345,241	2,340,859	6.78
cage15	5,154,859	99,199,551	19.24	nlpkkt120	3,542,400	95,117,792	26.85
				nlpkkt160	8,345,600	225,422,112	27.01

Unsymmetric Convection-Diffusion Problems (CDP). We considered the PDE $\varepsilon \Delta u + b * u = f$ in Ω, where $\Omega = [0, 1]^3$. For this example, we use homogeneous Dirichlet boundary conditions, i.e. $u = 0$ on $\partial \Omega$. The diffusion coefficient ε is set to 1, and the convective functions $b(x, y, z)$ are given by:

$$\begin{aligned} \text{conv. in } x\text{-direction:} \quad & [1, 0, 0], \\ \text{diagonal convection:} \quad & \tfrac{1}{\sqrt{3}}[1, 1, 1], \\ \text{circular convection:} \quad & [\tfrac{1}{2} - z, x - \tfrac{1}{2}, \tfrac{1}{2} - y]. \end{aligned}$$

The domain is discretized with a uniform mesh of size $h = \frac{1}{N+1}$ resulting in a linear system of size N^3. For the present experiments we chose a value of $N = 200$. For the diffusion part $-\varepsilon \Delta u$ we use a seven-point-stencil. The convective part $b * u$ is discretized using up-wind differences.

Symmetric Indefinite PDE. We considered the Laplacian equation $\Delta u = f$ in a 3D unit cube $\Omega = [0,1]^3$ with Dirichlet boundary conditions $u = g$ on $\delta\Omega$. The discretization consists in a uniform mesh of size $h = \frac{1}{N+1}$ and a seven-point stencil is used. The resulting symmetric positive definite (SPD) linear system $Au = b$ has a sparse SPD coefficient matrix with seven nonzero elements per row, and $n = N^3$ unknowns. We performed experiments with $N = 50$, 100, 159, 200, 252, which results in five benchmark SPD linear systems of order $n \approx$ 1M, 1.9M, 3.3M, 8M and 16M. These matrices were then modified so that the resulting problem becomes indefinite.

4.2 Evaluation of GMRES and BiCG

We first applied the BiCG and GMRES methods to the SPD matrices associated with the Laplacian PDE, treating them as if they were unsymmetric. The test instances in this benchmark can be scaled up arbitrarily while preserving certain pattern in the non-zeros structure of the factorization. The results in Table 2 show an important improvement in the performance of the two GPU-accelerated solvers, though this is more notorious for BiCG. The reason is that the only stages of the solver that are off-loaded to the accelerator are the application of the preconditioner and SpMV. The first one occurs twice per iteration for BiCG (as the transposed preconditioner also has to be applied), but only once for GMRES. If we consider the stages that involve the preconditioner, the acceleration factor reaches up to 6× for the transposed preconditioner in the largest test case. This is not surprising given the memory-bound nature of the problem and that the GPU has a memory bandwith only 11× higher than the CPU. The matrices of this set are SPD and well-conditioned, allowing us to use a drop tolerance $\tau = 0.1$ and still converge in a few iterations. This arguably high value of τ produces a sparser preconditioner, exposing a larger volume of data-parallelism that is exploited by the GPU kernels.

To expose the performance of the unsymmetric solvers, we repeated the evaluation with a set of large unsymmetric problems from the UFMC. Table 2 reports fair acceleration factors for the GPU versions of the solvers. In some detail, the speed-up values for the application of the preconditioner are quite similar to those attained for the Laplace matrices set, but the improvement experienced by the SpMV kernel is larger in all cases.

Thirdly, we tested our solver on the unsymmetric CDP cases. In these experiments, the parallel versions outperform the serial CPU solvers, with speed-ups in the order of 2×, while the acceleration of the preconditioner is almost 3×.

Comparing both solvers, the acceleration attained by GMRES is always lower than that observed for BiCG. This can be easily explained by noting that, in BiCG, the GPU-accelerated stages (preconditioner application and SpMV) take most of the execution time. For GMRES, the time of the unaccelerated stages is more important, to the extent that, in some cases, the unaccelerated steps of the GPU versions consume a higher fraction of the time than the accelerated ones. A detailed analysis revealed that, in these cases, the bottleneck of the GMRES method is the modified Gram-Schmidt re-orthogonalization, which we plan to

Table 2. Performance evaluation of BiCG and GMRES. From left to right: problem case; target architecture (device); number of iterations; execution time required for SpMV, preconditioner application (with M^{-1} and its transpose M^{-T}), remainder, and total; relative residual error of the solution; and speed-up of the GPU version with respect to the original CPU code in ILUPACK.

Solver	Matrix	Device	#Iters.	Time SpMV	M^{-1}	M^{-T}	Rem	Total	$\mathcal{R}(x^*)$	Speed-up M^{-1}	M^{-T}	Total
BiCG	A050	CPU	16	0.010	0.016	0.017	0.008	0.05	1.80E-09	-	-	-
		GPU	16	0.009	0.012	0.010	0.008	0.04	1.80E-09	1.35	1.62	1.31
	A100	CPU	14	0.07	0.18	0.21	0.08	0.54	5.80E-09	-	-	-
		GPU	14	0.06	0.05	0.05	0.08	0.24	5.80E-09	3.25	4.60	2.25
	A159	CPU	14	0.29	0.67	0.63	0.31	1.90	4.90E-09	-	-	-
		GPU	14	0.24	0.20	0.18	0.32	0.93	4.90E-09	3.43	3.79	2.04
	A200	CPU	14	0.60	1.35	1.25	0.62	3.82	5.30E-09	-	-	-
		GPU	14	0.47	0.39	0.35	0.63	1.84	5.30E-09	3.45	3.78	2.08
	A252	CPU	14	1.15	3.40	4.13	1.23	9.92	5.70E-09	-	-	-
		GPU	14	0.93	0.77	0.69	1.22	3.62	5.80E-09	4.39	6.27	2.74
	cage14	CPU	12	0.60	0.72	0.75	0.13	2.20	2.70E-09	-	-	-
		GPU	12	0.21	0.19	0.16	0.10	0.68	2.70E-09	3.78	4.69	3.24
	Freescale1	CPU	292	15.24	29.52	45.98	5.71	96.44	1.00E-03	-	-	-
		GPU	292	6.92	5.04	10.17	4.82	26.96	1.00E-03	5.86	4.52	3.58
	rajat31	CPU	8	0.48	0.93	0.86	0.29	2.55	1.40E-06	-	-	-
		GPU	8	0.16	0.19	0.29	0.22	0.88	1.40E-06	4.89	2.97	2.90
	cage15	CPU	12	2.25	2.83	3.28	0.43	8.78	5.50E-09	-	-	-
		GPU	12	0.86	0.60	0.51	0.35	2.33	5.50E-09	4.72	6.43	3.77
	CDP/circ	CPU	286	18.61	82.22	107.58	11.27	219.68	1.20E-07	-	-	-
		GPU	286	14.18	18.86	42.58	11.35	86.97	1.20E-07	4.36	2.53	2.53
	CDP/diag	CPU	298	19.37	78.44	81.87	11.59	191.27	2.00E-07	-	-	-
		GPU	298	14.48	19.47	44.24	11.58	89.77	2.00E-07	4.03	1.85	2.13
	CDP/u-vec	CPU	316	20.50	83.05	86.71	12.29	202.55	4.10E-08	-	-	-
		GPU	316	15.46	20.59	46.85	12.42	95.33	4.10E-08	4.03	1.85	2.12
GMRES	A050	CPU	9	0.006	0.019	—	0.018	0.043	9.20E-10	-	-	-
		GPU	9	0.005	0.013	—	0.017	0.035	9.20E-10	1.43	-	1.23
	A100	CPU	8	0.04	0.22	—	0.15	0.42	4.60E-09	-	-	-
		GPU	8	0.03	0.06	—	0.15	0.24	4.60E-09	3.60	-	1.75
	A159	CPU	8	0.16	0.97	—	0.66	1.79	4.10E-09	-	-	-
		GPU	8	0.10	0.23	—	0.66	0.99	4.10E-09	4.22	-	1.81
	A200	CPU	8	0.33	1.90	—	1.34	3.57	4.00E-09	-	-	-
		GPU	8	0.20	0.45	—	1.34	1.99	4.00E-09	4.22	-	1.79
	A252	CPU	8	0.63	3.13	—	2.58	6.34	3.90E-09	-	-	-
		GPU	8	0.41	0.89	—	2.59	3.88	3.90E-09	3.52	-	1.63
	cage14	CPU	7	0.36	0.84	—	0.26	1.46	2.40E-09	-	-	-
		GPU	7	0.05	0.22	—	0.21	0.49	2.40E-09	3.82	-	2.98
	Freescale1	CPU	46	2.70	9.32	—	6.19	18.21	6.30E-03	-	-	-
		GPU	46	0.54	1.60	—	5.18	7.33	6.30E-03	5.83	-	2.89
	rajat31	CPU	4	0.27	0.93	—	0.53	1.74	3.60E-07	-	-	
		GPU	4	0.06	0.19	—	0.41	0.67	3.60E-07	4.89	-	2.60
	cage15	CPU	7	1.31	3.30	—	0.91	5.52	4.80E-09	-	-	-
		GPU	7	0.18	0.70	—	0.71	1.61	4.80E-09	4.65	-	3.43
	CDP/circ	CPU	203	12.84	116.44	—	63.32	192.61	1.40E-06	-	-	-
		GPU	203	5.65	26.75	—	62.97	95.37	1.40E-06	2.27	-	2.02
	CDP/diag	CPU	241	15.25	127.66	—	75.89	218.81	1.60E-06	-	-	-
		GPU	241	6.73	31.59	—	76.21	114.52	1.60E-06	2.27	-	1.91
	CDP/u-vec	CPU	251	15.69	131.47	—	79.67	226.85	1.40E-06	-	-	-
		GPU	251	7.00	32.70	—	79.91	119.61	1.40E-06	2.24	-	1.90

address as part of future work. Regarding the quality of the computed solution x^*, the GPU enabled solvers converge in the same number of iterations and present the same final relative residual error $\mathcal{R}(x^*) := ||b - Ax^*||_2/||x^*||_2$ as the original version of ILUPACK.

4.3   Evaluation of SQMR

The results for these problem cases are summarized in Table 3. The first part contains the experiments with the modified symmetric PDE of scalable size, and illustrates a performance advantage of the GPU solvers that grows with the size of the instances. For this set of matrices, the acceleration of the SpMV is about $3\times$, and the preconditioning stage is improved around $4\times$ for the larger test

Table 3. Performance evaluation of SQMR. From left to right: problem case; target architecture (device); number of iterations; execution time required for SpMV, preconditioner application, remainder, and total; relative residual error of the solution; and speed-up of the GPU version with respect to the original CPU code in ILUPACK.

Matrix	Device	#Iters.	Time				$\mathcal{R}(x^*)$	Speed-up
			SpMV	M^{-1}	Rem	Total		Total
A050	CPU	40	0.04	0.29	0.03	0.37	7.90E-09	
	GPU	40	0.02	0.28	0.04	0.34	7.90E-09	1.09
A100	CPU	72	0.79	5.00	0.71	6.51	3.00E-08	
	GPU	72	0.26	1.72	0.77	2.76	3.00E-08	2.35
A159	CPU	114	5.03	34.78	4.65	44.49	4.10E-08	
	GPU	114	1.67	9.32	4.88	15.89	4.10E-08	2.79
A200	CPU	137	12.27	85.07	11.19	108.56	3.00E-08	
	GPU	137	4.07	21.30	12.16	37.56	3.00E-08	2.89
A252	CPU	170	31.37	201.91	27.33	260.66	6.60E-08	
	GPU	170	9.81	51.89	28.59	90.35	4.50E-08	2.88
darcy003	CPU	88	0.68	2.73	0.26	3.68	4.00E-08	
	GPU	88	0.12	2.02	0.33	2.48	3.60E-08	1.48
F1	CPU	477	23.03	33.90	1.35	58.29	1.30E-07	
	GPU	477	1.74	38.72	1.55	42.01	1.40E-07	1.39
c-big	CPU	22	0.11	0.87	0.06	1.06	1.10E-09	
	GPU	22	0.12	0.72	0.09	0.93	1.10E-09	1.13
mario002	CPU	88	0.63	2.58	0.26	3.48	4.00E-08	
	GPU	88	0.13	2.03	0.34	2.51	3.90E-08	1.38
nlpkkt120	CPU	187	24.35	73.02	6.34	103.73	1.40E-06	
	GPU	176	3.67	24.24	6.86	34.78	4.40E-06	2.98
nlpkkt160	CPU	252	82.92	252.22	21.77	356.95	4.40E-06	
	GPU	252	12.34	73.26	22.51	108.14	4.50E-06	3.30

cases, but the unaccelerated stages of the solver represent more than 10% of the total runtime and keep the global speedups below 3×.

In most of the test cases extracted from the UFMC, shown in the second part of the table, the preconditioner is not able to converge for $\tau > 0.01$. Decreasing the value of τ introduces a large amount of fill-in in the preconditioner, reducing the degree of data-parallelism. Figure 1 shows the sparsity pattern of the L factor that corresponds to each level of the preconditioner for the problem c-big. The plots illustrate that the fill-in in the L factor increases dramatically from the first to the second level of the factorization. This has two main effects. On the one hand, the new non-zero elements are likely to generate data dependencies between the rows of the L factor during the solution of the triangular linear systems, which severely harms the performance of CUSPARSE's level-based solver. On the other hand, as the dimension of the systems grow, the important memory requirements turn increasingly difficult to store the necessary matrices in the GPU, and thus the symmetric instances presented in the middle section of the table are all of intermediate size. The little improvement obtained for this set of matrices is mostly due to the speedup of the SpMV.

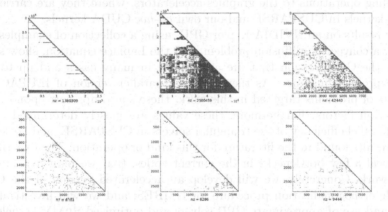

Fig. 1. L factor of each level of the LDL multilevel factorization of matrix c-big. Levels increase from left to right and from top to bottom.

The largest symmetric indefinite instance we were able to test was a non-linear programming problem from UFMC, also studied in [12]. The results for this benchmark are closer to those obtained in the symmetric indefinite PDE. There are four instances of this problem, which vary in size. When $\tau = 0.01$, the fill-in of the preconditioner allows only the three smaller instances to be executed in the GPU.

To close this discussion, we note that, contrary to the results obtained in the previous experiments, there are discrepancies in the number of iterations as well as residual errors for some of the tested instances.

5   Concluding Remarks and Future Work

ILUPACK provides an assorted number of sophisticated Krylov subspace-based routines for the iterative solution of general and symmetric (or Hermitian) positive definite/indefinite sparse linear systems. Unfortunately, this package contains sequential codes only. While there exist task-parallel versions of ILUPACK, these present a number of drawbacks: First, they compute a preconditioner different from that obtained with the original ILUPACK, with distinct numerical properties and convergence rate. Second, they incur a certain computational overhead, which increases with the amount of task-parallelism. Finally, they only cover the CG method for SPD linear systems in ILUPACK and, how to exploit task-parallelism for other types of systems, remains an open question.

In this paper we have continued our work in order to obtain a fully functional data-parallel version of ILUPACK, accelerated by means of GPUs, that preserves the most appealing properties of the sequential solver. For this purpose, we have extended our strategies, applied in the past to the CG method, to cover three new solvers: GMRES and BiCG for general systems, and SQMR for symmetric indefinite ones. All our data-parallel solvers off-load the most computationally-demanding operations to the graphics accelerators, where they are carried out via the kernels in CUSPARSE and our own *ad-hoc* CUDA kernels.

Our results on an NVIDIA Kepler GPU, using a collection of examples from UFMC, a convection-diffusion problem, and the Laplace equation, show speed-ups for the GPU version that are around 2× in many cases and up to 3.7× for one problem instance. As there exist no parallel version of ILUPACK for the class of problems targeted in this work, these speed-ups correspond to fair acceleration factors. Furthermore, these values are mostly determined by the scarce parallel efficiency of the triangular solvers in CUSPARSE, and are similar to the results found in the literature for this kind of operation. The experiments also reveal a few bottlenecks in the current codes, that we plan to address in future work. Concretely, we will develop an accelerated version of the Gram-Schmidt orthogonalization procedure for GMRES; and we will investigate the design and use of approximate GPU solvers and optimized SpMV kernels ([9]) for the preconditioner application that can replace CUSPARSE.

Acknowledgments. J.I. Aliaga and E.S. Quintana-Ortí were supported by project TIN2014-53495-R of the MINECO and FEDER. E. Dufrechou and P. Ezzatti were supported by *Programa de Desarrollo de las Ciencias Básicas* (PEDECIBA), Uruguay.

References

1. CUDA Toolkit 5.5. CUSPARSE Library. NVIDIA Corporation, Version 5.5, July 2013
2. Aliaga, J.I., Badia, R.M., Barreda, M., Bollhöfer, M., Dufrechou, E., Ezzatti, P., Quintana-Ortí, E.S.: Exploiting task and data parallelism in ILUPACK's preconditioned CG solver on NUMA architectures and many-core accelerators. Parallel Comput. **54**, 97–107 (2016)

3. Aliaga, J.I., Bollhöfer, M., Martín, A.F., Quintana-Ortí, E.S.: Exploiting thread-level parallelism in the iterative solution of sparse linear systems. Parallel Comput. **37**(3), 183–202 (2011)
4. Aliaga, J.I., Bollhöfer, M., Martín, A.F., Quintana-Ortí, E.S.: Parallelization of multilevel ILU preconditioners on distributed-memory multiprocessors. In: Jónasson, K. (ed.) PARA 2010. LNCS, vol. 7133, pp. 162–172. Springer, Heidelberg (2012). doi:10.1007/978-3-642-28151-8_16
5. Barrett, R., Berry, M., Chan, T.F., Demmel, J., Donato, J., Dongarra, J., Eijkhout, V., Pozo, R., Romine, C., Van der Vorst, H.: Templates for the Solution of Linear Systems: Building Blocks for Iterative Methods, 2nd edn. SIAM, Philadelphia (1994)
6. Bollhöfer, M., Saad, Y.: Multilevel preconditioners constructed from inverse-based ILUs. SIAM J. Sci. Comput. **27**(5), 1627–1650 (2006)
7. Davis, T.A., Hu, Y.: The University of Florida sparse matrix collection. ACM Trans. Math. Softw. **38**(1), 1–25 (2011)
8. Eijkhout, V.: LAPACK working note 50: distributed sparse data structures for linear algebra operations. Technical report, Knoxville, TN, USA (1992)
9. Greathouse, J.L., Daga, M.: Efficient sparse matrix-vector multiplication on GPUs using the CSR storage format. In: Proceedings of International Conference on High Performance Computing, Networking, Storage and Analysis, SC 2014 (2014)
10. Saad, Y.: A flexible inner-outer preconditioned GMRES algorithm. SIAM J. Sci. Comput. **14**(2), 461–469 (1993)
11. Saad, Y.: Iterative Methods for Sparse Linear Systems. SIAM Publications, Philadelphia (2003)
12. Schenk, O., Wächter, A., Weiser, M.: Inertia-revealing preconditioning for large-scale nonconvex constrained optimization. SIAM J. Sci. Comp. **31**(2), 939–960 (2009)

Performance and Power-Aware Classification for Frequency Scaling of GPGPU Applications

João Guerreiro[✉], Aleksandar Ilic, Nuno Roma, and Pedro Tomás

INESC-ID, Instituto Superior Técnico, Universidade de Lisboa, Lisboa, Portugal
joaoguerreiro@inesc-id.pt

Abstract. The increased adoption of Graphics Processing Units (GPUs) to accelerate modern computational intensive applications, together with the strict power and energy constraints of many computing systems, has pushed for the development of efficient procedures to exploit dynamic voltage and frequency scaling (DVFS) techniques in GPUs. Although previous works have applied several pattern recognition techniques for GPGPU application classification, these approaches often result in many misclassifications when trying to identify which applications can benefit from DVFS. To circumvent this limitation, a new lightweight methodology for classifying GPU applications based on their performance and power consumption in the presence of GPU core frequency scaling is presented. The proposed methodology is based on a set of performance counters, such as memory bandwidth utilization and memory-related stalls, which are extracted during the application execution. Experimental results for a set of 20 applications from the Parboil, Rodinia and Polybench benchmark suites show that the proposed classification approach is able to correctly identify applications that can benefit from frequency scaling.

1 Introduction

Modern high performance computing (HPC) systems are increasingly making use of general purpose accelerators, such as graphics processing units (GPUs), in order to increase the resulting system performance. This is confirmed by an analysis of the most recent version of the TOP500 list (November 2015), where 103 of these systems are equipped with accelerators (75 and 90 in the two previous editions of this list). However, with the established adoption of GPUs, it is gradually important to find mechanisms that ensure the maximum efficiency of the computing system, both in terms of performance and (most importantly) energy. Accordingly, significant research efforts are being put forth in the investigation of dynamic voltage and frequency scaling (DVFS) techniques, due to the inherent potential for significant power and energy savings in many of the computer system components, including the processor cores [4].

General-purpose applications can largely vary in the way they use the computational and memory resources of the devices where they are executing [10]. While some applications perform a large number of computational operations for

© Springer International Publishing AG 2017
F. Desprez et al. (Eds.): Euro-Par 2016 Workshops, LNCS 10104, pp. 134–146, 2017.
DOI: 10.1007/978-3-319-58943-5_11

each loaded data (more *compute-bound*), other applications may perform very few operations for each portion of fetched data (more *memory-bound*). Although in the former type of applications the resulting performance is more likely to scale proportionally with the frequency of the cores (highest frequency ≡ best performance), this behaviour is not guaranteed for the latter set of applications. This opens an interesting window of opportunity, since some of these applications can be executed at lower frequency levels with negligible performance drop-off. Consequentially, and considering that (under DVFS) power consumption increases with the operating frequency of the device, the identification of these classes of applications can potentially be considered as an interesting opportunity for energy savings. However, just as power scales up with the operating frequency, the execution time scales down, making the definition of the optimal operating frequency a non-trivial choice. Hence, to perform this type of analysis, it is therefore fundamental the adoption of appropriate methodologies that allow the proper classification of the applications workloads, in order to identify which cases could potentially result in power- or energy-savings.

Although some previous works have already addressed the topic of workload classification, they have mostly focused on CPUs [10], even though addressing many different goals, e.g. *characterization, diversity analysis, subsetting, etc.*. In particular, the majority of the previous works on workload characterization involves the combination of principal component analysis (PCA) and hierarchical clustering [9]. As a consequence, some previous studies on workload characterization in the GPU-domain have tried to use similar approaches to the ones that were applied to the CPUs. In particular, Kerr et al. [6] characterized PTX workloads using a GPU simulator with the purpose of optimizing these applications. Che et al. [3] also performed a diversity analysis on the Rodinia benchmark suite, by using a real GPU (NVIDIA GTX 480). However, when looking at the majority of the state-of-the-art works in the area of GPU workload classification, it can be seen that most of the research relies on the usage of GPU simulators instead of real hardware. Although this allows for a detailed profiling of the workloads, usually by considering performance counters that are non-existent in real hardware, this renders these approaches impossible to replicate in real systems. Additionally, the existing GPU simulators are based on the NVIDIA's Fermi microarchitecture, which has already been followed by Kepler (2013), Maxwell (late 2014) and more recently Pascal (2016).

In the same trend, Adhinarayanan et al. [1] also provided an automated framework for characterizing and subsetting GPU workloads, by also relying on PCA and hierarchical clustering. While this approach has the advantage of reducing the dimensionality of the problem, usually by transforming a large number of metrics into a smaller number of principal components, it makes the understanding of each resulting class harder (from the computing architecture perspective) and does not necessarily result in a energy-aware classification.

In contrast with the described approaches, this work specifically addresses the definition of alternate classification methodologies in order to unveil which workloads will benefit from the application of DVFS techniques to provide energy savings. In fact, while it makes sense to classify applications and workloads as compute-bound or memory-bound when analysing their performance on a given GPU, it is observed that these notions cannot be applied in the same way when the power consumption is considered. In particular, we show that classifying for performance and for power consumption may result in different application classifications, confirming the need for separate classification techniques that depend on the considered goal. Additionally, unlike the previous proposals, this work is performed by using real and modern hardware systems. Accordingly, the major contributions of this paper are the following:

- Analysis of different types of performance and power consumption metrics using several relevant GPU benchmarks on real hardware;
- novel application classification algorithms based on GPU performance and power metrics, able to characterize the execution of each application on a range of GPU frequencies based on its execution on a single core frequency;
- comparison with other state-of-the-art classification techniques for GPU applications.

To conduct this work, we study 20 applications from different relevant benchmark suites (Parboil [8], Rodinia [2] and Polybench [7]), and analyse how the core frequency scaling affects their performance and their power consumption. The obtained experimental results show that the proposed algorithms are able to accurately and consistently classify the considered GPU applications in terms of their behaviour in performance, power and energy consumption. Finally, the proposed approach is compared with other state-of-the-art classification methodologies, which result in classes of applications that do not exhibit similar performance/power behaviour in the presence of frequency scaling.

2   Application Classification for GPGPU DVFS

This work focuses on the classification of GPGPU applications, with the objective of identifying which applications can benefit from DVFS in order to provide energy-savings. The goal is to be able to properly classify one given application for all operating frequencies of a given GPU device, after the execution of that application on a single operating frequency.

However, changing the frequency of the GPU cores may affect an application execution in very different ways, depending on each application's characteristics. While it can be expected that a decrease in the core frequency (f) will cause the kernel execution time to increase ($T \propto \frac{1}{f}$) and power consumption to decrease ($P_{dynamic} \propto V^2 f$ and $P_{static} \propto V e^{\gamma V}$), the actual values for the application's performance and power consumption over different frequencies are highly dependent on the application. In fact, it has been shown that accurately predicting the impact of DVFS in the execution time or power consumption requires complex predictive models [5]. Hence, given that the energy (E) consumed by the GPU is computed as the product between power (P) and execution time (t), $E = P \times t$,

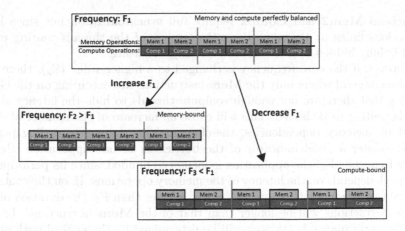

Fig. 1. Example of memory and compute operations overlap on three different core frequencies, with $F_2 > F_1 > F_3$. The instructions pairs (**Mem1**, **Comp1**) and (**Mem2**, **Comp2**) require full synchronization.

it is important to understand the effects of DVFS on both the execution time and power consumption of applications.

The DVFS impact on execution time is a complex problem that require a better understanding of the GPU architecture. In particular, one of the GPU main design goals concerns the use of multiple groups of parallel threads (*warps* in NVIDIA nomenclature) to hide instruction latency. However, in many general purpose applications, it is not always possible to hide the instruction latency with other warps. Therefore, when analysing the performance of applications, from the perspective of their bottleneck, most works tend to consider two main types of applications: *compute-bound* and *memory-bound*. Compute-bounded applications are defined as those where the execution time is mainly determined by the performance of the processing components, and is a direct consequence of an intensive utilization of the processing pipeline and functional units. On the other hand, memory-bound applications have their execution time mainly dependent on the bandwidth and latency of the memory hierarchy when satisfying the memory access requests.

Accordingly, when applying core level DVFS, the performance of a memory-bound kernel is limited by the communication with the GPU global memory, since the operating frequency of such component does not scale with the core frequency. However, such limitation is a consequence of the applied setup in terms of the core and memory operating frequencies. Hence, while one kernel may be compute-bound at one core operating frequency, it may become memory-bound if the operating frequency increases. To illustrate such condition, Fig. 1 presents a simplification of relative weight represented by the memory and compute operations of one given kernel at three different core frequencies. At frequency F_1, the threads start executing both the **Mem1** and **Comp1** instructions at the same time and both finish their execution at the same time. In this example, instructions **Mem2** and **Comp2** require full synchronization but since both instructions finish at the same time, the latency of the threads waiting to be issued is fully hidden by the threads currently executing.

However, if the core frequency is changed to a higher value (F_2), there will be a time interval where only the **Mem** instructions are executing on the GPU, meaning that there are not enough compute threads to hide the latency of the threads waiting to be issued. This will cause an increase of the number of stalls caused by memory dependencies, therefore making the corresponding performance counter a good indicator of the bottleneck of one application. Hence, at core frequency F_2, the application is memory-bounded, since its performance bottleneck depends on the latency of the memory operations. If, on the contrary, the core frequency is set to a value F_3 that is lower than F_1, the duration of the **Comp** instructions will be longer than that of the **Mem** instructions. In this case, the performance bottleneck will be determined by the critical path of the compute instructions, thus resulting in a compute-bounded classification.

However, although such classification strategy is valid for the application execution time, it is not entirely accurate for power classification. To demonstrate such conclusion, a set of benchmark applications from the previously referred Parboil, Rodinia and Polybench benchmark suites were executed on an NVIDIA Tesla K40c GPU at different core frequency levels, namely 875 MHz (default level), 810 MHz, 745 MHz and 666 MHz. Additionally, the DVFS impact on the execution time and energy consumption was measured (see Fig. 2). Also, the applications were hand-classified as *memory-bound* and *compute-bound* at the default operating frequency (Fig. 2, top-right), by considering the execution time increase when operating at the different frequencies, and each group's energy variation was analysed (Fig. 2, bottom-right). As can be observed, the presented compute/memory bound classification presents uninteresting results when energy consumption is considered. Hence, different methodologies must be employed. As a consequence, and keeping in mind that $E = P \times t$, a separate methodology to characterize effects of DVFS on the power consumption of applications is required.

In most GPUs (and in particular in modern NVIDIA GPUs) there are two independent frequency domains: (1) *Core domain*, which includes the streaming multiprocessors (SMs); and (2) *Off-chip domain*, which includes the off-chip DRAM. Accordingly, the power consumption can be expressed as

$$P(f_{\text{CORE}}, f_{\text{MEM}}) = P_{\text{CORE}}(f_{\text{CORE}}) + P_{\text{MEM}}(f_{\text{MEM}}) \tag{1}$$

where P_{CORE} is the power consumed by the components of the core domain, and P_{MEM} is the power consumed by the memory components, i.e. by the DRAM, which is herein assumed to remain constant. Based on Eq. 1, it is possible to characterize the applications depending on their usage of the core and memory components. Therefore, a given application shall be considered to have a high memory utilization (i.e. with high activity of the memory resources) if the power consumed by the GPU is dominated by the P_{MEM} parcel, i.e. if $P_{\text{MEM}} \gg P_{\text{CORE}}$. As a consequence, when the frequency of the core is changed, since the power

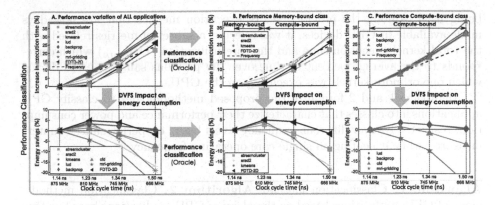

Fig. 2. Execution of the training set applications on NVIDIA Tesla K40c.

consumed by the memory is independent of the frequency of the core domain, the total power consumed will remain almost constant. On the other hand, if $P_{CORE} \gg P_{MEM}$, the GPU power consumption will scale linearly with the core frequency and the applications are considered to have a high core utilization. In order to perform the power-aware classification of GPU applications, a third scenario is also herein considered where both the memory and core components present a low utilization. Hence, since both components present a low activation of their resources, the average power consumption variation will be reduced when the core frequency is scaled.

Accordingly, when looking at the behaviour of the GPU power consumption over different operating frequencies, three different classes will be considered: *High Core Utilization*, *High Memory Utilization* and *Low Device Utilization*.

However, in order to perform such classification without having to execute the kernel at a different operating frequency, it is necessary to retrieve some profiling information regarding each application, which in this case must characterize its usage of the memory components (specifically, of the off-chip DRAM). One metric that gives a good indicator of the level of utilization of the memory resources is the percentage of stalls caused by memory dependencies (Eq. 2). However, it is still possible for one application to have other dominant causes for stalls and still a have high utilization of the memory components. In accordance, a complementary metric that quantifies the ratio of the achieved memory bandwidth over the device's peak (Eq. 3) is also considered.

$$Stalls_{mem} = \frac{Memory\ Dependency\ Stalls}{All\ Stalls} \tag{2}$$

$$Bandwidth_{mem} = \frac{Device\ memory\ transactions \times Transaction\ size}{Global\ memory\ bandwidth} \tag{3}$$

Hence, in order to perform the power-aware classification, additional metrics that characterize the utilization of the GPU resources are required, namely performance counters that characterize the amount of time the GPU resources are being used. Among the provided set of execution metrics that are nowadays made available in GPU devices, it was selected a subset of metrics related with the total kernel execution time and the core utilization (Util_{core}) which corresponds to the average percent of time over the previous sample period during which one or more kernels was executing on the GPU.

Algorithms 1 and 2 formalize the proposed methodologies to classify GPU applications into classes that characterize their performance and power consumption, respectively, over different frequency levels based on performance counters measured while executing on single core operating frequency.

Algorithm 1. Classification methodology of GPU applications based on the effects on execution time of DVFS.

Inputs: Bandwidth$_{mem}$ and Stalls$_{mem}$.
Output: Benchmark classification.

```
1: if Bandwidth_mem > α then
2:     memory-bound class.
3: else
4:     if Stalls_mem_depend > β then
5:         memory-bound class.
6:     else
7:         compute-bounded class.
8:     end if
9: end if
```

Algorithm 2. Classification methodology of GPU applications based on the DVFS effects on power consumption.

Inputs: Exec_time, Stalls$_{mem}$, Util$_{core}$.
Output: Benchmark classification.

```
1: if Exec_time < γ OR Util_core < δ then
2:     Low Device Utilization class
3: else
4:     if Stalls_mem > η then
5:         High Mem. Utilization class
6:     else
7:         High Core Utilization class
8:     end if
9: end if
```

For the performance-aware classification (Algorithm 1), a given application can be classified by executing it in the target GPU on a single chosen frequency level, during which the two mentioned performance counters are measured. The application under analysis is considered to be memory-bounded if one of the two measured values is higher than the corresponding respective thresholds, α and β, respectively, whose values were experimentally determined by using a training set to determine the combination of values that would result in the minimum misclassified applications. The power-aware classification (Algorithm 2), is similar to the performance one, with an additional class that selects the applications with low device utilization, according with a set of threshold γ, δ and η which were determined in the same way as before.

3   Experimental Results

To evaluate the proposed methodologies, several CUDA-based application benchmarks from the Parboil [8], Rodinia [2] and Polybench [7] suites (see Table 1) were executed on a NVIDIA Tesla K40c GPU (Kepler microarchitecture), which provides a user-level interface to scale the core operating frequency (f_{CORE}) in four non-idle levels, namely 875 MHz, 810 MHz, 745 MHz and 666 MHz.

Table 1. Summary of the considered application benchmarks.

Rodinia		Polybench			
Application	**Size**	**Application**	**Size**		
Backprop	655360	2MM	Default	**Parboil**	
CFD	missile.domn.0.2M	CORR	Default	**Application**	**Size**
Gaussian	2048×2048	COVAR	Default	CUTCP	Large
Hotspot	1024, 2, 10000	FDTD-2D	Default	Histo	Large
K-Means	3000000_34f.txt	GEMM	2048×2048	LBM	Long
Lud	8192×8192	GESUMMV	10240	MRI-Gridding	Small
SRAD2	4096	GRAMSCHM	Default		
Streamcluster	Default	SYRK	Default		

Each application was executed at the four allowed core frequency levels and their execution time was measured using CUDA events, together with the previously referred performance counters (see Sect. 2) for the reference (default) frequency level (875 MHz). Finally, in order validate the devised power-aware classification, the power consumption of each application executed on Tesla K40c GPU was obtained using NVML. Such power samples were obtained at a sample interval of 15 ms, and the final power consumption was computed as the average of all the kernels that constitute each application benchmark.

3.1 Classification Parameters

The previously proposed performance classification algorithm is dependent on two architecture-related parameters (α and β), which are determined using a randomly selected training set of applications. To assess such values Fig. 3a presents the number of misclassified benchmarks for different values of these parameters for the Tesla K40c GPU, when comparing the classifications resulting from the proposed algorithm with a manual classification of each application (oracle classifications), which confirms that $\alpha = 0.5$ and $\beta = 0.5$ correspond to the optimal setup. The values for the γ, δ and η parameters used in the proposed power classification methodology were also experimentally determined using the same approach. The obtained values are $\gamma = 170$ ms, $\delta = 50\%$ and $\eta = 22\%$.

3.2 Performance-Aware Algorithm Evaluation

Figure 3b and c depict the obtained values for the two metrics considered in the performance classification ($Stalls_{mem}$ and $Bandwidth_{mem}$), with the GPU cores set to 875 MHz. From these plots it can be observed that some applications have the majority of stalls caused by memory dependencies, while simultaneously achieving low usage of the device memory bandwidth. Some others display the opposite behaviour. Hence, after applying Algorithm 1, the two resulting classes correspond the ones presented in Fig. 4. To validate the obtained classification, all considered benchmarks were executed using the four allowed core

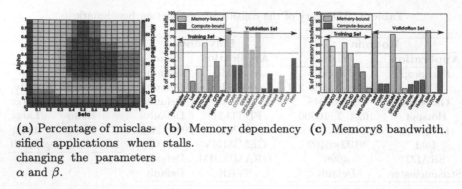

(a) Percentage of misclas-   (b) Memory dependency   (c) Memory8 bandwidth.
sified applications when   stalls.
changing the parameters
α and β.

Fig. 3. Considered metrics for the performance-aware classification on NVIDIA's Tesla K40c.

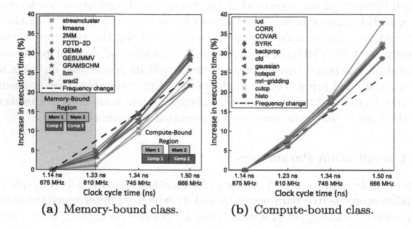

(a) Memory-bound class.   (b) Compute-bound class.

Fig. 4. DVFS effects on the execution time of the considered applications of the two performance classes in NVIDIA's Tesla K40c.

frequency levels for the considered GPU. The applications classified *memory-bounded* (see Fig. 4a) have a variation of their execution time lower than the frequency variation for frequencies above 810 MHz. Hence, at this core frequency the applications start behaving as compute-bound applications and have their execution time scaling approximately linearly with the core frequency. Furthermore, the *compute-bounded* applications (see Fig. 4b) always have their execution time scaling approximately linearly with the core frequency.

Again, it is important to stress that this methodology allows the classification of GPU applications into classes that characterize their performance at all frequency levels, by using the information obtained from their execution at a single core frequency in a real hardware device.

3.3   Power-Aware Algorithm Evaluation

Figure 5 presents the metrics considered in the devised power classification methodology (Exec_time, Util$_{core}$ and Stalls$_{mem}$) for the considered applications. By looking at their execution time (see Fig. 5a) it can be observed that there are many applications whose total kernel execution time is below the previously obtained γ parameter (170 ms), which will classify them in the *Low Device Utilization* class. By combining the values for these metrics for each of the workloads and applying Algorithm 2, the three classes presented in Fig. 6 are obtained. To validate the obtained classification, all considered applications were executed using the four allowed frequency levels for the considered GPU, resulting in distinct power curves. This is particularly noticeable by looking at the value of the power decrease at 666 MHz, since in the *Low Device Occupancy* class all applications have a decrease in power consumption below 10%; in the *High Memory Utilization* class have power savings between 10% and 20%; and finally in the *High Core Utilization* class the applications decrease their power consumption by more than 20%.

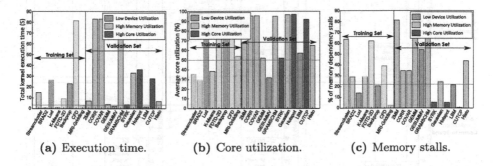

(a) Execution time.   (b) Core utilization.   (c) Memory stalls.

Fig. 5. Considered metrics for power classification on NVIDIA's Tesla K40c.

3.4   Energy Clusters

Since the proposed methodology depicts two performance classes and three power classifications for a given set of applications, it is possible to combine all this information, thus obtaining six energy classes, whose results is depicted in Fig. 7. Hence, when considering this classification methodology, it is not possible for one application to be simultaneously in the *memory-bounded* and *high core utilization* classes (it would require an application to simultaneously have $Stalls_{mem} > 0.5$ and $Stalls_{mem} < 0.22$).

When validating this classification by executing the applications at the GPU core levels and measuring the consumed energy (see Fig. 7), it can be seen that the applications within each class display a similar behaviour in the presence of DVFS. Hence, the result of those classification can be used to select the applications in which DVFS is more likely to generate greater energy-savings.

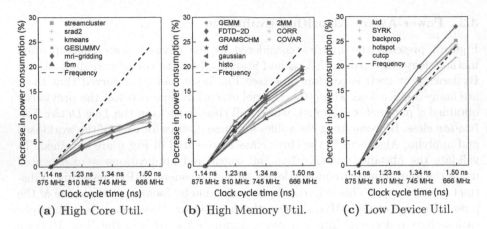

Fig. 6. DVFS effects on power consumption of applications in the three power classes in NVIDIA's Tesla K40c.

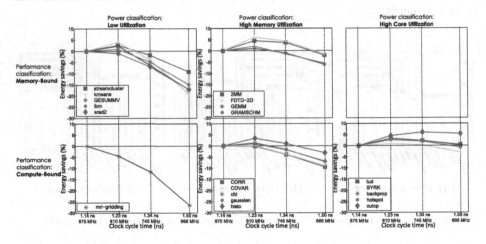

Fig. 7. Different energy classes resulting from the performance and power classes obtained for NVIDIA's Tesla K40c.

The proposed approach is considerable more versatile than other related approaches. As an example, Adhinarayanan et al. [1] perform a clustering of GPU applications using 13 performance counters, later reduced using Principal Component Analysis (PCA) into 6 principal components used in the hierarchical clustering stage. However, when their methodology is replicated in Tesla K40c using the applications benchmarks that were used in this work, and by considering six clusters during the hierarchical clustering stage, the results presented in Fig. 8 are achieved. As it can be seen, unlike the results from the proposed methodologies, this approach produces classes of applications that do not exhibit similar characteristics when DVFS is applied. Additionally, by using PCA and hierarchical clustering makes it harder to extract any architectural

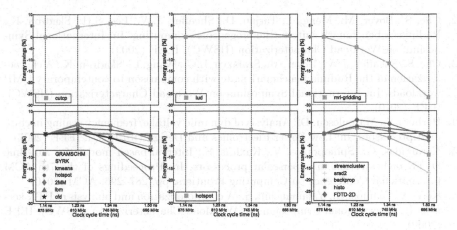

Fig. 8. Different classes resulting from the methodology proposed in [1].

meaning from the resulting classifications. In particular, it is hard to understand from Fig. 8 which of the resulting classes would correspond to the class composed by memory-bounded applications with high memory utilization.

4   Conclusion

A new methodology for GPU applications classification based on the resulting effects of DVFS on the application's execution time and power consumption was proposed. Such results from the fact that, existing classification techniques are not targeted for this specific goals, resulting in many wrongly classified applications when performance and power consumption are considered. To circumvent this absence, the proposed algorithms allow the classification of GPU applications into classes that characterize their performance (or power consumption) at all operating frequency levels, by solely using the information obtained from the execution of each application at a single core frequency. The performance and power classes define 6 distinct energy-aware classes of applications that present a similar behaviour in the presence of DVFS.

Acknowledgment. This work was partially supported by national funds through Fundação para a Ciência e a Tecnologia (FCT), under the project UID/CEC/50021/2013.

References

1. Adhinarayanan, V., Feng, W.C.: An automated framework for characterizing and subsetting GPGPU workloads. In: International Symposium on Performance Analysis of Systems and Software (ISPASS). IEEE (2016)

2. Che, S., Boyer, M., Meng, J., Tarjan, D., Sheaffer, J.W., Lee, S.H., Skadron, K.: Rodinia: a benchmark suite for heterogeneous computing. In: International Symposium on Workload Characterization (IISWC). IEEE (2009)
3. Che, S., Sheaffer, J.W., Boyer, M., Szafaryn, L.G., Wang, L., Skadron, K.: A characterization of the Rodinia benchmark suite with comparison to contemporary CMP workloads. In: International Symposium on Workload Characterization (IISWC). IEEE (2010)
4. Herbert, S., Marculescu, D.: Analysis of dynamic voltage/frequency scaling in chip-multiprocessors. In: Low Power Electronics and Design (ISLPED). IEEE (2007)
5. Keramidas, G., Spiliopoulos, V., Kaxiras, S.: Interval-based models for run-time DVFS orchestration in superscalar processors. In: Proceedings of the 7th ACM International Conference on Computing Frontiers, pp. 287–296. ACM (2010)
6. Kerr, A., Diamos, G., Yalamanchili, S.: A characterization and analysis of PTX kernels. In: International Symposium on Workload Characterization (IISWC). IEEE (2009)
7. Pouchet, L.N.: Polybench: the polyhedral benchmark suite. http://www.cs.ucla.edu/~pouchet/software/polybench/. Accessed 2012
8. Stratton, J.A., Rodrigues, C., Sung, I.J., Obeid, N., Chang, L.W., Anssari, N., Liu, G.D., Hwu, W.M.W.: Parboil: a revised benchmark suite for scientific and commercial throughput computing. Cent. Reliab. High-Perform. Comput. 127 (2012)
9. Yi, J.J., Sendag, R., Eeckhout, L., Joshi, A., Lilja, D.J., John, L.K.: Evaluating benchmark subsetting approaches. In: International Symposium on Workload Characterization (IISWC). IEEE (2006)
10. Zhuravlev, S., Blagodurov, S., Fedorova, A.: Addressing shared resource contention in multicore processors via scheduling. In: ACM SIGARCH Computer Architecture News. ACM (2010)

IWMSE - International Workshop on Multicore Software Engineering

A Context-Aware Primitive for Nested Recursive Parallelism

Herbert Jordan[1]($\boxtimes$), Peter Thoman[1], Peter Zangerl[1], Thomas Heller[2],
and Thomas Fahringer[1]

[1] University of Innsbruck, Innsbruck, Austria
{herbert,petert,peterz,tf}@dps.uibk.ac.at
[2] Friedrich-Alexander-Universität Erlangen-Nürnberg, Erlangen, Germany
thomas.heller@fau.de

Abstract. Nested recursive parallel applications constitute an important super-class of conventional, flat parallel codes. For this class, parallel libraries utilizing the concept of tasks have been widely adapted. However, the provided abstract task creation and synchronization interfaces force corresponding implementations to focus their attention to individual task creation and synchronization points – unaware of their relation to each other – thereby losing optimization potential.

Within this paper, we present a novel interface for task level parallelism, enabling implementations to grasp and manipulate the context of task creation and synchronization points – in particular for nested recursive parallelism. Furthermore, as a concrete application, we demonstrate the interface's capability to reduce parallel overhead within applications based on a reference implementation utilizing C++14 template meta programming techniques to synthesize multiple versions of a parallel task during the compilation process.

To demonstrate its effectiveness, we evaluate the impact of our approach on the performance of a series of eight task parallel benchmarks. For those, our approach achieves substantial speed-ups over state of the art solutions, in particular for use cases exhibiting fine grained tasks.

1 Introduction

For the development of parallel programs, various programming language extensions and libraries have been created. Many of these, including OpenMP, MPI, OpenCL, or CUDA, focus on the concept of parallel loops, and variations of those, as their primary use case. In general the associated data parallelism provides high degrees of concurrency, leading to scalable applications. Furthermore, the management overhead for distributing sub-ranges of parallel loops scales only with the number of processors, not the problem size itself – and is thus low.

© Springer International Publishing AG 2017
F. Desprez et al. (Eds.): Euro-Par 2016 Workshops, LNCS 10104, pp. 149–161, 2017.
DOI: 10.1007/978-3-319-58943-5_12

However, beyond the class of loop-parallel applications – also referred to as *flat* parallel applications – there is a large group of algorithms favoring nested parallelism. In those, concurrent control flows spawn further, *nested*, parallel control flows to obtain higher degrees of parallelism. In many cases, this nesting of parallel control flows, or *threads*, is even continued recursively.

Example algorithms benefiting from nested parallelism include divide and conquer approaches such as those found in sorting algorithms, the entire class of graph processing, as well as the wide range of problem space exploration algorithms, covering combinatorial problems, optimization problems, and decision problems (e.g. SAT or SMT problems). Also, many numerical problems have effective nested parallel implementations: matrix multiplication – in its 3-loop form a text book example for loop-level parallelism – can be more effectively solved by Strassen's algorithm, which exhibits a nested recursive parallel structure. Furthermore, conventional flat parallelism constitutes a special case of nested parallelism. Thus, the class of flat parallel algorithms is a true subset of the class of nested parallel algorithms.

Due to its benefits, existing languages and libraries have been modified to provide support for nested parallel codes. OpenMP introduced task-based parallelism in its version 3.0 [3] and CUDA supports nested parallelism since version 5.0 [8]. However, both superimpose nested parallelism on their otherwise flat execution model, resulting in management overhead for the runtime as well as for the developer. Cilk, on the other hand, has been specifically designed for nested, recursive parallelism, resulting in a (nearly) hands-off solution for the scheduling of nested (recursive) parallelism. However, as we will address in this paper, Cilk's fully general approach introduces overhead. Furthermore, as a compiler based approach, modifications and extensions to Cilk require modifications in the compiler and are thus not portable among different system software stacks.

The construct presented in this paper, the *prec* operator, provides a way to define nested parallel operations offering the flexibility of future based task systems, combined with the hands-off scheduling and load management qualities of Cilk, yet avoiding Cilk's inherent overhead for task-scheduling opportunities. Furthermore, all of those features are realized utilizing C++'s template-meta-programming feature – essentially a built-in, widely supported language feature to script C/C++ code generation in an early compilation stage. Thus, while being a code generation based solution, its implementation behaves like a library. It can therefore be flexibly extended or modified and is directly supported by every standard C++ compiler. Consequently, parallel codes developed utilizing *prec* are portable to all systems offering a C++ compiler.

2   Motivation and Main Idea

Our work was motivated by the unexpected low parallel performance observed when parallelizing nested recursive algorithms using state-of-the-art tools. For instance, Fig. 1 compares the execution time of various parallel codes computing Fibonacci numbers recursively similar to

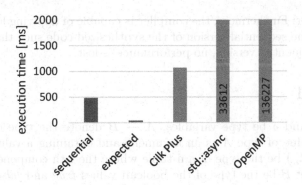

Fig. 1. Performance comparison of parallel `fib(40)` computations using parallel libraries integrated into GCC 5.3.0, compared to a desired linear speedup.

```
int fib(int n) {
    if (n <= 2) return 1;
    int a = spawn fib(n-1);
    int b = fib(n-2);
    sync;
    return a + b;
}
```

utilizing different parallel library and runtime implementations. Based on the parallel structure of the problem, an almost linear speedup would have been expected. However, as the data shows, none of the parallel implementations manages to provide any speedup over the sequential version. While the Cilk based version exhibits a slowdown by a factor of 2.2, the `std::async` and OpenMP variants lead to a slowdown by a factor of 70 and 284 respectively.

One common concept in all existing parallel libraries or program extensions is that each creation of at task is handled independently. While it is very prominent and explicit when using C++11's `std::async`, Cilk and OpenMP implementations also process each individual task-creation site independently of its context. Thus, if nested in a recursive function, each (potential) task-creation point has to be processed, and the cost for the thereby introduced overhead has to be paid.

With the `prec` operator, to be specified in detail in Sect. 3, we enable the parallel library implementation to grasp the context of a parallel task creation point – in particular in a nested recursive environment. Furthermore, we enable the parallel library to specialize the context around those task creation points. This capability is utilized by the `prec` operator to create multiple implementation versions of a given recursive operation – one processing sub-tasks in parallel and another processing sub-tasks sequentially. The runtime system may then switch between these two implementations depending on the system state.

As a result, when utilizing the `prec` operator for parallelizing nested recursive code, *the compiler is synthesizing an interleaved sequential and parallel version of the recursive function from a single specification.* Thus, the user only has to provide and maintain a single implementation. The multi-versioning is conducted

by the compiler. Furthermore, the compiler is capable of applying low-level optimizations to the sequential version of the synthesized code such that, compared
to a purely sequential version, no performance is lost.

3   Method

Let α, β, γ, and δ be type variables, $A \to B$ denote the type of a function
accepting a value of type A as an argument and obtaining a value of type B,
and $(A_1, \ldots, A_n)$ be the type of a n-tuple where the i-th component is of type
A_i. Further, let $\mathcal{B}$ be the type of the boolean values *true* and *false*, and $\mathcal{N}$ the
set of natural numbers.

3.1   The rec Operator

A recursive function can be defined by providing (i) a test for the base-case,
(ii) a function evaluating a base-case, and (iii) a function evaluating a step-case.
Furthermore, in a typed system, the parameter type and the result type of the
function has to be specified. For instance, for defining a recursive version of the
Fibonacci function fib, where

$$\text{fib}(x) = \begin{cases} 1 & x <= 2 \\ \text{fib}(x-1) + \text{fib}(x-2) & \text{otherwise} \end{cases}$$

the parameter and result type is $\mathcal{N}$ (natural numbers), the base-case test, the
base-case, and the step case are given (in C++11 lambda-like syntax) by the
three expressions

```
base_case_test = [](N x){ return x <= 2; };
base_case      = [](N x){ return 1; };
step_case      = [](N x, N → N fib){
                   return fib(x-1) + fib(x-2);
                 };
```

where the parameter `fib` is a token passed as an argument to conduct recursive
calls.

Let α and β be type variables representing the parameter type and result
type respectively. Then, in the general case, a definition requires

– a base-case test of type $\alpha \to \mathcal{B}$
– a base-case evaluation function of type $\alpha \to \beta$ and
– a step-case evaluation function of type $(\alpha, \alpha \to \beta) \to \beta$

To combine those parameters, a higher-order function `rec` of type

$$(\alpha \to \mathcal{B}, \alpha \to \beta, (\alpha, \alpha \to \beta) \to \beta) \to (\alpha \to \beta)$$

can be defined, such that a call `rec(a,b,c)` evaluates to the recursive function

```
β f ( α in ) {
    if (a(in)) return b(in);
    return c(in,f);
}
```

Thus, for our example above, we obtain after inlining

```
N f ( N in ) {
    if (in <= 2) return 1;
    return f(in-1) + f(n-2);
}
```

corresponding to a sequential implementation of the Fibonacci function.

3.2   The prec Operator

For the parallel case it would be desirable to process sub-tasks of the recursion in parallel. However, once sufficient concurrent control flows are present in the system, the individual tasks should avoid the overhead induced by allowing for task spawning by being processed sequentially. Thus, the scheme of the rec operator needs to be modified to enable the generation of sequential and parallel versions of the recursive function as well as to enable the task scheduler to decide which version to execute at every scheduling point.

Similar to the rec operator, the prec operator is a higher order function of type

$$(\alpha \rightarrow \mathcal{B}, \alpha \rightarrow \beta, (\alpha, \alpha \rightarrow \gamma\langle\beta\rangle) \rightarrow \beta) \rightarrow (\alpha \rightarrow \text{future}\langle\beta\rangle)$$

accepting three functions as arguments, and returning a new function as a result. The interpretation of α and β is the same as for the rec operator. Additionally, γ is a generic type to be substituted by a value wrapper providing access to a (potentially asynchronously processed) value. Two examples of such value wrappers are:

- value<δ> wrapping an immediately available value of type δ that has been computed synchronously, and
- future<δ> referencing a value of type δ asynchronously computed by a task

The result of the prec operator is a function asynchronously computing the recursive function defined by its parameters, thus returning a future to a value of type β.

Let $\text{expr}_1, \ldots, \text{expr}_n$ be $n \geq 1$ expressions of type T. Furthermore, let the expression spawn expr_1 or $\ldots$ or expr_n create a task evaluating asynchronously exactly one of the given n expressions and return a future of type $\text{future}\langle T\rangle$ as a handle to the resulting value. A call to $\text{prec}(a, b, c)$ is translated into the nested recursive parallel function f defined by

```
value<β> seq_f( α in ) {
    if (a(in)) return value(b(in));
    return value(c(in,seq_f));
}
```

```
future<β> par_f( α in ) {
  if (a(in)) return spawn b(in);
  return spawn c(in,f);
}
future<β> f( α in ) {
  return spawn seq_f(in).get() or par_f(in).get();
}
```

where `seq_f` is the sequential version of the recursion, `par_f` the parallel version and `f` a version serving as a dispatcher point between the sequential and parallel version upon each recursive invocation. Note that the functions `par_f` and `f` are mutually recursive, while `seq_f` is only invoking itself.

3.3 The Runtime System

A runtime system supporting the `prec` operator needs to provide efficient implementations for the `spawn` expression and the `future` class. It can rely on the fact that the `spawn` expression is called by passing (i) a single, nested parallel expression or (ii) two expressions, where the first is a sequential implementation and the second a parallel implementation. Thus, in case two implementations are provided, the first may be used in situations where the available parallel processing units are saturated and more parallelism is not beneficial, while the second implementation may be chosen if there are still idle resources in the system.

For the futures, any runtime implementation has to provide means to synchronize upon the completion of spawned tasks as well as to retrieve asynchronously computed values.

3.4 Implementation

We have implemented the `prec` operator in a reference implementation utilizing C++14 and its template meta-programming facilities. It is internally maintaining a pool of threads, each equiped with a local task queue. For load balancing, a task steeling policy has been integrated. The implementation is available online[1].

4   Evaluation

To evaluate the impact of our construct on the performance of task parallel applications we have conducted several experiments based on our reference implementation. The results are discussed in the following subsections.

4.1 Fibonacci

Our first evaluation concludes our motivational example. In Sect. 2 various parallel implementations of `fib`, based on state-of-the-art parallel libraries and

---

[1] https://github.com/HerbertJordan/parec commit 9aa5dac.

language extensions, have been presented. All of them fall short in providing acceptable performance results for computing our benchmark case fib(40). For a sequential execution time of ≈480 ms one would expect, presuming ideal scaling, an execution time of 40 ms on a 12-thread system, as illustrated in Fig. 1. Our prec based implementation obtains the result within 41 ms, corresponding to a 97.5% parallel efficiency. Clearly, our approach is able to mitigate the majority of overhead and to achieve acceptable performance for the given benchmark.

The evaluation of this fibonacci motivating example, as well as the comparison results shown in the motivation section, have been carried out using GCC 5.3.0, on a 6-core/12-thread Intel Core i7-5820K CPU at 3.3 GHz.

4.2   The prec Impact

In our second experimental setup, our goal was to identify the impact of considering the calling context like it is done by our prec operator compared to a purely localized task-generation code realized by utilizing a conventional async call. To eliminate any impact of the quality of an underlying runtime system, we utilized the same runtime implementation for both situations. Thus, we can exclude the effects of different scheduling policies, task queue lengths, stealing policies, or task handling overheads. To that end we compared two slightly different versions of our reference runtime:

- the parec::async configuration, where every call to spawn is treated like a std::async call, creating a new light-weight task to be scheduled by the runtime system
- the parec::prec configuration, where nested recursive tasks and their calling context are treated as described in Sect. 3

To compare those two setups, we ported the INNCABS [12] benchmark suite to the prec operator. The port can be obtained online[2].

Table 1 enumerates the eight benchmarks we have ported for our evaluation. The covered codes reach from numeric algorithms like Strassen and SparseLU, over combinatorial problems including QAP and NQueens, to standard utility algorithms like Sort. Table 1 also lists the problem sizes for our experiments. For practical reasons we decided to cancel all unfinished executions after 100 s and consider these to have timed out.

Our evaluation platform is a quad-socket shared-memory system equipped with Intel Xeon E5-4650 processors, each offering 8 cores clocked at a nominal frequency of 2.7 GHz (up to 3.3 GHz with Turbo Boost). The software stack consists of GCC 5.2.0 with -O3 optimizations, running on a Linux operating system with kernel version 2.6.32-473. The thread affinity for all benchmark runs was fixed using a fill-socket-first policy, and all reported numbers are medians over ten runs.

Figure 2 illustrates our experimental results. For each benchmark we show the median execution time for a varying number of threads. The execution times

---

[2] https://github.com/PeterTh/inncabs/tree/parec_port.

Table 1. Ported INNCABS benchmarks and problem sizes

Name	Description	Problem size
Fib	Fibonacci number	47
Health	Health care simulation	medium.input
NQueens	The N-Queens problem	13
Pyramids	2D cache-oblivious stencil solver	-
QAP	Quadratic assignment problem	chr15c.dat
Sort	Merge-sort	10^8 8192 2048 128
SparseLU	LU factorization	-
Strassen	Strassen algorithm	4096

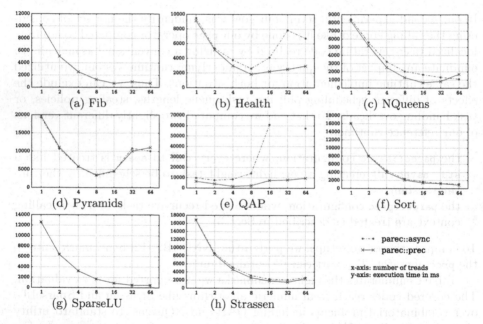

Fig. 2. Performance comparison of the `parec::async` and `parec::prec` operator mapped to the same runtime system.

for running in `parec::async` and in `parec::prec` mode are compared – with the exception of Fib, where the total run time of the `parec::async` configuration did not finish within a timeout of 100 s for any number of threads.

For benchmarks where task creation and spawning is clearly dominated by the actual workload of the task, no significant difference between the two configurations can be observed. This includes Pyramids, Sort, SparseLU, and Strassen. For all of those, both configurations produce almost identical results.

Benchmarks where the actual workload is small compared to the task spawning overhead however, benefit from context-awareness and specialization conducted by the prec. Those include

- Fib – with only one comparison, two function calls, and three arithmetic operations per task – here prec is faster by several orders of magnitude
- Health – where each task is a local operation on a single node in a graph
- NQueens – where each task conducts a small number of stack local operations
- QAP – where each task conducts stack local operations and a single access to a globally shared scalar value

Especially those benchmarks with a large, yet irregular fan out (Health and QAP) produce a large number of tasks in lower levels of the execution tree, the overhead of which can be significantly reduced by the prec approach.

For some of the benchmarks, increasing the number of threads beyond a single socket – thus exceeding 8 threads – shows a considerable change in their scaling behaviour. This is particularly prominent for Health, and QAP, in which each task accesses a single, globally shared scalar due to the branch-and-bound nature of the represented algorithms. Also, for some data intensive benchmarks like Pyramids, the data access order – and thus the efficient usage of caches – has a much higher impact on the execution performance of the benchmark than the task scheduling overhead. However, our reference runtime has not been specifically tuned to deal efficiently with this kind of challenges, which constitute large branches of research on their own.

As the data shows, the utilization of prec can provide substantial performance benefits, in particular for use cases with a low number of operations per tasks.

The raw data of this experiment, as well as all the sources and scripts used for their generation can be obtained online[3].

4.3   Application Benchmarks

For our final evaluation, we are comparing the absolute performance of our prec implementation with the performance obtainable by utilizing comparable parallel libraries – in particular GCC's Cilk Plus and std::async.

While Cilk Plus does not require additional tuning parameters, std::async does allow the user to specify a launch policy. According to the C++ standard, the following policies need to be supported:

- *async* – the spawned task is processed asynchronously
- *deferred* – the task is processed by the thread requesting the result (lazy evaluation)
- *default* – which is equivalent to either async or deferred, but leaves the choice to the implementation

For our comparison we evaluated all three of those policies and included the one providing the best performance for the respective number of threads. Furthermore, we utilized the same benchmarks and setup as in Subsect. 4.2.

---

[3] https://github.com/PeterTh/inncabs/tree/parec_port commit b3f87a2.

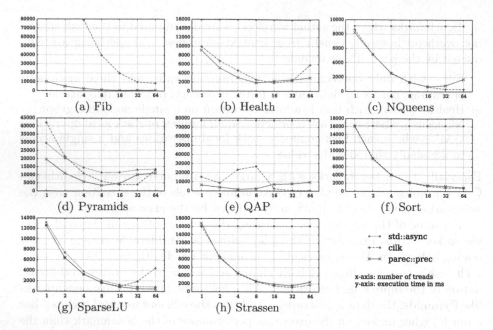

Fig. 3. Performance comparison of our `parec::prec` implementation, Cilk Plus, and C++'s `std::async`.

Figure 3 illustrates the obtained results. Similarly to our `parec::async` setup, `std::async` is not able to compute a solution for Fib within our time limit of 100 s.

In several cases the launch policy *deferred* turned out to be the fastest option, although leading to an effective serialization of the program code. As a result, for a set of benchmarks including NQueens, Sort, and Strassen, the execution time of `std::async` does not change with the number of threads.

Cilk Plus, on the other hand, also fails to obtain a result for Fib with only 1 or 2 threads within 100 s.

For NQueens, Sort, SparseLU, and Strassen, Cilk Plus and our reference runtime provide comparable results, while C++'s `std::async` only manages to obtain a speedup for SparseLU.

In particular for Fib, but also for the intra-socket QAP, our approach provides (highly) superior performance compared to the alternative libraries and/or language extensions.

For Pyramids, the Cilk and `std::async` implementation suffer from high sequential overhead due to their internal operation, which only Cilk manages to compensate due to almost linear scaling. However, within a single socket, our runtime manages to provide higher performance than both of them. Beyond the single-socket boundary, however, impacting factors like the evaluation order of sub-tasks and their effect on cache usage and NUMA effects become more important, weakening the performance of our runtime. However, those have not been the objectives of the presented work. These aspects will be further investigated by follow-up efforts.

The raw data for this experiment, as well as full sources and scripts to reproduce it, may be obtained online[4].

5   Related Work

Due to its status as a fundamental and easy to use parallel abstraction, there is a large body of existing work in optimizing task parallelism. Particular attention was previously paid to scheduling strategies [2,9] and alleviating task creation overhead [5,10]. What is common to all of these approaches is that they focus primarily on the runtime system level, while we employ C++ template programming in order to introduce a code-generation component evaluated at compile time. This allows us to generate more efficient parallel code, and to provide any given runtime system with the option of switching to a zero-overhead sequential implementation without requiring the user to manually create and maintain separate versions of their code. As such, our approach is orthogonal to and compatible with any further runtime-level adaptation and optimization – such as the lazy task creation scheme described by Duran et al. [5] or any of the hardware-aware or locality-based scheduling strategies [7].

Looking specifically at the C++ language, parallelism is primarily the domain of traditional tasking libraries [1,11], which are also inherently limited to runtime optimization due to the type of primitives they offer. Meanwhile, current compiler research related to C++11 parallelism has focused on the correctness of the memory model underlying the standard [4], not on the performance of its library function implementations. An exception is the authors' previous work on semantics-aware compilation techniques [13], however, unlike the template library based approach presented in this paper it requires a non-standard system software stack, limiting its applicability in real-world software deployments.

Existing C++ template libraries for parallelism which operate on a higher level of abstraction, such as Quaff [6], aim to support a wide variety of parallel patterns. However, unlike the work presented in this paper, they do not focus specifically on reducing overheads in recursive task parallel algorithm by compile-time multiversioned code generation.

6   Conclusion and Future Work

In this paper we presented a novel, abstract parallel construct enabling parallel task library implementations to grasp and manipulate the context of task spawning points. By utilizing the capabilities established by its design, we demonstrated its potential of reducing the task creation overhead within nested recursive parallel codes. Our reference implementation generally achieved comparable

---

[4] The files for the `std::async` reference implementation, the Cilk Plus port, and the `parec::prec` port are available at `https://github.com/PeterTh/inncabs/tree/[master,cilk_port,parec_port]` respectively (commits a87ed27, 6476d75 and b3f87a2).

or better performance than state-of-the art solutions. Crucially, for a class of use cases in which the computational effort of individual tasks is low, our approach was able to attain superior performance. Furthermore, unlike the best state of the art competitor (Cilk Plus), which depends on compiler extensions, our approach is a pure C++14 solution and thus portable to any compliant compiler.

Due to its library based nature, our approach is easy to customize e.g. in its scheduling and version selection policy. More sophisticated concepts for these will be investigated to improve the load balancing and scalability of our runtime implementation. Furthermore, additional high-level parallel constructs including parallel loops, stencils, or map-reduce like operators can be designed on top of prec to improve its usability.

Acknowledgement. This project has received funding from the European Union's Horizon 2020 research and innovation programme as part of the FETHPC AllScale project under grant agreement No. 671603.

References

1. An, P., et al.: STAPL: an adaptive, generic parallel C++ library. In: Dietz, H.G. (ed.) LCPC 2001. LNCS, vol. 2624, pp. 193–208. Springer, Heidelberg (2003). doi:10.1007/3-540-35767-X_13
2. Augonnet, C., Thibault, S., Namyst, R., Wacrenier, P.A.: StarPU: a unified platform for task scheduling on heterogeneous multicore architectures. Concurrency Comput.: Pract. Exp. **23**(2), 187–198 (2011)
3. Ayguadé, E., Copty, N., Duran, A., Hoeflinger, J., Lin, Y., Massaioli, F., Teruel, X., Unnikrishnan, P., Zhang, G.: The design of openMP tasks. IEEE Trans. Parallel Distrib. Syst. **20**(3), 404–418 (2009)
4. Batty, M., Memarian, K., Owens, S., Sarkar, S., Sewell, P.: Clarifying and compiling C/C++ concurrency: from C++11 to power. In: ACM SIGPLAN Notices, vol. 47, pp. 509–520. ACM (2012)
5. Duran, A., Corbalán, J., Ayguadé, E.: An adaptive cut-off for task parallelism. In: International Conference for High Performance Computing, Networking, Storage and Analysis, SC 2008, pp. 1–11. IEEE (2008)
6. Falcou, J., Sérot, J., Chateau, T., Lapresté, J.T.: Quaff: efficient C++ design for parallel skeletons. Parallel Comput. **32**(7), 604–615 (2006)
7. Guo, Y., Zhao, J., Cave, V., Sarkar, V.: SLAW: a scalable locality-aware adaptive work-stealing scheduler. In: 2010 IEEE International Symposium on Parallel & Distributed Processing (IPDPS), pp. 1–12. IEEE (2010)
8. Jones, S.: Introduction to dynamic parallelism. In: GPU Technology Conference Presentation, vol. 338 (2012)
9. Lakshmanan, K., Kato, S., Rajkumar, R.: Scheduling parallel real-time tasks on multi-core processors. In: 2010 IEEE 31st Real-Time Systems Symposium (RTSS), pp. 259–268. IEEE (2010)
10. Mohr, E., Kranz, D.A., Halstead Jr., R.H.: Lazy task creation: a technique for increasing the granularity of parallel programs. IEEE Trans. Parallel Distrib. Syst. **2**(3), 264–280 (1991)
11. Reinders, J.: Intel Threading Building Blocks: Outfitting C++ for Multi-core Processor Parallelism. O'Reilly Media Inc., Sebastopol (2007)

12. Thoman, P., Gschwandtner, P., Fahringer, T.: On the quality of implementation of the C++11 thread support library. In: 2015 23rd Euromicro International Conference on Parallel, Distributed and Network-Based Processing (PDP), pp. 94–98. IEEE (2015)
13. Thoman, P., Moosbrugger, S., Fahringer, T.: Optimizing task parallelism with library-semantics-aware compilation. In: Träff, J.L., Hunold, S., Versaci, F. (eds.) Euro-Par 2015. LNCS, vol. 9233, pp. 237–249. Springer, Heidelberg (2015). doi:10. 1007/978-3-662-48096-0_19

Achieving High Parallel Efficiency on Modern Processors for X-Ray Scattering Data Analysis

Abhinav Sarje[1(✉)], Xiaoye S. Li[1], and Nicholas Wright[2]

[1] Computational Research Division,
Lawrence Berkeley National Laboratory, Berkeley, USA
abhinav.sarje@gmail.com
[2] National Energy Research Scientific Computing Center,
Lawrence Berkeley National Laboratory, Berkeley, USA

Abstract. Modern processors have increasingly more parallelism available on-chip, which include simultaneous multithreading (SMT) and single-instruction multiple-data (SIMD) parallelisms. The former is typically available through multiple compute cores and the latter through long vector units. In this paper, we consider several compute kernels of a real-world scientific application, X-ray scattering data analysis, to demonstrate and analyze high performance through the exploitation of available SMT and SIMD parallelism on such modern processors, which form the base of current state-of-the-art supercomputers. We discuss various methods to effectively exploit the available on-node parallelism to increase parallel efficiency and provide detailed performance analysis on two leading Cray supercomputers. In addition, we also present performance results obtained on the Intel Knights Landing processor.

1 Introduction and Background

Modern processor architectures are being designed with increasing amount of on-chip parallelism available. These processors are designed to deliver higher computing power by exploiting multiple levels of parallelism. In high-performance scientific computing, these architectures play a central role in delivering the much needed compute and memory resources. In this paper, we consider performance analysis and optimization of an application code developed recently, *HipGISAXS* [2,3]. This is a high-performance code for X-ray scattering data analysis [4,5]. Such data analysis is useful to scientists for the characterization of macromolecules and nano-particle systems based on their structural properties, such as their shape and size, at the micro/nano-scales. Some of the major applications of these include the characterization of materials for the design and fabrication of energy-relevant nano-devices, such as photovoltaic cells, and development of high-density storage media.

In this paper, we consider some of the most compute-intensive kernels of the *HipGISAXS* code to demonstrate and analyze high-performance through the exploitation of simultaneous multi-threading (SMT) and single-instruction multiple-data (SIMD) parallelism on modern multi-core processors. We discuss

© Springer International Publishing AG 2017
F. Desprez et al. (Eds.): Euro-Par 2016 Workshops, LNCS 10104, pp. 162–174, 2017.
DOI: 10.1007/978-3-319-58943-5_13

various methods to effectively exploit the available on-node parallelism to increase parallel efficiency and provide detailed performance analysis on leading Cray supercomputers. We further provide performance analysis on Intel's Knights Landing manycore processor, which has even larger number of compute cores with 512-bit wide vector units.

2   Computational Kernels

In HipGISAXS simulation code, the kernels compute on a two-dimensional grid, with non-uniform positioning of the grid points. The simulated scattering light intensities are computed at each grid point. The computations at each grid point are independent of each other, which is amenable to efficient exploitation of parallelism. In each simulation, two types of routines are executed: Form Factor (FF) computations and Structure Factor (SF) computations. The former represent the scattering phenomenon due to individual nanoparticles in the sample model, while the latter represent the scattering due to all particles forming a structure (such as their three-dimensional arrangements) as a whole. Both types contain a number of kernels, each depending on the type of computations performed. The FF kernels could be either analytic, where computations are derived analytically for simple nanoparticle shapes, such as spheres, cylinders, cubes, etc., or numerical, which are generic and used for complex structures when they cannot be efficiently defined through simple shapes. In the following we focus on one of the analytical kernels and one of the numerical kernels for the purpose of demonstrating the exploitation of thread and vector parallelism. The form factor computation at a single q-point involves accessing data and performing independent calculations for each of the input shape triangles, followed by a reduction over all the triangles. This is done for all the q-points in the problem under consideration. The output matrix $\mathcal{F}$ of the same size as the Q-grid $\mathcal{Q}$, is constructed with the results of these computations. This is summarized in the following equation:

$$\mathcal{F} : f(q) = -\frac{i}{|q|^2} \sum_{t=1}^{n_t} e^{iq \cdot r_t} q_{n,t} s_t, \quad \forall q \in \mathcal{Q}. \tag{1}$$

2.1   An Analytical Form Factor Kernel

For certain simple nanoparticle shapes, such as spherical, cylindrical, cuboidal, etc., analytical formulae can be derived to calculate the form factor. In most cases, such analytical computations are significantly cheaper than performing the general-case computations through volume integrals. Hence, if a sample model can be described in terms of simple shapes, it is preferable to use the analytical method. The application under consideration includes a number of such analytical form factor computational kernels. We select one of these analytical kernels, the form factor for a cylindrical shape, for our study in the following sections.

Algorithm 1. Simplified structure of analytical cylinder form factor kernel

```
for(int z = 0; z < nqz; ++ z) {
  int y = z % nqy;
  vector3c_t mq = rotate(qx[y], qy[y], qz[z], rot);
  complex_t qpar = sqrt(mq[0] * mq[0] + mq[1] * mq[1]);
  // ... more computations ...
  complex_t temp_ff(0.0, 0.0);
  for(int i_r = 0; i_r < rsize; ++ i_r) {
    for(int i_h = 0; i_h < hsize; ++ i_h) {
      // ... more computations ...
      complex_t expo_val = exp(0.5 * mq[3] * h[i_h]);
      complex_t sinc_val = sinc(0.5 * mq[3] * h[i_h]);
      complex_t bess_val = cbesselj(qpar * r[i_r], 1) / (qpar * r[i_r]);
      temp_ff += sinc_val * expo_val * bess_val;
    }
  }
  // ... more computations ...
  complex_t temp2 = exp(temp1);
  ff[z] = temp_ff * temp2;
}
```

The basic computational loop structure of the cylinder form factor kernel is shown in Algorithm 1. The outermost loop is over all the q-points (n_{qz}). The number of q-points in a typical simulation is in over 1 million. All the kernels in this application make a heavy use of various transcendental functions, such as sine, cosine, exponential, Bessel, etc. Additionally, since the q-points are in the complex space, the computations are performed on complex numbers. The inner loop-nest in Algorithm 1 are over the two parameters defining the cylinderical shape, radius (**rsize**) and height (**hsize**). Total number of iterations for this loop-nest is typically small, on the order of tens, and in many cases, just one.

2.2   A Numerical Form Factor Kernel

For sample models where the nanoparticle shapes cannot be defined in terms of simple shapes, a full numerical integration over the particles' structure needs to be performed. This represents the general case, which can handle any kind of complex shapes. The shapes are defined through discretization of its surface, such as by triangulation. The higher the discretization resolution, the better the computed approximation, but with higher computational cost. The shape surface integration adds another dimension to the computational problem. A typical structure of a numerical form factor kernel is shown in Algorithm 2. As with the analytical kernels described previously, the outermost loop is over the q-points. The primary internal loop is over the set of triangles describing the corresponding structure in the sample. The number of triangles can vary from several hundreds to several millions depending on the structure complexity and discretization resolution.

Algorithm 2. A simplified structure of a numerical form factor kernel that uses triangulated structure definitions

```
for(int z = 0; z < nqz; ++ z) {
  int y = z % nqy;
  vector3c_t mq = rotate(qx[y], qy[y], qz[z], rot);
  // ... more computations ...
  complex_t ff_temp(0.0, 0.0);
  for(int t = 0; t < num_triangles; ++ t) {
    // ... load triangle data ...
    // ... more computations ...
    complex_t ff(0.0, 0.0);
    for(int e = 0; e < 3; ++ e) {
      // ... more computations ...
      vector3_t n_e = cross(edge[e], n_t); n_e = n_e / n_e.abs();
      vector3_t n_v = edge[e] / edge[e].abs();
      complex_t q_dot_ne = dot(mq, n_e);
      complex_t q_dot_v  = dot(mq, vertex[e]);
      complex_t q_dot_nv = dot(mq, n_v)
      // ... more computations ...
      complex_t c0 = CMPLX_MINUS_ONE_ * q_dot_nt * q_dot_ne * q_dot_nv;
      complex_t c1 = exp(CMPLX_MINUS_ONE_ * q_dot_v);
      ff += c0 * c1 / f0;
    }
    ff_temp += ff;
  }
  ff[z] = ff_temp;
}
```

3   Computational Platforms and Performance Modeling

In the work discussed in this paper, we perform experiments and performance analysis on the current Cray supercomputers installed at *NERSC* at Berkeley Lab:

1. Cray XC30 (*Edison*): Consists of dual-socket compute nodes with 12-core Intel Ivybridge processors, total 24 cores and 64 GB memory per node.
2. Cray XC40 (*Cori Phase 1*): Consists of dual-socket compute nodes with 16-core Intel Haswell processors, total 32 cores and 128 GB memory per node.

Additionally, we also analyze the performance on Intel's new Knights Landing (KNL) processor:

3. A single-socket compute node with 1.3 GHz 64-core Intel Knights Landing processor, 96 GB DRAM as well as 16 GB of MCDRAM (high-bandwidth memory).

In order to understand the performance of a code and identify bottlenecks before any optimization is performed, it is helpful to establish a performance model on which the code performance can be measured. In this paper, we present the analysis using the Roofline performance model [6]. The Roofline toolkit was used to obtain the empirical performance bounds for computations (GFLOPs/s) and memory bandwidths (GB/s) with respect to the first-level cache and DRAM. These are discussed in Sect. 6.

4   Threading

An effective way to exploit multiple compute cores available on a processor is through shared-memory threading. In our case, we utilize OpenMP to implement threading in each of the kernels. Since scattering light intensity computations at each q-point are independent of each other, a straight-forward threading of the loop over the q-points is the most efficient approach. The OpenMP threads do not require any significant synchronizations, making the kernel able to make full use of the available cores asynchronously. To achieve a higher threading performance, care should be taken while constructing data structures and buffers so as to minimize data movement overheads, cache line invalidation overhead and page thrashing. A node on typical supercomputers may have multiple NUMA regions. It is programmer's responsibility to minimize data traffic across these regions. The platforms we use to perform the experiments in this paper are dual-socket nodes (see Sect. 3), giving effectively two primary NUMA regions. Furthermore, to best affinities, we use the KMP_AFFINITY for setting the thread affinities to core-level and compact bindings with permute value of 1 (KMP_AFFINITY = granularity = core, compact, 1). Thread strong scaling performance are shown in Fig. 1 for the two systems under consideration.

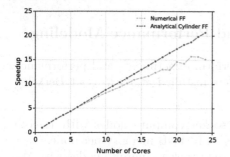 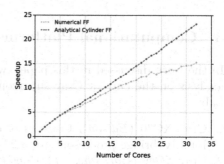

Fig. 1. Speedups for the two form factor kernels under consideration with increasing number of threads are shown on the Edison (left) and Cori-1 (right) systems, with Q-grid of size 125,000 q-points.

5   Vectorization

Data parallelism in modern processors is provided through wide vector units, which can have various widths such as 128, 256 or 512 bits. Typical multi-core processors, such as the Intel Ivybridge and Intel Haswell, provide 256-bit wide registers and support AVX2 vector instructions. Our application uses double precision computations, enabling the possibility of utilizing these vector units with a 4-way SIMD parallelism.

5.1   Compiler-Based Auto-Vectorization

Modern compilers are quite sophisticated and are able to automatically vectorize many codes. This alleviates the need for implementations that use vector datatypes directly in order to take advantage of the vector units. Typically compilers are able to auto-vectorize inner-most loops if they satisfy certain conditions such as, (1) the loop counts are known before its execution, (2) the loops are single block and do not have branching, particularly those which may break the loop short, (3) there are no backward loop dependencies, (4) computations involve simple operations which either have vector instructions or a vectorized libraries available, and the such. We use Intel compilers version 16 to compile our code for all the experiments presented in this paper. We used various compiler-directed pragmas, including Intel's `ivdep` and OpenMP `simd`. Unfortunately in our case, attempts to auto-vectorize the kernel codes failed. As we described in Sect. 2, the loop structures of the kernels in our application violate most of the requirements for auto-vectorization, since they: (1) make heavy use of transcendental functions, and subroutines with significant amounts of branching, (2) have inner-most loops which have either small iteration counts, such as in the analytical kernel presented previously, or complex structures, like those in the numerical kernels, (3) perform computations on complex number datatypes, which although can be generally auto-vectorized, may be inefficient with respect to non-basic operations.

5.2   Intel Math Kernel Library Vector Functions

Since the compilers are unable to auto-vectorize our codes, we utilized existing vectorized libraries such as the Intel Math Kernel Library's (MKL) Vector Math Library (VML) and CBLAS (level 1) vector functions to implement the kernels. CBLAS is the C-style interface to the BLAS library. Although use of these libraries enabled vectorization of a large fraction of the kernels, it presented a tradeoff between floating-point accuracy and performance. The default mode in VML is *High-Accuracy (HA)*[1]. Use of this mode resulted in a performance slowdown of our kernel codes on the Intel Ivybridge processors. The two other accuracy modes available in VML are *Low-Accuracy (LA)*[2] and *Enhanced-Performance (EP)*[3]. Using LA with our kernel code, we observed a slowdown as well. On the other hand, with the EP mode the code showed a performance speedup of up to 1.3×. Unfortunately, the precision provided by EP mode is too low to be used by our application to perform any useful simulations. These results on the use of Intel MKL are summarized in Table 1.

5.3   Hand-Vectorization

Highest performance efficiency can be achieved if the implementation can be done efficiently using vector instructions. Intel provides a set of vector

---

[1] High-Accuracy mode in VML provides an accuracy of 1 *ulp*.
[2] Low-Accuracy mode in VML provides an accuracy of 4 *ulp*.
[3] Enhanced-Performance mode in VML guarantees only 50% of the bits to be accurate.

168   A. Sarje et al.

Table 1. Performance comparisons on Cori-1 between different accuracy models of
Intel MKL VML applied to the analytical cylinder form factor kernel.

Version	Performance speedup	Rel. # instructions
Base (non-vectorized)	1.00	1.0
MKL VML Mode HA	0.73	3.8
MKL VML Mode LA	0.78	3.4
MKL VML Mode EP	1.28	0.6

instrinsics, which are low-level C functions, acting as a wrapper around the
assembly instructions, and allow a programmer to be more effective in the implementation by removing the need to directly implement in assembly language.
Given the low performance boost achieved by using the Intel MKL VML as
presented in the previous section, hand-vectorization is an obvious next step
to enable efficient vectorization. Additionally, since our kernels perform computations on complex numbers, hand-vectorization gives more flexibility on data
encoding and storage. In our implementation we follow the *AoSoA* (Array of
Structures of Arrays) model. The real and imaginary components of a complex
number are encoded with vector datatypes into a structure. Arrays of this 'complex vector' structure are used in implementing the kernels. This structure can
be written for AVX as shown in Fig. 2, where __m256d is defined as an AVX
datatype of packed four-double-precision length (256-bits). Hence, one complex
AVX vector holds four double precision complex numbers. This allows full use
of the available SIMD capabilities as opposed to the alternate approach where
the full complex numbers are encoded within the same vector with alternate
real and imaginary components. This alternative can hold two double precision
complex numbers in a single AVX vector, but would involve some redundancy
to perform operations on them. We implement all compute operations on vector complex numbers using the first approach and real number vector intrinsics.
One of the simplest operations, a complex-complex multiplication may be written using the real multiply and add/subtract intrinsics, also shown in Fig. 2,
where __mm256_ * _pd() intrinsics represent the AVX vector operations on the
packed double precision AVX datatype.

```
                              __m256c _mm256_mul_pc(__m256c a, __m256c b) {
                                __m256c vec;
                                __m256d t1 = _mm256_mul_pd(a.real, b.real);
typedef struct {                __m256d t2 = _mm256_mul_pd(a.imag, b.imag);
  __m256d real;                 vec.real = _mm256_sub_pd(t1, t2);
  __m256d imag;                 t1 = _mm256_mul_pd(a.real, b.imag);
} __m256c;                      t2 = _mm256_mul_pd(a.imag, b.real)
                                vec.imag = _mm256_add_pd(t1, t2);
                                return vec;
                              }
```

Fig. 2. (Left) AVX vectorized representation of a complex number using two double
precision AVX vector datatype __m256d. (Right) An example of a complex number
multiplication using the available AVX instrinsics for real numbers.

5.4   Vectorizing Analytical Cylinder Form Factor Kernel

We implement the entire analytical cylinder form factor kernel using the AVX vector intrinsics. The vectorization level is the same as the outer loop level for the code structure showed in Algorithm 1. A major performance bottleneck in this kernel is the first order Bessel function of the first kind, commonly denoted by J_1. Because of the two factors: need of a complex J_1 function, and, absence of any AVX vectorized implementation of J_1, we implemented this function following the sequential real-number implementation of this function as described in [1]. This function involves significant branching and loop breaks based on argument values, making it harder to vectorize efficiently. For example, to deal with branching based on the argument value, in the case of a vector, some arguments might satisfy one condition while others satisfying another. Hence, masking was used to handle such cases. Another example is the redundancy introduced with vectorization in the conditional loop breaks. For a given vector, the loop is executed for the largest number of iterations required among the vector entries, while masking the redundant computations.

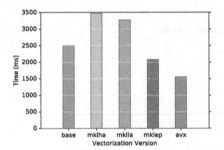 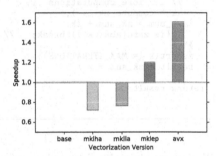

Fig. 3. Execution times (left) of the analytical cylinder form factor kernel and corresponding speedups (right) with various vectorized versions on Cori-1: base (non-vectorized), using Intel MKL with VML modes HA, LA and EP, and using AVX intrinsics. Performance is shown for this kernel with Q-grid of size 500,000 q-points.

A basic structure of the scalar J_1 function is shown in Algorithm 3. This function also takes form of a transcendental function with infinite series summations. This listing highlights the basic branching and conditional loop breaks. In a vectorized version, the input argument is a set of complex numbers, and the computations depend on the actual values of each of these numbers. Both the asymptotic and direct methods are executed in a call to this function. A masking vector is used to ensure that only the correct arguments are used in each method. For example, given an argument vector $\langle z_0, z_1, z_2, z_3 \rangle$ with $z_0, z_2, z_3 >$ THRESHOLD and $z_1 \leq$ THRESHOLD, a mask $\langle 1, 0, 1, 1 \rangle$ is used in the asymptotic method branch, and its complement $\langle 0, 1, 0, 0 \rangle$ is used in the direct method branch. Again, to ensure correctness with the conditional loop breaks, another mask vector, with

Algorithm 3. Simplified structure of Bessel function J_1 highlighting argument dependent branching and conditional loop breaks

```
complex_t cj1(complex_t z) {
  complex_t result;
  if(z > THRESHOLD) {                    // asymptotic method
    // ... initialize ak, xk, xk_sum, yk, yk_sum ...
    int k;
    for(k = 1; k < MAX_ITERATIONS; ++ k) {
      // ... more computations ...
      xk = compute_xk(...);
      xk_sum = xk_sum + xk;

      // ... more computations ...
      yk = compute_yk(...);
      yk_sum = yk_sum + yk;

      if(is_zero(abs(xk)) && is_zero(abs(yk))) break; // conditional break
    }
    assert(k != MAX_ITERATIONS);
    result = sqrt(...) * (cos(...) * xk_sum - sin(...) * yk_sum);

  } else {                               // direct method
    // ... initialize zk, zk_sum ...
    int k;
    for(k = 1; k < MAX_ITERATIONS; ++ k) {
      // ... more computations ...
      zk = compute_zk(...);
      zk_sum = zk_sum + zk;
      if(is_zero(abs(zk))) break;    // conditional break
    }
    assert(k != MAX_ITERATIONS);
    result = zk_sum * z / 2;
  }
  return result;
}
```

all elements initialized to 1, is used where an element is set to 0 when the corresponding element of the compute vectors satisfy the loop break condition. Finally, the loop break is taken when all the mask vector elements are set to 0. With this manual vectorization of the analytical kernel, we were able to achieve speedups of more than $1.5\times$ with respect to the baseline. The performance of all these versions of this kernel, vectorization using Intel MKL and with AVX intrinsics, are summarized in Fig. 3.

5.5   Vectorizing Numerical Form Factor Kernel

Due to the presence of an additional data dimension in the numerical form factor kernels, the vectorization approach used here is quite different from the one used for the analytical kernels. A single triangle is described by its three vertices, each with three coordinates, adding to nine real numbers. Constructing vectors with the previous approach would be quite inefficient in this case due to the need for excessive padding in describing a triangle using vectors. Hence, as seen in Algorithm 2 described previously, it is most efficient to vectorize at the level of the loop over triangles. The AoSoA model is followed to encode triangles into set of vector triangles, as shown in Fig. 4. Hence, a vector triangle encodes four triangles, without the need for any padding. The array of triangles is converted to an array of vector triangles, with possible padding needed only for the last vector in the array.

```
typedef struct {              typedef struct {
    __m256 x;                     avx_vertex_t a;
    __m256 y;                     avx_vertex_t b;
    __m256 z;                     avx_vertex_t c;
} avx_vertex_t;               } avx_triangle_t;
```

Fig. 4. AVX vectorized representation of triangles. Each triangle is described by its three vertices (right), and each vertex is described by its three coordinate values (left). Such an AVX vector triangle structure holds information about four triangles in double precision.

Table 2. Performance of the AVX vectorized numerical form factor kernel as the execution times and speedups with respect to the base (non-vectorized) kernel on Cori-1. The shape structure used for this set of experiments consists of 2,280 triangles. Performance is shown for three different Q-grid sizes.

Num. q-points	Base time (ms)	AVX time (ms)	Speedup
31,250	19243.1	3674.47	5.237
125,000	64637.6	14256.7	4.534
500,000	239881	52906.1	4.534

We have summarized the performance results for the final vectorized numerical kernel compared to the initial version in Table 2. The hand-vectorized version is able to achieve speedups of over 4.5× in most cases, with up to a maximum of 5.2×, over the initial baseline version showing that this vectorization approach is highly effective.

6 Roofline Performance Modeling

In order to analyze the performance of the final optimized kernels with threading and vectorization, we visit the Roofline performance modeling as mentioned earlier in Sect. 3. In Roofline performance modeling, the target is to achieve performance as close to the roofline plot as possible, depending on the arithmetic intensity of a given kernel. Since arithmetic intensity is defined as the ratio of FLOPs executed to bytes moved, different levels of the bandwidth bound can be shown with respect to the memory hierarchy. We utilize Intel SDE to calculate the FLOPs and L1-cache bandwidth of the kernels. It should be noted that the L1-cache data access are generally significantly higher than the off-chip data movement (DRAM). In Fig. 5, the performance of the analytical cylinder form factor kernel is shown. It can be observed that the use of Intel MKL vector

functions significantly decreased the kernel performance compared to the baseline, while the hand-vectorized version shows improved performance. It should
be noted that the performance of the various versions shown are all obtained
with same thread concurrency on the given systems: 24 threads on Edison and
32 threads on Cori-1 (single thread per core). Similarly in Fig. 6, we show the
performance of the numerical form factor kernel. In this case, the performance
improvement with the hand-vectorized version is significantly higher with respect
to the baseline kernel. In this case also performance of the two versions are
obtained with the same thread concurrencies.

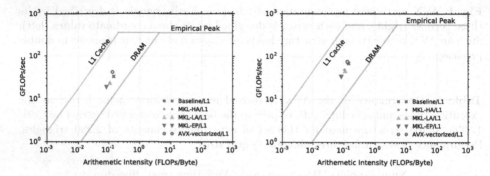

Fig. 5. The analytical cylinder form factor kernel performance plotted on the Roofline
model for the two systems, Edison (left) and Cori-1 (right), are shown. The baseline
(non-vectorized) version and the various vector versions, Intel MKL with VML mode
HA, LA and EP, and AVX-instrinsics are all shown for comparison.

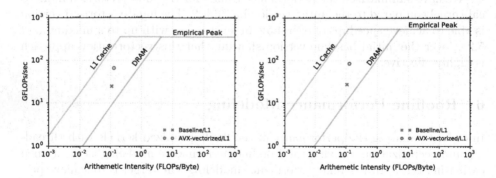

Fig. 6. Performance of the numerical form factor kernel with respect to the Roofline
model are shown for the two systems, Edison (left) and Cori-1 (right), with the baseline
and the AVX-intrinsics vectorized versions.

With the increase in the number of compute cores on emerging architectures, we analyze the performance of the two kernels under study on Intel's new
Knights Landing processor testbed. The corresponding results plotted on the

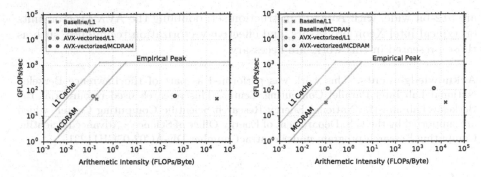

Fig. 7. Roofline performance modeling of the analytical cylinder (left) and the numerical form factor kernels are shown for the Intel Knights Landing processor. Performance of the baseline and the optimized versions are shown with respect to L1-cache and MCDRAM memory bandwidths. It can be seen that use of MCDRAM is highly beneficial for these kernels in increasing the arithmetic intensities significantly.

Roofline model are shown in Fig. 7. On this processor, we utilize the available high-bandwidth MCDRAM for the entire runs since the complete working set for these runs fits into this memory. Use of this high-bandwidth memory is able to significantly improve the arithmetic intensities, opening up even more room for computational optimizations. It should be noted that the vectorized version used in these experiments is the AVX2 versions developed above with 256-bit wide vectors. Due to the available room for performance improvement, use of 512-bit wide vectors on the KNL is expected to increase the performance, and is the next step in our work. Nonetheless, the current vectorized version KNL is showing up to 1.2× the performance on a Cori-1 node.

7   Conclusions and Further Discussions

Although modern processors pack large performance potential, exploiting them to gain high parallel efficiency for scientific applications still remains a challenge. In this work, we primarily considered two parallelism levels, SMT and SIMD, to deliver higher-performance with a real-world scientific application code. Even though current compiler technology is able to significantly optimize code performance, there remains a large class of computations for which these technologies fail. Our application code has such computational kernels where compilers are unable to significantly optimize them for effective exploitation of on-chip parallelisms. In such cases, it is inevitable to carry out implementations in much low-level vector intrinsics if high efficiency is desired.

The work presented in this paper is highly applicable to near-future processor architectures because the two parallelism levels addressed here are among the primary areas which these new processors target to deliver higher performance. For example, Intel's new Knights Landing manycore processor has much higher number of compute cores (≥ 64). Similarly, the vector units on these processors are 512-bit wide, with AVX512 instruction set, doubling the AVX2 vector units on typical Intel Xeon processors, and effective vectorization techniques, such as those presented in this work, are necessary.

Acknowledgements. This work was performed as part of the Lawrence Berkeley National Lab Intel Parallel Computing Center. This research used resources at the Berkeley Lab and the National Energy Research Scientific Computing Center, which are supported by the U.S. Department of Energy Office of Science's Advanced Scientific Computing Research program under contract number DE-AC02-05CH11231.

References

1. Bailey, D.H.: MPFUN2015: a thread-safe arbitrary precision package (2015)
2. Chourou, S., Sarje, A., Li, X., Chan, E., Hexemer, A.: HipGISAXS: a high performance computing code for simulating grazing incidence X-ray scattering data. J. Appl. Crystallogr. **46**(6), 1781–1795 (2013)
3. Sarje, A., Li, X., Chourou, S., Chan, E., Hexemer, A.: Massively parallel X-ray scattering simulations. In: International Conference for High Performance Computing, Networking, Storage and Analysis (Supercomputing) (2012)
4. Sarje, A., Chourou, S., Li, X., Hexemer, A.: Analysis of X-Ray Scattering Data using HipGISAXS (2016, in preparation)
5. Sarje, A., Li, X.S., Hexemer, A.: Tuning HipGISAXS on multi and many core supercomputers. In: Jarvis, S.A., Wright, S.A., Hammond, S.D. (eds.) PMBS 2013. LNCS, vol. 8551, pp. 217–238. Springer, Cham (2014). doi:10.1007/978-3-319-10214-6_11
6. Williams, S., Waterman, A., Patterson, D.: Roofline. Commun. ACM **53**(4), 65–76 (2009)

Exploiting a Parametrized Task Graph Model for the Parallelization of a Sparse Direct Multifrontal Solver

Emmanuel Agullo[1], George Bosilca[5], Alfredo Buttari[2(✉)],
Abdou Guermouche[3], and Florent Lopez[4]

[1] INRIA - LaBRI, Bordeaux, France
[2] CNRS - IRIT, Toulouse, France
alfredo.buttari@enseeiht.fr
[3] Université de Bordeaux - LaBRI, Bordeaux, France
[4] RAL - STFC, Didcot, UK
[5] University of Tennessee, Knoxville, USA

Abstract. The advent of multicore processors requires to reconsider the design of high performance computing libraries to embrace portable and effective techniques of parallel software engineering. One of the most promising approaches consists in abstracting an application as a directed acyclic graph (DAG) of tasks. While this approach has been popularized for shared memory environments by the OpenMP 4.0 standard where dependencies between tasks are automatically inferred, we investigate an alternative approach, capable of describing the DAG of task in a distributed setting, where task dependencies are explicitly encoded. So far this approach has been mostly used in the case of algorithms with a regular data access pattern and we show in this study that it can be efficiently applied to a higly irregular numerical algorithm such as a sparse multifrontal QR method. We present the resulting implementation and discuss the potential and limits of this approach in terms of productivity and effectiveness in comparison with more common parallelization techniques. Although at an early stage of development, preliminary results show the potential of the parallel programming model that we investigate in this work.

Keywords: Multicore architectures · Programming models · Runtime system · Parametrized task graph · Numerical scientific library · Sparse direct solver · Multifrontal QR factorization

1 Introduction

Since their introduction, multicore processors have become increasingly popular and are nowadays a commodity used beyond the high performance computing (HPC) community. However, there is no clear consensus on the best practices for programming such architectures and developers often have to make a trade-off between productivity (the pace at which a code may be written and maintained) and performance (the pace at which the code is eventually executed).

© Springer International Publishing AG 2017
F. Desprez et al. (Eds.): Euro-Par 2016 Workshops, LNCS 10104, pp. 175–186, 2017.
DOI: 10.1007/978-3-319-58943-5_14

For instance, some software developers may choose to limit the parallelization of their code to the introduction of a few OpenMP pragma directives within the main computational-intensive loops of their algorithms. On the other end of the spectrum, highly optimized libraries such as linear algebra numerical kernels are often written with low-level synchronizations schemes relying on POSIX threads (pthread) primitives at a possible high cost in terms of development and maintenance. One of the most promising approach for enhancing the productivity while maintaining high performance consists in abstracting an application as a directed acyclic graph (DAG) of tasks and delegating the orchestration of the task to a runtime system.

Whereas task-based runtime systems were mainly research tools in the past years, their recent progress make them now a solid candidates for designing advanced scientific software. They provide programming paradigms that allow the programmer to express concurrency in a simple yet effective way and relieve her from the burden of dealing with low-level architectural details. Runtime systems offer a uniform programming interface for a specific subset of hardware or low-level software entities (e.g., pthread implementations). They are designed as thin user-level software layers that complement the basic, general purpose functions provided by the operating system. Applications then target these uniform programming interfaces in a portable manner and low-level, hardware dependent details are hidden inside runtime systems. The adaptation of runtime systems is commonly handled through drivers. Portability is thus enabled by the abstraction provided by the runtime system.

All the above mentioned efforts have contributed to proving the ease of use, the effectiveness and portability of general purpose runtime systems to the point where the OpenMP board has decided to include similar features since the 4.0 standard: the `task` construct was extended with the `depend` clause which enables the OpenMP runtime to automatically detect dependencies among tasks and consequently schedule them accordingly. While task-based programming has been popularized with OpenMP 4.0 where dependencies between tasks are automatically inferred, the concept itself is much older, and provided in varied forms by several research projects. In the context of this work we investigate an alternative approach consisting of explicitly encoding the dependencies between tasks. Many studies [1,3,11,19] have shown the potential of the approach in the case of relatively regular algorithms such as dense linear algebra. On the other hand, the effort for assessing it on irregular algorithms is much more narrow [20,21]. In this paper, we consider a highly irregular numerical algorithm, namely the sparse multifrontal QR method, and we show how we can turn it out into a DAG of tasks with explicit dependencies. We present the resulting code and discuss the potential and limits it delivers in terms of productivity and effectiveness in comparison with more common parallelization techniques.

The rest of the paper is organized as follows. Section 2 presents the related work on task-based programming models and runtime systems as well as numerical libraries that have been developed on top of them, including the model we want to highlight in this paper (consisting in explicitly defining the dependencies of the DAG) together with the runtime system we use (PaRSEC [9,10]) to support it. We then present the highly irregular numerical method we want to implement (namely, the multifrontal QR method) to illustrate our discussion in Sect. 3. We show how it can be written as a DAG of tasks with explicit dependencies in Sect. 4 and present preliminary (but encouraging!) performance results in Sect. 5. Section 6 concludes the paper and present perspectives.

2 Related Work

2.1 Parallel Programming Models for Task-Based Algorithms

The most common strategy for the parallelization of task-based algorithms consists in traversing the DAG sequentially and submit the tasks, as discovered, to the runtime system using a non blocking function call. The dependencies between tasks are automatically inferred by the runtime system through a data dependency analysis [4] and the actual execution of the task is then postponed to the moment when all its dependencies are satisfied. This programming model is known as a *Sequential Task Flow* (STF) model as it fully relies on `sequential consistency` for the dependency detection. This paradigm is also sometimes referred to as *superscalar* since it mimics the functioning of superscalar processors where instructions are issued sequentially from a single stream but can actually be executed in a different order and, possibly, in parallel depending on their mutual dependencies. As mentioned above, the popularity of this model encouraged the OpenMP board to include it in the 4.0 standard. The simplicity of the STF model facilitates the design of numerical algorithms in a concise manner and can be exploited to efficiently target multicore architectures [2].

One challenge in scaling to large scale distributed many-core systems is how to represent extremely large DAGs of tasks in a compact fashion. The *Parameterized Task Graph* (PTG) model introduced in [14] addresses this issue. In this model, tasks are not enumerated as in the STF model but parametrized and the dependencies between tasks are explicitly expressed. This property can be used to encode the DAG in a compact, size independent, way inducing a lower memory footprint for its representation as well as ensuring limited complexity for parsing it as the problem size grows. For this reason the memory consumption overhead in the runtime system for representing the DAG is much lower for the PTG model than for the STF model. In addition with a STF model the DAG has to be completely unrolled on all participating processes whereas with a PTG the DAG is only partially unfolded during the execution following the task progression. From this point of view, the advantage of the PTG approach over the STF can be crucial when exploiting processors with a very large number of cores. We address this particular model in the present paper.

2.2 Task-Based Runtime Systems for Modern Architectures

Many initiatives have emerged in the past years to develop efficient task-based runtime systems for modern platforms. Their review is out of the scope of this paper. We mention two important projects supporting the STF model. The StarSs project is actually an umbrella term that describes both the StarSs language extensions and a collection of runtime systems targeting different types of platforms [6,7]. StarSs provides an annotation-based language which extends C or Fortran applications to offload pieces of computation on the architecture targeted by the underlying runtime system. The StarPU runtime system provides a generic interface for developing parallel, task-based applications. It supports multicore architectures equipped with accelerator as well as distributed memory systems. This runtime is capable of transparently handling data and provides a rich panel of features.

The PaRSEC runtime system provides a distributed generic task scheduler supplemented by programming interface complying to the two main programming models presented in Sect. 2.1. In particular, it is one of the few (and certainly the most popular) runtime systems supporting the PTG model. The embedded scheduler is dynamic, designed to exploit the memory hierarchy of modern architectures and capable of maximizing computation to communication overlap, exploiting data locality and achieving load-balancing between the resources. PaRSEC provides a language called Job Data Flow (JDF) providing an extended PTG expressivity to parallel codes. During the compilation process, the files containing the JDF code are translated into C-code files by a specific compiler distributed with PaRSEC called *daguepp*. The DAG is defined by a set of *task types* that can be associated with several *parameters* defined on a given *range* of values. The tasks are associated with a list of *predecessors* and *successors* that define the dependencies in the DAG. These dependencies are generally based on data but may also represent precedence constraints. Tasks are associated with a code that will be executed for each task instance. This task code can have multiple instances, each tied to specific hardware resources (accelerators, FPGA, ...), and the runtime will select the most appropriate one dynamically depending on the availability of resources and the needs of the algorithm. For more information we redirect the interested reader to [8–11].

3   Multifrontal QR Method

The multifrontal method, introduced by Duff *et al.* [17] is a method for the factorization (either Cholesky, LDL^T, LU or QR) of sparse, linear systems. This algorithm is based on the concept of *elimination tree* [22] expressing the dependencies between the operations which eliminate the unknowns of the input matrix A, each vertex f of the tree being associated with k_f of these unknowns. The coefficients of the corresponding k_f columns and all the other coefficients concerned by their elimination are assembled together into a dense matrix, called *frontal matrix* or, simply, *front*, associated with the tree node. An edge of the tree represents a dependency between such fronts. The elimination tree is thus a topological order for the elimination of the unknowns: a front can only be eliminated after its children. The multifrontal QR factorization then consists in a tree traversal following a **topological order** for eliminating the fronts.

When a front is visited, first, the **activation** operation allocates and initializes the front data structure. Next, the front can then be **assembled**, i.e., filled up with the coefficients in the associated k_f rows of the matrix A and with coefficients resulting from the factorization of child nodes. Once assembled, the k_f unknowns are eliminated through a **complete, dense QR factorization** of the front. This produces k_f rows of the global R factor, a number of Householder reflectors that implicitly represent the global Q factor and a *contribution block* formed by the coefficients that will be assembled into the parent front together with the contribution blocks from all the sibling fronts.

One distinctive feature of the multifrontal QR factorization is that frontal matrices are not entirely full but, prior to their factorization, can be permuted into a staircase structure that allows for moving many zero coefficients in the bottom-left corner of the front and for ignoring them in the subsequent computation; this allows for a considerable saving in the number of operations. It must be noted that when handling matrices from real-life applications, elimination trees can be quite large (i.e., contain up to $O(10^4)$ nodes), irregular and unbalanced, frontal matrices can be of varying sizes (from a few units up to $O(10^4)$ rows or columns) and shapes (either over or under-determined). We refer to [5,12,15] for further details on the multifrontal QR method.

Because of what said above, the multifrontal factorization results in an extremely irregular, heterogeneous and unpredictable workload even in the case where a regular partitioning is applied to fronts. Therefore its implementation on modern supercomputers is a challenging task. In this work we investigate the use of PTG based runtime systems for this method and assess their ease of use and effectiveness.

4   Design of a Task-Based Multifrontal QR Factorization with Explicit Dependencies

The multifrontal method provides two distinct sources of concurrency: **tree-level** and **node-level** parallelism. The first one stems from the fact that fronts in separate branches are independent and can thus be processed concurrently; the second one from the fact that, if a front is large enough, multiple processes can be used to assemble and factorize it.

In order to exploit both sources of parallelism; in the proposed implementation of our PTG-based parallel multifrontal factorization, which we refer to as qrm_parsec, we use an approach based on hierarchical DAGs. We consider a two-level hierarchy with an outer DAG and multiple inner DAGs spawned by the tasks in higher level DAG. The outer DAG contains tasks related to the activation, assembly and deactivation of fronts in the elimination tree whereas each inner DAG contains the tasks related to the factorization of the frontal matrix. This approach is illustrated in Fig. 1 where three different DAGs denoted by 1, 2 and 3 are spawned by tasks in the outer DAG.

The PaRSEC implementation of our solver is split into three JDF files described in the next sections.

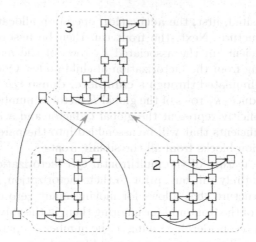

Fig. 1. Two levels hierarchical DAGs implemented in PaRSEC. The inner DAGs are spawned by tasks contained in the top level DAG.

4.1 The Factorization

This JDF file represents the DAG operating at the elimination tree level and contains the description of four tasks:

- **activate:** allocates the memory needed for assembling and factorizing a frontal matrix. The activation of a node depends on the activation of its children.
- **assemble:** spawns a lower level DAG of tasks performing the assembly of the frontal matrix in parallel; this DAG is defined in the `assembly.jdf` file described below. It depends on the activation of the related node and is completed when all the spawned tasks have been executed.
- **init:** initializes the frontal matrix data structure and spawns the lower level DAG performing the front factorization which is described below. This task depends on the assemble tasks as the front factorization can only start once it has been assembled. As for the assemble task, its completion is achieved when the DAG it spawn is completely executed.
- **deactivate:** stores apart the result of a front factorization and frees the memory allocated by the activate task. It can be executed only after its contribution block has been assembled into the parent node.

An excerpt of the `factorization.jdf` file is shown in Fig. 2 where, for the sake of simplicity, we only describe the **init** task. This task needs a set of symbolic data denoted S in the data-flow which is provided by the **assemble** task. Note that in the case were the front has no children, the **assemble** task perform no operations apart from passing the symbolic data to the init task. When the **init** tasks is completed, the front is factorized and can be assembled into the parent node. Therefore we transfer the symbolic data to the assembly operation of the parent node.

```
init(n)

  n = 1 .. NN

  /* get info on frontal matrix */
  front = inline_c %{ return get_front(n); %}
  p     = inline_c %{ return get_front_parent(n); %}
  prio  = inline_c %{ return get_front_prio(front); %}

  RW S <- S assemble(n) /* initialize the front  assembly */
       -> (p != 0) ? S assembly(p)

BODY
{
   /* initialize frontal matrix*/
   _qrm_init_front(front);
   /* create qr factorization DAG for frontal matrix */
   qr_handle = qr_initialize(front);
   /* submit front factorization to PaRSEC */
   dague_enqueue(qr_handle);
}
END
```

Fig. 2. Excerpt of code for performing operation at elimination tree level with PaRSEC.

Each of these tasks are executed once for every node in the elimination tree.

4.2 qr_1d.jdf, qr_2d.jdf

Once assembled, a frontal matrix can be factorized using any QR factorization algorithm for dense matrices. For this operation, we have chosen two different variants, namely, a LAPACK-style factorization based on a 1D partitioning of the front in block-columns and a Communication Avoiding method based on a 2D partitioning into tiles [13,18]. For a matter of conciseness we only present the 1D version (qr_1d.jdf) of the code. These implementations are based on the ones found in the DPLASMA library [8] which provide dense linear algebra kernels routine for distributed systems built on top of the PaRSEC runtime systems. We adapted those kernels to the specific staircase structure of frontal matrices described in Sect. 3.

The JDF code for the QR factorization with a 1D block-column partitioning is presented in Fig. 3. In this JDF we have two type of task: the geqrt task corresponding to the panel operations and the gemqrt corresponding to update operations with respect to panel reductions. Note that this JDF is similar to the DPLASMA implementation except that we used the _geqrt_stair and _gemqrt_stair kernels, respectively for the panel and update operations, capable of exploiting the staircase structure of block-columns. The geqrt tasks are associated with the panel index represented by the parameter p which has values in the range 0..NP-1 where NP represents the number of panel operations in the front. Similarly, the gemqrt task is defined by two parameters. The first represents the panel operations and the second represents the subsequent update operations depending on each panel operation. For each panel operation p we perform update operations on block-columns p+1..NC-1 where NC is the total

```
geqrt(p)

  p = 0 .. (NP-1)

  RW A_p <- (p==0) ? A(0,p) : C_u gemqrt(p-1, p)
          -> (p < NC-1) ? V_p gemqrt(p, (p+1)..(NC-1))
          -> A(p)

  RW T_p <- T(p)                                        [type = LITTLE_T]
          -> (p < NC-1) ? T_p gemqrt(p, (p+1)..(NC-1))  [type = LITTLE_T]
          -> T(p)

BODY
{
    _geqrt_stair(&m, &n, &ib, &stair[off], &off, A_p + off,
                 &lda, T_p, &ldt, work, &info);
}
END

gemqrt(p, u)

  p = 0..(NP-1)
  u = (p+1)..(NC-1)

  READ  V_p <- A_p geqrt(p)
  READ  T_p <- T_p geqrt(p)                             [type = LITTLE_T]
  RW    C_u <- (p==0) ? A(0,u) : C_u gemqrt(p-1, u)
            -> ((u == p+1) && (u <= (NP-1))) ? A_p geqrt(u)
            -> ((u > p+1) && (p < (NP-1))) ? C_u gemqrt(p+1, u)

BODY
{
    _gemqrt_stair("l", "t", &m, &j, &k, &ib, &stair[off], &off, V_p + off,
                  &ldv, T_p, &ldt, C_u  + off, &ldc, work, &info);
}
END
```

Fig. 3. Code for the 1D block-column dense QR factorization with PaRSEC.

number of block-columns in the frontal matrix. Along with a R factor resulting from the geqrt_stair operation, the geqrt task produce a V and T data that are sent to the subsequent update tasks which are represented by gemqrt(p, p+1..NC-1) in the JDF code. Concerning the gemqrt tasks, for a given a block-column u, it retrieves the V and T matrices of the corresponding panel p along with the block-column issued by the update with respect to the previous panel task denoted gemqrt(p-1,u). Once the update operation has been executed, the block-column is sent either to the next update operation denoted gemqrt(p+1,u) or to the panel operation denoted geqrt(u) if the block-column is up-to-date.

As for the 2D code, because of the fronts staircase structure, some tiles are equal to zero and must be skipped in the computation which alters the data-flow with respect to the methods described in the literature. In PaRSEC this can be conveniently handled by using conditional expressions in the JDF.

4.3   assembly.jdf

In the DAG instantiated by this assembly operations, each task corresponds to the assembly of a block from all the blocks in children's frontal matrices contributing to it. Note that in order to express the data-flow for these assemblies, we need to compute, for every block in a frontal matrix, a list of contributing blocks in children node. This mapping is computed upon front activation and is not required when using a STF model.

4.4 Discussion

It must be noted that it is possible to execute some of the factorization tasks related to a node before the handling of its child nodes is completed; this additional concurrency, which we refer to as *inter-level parallelism*, may lead to considerable benefits especially in the case of narrow and unbalanced elimination trees where tree parallelism is scarce. qrm_parsec cannot use inter-level parallelism because the factorization DAG is spawned only once the front is fully assembled due to the dependency between the init and the assemble tasks described above. Although technically possible, using inter-level parallelism is more complex to achieve with the PTG model than with the STF one where the expression of dependencies is simpler when the DAG is defined dynamically, as it's partially the case in the multifrontal method. This is the subject of ongoing research.

In practical cases the elimination tree may have thousands of nodes and thus the DAG may contain millions of tasks; this much concurrency is clearly useless for the systems targeted by this work which only include few cores. In order to reduce the size of the DAG, entire subtrees at the bottom of the elimination tree are handled at once within a single task. This technique is very well known in the domain of sparse, direct methods and provides considerable benefits in terms of reduced runtime overhead as well as improved data locality.

Most of the execution time is spent in BLAS-3 operations (like dense matrix multiplications). Because these have a favorable ratio between computations and data access, the whole multifrontal factorization can be considered as *compute bound* and thus the effects of memory contention can be considered light.

5   Early Experimental Results

We evaluate the PTG implementation of our solver on a set of test matrices presented in Table 1 from real world applications publicly available in the University of Florida Sparse Matrix Collection [16]. We also use the hirlam matrix, from the HIRLAM[1] research program. The PaRSEC runtime system is used to support the PTG model. The COLAMD fill-reducing column permutation was applied to all the matrices. The runs were performed on the Dude system which is a shared-memory machine equipped with four AMD Opteron(tm) Processor 8431 (six cores) and 72 GB of memory. As a reference, we also report on the performance of the STF implementation of the solver from [2], which is supported with StarPU and named qrm_starpu below.

---

[1] http://hirlam.org.

Table 1. The set of matrices used for the experiments along with the associated sequential factorization time and memory consumption.

id	Mat. name	m	n	nz	op. count (Gflop)	Time (sec)	Mem (GB)
1	karted	46502	133115	1770349	257	46.3	0.7
2	degme	185501	659415	8127528	591	103.2	1.4
3	cat_ears_4_4	19020	44448	132888	716	134.9	1.2
4	hirlam	1385270	452200	2713200	2339	392.0	3.5
5	e18	24617	38602	156466	3399	474.5	3.5
6	flower_7_4	27693	67593	202218	4261	774.7	3.6
7	Rucci1	1977885	109900	7791168	12764	1786.0	5.1
8	TF17	38132	48630	586218	38209	5185.0	15.3

The experimental results are presented in Fig. 4. They show the scalability of qrm_parsec using both the 1D and 2D front factorization algorithms; the speedups are computed with respect to the sequential running time reported in Table 1. These are compared to the results obtained with an equivalent implementation based on the Sequential Task Flow model and the StarPU runtime system [2]. The results show that qrm_parsec achieves a satisfactory performance on all the tested matrices, including the smallest ones (on the left side of the plot) with speedups close to 20 (out of 24) for the largest size ones. Figure 4 also shows that the 2D Communication Avoiding front factorization variant achieves much better speedups than the 1D block-column one; this is expected since most of the frontal matrices in the multifrontal QR method are (strongly) overdetermined and thus the 1D method simply does not provide enough concurrency (especially for smaller size matrices).

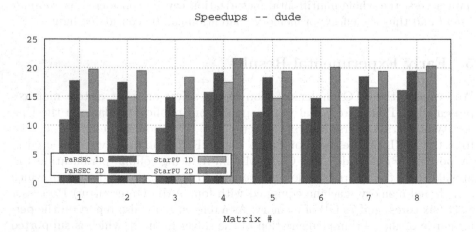

Fig. 4. Speedup of qrm_starpu and qrm_parsec on the Dude system (24 cores).

Finally, the STF implementation consistently achieves better performance than the PTG-based one. This difference comes mostly from the fact that the STF code exploits the inter-level parallelism mentioned in Sect. 4.4. Note, also, that `qrm_parsec` is a proof of concept code whereas the StarPU-based implementation is fully optimized; therefore the performance gap could be partly reduced through code optimization.

6   Concluding Remarks

In this paper, we have investigated the impact on programmability and discussed the potential in terms of performance of programming a highly irregular numerical algorithm as a task-based DAG of tasks with explicit dependencies. We have shown that providing the dependencies is not trivial and requires a deep understanding of the parallelism available in the algorithm. However, thanks to the task-based abstraction, this model provides an interesting alternative to STF as it allows to write the high-level algorithm independently of the underlying processor, delegating the burden of handling synchronizations to the runtime system. Furthermore, we have shown that the considered model provides a lot of flexibility at runtime to instantiate the most appropriate variant of an algorithm (such as 1D and 2D kernels in this study). Although the performance results are preliminary, they are very encouraging. We would be delighted to present them and discuss them in a workshop that aims at making parallelism available to a wide range of applications using systematic software engineering methodology, beyond the scope of numerical, scientific libraries.

References

1. Agullo, E., Augonnet, C., Dongarra, J., Ltaief, H., Namyst, R., Thibault, S., Tomov, S.: A hybridization methodology for high-performance linear algebra software for GPUs. In: GPU Computing Gems, vol. 2, pp. 473–484. Jade Edition (2011)
2. Agullo, E., Buttari, A., Guermouche, A., Lopez, F.: Implementing multifrontal sparse solvers for multicore architectures with sequential task flow runtime systems. In: ACM Transactions on Mathematical Software (2016, to appear)
3. Agullo, E., Demmel, J., Dongarra, J., Hadri, B., Kurzak, J., Langou, J., Ltaief, H., Luszczek, P., Tomov, S.: Numerical linear algebra on emerging architectures: the PLASMA and MAGMA projects. J. Phys.: Conf. Ser. **180**(1), 012–037 (2009)
4. Allen, R., Kennedy, K.: Optimizing Compilers for Modern Architectures: A Dependence-Based Approach. Morgan Kaufmann, Burlington (2002)
5. Amestoy, P.R., Duff, I.S., Puglisi, C.: Multifrontal QR factorization in a multiprocessor environment. Int. J. Num. Linear Alg. Appl. **3**(4), 275–300 (1996)
6. Ayguadé, E., Badia, R.M., Igual, F.D., Labarta, J., Mayo, R., Quintana-Ortí, E.S.: An extension of the StarSs programming model for platforms with multiple GPUs. In: Sips, H., Epema, D., Lin, H.-X. (eds.) Euro-Par 2009. LNCS, vol. 5704, pp. 851–862. Springer, Heidelberg (2009). doi:10.1007/978-3-642-03869-3_79

7. Badia, R.M., Herrero, J.R., Labarta, J., Pérez, J.M., Quintana-Ortí, E.S., Quintana-Ortí, G.: Parallelizing dense and banded linear algebra libraries using SMPSs. Concurr. Comput.: Pract. Exp. **21**(18), 2438–2456 (2009)
8. Bosilca, G., Bouteiller, A., Danalis, A., Faverge, M., Haidar, A., Hérault, T., Kurzak, J., Langou, J., Lemarinier, P., Ltaief, H., Luszczek, P., Yarkhan, A., Dongarra, J.J.: Distibuted dense numerical linear algebra algorithms on massively parallel architectures: DPLASMA. In: Proceedings of the 25th IEEE International Symposium on Parallel and Distributed Processing Workshops and Phd Forum (IPDPSW 2011). PDSEC 2011, Anchorage, United States, pp. 1432–1441 (2011)
9. Bosilca, G., Bouteiller, A., Danalis, A., Faverge, M., Hérault, T., Dongarra, J.J.: Parsec: exploiting heterogeneity to enhance scalability. Comput. Sci. Eng. **15**(6), 36–45 (2013)
10. Bosilca, G., Bouteiller, A., Danalis, A., Hérault, T., Lemarinier, P., Dongarra, J.: DAGuE: a generic distributed DAG engine for high performance computing. Parallel Comput. **38**(1–2), 37–51 (2012)
11. Bosilca, G., Bouteiller, A., Danalis, A., Herault, T., Luszczek, P., Dongarra, J.: Dense linear algebra on distributed heterogeneous hardware with a symbolic DAG approach. In: Scalable Computing and Communications: Theory and Practice, pp. 699–733 (2013)
12. Buttari, A.: Fine-grained multithreading for the multifrontal QR factorization of sparse matrices. SIAM J. Sci. Comput. **35**(4), C323–C345 (2013)
13. Buttari, A., Langou, J., Kurzak, J., Dongarra, J.: A class of parallel tiled linear algebra algorithms for multicore architectures. Parallel Comput. **35**, 38–53 (2009)
14. Cosnard, M., Loi, M.: Automatic task graph generation techniques. In: Proceedings of the Twenty-Eighth Hawaii International Conference on System Sciences 1995, Vol. 2, pp. 113–122, January 1995
15. Davis, T.A.: Algorithm 915, SuiteSparseQR: multifrontal multithreaded rank-revealing sparse QR factorization. ACM Trans. Math. Softw. **38**(1), 8:1–8:22 (2011)
16. Davis, T.A., Hu, Y.: The university of Florida sparse matrix collection. ACM Trans. Math. Softw. **38**(1), 1:1–1:25 (2011)
17. Duff, I.S., Reid, J.K.: The multifrontal solution of indefinite sparse symmetric linear systems. ACM Trans. Math. Softw. **9**, 302–325 (1983)
18. Hadri, B., Ltaief, H., Agullo, E., Dongarra, J.: Tile QR factorization with parallel panel processing for multicore architectures. In: IPDPS, pp. 1–10. IEEE (2010)
19. Igual, F.D., Chan, E., Quintana-Ortí, E.S., Quintana-Ortí, G., van de Geijn, R.A., Zee, F.G.V.: The flame approach: from dense linear algebra algorithms to high-performance multi-accelerator implementations. J. Parallel Distrib. Comput. **72**(9), 1134–1143 (2012)
20. Kim, K., Eijkhout, V.: A parallel sparse direct solver via hierarchical DAG scheduling. ACM Trans. Math. Softw. **41**(1), 1–27 (2014)
21. Lacoste, X.: Scheduling and memory optimizations for sparse direct solver on multi-core/multi-GPU cluster systems. PhD thesis, LaBRI, Université Bordeaux, Talence, France, February 2015
22. Schreiber, R.: A new implementation of sparse Gaussian elimination. ACM Trans. Math. Softw. **8**, 256–276 (1982)

Parallel String Matching

Philip Pfaffe[✉], Martin Tillmann, Sarah Lutteropp, Bernhard Scheirle,
and Kevin Zerr

Karlsruhe Institute of Technology, Karlsruhe, Germany
{philip.pfaffe,martin.tillmann}@kit.edu,
{sarah.lutteropp,bernhard.scheirle,kevin.zerr}@student.kit.edu

Abstract. We explore the benefits of parallelizing 7 state-of-the-art
string matching algorithms. Using SIMD and multi-threading techniques
we achieve a significant performance improvement of up to 43.3× over
reference implementations and a speedup of up to 16.7× over the string
matching program `grep`.

We evaluate our implementations on the smart-corpora and the full
human genome data set. We show scalability over number of threads and
impact of pattern length.

1 Introduction

String matching is a fundamental tool in a wide range of practical software.
Molecular biology, data compression and information retrieval all rely on efficient string matching algorithms on challenging amounts of input data. For over
35 years string matching algorithms have been studied extensively. Speed and
memory constraints are the crucial attributes of state-of-the-art matching algorithms.

Parallelization has become an essential part of algorithm design. Multi-
threading, heterogeneous computing and SIMD (single instruction stream, multiple data stream) instructions are the current tools of the trade. Due to the
data-parallel nature of most string matching algorithms, these techniques can
be used to achieve significant performance gains.

In this paper, we propose parallelization improvements to existing state-of-
the-art string matching algorithms. We explore a chunking approach, partitioning the input data and distributing the workload with a thread pool. We utilize
modern SIMD-instructions to improve throughput in computational intensive
situations and optimize data structures for parallel access. Our implementations are evaluated on the smart-corpora [11] and the human genome[1] [20].
To demonstrate the effectiveness of our approach, we compare the runtime of
our implementations with sequential reference implementations provided by the

---

[1] Dec. 2013 (GRCh38/hg38) assembly of the human genome (hg38, GRCh38 Genome
Reference Consortium Human Reference 38 (GCA_000001405.2)). See http://
genome.ucsc.edu/ for details on the data set.

© Springer International Publishing AG 2017
F. Desprez et al. (Eds.): Euro-Par 2016 Workshops, LNCS 10104, pp. 187–198, 2017.
DOI: 10.1007/978-3-319-58943-5_15

smart-corpora as well as the string matching program `grep`[2] of the GNU/Linux operating system.

Pattern length and alphabet size influence the effectiveness of different algorithms, choosing the optimal implementation therefore depends on those two parameters. Our evaluation considers different combinations of pattern length and alphabet size. When both parameters are known at runtime this information can be used to choose the optimal algorithm.

2   Problem Definition

We define the problem of string matching as the task of finding a pattern P of length $m = |P|$ in a text T of length $n = |T|$. Pattern and text are based on an alphabet Σ. The results are the absolute positions of every occurrence of P in T. The input is dynamic, preprocessing of pattern or text have to take place at runtime. Only exact matches are returned, approximate matches or regular expression patterns are not considered.

3   Related Work

The introduction of the Knuth et al. [17] and Boyer and Moore [4] algorithms which are, respectively, the first linear and the first sublinear string matching algorithms, initiated the ongoing search for ever faster matching approaches. Both of these inspired many variations. Prominent examples are Horspool [15] and QuickSearch [25], simplifying variations of Boyer-Moore, which have proven to be efficient in practice. The Rabin and Karp [16] algorithm is an alternative solution to the string matching problem, testing for matches based on hashes computed from the input text and pattern.

In more recent years, many more variations and combinations of the classical matching algorithms have been proposed. Faro and Lecroq [11] report on more than 50 new algorithms that have been published since 2000. One example is the Average Optimal Shift-Or algorithm by Fredriksson and Grabowski [12], an extension of the original Shift-Or [2], which leverages bit-parallelism within pattern and text comparison. The BNDM algorithm by Navarro and Raffinot [23] is based on the same principle, and combines it with suffix automata to find matches by efficiently identifying all subpatterns of a word. Another family of algorithms which relies on finding subpatterns is BOM [1] and its variations (cf. e.g. [10]).

For a more detailed and more complete overview of recent advances in string matching algorithms we direct the interested reader to Faro's and Lecroq's review article [11].

Despite the global trend in industry and research to increase performance by parallelizing algorithms, to the best of our knowledge, only few parallel approaches to string matching exist, even though efficient theoretical solutions have been

---

[2] GNU grep 2.20, Copyright (C) 2014 Free Software Foundation, Inc. http://www.gnu.org/software/grep/.

proposed: The optimal parallel algorithm for a CREW-PRAM (concurrent-read, exclusive write parallel random access machine) runs in $O(\log^2 n)$ [13]. For a CRCW-PRAM, even a constant time solution has been proposed [14]. There are, however, no practical implementations available for these theoretical algorithms. Nevertheless, there are several published approaches that in some sense rely on inherently parallel properties of string comparisons, such as by exploiting bit-parallelism [5] in comparing strings (cf. e.g. the Shift-Or algorithm [2] and its derivatives, or the works of Cantone et al. [6] or Peltola and Tarhio [24], among many others). Faro and Kúlekci, on the other hand, further increase the benefits of these approaches by using modern processor's SIMD extensions [9,19].

Although there is a surprising lack of approaches leveraging classical threading parallelism, there are some works which explore the benefits provided by the massive parallel computing power within modern GPUs. Kouzinopoulos and Margaritis evaluate the performance of GPU implementations of the classical matching algorithms [18] and report on a possible speedup of more than $10\times$. Vasiliadis et al. [26] and Cascarano et al. [7] present solutions for regular expression matching in GPUs, which is a superset of the string matching problem. These approaches create finite state machines from the input patterns and execute them in parallel on partitioned input data. Another problem related to string matching is the approximate string matching problem, which allows for missing some possible matches in exchange for speed. Liu et al. [22] present GPU-based solutions and report on up to $80\times$ speedups.

4   Implementation

We implement a general chunking approach for all of our string matching implementations. The initial text T is split into chunks of size $s = \max(2*m, s_a)$ where s_a is 4MiB for the SSEF algorithm and 1MiB for all other algorithms. A thread pool runs string matching tasks on these chunks in parallel. The string matching tasks examine an additional overlap of $m - 1$ characters after each chunk to ensure matches that cross chunk boundaries are found. This also avoids inter-chunk synchronization in the matching algorithm. If the text size is not large enough to create at least one chunk per thread, we reduce the chunk size to $s = n/thread\_count$. To preserve global ordering the matching results are written to a synchronized set.

We employ SSE (streaming SIMD extensions) in the appropriate implementations. We use the SSE instruction set (up to version 4.1), as it is supported by Intel and AMD CPUs. The resulting bit-parallelism is essential for high throughput on modern CPU cores.

Our implementations can be found on our project page[3]. We provide a unified C++ interface for all discussed algorithms.

The following subsections give a brief overview of the implemented algorithms. Of particular interest are our modifications to the SSEF algorithm. For a more detailed discussion we refer to the referenced articles.

---

[3] https://code.ipd.kit.edu/pmp/pgrep.

4.1 Knuth-Morris-Pratt

The well-known Knuth-Morris-Pratt (KMP) algorithm was first published in 1977 [17]. It uses a preprocessing phase on the pattern to build a partial match table. This table can be used to skip known matching prefixes after a partial match was found. Once matched characters are therefore never visited again. The preprocessing phase runs in $O(m)$ and the actual matching in $O(n)$, resulting in an asymptotic runtime of $O(n + m)$.

4.2 Shift-Or

The Shift-Or algorithm proposed by Baeza-Yates and Gonnet in 1992 uses efficient bitwise operations [2]. For each character c in the alphabet Σ an occurrence bit-vector o_c is calculated in a preprocessing phase.

$$o_c[i] = \begin{cases} 1, & \text{if } P[i] = c \\ 0, & \text{otherwise} \end{cases}$$

In the matching phase a result bit-vector r is iteratively and-combined with the occurrence vector of the current character. Vector r is then bit-shifted by one position and incremented by one. A match is found when $r[m] = 1$. We use a word size of 64bit for the bit-vectors. The runtime is deterministic and in $O(n * m)$.

4.3 Hash3

Lecroq's Hash$q$ algorithm from 2007 [21] is based on hash values for q-grams. The preprocessing phase computes a shift table for each hashed q-gram in the pattern. The search algorithm then hashes sub-strings of length q and skips characters according to the precomputed shift table. Potential matches are checked naively. Choosing $q = 3$ promises the best results for medium length patterns. Hash3 requires a minimum pattern length of $m = 3$.

4.4 SSEF

The SSEF algorithm [19] precomputes 65536 filter lists based on the kth bit of each character on the pattern. These filters are then applied efficiently, utilizing SSE instructions, on shifting alignments of pattern and text. SSEF is restricted to patterns with a minimum length of $m \geq 32$. The worst case runtime is in $O(n*m)$. If we consider the probability to filter possible matches, SSEF achieves an average runtime in $O(n * m/65536)$.

In the original SSEF algorithm parameter k has to be specified by the user. The smart-corpora implementation chooses a fixed value of $k = 7$. We improved on this by finding the bit that carries the most information in the pattern. We count the set bit positions in each character of the pattern and choose the bit

Table 1. Finding the bit that carries the most information. For the pattern 'acaf' the second bit is set in 50% of the characters.

Character	Bits						
	7	6	5	4	3	2	1
a	1	1	0	0	0	0	1
c	1	1	0	0	0	1	1
a	1	1	0	0	0	0	1
f	1	1	0	0	1	1	0
Ratio	1.00	1.00	0.00	0.00	0.25	0.50	0.75

that carries the most information, see Table 1 for an example. Optimally the kth bit is set 50% of the time.

A second optimization is the filter list itself. The original algorithm and the smart-corpora implementation use a linked list and allocate each entry dynamically. The reference performs separate heap allocations for each individual entry. As the number of entries in this linked list is fixed for a given pattern size, we only allocate a single chunk of memory. This allows us to use simple offsets (instead of pointers) to address the list entries. Also we minimize the total memory footprint of the filter list by automatically using the smallest data type possible to store the offsets inside the list. This has the fortunate side effect of improved cache locality.

4.5   Variants of the Backward-Oracle-Matching

Faro and Lecroq presented Extended-Backward-Oracle-Matching (EBOM) and Forward-Simplified-Backward-Nondeterministic-DAWG-Matching (FSB-NDM) in 2009 [10]. Both are variants of the Backward-Oracle-Matching algorithm and based on finite automata.

Extended-Backward-Oracle-Matching. The EBOM algorithm extends Backward-Oracle-Matching with a fast-loop. The fast-loop technique iterates a matching heuristic in a non-branching cycle. This is used to quickly locate the last character of the pattern in the currently observed text window. In each iteration two consecutive characters are handled. EBOM requires a preprocessing phase in $O(|\Sigma|^2)$.

Forward-Simplified-Backward - Nondeterministic - DAWG - Matching. The FSBNDM algorithm uses bit-parallelism to implement a non-deterministic forward automaton on the reversed pattern. The preprocessing phase can be performed in $O(|\Sigma| + m)$.

4.6   Exact-Packed-String-Matching

Exact-Packed-String-Matching (EPSM) was presented in 2013 by Faro and Külekci [8]. EPSM makes use of bit-parallelism by packing several characters into a bit-word and partitioning text T into chunks T_i. These bit-word sized chunks are compared with a packed pattern bit-word. Shift and bitwise-and operations are used to efficiently compare text chunks with the pattern. Our implementation uses SSE registers as 128 bit words. We limit the usage of EPSM to cases with short patterns ($m \leq 8$). Under these restrictions EPSM is very fast and runs in $O(n)$. The asymptotic runtime for the general case remains $O(n * m)$.

5   Evaluation

In the following section we present the evaluation of the performance of our parallelized string matching algorithms. We show experimental results obtained from two benchmarks using the smart-corpora [11] and the human genome [20]. The human genome benchmark input text is the assembly of the human genome, which is 3.1 GB in size and uses an alphabet of four characters. The smart-corpora benchmark is comprised of seven input texts from the smart-coprora archive:

- The text of the English King James Bible, containing natural English language with a complete alphabet of 63 characters.
- A set of genome sequences for the E. Coli bacterium. The DNA is encoded over an alphabet of size 4.
- Four protein sequences hi, hs, mj, sc, with an alphabet of 20 characters (19 characters for the hs protein).
- The CIA world fact book. Natural English language with a few special characters. Alphabet size of 94.

For both benchmarks, we generate 10 patterns for every input file of the lengths 2, 4, 8, 16, 32, 64, 128, 256, 512, and 1024. The patterns for an input file are generated by randomly picking sequences of the respective length from the file, thus ensuring that there actually are matches for every file and pattern. The benchmark results shown in the remainder of this chapter are averaged over all 10 patterns for every file and configuration. To assess the benefits of parallelization, all experiments are conducted using 1,2,4, and 8 threads.

Additionally, we compare the performance results of our implementations with sequential reference implementations of the respective algorithm provided by the smart-corpora as well as the string matching program grep of the GNU/Linux operating system.

Input files are directly mapped into the application's memory to reduce I/O latencies. We ensured that input files are completely cached by the operating system. To get comparable results we used an equivalent memory-mapping interface for the smart-corpora algorithms. Memory-mapping is used in grep as well. We invoke grep with the parameters grep <pattern> <file> -c. To benchmark the actual string matching we use the additional switch -c to suppresses output of the individual matches and instead print the count of matching lines. The runtimes of grep and our implementations thus encompass the matching algorithm including all synchronization but minimize file and screen I/O. To run the benchmarks we used `temci` [3], a benchmarking helper tool, in combination with `perf`, a tool for profiling with performance counters. All experiments were performed on an Intel Xeon E5 system, with 4 CPU cores (8 hardware threads) at 3.7 GHz.

In the following subsection we discuss an excerpt of our result data.

5.1   Results

Figure 1 shows the average time to match a pattern of length 32 on the genome data set for six algorithms on a logarithmic scale. We can observe linear scalability with increased thread count. Our FSBNDM implementation requires a minimum of two threads due to space limitations exceeded by the genome data set and the EPSM algorithm is not applicable due to $m > 8$. The content of the patterns has an insignificant impact on performance. The maximum relative standard deviation over the patterns is 3% with a relative range of 9%.

Figure 2 shows the average absolute runtimes of six algorithms on the smart-corpora. The algorithms use up to 8 threads. The pattern length is 32. Both SSEF and Hash3 are consistently fast on all seven texts. The relative performance between the algorithms is surprisingly stable.

In Fig. 3 we see the average performance of seven algorithms over different pattern lengths. We use the bible text and our implementations use up to 8 threads. Several algorithms are restricted to specific pattern sizes. With increasing pattern length algorithm performance increases as well with the exception of EPSM which is optimal for $m = 2$. The maximum relative standard deviation

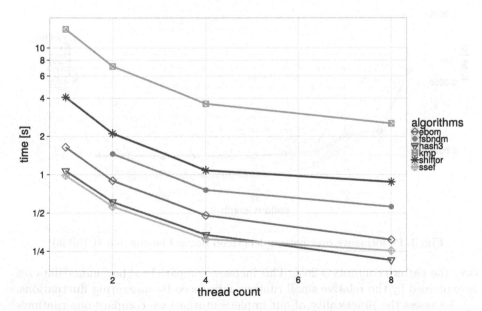

Fig. 1. Runtime scalability of six algorithms for 1, 2, 4, and 8 threads. Human genome data set, pattern length of 32.

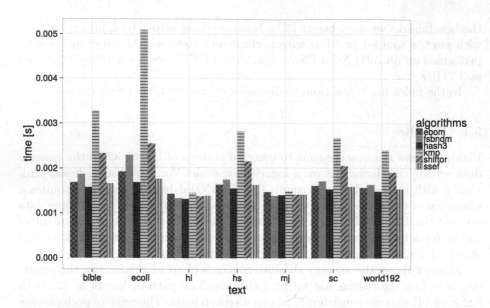

Fig. 2. Absolute runtimes of six parallelized algorithms for the seven texts of the smart-corpora. Pattern length is 32.

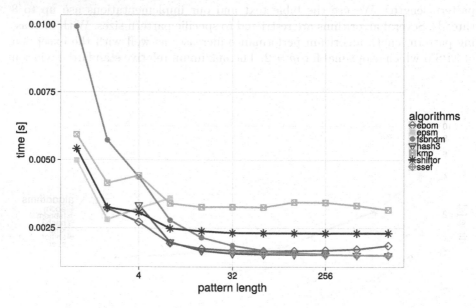

Fig. 3. Performance over pattern length on natural language text (bible).

over the pattern contents is 26%. This increase compared to the genome data set is explained by the relative small runtime influenced by measuring fluctuations.

To assess the practicality of our implementations we compare our runtimes against the performance of grep. In Fig. 4 we show the relative speedups over different pattern lengths on the human genome data set on a logarithmic scale. In the case where we are limited to one thread, we can achieve a performance increase for pattern lengths between 4 and 128. However `grep` outperforms our

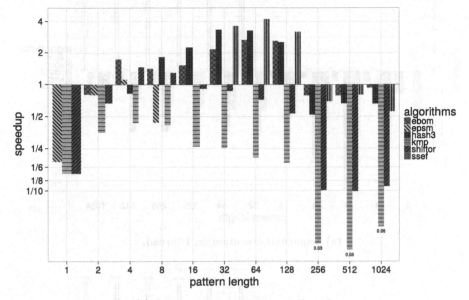

(a) Sequential execution on 1 thread.

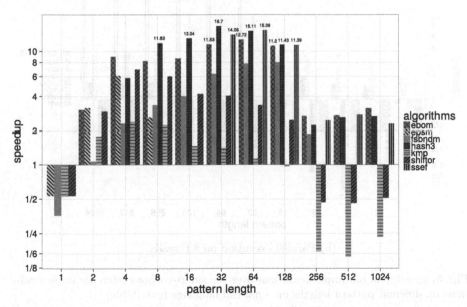

(b) Parallel execution on 8 threads.

Fig. 4. Speedup of our implementations over `grep` on different pattern lengths on the human genome data set.

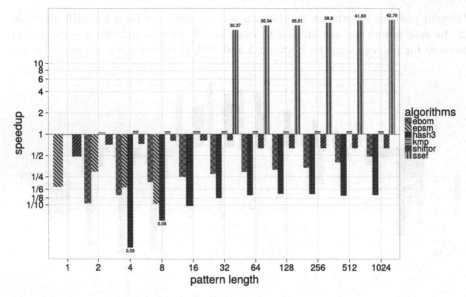

(a) Sequential execution on 1 thread.

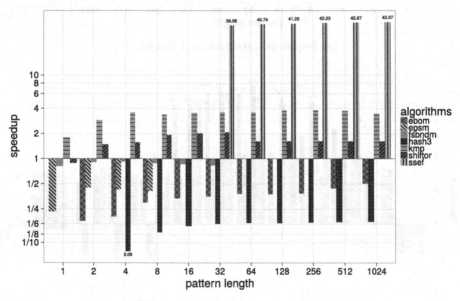

(b) Parallel execution on 8 threads.

Fig. 5. Speedup of our implementations over the smart-corpora reference implementations on different pattern lengths on a natural language text (bible).

implementations for patterns with $m \leq 2$ or $m \geq 256$. If we utilize eight threads we can achieve significant speedups of up to $16.7\times$ for all patterns with $m \geq 2$. SSEF, EBOM and Hash3 all perform consistently well on this data set.

Figure 5 shows the speedups of our implementations over the reference implementations found in the smart-corpora. The speedups are displayed on a logarithmic scale. The baseline for each algorithm is the corresponding reference implementation. In contrast to speedups on the human genome data set, only the EPSM, KMP and Shift-Or implementations benefit from an increased thread count on this smaller data set. However our modifications to the SSEF implementation result in a significant speedup even in the sequential case.

6   Conclusion

We used a chunking approach to parallelize seven state-of-the-art string matching algorithms. We have shown linear scalability on the number of threads for large input data. We observed the influence of pattern size on string matching algorithms. For short patterns EPSM and EBOM are the algorithms of choice, while bigger patterns favor Hash3, SSEF and FSBNDM.

SSEF is consistently fast over different alphabet sizes and the supported pattern lengths. With our modifications to SSEF we achieved a 43× speedup over the reference implementation. Compared with grep we achieve significant speedups in all cases where the pattern has two or more characters. On the human genome data set the maximal speedup of SSEF compared to grep is 15×.

In the future we plan to explore a heterogeneous approach by distributing text chunks on CPUs, GPUs and Intel MICs.

References

1. Allauzen, C., Crochemore, M., Raffinot, M.: Factor oracle: a new structure for pattern matching. In: Pavelka, J., Tel, G., Bartošek, M. (eds.) SOFSEM 1999. LNCS, vol. 1725, pp. 295–310. Springer, Heidelberg (1999). doi:10.1007/3-540-47849-3_18
2. Baeza-Yates, R., Gonnet, G.H.: A new approach to text searching. Commun. ACM 35(10), 74–82 (1992)
3. Bechberger, J.: temci (2016). http://temci.readthedocs.io
4. Boyer, R.S., Moore, J.S.: A fast string searching algorithm. Commun. ACM 20(10), 762–772 (1977)
5. Cantone, D., Faro, S., Giaquinta, E.: Bit-(parallelism)^2: getting to the next level of parallelism. In: Boldi, P., Gargano, L. (eds.) FUN 2010. LNCS, vol. 6099, pp. 166–177. Springer, Heidelberg (2010). doi:10.1007/978-3-642-13122-6_18
6. Cantone, D., Faro, S., Giaquinta, E.: A compact representation of nondeterministic (suffix) automata for the bit-parallel approach. In: Amir, A., Parida, L. (eds.) CPM 2010. LNCS, vol. 6129, pp. 288–298. Springer, Heidelberg (2010). doi:10.1007/978-3-642-13509-5_26
7. Cascarano, N., Rolando, P., Risso, F., Sisto, R.: iNFAnt: NFA pattern matching on GPGPU devices. SIGCOMM Comput. Commun. Rev. 40(5), 20–26 (2010)
8. Faro, S., Külekci, M.O.: Fast packed string matching for short patterns. In: Proceedings of the Meeting on Algorithm Engineering & Expermiments. Society for Industrial and Applied Mathematics (2013)

9. Faro, S., Külekci, M.O.: Fast and flexible packed string matching. J. Discret. Algorithms **28**, 61–72 (2014)
10. Faro, S., Lecroq, T.: Efficient variants of the backward-oracle-matching algorithm. Int. J. Found. Comput. Sci. **20**(6), 967–984 (2009)
11. Faro, S., Lecroq, T.: The exact online string matching problem: a review of the most recent results. ACM Comput. Surv. **45**(2), Article no. 13 (2013)
12. Fredriksson, K., Grabowski, S.: Practical and optimal string matching. In: Consens, M., Navarro, G. (eds.) SPIRE 2005. LNCS, vol. 3772, pp. 376–387. Springer, Heidelberg (2005). doi:10.1007/11575832_42
13. Galil, Z.: Optimal parallel algorithms for string matching. Inf. Control **67**(1), 144–157 (1985)
14. Galil, Z.: A constant-time optimal parallel string-matching algorithm. J. ACM **42**(4), 908–918 (1995)
15. Horspool, R.N.: Practical fast searching in strings. Softw.: Pract. Exp. **10**(6), 501–506 (1980)
16. Karp, R.M., Rabin, M.O.: Efficient randomized pattern-matching algorithms. IBM J. Res. Dev. **31**(2), 249–260 (1987)
17. Knuth, D.E., Morris Jr., J.H., Pratt, V.R.: Fast pattern matching in strings. SIAM J. Comput. **6**(2), 323–350 (1977)
18. Kouzinopoulos, C.S., Margaritis, K.G.: String matching on a multicore GPU using CUDA. In: 13th Panhellenic Conference on Informatics, 2009, PCI 2009 (2009)
19. Külekci, M.O.: Filter based fast matching of long patterns by using SIMD instructions. In: Stringology (2009)
20. Lander, E.S., Linton, L.M., Birren, B., Nusbaum, C., Zody, M.C., Baldwin, J., Devon, K., Dewar, K., Doyle, M., FitzHugh, W., et al.: Initial sequencing and analysis of the human genome. Nature **409**(6822), 860–921 (2001)
21. Lecroq, T.: Fast exact string matching algorithms. Inf. Process. Lett. **102**(6), 229–235 (2007)
22. Liu, Y., Guo, L., Li, J., Ren, M., Li, K.: Parallel algorithms for approximate string matching with k mismatches on CUDA. In: Parallel and Distributed Processing Symposium Workshops PhD Forum (2012)
23. Navarro, G., Raffinot, M.: Fast and flexible string matching by combining bit-parallelism and suffix automata. ACM J. Exp. Algorithmics **5**, Article no. 4 (2000)
24. Peltola, H., Tarhio, J.: Alternative algorithms for bit-parallel string matching. In: Nascimento, M.A., Moura, E.S., Oliveira, A.L. (eds.) SPIRE 2003. LNCS, vol. 2857, pp. 80–93. Springer, Heidelberg (2003). doi:10.1007/978-3-540-39984-1_7
25. Sunday, D.M.: A very fast substring search algorithm. Commun. ACM **33**(8), 132–142 (1990)
26. Vasiliadis, G., Polychronakis, M., Ioannidis, S.: Parallelization and characterization of pattern matching using GPUs. In: IEEE International Symposium on Workload Characterization (2011)

Speed-Up Computational Finance Simulations with OpenCL on Intel Xeon Phi

Michail Papadimitriou[1], Joris Cramwinckel[2], and Ana Lucia Varbanescu[3(✉)]

[1] Delft University of Technology, Delft, The Netherlands
m.papadimitriou@student.tudelft.nl
[2] Ortec Finance, Rotterdam, The Netherlands
joris.cramwinckel@ortec-finance.com
[3] University of Amsterdam, Amsterdam, The Netherlands
a.l.varbanescu@uva.nl

Abstract. Computational finance is a domain where performance is in high demand. In this work, we investigate the suitability of Intel Xeon Phi for computational finance simulations. Specifically, we use a scenario based ALM (Asset Liability Management) model and propose a novel OpenCL implementation for Xeon Phi. To further improve the performance of the application, we apply several optimization techniques (data layout and data locality improvement, loop unrolling) and study their effects. Our results show that the optimized OpenCL code deployed on the Phi can run up to 135x faster than the original scalar code running on an Intel i7 GPP. Furthermore, we also show that choosing the optimal work-item/work-group distribution has a compelling effect on massively parallel and heavily-branching code. Overall, these results are significant for the computational finance specialists, as they enable a major increase in model accuracy, because 10x more simulations can be performed in less than a 10th of the original time.

Keywords: OpenCL · Computing · Accelerated architectures · Intel Xeon Phi · MIC · GPGPU · Parallel computing · Asset Liability Management

1 Introduction

Modern applications targeting the finance industry become popular candidates for using high performance computing (HPC) platforms and techniques. Almost 10% of the TOP500 supercomputers, are dedicated for computational finance purposes [5]. This trend occurs because of the nature of applications that the financial sector has to offer and the increasing amount of data related to these applications. Examples of such applications are stock market data streaming, option pricing, high frequency trading, or risk management. They are loosely clustered in the fast-growing field of computational finance.

A computational finance instrument is the OPAL platform offered by Ortec-Finance, which provides goal based financial planning for private investors. The

© Springer International Publishing AG 2017
F. Desprez et al. (Eds.): Euro-Par 2016 Workshops, LNCS 10104, pp. 199–208, 2017.
DOI: 10.1007/978-3-319-58943-5_16

feasibility of potential goals is estimated based on high-quality scenario projections. These projections are influenced by investment decisions, market changes, clients financial situation and future goals [15]. Therefore, being able to increase efficiently the number of projections of the future can result into a more accurate investment plan. For this work, we have extracted from OPAL a test case of Asset Liability Management (ALM), to investigate the potential performance and/or accuracy increase when utilizing HPC platforms such as Intel Xeon Phi. ALM was chosen because it can have several applications within the finance industry such as risk management and it's need to comply with regulations. Typical regulations are Solvency II[1] and MiFID[2].

In general, the vast majority of accelerated applications from computational finance are using GPUs [2,6,11] and highly parallelizable (Monte Carlo and PDEs) methods [4,17]. Because of the prevalence of GPUs, some areas of computational finance, such as risk management, are less likely to be accelerated, as they contain extensive branching.

To address performance, OpenCL solution of the extracted test case was implemented. Then, a series of optimizations were applied for increasing its potential performance. As this model works with several conditional statements, GPU implementation approach can be very challenging. Therefore, Intel Xeon Phi due to it's CPU like behaviour, was chosen as the implementation platform. The performance on the Intel Xeon Phi was evaluated, as well as the individual effect for each of the optimization. In addition, solutions scalability was studied to determine the correlation between the effective speed-up and the number of future projections (scenarios).

Our results show that there is an great improve in performance which varied from x17 to x135 depending on the number of future projections. In addition, we studied the optimizations that lead to these speed-ups and their contributions to this performance.

The main contributions of our work are as follows:

- We chose a case study extracted from the financial sector industry, where improve in performance is in high demand.
- We propose a novel OpenCL implementation of the chosen case study.
- We applied various optimizations on the OpenCL implementation.
- We evaluate its performance on Intel Xeon Phi co-processor and the effect of the individual optimizations.

The rest of the paper is organized as follows: Sect. 2 provides the necessary background information on the test case model, programming language and development platform. Section 3 introduces the model, the OpenCL implementation and the different optimizations techniques used. Section 4, presents the obtained results on the Intel Xeon Phi along with the individual effect of each optimization. Finally, conclusion and future work is featured in Sect. 5.

---

[1] Solvency II is a new regulatory framework for insurance companies.
[2] MiFID is a directive that ensures investors protection in financial instruments, such as bonds, shares and derivatives.

2   Background

This section contains a brief introduction to Scenario based ALM case used, the OpenCL programming language and the Intel Xeon Phi which is proposed implementation platform.

2.1   Scenario Based ALM

The private investor has to make a decision about investments and chose an optimum investment strategy. The investment strategy usually lies between the balance of risk and reward. It is a plan of attack based on individual goals, risk tolerance, future capital needs and potential hazards [12]. In addition, these investments strategies taking in account asset allocation, buy and sell guidelines and risk guidelines. Therefore, the combination of this factors leads to changes in the chosen investment strategy.

An analysis using various different economic scenarios is crucial to get an accurate insight in risk and return. Thus, simulation techniques are clearly favored above analytical formulas here, because simulation can take into account a multitude of different variables, such as deposits, withdrawals, taxes, inflation, etc., and do so across a range of investment strategies and portfolios. Therefore, scenario based analysis instead of predicting the economic future, tries to assemble as realistic as possible projections of it.

Consider, for example, a typical pension fund case where 10,000 real world scenarios with a horizon of 64 years (monthly frequency), then 768000 evaluations are required in total. Assuming that this computation is the most computational intensive part of a larger process pipeline (scenario generation, pattern extraction etc.), it can take up to several minutes for completion. Therefore, the number of scenarios is the primary constraint for future development of the model and its accuracy.

2.2   The OpenCL Programing Lanaguage

OpenCL (Open Computing Language) is a framework which allows the composition of programs aiming for heterogeneous platforms. These platforms can consist of CPUs, GPUs, FPGAs, DSPs and other hardware such as co-processors (Intel Xeon Phi, Cell) [7].

In the early stages of development, OpenCL was initially a side project of Apple Inc. Later, Khronos Compute Working Group consisting of CPU, GPU, embedded-processor and other vendors. Therefore, in the OpenCL Ecosystem hardware (IBM, AMD, Intel, ARM, NVIDIA, ALTERA, XILINX) and software (codeplay, Sony, vmware, Adobe) dedicated members can be found. Finally, in 2008 an approved technical specification was released [7].

Figure 1 represents an overview of the OpenCL architecture. There is a host device which is able to control more than one of Compute Devices. For instance, these Compute devices can be either CPUs or GPUs. Each of these devices

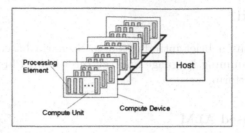

Fig. 1. Opencl architecture overview [7]

contains several Compute Units such as cores. Eventually, every Processing Unit contains several Processing Elements which execute the OpenCL kernels.

One of the greatest advantages of OpenCL is portability. Although, even with the code to be highly portable, the performance is not working in the same manner. Therefore, with OpenCL code which is cross-platform executable, unique optimizations need to performed for each platform.

2.3   Intel Xeon Phi Co-processor

The Intel Xeon Phi co-processor [9,10], is equipped with 60 general purposed cores. These cores are connected with a high speed bidirectional ring. Also, the cores are based on an updated Intel Pentium architecture (P54C), enhanced with 64-bit instructions and 512-bit vector instructions. These instructions are able to perform 16 single-precision operations or 8 double precision operations per instruction. In addition, the co-processor contains two levels of cache memory. The cache structure corresponds to a 32KB L1 for data, 32KB L1 for instructions and a 512KB L2 cache for every core [3]. The co-processor is able to provide 1.1 Tflops and 2.1 TFlops, peak performance for double and single precision operations, respectively. Additional features of the co-processor are the PCI express system interface, the 16 memory channels that it offers and it's Linux based micro OS. Also, The it offers two main modes, where applications can run on either native or offload mode. This allows application to run independently on the device or offloading highly computational and parallel parts from the CPU.

In terms of programming, Intel Xeon Phi offers a broad range of tools and programming tools, very similar to the ones available for a regular CPU [18]. In more detail, OpenCL [20], OpenMP [14], Intel Cilk Plus [16], Pthreads [13] and specialized math libraries like Intel Math Kernel Library [1] are available.

3   OpenCL Implementation

In this section, the Scenario based ALM, extracted from OPAL, is presented. Also, the proposed OpenCL implementation is outlined, along with the individual optimizations that applied.

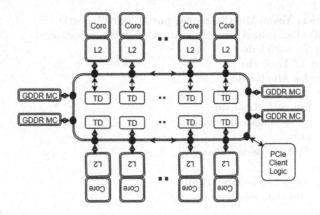

Fig. 2. Intel Xeon Phi architecture

3.1 Scenario Based ALM

The Scenario based ALM kernel, is a part of a larger process pipeline (scenario generation, statistical interpretation etc.), but still the most computationally expensive one. As it can be seen from Algorithm 1, the given application allows a level of parallelism among the different scenarios. Each scenario, has zero inference with the rest and therefore provide us with an initial degree of parallelization freedom.

Each scenario performs a number of computations for a given portfolio. Each portfolio can contain several assets (up to 20). Usually, these assets represent cash, bonds, stocks and equities from different regions (UK, US, JPN). Also, as each scenario needs to comply with real world financial needs such as taxation and rebalancing of the capital between the assets, extensive branching is present in that kernel. Eventually, the value of each asset of each portfolio and the level of taxes needs to be recorded at every iteration of every scenario.

$$PortfolioValue = \sum_{i=1}^{n} = scenAssetweight(i) * currentAssetValue(i) \quad (1)$$

Equation 1, represents how the total value of each portfolio is calculated. The value of each is multiplied by a weight correspond to the current iteration of the current scenario. Therefore, it contributes on increasing significantly the number of accesses to global memory. Each weight is different for each scenario as it is related to a different projection of the economy and a different financial decision.

3.2 OpenCL Implementation

The Scenario based ALM model, presented in Sect. 3.1 is implemented as a single kernel. Each individual scenario is simulated by a work item, in 1D work groups. OpenCL allows the compilation of kernels to take place during the execution time. Therefore, a very large part of the parameters can be passed as preprocessed constants and save resources from parameter passing. Under this

Input: Scenarios, Years, Months, portA, portB, portC, portD
Output: totalValue, valueA, valueB, cvalueC, valueD, valueTax
for *Number of Scenarios* **do**
   for *Number of Years* **do**
      for *Twelve Months* **do**
         for *each Portfolio* **do**
            for *each Asset* **do**
               | Calculate new value;
            end
            Sum of Assets value;
         end
         if *Month is December* **then**
            | Calculate amount of taxes;
         end
         Store Current Value of each Portfolio and each Asset;
         Store Tax Value;
         Store Total Value of Portfolios;
      end
   end
end
return totalValue, valueA, valueB, cvalueC, valueD, valueTax

Algorithm 1. Abstract representation of Scenario based ALM

structure all of the required constants by the model can be passed at a minimum cost. For this first OpenCL implementation, we tried to keep as simple as possible, without utilizing specific hardware or OpenCL features.

3.3 Optimizations

For increasing the performance of the proposed OpenCL implementation, a selection of four different optimizations were applied. By experimenting with this optimization space, some key observations were made regarding the effect and the possible improvement in terms of performance.

Workgroup Configuration. For any OpenCL kernel, the recommend work group size should be equal to the SIMD width. Therefore, for Intel Xeon Phi and float data type, the kernel width should be in multiplies of 16. This structure exploits the auto vectorization module in an optimum way while for non multiplies of 16, the items are packaged in a traditional scalar way [21].

Compiler Optimizations. In most GPGPU architectures, several hardware specific optimizations are available by the compiler. These optimizations may have the form of specific "expensive" mathematical functions such as square roots. In the same manner OpenCL allows a certain number of such flags for allowing better exploitation of the hardware. The optimizations chosen relevant to the nature of the model where *-cl-fast-relaxed-math*, *-cl-no-signed-zeros* and *-cl-denorms-are-zero*.

Data Layout. Data layout can have significant impact in an applications performance. Memory access patterns of the kernel can be converted from array of structures (AoS) to structure of arrays (SoA). This conversion results to a more cache friendly layout which can be benefited by the vectorization module. [22] Thus, the resulted performance can be improved with the used of a more SIMD friendly layout like the SoA [19]. The vectorization module transforms scalar data type operations on adjacent work-items into an equivalent vector operation. If vector operations already exist in the kernel source code, the module scalarizes (breaks into component operations) and revectorizes them.

Constant Memory. The use of constant memory can allow all compute units of the device to have access on the same data. Any constant memory element can be accessible on the same time by all work-items. Although, use of constant memory is strongly relative to the nature of the problem and work-group dimensions. Moreover, constant memory is expected to effect performance only for small problem sizes, where data can fit in the small constant memory.

4   Results

In this section, the results obtained after applying various optimizations will be presented. All the experiments performed in an Intel i7 GPP and Intel Xeon Phi co-processor.

4.1   Performance Impact of the Optimizations

In Table 1, the individual and relevant impact of each optimization are presented. The final performance yield a speed-up in magnitude of 109 times compared with our initial scalar implementation.

Initially, a naive OpenCL implementation was tested on the Phi. The out of the box performance was x21 faster than the original scalar code. This extend of improvement in performance was satisfying, but still not any specific architecture or programming features were exploit.

Further results demonstrate that while choosing the optimum workgroup configuration, the impact in performance can be significant. By tuning the application for a global size of 10240 over 1D range, demonstrate an extensive effect in performance. For the optimum work-group/work-item arrangement (128×80), the overall speed-up increases to x80.1, while the relative speed-up compared to the naive OpenCL solution increases by a factor of x3.8.

Enabling the compiler flags mentioned in Sect. 3.2, increase the relative speedup by just x1.06. On the other hand, converting the data access patterns to structure of arrays (SoA) gives almost 20 times faster performance in comparison with the original version. In addition, using constant memory intead of global for the different work-items to have access to independent scenario weights, gives an additional x1.05 speed-up. Although, for larger number of scenarios (more than 10240), data cannot fit in constant memory.

Table 1. Single precision OpenCL implementation: speed-up and relative speed-up for various optimizations and input of 10240 scenarios

Version	Time [s]	Speed-up	rSpeed-up
Scalar	3.1245	1	-
Naive	0.1500	20.8	1
Workgroup dim	0.0390	80.1	3.8
Compiler flags	0.0368	85	1.06
SoA	0.0304	103	1.21
Constant memory	0.0287	109	1.05

4.2 Speed-Up Scalability

After evaluating the peak performance under a specific knob of optimizations, we evaluate the scalability of these results under different number of scenarios. For each number of scenarios, the optimum work group configuration was determined and used.

In Table 2, the results obtained from our novel OpenCL implementation compared to the scalar baseline are presented. These results provide us with enough information to evaluate the potential benefits of using Intel Xeon Phi. Firstly, we note that in 2/3 of the simulation time for 1024 scenarios, we were able to simulate 80 times more scenarios. In addition, we shown that for very large number of scenarios, we were able to achieve speed-ups, up to x135 compared to our scalar implementation running on a GPP.

Finally, we verified that for larger scenario inputs, we achieved the best performance while using work groups in multiplies of 16 [8]. This behaviour was due to the fact that SIMD, deploys the work-group items in groups of 16. On the other hand, for very small group scenarios, the work-group parallelism couldn't exploited in it's fullest potential and thus, smaller speed-ups were achieved.

Table 2. Single precision execution time results: Intel Xeon Phi vs Intel i7-5600U

Scenarios	Execution time (s)		Speed-up
	Intel i7-5600U	Intel Xeon Phi	
1024	0.2853	0.01719	x17
4096	1.1381	0.01339	x85
8192	2.1431	0.02547	x86
10240	3.1245	0.02873	x109
40960	9.8645	0.09031	x112
81920	26.06165	0.19205	x135

5   Conclusion and Future Work

Due to the continuous need for faster and more accurate models, the financial sector offers a broad range of applications in need for acceleration. Therefore, we chose a scenario based ALM application, where speed and increase in accuracy are in particular needs. We proposed a novel OpenCL implementation of the Scenario based ALM and we tested on Intel Xeon Phi co-processor. We evaluate its out of the box performance and the effects of different optimizations.

In general, we proved that utilizing Intel Xeon Phi and OpenCL for scenario based ALM simulations, can yield to significant improvements in performance (up to x135). Also, we clarify that for application in which extensive branching is present, Intel Xeon Phi expected to offer a more efficient solution compared to a GPU. In addition, we shown that when optimizations are applied, the out of the box performance can be increased up to four times.

In terms of future, work we are working on investigating the performance portability for our OpenCL scenario based ALM solution. This investigation will focus on the OpenCL portability among different platforms, as well as the individual effects of different optimizations in every platform. This study will aim to find a minimum set of optimization knobs, for which a certain level of performance can be kept among different platforms.

References

1. Intel Math Kernel Library: Reference Manual. Intel Corporation, Santa Clara (2009). ISBN 630813-054US
2. Cramwinckel, J., Singor, S., Varbanescu, A.L.: FiNS: a framework for accelerating nested simulations on heterogeneous platforms. In: Hunold, S., et al. (eds.) Euro-Par 2015. LNCS, vol. 9523, pp. 246–257. Springer, Cham (2015). doi:10.1007/978-3-319-27308-2_21
3. Fang, J., Sips, H., Zhang, L., Xu, C., Che, Y., Varbanescu, A.L.: Test-driving intel xeon phi. In: Proceedings of the 5th ACM/SPEC International Conference on Performance Engineering, ICPE 2014, pp. 137–148. ACM, New York (2014). http://doi.acm.org/10.1145/2568088.2576799
4. Gaikwad, A., Toke, I.M.: Parallel iterative linear solvers on GPU: a financial engineering case. In: 2010 18th Euromicro Conference on Parallel, Distributed and Network-based Processing, pp. 607–614, February 2010
5. Giles, M.: From CFD to computational finance and back again, November 2009. https://people.maths.ox.ac.uk/gilesm/talks/princeton.pdf
6. Giles, M., Lszl, E., Reguly, I., Appleyard, J., Demouth, J.: GPU implementation of finite difference solvers. In: 2014 Seventh Workshop on High Performance Computational Finance (WHPCF), pp. 1–8, November 2014
7. group, K.: The open standard for parallel programming of heterogeneous systems, January 2016. https://www.khronos.org/opencl/
8. Intel: Work-group size considerations for intel xeon phi coprocessors (2015). https://software.intel.com/en-us/node/540512
9. Intel: Intel xeon phi co-processor. April 2016. http://www.intel.com/content/www/us/en/processors/xeon/xeon-phi-detail.html

10. Jeffers, J., Reinders, J.: Intel Xeon Phi Coprocessor High Performance Programming, 1st edn. Morgan Kaufmann Publishers Inc., San Francisco (2013)
11. Liu, R.S., Tsai, Y.C., Yang, C.L.: Parallelization and characterization of garch option pricing on GPUS. In: 2010 IEEE International Symposium on Workload Characterization (IISWC), pp. 1–10, December 2010
12. Dempster, M.A.H., Medova, E.A..: Asset liability management for individual households. Br. Actuar. J. 405–439 (2011)
13. Nichols, B., Buttlar, D., Farrell, J.P.: Pthreads Programming. O'Reilly & Associates Inc., Sebastopol (1996)
14. OpenMP Architecture Review Board: OpenMP application program interface version 3.0, May 2008. http://www.openmp.org/mp-documents/spec30.pdf
15. Ortec-Finance: Goal-based financial planning, April 2016. http://www.ortec-finance.com/Private-Wealth/Online-Financial-Services.aspx
16. Robison, A.D.: Composable parallel patterns with intel cilk plus. Comput. Sci. Eng. 15(2), 66–71 (2013)
17. Rocki, K., Suda, R.: Large-scale parallel monte carlo tree search on GPU. In: 2011 IEEE International Symposium on Parallel and Distributed Processing Workshops and Ph.D. Forum (IPDPSW), pp. 2034–2037, May 2011
18. Heinecke, A., Pflüger, D., Budnikov, D., Klemm, M., Narkis, A., Shevtsov, M., Zaks, A., Lyalin, S.: Demonstrating performance portability of a custom opencl data mining application to the intel r xeon phi (2013). http://dx.doi.org/10.13140/2.1.4212.6084
19. Smelyanskiy, M., Sewall, J., Kalamkar, D.D., Satish, N., Dubey, P., Astafiev, N., Burylov, I., Nikolaev, A., Maidanov, S., Li, S., Kulkarni, S., Finan, C.H., Gonina, E.: Analysis and optimization of financial analytics benchmark on modern multi- and many-core IA-based architectures. In: 2012 SC Companion: High Performance Computing, Networking Storage and Analysis, pp. 1154–1162 (2012). http://ieeexplore.ieee.org/lpdocs/epic03/wrapper.htm?arnumber=6495921
20. Stone, J.E., Gohara, D., Shi, G.: Opencl a parallel programming standard for heterogeneous computing systems. IEEE Des. Test 12(3), 66–73 (2010). http://dx.doi.org/10.1109/MCSE.2010.69
21. Tian, X., Saito, H., Preis, S.V., Garcia, E.N., Kozhukhov, S.S., Masten, M., Cherkasov, A.G., Panchenko, N.: Practical SIMD vectorization techniques for intel® xeon phi coprocessors. In: Proceedings of the 2013 IEEE 27th International Symposium on Parallel and Distributed Processing Workshops and Ph.D. Forum, IPDPSW 2013, pp. 1149–1158 (2013). http://dx.doi.org/10.1109/IPDPSW.2013.245
22. Zhang, Y., Sinclair, M., Chien, A.A.: Improving performance portability in OpenCL programs. In: Kunkel, J.M., Ludwig, T., Meuer, H.W. (eds.) ISC 2013. LNCS, vol. 7905, pp. 136–150. Springer, Heidelberg (2013). doi:10.1007/978-3-642-38750-0_11

LSDVE - Workshop on Large-Scale Distributed Virtual Environments

TallyNetworks: Protecting Your Private Opinions with Edge-Centric Computing

Marc Ruiz Rodríguez(✉), Pedro García López, and Marc Sánchez-Artigas

Universitat Rovira i Virgili, Tarragona, Spain
marc.ruiz@urv.cat

Abstract. In this paper we claim that your private opinions cannot be controlled by a single centralized entity. Some examples of this are user participation in open polls or rating (`stars`, `like/dislike`) services and persons in a community. To this aim, we present TallyNetworks, an edge-centric distributed overlay that aims to provide end-to-end verifiability of online opinions by leveraging the computing resources (TallyBoxes) of users and third-party organizations.

Thanks to blind signatures, pseudonyms and anonymous channels, we ensure that the edge nodes (TallyBoxes) are blind and guarantee anonymity and privacy. Thanks to a one-hop structured overlay and a global membership protocol using redundant broadcasting and syncing, we ensure that messages reach all nodes in the network (integrity, robustness), and that vote information can be obtained and checked from different points (end-to-end verifiability).

1 Introduction

We live in a post-privacy world where our opinions are controlled by a few big players in the market. The business models of companies like Facebook or Google rely on analyzing user opinions and behaviors and trade this valuable information with advertisers. Furthermore, a flourishing market of data brokers [4] is emerging to analyze consumer's data to create consumer's profiles which may contain sensitive user information. Every time you like a post in Facebook, every time you like or dislike something in Google or Youtube, every time you rate something in Amazon, or every time you participate in a poll, you are giving away valuable information about yourself.

Following the claim of edge-centric computing, we believe that key personal and social communication services should be decentralized and human-driven. In this article, we introduce *TallyNetworks*, an edge-centric distributed architecture designed to preserve your opinions/votes's privacy in large online communities. The core idea of our system is to move opinion counting and storage to the edges of the network. A key assumption is that we cannot trust a single centralized entity to store and count our opinions. Instead, we will rely on a decentralized overlay of TallyBoxes controlled by users.

Our model is inspired in the remote voting paradigm where participants receive blindly signed voting credentials that permit them to vote anonymously.

F. Desprez et al. (Eds.): Euro-Par 2016 Workshops, LNCS 10104, pp. 211–223, 2017.
DOI: 10.1007/978-3-319-58943-5_17

Like remote voting systems, we provide: 1. *Privacy:* the identity of a voter cannot be linked to his vote; 2. *Integrity:* the result of the election cannot be altered in any way; 3. *Robustness:* the tolerance to the misbehavior of users or external parties; and 4. *End-to-end verifiability:* the check that the reception and tallying of the votes is correct.

The key insight behind our approach is to leverage the services provided by a decentralized, one-hop overlay of Tallyboxes and combine it with cryptographic techniques such as blind signatures, pseudonyms and anonymous channels. The stability and capacity of edge nodes, mainly, stable home devices, datacenter edge services and nanodatacenters, permits the management of a global routing table and the one-hop abstraction.

As a proof-of-concept of TallyNetworks, we implemented a global membership service based on a robust and reliable broadcast and synchronization algorithm for Kademlia. Our algorithm permits to set the targeted robustness to attacks and churn by tuning redundancy across both the broadcast and synchronization phases.

2   Related Work

Edge-centric computing has been recently proposed as the natural evolution of peer-to-peer (P2P) systems. One of the major claims of this new paradigm is to move the control to the edges of the system (human-controlled) in order to preserve user's privacy. Edge-centric systems may combine centralized and decentralized components in order to overcome the limitations of P2P systems.

In this new paradigm, TallyNetworks is one of the first Internet distributed services following the edge-centric paradigm. TallyNetworks combines centralized (Authenticator) and decentralized (TallyBox one-hop overlay) components to avoid security problems (like the Sybil attack) and to simplify architecture services (opinion voting and opinion retrieval, user membership, global knowledge of the routing table).

TallyNetworks cannot be directly compared with traditional e-voting systems as used in public elections. Such systems are normally based on centralized trusted components [5] managed by a public institution. The security requirements in these systems are extremely high; for example, voting from mobile devices cannot be considered without secure hardware devices.

More specifically, our proposal is more related with previous approaches of remote voting [7] or [8] using blind signatures [10]. In our case, the Authenticator component uses blind signatures to create an anonymous pseudonym (public key) that can later be used for voting or for participating in the network. By combining blind signatures and anonymous channels, we provide a level of pseudoanonimity that is by far sufficient for the problem of distributed management of personal opinions.

Another relevant related work is the literature on one-hop structured overlays [11]. Such overlays are highly suitable in networks of relatively stable peers like the ones proposed by edge-centric computing. In this case, the widespread adoption of stable home appliances (storage and compute sticks, media centers, nanodatacenters) and the improvements in residential bandwidth can create very efficient Internet services like the one proposed in this paper.

An important difference with previous related works on one-hop overlays is the algorithm employed for the efficient management of a huge up-to-date routing table. Previous works [11] aim to reduce the bandwidth imposed to nodes due to the event dissemination of active peers in the routing table. In our case, our global membership service will only send events about permanent joins or leaves from the network, and not about transient churn. Our novel approach efficiently combines a redundant broadcast algorithm for Kademlia with a syncing protocol.

Finally, previous works like [9] have linked networks of edge web servers using structured overlays. Interconnecting stable web servers using HTTP in structured overlays offer interesting value-added services to applications such as indexing or efficient content dissemination. Like in [9], our implementation also interconnects edge servers in a structured overlay. But in this case, our efficient one-hop overlay considerably reduces the communication overhead for the servers thanks to the adaptive broadcast/sync membership model.

3   Background: Blind Signatures

In this section, we revisit the concept of *blind signature*. A blind signature [6] allows a user to get a signature on a hidden message without the signer learning the message in question. A secure blind signature scheme ensures that nobody can fake a new signature for a new message (unforgettably) and that the signer will never be able to learn the message he is signing nor be able to link a signature to the protocol run where it was obtained (blindness).

We can define an analogy in order to make things clearer. Consider Alice has a letter which should be signed by an authority, Bob. But, Alice does not want Bob can read the letter. So, she finds a clever solution, she can place the letter in an envelope lined with carbon paper and ask Bob to sign it. Bob will sign the outside of the carbon envelope without being able to open it, so when he sends it back to Alice, she will be able to open the envelope and find the letter signed by Bob, without him seeing the contents.

We distinguish two operations: blinding $\mathcal{B}(m)$, the process to put the letter m into the envelope to avoid Bob seeing the content, and the unblinding $\mathcal{UB}(m)$, the process to taking out the signed letter m from the envelope.

4   TallyNetworks

In this section, we explain the key insights of our idea and the overall architecture of our solution, the life-cycle of the system and our novel global membership protocol based on Kademlia.

4.1 Main Idea

We aim to build a system that allows people to participate in any kind of poll or rating without disclosure of their real identities. But we want also to ensure the integrity of the result of any poll in the presence of malicious behavior. And very importantly, we want to provide *end-to-end verifiability*, i.e., the property that both the reception and tallying of votes is correct.

Instead of pure cryptographic solution, we propose *TallyNetworks*, a system that meets this challenge through a novel integration of cryptographic techniques with a one-hop Distributed Hash Table (DHT). For a given poll, the basic idea is to leverage the underlying one-hop DHT to assign the task of tallying to a subset of TallyBoxes with enough redundancy to ensure the correctness of the result. To guarantee the correct delivery of the votes to the responsible TallyBoxes, we will combine a broadcast algorithm with a pull based approach, recasting our problem as a secure distribution of votes.

4.2 Entities

The entities involved in our proposal are the following:

- **Participant:** A registered user who can emit opinions (`like`/`dislike`) or participate in public polls anonymously from a mobile terminal. It can also query the system about the current state (votes, opinions) of specific polls or items.
- **TallyBox edge server:** It is a node of the TallyNetworks overlay. It can cast votes but also retrieve and query them using the one-hop DHT. It receives votes from participants and redirects them to the appropriate TallyBoxes using the opinion identifier. The responsible nodes will then count and store the votes if they are valid according to their credentials.
- **Authenticator server:** It authenticates participants and TallyBoxes based on an admission policy and blindly signs their credentials. For participants, it can check whether they are members of the community or real authenticated users. When a TallyBox edge server is accepted, then the Authenticator server will assign a unique identifier to it, in order to avoid Sybil attacks.

4.3 Security Threats

We assume that the goal of a malicious participant is to try to tamper with the poll results, for instance, by emitting multiple votes to favor some option, or even by emitting contradictory votes for the same poll. Our system will have to handle these situations in order to ensure one vote per user and that all participants have seen the same vote counting result.

Further, we assume that a malicious TallyBox can drop messages, flood the network with fake messages or try to disconnect other TallyBox servers from the network. Our system must mainly prevent the loss of votes in addition to thwart DoS attacks and overlay partitions.

4.4 Protocol Steps

We can distinguish different steps for participants and for TallyBoxes.

A TallyBox follows these protocol steps depicted in Fig. 1:

- *Obtaining the node identifier:* To register a new TallyBox in the network, the first step is to contact the Authenticator server and request a node credential. If accepted, it will receive a signed credential including the node identifier and URL.
- *Entering the network:* Since the network of TallyBoxes is a one-hop overlay, a joining node only needs to contact a group of TallyBoxes in the system, and then broadcast its signed join request to the rest of them. The joining node will also retrieve the one-hop routing table of the contacted TallyBoxes and the information for the active polls it is responsible for. This is transparently handled by the underlying DHT itself.
- *Participating in the network:* Every TallyBox can fine tune its activity in the broadcast and synchronization protocols depending upon its resources. For example, a weak node might decide to avoid participating in the broadcast algorithm, and only periodically synchronize on a per-day or per-week basis.

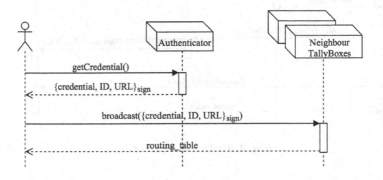

Fig. 1. TallyBox protocol

A participant follows these protocol steps shown in Fig. 2:

- *Obtaining a user credential:* For a participant to register in the system, the first step is to contact the Authenticator server to request a user credential. To do so, the joining participant sends his public key PK in blinded form $\mathcal{B}(PK)$. If admitted, he will receive a blindly signed credential $\{\mathcal{B}(PK)\}_{sign}$ from the Authenticator to participate in TallyNetworks. Upon reception, the joining participant will unblind the signature to get $\{PK\}_{sign}$.
- *Voting process:* The participant can now use an anonymous channel (e.g., Tor) to cast a vote in any TallyBox using his public key PK as pseudonym. For robustness, the vote is cast to more than one TallyBox. To actually cast a

vote v, the vote itself, its signature $\{v\}_{SK,sign}$ with the participant's private key SK, and the authentication credential $(PK, \{PK\}_{sign})$ must be sent via the one-hop overlay to the TallyBoxes responsible for the poll. For example, if a participants wants to add a Like to "Hans", this Like vote will be addressed to the TallyBoxes responsible for the key "Hans". The number of nodes responsible for each key can be configured to ensure the robustness of the voting process.

- *Tallying:* Unlike traditional voting systems, the voting period can be always open and a participant can retrieve the current state at any time. Tallyboxes will receive votes for the polls they manage. For each vote, they will verify that the signature comes from a valid participant. Then, they will check that the vote is not a duplicate one. For keeping the vote counting up to date, the TallyBoxes responsible for the same key will also be "in sync" so that vote counting will eventually converge.

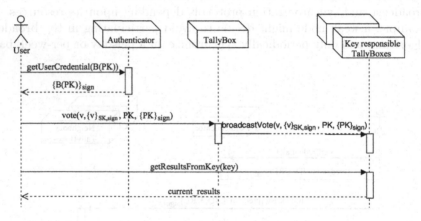

Fig. 2. Participant protocol

4.5   One-Hop Architecture: Membership

To build a system capable of satisfying all of the goals listed in the introduction of this paper, it is necessary to implement an efficient DHT of stable TallyBox edge servers. Since servers do not maintain active connections (HTTP) and they have enough resources, they can maintain in disk a huge amount of contacts in the network. This is clearly in line with previous one-hop or two-hop overlays that maintain big routing tables.

The fundamental difference of our approach is that we only handle permanent joins or leaves (and not transient churn), avoiding active checks or keep-alives to detect and propagate the availability of nodes in the system. As explained below, our network is designed with sufficient redundancy to overcome transient churn and malicious participants.

We chose Kademlia as the structured overlay, mainly for its resilient design and ability to issue parallel queries. To maintain the routing tables up to date, we propose a novel Kademlia CAST & SYNC algorithm that leverages an existing broadcast algorithm over the Kademlia tree overlay. Our algorithm is adaptive to the size of the network and capabilities of each TallyBox. It also permits the configuration of the redundancy level across the broadcast and synchronization phases.

4.6   Kademlia CAST and SYNC

Our membership protocol aims to be adaptive to the size and persistent churn of the network. In a very small network, the broadcast (CAST) algorithm may become a star topology. In fast-growing networks, the broadcast traffic might be very costly, so the synchronization (SYNC) phase should prevail.

The combination of CAST & SYNC algorithms is ideal for large steady-state networks. In this case, the broadcast algorithm will accelerate convergence time and interactivity, and the SYNC phase will guarantee 100% coverage.

Broadcast. We build upon a previous Kademlia broadcast algorithm [2,3]. This algorithm divides the key space using the Kademlia k-bucket routing tables. The initiator of the broadcast will send a message to a contact in each bucket. Then, recipients will forward it to their contacts in their buckets but only to those within their own region. This solution is the most natural and reliable way of dividing the key space in Kademlia for broadcasting. And it has been widely proven by the referred authors.

However, a simple Kademlia broadcast cannot assure the total coverage of the network, because messages can be lost due to churn and malicious participants. In our case, because malicious and offline TallyBoxes have the same effect on the network, we will treat them equally.

To overcome message losses, one typical solution is to increase the redundancy of the broadcast algorithm. This can be simply achieved by choosing more than one representative contact in each bucket. This really improves the reliability of the broadcast, but its communication cost quickly increases. As redundancy increases, the traffic grows with it, compromising scalability. Moreover, a network that is handling popular opinions is very susceptible to be attacked. So high packet loss ratios should be tolerated.

To give some simple numbers: If each node had 160 buckets, the initiator of the broadcast would send $n * 160$ messages, where n is the redundancy level. In our case, the messages size would be: TallyBox server ID (160 bits) + IP address (32 bits) + port number (16 bits) + signature of the server ID (2048 bits), the latter depending on the chosen cryptographic system. With $n = 3$, only the initiator of the broadcast would send around 1 MB. If this number is ported to huge networks, it is obvious that scalability will be severely undermined.

We must then disseminate information efficiently and with high resiliency to packet losses, but also minimizing the communication traffic in the network. In order to reduce redundancy, we will complement this protocol with a SYNC phase.

Redundancy Analysis. Let us first study the analytical model presented and validated by [2]. Later, we will extend it with the SYNC protocol. Now, let B be the number of nodes receiving the message over all nodes in the overlay. The expected coverage of the broadcast depending on packet loss ratio is then:

$$B = (1 + P)^d, \tag{1}$$

where P is the probability of correct delivery of a message and d is the length of the message path, which can be estimated as $\log_2 N$ (height of the broadcast tree), where N is the total number of nodes.

By dividing the above expression by the number of nodes 2^d, in order to get the ratio of nodes receiving the message m, we get:

$$m = \left(\frac{1 + P}{2}\right)^d \tag{2}$$

In order to add redundancy, we will consider P as $1 - P_l^{k_d}$, where P_l is the packet loss ratio and k_d is the level of redundancy. Substituting it into the previous expression, we get:

$$\left(\frac{2 - P_l^{k_d}}{2}\right)^d \tag{3}$$

These equations were validated by their authors, getting even better results in the experimentation when using the redundant algorithm, among other things because when messages are duplicated, each node can receive the message from multiple paths, which can be shorter than the estimated.

Broadcast + SYNC. Broadcast alone cannot make sure that every TallyBox maintains a perfect membership of system, even with high redundancy. For this reason, we propose a solution that uses less redundancy without (negligible) loss of robustness based on periodic reconciliation or anti-entropy. More concretely, the SYNC phase contacts periodically a number of random TallyBox servers and ask them for the last received updates. In this way, if a membership message is lost during the broadcast phase, it will be recovered from the nodes that received it. The synchronization period can be adapted depending on the network activity and the desired refresh rate.

We assume that malicious TallyBoxes will be evenly distributed as their IDs are assigned by the Authenticator server. So now, we analyze not only the reliability of the broadcast, but the reliability of combining the CAST with the SYNC phase.

Obviously the SYNC phase will depend directly on the redundant broadcast, so we will use its equation. There are two possible situations to fail when syncing. The first one is that the packet gets lost with probability P_l as before. The second one is that the packet arrives to a node that will respond, but the contacted node does not have the message because it got lost in the broadcast phase. Taking both situations into account, we defined the reliability S of the SYNC phase as:

$$S = 1 - (P_l + (1 - m)(1 - P_l)) \tag{4}$$

But, as above, sending a single SYNC message is clearly insufficient to re-synchronize correctly, so redundancy, k_s, is added to the equation which yields

$$S = 1 - (1 + m * (P_l - 1))^{k_s}$$ (5)

In summary, a message can be received in two ways in our proposal, through the broadcast or if it was not received, it will be obtained it in the SYNC phase. So, the total system reliability M is given by:

$$M = m + (1 - m) * S$$ (6)

5 Analysis

5.1 Security Analysis

Now we analyze how our proposed protocol maintains the four security requirements:

- **Privacy:** This property guarantees that the relation between a vote and the identity of the person who cast it cannot be discovered. We ensure this property thanks to the untraceability of the blind signature scheme and the use of an anonymous bidirectional channel between participants and TallyBoxes. Our model only provides *pseudoanonimity* since the entire voting history of a given pseudonym is stored in the network. If the participant is identified in any of the communications with a TallyBox, the whole voting history will be linked to his real identity.
- **Integrity:** This property guarantees that the result of the election cannot be altered in any way. This includes: (1) allowing only registered users to cast votes; (2) allowing users only to vote once; and (3) making sure that votes are correctly tallied. The first property is ensured thanks to the Authenticator's signature of the pseudonym. If the pseudonym is not signed, the vote will not be propagated into the network. The second property is ensured thanks to the user's signature of each vote. If a vote signed with an already used key is emitted, it will be discarded. And the third property is ensured thanks to the redundancy of TallyBoxes that cover each key. This allows TallyBoxes to wait for a minimum number of messages before considering the vote as valid. If two different votes signed with the same key are received at the same time, both are discarded.
- **Robustness:** This property guarantees that the protocol is robust against external attacks or malicious nodes that try to disrupt the overall process. In our case, our distributed overlay is designed with sufficient redundancy and communication to overcome such attacks. The most vulnerable part of our architecture is the centralized Authenticator component. If this component is not working due to attacks, the entrance of new nodes and users to the network is compromised, but in any case, the distributed TallyNetwork can continue working independently from the Authenticator.

– **Verifiablity:** Our system provides individual verifiability, since a user can recover (via a GET request for a key) the votes of a poll from different Tally-Boxes (key managers), and check if his vote is present and counted. A user can also check if all votes in a poll are correct according to their signatures and if the global count is consistent in the different TallyBoxes.

5.2 Experimental Analysis

Broadcast + Sync Simulation. As shown in Fig. 3, it can be easily seen how synchronization improves the overall system reliability M, according to the redundancy level determined by our equations. We simulated a network of 10, 000 TallyBoxes with Peersim.

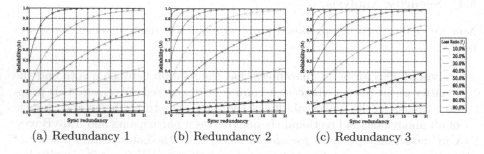

| (a) Redundancy 1 | (b) Redundancy 2 | (c) Redundancy 3 |

Fig. 3. Broadcast + Sync evaluation

As shown in Fig. 3, the obtained results (crosses) faithfully follow our analytical model (lines). However, our evaluation is rather pessimistic, as our equations capture only the worst-case scenario when all out-of-sync TallyBoxes try to re-sync at the same time, just after a broadcast. However, in a real situation, all nodes will not sync at the same time, which means that the probability of re-synchronizing increases after any other node has already synced. Therefore, a better reliability M will be achieved in practice.

The initial reliability of the broadcast is the one that corresponds to the value 0 of the x axis (sync redundancy).

Analyzing Fig. 1(a), the most relevant result obtained is that with $P_l = 10\%$ of loss ratio and no redundancy, reliability improves from 50% to 100% by just contacting 8 nodes. In order to achieve the same result with just broadcasting, a minimum of 3 levels of redundancy would be required as shown in [2].

Figure 1(b) illustrates that with redundancy 2, we only need to contact 2 nodes when $P_l = 10\%$ to achieve 100% reliability, and only 4 nodes to obtain 100% reliability with $P_l = 20\%$. Even 30% of losses can be overcome by simply contacting 10 nodes, improving from 50% to 100% the level of reliability. To achieve this with just broadcasting, at least a redundancy level of 4 would be required.

Finally, compared with the previous figure, Fig. 1(c) shows that the number of nodes required to ask for synchronization is smaller up to $P_l = 30\%$. But it also shows that a reliability of 100% can be achieved with a loss ratio of 40% by only contacting 10 nodes. Furthermore, even a loss ratio of 50% could be supported by just contacting 20 nodes or even less.

Those results clearly show that our network is more tolerant to failures with less resources, thus saving significant amounts of bandwidth. Moreover, the syncing phase makes our network much less fragile in front any attack that wants to silence the public opinion, thanks to a our greater reliability.

Notice that both the broadcast redundancy and the syncing redundancy are not static parameters and can evolve with the network, i.e., increasing or decreasing their values according to the network state. The state of the network and its loss ratio can be estimated by the nodes themselves by calculating the ratio of their unanswered requests sent to other TallyBoxes. So the algorithm can be adaptive to optimize system resources.

Protocol Cryptographic Operations Validation. We evaluated the cost of each protocol operation. We implemented them in Python using the Pycrypto library. We ran more than 10, 000 tests in an Intel Core i5-3470@3.20GHz with Debian 7.8. The obtained results are shown in the table below.

Table 1. Protocol simulation

Operations/second (depending on key size)			
Stage	1024	2048	4096
1. Participant join			
1.1 P: Key generation	4,23	1,06	0,16
1.2 P: Public key hashing	12500	10000	7142
1.3 P: Hash blinding	20000	7142	2857
1.4 A: Blind signature	657,89	110	18,16
1.5 P: Signature unblinding	100000	40000	16666
2. TallyBox join			
2.1 A: Credential signature	657,89	110	18,16
2.2 T: Signature verification	16666,66	5000	1538,46
3. Voting			
3.1 P: Vote signature	657,89	110	18,16
3.2 T: Vote signature verification	16666,66	5000	1538,46

P: Participant, A: Authenticator, T: TallyBox

As showed in Table 1, the most limiting operations are signing and key generation. The latter is not a problem, as it is performed only once by each participant when joining. Consequently, the Authenticator is the only limiting entity. But because it is a trusted and controlled entity, it can be easily scaled to perform much more operations per second. Also, the Authenticator can rate limit the joining process to the network in order to reduce pronounced joining peaks.

Membership Storage Cost Evaluation. We also evaluated the space cost of storing the membership info. We assume a 160-bit TallyBox server ID, an IP address of 32 bits, a port of 16 bits and a signature of variable size. A TallyBox stores this information for each TallyBox in the network. As it can be seen in the following results Table 2 in MB and assuming 4096-bit signatures, it would take only around 513 MB of disk space, so space is not a problem.

Our combined SYNC & CAST algorithm is adaptive and resilient and can scale to big networks. Furthermore, thanks to full membership, we know the size of the network and depth of the tree, so that the aforementioned broadcast algorithm is efficient and feasible to implement in real networks.

Table 2. Storage cost evaluation (MB)

Network size	Signature size (bits)		
	1024	2048	4096
10.000	1,47	2,69	5,13
100.000	14,69	26,89	51,31
1.000.000	146,87	268,94	513,08

6 Conclusion

In this paper we have presented TallyNetworks, an edge-centric distributed overlay for protecting the privacy of your online opinions. It is aimed for typical user online participation tools like open polls or item rating (stars, like/dislike).

A TallyNetwork must count opinions but also assure their correct retrieval under attacks or censorship attempts. We show in this work how it is possible to provide privacy, integrity, robustness, and end-to-end verifiability through the combination of secure technologies (blind signatures, anonymous channels) with a one-hop DHT of edge servers.

Acknowledgments. This work has been partly funded by the EU project IOStack (H2020-644182) and Spanish research project Cloud Services and Community Clouds (TIN2013-47245-C2-2-R) funded by the Ministry of Science and Innovation.

References

1. Maymounkov, P., Mazières, D.: Kademlia: a peer-to-peer information system based on the XOR metric. In: Druschel, P., Kaashoek, F., Rowstron, A. (eds.) IPTPS 2002. LNCS, vol. 2429, pp. 53–65. Springer, Heidelberg (2002). doi:10.1007/3-540-45748-8_5

2. Czirkos, Z., Hosszú, G.: Solution for the broadcasting in the Kademlia peer-to-peer overlay. Comput. Netw. **57**(8), 1853–1862 (2013)
3. Peris, A.D., Hernández, J.M., Huedo, E.: Evaluation of alternatives for the broadcast operation in Kademlia under churn. Peer-to-Peer Netw. Appl. 1–15 (2015)
4. Ramirez, E., et al.: Data Brokers: A call for Transparency and Accountability. Federal Trade Commission, US, May 2014
5. Peng, K.: An efficient shuffling based eVoting scheme. J. Syst. Softw. **84**(6), 906–922 (2011)
6. Chaum, D.: Blind Signatures for Untraceable Payments. Advances in Cryptology. Springer, US (1983)
7. Radwin, M.J., Klein, P.: An untraceable, universally verifiable voting scheme. In: Seminar in Cryptology (1995)
8. Mu, Y., Varadharajan, V.: Anonymous secure e-voting over a network. In: Proceedings of 14th Annual IEEE Computer Security Applications Conference (1998)
9. Sanchez-Artigas, M., et al.: p2pWeb: an open, decentralized infrastructure of Web servers for sharing ephemeral Web content. Comput. Netw. **54**(12), 1968–1985 (2010)
10. Chaum, D.: Security without identification: transaction systems to make big brother obsolete. Commun. ACM **28**(10), 1030–1044 (1985)
11. Gupta, A., Liskov, B., Rodrigues, R.: One hop lookups for peer-to-peer overlays. In: HotOS (2003)

Balancing Speedup and Accuracy in Smart City Parallel Applications

Carlo Mastroianni(✉), Eugenio Cesario, and Andrea Giordano

ICAR-CNR, Rende, CS, Italy
{mastroianni,cesario,giordano}@icar.cnr.it

Abstract. Smart city and Internet of Things applications can benefit from the use of distributed computing architectures, due to the large number and pronounced territorial dispersion of the involved users and devices. In this context, a natural method to parallelize the computation is to consider the territory as partitioned into regions, e.g., city neighborhoods, and associate a computing entity with each region. The application considered in this paper is the prediction of the amount of internet traffic generated within a given region, which requires to consider not only the devices located in the region but also the mobile devices that are expected to enter the local region in the future. When setting the number of neighbor regions included in the computation, it must be considered that this parameter has opposite effects on two important objectives: increasing the number of neighbors tends to improve the accuracy of the prediction but slows down the computation because more computing entities need to synchronize among each other. Similar considerations apply when setting the size and number of regions that partition the territory. This paper offers an insight onto these important tradeoff issues.

1 Introduction

In the last few years, increasing attention is devoted to the field of the so-called "Internet of Things" (IoT), an emerging paradigm built upon the research and development advances in a wide range of areas including wireless and sensor networks, mobile and distributed computing, embedded systems, agent technologies, autonomic communication, Cloud computing. The variety of involved application domains is also wide [10]: transportation and logistics, smart electrical grids, big data and business analytics, social sciences, etc. The intelligent management of "smart cities" is one of the most important application scenarios of the Internet of Things paradigm. Sustainable development of urban areas is a challenge of key importance and requires new, efficient, and user-friendly technologies and services [3]. The challenge is to harness the collaborative power of ICT networks (networks of people, of knowledge, of sensors) and use the resulting collective intelligence to implement better informed decision-making processes and empower citizens, through participation and interaction, to adopt more sustainable individual and collective behaviors and lifestyles [12]. High-quality can

F. Desprez et al. (Eds.): Euro-Par 2016 Workshops, LNCS 10104, pp. 224–235, 2017.
DOI: 10.1007/978-3-319-58943-5_18

be obtained by cross-correlating data retrieved from a number of sensors and objects and by analyzing such data with sophisticated algorithms.

Due to the specific nature of smart city applications, data and objects are strictly related to the space or territory on which they are defined and used: for example, environmental information extracted from sensors, data inherent to the neighborhoods and residential units in a city, etc. It is then natural to manage such data through the use of computing entities distributed over the territory, in order to perform the computation as close as possible to data sources and to improve the performances by increasing the degree of parallelization [4]. Cloud computing provides an ideal back-end solution for handling the data produced by such a large number of heterogeneous devices. However, because of the inherent dispersion of data and computing entities, it can be unfeasible or inconvenient to bring computation to a single Cloud infrastructure, e.g., a big centralized data center. A better support to tackle mobility and geo-distribution of data, embrace location awareness and ensure low latency, can be provided by a variant of Cloud, referred to as *Fog Computing* [2,9], which is composed by a number of distributed Cloud facilities located close to data sources, i.e., a cloud close to the ground. The computation related to smart city applications can be partitioned and parallelized by assigning different areas of the city to different computing entities, for example servers or smart sensors, all connected through a Fog Computing infrastructure.

Most parallel applications are designed so that the computation advances through successive steps, and all the nodes need to synchronize before proceeding to the computation related to the next step. For example, when using the master-slave model, the computation is "embarrassingly parallel" [5], i.e., the parallel tasks do not need to exchange data during the execution. When completing every step, however, the nodes must communicate the results to a central node that, after collecting all the data, gives the nodes the permission to execute the next step. Smart city applications differ from this model because they typically require that the computation regarding a specific region of the city is performed using the information received from a subset of neighbor regions. This corresponds to the necessity of synchronizing the computation only among a limited number of parallel nodes, without the need for a coordinator node.

Depending on the specific application, it is possible to tune the number of regions that partition the territory – and consequently their size – and the "synchronization degree", i.e., the number of neighbor regions that must communicate data among them and synchronize. The main objective of this paper is to show that the proper setting of these parameters is of paramount importance to balance the efficiency and effectiveness of computation. This is evaluated for the specific case of a "smart avenue" traversed by mobile devices held by vehicles and pedestrians, in which the goal of the computation is to predict the amount of internet traffic generated in each region of the avenue. The prediction of internet traffic is an important application scenario today [6,14], as numerous vehicles possess powerful sensing, networking, communication, and data processing capabilities, and can exchange information with each other (Vehicle to Vehicle,

V2V) or exchange information with the roadside infrastructure such as camera and street lights (Vehicle to Infrastructure, V2I) over various protocols, including HTTP, SMTP, TCP/IP, WAP, and Next Generation Telematics Protocol (NGTP) [7].

In particular, increasing the synchronization degree allows the accuracy of the prediction to be improved, because more devices are included in the computation, but can slow down the computation because of the larger overhead related to synchronization. Furthermore, increasing the degree of parallelization, i.e., the number of regions in which the avenue is partitioned, allows the computation to be fastened but generates the necessity of increasing the synchronization degree to keep the same accuracy, since each region covers a smaller fraction of the avenue. The proper tradeoff between computation and accuracy should take into account the characteristics of the specific scenario, and can be formulated as an optimization problem with given constraints. For example, the system manager could be asked to maximize the accuracy of the computation given that it is completed within a given interval of time.

The rest of the paper is organized as follows: Sect. 2 describes the smart avenue scenario considered for this work; Sect. 3 illustrates how the synchronization among neighbor regions can be modeled through a Petri net; Sect. 4 reports performance results, in terms of computation time, speedup and accuracy of the computation, when varying the number of parallel nodes and the synchronization degree; finally, Sect. 5 concludes the paper.

2 Smart Avenue Scenario

The smart city application used as a test case in this work is the analysis of the internet traffic generated by the devices located and moving over a city avenue. This choice allows us to start with a mono-dimensional scenario, as this kind of scenario is simpler to model and the related results are easier to be analyzed. Afterward, the analysis can be naturally extended to a two- or three-dimensional scenario. The smart avenue model consists in a large road on which pedestrians and vehicles generate internet traffic to use classical audio/video applications, for example social applications or navigators. In addition, as envisioned by the Cloud of Things paradigm, in particular by the vehicular Cloud scenario [7], smart devices can offer their computing and storage capabilities to perform computations in combination with the facilities of the fixed Cloud infrastructure. The goal of the smart avenue application is to predict the amount and characteristics of the data network traffic and the required computing and storage capabilities of devices in a future interval of time, starting from the past behavior of mobile devices. In this context, past behavior concerns both the usage of internet applications and the mobility behavior of the users. The accurate prediction of internet traffic can be used for several goals: to anticipate possible bottlenecks in some portions of the avenue, to save energy and batteries consumption by dynamically redistributing the workload between fixed and mobile devices, as recently described in [1], to design traffic-aware energy-efficient cellular networks [11], to improve the Quality of Service offered to the users, etc. To this aim, the use of machine learning algorithms for traffic forecasting through behavior modeling of mobile users is becoming a challenging issue to improve service effectiveness and efficiency [6,14]. For instance, usage pattern prediction of requests can be used to influence the admission/denial of service demands made by priority and non-priority users, in order to match their respective Quality of Service agreements [14]. As another example, the bandwidth provided in a given area can be dynamically adapted according to the predicted volume of requests, thus saving energy consumption in the overall network [6].

The parallelization of the computation is achieved by partitioning the avenue into N regions, and by assigning each region to a computing entity or "node", for example a smart device or a server. Each node has detailed information about the behavior of the users included in the region and receives summarized information about the users located in a number of neighbor regions. For example, information about the number and type of mobile devices that will probably enter the local region. We define the *visibility radius* R_V as the number of regions, on each of the two sides, from which a computing node receives information. The computation is performed at every given interval of time, or time step, whose duration depends on the applications requirements. An essential requirement is that the duration of the time step is longer than the time needed by the nodes to perform the computation and transmit related data among them, so that the nodes are able to keep the pace and complete the computation in time, i.e., before the beginning of the next step.

At the end of a time step, each computing node sends information about the local region to the computing nodes up to R_V regions away. Only when a node receives the information from all the neighbor nodes it can start predicting the internet traffic for the next time step. In the section devoted to performance results, we will see that the number of nodes and the visibility radius are essential parameters to establish the proper tradeoff between computation time, speedup and accuracy of the result. The scenario of interest, outlined in Fig. 1, is completed with the following assumptions:

- the length of the avenue under consideration is L, which is set to 10 km in this work. The width of the avenue is a constant, therefore all the quantities that are assumed to be proportional to the area covered by a section of the avenue, are also proportional to the length of the section;
- to simplify the scalability analysis, all the N computing nodes are assumed to have the same computation power;
- the time that would be needed by a single node to perform the overall computation for the entire avenue is T_{serial}, assumed to be equal to 10 min in the case that $L = 10$ km;
- the computational load is uniformly distributed over the avenue, and the average time needed to perform the computation on a single node, T_{node}, is proportional to the length of the corresponding avenue portion, i.e., $T_{node} = T_{serial}/N$. The time is assumed to be distributed with negative exponential distribution. The variability can depend on many factors, among which the variable workload on the nodes and the variable number of involved devices.

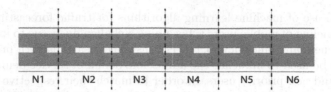

Fig. 1. Smart avenue scenario.

- the time needed to communicate (transmit and receive) data with the neighborhood nodes is negligible with respect to the computation time. This assumption is coherent in the case that only summary and aggregated data are communicated, such as the number and type of mobile devices, the estimation about the global data that will be transmitted by such devices, etc.
- the mobile devices are assumed to belong to two classes: those held by pedestrians and those held by vehicles. They move along the two directions with equal probabilities, and their average speed is 50 km/h for vehicles and 5 km/h for pedestrians. Clearly, this is a very simple mobility model. It is possible to use much more complex models, such as those defined in [6,14], but we use a simple model for two reasons: (i) it is sufficient to understand the basic behavior of the system; (ii) the analysis is not influenced and biased by additional assumptions that are often related to a specific domain or city.

In this scenario, there is a clear tradeoff to achieve when setting the number of nodes N. Indeed, parallelizing the computation on a larger number of nodes reduces the time T_{node} and therefore the time to complete the parallel computation related to a single step. However, a larger number of nodes corresponds to smaller regions: it means that the input data used by the computation is related to a smaller portion of the avenue (if the value of R_V is kept constant) and a smaller fraction of involved mobile devices, which can lead to a reduced accuracy of the results.

The second important tradeoff concerns the value of R_V. On the one hand, a higher value of R_V is expected to slow down the computation, due to the stronger impact of the involved *synchronization barrier*. Indeed, before executing the computation at step s, a node n must wait until $2 \times R_V$ neighbor nodes terminate their computation at step $s-1$ and send to n the related computation results. The time needed for the synchronization is expected to increase with the number of involved nodes, $2 \times R_V$. On the other hand, a larger value of R_V (if the value of N is kept constant) allows the accuracy of the computation to be increased, because the computation can be based on information about a larger portion of the avenue.

3   Petri Net Model for the Computation

The parallel computation process for the described smart avenue application, and the synchronization barrier among the nodes, can be represented by the

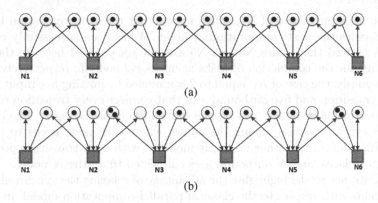

Fig. 2. Petri net representing the execution of tasks at six parallel nodes, with R_V equal to 1. In (a) all the nodes are ready to execute. After execution at nodes N3, N4 and N5, the state of the Petri net is depicted in (b): now N1, N2 N4 and N6 are ready to execute, while N3 and N5 must wait for the execution at nodes N2 and N6, respectively.

Petri net model depicted in Fig. 2, in a sample scenario with six parallel nodes and the visibility radius R_V set to 1. Six Petri net *transitions*, labeled as N1–N6, are associated with the parallel nodes, and the *firing* of a transition corresponds to the execution of the computation at the corresponding node. Every transition is connected by inbound arcs to three input *places*, and in accordance to Petri net rules [13], the transition is *enabled*, and the computation can start, if all the input places hold at least one *token*. When a transition fires (i.e., the computation is performed at the current step), one token is *consumed* at each input place, and one token is *produced* on each of the output places, i.e., the places connected to the three outbound arcs leaving the transition. One of these output place coincides with the input place of the same transition. The other two output places are input places of the two neighbor nodes: the production of a token on these two places models the delivery of the computation results to the neighbor nodes and the permission to such nodes to execute their computation at the next time step[1].

Figure 2(a) represents the state of the system in a situation where all the Petri net transitions are enabled, i.e., all the nodes are ready to execute the computation at the current step. The ability to perform the computation is represented by the presence of a red border on the square representing the transition. Figure 2(b) represents the situation after the execution of tasks at nodes N3, N4 and N5. N4 is now enabled to execute the next task, because it has performed the previous task and has received permissions by its neighbor nodes N3 and N5. In the Petri net model, this corresponds to the presence of three new

---

[1] The two transitions that correspond to the two extreme regions of the avenue are modeled differently, as depicted in the figure, and only two outbound arcs depart from those transitions.

tokens at the input places of N4, which means that the synchronization barrier which precedes the next computation at node N4 has been successfully passed. It is also noticed that nodes N3 and N5 are not yet enabled because they are still waiting for the completion of tasks at nodes N2 and N6, respectively.

Analogously, the case of R_V equal to 2 is modeled by putting five input places at every transition and five outbound arcs that connect every transition to itself and to four neighbor nodes, two on the left and two on the right. The case of all–to–all synchronization among the nodes, where each node needs to receive the results from all the other nodes, is modeled with each transition preceded by N input places, and N outbound arcs connected to all the N nodes.

The Petri net model highlights the advantage of relaxing the synchronization requirements with respect to the classical parallel computation model, in which the synchronization involves all the nodes. When a node needs to synchronize with a limited number of neighbor nodes, different nodes are allowed to execute different time steps. For example, with R_V set to 1, each node can be one step ahead than its direct neighbors, and the gap between the time steps executed by the two nodes located at the two ends of the avenue can be as large as N. This is a notable advantage in the case that the computation time varies from node to node and from step to step, as in the smart avenue case. The advantage resides in the fact that a longer execution time at one node does not slow down the execution at all the other nodes, but only at the neighbor nodes. As an example, if the nodes located at one end of the avenue are slower for a period of time (e.g., due to the presence of a larger number of vehicles), the nodes located at the other end can proceed and execute some additional time steps. In the future, the nodes that are some steps behind can become faster and reach the other nodes, and so on. This is true if the assumption holds that the computation load is evenly distributed on the territory. If this does not hold, it is possible to divide the territory in a non-uniform fashion, for example, by assigning more nodes to the regions with the highest computational load. Overall, this allows the global computation to proceed faster, as will be shown in the next section, devoted to performance results. The results have been obtained in two ways: by using the well-known Petri net simulator Yasper [8], specifically its "automatic simulation" tool, and through an ad hoc simulator written in Matlab, which reproduces the same computation modeled by the Petri nets. Results are statistically identical, with the correlation factor always larger than 0.99.

4　Performance Results: Speedup and Accuracy of Computation

When setting the number of nodes N and the visibility radius R_V, a tradeoff emerges between minimizing the computation time and maximizing the accuracy of the computation. The next two subsections focus on these two aspects.

4.1   Computation Time and Speedup

To analyze the efficiency of the computation, we performed a scalability evaluation, by considering an avenue with length L of 10 km, partitioned into a number of regions N. As described in Sect. 2, the average computation time at a single node, T_{node}, is proportional to the length of the region, $l = L/N$, and is equal to T_{serial}/N, where T_{serial} is assumed to be equal to 10 min. We also tested three different values of the visibility radius R_V, from 1 to 3, and considered the case of all–to–all synchronization as a reference, i.e., the visibility radius extends over the entire avenue. We simulated the computation for a time equal to 30 days and obtained the average time needed to execute a single step on all the nodes, T_{step}, by dividing the 30-days time interval by the number of completed steps[2].

Figure 3 reports the values of T_{step}, the average time needed to perform a step on all the nodes. When N increases, the value of T_{step} decreases because the

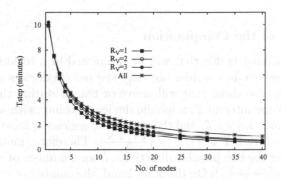

Fig. 3. Values of T_{step} in the case of an avenue with fixed length and partitioned among a variable number of regions.

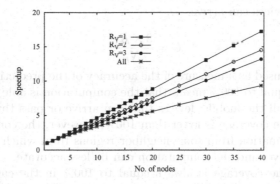

Fig. 4. Values of the speedup in the case of an avenue with fixed length and partitioned among a variable number of regions.

---

[2] As explained in Sect. 3, there can be a gap between the steps executed at different nodes. Therefore, we consider the node that has executed the minimum number of steps.

computation is partitioned among a larger number of nodes. Figure 4, reporting the speedup – i.e., the ratio between T_{serial} and T_{step} – is more useful to analyze the effect of the visibility radius R_V on the scalability. The effect is remarkable: as an example, when N is set to 40, with all–to–all synchronization the speedup is equal to about 9.3, while it increases to 13.2, to 14.5 and to 17.2 with values of R_V equal, respectively, to 3, 2 and 1. The corresponding speedup increments, in percentage, are 42%, 56% and 85%.

Ongoing experiments are showing that the speedup value greatly depends on the type of random distribution of the computation time, specifically on the coefficient of variation, i.e., the standard deviation/average ratio. With larger values of this ratio, the time needed for the synchronization increases, and the speedup decreases. Interestingly, however, we are also noticing that the improvement obtained when restricting the synchronization to a few neighbor nodes (with respect to all–to–all synchronization) increases with the value of the coefficient of variation.

4.2   Accuracy of the Computation

To predict the internet traffic that will be originated in a region during a time interval, it is necessary to consider not only the mobile devices already located in the region, but also those that will arrive or transit during the time interval of interest. In a time interval T, a mobile device traveling with average speed v can travel a distance $s = v \times T$, and the number of regions of length $l = L/N$ that can be traversed during T is $\lceil s/l \rceil = \lceil \frac{v \times T \times N}{L} \rceil$. Therefore, mobile devices can arrive, considering the two possible directions, from a number of regions equal to $N_R = min(N, 2 \times \lceil \frac{v \times T \times N}{L} \rceil)$. On the other hand, the number of "visible" regions, i.e., the number of the neighbor regions that transmit data to the local region, is equal to $2 \times R_V$. We then define the *coverage ratio* C, or simply *coverage*, as the ratio between the number of visible regions and the number of regions from which mobile devices can arrive:

$$C = \frac{2 \times R_V}{N_R} \tag{1}$$

This ratio is used as a measure of the accuracy of the prediction. Indeed, the coverage ratio equal to 100% means that the computation is able to consider the data related to all the mobile devices that can arrive or pass through the local region. When the coverage is lower than 100%, however, the computation does not receive information from some neighbor regions from which mobile devices can actually arrive, and the computation can be less accurate.

Of course, the coverage is always equal to 100% in the case of all–to–all synchronization, since each node receives information from all the other regions. In all the other cases, the value of C depends on the speed of mobile devices, the number of nodes N and the visibility radius R_V. Figures 5 and 6 show the values of the coverage ratio computed for the devices held, respectively, by pedestrians traveling at 5 km/h and by vehicles traveling at 50 km/h, in the case that the length L of the avenue is 10 km and the time interval T is set to 10 min. Of course,

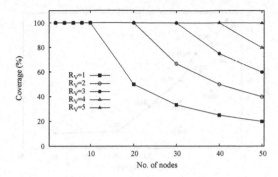

Fig. 5. Coverage ratio for mobile devices held by pedestrians.

with the same values of N and R_V, the coverage is lower for vehicles than for pedestrians, as vehicles can reach farther regions in the same amount of time, and the value of N_R, in the denominator of expression (1), is higher. In addition, it clearly appears that the coverage decreases with larger values of N and with smaller values of R_V. Figures 5 and 6 can be used by administrators to set the value of parameters needed to achieve a desired goal with given constraints. For example, if N is set to 10, the two figures shows that the value of R_V must be set to a value equal or larger than 3 if the desired coverage is at least 50% for both vehicles and pedestrians.

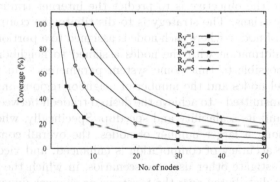

Fig. 6. Coverage ratio for mobile devices held by vehicles.

As speedup and coverage are heterogenous objectives, they cannot be easily combined in a single optimization function. However, the analysis of Pareto frontiers can help to tune the values of the parameters, in our case N and R_V. Figure 7 reports the values of speedup and coverage, measured for vehicles, obtained with different values of the couple (N, R_V), and shows the Pareto frontier. Values of N and R_V that are not positioned on the frontier are not acceptable, because other choices of the parameter values allow both the objectives to be improved. Values that are positioned on the frontier, however, can

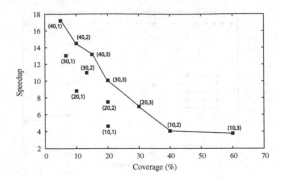

Fig. 7. Values of coverage and speedup for different values of the couple $(N,\ R_V)$. The Pareto frontier is shown.

be considered by the administrator and can be chosen depending on the relative importance of the two objectives.

5 Conclusion and Future Work

This paper addresses the issue of efficiently managing the parallel and concurrent execution of smart city applications, where the computation is driven by space-aware information. We focused on the sample mono-dimensional scenario of a city avenue where the objective is to predict the internet traffic generated by vehicles and pedestrians. The strategy is to distribute the computational load among a number of nodes, where each node is assigned to a portion of the avenue and exchanges information with the nodes assigned to neighbor portions. We showed that is possible to tune some system parameters – in particular, the number of parallel nodes and the number of neighbor regions among which the information is transmitted – to achieve the desired tradeoff between the accuracy of computation and its scalability and speedup. Specifically, when information is exchanged among a larger number of nodes, the overall computation time increases but the accuracy of computation is enhanced, and vice versa. Future work aims to investigate other use case scenarios, in which the computational load is not evenly distributed over the territory, or changes dynamically.

References

1. Altomare, A., Cesario, E., Talia, D.: Energy-aware migration of virtual machines driven by predictive data mining models. In: Proceedings of the 23rd Euromicro International Conference on Parallel, Distributed and Network-Based Computing (PDP 2015), Turku, Finland, pp. 549–553 (2015)
2. Bonomi, F., Milito, R., Zhu, J., Addepalli, S.: Fog computing and its role in the internet of things. In: Proceedings of the 1st ACM MCC Workshop on Mobile Cloud Computing, pp. 13–16 (2012)

3. Botta, A., de Donato, W., Persico, V., Pescapé, A.: Integration of cloud computing and internet of things: a survey. Future Gen. Comput. Syst. **56**, 684–700 (2016)
4. Cicirelli, F., Forestiero, A., Giordano, A., Mastroianni, C., Spezzano, G.: Parallel execution of space-aware applications in a cloud environment. In: 24th Euromicro International Conference on Parallel, Distributed and Network-Based Computing (PDP 2016), Heraklion, Crete, Greece, February 2016
5. Ekanayake, J., Fox, G.: High performance parallel computing with clouds and cloud technologies. In: Avresky, D.R., Diaz, M., Bode, A., Ciciani, B., Dekel, E. (eds.) CloudComp 2009. LNICSSTE, vol. 34, pp. 20–38. Springer, Heidelberg (2010). doi:10.1007/978-3-642-12636-9_2
6. Göndör, S., Uzun, A., Rohrmann, T., Tan, J., Henniges, R.: Predicting user mobility in mobile radio networks to proactively anticipate traffic hotspots. In: Proceedings of the 2013 International Conference on Mobile Wireless MiddleWARE, Operating Systems, and Applications (Mobilware 2013), Bologna, Italy, pp. 120–129 (2013)
7. Hank, P., Müller, S., Vermesan, O., Van Den Keybus, J.: Automotive ethernet: in-vehicle networking and smart mobility. In: Proceedings of the Conference on Design, Automation and Test in Europe (DATE 2013), San Jose, CA, USA, pp. 1735–1739 (2013)
8. van Hee, K., Oanea, O., Post, R., Somers, L., van der Werf, J.M.: Yasper: a tool for workflow modeling and analysis. In: Proceedings of the Sixth International Conference on Application of Concurrency to System Design (ACSD 2006), pp. 279–282. IEEE Computer Society, Washington, DC (2006)
9. Krishnan, Y.N., Bhagwat, C.N., Utpat, A.P.: Fog computing- network based cloud computing. In: 2nd IEEE International Conference on Electronics and Communication Systems (ICECS), pp. 250–251 (2015)
10. Lee, I., Lee, K.: The internet of things (IoT): applications, investments, and challenges for enterprises. Bus. Horiz. **58**(4), 431–440 (2015)
11. Li, R., Zhao, Z., Zhou, X., Palicot, J., Zhang, H.: The prediction analysis of cellular radio access network traffic: from entropy theory to networking practice. IEEE Commun. Mag. **52**(6), 234–240 (2014)
12. Mitton, N., Papavassiliou, S., Puliafito, A., Trivedi, K.S.: Combining cloud and sensors in a smart city environment. EURASIP J. Wireless Commun. Netw. **2012**(1), 1–10 (2012)
13. Peterson, J.L.: Petri nets. ACM Comput. Surv. **9**(3), 223–252 (1977)
14. Singh, R., Srinivasan, M., Murthy, C.: A learning based mobile user traffic characterization for efficient resource management in cellular networks. In: 12th Annual IEEE Consumer Communications and Networking Conference (CCNC), pp. 304–309, January 2015

Multi-objective Optimization Framework for VMI Distribution in Federated Cloud Repositories

Dragi Kimovski[1]([⊠]), Nishant Saurabh[1], Sandi Gec[2], Vlado Stankovski[2], and Radu Prodan[1]

[1] Distributed and Parallel Systems, Institute of Informatics, University of Innsbruck, Innsbruck, Austria
dragi@dps.uibk.ac.at
[2] Faculty of Civil and Geodetic Engineering and Faculty of Computer and Information Science, University of Ljubljana, Ljubljana, Slovenia

Abstract. Cloud Federation facilitates the concept of aggregation of multiple services administered by different providers, thus opening the possibility for the customers to profit from lower cost and better performance, while allowing for the cloud providers to offer more sophisticated services. Unfortunately, current state-of-the-art does not provide any substantial means for streamlined adaptation of federated Cloud environments. One of the essential barriers that prevents Cloud federation is the inefficient management of distributed storage repositories for Virtual Machine Images (VMI). In such environments, the VMIs are currently stored by Cloud providers in proprietary centralised repositories without considering application characteristics and their runtime requirements, causing high deployment and instantiation overheads. In this paper, a novel multi-objective optimization framework for VMI placement across distributed repositories in federated Cloud environment has been proposed. Based on the communication performance requirements, VMI use patterns, and structure of images or input data, the framework provides efficient means for transparent optimization of the distribution and placement of VMIs across distributed repositories to significantly lower their provisioning time for complex resource requests and for executing the user applications.

Keywords: Federated Cloud environment · Distributed storage repositories · Multi-objective optimization

1 Introduction

The rapid growth and development of Cloud computing platforms has brought high level of operational efficiency, thus provoking the appearance of multitude public cloud providers. Therefore, the increased availability of wide range of

© Springer International Publishing AG 2017
F. Desprez et al. (Eds.): Euro-Par 2016 Workshops, LNCS 10104, pp. 236–247, 2017.
DOI: 10.1007/978-3-319-58943-5_19

different providers has prompted the idea of federating Clouds infrastructures [2]. The core aspect of Cloud federation can be considered the possibility for aggregation of complementary resources, which can be bundled together to allow boundless availability. The particular incentive for forming Cloud federations can be of different nature, such as application driven or community driven. In this sense, cloud federation can be viewed from the perspective of the Cloud providers or from the user's point of view. It may allow for the customers to profit from lower cost and better performance, and at the same time it can open the opportunity for the cloud providers to offer more sophisticated services [1]. Besides, this symbiosis can empower the formation of smart communities with decentralized infrastructures at the edge of the global network.

Unfortunately, current state-of-the-art does not provide any substantial means for streamlined adaptation of federated Cloud environments [5]. One of the essential barriers that prevents Cloud federation is the inefficient management of distributed storage repositories for Virtual Machine Images (VMI). In such environments, the VMI are currently stored by Cloud providers in proprietary centralised repositories without considering application characteristics and their runtime requirements, causing high deployment and instantiation overheads. Moreover, users are expected to manually manage the VMI storage, which is tedious, error-prone and time-consuming process, especially if working with multiple Cloud providers. Formerly, limited research has been conducted on the optimization of file distribution in relatively tightly coupled systems. Regrettably, those strategies are not suitable for federated Cloud environment.

In this paper, a novel multi-objective optimization framework for VMI placement across distributed repositories in federated Cloud environment has been proposed. Based on the communication performance requirements, VMI use patterns, and structure of images or location of input data, the framework provides efficient means for transparent optimization of the distribution and placement of VMI across distributed repositories to significantly lower their provisioning time for complex resource requests and for executing the user applications.

The optimization framework can be applied on two distinctive levels within a federated environments: (i) initial VMI distribution and (ii) offline VMI redistribution. Diverse heuristic tracks have been pursued for the implementation of the distinctive application levels of the framework, such as NSGA-II and other population based algorithms. Above all, a consolidated service based application program interface has been provided for easy integration of the framework within heterogeneous environments. The proposed framework has been developed by leveraging the jMetal Multi-objective optimization library and it's behaviour has been evaluated in multiple different scenarios [3].

2   Background

In this section a brief overview of all concepts pertaining to this research work will be presented. Significant attention has been directed towards the basic concepts of multi-objective optimization and to the NSGA-II algorithm implemented in the proposed optimization framework.

2.1 Multi-objective Optimization

Optimization is a process of denoting one or multiple solutions that relate to the extreme values of multiple specific objective functions within given constraints. When the optimization task encompasses a single objective function it typically results in a single solution, called an optimal solution. Furthermore, the optimization also considers several conflicting objectives simultaneously. In such circumstances, the process will result in a set of alternative trade-off solutions, so-called Pareto solutions, or simply non-dominated solutions. The task of finding the optimal set of non-dominated solutions is known as multi-objective optimization [4].

A multi-objective optimization problem usually involves a number of objective functions which have to be minimized or maximized. In the most generic form, the problem can be formulated as:

$$min(f_1(x), f_2(x), ..., f_v(x)) \tag{1}$$

subject to x $\in$ X where $v \geq 2$ is the number of conflicting objectives functions f_i that we want to minimize, while X is a nonempty feasible region enclosing the set of variable (decision) vectors $x = (x_1, x_2, ..x_n)$.

The generic formulation of the multi-objective optimization is free from any constraints. However, this is hardly the case when real life optimization problems are being solved, which are typically constrained by some bounds. Constraints divide the search space into two distinctive regions: feasible and infeasible.

The multi-objective optimization consist of three distinctive phases: problem modeling, optimization and lastly decision making. Each of these phases is of paramount importance for attaining the optimal set of feasible solutions.

2.2 Elitist Non-dominated Sorting Genetic Algorithm - NSGA-II

The Elitist Non-dominated Sorting Genetic Algorithm (NSGA-II) is an evolutionary multi-objective optimization procedure which attempt to find multiple Pareto-optimal solutions in a multi-objective optimization problem [6]. NSGA-II is characterised by the following three features: (i) it uses the principle of elitism, which dictates that the best solutions in the population should always be preserved and never deleted, (ii) it implements an explicit mechanism for diversity preserving in the population, (iii) and it emphasizes the non-dominated solutions on each iteration. Like with every genetic algorithm, the offspring population Op is created by using the parent population Pp and applying the proper crossover and mutation operators. Afterwards, the two populations are combined together to form Rt, which has double the initial population size. Only then a non-dominated sorting algorithm is applied to classify the full Rt population. Even though, this process induces higher computational costs, it allows for global non-dominated check to be performed both on parent and children populations. After the non-domination sort has been performed, the new population is created by adding solutions from different non-dominated fronts. The filling starts with the best non-dominated front and continues with addition of solutions from the other fronts. It is important to note that since the overall population of Rt is $2N$, not all fronts will be accommodated in the new population. Lastly, when the final allowed front is considered, if the number of solutions is bigger than the available population slots, a strategy called crowding distance sorting is applied to select solutions from the least crowded region in the Pareto front.

3 Multi-objective Optimization Framework for VMI Distribution

In this section a detailed description of the multi-objective optimization framework for VMI distribution in Federated Cloud repositories will be presented. The optimization framework has been applied on two distinctive application levels: (i) initial VMI distribution and (ii) offline VM image redistribution.

3.1 Framework Description

The framework is encompassed around unified multi-objective optimization module, which can be utilized for multiple different optimization purposes. Internally, the optimization module is branched in two distinctive sub-modules. Each of the sub-modules has been tailored specifically for a given task. The "Initial Distribution" sub-module covers the multi-criteria evaluation of the possible repository sites where the VMIs or associated data sets can be initially stored. Afterwards, the "Offline VMI Redistribution" sub-module encapsulates the optimization of the VM images distribution within the federated repository sites. By taking into account the VMIs usage patterns, the algorithm is capable of providing multiple trade-off solutions, where each solution represents a possible mapping between the stored images and available repository sites.

The framework is dependent on the repository's usage patterns to properly optimize the distribution of the VM images. To this aim a specific module is required to store information on the previous transfers within the federation and to provide the collected data in a proper format. The module has been realized as an ontology-based knowledge base [8]. The framework has been designed to acquire input data from the knowledge base, and also to return the output results there. Moreover, a specific monitoring agent is required for proper documentation of the data transfers. The monitoring tool itself can be realized in multiple different manners, and it is dependent on the specifics of the Cloud infrastructure.

Furthermore, the framework provides a service based API, through which the Decision Maker (DM) can access the list of optimal Pareto solutions in a guided manner, thus reducing the complexity of the VMI storage management process. The high level structure of the optimization framework is presented on Fig. 1.

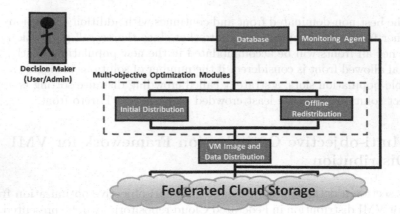

Fig. 1. Top level view of the multi-objective optimization framework for VM image distribution

3.2 Initial VM Image Upload

It is of paramount importance to properly store new VMIs and related data sets in federated Cloud repositories. In this section we introduce concepts from the field of Multiple-criteria decision making, to assist image providers and users to efficiently store new VMIs in accordance with their needs and repository characteristics. The described module, provides a tool which mitigates the process of initial VMI upload, when the available storage sites possibilities are so large that can overwhelm the user during the decision process.

The problem of initial VM image upload consist of a finite number of combinatorial alternatives, which are explicitly known in the beginning of the solving process. In this case, each alternative solution represents one storage site in the federated repository, where the image or data-sets can be stored. Every solution is evaluated on the basis of two conflicting objectives. For the specific problem, the following objectives have been defined:

$$f(P) = B_r \qquad (2) \qquad\qquad f(C) = C_{st} + C_{tr} \qquad (3)$$

where B_r represents the maximal theoretical performance of the interconnections of the repository, while C_{st} is the cost for storing data on the given repository and C_{tr} is the cost for transfer. Based on the given objectives, all possible storage sites in the repository, are then evaluated. It is important to be noted, that the evaluation is performed only on the feasible solutions, i.e. only on the list of available repository sites. This means that prior to evaluation, all constraints for storing the VMI are taken into account. Afterwards, by introducing the concept of domination all evaluated solutions are sorted. The solutions which are non-dominated by any other solution are presented to the user in the form of Pareto front. In a sense, those solutions represent multiple optimal storage sites for storing a single VM image within the federated repository. Next, the user, as a decision maker, can choose where to initially store it's own images.

It also worth mentioning, that due to the static nature, this type of evaluation should only be performed when new storage sites have been added or removed from the federated repository. Afterwards, if there are no changes in the structure of the federated repository, the evaluation data can be used for selecting the appropriate storage site for every VM image that might be uploaded in future.

3.3 Offline VM Image Redistribution

Unlike the initial image upload, the problem of offline VMI redistribution consist of a finite, but very large, number of combinatorial alternatives, which are not known in the beginning of the solving process. The optimization process is conducted by utilizing two conflicting objectives: cost for storing and transferring of the data, which we simply call Cost objective and Performance objective. This process is performed by analyzing the repositories usage patterns, and results in optimized distribution of the VMIs and the associated data-sets across the federated environment. In what follows the exact sequence of steps of the offline VMI redistribution sub-module is presented.

Objective Functions Modeling. The cost model is described around the notion of the financial expenses which are needed to store a unit of data in a given repository site C_{st} and the economical burden for transferring the data from the initial to the optimal site C_{trnew}. The exact values of the financial expenses for data storage and transfers should be provisioned by all Cloud providers within the federation. For each VM image the cost objective can be calculated by using the formula below:

$$f(C) = C_{st} + C_{trnew} \tag{4}$$

The performance model includes much more complex reasoning behind it. It is based on the VM image usage patterns and it requires proper monitoring tool for efficient execution. The raw theoretical throughput of the interconnecting structure within a Cloud federation does not properly describe the factual communication performance, as it is difficult to predict the actual route the packets may take to reach the destination and the load on the intermediate communication channels. Opportunely, it is possible to leverage the data from the framework's monitoring module to perform a coarse but sufficient estimation on the actual throughput between any pair of end points in the federation. In this way, if there is a sufficient information on the previous transfers among the repository sites and the Cloud computing instances, a direct "virtual" links between the above mentioned entities can be abstracted over the physical network and their bandwidth can be estimated.

Furthermore, it is possible to model an undirected weighted graph, where the vertices correspond to either a repository site or a computational Cloud instance and the edges of the graph are represented by the "virtual" links. The weighted graph actually enclosed a union of multiple neighboring subgraphs, where each storage site vertex, as direct neighbor, is linked to all known computational cloud vertices. The weights of the edges in the graph are determined by leveraging the estimated average bandwidth B_{rc_i} on the corresponding "virtual" links. The weights are calculated dynamically, based the VMI distribution that is being considered. To properly model the weight of the edges, we introduce weight function, which considers the total number of downloads of the VMI to all neighbours G_{tv} and the number of downloads to particular Cloud neighbor G_i. The ratio of those two values is then multiplied with the estimated bandwidth of the particular "virtual" link to provide the final value of the edge's weight. The structure of the neighbouring sub-graph has been represented on Fig. 2.

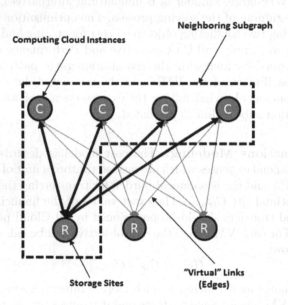

Fig. 2. An example of a neighbouring sub-graph in a structure with 3 repository sites and 4 different cloud providers

Subsequently, for modeling of the performance objective, the sum of the weights of the edges in the neighbouring subgraph is exploited, thus the performance can be described as:

$$f(P) = \sum_{i=1}^{n} B_{rc_i}\left(\frac{G_i}{G_{tv}}\right) \tag{5}$$

Search Algorithm and Decision Making. The core of the offline VMI redistribution sub-module is constructed over the NSGA-II multi-objective optimization algorithm. As with any population based genetic heuristic the basic entity is the individual. Within the given problem description the individual has been represented as vector with a size equal to the number of stored VMIs. The value kept in every element of the vector corresponds to a single storage repository where a particular VMI can be stored. For accomplishing the above statement, within the proposed framework, each VMI is assigned with a unique ID value, which correspond to the index of the vector element. Respectively, all storage sites in the federation are also assigned with unique IDs that are parallel to the appropriate values saved in the vector elements. In such way, each individual corresponds to a solution vector that represents unique global mapping of all VMIs to storage sites in the federated repository.

Afterwards, multiple solutions vectors are created and then randomly populated with values in the range from one to the number of available storage sites, thus creating the initial population. Every single individual represents one possible distribution solution that has to be evaluated. Then, the evaluation of each individual is performed by reading the values stored in the vector fields. Based on those values, starting from every element in the vector, a neighboring subgraph is constructed and the appropriate objective functions are applied. Those values are then grouped together and the median value is selected as the overall fitness of the given individual. An example of a single individual that correspond to a solution vector for mapping 9 VMIs to 3 storage repository sites in a given federation is presented on Fig. 3. When all individuals in the initial population have been successfully evaluated, the proper mutation and crossover operators are applied to create the children population. Then, the parents and children populations are grouped together and sorted according to dominance. Afterwards, only the best solution of the newly formed group are selected for the next iteration. This process is then repeated for a predefined number of iterations. The solutions which have been acquired after the last iteration are sorted based on the dominance. The non-dominated solutions are then presented to the administrative entity of the federation, which acts as a DM, and should select the most appropriate solution based on the pre-defined decision making policy.

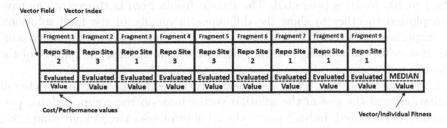

Fig. 3. An example individual represented as a solution vector

Decision making on the alternatives discovered by the optimization algorithm requires an explicit model of the decision maker preferences. For the case of offline VMI redistribution the DM model will depend on the implementation of the federated infrastructure. As the offline image redistribution envelops federation wide distribution of the VMIs we envision that the DM will be an administration entity, which will implement the federation storage policy based on the decision making model.

4   Experimental Evaluation

In this section, the proposed framework has been experimentally evaluated based on a synthetic set of benchmark data. As our research deals with the implementation of a combinatorial multi-objective problem in federated Cloud environment, we present an experimental results that demonstrate the ability of our approach to provide an adequate VMI distribution across federated repositories.

With respect to the different application levels of the multi-objective optimization framework, distinctive set of experiments were conducted. The initial VMI upload module has been evaluated on the basis of the degree of scalability, while the behaviour of the redistribution module has been examined from multiple aspects, such as accuracy, scalability and computational performance.

To begin with, the scalability and computational performance of the initial VMI upload module have been evaluated by varying the number of repository sites in the federation from 10 up to 10000 sites. Figure 4 shows the correlation between the average execution time and the number of storage sites in the federation. It is evident that the module can be lightly scaled up to large sizes. For relatively small federations the module can be invoked at each VMI upload, as it requires only few milliseconds to be executed.

On the other hand, the VMI redistribution module encloses diverse operations that can affect its behavior to a various degree. Due to the nature of the algorithm it is not adequate to evaluate it's computational performance based on the number of repositories in the federation. Increasing the number of storage sites, influences on the number of possibilities where to store a single VMI image, which translates into reduced quality of the proposed solutions, but relatively constant execution time. For example, on Fig. 5 a scenario in which the vector size (number of fragments) and number of evaluations have been kept constant, while the number of available repositories has been increased from 10 (blue) to 100 (red), is presented. The Pareto fronts from both executions have been plotted together to show the difference in quality of the final solutions. The experimental scenario clearly shows that if we increase the number of storage sites, while maintaining constant number of evaluations, the quality of the solutions will decrease.

Furthermore, on Figs. 6 and 7, respectively, the influence that the number of evaluations and the size of the solution vector have on the computational performance is presented. In both cases, the number of associated cloud computing instances and storage sites were maintained constant; only the corresponding parameters were increased gradually. The presented results support the assumption of satisfactory scalability, both in a sense of increased number of stored VMIs and number of iterations needed to provide mapping solutions with good quality.

Lastly, Tables 1 and 2 are providing a comprehensive review of the quality values for the trade-off mapping solutions calculated by the redistribution module. Moreover, a comparison has been presented with a set of mapping solutions determined by using "round robin" mapping model for storing VMIs in the federation. The statistical significance of the results has been analyzed by applying

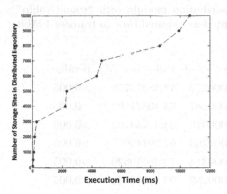

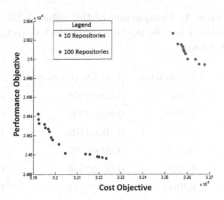

Fig. 4. Execution time in comparison with the number of storage sites in case of initial distribution

Fig. 5. Comparison of two Pareto fronts during redistribution with varying storage sites (Color figure online)

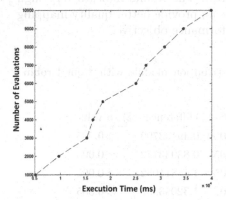

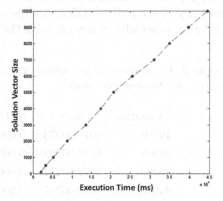

Fig. 6. Execution time in comparison with the number of evaluations during offline redistribution

Fig. 7. Execution time in comparison with the size of solution vector during offline redistribution

ANOVA test, which has shown significant difference between the proposed algorithm and the "round robin" mapping strategy, both in respect with the cost and performance objective. The cost objective has been calculated based on the publicly provided price list for storing data in the Cloud by Amazon. The performance objective has been modelled based on the reported communication performance measures for 10 Gbit and 1 Gbit Ethernet [7]. For readability reasons, the bandwidth values, were converted to delivery time needed for 1 Mbit of data to be transferred from the source to the destination.

With respect to the parameters of the evolutionary algorithms, we have used a population of 1000 individuals, that iterates from 1 to 6 generations across populations. Every single individual (solution vector) is comprised of 1000 chromosomes, thus inducing mapping solutions for 1000 VMIs. Taking into account

Table 1. Comparison of the offline VMI redistribution module with "round robin" strategy for the performance objective (represented as required time to transfer 1 Mbit of data).

Evaluations	Average performance	STD (+/−)	Difference (%)	p-value
10000	0.00005356	0.00000272	18.48472759	>0.005
20000	0.00004732	0.00000287	34.10821694	>0.005
30000	0.00004109	0.00000316	54.42734792	>0.005
40000	0.00003793	0.00000263	67.29142067	>0.005
50000	0.00003526	0.00000314	79.98110620	>0.005
60000	0.00003281	0.00000259	93.39303541	>0.005

the results obtained in preliminary experiments, we have used simulated single point crossover with a crossover probability of 0.9, a mutation probability equal to $1/n$ (n is the number of decision variables). The results indicate very high efficiency of the redistribution module, as it can provide better quality mapping solutions, especially in regards with the performance objective.

Table 2. Comparison of the offline VMI redistribution module with "round robin" strategy for the cost objective.

Evaluations	Average cost	STD (+/−)	Difference (%)	p-value
10000	0.00003273	0.00000005	0.49133799	>0.005
20000	0.00003262	0.00000005	0.83933772	>0.005
30000	0.00003251	0.00000005	1.16811082	>0.005
40000	0.00003247	0.00000006	1.32053992	>0.005
50000	0.00003240	0.00000006	1.52613233	>0.005
60000	0.00003237	0.00000005	1.62638639	>0.005

5   Conclusion and Future Work

In this paper a novel approach for multi-objective optimization of the distribution of VMIs, as an essential storage resources, across distributed repositories in federated Cloud environment has been proposed. The research work has resulted in development of a optimization framework that exploits multiple different factors, such as communication performance requirements, VMI use patterns, and structure of images, in order to optimize the distribution and placement of VMI across distributed repositories and to significantly lower their provisioning time for complex resource requests and for executing the user applications. The optimization framework has been evaluated based on synthetic simulation benchmark. As our research deals with the implementation of a combinatorial multiobjective problem, where the main incentive is to find the proper mapping of VMIs across storage sites, we present an experimental results that demonstrate the ability of our approach to provide an adequate VMI distribution across federated repositories.

There are multiple opportunities for future work in this research field. Novel heuristic algorithms can be implemented to further improve the performance and quality of the redistribution process. Furthermore, lightweight optimization algorithms can be utilized for performing time sensitive fine-grained optimization of the distribution of the VMIs and the associated data-sets during application execution.

Acknowledgments. This work is being accomplished as a part of project *ENTICE:* *"dEcentralised repositories for traNsparent and efficienT vIrtual maChine opErations"*, funded by the European Union's Horizon 2020 research and innovation programme under grant agreement No. 644179.

References

1. Goiri, I., Guitart, J., Torres, J.: Characterizing cloud federation for enhancing providers' profit. In: 2010 IEEE 3rd International Conference on Cloud Computing (CLOUD), pp. 123–130. IEEE, July 2010
2. Villegas, D., Bobroff, N., Rodero, I., Delgado, J., Liu, Y., Devarakonda, A., Parashar, M.: Cloud federation in a layered service model. J. Comput. Syst. Sci. **78**(5), 1330–1344 (2012)
3. Durillo, J.J., Nebro, A.J.: jMetal: a Java framework for multi-objective optimization. Adv. Eng. Softw. **42**(10), 760–771 (2011)
4. Branke, J., et al. (eds.): Multiobjective Optimization: Interactive and Evolutionary Approaches, vol. 5252. Springer, Heidelberg (2008)
5. Kurzo, T., Klems, M., Bermbach, D., Lenk, A., Tai, S., Kunze, M.: Cloud federation. Cloud Comput. **2011**, 32–38 (2011)
6. Deb, K., Pratap, A., Agarwal, S., Meyarivan, T.A.M.T.: A fast and elitist multiobjective genetic algorithm: NSGA-II. IEEE Trans. Evol. Comput. **6**(2), 182–197 (2002)
7. Feng, W.C., Balaji, P., Baron, C., Bhuyan, L.N., Panda, D.K.: Performance characterization of a 10-Gigabit Ethernet TOE. In: 2005 of Proceedings 13th Symposium on High Performance Interconnects, pp. 58–63. IEEE, August 2005
8. Abburu, S.: A survey on ontology reasoners and comparison. Int. J. Comput. Appl. **57**(17) (2012)

Adgt.js: A Web Application Framework for Peer-to-Peer Location-Based Services

Giacomo Brambilla[✉], Michele Amoretti, and Francesco Zanichelli

Dipartimento di Ingegneria dell'Informazione,
Università degli Studi di Parma, Parco Area delle Scienze 181a, 43124 Parma, Italy
giacomo.brambilla@studenti.unipr.it,
{michele.amoretti,francesco.zanichelli}@unipr.it
http://dsg.ce.unipr.it

Abstract. Mobile applications are increasingly taking advantage of user geographic location to provide sophisticated Location-Based Services (LBSs). Unfortunately, most LBSs rely upon centralized infrastructures, with serious problems as regards user privacy. For this reason, the research community has proposed a number of decentralized protocols and studied their effectiveness and efficiency by means of simulations.

In this paper, we describe Adgt.js, a truly cross-platform, WebRTC-based implementation of the ADGT georeferenced peer-to-peer overlay scheme. Moreover, we present a concrete LBS example, realized with Adgt.js, to illustrate how simple and powerful such a framework is.

Keywords: WebRTC · Peer-to-peer · Location-based service

1 Introduction

In recent years, there has been a growing attention to Location-Based Services (LBSs), *i.e.*, services that take advantage of user geographic location, especially owing to the expansion of the smartphone and tablet markets. LBSs allow, for example, to locate people on a map, discover nearby social events or receive geolocalized alerts (such as warnings of traffic jams along the user route).

If, on the one hand, large IT companies such as Google and Facebook are pushing more and more their LBSs without worrying too much about user privacy, on the other hand, researchers are investigating to provide such services while preserving user privacy. In particular, various peer-to-peer (P2P) overlay schemes that enable completely decentralized LBSs have been presented [1,2].

These P2P protocols, in addition to safeguard privacy of users inasmuch the data are not in the hands of a single possibly untrustworthy company, support the realization of bottom-up LBSs, not requiring large and expensive infrastructures. Despite the many benefits of a P2P approach, often these solutions have been studied only in simulative environment and truly usable implementations have never been released.

F. Desprez et al. (Eds.): Euro-Par 2016 Workshops, LNCS 10104, pp. 248–259, 2017.
DOI: 10.1007/978-3-319-58943-5_20

In this paper we present a working implementation of the ADGT overlay scheme [2]. The objective behind the development is the software interoperability between all possible and heterogeneous devices, to make sure that the adoption is high. For this reason, we turned to real cross-platform technologies, such as WebRTC, WebSocket and JavaScript to build a framework that supports the development of P2P-based LBSs. To the best of our knowledge, our implementation is the first of its kind in the area of P2P protocols for LBSs.

The paper is organized as follows. Section 2 provides an overview of the ADGT overlay scheme. Web technologies adopted for the cross-platform implementation of ADGT are described in Sect. 3. In Sect. 4 we describe how the ADGT has been implemented and in Sect. 5 it is explained how to realize LBSs using the developed framework, with reference to a concrete example. Related work are presented in Sect. 6. Finally, in Sect. 7, we present our conclusions and future work.

2 Adaptive Distributed Geographic Table (ADGT)

ADGT is a location-aware P2P overlay scheme designed with the objective to fully take into account peer mobility [2]. What mainly characterizes ADGT is its particular data structure for the management of neighborhood, based on the idea that a peer should be directly connected to those peers from which it is most likely to obtain contents of its interest, using an adaptive topology that reacts to peers' movements.

In the ADGT overlay scheme, the distance between two peers is evaluated as the great-circle distance, which is the shortest distance between two points on the surface of a sphere, measured along the surface of the sphere itself.

The neighborhood of a geographic location is defined as the set of peers that are geographically close to that specific location. In other words, those peers which are located inside a given surrounding region.

In the ADGT, each peer stores a set of lists of neighbors, called GeoBucket, each list being sorted according to the distance from the center that the GeoBuckets have in common. Such lists are regularly updated in order to have the latest peers' positions. As shown in Fig. 1, the shape of GeoBuckets is elliptical, where both the semi axes of the ellipse depend on the velocity of the peer, *i.e.*, depend both on the direction and speed of the peer.

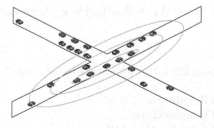

Fig. 1. ADGT GeoBucket example.

The idea behind such elliptical GeoBuckets is that the higher is the speed of the peer, the higher is the eccentricity of the ellipses: when the peer is stationary, its speed is 0 and the eccentricity of the ellipses is also 0, so the GeoBuckets are circular. On the other hand, when the peer reaches the maximum speed, the eccentricity of the ellipses is high, so the GeoBuckets have an elongated shape. Also, the direction of the semi-major axis coincides with the direction of movement of the peer.

3   Technologies

As the idea behind our implementation is the complete interoperability among devices as much as possible different – both from the hardware point of view, and in terms of installed software – we have turned to those technologies that constitute the Open Web Platform (OWP).[1] The OWP is a collection of open royalty-free Web technologies, such as HTML5 and JavaScript, developed by the World Wide Web Consortium (W3C) and other Web standardization bodies such as the Unicode Consortium, the Internet Engineering Task Force (IETF), and ECMA International, with the objective to obtain a platform that works on all browsers, operating systems and devices, without requiring any approvals or waiving license fees.

Although the standards of the Open Web Platform are at different maturity levels, and the development of most standards is still in progress, the web browser has become the main access interface to the Internet and has actually become synonymous with the Internet itself for a large portion of Internet users. While initially web browsers were designed only to display information provided by web servers, thanks to this standardization process, they are becoming the real cross-platform technology, being able to truly realize the "write once, run everywhere" unfulfilled promise of Java related technologies.

Among the many technologies that are encompassed under the umbrella of Open Web Platform, one of the most interesting definitions the W3C has worked on is the Web Real-Time Communication (WebRTC[2]), a free and open API that supports browser-to-browser applications for voice calling, video chat, and P2P data sharing without the need of either internal or external plugins. Its aim is to enable rich, high quality, real-time applications to be developed for browsers, mobile platforms, and IoT devices, allowing them all to communicate via a common set of protocols. WebRTC, WebSocket API[3], Geolocation API[4] and ECMAScript[5] are the OWP technologies we have embraced to implement the ADGT protocols.

---

[1] http://www.w3.org/blog/2014/10/application-foundations-for-the-open-web-platform.
[2] http://www.w3.org/TR/webrtc/.
[3] http://www.w3.org/TR/websockets/.
[4] http://www.w3.org/TR/geolocation-API/.
[5] http://www.ecma-international.org/ecma-262/6.0/index.html.

3.1 WebRTC

The Internet is no stranger to audio and video. Nowadays, speaking to someone over a video stream is a simple task for an everyday user, with technologies such as Apple FaceTime, Google Hangouts and Skype video calling. Together with these applications, a wide range of techniques and solutions to problems have been developed and engineered, such as packet loss, recovering from disconnections, and reacting to changes in network, to ensure a high quality of the communication.

The aim of Web Real-Time Communication (WebRTC) is to bring all of this technology into the browser. Differently from those solutions that require the installation of plugins which can be difficult to deploy, test and mantain, and may necessitate licensing fees from developers, WebRTC brings high-quality audio and video to the open Web [3].

Moreover, WebRTC supports data transfer: since a high-quality data connection is needed between two clients for audio and video, it also makes sense to use this connection to transfer arbitrary data. Indeed, WebRTC enables data streaming between browser clients without the need to install plugins or third-party software, implying a strong integration between the content presented by the browser and the real-time content. With WebRTC, web browsers become peers of a real P2P network, being capable to exchange data in an unmediated fashion.

To acquire and communicate streaming data, WebRTC implements the following APIs:

- **MediaStream**, which represents synchronized streams of media such as user's camera and microphone;
- **RTCPeerConnection**, which handles stable and efficient communication of streaming data between peers, with facilities for encryption and bandwidth management;
- **RTCDataChannel**, which enables P2P exchange of arbitrary data, with low latency and high throughput.

The **MediaStream** interface represents a stream of data of audio and/or video. A **MediaStream** may be extended to represent a stream that either comes from or is sent to a remote node, and not just the local camera. This API will not be detailed further here because it is not strictly relevant to the presented work.

The **RTCPeerConnection** interface represents a WebRTC connection between the local computer and a remote peer. It is used to handle efficient data streaming between the two peers.

Differently from most Web applications that choose the Transmission Control Protocol (TCP), WebRTC relies on User Datagram Protocol (UDP) as the default transport protocol. In fact, if on the one hand TCP guarantees delivery of data in the exact order and without duplication, on the other hand in streaming applications most data quickly become obsolete and, if any data were to be ensured in the reception, there would be a bottleneck in case of data loss. Since a completely reliable connection is not a requirement for audio, video and data streaming transmissions, while a very fast connection between the two browsers is highly desirable, UDP has been chosen as the default transport protocol in WebRTC. In particular, WebRTC transports audio and video streams using the Secure Real-Time Transport (SRTP) protocol, which is real-time, and provides encryption, message authentication and integrity to transmitted data. RTCPeerConnection hides all the complexities of WebRTC to web developers. WebRTC uses codecs and protocols to make real-time communication possible, even over unreliable networks, adopting techniques for packet loss concealment and noise reduction and suppression, in a completely transparent manner to developers.

Another feature that RTCPeerConnection offers to web developers is the Interactive Connectivity Establishment (ICE), a technique developed by the Internet Engineering Task Force [4] to overcome the complexities of real-world networking, where most devices live behind one or more NAT layers, some have anti-virus software that blocks certain ports and protocols, and many are behind proxies and corporate firewalls. First, ICE tries to make a connection using the host address obtained from the operating system and the network card. In case of failure, ICE uses the Session Traversal Utilities for NAT (STUN) [5] protocol to discover the public address of the device and then pass that on. If also this attempt fails and a direct communication between peers over UDP cannot be established, ICE falls back on Traversal Using Relays around NAT (TURN) [6], rerouting the traffic via a TURN relay server using TCP.

The RTCDataChannel interface allows us to transfer arbitrary data directly from one peer to another. RTCDataChannel works with the RTCPeerConnection API, which enables P2P connectivity with lower latency, and uses Stream Control Transmission Protocol (SCTP), allowing configurable delivery semantics: out-of-order delivery and retransmit configuration.

SCTP is a transport-layer protocol, serving in a similar role to the popular protocols TCP and UDP that provides some of the same service features of both: it is message-oriented like UDP and ensures reliable, in-sequence transport of messages with congestion control like TCP.

RTCDataChannel can work in either reliable mode (analogous to TCP) or unreliable mode (analogous to UDP). The first guarantees the transmission of messages and also the order in which they are delivered. This takes extra overhead, thus potentially making this mode slower. The latter does not guarantee every message will get to the other side nor what order they get there. This removes the overhead, allowing this mode to work much faster.

Furthermore, in the case of WebRTC, SCTP sits on top of the Datagram Transport Layer Security (DTLS) protocol, which is derivative of SSL, and provides communication security for datagram protocols. In particular, using DTLS, WebRTC guarantees that every peer connection is automatically encrypted and, in particular (Fig. 2):

- messages are not readable if they are stolen while in transit between peers;
- a third party cannot publish messages within the ADGT overlay network;
- messages can not be altered while in transit;
- the encryption algorithm is fast enough to support the highest possible bandwidth between peers.

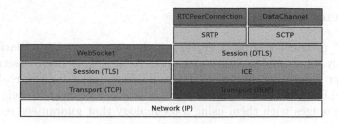

Fig. 2. WebRTC and WebSocket protocol stack.

3.2 WebSocket

The Web has been traditionally tied to the request/response paradigm of HTTP. Nevertheless, with the need to have a more and more dynamic web, new technologies such as AJAX have emerged. However, all of these technologies are not well suited for low latency applications, carrying the overhead of HTTP.

The WebSocket specification defines an API establishing an interactive communication session between a web browser and a server. With this API, the client and the server can make a persistent full-duplex connection between them and send data to each other at any time. The main advantage is that the client can send messages to a server and receive event-driven responses without having to poll the server for a reply.

3.3 Geolocation

The Geolocation API defines a high-level interface to location information associated with the device. The API itself is agnostic of the underlying location information sources: location can be indiscriminately obtained from a Global Positioning System (GPS), inferred from network signals such as IP address, RFID, Wi-Fi and Bluetooth MAC addresses, and GSM/CDMA cell IDs, as well as user input.

The API provides the location information represented by latitude and longitude coordinates. The API is designed to enable both "one-shot" position requests and repeated position updates, as well as the ability to explicitly query the cached positions.

3.4 ECMAScript

ECMAScript is a scripting language specification standardized by ECMA International. JavaScript is one of the most known implementation of the language.

The current version of the ECMAScript Language Specification standard is ECMAScript 2015 (6th Edition) and introduces language support for classes, constructors, and the `extend` keyword for inheritance. Moreover, it provides a way to load and manage module dependencies, new `Map` and `Set` objects, `Promise` objects and many other features.

4   Implementation

The ADGT protocol has been implemented using Open Web Platform technologies only. Our implementation, named Adgt.js, has been designed as an ECMAScript 6 software library that can be freely used for the realization of P2P-based LBSs, where it is important to discovery geographic neighbors and exchange messages with them using a technology that guarantees security and data encryption.

In particular, we have defined and written a JavaScript `Peer` class that represents the ADGT peer. This class is characterized by a `Descriptor`, *i.e.*, an unique identifier of the peer in the network and its geographic location. This latter implements the `Position` interface defined in the Geolocation API and represents the position of the peer at a given time, but also its altitude and its speed.

Furthermore, the `Peer` class contains a reference to a `GeoBucket` object that, as the name says, implements the peculiar routing table of the ADGT protocol. Our GeoBucket implementation consists of a wrapper of the new ECMAScript 6 `Set` class, whose elements are nodes of the network. The `GeoBucket` class, in addition to being a collection of nodes, presents functionalities for the management of geographic neighborhood, therefore to add and remove nodes that approach and move away from the peer, and to update the information about the geographic locations of the neighbors.

In Adgt.js, neighbors are represented by the `RemoteNode` class, which actually realizes the P2P connection with other peers, through WebRTC technologies. More specifically, this class allows to connect to another peer of the ADGT network using the `RTCPeerConnection` interface, and to directly send a message to it with the `DataChannel` interface. In this way, all data exchanges between network nodes—such as position updates as well as peer discovery messages—are realized using WebRTC.

`DataChannel`s are also used as signaling channels. In fact, signaling methods and protocols, *i.e.*, the mechanisms required to coordinate communication and to send control messages, are not specified by WebRTC. WebRTC assumes the existence of a communication coordination process, allowing clients to exchange session control messages (outlined by the JavaScript Session Establishment Protocol [7]), error messages, media metadata such as codecs and codec settings, bandwidth and media types, key data, used to establish secure connections, and network data, such as a IP address and port, without placing constraints on the signaling technology.

Although a signaling service consumes relatively little bandwidth and CPU per client, signaling servers for a popular application may have to handle a lot of messages, from different locations, with high levels of concurrency. For this reason, we have decided to distribute the responsibility to act as signaling servers among all the peers of the network, using `DataChannel`s. In particular, the peer discovery operation has been implemented in a way that when a peer receives the list of neighbors from the peer that has contacted, the latter acts also as a signaling server between the first and the possible peers which have to be contacted.

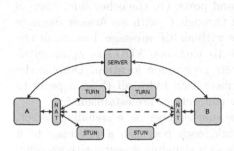

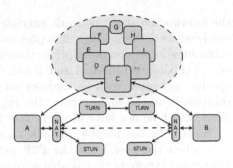

Fig. 3. Using ICE to cope with NATs and firewalls.

Fig. 4. Peers of the network act as signaling servers in our implementation.

A direct connection between two peers can be achieved by means of a signaling server that coordinates the communication. Actually, a signaling server by itself is not sufficient to overcome the complexities of real-world networking, that can be solved with the use of ICE technology, as shown in Fig. 3.

To increase system scalability, Adgt.js has been designed to be architecturally different from what depicted in Fig. 3, inasmuch the operations of signaling between two peers that are attempting to establish a connection are provided by an intermediary peer rather than from a centralized server. Figure 4 represents the architecture of our implementation.

In particular, the peer designed to act as a signaler between two other peers is the one that allowed the other two to get to know each other, at the end of the discovery process. Figure 5 shows the sequence of messages exchanged during a discovery operation, in the event that peer A wants to start a conversation with peer B, just discovered by means of peer C. After peers A and C have exchanged discovery messages, where A asks for a specific geographic location and C returns a list of known peers near the location indicated including B, if peer A wants to add peer B to its GeoBucket, peer C will be the signaler among them. The first message that A has to send to B through C is an Offer message, which is a serialized session description message, followed by an ICE message with

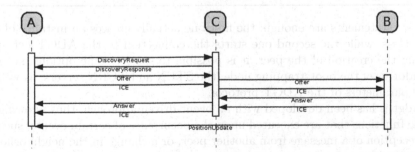

Fig. 5. Messages exchanged during discovery operation.

the information about network interfaces and ports. On the other side, when B receives the Offer message, it replies to A through C with an Answer message containing its session description, therefore with an ICE message. Finally, at the end of this initialization, A and B can directly exchange ADGT or application-specific messages, such as updates on their geographic location. Despite the complexity of the architecture, the implementation hides all these aspects to users, which do not have to worry how the connections are established.

Since it is not always possibile to use another peer as a signaling server, e.g., when the peer joins the P2P network, each peer has a reference to a BootstrappingNode that is able to operate as a signaling server for those peers that log on to the network for the first time. We have implemented this kind of signaling server using the Node.js framework[6] and the WebSocket protocol. The choice of adopting Node.js, which is an open-source runtime environment based on Google's V8 JavaScript engine, has allowed to reuse most of the code written for the ADGT implementation. Furthermore, the WebSocket protocol allowed us to encrypt the signaling and negotiation communication like the standard HTTPS protocol works, ensuring that no one can intercept messages sent to the server to figure out which peers are talking to whom.

Adgt.js has been released online[7] with a free and open-source software license and can be used as a web application framework without restrictions.

5   Realizing LBSs with Adgt.js

To design and implement LBSs with Adgt.js is easy, not much different from making a simple web page. Moreover, being Adgt.js an implementation of a P2P protocol, it is affordable by whoever, as it may run over any type of device, not being particularly demanding in terms of computing and memory resources.

In order to use the Adgt.js web application framework, it is sufficient to include the JavaScript file in the HTML page using the src attribute in the <script> tag. Once the Adgt.js is included, it is already possible to create a new ADGT peer, as shown in Listing 1.1.

Listing 1.1. Creating a new ADGT peer.

```
1  var peer = new Peer(options);
2  peer.connect();
```

Two statements are enough: the first one actually creates an instance of the Peer class, while the second one starts the connection to the ADGT network. During the creation of the peer, it is possible to specify some options, such as the address of the bootstrapping node, the STUN and TURN servers, as well as some parameters of the ADGT protocol.

Adgt.js has been developed with an event-driven approach, thus allowing to define functions that are executed upon the occurrence of certain events, such as the reception of a message from another peer, or a change in the neighborhood.

---

[6] https://nodejs.org.

[7] https://github.com/brambilla/adgt.js.

In Listing 1.2, it is reported how to set listener functions for two kinds of events: `neighbors` and `data`. The first event occurs when the neighborhood of the peer changes, while the second one fires when the peer receives any type of data from near peers. The callback functions allow us to manage the set of neighbor `descriptors` and received `data`, respectively.

Listing 1.2. Setting listeners for peer events.

```
1  peer.on('neighbors', function(descriptors) {  });
2  peer.on('data', function(data) {  });
```

To send `data` to the geographic neighbors of the peer, it is sufficient to invoke the `send` method, as in Line 1 of Listing 1.3.

Listing 1.3. Sending data to neighbors and updating peer's position.

```
1  peer.send(data);
2  ...
3  peer.move(position);
```

In case the geographic location of the peer changes, it is sufficient to use the `move` method to automatically trigger the position update process, that involves the transmission of a message to the neighbors and the removal of peers no longer included in the GeoBucket (Line 3 of Listing 1.3).

Fig. 6. The LBS developed with ADGT.js, running on Firefox for Android.

We have implemented and published online[8] a simple LBS that illustrates the ease of use of Adgt.js and represents a building block for more sophisticated applications. The LBS shows on a map the peers connected to the network, *i.e.*, visitors of the web page, that are at a maximum distance of 40 km. Neighbor discovery and connection establishment is entrusted to Adgt.js. Regarding the map, we have adopted Leaflet.js[9], a widely used open-source JavaScript library used to build web mapping applications. Figure 6 is a screenshot taken from an Android smartphone running the LBS on Firefox for mobile.

---

[8] https://brambilla.github.io/map/index.html.

[9] http://leafletjs.com.

This LBS only requires to update the geographic location of the peer and change the marker on the map with the position of the browser obtained with the Geolocation API, as shown in Listing 1.4.

Listing 1.4. Managing current position of the device.

```
1  navigator.geolocation.watchPosition(function(position) {
2    peer.move(position);
3    var latLng = L.latLng(position.coords.latitude, position.coords.longitude);
4    marker.setLatLng(latLng);
5    if (position.coords.speed > 0) { marker.setIcon(icon_heading); }
6    marker.setRotationAngle(position.coords.heading);
7    map.panTo(latLng);
8  });
```

In addition, when a change in the neighborhood happens, all the markers on the map representing neighbors are updated as in Listing 1.5.

Listing 1.5. Managing changes of neighborhood.

```
1   peer.on("neighbors", function(descriptors) {
2     markers.clearLayers();
3     for (var index in descriptors) {
4       var position = descriptors[index].position;
5       var latLng = L.latLng(position.coords.latitude, position.coords.longitude);
6       var rotationAngle = position.coords.heading;
7       if (position.coords.speed > 0) {
8         markers.addLayer(L.marker(latLng, {rotationAngle: rotationAngle, icon: icon_heading}));
9       } else {
10        markers.addLayer(L.marker(latLng, {rotationAngle: rotationAngle, icon: icon}));
11      }
12    }
13  });
```

6   Related Work

As WebRTC has reached a good level of maturity and has been adopted by major web browsers, researchers have started to investigate the potentiality of this technology. Tindall and Harwood presented an implementation of an unstructured P2P protocol using WebRTC [8]. Bevilacqua *et al.* described a network architecture for the development of browser-based P2P web applications [9]. Such a work has the disadvantage of requiring a nonstandard browser plugin for signaling. A framework for decentralized online social networks is presented by Disterhoft and Graffi [10]. The main differences between our implementation and the above-mentioned ones, apart from the fact that the P2P schemes are different, reside in the signaling process. Indeed, in Adgt.js, signaling is a distributed mechanism, not supplied by a single central server.

7   Conclusion

In this paper we have presented Adgt.js, a web application framework that enables the realization of completely decentralized LBSs, being a cross-platform implementation of the ADGT georeferenced P2P overlay scheme.

We have described the implementation and the architecture of the developed framework, paying particular attention to the adopted technologies. It has also been accurately described how to use the framework, with reference to a concrete example. Moreover, the framework has been published online, together with the example, which is freely usable.

Regarding future work, we will investigate the performance of the implemented framework, with respect to technological aspects such as battery drain of mobile devices, also compared with previous results obtained in simulation. Furthermore, we will evaluate the adoption of even more innovative technologies, such as Web Workers[10] and Object Real-Time Communications for WebRTC.[11]

References

1. Florian, M., Pieper, F., Baumgart, I.: Establishing location-privacy in decentralized long-distance geocast services. Ad Hoc Netw. **37**, 110–121 (2016)
2. Brambilla, G., Picone, M., Amoretti, M., Zanichelli, F.: An adaptive peer-to-peer overlay scheme for location-based services. In: IEEE 13th International Symposium on Network Computing and Applications (NCA), Cambridge, MA, August 2014
3. Grigorik, I.: High Performance Browser Networking. O'Reilly Media, Sebastopol (2013)
4. Rosenberg, J.: Interactive Connectivity Establishment (ICE): A Protocol for Network Address Translator (NAT) Traversal for Offer/Answer Protocols, Internet Engineering Task Force (IETF). Request for Comments **5245**, April 2010
5. Rosenberg, J., Mahy, R., Matthews, P., Wing, D.: Session Traversal Utilities for NAT (STUN), Internet Engineering Task Force (IETF). Request for Comments **5389**, October 2008
6. Mahy, R., Matthews, P., Rosenberg, J.: Traversal Using Relays around NAT (TURN): Relay Extensions to Session Traversal Utilities for NAT (STUN), Internet Engineering Task Force (IETF). Request for Comments **5766**, April 2010
7. Uberti, J., Jennings, C.: Javascript Session Establishment Protocol, Internet Engineering Task Force (IETF), Network Working Group, February 2012
8. Tindall, N., Harwood, A.: Peer-to-peer between browsers: cyclon protocol over WebRTC. In: IEEE International Conference on Peer-to-Peer Computing (P2P) (2015)
9. Bevilacqua, A., Boemio, P., Romano, S.P.: Introducing ufo.js: a browser-oriented P2P network. In: International Conference on Computing, Networking and Communications (ICNC) (2014)
10. Disterhoft, A., Graffi, K.: Protected chords in the web: secure P2P framework for decentralized online social networks. In: IEEE International Conference on Peer-to-Peer Computing (P2P) (2015)

---

[10] https://html.spec.whatwg.org/multipage/workers.html.
[11] https://www.w3.org/community/ortc/.

VM Image Repository and Distribution Models for Federated Clouds: State of the Art, Possible Directions and Open Issues

Nishant Saurabh[✉], Dragi Kimovski, Simon Ostermann, and Radu Prodan

Distributed and Parallel Systems, Institute of Informatics,
University of Innsbruck, 6020 Innsbruck, Austria
{nishant,dragi,simon,radu}@dps.uibk.ac.at
http://www.dps.uibk.ac.at

Abstract. The emerging trend of Federated Cloud models enlist virtualization as a significant concept to offer a large scale distributed Infrastructure as a Service collaborative paradigm to end users. Virtualization leverage Virtual Machines (VM) instantiated from user specific templates labelled as VM Images (VMI). To this extent, the rapid provisioning of VMs with varying user requests ensuring Quality of Service (QoS) across multiple cloud providers largely depends upon the image repository architecture and distribution policies. We discuss the possible state-of-art in VMI storage repository and distribution mechanisms for efficient VM provisioning in federated clouds. In addition, we present and compare various representative systems in this realm. Furthermore, we define a design space, identify current limitations, challenges and open trends for VMI repositories and distribution techniques within federated infrastructure.

Keywords: VMI storage repository · VMI distribution · Federated cloud

1 Introduction

The *Cloud Computing* is a ubiqutous global paradigm, empowering users to acquire on demand compute resources without the onus of owning, managing or maintaining them. In this context, one of the important concept is *Infrastructure as a Service* (IaaS) [8] cloud model. Virtualization [9] is a key technology employed in cloud data centers to support IaaS, allowing users to instantiate multiple Virtual Machines (VM). The instantiated VMs constitute users application environment to be adequately scaled by elastic on-demand provisioning in response to variable load to achieve increased utilization efficiency at lower operational cost, while guaranteeing *Quality of Service* (QoS) [7] to end users.

VMs in general, are instantiated using specific templates termed as *VM Images* that are stored in proprietary repositories, leading to provider lock-in [10] and hampering portability or simulataneous usage of multiple federated Clouds.

© Springer International Publishing AG 2017
F. Desprez et al. (Eds.): Euro-Par 2016 Workshops, LNCS 10104, pp. 260–271, 2017.
DOI: 10.1007/978-3-319-58943-5_21

In addition, the proprietary repositories do not take into account underlying application characterstics resulting to deployment and instantiation overheads.

To this end, VMI repository research extends to a novel operational environment aiming to mitigate limitations with regard to VMI storage and distribution for federated cloud infrastructures. Such a Large Scale Distributed Virtual Environment for VMI repository imminently benefit the elastic auto-scaling of diverse applications on cloud resources based on their fluctuating load. Henceforth, VM interoperability across multiple cloud infrastructures is achieved without provider lock-in, only to justify the virtualization technology as a universal cloud IaaS model.

In this paper, we split the state of the art contention into two parts, namely VMI Repository and VMI Distribution. Initially, we emphasize the required consideration to treat image repository beyond the typical storage systems and henceforth, detail the factors defining the VMI Repository with respect to functionality, architecture, VMI management and cloud federation aspects. Furthermore, we discuss the existing VMI distribution tecnhiques and suitability of each with regard to varying VMI repository architecture meant to provide middleware services in federated cloud models.

To examine current advances corresponding to our discussion, we consider as case studies, various production systems, in particular namely: Virtual Machine Repository Catalog (VMRC)[1] [11], Amazon Image Service[2] and Openstack Glance[3]. In our view, these three systems define the closest state of the art of VMI Repository and furthermore, each of the systems has some common and unique set of functionalities to offer. Our discussion focusses on VMI repository service's rationales, distribution models and their respective usage scenario in case of multiple cloud providers. To be concise, we have investigated possible measures required to allow flexibility for rapid VM provisioning appropriated by image repository and distribution models. Finally, we identify open issues and suggest future research directions regarding federated VMI middleware repository.

The contributions of the paper are:

- An overview of the existing storage modelling factors and its application to VM Image repository design.
- An analysis and classification of VM Image storage and distribution techniques applicable to federated cloud models.
- A synopsis of the current state of the research area, identifying trends and open issues.
- A vision on possible future directions.

The remainder of this paper is organized as follows. Initially, Sect. 2 surveys the existing production systems. Section 3 outlines possible state of the art to

---

[1] http://www.grycap.upv.es/vmrc/index.php.
[2] http://docs.aws.amazon.com/AWSEC2/latest/UserGuide/AMIs.html.
[3] http://docs.openstack.org/developer/glance/.

design the VM image repository along with the distribution mechanisms in federated cloud infrastructures. We discuss and analyze the quality rationales of surveyed image repository systems in Sect. 4, followed by possible future directions and open issues. We conclude the paper in Sect. 5.

2 Existing VMI Repository Systems

The design of most of the existing VMI repositories are subjected to specific hypervisor technology concerning the cloud architecture. In general, users interaction is provided through a web interface and corresponding attached APIs to these repository systems with very basic functionalities. Hence, the VMI and associated metadata management are left onto the user based manual actions instead of allowing automated query executions leading to error-prone usage.

To mention a few such systems, VMware[4] repository system at its disposal allows upload and download of images by authorized users. In addition, a weak virtual management system for existing VMI categorization is intact, enabling to search for the required images corresponding to the target application of the user. Another VMI specific repository by Science Clouds[5] only allow download of exisiting stored images and evades the upload or indexing functionality of any user specific VMIs. FutureGrid [15], an experimental system for HPC and cloud based applications provisions another image repository with federated storage systems empowering the users to avail upload, download and update functionality with limited metadata informations through REST interface.

Apart from above mentioned systems, in this section, we give a detailed account of some VMI repositories adopted by private and public cloud infrastructures, namely *VMRC* (Virtual Machine Repository Catalog) [11], *Openstack Glance*[6] and *Amazon Image Service*[7]. In our view, these three systems are closest to the state of the art in the field of VMI repository service with respect to image storage and corresponding image functionalities as a middleware service.

2.1 VMRC

The *VMRC* (Virtual Machine Repository Catalogue) [11] modelled as a client-server based architecture enables user to upload, store and catalog VMIs. It also serves as a matchmaking collaborative system to facilitate sharing of images availing through the usage of extensive metadata, where independent users can search and retreive appropriate stored VMI using the catalog functionality.

In general, VMRC is represented into four modules namely *Storage, Repository, Catalog and Client*. The *Storage* module handles the appropriate mediums to store VMIs, while *Repository* provisions support for transfer of VMIs within different storage mediums. In addition, *Repository* module also facilitates user

---

[4] http://www.vmware.com/appliances.
[5] http://scienceclouds.org/marketplace.
[6] http://docs.openstack.org/developer/glance/.
[7] http://docs.aws.amazon.com/AWSEC2/latest/UserGuide/AMIs.html.

authorizations in case of VMI uploads. In order to index the stored images, *Catalog* module is used accompanied by unique matchmaking algorithms to retreive the appropriate images suiting the users requirement. The easy usage of the mentioned functionalities are supported with an end-user command line application *Client* module.

2.2   OpenStack Glance

Glance[8] in general, is a middleware service enabling users to upload independent data assets including VMI. In particular, glance image service provisions various functionalities including discovering, registering and retrieving images. In order to provide respository based service, federation of storage systems are attached. These storage systems with varying capabilities ranging from simple file systems to object based storage are located within varying regions to manage VMI services.

Glance integrated with Openstack virtualized infrastructure, follows a client-server based centralized architecture which provides a REST API for its users to access image functionality. Furthermore, it provides an interface to its various components managing internal operations as shown in Fig. 1 to openstack. Any REST API based request from the client is accessed through *domain controller* component which handles services corresponding to different layers, where each layer appropriates to perform a specific task. These tasks include authorization governing policies regarding the actions of a user to a particuar image such as verifying access rights to add, update or delete a VMI or checking quota of storage capacity attached to a user for adding an image at a particular region etc. It is to be observed that policies regarding the authorization, storage quota could

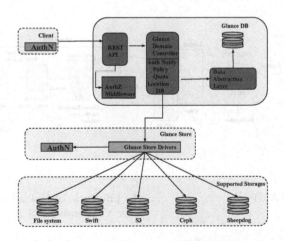

Fig. 1. Glance architecture

---

[8] http://docs.openstack.org/developer/glance/.

vary and depend upon the organization implementing glance domain controller component specific to its infrastructure.

Another component *Glance Store*, handling VMI storage provides an uniform access to various attached storage systems. It provides a series of library functions to execute VMI operations requested by the user with regards to authorization inputs received from *Domain Controller*. The library functions are basically file based operations such as upload, update, delete etc.

The *Domain Controller* also provides an interface to centralized *Glance Database* API, which contains several methods for moving image metadata to and from attached persistent storage systems. These methods basically references to metadata regardging creating, updating, retreiving VMI with respect to parameters like image identifier, image location, image context etc. Once image is registered onto the centralized database, it is deemed appropriate to be instantiated with specific configurations within a particular region or loaction.

2.3   Amazon Image Service

Amazon Elastic Compute Cloud (EC2) services is one of the most poular commerical public cloud infrastructure. In the early stages, *Amazon Web Services* (AWS) only provided functionality to create *Amazon Machine Images* (AMI)[9] onto its own infrastructure instead of allowing upload of user specific images as shown in Fig. 2a. The AMI is similar to VMI, which includes a template for the root volume for VM to be instantiated consisting of OS, application server and underlying target application services. Furthermore, AMI also comprise of permisssion authorizations to launch corresponding AMI.

However, recently AWS added a VM export/import functionality to import and export VMI from user specific environment onto Amazon EC2. This

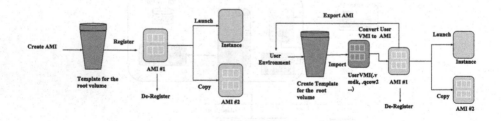

(a) Life Cycle of AMI creation onto AWS.

(b) Life cycle of Upload of User VMI onto AWS

Fig. 2. AWS VM image services depicting creation and upload of amazon infrastructure supported user VMI.

---

[9] http://docs.aws.amazon.com/AWSEC2/latest/UserGuide/AMIs.html.

functionality enables a user to include its own configurations, security and compliance requirement within image intended for target VM instance.

AWS provides a client interface to upload VMI. As a part of import functionality, user specific images are converted to AWS EC2 AMI and stored onto *Elastic Block store* or *S3* data store of Amazon. The AMI identifier is further mapped onto a region as specified by the user, hence facilitating the instatiation of VMs. AWS also allows the user to have the authority of enabling the stored images to be either private, shared with specific AWS users or to be public to whole community.

3   State of the Art

In Sect. 2, we overviewed the existing image repository systems. Although most of them support the basic functionalities of upload and download of VMIs, the eminent federation functionalities including repository management, interoperability etc. are left onto the user based manual actions. In this section, we focus on the possible state of the art in terms of VMI storage and distribution for federated clouds. While we state some of the common functionalities, we also define the VMI and corresponding repository operations, currently missing in the existing production systems.

3.1   VM Image Storage Repository

VM Image usually in size of GigaByte (GB) contains a bare operating system (OS), or an operating system with user defined software and applications. In specific cases, additional data is also attached to corresponding image template. A typical example of such VMI is running an Earth Observational Data processing cloud application [12] with large sized sattelite imagery data. The storage of such diverse images require a scalable and elastic storage model for optimized VMI distribution across the multiple cloud providers. Furthermore, image repository is also necessitated to act as a middleware providing services beyond the typical storage repositories. Placek and Buyya et al. [6] defines storage systems taxonomy built upon a number of factors. To this extent, we discuss the state of the art of VMI storage Repository including functionality, architecture and federated interoperability concerning VMI application characteristics.

Functionality. The VMI Repository is customary to have a wide array of behavioral functions beyond the typical storage and retreival offered by general purpose storage systems. In custom, a VMI is a collection of complex set of bytes with a sequence of functional descriptions specific to user defined applications. A large sized VMI can also be splitted into fragments, where each fragment refers to a specific functionality [13]. These attributes make it difficult to inject updates if any, directly to the stored VMI or functional fragments. In case of decentralized repository with geographically distributed storage systems, propagating updates to various stored image replicas is even more of a gruelling task. Hence, VMI repository is specifically to be characterised as a persistent storage system restricted to the write-once and read-many feature. In this category of storage, any updates to the VMI propells the removal of old image and creating a new image onto the repository. However, the concept of VM contextualization can be utilized by the incorporation of existing tools like *Chef*[10] and *Puppet*[11], hence facilitating VMI size optimization by synthesizing and pruning the un-necessary files or analyzing and fragmenting the VMI with respect to functionality in case of large sized images encompassed with various services. This feature indeed helps in reducing the storage cost with faster distribution and VM provisioning across cloud boundaries.

In addition, the modern cloud providers maintains a list of VMI's provisioned for sharing amongst users. These images are typically not user specific, instead consists of some most commonly used OS platforms or applications. The repositories facilitating sharing of such images deliver pubish/share functional service, inhibiting the censorship of stored VMI.

One of the other interesting functionality of VMI repository is providing a homogenous interface to an array of attached storage systems. These evident systems either coupled or decoupled to cloud storage are accomplished with varying capabilities which provide unique interface to interact with. In such cases VMI Repository has much of a task to act as a middleware entity instead of just a storage service.

Repository Architecture. The repository architecture in general, determines the operational boundaries of stored resource, ultimately forging behavior and functionality corresponding to the application services, a resource provide [6]. In our paper, VMI is the stored resource and the operational boundary corresponds to the factors affecting distribution of images to multiple cloud providers. Typically, image storage repository can be classified as *Centralized* or *Distributed* on the basis of the architecture it follows. In this section, we discuss the functional capabilities and limitation of pre-mentioned architectural models to the applications of VMI.

Centralized. In most of cloud infrastructures, a centralized image server serves as a repository to host a catalog of VMIs. These repositories maintain a central index of stored images which are either produced locally or imported from user specific environment.

In general, Centralized repository can be either classified as globally or locally central [6]. The globally centralized model contains a single image server handling requests for many users related to VMI functionality such as upload, update, download etc. Such architecture has limited scalability with a single point of failure.

The image repositories within cloud data centres broadly come into category of locally centralized architectures which alleviate independent functionalities

---

[10] http://www.opscode.com/chef.
[11] http://www.puppetlabs.com.

across multiple attached servers. However, VMI repositories under this category as well, faces scalability bottlenecks and failure centric issues, specifically in the case of supporting federated cloud models, where each provider regulate its own trust policies.

Distributed. The recent advances in storage repository architecture has observed existing centralized models evolving into decentralized approaches to achieve scalability and reliability. The reason being, centralized structured models often encounter bandwidth and scalability bottleneck, hence influencing the quality of service.

The essential feature of distributed repository is to compound the image stores within multiple cloud providers interfaced with independent APIs, to be precise a middleware service providing user transparency for the VMI storage at different attached storage systems. Another essential characterstic is to maintain the VMI replicas or chunks placement with respect to fault tolerance techniques used such as *Replication* and *Erasure Coding* [14] respectively in consireation to reduce distribution times aross cloud sites.

VMI Repository Management. The distributed VMI repository enables to maintain a set of VMI replicas or erasure coded chunks to enhance fault tolerance. However, it is as imminent to decide the repository nodes at which replicas should be placed. Initially, the user provides a set of metrics including storage cost, performance based metrics while uploading the image. Moreover, the attached storage systems are accomplished with varying capabilities, hence exists different cost policies and performance metrics for each. The VMI repository system applies a decision making process, placing the replicas onto the storage repositories satisfying the user specifications for initial upload.

Furthermore, every time a user requests for distribution of image to a cloud provider, a learner module track the statistics of the frequency of distribution of image to a specific provider. To this extent, the placement of VMI replicas or chunks concerning factors like image popularity at a particular cloud provider or across cloud boundaries, avoiding vendor lock-in etc. is reshuffled to the image storage repository closer to the region corresponding to the provider with frequent distributions. This greatly improves the geographical scalability of stored images with respect to faster distribution and provisioning.

Federation. VM Images are currently stored by cloud providers in proprietary centralized repositories without considering application characterstics and their runtime requirements, causing high deployment and instantiation overheads. Moreover, users are expected to manually manage the VM Image storage which is tedious, error-prone and time-consuming especially if working with multiple cloud providers. Every cloud provider is highly interested in attracting new customers from other providers. Unfortunately, current users must be familiar with providers repository interfaces and specific VMI formats in order to use them, which is unsurpassable barrier in deploying new images and exploiting provider resources.

The VMI repository for federated cloud models mitigate the user limitations and manages the interoperability of user created images across multiple providers. Once a request is received by the repository to distribute a corresponding VMI onto a cloud provider, an image conversion module is executed to convert VMI to the format suited for the cloud infrastructure, it has to be instantiated on. Hence, facilitating the user with a federation middleware VMI repository, servicing storage and distribution requests of images across a federation of cloud providers to achieve globalised Infrastructure as a Service paradigm.

3.2   VMI Distribution

Modern cloud computing data centers face the key challenge to provide rapid VM provisioning in elastic and scalable manner. To this extent efficient VMI distribution [1–5] onto the physical compute node across cloud providers is an imminent aspect. The distribution process essentially suffers a handicap in case of federated cloud models owing to the inconsiderate VMI Repository architecture offering unscalable services to increasing user requests, and lack of VMI interoperability across multiple clouds as discussed earlier. In this section we discuss some of the popular VMI distribution techniques, focussing to its appropriateness and limitation with reference to repository models for federated clouds.

3.3   Unicast Distribution

Unicast distribution [3], a fairly simple method for distributing VMI works for centralized as well as decentralized image repositories. The VMIs of appropriate format are transferred from the image repository to the destined cloud provider in a sequential manner. This method has a huge drawback in terms of transfer rate specific to increased number of requests within a time interval.

Binary Tree Distribution. In contrast to the naive sequential approach used by Unicast Distribution, binary tree based distribution [3] model follows the parallelized transfer of images. The technique arranges the compute nodes as balanced binary tree. The parent node initiates the image transfer in a sequential fashion followed by the transmission from child nodes at respective levels. However, the transfers are synchronized at every level of the tree to avoid the initiation of transmission from child node until parent's node data is available. Once the intial image transfer from the parent node completes, the receiving node becomes parent itself.

Binary tree distribution of images optimizes the throughput at a lower distribution rate. This technique suits the distrbuted VMI repository architecture, however application within a cross cloud environment is an area of concern with regard to trust policies between multiple infrastructures.

Multicast Distribution. The multicast distribution [3] technique is mostly preferred in local environment. The image chunk packets are distributed to compute nodes registered onto the host node subscribed for multicast transfer. However multicasting of image is not preferred in case of transferring data over network boundaries specifically in the case of multple cloud providers requiring special multicast protocol support at the core of their internal network.

Peer-to-Peer Distribution. In case of Peer-to-Peer distribution [3], a popular bit-torrent protocol [4] is used to distribute VMI to corresponding compute nodes. Using this technique, a torrent file is generated comprising of the URL of the tracker node storing the VMI. Furthermore, the storage node executes the seeder module, to which bit-torrent client started on specific compute nodes across multiple cloud providers interface with. To this end, the compute nodes connect to the tracker using URL and seed images from the host storage node completing efficient transmission.

4 Discussion

In this section, we summarize the main features of three Image repository systems surveyed in Sect. 2. We lead our discussion further by focusing on system-wise decision rationales and possible future research directions.

4.1 Summary

In terms of typical storage systems, the systems we overviewed does provide basic functionalities including upload, store and update VMI. On one hand, VMRC provisions indexing of images via *Catalog* functionality, while Amazon allows publish/share of VMIs with respect to appropriate authorization in each case. Although, the discussed production systems qualify for the VMI storage functionality, none of them provide service to facilitate interoperability of images over multiple cloud providers. As mentioned, Openstack Glance and Amazon comprise of proprietary image repository, while VMRC doesnt contribute to interoperability issue, instead has a unique VM matchmaking service for sharing of images. Moreover, the locally centralized architectural model of defined systems inhibit scalable image distribution and hence amounts to delayed VM provisioning. Specifically, the current state of the art in consideration with these respective systems represents a wide gap compared to the possible state of the art for VMI Repository and Distribution models for federated clouds.

4.2 Possible Directions and Open Issues

Based on the survey of studied systems and possible state of the art presented in the paper, we propose visions on directions and open issues. One of the promising orientation in this domain, in our view, is interoperability and portability support of VMIs over multiple providers by image repositories. This is particularly important to realise the Cloud IaaS as an all-inclusive paradigm. One way of enhancing interoperability lies in the managment of images by introducing the vendor lock-in objective in consideration to trade-off establishment with *QoS* cloud metrics and providing a set of optimal solutions to the user with image store options to avoid vendor lock-in. This would require extensive analysis of metadata informations of specific VMIs including funtional descriptions and requirements. An another way of solving interoperability lies in VM contextualization, where VMIs stored functional fragments can be assembled by minimal virtual machines running at destination cloud sites with specific requirements.

Secondly, VMI repository is required to enforce optimization techniques for VMI replica management over the distributed repository to enhance the distribution of images for rapid VM provisioning. In particular, the distribution techniques and its application in different cloud environments, to be precise within same and cross cloud networks is needed to be included as an optimization objective.

5   Conclusion

VMI Repository systems and distribution mechanisms attibuted to underlying VMI characteristics is a promising and essential research area. However, there is a need to look beyond the typical storage systems with regard to VMI operational boundaries in terms of efficient distribution and VM provisioning. Henceforth, realizing IaaS as a cloud service beyond a specific provider. In this regard, we discussed the possible state of the art in VMI Repository and Distribution models. We pointed out various factors to define a design space for image repository and prior contributing scenarios to federated infrastructure. We also compared three representative image repository systems identiying the existing gap between current state of the art and the possible design space. Hence, highlighting some of the open issues and possible future directions, including VMI management as a repository service for enhanced distribution, image interoperability support across multiple providers.

Acknowledgments. This work was accomplished as a part of project *ENTICE: "dEcentralised repositories for traNsparent and efficienT vIrtual maChine opErations"* (http://www.entice-project.eu/), funded by the European Unions Horizon 2020 research and innovation programme under grant agreement No. 644179. The authors would also like to thank anonymous reviewers for their valuable comments.

References

1. Freimuth, D.M., Pappas, V., Sathaye, S.: Virtual machine image distribution network. US Patent Ap. 13/542,421, 9 January 2014
2. Peng, C., Kim, M., Zhang, Z., Lei, H.: VDN: virtual machine image distribution network for cloud data centers. In: Greenberg, A.G., Sohraby, K. (eds.) INFOCOM, pp. 181–189. IEEE (2012)

3. Schmidt, M., Fallenbeck, N., Smith, M., Freisleben, B.: Efficient distribution of virtual machines for cloud computing. In: Proceedings of the 2010 18th Euromicro Conference on Parallel, Distributed and Network based Processing, PDP 2010, Washington, DC, USA, pp. 567–574. IEEE Computer Society (2010)
4. Wartel, R., Cass, T., Moreira, B., Roche, E., Guijarro, M., Goasguen, S., Schwickerath, U.: Image distribution mechanisms in large scale cloud providers. In: CloudCom, pp. 112–117. IEEE Computer Society (2010)
5. Wu, D., Zeng, Y., He, J., Liang, Y., Wen, Y.: On P2P mechanisms for VM image distribution in cloud data centers: modeling, analysis and improvement. In: CloudCom, p. 5057. IEEE Computer Society (2012)
6. Placek, M., Buyya, R.: A Taxonomy of Distributed Storage Systems. www.cloudbus.org/reports/DistributedStorageTaxonomy.pdf
7. Bardsiri, A.K., Hashemi, S.M.: Qos metrics for cloud computing services evaluation. Int. J. Intell. Syst. Appl. (IJISA) 6, 27 (2014)
8. Iosup, A., Prodan, R., Epema, D., Benchmarking, I.C.: Approaches, challenges, and experience. In: Proceedings of 5th Workshop on Many-Task Computing on Grids and Supercomputers (MTAGS) (2012)
9. Uhlig, R., Neiger, G., Rodgers, D., Santoni, A.L., Martins, F.C.M., Anderson, A.V., Bennett, S.M., Kagi, A., Leung, F.H., Smith, L.: Intel virtualization technology. Computer 38(5), 48–56 (2005)
10. Opara-Martins, J., Sahandi, R., Tian, F.: Critical analysis of vendor lock-in and its impact on cloud computing migration: a business perspective. J. Cloud Comput. 5(1), 18 p. (2016). Article No. 54
11. Carrin, J.V., Molt, G., De Alfonso, C., Caballer, M., Hernndez, V.: A generic catalog and repository service for virtual machine images. In: 2nd International ICST Conference on Cloud Computing (CloudComp 2010) (2010)
12. Dana, P., Silviu, P., Marian, N., Marc, F., Daniela, Z.: Earth observation data processing in distributed systems. Informatica 34(4), 463–476 (2010)
13. Kecskemeti, G., Attila, K., Zsolt, N.: Developing Interoperable and Federated Cloud Architecture, pp. 1–398. IGI Global (2016). Web: 15 May 2016. doi:10.4018/978-1-5225-0153-4
14. Aguilera, M.K., Janakiraman, R., Xu, L.: Using erasure codes efficiently for storage in a distributed system. In: Proceedings of the 2005 International Conference on Dependable Systems and Networks, DSN 2005, Washington, DC, USA, pp. 336–345. IEEE Computer Society (2005)
15. Diaz, J., von Laszewski, G., Wang, F., Younge, A., Fox, G.: Futuregrid Image repository: a generic catalog and storage system for heterogenous virtual machine images. In: Third IEEE International Conference on Coud Computing Technology and Science (CloudCom2011) (2011)

TRACE: Generating Traces from Mobility Models for Distributed Virtual Environments

Emanuele Carlini[1](✉), Alessandro Lulli[1,2], and Laura Ricci[1,2]

[1] Istituto di Scienza e Tecnologie dell'Informazione (ISTI),
Consiglio Nazionale delle Ricerche (CNR), Rome, Italy
{emanuele.carlini,alessandro.lulli,laura.ricci}@isti.cnr.it,
{lulli,ricci}@di.unipi.it
[2] Dipartimento di Informatica, Università di Pisa, Pisa, Italy

Abstract. The development and evaluation of a proper mobility model is an essential feature to evaluate a system that manages a virtual world. In distributed virtual environments, this is also more important because each avatar requires a consistent view of the world that usually is splitted on multiple machines. Several models have been proposed in the literature to describe avatars' mobility, but a single environment supporting the generation of traces from different models to enable a simple comparison of them is still lacking. In this work we present a tool that implements popular mobility models and supports the generation of traces generated by them. This may help developers to easily validate their systems using several mobility models. Our tool provides a unified format to describe the traces, enables the generation of traces for thousands of avatars and defines an API enabling the integration of additional models.

1 Introduction

A common trait of many virtual environments is the fact that the behaviour of avatars depends mostly on what happen in their immediate surroundings. This fact, referred to as *locality*, has been widely exploited to optimize the management of the virtual environments operations at system level. In the last decade many approaches have been proposed to foster the transition of virtual environments from client-server to distributed applications, referred to as Distributed Virtual Environments (DVEs) [14]. Most DVEs architectures heavily rely on the concept of locality to split the virtual world and distribute each part of the world to different machines. In this scenario, each avatar needs to reconstruct its local view of the virtual world by interacting with the host of the nearby avatars. Also, the machines that handle the world need to cooperate to provide a consistent view of the virtual environment. This kind of approach holds for approaches based on unstructured [9,15] and structured [2,10] peer-to-peer technologies, as well as more centralized technologies like cloud computing [13]. For example, in Voronoi-based DVE approaches, the world is assigned to the hosts of the avatars according to a tessellation of the virtual world, which depends on the position of the avatars [9,15]. When avatars move, the assignments change accordingly.

© Springer International Publishing AG 2017
F. Desprez et al. (Eds.): Euro-Par 2016 Workshops, LNCS 10104, pp. 272–283, 2017.
DOI: 10.1007/978-3-319-58943-5_22

Therefore, the description of how avatars move in a DVE is essential to design, validate and compare different DVE architectures.

Performing the above actions in a real setting is an expensive and difficult task, since it requires to organize the setting on multiple machines and involve multiple persons each moving an avatar in the virtual world. Therefore, the solution adopted by the researchers is to simulate avatars' movement in order to validate the specific DVE architecture. Normally, two common ways are considered to simulate avatars' movements, i.e. traces taken from an instance of a real virtual environment application, or synthetic traces generated from mobility models. Real traces are usually a good mean of validation, as they represent what is the actual behaviour of avatars in the virtual worlds [7]. However, they suffer from the same issues of testing a DVE in a real setting: it is difficult to collect real traces and, in particular, they may be not suitable to validate the system on an extreme or specific scenario. Synthetic traces are usually not extremely precise in simulating avatars' movement but present many clear advantages in contrast with real traces [17], such as (i) *scalability*, to stress the DVE support in limit situations, (ii) *reproducibility*, as synthetic traces can be reused on different systems in order to have a common ground for comparison.

As a consequence the best way to evaluate a DVE architecture is to exploit a combination of real and synthetic traces. In this paper we focus on the latter, and we provide the description of a software library we developed to generate synthetic traces using mobility models. Mostly, all the approaches generate synthetic traces with custom specifically developed solutions. This has several drawbacks: (i) it is hard to compare different systems on the same scenario, as exact details on how the traces are generated are usually not released; (ii) researchers spend time to code and test traces and trace generators; (iii) there are no clear reference mobility models that are targeted by the DVE community; (iv) it is difficult to reuse traces because usually they are encoded using specific formats. In order to overcome these drawbacks, we developed TRACE, a software library that generate avatar positions according to mobility models. Initially, we have used TRACE for internal research (such as in [4,5]) but eventually we have made it available for the whole DVE community. TRACE: (i) provides means to generate traces for a wide variety of DVE-based mobility models; (ii) allows to export and reload traces for later uses and comparisons; (iii) works in memory (Java) and with a separate visual tool; (iv) is fully configurable, both on mobility models and the map; (v) is designed for an easy integration of new and personalized mobility models; (vi) uses a unified format in all the mobility models used.

In this paper we present the main features and characteristics of the tool, unravelling important under-the-hood decisions that makes it easy and practical to use. We provide an overview of the tool's API. We show an example of integration of TRACE in an existing DVE support, showing how different traces can be used to test and validate the support.

2   Related Works

Although mobility models have been extensively used, in the last years, in several applicative domains, and in particular for DVE, no tool able to generate multiple models on demand currently exists. A mobility model is usually implemented and used in isolation. For instance, mobility models are one of the most important factors to validate gaming overlays. VON [9], Mopar [18], pSense [16] and Gross et al. [6] is only a brief list of the most popular P2P game overlays that use just random based walker models or random walk between hotspots. Those models are popular thanks to their simplicity: a random walk model only requires a few lines of code and the community generally accepts it as a model able to describe several gaming scenarios. However, different and more complex models exist, that are able describe specific scenarios more precisely. BlueBanana [12] is inspired by the virtual world defined by Second Life. In this world, players gather around a set of hotspots, which usually correspond to towns, or, in general, to points of interest of the virtual world. Using the Least Action Planning trip (LAPT) [11] the avatars select hotspots in close proximity with higher probability. When an avatar visits an hotspot, it stays there for a time drawn from a truncated-Pareto distribution and then moves to another hotspot. In RPGM [8], each player belongs to a group and it moves by following the movement of its group, in order to model the players habit to gather in teams. Similar to the previous, a subset of the authors of this work defined a mobility model called WOW [3]. wow considers also hotspots where players are placed at the start of the game and spawn after death. This model takes into account the team-oriented nature of the scenario, where moving in group is encouraged by the game semantics. However, an avatar may decide to move alone by itself, for instance to take the enemy by surprise. All the above models have been defined and used on specific scenarios. However we think it is important to unify how the models are generated and how they are used.

An interesting approach is that of the game trace archive [7], which collects different real traces with the main aim of defining a common format to collect and record game traces so that these can be easily used. In April 2016 the archive includes 12 traces. Even if this environment presents some similarity with our work, it does not include a mobility model generator.

Triebel et al. [17] study both the mobility of avatars and their interactions. They compare the movement of avatars guided by mobility models versus movements generated by artificial intelligence techniques. Although the latter provides better results, using simple mobility model such as random way point and a random model based on hot spots, give close results, in particular the one based on hot spots. Artificial intelligence movements take into account also the context of the game, must be built specifically for each game and they base their movement on the mobility models. For all these reasons, although specific solutions may get marginal improvements on the validation, we think that the generality of the mobility models is an important way to validate games.

3   The Tool

TRACE is a open-source Java library[1] specifically designed for the experimentation of DVEs that generate traces from mobility models, unifies the output of the models and provides an API to enrich TRACE with additional mobility model implementations. In the following of this section we describe the main characteristics of TRACE, its architecture and the functionalities provided.

TRACE has been primarily designed with the idea of focusing on experimentation and evaluation of distributed virtual environments, therefore most of the terminology used in this section refers to such field. However, we believe that TRACE is flexible enough to be used in other contexts in which a number of entities move across a (virtual) area. In DVEs, avatars are the digital agents of the users in the virtual environment and are associated with a position in the virtual world. They are the moving unit considered in TRACE. Other than avatars, TRACE gives the possibility to specify *static* entities, namely passive objects and hotspots. Passive objects are entities that have a state and can be interacted by avatars (e.g. doors), but unlike avatars are not controlled by an human user. The hotspots are those areas of the virtual environment corresponding to places of interest and where usually is present an higher density of passive and active entities.

In a nutshell, TRACE (Fig. 1 provides an high-level overview of TRACE and Table 1 provides a list of the most important classes of TRACE) takes in input the definition of the virtual environment and the mobility model and outputs

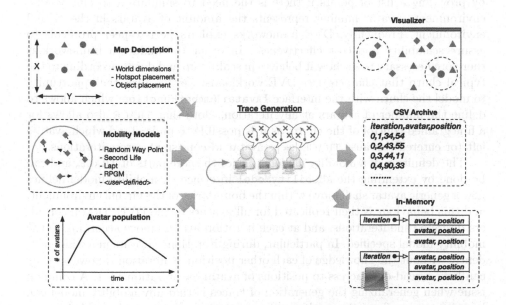

Fig. 1. TRACE overview: inputs and outputs

---

[1] Publicly available at: https://github.com/hpclab/trace.

Table 1. Notable interfaces and classes of TRACE

`AMobilityModel`	Abstract class to define mobility models. The core method is `move` in which the movement of the generic avatar is defined according to the iteration
`AStaticPlacement`	Abstract class to define placement function for static entities, such hotspots and passive objects. This class is called once during the initialization of the virtual environment
`IAvatarNumberFunction`	Interface to define the amount of avatars at any iteration. It is called by the engine before the computation of each iteration to adjust the avatar population

the resulting traces. All the inputs are defined in a *configuration* file composed by a list of key-value tuples that contains all the necessary information for the generation of the traces. Map description defines the rectangular area of the virtual environment, including its size, hotspots and how to assign the position of the passive objects. Note, both hotspots and passive objects can influence the movements of the avatars, but they are not essential for the generation of the traces. Nevertheless, the placements of hotspots and passive objects is totally configurable via the class `AStaticPlacement`, which can be extended to place static entities according to a user-defined function (e.g. randomly across the area of the environment or with high probability placement in hotspots) or by providing a list of points if there is the need to simulate a specific virtual environment. Avatar number represents the amount of avatars in the virtual environment. Frequently, DVE frameworks exploits peer-to-peer protocols to assure scalability and cost effectiveness. In order to validate a framework is therefore necessary to see how it behaves in scaling up and down, according to the typical churn that characterizes DVE workloads. TRACE gives the opportunity to model the churn with the interface `IAvatarNumberFunction`, which allows to define the number of avatars at any iteration. Note that TRACE also allows for a fine grained control of the churn, as it is possible to understand which avatars left (or entered) because TRACE keeps avatar id consistent across iterations.

The definition of a mobility model is one of the core parts of TRACE, and can be done by extending the `AMobilityModel` interface. A mobility model defines how a generic avatar shall move within the boundaries of the virtual environment, and this behaviour is then replicated for all avatars in the DVE. TRACE considers discrete time iterations, and at each iteration avatars move according to the mobility model specified. In particular, during iteration t avatars move independently without the knowledge of each other position at iteration t; however they can have a read-only access to positions of avatars at iteration $t-1$. A common issue when generalizing the generation of traces is that any mobility model can have its own configuration with specific parameter. TRACE resolves this issue by allowing a free definition of the parameters inside the configuration file, leaving to the developer the responsibility of matching the correct parameter within the implementation of the mobility model. For example, the Blue Banana mobility model (whose implementation is described in detail in Sect. 4) is heavily focused on hotspots and therefore define specific properties such as the probability for an avatar of being inside the area of an hotspot.

According to the configuration file, TRACE creates the mobility traces, iteration by iteration, completing each avatar movements before dealing with the next iteration. The `MapVirtualEnvironment` object stores all the information about movements of the avatar, hotspots and passive objects. This class can be accessed in a read-only fashion to be used right away when the generation of the traces is done contextually to the experimentation. Apart from such in-memory data structure, TRACE provides two additional and optional output features, namely *logfile archive* and *visualizer*. These two features can be active at the same time.

With logfile activated, a dump of `VEMap` is saved on disk in a format that represents the movement of all the entities in the virtual environment. Regardless of the model used, TRACE builds a compressed archive consisting of the following files: *(i) configuration*, which contains all the variables to replicate the scenario; *(ii) avatars*, which stores the movement of the avatars; *(iii) hotspots*, which stores the position of the hotspots; *(iv) objects*, which stores the position of the passive objects in the game; *(v) bandwith*, which provides statistics regarding the number of objects in the AoI of each avatar; *(vi) aoiStat*, which provides statistics regarding the number of avatars in the AoI of each avatar. The avatars file contains a snapshot of the position of all the avatars in each time step in a CSV format containing the following values: time step, unique avatar identifier, position of the avatar in the map as a couple (x, y). The resulting file can be loaded at a later time to be used in different experimental evaluation. With the visualizer activated, TRACE provides a graphical representation of the avatars moving across the map. Although this option may slow down the generation of the traces, it results very useful to tune the parameters of a mobility model in order to obtain specific behaviour from avatars.

TRACE comes bundled with the following mobility models already implemented and ready to be used[2]: (i) Random Way Point [1], (ii) RandomWalk, (iii) Lapt [11], and (iv) Blue Banana [12]. In order to provide an hand-on overview on the utilization of TRACE, the next section describes in details BlueBanana and how it has been implemented within TRACE.

4   Case Study: Blue Banana

Avatars move on the map according to realistic mobility traces that have been computed according to the mobility model presented by Legtchenko et al. [12], which simulates avatars movement in a commercial MMOG, Second Life[3]. We provided a preliminary implementation of this mobility model, as well as a comparison with other mobility models in [3], In the model, avatars gather around

---

[2] More mobility models are under development and will be added in the future.
[3] http://secondlife.com/.

Algorithm 1. *AMobilityModel.move()* implementation: BlueBanana

---

Input : *map*: a Map representing the virtual world
    t: the current time
    avatarList: the avatars position at time $t - 1$
Output: the position of the avatars at time t
1 List next = avatarList
2 **forall** *Avatar a∈avatarList* **do**
3   State nextState = markovChain.getNextState(a, markovChain.getState(a))
4   **if** *nextState = E* **then**
5   Point current = a.getPosition()
6   next(a) = current.explore()
7   **else if** *nextState = T* **then**
8   Point t = map.getRandomPoint()
9   Point current = a.getPosition()
10   next(a) = current.moveToward(t)
11   **else**
12   do nothing
13   **end**
14 **end**
15 **return** *next*

---

a set of *hotspots*, which usually correspond to towns, or in general to points of interest in the virtual world. Each hotspot has a circular area characterized by a center and by a radius. Traces generation goes through two phases: *initialization* and *running*.

In the initialization phase, the area of the virtual environment is divided in *hotspot area* and *outland area*. The percentage of the hotspot area is defined by p_{hot} and, consequently $1 - p_{hot}$ represents the outland area. The hotspots are placed randomly in the virtual environment. The number of hotspot is defined by the parameter H_{num}. Their radius is computed such that the total area covered by the hotspots is in accordance to p_{hot}. The parameter p_{den} defines the probability that an avatar would be initially placed in an hotspot, whereas $1 - p_{den}$ defines the probability for an avatar to be initially placed in outland. If the avatar is placed in the outland, its position is chosen uniformly at random on the whole map. Otherwise, an hotspot for the avatar is randomly selected and the avatar is positioned inside the hotspot. The position inside the hotspot is chosen by considering a Zipfian distribution, so to ensure an higher density of players near the center of the hotspot.

The running phase moves the avatars across the virtual environment. The movements are driven by a Markov chain, whose transition probabilities are taken from the original paper [12]. The possible states for an avatar is the following:

- *Halt*(H): the avatar remains in place;
- *Exploration*(E): the avatar explores a specific area. If the avatar is moving inside an hotspot, the new position is chosen according to a power law distribution. Otherwise, the new position is chosen at random;
- *Travelling*(T): the avatar moves straight toward another point in the virtual environment. The new point is chosen in accordance with p_{den}.

Initially every avatar is in state H. At each step t, the model decides the new state according to the probability of moving between states defined in the Markov chain. This mobility model exposes a fair balance between the time spent by avatars in hotspots and outland.

To integrate such model in TRACE the following steps are required:

- *configuration*: it is required to load all the model specific configuration variables such as p_{hot}, H_{num} and p_{den};
- *additional functionalities*: since this model requires a Markov Chain to move the avatars between different states, i.e. (H, E, T), we implemented an utility class to easily know, given a state, which is the next state of the avatar;
- *AMobilityModel*: the core of the model is the implementation of the *AMobilityModel* interface. Specifically, it is required to implement the *move* method where TRACE provides the position of the avatars at time $t - 1$ as well as an object describing the virtual environment where is possible to find the position and size of the hotspots and objects. The model must return the position of the avatars at time t. Refer to Algorithm 1 to an example of the method's definition and implementation.

For what concerns the initialization phase, our implementation at time 0 follows the specification of the initialization phase provided in the original paper. During the running phase, we generate a new position for each avatar (Line 2) and the new state of the avatar according to its previous state (Line 3). Based on the next state, we follow the specification of the model for the *Travelling* state (Line 7), *Exploration* state (Line 4) and *Halt* state (Line 11). We collect all the new positions in a list and we return all the new positions (Line 15).

Finally, to use the new implemented model, it is required to modify the configuration of TRACE, giving a name to the new model, for instance "BlueBanana", and providing the package and class name where it is implemented. Next, it is necessary to set, in the configuration, the property "model BlueBanana", as well as all the configuration parameters required by the model. The execution will use the selected model and generate the traces accordingly.

5   Experimental Results

We implemented TRACE in Java and we make the code publicly available[4]. For all the experiments, we considered a virtual environment composed by a squared region with side having 1500 points. Each avatar has a circular AoI, whose

---

[4] https://github.com/hpclab/trace.

radius is 15 points. Each hotspot has a circular shape, whose radius is 100 points. The simulations ran on a machine equipped with Java 7, 128 Gb of RAM, an AMD Opteron(TM) Processor 6276 with 32 cores @1.4 Ghz. In the following, we present results showing some properties of the models implemented in TRACE. In particular, the avatars' crowding in the virtual world (Sect. 5.1) and the estimated bandwidth consumption to transmit objects of the virtual world (Sect. 5.2). We conclude our experiments with an evaluation of the computational time to generate a mobility model and the scalability of TRACE (Sect. 5.3).

5.1   Evaluating the Crowding Generated

With the terms crowding we refer to the evaluation of the number of avatars present in each avatar's AoI. This metric assesses how much communication is required to keep updated the vision of the avatars with respect to the other players in the game.

Figure 2a shows the average number of avatars in the AoI of each avatar for all the models produced by TRACE. On the X axis is represented the number of avatars present in the virtual world, on the Y axis the average number of avatars in a AOI. We generate for each model a trace having a number of avatars in the range [100, 1600]. It is interesting to note that with RPGM we obtain similar results in all the configurations. This result is expected because we configure RPGM in order to keep the number of groups equals to 1/20 of the number of avatars. The two models based on random movements are the ones having the less number of avatars in the AoI. Instead, LAPT is the model having the larger increase of crowding as the number of avatars grows, because all the avatars move only between hotspots. With BLUEBANANA this effect is mitigated because a percentage of the avatars is free to move outside the hotspots.

For what concerns LAPT and BLUEBANANA, the models that take in consideration the hotspots, Fig. 2b shows the impact of the number of hotspots using

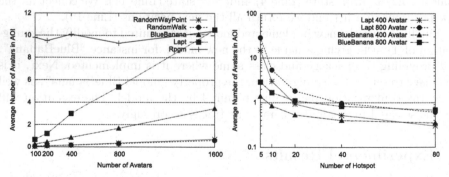

(a) Average number of avatars in AOI (b) Average number of avatars in AOI
with different number of hotspots

Fig. 2. Evaluation of Optimizations

the same metric of the previous figure. Note the log scale on the Y axis. When the number of hotspots is kept low, LAPT is, in both the configurations, the model having a larger crowding factor. However, when the number of hotspots increases, the two models behave similarly.

5.2   Evaluating the Bandwidth to Transmit Objects

In this set of experiments, we evaluate the ability of TRACE to model the avatars and objects placement. In particular, when an object enters the AoI of an avatar, a transmission of the object to the avatar is required, resulting in a bandwidth consumption. We measure the total number of objects transmitted when increasing the total number of objects in the virtual world. We test the two methodologies to distribute the objects, respectively the uniformly at random in Fig. 3a, and higher probability in the hotspots in Fig. 3b. For the uniformly at random placement, all the models behave similarly and have a linear increase of the bandwidth with respect to the number of objects. Only LAPT have a little more bandwidth requirement but in the same order of magnitude. Instead, when the objects are more present in the hotspots area, Fig. 3b, the two models, LAPT and BLUEBANANA, as expected, require more bandwidth, because the avatars are more present in the hotspots area.

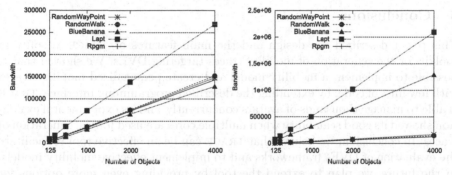

(a) Object placement: uniformly at random

(b) Object placement: higher probability in hotspots

Fig. 3. Evaluation of Bandwidth consumption

5.3   Evaluating the Computational Time and Scalability

Finally, we test the computational time required by TRACE to generate the traces. Figure 4a depicts the computational time when requesting a different number of avatars moving in the virtual world. As expected, the time increases when increasing the number of avatars but it is acceptable also with a large number of avatars, as well as 51 200 avatars. All the mobility models behaves similarly. Due to this, we perform the scalability of TRACE only with the RW model

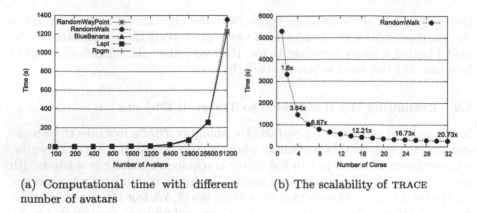

(a) Computational time with different number of avatars

(b) The scalability of TRACE

Fig. 4. Evaluation of computational time

(we confirm that with other models the shape of the curve is identical). We are able to test our tool with a scenario having a number of cores in the range [1, 32]. We obtain a good scalability of TRACE. For instance, with 8 cores we obtain a speed-up of 6.67 to a maximum of 8 and with 12 cores a speed-up of 12.21 to a maximum of 16.

6 Conclusions

This paper described the design and the main features of TRACE, a software toolkit for the generation of mobility traces targeting DVEs. We showed that is possible to implement a mobility model and create personalized mobility traces with few lines of code, by extending the described programming interface. TRACE is able to manage thousands of avatars concurrently, and its experimental evaluation showed its good scalability when multiple cores are used for the generation of traces. In conclusion, we believe that TRACE can be an effective tool to facilitate the evaluation of DVEs frameworks and to implement effective mobility models. In the future, we plan to extend the tool by providing even more options for the generation of traces, as for example an command-line interface to generate traces in a programmatic way.

References

1. Bai, F., Helmy, A.: A Survey of Mobility Models. Wireless Adhoc Networks, vol. 206. University of Southern California, USA (2004)
2. Bharambe, A., Douceur, J.R., Lorch, J.R., Moscibroda, T., Pang, J., Seshan, S., Zhuang, X.: Donnybrook: enabling large-scale, high-speed, peer-to-peer games. ACM SIGCOMM Comput. Commun. Rev. **38**(4), 389–400 (2008)
3. Carlini, E., Coppola, M., Ricci, L.: Evaluating compass routing based aoi-cast by mogs mobility models. In: Proceedings of the 4th International ICST Conference on Simulation Tools and Techniques, pp. 328–335. ICST (Institute for Computer Sciences, Social-Informatics and Telecommunications Engineering) (2011)

4. Carlini, E., Dazzi, P., Mordacchini, M., Lulli, A., Ricci, L.: Community discovery for interest management in DVEs: a case study. In: Hunold, S., Costan, A., Giménez, D., Iosup, A., Ricci, L., Gómez Requena, M.E., Scarano, V., Varbanescu, A.L., Scott, S.L., Lankes, S., Weidendorfer, J., Alexander, M. (eds.) Euro-Par 2015. LNCS, vol. 9523, pp. 273–285. Springer, Cham (2015). doi:10. 1007/978-3-319-27308-2_23

5. Carlini, E., Ricci, L., Coppola, M.: Flexible load distribution for hybrid distributed virtual environments. Futur. Gener. Comput. Syst. **29**(6), 1561–1572 (2013)

6. Gross, C., Lehn, M., Münker, C., Buchmann, A., Steinmetz, R.: Towards a comparative performance evaluation of overlays for networked virtual environments. In: 2011 IEEE International Conference on Peer-to-Peer Computing (P2P), pp. 34–43. IEEE (2011)

7. Guo, Y., Iosup, A.: The game trace archive. In: Proceedings of the 11th Annual Workshop on Network and Systems Support for Games, p. 4. IEEE Press (2012)

8. Hong, X., Gerla, M., Pei, G., Chiang, C.C.: A group mobility model for ad hoc wireless networks. In: Proceedings of the 2nd ACM International Workshop on Modeling, Analysis and Simulation of Wireless and Mobile Systems, pp. 53–60. ACM (1999)

9. Hu, S.Y., Chen, H.F., Chen, T.H.: VON: a scalable peer-to-peer network for virtual environments. IEEE Netw. **20**(4), 22–31 (2006)

10. Kavalionak, H., Carlini, E., Ricci, L., Montresor, A., Coppola, M.: Integrating peer-to-peer and cloud computing for massively multiuser online games. Peer-to-Peer Netw. Appl. **8**(2), 301–319 (2015)

11. Lee, K., Hong, S., Kim, S.J., Rhee, I., Chong, S.: Slaw: a new mobility model for human walks. In: INFOCOM 2009, pp. 855–863. IEEE (2009)

12. Legtchenko, S., Monnet, S., Thomas, G.: Blue banana: resilience to avatar mobility in distributed MMOGs. In: 2010 IEEE/IFIP International Conference on Dependable Systems and Networks (DSN), pp. 171–180. IEEE (2010)

13. Nae, V., Prodan, R., Fahringer, T.: Cost-efficient hosting and load balancing of massively multiplayer online games. In: 2010 11th IEEE/ACM International Conference on Grid Computing (GRID), pp. 9–16. IEEE (2010)

14. Ricci, L., Carlini, E.: Distributed virtual environments: from client server to cloud and P2P architectures. In: 2012 International Conference on High Performance Computing and Simulation (HPCS), pp. 8–17. IEEE (2012)

15. Ricci, L., Carlini, E., Genovali, L., Coppola, M.: AOI-cast by compass routing in delaunay based DVE overlays. In: 2011 International Conference on High Performance Computing and Simulation (HPCS), pp. 135–142. IEEE (2011)

16. Schmieg, A., Stieler, M., Jeckel, S., Kabus, P., Kemme, B., Buchmann, A.: pSense-maintaining a dynamic localized peer-to-peer structure for position based multicast in games. In: Eighth International Conference on Peer-to-Peer Computing P2P 2008, pp. 247–256. IEEE (2008)

17. Triebel, T., Lehn, M., Rehner, R., Guthier, B., Kopf, S., Effelsberg, W.: Generation of synthetic workloads for multiplayer online gaming benchmarks. In: Proceedings of the 11th Annual Workshop on Network and Systems Support for Games, p. 5. IEEE Press (2012)

18. Yu, A.P., Vuong, S.T.: MOPAR: a mobile peer-to-peer overlay architecture for interest management of massively multiplayer online games. In: Proceedings of the International Workshop on Network and Operating Systems Support for Digital Audio and Video, pp. 99–104. ACM (2005)

Towards a Methodology to Form Microservices from Monolithic Ones

Gabor Kecskemeti[1]([⊠]), Attila Kertesz[2,3], and Attila Csaba Marosi[2]

[1] Liverpool John Moores University, Liverpool, UK
g.kecskemeti@ljmu.ac.uk
[2] Institute for Computer Science and Control,
Hungarian Academy of Sciences, Budapest, Hungary
{kertesz.attila,marosi.attila}@sztaki.mta.hu
[3] University of Szeged, Szeged, Hungary
keratt@inf.u-szeged.hu

Abstract. Cloud computing is the cornerstone for elastic and on-demand service provisioning to achieve more efficient resource utilisation and quicker responses to varying application loads. Virtual machines, one of the building blocks of clouds, can be created using provider specific templates stored in proprietary repositories, which may lead to provider lock-in and decreased portability. Despite these enabling technologies, large scale service oriented applications are still mostly inelastic. Such applications often use monolithic services that limit the elasticity (e.g., by obstructing the replicability of parts of a monolithic service). Decomposing these services to smaller, more targeted and more modular services would open towards elasticity, but the decomposition process is mostly manual. This paper introduces a methodology for decomposing monolithic services to several so called microservices. The proposed methodology applies several achievements of the ENTICE project: its image synthesis and optimisation tools. Finally, the paper provides insights on how these achievements help revitalise past monolithic services, and what techniques are applied to aid future microservice developers.

1 Introduction

Cloud computing enables elastic and on-demand service provisioning by building on the achievements of virtualisation technologies. Virtual machines, or in short VMs, are software constructs that mimic real-life hardware with the help of hypervisors, also known as virtual machine monitors. VMs open up possibilities like improving resource utilisation (e.g., by server consolidation) and adapting applications to varying application loads by scaling them up or down. VMs can be created using provider specific templates and virtual hard disk files (so called virtual machine images) stored in proprietary repositories. The creation process

This research work has received funding from the European Union's Horizon 2020 research and innovation programme under grant agreement No. 644179 (ENTICE).

© Springer International Publishing AG 2017
F. Desprez et al. (Eds.): Euro-Par 2016 Workshops, LNCS 10104, pp. 284–295, 2017.
DOI: 10.1007/978-3-319-58943-5_23

of VMs depends on the applied cloud and virtualisation technique in particular, but as well as on the application to be hosted in the VM.

These virtualised environments host a wide range of services, but are mostly delivered as a monolithic block composed of multitude of sometimes vaguely related functionalities. Unfortunately, because of the monolithic nature of these services, creating VMs hosting them costs significant amounts of time. Also, the user needs to instantiate a VM that host a complete monolithic service regardless of whether he/she needs only a subset or one of the offered functionalities. This results in large portions of the VM left unused, since the rest of the functionalities are not needed by users. The concept of microservices were proposed [13] to avoid these problems. This concept ensures that there is only a single, well defined functionality offered by a particular VM and its image is optimised just to host this functionality.

Namiot and Sneps-Sneppe [8] defined microservices as lightweight and independent services that perform single functions collaborating with other similar services through a well-defined interface. On the contrary, in monolithic architecture, services are deployed as united solution called a monolith. Its main drawback is the large code base and complexity, which erodes modularity and hinders productivity. The authors also argued that splitting up monoliths to microservices can result in a more manageable and scalable application.

Creating virtual machine images for such microservices is mostly done manually by skilled developers and it is a tedious task. Generally, the building process is done through the following distinct approaches: (i) developing a new system just for the necessary functionality, (ii) manually selecting parts of a previously created and widely used monolithic service (that is often integral part of a company's business process) until it mostly contains the desired functionality. In the first case, the past legacy service functionality is replaced with a new one, which might not fit well into the current business processes. In the second case, the manual code clean-up procedure often overlooks significant parts of the monolithic service thus the procedure does not necessary lead to the level of microservices (i.e., the resulting VM image might retain some unrelated features).

The goal of this research is to propose a methodology that can be used to split up a monolithic service to small microservices. These later can be used to increase the elasticity of large scale applications, or to allow more flexible compositions with other services. To achieve this, we incorporate several techniques to the microservice creation process: (i) we present a recipe based generic image creation service that is capable to create VM and container images crafted for particular cloud systems, (ii) we reveal how a dynamic, live-evaluation based image size optimisation technique could be utilised to create a family of images based on the previous monolithic service, and (iii) we show how this image family can be turned to a set of microservices within the ENTICE environment.

The remainder of this paper is as follows: Sect. 2 presents related work, then Sect. 3 introduces the ENTICE project. Section 4 introduces the proposed methodology, detailing the recipe-based image synthesis and image size optimizations. Finally, the contributions are summarised in Sect. 5.

2   Related Work

To foster a more efficient and scalable cloud application management, the approach of composing microservices can be used [13]. Microservice building can be done by different tools, such as Puppet [10], Chef [2], and Docker [3]. These tools can cover the development and operation aspects of system administration tasks, such as delivery, testing and maintenance to improve reliability, security and so on. For example, Tihfon et al. [12] used Docker to deploy applications based on microservices. Gabbrielli et al. [5] proposed an automatic and optimised deployment of microservices written in the Jolie language. Their tool can automatically generate a fully detailed Service-Oriented Architecture configuration starting from an abstract description of the target application. In this paper, we focus on microservice image synthesis and optimisations during the creation process instead of optimisations applied during the deployment of the services.

Existing methods for VM image creation do not provide size and functional optimisation features other than dependency management, which is based on predefined dependency trees produced by third-party software maintainers. If a complex software is not annotated with dependency information, it requires manual dependency analysis upon VM image creation based on worst case assumptions and consequently. The resulting VM images are far from optimal size in most cases. On the other hand, optimising the size of existing images by aiming at providing only particular functionalities can be addressed with two approaches:

1. *The pre-optimising approach* requires the VM image developer to provide the application and its known dependencies prepared as reusable VM image components. The image developers select from these components so that they can form the base of the user application. These approaches then form the VM image with the selected reusable components and the service itself. For example, the company SAS [11] applied this algorithm with an extension that supports creating custom VM images by building from the source code. Other pre-optimising approaches determine dependencies within the VM image by using its source code using Software clone and dependency detection techniques [1]. Once the dependencies are detected, these approaches leave only those components that are required for serving the key functionality of the VM image. Optimising a VM image with these techniques requires the source code of all the software encapsulated within the image and to analyse the underlying systems.
2. *The post-optimising approach* uses existing but unoptimised VM images or, in the extreme case, optimised VM images with known software. To support this approach, several OS and application vendors offer the minimalist versions of their products packaged together with their Just-enough Operating System [6] using the Virtual Appliance approach. However, this approach requires the image developer to manually install its application to a suitable optimised VM image. The advantage of these approaches is the fast creation of the images but at the price that the developer has to trust the optimisation attempt of the used VM image's vendor. If the image is not well optimised, or the vendor

offers a generic image for all uses then the descendant VM images cannot be optimal without further efforts.

Existing research mostly focuses on pre-optimising approaches, which are not applicable to already available VM images. In ENTICE we use an VM synthesiser to extend pre-optimising approaches so that image dependency descriptions are mostly automatically generated.

3   The ENTICE Project

The ENTICE project [4] is a multidisciplinary team of computer scientists, application developers, cloud providers and operators with the aim to research a ubiquitous repository-based technology for VM and container image management called ENTICE environment. This environment proves a universal backbone for IaaS VM/container image management operations, which accommodate the needs for different use cases with dynamic resource (e.g., requiring resources for minutes or just for a few seconds) and other QoS requirements. As the discussed concepts are not dependent on the applied virtualisation technology, the rest of the paper uses the terms VM image and container image interchangeably.

The technologies developed by the ENTICE project are completely decoupled from the particular applications and their runtimes. Despite the decoupling, ENTICE still provides constant support for applications via optimised VM image creation, assembly, migration and storage. ENTICE expects users to provide their original and functionally complete VM or container images. Then it transparently tailors and optimises the images for user targeted Cloud infrastructures with respect to their size, configuration, and geographical distribution. As a result of the optimisation, these images are dispatched to the clouds (even across Clouds), executed faster and they have a potential for QoS improvement. ENTICE stores metadata about the images and fragments in a distributed knowledge base to be used for interoperability, integration, reasoning and optimisation purposes (e.g., supporting decisions about replica locations for high demand images and also decisions about the time instances at which an image should be replicated).

In the following we list the main ENTICE objectives:

1. The distributing Virtual Machine and Container Images (VMIs) with the ENTICE repository;
2. The analysis and synthesis of VMIs for already existing services and functionalities;
3. An image portal in association with a knowledge base, composing together the components of the projects' distributed, highly optimised repository.

Albeit there could be numerous stakeholders in the cloud computing context, the project aims at the following list of stakeholders specifically who should directly benefit from the distributed image repository built by ENTICE:

– End-customers, such as the users of the satellite image service of Deimos[1]
  should not be aware of the Deimos's use of the ENTICE repository environment. On the other hand, they should still benefit from the better Quality
  of Service (QoS) in the runtime of Deimos's applications as a result of the
  ENTICE applied optimisations.
– Cloud Application Providers and/or Software as a Service (SaaS) providers,
  such as the company Wellness Telecom[2], are offering SaaS applications utilizing the Cloud to serve many of their customers;
– Application Developers, such the above mentioned Deimos, who aim at deploy
  and run their applications with high efficiency. For example, Deimos is operating a satellite and is in great need for such deployment optimisations for its
  Earth observation platform and its customers (i.e. the previously discussed
  end-customers);
– Cloud Operators, such as the well-known company Flexiant[3] which has several offerings in the area of managing cloud applications across multiple
  clouds;
– Cloud Providers, such as Amazon EC2[4] could benefit through incorporating
  ENTICE technologies in their VMI storage and management solution, or even
  if just their customers are applying ENTICE optimizations on their images.

4 The Proposed Methodology

Our goal set out for this research was to identify a simple to follow methodology
usable fragment a monolithic application alongside its sub-service boundaries.
Allowing these sub-services to act as small micro-services that later can be composed to other services (without the need of the entire monolithic application).
The original monolithic image can then act as an shared base for its derived
micro-service family. To achieve this, we use image synthesis and image analysis
methods which both have pivotal roles within the architecture of the ENTICE
project.

Our VMI synthesis mechanism enables users to build new images with several
approaches. First, it allows the use of generic user provided images or software
recipes to act as the foundation before specialising them into micro services.
Next, VMI synthesis cooperates with the ENTICE image portal (the main GUI
for image creation and distribution procedures) to identify the functional requirements a newly created image must meet (this must be done on a per micro service
basis - i.e., resulting a new image from every functional requirement specified).
Then, our synthesis tool modifies the generic images (from the first step) either
directly (by altering the image file(s)) or indirectly (through creating alternative
recipes that lead to more compact images). These alterations aim at removing
contents from the original images. Thus the alterations lead the generic images

---

[1] http://www.deimos-space.com/.
[2] http://www.wtelecom.es/.
[3] https://www.flexiant.com/.
[4] http://aws.amazon.com/ec2.

towards their single purpose: namely, the functional requirements listed against the image in the portal. For optimised images, VMI Synthesis offers image maintenance operations (e.g., allowing software updates to be done on the original image and transforming those updates to the optimised image).

Alongside synthesis, ENTICE also delivers VMI analysis allowing the discovery of equivalent pieces in apparently non-related VM images which were sometimes even received from different stakeholders or communities. Analysis operates independently of the cloud provider where the image is stored. Equivalence information then stored in the ENTICE knowledge base for later use. ENTICE also allows splitting VM images into smaller fragments allowing the storage of the frequently shared image components only once (e.g., a particular flavour of Linux used by two different images). Fragmenting fosters the VM image distribution and enables the optimization of overall storage space throughout the distributed repository.

As fragmented images would not be directly usable in clouds, the ENTICE environment offers virtual machine management templates (so called VMMTs) to be stored in the repositories of the connected cloud systems. These VMMTs allow the fragmented images to be reconstructed at runtime. For optimal VM instantiation performance, the templates are formulated as stand-alone VM/Container images solely having functionality to access and build fragments from the project's distributed repository. After a VM is instantiated using a VMMT, it will ensure fragments (needed for a particular functionality specified by the user) are placed and enabled for use in the instantiated VM. VMMTs even allow customisation of files/directories for specific VMs in accordance of the needs of various stakeholders. The functions of the VMMTs are underpinned by user-defined functional and non-functional descriptions about the application to be deployed with the help of the ENTICE knowledge base and its reasoning mechanisms.

In Fig. 1, we reveal the use case diagram for ENTICE's image synthesis. The nodes (use cases) of the diagram were derived from the comprehensive requirement set (i.e., both originated from pilot cases and architectural ones) and the foundational principles of the project objectives. As a result, these use cases are expected to cover the requirements and project objectives where applicable, while they are strictly limited to image synthesis and analysis aspects. The Application Developer is expected to behave as the key actor who interacts with most use cases and can initiate most activities. Apart from the developer, we also expect Service Providers to use our image synthesis solution when they decide whether they should to adopt a particular service and image version. We also expect ENTICE's image distribution component to interact with the optimiser if it foresees potential for more optimal delivery by automatically continuing the optimization of not yet completely optimised images. In the coming subsections, we describe the most relevant use cases by considering and discussing their requirements (and some of their specific aspects), and then revealing our plans to fulfil them.

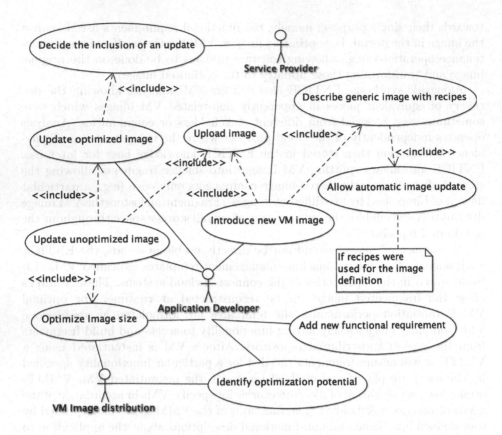

Fig. 1. Detailed use cases of image synthesis

4.1 Recipe Based Image Synthesis

This section mainly focuses on the use cases of "Describe generic image with recipes" and "Introduce new VM image" (see Fig. 1). These use cases focus on the application developer's activities when he/she wishes to build a set of cloud provider specific VM/Container images. The use cases discuss the ways developer provided recipes used to create new images with the help of devops concepts. On this use case level, the recipes are expected to guide the creation of the developer's original monolithic service on a generic way.

The recipe based image synthesis process of ENTICE can be seen in Fig. 2. It depicts 7 steps starting by creating an image, and ending with an optional cancel request. ENTICE provides APIs in a REST interface to use the services covered by these steps. There is also a backend part of this Synthesis service that uses other subcomponents to create the requested images. The images that can be managed in these processes may be of normal virtual machines (e.g. VMIs) or containers. The contents can also vary from microservices to complex ones. As they suggests, microservices in containers have smaller footprints, therefore they are easier to optimize. As shown in Fig. 2 the API enables the following processes:

- 1: submission of build requests;
- 5: retrieve build results;
- 6: query the status of the builds (optional);
- and 7: cancel ongoing builds (optional).

The image creation process at the backend consists of two parts. The first one is the building phase, while the second is the testing phase. First let's detail the building phase. It can be initiated with the create API call (step no. 1 in Fig. 2) by specifying the build target with its parameters, and the service description for the provisioning step, and the test cases for the testing phase.

The first part of the building phase is the bootstrapping step (no. 2). It is responsible to make a base image (in case of VMI's) or a container available for the provision step. It is possible to create them in the following ways:

- from scratch (with tools QEMU/QCOW2);
- targeting a container build (e.g., Docker);
- or using an existing one from a cloud image repository (e.g., Amazon Web-Services or OpenStack).

In case of QEMU/QCOW2, the build target Debian and Red Hat derived distributions are supported.

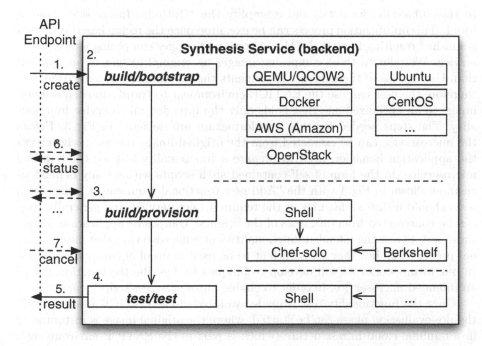

Fig. 2. Process of recipe based image synthesis

The first part of the building phase is the provisioning phase, which responsible for installing the requested microservice by the specified description. It can be done in two ways. First, a custom shell script can be provided containing sequential steps to be executed. Another option is to use Chef-solo, where Chef cookbooks must be provided (e.g. retrieved via Berkshelf) or a custom one. These targets can also be used together when needed, e.g., performing basic maintenance via Shell and deploying the requested microservice components to the image via Chef.

In the testing phase, the image is duplicated, and the supplied test script is executed in the copied image. The testing methods can be of any type, only the exit status is what matters: zero means everything went fine, non-zero denotes an error. The script can deploy any packages from the Linux distribution repository and beside the shell script a custom zip file can be supplied containing additional testing tools, but no other external access is allowed for security reasons. The methods to be used in the testing phase are very flexible, since different services require different methods or tools to be tested. The copied test image is discarded after the tests, and the original one will be available for download. Currently there is no option to link the image to another location or repository, this feature will be considered for future work. Our current implementation relies on ImageFactory [7] and Packer [9].

4.2 Targeted Size Optimisation

In this subsection we detail and exemplify the "Optimize Image size" case of Fig. 1. This optimization process can be executed once the recipe based synthesis is finished resulting in several VMIs or container images composing a monolithic service. We refer to these composing images as original images of an application. Usually one of these images implements the functionality of a microservice, therefore the user can use the ENTICE environment to transform such original image to an optimized one that holds only the intended microservice functionality. The steps needed for this transformation are depicted in Fig. 3. Before the microservice can be extracted from the original image the user, who knows the application behavior, need to prepare a functionality test for the required microservice (in the form of self-contained shell scripts without any dependencies), as shown in Fig. 1 with the "Add new functional requirement" case. Such tests should utilise all features of the required microservice, and generally they can be constructed from unit tests of the original, composing application. Hence these scripts test the intended functionalities of a microservice, they needs manual preparation, but they are sufficient to be used in proof of concept scenarios. In our future works we will develop techniques to describe the functionality of an intended microservice, in order to enable automatic test script generation.

Once the functionality test is made available in the ENTICE Image portal, the pre-evaluation phase can be started, where the original image is instantiated in a minimal cloud infrastructure (which is part of the ENTICE environment), as depicted in step 1 of Fig. 3. To this end a virtualised environment (VE) is set up by instantiating a new VM or container with its filesystem instrumented for

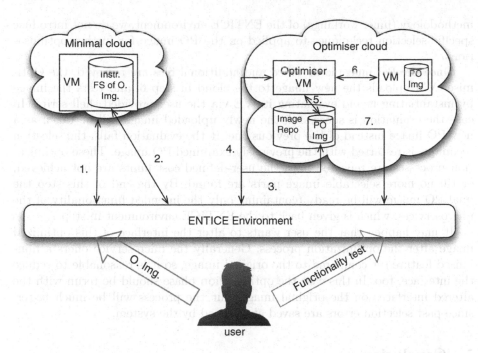

Fig. 3. Steps to transfrom an image to host only the intended microservice

read operations (called Instr. FS in the figure). Once the ENTICE environment starts, it collects the VE's read access operations to its disks (step 2 in Fig. 3).

Besides this data collection process, the microservice's functionality test is also executed by pointing its shell script to the VE's host. If the test fails after the execution, the collected data is discarded and the user is notified about the incorrect test result for the original image. If the test is successful, the collected data (representing the list of read blocks in the VE) is transformed to reflect individual files in the original image. The list of files acquired during this transformation is the so called restricted list.

The next step is the image optimisation phase. From now on, we assume that files that are not referenced by the restricted list are not relevant for the actual microservice. This means that in step 3 of Fig. 3 the system uploads a partially optimised image (PO image) that contains only the registered files (thus all unreferenced files are deleted from it). In step 4, an Optimizer VM is deployed and contextualized to use this image, and to perform the optimisation procedure by executing a test script in step 5. Here it analyses the remaining contents of the PO image and selects parts of the image that can still be removed. These newly selected parts should also be not relevant for the microservice's intended functionality, instead they are believed to be used by background activities of the original image (e.g., startup procedures and periodic activities unrelated to the core functionality). Since in this paper we present and describe the methodology (inner workings) of the ENTICE environment, we do not introduce specific selection techniques to applied on the PO image for further optimisations.

Once the PO image is modified and additional files are removed, the Optimiser VM uploads the new image to the cloud in step 6, and tests the image by instantiating it and evaluating its VE via the user-provided shell script. In case the evaluation is successful, the newly uploaded image will be taken as a new PO image instead of the previous one. It the evaluation fails, the selection technique is restarted with the previously examined PO image. These optimization processes are repeated until the user-defined cost limits are not achieved, or till no more selectable image parts are found. By the end of this step the final PO image will be ready (containing only the intended functionality of the microservice), which is given back to the ENTICE environment in step 7.

It may happen that the user wants to alter the interface of this optimized image after the optimization process. Generally the microservice offers a minimised feature set compared to the original image, so it is reasonable to reduce the interface, too. In this case the optimisation phase should be rerun with the altered interfaces on the original image, but the process will be much faster, since past selection errors are saved and reused by the system.

5   Conclusion

Virtual machine and container images are generally created by provider-specific templates stored in proprietary repositories, which may lead to provider lock-in and decreased portability. Despite these enabling technologies, large-scale service-oriented applications are still mostly inelastic due to the robust services they create. In this paper we introduced image repository management of multiple federated clouds in the frame of the ENTICE project, which tries to address this issue by transfroming monolithic services to microservices. Hence, we provided a methodology for microservice creation with an image synthesis approach, which can be used to create optimized images in a distributed repository.

In the future we will work on generalizing monolithic service fragmentation to support such monolithic services that cannot be decomposed without introducing alternative protocols in the communication between the fragmented microservices. We also envision further optimisations of microservice delivery by identifying common parts of microservice in the form of custom virtual machine management templates. Such templates would allow better image part selection and faster optimisations.

References

1. Belguidoum, M., Dagnat, F.: Dependency management in software component deployment. Electr. Notes Theor. Comput. Sci. **182**, 17–32 (2007)
2. Chef: http://www.getchef.com, May 2016
3. Docker: https://www.docker.io, May 2016

4. ENTICE consortium: Entice project website. http://www.entice-project.eu/, May 2016
5. Gabbrielli, M., Giallorenzo, S., Guidi, C., Mauro, J., Montesi, F.: Self-reconfiguring microservices. In: Ábrahám, E., Bonsangue, M., Johnsen, E.B. (eds.) Theory and Practice of Formal Methods, pp. 194–210. Springer, Heidelberg (2016)
6. Geer, D.: The OS faces a brave new world. Computer **42**, 15–17 (2009)
7. Image Factory: http://imgfac.org/, May 2016
8. Namiot, D., Sneps-Sneppe, M.: On micro-services architecture. Int. J. Open Inf. Technol. **2**(9) (2014)
9. Packer: https://www.packer.io/, May 2016
10. Puppet: http://puppetlabs.com, May 2016
11. SAS: rBuilder. http://www.sas.com/en_us/software/sas9.html, May 2016
12. Tihfon, G.M., Kim, J., Kim, K.J.: A new virtualized environment for application deployment based on Docker and AWS. In: Kim, K., Joukov, N. (eds.) ICISA 2016. LNEE, vol. 376, pp. 1339–1349. Springer, Heidelberg (2016)
13. Toffetti, G., Brunner, S., Blöchlinger, M., Dudouet, F., Edmonds, A.: An architecture for self-managing microservices. In: Proceedings of the 1st International Workshop on Automated Incident Management in Cloud, pp. 19–24. ACM (2015)

Misrouted Prophecy – On the Impact of Security Attacks on PRoPHET

Raphael Bialon[(✉)] and Kalman Graffi

Heinrich-Heine-University Düsseldorf, Universitätsstraße 1,
40225 Düsseldorf, Germany
{bialon,graffi}@cs.uni-duesseldorf.de

Abstract. In opportunistic networking, the wireless connectivity of mobile nodes is used to engage in opportunistic contacts, to exchange messages and thus to forward message in a store-carry-forward approach to a destination. Routing algorithms were developed with regards to the characteristics of these regularly partitioned networks. Network partitioning, no guarantee on device availability, and long delivery delays make these networks outstanding from traditional networks. In this paper, we investigate the behaviour of the prominent routing algorithm PRoPHET in opportunistic networks under different attack strategies. The attacks are performed by malicious nodes aimed at sabotaging the routing process in the network. Utilising ONE, the opportunistic network environment simulator, we conduct tests on these attacks and evaluate the outcomes of networks with malicious nodes compared to regular network behaviour. Through characteristic scenarios we document the behaviour of the network under attack. While in most cases the impact is tremendous, we also observe an interesting case of an attack causing an improved result in the network under attack.

Keywords: Opportunistic networks · Security · Attacks · PRoPHET routing

1 Introduction

Smartphones and small high-performance gadgets have become a ubiquitous part of our everyday life. Eminently mobile and connected through various wireless interfaces, these devices are perfect applicants to participate in opportunistic networks [2]. Establishing connections while their owners encounter each other, deliberately or not, they can be parts of a large amount of small, segregated wireless mesh networks. Utilising their mobility, one can bring information from all these segregated networks into a large time-delay network, where data exchange happens between intermediate devices, allowing for a delayed routing of messages over large distances.

The scenario of opportunistic networks is applicable to Android-based wireless networks, such as presented in [7,20]. These approaches, build on casual, not necessarily rooted Android devices, i.e. a basis of 82.8% of all smartphones in

© Springer International Publishing AG 2017
F. Desprez et al. (Eds.): Euro-Par 2016 Workshops, LNCS 10104, pp. 296–308, 2017.
DOI: 10.1007/978-3-319-58943-5_24

the year 2015[1]. Application areas range from wireless multi-chat Apps, to local file sharing networks as well as fully decentralized, private and local collaborative applications, for e.g. such as computer supported collaborative work or local distributed virtual world for gaming or enterprise applications.

The most prominent routing protocol in literature for the opportunistic networks is *Probabilistic Routing using History of Encounters and Transitivity* (PRoPHET) [12]. It provides a probabilistic routing without having an omniscient view on the network and its participants. While it focuses on a best probability routing, security counter-measures were not included in the original design of the protocol and also have been rarely discussed up to now in literature.

In this paper, we provide an analysis of the outcomes of security attacks on PRoPHET. In Sect. 2, we give a short description of the PRoPHET protocol that is essential to understand the attacks. Section 3 presents related work focusing on security attacks and counter-measures on PRoPHET Then, in Sect. 4, we propose seven different attacks on PRoPHET. These attacks are evaluated utilising an opportunistic network simulation in Sect. 5. Finally, we conclude on our observations and give an outlook on future work in Sect. 6.

2   PRoPHET Routing Protocol

PRoPHET, as presented in [5,12], is a probabilistic routing protocol which can be applied onto opportunistic networks. Because of the nature of opportunistic networks, paths for message routing are not known before a message is sent or even during transmission, there is also no guaranteed comprehensibility after a successful transmission. Message routing is conducted on single nodes' decisions for the next hop to forward the message to. Nodes utilising PRoPHET consult a probabilistic function to determine the suitability of a potential next hop. For the calculation of this function, PRoPHET takes node encounter history and transitivity between nodes into account. A *delivery predictability* is calculated for each encountered node utilising the number and duration of encounters. Different versions of PRoPHET take different information on the encounters into account.

Because encounters may be singular and not happen all the time, *information aging* is performed on calculated values to favour more recent and active encounters instead of less recent ones. Another important characteristic of PRoPHET is the application of transitivity of node connections. Utilising connections between multiple nodes, a probable route for the packet can be sought.

PRoPHET then uses the delivery predictability and a given amount of copies of the message to distribute it along suitable encounters. The PRoPHET-RFC describes a default strategy for message distribution as follows: If an encountered node has a higher delivery predictability than the current node and the maximum amount of copies is not yet reached, the message is forwarded to the encountered node for further routing.

---

[1] See https://www.idc.com/prodserv/smartphone-os-market-share.jsp.

3 Related Work

While PRoPHET is very prominent, only few work in literature addresses its security issue.

In [6], the authors introduce the concept of a trust-based security protocol in PRoPHET. The only attack considered in [6] is the *Black hole Attack* where a node imposes itself into an important network position by propagating false information on its capacities or other features. It is then a main actor in the routing process and misuses its position to drop received packets. This way it breaks down a part of the network by not delivering data. In our work, we do not focus on only one attack, but on a larger amount of attacks on the PRoPHET protocol in opportunistic networks.

In [15], the authors describe a security analysis of two opportunistic network models using *Complex Network Properties*, such as Average Shortest Distance, Degree Distribution, and Clustering Coefficients. The authors are interested in network robustness against attacks, specifically a *Wormhole Attack*. While they focus on the effects of network properties using a wormhole attack, we utilise an attack tree according to the definitions in [18] to define different categories of attacks, whose effects on message transmission are observed. We then investigate the outcomes of this variety of attacks carried out by a varying number of malicious nodes.

4 Attack Tree

In this paper, we aim at a comprehensive analysis of various attack classes on performed by selfish and/or malicious nodes on the PRoPHET protocol. An overview of these attacks is given in Table 1, the attacks are defined according to the methodology of attack trees described in [18].

Table 1. Attack tree

OR 1.1 Nodes hinder the routing process
OR 1.1a No data routing
1.1a.1 No forwarding of messages (possible direct delivery)
1.1a.2 No forwarding and no direct delivery to other nodes
1.1a.3 Set TTL to smallest possible value
OR 1.1b Modification of routing information
1.1b.1 Modifying the predictability table to small values or 0
1.1b.2 Modifying the predictability table to high values
OR 1.1c Overloading other nodes
1.1c.1 Direct Neighbor flooding
1.1c.2 Routing over not optimal paths

4.1 Attack Types

In the following we give a short overview on the defined attack types and their operations. Please note, that for all attacks, nodes still dispatch their own messages in the aforementioned manner. The attacks can be divided into three groups containing similar attack types.

No Data Routing. Attack 1.1a.1, Attack 1.1a.2 and Attack 1.1a.3 belong to the attacks that hinder the routing by disabling the routing process partially or completely.

In *Attack 1.1a.1*, malicious nodes do accept messages and carry them with them, but only deliver a message to its direct destination. No in-between routing is performed by these nodes.

This behaviour is extended in *Attack 1.1a.2*, where malicious nodes accept all messages but do not deliver any message at all.

Malicious nodes acting according to *Attack 1.1a.3* carry and forward messages as defined by PRoPHET, but manipulate the *Time-to-Live* (TTL) field by setting it to the smallest possible values, thus decreasing the possibility of a successful message delivery.

Modification of Routing Information. As PRoPHET relies on node delivery probabilities for message routing, manipulating delivery probabilities result in either malicious nodes not being used or mostly malicious nodes being used for message routing.

For *Attack 1.1b.1*, malicious nodes declare a small or zero probability for node encounters. This way these node are not chosen for message routing or only chosen for a small amount of messages to be forwarded. Similar to an eclipse attack in overlay networks, as described in [19], this kind of attack allows malicious nodes to exclude other nodes from participating with the network.

Attack 1.1b.2 propagates high probabilities of node encounter, leading to more nodes relying on these malicious nodes for message routing. The malicious node then can act as a black hole as in *Attack 1.1a.1* or *Attack 1.1a.2*.

Overloading Other Nodes. These attacks try to overload the network by either flooding other nodes or manipulating optimal routing paths.

A malicious node performing an attack according to *Attack 1.1c.1* floods a passing neighbour with either manipulated or invalid messages. The receiving node dissipates its resources and is not active in the network for the duration of attack.

Attack 1.1c.2 manipulates routing paths by choosing the worst next hop for message routing according to delivery probabilities. Messages affected by this attack may take longer to reach their destination or not be able to be delivered at all.

5   Evaluation

In this section we analyse and explain the outcomes of the attacks defined in Sect. 4. As we analysed the effects of our attacks using simulations, we depict the simulation environment in Sect. 5.1. To compare the outcomes of different simulations, relevant metrics are defined in Sect. 5.2 which are then executed and evaluated on the simulation results in Sect. 5.3.

5.1   Simulation Setup

Several simulators are available for simulating opportunistic networks, such as *Opportunistic Network Environment* (ONE) [10], DTN-Agent [21] or recently PeerfactSim.KOM [3]. We performed our tests by simulating nodes in the *Opportunistic Network Environment* (ONE) simulator after a thoughtful comparison of the simulators in [1].

Our scenarios include 100 nodes with different proportions of these acting malicious according to the examined attack. For the simulation area we use a 1500 m × 500 m rectangle on which nodes are simulated by using a random waypoint model as described in [8]. The size of the simulation area allows for a high delivery ratio of messages at a constant message size. This high delivery ratio in a regular PRoPHET network without malicious nodes provides a good standard for comparison against networks with malicious nodes present.

Nodes travel at a speeds randomly chosen between 0.5 m/s and 1.5 m/s. Simulation duration is 43200 s and randomness is initialised with a seed, so that simulation results can be reproduced deterministically.

All nodes are equipped with Bluetooth modules having a transmission range of 10 m. Transmission speed is constant at 250 kB/s. Each node has a 50 MB message buffer for message carrying and dispatches a new 50 kB message with a TTL of 360 s every 30 to 60 s. This represents a network with low message activity but the highest possible number of nodes being active, similar to a sensor network. As all nodes are active throughout the whole simulation, they scan for present neighbours all the time and are able to transmit matching messages upon every encounter.

As these simulations only focus on the effects of malicious nodes, no effects on a node's resources and/or lifetime in the network due to power consumption or overload have been investigated.

5.2   Metrics

To be able to compare the effects of the different attacks on the simulation we define comparable metrics in this section.

Delivery Ratio. One of the largest effects of our performed attacks is the impact on message delivery. Message delivery is not guaranteed in opportunistic networks. The delivery probability in a network without malicious nodes is 92.05% in our simulations. This value is always included in our graphs to allow easy comparison within one attack and between attacks.

Average Latency. As no connected path for a route is given to a message's transmission, transmission latencies vary due to different nodes forwarding messages. The average transmission latency in a simulation without malicious nodes is 3371 s for our simulations.

5.3 Simulation Results

Simulations were conducted for a varying number of malicious nodes of 0%, 20%, 40%, 60%, 80% and 100%. For some simulations no results were received after a certain amount of malicious nodes. In these cases, no results for a higher amount of malicious nodes are shown. The average transmission latency is always shown in thousands of seconds.

As we cannot explain the simulation result of every attack in detail, we explain every simulation outcome by giving a short summary of the results and focus on the most interesting result by giving a more detailed analysis.

Simulation 1.1a.1: No Data Routing. As can be seen in Fig. 1, the outcome of this simulation is as expected: The larger the amount of malicious nodes gets, the larger the average latency and the smaller the delivery ratio become. Because nodes still perform direct delivery of messages to the destination, the delivery ratio is still close to 50% with only malicious nodes.

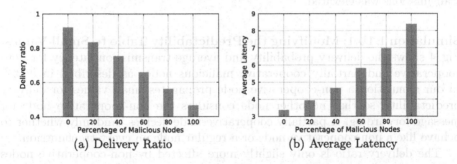

Fig. 1. Delivery ratio and average latency in simulation 1.1a.1 – no data routing

Simulation 1.1a.2: No Forwarding and No Direct Delivery to Other Nodes. Similar to Fig. 1, but far more extreme, Fig. 2 shows the simulation outcomes for up to 60% of all nodes being malicious for this attack. A higher amount of malicious nodes results in an arbitrarily low number of transmissions. Malicious nodes accept only messages they are the destination for. This results in more and more transmissions being successful only if the next hop is the destination, too.

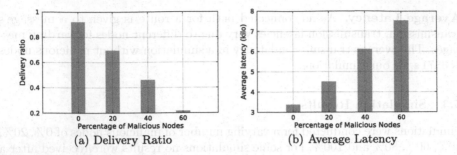

(a) Delivery Ratio   (b) Average Latency

Fig. 2. Delivery ratio and average latency in simulation 1.1a.2 – no forwarding and no direct delivery to other nodes

Simulation 1.1a.3: Set TTL to Smallest Possible Value. As malicious nodes in this attack act as black holes, the decrease in the delivery ratio and the increase in average latency is to be expected. Surprisingly, though, the outcome is better as in simulation 1.1a.2 because the simulation maintains a higher delivery ratio and lower average latency at the same percentage of malicious nodes. This happens at the expense of the number of transmissions, as can be seen in Fig. 3(c). Without malicious nodes, only 69 606 transmissions took place and usually decreased with the amount of malicious nodes increasing. In this scenario PRoPHET was able to cope with some malicious nodes because the number of transmissions was elevated.

Simulation 1.1b.1: Modifying the Predictability Table to Small Values. Fig. 4 shows the delivery probability and average transmission latency for non-cooperative and partially cooperative malicious nodes as described in [9,16]. In our simulation a non-cooperative node propagates small values for delivery predictability, so that no other node considers the non-cooperative node for message forwarding. A partially cooperative node decides randomly whether to behave like a non-cooperative node or a regular node on every transmission.

The delivery ratio is only slightly more affected by non-cooperative nodes compared to partially cooperative nodes. Both types show a similar progress of the delivery ratio as can be observed in the preceding simulation results.

With partially cooperative nodes the average latency is more gradual than with non-cooperative nodes. In contrast to non-cooperative nodes, partially cooperative nodes are sometimes chosen for message forwarding, which helps reduce latency as no other next hop has to be found.

The better score of partially cooperative nodes is caused by a slightly higher amount of transmissions. Due to the difference between these two node behaviours', this outcome can be expected.

Simulation 1.1b.2: Modifying the Predictability Table to High Values. For this attack, malicious nodes always propagate a high delivery probability

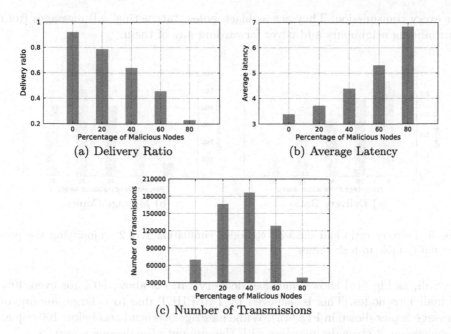

(a) Delivery Ratio   (b) Average Latency

(c) Number of Transmissions

Fig. 3. Delivery ratio and average latency in simulation 1.1a.3 – set TTL to smallest possible value

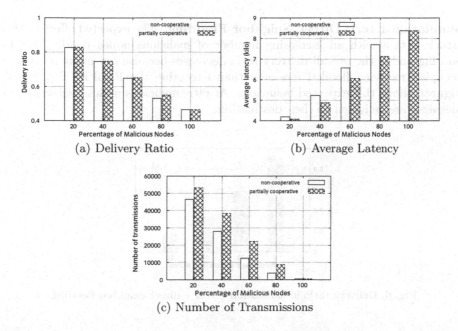

(a) Delivery Ratio   (b) Average Latency

(c) Number of Transmissions

Fig. 4. Delivery ratio, average latency, and number of transmissions of simulation 1.1b.1 – modifying the predictability table to small values

for every transmission. They act as black holes, "attracting" all messages from surrounding neighbours and never forwarding any of them.

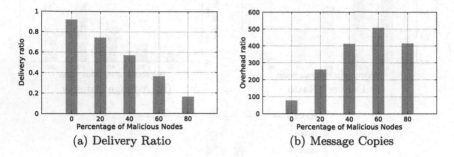

(a) Delivery Ratio   (b) Message Copies

Fig. 5. Delivery ratio and message copies of simulation 1.1b.2 - modifying the predictability table to high values

Still, as Fig. 5(a) shows, message delivery ratio is above 50% for even 40% of malicious nodes. This is achieved by PRoPHET due to a large amount of message copies shown in Fig. 5(b). While message overhead was below 100 copies per message, it strongly increases with the amount of malicious nodes.

The higher message delivery ratio can only be maintained at the cost of multiple message copies being present in the network.

Simulation 1.1c.1: Direct Neighbor Flooding. The expected effect of this attack is that with an increasing number of malicious nodes flooding neighbouring nodes, the overall delivery ratio decreases because too many nodes are occupied receiving flooded messages than executing the PRoPHET protocol. Figure 6 shows this expected behaviour. At 60% malicious nodes, below 20% of messages are delivered to their destination.

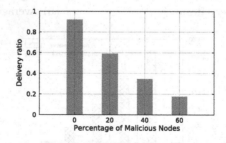

Fig. 6. Delivery ratio in simulation 1.1c.1 – direct neighbor flooding

Simulation 1.1c.2: Routing over Not Optimal Paths. The outcome of this attack, shown in Table 2, is the most interesting. Malicious nodes acting

Table 2. Simulation results for attack 1.1c.2 – routing over not optimal paths

Malicious nodes	0%	20%	40%	60%	80%	100%
No of started	69 606	85 763	87 669	88 524	87 449	80 379
Delivery ratio	0.9205	0.9329	0.9340	0.9391	0.9288	0.9185
Avg copy count	58	78	82	83	82	70
Avg latency	3371	2774.46	2526.47	2501.62	2718.81	3188
Avg hop count	2.6984	3.4790	3.7381	3.7242	3.4500	2.7978

according to this attack conform to the PRoPHET protocol, but with one difference: Instead of choosing the next hop with the highest delivery probability, these nodes chose the next hop with the lowest delivery probability.

Although messages should now travel along a non-optimal routing path as defined by PRoPHET, their delivery ratio increases and average latency decreases over the amount of malicious nodes rising.

This all happens at the expense of message copy count and hop count. Because no optimal next hop is chosen, the probability for an optimal routing decreases. The average hop count increases and so does the average copy count. As nodes in our simulation travel over a manageable sized simulation area, even the nodes with the lowest delivery probability happen to meet other nodes whom they can forward the message as a next hop to.

6   Summary

In this paper we have seen various attacks on the PRoPHET protocol conducted using the ONE simulator. These attacks aim at different points of attack and thus result in divergent changes of network behaviour. Classified using an attack tree, their goals and possible techniques were outlined.

We then introduced our simulator and simulation environment by stating configuration parameters consulted for our simulations in the *Opportunistic Network Environment* (ONE) simulator. After conducting simulations for each attack and different constellations of malicious and regular nodes, gathering their results and plotting the simulation outcomes with regards to our defined metrics, we are now able to conclude on our observations.

6.1   Conclusion

The attacks belonging to the *No data routing* type and attack 1.1c.1 present an expectable simulation outcome. The influence of their manipulations are reflected by the PRoPHET protocol as one would suppose.

Attacks of type *Modification of Routing Information* emphasize PRoPHETs' counter-measures, intended or not, against such types of attack. They lead to an increase of message copy overhead, thus compensating for wrong routing information.

For the last category of attacks, *Overloading other nodes*, 1.1c.1 shows an expected behaviour towards nodes being flooded with messages. PRoPHET does not include any resistance against such attacks as it only concentrates on routing through an opportunistic network. Interestingly, attack 1.1c.2 – which should break PRoPHET's routing with least optimal next hop choices – led to an even higher delivery ratio and lower average latency in our scenario. Nodes also reacted to the attack by elevating the amount of message copies, which then travelled longer paths. Still, these reactions lead to an improvement of some simulation results while only slightly impairing others.

With this paper we have shown and explained the effects of attacks on the PRoPHET routing protocol with regards to two metrics and additional observations. Most simulation outcomes of the attacks confirm the expected behaviour, others led to performance drops in the network – with which PRoPHET was able to cope for a while by producing a larger amount of message copies –, but one attack surprisingly shows an improvement with regards to our two metrics at the cost of the amount of message copies.

6.2   Future Work

The simulations conducted for this paper evince some interesting behaviour of the opportunistic network and results. It has to be differentiated between influence of the attacks and influence of the simulation scenario. As our simulations were all conducted using the same scenario to provide comparable results, thus an influence caused by the simulation scenario cannot be precluded.

PRoPHET does not include counter measures against malicious or selfish nodes itself, it only tries to cope with different network characteristics by shifting its performance between delivery ratio, latency and resource allocation. Techniques mentioned in [11] or in solutions for wireless mesh networks such as in [13,14] can be implemented in PRoPHET and possible changes in the behaviour of PRoPHET with regards to our attacks can be investigated.

Additional checks like plausibility of routing over nodes, trust between nodes or even a proof of work for message forwarding promise to improve PRoPHET's behaviour against the attacks defined in this paper.

The scheduling policy and drop policy used for buffer management, as analyzed for opportunistic networks in [17] or peer-to-peer networks in [4] show lots of potential both for improved routing, but also for security attacks, such as through the priorization of packets that have low chances to arrive at their destination within the remaining time to live. Options for optimization should be harnessed here while mitigating undesired behavior.

References

1. Cheraghi, A., Amft, T., Sati, S., Hagemeister, P., Graffi, K.: The state of simulation tools for p2p networks on mobile ad-hoc and opportunistic networks. In: IEEE ICCCN 2016 Proceedings of the International Conference on Computer Communication and Networks, pp. 1–7 (2016)

2. Conti, M., Giordano, S., May, M., Passarella, A.: From opportunistic networks to opportunistic computing. IEEE Commun. Mag. **48**(9), 126–139 (2010)
3. Graffi, K.: PeerfactSim.KOM: a P2P system simulator - experiences and lessons learned. In: IEEE P2P 2011 Proceedings of the International Conference on Peer-to-Peer Computing, pp. 154–155 (2011)
4. Graffi, K., Pussep, K., Kaune, S., Kovacevic, A., Liebau, N., Steinmetz, R.: Overlay bandwidth management: scheduling and active queue management of overlay flows. In: IEEE LCN 2007 Proceedings of the International Conference on Local Computer Networks (2007)
5. Grasic, S., Davies, E., Lindgren, A., Doria, A.: The evolution of a DTN routing protocol - PRoPHETv2. In: Proceedings of Workshop on Challenged Networks (CHANTS), pp. 27–30. ACM (2011)
6. Gupta, S., Dhurandher, S.K., Woungang, I., Kumar, A., Obaidat, M.S.: Trust-based security protocol against blackhole attacks in opportunistic networks. In: Proceedings of International Conference on Wireless and Mobile Computing, Networking and Communications (WiMob), pp. 724–729. IEEE (2013)
7. Ippisch, A., Graffi, K.: An android framework for opportunistic wireless mesh networking. In: NetSys 2015 Proceedings of the Conference on Networked Systems (2015)
8. Johnson, D.B., Maltz, D.A.: Dynamic source routing in ad hoc wireless networks. In: Imielinski, T., Korth, H.F. (eds.) Mobile Computing, pp. 153–181. Kluwer Academic Publishers, Dordrecht (1996)
9. Keränen, A., Pitkänen, M., Vuori, M.: Effect of non-cooperative nodes in mobile DTNs. In: Proceedings of World of Wireless, Mobile and Multimedia Networks (WoWMoM). IEEE (2011)
10. Keränen, A., Ott, J., Kärkkäinen, T.: The ONE simulator for DTN protocol evaluation. In: SIMUTools 2009 Proceedings of the 2nd International Conference on Simulation Tools and Techniques. ICST, New York (2009)
11. Lilien, L., Kamal, Z.H., Bhuse, V., Gupta, A.: The concept of opportunistic networks and their research challenges in privacy and security. In: Makki, S.K., Reiher, P., Makki, K., Pissinou, N., Makki, S. (eds.) Mobile and Wireless Network Security and Privacy, pp. 85–117. Springer, Boston (2007). doi:10.1007/978-0-387-71058-7_5. ISBN 978-0-387-71058-7
12. Lindgren, A., Doria, A., Davies, E., Grasic, S.: RFC 6693: probabilistic routing protocol for intermittently connected networks. IETF (2012)
13. Mogre, P., Graffi, K., Hollick, M., Steinmetz, R.: AntSec, WatchAnt and AntRep: innovative security mechanisms for wireless mesh networks. In: IEEE LCN 2007 Proceedings of the International Conference on Local Computer Networks (2007)
14. Mogre, P.S., Graffi, K., Hollick, M., Steinmetz, R.: A security framework for wireless mesh networks. Wireless Commun. Mobile Comput. **11**(3), 371–391 (2011)
15. Mohan, S., Qu, G., Mili, F.: Security analysis of opportunistic networks using complex network properties. In: Wang, X., Zheng, R., Jing, T., Xing, K. (eds.) WASA 2012. LNCS, vol. 7405, pp. 462–478. Springer, Heidelberg (2012). doi:10.1007/978-3-642-31869-6_40
16. Panagakis, A., Vaios, A.: On the effects of cooperation in DTNs (2007)
17. Sati, S., Probst, C., Graffi, K.: Analysis of buffer management policies for opportunistic networks. In: IEEE ICCCN 2016 Proceedings of the International Conference on Computer Communication and Networks, pp. 1–7 (2016)
18. Schneier, B.: Modeling security threats. Dr Dobb's Journal (1999). https://www.schneier.com/cryptography/archives/1999/12/attack_trees.html

19. Singh, A., wan Johnny Ngan, T., Druschel, P., Wallach, D.S.: Eclipse attacks on overlay networks: threats and defenses. In: Proceedings of International Conference on Computer Communications (INFOCOM). IEEE (2006)
20. Trifunovic, S., Kurant, M., Hummel, K.A., Legendre, F.: WLAN-Opp: ad-hoc-less opportunistic networking on smartphones. Ad Hoc Netw. **25**, Part B, 346–358 (2015)
21. Vardalis, D., Tsaoussidis, V.: DTN Agent for ns-2 (2010). http://www.spice-center.org/dtn-agent/

PADABS -Workshop on Parallel and Distributed Agent-Based Simulations

A Standardised Benchmark for Assessing the Performance of Fixed Radius Near Neighbours

Robert Chisholm[✉], Paul Richmond, and Steve Maddock

Department of Computer Science, The University of Sheffield, Sheffield, UK
{r.chisholm,p.richmond,s.maddock}@sheffield.ac.uk

Abstract. Many agent based models require agents to have an awareness of their local peers. The handling of these fixed radius near neighbours (FRNNs) is often a limiting factor of performance. However without a standardised metric to assess the handling of FRNNs, contributions to the field lack the rigorous appraisal necessary to expose their relative benefits.

This paper presents a standardised specification of a multi agent based benchmark model. The benchmark model provides a means for the objective assessment of FRNNs performance, through the comparison of implementations. Results collected from implementations of the benchmark model under three agent based modelling frameworks show the 64-bit floating point performance of each framework to scale linearly with agent population, in contrast the GPU accelerated framework's 32-bit floating point performance only became linear after maximal device utilisation around 100,000 agents.

Keywords: Parallel agent based simulation · OpenAB · Benchmarking · Fixed radius near neighbours · FLAMEGPU · MASON · Repast simphony

1 Introduction

Many complex systems have mobile entities located within a continuous space such as: particles, people or vehicles. Typically these systems are represented via Agent Based Simulations (ABS) where entities are agents. In order for these mobile agents to decide actions, they must be aware of their neighbouring agents. This awareness is typically provided by fixed radius near neighbours (FRNNs) search, whereby each agent considers the properties of every other agent located within a spatial radial area about their simulated position. This searched area can be considered the agent's neighbourhood and must be searched every timestep of a simulation, ensuring the agent has access to the most recent information about their neighbourhood. In many cases such as flocking, pedestrian interaction and cellular systems, the majority of time is spent performing this neighbourhood search, as opposed to agent logic. It is hence often the primary performance limitation.

F. Desprez et al. (Eds.): Euro-Par 2016 Workshops, LNCS 10104, pp. 311–321, 2017.
DOI: 10.1007/978-3-319-58943-5_25

The most common technique utilised for accelerating FRNNs is one of uniform spatial partitioning. Within uniform spatial partitioning, the environment is decomposed into a regular grid, partitioned according to the interaction radius. Agents are then stored or sorted according to the grid cell they are located within. Agents consider their neighbourhood by performing a distance test on all agents within their own grid partition and any directly adjacent neighbouring grid cells. This has caused researchers to seek to improve the efficiency of FRNNs handling, primarily by approaching more efficient memory access patterns [3,5,11]. However without a rigorous standard to compare implementations, exposing their relative benefits is greatly complicated.

With ABS reliance on FRNNs, there are many capable available frameworks, providing initial FRNNs implementations for assessment. The Open Agent Benchmark Project (OpenAB)[1] exists for the wider assessment of ABS and to pool the research community's ABS knowledge and resources. This paper uses the OpenAB's process of publishing a simulator independent benchmark model in a format which allows the performance of implementations across multiple ABS frameworks to be compared. By unifying the process of benchmarking ABS it is hoped that the OpenAB project will foster the necessary transparency and standards among the ABS community, ensuring that rigorous benchmarking standards are adhered to.

This paper formalises and standardises a benchmark model named circles, previously implemented by frameworks such as FLAMEGPU [10]. The model is specifically standardised and designed to assess the performance of FRNNs implementations. A formal specification of the benchmark and it's applications is provided alongside a preliminary comparison of results obtained from the single node agent modelling frameworks: FLAMEGPU, MASON and REPAST Simphony. Single machine frameworks have been targeted as they provide a simpler and more accessible platform than distributed for initial development. This work has been published to the OpenAB website[2] and provides a foundation for the future assessment of ABS frameworks.

The results within this paper assess each framework's FRNNs implementation against the metrics of problem size and neighbourhood size, which can be measured using the circles benchmark. Most apparent from these results is how the runtime scales linearly with problem size after maximal hardware utilisation. However, a much larger problem size is required to fully utilise Graphics Processing Unit (GPU) hardware when working with 32-bit floating point data.

The remainder of this paper is organised as follows: Sect. 2 provides an overview of related research; Sect. 3 lays out a clear specification of the circles benchmark model and how it can be utilised effectively; Sect. 4 details the frameworks which have been assessed using the benchmark; Sect. 5 discusses the results obtained from the application of the circles benchmark to each framework; Finally Sect. 6 presents the concluding remarks and directions for further research.

---

[1] http://www.openab.org.

[2] http://www.openab.org/benchmarks/models/submit/circles/.

2   Related Research

FRNNs searches are most often found within agent-based models. They have also been used alongside similar algorithms within the fields of Smoothed-Particle Hydrodynamics (SPH) and collision detection. FRNNs is the process whereby each agent considers the properties of every other agent located within a radial area about their location. This searched area can be considered the agent's neighbourhood and must be searched every timestep of a simulation to ensure agents have live information. Whilst various spatial data-structures such as kd-trees and R-trees are capable of providing efficient access to spatial neighbourhoods, in order to achieve high performance in a problem as general as FRNNs they must sacrifice accuracy [6].

The naive approach for carrying out a neighbourhood search is via a brute-force technique, individually considering whether each agent is located within the target neighbourhood. This technique may be suitable for small agent populations, however the overhead quickly becomes significant as agent populations increase, reducing the proportional volume of the neighbourhoods with respect to the volume of the environment.

The most common technique that is used to reduce the overhead of FRNNs handling is that of uniform spatial partitioning (Fig. 1), whereby the environment is partitioned into a uniform grid, whereby grid cells have dimensions equal to the interaction radius. Agents are then (sorted and) stored according to the ID of their containing cell within the grid. Serial implementations are likely to utilise linked list's to store the agents within each bin. Parallel implementations in contrast are likely to store agents within a single compact array which is sorted in a distinct step after agent locations have been updated, following which an index to provide direct access to the storage of each cell's agents is produced. This allows the Moore neighbourhood[3] of an agent's cell to be accessed, ignoring agents within cells outside of the desired neighbourhood. This method is particularly suitable for parallel implementations [4] and several advances have been suggested to further improve their performance: Goswami et al. proposed the use of Z-order curves to improve memory locality

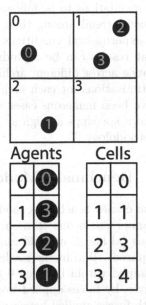

Fig. 1. A representation of a data structure that can be used for uniform spatial partitioning. The Cells table denotes the index within the agents table that data for the corresponding cell begins.

---

[3] The collection of cells inclusively bounded by the ring of adjacent cells surrounding the target cell.

[3]; Hoetzlein considered the effect of changing the partition cell dimensions [5]; and Sun et al. proposed the use of a parallel ordered sort to improve sorting efficiency [11].

Recent FRNNs publications have either provided no comparative performance results, or simply compared with their prior implementation lacking the published innovation [3,5,11]. With numerous potential innovations which may interact and overlap it becomes necessary to standardise the methodology by which these advances can be compared both independently and in combination. When assessing the performance of High Performance Computation (HPC) algorithms there are various approaches which must be taken and considered to ensure fair results.

When comparing the performance of algorithms there are a plethora of recommendations to be followed to ensure that results are not misleading [1]. The general trend among these guidelines is the requirement of explicit detailing of experimental conditions and ensuring uniformity between test cases such that results can be reproduced. Furthermore, if comparing algorithm performance across different architectures it is important to ensure that appropriate optimisations for each architecture have been implemented. Historically there have been numerous cases whereby comparisons between CPU and GPU have shown speedups as high as 100x which have later been debunked due to flawed methodology [7].

3   Benchmark Model

The circles benchmark model is designed to utilise neighbourhood search in a manner analogous to a simplified particle simulation in two or three dimensions (although it could easily be extended to higher levels of dimensionality if required). Within the model each agent represents a particle whose location is clamped within between 0 and $W - 1$ in each axis.[4] Each particle's motion is driven by forces applied from other particles within their local neighbourhood, with forces applied between particles to encourage a separation of r.

The parameters (explained below) of the circles benchmark allow it to be used to assess how the performance of FRNNs search implementations are affected by changes to factors such as problem size and neighbourhood size. This assessment can then be utilised in the research of FRNNs ensuring comparisons against existing work and to advise design decisions when requiring FRNNs during the implementation of ABS.

3.1   Model Specification

The benchmark model is configured using the parameters in Table 1. In addition to these parameters the dimensionality of the environment (E_{dim}) must be

---

[4] All frameworks tested utilised an environment of $0 <= x < W$, as it is not possible to cleanly clamp a floating point value within a less than bound, the nearest valid whole number was instead used to ensure the correct operation of each framework.

Table 1. The parameters for configuring the circles benchmark model.

Parameter	Description	Fig. 2	Fig. 3
k_{rep}	The repulsion dampening argument. Increasing this value encourages agents to repel	1×10^{-3}	1×10^{-3}
k_{att}	The attraction dampening argument. Increasing this value encourages agents to attract	1×10^{-3}	1×10^{-3}
r	The radial distance from the particle to which other particles are attracted. Twice this value is the interaction radius	5	1–15
ρ	The density of agents within the environment	1×10^{-2}	1×10^{-2}
W	The diameter of the environment. This value is shared by each dimension therefore in a two dimensional environment it represents the width and height. Increasing this value is equivalent to increasing the scale of the problem (e.g. the number of agents) assuming ρ remains unchanged	50–300	100

decided, which in most cases will be 2 or 3. The value of E_{dim} is not considered a model parameter as changes to this value are likely to require implementation changes. The results presented later in this paper are all from 3D implementations of the benchmark model.

Initialisation. Each agent is solely represented by their location. The total number of agents A_{pop} is calculated using Eq. 1.[5] Initially the particle agents are randomly positioned within the environment of diameter W and E_{dim} dimensions.

$$A_{pop} = \left\lfloor W^{E_{dim}} \rho \right\rfloor \tag{1}$$

Single Iteration. For each timestep of the benchmark model, every agent's location must be updated. The position x of an agent i at the discrete timestep $t + 1$ is given by Eq. 2, whereby F_i denotes the force exerted on the agent i as calculated by Eq. 3.[6] Within Eq. 3 F_{ij}^{rep} and F_{ij}^{att} represent the respective attraction and repulsion forces applied to agent i from agent j. The values of F_{ij}^{att} and F_{ij}^{rep} are calculated using Eqs. 4 and 5 respectively, the relevant force parameter is multiplied by the distance from the force's boundary and the unit vector from x_i to x_j in the direction of the respective force. After calculation, the agent's location is then clamped between 0 and $W - 1$ in each axis.

$$\overrightarrow{x_{i(t+1)}} = \overrightarrow{x_{i(t)}} + \overrightarrow{F_i} \tag{2}$$

---

[5] $\lfloor \ \rfloor$ represents the mathematical operation floor.
[6] The square Iversion bracket notation [ ] denotes a conditional statement; when the statement evaluates to true a value of 1 is returned otherwise 0.

$$\vec{F_i} = \sum_{i \neq j} \overrightarrow{F_{ij}^{rep}} [\|\overrightarrow{x_i x_j}\| < r] + \overrightarrow{F_{ij}^{att}} [r <= \|\overrightarrow{x_i x_j}\| < 2r] \qquad (3)$$

$$\overrightarrow{F_{ij}^{att}} = k_{att}(2r - \|\overrightarrow{x_j x_i}\|) \frac{\overrightarrow{x_j x_i}}{\|\overrightarrow{x_j x_i}\|} \qquad (4)$$

$$\overrightarrow{F_{ij}^{rep}} = k_{rep}(\|\overrightarrow{x_i x_j}\|) \frac{\overrightarrow{x_i x_j}}{\|\overrightarrow{x_i x_j}\|} \qquad (5)$$

Algorithm 1 provides a pseudo-code implementation of the calculation of a single particles new location, whereby each agent only iterates their agent neighbours rather than the global agent population.

Algorithm 1. Pseudo-code for the calculation of a single particle's new location

```
vec myOldLoc;
vec myNewLoc = myOldLoc;
float r2 = 2*RADIUS;
foreach neighbourLoc
{
  vec toVec = neighbourLoc-myOldLoc;
  float separation = length(toVec);
  if(separation < r2)
  {
    float k = (separation<RADIUS)?REP_FORCE:ATT_FORCE;
    toVec = (separation<RADIUS)?-toVec:toVec;
    separation = (separation<RADIUS)?separation:(r2-separation);
    myNewLoc += k * separation * normalize(toVec);
  }
}
myNewLoc = clamp(myNewLoc, envMin, envMax);
```

Validation. There are several checks that can be carried out to ensure that the benchmark has been implemented correctly, the initial validation techniques rely on visual assessment. During execution if the forces F_{att} & F_{rep} are both positive particles can be expected to form spherical clusters. Due to the force drop-off (switching from the maximal positive force, to the maximal negative force) when a particle crosses the force boundary, these clusters oscillate, this effect is amplified by agent density and force magnitude. If these forces are however both negative, particles will spread out, with some particles overlapping each other.

More precise validation can be carried out by seeding two independent implementations[7] with the same initial particle locations. With appropriate model parameters (such as those in Table 1), it is possible to then export agent positions after a single iteration from each implementation[8]. Comparing these exported

---

[7] The implementations used within this paper are available within this projects repository. https://github.com/Robadob/circles-benchmark.

[8] It is recommended to export agents in the same order that they were loaded, as sorting diverged agents may provide inaccurate pairings.

positions should show a parity to several decimal places, whilst significant differences between the initial state and the exported states. Due to the previously mentioned force fall-off and floating point arithmetic limitations, it was found that a single particle crossing a boundary between two models, snowballs after only a few iterations, causing many other particles to differ between simulation results.

The 3 agent framework implementations tested within this paper were all tested with shared initial particle locations states to ensure that their models were performing the same operations.

3.2 Effective Usage

The metrics which may affect the performance of neighbourhood search implementations are agent quantity, neighbourhood size, agent speed and location uniformity. Whilst it is not possible to directly parametrise all of these metrics within the circles benchmark, a significant number can be controlled to provide understanding of how the performance of different implementations is affected.

To modify the scale of the problem, the environment width W can be changed. This directly adjusts the agent population size, according to the formula in Eq. 1, whilst leaving the density unaffected. Modulating the scale of the population is used to benchmark how well implementations scale with increased problem sizes. In multi-core and GPU implementations this may also allow the point of maximal hardware utilisation to be identified, whereby lesser population sizes do not fully utilise the available hardware.

Modifying either the density ρ or the radius r can be used to affect the number of agents found within each neighbourhood. The number of agents within a neighbourhood of radius r can be estimated using Eq. 6, this value assumes that agents are uniformly distributed and will vary slightly between agents.

$$N_{size} = \rho\pi(2r)^{E_{dim}} \tag{6}$$

Modifying the speed of the agent's motion affects the rate at which the data structure holding the neighbourhood data must change (referred to as changing the entropy, the energy within the system). Many implementations are unaffected by changes to this value. However optimisations such as those by Sun et al. [11] should see performance improvements at lower speeds, due to a reduced number of agents transitioning between cells within the environment per timestep. The speed of an agent within the circles model is calculated using Eq. 3. There are many parameters which impact this speed within the circles model. As a particles motion is calculated as a result of the sum of vectors to neighbours it clear that the parameters affecting neighbourhood size (ρ & r) impact particle speed in addition to the forces F_{att} & F_{rep}.

The final metric location uniformity, refers to how uniformly distributed the agents are within the environment. When agents are distributed non-uniformly, as may be found within many natural scenarios, the size of agent neighbourhoods are likely to vary more significantly. This can be detrimental to the performance of implementations which parallelise the neighbourhood search such that each agents search is carried out in a separate thread via single instruction multiple thread (SIMT) execution. This is caused by sparse neighbourhood threads spending large amounts of time idling whilst waiting for larger neighbourhood threads searching simultaneously within the shared thread-group to complete. It is not currently possible to suitably affect the location uniformity within the circles model.

Independent of model parameters, the circles benchmark is also capable of assessing the performance of FRNNs when scaled across distributed systems, however that is outside the scope of the results presented within this paper.

4   Assessed Frameworks

The benchmark implementations assessed within this paper all target execution on a single machine. Care has been taken to follow best practices as expressed in the relevant documentation and examples provided with each framework to ensure that the optimisation of model implementations is appropriate. The associated model implementations are publicly available on this projects repository[9] and further details regarding the frameworks can be found on the OpenAB website[10]. The frameworks targeted within this research are:

- Inspired by the FLAME agent-based modelling framework, FLAMEGPU was developed to utilise GPU computation via a combination of XML and CUDA [10].
- MASON is a Java multiagent simulation toolkit capable of executing models with a large numbers of agents on a single machine, providing an additional suite of visualisation tools [8].
- The Repast collective of modelling tools has now been under development for over 15 years. Repast Simphony targets computation on individual computers and small clusters, facilitating the development of agent-based models using Java and Relogo [9].

Notably FLAMEGPU supports the usage of both 32-bit and 64-bit floating point values, whereas both MASON and Repast Simphony use 64-bit floating point values exclusively within their frameworks. This is likely influenced by the negative impact 64-bit floating point values have on GPU performance being significantly greater to that of CPUs.

5   Results

Results presented within this section were collected on a single machine running Windows 7 × 64 with a Quad core Intel Xeon E3-1230 v3 running at 3.3 GHz[11].

---

[9] https://github.com/Robadob/circles-benchmark.

[10] http://www.openab.org/benchmarks/simulators/.

[11] The processor supports hyper-threading, enabling 4 additional concurrent logical threads.

Additionally the FLAME-GPU framework utilised an Nvidia GeForce GTX 750 Ti GPU which has 640 CUDA cores running at 1 GHz.

Each of the parameter sets utilised targeted a different performance metric identified in Sect. 3.2. Results were collected by monitoring the total runtime of 1000 iterations of 3D implementations of the benchmark (executed without visualisation) and are presented as the per iteration mean. Initialisation timings are excluded as the benchmarks focal point is the performance of the near neighbours search carried out within each iteration.

The results in Fig. 2 present the variation in performance as the scale of the problem increases. This is achieved by increasing the parameter W, which increases the volume of the environment and hence the agent population. Most apparent from these results is that both the FLAMEGPU implementations, which utilise GPU computation as opposed to the other frameworks which utilise a multi-threaded CPU approach, consistently outperform the best multi-core framework by a margin which at the largest test-case increases to greater than 6x with 64-bit floating point computation and 10x with the lower precision 32-bit floating point. This is slightly better than the expectations of GPU accelerated computation [7], suggesting their may be further room for optimisation. Although MASON and Repast Simphony are both Java based frameworks, Repast's performance trailed that of MASON by around 3x, investigating this showed Repast's separate operations for updating a particle's spatial and grid locations to be slower than that of MASON which handles both in a single operation. Notably the operation of updating a particles location could not be handled in parallel by MASON or Repast.

The MASON, Repast and 64-bit floating point FLAMEGPU results both have a Pearson correlation coefficient (PCC) [2] of 0.99. This is indicative of a linear relationship. Similarly 32-bit floating point FLAMEGPU has a PCC of 0.99 when only agent populations of 100,000 and higher are considered, this suggests that smaller agent populations did not fully utilise the GPU during 32-bit floating point computation.

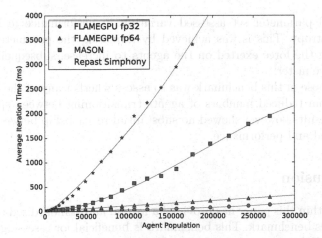

Fig. 2. The average iteration time of each framework against the agent population.

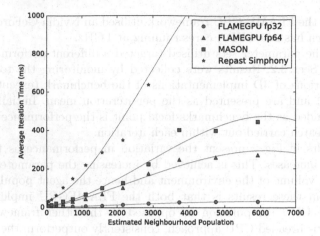

Fig. 3. The average iteration time of each framework against the estimated neighbour-hood population. The estimated neighbourhood population is the calculation of agents within a neighbourhood where agents are uniformly distributed, providing a clearer interpretation of changes to the interaction radius (r).

The next parameter set, shown in Fig. 3, assessed the performance of each framework in response to increases in the agent populations within each neighbourhood. The purpose of this benchmark set was to assess how each framework performed when agents were presented with a greater number of neighbours to survey. This was achieved by increasing the parameter r, hence increasing the volume of each agent's radial neighbourhood. All results have a PCC [2] of 0.96. This is indicative of a linear relationship, albeit much weaker correlation than that seen within the prior experiment. It is likely that this weaker relationship can be explained by how the agent density becomes more non-uniform as the model progresses, causing the number of agents within each neighbourhood to grow.

The final parameter set assessed variation in performance in response to increased entropy. This is was achieved by adjusting the parameters k_{att} and k_{rep}, causing the force exerted on the agents to increase, subsequently causing them to move faster.

The purpose of this benchmark was to assess whether any of the frameworks benefited from reduced numbers of agents transitioning between spatial partitions. The results however showed no substantial relationship between increased particle speed and performance.

6   Conclusion

The work within this paper has provided a formal and standardised specification for the circles benchmark. This benchmark is beneficial for assessing the performance of FRNNs search implementations in response to changes to problem size, neighbourhood size and agent entropy. The results within this paper have shown the linear performance relationships of the tested ABS frameworks in response to changing agent populations and neighbourhood sizes. This provides a guide for those looking to implement ABS reliant on FRNNs and a metric to improve FRNNs search implementations.

The next stages of this research are: further evaluation of standalone FRNNs implementations utilising the most recent research advances, improving the benchmark model to further isolate assessment criteria of FRNNs and reduce the effects of force fall-off, developing a statistical method of validating model outputs, assessing how distributed systems affect the scalability of FRNNs and considering the implications of wrapped (torodial) environments.

References

1. Bailey, D.H.: Misleading performance in the supercomputing field. In: Proceedings of the 1992 ACM/IEEE Conference on Supercomputing, pp. 155–158. IEEE Computer Society Press (1992)
2. Edwards, A.: The correlation coefficient. In: An Introduction to Linear Regression and Correlation, pp. 33–46 (1976)
3. Goswami, P., Schlegel, P., Solenthaler, B., Pajarola, R.: Interactive SPH simulation and rendering on the GPU. In: Proceedings of the 2010 ACM SIGGRAPH/Eurographics Symposium on Computer Animation, pp. 55–64. Eurographics Association (2010)
4. Green, S.: Particle simulation using cuda. Nvidia whitepaper 6, 121–128 (2010)
5. Hoetzlein, R.: Fast fixed-radius nearest neighbors: interactive million-particle fluids. In: GPU Technology Conference (2014)
6. Kofler, K., Steinhauser, D., Cosenza, B., Grasso, I., Schindler, S., Fahringer, T.: Kd-tree based n-body simulations with volume-mass heuristic on the GPU. In: 2014 IEEE International on Parallel and Distributed Processing Symposium Workshops (IPDPSW), pp. 1256–1265. IEEE (2014)
7. Lee, V.W., Kim, C., Chhugani, J., Deisher, M., Kim, D., Nguyen, A.D., Satish, N., Smelyanskiy, M., Chennupaty, S., Hammarlund, P., et al.: Debunking the 100X GPU vs. CPU myth: an evaluation of throughput computing on CPU and GPU. In: ACM SIGARCH Computer Architecture News. vol. 38, pp. 451–460. ACM (2010)
8. Liu, J., Chandrasekaran, B., Yu, W., Wu, J., Buntinas, D., Kini, S., Panda, D.K., Wyckoff, P.: Microbenchmark performance comparison of high-speed cluster interconnects. IEEE Micro 24(1), 42–51 (2004)
9. North, M.J., Collier, N.T., Ozik, J., Tatara, E.R., Macal, C.M., Bragen, M., Sydelko, P.: Complex adaptive systems modeling with repast simphony. Complex Adapt. Syst. Model. 1(1), 1–26 (2013)
10. Richmond, P., Romano, D.: A high performance framework for agent based pedestrian dynamics on GPU hardware. In: European Simulation and Modelling, vol. 3 (2008)
11. Sun, H., Tian, Y., Zhang, Y., Wu, J., Wang, S., Yang, Q., Zhou, Q.: A special sorting method for neighbor search procedure in smoothed particle hydrodynamics on GPUs. In: 44th International Conference on Parallel Processing Workshops (ICPPW), pp. 81–85. IEEE (2015)

D-MASON on the Cloud: An Experience with Amazon Web Services

Michele Carillo[1], Gennaro Cordasco[2], Flavio Serrapica[1],
Carmine Spagnuolo[1(✉)], Przemysaw Szufel[3], and Luca Vicidomini[1]

[1] ISISLab–Dipartimento di Informatica,
Università degli Studi di Salerno, Fisciano, Italy
michele.carillo@gmail.com, flavio.serrapica@gmail.com
{cspagnuolo,lvicidomini}@unisa.it
[2] Dipartimento di Psicologia, Seconda Università degli Studi di Napoli,
Caserta, Italy
gennaro.cordasco@unina2.it
[3] Warsaw School of Economics (WSE - SGH), Warsaw, Poland
pszufe@gmail.com

Abstract. D-MASON framework is a parallel version of the MASON library for writing and running Agent-based simulations – a class of models that, by simulating the behavior of multiple agents, aims to emulate and/or predict complex phenomena. D-MASON has been conceived to harness the amount of unused computing power available in common installations like educational laboratory. Then the focus moved to dedicated installation, such as massively parallel machines or supercomputing centers. In this paper, D-MASON takes another step forward and now it can be used on a cloud environment.

The goal of the paper is twofold. Firstly, we are going to present D-MASON on the cloud – a D-MASON extension that, starting from an IaaS (Infrastructure as a Service) abstraction, and exploiting Amazon Web Services and StarCluster, provides a SIMulation-as-a-Service (SIMaaS) abstraction that simplifies the process of setting up and running distributed simulations in the cloud. Secondly, an additional goal of the paper is to assess computational and economic efficiency of running distributed multi-agent simulations on the Amazon Web Services EC2 instances. The computational speed and costs of an EC2 cluster will be compared against an on-site HPC cluster.

Keywords: Agent-Based simulation Models · Cloud computing ·
D-MASON · Parallel computing · Distributed systems · High performance computing

1 Introduction

Computational science is a rapidly growing novel field that uses advanced computing in order to solve complex problems. This new discipline combines new

© Springer International Publishing AG 2017
F. Desprez et al. (Eds.): Euro-Par 2016 Workshops, LNCS 10104, pp. 322–333, 2017.
DOI: 10.1007/978-3-319-58943-5_26

technologies, modern computational methods and simulations to address problems too complex to be reliably predicted by theory and too dangerous or expensive to be reproduced in the laboratory.

Many simulation paradigms have been proposed. Among them, Agent-Based simulation Models (ABMs) are an increasingly popular tool in terms of expressiveness and easy to understand for the developer of simulation models [9].

Successes in computational sciences over the past ten years have caused demand for supercomputing resources, to improve the performance of the system and to allow the growth of the models, in terms of sizes and quality. From a computer scientist's perspective, it is natural to think to distribute the execution of the simulations among multiple machines: it is well known that the speed of single-processor computers is reaching some physical limits. For these reasons, parallel computing has become the dominant paradigm for computational scientists who need the latest development on computing resources in order to solve their problems.

The cloud computing paradigm [1] is becoming very popular these days. With cloud computing, the cloud vendors provide IT resources to users as a utility like the electricity; the user accesses the IT resources easily and pays only for the ones they consumed. Cloud providers offer managed infrastructures (IaaS - Infrastructure as a Service) as well as managed platforms such as a key-value storage or a relational database (PaaS - Platform as a Service). The offered IaaS and PaaS services enable Cloud computing services that range from simple data backup to the possibility of deploying entire computing clusters or data centers in a remote environment.

The goal of cloud computing is to allow users to take benefit from IT resources, without the need for deep knowledge about or expertise with each one of them. Moreover, individual user or small groups do not need to provide and maintain IT-infrastructure on their own, but instead rely on cloud services to satisfy their needs. The flexibility, cost-efficiency, scalability, accessibility as well as user-friendliness of cloud services make it also an attractive model to address computational challenges in the scientific community. The design of ABMs is usually done by domain experts who seldom are computer scientists and have limited knowledge of managing a modern parallel infrastructure. In this context, there is the need of tools that allow, in a transparent way, the use of cloud resources to non-expert users [7,8].

In this paper, we introduce D-Mason on the cloud – a D-Mason extension that provides a SIMulation-as-a-Service (SIMaaS) infrastructure that simplifies the process of setting up and running distributed simulations in the cloud. We will present a preliminary evaluation of the novel infrastructure in order to assess computational and economic efficiency of running distributed multi-agent simulations on the Amazon Web Services EC2 instances. The computational speed and costs of an EC2 cluster will be compared against an on-site HPC cluster.

2   Background

2.1   D-Mason

D-MASON [3,4] is the distributed version of MASON [10,11], a discrete-event simulation core and visualization library written in Java, designed to be used for a wide range of ABMs. MASON is composed of two independent layers: the *simulation* layer and the *visualization* layer. D-MASON adds a new layer named *D-simulation*, which extends the MASON simulation layer. The new layer adds some features that allow the simulation work distribution on multiple, even heterogeneous, Logical Processors (LPs). D-MASON has been designed to enable the porting of existing applications to a distributed platform in a transparent and easy way.

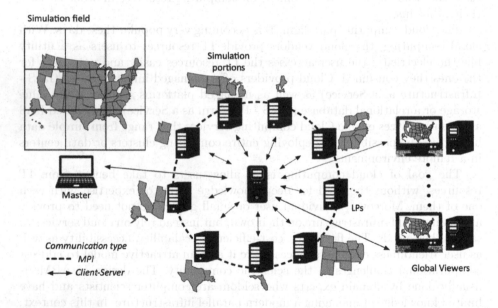

Fig. 1. D-MASON scheme.

D-MASON is based on a Master/Workers paradigm that exploits a space partitioning approach: the master partitions the space to be simulated (i.e., the field) into cells (see Fig. 1). Each cell, together with the agents it contains, is assigned to an LP; then each LP is in charge of:

- simulating the agents that belong to the assigned cell;
- handling the migration of agents;
- managing the synchronization between neighboring cells (this information exchange is required in order to let the simulation run consistently).

D-Mason LPs communicate via a well-known mechanism, based on the Publish/Subscribe paradigm: a multicast channel is bound to each cell; LPs then simply subscribe to the topics associated with the cells, which overlap with their Area of Interest (AOI) in order to receive relevant message updates. Other topics are also used for system management and visualization.

D-Mason has been conceived to harness the amount of unused computing power available in common installations like educational labs, that is, a loosely coupled environment with heterogeneous machines. To take advantage of this environment, the former version of D-Mason used a centralized communication mechanism (JMS), while the main emphasis was represented by load balancing [6]. Indeed, when the number of LPs available is limited, a centralized communication is, at the same time, easy to develop/manage and efficient. Then the initial design idea has spanned beyond this. The focus moved to dedicated installation, such as massively parallel machines or supercomputing centers. These platforms usually offer a large number of homogeneous machines that, on one hand, simplify the issue of balancing the load among LPs, but, on the other hand, the considerable computational power provided by the system weakens the efficiency of the centralized communication server. For this reasons, a novel decentralized communication mechanism, which realizes a Publish/Subscribe paradigm through a layer based on the MPI standard, was implemented in D-MASON [5].

2.2 Amazon Web Services

Amazon Web Services (AWS) is a scalable and highly reliable cloud infrastructure for deploying applications on demand. The main idea is to let the user building its services with minimal support and administration costs. AWS provides different services on the cloud. In this work, we are interested to the web services that enable either the modeler or the developer to run their simulation on the cloud. Amazon Elastic Compute Cloud (Amazon EC2) provides resizable computing capacity in the cloud. In terms of abstraction layers, the Amazon EC2 is an instance of the Infrastructure as a Service (IaaS) model, where the Amazon infrastructure is seen as a complete virtual environment which allows to execute different instances of virtual machines. Specifically, Amazon allows bundling operating system, application software and configuration settings into an Amazon Machine Image (AMI). Then each user can configure and deploy a cluster of machines using a specific AMI instance to run distributed simulations. Advanced users may also create their own AMIs and publish them on the Amazon Marketplace Web Service (Amazon MWS).

In terms of business model, Amazon offers three different purchasing mechanisms: On-Demand Instances, Reserved Instances and Spot Instances. On-Demand Instances have fixed price (per hour) and allow using the resources immediately. With Reserved Instances, it is possible to reserve the utilization of some instances for a predefined period (from 1 to 3 years) with lower payment. Finally, when the timing is not crucial, with Spot Instances, it is also possible to bid for unused resources in order to reduce drastically the costs.

2.3 StarCluster

The main issue a user needs to solve in order to use an IaaS service, to run a distributed application, is the configuration and management of each machine. Even using a dedicated AMI, which bundle the basic software components, there are still several parameters that have to be configured separately on each machine. Moreover, the management of the machines is usually time-consuming and requires repetitive tasks that need to be executed for each instance and therefore should be automate to avoid human mistake. To face this issue, a cluster-computing toolkit, StarCluster [15], released under the LGPL license, has been deployed to configure and manage Amazon EC2 instances. StarCluster enables users to easily setup a cluster computing environment in the cloud, suited for distributed and parallel computing applications and systems.

StarCluster is useful to configure the network of the cluster, create user accounts, enable password-less connections sharing the SSH password between the cluster's nodes, setup NFS shares and the queuing system for the jobs. StarCluster is also customizable via plug-ins, which allow users to configure further the cluster with their specific configuration. Plugins are written in Python exploiting StarCluster API to interact with the nodes. The API supports executing commands, copying files, and other OS-level operations on the nodes. StarCluster supports also the use of Spot instances allowing the user to run on-demand experiments in easy way and at affordable prices.

3 D-Mason on the Cloud

D-MASON on the cloud has been realized with the purpose to provide a SIMulation-as-a-Service (SIMaaS) environment. The architecture of the system is depicted in Fig. 2. D-MASON on the cloud is based on a modular approach, which comprises three levels: The Infrastructure is given by Amazon EC2 which provides a wide portfolio of instance types [13] designed to be adopted for different use cases. Instance types vary by CPU performances, memory, storage (size and performance), and networking capacity. The user is free to select an AWS cell according to prices and availability or resources. Starting with a free available Amazon AMI (ami-52a0c53b) that includes a minimal software stack for distributed and parallel computing [15], we realized an AMI specifically configured for executing D-MASON on the cloud. The D-MASON AMI, public available on Amazon Infrastructure, provides also Java 8, Maven, D-MASON 3.1. On top of that, we developed a StarCluster plugin, which exploits all the functionality provided by StarCluster in order to create automatically a runnable D-MASON environment based on the D-MASON AMI. With more details, the StarCluster plugin:

- configure the cluster network environment (users account, hostnames setting, SSH key share, NFS setup);
- appoint one of the machines as a Master node;
- install and configure the D-MASON environment.

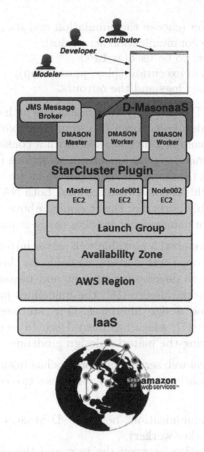

Fig. 2. D-MASON on the cloud: architecture.

The master node runs the D-MASON Master application, the JMS message broker (ActiveMQ) and the web system management server (see Sect. 3.1). The other machines run the D-MASON Worker applications, which communicate using the JMS message broker running on the Master node. Each D-MASON Worker application provides a simulation slot for each core available on the machine. The StarCluster D-MASON Plugin is freely available on GitHub D-MASON source code repository [14].

The D-MASON tier did not require any particular change but, since now the system will be executed on a cloud environment, a novel Web system management interface has been developed in order to manage the system.

3.1 D-Mason Web System Management

The former version of D-MASON system management was introduced in [2]. Briefly, it is a console written in Java, using *Java swing* framework, for managing and monitoring D-MASON simulations. In details, D-MASON system management enables to:

- configure a simulation (choose the simulation and its parameters, define the partitioning and the communication strategies);
- select a set of workers to be used as LPs;
- manage the simulation execution (play/pause/stop);
- collect the simulations' logs and the outputs.

The former version of D-MASON system management had two disadvantages: First, it was not fully decoupled from the simulation part. Hence, adding new features often requires complex interventions with a considerable waste of time. Moreover, the system was designed for local interactions (that is assuming that both the simulation and the management applications are reachable on several IP ports). Unfortunately, this is not always the case, both NAT and firewall services may result in unreachable ports. For the reasoning above, we decided to develop a fully decoupled system management services easily available via web services.

Design. We decided to embed a portable web server into our architecture. After a deep analysis of the open web servers available for Java, we decided to opt for Jetty [18]. In order to develop an efficient and pleasant interface, we were inspired by Google material design [16], the guidelines provided by Google for the development of good design interfaces. Our interface is based on a useful library named Polymer [17], which has been designed to create components for the modern web, following the material design guideline.

Architecture. The novel web server components has been encapsulated into the D-MASON Master application, which now comprises two communication components:

- ActiveMQ, for communication between D-MASON applications (either master-worker or worker-worker)
- Jetty, for communication between the user and the master application (via web interface)

When the user starts the Master application, both the ActiveMQ and the Jetty server will run on the host. In particular the Jetty server is reachable on a TCP port (default is 8080) and the user can access the management console via browser. Using this approach the user can manage and monitor its simulation, provided that the port 8080 of the Master node is reachable on the Internet.

We posit that the load of the Jetty Server will have no impact on the overall performances of the system. This is true especially when the number of users is small and the user interaction is limited. Indeed, the load of the Jetty server is only due to the activity of discovering and monitoring of LPs. In any case, when this load increases (i.e., a huge number of users continuously interacting with the master and/or the number of LPs to be monitored is large) the master node can be configured to use an external ActiveMQ communication server.

A dedicated hand-shaking mechanism allows bonding the Master application with the workers available. When a worker joins the system, it communicates how many slots (LPs) it can afford. As soon as the master realizes that he has enough LPs to start the simulation, the system enables the user to interact with the simulation.

The web system management enables also the user to monitor the resources available on all connected workers (see Fig. 3). Using such information the user is able to choose appropriately the workers to be engaged for future simulations.

The system management provides a library of preloaded simulation but at the same time, it is possible to upload a novel simulation as a jar file. Once a simulation has been chosen, the user has to select the simulation's parameters and submit it to the selected workers. The simulations page shows the list of all the simulations running on the system; for each simulation, using the *Simulation Controller* (see Fig. 4 (left)), the user can start, pause or stop the execution until the end of the simulation. In order to monitor the evolution of a simulation, a logging mechanism has been implemented. All the log files are available at run-time on the Simulation Info panel (see Fig. 4 (right)). Moreover, a history page is available in order to get all the information available about executed simulations. The history page allows also downloading log files.

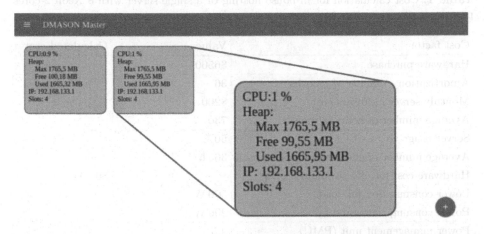

Fig. 3. Workers seen from master

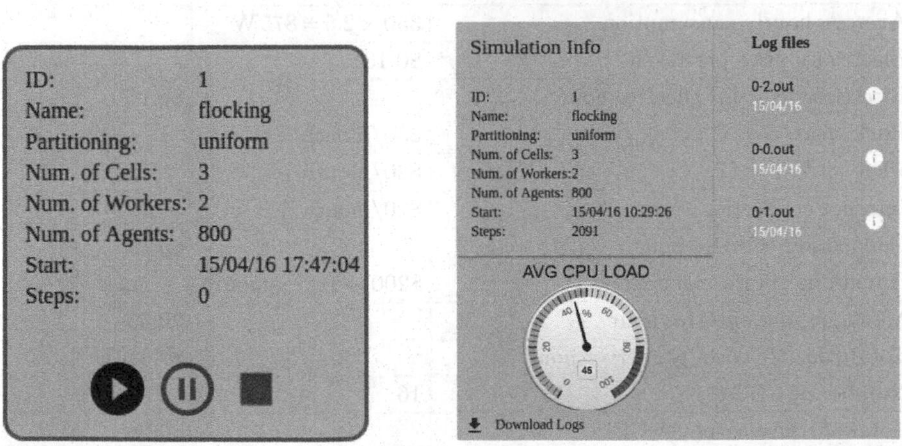

Fig. 4. Simulation Controller (left) and Simulation Info (right)

4 Performance and Cost Evaluation

We performed several benchmarks in order to evaluate the performance of D-MASON on the cloud. All the tests have been performed on *D-Flockers*, which is the distributed version of *Flockers* MASON model and represents an implementation of the Boids model [12]. Boids/Agents have been simulated on a 2D geometric field having size 6400 × 6400. For each test we executed a reproducible simulation with 1 million agents for 15 min. At the end of the simulation, we computed the number of simulation steps performed. We used the novel system management, to start and stop the simulation and to collect the log files.

Five 2D space partitioning strategies (2 × 2, 2 × 4, 3 × 4, 4 × 4, 4 × 5) which generate respectively 4, 8, 12, 16 and 20 cells have been considered. All the simulations have been performed with a number of LPs (cores) equal to

Table 1. Cost calculation for in-house hosting of a single server with 8 Xeon 2-cores processors.

Cost factor	Value	Calculated cost
Hardware purchase	$6500	
Amortization - number of months	36	
Monthly server hardware cost	$200	
Average number of hours in month	730	
Server usage %	50%	
Average number of effective hours in month	365 h	
Hardware cost for effective hour		0.49
Power consumption full load	500 W	
Power consumption stand by	200 W	
Power management unit (PMU)	2.5	
Server usage %	50%	
Average hourly consumption	$350 \times 2.5 = 875$ W	
Electricity price per KWh	$0.13	
Electricity cost for effective hour		$0.11
Rack space	$30/month	
UPS	$20/month	
Internet connection	$20/month	
Collocation effective hour		$0.19
Human hardware maintenance	$200/server × month	
Managing per effective hour		$0.55
Total effective costs per server hour		$1.34
Number of CPUs	16	
Total effective costs per CPU		$0.08

the number of cells described by the partitioning strategy on four instance type (either cloud or HPC). Specifically we tested two cloud instances available on Amazon EC2:

c3.large, processor Intel Xeon E5-2680 v2 (Ivy Bridge) with 2 vCPU, 3.75 GB of memory and 2 × 16 GB SSD storage (cost $0.105/h — or 0.019/h for spot at the low price range);

c3.xlarge, processor Intel Xeon E5-2680 v2 (Ivy Bridge) with 4 vCPU, 7.5 GB of memory and 2 × 40 GB SSD storage. (cost $0.210/h — or 0.039/h for spot at the low price range).

In order to compare the results against a dedicated on–site environment, we performed the same tests on an HPC cluster. The HPC cluster consists of 16 nodes – each one equipped with 2 × Intel(R) Xeon(R) CPU E5-2430 with 12 vCPU, 16 GB of memory and 1 TB HDD storage – interconnected through a Gigabit Ethernet. Each node is running Ubuntu 14.04 operating system with latest updates. The (per node) cost of the considered HPC environment is reported in Table 1.

We considered two different configurations. In the former one, named **HPC1**, all the LPs are executed using a single node, while in the latter, named **HPC***,

Table 2. Performance and costs comparison.

Instance type	# of instances	# of LPs	Partitioning	Performed steps in 15 min (Avg)	Overall cost	Overall EC2 spot	Cost (x step) $/1000
c3.large	2	4	2 × 2	110	$0.210/h	$0.038/h	0.48
c3.large	4	8	2 × 4	271	$0.420/h	$0.076/h	0.39
c3.large	6	12	3 × 4	408	$0.630/h	$0.114/h	0.39
c3.large	8	16	4 × 4	601	$0.840/h	$0.152/h	0.35
c3.large	10	20	4 × 5	846	$1.05/h	$0.19/h	0.31
c3.xlarge	1	4	2 × 2	139	$0.210/h	$0.038/h	0.38
c3.xlarge	2	8	2 × 4	325	$0.420/h	$0.076/h	0.32
c3.xlarge	3	12	3 × 4	555	$0.630/h	$0.114/h	0.28
c3.xlarge	4	16	4 × 4	598	$0.840/h	$0.152/h	0.35
c3.xlarge	5	20	4 × 5	955	$1.05/h	$0.19/h	0.27
HPC1	1	4	2 × 2	245	$1.34/h	N/A	1.37
HPC1	1	8	2 × 4	336	$1.34/h	N/A	1
HPC1	1	12	3 × 4	375	$1.34/h	N/A	0.89
HPC1	1	16	4 × 4	387	$1.34/h	N/A	0.87
HPC1	1	20	4 × 5	389	$1.34/h	N/A	0.86
HPC*	2	4	2 × 2	326	$2.68/h	N/A	2.05
HPC*	4	8	2 × 4	651	$5.36/h	N/A	2.06
HPC*	6	12	3 × 4	966	$8.04/h	N/A	2.08
HPC*	8	16	4 × 4	1293	$10.72/h	N/A	2.07
HPC*	10	20	4 × 5	1591	$13.4/h	N/A	2.11

we executed exactly 2 LPs for each machine. Hence in this last configuration the system uses up to 10 nodes.

We tested the four instances (**c3.large, c3.xlarge, HPC1, HPC***) with 5 partitioning configuration (20 tests overall). We notice that all the tests have been executed on a reproducible deterministic simulation using the same JVM (version 1.8.0_72). We executed each test 10 times. The results are compared using means of simulation steps performed (we observed a minimum variance in the cloud instance results, while on the HPC instances the variance was negligible). Results about performance and costs are reported in Table 2.

Analyzing the results from Table 2, we notice that D-MASON on the cloud scales pretty well. In general, we provide the following observations. The **HPC*** instance provides the best performance. This result was expected and we believe that it is mainly due to the quality of the dedicated interconnection network. It should be highlighted, however, that the **HPC*** configuration is considerably more expensive. On the other hand the cloud instances are much cheaper than the **HPC** ones. Moreover, both the cloud instances scale better than the **HPC1**, which have comparable costs. Finally, in order to measure the trade-off between performances and cost, we computed the cost (per step) of each test setting (see last column of Table 2). The results show that the cloud instances are much cheaper than dedicated instances.

5   Conclusion

The performance results described in Sect. 4 show that the proposed SIMulation-as-a-Service (SIMaaS) infrastructure provides a very attractive price-performance ratio. As a future work, it would be interesting to analyze the performance of other cloud instances also on much more demanding simulations (both in terms of computation and communication requirements).

References

1. Buyya, R., Yeo, C.S., Venugopal, S., Broberg, J., Brandic, I.: Cloud computing and emerging IT platforms: vision, hype, and reality for delivering computing as the 5th utility. Future Gen. Comput. Syst. **25**(6), 599–616 (2009). http://www.sciencedirect.com/science/article/pii/S0167739X08001957
2. Cordasco, G., Chiara, R., Fulgido, F., Vitale, M.F.: Supporting the exploratory nature of simulations in D-MASON. In: Mey, D., et al. (eds.) Euro-Par 2013. LNCS, vol. 8374, pp. 555–564. Springer, Heidelberg (2014). doi:10.1007/978-3-642-54420-0_54
3. Cordasco, G., Chiara, R., Mancuso, A., Mazzeo, D., Scarano, V., Spagnuolo, C.: A framework for distributing agent-based simulations. In: Alexander, M., et al. (eds.) Euro-Par 2011. LNCS, vol. 7155, pp. 460–470. Springer, Heidelberg (2012). doi:10.1007/978-3-642-29737-3_51
4. Cordasco, G., De Chiara, R., Mancuso, A., Mazzeo, D., Scarano, V., Spagnuolo, C.: Bringing together efficiency and effectiveness in distributed simulations: The experience with D-MASON. SIMULATION: Trans. Soc. Model. Simul. Int. **89**(10), 1236–1253 (2013)

5. Cordasco, G., Milone, F., Spagnuolo, C., Vicidomini, L.: Exploiting D-MASON on parallel platforms: a novel communication strategy. In: Lopes, L., et al. (eds.) Euro-Par 2014. LNCS, vol. 8805, pp. 407–417. Springer, Cham (2014). doi:10.1007/978-3-319-14325-5_35

6. Cosenza, B., Cordasco, G., De Chiara, R., Scarano, V.: Distributed load balancing for parallel agent-based simulations. In: Proceedings of the 19th International Euromicro Conference on Parallel, Distributed, and Network-Based Processing, (PDP 2011), pp. 62–69 (2011)

7. D'Angelo, G., Marzolla, M.: New trends in parallel and distributed simulation: from many-cores to cloud computing. Simul. Model. Pract. Theory **49**, 320–335 (2014). http://www.sciencedirect.com/science/article/pii/S1569190X14001014

8. Fujimoto, R., Malik, A., Park, A.: Parallel and distributed simulation in the cloud. Int. Simul. Mag. Soc. Model. Simul. **3**(1) (2010)

9. López-Paredes, A., Edmonds, B., Klugl, F.: Editorial of the special issue: agent based simulation of complex social systems. SIMULATION: Trans. Soc. Model. Simul. Int. **88**(1), 4–6 (2012)

10. Luke, S., Cioffi-Revilla, C., Panait, L., Sullivan, K.: MASON: a new multi-agent simulation toolkit. In: Proceedings of the 2004 SwarmFest Workshop (2004)

11. Luke, S., Cioffi-Revilla, C., Panait, L., Sullivan, K., Balan, G.: MASON: a multiagent simulation environment. Simulation **81**(7), 517–527 (2005). http://dx.doi.org/10.1177/0037549705058073

12. Reynolds, C.W.: Flocks, herds and schools: a distributed behavioral model. SIGGRAPH Comput. Graph. **21**(4), 25–34 (1987). http://doi.acm.org/10.1145/37402.37406

13. Amazon EC2. https://aws.amazon.com/ec2

14. D-MASON Official GitHub Repository. https://github.com/isislab-unisa/dmason. Accessed May 2016

15. StarCluster. http://star.mit.edu/cluster/index.html

16. Google Material Design. https://www.google.com/design/spec/material-design

17. Polymer. https://www.polymer-project.org/1.0/

18. Jetty. http://www.eclipse.org/jetty/

Load-Sharing Policies in Parallel Simulation of Agent-Based Demographic Models

Alessandro Pellegrini[1]([⊠]), Cristina Montañola-Sales[2], Francesco Quaglia[1], and Josep Casanovas-García[2]

[1] DIAG, Sapienza University of Rome, Rome, Italy
{pellegrini,quaglia}@dis.uniroma1.it
[2] inLab FIB, Barcelona School of Informatics, Barcelona, Spain
cristina.montanola@upc.edu, josepk@fib.upc.edu

Abstract. Execution parallelism in agent-Based Simulation (ABS) allows to deal with complex/large-scale models. This raises the need for runtime environments able to fully exploit hardware parallelism, while jointly offering ABS-suited programming abstractions. In this paper, we target last-generation Parallel Discrete Event Simulation (PDES) platforms for multicore systems. We discuss a programming model to support both implicit (in-place access) and explicit (message passing) interactions across concurrent Logical Processes (LPs). We discuss different load-sharing policies combining event rate and implicit/explicit LPs' interactions. We present a performance study conducted on a synthetic test case, representative of a class of agent-based models.

1 Introduction

Agent-based modeling (ABM) is a simulation technique which provides abstract representations of a scenario via a descriptive model to reproduce its evolution through its components, including their decision-making capabilities and interaction patterns. An agent can be defined as an entity (theoretical, virtual or physical) capable of acting on itself, on the environment in which it evolves, and capable of interacting with other agents [13]. ABM is very useful in capturing interactions at a macro scale coming from the way agents behave at a micro level. This intrinsic expressive power makes it a proven solution to explore complex real-world scenarios, such as disaster rescue [29], ancient societies resilience [2], epidemiology [27], and economic analysis [23].

Supporting the execution of simulation models expressed using such a versatile formalism is a task which requires a substantial methodological effort. In fact, a large number of widely-adopted ABM frameworks [17,20,22,30] is intrinsically serial, and can therefore handle a *population* which is significantly limited in its size. To avoid limiting the speed and scalability of simulations, efficient parallelization techniques must be employed. On this trend, several works aim at exploiting the high parallelism offered by GPU computing [18,24] or cluster-based parallel computing [7]. More in general, Discrete Event Simulation (DES) can be considered as a mainstream formalism to describe agent-based models.

© Springer International Publishing AG 2017
F. Desprez et al. (Eds.): Euro-Par 2016 Workshops, LNCS 10104, pp. 334–346, 2017.
DOI: 10.1007/978-3-319-58943-5_27

The reason is that agents' interactions can be abstracted as occurring at particular time instants—interactions having a specific duration can be mapped to a couple of *begin* and *end* discrete events. The mapping from ABM to DES is trivial, as the entities (agents and the environment) can be easily mapped to the general notion of Logical Process (LP) proper of DES. This is an important aspect, given the existence of a plethora of techniques globally referred to as Parallel Discrete Event Simulation (PDES) [9], which provide protocols and mechanisms to run complex DES models in parallel, allowing for model speedup and tractability of more complex and large models.

In this paper, we discuss a reference programming model for agent-based demographic models to be run on top of shared-memory PDES systems. In particular, we target the speculative paradigm incarnated by the well-known Time Warp synchronization protocol [12], which has been recently shown to provide scalability up to thousands or millions of CPU-cores [3]. Our goal is to give the highest degree of freedom to the programmer, and to ensure an efficient execution of the simulation. We target symmetric-multithread PDES environments for shared-memory multicore systems [34]. LPs are allowed to interact in a twofold way: (i) *explicitly*, namely via traditional message passing, or (ii) *implicitly*, i.e. relying on in-place memory accesses of their respective simulation states. This latter interaction is based on *cross-state synchronization* [26] to track memory areas accessed by threads scheduling LPs, and it has already been proven a good facility to enhance the programmability of agent-based models [25].

Moreover, we present three *load-sharing policies* to optimize the *binding* between LPs and worker threads of the simulation platform. As discussed in [34], this is a fundamental aspect to offer competitive performance. The binding temporarily assigns computing resources (i.e., worker threads stick to certain cores) to groups of LPs. Their composition can significantly affect the overall performance due to, e.g., reduced rollback frequency. The policies are based on: (i) *density of events* in the future event list of LPs; (ii) implicit interactions among different LPs; (iii) both implicit and explicit interactions among the LPs. Different simulative scenarios can benefit from these policies, depending on the events' generation pattern and/or the amount and the nature of the interactions. A synthetic benchmark, representative of a wide range of ABM demographic models, is used to study these policies under different workload scenarios.

The load-sharing policies can bias synchronization dynamics to let a Time Warp system improve its performance when different portions of the simulation model exhibit stricter interdependencies. This can improve the usage of computing resources while carrying out speculative processing of DES models, by reducing negative effects of speculation, such as the rollback frequency. This is the objective of classical load balancing/sharing approaches proposed in literature (see, e.g., [5,10,33]). However, these proposal consider only explicit interactions supported via the classical event cross-scheduling approach.

The remainder of this paper is structured as follows. Section 2 discusses related work. In Sect. 3 we present our programming model. Section 4 introduces our load-sharing policies. The experimental assessment is provided in Sect. 5.

2 Related Work

In the literature, there are several frameworks to efficiently support agent-based simulation, both on distributed and shared-memory systems, or on GPUs.

The MASON framework [17] pays special attention to the performance of simulation execution, addressing computing-intensive models (i.e., large scenarios with many agents), along with portability and reproducibility of the results across different hardware architectures. A parallel/distributed version (D-MASON) has been presented in [7], which relies on time-stepped synchronization and on the master/slave paradigm. We similarly address the performance of agent-based simulation execution, yet we do this for the case of speculative asynchronous (non-time-stepped) PDES, reducing the negative effects of optimism by finding proper binding between LPs and threads.

AnyLogic [14] is a commercial multi-method general-purpose simulation modeling and execution framework, offering at the same time the possibility to support discrete-event, system dynamics, and agent-based simulation. The simulation model developer can rely on graphical modeling languages to implement the simulation models, along with Java code. Differently from this framework, we target C technology and explicitly provide self-tuning capabilities in the load-sharing policies, which allow to optimize at runtime the simulation performance.

FLAME [11] is a simulation framework targeting large, complex models with large agent populations to be run on HPC platforms using MPI and OpenMP. The counterpart FLAME GPU [28] targets 3D simulations of complex systems with a multi-massive number of agents on GPU devices. We keep the ability to deal with large amount of agents (bound by the simulation state size), yet we rely on traditional CPU-based execution of the simulation model.

In the context of PDES, several works have studied the problem of finding the best binding between LPs and worker threads—see, e.g., [19,31–34]. Nevertheless, none of these works has ever used information related to the interaction between LPs to explicitly reduce the (possible) negative effects of optimistic simulation runs.

The proposal in [4], still targeting multi-core architectures as we do, proposes a technique called Dynamic Local Time Window Estimates (DLTWE), in which each processor communicates time estimates of its next inter-processor event to its neighbors, which use the estimates as bounds for advancement. The proposal specifically targets spatial simulations, in which different (close) sub-volumes could be interested by a rollback operation. A selective rollback function is described, which allows to reduce the effects of rollbacks at LPs managing "close" entities. Contrarily, we do not impose any topology or predetermined relation across the LPs, which is an implicit outcome thanks to the different supported programming model (based on in-place state access everywhere). Moreover, we limit the effect of a rollback too for applications exploiting such a programming model by explicitly avoiding causal inconsistencies across LPs that are dynamically granulated together.

3   Reference Programming Model

In the most general case, the core element of a demographic model is the life course of *individuals*, while their behaviour and their decisions strongly depend on the *environment* they act into [1]. ABM is interesting for demography due to its ability to generate personal-event histories and to produce estimates of the full distribution outcome [21]. Only two elements are required by any demographic agent-based model: the environment and the agents (with their interactions). Borrowing from the discussion in [6], we map environment portions or places to LPs, and agents to specific data structures managed by LPs' handlers.

Indeed, an agent can be described in terms of *individual-specific explanatory variables*. Changes in its state can be expressed as transitions (implemented within the LPs' event handlers) on some variables. In this way, different LPs can manipulate the same agent differently, giving more expressive power at no additional cost. The movement of an agent from a portion of space to another can be encoded by having the origin LP schedule an event carrying the agent's data structure(s) at the destination LP. This LP can then register the agent's records within its simulation state. A LP might implement any logic within its event handlers, and can therefore access any agent currently registered at it.

Nothing prevents multiple LPs from keeping in their states the records of the same agents. This reflects a scenario where LPs represent non-disjoint places, e.g., one LP might logically represent a city, while another LP might represent a workplace within it. Both LPs can manage a subset of the state transitions which involve an agent, and this organization clearly simplifies the implementation of the model, allowing for reuse/interoperability of different models. In this scenario, cross-state synchronization [26] becomes a mandatory aspect to deal with the correctness of the parallel simulation run.

By relying on cross-state synchronization, we can schematize our programming model for demography as in Fig. 1. Each LP can describe a geographical

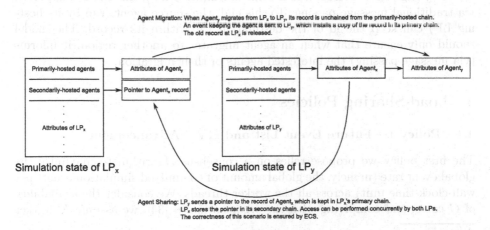

Fig. 1. Cross state-enabled programming model for agent-based demographic models.

region or a specific place (e.g., a workplace or a hospital) within one of the geographical regions. Both kinds of LPs keep two lists of records, a *primary list* and a *secondary list*. The primary list keeps track of the agents currently in the region represented by the LP, and therefore the LP's handlers can manipulate their attributes. Each agent is identified by a system-wide unique id, so that a LP's handler can manipulate subsets of the currently-hosted agents. Similarly, the secondary list keeps track of the agents which can be managed (in terms of record update) by the LP, yet are not *primarily hosted* at the region. This is a list of *pointers* to some agent records kept in the primary list of any other LP in the system. In this way, multiple LPs share a portion of their simulation state, and concurrently access the records of the agents of interest for the execution of the model, decoupling different logical aspects of the model. For example, if a LP represents a workplace, all agents working there could have their salary updated via a simple chain traversal—this operation is independent of any other action involving the agents, and is thus realized on a separate module of the model.

By this organization of the LPs' states, we envisage two different operations on agents which are of general usability for demographic agent-based models:

- *Agent sharing*: if a LP wants to share an agent with other LPs, it simply sends an event carrying a pointer to the record chained to its primary list.
- *Agent migration*: when an agent physically moves from one spatial region to another, the source LP creates a copy of the agent's record into a message, which is scheduled to the destination LP with a model-specific timestamp increment. The record currently chained to the origin LP's primary list is detached and `free()`'d[1], and all the LPs keeping a pointer to the record are instructed via message passing to removed pointers from the secondary list.

If two agents want to interact, this is likely due to them being registered at the same LP (or shared across the same LPs), and their records can be easily retrieved from LPs' lists. In the more unlikely case that two agents interact *remotely* (e.g., they interact due to some kinship relation), this can be supported via traditional message passing. To this end, the source agent (run by its hosting LP) can keep the id of the destination LP within its record. The model should only ensure that when an agent migrates to another region, it informs (via message passing) the interested agents of their migration.

4   Load-Sharing Policies

4.1   Policy 1—Future Event List and GVT Advancement

The first policy we propose relies on a consensus algorithm to maximize the global event rate (namely, the global amount of committed simulation events per wall-clock-time unit) across all the worker threads. We consider the availability of C cores, and complying with the organization in [34], we assume K worker

---

[1] This pattern is compliant with traditional PDES environments, in which the virtual address of a buffer identifies its ownership with respect to a certain LP.

threads ($K \leq C$) are available for event processing. To determine what LPs should be bound to the available worker threads, we follow these steps:

Step 1. Each worker thread k_i, $i \in [1, K]$, hosts a set of LPs with cardinality $numLP^{k_i}$. We associate each LP_l, $l \in [1, numLP^{k_i}]$, with a *workload factor* L_l, defined as the wall-clock time needed to advance LP_l's local virtual time of one unit. The factor L_l is computed considering the number of events registered into the LP's future event list which fall within a distance in the future equal to the last GVT advancement normalized to the local virtual time advancement they would produce, weighted by the average CPU time for event processing by LP_l, that is:

$$L_l = \frac{q_l \cdot \delta_l}{LVT_l^{q_l} - LVT_l^1} \tag{1}$$

where q_l is the amount of events falling within the interval of interest, LVT_l^i is the timestamp of the i-th pending event in the queue, and δ_l is the average CPU time requirement for event processing by LP_j. Among the above parameters, q_l and LVT_l^i are known in advance, since they depend on the state of the input queue. Instead, δ_l is unknown since it expresses the average cost for events that have not yet been processed. Anyhow, it can be approximated by an exponential mean over already-processed events.

Step 2. The worker thread k_i computes its total workload as:

$$L^{k_i} = \sum_{l=1}^{numLP^{k_i}} L_l \tag{2}$$

Step 3. The actual bindings are determined, accounting for the highest workload factor found among LPs. This is done in several sub-steps based on *knapsack*:

- Workload factors for the LPs hosted by k_i are non-increasingly ordered (let us call them in this order as $L_{l_1}, L_{l_2}, \ldots, L_{l_H}$);
- The highest factor L_{l_1} is taken as the reference value, and the knapsack formed by LP_{l_1} is defined;
- The other knapsacks are built by aggregating the remaining LPs according to a *0–1 one-dimensional multiple knapsack* problem-solving algorithm. This problem is NP-hard, whose integral solution is non-trivial. So we rely on a *greedy approximation approach* [8], considering K knapsacks. At each step of the algorithm, $\forall i \in [2, H]$, the k-th knapsack's size is updated as $S_k = S_k + L_{l_i}$, and it is considered full if the size constraint is violated. We then switch to the $k + 1$ knapsack, and begin to fill it. Once all K knapsacks are full, the remainder LPs (if any) are distributed in a round-robin fashion.

4.2 Policy 2—Implicit Synchronization

The memory management architecture in [26], allows to materialize cross-state accesses by leveraging a Linux kernel module which installs sibling page tables in x86 MMU registers. In this way, whenever a LP accesses a memory page bound

Algorithm 1. LP Grouping

```
 1: procedure REGROUP(LpGroup GLP, int LPid, int group)
 2:     if GLP[LPid].group ≠⊥ then
 3:         return GLP[LPid].group
 4:     end if
 5:     if group ≠⊥ then
 6:         GLP[LPid].group ← group
 7:     else
 8:         GLP[LPid].group ← LPid
 9:     end if
10:     if GLP[LPid].MaxDep ≠⊥ then
11:         GLP[LPid].group = REGROUP(GLP, GLP[LPid].MaxDep, GLP[LPid].group)
12:     end if
13:     return GLP[LPid].group
14: end procedure
```

to another LP, we can determine a cross-LP relation which we use to rebind LPs to worker threads. We rely on the *LpDependencies* matrix, which gets incremented at elements $[i, j]$ and $[j, i]$ whenever a cross-state access between LP_i and LP_j is detected. We map *LpDependencies* to an incidence matrix of a directed multigraph $G = (V, E)$ where the set of vertices V keeps the identifiers of the LPs in the system, and the set of edges E is defined as $E = \{\{i, j\} : i, j \in V \wedge LpDependencies[i, j] > 0\}$. Before converting it to an incidence matrix, we filter the values to reduce the possibility of capturing spurious cross-state relations, by using a threshold τ_{dep}. We thus build a *cross-state dependency multigraph* $G = \{\{i, j\} : i, j \in V \wedge LpDependencies[i, j] \geq \tau_{dep}\}$ and derive its incidence matrix IMG. If no edge exists in G between two LPs LP_i and LP_j, then the (i, j) IMG element's value is set to the special value $\perp$. Periodically, IMG is accessed to identify the highest cross-state access counter:

$$MaxDep_k = \max_{i\in[0,numLPs-1],i\neq k}\{IMG[k,i]\} \tag{3}$$

where $\perp$ is assumed to be the lowest value in the domain where the maximum is searched. These indices are used to build a vector of tuples, each one structured as $\langle MaxDep_k, group \rangle$ $\forall k \in [0, numLPs - 1]$. Initially, the value *group* for all the elements is set to $\perp$, telling that LP_k has its highest dependency counter set to $MaxDep_k$ and belongs to the special group $\perp$ (no group).

This construction transforms the multigraph G into another oriented multigraph $\bar{G}$ such that $\bar{V} \equiv V$, but if $\{i, j\} \in \bar{V}$, then $\{i, k\} \notin \bar{V}$ $\forall k \neq j$. This means that every node $i \in \bar{V}$ has at most one edge connecting it to another node $j \in \bar{V}$, with $i \neq j$, and by construction $j = MaxDep_i$.

A graph visiting algorithm on $\bar{G}$ is then used to group LPs together. We iterate over all indices $k \in [0, numLPs - 1]$, and for each value k we execute the recursive function REGROUP(*LpGroup*, k, $\perp$) shown in Algorithm 1. Its goal is to determine whether the selected LP already belongs to a group or, in the negative case, either the target LP is aggregated into the passed group (line 6) or a new group is created (line 8). In the positive case, only the group the LP belongs to is returned (line 3). Both cases are associated with *tentative groups*, which could be later confirmed or discarded. If the LP was associated with a tentative group, a recursive call is issued to REGROUP() (line 11), selecting as the target LP the *MaxDep* one of the current LP, and passing the ID of the group which the current LP belongs to. The group ID of the current LP is then updated with the return value of this call, which is done to backwards propagate the creation of new groups or the agglomeration to existing ones (line 13).

Once the graph visiting algorithm is completed, we apply Policy 1, taking into account the groups of LPs rather than single LPs. We note that in the scenario where no dependencies at all are detected, Algorithm 1 creates $numLPs$ groups, each one keeping a single LP. In this case, Policy 2 boils down to Policy 1.

4.3 Policy 3—Implicit and Explicit Synchronization

To account for both implicit and explicit synchronization, we must optimize towards multiple variables. For each LP_i of the system, we rely on a set of counters, identifying the volume of implicit and explicit interactions. Particularly, each LP_i is associated with a tuple $\langle I_0, I_1, \ldots, I_{numLP-1}, E_0, E_1, \ldots E_{numLP-1} \rangle$ where each component I_j is the amount of implicit accesses from LP_i to LP_j—measured in terms of cross-state synchronizations. Each E_j is the amount of events scheduled from LP_i to LP_j. For the case $i = j$, we arbitrarily set the value I_i to the number of events executed by LP_i, under the assumption that the likelihood that one LP accesses its own state is very high. This decision prevents the introduction of any bias in the general algorithm which is used for load-sharing.

Each tuple $\langle I_0, I_1, \ldots, I_{numLP-1}, E_0, E_1, \ldots E_{numLP-1} \rangle$ can be regarded as a point in an n-dimensional space, referred to as the *LPs interaction space*. The third policy aims at identifying a set of *clusters* of LPs with high interdependence. Indeed, if two LPs have similar coordinates in the n-dimensional space, they are very likely to interact. In particular, we want to identify K clusters, where K is the number of active worker threads. To this end, we rely on a variant of the Lloyd's solution [16] to the problem of finding evenly-sized Voronoi regions in an Euclidean space. This variant, known as the *k-medoids clustering algorithm* [15], tries to partition the available $numLP - 1$ LPs into K different clusters trying to minimize the effect of outliers. Specifically, if we call **i** and **j** the n-dimensional vectors associated with the coordinates of LP_i and LP_j in the n-dimensional interaction space, we define the *distance* between the two LPs as the Manhattan distance $d(\mathbf{i}, \mathbf{j}) = \|\mathbf{i} - \mathbf{j}\| = \sum_{i=1}^{n} |i_i - j_i|$. This distance is used in the objective function of the algorithm, which is defined as:

$$D = \sum_{k=1}^{K} \sum_{i \in C_k} \sum_{j \in C_k} d_{i,j} \qquad (4)$$

where C_k is the set of all LPs in cluster k. When the load-sharing resource allocation is recomputed, an initial LP is selected having the shortest distance to any other LP in the n-dimensional space—it is *approximately* in the center. Then, other $k - 1$ LPs are selected so that they decrease the value of D as much as possible. In a second phase, possible alternatives for the k objects are selected, by picking an unselected LP and trying to exchange it with one of the k

objects. The choice is kept if and only if it produces a decrease in the value of D. This step is repeated until no exchange can be found that lowers the objective function's value. We anyhow impose a maximum number of refinement steps, which can be tuned at compile time.

The selected k LPs define the centroids of the k Voronoi regions of the n-dimensional interaction space. The LPs belonging to each group can then be picked minimizing the distance $d(\mathbf{i}, \mathbf{j})$ with respect to the centroids.

5   Experimental Results

To study our policies, we rely on a synthetic benchmark which is representative of a wide range of agent-based models. Upon simulation startup, a pre-determined number of LPs acting as non-disjoint hexagonal cell regions is set up. They implement event handlers which, with a certain probability, operate changes on the hosted agents, execute an agent migration, or schedule to any other LP an *operative event*, i.e. an event associated with an operation correlating two agents hosted by different LPs.

As described, we map agents to data structures. An agent is described by a bitmask of attributes and a payload which is updated by the event handler implemented at any LP. In particular, we define three operations:

- *State-machine update*: with a certain probability p_{smu}, a bit in the bitmask is negated, mimicking a state transition;
- *Memory update*: with a certain probability p_{mu}, a portion of the payload of the agent's structure is written with random data, mimicking the update of less-concise metadata describing the agent;
- *Remote agent interaction*: with a certain probability p_{rai}, a random LP is scheduled an event piggybacking random data. Upon its receipt, a random agent is picked and the content of the event is copied into its state, mimicking kinship or family interactions with relatives who live in separate places.

Upon simulation startup, each LP instantiates the same number of agents, to have an even distribution, and links them to the primary list. Each LP schedules to itself separate chains of events, exponentially distributed, which trigger the state-machine and memory update operations. Once one of these operations is triggered, the LP scans the whole list of records so as to randomly select agents which undergo the corresponding operation. After a certain residence time, an agent is migrated towards one remote region, and a new agent migration event is scheduled, so that its lifetime within a certain region is pre-determined. Upon installation, with a certain probability p_{sh} the agent is shared (via message passing) with another region as well.

We have varied the probability p telling whether two LPs interact via message passing—$p = 0.5$ shows an even amount of in-place accesses vs message passing. We set $p_{smu} = 0.3$, $p_{mu} = 0.5$, $p_{rai} = 0.2$, and $p_{sh} = 0.1$, we use 1024 regions, with a population of 100.000 agents, and run the experiments on ROOT-Sim [34] on a 32-cores NUMA machine with 32 GB of RAM. The payload buffer of an

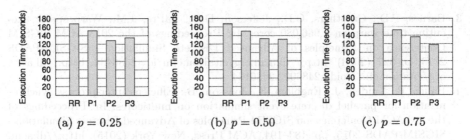

(a) $p = 0.25$ (b) $p = 0.50$ (c) $p = 0.75$

Fig. 2. Experimental results with different in-place state access probability p.

agent is 16 KB, for a total of $\sim$1.6 GB of live simulation state (i.e., without considering checkpoints). Additionally, we compare to an "agnostic" load sharing, where LPs are bound to threads in a round robin fashion (RR in the plots). By the results in Fig. 2, we can see that when the amount of message-passing interactions is non-minimal (Fig. 2(c)), Policy 3 offers the better results. In fact, this is the only policy which accounts for both implicit and explicit interaction among LPs. On the other hand, when the vast majority of the interactions rely on in-place accesses (Fig. 2(a)), Policy 2 gives better results, although in a slightly reduced way since the graph visiting algorithm is not able to capture a large amount of mutual dependencies. Policy 1 is interaction-agnostic, and is not therefore able to compete with the other two policies.

In the best case, there is a performance speedup of around 30% with respect to the RR policy. This evidences that load-sharing policies are fundamental to offer a competitive simulation when run on shared-memory systems.

6 Conclusions

In this paper we have discussed a parallel ABM programming model for demography, using the DES formalism. Additionally, we have proposed three different policies to support efficient load balancing under different workloads. By our results, we showed how load balancing is fundamental when running simulations on shared-memory machines. Moreover, policies which explicitly account for (implicit and explicit) interactions can find a binding between LPs and threads which allows to better capture the parallelism degree of the model, and thus increase performance.

References

1. Andrew, H.: Demographic Methods. Routledge, London (1998)
2. Balbo, A.L., Rubio-Campillo, X., Rondelli, B., Ramírex, M., Lancelotti, C., Torrano, A., Salpeteur, M., Lipovetzky, N., Reyes-García, V., Montañola-Sales, C., Madella, M.: Agent-based simulation of Holocene monsoon precipitation patterns and hunter-gatherer population dynamics in semi-arid environments. J. Archaeol. Method Theory **21**(2), 426–446 (2014)

3. Barnes, P.D., Carothers, C.D., Jefferson, D.R., LaPre, J.M.: Warp speed: executing time warp on 1,966,080 cores. In: Proceedings of the 2013 ACM SIGSIM Conference on Principles of Advanced Discrete Simulation - SIGSIM-PADS 2013, p. 327 (2013). http://dl.acm.org/citation.cfm?id=2486134, http://dl.acm.org/citation.cfm?doid=2486092.2486134

4. Bauer, P., Lindén, J., Engblom, S., Jonsson, B.: Efficient inter-process synchronization for parallel discrete event simulation on multicores. In: Proceedings of the 3rd ACM Conference on SIGSIM-Principles of Advanced Discrete Simulation - SIGSIM-PADS 2015, pp. 183–194. ACM Press, New York (2015). http://dl.acm.org/citation.cfm?doid=2769458.2769476

5. Carothers, C.D., Fujimoto, R.M.: Efficient execution of time warp programs on heterogeneous, NOW platforms. IEEE Trans. Parallel Distrib. Syst. **11**(3), 299–317 (2000)

6. Cingolani, D., Pellegrini, A., Quaglia, F.: RAMSES: reversibility-based agent modeling and simulation environment with speculation-support. In: Hunold, S., et al. (eds.) Euro-Par 2015. LNCS, vol. 9523, pp. 466–478. Springer, Cham (2015). doi:10.1007/978-3-319-27308-2_38

7. Cordasco, G., Chiara, R., Mancuso, A., Mazzeo, D., Scarano, V., Spagnuolo, C.: A framework for distributing agent-based simulations. In: Alexander, M., et al. (eds.) Euro-Par 2011. LNCS, vol. 7155, pp. 460–470. Springer, Heidelberg (2012). doi:10.1007/978-3-642-29737-3_51

8. Dantzig, G.B.: Discrete-variable extremum problems. Oper. Res. **5**, 266–288 (1957)

9. Fujimoto, R.M.: Parallel discrete event simulation. Commun. ACM **33**(10), 30–53 (1990)

10. Glazer, D.W., Tropper, C.: On process migration and load balancing in time warp. IEEE Trans. Parallel Distrib. Syst. **4**(3), 318–327 (1993)

11. Holcombe, M., Coakley, S., Smallwood, R.: A general framework for agent-based modelling of complex systems. In: Proceedings of the 2006 European Conference on Complex Systems. European Complex Systems Society Paris, France (2006)

12. Jefferson, D.R.: Virtual time. ACM Trans. Progr. Lang. Syst. **7**(3), 404–425 (1985)

13. Jennings, N.R., Sycara, K., Wooldridge, M.: A roadmap of agent research and development. Auton. Agents Multi-agent Syst. **1**(1), 7–38 (1998). http://eprints.soton.ac.uk/252112/

14. Karpov, Y.G.: AnyLogic – a new generation professional simulation tool. In: Proceedings of the 6th International Congress on Mathematical Modeling, MATHMOD (2004)

15. Kaufman, L., Rousseeuw, P.J.: Clustering by means of medoids. In: Statistical Data Analysis Based on the L1-Norm and Related Methods, pp. 405–416 (1987)

16. Lloyd, S.: Least squares quantization in PCM. IEEE Trans. Inf. Theory **28**(2), 129–137 (1982). http://ieeexplore.ieee.org/lpdocs/epic03/wrapper.htm?arnumber=1056489

17. Luke, S., Cioffi-Revilla, C., Panait, L., Sullivan, K., Balan, G.: MASON: a multi-agent simulation environment. Simulation **81**(7), 517–527 (2005)

18. Lysenko, M., D'Souza, R.M.: A framework for megascale agent based model simulations on the GPU. J. Artif. Soc. Soc. Simul. **11**(4), 10 (2008). http://jasss.soc.surrey.ac.uk/11/4/10.html

19. Marziale, N., Nobilia, F., Pellegrini, A., Quaglia, F.: Granular time warp objects. In: Proceedings of the 2016 ACM/SIGSIM Conference on Principles of Advanced Discrete Simulation, PADS, pp. 57–68. ACM Press, New York (2016). http://dl.acm.org/citation.cfm?doid=2901378.2901390

20. Minar, N., Burkhart, R., Langton, C., Askenazi, M.: The SWARM simulation system: a toolkit for building multi-agent simulations. Technical report, Santa Fe Institute (1996)
21. Montañola-Sales, C., Casanovas-Garcia, J., Kaplan-Marcusán, A., Cela-Espín, J.M.: Demographic agent-based simulation of Gambians immigrants in Spain. In: Proceedings of the 10th Social Simulation Conference. European Social Simulation Association (2014)
22. North, M.J., Howe, T.R., Collier, N.T., Vos, J.R., M.J. North, T.R. Howe, N.T. Collier, J.V.: The repast simphony runtime system. In: Proceedings of the Agent 2005 Conference on Generative Social Processes, Models and Mechanisms, pp. 151–158. Argonne National Laboratory (2005)
23. Page, S.E.: Agent-based models. In: Durlauf, S.N., Blume, L.E. (eds.) The New Palgrave Dictionary of Economics, pp. 47–52. Nature Publishing Group (2008). http://www.dictionaryofeconomics.com/article?id=pde2008_A000218
24. Park, H.K., Han, J.H.: Fast rendering of large crowds using GPU. In: Stevens, S.M., Saldamarco, S.J. (eds.) ICEC 2008. LNCS, vol. 5309, pp. 197–202. Springer, Heidelberg (2008). doi:10.1007/978-3-540-89222-9_24
25. Pellegrini, A., Quaglia, F.: Programmability and performance of parallel ECS-based simulation of multi-agent exploration models. In: Lopes, L., et al. (eds.) Euro-Par 2014. LNCS, vol. 8805, pp. 395–406. Springer, Cham (2014). doi:10.1007/978-3-319-14325-5_34
26. Pellegrini, A., Quaglia, F.: Transparent multi-core speculative parallelization of DES models with event and cross-state dependencies. In: Proceedings of the 2014 ACM/SIGSIM Conference on Principles of Advanced Discrete Simulation, PADS, pp. 105–116. ACM Press (2014). http://dl.acm.org/citation.cfm?doid=2601381.2601398
27. Prats, C., Montañola-Sales, C., Gilabert-Navarro, J.F., Valls, J., Casanovas-Garcia, J., Vilaplana, C., Cardona, P.J., López, D.: Individual-based modeling of tuberculosis in a user-friendly interface: understanding the epidemiological role of population heterogeneity in a city. Front. Microbiol. **6**, 1564 (2016). http://journal.frontiersin.org/Article/10.3389/fmicb.2015.01564/abstract
28. Richmond, P., Romano, D.: Agent based GPU, a real-time 3D simulation and interactive visualisation framework for massive agent based modelling on the GPU. In: Proceedings International Workshop on Supervisualisation (2008)
29. Takahashi, T., Tadokoro, S., Ohta, M., Ito, N.: Agent based approach in disaster rescue simulation - from test-bed of multiagent system to practical application. In: Birk, A., Coradeschi, S., Tadokoro, S. (eds.) RoboCup 2001. LNCS, vol. 2377, pp. 102–111. Springer, Heidelberg (2002). doi:10.1007/3-540-45603-1_11
30. Tisue, S., Wilensky, U.: Netlogo: a simple environment for modeling complexity. In: Proceedings of the International Conference on Complex Systems, ICCS, pp. 1–10. NECSI (2004). http://ccl.sesp.northwestern.edu/papers/netlogo-iccs2004.pdf
31. Vitali, R., Pellegrini, A., Quaglia, F.: A load sharing architecture for optimistic simulations on multi-core machines. In: Proceedings of the 19th International Conference on High Performance Computing, HiPC, pp. 1–10. IEEE Computer Society (2012)
32. Vitali, R., Pellegrini, A., Quaglia, F.: Assessing load sharing within optimistic simulation platforms. In: Proceedings of the 2012 Winter Simulation Conference, WSC. Society for Computer Simulation (2012)

33. Vitali, R., Pellegrini, A., Quaglia, F.: Load sharing for optimistic parallel simulations on multi core machines. ACM SIGMETRICS Perform. Eval. Rev. **40**(3), 2–11 (2012). http://dl.acm.org/citation.cfm?doid=2425248.2425250
34. Vitali, R., Pellegrini, A., Quaglia, F.: Towards symmetric multi-threaded optimistic simulation kernels. In: Proceedings of the 26th Workshop on Principles of Advanced and Distributed Simulation, PADS, pp. 211–220. IEEE Computer Society, July 2012. http://ieeexplore.ieee.org/articleDetails.jsp?arnumber=6305914, http://ieeexplore.ieee.org/lpdocs/epic03/wrapper.htm?arnumber=6305914

Computational Considerations for a Global Human Well-Being Simulation

Aaron Howell[1] and Paul Brenner[2](✉)

[1] Indiana University South Bend, South Bend, IN 46615, USA
aarohowe@umail.iu.edu
[2] The University of Notre Dame, Notre Dame, IN 46556, USA
paul.r.brenner@nd.edu

Abstract. Global scale human simulations have application in diverse fields such as economics, anthropology and marketing. The sheer number of agents, however, makes them extremely sensitive to variations in algorithmic complexity resulting in potentially prohibitive computational resource costs. In this paper we show that the computational capability of modern servers has increased to the point where billions of individual agents can be modeled on moderate institutional resources and (in a few years) on high end consumer systems. We close with the proposition of future frameworks to enable collaborative modelling of the global human population.

Keywords: Agent-based modeling · Parallel programming · Human well-being · Computational social science

1 Introduction

Effective social planning and behavioural understanding is essential to improving global human well-being. Given changing global economic, social and political landscapes, how will organizations and nations forecast and prioritize their internal and external actions? It is difficult for governments and organizations to effectively prioritize their policies and resource spending due to the complex nature of human interaction–especially on a global scale. Despite libraries full of expert strategic guidance and lessons learned in diplomatic, military, and development efforts, a major portion of the human population lacks basic physical and social resources for personal well-being. In a rapidly evolving and complex landscape, we must develop new tools to better leverage our accumulated knowledge, experience, and the myriad of new data sensors and emerging computational technologies.

One such tool is our ability to now produce large scale social simulations to model behavioral patterns. In this work we specifically focus on computational social science simulation tools in relation to modeling the global human population given current computer systems capabilities. Fortunately for us, computational capability is growing at a faster rate than the human population of Earth,

© Springer International Publishing AG 2017
F. Desprez et al. (Eds.): Euro-Par 2016 Workshops, LNCS 10104, pp. 347–355, 2017.
DOI: 10.1007/978-3-319-58943-5_28

which will allow us to increase the complexity (and accuracy) of the models and make global scale simulations more tractable on increasingly less expensive IT infrastructure.

1.1 Related Work

Over the past decade a number of researchers have demonstrated that large scale agent-based simulations are viable. In 2008, Lysenko and D'Souza [1] used GPGPU accelerated techniques to model up to 16 million agents spatially using an AMD Athlon64 3500+ with 1 GB RAM and an NVidia GeForce 8800 GTX GPU. In 2010, Rakowski et al. [2] created a grid-based framework to simulate the 38 million human population of Poland using data from LandScan and the Polish National Census Bureau. In 2011, Parker and Epstein [3] used GSAM to implement a graph-based model of disease propagation amongst 6.75 billion people using 32 CPU cores and 256 GB of memory. In 2014, Richmond [4] used FLAME GPU [5,6] 1.3 to simulate up to 16.7 million simple agents with SugarScape on an Intel Core i7-2600K Machine using an NVIDIA K40 GPU with CUDA 6.0. In 2015, Collier et al. [7] simulated the spread of CA-MRSA throughout the population of Chicago (2.9 million people) using a graph-based representation and Repast HPC. Also in 2015, Lettieri et al. [8] modeled the spread of social norms using D-MASON [9] amongst a graph-based population of 2.5 million commuters on a cluster of 8 16 core servers. Their work serves as a foundation of demonstrated computational capability motivating the evolution of global scale models.

2   Creating a Global Scale Human Well-Being Simulation

2.1   A Target Framework

Our societies have developed advanced technologies to meet diverse needs (advanced medicines, self driving cars, new energy sources) but we have yet to solve global grand challenges such as hunger, violence and economic inequality. Understanding global complexities with increased accuracy and resolution is essential to formulating effective global strategy, policy and plans. If the computational capability of our devices continues to double every two years (leveraging parallelism to complement deviations from Moore's Law) we must start developing software frameworks (and parallel algorithms) for 2025 that leverage highly parallel systems 30× more capable than today's leading technology. The ability to globally model 10 billion human agents should not be a hurdle, we must make it part of the solution.

As one example framework (Fig. 1), a Global Open Simulator (GOS) would provide a dynamically re-scalable platform on which to develop, test, verify and validate strategy and plans at a speed, breadth, complexity and depth of resolution previously deemed intractable. The open nature of the framework is a differentiator from prior attempts which became unsustainably mired in licensing restrictions and limited support/expertise. A modular GOS framework will

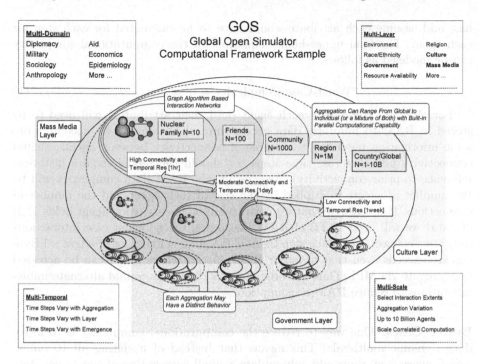

Fig. 1. A visual representation of a target GOS framework.

allow for layered application of influential factors on human behavior such as culture, government and media. The level of aggregation can vary from a global scale of 10 billion agents (humans) down to an individual. Additionally, temporal modeling variance allows the strategic analyst to set the time horizon (hour, day, month, etc.) and dynamically change resolution if an emergent behavior is triggered (agents reach a certain hunger or insecurity level).

2.2 Algorithm Analysis

Before we started running actual tests at the scale of 1 billion agents (as discussed in the next section) we wanted to evaluate the basic algorithmic bounds for our simulation in terms of computational requirement, data size requirements (both transient RAM and persistent disk storage) and, ultimately, the potential computational platforms on which to run our tests.

In the Worst Case: First, assume every person on the planet interacts with everyone else (in a single time step), we can thus use η^2 as an upper bound, where η is the number of agents (order 10 billion). Second, assume every agent in the simulation is updated at every step (σ). For instance, if we want each step to represent an hour, we would need to have 365×24 steps to study one year. Third, we would need to account for the number of attributes (α) each agent has; and assume each attribute would have to be calculated for each step for each agent. The final upper bound equation for the computational complexity can be modeled as follows:

$$\text{Worst Case Complexity} = \eta^2 \times \sigma \times \alpha \tag{1}$$

For the data complexity each agent (and their attributes) will need to be stored in RAM to minimize data access time. Additionally, we need to store some information regarding the degree of connectivity between agents, should connectivity persist across time steps (or should the model require historical reference to prior connectivity). As a result, the RAM data complexity will be the number of agents multiplied by the size of each agent and the number of connections. If we assume that we have 10 billion agents (each agent holds 1KB of data) we will need 10 TB of RAM. Assuming the η^2 worst case interactions indicate a connection at each step the WC RAM for connecting η^2 edges $\times$ 1 Byte quickly exceeds even that of major HPC clusters where RAM can be accessed in aggregate via MPI. Thus our brief analysis directs us to find alternate implementations to reduce RAM consumption.

Better Cases: One way to reduce the computational complexity is to introduce dynamic multiscale. This means that instead of updating all 10 billion agents every step, we would only update a small aggregation of agents per step, with the entire population being recalibrated only after several steps. Another way to greatly reduce the computational complexity is to reduce the number of interactions per step. It is likely unrealistic to assume that everyone on the planet interacts with every other person on the planet at each step (note: this paper explicitly makes no argument in terms of the most realistic models). A better model will reduce the number of interactions from order η^2 to something smaller, such as order $\eta \log \eta$ or just order η. For instance, if we assume that people will only interact with the members in their nuclear family of 10 people (or 10 random people) at each step, the number of interactions per step would be reduced to $10 \times \eta$.

To save memory all of each agent's attributes could be in a large group array, instead of in each individual agent's object as indicated by Parker et al. [3]. Each agent is not stored as its own separate object, but rather just an entry in each array in the group class, saving memory on object overhead. Another method is to use agent compression, which is when similar agents are grouped together as an aggregate agent that will behave as a single agent [1]. Finally one could simplify edges via an integer representation such that storing similar edges as value '4' results in a lookup to the specification of 4's properties rather than each edge actually storing the full property set.

Ultimately the choice of "better case" algorithmic reductions has varying impact depending upon the computational platform. In this case we typically refer to enterprise cluster, server or high end consumer parallel programming platforms and architectures. For instance, in 2008, a GPU-based framework for agent-based modeling yielded over a 9000× speed increase when compared to the contemporary CPU-based frameworks of SugarScape [1]. With equally impressive scale and speed on a totally different (non-GPU) architecture Repast HPC enables scalable tightly coupled MPI and MPI+OpenMP based simulations on HPC clusters [10]. Other less tightly coupled simulation techniques have run on highly distributed commercial cloud infrastructures to potentially facilitate more cost-effective or accessible simulation infrastructure [11].

2.3   Tests at 1 Billion

To test the practicality of our global human well-being modeling objectives, we set an initial goal to simulate up to 1 billion agents. We used RepastHPC version 2.1 as a framework for our simulations, using Open MPI version 1.8.7 and the Intel v15 compiler. Our server was a Dell PowerEdge R920 with 4 12 core 2.3 GHz Intel Xeon CPUs (E7-4850v2) with 3 TB RAM running the RHEL6 OS.

We used the well-known prisoner's dilemma model [12] as provided as part of a Repast tutorial. In this implementation pairs of interacting agents randomly decide whether to cooperate with their partner. Points are then assigned to each agent based on whether they chose to cooperate, and whether their partner chose to cooperate. The model was a bit too computationally simplistic to accurately represent calculations over multiple human attributes, so we increased the computational complexity by adding 1000 floating point operations per agent interaction per step. We also made some small changes to the model's graph instantiation (prior to the first step) which allowed for the same number of paired interactions per step but removed a non-linear instantiation computational cost.

We started by testing how well runtime reduced with increasing core counts. According to our trials, when modeling 1 million agents for 100 steps, doubling the core count generally halved the runtime in linear fashion up to 32 cores. Bridging multiple servers for more cores showed some significant MPI communication overhead, and as our focus was shifting to RAM limitations, we therefore decided to use 32 cores on a single large memory server for the remainder of the tests. We then started running our simulations on varying numbers of agents in order to test scalability. After our edits to the original RepastHPC code, we were able to achieve linear scaling for both runtime and RAM usage for increasing numbers of agents. As a result, we were able to run a 100 step simulation of 1 billion agents in 29 h using 800 GB of RAM as shown in Fig. 2.

3   Toward a Modular Framework for 10 Billion

3.1   Computational Limits

In this work we successfully performed a social simulation (based on the prisoner's dilemma) of 1 billion human agents over 100 steps using a graph representation in roughly one day's compute time (29 h). This was possible on a single enterprise class large memory server. The primary resource limitation was RAM

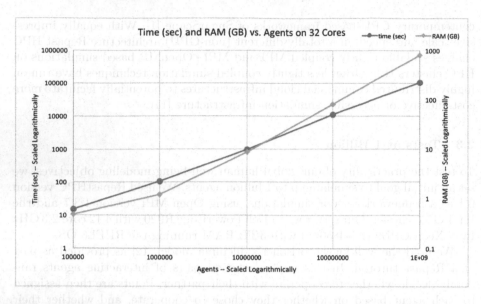

Fig. 2. Runtime and RAM usage for varying agent counts using 32 cores for 100 steps.

consumption which would have been 8 TB for a 10 billion agent system. It is feasible to aggregate 8 TB of RAM across numerous HPC cluster compute nodes but the MPI communication overhead and cost of the numerous cluster nodes would be prohibitive compared to a single large memory server. Based on our findings it was more important to re-organize code for minimal memory footprint than to modify the computations at each step to reduce runtime. This of course is entirely dependent upon the interaction model you choose but still highlights the fact that memory requirements are a first class design consideration when designing a platform to handle 10 billion human agents.

3.2 Vision of a Global Collaboration Platform

The authors have a vision for a community evolved platform on which to develop and share human-well being models that scale up to the global population. Certainly, smaller scale or multi-scale models would also be supported, but we want to focus design efforts on developing infrastructure over the next 10 years that will facilitate increasingly accurate and complex models up to 8 billion (the 2025 mean world population per 2015 United Nations estimates). The computational estimates we presented, simulation results at 1 billion and peer publications provide the foundation to enable the continued project evolution. In Fig. 3 we provide one example vision of the distributed infrastructure that will allow for community driven evolution of the models.

The following are critical steps in initial development and implementation:

- Establish an Initial Team of (subject matter experts) SMEs
- Scope Phase One Human Behavior Layers

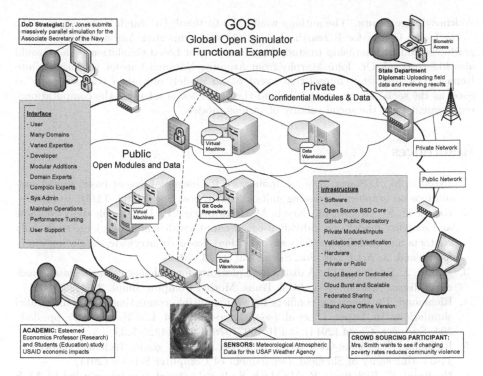

Fig. 3. Infrastructure for community driven human well-being simulation.

- Scope Phase One Aggregate Population Measures
- Design Prototype Computational Architecture and Portal Interface
- Public Messaging and Coordination Plan for Volunteer Participants
- Identify verification and validation measures to include regression testing on historical data outcomes and integration of realtime incites from deep learning as applied to various big data sources

3.3 Future Work

Our team plans to extend more human simulation models to the 1–10 billion agent scale over multiple computer architectures to better classify the computational resource requirements of various model representations (geospatial, graph, aggregated objects, etc.) Our plan is to use open models publically posted via the Open Agent Based Modeling Consortium (we are currently scaling up a model posted by Dr. Christopher Thron). Similarly we hope to cross reference the varied model representations across common HPC, enterprise and high end consumer architectural platforms. The architectural cross comparison will likely be more challenging as some open codes written for MPI may not be naturally algorithmically portable to accelerators (GPUs, FPGA, etc.) and vise versa.

Acknowledgements. The authors would like to thank Dr. Jarek Nabrzyski and the Notre Dame Center for Research Computing who supported Aaron Howell's undergraduate student internship to study large scale agent based simulations. They would also like to thank Dr. John Murphy from Argonne National Lab for his insights into Repast HPC and wise counsel that agent based models of greater scale are only as good as the social science models behind them. We focus solely on the computational requirements; not the social validity of various models.

References

1. Lysenko, M., D'Souza, R.M.: A framework for megascale agent based model simulations on graphics processing units. J. Artif. Soc. Soc. Simul. **11**(4), 10 (2008)
2. Rakowski, F., Gruziel, M., Krych, M., Radomski, J.P.: Large scale daily contacts and mobility model - an individual-based countrywide simulation large scale daily contacts and mobility model - an individual-based countrywide simulation study for Poland. J. Artif. Soc. Soc. Simul. **13**(1), 13 (2010)
3. Parker, J., Epstein, J.M.: A distributed platform for global-scale agent-based models of disease transmission. ACM Trans. Model. Comput. Simul. **22**(1), 2 (2011)
4. Richmond, P.: Resolving conflicts between multiple competing agents in parallel simulations. In: Lopes, L., et al. (eds.) Euro-Par 2014. LNCS, vol. 8805, pp. 383–394. Springer, Cham (2014). doi:10.1007/978-3-319-14325-5_33
5. Richmond, P.: Flame GPU technical report and user guide. Technical report CS-11-03. University of Sheffield, Department of Computer Science (2011)
6. Heywood, P., Richmond, P., Maddock, S.: Road network simulation using FLAME GPU. In: Hunold, S., et al. (eds.) Euro-Par 2015. LNCS, vol. 9523, pp. 429–441. Springer, Cham (2015). doi:10.1007/978-3-319-27308-2_35
7. Collier, N., Ozik, J., Macal, C.M.: Large-scale agent-based modeling with repast HPC: a case study in parallelizing an agent-based model. In: Hunold, S., et al. (eds.) Euro-Par 2015. LNCS, vol. 9523, pp. 454–465. Springer, Cham (2015). doi:10.1007/978-3-319-27308-2_37
8. Lettieri, N., Spagnuolo, C., Vicidomini, L.: Distributed agent-based simulation and GIS: an experiment with the dynamics of social norms. In: Hunold, S., et al. (eds.) Euro-Par 2015. LNCS, vol. 9523, pp. 379–391. Springer, Cham (2015). doi:10.1007/978-3-319-27308-2_31
9. Balan, G.C., Cioffi-Revilla, C., Luke, S., Panait, L., Paus, S.: MASON: a Java multi-agent simulation library. In: Proceedings of the Agent 2003 Conference (2003)
10. Park, B.H., Allen, M.R., White, D., Weber, E., Murphy, J.T., North, M.J., Sydeko, P.: MIRAGE: a framework for data-driven collaborative high-resolution simulation. In: Proceedings of the 13th International Conference on GeoComputation, Richardson, Texas, USA, pp. 343–348 (2015)
11. Wittek, P., Rubio-Campillo, X.: Scalable agent-based modelling with cloud HPC resources for social simulations. In: IEEE 4th International Conference on Cloud Computing Technology and Science, Taipei, Taiwan, pp. 355–362 (2012)
12. Rapoport, A., Chammah, A.M.: Prisoner's Dilemma: A Study in Conflict and Cooperation. The University of Michigan Press, Ann Arbor Paperbacks (1970)

13. Cordasco, G., Chiara, R., Mancuso, A., Mazzeo, D., Scarano, V., Spagnuolo, C.: A framework for distributing agent-based simulations. In: Alexander, M., et al. (eds.) Euro-Par 2011. LNCS, vol. 7155, pp. 460–470. Springer, Heidelberg (2012). doi:10. 1007/978-3-642-29737-3_51
14. Collier, N., North, M.: Repast HPC: a platform for large-scale agent-based modeling. In: Large-Scale Computing Techniques for Complex System Simulations. Wiley, Hoboken (2011)

PBIO - International Workshop on Parallelism in Bioinformatics

High Performance Small RNA Detection with Pipelined Task Parallel Computation Model

Linqiang Ouyang and Jin H. Park(✉)

Computer Science Department, California State University, Fresno, CA 93740, USA
jimmyou587@gmail.com, jpark@csufresno.edu

Abstract. We present efficient parallel computation models for accelerating secondary structure based RNA sequence searching tool Infernal cmsearch, which processes covariance models representing small RNA families in a serial manner with high time complexity. The proposed computation models are based on the pipelined task parallel strategy and both static and dynamic load balancing schemes are developed and used to exploit the maximum parallelism. For the dynamic load balancing, regression model based heuristic is used and tested. The computation models are implemented with Pthreads and OpenMP and tested for performance within the scope of searching Rfam bacterial small RNA families in HMP (Human Microbiome Project) gastrointestinal_track database. Our experimental results show that the proposed computation models yield 1.56×–3.41× speedup, depending on the versions of the models. The proposed computation models are scalable and flexible to be used with other trivial data parallel approaches.

Keywords: RNA prediction · High performance computing · Thread · Pipeline · Load balancing

1 Introduction

High performance computation has always been demanded in the fields of bioinformatics and computational biology since the volume of biological database has been increasing explosively in recent years. To achieve high performance in bioinformatics applications researchers have proposed diversified approaches of accelerating popularly used tools including software- and hardware-oriented approaches [1–7]. Besides, recent technology of clustered or cloud systems makes naive users attain the power of parallel systems without using specialized parallel codes, e.g., OpenMP, MPI, etc., but simply running multiple copies of an application with divided data through job submission queuing system, e.g., condor [8,9]. Regardless of the system environment including stand-alone, clustered/cloud and specialized systems, developing high performance versions of applications is ever demanded and beneficial.

In this paper, we propose and describe an efficient high performance approach of accelerating RNA sequence searching tool Infernal [10], more specifically, the

© Springer International Publishing AG 2017
F. Desprez et al. (Eds.): Euro-Par 2016 Workshops, LNCS 10104, pp. 359–371, 2017.
DOI: 10.1007/978-3-319-58943-5_29

cmsearch module in the Infernal package, based on task parallel and pipelined parallel processing methodologies. We name this model 'pipelined task parallel' computation model in this paper. Infernal cmsearch module is implemented as a filter pipeline, which consists of seven major filtering stages [10]. Each stage in the filtering pipeline is designed to yield reduced data to be processed in the following stages. However, even with this series of filtering operations, the execution time of the cmsearch module is considerably long in many cases. To address this, Infernal cmsearch provides MPI and Pthread mode options, which are based on a straightforward data parallel methodology, i.e., providing multiple copies (paths) of the serial pipeline with divided input data. However, this simple and static data parallel approach cannot exploit highly efficient parallelism since the code in each pipeline path is same as the original serial code. This becomes the motivation of our research. Our aim is parallelizing the serial operations in the filtering pipeline. Our proposed 'pipelined task parallel' computation model can be deployed in either a stand-alone multicore workstation/server environment or a clustered/cloud system environment in which each node is a multicore machine. Also, the proposed approach is suitable to be integrated with the straightforward data parallel approach used in the cmsearch code. In our current practice, the proposed approach is implemented with Pthread and OpenMP, and sophisticated load balancing methodologies are developed and used. The stages in the filtering pipeline are executed in a pipelined parallel manner, i.e., after the initial trigger time slices, all stages in the filtering pipeline work in parallel with a different segment of input data to each stage - a kind of systolic processing.

The rest of this paper is organized as follows. In Sect. 2, we briefly review related work on the Infernal tool and background knowledge. In Sect. 3, detailed description of the cmsearch program is provided. In Sect. 4, our proposed approaches of achieving the maximum parallelism is described in detail. In Sect. 5, experimental results and discussion are provided, and Sect. 6 concludes the paper.

2   Related Work and Background

Before the emergence of Infernal, some heuristic sequence homology searching tools, e.g., FASTA, BLAST, BLAT, etc., had already appeared, but the alignment processing is based on the RNA primary structure, which is not able to detect homology in a group of samples having homologous secondary structures. This became the motivation of developing Infernal tool [10]. Inspired by the method of formalizing the linear sequence alignment proposed in [11], a structural RNA model is used as the query in Infernal.

The first version of the Infernal package was released in 2002 [12]. In this tool, a memory-efficient dynamic programming algorithm is used with a divide-and-conquer strategy [12]. To achieve a better time complexity, a query dependent banded method was introduced in Infernal in 2007 and it was able to obtain the average time complexity of $O(LN^*2.4) \sim O(LN^*1.3)$, where L and N are the numbers of base pairs in the query and database sequences, respectively [13].

Researchers considered Infernal 1.0 (released in 2009) as the first reasonably complete version of the tool [14,15]. In this version, two levels of filtering operations are used to reduce the data to be processed. The HMM (Hidden Markov Model) based filtering described in [16] was used as the primary filter and the QDB CYK maximum likelihood searching algorithm is used as the secondary filter. Subsequences that passed through the two filters are searched with Inside algorithm [17] for the final alignment. Although later versions provide considerably improved performance, Infernal cmsearch program remains as a computationally expensive module. The current version of Infernal cmsearch (version 1.1) is claimed to be 100-fold faster than the previous version [10,18]. This improvement is achieved by using a new filtering pipeline, which takes advantages of using profile HMM based filtering operations originated from HMMER3 project [19] together with banded covariance model based dynamic programming algorithms [20].

2.1   Covariance Model Based Alignment

Infernal cmsearch module processes two input files, a CM (covariance model) file representing an RNA secondary structure and a database sequence file in the fasta format. A CM file consists of both profile HMM and CM representations derived from the consensus structure of the multiple RNA sequence alignments found in an RNA family (refer to the Rfam CM models [21]). Infernal package provides a module named 'cmbuild' for this and how a CM file is constructed is described in [10] in detail. Cmsearch program scans the database sequence file to align the profile HMM and the CM provided in a CM file using multiple dynamic programming algorithms. In this subsection, we briefly describe the structure of a CM file.

A CM is a specific repetitive profile SCFG architecture, which models a consensus secondary structure of an RNA family. Each CM has a group of states that are mapped to consensus and non-consensus positions in the RNA secondary structure from a given group of multiple sequence alignments in an RNA family. The final CM becomes a list of states connected in a directed graph in which each state has both position specific emission and transition probability scores [10]. A profile HMM is a repetitive HMM architecture that associates with each consensus column of a multiple alignment with a single type of model node. A profile HMM could be thought as a special case of a CM.

Each CM file built from the cmbuild module consists of both CM and profile HMM sections each of which contains header and state parts as illustrated in Fig. 1. The CM header part includes metadata such as model name, RNA family, number of nodes, number of states, etc. The CM states part contains the representation of the entire model. Each node in the CM model is denoted by a line of node type and node index followed by a couple of lines of state information. Each state line consists of state type, state index, indices of parent/child states that can transit, bit scores, etc. Analogously, the profile HMM header includes HMM related metadata. Finally, in the profile HMM states part, each node has a line of match emission scores and a line of insertion emission scores and state

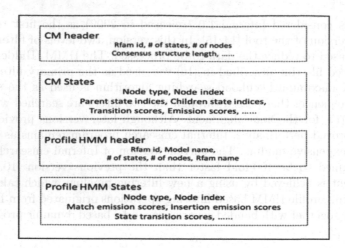

Fig. 1. CM file structure

transition scores. The cmsearch program code is tightly related to the node and state data in the CM file.

3   Cmsearch Filtering Pipeline

The filtering pipeline used in the cmsearch program consists of profile HMM based filtering stages and CM based filtering stages. Profile HMM stages use a combination of Viterbi algorithm, forward algorithm and backward algorithm to align the sequence with the profile HMM to find qualified sequence fragments, which pass the threshold values set by the program. All profile HMM stages yield considerably higher efficiency than those CM based stages since a profile HMM structure is much simpler than its equivalent CM structure. Thus, the profile HMM stages are positioned in the front part of the pipeline to prune relatively higher volume of the subsequences from the target sequences to alleviate the processing time in the following complex CM based stages. Figure 2 illustrates the filtering pipeline, in which seven filters are organized into four stages. We describe briefly the operation performed in each filter in the pipeline, and more detailed descriptions can be found in [10].

3.1   Stage 1

Stage 1 consists of the front end three filters, which perform vector mode operations [10,22].

Local Scanning SSV Filter. A local un-gapped Viterbi algorithm is used in this filter to find a set of high-scoring subsequences, defined as 'windows', from a given input sequence. Each alignment can start from any position in the

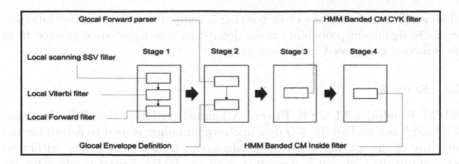

Fig. 2. Infernal cmsearch filtering pipeline

model and the sequence, and overlapped subsequences are combined into a SSV (single-segment Viterbi). Very long windows are split into multiple windows [10] and all qualified windows are passed to the next filter.

Local Viterbi Filter. In this filter, each forwarded window is aligned with the profile HMM model using the local Viterbi algorithm for finding the optimal gapped alignment, which calculates the maximum likelihood score of the state sequence in the profile HMM. Note that this filter is set to be in the local mode since each alignment can start/end at any position in the model. The same mechanism applies to the next filter.

Local Forward Filter. Windows passed through the local Viterbi filter are aligned with the profile HMM via a local forward algorithm in this filter. With the forward algorithm, the maximum likelihood score for the given sequences and the profile HMM is computed by summing up the probabilities of all possible paths in the model.

3.2 Stage 2

In this stage, 2-D dynamic programming based forward and backward algorithms are used to detect further shorter high-scoring subsequences from the windows.

Glocal Forward Parser Filter. The full forward algorithm is used to align the remaining (qualified) windows to the profile HMM in the 'glocal' mode - global to the profile HMM but local to the windows, i.e., each alignment can start/end at any position in the sequence window.

Glocal Envelop Definition Filter. From the windows, which passed the glocal forward parser filter, further shorter hits are identified in this filter. First, the glocal backward algorithm is applied to the windows. Second, by combining the results from the glocal forward algorithm the posterior probability that a target window starts and ends at a given position is computed. Lastly, shorter hits having more significant probability mass, defined as 'envelopes' are extracted from the windows and passed to the next stage.

3.3 Stage 3

HMM Banded CM CYK Filter. A banded version of the CYK algorithm [21], which is based on the 3-D dynamic programming, is used to determine the bit score of the maximum likelihood alignment of any subsequence within an envelope to the CM that is consistent with the HMM-derived bands. This bit score is checked with a threshold value and only qualified sequence envelopes are passed to the next stage. The time complexity of this stage (and the next stage) is relatively high since the CM model is processed, but the number of input envelopes is greatly reduced by the previous HMM based light-weight filters.

3.4 Stage 4

HMM Banded CM Inside Filter. The full likelihood of each profile/sequence envelope is evaluated in this filter using the CM Inside algorithm [17]. For each envelope, the entire alignments are summed. Similar to the CYK algorithm, HMM bands are used to constrain the CM dynamic programming calculations. This filter identifies possible non-overlapping high-scoring alignments and adds them to the final output.

4 Proposed Approaches: Pipelined Task Parallel Computation Models

In this section, we describe our proposed approaches of exploiting maximum parallelism in the filtering pipeline path with multiple threads. Since the proposed approaches accelerate the operation of the filtering pipeline internally, i.e., within the pipeline, they can be integrated with the original cmsearch data parallel approach or any other data parallel approaches without difficulties for further performance gain.

4.1 Pipelined Task Parallel (PTP) Computation Model

Our first trial is developing a 'pipelined parallel' computation model within the filtering pipeline of the cmsearch program. This strategy is inspired by the hardware pipelining used in the datapath of modern processors. In this parallel computation model, each stage of the filtering pipeline is assigned to a thread and all the threads work in parallel after the initial trigger time of the depth 4 pipeline (refer to Fig. 2). Since the task of each pipeline stage is different from others', we name this model 'pipelined task parallel computation model' there after, 'PTP computation model'. Input database sequences are divided into small blocks and a series of the divided blocks enter the pipeline in a systolic manner.

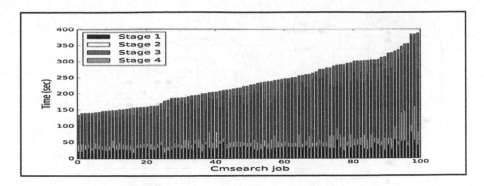

Fig. 3. Execution times of four stages in the cmsearch pipeline

In the ideal case in which the processing times of the four stages are identical, this model can achieve 4-fold performance gain. However, in the reality, time complexities of the four stages are not identical and the actual speedup of the computation model tightly depends on the most time consuming stage. The graph shown in Fig. 3 reveals this. From our primitive study with 200 randomly selected cmsearch jobs (200 CM files with a fixed database), stage 3 (HMM banded CM CYK filter) usually takes the longest time as shown in the figure in which random 100 (from 200) cmsearch jobs are shown in the ascending order of the total execution time. Thus, we need to employ a load balancing mechanism in the pipeline.

4.2   PTP Computation Model with Static Load Balancing

Our first load balancing strategy is based on the observation as partly illustrated in Fig. 3. Within our practice of searching Rfam [21] bacterial small RNA families in the divided HMP [24] database, we randomly selected 200 relatively time consuming cmsearch jobs and tested for time consumption in each stage. To resolve the bottleneck of the pipelining caused by the stage 3 (CYK filter), we included a parameter for setting the desired number of threads for the stage 3. This model is illustrated in Fig. 4(a). Although this statically load balanced version yields much better performance than the original PTP computation model, it is still difficult to exploit the maximum parallelism due to the lack of the information, which predicts the relative execution time differences among the stages in the pipeline. This became the motivation of developing a dynamic load balancing strategy described in the following subsection.

4.3   PTP Computation Model with Dynamic Load Balancing

Our further testing practices with more diversified cmsearch jobs revealed that there exist some abnormalities in which stage 3 is not the longest stage. This is due to the fact that the cmsearch execution time not only depends on the

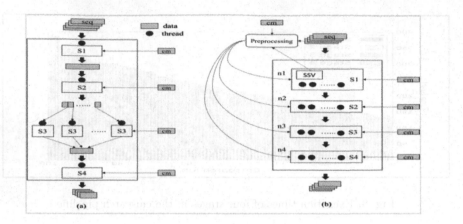

Fig. 4. Concepts of pipelined task parallel (PTP) computation models (a) with static load balancing (b) with dynamic load balancing

CM file to process, but also depends on the segment of the database processed. To balance the load maximally/equally on each stage of the PTP computation model, we need to develop a sophisticated heuristic prediction scheme to determine the relative weight of each stage upon receiving the input to the pipeline, i.e., a CM file and a database sequence file. Based on the prediction result for each cmsearch job, appropriate numbers of threads are assigned to each stage in the pipeline dynamically as illustrated in Fig. 4(b).

The methodology of our prediction scheme is based on the linear/polynomial regression model. The initial linear regression model that we started with is shown below:

$$t = \theta_0 + \theta_1 s + \theta_2 n + \theta_3 c + \theta_4 l + \theta_5 k \tag{1}$$

where, t is the execution time to predict, s is the number of states in the CM, n is the number of nodes in the CM, c is the length of the consensus string (same as the number of states in the profile HMM), l is the number of residues in the target sequence file, k is the number of sequences in the target sequence file, and $\{\theta_0, \theta_1, \theta_2, \theta_3, \theta_4, \theta_5\}$ are coefficients. We collected over 2,000 cmsearch job running results as the training dataset and extracted those dependent and independent variables. The next step is computing a set of coefficients $\{\theta_0, \theta_1, \theta_2, \theta_3, \theta_4, \theta_5\}$ that could minimize the average difference between the actual execution time and the predicted execution time of each stage in the pipeline. We utilized the linear regression model provided in the Python machine learning library, scikit-learn, to build the regression model and we measured the model using the R^2 (coefficient of determination) score, which ranges from 0 to 1 - the closer R^2 score is to 1, the better the model fits the training data. This primitive regression model yields good predictions on the execution time of the stage 1 in the pipeline, i.e., R^2 score is over 0.8 in average, but fails to make good predictions for other three stages.

Since both profile HMM and CM are position dependent statistic models, the performance of the cmsearch program heavily depends on the scoring model used in the CM file and the residue distribution used in the database sequence file. To improve the accuracy of our prediction scheme, we modify the primitive regression model shown in (1) as follows:

$$t = \theta_0 + \theta_1 s + \theta_2 n + \theta_3 c + \theta_4 l + \theta_5 k + \theta_6 nwin + \theta_7 lwin \qquad (2)$$

where, $nwin$ and $lwin$ are the number of windows and the number of residues passed through the local scanning SSV filter, and $\{\theta_6, \theta_7\}$ are two new coefficients. With this modification, the average R^2 score of all stages are increased, but it still is considered as under-fitting [23] in terms of the R^2 scores for stage 2, stage 3 and stage 4. To resolve the under-fitting problem, we finally convert our linear regression model to a polynomial regression model in which some polynomial variables are added to the dependent variables used in (2). For example, if we set the degree of the polynomial regression to 2, the regression model (2) becomes:

$$t = \theta_0 + \theta_1 s^2 + \theta_2 n + \theta_3 c + \theta_4 l + \theta_5 k + \ldots + \theta_{34} lwin^2 + \theta_{35} lwin \qquad (3)$$

As we increase the polynomial degree, the R^2 score on the training dataset is increased. However, fitting the training dataset better doesn't mean that it is a well-established model in general. A regression model falls into over-fitting when it fits to the training dataset well but fails to fit to the testing dataset. We developed and tested more polynomial regression models with degree 3–5 and realized that the higher degree yields worse cross validation scores. Our testing results showed that the modified linear regression model (2) and the polynomial model with degree 2 (3) yield analogously the best performance.

5   Experimental Results

To measure performance, our proposed PTP computation models were implemented in the Infernal cmsearch code, which is written in C, with both Pthreads and OpenMP. Our experiment was conducted on a server, PowerEdge T620 with two 8-core Intel Xeon processors (2.60 GHz) and 32 GB memory. Data used are HMP (Human Microbiome Project) [24] gastrointestinal_track database (Dec. 2012 version, 61,238 sequences, 2.49 GB) and Rfam [21] bacterial small RNA families (1,105 CM files from Rfam version 12.0). The HMP database is divided into 20 approximately equal sized pieces (~125 MB each) and we randomly selected 200 combinations, each of which consists of a CM file and a piece of the HMP database, in our experiment. To develop the regression models described in Sect. 4, we tested 2,000 randomly selected combinations (cmsearch jobs). Since the PTP computation model is pipelined parallel, we tested and determined the optimum size of the pipelined data, which is ~10% (~12 MB) of the given input database file (~125 MB each), to yield the maximum performance.

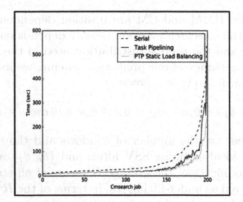

Fig. 5. Performances of the pipelined task parallel (PTP) computation models

Figure 5 shows performances of the pipelined task parallel (PTP) computation model described in Sect. 4.1 and the PTP computation model with static load balancing described in Sect. 4.2. We use the original Infernal cmsearch serial pipeline as the baseline for the comparison purpose since the PTP computation model accelerates the operation within the pipeline. As shown in the figure, the proposed PTP computation models yield a considerable amount of performance gain. In average, the PTP computation model in which each of the four pipeline stages is assigned to a thread (so, total 4 threads) yields 1.56× speedup and the PTP model with static load balancing in which the stage 3 is assigned to 3 threads (so, total 6 threads) yields 2.04× speedup over the baseline serial pipeline.

Figure 6 shows the performance difference between the PTP with static load balancing and the PTP with dynamic load balancing described in Sect. 4.3. As shown in the figure, the dynamic load balancing method achieves higher

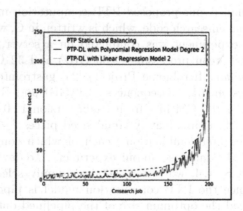

Fig. 6. Performance comparison of PTP with static/dynamic load balancing

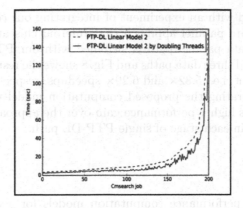

Fig. 7. Performance from doubling the threads in each stage of PTP-DL

performance than the static approach in general, and the modified linear regression model (2) and the polynomial regression model with degree 2 yield pretty similar results, i.e., 3.41× and 3.20× speedups, respectively. The average number of threads used in the PTP-DL model is 8. Some abnormalities shown in the figure are due to the accuracy of the current prediction scheme used in the dynamic load balancing. As described in [10], prediction of the execution time of the cmsearch job is highly difficult and complex task and we work towards making further accurate prediction scheme.

Lastly, we checked the scalability and flexibility (compatibility) of the PTP computation model, specifically the PTP with dynamic load balancing model (PTP-DL, there after) with the modified linear regression model (2). In the experiment of checking the scalability, we compared the PTP with the dynamic load balancing model to the version with doubled number of threads in each stage. Figure 7 shows the result from this experiment, i.e., 4.90× speedup. The

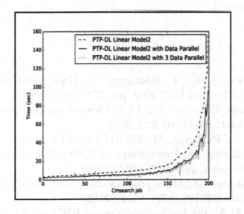

Fig. 8. Performance with multiple data parallel paths with PTP-DL

flexibility is checked with an experiment of integrating our computation model into the original data parallel approach that Infernal cmsearch provides as an option, i.e., each data parallel path is switched with our PTP-DL. We implemented with two and three data paths and Fig. 8 shows the resulting performance from this experiment, i.e., 5.32× and 6.29× speedups, respectively. As shown in Figs. 7 and 8, integrating the proposed computation model with doubled data parallel paths yields higher performance gain over the approach of doubling the number of threads in each stage of single PTP-DL path.

6 Conclusion

We proposed high performance computation models for accelerating Infernal cmsearch module, which is an RNA sequence prediction tool based on the secondary structure of RNA. The proposed approach is based on a pipelined task parallel strategy in which serial steps of the operations used in the original tool are parallelized in a pipelined parallel manner, i.e., systolic. To exploit the maximum parallelism, we included both static and dynamic load balancing strategies to alleviate heavy loaded stages in the pipeline. To develop the dynamic load balancing strategy we used heuristic regression models to predict the execution time of each stage in the pipeline.

In our practice, we implemented and tested several versions of the proposed high performance computation model with Rfam bacterial small RNA CM files and HMP gastrointestinal_track database as input to the program. Experimental results showed that 1.56× and 2.04× speedups in average were achieved with the model with simple pipelining and pipelining plus static load balancing, respectively. With the model with the dynamic load balancing, 3.41× speedup in average was achieved. The proposed computation models are scalable and flexible to be integrated with other trivial data parallel approaches, i.e., hybrid model of data parallel and our proposed pipelined task parallel approaches. With the hybrid model with 2 and 3 data paths, 5.32× and 6.29× speedups, respectively, in average were achieved.

References

1. Yamaguchi, Y., Maruyama, T., Konagaya, A.: High speed homology search with FPGAs. In: Proceedings of PSB 2002, pp. 271–282 (2002)
2. Blas, A.D., Karplus, K., et al.: The UCSC kestrel parallel processor. IEEE Trans. Parallel Distrib. Syst. **16**(1), 80–92 (2005)
3. Park, J.H., Qiu, Y., Herbordt, M.: CAAD BLASTn: accelerated NCBI BLASTn with FPGA prefiltering. In: Proceedings of 2010 IEEE International Symposium on Circuits and Systems, pp. 3797–3800 (2010)
4. Chitty, D.M.: Fast parallel genetic programming: multi-core CPU versus many-core GPU. Soft. Comput. **16**(10), 1795–1814 (2012)
5. Lenis, J., Senar, M.A.: On the performance of BWA on NUMA architectures. In: 2015 IEEE Trustcom/BigDataSE/ISPA, Helsinki, pp. 236–241 (2015)

6. Mahram, A., Herbordt, M.C.: NCBI BLASTP on high-performance reconfigurable computing systems. ACM Trans. Reconfig. Technol. Syst. **7**(4), 33 (2015)
7. Rubio-Largo, A., Vega-Rodríguez, M.A., González-Álvarez, D.L.: Parallel H4MSA for multiple sequence alignment. In: Proceedings of 2015 IEEE Trustcom/BigDataSE/ISPA, vol. 3, pp. 242–247 (2015)
8. Thain, D., Tannenbaum, T., Livny, M.: Distributed computing in practice: the condor experience. Concurr. Comput.: Pract. Exp. **17**(2–4), 323–356 (2005)
9. Computing with HTCondor. https://research.cs.wisc.edu/htcondor/index.html. Accessed Apr 2016
10. Nawrocki, E.P., Eddy, S.R.: The Infernal 1.1 User's Guide. (2012) http://infernal.janelia.org
11. Krogh, A., Brown, M., Mian, I., et al.: Hidden Markov models in computational biology: applications to protein modeling. J. Mol. Biol. **1994**(235), 1501–1531 (1994)
12. Eddy, S.R.: A memory-efficient dynamic programming algorithm for optimal alignment of a sequence to an RNA secondary structure. BMC Bioinform. **3**, 18 (2002)
13. Nawrocki, E.P., Eddy, S.R.: Query-dependent banding (QDB) for faster RNA similarity searches. PLoS Comput. Biol. **3**, E56 (2007)
14. Nawrocki, E.P.: Structural RNA homology search and alignment using covariance models. Ph.D. thesis, School of Medicine, Washington University (2009)
15. Nawrocki, E.P., Kolbe, D.L., Eddy, S.R.: Infernal 1.0: inference of RNA alignments. Bioinformatics **25**, 1335–1337 (2009)
16. Weinberg, Z., Ruzzo, W.L.: Sequence-based heuristics for faster annotation of noncoding RNA families. Bioinformatics **22**, 35–39 (2006)
17. Durbin, R., Eddy, S.R., et al.: Biological Sequence Analysis: Probabilistic Models of Proteins and Nucleic Acids. Cambridge University Press, Cambridge (1998)
18. Nawrocki, E.P., Eddy, S.R.: Infernal 1.1: 100-fold faster RNA homology searches. Bioinformatics **29**, 2933–2935 (2013)
19. Eddy, S.R.: HMMER: Biosequence Analysis Using Profile Hidden Markov Models (2008). http://hmmer.janelia.org
20. Eddy, S.R.: Profile hidden Markov models. Bioinformatics **1998**(14), 755–763 (1998)
21. Rfam 12.1. http://rfam.xfam.org/. Accessed Apr 2016
22. Eddy, S.R.: Accelerated profile HMM searches. PLoS Comput. Biol. **7**(10), E1002195 (2011)
23. Model Fit: Underfitting vs. Overfitting. http://docs.aws.amazon.com/machine-learning/latest/dg/model-fit-underfitting-vs-overfitting.html. Accessed Apr 2016
24. NIH Human Microbiome Project. http://hmpdacc.org/. Accessed Apr 2016

Improving Memory Accesses for Heterogeneous Parallel Multi-objective Feature Selection on EEG Classification

Juan José Escobar, Julio Ortega$^{(\boxtimes)}$, Jesús González, and Miguel Damas

Department of Computer Architecture and Technology, CITIC,
University of Granada, Granada, Spain
{jjescobar,jortega,jesusgonzalez,mdamas}@ugr.es

Abstract. Bioinformatics applications that analyze large volumes of high-dimensional data and present different implicit parallelism can benefit from the efficient use, in performance terms, of heterogeneous parallel architectures, including accelerators such as graphics processing units (GPUs). This paper aims to take advantage of parallel codes to accelerate electroencephalogram (EEG) classification and feature selection problems in the context of Branch-Computing Interface (BCI) tasks. As the approaches to tackle these applications usually involve optimized codes that implement different types of parallelism, the use of heterogeneous architectures with multicore microprocessors along with GPUs could provide relevant performance improvements after careful code optimizing. More specifically, the memory access patterns have been taken into account to improve the performance of data-parallel GPU kernels.

Keywords: EEG classification · Feature selection · GPU · Heterogeneous parallel architectures · Multi-objective optimization

1 Introduction

Many bioinformatics applications involve high-dimensional data mining problems that comprise tasks such as classification, clustering, optimization, feature selection and optimization. EEG classification is a good example of such applications that process high-dimensional patterns and require feature selection techniques to remove noisy or irrelevant features or to improve the learning accuracy and result comprehensibility, especially when the number of features in the input patterns is higher than the number of available patterns. The proposed approach to EEG classification for BCI tasks [16], includes an evolutionary multi-objective optimization algorithm and a clustering algorithm applied to a set of high-dimensional patterns usually requiring high-volume storage. Thus, as many other bioinformatics applications, the application here considered requires solving problems with different kinds of inherent parallelism.

This paper aims to provide an insight into the design of efficient parallel procedures for high-dimensional classification and optimization tasks, in heterogeneous parallel architectures involving multiple general-purpose superscalar

© Springer International Publishing AG 2017
F. Desprez et al. (Eds.): Euro-Par 2016 Workshops, LNCS 10104, pp. 372–383, 2017.
DOI: 10.1007/978-3-319-58943-5_30

multicore CPUs and accelerators (mainly GPUs). As they constitute the present mainstream approach to take advantage of technology improvements [5] their use has been proposed in many previous papers on parallel metaheuristics and evolutionary computation [1]. Nevertheless, the parallelization on a heterogeneous platform of a whole data mining application with the characteristics of our target application is less frequent in the literature.

After this introduction, Sect. 2 describes the evolutionary multi-objective optimization approach to feature selection whose implementation we have parallelized. Section 3 analyzes the main issues to develop efficient parallel codes in heterogeneous platforms and also details our proposed OpenCL codes. Then, Sect. 4 describes the experimental results and compares the behavior of different considered alternatives and finally, Sect. 5 summarizes the conclusions.

2   Multi-objective Feature Selection

This paper deals with feature selection in unsupervised classification of patterns characterized by a high number of features. As the number of patterns to classify is usually lower than the number of features, we have to cope with a curse of dimensionality problem [4]. Thus, the most relevant features should be selected to achieve an adequate performance of the classifier, decrease the computational complexity of the classification, and remove irrelevant/redundant features. Nevertheless, optimal feature selection is an NP-hard problem that requires efficient metaheuristics, especially in high-dimensional classification problems. Here, we apply multi-objective optimization to feature selection and propose the use of heterogeneous parallel architectures to accelerate it.

The use of multi-objective optimization in data mining applications is shown in [14,15], and the benefits from a multi-objective approach to feature selection in both supervised and unsupervised classification have been reported elsewhere [12]. Moreover, as the number of features involved in the applications here considered is large, a multi-objective optimization approach would imply high computational costs, and execution time is an important issue to consider. The main contribution of this paper deals with parallel processing, on CPU and GPU architectures, of feature selection approached by multi-objective optimization in applications with a large number of features.

Figure 1 describes our approach for feature selection in unsupervised classification of EEG patterns. A multi-objective evolutionary procedure, in our case the well-known NSGA-II algorithm [6], evolves a population of individuals that codify different feature selections. Given a feature selection (an individual in the population of the evolutionary algorithm), the NP patterns included in the database, DS, will be used to define the set training patterns by choosing the components corresponding to the number of features, NF, selected. This way, the K-means algorithm will be applied to the NP patterns $P_i = (p_i^1, \ldots, p_i^{NF})(i = 1, \ldots, NP)$ to determine the centroids $K(j)(j = 1, \ldots, W)$ of the W clusters we have (W is known in our classification problems, and it is equal to the number of classes). The K-means algorithm has the following steps:

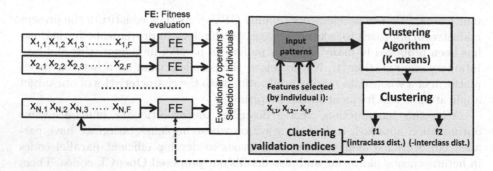

Fig. 1. Wrapper procedure for unsupervised feature selection by evolutionary multi-objective optimization (and K-means as clustering algorithm)

1. Generate W initial centroids (as many centroids as clusters or classes).
2. Assign each pattern to the cluster corresponding to the nearest centroid.
3. Calculate the new cluster centroids.
4. If the end condition is not met (either changes in the centroids or a maximum number of iterations have not been completed yet) repeat steps 2 and 3.

Once the clusters are built, the fitness of each individual in the population is evaluated by using two clustering validation indices (CVI) [2], defined as:

$$f_1 = \sum_{j=1}^{W} \frac{1}{|C(j)|} \left(\sum_{P_i \in C(j)} \|P_i - K(j)\| \right) \tag{1}$$

$$f_2 = - \sum_{j=1}^{W-1} \left(\sum_{i>j} \|K(i) - K(j)\| \right) \tag{2}$$

where (1) and (2) correspond, respectively, to the intraclass and minus the inter-class distances. In these equations, $|C(j)|$ is the number of patterns in cluster $C(j)(j = 1, \ldots, W)$ whose centroid is $K(j)$, and $\|P_i - K(j)\|$ is the Euclidean distance between the pattern P_i and the centroid $K(j)$.

The papers of Sharma and Collet [17] and Wong and Cui [18] show implementations of evolutionary multi-objective procedures. Others [19,20] have approached the parallelization of the K-means algorithm for high-dimensional data on GPUs using large datasets. Our procedure, not only distributes the individuals to evaluate their fitness but also parallelizes the clustering algorithm and the computation of the cost functions required to complete the fitness evaluation for each individual.

3   OpenCL Codes for Multi-objective Feature Selection

In this section, we will describe the parallel implementations we have considered to take advantage of heterogeneous CPU-GPU architectures. The GPU plays the role of a coprocessor connected, through a bus, to a host including multiple superscalar cores that share the main memory. The basic computing elements or cores of the GPU are the so called *Stream Processors* (SP). They do not contain instruction units and are able to execute scalar operations. Several SP along with one or several instruction units and a register file comprise a multiprocessor, also called *Streaming Multiprocessor* (SMX). A GPU can include several SMX and allows the simultaneous execution of the same program on different data (i.e. the SPMD model). The threads are organized within thread blocks in such a way that all the threads in a block are assigned to a single SMX. Moreover, the blocks are also partitioned into *warps* containing threads with consecutive and increasing identity number that start together at the same program address. While the threads in a block are able to cooperate and share the instruction unit, the register file and some low latency memory, threads in different blocks can only communicate among themselves through the *global memory*.

Codes have been developed on OpenCL, which allows platform-independent parallel programming through programs executed in a host that launch functions, called *kernels*, to other OpenCL devices, such as multicore CPUs or GPUs. A device in OpenCL is an array of functionally independent *computing units* divided into *processing elements*. For example, in the GPU previously described, the SMX processors are computing units and the SP cores processing elements. The units of concurrent execution are called *work-items*, which are mapped to the processing elements. The abstract memory model of OpenCL also defines memory spaces that also resemble the usual memory hierarchies. Thus, the global memory is visible to all computing units in the device, as the *constant memory*, included in the global memory to store variables whose values do not change. All the processing elements in a given computing unit share the corresponding *local memory*, while the *private memory* is only accessed by a processing element.

From Fig. 1 of Sect. 2, it is clear that our application involves both evolutionary multi-objective and clustering algorithms. In [13] we have proposed several approaches to parallelize the application through different parallel evolutionary multi-optimization options, although we did not parallelize the fitness computation for the individuals in the population. This issue is considered here by taking advantage of the GPU resources to run data parallel codes. Thus, a core in the CPU (i.e. the host) launches a kernel in the GPU to evaluate the fitness (the two cost functions) of the individuals in the population. The GPU kernel implements two levels of parallelism: parallel evaluation of the population (implemented as a master-worker parallel evolutionary algorithm) and the data parallel evaluation of the cost functions for each individual. The paper [9] shows another OpenCL implementation of a genetic algorithm for feature selection in a biometric recognition application. Although that paper does not implement a multi-objective algorithm and the fitness function differs from the one here considered, its approach follows a quite similar strategy.

This way, the patterns have to be transferred from the host memory to the GPU memory at the beginning and, each iteration, individuals of the population and their computed fitness have to be transferred between host and GPU and

---

Algorithm 1. Kernel pseudocode for the evaluation of the individuals

---

1 **Kernel function** evaluation($S(i), DS, K, DS_t$)

    Input   : A possible solution for the problem, $S(i)$
    Input   : Dataset $DS(j); \forall j = 1, ..., P$ training patterns of F components)
    Input   : The set K of W centroids randomly chosen from the dataset DS
    Input   : Dataset DS_t is DS in column-major order (only for GPU kernel)
    Output: $f_1(S(i))$, the intraclass distances in $S(i)$ according to (1)
    Output: $f_2(S(i))$, the interclass distances in $S(i)$ according to (2)

2    $<<$ *All work-groups, All work-items* $>>$
3   **for** $i \leftarrow 1$ **to** N individuals **do**

4        $<<$ *work-groupID, All work-items in work-groupID* $>>$
5        $K_l \leftarrow$ Copy the centroids from global memory to local memory
6        $I \leftarrow$ Copy the individual $S(i)$ from global memory to local memory
7   Initialization of the mapping table, $MT \leftarrow 0$
8   **repeat**

9            $<<$ *work-groupID, work-itemID* $>>$
10           $MT \leftarrow$ Each pattern is assigned to the nearest cluster using DS_t
11           $D \leftarrow$ Nearest Euclidean distance is stored for each pattern
12   Check if the pattern has been assigned to another centroid

13           $<<$ *work-groupID, All work-items in work-groupID* $>>$
14           $K_l \leftarrow$ Update the centroids using the dataset DS
15   **until** *stop criterion is not reached*;

16        $<<$ *work-groupID, Work-item number 0* $>>$
17        $f_1(S(i)) \leftarrow$ intraclass(K_l, DS)
18        $f_2(S(i)) \leftarrow$ interclass(K_l, DS)
19   **end**
20   **return** $(f_1(S(i)), f_2(S(i)))$
21 **End**

---

vice versa. The drawback of this scheme is the number of copies (in each direction per iteration) through a bus with worse bandwidth and latency than those provided by the memory buses in CPU cores and GPU. It could be an important bottleneck as in the application here considered the size of the dataset is usually big and the GPU memory hierarchy should be carefully managed. Thus, the local memory (i.e. the shared memory in the NVIDIA GPUs), available for the threads of a thread block, should be used to store the data structures corresponding to the subpopulation of individuals assigned to each thread block.

Algorithm 1 shows the kernel pseudocode to evaluate the fitness of the individuals (the intraclass and interclass distances defining the two cost functions of the multi-objective optimization procedure). As it has been said, in the OpenCL GPU kernel, individuals are evaluated in parallel by different work-groups, thus implementing the first level of parallelism of the algorithm (line 3 in Algorithm 1). Moreover, the GPU kernel also implements a second level of parallelism as each work-group is composed by warps of 32 work-items each in the case of the

NVIDIA GPUs for example. This second level of parallelism corresponds to the parallel implementation of the K-means algorithm (lines 5–15 in Algorithm 1). The expression $<<work\text{-}groupID, work\text{-}itemID>>$ defines the distribution of work-items in each work-group through the different steps of the K-means algorithm in the GPU. For comparison purposes in Sect. 4, we have also implemented the first parallel approach in a CPU kernel to be executed in the multicore host. In this CPU kernel case, a work-group is composed by only one work-item (the CPU kernel does not implement data parallel processing).

In what follows, we describe the main details of the proposed GPU kernel. Relevant optimizations have been implemented with respect to our first approach described in [8]. As it will be demonstrated in Sect. 4, these optimizations have allowed efficient data parallel performances.

1. The CPU/GPU kernels receive the input parameters provided by the host code: the individuals of the population, the dataset, and the initial centroids for the K-means algorithms. An individual, $S(i)$, is a one-dimensional array of contiguous 0's and 1's (according to the selection or not of the corresponding feature) stored in global memory. It will be copied into local memory (line 6 in Algorithm 1) as this on-chip memory is faster. The global memory used is $S_{Pop} = N \times F$ bytes, where N is the number of individuals and F is the number of features (among which the selection is to be done). The datasets DS and DS_t include the P training patterns, each characterized by F features. Both sets are stored in the global memory due to their large sizes, in a one-dimensional array of $P \times F$ elements normalized by the host program. In DS the patterns are organized in row-major order while column-major order is used in DS_t. Each dataset needs $S_{DB} = 4 \times P \times F$ bytes of memory. Instead the W centroids randomly selected from the dataset, the indices of these centroids are copied from the host memory to the GPU constant memory: the amount of constant memory used is $S_W = 4 \times W$ bytes.

2. As the positions of the centroids are modified along the iterations of the K-means algorithm (otherwise K-means ends), it is necessary to copy each centroid from global memory to local memory whenever a new individual is going to be evaluated (line 5). The operations of lines 5 and 6 in Algorithm 1 are executed in parallel by all work-items of the corresponding work-group. Thus we can benefit from coalescence, a technique in which consecutive threads of a warp request data stored in global memory, in consecutive logical addresses. This technique aims to minimize the number of transaction segments requested from the global memory by taking advantage of memory bus width to get multiple data in a single transaction. We have been able to use coalescence as consecutive work-items in the same work-group request data stored in consecutive logical addresses of the global memory. As Fig. 2 shows, the memory bank conflicts in the local memory are minimized. When the WI work-items in the work-group process the first WI data, the next WI data are repeatedly requested and processed, until finish. In the CPU kernel, the only work-item in a work-group sequentially performs the copy of the centroids and individuals of the population. The centroids need $S_{K_l} = 4 \times W \times F$ bytes

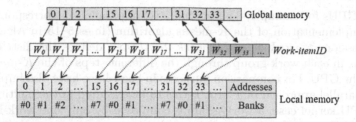

Fig. 2. Work-items of different warps (in white and shaded) copy from global memory to local memory providing coalescent access and minimizing the memory bank conflicts

of memory and each individual $S_{ind} = F$ bytes (W centroids, F features and 4 bytes per floating-point data).

3. The mapping table MT needs $S_{MT} = P$ bytes of local memory (P is the number of patterns in the dataset DS). This table contains the centroid assigned to each pattern along the K-means iterations. The initialization (line 7) is carried out by all work-items in the same way as the previous initialization of centroids and individuals. Each pattern only stores the index of its corresponding centroid, K_i. Moreover, through the mapping table MT, it is easier to check the algorithm convergence by taking into account whether a pattern has been assigned to another centroid (line 12), instead of at the end of the iteration (if there are not changes in the centroid assignments).

4. Each work-item has to find the nearest centroid for a specific pattern by using the Euclidean distances between patterns and centroids. The dataset DS_t is stored in the GPU global memory to accelerate this task. The P first memory addresses of DS_t store the values of the first feature for all patterns, the following P memory addresses store the values of the second feature, and so on. Therefore, as each work-item handles a different pattern in a given time, consecutive work-items will request consecutive memory addresses, thus allowing full coalescence of the accesses to global memory. Moreover, when the nearest centroid to a given pattern and the corresponding distance are obtained, they can be written in, respectively, MT and D with the minimum number of memory bank conflicts. As MT, the array D is stored in local memory including the Euclidean distances between each pattern and its closest centroid, occupying a total of $S_D = 4 \times P$ bytes.

5. Update the centroids (line 14) is the most complex step of K-means in terms of data parallelization. Some approaches [7,11] propose to perform this step sequentially in the host, although the cost per iteration associated to transfer the centroids to the host, process them, and return them could be too high, especially in applications with high-dimensional patterns. Thus, we use our GPU kernel and assign each work-item to add the same feature of all patterns belonging to the centroid in question. The dataset DS_t is not adequate as consecutive work-items compute consecutive features. Now, DS is used because its first F memory addresses contain all the features of the first

pattern, the following F addresses contain the features of the second pattern, and so on. Thus, the coalescence of global memory accesses can be achieved and the memory bank conflicts are minimized when a centroid is updated.
6. The GPU and CPU kernels return the fitness values of the individuals (lines 17 and 18), built from two components, the intra-cluster and the inter-cluster distances given in (1) and (2) of Sect. 2.

4   Experimental Results

In this section, we analyze the performance of our OpenCL (version 1.2) codes running on Linux CentOS 6.7 operating system, in a platform comprised of two NUMA (Non-Uniform Memory Access) nodes connected by Gigabit Ethernet. Each node has 32 GB of DDR3 memory and two Intel Xeon E5-2620 processors at 2.1 GHz including six cores per socket with Hyper-Threading, thus comprising 24 threads. One of the nodes of this NUMA platform also includes a Tesla K20c with 5 GB of global memory, 208 GB/s as maximum memory bandwidth and 2496 CUDA cores at 705.5 MHz, distributed into 13 SMXs, thus including 192 cores per SMX. In our experiments, we have used two benchmarks extracted from the datasets recorded in the BCI Laboratory at the University of Essex and described in [3]. The data benchmark b480a includes 178 patterns (EEGs) with 480 features corresponding to the subject coded as 110 in the dataset. We have also considered another larger data file for the same subject, the b3600a, including 178 patterns (EEGs) with 3600 features. We have made 10 repetitions of each experiment, to apply Kolmogorov-Smirnov tests in order to determine whether the data follow a standard normal distribution. According to these tests, we then apply either an ANOVA test if the data follow a normal distribution or a Kruskal-Wallis test otherwise.

The implemented multi-objective optimization algorithm NSGA-II [6] uses two point crossover with a probability of 0.9, a mutation by inversion of the selected bit with probability of 0.1, and selection by binary tournament. The hypervolumes are obtained with $(1, 1)$ as reference point, and the minimum values for the cost functions f_1 and f_2 are respectively 0 and -1, i.e. $(0, -1)$.

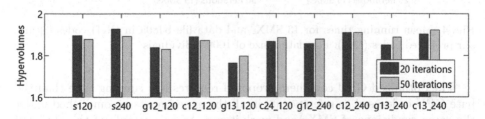

Fig. 3. Mean hypervolumes for 20 and 50 iterations (sY = sequential; cX_Y/gX_Y = CPU/GPU kernels; X = number of cores/SMXs; Y = population size) with b3600a

Table 1. Memory (in bytes) used by (Ref) code [8] and our proposed code (Opt). N, W, F and P are the number of individuals, centroids, features and patterns respectively

Mem. type		Global		Constant	Local			
Description		Population	Databases	Centroids		Indiv.	Tables	Distances
Array		S_{pop}	S_{DB}	S_W	S_{K_l}	S_{ind}	S_{MT}	S_D
Size	Ref	$N \times F$	$4 \times P \times F$	$4 \times W \times F$	$4 \times W \times F$	F	$3 \times W \times P$	$4 \times W \times P$
	Opt		$8 \times P \times F$	$4 \times W$			P	$4 \times P$
Total size	Ref	$N \times F + 4 \times P \times F$		$4 \times W \times F$	$4 \times W \times F + 7 \times W \times P + F$			
	Opt	$N \times F + 8 \times P \times F$		$4 \times W$	$4 \times W \times F + 5 \times P + F$			

Figure 3 shows the mean hypervolumes [10] obtained after 10 experiments for different codes and configurations. After analyzing the obtained hypervolume results, it has been observed that there are not statistically significant differences with respect to the results obtained by the sequential procedures with the same number of individuals in the population and generations. This is expected, as our OpenCL codes correspond to alternative parallel implementations that keep the behavior of the sequential algorithm. In what follows, we analyze the behavior of the parallel codes here proposed. These codes implement the optimizations described in Sect. 3 with respect to a basic parallel code evaluated in [8]. Table 1 compares the memory requirements of both codes and shows the decrease in the memory requirements achieved by the optimizations previously described.

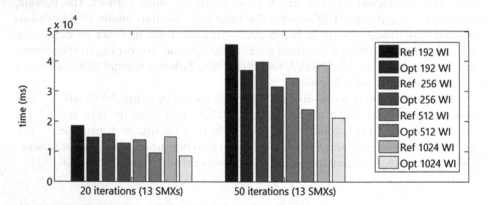

Fig. 4. Mean running times for 13 SMXs and data file b480a in (Ref) codes [8] and our proposed codes (Opt). Population size of 1000 individuals

The optimized GPU code here proposed requires less running time than the base GPU code used as reference [8] in all the experiments accomplished under the same conditions of SMXs and work-items. As an example of the obtained results, Fig. 4 shows the mean running times for 13 SMXs multiprocessors (the maximum number of SMXs in our GPU) and different number of work-items.

As can be seen, contrary to the optimized code here proposed, in the reference code the time does not decrease from 512 to 1024 work-items. Indeed, not

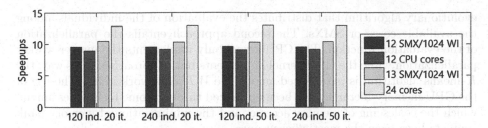

Fig. 5. Mean speedups in (opt) GPU and CPU kernels for b3600a and 1000 individuals

only the running time decreases as more work-items are used in all the cases, but also the amount of time-cutting provided by the optimized GPU-kernel grows as more work-items are used due to the effect of the applied coalescence technique. Moreover, it has not been possible to compare both codes by using the benchmark b3600a due to its local memory requirements for the not optimized code. Figure 5 compares the speedups obtained by a CPU kernel and those obtained by the proposed optimized GPU kernel with a population of 1000 individuals. While the CPU kernel implements the parallel evaluation of individuals, the GPU kernel takes advantage of both, and also implements the data parallel implementation of the evaluation function based on K-means. The sequential time used in all the speedup measures corresponds to the execution of the procedure in one of the host cores. This way, the speedups also allow us to compare the corresponding running times. If we only consider the maximum number of available CPU cores and SMXs multiprocessors (24 and 13 respectively), the CPU kernel provides better results.

5 Conclusions

Many works in the literature have shown important speedups achieved by different parallel evolutionary algorithms implemented on GPUs, but fewer details have been reported about the benefits of such many-core architectures in data mining applications with irregularities in the codes or in the data accesses, along with high-dimensional patterns and/or high volume data. This paper compares parallel implementations for heterogeneous platforms including multicore CPU and GPU architectures of a multi-objective approach to a high-dimensional feature selection problem related with EEG classification on BCI tasks. Thus, OpenCL CPU and GPU kernels have been implemented to analyze the behavior of different parallel approaches to take advantage of heterogeneous architectures.

More specifically, the parallelized application is based on a multi-objective optimization evolutionary algorithm with two cost functions. Thus, the fitness evaluation for a given individual implies the computation of two validation indices through a K-means algorithm applied to the patterns of the dataset.

Two parallelization approaches have been implemented in the GPU kernel. The first one corresponds to a master-worker parallel multi-objective evolutionary algorithm that distributes the evaluation of the individuals among the available cores or SMXs. The second approach entails the parallelization of the evaluation function. The CPU kernel only implements the master-worker parallelization while the GPU kernel implements both approaches. This way, the K-means algorithm is parallelized among the $WILocal$ work-items. The use of the GPU memory hierarchy has been optimized through some techniques among which the coalescing of memory accesses and the minimization of memory bank conflicts have been the most efficient ones.

The experimental results show a relevant time reduction in the optimized GPU kernel here proposed compared to a first GPU kernel previously provided in [8]. Moreover, our proposed GPU kernel also provides an efficient use of the work-items as more of them are used. Nevertheless, despite the relatively good results shown in this paper, more alternatives should be also explored to take advantage of the heterogeneous parallelism. Among them, parallel implementations with load-balancing between CPUs and GPUs in the present computing platforms, and the implementation of evolutionary subpopulations through island approaches could offer new insights about the possibilities of heterogeneous parallel architectures in the kind of applications here considered.

Acknowledgements. This work has been funded by project TIN2015-67020-P (Spanish "Ministerio de Economía y Competitividad" and FEDER funds). We also thank the BCI laboratory of the University of Essex, and especially Prof. John Q. Gan, for allowing us to use their databases.

References

1. Alba, E., Luque, G., Nesmachnow, S.: Parallel metaheuristics: recent advances and new trends. Int. Trans. Oper. Res. **20**(1), 1–48 (2013)
2. Arbelaitz, O., Gurrutxaga, I., Muguerza, J., Pérez, J., Perona, I.: An extensive comparative study of cluster validity indices. Pattern Recogn. **46**(1), 243–256 (2013)
3. Asensio-Cubero, J., Gan, J., Palaniappan, R.: Multiresolution analysis over simple graphs for brain computer interfaces. J. Neural Eng. **10**(4), 046014 (2013)
4. Bellman, R.: Adaptive Control Processes: A Guided Tour. Princeton University Press, Princeton (1961)
5. Collet, P.: Why GPGPUs for evolutionary computation? In: Tsutsui, S., Collet, P. (eds.) Massively Parallel Evolutionary Computation on GPGPUs. NCS, pp. 3–14. Springer, Heidelberg (2013). doi:10.1007/978-3-642-37959-8_1
6. Deb, K., Agrawal, S., Pratap, A., Meyarivan, T.: A fast elitist non-dominated sorting genetic algorithm for multi-objective optimization: NSGA-II. In: Schoenauer, M., Deb, K., Rudolph, G., Yao, X., Lutton, E., Merelo, J.J., Schwefel, H.-P. (eds.) PPSN 2000. LNCS, vol. 1917, pp. 849–858. Springer, Heidelberg (2000). doi:10.1007/3-540-45356-3_83
7. Dhanasekaran, B., Rubin, N.: A new method for GPU based irregular reductions and its application to k-means clustering. In: Proceedings of 4th Workshop on General Purpose Processing on Graphics Processing Units (GPGPU-4), pp. 729–737. ACM, Newport Beach, March 2011

8. Escobar, J.J., Ortega, J., González, J., Damas, M.: Assessing parallel heterogeneous computer architectures for multiobjective feature selection on EEG classification. In: Ortuño, F., Rojas, I. (eds.) IWBBIO 2016. LNCS, vol. 9656, pp. 277–289. Springer, Cham (2016). doi:10.1007/978-3-319-31744-1_25

9. Fazendeiro, P., Padole, C., Sequeira, P., Prata, P.: OpenCL implementations of a genetic algorithm for feature selection in periocular biometric recognition. In: Panigrahi, B.K., Das, S., Suganthan, P.N., Nanda, P.K. (eds.) SEMCCO 2012. LNCS, vol. 7677, pp. 729–737. Springer, Heidelberg (2012). doi:10.1007/978-3-642-35380-2_85

10. Fonseca, C., López-Ibáñez, M., Paquete, L., Guerreiro, A.: Computation of the hypervolume indicator. http://lopez-ibanez.eu/hypervolume. Accessed 30 Nov 2015

11. Gunarathne, T., Salpitikorala, B., Chauhan, A., Fox, G.: Optimizing OpenCL kernels for iterative statistical algorithms on GPUs. In: Proceedings of 2nd International Workshop on GPUs and Scientific Applications (GPUScA 2011), Galveston Island, Texas, USA, pp. 33–44, October 2011

12. Handl, J., Knowles, J.: Feature subset selection in unsupervised learning via multiobjective optimization. Int. J. Comput. Intell. Res. 2(3), 217–238 (2006)

13. Kimovski, D., Ortega, J., Ortiz, A., Baños, R.: Leveraging cooperation for parallel multi-objective feature selection in high-dimensional EEG data. Concurr. Comput.: Pract. Exp. 27(18), 5476–5499 (2015)

14. Mukhopadhyay, A., Maulik, U., Bandyopadhyay, S., Coello Coello, C.: A survey of multiobjective evolutionary algorithms for data mining: part i. IEEE Trans. Evol. Comput. 18(1), 4–19 (2014)

15. Mukhopadhyay, A., Maulik, U., Bandyopadhyay, S., Coello Coello, C.: A survey of multiobjective evolutionary algorithms for data mining: part ii. IEEE Trans. Evol. Comput. 18(1), 20–35 (2014)

16. Rupp, R., Kleih, S.C., Leeb, R., Millan, J., Kübler, A., Müller-Putz, G.R.: Brain–computer interfaces and assistive technology. In: Grübler, G., Hildt, E. (eds.) Brain-Computer-Interfaces in their ethical, social and cultural contexts. TILELT, vol. 12, pp. 7–38. Springer, Dordrecht (2014). doi:10.1007/978-94-017-8996-7_2

17. Sharma, D., Collet, P.: Implementation techniques for massively parallel multi-objective optimization. In: Tsutsui, S., Collet, P. (eds.) Massively Parallel Evolutionary Computation on GPGPUs. NCS, pp. 267–286. Springer, Heidelberg (2013). doi:10.1007/978-3-642-37959-8_13

18. Wong, M.L., Cui, G.: Data mining using parallel multi-objective evolutionary algorithms on graphics processing units. In: Tsutsui, S., Collet, P. (eds.) Massively Parallel Evolutionary Computation on GPGPUs. NCS, pp. 287–307. Springer, Heidelberg (2013). doi:10.1007/978-3-642-37959-8_14

19. Wu, R., Zhang, B., Hsu, M.: Clustering billions of data points using GPUs. In: Hast, A., Buchty, R., Tao, J., Weidendorfer, J. (eds.) Proceedings of Combined Workshops on UnConventional High Performance Computing Workshop Plus Memory Access Workshop (UCHPC-MAW 2009), pp. 1–6. ACM, Ischia, May 2009

20. Zechner, M., Granitzer, M.: Accelerating k-means on the graphics processor via cuda. In: Proceedings of 1st International Conference on Intensive Applications and Services (INTENSIVE 2009), pp. 7–15. IEEE, Valencia, April 2009

Improving Multiobjective Phylogenetic Searches by Using a Parallel ε-Dominance Based Adaptation of the Firefly Algorithm

Sergio Santander-Jiménez[✉] and Miguel A. Vega-Rodríguez

Department of Computer and Communications Technologies,
Escuela Politécnica, University of Extremadura,
Campus Universitario s/n, 10003 Cáceres, Spain
{sesaji,mavega}@unex.es

Abstract. One of the current trends of research in bioinformatics focuses on the application of multiobjective techniques to solve biological optimization problems involving multiple criteria. In this sense, the combination of parallelism and multiobjective bioinspired computing represents a relevant approach to tackle challenging NP-hard problems in this area. In this work, we aim to improve a previous multiobjective proposal based on the Firefly Algorithm to infer multiobjective phylogenetic hypotheses. We study the integration of the ε-dominance mechanism, along with other multiobjective strategies, to improve the overall quality of the Pareto fronts generated by the algorithm. The resulting approach is parallelized with OpenMP to exploit the capabilities of a multicore system composed of 32 execution cores. Experiments over four real nucleotide data sets give account of significant parallel and multiobjective results, pointing out the benefits of the applied strategies in comparison to our original proposal and other biological tools from the literature.

Keywords: Multiobjective optimization · OpenMP · Firefly Algorithm · Bioinformatics

1 Introduction

Recent advances in algorithmic and hardware development have allowed the inclusion of more realistic assumptions in the modelling of biological optimization problems. As a result, a significant increase in the proposal of parallel and multiobjective approaches to solve bioinformatics problems has been observed [9,18]. A representative NP-hard problem in this context is given by the reconstruction of phylogenetic histories describing the evolution of living organisms [11]. The literature gives account of successful applications of multiobjective bioinspired computing to solve incongruence issues during the inference process. Poladian and Jermiin applied multiobjective optimization with the aim of performing phylogenetic analyses when conflicting sources of information are considered [14].

© Springer International Publishing AG 2017
F. Desprez et al. (Eds.): Euro-Par 2016 Workshops, LNCS 10104, pp. 384–396, 2017.
DOI: 10.1007/978-3-319-58943-5_31

Other proposals focused on tackling the problem according to multiple optimality criteria. We can highlight the works from Coelho et al. [4], who proposed immune-inspired strategies according to distance-based criteria, and Cancino and Delbem [1], who designed the PhyloMOEA tool to perform phylogenetic searches attending to parsimony and likelihood. The additional challenge that represents the multiobjective treatment of this problem has motivated the application of parallel computing to minimize execution times. For example, Cancino et al. reported in [2] MPI and MPI+OpenMP parallelization schemes to their proposal, while Santander-Jiménez and Vega-Rodríguez evaluated evolutionary and swarm intelligence parallel designs for multicore clusters in [15].

When solving multiobjective optimization problems, the output of the algorithm is given by a set of solutions which represent a compromise between $n \geq 2$ objective functions [5]. The Pareto dominance concept is often used to distinguish solution quality throughout the search. It states that, given two solutions s_1 and s_2, s_1 dominates s_2 iff $\forall \, i \in [1, 2...n]$, $f_i(s_1)$ is not worse than $f_i(s_2)$ and $\exists \, i \in [1, 2...n]$ such that $f_i(s_1)$ is better than $f_i(s_2)$. In this optimization context, we can define two key properties to measure the quality of the output provided by a multiobjective algorithm: convergence to the Pareto-optimal front and solution diversity. Accomplishing these two goals is considered a challenging issue in real optimization scenarios, so multiobjective searches can be boosted by using a variety of strategies. A representative approach is given by the ε-dominance proposal [10], which extends Pareto dominance by not allowing two solutions with a difference (or proportion) less than ε_i in the i-th objective to be non-dominated to each other. This mechanism can be useful i.e. to identify promising individuals in the population, considering them in the learning strategies of the algorithm to support the generation of improved candidate solutions.

In this work, we study the application of ε-dominance and other strategies to improve a Multiobjective Firefly Algorithm (MO-FA) [15] for inferring phylogenies according to parsimony and likelihood. We also propose a parallel adaptation of the resulting algorithm, named as ε-MO-FA, to exploit multicore machines with OpenMP [3]. The main goal lies on assessing the performance of the proposed algorithm from both parallel and multiobjective perspectives. We will evaluate firstly the scalability of the algorithm in a multicore system up to 32 cores attending to the metrics of speedup and efficiency. Secondly, we will introduce a comparative study to assess ε-MO-FA with regard to our previous proposal, using three multiobjective metrics: hypervolume, set coverage and spacing. This experimental analysis will be conducted over four real nucleotide data sets, making comparisons with other phylogenetic tools from the literature.

This paper is organized in the following way. The next section details the definition of the problem and formulates the considered objective functions. Section 3 highlights the main features of ε-MO-FA and describes its parallelization with OpenMP. Section 4 contains the experimental evaluation of the proposal. Finally, concluding remarks and future work lines are included in Sect. 5.

2   Phylogenetic Reconstruction Problem

Phylogenetic reconstruction methods are aimed at describing the evolutionary history of species by modelling ancestor-descendant relationships between living and hypothetical organisms. A phylogenetic hypothesis is given by a tree data structure $T = (V, E)$. Here, V represents the node set containing ancestral organisms at the internal nodes, while the results of the evolutionary process are given in the shape of leaf nodes. On the other hand, E contains the branches used to link related organisms throughout the course of evolution. This evolutionary history is inferred by processing the similarities and divergence observed in a dataset composed of N aligned sequences (i.e. nucleotide sequences in the case of DNA-based analyses, represented by character strings following the state alphabet $\Lambda = \{A,C,G,T\}$) with M sites per sequence.

Phylogenetic inference can be modelled as an optimization problem which seeks to obtain an optimal phylogeny attending to certain biological criteria (implemented as objective functions). However, different phylogenetic functions can give rise to conflicting phylogenies for the same biological data [12]. To address this issue, we tackle the problem from a multiobjective perspective, considering two popular objective functions: parsimony and likelihood. On the one hand, the maximum parsimony principle applies Ockham's razor to give preference to the simplest evolutionary hypothesis, given by a phylogenetic topology which minimizes the number of changes observed between related organisms (that is, the one showing a minimal number of mutation events per generation). The parsimony score for a phylogenetic tree $T = (V, E)$ is calculated as [11]:

$$P(T) = \sum_{i=1}^{M} \sum_{(a,b)\in E} C(a_i, b_i),   \tag{1}$$

where $(a, b) \in E$ defines the evolutionary relationship between two nodes $a, b \in V$, a_i and b_i are the state values at the i-th site of the sequences related to a and b, and $C(a_i, b_i)$ quantifies the state divergence observed between a_i and b_i.

On the other hand, maximum likelihood approaches conduct the inference process under the assumptions provided by an evolutionary model, which defines the probabilities of observing mutation events. The main idea focuses on using these probabilities to infer the most likely evolutionary hypothesis that explains the features observed in the input organisms. Considering the probabilities defined by a model μ, the maximum likelihood hypothesis is described by the evolutionary tree $T = (V, E)$ which maximizes the following expression [11]:

$$L[T, \mu] = \prod_{i=1}^{M} \sum_{x,y\in\Lambda} \pi_x \left[P_{xy}(t_{ru}) L_p \left(u_i = y \right) \right] \times \left[P_{xy} \left(t_{rv} \right) L_p \left(v_i = y \right) \right],   \tag{2}$$

where π_x is the stationary probability of the state $x \in \Lambda$, $P_{xy}(t)$ the probability of observing a mutation from x to a different state y within a time t, $r \in V$ the root node of the tree with descendants $u, v \in V$, and $L_p(u_i = y)$, $L_p(v_i = y)$ the partial likelihoods of observing y at the i-th site in u and v, respectively.

Tackling phylogenetic inference as an optimization problem represents a significant challenge from a computational perspective. This is due to the fact that the reconstruction of optimal phylogenies (i.e. under parsimony and likelihood) shows an NP-hard complexity. This hardness is closely related to the dimensions N and M of the input dataset. Firstly, the size of the tree search space depends on the number of species N in such a way that a exponential growth in the number of possible phylogenetic topologies is verified for increasing values of N. Secondly, the evaluation times required by the computation of objective functions depend on the sequence size M, showing a linear growth with M which can represent a significant time-consuming factor in current biological alignments. These two key issues explain why phylogenetic inference represents a grand computational challenge and the need to undertake real-world analyses upon the basis of high performance computing and bioinspired computing.

3   A Parallel ε-Dominance Based Proposal

To address the phylogeny inference problem, we propose a parallel approach which implements ε-dominance and other multiobjective techniques to improve search capabilities. This section describes the main features of the proposal.

ε-Based Multiobjective Firefly Algorithm. The Firefly Algorithm (FA) [17] is a bioinspired algorithm built upon the bioluminescence of fireflies to solve optimization problems. The basic idea lies on modelling the interactions performed by these organisms, based on the emission of flashing lights to attract potential partners. The decision on moving to the position of another firefly according to this attraction system depends on multiple factors, such as the light intensity, the distance between fireflies and the environmental light absorption. A previous multiobjective adaptation of this algorithm (MO-FA) was reported in [15], in which we applied the dominance concept to distinguish which fireflies showed the most attractive light patterns, that is, which solutions showed the best quality from a multiobjective perspective. Although high-quality solutions were obtained by this approach (improving the standard Non dominated Sorting Genetic Algorithm II, NSGA-II [6]), the overall shape of the obtained Pareto fronts could be improved from both convergence and diversity perspectives. This is the reason why we propose here a new adaptation ε-MO-FA based on ε-dominance to promote improved search capabilities by making more flexible the learning patterns in this algorithm. The input parameters for ε-MO-FA include the number of fireflies in the population ($popSize$), the maximum number of evaluations established as stop criterion ($maxEval$), an attractiveness factor (β_0), an environmental light absorption coefficient (γ), a randomization factor (α), and the epsilon values for each objective (ε_1, ε_2).

In order to apply this algorithm to phylogenetics, solutions are encoded by means of NxN symmetric floating-point distance matrices, where N is the number of input species. These structures contain in each entry $m[x,y]$ a measure of the evolutionary distance between the organisms x and y. This indirect encoding allows us to perform searches in an auxiliary matrix space which is suitable to be processed by using the operators defined in the original FA design, applying the BIONJ tree-building method to map the matrices into the corresponding phylogenetic trees. Starter matrices at the population initialization stage are obtained from the processing of randomly selected starter phylogenetic topologies taken from a repository generated by bootstrapping techniques, using the Bio++ bioinformatics library [7] for implementation purposes.

At each generation, fireflies in the population are compared with each other under ε-dominance. Let P_i be a firefly with distance matrix $P_i.m$ which is ε-dominated by another firefly P_j with matrix $P_j.m$ ($P_j \succ_\varepsilon P_i$). The attraction procedure in ε-MO-FA generates a new solution P_i' by moving P_i towards P_j, computing in a first step the overall distance δ_{ij} that separates P_i from P_j:

$$\delta_{ij} = \sqrt{\sum_{x=1}^{N}\sum_{y=1}^{x}(P_i.m[x,y] - P_j.m[x,y])^2}. \tag{3}$$

Once we have calculated δ_{ij}, the new distance matrix is computed by using the firefly movement formula, which is governed by the parameters of attractiveness β_0, environmental absorption γ and movement randomization α:

$$P_i'.m[x,y] = P_i.m[x,y] + \beta_0 e^{-\gamma\delta_{ij}^2}(P_j.m[x,y] - P_i.m[x,y]) + \alpha(rnd[0,1] - \frac{1}{2}), \tag{4}$$

where $rnd[0,1]$ is a random number taken from a uniform distribution in the interval [0,1]. While the second term in this formula denotes the degree P_i learns from P_j, the third term introduces randomness to support the exploration capabilities of the algorithm. These steps are repeated for each firefly in the population that ε-dominates P_i, so the new matrix $P_i'.m$ is generated according to the information provided by multiple individuals hence modelling the collective behaviour of swarm intelligence. As the resulting matrix must be symmetric, a blend crossover operator BLX-α [13] is applied over those entries $m[x,y] \neq m[y,x]$. Afterwards, we infer and evaluate the corresponding phylogenies, repeating the movement calculations over each ε-dominated firefly in the population.

At the end of each generation, the new solutions compete with the original fireflies with the aim of preserving the most promising *popSize* solutions. For this purpose, we apply fast non-dominated sorting and crowding computation to classify and sort our solutions by means of Pareto ranks and density values [6]. Then, the Pareto front is updated and a new generation takes place.

Parallel Design. Algorithm 1 provides an OpenMP-based parallel design of ε-MO-FA for shared-memory multicore systems. When parallelizing this algorithm, the main challenge from a parallel perspective is given by the fact that firefly movements are affected by two main sources of load imbalance. Firstly, the attraction procedure checks the whole population under ε-dominance, so the movements are only applied over those solutions which are ε-dominated by at least another solution in the population. Secondly, as solutions can be ε-dominated by multiple, different fireflies at the current generation, the movement

---

Algorithm 1. ε-MO-FA - OpenMP Parallel Design

```
1:  #pragma omp parallel (num_threads)
2:  P ← Initialize Population (popSize, dataset, num_threads), ParetoFront ← 0
3:  while ! stop criterion reached (maxEval) do
4:     #pragma omp single
5:        /* Obtaining information about ε-dominated fireflies */
6:        idεDominatedFireflies ← 0
7:        numεDominatedFireflies ← 0
8:        εDominatingFireflies ← 0
9:        for i = 1 to popSize do
10:          if ∃ P_j: P_j ≻_e P_i then
11:             idεDominatedFireflies[numεDominatedFireflies] ← i
12:             εDominatingFireflies[i] ← εDominatingFireflies[i] ∪ P_j
13:             numεDominatedFireflies ← numεDominatedFireflies + 1
14:          end if
15:       end for
16:    #pragma omp for schedule (dynamic) /* Parallelizing the firefly movement loop */
17:    for i = 1 to numεDominatedFireflies do
18:       idDom ← idεDominatedFireflies[i]
19:       P_{popSize+i}.m ← Attract Firefly (P_{idDom}.m, εDominatingFireflies[idDom], β_0, γ, α)
20:       P_{popSize+i}.T ← Infer Phylogenetic Tree (P_{popSize+i}.m, dataset)
21:       P_{popSize+i}.scores ← Evaluate Solution (P_{popSize+i}.T, dataset)
22:    end for
23:    #pragma omp single
24:       P ← Fast Non-Dominated and Crowding Sorting (P, popSize+numεDominatedFireflies)
25:       ParetoFront ← Update Pareto Front (P, ParetoFront)
26: end while
```

---

operators must be applied a variant number of times, thus leading to different processing times for each ε-dominated firefly.

Our parallel proposal deals with these two issues in the following way. At the beginning of each generation, we calculate the number of ε-dominated fireflies in the population (lines 4–15 in Algorithm 1), storing their identifiers along with the ones from the ε-dominating fireflies. Once we have identified which fireflies must be processed, we apply the movement loop over the number of ε-dominated fireflies detected. In this way, we are able to remove the if-condition which governed the calculation of new fireflies in the original movement loop from the serial version, addressing the first source of load imbalance. The movement loop (lines 16–22) is parallelized by using *#pragma omp for*, enabling a dynamic scheduling policy to address the second source of imbalance, mainly related to the changing number of ε-dominating fireflies that must be considered per iteration. The final steps of the generation (lines 23–25) are enclosed in a *#pragma omp single* directive due to the presence of data dependences in the management of the population and Pareto front data structures. Please observe that this parallelization scheme, in which we define a parallel region at the beginning and apply single/for directives to define serial/parallel fractions of code, is aimed at minimizing the additional thread management overhead that would imply the use of *#pragma omp parallel for* inside the main loop of the algorithm.

4   Experimental Results

This section reports the results of the experiments conducted to evaluate ε-MO-FA from both parallel and multiobjective perspectives. Our experimentation involves the analysis of four real nucleotide data sets from the literature [1]: rbcL_55 (rbcL plastid gene data, $N = 55$ sequences, $M = 1314$ nucleotides per sequence), mtDNA_186 (human mitochondrial DNA, $N = 186$, $M = 16608$), RDPII_218 (prokaryotic RNA, $N = 218$, $M = 4182$), and ZILLA_500 (rbcL gene, $N = 500$, $M = 759$). Our hardware setup comprises two 16-core processors AMD Opteron 'Abu Dhabi' 6376 (a total of 32 execution cores) running at 2.3 GHz with 48GB DDR3 RAM, using Ubuntu 14.04 LTS and GCC 5.3.0.

In order to evaluate the behaviour of the proposal on these real-world scenarios, we have used different metrics to measure parallel performance and solution quality. Firstly, the speedup and efficiency metrics have been used to study how the algorithm scales over different problem and system sizes, taking as reference the serial times reported in Table 1. Secondly, the multiobjective quality of the generated Pareto fronts has been assessed by using three multiobjective metrics [5]: the hypervolume I_H of the objective space covered by the reported solutions, the coverage relation $SC(X, Y)$ which allows to make pairwise comparisons between two algorithms X and Y by calculating the fraction of solutions in Y which are weakly-dominated by X, and the spacing SP between solutions in the Pareto front. The configuration of input parameters in ε-MO-FA has been performed by studying different uniformly-distributed values for each one, using hypervolume to measure the quality of the generated outputs. This parametric study reported the following best values for each parameter: $popSize = 128$, $\beta_0 = 1$, $\gamma = 0.5$, $\alpha = 0.05$, and the epsilon values $\varepsilon_1 = 0.005$ (parsimony objective) and $\varepsilon_2 = 0.0005$ (likelihood objective). The stop criterion was set to 10000 evaluations and the analyses were conducted under the $GTR + \Gamma$ evolutionary model.

Table 1. Serial times (in seconds) for ε-MO-FA

	rbcL_55	mtDNA_186	RDPII_218	ZILLA_500
T_{exec}	5008.131	44927.917	45576.534	70179.939

Parallel Results. The evaluation of parallel performance for ε-MO-FA has been conducted by considering increasing system configurations involving 8, 16, 24 and 32 cores. For each configuration and dataset, 11 independent runs were carried out in order to obtain statistically meaningful samples of execution time. Table 2 shows the median speedups (columns 2, 4, 6 and 8) and efficiencies (columns 3, 5, 7, and 9) observed over the serial times reported in Table 1 for each dataset. In addition, columns 10–11 in Table 2 summarize the mean behaviour of the algorithm under these two parallel metrics, taking into account the results obtained in all the data sets under study.

In overall terms, our parallel proposal is able to take effective advantage of the parallel resources available in the architecture. In short, ε-MO-FA obtains speedup values in the ranges 7.2–7.8 (8 cores), 12.3–14.4 (16 cores), 16.3–19.8 (24 cores), and 19.6–24.0 (32 cores). The efficiencies point out that the algorithm

Table 2. Speedups and efficiencies achieved by ε-MO-FA

	rbcL_55		mtDNA_186		RDPII_218		ZILLA_500		Mean	
Cores	Speedup	Eff.(%)	Speedup	Eff.(%)	Speedup	Eff.(%)	Speedup	Eff.(%)	Speedup	Eff.(%)
8	7.209	90.114	7.291	91.141	7.294	91.180	7.818	97.727	7.403	92.541
16	12.255	76.592	13.123	82.018	13.383	83.645	14.385	89.905	13.286	83.040
24	16.257	67.736	17.821	74.256	18.423	76.762	19.782	82.424	18.071	75.295
32	19.568	61.150	21.190	66.219	22.029	68.841	24.042	75.131	21.707	67.835

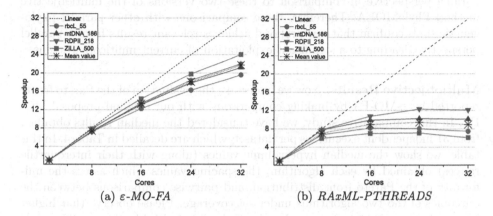

(a) ε-MO-FA   (b) RAxML-PTHREADS

Fig. 1. Parallel performance - speedup comparisons

attains a satisfying exploitation of the underlying hardware, reporting in the dataset with the highest number of species (ZILLA_500) a significant efficiency value of 75.1% when using the whole system (32 cores). It is also remarkable to point out that the attained speedups are closely related to the complexity of the input dataset, as growing problem sizes imply more computations over matrix and tree data structures of growing size, motivating in this way an increase in the parallelizable fraction of the application.

With the aim of assessing these parallel results, we have conducted comparisons with two parallel tools for phylogenetic reconstruction: RAxML [16] (maximum likelihood inference) and PhyloMOEA [2] (multiobjective inference). Figure 1 provides a graphical comparison between the speedups obtained by ε-MO-FA and RAxML in its multicore POSIX-based release. For system

Table 3. Speedup comparisons with PhyloMOEA (16 cores)

	rbcL_55	mtDNA_186	RDPII_218	ZILLA_500
ε-MO-FA	**12.26**	**13.12**	**13.38**	**14.39**
PhyloMOEA MPI	7.30	7.40	9.80	6.70
PhyloMOEA Hybrid	8.30	8.50	10.20	6.30

configurations involving 16 or more execution cores, a significant improvement in the way ε-MO-FA scales can be verified with regard to RAxML-PTHREADS. In fact, when using the whole system, ε-MO-FA is able to obtain a mean speedup value of 21.7, in comparison to the speedup of 8.95 reported by this likelihood-based parallel tool. Regarding PhyloMOEA, Table 3 introduces a comparison with the speedup results reported (16 cores) for the MPI-based and hybrid MPI+OpenMP parallel versions of this tool [2]. This table gives account of how the parallel implementation of ε-MO-FA shows an improved behaviour from a parallel perspective in comparison to these two versions of the multiobjective method PhyloMOEA. Therefore, these comparisons with other parallel phylogenetic tools confirm that our proposal achieves relevant results from a parallel perspective, leading to a significant exploitation of current multicore systems.

Multiobjective Results. Now we undertake the evaluation of the Pareto fronts reported by ε-MO-FA by making comparisons with our original proposal MO-FA. In this comparative study, we have considered the median results obtained from 31 independent executions per dataset, which are detailed in Table 4. In this table, we show the median hypervolume values (along with their interquartile ranges) obtained by each algorithm, the spacing values which assess the uniformity of the Pareto front distribution, and pairwise comparisons between the outcomes of the two algorithms under set coverage. Please observe that higher hypervolume and set coverage values imply better multiobjective quality, while spacing is a metric to be minimized. In addition, we report in Fig. 2 a graphical comparison of the Pareto fronts obtained by ε-MO-FA and MO-FA in the median-hypervolume execution for each dataset under study.

Attending to the overall quality of the inferred Pareto fronts, Table 4 points out that the new ε-based proposal outperforms the original adaptation of the algorithm in all the data sets under study. While the differences in hypervolume scores might not be too high, both spacing and set coverage give account of the success of ε-MO-FA in achieving more satisfying outcomes than MO-FA from a multiobjective perspective. In fact, spacing confirms that ε-MO-FA is able to obtain a more relevant spread of solutions in the Pareto fronts, overcoming the diversity issues originally shown by MO-FA. In addition, the coverage relation suggests better convergence properties in the fronts obtained by ε-MO-FA, according to the fact that the new proposal is able to cover, in average terms, over 70% of the solutions reported by MO-FA. These two statements are verified by the representation of Pareto fronts in Fig. 2, where a noticeable improvement in both solution quality and spread can be observed. In conclusion, ε-MO-FA succeeds in attaining significant results attending to multiobjective quality, addressing the problems shown by the previous version of the algorithm.

Once multiobjective results have been analyzed, we now undertake the evaluation of the inferred phylogenetic trees by introducing comparisons with other state-of-the-art phylogenetic tools. More specifically, Table 5 reports the parsimony and likelihood scores of the extreme points in our median Pareto fronts and compare them with the tools TNT [8] (for maximum parsimony), RAxML

Table 4. Multiobjective performance - comparisons between ε-MO-FA and MO-FA

	rbcL_55	mtDNA_186	RDPII_218	ZILLA_500
Hypervolume				
$I_H(\varepsilon$-MO-FA)	**71.55 ± 0.01**	**70.02 ± 0.01**	**74.81 ± 0.13**	**73.00 ± 0.08**
I_H(MO-FA)	71.47 ± 0.08	70.00 ± 0.01	74.73 ± 0.08	72.96 ± 0.02
Spacing				
SP(ε-MO-FA)	**0.097**	**0.078**	**0.028**	**0.037**
SP(MO-FA)	0.128	0.103	0.033	0.051
Set coverage				
SC(ε-MO-FA, MO-FA)	**62.50%**	**85.71%**	**57.32%**	**81.25%**
SC(MO-FA, ε-MO-FA)	30.00%	18.75%	22.12%	13.24%

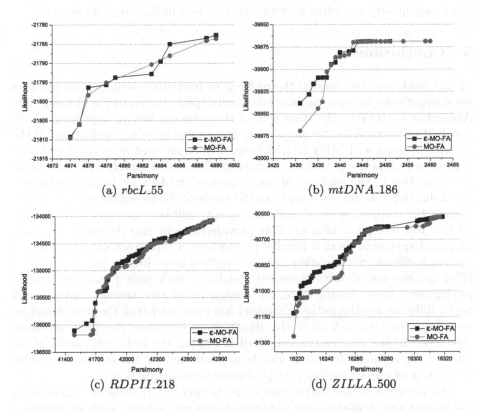

(a) $rbcL\_55$

(b) $mtDNA\_186$

(c) $RDPII\_218$

(d) $ZILLA\_500$

Fig. 2. Multiobjective performance - Pareto front comparisons

(under the GTR+Γ model) and PhyloMOEA (under the HKY85+Γ model). With regard to parsimony results, ε-MO-FA matches the quality of TNT in all the data sets under study, while outperforming PhyloMOEA in mtDNA_186,

Table 5. Evaluation of parsimony and likelihood results

Dataset	Parsimony score			Likelihood score (GTR+Γ)		Likelihood score (HKY85+Γ)	
	ε-MO-FA	TNT	PhyloMOEA	ε-MO-FA	RAxML	ε-MO-FA	PhyloMOEA
rbcL_55	**4874**	**4874**	4874	**−21782.64**	−21788.57	**−21813.81**	−21889.84
mtDNA_186	**2431**	**2431**	2437	**−39868.64**	−39868.07	**−39889.23**	−39896.44
RDPII_218	**41488**	**41488**	41534	**−134080.68**	−134085.14	**−134154.31**	−134696.53
ZILLA_500	**16218**	**16218**	16219	**−80568.24**	−80599.77	**−80967.27**	−81018.06

RDPII_218, and ZILLA_500. As for likelihood, our proposal is also able to obtain significant solutions attending to this phylogenetic function, improving the scores reported by RAxML in three data sets and PhyloMOEA in all of them. In conclusion, our experimentation confirms the success of the new strategies introduced in ε-MO-FA to boost its search capabilities, leading to Pareto fronts with significant quality attending to multiobjective and biological performance.

5 Conclusions

In this work, we have tackled the problem of inferring multiobjective phylogenetic hypotheses by using an improved multiobjective adaptation of the Firefly Algorithm, ε-MO-FA. The main goal of the proposal lies on improving search capabilities by applying ε-dominance to govern the learning mechanisms of the algorithm, along with other multiobjective strategies (fast non-dominated sorting and crowding computations) to distinguish solution quality in a more accurate way. Due to the hardness of the addressed problem, we have introduced a parallelization scheme based on OpenMP to allow the algorithm to take advantage of the computing capabilities of current multicore systems. Experiments on four real biological data sets have provided insight into the relevance of the proposed approach. From a parallel perspective, a significant exploitation of a 32-core hardware configuration has been verified according to the speedup and efficiency metrics, showing improved scalability with regard to other parallel phylogenetic tools. Furthermore, the evaluation of the inferred Pareto fronts under different multiobjective indicators has confirmed that the new strategies introduced in ε-MO-FA allow the algorithm to overcome the main problems shown by the previous adaptation, MO-FA. Finally, the biological quality of the inferred phylogenetic trees has also been confirmed by the comparisons with other state-of-the-art methods for phylogenetic reconstruction.

Our future work lines aim to explore in a deeper way the relationship between parallelism and multiobjective metaheuristics when solving NP-hard problems like phylogenetic reconstruction. Particularly, we will undertake the analysis of multiple algorithmic designs (including evolutionary algorithms and swarm intelligence), evaluating the impact in parallel performance which implies the use of alternative multiobjective strategies. In addition, advanced parallel designs for improving multiobjective quality and parallel scalability will be studied.

Acknowledgments. The authors thank the University of Extremadura for the postdoc grant ACCION-III-04 provided to Sergio Santander-Jiménez (Plan de Iniciación a la Investigación, Desarrollo Tecnológico e Innovación 2015). Thanks to the Junta de Extremadura for the GR15011 grant provided to the group TIC015.

References

1. Cancino, W., Delbem, A.C.B.: A multi-criterion evolutionary approach applied to phylogenetic reconstruction. In: New Achievements in Evolutionary Computation, pp. 135–156. InTech (2010)
2. Cancino, W., Jourdan, L., Talbi, E.-G., Delbem, A.C.B.: Parallel multi-objective approaches for inferring phylogenies. In: Pizzuti, C., Ritchie, M.D., Giacobini, M. (eds.) EvoBIO 2010. LNCS, vol. 6023, pp. 26–37. Springer, Heidelberg (2010). doi:10.1007/978-3-642-12211-8_3
3. Chapman, B., Jost, G., van der Pas, R.: Using OpenMP: Portable Shared Memory Parallel Programming. The MIT Press, Cambridge (2007)
4. Coelho, G.P., Silva, A.E.A., Zuben, F.J.V.: An immune-inspired multi-objective approach to the reconstruction of phylogenetic trees. Neural Comput. Appl. **19**(8), 1103–1132 (2010)
5. Coello, C., Dhaenens, C., Jourdan, L.: Advances in Multi-Objective Nature Inspired Computing. Springer, Heidelberg (2010)
6. Deb, K., Pratap, A., Agarwal, S., Meyarivan, T.: A fast and elitist multi-objective genetic algorithm: NSGA-II. IEEE Trans. Evol. Comput. **6**(2), 182–197 (2002)
7. Dutheil, J., et al.: Bio++: a set of C++ libraries for sequence analysis, phylogenetics, molecular evolution and population genetics. BMC Bioinform. **7**, 188–193 (2006)
8. Goloboff, P.A., Farris, J.S., Nixon, K.C.: TNT, a free program for phylogenetic analysis. Cladistics **24**(5), 774–786 (2008)
9. Handl, J., Kell, D.B., Knowles, J.D.: Multiobjective optimization in bioinformatics and computational biology. IEEE/ACM Trans. Comput. Biol. Bioinf. **4**(2), 279–292 (2007)
10. Laumanns, M., Thiele, L., Deb, K., Zitzler, E.: Combining convergence and diversity in evolutionary multi-objective optimization. Evol. Comput. **10**(3), 263–282 (2002)
11. Lemey, P., Salemi, M., Vandamme, A.M.: The Phylogenetic Handbook: A Practical Approach to Phylogenetic Analysis and Hypothesis Testing. Cambridge University Press, Cambridge (2009)
12. Macey, J.R.: Plethodontid salamander mitochondrial genomics: a parsimony evaluation of character conflict and implications for historical biogeography. Cladistics **21**(2), 194–202 (2005)
13. Poladian, L.: A GA for maximum likelihood phylogenetic inference using neighbour-joining as a genotype to phenotype mapping. In: Genetic and Evolutionary Computation Conference, pp. 415–422 (2005)
14. Poladian, L., Jermiin, L.: Multi-objective evolutionary algorithms and phylogenetic inference with multiple data sets. Soft. Comput. **10**(4), 359–368 (2006)
15. Santander-Jiménez, S., Vega-Rodríguez, M.A.: Parallel multiobjective metaheuristics for inferring phylogenies on multicore clusters. IEEE Trans. Parallel Distrib. Syst. **26**(6), 1678–1692 (2015)
16. Stamatakis, A.: RAxML Version 8: A Tool for Phylogenetic Analysis and Post-Analysis of Large Phylogenies. Bioinformatics **30**(9), 1312–1313 (2014)

17. Yang, X.S.: Firefly algorithm, stochastic test functions and design optimisation. Int. J. Bio-Inspired Comput. **2**(2), 78–84 (2010)
18. Zomaya, A.Y.: Parallel Computing for Bioinformatics and Computational Biology: Models, Enabling Technologies, and Case Studies. Wiley, Hoboken (2006)

Evaluation of Parallel Differential Evolution Implementations on MapReduce and Spark

Diego Teijeiro[1], Xoán C. Pardo[1], David R. Penas[2], Patricia González[1(✉)], Julio R. Banga[2], and Ramón Doallo[1]

[1] Grupo de Arquitectura de Computadores,
Universidade da Coruña, A Coruña, Spain
{diego.teijeiro,xoan.pardo,patricia.gonzalez,doallo}@udc.es
[2] BioProcess Engineering Group, IIM-CSIC, Vigo, Spain
julio@iim.csic.es

Abstract. Global optimization problems arise in many areas of science and engineering, computational and systems biology and bioinformatics among them. Many research efforts have focused on developing parallel metaheuristics to solve them in reasonable computation times. Recently, new programming models are being proposed to deal with large scale computations on commodity clusters and Cloud resources. In this paper we investigate how parallel metaheuristics deal with these new models by the parallelization of the popular Differential Evolution algorithm using MapReduce and Spark. The performance evaluation has been carried out both in a local cluster and in the Amazon Web Services public cloud. The results obtained can be particularly useful for those interested in the potential of new Cloud programming models for parallel metaheuristic methods in general and Differential Evolution in particular.

Keywords: Parallel metaheuristics · Differential Evolution · Cloud computing · MapReduce · Spark

1 Introduction

Many key problems in computational systems biology can be formulated and solved using global optimization techniques. Metaheuristics are gaining increased attention as an efficient way of solving hard global optimization problems. Differential Evolution (DE) [12] is one of the most popular heuristics for global optimization, and it has been successfully used in many different areas [4]. However, in most realistic applications, like parameter estimation problems in systems biology, this population-based method requires a very large number of evaluations (and therefore, large computation time) to obtain an acceptable result. Therefore, several parallel DE schemes have been proposed, most of them focused on traditional parallel programming interfaces and infrastructures.

The aim of this paper is to investigate how parallel metaheuristics could be handled based on the recent advances in Cloud programming models. Distributed

F. Desprez et al. (Eds.): Euro-Par 2016 Workshops, LNCS 10104, pp. 397–408, 2017.
DOI: 10.1007/978-3-319-58943-5_32

frameworks like MapReduce or Spark, provide advantages such as higher-level programming models to easily parallelize user programs, support for data distribution and processing on multiple nodes/cores, and run-time features such as fault tolerance and load-balancing. The goal of this paper is to explore this direction further considering a parallel implementation of DE in both frameworks and evaluating their performance in a real testbed using both a local cluster and the Amazon Web Services (AWS) public cloud.

The organization of the paper is as follows. Section 2 presents the background and related work. The proposed implementations of DE using both MapReduce and Spark are described in Sect. 3. The performance of these implementations and a comparison between them are assessed in Sect. 4. Finally, Sect. 5 concludes the paper.

2   Background and Related Work

Since its appearance, MapReduce [5] (MR from now on) has been the distributed programming model for processing large scale computations that has attracted more attention. In short, MR executes in parallel several instances of a pair of user-provided *map* and *reduce* functions over a distributed network of *worker* processes driven by a single *master*. Executions in MR are made in batches, using a distributed filesystem to take the input and store the output. MR has been applied to a wide range of applications, including distributed sorting, graph processing or machine learning. But for iterative algorithms, as those typical in parallel metaheuristics, MR has shown serious performance bottlenecks [6] because there is no way of reusing data or computation from previous iterations efficiently when several of these single batches are executed inside a loop.

Spark [15] is a recent proposal designed from the very beginning to provide efficient support for iterative algorithms. Spark provides a distributed memory abstraction denominated *resilient distributed datasets* (RDDs) for supporting fault-tolerant and efficient in-memory computations. Formally, an RDD is a read–only fault–tolerant partitioned collection of records. RDDs are created from other RDDs or from data in stable storage by applying coarse-grained *transformations* (e.g., *map*, *filter* or *join*) that can be pipelined to from a *lineage*. Once created, RDDs are used in *actions* (e.g. *count*, *collect* or *save*) which are operations that return a value to the application or export data to a storage system. Spark runtime is composed of a single *driver* program and multiple long-lived *workers* that persist RDD partitions in RAM across operations. Developers write the driver program where they define one or more RDDs and invoke actions on them. Lineages are used to compute RDDs lazily whenever they are used in actions or to recompute them in case of failure.

There are some proposals which investigate how to apply MR to parallelize the DE algorithm. In [16] the Hadoop framework (the most widely used open source implementation of MR) is used to perform in parallel the fitness evaluation. However, the experimental results reveal that HDFS (Hadoop Distributed File System) I/O and system bookkeeping overhead significantly reduces the benefits of the parallelization. In [13], a concurrent implementation of the DE based on MR is proposed which was only evaluated on a multi-core CPU taking advantage of the shared-memory architecture. In [3] a parallel implementation of DE based clustering using MR is also proposed. This algorithm was implemented in three levels, each of which consists of DE operations. To the best of our knowledge, there is no previous work that explores the use of Spark for parallel metaheuristics.

There are also a few references comparing MR and Spark performance for iterative algorithms. In [15] Spark authors compare their proposal to MR (using Hadoop) for different types of iterative algorithms on Amazon EC2. They implemented two machine learning algorithms, logistic regression which is more I/O-intensive and k-means which is more compute-intensive, and found that scaling up to 100 nodes Spark outperformed MR from 12.3x up to 25.3x for logistic regression and from 1.9x up to 3.2x for k-means. They also tested the well-known PageRank algorithm finding that Spark outperformed MR by up to 7.4x, scaling well in up to 60 nodes. In [8] performance of several distributed frameworks including Hadoop (v.1.0.3) and Spark (v.0.8.0) were assessed in Amazon EC2 for iterative scientific algorithms. The Partitioning Around Medoids (PAM) clustering algorithm and the Conjugate Gradient (CG) linear system solver were implemented for evaluation. Results show that scaling up to 32 nodes and using 3 datasets of different sizes, Spark outperformed MR from 1.3x up to 48x for PAM and from 23x up to 99x for CG. Authors concluded that Spark results seemed to be greatly affected by the characteristics of the benchmarking algorithms and their dataset composition. In [11] Hadoop (v.2.4.0) and Spark (v.1.3.0) major architectural components are thoroughly compared using a set of analytic workloads. Results show that, using a 4 node (32 cores, 190 GB RAM, 9x1TB disk each) cluster with a 1GB Ethernet network, Spark outperformed MR by 5x for k-means, linear regression and PageRank. Authors conclude that, for iterative algorithms, caching the input as RDDs in Spark can reduce both CPU and disk I/O overheads for subsequent iterations and that RDD caching is much more efficient than other low-level caching approaches such as OS buffer caches, and HDFS caching, which can only reduce disk I/O.

3   Implementing DE on MR and Spark

Differential Evolution [12] is an iterative mutation algorithm where vector differences are used to create new candidate solutions. Starting from an initial population matrix composed of NP D-dimensional solution vectors (individuals), DE attempts to achieve the optimal solution iteratively through changes in its vectors. Algorithm 1 shows the basic pseudocode for the DE algorithm. For each iteration, new individuals are generated in the population matrix through operations performed among individuals of the matrix (mutation - F), with old solutions replaced (crossover - CR) only when the fitness value of the objective function is better than the current one. A population matrix with optimized individuals is obtained as output of the algorithm. The best of these individuals are selected as solution close to optimal for the objective function of the model.

Algorithm 1. Differential Evolution algorithm

---

input : A population matrix P with size D x NP
output: A matrix P whose individuals were optimized
repeat
    for *each element x of the P matrix* **do**
        $\vec{a}, \vec{b}, \vec{c}$ ⇐ different random individuals from P matrix
        for k ⇐ 0 **to** D **do**
            if *random point is less than* CR **then**
                | $\overrightarrow{Ind}(k)$ ⇐ $\vec{a}(k) + F(\vec{b}(k) - \vec{c}(k))$
            end
        end
        if *Evaluation*($\overrightarrow{Ind}$) *is better than Evaluation*($\overrightarrow{P(x)}$) **then**
        | Replace_Individual($P,\overrightarrow{Ind}$)
        end
    end
until *Stop conditions*;

However, typical runtimes for many realistic problems are in the range from hours to days due to the large number of objective function evaluations needed, making the performance of the classical sequential DE unacceptable. In the literature, different parallel models can be found [2] aiming to improve both computational time and number of iterations for convergence. The *master-slave* and the *island-based* models are the most popular. In the *master-slave* model the behavior of the sequential DE is preserved by parallelizing the inner-loop of the algorithm, where a master processor distributes computation between the slave processors. In the *island-based* model the population matrix is divided in subpopulations (*islands*) where the algorithm is executed isolated. Sparse individual exchanges are performed among islands to introduce diversity into the subpopulations, preventing search from getting stuck in local optima.

The implementation of the DE master-slave model does not fit well with the distributed nature of programming models like MR or Spark [14]. The reason is that when the mutation strategy is applied to each individual, random different individuals have to be selected from the whole population. Considering that the population would certainly be partitioned and distributed among slaves, any solution to this problem would introduce an unfeasible communications overhead. In the rest of this section we briefly describe our island-based parallel implementations of the DE algorithm, which in advance seemed to be a more promising approach, for both MR and Spark.

Algorithm 2 shows the pseudocode for the *driver* (the user-provided code run by the master) of our island-based parallel implementation of the DE algorithm using MR. The driver is responsible for randomly generating the initial population and for evolving it repeating a loop until the termination criterion is met.

Algorithm 2. Driver pseudocode

---

input : DE configuration parameters
output: A population P whose individuals were optimized

$P \Leftarrow$ initial random population
$\#i \Leftarrow$ number of islands

repeat
　　$\overrightarrow{Islands} \Leftarrow$ PartitionPopulation$(P, \#i)$ // with shuffling
　　$P \Leftarrow$ EvolveIslands$(\overrightarrow{Islands})$ //the MR job
until *Stop conditions*;

Algorithm 3. Map pseudocode

---

inputs : An island I; DE configuration parameters
output: An island I whose individuals were optimized

repeat
　　$I \Leftarrow$ EvolveIsland(I) // apply the DE mutation strategy
until *number of evolutions*;

for *each individual $\overrightarrow{Ind}$ of the island I* **do**
　　Emit(Evaluation($\overrightarrow{Ind}$), $\overrightarrow{Ind}$)
end

In each loop iteration the population is randomly partitioned into islands all with the same number of individuals, islands are written to HDFS one file each, a MR job for evolving the islands is configured and launched and the evolved global population is gathered from HDFS after the MR job finished. Algorithm 3 shows the pseudocode of the map functions executed in each MR job. Each map is responsible for the evolution of exactly one island isolated from the rest during a predefined number of evolutions, the same for all islands. The map starts by reading the island individuals from HDFS and storing them in local memory, then applying the DE mutation strategy taking random individuals only from its island until the predefined number of evolutions is reached and, finally, emitting an output record for each individual of the evolved island using its fitness value as key. The MR job implementation is completed with a single identity reducer which simply receives the individuals from all the islands ordered by their fitness value and writes them to an HDFS file. Note that, as individuals are ordered by fitness, the first record in the output file will be the best individual. To introduce diversity a migration strategy that randomly shuffles individuals among islands without replacement is applied by the driver during the partition of the population in islands. This is a naive strategy intended only to evaluate the migration overhead and not to improve the searching quality of the algorithm.

Figure 1 shows the scheme of our island-based parallel DE implementation using Spark. In the figure, boxes with solid outlines are RDDs. Partitions are

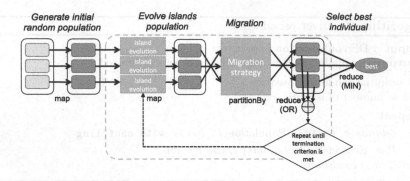

Fig. 1. Spark-based island implementation of the DE algorithm.

shaded rectangles, darker if they are persisted in memory. A key-value pair RDD has been used to represent the population where each individual is uniquely identified by its key. The algorithm starts by distributing the random generation and initial evaluation of individuals that form the population using an Spark map transformation, then an evolution-migration loop is repeated until the termination criterion implemented as an Spark reduce action (a distributed OR operation) is met and, finally, the selection of the best individual is done by using an Spark reduce action (a distributed MIN operation). In the evolution-migration loop every partition of the population RDD has been considered to be an island, all with the same number of individuals. Islands evolve isolated during a predefined number of evolutions, the same for all islands, and in order to introduce diversity the same migration strategy as in the MR implementation is executed after an evolution. We have developed a custom Spark *partitioner* that randomly and evenly shuffles elements among partitions for implementing the migration strategy.

It must be noted that although the migration strategy is the same for both implementations, the overhead they add is not. In MR migration is implemented in the driver that reads the population from HDFS, shuffles the individuals among islands and writes back the islands to HDFS, so the overhead is mainly caused by accessing HDFS. In Spark migration is implemented as a *partitionBy* operation, so the overhead is mainly caused by communications.

4   Experimental Results

In order to evaluate and compare the island-based implementation of DE using MR and Spark, different experiments have been carried out. Their behavior, in terms of execution time and overhead, has been compared with the sequential implementation. Programming languages used have been Scala (v2.10) for the sequential and Spark implementations, and Java (v1.7.0) for the MR implementation. Spark (v.1.4.1) and Hadoop (v2.7.1) frameworks were used for the experiments.

Two sets of benchmark problems were used: on the one hand, two problems out of an algebraic black-box optimization testbed, the Black-Box Optimization Benchmarking (BBOB) data set [7]: Rastrigin function (f_{15}) and Gallagher's Gaussian 21-hi Peaks function (f_{22}); on the other hand, a challenging parameter estimation problem in a dynamic model of the *circadian* clock in the plant *Arabidopsis thaliana*, as presented in [9]. Table 1 shows the configurable parameters used for the reported experiments.

Table 1. Benchmark functions. Parameters: dimension (D), population size (NP), crossover constant (CR), mutation factor (F), mutation strategy (MSt), value-to-reach/*ftarget* (VTR).

B	Function	D	NP	CR	F	MSt	VTR
f_{15}	Rastrigin function	5	1024	.8	.9	DE/rand/1	1000
f_{22}	Gallagher's Gaussian	10	1600	.8	.9	DE/rand/1	−1000
circadian	Circadian model	13	640	.8	.9	DE/rand/1	1e−5

For the experimental testbed two different platforms has been used. First, experiments were conducted in our multicore local cluster Pluton, that consists of 16 nodes powered by two octa-core Intel Xeon E5-2660 CPUs with 64 GB of RAM, and connected through an InfiniBand FDR network. Second, experiments were deployed with default settings in the AWS public cloud using virtual clusters formed by 2, 4, 8 and 16 nodes communicated by the AWS standard network (Ethernet 1 GB). For the nodes the m3.medium instance (1 vCPU, 3.75 GB RAM, 4 GB SSD) was used. In both testbeds, each experiment was executed a number of 10 independent runs, and the average and standard deviation of the execution time are reported in this section. Note that, since Spark and MR programs run on the Java Virtual Machine (JVM), usual precautions (i.e. warm-up phase, effect of garbage collection) have been taken into account to avoid distortions on the measures.

Comparing the sequential and the parallel metaheuristics is not an easy task, therefore, guidance of [1,7] has been followed when analyzing the results of these experiments. Since the parallel strategy followed is the same in both MR and Spark implementations, the best way to fairly compare the performance of both implementations is to stop at a predefined effort, that is, for a vertical view. Results obtained in the local cluster Pluton and in the AWS public cloud, both in terms of execution times and speedups, are shown in Fig. 2 using a predefined number of evaluations as stopping criterion. All the experiments execute two iterations of the algorithm (each iteration corresponding to an evolution-migration). To assess the scalability up to 16 islands have been used for the parallel implementations. We do not use more than 16 islands due to the small population size in this benchmarks. As it can be seen, the Spark implementation achieves good results, both in time and speedup, versus the sequential algorithm, and a good scalability when the number of islands grows. However, the

MR implementation presents poorer results, specially for f_{15}, the shortest of the two benchmarks, because it introduces a high overhead. Note that the execution times are larger in AWS than in cluster Pluton, even for sequential executions. Virtualization overhead, use of non-dedicated resources in a multi-tenant platform, and differences in node characteristics can explain these results. Even so, the Spark implementation achieves good results in terms of speedup versus the sequential implementation in AWS. However, the MR implementation presents even poorer results than in the experiments carried out in the local cluster.

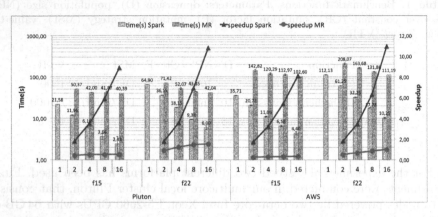

Fig. 2. Execution time and speedup results comparing MR vs Spark implementation in cluster Pluton and the AWS public cloud. Stopping criterion: $Nevals_{f15} = 1,025,024$ and $Nevals_{f22} = 3,200,000$.

To evaluate the overhead introduced by MR and Spark we have used modified versions of our implementations in which the evolution of the population was removed. Each modified implementation was executed for a total of 8 *evolution-migration* iterations and the overhead of each iteration was measured separately in order to assess differences between them. Figure 3 shows the results obtained. The first iteration in the Spark implementation is always the most time consuming (it corresponds to the outliers in the box plots), being the mean of the experiments 0.050 ± 0.009 s in the local cluster. However, the rest of the iterations present even lower overhead and lower dispersion in the results, being the mean overhead of each iteration of 0.023 ± 0.004 s. In the case of MR there is no significant difference between iterations, and the figures clearly indicate a higher overhead and large dispersion in the results, being the mean overhead of each iteration 17.95 ± 2.50 s in Pluton. This explains why, in Fig. 2, execution times of MR implementation stagnate around 40 s (close to the overhead of the two iterations) when the number of cores grows. The experiment confirms that Spark has lower overhead and better support for iterative algorithms than MR.

Figure 3 shows also that, both for MR and Spark, the overhead in AWS is larger than in the local cluster. The first iteration in Spark is again the most time consuming, being the mean of the experiments of 0.26 ± 0.12 s. However,

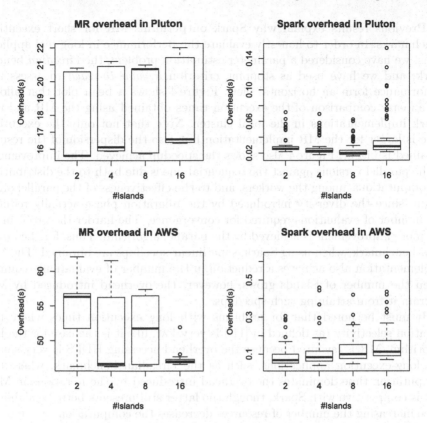

Fig. 3. Box plot of the overhead times per evolution-migration iteration in MR and Spark.

the rest of the iterations present low overheads, being the mean overhead of each iteration of 0.09 ± 0.04 s. Also, it must be noted that the Spark overhead slightly increases when the number of nodes grows, which is in tune with what was expected. Results in the local cluster does not clearly show this increase, but it should be noted that differences are very small and we are shuffling very few data among a small number of physically close nodes using a high-throughput and low-latency InfiniBand network.

In the case of MR there is again no significant difference between the first and the subsequent iterations, but overheads are higher than in the local cluster, being the mean overhead for each iteration of 51.03 ± 5.07 s. In addition to the overhead due to the virtualization and the differences in node characteristics, these results could be explained by the use of HDFS with Amazon EBS volumes which are mounted over a non-dedicated 1GB Ethernet network. These boxplots also show that the variability in the MR overhead between independent experiments is much more noticeable in AWS. For instance, experiments with 2, 4, 8 and 16 nodes were performed at different moments and, although they obtain similar mean overhead, the standard deviation is significantly different.

Previous results explain why Spark outperforms MR for short execution benchmarks. In order to honestly evaluate the performance in long real applications, we have considered a parameter estimation problem, the *circadian* benchmark, and we have used as stopping criterion a *value-to-reach* to assess the performance form an horizontal view. Figure 4 shows a bean plot that allows for an easy comparison of the execution times obtained using the MR and the Spark implementations in the local cluster. Note that not only the execution time is larger for the MR implementation but also the dispersion of the results obtained is bigger. Figure 4 also shows the speedup achieved. The improvement of the parallel versions against the sequential one is due both to the distribution of computations among the workers, and to the effectiveness of the parallel algorithm, since the diversity introduced by the migration phase actually reduces the number of evaluations required for convergence. The harder the problem is, the more improvement is achieved by the parallel algorithm. Thus, for the *circadian* benchmark, when using Spark, superlinear speedups are obtained. The MR implementation also achieves a reduction in the number of evaluations required when the number of islands grows, however, the overhead introduced by MR restrain it from attaining such speedups.

It must be noted that for problems with long execution times where the iteration selectivity (as defined in [11]) is very low, like it is the case for the DE algorithm, MR is favoured because the overhead accessing HDFS is very small. For long-execution applications, such as the circadian benchmark, where the computation time dominates the overhead introduced by the iterations in MR, MR is competitive with Spark, though the latter still presents better scalability, since increasing the number of resources decreases the computation time but, as we have seen, the overhead does not decrease.

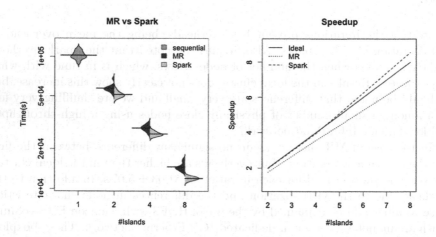

Fig. 4. Circadian benchmark. Comparing MR vs Spark implementation in cluster Pluton: bean plots of the execution time and speedup results vs the sequential implementation in Scala.

Finally, although it is not the aim of this work, we have performed several preliminary tests to assess how competitive the Spark parallel implementation can be with respect to traditional HPC solutions. The same previous experiments were carried out with the implementation of the asynchronous parallel DE described in [10]. This implementation is coded in C and uses the OpenMPI library. Directly comparing the execution times of both implementations is not fair, since the implemented algorithms are not the same: (i) the MPI implementation includes some heuristics to improve the convergence rate of the DE, and (ii) the migration strategy is not the same in both algorithms. Thus, we have estimated the execution time per evaluation such as $T_{eval} = T_{total}/N_{evals}$. Note that this estimated T_{eval} includes not only the CPU time for the evaluation itself but also the communication time and other overheads introduced by the algorithm implementation. We encountered that execution time per evaluation of the Spark implementation was between 2.24x and 2.57x the execution time per evaluation of the MPI implementation. It must be noted that, as already available implementations in C/C++ and/or FORTRAN existed for all the benchmarks, we have wrapped them in our code by using Java/Scala native interfaces (i.e. JNI, JNA, SNA). Further studies to determine a more accurate interpretation of this overhead are left for future work.

5 Conclusions

In order to explore how parallel metaheuristics could take advantage of the recent advances in Cloud programming models, in this paper MR and Spark island-based implementations of the DE algorithm are proposed and evaluated. The performance evaluation of both implementations was conducted on a local cluster and on the AWS public cloud. Both synthetic and real biology-inspired benchmarks were used for the testbed.

The experimental results show that MR has significant higher overhead per iteration than Spark mainly caused by longer task initialization times and HDFS access, and that Spark has best support for iterative algorithms as it reduces the overhead between the first and subsequent iterations. For short benchmarks Spark clearly outperforms MR, which speedup is limited by its overhead. For long running benchmarks, in which computation time prevails over iteration overhead, MR is competitive with Spark. In addition, MR would be favoured by algorithms with low iteration selectivity (i.e. small population size) like DE, but on the contrary, it would be harmed by algorithms with short iterations and higher iteration selectivity.

Acknowledgements. Financial support from the Spanish Government (and the FEDER) through the projects DPI2014-55276-C5-2-R, TIN2013-42148-P, and from the Galician Government under the Consolidation Program of Competitive Research Units (Network Ref. R2014/041 and Project Ref. GRC2013/055) cofunded by FEDER funds of the EU.

References

1. Alba, E., Luque, G.: Evaluation of parallel metaheuristics. In: PPSN-EMAA 2006, pp. 9–14. Reykjavik, Iceland, September 2006
2. Alba, E., Luque, G., Nesmachnow, S.: Parallel metaheuristics: recent advances and new trends. Int. Trans. Oper. Res. **20**(1), 1–48 (2013)
3. Daoudi, M., Hamena, S., Benmounah, Z., Batouche, M.: Parallel differential evolution clustering algorithm based on MapReduce. In: 6th International Conference of Soft Computing and Pattern Recognition (SoCPaR), pp. 337–341. IEEE (2014)
4. Das, S., Suganthan, P.N.: Differential evolution: a survey of the state-of-the-art. IEEE Trans. Evol. Comput. **15**(1), 4–31 (2011)
5. Dean, J., Ghemawat, S.: MapReduce: simplified data processing on large clusters. In: The 6th USENIX Symposium on Operating Systems Design and Implementation (2004)
6. Ekanayake, J., Li, H., Zhang, B., Gunarathne, T., Bae, S.H., Qiu, J., Fox, G.: Twister: a runtime for iterative MapReduce. In: The First International Workshop on MapReduce and its Applications (2010)
7. Hansen, N., Auger, A., Finck, S., Ros, R.: Real-parameter black-box optimization benchmarking 2009: experimental setup. Technical report, RR-6828, INRIA (2009)
8. Jakovits, P., Srirama, S.N.: Evaluating MapReduce frameworks for iterative scientific computing applications. In: International Conference on High Performance Computing & Simulation, HPCS 2014. IEEE (2014). http://ieeexplore.ieee.org/xpl/articleDetails.jsp?arnumber=6903690
9. Locke, J., Millar, A., Turner, M.: Modelling genetic networks with noisy and varied experimental data: the circadian clock in Arabidopsis thaliana. J. Theor. Biol. **234**(3), 383–393 (2005)
10. Penas, D.R., Banga, J.R., González, P., Doallo, R.: Enhanced parallel differential evolution algorithm for problems in computational systems biology. Appl. Soft Comput. **33**, 86–99 (2015). http://www.sciencedirect.com/science/article/pii/S1568494615002525
11. Shi, J., Qiu, Y., Minhas, U.F., Jiao, L., Wang, C., Reinwald, B., Özcan, F.: Clash of the titans: MapReduce vs. spark for large scale data analytics. In: Proceedings of the Very Large Data Bases (VLDB) Endowment, vol. 8, pp. 2110–2121 (2015)
12. Storn, R., Price, K.: Differential evolution - a simple and efficient heuristic for global optimization over continuous spaces. J. Glob. Optim. **11**(4), 341–359 (1997)
13. Tagawa, K., Ishimizu, T.: Concurrent differential evolution based on MapReduce. Int. J. Comput. **4**(4), 161–168 (2010)
14. Teijeiro, D., Pardo, X.C., González, P., Banga, J.R., Doallo, R.: Implementing parallel differential evolution on spark. In: Squillero, G., Burelli, P. (eds.) EvoApplications 2016. LNCS, vol. 9598, pp. 75–90. Springer, Cham (2016). doi:10.1007/978-3-319-31153-1_6
15. Zaharia, M., et al.: Resilient distributed datasets: a fault-tolerant abstraction for in-memory cluster computing. In: The 9th USENIX Symposium on Networked Systems Design and Implementation, NSDI 2012 (2012)
16. Zhou, C.: Fast parallelization of differential evolution algorithm using MapReduce. In: Proceedings of the 12th Annual Conference on Genetic and Evolutionary Computation, pp. 1113–1114. ACM (2010)

Performance Analysis and Optimization of SAMtools Sorting

Nathan T. Weeks[1,2]($\boxtimes$) and Glenn R. Luecke[2]

[1] Department of Computer Science, Iowa State University, Ames, USA
[2] Department of Mathematics, Iowa State University, Ames, USA
weeks@iastate.edu

Abstract. SAMtools is a suite of tools that is widely-used in genomics workflows for post-processing sequence alignment data from large high-throughput sequencing data sets. A common use of SAMtools is to sort the standard Binary Alignment/Map (BAM) format emitted by many sequence aligners. This can be computationally- and I/O-intensive: BAM files can be many gigabytes in size, and may need to be decompressed before sorting and compressed afterwards. As a result, BAM-file sorting can be a bottleneck in genomics workflows. This paper presents a case study on the performance characterization and optimization of BAM sorting with SAMtools. OpenMP task parallelism to enhance concurrency and memory optimization techniques were employed in both SAMtools and the underlying library HTSlib. Utilizing all 32 processor cores on the benchmark system, the optimizations resulted in a speedup of 3.92X for an in-memory sort of 24.6 GiB of BAM data (102.6 GiB uncompressed), while a 1.55X speedup was achieved for an out-of-core sort.

Keywords: Bioinformatics · High-throughput sequencing · OpenMP

1 Introduction

The rapid decline in DNA sequencing costs has outpaced the growth in transistor density from Moore's Law since 2007 [9]. The resulting increase in genomics data generation is predicted to potentially dwarf Twitter, YouTube, and astrophysics data combined by the year 2025 [7]. Furthermore, application performance has generally not even kept pace with Moore's Law, as many applications are ill-equipped to express the parallelism needed to utilize the extra performance potential. As a result, storing, processing, and analyzing genomics data have already become problematic for many institutions. Improvements in algorithms, computing hardware, and storage technology are needed to prevent this trend from worsening.

Most genomics data being generated is high-throughput sequencing (HTS) comprising numerous, relatively-short sequencing reads. HTS is commonly aligned against a reference sequence, typically resulting in sequence alignment data in the standard text-based Sequence Alignment/Map (SAM) format; its

© Springer International Publishing AG 2017
F. Desprez et al. (Eds.): Euro-Par 2016 Workshops, LNCS 10104, pp. 409–420, 2017.
DOI: 10.1007/978-3-319-58943-5_33

binary analog, the Binary Alignment/Map (BAM) format; or the relatively-recent CRAM format. These formats can be consumed by a number of bioinformatic tools for downstream analysis.

SAMtools is a utility for working with sequence alignment data in the SAM, BAM, and CRAM formats [5]. SAMtools supports operations such as sorting, merging sorted files, indexing, selecting subsets of records, compressing, and reporting various statistics. SAMtools makes use of the code-veloped HTSlib library for reading, parsing, and compressing/decompressing SAM/BAM/CRAM data. As SAMtools and HTSlib are developed in lockstep with the SAM/BAM/CRAM specifications, they are considered to be the reference implementations among software tools/libraries that work with these formats.

While SAMtools is partially parallelized using the pthreads API, this implementation is inefficient in some cases (as illustrated by performance profiling of SAMtools 1.3 in Sect. 3 compared with in performance profiling post-optimization in Sect. 4), and there are other parts of the code that could benefit from multithreading. Performance optimization of this foundational tool could benefit many genomics workflows and many users.

The rest of this paper is organized as follows. Section 2 describes other attempts to improve the performance of SAMtools, as well as other software that exists with the explicit goal of implementing performance-critical SAMtools functionality more efficiently. Section 3 characterizes the performance of a SAMtools sort workflow, and identifies performance bottlenecks. Section 4 describes the various categories of optimizations implemented in this work to address the performance bottlenecks identified in Sect. 3. The impact of the performance optimizations on a benchmark data set is analyzed in Sect. 5. Section 6 lists additional opportunities for performance optimization. Section 7 discusses the significance of this work in the context of other work that has been done to address the performance limitations of SAMtools.

2   Related Work

SAMtools uses the HTSlib library for SAM/BAM/CRAM I/O. HTSlib supports multi-threaded reading/writing of CRAM data using a custom pthreads-based thread pool (originally adapted from the Scramble [2] I/O library). Though HTSlib supports multi-threaded BAM compression/output, it supports only single-threaded BAM decompression/input. While it should be feasible to extend HTSlib to accommodate concurrent compression/output of BAM data using the method implemented by Scramble, this paper presents an alternative approach using OpenMP, a high-level API for shared-memory parallel programming that is widely supported by most C, C++, and Fortran compilers.

Other software projects exist with the explicit goal of providing better performance over SAMtools for performance-critical tasks. Sambamba [8] is intended to be a high-performance replacement for a subset of the SAMtools functionality (including BAM sorting, the focus of this paper). Written in the D programming language with parallelism as explicit design goal, Sambamba aims to exploit multi-core CPUs better than SAMtools.

elPrep [4] is a multi-threaded Lisp application that focuses on high-performance, in-memory execution of a subset of SAMtools functionality useful for preparing SAM/BAM/CRAM data for variant calling. elPrep has large memory requirements for sorting, however: the elPrep 2.4 documentation states "As a rule of thumb, elPrep requires 6x times more RAM memory than the size of the input file in .sam format when it is used for sorting". In contrast, the BAM data set described in Sect. 3, which is ∼85.5 GiB when converted to SAM, is sorted in-memory by SAMtools on the 128 GiB-memory compute node. elPrep uses SAMtools internally for reading and writing BAM files, and so could benefit from the decompression and compression optimizations to SAMtools described herein.

DNANexus has submitted a patch to SAMtools that improves concurrency in the BGZF compression/writing code[1] (this paper describes a different method in Sect. 4), as well a fork that leverages RocksDB for improved sorting/merging performance[2]. Neither of these contributions have been accepted into the SAMtools code base.

Intel- and CloudFlare-optimized versions of the zlib compression library have been shown to improve compression performance in SAMtools[3].

3   Performance Profiling

A single compute node of the NERSC Cori (phase 1/Data Partition) supercomputer was used for performance profiling and benchmarking. Each compute node contains two 16-core 2.3 GHz Intel "Haswell" Xeon processors (with each processor core supporting two hardware threads), and 128 GiB 2133 MHz DDR4 memory. While there is no local storage on a compute node, a high-speed Aries interconnection network provides a fast path to a Lustre parallel file system capable of >700 GB/s aggregate bandwidth. Using the dd command with a 4 MiB block size (optimal per st_blksize from the stat() system call) to test single-threaded read performance on the data set described below resulted in a throughput of over 500 MiB/s.

SAMtools 1.3 and HTSlib 1.3 were compiled with the gcc 5.2.0 compiler[4] using the default compiler options specified in the SAMtools/HTSlib makefile, with the exception of using the Cray compiler driver to invoke gcc, overridden to use dynamic linking (cc -dynamic).

---

[1] https://github.com/samtools/htslib/pull/51.
[2] http://devblog.dnanexus.com/faster-bam-sorting-with-samtools-and-rocksdb/.
[3] http://www.htslib.org/benchmarks/zlib.html.
[4] The Intel 16.0.2 compiler was initially used, but due to a potential compiler bug affecting subsequently-implemented OpenMP-based optimizations, the gcc compiler was used for the benchmarking described in this paper.

SAMtools was benchmarked with the 19.9 GiB (102.6 GiB uncompressed) BAM for individual HG00109 from the 1000 Genomes Project [3]. As this BAM file was already sorted by position, it was first sorted by query name to "shuffle" it. The resulting BAM had a considerably worse compression ratio: the file size increased to 24.6 GiB.

SAMtools was run with 32 threads under two scenarios:

1. Out-of-core: the default memory per thread (768MiB) results in sublists sorted in-memory, then written to disk for an out-of-core merge at the end.
2. In-memory: using 3664MiB per thread is enough to store and sort the entire uncompressed BAM data set in memory.

HPCToolkit 5.4.2 [1] was used to generate a profile trace for the in-memory sort (Fig. 1). This profile revealed that program execution (~16 min) is divided into four main phases, in which (1) the compressed BAM data is read and decompressed (~35% run time), (2) the BAM records are sorted by a single thread (~24% run time), (3) the sorted BAM is compressed and written to disk (~25% run time), and (4) data structures allocated during program execution are deallocated (~16% run time). Only the compress/write phase is performed by multiple threads.

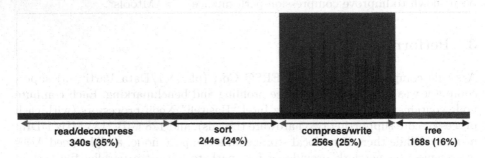

read/decompress	sort	compress/write	free
340s (35%)	244s (24%)	256s (25%)	168s (16%)

Fig. 1. HPCToolkit performance summary of SAMtools 1.3 for a sort (16 threads) of HG00109 BAM alignment data (102.6 GiB uncompressed). This represents the number of threads that are in a particular procedure at a given time. The white area indicates that only one thread is active in three of the four phases. In the compress/write phase, the magenta area represents the compression routine (`bgzf_compress()`), while the green area phase represents idle threads waiting on a condition variable (`pthread_cond_wait()`). (Color figure online)

The out-of-core sort cycles between phases 1–3 until all input has been processed. Unlike the in-memory sort, the sort phase for the out-of-core sort is multi-threaded, where each thread sorts a separate sublist of BAM records and writes its sublist to disk. Finally, the on-disk sorted BAM files are merged and written to a single sorted BAM file.

The run time of the out-of-core sort (~15 min) is actually less than the run time of the in-memory sort. This is due to reductions in run time from added parallelism in the sort phase ($\sim$6% of the run time is spent sorting sublists and writing to temporary files), and in the time spent freeing dynamically-allocated memory associated with BAM data (<3%). The additional I/O overhead from writing the sorted sublists to disk and reading them in again during the final merge did not outweigh the benefit of the parallel sort, at least in part because of the high-bandwidth of the underlying Lustre parallel file system. A conventional (non-parallel) file system might not handle I/O from multiple data streams so effectively.

As a result of performance profiling, a goal was formulated to optimize the performance of each of the four phases of the in-memory sort, with the recognition that many of the optimizations would also benefit the out-of-core sort. These optimizations are described in the next section.

4   Optimizations

Read/Decompress. The HTSlib routines for reading BGZF-compressed BAM data are sequential. While reading an input stream is inherently sequential, in this case the input stream consists of compressed BGZF[5] blocks that can be decompressed independently.

Previously there was an effort to parallelize the decompression of the input BGZF blocks[6]. In this approach, the master thread reads the input data stream, assigning a fixed number of BGZF blocks to each worker thread, while the worker threads wait on a condition variable. When all input buffers have been filled, the master thread executes `pthread_cond_broadcast()` to start the worker threads. Each worker thread inflates each assigned compressed BGZF block into a temporary buffer before copying it into the origin buffer, overwriting the compressed BGZF block. When all worker threads are complete, the master thread adds each buffer pointer to a hash-based cache, allocates new buffers, and repeats the process on new input data. A drawback of this approach is that it limits concurrency: worker threads are idle while the master thread reads input data into the workers' input buffers.

Using the previous effort as a guide for safely adding concurrency to the relevant HTSlib routines, the code was modified so that the master thread generates OpenMP tasks to decompress BGZF blocks as they are read. The next consideration was how many BGZF blocks should be decompressed by each task. A finer level of granularity (i.e., fewer BGZF blocks per task) would improve load balancing, while a coarser level of granularity (coalescing more adjacent BGZF blocks into a single payload for each task) would reduce synchronization overhead. A microbenchmark was constructed to approximate *task creation overhead* from the time elapsed between the last statement before and the first statement

---

[5] Each BGZF block is effectively a gzip file of size $\leq$64K (compressed or uncompressed), with a user-defined field in the gzip header used to represent the length of the BGZF block. The BGZF file format is described in more detail in the SAM/BAM specification.

[6] https://github.com/smowton/htslib/compare/parallel_read.

inside the OpenMP task construct. With 505,455 tasks (the number of BGZF blocks in the HG00109 BAM file) and a 64 KiB OpenMP `firstprivate` payload (the maximum size of a BGZF block) per task, the aggregate task creation overhead for all 32 threads less than 4 s—an average of less than $\frac{1}{8}$ of a second per thread. This indicated that the fine-grained approach of one BGZF block per task would facilitate load balancing without introducing significant synchronization overhead. To eliminate a `memcpy()` for each BGZF block, a new target buffer is dynamically allocated, and a pointer to this buffer is cached.

Memory Allocation. Profiling revealed that a significant fraction (~4%) of the run time for the in-memory SAMtools 1.3 sort was due to a single line of code that allocated an array to store the variable-length data for each BAM record. In the benchmark data set, this meant almost 207 million calls to `realloc()` (each of which was subsequently paired with a corresponding `free()` upon data structure deallocation).

The original data structure used to represent a single BAM record is listed in Fig. 2.

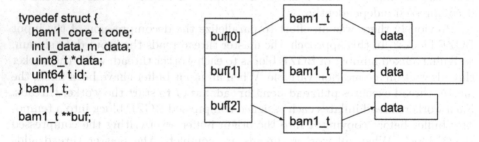

```
typedef struct {
    bam1_core_t core;
    int l_data, m_data;
    uint8_t *data;
    uint64 t id;
} bam1_t;

bam1_t **buf;
```

Fig. 2. The original SAMtools represented each BAM record as a dynamically-allocated bam1_t struct, each containing a dynamically-allocated `data` member. The length of each BAM record is stored in the `l_data` member. An array of pointers (`buf[]`) to the BAM records is sorted during the BAM sort.

This memory allocation overhead was addressed by allocating a single, contiguous array of approximately the maximum memory size requested by the user, as well as an ancillary array of pointers of type `bam1_t` into this array to indicate the start of each BAM record. Each subsequent BAM record starts at the address of the previous BAM record + `l_data`, rounded up to the nearest 8-byte boundary to ensure proper memory alignment of all structure members.

To accomplish the partitioning of the contiguous memory region into an array of variable-length structs, a flexible array member (`fam[]`) was added to bam1_t (Fig. 3). For backwards compatibility with other HTSlib code, the `data` member was retained, pointing to `fam[]`. Reworking the HTSlib code to remove the dependence on the `data` member could save 8 bytes per `bam_t` BAM record (the flexible array member is not a pointer, and consumes no storage beyond the data contained in the array).

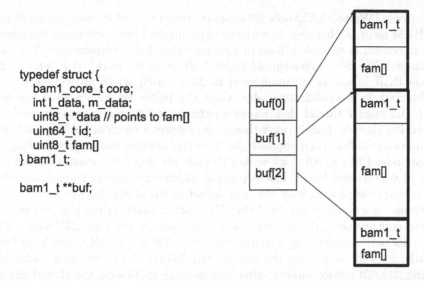

```
typedef struct {
    bam1_core_t core;
    int l_data, m_data;
    uint8_t *data // points to fam[]
    uint64_t id;
    uint8_t fam[]
} bam1_t;

bam1_t **buf;
```

Fig. 3. The use of a flexible array member (fam[]) for variable-length data allows BAM records to be stored consecutively in a contiguous memory region. The array of pointers (buf[]) points to the beginning of each (8-byte aligned) bam1_t record in the array. For backwards compatibility, the data member points to fam.

Sort. In SAMtools 1.3, if the input BAM records do not fit within the user-specified memory limit, then the BAM records in memory are partitioned into N sublists, where N is the number of threads. Each thread sorts its sublist, then writes it to a separate temporary BAM file. After all input data has been processed in this manner, the master thread merges the sorted temporary BAM files to produce a single sorted output stream.

A shortcoming with the SAMtools 1.3 implementation is that if the BAM input fits within the user-specified memory limit, then the sort will be performed by only a single thread. To address this issue, the merge sort was implemented on the entire in-memory array of BAM records, which dramatically reduced the amount of time spent in the sort phase. However, it was recognized much of the sort phase could be overlapped with the read/decompression phase to make use of the spare computational capacity. This idea was implemented by creating a sort task after reading/decompressing every 2^{20} BAM records (an empirically-chosen value). For the benchmark data set, this approach resulted in more sublists to merge (in-memory), but the result was still faster than the previous approach.

An additional I/O optimization was implemented for the out-of-core sort. Instead of writing each in-memory sorted sublist to a separate file, the sorted sublists are merged while writing to a single file. This reduces both the number of temporary BAM files that must be written and subsequently merged, potentially improving performance on storage systems that benefit from fewer, larger I/O streams.

Compress/Write. SAMtools 1.3 supports multi-threaded compression of output BAM records. However, as with the experimental pthreads read/decompress code, a condition variable is used in a manner that limits concurrency. The master thread fills per-worker-thread input buffers with "work" (by default, 256 up-to-64KiB blocks of uncompressed BAM records) while all worker threads are blocked on a condition variable. Once the buffer for each worker has been filled, the master thread then issues a `pthread_cond_broadcast()` to unblock the worker threads. Each worker thread compresses a block of BAM records into a temporary buffer, then copies it back to the original buffer, overwriting the uncompressed block. After all worker threads are done, the master thread outputs all compressed BGZF blocks (during which time worker threads are idle), and repeats the process with the next subset of the sorted BAM data.

To increase concurrency (and thus CPU utilization) during this process, the limited-concurrency pthreads code was refactored to use OpenMP tasks, with each task both compressing a contiguous list of 256 up-to-64KiB blocks of BAM records, as well as writing the compressed BGZF blocks in input order (see Listing 1.1). To reduce latency, after compressing its blocks, the thread executing the task spins until its turn to write the output (effectively implementing a ticket lock [6]). Because OpenMP `atomic` directives are effectively used for synchronization, an OpenMP `flush` directive must be used before and after the routine that writes the compressed BGZF blocks to ensure memory consistency between threads of any referenced shared data structures. Alternatively, compilers supporting OpenMP 4.0 or newer could specify the `seq_cst` clause to the `atomic` directive, which makes the atomic construct sequentially consistent (implying the `flush`).

Listing 1.1. Conceptual routine invoked by the master thread to concurrently BGZF compress ≤ 64 KiB blocks of BAM records and serialize output in input order

```
void compress_and_output (BAM *master_thread) {
  char blocks [SIZEOF_BLOCK*NUM_BLOCKS_PER_TASK];
  static uint64_t now_serving_shared = 0;
  memcpy( blocks, master_thread->blocks, sizeof( blocks ));
  uint64_t my_ticket = master_thread->ticket++;
  #pragma omp task firstprivate(blocks, my_ticket)
  { uint64_t now_serving_private;
    compress(blocks); // concurrent with other tasks
    do { // wait until this task's turn to output
      #pragma omp atomic read
      now_serving_private = now_serving_shared;
    } while ( now_serving_private != my_ticket );
    #pragma omp flush
    output(blocks); // serialized
    #pragma omp flush
    #pragma omp atomic update
    now_serving_shared++; // let the next task output
} }
```

The task generation is continuous until input (uncompressed blocks) has been exhausted.

Memory Deallocation. Approximately 16% of the 32-thread in-memory SAMtools 1.3 sort runtime was spent deallocating over 100 GiB of dynamically-allocated memory comprising approximately 207 million BAM records. This required two calls to `free()` for each BAM record: one for the (fixed-size) `bam1_t` data structure, and one for the variable-length `data` member. As this was done at the end of execution, an initial workaround to avoid this excessive memory deallocation overhead was to not explicitly free the memory, instead allowing the operating system to reclaim allocated memory upon process termination. However, storing the BAM records in a single contiguous memory region (allocated with a single `malloc()`, and deallocated with a single `free()`) as described in the *Memory Allocation* subsection obviated the need for this workaround.

5   Benchmark Results

The benchmark hardware/software environment and data set are described in Sect. 3. Minor optimizations to avoid the overhead of dynamic memory allocation with multiple threads were implemented in several places using automatic variables on the stack. To accommodate the extra per-thread stack usage, the `OMP_STACKSIZE` environment variable was set to 64M. Approximately 112 GiB total, divided by the number of threads, was specified for the per-thread memory argument to the `samtools sort` command to allow the in-memory sort.

Both the original SAMtools 1.3 and SAMtools with the optimizations described in Sect. 4 were used to perform `samtools sort` on the benchmark data set with 1, 2, 4, 8, 16, 32, and 64 threads. The 64-thread run utilized both hardware threads in each core (HyperThreading).

Single-threaded performance was similar for both SAMtools 1.3 and the optimized SAMtools. Moving to two threads activated different code paths in each code base, and resulted in a performance regression in the optimized SAMtools. The reason for this regression may be due to a combination of overhead associated with creating OpenMP tasks, and lack of work stealing in the GNU OpenMP runtime, leading to load imbalance with one dedicated task "producer" and one dedicated "consumer". With ≥ 4 threads, the optimized SAMtools performed between 29% and 73% faster than the SAMtools 1.3. The performance of the optimized SAMtools was slightly slower with HyperThreading (64 threads, or 2 threads per core) than without (32 threads), whereas the performance of the original SAMtools was slightly better with HyperThreading than without.

For the in-memory sort, the optimized SAMtools saw a modest single-threaded performance boost (7%) over the SAMtools 1.3, likely due to the memory optimizations described in Sect. 4. As with the out-of-core sort, the performance of the optimized SAMtools with 2 threads was worse than SAMtools 1.3. With more than 2 threads, the optimized SAMtools demonstrated significant speedups: 1.58X at 4 threads, 2.41X at 8 threads, 3.6X at 16 threads,

3.92X at 32 threads, and 3.49X at 64 threads. Performance at 32 threads was not substantially better than performance at 16 threads, as the extra computational capacity was mostly idle (Fig. 5). Profiling with 32 threads (Fig. 5) revealed that code for performing the N-way merge of sorted sublists using a heap data structure became a bottleneck (~15% of total thread 0 run time). Thus, thread 0 could not generate sorted blocks for the merge/compress/write tasks fast enough to keep the remaining threads busy.

The profiled times for the in-memory sort (Figs. 4 and 5) exclude 30–35 s after the call to exit(). The timings in Fig. 6 time the SLURM srun command, and thus include this time not counted by HPCToolkit. Subsequent testing with a microbenchmark that allocated a large amount of memory indicated that the extra time was likely due to operating system overhead (e.g., freeing large page tables). Specifying huge pages (via the cray-hugepages2M environment module) at compile time reduced the time to process termination on the microbenchmark; however, a libhugetlbfs error occurred at run time when this was attempted with samtools on the HG00109 data set.

Interestingly, there wasn't a substantial performance difference between the in-memory and out-of-core sorts for SAMtools 1.3 with ≥8 threads, indicating that the added parallelism in the sort phase in the out-of-core version compensated for the extra I/O. As mentioned previously, this is due to the reduction in

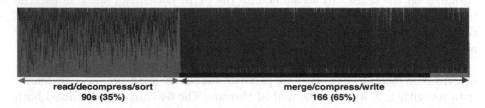

read/decompress/sort
90s (35%)   **merge/compress/write**
                             166 (65%)

Fig. 4. HPCToolkit performance summary of the optimized SAMtools for the in-memory sort (16 threads). The green area represents overall time among all threads spent "idle" (waiting in gomp_barrier_wait_end()). In the merge/compress/write phase, the magenta area indicates that most of the time is spent in the compression routine. (Color figure online)

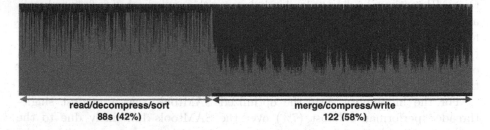

read/decompress/sort
88s (42%)   **merge/compress/write**
                             122 (58%)

Fig. 5. HPCToolkit performance summary of the optimized SAMtools for the in-memory sort with 32 threads. Unlike with 16 threads, there is noticeable thread idle time (green area) in the merge/compress/write phase. (Color figure online)

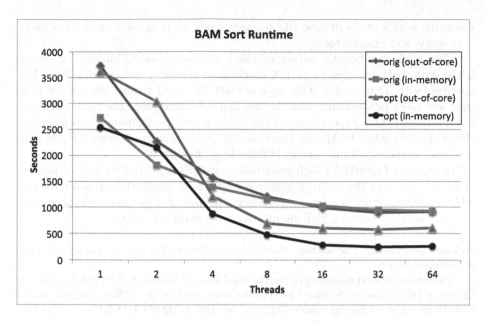

Fig. 6. Runtimes in seconds of SAMtools sort on HG00109 BAM for SAMtools 1.3 (labeled "orig") and the optimized SAMtools (labeled "opt"). The average of 3 timings for each thread count is reported.

time spent deallocating data structures and added parallelism in the sort phase, with the cost of extra I/O to temporary files offset by the large amount of I/O bandwidth afforded by the Lustre parallel file system.

6 Future Work

A dedicated read-ahead thread could improve concurrency and allow greater processor utilization while reading/decompressing sequentially-read BAM files. Similarly, a dedicated writer thread with a work queue could reduce busy-waiting and thus improve concurrency while compressing/writing BAM data.

The out-of-core sort implementation requires all sorted BAM sublists to be written to disk before the final merge. A more efficient approach would be to allow as much data as possible to remain in memory.

7 Conclusions

As an important component in many HTS pipelines, SAMtools processes large amounts of HTS data every day worldwide. Therefore, improvements to this fundamental tool have the potential to positively affect a vast audience. In particular, performance improvements collectively reduce time to solution for many scientific workflows in diverse life sciences fields such as agriculture, oncology, pathology, and pharmacology.

This work significantly enhanced the performance of SAMtools for sorting BAM data, both in-memory (3.92X speedup 32-threads) and out-of-core (1.55X speedup with 32 threads). This may obviate the need to use alternative tools that are more performant than the original SAMtools for this task. Although not analyzed in this paper, many of the implemented performance improvements should benefit other SAMtools functionality (including in-memory CRAM sorting) and applications that utilize HTSlib (e.g., bgzip).

Leveraging OpenMP's high-level task parallelism proved to have a number of advantages over the existing pthreads-based implementation. Besides offering additional opportunities for concurrency, the use of OpenMP enhanced code conciseness and clarity, which should facilitate maintainability.

Acknowledgment. The authors thank Marina Kraeva for her careful proofreading of the manuscript.

This research used resources of the National Energy Research Scientific Computing Center, a DOE Office of Science User Facility supported by the Office of Science of the U.S. Department of Energy under Contract No. DE-AC02-05CH11231.

References

1. Adhianto, L., Banerjee, S., Fagan, M., Krentel, M., Marin, G., Mellor-Crummey, J., Tallent, N.R.: HPCToolkit: tools for performance analysis of optimized parallel programs. Concurr. Comput.: Pract. Exp. **22**(6), 685–701 (2010). http://dx.doi.org/10.1002/cpe.1553
2. Bonfield, J.K.: The scramble conversion tool. Bioinformatics **30**(19), 2818–2819 (2014). http://bioinformatics.oxfordjournals.org/content/30/19/2818.abstract
3. 1000 Genomes Project Consortium, et al.: A global reference for human genetic variation. Nature **526**(7571), 68–74 (2015)
4. Herzeel, C., Costanza, P., Decap, D., Fostier, J., Reumers, J.: elPrep: high-performance preparation of sequence alignment/map files for variant calling. PLoS ONE **10**(7), 1–16 (2015). http://dx.doi.org/10.1371/journal.pone.0132868
5. Li, H., Handsaker, B., Wysoker, A., Fennell, T., Ruan, J., Homer, N., Marth, G., Abecasis, G., Durbin, R., Subgroup, G.: The sequence alignment/map format and SAMtools. Bioinformatics **25**(16), 2078–2079 (2009). http://bioinformatics.oxford journals.org/content/25/16/2078.abstract
6. Mellor-Crummey, J.M., Scott, M.L.: Algorithms for scalable synchronization on shared-memory multiprocessors. ACM Trans. Comput. Syst. **9**(1), 21–65 (1991). http://doi.acm.org/10.1145/103727.103729
7. Stephens, Z.D., Lee, S.Y., Faghri, F., Campbell, R.H., Zhai, C., Efron, M.J., Iyer, R., Schatz, M.C., Sinha, S., Robinson, G.E.: Big data: astronomical or genomical? PLoS Biol. **13**(7), 1–11 (2015). http://dx.doi.org/10.1371/journal.pbio.1002195
8. Tarasov, A., Vilella, A.J., Cuppen, E., Nijman, I.J., Prins, P.: Sambamba: fast processing of NGS alignment formats. Bioinformatics **31**(12), 2032–2034 (2015). http://bioinformatics.oxfordjournals.org/content/31/12/2032.abstract
9. Wetterstrand, K.: DNA Sequencing Costs: Data from the NHGRI Genome Sequencing Program (GSP). http://www.genome.gov/sequencingcostsdata

Ultra-Fast Detection of Higher-Order Epistatic Interactions on GPUs

Daniel Jünger[1], Christian Hundt[1], Jorge González-Domínguez[2(✉)], and Bertil Schmidt[1]

[1] Institut für Informatik, Johannes Gutenberg-Universität Mainz, Mainz, Germany
djuenger@students.uni-mainz.de, {hundt,bertil.schmidt}@uni-mainz.de
[2] Grupo de Arquitectura de Computadores, Universidade da Coruña, A Coruña, Spain
jgonzalezd@udc.es

Abstract. Detecting higher-order epistatic interactions in Genome-Wide Association Studies (GWAS) remains a challenging task in the fields of genetic epidemiology and computer science. A number of algorithms have recently been proposed for epistasis discovery. However, they suffer from a high computational cost since statistical measures have to be evaluated for each possible combination of markers. Hence, many algorithms use additional filtering stages discarding potentially non-interacting markers in order to reduce the overall number of combinations to be examined. Among others, Mutual Information Clustering (MIC) is a common pre-processing filter for grouping markers into partitions using K-Means clustering. Potentially interacting candidates for high-order epistasis are then examined exhaustively in a subsequent phase. However, analyzing real-world datasets of moderate size can still take several hours when performing analysis on a single CPU. In this work we propose a massively parallel computation scheme for the MIC algorithm targeting CUDA-enabled accelerators. Our implementation is able to perform epistasis discovery using more than 500,000 markers in just a couple of seconds in contrast to several hours when using the sequential MIC implementation. This runtime reduction by two orders-of-magnitude enables fast exploration of higher-order epistatic interactions even in large-scale GWAS datasets.

Keywords: Bioinformatics · GWAS · Epistasis · High performance computing · CUDA

1 Introduction

Discovering genotype-phenotype associations between genetic markers and certain diseases has become an increasing field of interest in recent years. Case-control studies, such as Genome Wide Association Studies (GWAS), search for genetic factors that influence common complex traits. Some of these studies have

© Springer International Publishing AG 2017
F. Desprez et al. (Eds.): Euro-Par 2016 Workshops, LNCS 10104, pp. 421–432, 2017.
DOI: 10.1007/978-3-319-58943-5_34

explored single-locus associations between specific markers and a certain disease [4,5]. However, most complex diseases are suspected to have more sophisticated association patterns [1]. One cause of complex association patterns arises from the existence of epistasis; i.e. interactions among k markers ($k \geq 2$). A variety of algorithms has been proposed using different approaches for finding such epistatic interactions in GWAS. Exhaustive search approaches [6,7,10,11] examine every possible k-combination of markers. Hence, these approaches promise high accuracy but often lack scalability, since the number of possible combinations grows exponentially with the order of interaction k. Stochastic random sampling methods [14] usually need to specify many parameters that heavily influence their execution time. Machine learning algorithms [9,12] are often faster than exhaustive approaches, but may only find local extrema instead of globally optimal solutions.

Approaches for finding higher-order epistasis in GWAS use filter cascades such as SNPHarvester [13] or MIC [8]. These approaches utilize filters to prune unpromising markers that are unlikely to exhibit high interactions. Subsequently, the markers that have survived the filtration stage are examined exhaustively for k-locus interactions. The MIC algorithm uses K-Means clustering in combination with mutual information as distance measure for the filtering to determine sets of markers that are potentially interacting. Afterwards, the obtained candidates are examined exhaustively. Using a CPU-only implementation of MIC, it is possible to search for six-SNPs epistasis in the well-known Wellcome Trust Case-Control Consortium (WTCCC) dataset with over 500,000 markers in a couple of hours.

The main contributions of this paper are the design of fine-grained parallelization schemes for the sequential MIC algorithm targeting massively parallel architectures and their implementation on CUDA-enabled accelerators providing speedups of around two orders-of-magnitude in comparison to single-threaded CPU code. Consequently, we are able to reduce the runtime of MIC drastically from hours to seconds enabling researchers to perform exploratory analysis in an interactive manner.

The rest of the paper is organized as follows. Section 2 gives a brief overview of the sequential MIC algorithm. Section 3 describes our parallelization scheme. Performance is evaluated in Sect. 4. Section 5 concludes the paper.

2   Background

Mutual Information Clustering (MIC) performs fast candidate selection for higher-order epistatic interactions in GWAS. It consists of two stages for detecting k-locus interactions. The first stage filters single-nucleotide polymorphisms (SNPs) that are unlikely to interact using a variant of K-Means clustering that determines a notion of similarity by the pairwise computation of mutual information between the individual markers. After the clustering step a user-defined number of m SNP candidates are selected from each cluster. These candidates are examined to find the causative SNPs of k-locus interactions.

Based on [8], mutual information I is used as similarity measure of association between genotypes and susceptibilities of diseases. Let $X = \{A_1, A_2, \ldots, A_n\}$ be a partition of a set S, meaning that $S = A_1 \cup A_2 \cup \ldots \cup A_n$ and $A_i \cap A_j = \emptyset$ for all distinct pairs of i and j. The entropy $H(X)$ can be expressed as

$$H(X) = -\sum_{i=1}^{n} \frac{|A_i|}{|S|} \cdot \log \frac{|A_i|}{|S|} \tag{1}$$

where $|\cdot|$ denotes the number of elements in a set. Note that $\frac{|A_i|}{|S|}$ can be interpreted as the probability mass function of the partition X. An extension of this definition to an arbitrary number of partitions is straightforward. Let $X_j = \{A_1^{(j)}, A_2^{(j)}, \ldots, A_n^{(j)}\}$ for $j = 1, \ldots, k$ be k partitions of a set S. Then the joint entropy of k partitions $H(X_1, X_2, \ldots, X_k)$ is defined as

$$H(X_1, X_2, \ldots, X_k) = -\sum_{i_1=1}^{n_1} \sum_{i_2=1}^{n_2} \cdots \sum_{i_k=1}^{n_k} P_{i_1 i_2 \cdots i_k} \cdot \log P_{i_1 i_2 \cdots i_k}$$

$$\text{where} \quad P_{i_1 i_2 \cdots i_k} = \frac{|A_{i_1}^{(1)} \cap A_{i_2}^{(2)} \cap \ldots \cap A_{i_k}^{(k)}|}{|S|}. \tag{2}$$

The mutual information between the joined partition of $X_1, X_2, \ldots, X_k$ and a partition Y can be expressed as:

$$I(X_1, X_2, \ldots, X_k; Y) = H(Y) + H(X_1, X_2, \ldots, X_k)$$
$$- H(X_1, X_2, \ldots, X_k, Y) \tag{3}$$

Let $X_1, X_2, \ldots, X_k$ be partitions for the set of samples induced by the genotypes of $\text{SNP}_1, \text{SNP}_2, \ldots, \text{SNP}_k$, respectively, and Y be the partition by disease state (case or control) then $I(X_1, X_2, \ldots, X_k; Y)$ represents the degree of associations between genotypes of $\text{SNP}_1, \text{SNP}_2, \ldots, \text{SNP}_k$ and the disease state. The objective is to find the set of k SNPs that maximizes the value of $I(X_1, X_2, \ldots, X_k; Y)$. Examining every possible k-combination of n SNPs is considered computational intractable for more than half a million SNPs in GWAS for $k \geq 3$ [6,7]. In order to reduce the number of SNPs to be considered in the exhaustive step, MIC uses K-Means which scales linearly in the number of processed markers. The clustering procedure is a modification of Lloyd's algorithm:

1. *Assignment step.* The pair-wise distance $\text{dist}(X_i, X_j)$ between two SNPs X_i and X_j is defined as the mutual information $I(X_i, X_j; Y)$. This implies that SNPs that are strongly interacting tend to be placed into different clusters.
2. *Update step.* The process of selecting the centroid of each cluster works as follows. Each SNP generates a contingency table consisting of genotype frequencies among samples. The average contingency table $T_{\text{avg}}^{(j)}$ of a cluster j is defined as follows: each entry of $T_{\text{avg}}^{(j)}$ is the average of the corresponding entries of all contingency tables generated by the SNPs belonging to the cluster j. A centroid c_j of a cluster j is defined as the nearest neighbour of $T_{\text{avg}}^{(j)}$ with respect to the sum of squared errors

$$c_j = \underset{q}{\text{argmin}} \|T_q - T_{\text{avg}}^{(j)}\|^2. \tag{4}$$

After the clustering step, m candidates are selected from each cluster. A candidate in a cluster is a SNP that is far apart (in terms of pairwise mutual information) from SNPs in other clusters. MIC makes use of this similarity measure to define a score value for SNPs. Let $x^{(i)}$ be a SNP in the i-th cluster with c_i as the corresponding centroid then the score value is determined by:

$$\begin{aligned}
\text{score}(x^{(i)}) &= \sum_{j \neq i} \text{dist}(x^{(i)}, c_j) \\
&= I(x^{(i)}, c_1 \; ; Y) + \ldots + I(x^{(i)}, c_{i-1}; Y) \\
&\quad + I(x^{(i)}, c_{i+1}; Y) + \ldots + I(x^{(i)}, c_k; Y).
\end{aligned} \tag{5}$$

From each cluster MIC selects the top m SNPs in terms of their scores as candidates for further processing. Thus, a total of $k \cdot m$ candidates are chosen. Among these candidates, MIC exhaustively searches the k-tuple with the highest mutual information value $I(X_1, X_2, \ldots, X_k; Y)$. This implies that it only has to probe $\binom{m \cdot k}{k}$ combinations instead of $\binom{n}{k}$, where $m \cdot k \ll n$.

3 CUDA Implementation

In this section, we discuss the details of our parallel implementation of the MIC algorithm using CUDA. Besides native CUDA, we also utilize the CUDA Unbound (CUB) library [3] which provides a set of highly optimized parallel primitives. We subdivide the MIC algorithm into the following four distinct phases.

3.1 Data Preparation

Our implementation stores the genotype information in form of a C++ standard library vector containing SNP elements. A SNP is represented by a struct containing the genotype information for both cases and controls. SNPs are expressed in three different genotypes for both cases and controls. Hence, the SNP-struct has six sub-elements. Each of these sub-elements is a bit-array where the bit at index i encodes whether the ith individual (case or control) has the particular genotype. For simple enumeration we will label genotype AA as 0, AB as 1, and BB as 2. Hence, we can refer to the genotype arrays of the SNP-struct as case0, case1, case2, ctrl0, ctrl1, and ctrl2. For later use in the clustering step we pre-compute the genotype frequencies of each SNP for cases and controls respectively, by determining the population count of each bit array. This step takes linear time. We refer to the structure of combinations of the six genotype frequencies as the *contingency table*.

In order to use the genotype information on the GPU in an efficient manner, we use six global bit-arrays on the CUDA device, each of which combines one genotype case/control bit array from all SNPs one after another. Subsequently, we transpose each bit-array, assuring coalesced access between CUDA threads in a warp if threads are assigned to SNPs within the SNP set consecutively. Transposition is achieved using one CUDA-stream per array using a shared memory-based out-of-place transposition algorithm. We compute the genotype frequency of each SNP using the vectorization capabilities of the GPU along with coalesced data access patterns.

3.2   Clustering

The modified K-Means algorithm can be split into three subroutines that are parallelized separately using dedicated CUDA kernels.

First, the cluster assignment step compares each SNP with the set of centroids c_j and subsequently assigns the nearest neighbour. Since this can be determined for each of the SNPs independently, we map individual SNPs to CUDA-threads exploiting the optimized data alignment discussed in the previous subsection. As a result, the cluster indices of each SNP are stored in an array residing in the global memory of the GPU.

Second, the mean contingency table of each cluster is computed by pointwise addition of all contingency tables of SNPs that are assigned to that cluster and subsequent division by the number of SNPs in the cluster. The applied reduction algorithm utilizes different memory spaces of the GPU. On the lowest level each warp (consisting of 32 threads) computes its partial result using warp intrinsics and stores the result in the shared memory of its block. Subsequently, each block uses a tree-based reduction to accumulate partial sums and stores the final result in global memory using atomic operations. We then divide the per-cluster accumulated contingency table by the number of SNPs in each cluster in parallel using the device-wide `cub::DeviceHistogram` primitive from the CUB library on the cluster array in order to determine the cluster sizes.

The third subroutine determines the updated centroids for the next iteration of Lloyd's algorithm by computing the nearest neighbour SNP of each centroid in terms of sum of squared errors to the mean contingency table of the corresponding cluster. In order to update the centroids in parallel, we first compute the distance of each SNP to its corresponding cluster mean using one thread per SNP. Subsequently, the obtained distance values are stored as 32-bit unsigned integer into the lower half of a 64-bit unsigned integer and consecutively write the 8-bit cluster identifier of a SNP into the upper half. This step is visualized in Fig. 1(a). We can now define a lexicographical ordering over these elements with the cluster identifier as major order and the distance value as minor order. Using this relation, we sort this array using a device-wide call to `cub::DeviceRadixSort`. A schematic overview of this step is illustrated in Fig. 1(b). Note that CUB provides the ability to run radix-sort only on a sub-set of bits of an integer. Hence, we just consider the first 40 bits of an element for the sorting step. The SNP of cluster c_j with minimal distance to the mean contingency table is placed at index $\sum_{i=1}^{j-1} |c_i|$. We then use a `cub::DeviceExclusiveSum` primitive on the clustering histogram to determine the starting indices of each cluster. Finally, we select the first SNP of each cluster from the sorted array as the new centroid.

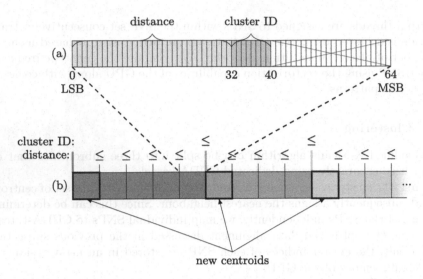

Fig. 1. Selection of centroids using lexicographical ordering. (a) Shows a 64-bit unsigned integer which represents a SNP. The distance from the SNP to its centroid is stored as a 32-bit unsigned integer in the lower half of the 64-bit datatype. The 8-bit long identifiers of the corresponding cluster are stored consecutively. Overall the struct holds 40 bits of information. (b) Shows the result of `cub::DeviceRadixSort` on an array of the datatype depicted in (a). The new centroid elements are the first elements of each cluster section (denoted by different color shading).

3.3 Candidate Selection

The score computation of each SNP can be performed independently by utilizing CUDA-threads. The candidates of each cluster are those m SNPs with the highest scores. For this purpose, we use a slight modification of the major-minor radix-sort approach as shown in Fig. 1. Different from our initial definition, we now pack the score value of type float into the lower half of a 64-bit unsigned integer together with the 8-bit cluster ID stored consecutively. Since we want to sort the elements of this array ascending by the cluster ID (major ordering) but descending by the score values (minor ordering), we negate the score values before sorting the array. The selection step is analogous to Fig. 1(b): the first m SNPs of each cluster are selected in the sorted array rather than just one. As a result of this phase we have selected $k \cdot m$ SNPs that are exhaustively examined in the final phase.

3.4 Exhaustive Search

Algorithm 1 represents the implementation of Eq. 3. As a subtask of this calculation, we probe each of the 3^k possible genotype combinations of the given SNP combination in order to determine the joint entropies $H(X_1, X_2, \ldots, X_k)$ and $H(X_1, X_2, \ldots, X_k, Y)$ as given in Eq. 2. For one of these genotype combinations

$i_{geno} \in \{0, \ldots, 3^k - 1\}$ the genotype $g_{i_k} \in \{0, 1, 2\}$ to choose for one SNP snp_{i_k} with $i_k \in \{0, \ldots, k - 1\}$ of this SNP combination can be calculated by:

$$g_{i_k} = \lfloor \frac{i_{geno}}{3^{i_k}} \rfloor \mod 3 \tag{6}$$

Using this extension we can now implement the k-locus mutual information for one SNP combination as follows:

Algorithm 1. Mutual Information of k loci

1: **procedure** KMI
2:     pCase← 0.0
3:     pCtrl← 0.0
4:     $H_{xy} \leftarrow 0.0$
5:     $H_x \leftarrow 0.0$
6:     $H_y \leftarrow H(Y)$ ▷ computation according to Eq. 1
7:
8:     **for** $i_{geno} \in [0, 3^k)$ **do**   ▷ 3^k combinations of genotypes
9:         f_case←POPC(snp_0.cases$[g_0] \cap snp_1$.cases$[g_1] \cap \ldots \cap snp_{k-1}$.cases$[g_{k-1}]$)
10:        f_ctrl←POPC(snp_0.ctrls$[g_0] \cap snp_1$.ctrls$[g_1] \cap \ldots \cap snp_{k-1}$.ctrls$[g_{k-1}]$)
11:
12:        pCase← $f\_case/(|cases| + |ctrls|)$
13:        pCtrl← $f\_ctrl/(|cases| + |ctrls|)$
14:
15:        $H_x - = (pCase + pCtrl) \cdot \log(pCase + pCtrl)$ ▷ computation according to
   Eq. 2
16:        $H_{xy} - = pCase \cdot \log pCase + pCtrl \cdot \log pCtrl$
17:     **end for**
18:     **return** $H_y + H_x - H_{xy}$ ▷ computation according to Eq. 3
19: **end procedure**

Note that the computation of the joint frequencies is performed efficiently by using bitwise AND-operations followed by a CUDA-intrinsic population count on the SNP bit-sets (see Lines 9 and 10 in Algorithm 1). The parallelization-scheme for this task assigns each SNP combination to one CUDA-thread.

The task of computing the k-locus mutual information for each k-combination is computationally demanding. We reduce the computational load per CUDA core by pre-computing the SNP combinations of the given candidates as follows.

First, we need to find a mapping that associates each combination index $i_{comb} \in \{1, \ldots, \binom{k \cdot m}{k}\}$ with a distinct k-combination from the set of $k \cdot m$ candidates. This can be implemented by decomposing binomial coefficients using their recursive definition:

$$(I) : \quad \binom{n}{n} = \binom{n}{0};$$

$$(II) : \quad \binom{n+1}{k+1} = \binom{n}{k} + \binom{n}{k+1}; \tag{7}$$

If we substitute n by $(km - 1)$ and k $b < (k - 1)$ we can rewrite (II) as

$$\binom{k \cdot m}{k} = \binom{km - 1}{k - 1} + \binom{km - 1}{k}$$

(8)

Using this representation we can apply a recursive binary tree decomposition. Each level of the tree represents one element of the set of km elements. Additionally, each distinct path through the tree represents a distinct SNP combination. Algorithm 2 computes one path given the index i_{comb} of the combination to be formed and returns the corresponding k-combination. We will execute this algorithm on $\binom{k \cdot m}{k}$ CUDA-threads, each one processing a single combination.

Algorithm 2. Computation of k-combination

```
1: procedure GETSNPCOMBINATION(i_comb)
2:     combination[]
3:     index← i_comb
4:     local_n← k · m
5:     local_k← k
6:     j ← 0
7:
8:     for i ∈ [0, km) do
9:         lower← (local_n−1 / local_k)
10:
11:        if index ≥ lower then
12:            local_k -= 1
13:            combination[j]← i
14:            j++
15:            index -= lower
16:        end if
17:        local_n -= 1
18:    end for
19:    return combination[]
20: end procedure
```

Algorithm 2 calls the binomial coefficient function $k \cdot m$ times per thread in Line 9. To further reduce the workload of each CUDA-core, we pre-compute the values of the binomial coefficients and cache them in a look-up table residing in global memory. Finally, we determine the highest epistatic interaction candidate using a device-wide key-value sort primitive form the CUB library.

4   Experimental Evaluation

In order to measure the time benefits of our CUDA-parallelized version of MIC compared to the single- and multi-core CPU version, we use a real-world dataset from WTCCC. The dataset consists of the genotype information of roughly

500,000 SNPs that were gathered from 3,000 controls drawn from the British population and 2,000 cases which are all affected by *inflammatory bowel disease*. The system configuration used for benchmarking is listed in Table 1.

Table 1. Benchmark system.

Host system	CPU	Intel Core i7-3970X, 64-bit, HT
	CPU cores	6 cores @ 3.50 GHz (max. 4.0 GHz)
	RAM	32 GB DDR3
	OS	Ubuntu 14.04.4 LTS, 64-bit
CUDA device	Device	NVIDIA GeForce GTX Titan X
	GPU	NVIDIA GM 200
	GPU cores	3072 SPs @ 1GHz
	DRAM	12 GB GDDR5
	CC	5.2
Compilers	Host	g++ v4.8.4
	Device	nvcc v7.5.17
Compiler flags	g++	-O3 -std=c++11 -fopenmp
	nvcc	-O3 –expt-relaxed-constexpr -use_fast_math
		-std=c++11 -rdc true
		-gencode=arch=compute_52,code=sm_52

In this work we focus on testing the performance improvement of our GPU-based parallel implementation as the accuracy is the same as the original MIC which has already been assessed in [8]. The MIC algorithm can be divided into two major phases. The first phase represents the K-Means clustering step. This step takes $\mathcal{O}(lkn)$ time, where l denotes the number of samples (cases/controls), k the number of clusters, and n the number of SNPs to be examined. The second phase performs exhaustive search and examines $\binom{k \cdot m}{k}$ k-combinations of SNPs for epistasis. The computation of the mutual information of each k-SNP combination and disease state takes linear time i.e. $\mathcal{O}(l)$. Thus, this phase takes $\mathcal{O}(l(km)^k)$ time. Since k occurs in the asymptotical runtime of both phases, we choose k as the varying parameter for our benchmark. The value of n is given by the WTCCC dataset and therefore fixed. We also set $m = 5$ throughout the experiments.

Table 2 shows the benchmark results for varying values of k (from one to six). As the original MIC implementation [8] is not publicly available, we developed a CPU-based C implementation and parallelized it using Open Multi-Processing (OpenMP or OMP)[2] for comparison purposes. We use the average of 50 executions for the GPU implementation and 30 executions for the CPU implementations. However, sequential execution for the highest k takes more than two hours and is not very stable at runtime. Hence, we were only able to measure two executions for this configuration with the sequential implementation.

Table 2. Average runtimes in seconds and speedups of the CUDA implementation on a GTX Titan X GPU over a single- and multi-core CPU-based version for $m = 5$.

	k	2	3	4	5	6
Runtime	t_{seq}	11.39	26.97	183.75	386.58	7865.17
	t_{omp}	4.25	5.11	6.67	49.44	1926.42
	t_{cuda}	0.69	0.74	0.83	1.36	16.41
Speedup	t_{seq}/t_{omp}	2.68	5.28	27.55	7.82	4.08
	t_{seq}/t_{cuda}	37.85	36.41	221.66	285.00	479.30
	t_{omp}/t_{cuda}	6.16	6.91	8.04	36.35	117.39

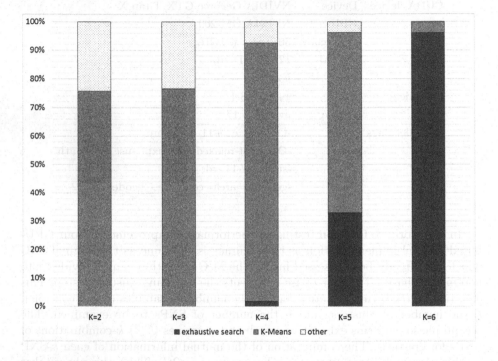

Fig. 2. Execution time proportions of K-Means and exhaustive step.

The benchmark results show that the speedups grow when k is increased. This is due to the fact that the number of combinations in the exhaustive search step grows exponential, as the asymptotic runtime is given by $\mathcal{O}(l(km)^k)$. Figure 2 illustrates the proportions between the K-Means step and the exhaustive step to the execution time when k is increased. We observe that K-Means holds the largest share for $k \leq 5$, whereas the exhaustive step, by far, holds the biggest share for $k > 5$. Our CUDA-based approach obtains more benefit for experiments where the exhaustive search has a significant impact on the total runtime.

5   Conclusion

We have developed an efficient parallel implementation of the MIC algorithm for finding higher-order epistasis in GWAS using CUDA-enabled accelerator cards. Concretely, we have proposed a parallel GPU-only implementation of a modified K-Means clustering algorithm. In addition to the clustering step, we also make extensive use of the GPU for the remaining parts, leaving the host CPU only for organizational purposes during execution.

Using our implementation it is possible to examine moderately-sized GWAS datasets in just a few seconds on a modern consumer-grade workstation. Our benchmark results indicate speedups of about two orders-of-magnitude compared to the sequential solution. The benefits of our parallel implementation are more significant when increasing the order of the interactions, i.e. when the exhaustive phase has more impact on the total execution time.

As part of our future work, we are planning to further improve the CUDA-implementation of the exhaustive search step. For now, this computation is done by a so-called *heavy kernel*, where each thread has to compute a rather big portion of the overall task. The CUDA architecture, however, is designed and optimized for *lightweight threads*. Hence, we have to develop a parallelization-scheme that implements the concept of lightweight threads by further splitting each computation into independent subtasks. A further possible direction of future research is the design and comparison of novel lightweight candidate selection algorithms on CUDA-enabled accelerators in order to robustly prune non-interacting markers at even higher speed.

Acknowledgments. This study makes use of data generated by the Wellcome Trust Case-Control Consortium. A full list of the investigators who contributed to the generation of the data is available from www.wtccc.org.uk. Funding for the project was provided by the Wellcome Trust under award 076113 and 085475.

References

1. Cordell, H.J.: Detecting gene-gene interactions that underlie human diseases. Nat. Rev. Genet. **10**(6), 392–404 (2009)
2. Dagum, L., Menon, R.: OpenMP: an industry standard API for shared-memory programming. IEEE Comput. Sci. Eng. **5**(1), 46–55 (1998)
3. Duane Merrill, N.C.: Cub documentation (2016). https://nvlabs.github.io/cub/
4. Easton, D.F., Pooley, K.A., et al.: Genome-wide association study identifies novel breast cancer susceptibility loci. Nature **447**(7148), 1087–1093 (2007)
5. Frayling, T.M., Timpson, N.J., et al.: A common variant in the FTO gene is associated with body mass index and predisposes to childhood and adult obesity. Science **316**(5826), 889–894 (2007)
6. González-Domínguez, J., Schmidt, B.: GPU-accelerated exhaustive search for third-order epistatic interactions in case-control studies. J. Comput. Sci. **8**, 93–100 (2015)
7. Kässens, J.C., Wienbrandt, L., González-Domínguez, J., Schmidt, B., Schimmler, M.: High-speed exhaustive 3-locus interaction epistasis analysis on FPGAs. J. Comput. Sci. **9**, 131–136 (2015)

8. Leem, S., Jeong, H.H., et al.: Fast detection of high-order epistatic interactions in genome-wide association studies using information theoretic measure. Comput. Biol. Chem. **50**, 19–28 (2014)
9. Meng, Y.A., Yu, Y., et al.: Performance of random forest when SNPS are in linkage disequilibrium. BMC Bioinf. **10**(1), 1 (2009)
10. Nelson, M., Kardia, S., et al.: A combinatorial partitioning method to identify multilocus genotypic partitions that predict quantitative trait variation. Genome Res. **11**(3), 458–470 (2001)
11. Wan, X., Yang, C., et al.: Boost: a fast approach to detecting gene-gene interactions in genome-wide case-control studies. Am. J. Hum. Genet. **87**(3), 325–340 (2010)
12. Wan, X., Yang, C., et al.: Predictive rule inference for epistatic interaction detection in genome-wide association studies. Bioinformatics **26**(1), 30–37 (2010)
13. Yang, C., He, Z., et al.: SNPHarvester: a filtering-based approach for detecting epistatic interactions in genome-wide association studies. Bioinformatics **25**(4), 504–511 (2009)
14. Zhang, Y., Liu, J.S.: Bayesian inference of epistatic interactions in case-control studies. Nature Genet. **39**(9), 1167–1173 (2007)

A Framework for Accessible Cluster-Enabled Epistatic Analysis

Alex Upton[1(✉)], Johan Karlsson[2], Oswaldo Trelles[1],
Miguel Hernandez[2], and Juan Elvira[2]

[1] Department of Computer Architecture, University of Malaga, Málaga, Spain
{aupton, ortrelles}@uma.es
[2] Perkin Elmer, 18100 Armilla, Granada, Spain
{johan.karlsson, miguel.hernandez,
juan.elvira}@perkinelmer.com

Abstract. Complex diseases are typically caused by joint effects of multiple genetic variations, rather than a single variant. Multiple single nucleotide polymorphism (SNP) interactions, epistatic interactions, potentially provide information about the causes of complex diseases, building on studies that focus on the association between single SNPs and phenotypes. However, execution of epistatic methods on desktop computers is not practical, owing to the huge number of interactions that have to be calculated. These models have tended to be command line based, presenting a barrier for users such as biologists that are not comfortable with this environment. To overcome this, we present a framework with a front-end GUI deployed on a cluster that allows users to analyse genotype/phenotype correlations using computationally accelerated epistatic models. The parallel processing of the data results in a typical epistatic analysis taking a few days, presenting a feasible approach for the analysis of genetic variants associated with disease.

1 Introduction

Technological advancements in the last decade have led to a remarkable increase in the amount of biological data produced. These data can be used to investigate human disease, with one particular data type, single nucleotide polymorphisms (SNPs), widely used to uncover genetic variations that are associated with phenotypes of interest. By comparing the frequency of variants between cases and controls in genome wide association studies (GWASs), SNPs have been linked to a number of diseases, such as breast cancer [1] and hypertension [2]. However, it is widely agreed that complex diseases are due to the joint effects of multiple genetic variations, rather than a single variation [3], and this might explain why numerous studies have only uncovered alleles with a low genotype risk. As such, epistatic interactions, interactions between SNPs, can potentially provide insight about the causes of complex diseases, and build on GWASs that investigate the association between single SNPs and phenotypes.

A number of models have been proposed to search for epistasis e.g. [4, 5]. However, implementation of these methods on typical desktop computers is generally not practical, as a large number of interactions have to be calculated. For example, a

© Springer International Publishing AG 2017
F. Desprez et al. (Eds.): Euro-Par 2016 Workshops, LNCS 10104, pp. 433–444, 2017.
DOI: 10.1007/978-3-319-58943-5_35

relatively small GWAS dataset with 100,000 SNPs has 5×10^9 pairwise interactions. Using the FaST-LMM method [5], the search for these pairwise interactions would take approximately two years on a desktop computer. This does not present a viable approach for researchers. In order to overcome this, high performance computing (HPC) and cloud computing facilities can be taken advantage of, and the analysis can be deployed across multiple cores or instances. By splitting the analysis into various tasks, these can be executed in parallel, resulting in a significant speedup in the execution time. As a result, the exhaustive search for epistasis can be carried out in a relative short time span, presenting a feasible analysis tool.

It should also be noted that the majority of these epistatic models are deployed using command line interfaces. One of the main challenges facing bioinformatics is to ensure that experts from across all biomedical domains are able to process biological data via user-friendly solutions [6]. In response to this, there has been an increase in recent years in the popularity of workflow management systems (WMSs) that allow the deployment of workflows that piece together separate analyses often carried out by different software packages. Workflows are becoming increasingly important in the area of bioinformatics, allowing complex analyses to be carried out and shared. A number of WMSs have gained prominence, with Chipster [7], and Galaxy [8] amongst those widely used. By offering increased usability and accessibility typically via a GUI, they allow users that do not possess specialist programming skills to run tools and workflows that would otherwise require command line operation or competence in programming language skills. Additionally, as users are able to publish and share their analyses via the internet, WMSs offer robustness, transparency, re-usability, and reproducibility [9, 10].

In this work, we present a prototype implementation of a Galaxy-based framework that uses a HPC cluster in order to reduce the time needed to analyse the data, and Spotfire for creating Galaxy-embedded visualisations that allow the user to interactively explore the results. Galaxy has been chosen due to its wide user base and active developer community; thereby allowing tools and workflows to be easily shared with other researchers via tool sheds. These tools sheds are open resources that function in a similar way to "app stores", and allow resources such as Galaxy tools and workflows to be shared amongst researchers. The main Galaxy tool shed is found at: https://toolshed. g2.bx.psu.edu/. In addition, the creation of a custom instance avoids issues such as long wait times for job execution, storage quotas, and bottlenecks uploading and downloading data associated with the main server. The custom instance offers a standardised, easy-to-use interface, allowing users such as clinicians and biologists that are not comfortable with command line and programming language environments to easily deploy epistatic analysis tools. In addition, these tools in the framework have already been configured to run on the HPC cluster, thereby enabling the analysis to be carried out with the required computational power. Furthermore, a number of pre-defined execution options are provided, removing the need for the end user to configure resource allocation scripts, and the authentication step is also simplified through the use of certificates. More details about the underlying infrastructure can be seen in Figs. 2 and 3 in the Infrastructure section, whilst further details about the framework are provided in the following section.

Finally, it should be noted that the HPC facilities at the University of Malaga have been used to validate the cluster-based deployment of the framework, and that the framework can be easily adapted to other computational resources. In the same vein, the use of the epistasis tools also provides a means by which to validate the 'generic' framework of Galaxy with Amazon S3 for data storage, and Spotfire for visualisation and exploration.

2 Galaxy Implementation

Two widely used epistatic analysis tools are implemented in the custom Galaxy instance; the linear regression based method BOOST [4], and the linear mixed model based FaST-LMM [5]. These two models have been chosen as they both test all pairs of SNPs in the dataset for association with phenotypes, typically case and control, returning a *p-value* for each tested pair. Therefore, they both require substantial computational power. In addition, they are both deployed via the command line, and have also been used in a number of previous studies, such as those by Lippert et al. [11] and Tao et al. [12]. An all-in-one easy-to-use workflow is also available for end users seeking a complete analysis protocol. This workflow is shown in Fig. 1, starting with data in the raw .CEL format. Subsect. 2.1 details the steps that make up this workflow, as well as detailing the software that would typically be used for each step, thereby highlighting the advantages of an all-in-one approach, rather than multiple software steps required.

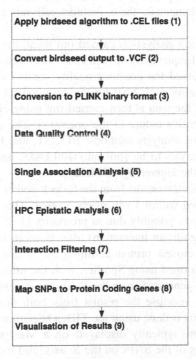

Fig. 1. Steps in the workflow

2.1 Workflow Steps

The workflow above also incorporates single association analysis. This has been incorporated as it is probable that the end user will be interested in comparing the single association results with the epistatic results, and also in case the user has the data in raw format. The main advantage of carrying out the workflows using Galaxy is that the end-user can perform all these steps in just one click, instead of having to use different programming languages and command line tools. The individual steps involved are detailed below.

(1) The first step is for the end user to upload raw .CEL files, and apply the birdseed v2 algorithm, using Affymetrix Power Tools. The first two steps that take the .CEL files and convert them to .VCF format is a Galaxy implementation of genCloud [13], a pipeline for converting .CEL to .VCF files suitable for analysis. This has been provided as it is likely that a number of researchers will have raw data, but will not be comfortable with the computational steps required to convert this to a suitable analysis format. By taking advantage of the facilities offered by the cluster, this step can be greatly speeded up by processing each of the .CEL files in parallel, rather than serially.

(2) The next step is to convert the birdseed output to .VCF format. Along with the previous step, this step is also part of the genCloud pipeline [13].

(3) It is also possible that the end user might already have the data as .VCF files. The next step is to convert this to PLINK [14] binary format, using PLINK.

(4) Next, a number of quality control procedures are carried out on the data. Various procedures are implemented; these include call rate >98%, and minor allele frequency >0.05.

(5) Single SNP association analysis is carried out using the default PLINK settings, that compares allele frequencies between cases and controls. The output is a list of all the SNPs that passed the previous quality control steps with various fields, including the *p-value* for each SNP for the case-control test.

(6) Epistatic analysis of the data is then carried out using HPC facilities, due to the computationally intensive nature of the operation. The end-user can select from two available epistatic analysis methods; BOOST, and FaST-LMM. The default setting is for the analysis to be split into 400 tasks, and deployed on the HPC Picasso facilities at the University of Malaga.

(7) The next step is to join the results from the tasks together, and remove interactions between SNPs located within 1 Mb of each other. This step is taken to remove potential false positives possibly due to proximity [15].

(8) SNPs involved in significant interactions after Bonferroni correction and filtering are mapped to the closest protein-coding gene within a flanking distance of 500 Kb. This is performed using Spotfire, with the information about the closest protein coding gene generated from the R library Postgwas [16].

(9) The final step is to visualise the results from both the single association, and epistatic analysis. This is done using the TIBCO Spotfire Web Player [17]. Single association results are typically displayed on a Manhattan plot; this plots the genomic co-ordinates of the SNPs on the X axis, and the negative $\log_{10}$ value of

the single association *p-values* for each SNP on the Y axis. Figure 5 shows a Manhattan plot obtained from a previously published dataset. This interactive Manhattan plot allows the end user to specify a threshold based on $-\log_{10} p\text{-}value$, and in addition to displaying the SNPs that have a *p-value* greater than this threshold, will also display additional information such as the closest protein coding gene to the SNP. The interactions of the protein-coding genes that the SNPs map to is visualised using the D^3 JavaScript library [18], and displayed in a Galaxy frame with the Manhattan plot underneath. This enables the user to easily compare the single association and epistatic analysis results visually.

3   Infrastructure

In order to carry out steps 1–7 shown in Fig. 1, a number of underlying infrastructure processes have to be carried out. These are shown in the diagram below.

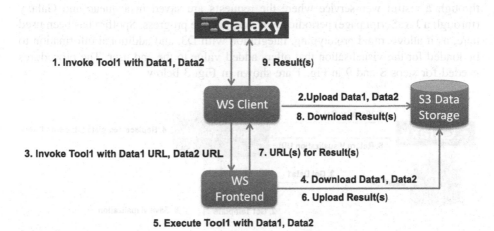

Fig. 2. Underlying infrastructure for single association and epistatic analysis

(1) Galaxy executes a Web-Service client with the tool to execute (must be in pre-configured white-list) and the parameters (files).
(2) The client uploads the parameters to an Amazon S3 compatible storage. This could be Amazon S3 instance or any of the many S3 API compatible data storages (e.g. OpenStack). Client requests a temporary URL which is valid for a specified time-frame.
(3) The client invokes the Web-Service Frontend (pre-configured) with the tool to invoke and a list of URLs where the data is available. Before accepting the job, the WS Frontend confirms that the tool is in the white-list of available tools and that the parameters are valid. If so, the Frontend places the job in a queue and returns a job identifier which the client will use to check for status and retrieve the results (status polling not shown in this figure).

(4) The Frontend downloads the parameters specified from the S3 data storage.
(5) When the job is in the front of the queue, the Frontend executes the tool. Note that the execution could be local or remote (e.g. in a HPC machine).
(6) Once ready, Frontend uploads results to an S3 Data Storage. Depending on the configuration, could be a different storage than used by the client. Once uploaded, the Frontend requests temporary URL and sets job-status to ready.
(7) Once the client has determined that the job has finished, it requests the Result(s) URL(s) generated in step 6.
(8) Client downloads data from the S3 Data Storage using temporary URL(s).
(9) The client finishes the execution and reports the results to Galaxy.

Galaxy can be extended with visualisations for specific datatypes. In this case, we configured Galaxy to visualise the single association and epistatic analysis results using the Spotfire WS API. The Spotfire WS API is a flexible component, developed as part of the Mr. SymBioMath project, which extends the Spotfire visualisation platform with automatisation features; specifically it allows the remote, programmatic control of Spotfire using IronPythonscripts. The communication between Galaxy and Spotfire is through a restful web-service where the requests are saved in a queue and Galaxy (through a JavaScript page) periodically checks for the progress. Spotfire has been used here, as it allows rapid prototyping, integration with D3, and additional information to be loaded for the visualisation that offers added value to the end user. The procedures needed for steps 8 and 9 in Fig. 1 are shown in Fig. 3 below.

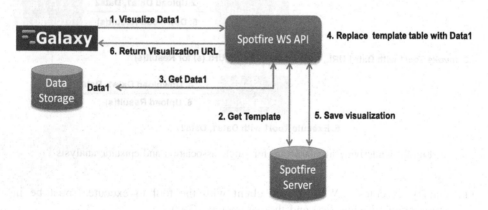

Fig. 3. Infrastructure for visualisations created by Spotfire

(1) Galaxy requests the visualisation from the Spotfire WS API, with the URL of the single associations from PLINK and the multiple SNP associations, i.e. epistatic analysis from FaST-LMM, together with the name of a pre-configured script which will generate the visualisation. This script performs steps 2–6 below.
(2) The script loads a prepared visualisation from the Spotfire Server.
(3) Data are then loaded from Galaxy using specified URL into the visualisation.

(4) Once the data are available, the script replaces the data table in the visualisation with the new data.
(5) The new visualisation is saved in the Spotfire Server.
(6) The Spotfire WS returns a URL to a Spotfire Web-Player document. This document can be loaded in standard Web-Browsers in most platforms (Windows, Linux, Mac OSX).

4 Validation

In order to test the implementation of the Galaxy tools, two testing stages are employed, each with a different dataset. First, in order to measure speedup of the epistatic analysis obtained by using the epistatic tools deployed on the cluster that are accessed via Galaxy, a simulated dataset of 10,000 SNPs much lower than typically found is used. This reduced dataset permits the epistatic analysis to be carried out in a reasonable time frame using a single core on the cluster, providing a benchmark figure against which to compare the execution times with multiple cores, and also simulating the performance of a single core desktop computer. This implementation is compared against 50, 100, 200, and 400 cores for both epistatic methods. Table 1 below shows FaST-LMM and BOOST execution times for this 10,000 SNP dataset for the different configurations on the HPC facilities, with speedup shown in brackets.

Table 1. Execution times for simulated data set

Computational environment	BOOST execution time (s)	FaST-LMM execution time (s)
HPC deployment (a)	38.4	15212
HPC deployment (b)	1.9 (20.2)	306 (49.7)
HPC deployment (c)	1.6 (24)	153 (98.8)
HPC deployment (d)	1.4 (27.4)	77 (197.6)
HPC deployment (e)	1.2 (32)	39 (390.1)

(a) Analysis carried out using 1 GB RAM and one core on the cluster Analysis split into (b) 50 tasks, (c) 100 tasks, (d) 200 tasks, (e) 400 tasks, with one core and 1 GB RAM assigned to each task

Note that a maximum speedup of 390 for FaST-LMM execution is obtained with 400 cores compared to the single core execution, with almost linear speedups for all of the different FaST-LMM configurations. This is not the case for BOOST, possibly due to the time taken for data transfer, and also the short execution time of the method using a single core. This is reflected in the noticeably different execution times of the epistatic methods, due to the different underlying models used by both; linear regression compared to a linear mixed model. Having obtained considerable speedups for the simulated dataset, particularly for FaST-LMM, the next step is to test the tools with a typical dataset. For this, we will repeat the analysis of a previously published epistatic study [19]. After carrying out quality control procedures, as detailed in step 4 in Subsect. 2.1, 764,537 SNPs remain. One of the advantages of using a dataset from a previously published study is that it is possible to compare the results obtained with those published. In this case, it is possible to validate the results obtained for the single association analysis from the original study [20]. As there are 764,537 SNPs, the association for 2.92×10^{11} SNP pairs will have to be calculated. The execution times for the epistatic analysis for this dataset are shown in Table 2 below. As oppose to the previous dataset, a comparison will only be made for single core execution against 400 cores due to the time this would take with all of the core configurations.

From Table 2 above, almost linear speedups are obtained for both methods. Note that epistatic analysis for this dataset using FaST-LMM is not carried out due to the estimated execution time, highlighting the need for HPC. Having verified that the implemented epistatic analysis tools are capable of analysing a previously published dataset in a reasonable timeframe, the final verification is to compare the visualisation against a previously published example. The Manhattan plot in the paper by Xie et al. [20], will be compared to the Manhattan plot produced by the workflow. Figure 4 shows the single association and epistatic analysis visualisations. Figure 5 shows the Manhattan plot above in more detail. Note the similarity of this plot with the Manhattan plot from the original Clarkson study; minor differences in the two plots are due to slightly different quality control procedures used in the workflow compared to the original study, resulting in 764,537 SNPs passing quality control compared to 875,967 for the original study.

Table 2. Execution time results for the previously published Clarkson dataset. As noted before, FaST-LMM epistatic analysis of this dataset using a single core is not feasible.

Computational environment	BOOST execution time (s)	FaST-LMM execution time (s)
HPC deployment (a)	158896	45401792*
HPC deployment (b)	405	113704
Speedup	392.3	399.3

(a) Analysis carried out using 1 GB RAM and one core on the cluster
(b) Analysis split into 400 tasks, with one core and 1 GB RAM assigned to each task
*estimated based on previous dataset, not carried out due to long execution time

As can be seen in Fig. 4, information on the closest protein coding gene for the SNP selected is presented to the end user underneath the plot within Galaxy. Information on the closest protein coding genes for all the SNPs above the threshold, in Fig. 5 those with $-\log_{10} p\text{-}value > 4.5$, is automatically loaded by Spotfire from the values returned by the Postgwas R library. This provides added value to the end user by providing additional information about the markers in the plot, thus aiding in downstream analysis such as gene set enrichment analysis as the end user does not have to manually annotate SNPs of interest. In addition, clicking the gene name takes the end user to the NCBI gene record, providing additional information of interest.

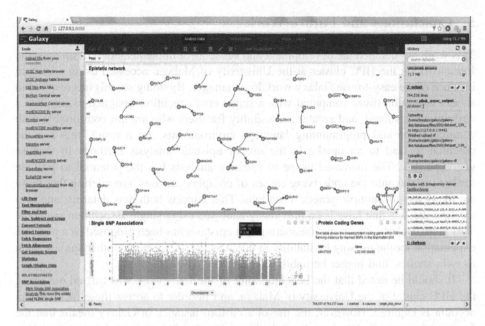

Fig. 4. Manhattan plot and network visualisations created by Spotfire Web Player

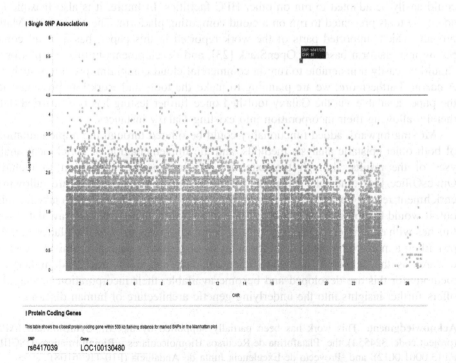

Fig. 5. TIBCO Spotfire Web Player Manhattan Plot

5   Conclusions and Future Work

This work has detailed the development and subsequent implementation of an epistatic framework on the HPC cluster at the University of Malaga, accessed using a custom instance of the easy-to-use Galaxy workflow manager. By doing so, this has resulted in shorter execution times compared with a single core execution designed to simulate a desktop environment, and greater accessibility for users who are not comfortable with command line and programming language environments. As a result, this has the potential to lead to an uptake in the use of epistatic analysis methods to analyse genotype data. The increased usage of epistatic analysis has the potential to provide further insights into the underlying causes of complex diseases, considering that these are likely due to multiple genetic variations. This impacts both new datasets, and also existing datasets that have been previously analysed using single association methods. This is particularly important considering that epistasis has been proposed as a possible explanation for the missing heritability in GWASs [21, 22], i.e. why other studies, such as twin studies, find higher heritability.

It should be noted that the benchmarking of the framework was carried out using the HPC cluster at the University of Malaga, and in order to access these facilities, an account is required. However, the use of a custom instance of Galaxy means that the framework can easily be adapted and deployed on other computing infrastructures. Due to the use of SLURM as the resource manager, the scripts for the epistatic analysis could easily be adapted to run on other HPC facilities. In future, it is also feasible to adapt the tools presented to run on a cloud computing platform. The Mr.SymBioMath project, which supported parts of the work reported in this paper, has a cloud computing test platform based on OpenStack [23], and developments in this test platform should be easily transferable to run on commercial cloud computing providers such as Amazon. Furthermore, we are planning to make the tools and workflow presented in the paper available via the Galaxy toolshed once further testing has been carried out, thereby allowing their incorporation into existing Galaxy instances.

Moving forward, added functionality could be offered through the implementation of both other epistatic analysis methods, and the implementation of enrichment analyses of the results, through the extension of the Spotfire integration to include OmicsOffice [24], and take advantage of the annotation manager feature, allowing enrichment results obtained to be directly displayed within Galaxy. By carrying this out, it would be possible to offer an all-in-one workflow that starts with raw data, and finishes with enrichment analysis results all from within one easy-to-use platform, thus providing a more complete tool-set for analysis of genotype data. A promising area of research is the detection of higher order epistasis, i.e. third order and higher; as methods for this are developed and become available, their incorporation potentially offers further insights into the underlying genetic architecture of human disease.

Acknowledgment. This work has been partially supported by the Mr. SymBioMath IAPP (project code: 324554), the 'Plataforma de Recursos Biomoleculares y Bioinformaticos (ISCIII-PT13.0001.0012)' and 'Proyecto de Excelencia Junta de Andalucía (P10-TIC-6108)'.

References

1. Low, S.-K., Takahashi, A., Ashikawa, K., Inazawa, J., Miki, Y., Kubo, M., Nakamura, Y., Katagiri, T.: Genome-wide association study of breast cancer in the Japanese population. PLoS ONE **8**, e76463 (2013)
2. Adeyemo, A., Gerry, N., Chen, G., Herbert, A., Doumatey, A., Huang, H., Zhou, J., Lashley, K., Chen, Y., Christman, M., Rotimi, C.: A genome-wide association study of hypertension and blood pressure in African Americans. PLoS Genet. **5**, e1000564 (2009)
3. Upton, A., Trelles, O., Cornejo-García, J.A., Perkins, J.R.: Review: high-performance computing to detect epistasis in genome scale data sets. Brief. Bioinform. **17**, bbv058 (2015)
4. Wan, X., Yang, C., Yang, Q., Xue, H., Fan, X., Tang, N.L.S., Yu, W.: BOOST: a fast approach to detecting gene-gene interactions in genome-wide case-control studies. Am. J. Hum. Genet. **87**, 325–340 (2010)
5. Lippert, C., Listgarten, J., Liu, Y., Kadie, C.M., Davidson, R.I., Heckerman, D.: FaST linear mixed models for genome-wide association studies (2011)
6. Kouskoumvekaki, I., Shublaq, N., Brunak, S.: Facilitating the use of large-scale biological data and tools in the era of translational bioinformatics. Brief. Bioinform. **15**, 942–952 (2013)
7. Kallio, M.A., Tuimala, J.T., Hupponen, T., Klemelä, P., Gentile, M., Scheinin, I., Koski, M., Käki, J., Korpelainen, E.I.: Chipster: user-friendly analysis software for microarray and other high-throughput data (2011)
8. Giardine, B., Riemer, C., Hardison, R.C., Burhans, R., Elnitski, L., Shah, P., Zhang, Y., Blankenberg, D., Albert, I., Taylor, J., Miller, W., Kent, W.J., Nekrutenko, A.: Galaxy: a platform for interactive large-scale genome analysis. Genome Res. **15**, 1451–1455 (2005)
9. Wolstencroft, K., Haines, R., Fellows, D., Williams, A., Withers, D., Owen, S., Soiland-Reyes, S., Dunlop, I., Nenadic, A., Fisher, P., Bhagat, J., Belhajjame, K., Bacall, F., Hardisty, A., de la Hidalga, A.N., Balcazar Vargas, M.P., Sufi, S., Goble, C.: The taverna workflow suite: designing and executing workflows of web services on the desktop, web or in the cloud. Nucleic Acids Res. **41**, W557–W561 (2013)
10. Goecks, J., Nekrutenko, A., Taylor, J.: Galaxy: a comprehensive approach for supporting accessible, reproducible, and transparent computational research in the life sciences. Genome Biol. **11**, R86 (2010)
11. Lippert, C., Listgarten, J., Davidson, R.I., Baxter, S., Poon, H., Poong, H., Kadie, C.M., Heckerman, D.: An exhaustive epistatic SNP association analysis on expanded Wellcome Trust data. Sci. Rep. **3**, 1099 (2013)
12. Tao, S., Feng, J., Webster, T., Jin, G., Hsu, F.C., Chen, S.H., Kim, S.T., Wang, Z., Zhang, Z., Zheng, S.L., Isaacs, W.B., Xu, J., Sun, J.: Genome-wide two-locus epistasis scans in prostate cancer using two European populations. Hum. Genet. **131**, 1225–1234 (2012)
13. Heinzlreiter, P., Perkins, J.R., Tirado, O.T., Karlsson, J., Ranea, J.A., Mitterecker, A., Blanca, M., Trelles, O.: A cloud-based GWAS analysis pipeline for clinical researchers. In: Proceedings of the Fourth International Conference on Cloud Computing and Services Science, pp. 378–394 (2014)
14. Purcell, S., Neale, B., Todd-Brown, K., Thomas, L., Ferreira, M.A.R., Bender, D., Maller, J., Sklar, P., de Bakker, P.I.W., Daly, M.J., Sham, P.C.: PLINK: a tool set for whole-genome association and population-based linkage analyses. Am. J. Hum. Genet. **81**, 559–575 (2007)
15. Wood, A.R., Tuke, M.A., Nalls, M.A., Hernandez, D.G., Bandinelli, S., Singleton, A.B., Melzer, D., Ferrucci, L., Frayling, T.M., Weedon, M.N.: Another explanation for apparent epistasis. Nature **514**, E3–E5 (2014)

16. Hiersche, M., Rühle, F., Stoll, M.: Postgwas: advanced GWAS interpretation in R. PLoS ONE **8**, e71775 (2013)
17. Anonymous: TIBCO Software Inc releases new version of Spotfire. Telecomworldwire (2008)
18. Bostock, M., Ogievetsky, V., Heer, J.: D3; Data-Driven Documents. IEEE Trans. Vis. Comput. Graph. **17**, 2301–2309 (2011)
19. Upton, A., Trelles, O., Perkins, J.: Epistatic analysis of clarkson disease. Procedia Comput. Sci. **51**, 725–734 (2015)
20. Xie, Z., Nagarajan, V., Sturdevant, D.E., Iwaki, S., Chan, E., Wisch, L., Young, M., Nelson, C.M., Porcella, S.F., Druey, K.M.: Genome-wide SNP analysis of the systemic capillary leak syndrome (clarkson disease). Rare Dis. (Austin Tex) **1**, e27445 (2013)
21. Manolio, T.A., Collins, F.S., Cox, N.J., Goldstein, D.B., Hindorff, L.A., Hunter, D.J., McCarthy, M.I., Ramos, E.M., Cardon, L.R., Chakravarti, A., Cho, J.H., Guttmacher, A.E., Kong, A., Kruglyak, L., Mardis, E., Rotimi, C.N., Slatkin, M., Valle, D., Whittemore, A.S., Boehnke, M., Clark, A.G., Eichler, E.E., Gibson, G., Haines, J.L., Mackay, T.F.C., McCarroll, S.A., Visscher, P.M.: Finding the missing heritability of complex diseases. Nature **461**, 747–753 (2009)
22. Cho, J.H.: Genome-Wide association studies: present status and future directions. Gastroenterology **138**, 1668–1672 (2010)
23. Sefraoui, O., Aissaoui, M., Eleuldj, M.: OpenStack: toward an open-source solution for cloud computing. Int. J. Comput. Appl. **55**, 38–42 (2012)
24. OmicsOffice (2014). https://www.integromics.com/omicsoffice-suite/

Two-Level Parallelism to Accelerate Multiple Genome Comparisons

Oscar Torreno[✉] and Oswaldo Trelles

Department of Computer Architecture, University of Málaga,
Campus de Teatinos, 29071 Málaga, Spain
{oscart,ortrelles}@uma.es

Abstract. We present a two-level parallel strategy focused in the enhancement of GECKO software for multiple and pairwise genome comparisons. GECKO was developed to break the computational barriers on search space and memory demands faced by equivalent software. However, although being faster than equivalent software for comparing long sequences, its execution time attracted our interest to develop a parallel strategy. Additionally, the execution time is even higher in multiple genome comparisons where several independent pairwise comparisons are typically performed sequentially. After a careful study of the internal data dependencies of the GECKO modules, we noticed that most of them were subject to an easy and efficient parallelization. The result is a two-level parallel approach to accelerate multiple genome comparisons. The first level is aimed at parallelizing each independent pairwise genome comparison of a multiple comparison study to a different core. This level is application-independent, we are using GECKO but any other equivalent software can be used. The second level consists on the internal parallelization of GECKO modules with evident enhancements in performance while results remain invariant. After solving the problems of combining the big amount of I/O operations overlapped with computation, the obtained speedups reflect the good efficiency of the devised strategy.

1 Introduction

Two-level and more generally multi-level parallelism have been already applied in a number of different fields including video coding, aerodynamics and shape design [3,6,7]. After analysing the specifics of the application to be parallelized, these multi-level approaches use either only message passing implementations applied to the different levels, or merge the usage of MPI with OpenMP for multi-core shared memory machines. In addition, some approaches such as [7] use hybrid CPU-GPU implementations to accelerate the computation. Examples of reasons motivating the use of these multi-level strategies are the mixture of lightweight and heavyweight tasks or the dissimilar combination of computation and I/O operations.

We have found that multiple and pairwise genome comparisons have the mentioned computation patterns and are therefore suitable to be parallelized

© Springer International Publishing AG 2017
F. Desprez et al. (Eds.): Euro-Par 2016 Workshops, LNCS 10104, pp. 445–456, 2017.
DOI: 10.1007/978-3-319-58943-5_36

in multiple levels. The computational space and memory demands of current software is significantly high for just comparing two long sequences. GECKO [9] was designed to overcome these limitations of equivalent software. However, although reporting shorter execution time compared to equivalent software, its execution time is still big enough to study potential parallel approaches.

The problem becomes even more notorious when we aim at comparing a set of genome sequences in what is referred as a multiple genome comparison study. For such studies, pairwise genome comparison software is used, executing it sequentially several times depending on the number of genomes under study. If already at pairwise genome comparison level the execution time is important, at the multiple genome comparison level it becomes even higher and therefore more interesting from the computational point of view.

After analysing in more detail the parallelization possibilities, we noticed it was possible to apply a two-level strategy. First, we observed that each pairwise genome comparison inside a multiple genome comparison is independent so it represents an embarrassingly parallel problem. Second, and less obvious, we detected that some of the GECKO modules were subject to be parallelized. For instance, the first step of GECKO calculates a dictionary of K-mers (words of length K), which may consume a significant amount of time for long sequences. In this case, splitting the calculation of given word prefixes to different processors could be a solution. Similarly, the rest of GECKO steps could be parallelized with relatively simple strategies.

In this work, we present a two-level parallelization strategy designed to speed up multiple and pairwise genome comparisons. Efficiency in both levels has been obtained by using dynamic scheduling algorithms which generate the sufficient number of tasks to overlap I/O and computation. Hybrid solutions using GPUs are not considered in this work (but will be possibly considered in the future) because the application is data intensive and the loading time to GPU memory would govern the performance. The resulting strategy reduces the execution time when the number of processors increase, especially while working with long sequences. The code has been developed in C using the Open MPI library [1] (it will be available under request). The associated binaries can be obtained from http://bitlab-es.com/gecko.

2   Related Work

In the literature, several papers provide a review on HPC solutions applied to pairwise and multiple sequence comparisons such as [8]. The solutions mentioned in these papers use different architectures such as GPUs, FPGAs, multicores and/or Intel Xeon Phi being able to compare at most sequences of up to hundreds of millions of characters (10^8), as stated in [8]. The CPU implementations employ fine-grained parallelism using different data distribution techniques. Some of the CPU techniques report memory consumption of quadratic order, thus limiting the size of the input sequence. FPGA implementations clearly accelerate the process but they have important limitations. First, they can only handle sequences up to 10^5 base pairs (bp), and second, almost all of them only report the alignment score as output. GPU-based solutions accelerate the process as well, but they also are limited in the length of the input sequence (10^8 bp). In addition, most GPU implementations require quadratic space to report the alignment. A small number of Intel Xeon Phi implementations exist, which already report better performance than GPU implementation in some cases.

Trying to benefit from the best part of each architecture, there already exist a number of hybrid approaches using various devices simultaneously. Such solutions implement two-level parallelization, in which in a first coarse-grained level a set of sequences is assigned to each device. The second level (i.e. fine-grained) often uses previously proposed algorithms/tools to compare the sequences. We considered this two-level approach suitable to multiple genome comparisons using GECKO. The reason why we are not using GPUs, FPGAs or Intel Xeon Phi in this work is because of the mentioned input sequence size limitation faced in such devices.

As reported in [8], even with the performance improvement of the HPC techniques applied to the research field, the comparison of long sequences such as human chromosomes still takes more than 9 h to complete. Therefore, our effort in this paper concentrates in both reducing such execution time, removing the input sequence size limitation and reporting the alignment together with quality information such as the score (i.e. the main limitations of related approaches).

3   System and Methods

3.1   The Pairwise Genome Comparison Application

The latest release of GECKO program has been used in this work as the base sequences comparison algorithm (see Algorithm 1). GECKO is a modular application which calculates a set of conserved segments or High-scoring Segment Pairs (HSPs) shared by two given input sequences. It has not been modified in terms of functionality, however a number of minor changes were introduced in order to be able to parallelize it.

The program starts by calculating a dictionary of words of length K (K-mers) for each of the input sequences to be compared. The dictionary calculation scans the sequence with a sliding window of length K and a step of 1 producing an alphabetically sorted dictionary of K-mers together with their frequencies and occurrence positions.

Using the dictionaries of both input sequences, a set of exact word matches (seed points or hits) is produced. A hit is defined by the coordinates of the same word in the input sequences, therefore, a given word W_i with frequencies f_1 and f_2 in sequences 1 and 2 respectively, will produce $f_1 \times f_2$ hits following all the combinations.

In order to reduce the previously generated hits set, hits are sorted and optionally filtered based on proximity. The next program compares the residues present at each sequence starting where each hit occurs, adding or subtracting a given value depending if the residues match or not. When the alignment score becomes negative, the calculated alignment (using the maximum score reached) is reported in case it passes the threshold parameters.

Algorithm 1. GECKO

1: Calculate a dictionary of K-mers for each input sequence.
2: Calculate a set of seed points based on the previously calculated dictionaries.
3: Sort (and optionally filter) the produced set of seed points.
4: Calculate the final set of HSPs based on the previous set of seed points.

As described in GECKO documentation, CPU time is mostly concentrated in the sorting procedures ((1) and (3)) due to the amount of data to be sorted what forces the program to use the hard disk. Therefore, our main effort will be in the parallelization of such steps. Besides, steps (2) and (4) are also subject to parallelization although they do not concentrate the major CPU time. The parallelization speedup for these steps will be noticed mostly for long similar sequences. All the steps (from (1) to (4)) have to be executed sequentially since each step is using the output of the previous. However, there is still room to internally parallelize each step.

3.2   Generic Overview of the Parallelization Approaches

Master-Slave. This approach has been applied to the two parallelization levels. In the first level, we have applied a master-slave tasks distribution approach to perform each pairwise genome comparison of a multiple genome comparison study in a different core (see Fig. 1.A). In the second level, the slaves calculate the partial result of the modules composing GECKO (see Fig. 1.B). This approach considers at both levels as many slave processes as cores being used. The master process reads the set of tasks from a workload file, which is generated by a previous mapping process. Later the master distributes the tasks, assigning the cores more tasks as soon as they become idle.

Considering the high number of I/O operations performed by GECKO modules, the master is assigning more than one task per core in order to overlap I/O and computation. Additionally, this is done to reduce the overhead introduced by sending tasks in separated messages. Depending on the number of processes and the selected prefix size (as explained in Sect. 3.3), the *task_per_core* value is either 2 (for number of cores power of 2) or 4 (for number of cores power of 4) in order to always have more than 1 task per core.

Balanced Splits Distribution. This strategy is similar to the master-slave approach, but in this case the master and slaves are customised for the specific parallelized module, what contrasts with the generic ones of the previously described strategy. Besides, the master calculates the offset coordinates of a balanced set of independent data chunks, which are later processed by the slaves.

Once all the partial results become available, the master produces the final output. As in the previous approach, each processor is assigned either with 2 or 4 data chunks depending on the number of cores.

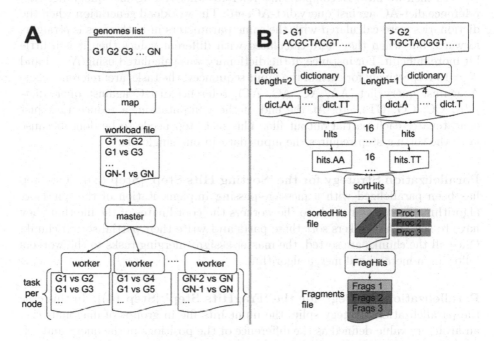

Fig. 1. Overview of the parallelization levels. Sub-figure A outlines how the strategy starting from a list of genomes ends performing each independent pairwise genome comparison in a separate worker. Sub-figure B shows the performed parallelization within the internal modules of GECKO.

3.3 Details of the Parallelization Strategies of the Second Level

Parallelization Strategy for the 'Dictionary Step' [Step (1)]. The parallelization of this step is performed in two levels. The first and simpler level, is the parallelization at sequence level, since the dictionary calculation of each sequence is independent. The second level, splits the dictionary calculation in N tasks, being $N = 4^{PrefixSize}$. $PrefixSize$ indicates the size of the prefix to be used to split the work, so special care with its value must be taken in order to have the correct number of tasks as explained in the Sect. 3.2. The alphabet used for the K-mers is $\Sigma = \{A, C, G, T\}$, so when the parallelization is made with $PrefixSize = 2$, 16 tasks are generated. Such tasks calculate words starting with the following prefixes (in alphabetical order): $AA, AC, AG, AT, ..., CA, CC, ..., TT$.

Parallelization Strategy for the 'Hits Step' [Step (2)]. This step calculates the matches between the N previously calculated sub-dictionaries suitable to produce matches. For example, if the dictionaries were calculated with $N = 16$ then we have 16 comparisons, reference.dict-AA against query.dict-AA, reference.dict-AC against query.dict-AC, etc. The workload generation when the dictionaries were calculated with the same parameters in both cases is straightforward, but when they were calculated with different values then it is a little bit more difficult. For instance, if the dictionary was calculated using $N = 4$ and $N = 16$ respectively for each of the input sequences, the tasks are: reference.dict-A against query.dict-(AA, AC, AG, AT), reference.dict-C against query.dict-(CA, CC, CG, CT), etc. At the end of the computation, a reduce task just concatenates each partial output file. This last step needs to be done because later the sorting step requires the input data in one single file.

Parallelization Strategy for the 'Sorting Hits Step' [Step (3)]. This step has been parallelized with a message-passing implementation of the quicksort algorithm. The master sends to the workers the coordinates of the file that they have to sort. The workers sort these parts and write their partial sorted chunk. Once all the chunks are sorted, the master assigns merging tasks to the workers following a hierarchical merge algorithm.

Parallelization Strategy for the 'FragHits Step' [Step (4)]. In this case the parallelization strategy splits the input hits file in groups of diagonals (i.e. an arbitrary value defined as the difference of the positions in the query and reference sequences respectively). The reason behind this data splitting strategy is that hits belonging to the same diagonal have data dependencies. The extension of a hit could cover a further one within the same diagonal and this covered hit should in turn not be extended because it will produce a fragment contained in the previous one. In order to have a balanced set of tasks the number of diagonals varies depending on the numer of hits they contain. A final reduce step concatenates the partial results producing a unique HSPs file equivalent to the one generated by the sequential version.

4   Results

In this section, the performance of the applied paralellization strategies in terms of speedup and reduced time is illustrated. All the speedup curves contained in this document reflect the average execution time of 10 runs. A number of different tests are used to illustrate the performance achievement on each of the parallelized levels. These tests are using input data ranging from short to large sequences and also different *tasks_per_core* values due to the high number of I/O operations performed by some modules. In addition to the performed tests to each step of the second parallelization level, the multiple genome comparison and overall application speedups are shown to illustrate the gains achieved by the presented two-level parallelization strategy.

4.1   Infrastructure

This new implementation has been tested in the fat nodes of the Picasso supercomputer located at the University of Málaga (Málaga, Spain). Each fat node has 2 TB of RAM and eight Intel E7-4870 processors, which deliver 96 Gflop/s. For the first parallelization level only one node has been used until the measurement of 64 cores and two nodes for the 128 cores measurement. For the second parallelization level only one node has been used, requiring no MPI communication over the network, since each node has 80 cores and the speedup measurements are made until 32 cores.

4.2   Dataset

The selected test datasets contain several public available sequences[1] of different sizes in order to thoroughly study the speedup of the two parallelization levels. In the first level, we are using two sets of 30 and 40 small sequences of Mycoplasma genus with an average length of 1 Mbp. Both sets contain sequences sharing different level of similarity ranging from closely to remotely related sequences. The dataset to test the internal parallelization level is composed of bacteria and mammalian sequences ranging from 5 to 410 Mbp. The large mammalian sequences (Homo sapiens (HS) and Macaca Mulatta (MM)) are used in two tests. The first test uses the chromosome 1 of both mammalian sequences (from now on the test will be referred as HS-MM(chr1)), while the second one compares the concatenation of chromosomes 1 and 2 of each species in order to conform a longer sequence (the test will be referred as HS-MM(chr1+2)).

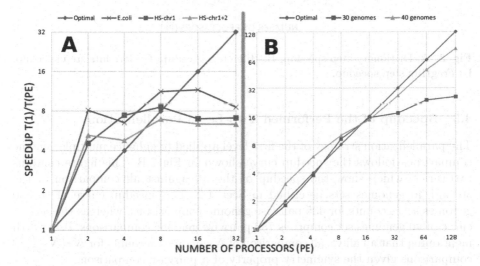

Fig. 2. A: Total application speedup; B: Multiple genome comparison speedup

---

[1] http://www.ncbi.nlm.nih.gov/genome/.

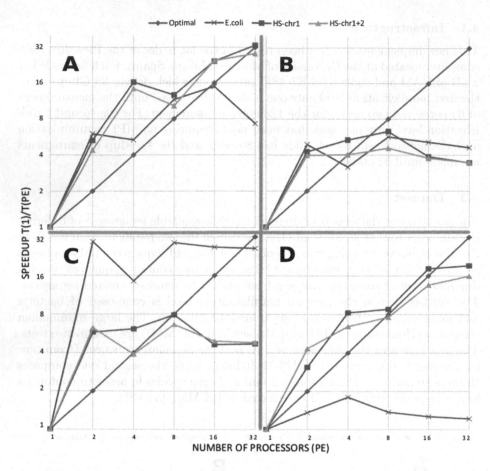

Fig. 3. A: Dictionary step speedup; B: Hits step speedup; C: Sort hits step speedup; D: FragHits step speedup.

4.3   Speedup of the Performed Two-Level Parallelization

The parallelization strategy of the first level applied to enhance multiple genome comparisons follows the speedup curve shown in Fig. 2.B. This figure contains two series, which show the speedup of the all against all comparison of the 30 and 40 genomes sets described in Sect. 4.2. The speedup curve of the 30 genomes set accounts for 435 pairwise genome comparisons, whereas the second curve of 40 genomes set comprises 780 pairwise genome comparisons. It is worth mentioning that an all vs. all comparison of N genomes accounts for $N*(N-1)/2$ comparisons given the symmetry property of a pairwise comparison.

The devised strategies in the second parallelization level follow the speedup curves shown in Figs. 3 (A, B, C and D; which relates in order to the steps of Algorithm 1) and 2.A, which shows the overall application speedup.

5   Discussion

5.1   Speedup of the Multiple Genome Comparison Study

The speedup of the first parallelization level (see Fig. 2.B) indicates that the application is scalable. It is worth noting that until 16 PE, both series (i.e. 30 and 40 genomes) have a speedup close to the theoretical one or even super-linear because of the overlap between I/O and computation produced while executing several comparisons at the same time. From 32 PE onwards, the speedup of the 30 genomes series degrades because there are not enough tasks for the available cores. In contrast, the 40 genomes series, which generates a higher number of tasks, keeps scaling closer to the theoretical speedup with an efficiency of 65.98% in the worst case.

5.2   Dictionary Step Speedup

Results are good when the sequence size is big enough as can be observed in Fig. 3.A, having reached accelerations above the theoretical until 8 PE for E.coli, 32 PE for HS-MM(chr1) and 16 PE for HS-MM(chr1+2). The performance reduction that can be observed in the E.coli series is produced by its short length, which is on of the parameters that conducts the compute time. It is worth noting that the speedup of the longest sequence (HS-MM(chr1+2)) is not the best as it is supposed to be, based on previous assumptions, mainly because of the higher I/O load. It is also important to note that the application scales good until 16 PE, from where the super-linear speedup turns into normal speedup. We believe that the cause of this behaviour could be that the required number of I/O operations is very high, what is not giving a good computation-I/O ratio. Furthermore, since processes within the same physical node share the filesystem, this could be also a bottleneck in this case.

5.3   Hits Step Speedup

We can observe two interesting aspects in the speedup curves of the hits step (see Fig. 3.B). First, the super-linear speedup achieved in the cases of 2 and 4 PE for the longer sequences (HS-MM(chr1+2) and HS-MM(chr1)). This is caused again by the fact of having simultaneous executions in each node overlapping computation and I/O operations. The second aspect, the reduction of the speedup just after obtaining the super-linear one (after 4 PE in one case and 2 PE in the other cases). Here, we believe that writing the output file is consuming most of the time due to its size (around 78 GB for HS-MM(chr1) and 252 GB for HS-MM(chr1+2)). In consequence, adding more cores, which provide processing power, does not speed up the process. With regards to the shortest sequence (E.coli), the output file is much smaller, but the situation remains the same, because in essence the ratio between compute and I/O is similar.

5.4   Sort Hits Step Speedup

Similarly to the hits step, we can also observe in the speedup of this module (see Fig. 3.C) a super-linear speedup until 16 PE for E.coli, 4 PE for HS-MM(chr1) and 2 PE for HS-MM(chr1+2). However, in this case the reason resides in the data fitting in main memory instead of working with it stored on the hard disk. Although the curve shapes are similar, the speedup achieved in the case of HS-MM(chr1) for 4 PE (6.13) is higher than the obtained in the hits step (5.34). Besides super-linearity, the speedup is again reduced due to the size of the files to be read and written. In constrast, in the short sequences series, the super-linear speedup is also achieved for 16 PE, what confirms our assumption of the bottleneck caused by the size of the output file.

5.5   FragHits Step Speedup

For this step, in the case of long sequences, the speedup is again super-linear until 4 PE for the HS-MM(chr1+2) case and until 16 PE for HS-MM(chr1). Although the speedup is super-linear at the beginning, the efficiency level degrades, resulting in 60.06% in HS-MM(chr1) and 49.84% in HS-MM(chr1+2) with 32 PE. Again the results for short sequences demonstrate that the computational workload is not big enough in such case to take profit of a parallel strategy.

5.6   Overall Application Speedup in a Pairwise Comparison

The speedup curves shown in Fig. 2.A confirm what we explained in previous sections. The application reports super-linear speedup until 8 PE (except for HS-MM(chr1+2), reasons in Sects. 5.3 and 5.4). In addition, starting from 16 PE, the performance does not improve, what is normal due to parallelization overheads compared to the actual computation as well as the high I/O load the application has. It is important to note that although for many steps the speedup for the shortest sequence was not that good, the efficiency of the overall application is acceptable until 16 PE (61.25%) and the speedup is even better than the one of the two long sequences, mostly because the speedup is better in the most time consuming step (i.e. sort hits).

5.7   Time Reduction

Although the speedup curves in some cases suggest not particularly good efficiency levels, the time reduction has been considerable. In the first parallelization level, although the efficiency for the 30 genomes series is not good, the execution time has been reduced to 10 s compared to the 250 s of the sequential execution. In the second parallelization level we can observe a similar situation. Although for some GECKO modules the speedup is not good, the overall time reduction is significant. For instance, for the case of HS-MM(chr1+2) using 16 PE the time has been reduced to 49 min from the 5 h and 11 min of the sequential execution.

6 Conclusions

In this work we have approached the parallelization of multiple genome comparisons following a two-level strategy. The first level is aimed at parallelizing each independent pairwise genome comparison of the multiple comparison study to a different core. The second level consists on the parallelization of GECKO modules with evident time reduction while results remain invariant. Although the second parallelization level is customised for GECKO, the first one is generic enough to be used with any of the GECKO equivalent applications. The reason behind selecting GECKO is that it produces results of higher quality without computational barriers compared to current top methods such as MUMmer [5] or Mauve [2] as stated in [9].

To decrease the scheduling cost in the master process we implement a simple mapping of tasks to the available workers, assigning them a new set of tasks as soon as they became idle. This scheduler introduces a tasks per core parameter which allows the user to overlap the execution of tasks, what we found specially useful in terms of performance while working with a disparate combination of CPU and I/O bounded applications. In fact, the overlapping of I/O and computation is producing the super-linear speedups shown in the figures included in this document.

Tests in the first parallelization level have been performed using two different datasets of 30 and 40 genomes respectively. The selected dataset in this case represents the most typical multiple genome comparison study, which is the comparison of short sequences given that around 75% of the available sequences are short sequences[2]. However, the obtained results indicate that it would be possible to use long sequences as well. The obtained speedup in the 30 genome sequences set indicates that from 32 PE onwards the number of tasks is not sufficient. However, in the 40 genomes set the speedup maintains good efficiency levels beyond that point.

In the second parallelization level, tests using different sequence lengths have been performed, since this is one of the parameters governing the execution time. The obtained results show that all GECKO modules reduce significantly their execution time, although in terms of speedup with a high number of cores the results are not specially prominent. Analysing the speedup, we can extract the correct number of PE for each of the modules. In the case of the dictionary module this value is 32 PE (although for the short sequence the efficiency is not good). The hits and sort hits steps report asymptotic speedups, which are good in terms of efficiency until 8 PE in both cases. For the last application module (i.e. FragHits), the efficiency is acceptable until 32 PE for the long sequences cases and clearly not worthing to be parallelized for the short sequences case. The different values of number of PE suggest that the use of auto-scaling architectures such as cloud computing could be suitable for this application.

It is worth noting that the biological problem addressed here is really important. In fact, in comparative genomics the core applications include the

---

[2] https://gold.jgi.doe.gov/statistics.

competitors of GECKO (e.g. MUMmer, Mauve, Lastz [4]). Using this two-level parallel strategy for multiple genome comparisons, the researchers have a faster way to study a given sequence. The original version of GECKO was already able to compare two concatenated chromosomes in less time than parallel methods, which take 9 h as reported in [8]. The parallel version presented in this document reduces the execution time even further reducing it to 49 min. Additionally, this faster way of comparing multiple genomes allow users contrasting the current evolutionary models.

As future work, we plan to test it with more input sequences and in a different system in terms of number of processors and underlying filesystem. We sincerely hope, that this tests will reinforce the fact of the results obtained with the devised parallelization strategies described in this document.

Acknowledgements. This work has been partially supported by the European projects Mr. Symbiomath (grant no. 324554) and Elixir-Excelerate (grant no. 676559), and the Spanish national projects "Plataforma de Recursos Biomoleculares y Bioin-formáticos" (ISCIII-PT13.0001.0012) and RIRAAF (ISCIII-RD12/0013/0006).

References

1. Open MPI. https://www.open-mpi.org/
2. Darling, A.E., Mau, B., Perna, N.T.: progressivemauve: multiple genome alignment with gene gain, loss and rearrangement. PLoS One **5**(6), e11147 (2010)
3. Duvigneau, R., Kloczko, T., Praveen, C.: A three-level parallelization strategy for robust design in aerodynamics. In: Proceedings of 20th International Conference on Parallel Computational Fluid Dynamics, pp. 379–384 (2008)
4. Harris, R.: Improved pairwise alignment of genomic DNA. Ph.D. dissertation, The Pennsylvania State University (2007)
5. Kurtz, S., Phillippy, A., Delcher, A.L., Smoot, M., Shumway, M., Antonescu, C., Salzberg, S.L.: Versatile and open software for comparing large genomes. Genome Biol. **5**(2), R12 (2004)
6. Marco, N., Lanteri, S.: A two-level parallelization strategy for genetic algorithms applied to optimum shape design. Parallel Comput. **26**(4), 377–397 (2000)
7. Momcilovic, S., Roma, N., Sousa, L.: Multi-level parallelization of advanced video coding on hybrid CPU+GPU platforms. In: Caragiannis, I., et al. (eds.) Euro-Par 2012. LNCS, vol. 7640, pp. 165–174. Springer, Heidelberg (2013). doi:10.1007/978-3-642-36949-0_19
8. Sandes, E., Boukerche, A., Melo, A.: Parallel optimal pairwise biological sequence comparison: algorithms, platforms, and classification. ACM Comput. Surv. (CSUR) **48**(4), 63 (2016)
9. Torreno, O., Trelles, O.: Breaking the computational barriers of pairwise genome comparison. BMC Bioinf. **16**(1), 1 (2015)

Improving Bioinformatics Analysis of Large Sequence Datasets Parallelizing Tools for Population Genomics

Javier Navarro[1], Gonzalo Vera[2], Sebastián Ramos-Onsins[2], and Porfidio Hernández[1(✉)]

[1] Universitat Autonòma de Barcelona, Bellaterra, Spain
{javier.navarro,porfidio.hernandez}@uab.es
[2] Center for Research in Agricultural Genomics, Barcelona, Spain
{gonzalo.vera,sebastian.ramos}@cragenomica.es

Abstract. Next-generation sequencing (NGS) technologies initiated a revolution in genomics, producing massive amounts of biological data and the consequent need for adapting current computing infrastructures. Multiple alignment of genomes, analysis of variants or phylogenetic tree construction, with quadratic polynomial complexity in the best case are tools that can take days or weeks to complete in conventional computers.

Most of these analysis, involving several tools integrated in workflows, present the possibility of dividing the computational load in independent tasks allowing parallel execution. Determining adequate load balancing, data partitioning, granularity and I/O tuning are key factors for achieving suitable speedups.

In this paper we present a coarse-grain parallelization of GH caller (Genotype/Haplotype caller), a tool used in population genomics workflows that performs a probabilistic identification process to account for the frequency of variants present between population individuals. It implements a master-worker model, using the standard Message Passing Interface (MPI), and concurrently and iteratively distributes the data among the available worker processes by mapping subsets of data and leaving the orchestration to the master process. Our results show a performance gain factor of 260x using 64 processes and additional optimizations with regard to the initial non-parallelized version.

Keywords: Bioinformatics · NGS · Population genomics · Variant analysis · Parallelization · Scalability

1 Introduction

More than a decade ago bioinformatics analysis experienced a major revolution with the introduction of NGS technologies, able to produce millions of DNA fragments at very high speed [11,12]. Higher volumes of experimental data have a great impact in multiple areas, where an increase in the amount of observations improves the statistical power and hence the accuracy of results. Variability analysis in population genomics is an example where researchers take

© Springer International Publishing AG 2017
F. Desprez et al. (Eds.): Euro-Par 2016 Workshops, LNCS 10104, pp. 457–467, 2017.
DOI: 10.1007/978-3-319-58943-5_37

advantage of large-scale data volumes by incorporating more individuals and increasing DNA coverage in their experiments [16]. Originally driven by theoretical approaches, population genomics needs to test their models and validate its hypothesis using large amounts of sequencing data which require high performance technologies for its processing. In this context, population genomics has become a data-driven discipline. By contrast, there is a wide gap between data production and current processing capabilities. This divergence results in the need of providing new methods and solutions in the field of high performance computing. A typical case of variant analysis involves the identification, catalog, and map of variations at a single position (locus) in a DNA sequence among individuals, also known as single nucleotide polymorphism or SNP. The number of tools and its relation inside analytical workflows depends on each specific study [13], but we can identify three common stages illustrated in Fig. 1. First stage is performed to prepare raw input data (preprocess), followed by a main processing stage like SNP calling (process), and a final stage where results are arranged for its review.

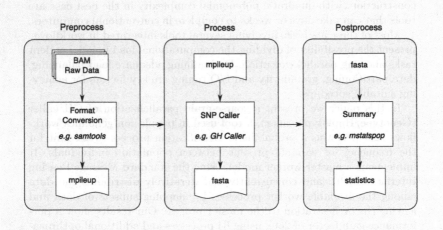

Fig. 1. An example of generic workflow used in variant analysis.

Bioinformatics tools like Samtools [8], GATK [1] or ANGSD [7] have been mainly designed for detecting SNPs while keeping lower false discovery rates, but not for the analysis of variability. In this work we present a coarse-grain parallelization of the software *Genotype/Haplotype caller (GH caller)* [13]. This program is developed for the analysis of variability and implements the Roesti et al. [14] algorithm to accurately account the number of effective positions and the frequency of the variants, making this tool highly suitable for population genomics studies. We show that our parallel implementation can provide a performance advantage when using a data-intensive computing system (cluster).

The remaining of the paper is organized as follows. Section 2 reviews the original serial application GH caller. Our proposal and MPI implementation are described in Sect. 3 while its performance is analyzed in Sect. 4. Final conclusions and outlines of our future work are described in Sect. 5.

2   GH Caller

GH caller implements the Roesti algorithm [14], which is based in the algorithms proposed by Hohenhole et al. [4] and Lynch [10]. The main difference with other SNP callers is that *GH caller* counts the number of chromosomes that are effectively read per site, so that it makes unbiased in relation to the frequency of the variants for neutrality tests and to the calculation of the nucleotide variability.

As input, *GH caller* takes *pileup* or *mpileup* file formats obtained from *bam* files [9] produced in previous steps of a variant analysis workflow. The *pileup* or *mpileup* format is a text-based format for summarizing the base calls of aligned reads to a reference sequence. This format describes the base-pair information at each chromosomal position, and one line contains the information of all the individuals at this position (locus). The output of *GH caller* is a *fasta* file with two sequences per individual and a length equal to the total length of the input sequence in *mpileup*.

Table 1 shows an example of sizes used as input and output data, and execution time of GH caller using these data sets. First column represents the number of individuals (*bam* files) used to create the *mpileup* input file; second column indicates the total size of the resulting *mpileup*. These files were obtained from 50 different *bam* files, and represent only one chromosome (chromosome 1) from the pig genome. Third column shows the size of the output *fasta* file. Last column shows the elapsed execution time using the original application. These figures show that the execution time increases with the problem size. For the case of 50 individuals and one chromosome (an input file of 283 GBytes) the time elapsed exceeds 60.000 s. It is not hard to foresee that as soon as NGS costs drop another fraction, researchers will be willing to analyze full genomes what it will easily require several days to process. These evidences make this problem worth to be analyzed in order to reduce execution times and improve resource usage.

Table 1. Execution time obtained by running the original application using different data sets.

Individuals	Input (GB)	Output (GB)	Time (s)
10	67	6	13,058
20	125	12	24,961
30	182	18	37,991
40	231	24	51,793
50	283	50	63,626

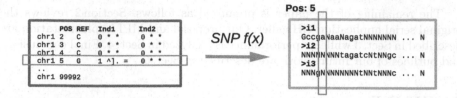

Fig. 2. Independent rows from the input *mpileup* file can be processed to generate known positions of the output *fasta* file.

In order to analyze the original application (serial), Fig. 2 shows the schema of how data is processed through the main flow of execution. The main steps are: First, it obtains all the information needed to apply the SNP algorithm at a given position (locus), reading a full line from the *mpileup* file. Next, for each locus GH caller applies the SNP calling algorithm and generates the corresponding output. Finally, all results are stored in memory and, at the end of execution, they are written to disk. Because all information is self-contained in each locus and there is no data dependency to apply the SNP calling algorithm, we can ensure that this problem is *embarrassingly parallel*, and hence it can be divided into components that can be executed concurrently. Next section will shows the strategy applied to parallelize this application.

3 Parallelization

The parallel implementation takes advantage of the inherent data parallelism found in the Roesti algorithm [14]. As we shown in previous section, this algorithm is applied independently in each site (locus), so this problem is *embarrassingly parallel*. Thanks to this property, we can split input data in groups of n loci and distribute them in chunks among the available processing units, where all the computations will be performed in parallel. The main parallelization phases are the following:

(1) All processors initialize the parallel environment;
(2) the main process (master) indexes the input file and maps the input data to other processes (workers);
(3) the parallel computations start asynchronously on each worker. Locally, each process reads and parses a subset of data (*'Read' and 'Parse'*), applies the base calling algorithm to these data (*'Process'*), and finally writes his partial results to the final *fasta* output file (*'Write'*);
(4) if it was selected as a command line option, a synchronization point (barrier) is used to allow the master process append a reference/outgroup sequence.

Phases 1 and 3 are independent and only need synchronization, hence are performed in parallel, while phases 2 and 4 are serial and must be performed in order. The master-worker model implemented is illustrated in Fig. 3.

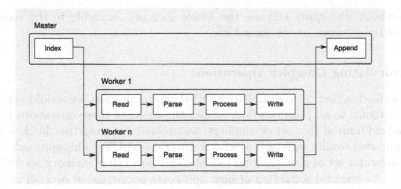

Fig. 3. Master starts indexing the input file and it generates tasks. For each task, a worker reads and parses its data, applies the SNP calling algorithm and writes down its output. Finally, if set, the master appends a reference sequence to the output file.

Domain Decomposition

Our application uses the standard Message Passing Interface (MPI) [3] and distributes the data among the available processors by mapping subsets of data (hereinafter "chunks") in an uniform way, giving one to each worker process at a time. Index and map operations are carried out by the master process. All workers open the input file and read the part of the assigned data. Finally, they process its data using the algorithm described in the previous section (Fig. 4).

This master-worker model provides two main advantages: First, it allows the implicit parallelization of input/output operations along all workers. Second, as not all these chunks needs the same time to be processed, the master process can apply a load balancing strategy that distributes chunks dynamically across multiple workers. Futhermore, each chunk does not need to be replicated at the local memory of any other process, so memory used is released when data is written to disk: this allows GH caller to take advantage of working with data

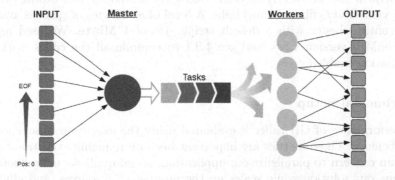

Fig. 4. Master performs a domain decomposition process mapping subsets of data to each worker.

sets without size limits and use the whole memory available to the bunch of allocated processors, at the same time.

Pre-calculating Complex Operations

As described in Sect. 2, to complete the SNP calling process, we should apply the same formulas to all positions (loci). Since the scope of these operations is well-known and limited to a set of numbers, we created an array that holds a set of pre-computed results and use it as a Look-Up-Table (LUT). This approach allows to transform a set of slow complex calculations into faster memory accesses. As a result, we reduced a fraction of high cpu costs accumulated over all the SNP calling iterations.

4 Experimentation and Results

The main objective of the experiments proposed here are to evaluate the benefits obtained in our parallel approach by comparing both applications, serial and parallel versions, in terms of effective usage of variable computational resources using the same data.

Experimental Platform

The experimental platform used is a cluster composed by 8 nodes. Each node has 12 cores in 2 Intel Xeon X5660 processors with a frequency of 2.8 GHz, and 96 GBytes of RAM. The total number of available cores on this platform is 96 with 768 GBytes of RAM. These nodes are connected via 10 Gbit Ethernet links and run Scientific Linux version 6.3.

Our application was evaluated using the parallel file system Lustre, version 2.5.3 configured with 1 Metadata Server (MDS) and 2 object storage servers (OSS), which were connected to the same 10 Gbit Ethernet network. These Lustre servers manage up to 8 Object Storage Target (OST, that stores the data) with a size of 10 TBytes each. OSTs are served by two Storage Arrays (SAN) via 8 Gbit/s fiber channel links. A total of 80 TBytes of space is available to the entire cluster with a default stripe size of 1 Mbyte. We used mpicxx for OpenMPI version 1.8.8, and gcc 4.9.1 to compile all the codes, with −03 optimization enabled.

Experimental Setup

The performance of GH caller is evaluated using the execution time, speedup, and efficiency. These metrics are important because reducing execution time is the main concern to parallelize our application, speedup allows us to know how performs our solution while scales up the number of resources, and efficiency indicates how much of the resources are being used by our implementation.

First, we obtain the execution time of the original GH caller (serial) using only one core as computational resources (T_1). This value is used as a baseline to compare gains obtained regarding with the execution time used by our new parallel version (T_N). Although there are different definitions of speedup [15], we define the relative speedup obtained by the parallel program, Q, when solving a instance of instance I of size i, using NP processes as follows:

$$RelativeSpeedup(I, Q) = \frac{T_{(I,1)}}{T_{(I,NP)}} \qquad (1)$$

Where $T_{(I,1)}$ is the time to solve I using program Q and 1 process. Because our application uses a master-worker scheme, this value corresponds to $T_{I,2}$ (2 processes using 2 cores). $T_{(I,NP)}$ is the time to solve I using program Q and NP processes.

We performed each experiment ten times and kept the average execution time. In all the experiments performed we used the case of 10 individuals, all from the chromosome 1 of the pig genome. Sizes of input and output files used in this example are show in first row of Table 1.

Execution Time and Scalability

Table 2 shows all results obtained from serial and parallel execution, scaling up the parallel implementation from 2 to 96 cores, and showing the obtained execution times, relative speedup, efficiency and gains with respect to the original version. As we can observe, execution times has been dramatically reduced thanks to the parallelization, while maintaining high efficiency figures (above 80%) until it reaches 64 processes, where the benefits of adding more resources begins to decrease.

In order to clearly show and appreciate gains obtained respect the original version, Fig. 5 plots and compares execution time of different implementations of GH caller. First column represents the original serial implementation, whereas next columns are results from parallel executions. As can be observed, using

Table 2. Results obtained running GH caller scaling up to 96 cores.

NP	Workers	Time (s)	Speedup	Efficiency	Gain factor
1	–	13058.0	–	–	1
2	1	2162.6	1.00	1.00	6.0
4	3	725.6	2.98	0.99	17.9
8	7	327.2	6.61	0.94	39.9
16	15	161.9	13.36	0.89	80.6
32	31	84.6	25.56	0.82	154.3
64	63	49.7	43.47	0.69	262.7
96	95	54.8	39.46	0.42	238.2

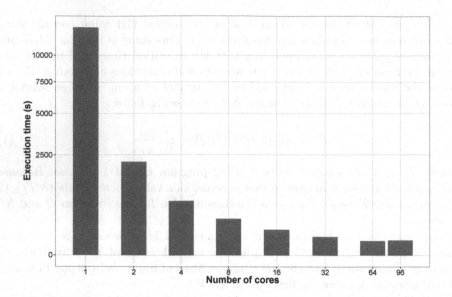

Fig. 5. Execution time increasing the number of workers on cluster up to 96 processes.

only 2 processes - a Master and a Worker - using this parallel implementation it reduces in 6x total execution time, due to improvements made in SNP algorithm internal calculations, parallelization of input/output tasks, and use of buffers to reduce total number of input/output operations. Furthermore, if we compare execution time using 64 cores, our results show a significant reduction in the time with respect to the original version, from 13,000 s to nearly 50 s. Looking at these results, we can observed that the execution time can be reduced by adding computational resources up to 260x, by using 64 cores and MPI processes. Nevertheless, these gains start to decrease when using all the available computational resources, a total of 96 cores, proving that there are some scalability issues.

In order to show plainly these issues, at Fig. 6 we plot relative speedup and efficiency. Dashed lines at these figures represent linear speedup and ideal efficiency, respectively. As described above, there are no data dependencies processing each chunk, as a result we can expect a linear speedup when scaling up the number of resources. However, we observe scalability issues using more than 64 processes, and these problems can be appreciate more clearly observing the efficiency values obtained. In fact, relative speedup obtained with 96 processes is limited to 39, clearly showing a low efficiency, with a value obtained of 42% of effectiveness. This low efficiency will be discussed in the next section.

Bottleneck Analysis

The work done in this section should distinguish the overhead introduced by each phase and identify the main reasons. First, like other analysis tools [6], we intercept the MPI calls to instrument the application. We use the MPI Parallel

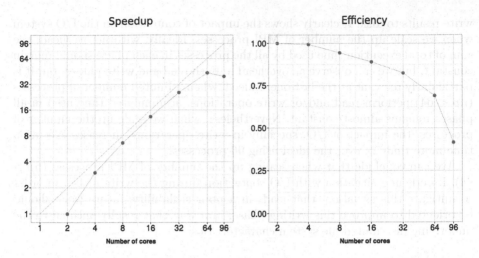

Fig. 6. Relative speedup and efficiency for an increasing number of workers on cluster. MPI configuration is started with 2 MPI processes with a process working as master, and one Worker to perform heavier computational tasks.

Environment (MPE) library [17] in our parallel application to log custom events and perform further analysis. Next, as MPE logging is accompanied by very precise time stamps, we used output log traces created by MPE in clog2 format to profile all executions and extract the execution time used in all application phases described in Sect. 3.

Figure 7 shows the total CPU time used by all processes in each phase: read the buffer from disk, parse data, apply SNP caller algorithm (process), and finally

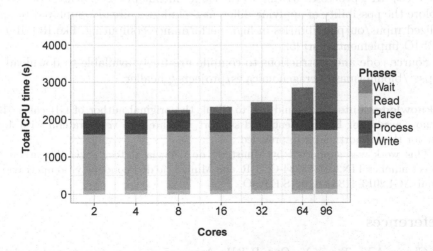

Fig. 7. Total CPU time used in each phase. Ideally, it should be equal in all executions independently of the number of processes.

write results to disk. It clearly shows the impact of contention on the I/O system when we scale up the number of MPI processes. Ideally, with no overhead, the sum of total execution time used by all the processes in each phase should remain constant, but we can observe an overhead in both read and write phases, but it is particularly relevant at the last one. Indeed, when a limited number of processes ($np < 64$) perform read and/or write operations, accumulated time used in all phases remains almost constant. Nevertheless, when we scale up the number of processes, the impact of I/O, specially in write operations, increases execution time more than 2x over the ideal using 96 processes.

We can conclude that when scaling up the number of MPI processes ($np > 64$), it ends in a situation with I/O contention during the write phase. In order to mitigate this situation, that leads in a poor scalability, future work should be oriented to improve this writing phase, in a way that results optimal to the underlying distributed file system characteristics.

5   Conclusions and Future Work

In this work we have described the parallelization of GH caller using a master-worker strategy with the MPI library. We have shown that our parallel implementation can provide a performance advantage using a data-intensive computing system (cluster), reaching a performance gain factor of 260x using 64 processes and additional optimizations with regard to the initial non-parallelized version. Although execution time can considerably be reduced by adding more computational resources, we measured a poor efficiency when we scale up the number of MPI processes above a certain limit. The main reason is that our implementation is not optimized for parallel I/O and cannot take advantage of existing advanced techniques in this field, thus leading to poor performance when there are many ($np > 64$) MPI processes writing to the same output file [2]. Future work could explore the possibility of applying different techniques already employed by specialized input/output libraries in high performance computing, like ROMIO (a MPI-IO implementation) [5].

Source code and instructions to compile are freely available to download at https://bioinformatics.cragenomica.es/projects/ghcaller.

Acknowledgments. We would like to thank the original author of GH caller [13], Bruno Nevado, for his comments and support. We are also very grateful with Joan Jené for the support and help provided.

This work was supported by Ministerio de Ciencia y Tecnología (Spain) under project number TIN2014-53234-C2-1-R, and Ministerio de Economía y Competitividad (grant AGL2013-41834-R) to S.E.R.-O.

References

1. Cheng, A.Y., Teo, Y.Y., Ong, R.T.H.: Assessing single nucleotide variant detection and genotype calling on whole-genome sequenced individuals. Bioinformatics **30**(12), 1707–1713 (2014)

2. Corbett, P., et al.: Overview of the MPI-IO Parallel I/O Interface. In: Jain, R., Werth, J., Browne, J.C. (eds.) Input/Output in Parallel and Distributed Computer Systems, vol. 362, pp. 127–146. Springer, Heidelberg (1996). doi:10.1007/978-1-4613-1401-1_5

3. Forum, M.P.: MPI: a message-passing interface standard. Technical report, Knoxville, TN, USA (1994)

4. Hohenlohe, P.A., Bassham, S., Etter, P.D., Stiffler, N., Johnson, E.A., Cresko, W.A.: Population genomics of parallel adaptation in threespine stickleback using sequenced RAD tags. PLoS Genet 6(2), e1000862 (2010)

5. Liao, W.K., Choudhary, A.N.: Dynamically adapting file domain partitioning methods for collective I/O based on underlying parallel file system locking protocols. In: SC 2008, p. 3. IEEE/ACM (2008). http://dblp.uni-trier.de/db/conf/sc/sc2008.html#LiaoC08

6. Knüpfer, A., Brunst, H., Doleschal, J., Jurenz, M., Lieber, M., Mickler, H., Müller, M.S., Nagel, W.E.: The vampir performance analysis tool-set. In: Resch, M., Keller, R., Himmler, V., Krammer, B., Schulz, A. (eds.) Tools for High Performance Computing, pp. 139–155. Springer, Heidelberg (2008). doi:10.1007/978-3-540-68564-7_9

7. Korneliussen, T., Albrechtsen, A., Nielsen, R.: ANGSD: analysis of next generation sequencing data. BMC Bioinform. 15(1), 356 (2014)

8. Li, H.: A statistical framework for SNP calling, mutation discovery, association mapping and population genetical parameter estimation from sequencing data. Bioinformatics 27(21), 2987–2993 (2011)

9. Li, H., Handsaker, B., Wysoker, A., Fennell, T., Ruan, J., Homer, N., Marth, G., Abecasis, G., Durbin, R.: 1000 genome project data processing subgroup: the sequence alignment/map format and samtools. Bioinformatics 25(16), 2078–2079 (2009)

10. Lynch, M.: Estimation of nucleotide diversity, disequilibrium coefficients, and mutation rates from high-coverage genome-sequencing projects. Mol. Biol. Evol. 25(11), 2409–2419 (2008)

11. Mardis, E.R.: A decade's perspective on DNA sequencing technology. Nature 470(7333), 198–203 (2011). http://dx.doi.org/10.1038/nature09796

12. Metzker, M.L.: Sequencing technologies - the next generation. Nat. Rev. Genet. 11(1), 31–46 (2010)

13. Nevado, B., Ramos-Onsins, S.E., Perez-Enciso, M.: Resequencing studies of non-model organisms using closely related reference genomes: optimal experimental designs and bioinformatics approaches for population genomics. Mol. Ecol. 23(7), 1764–1779 (2014)

14. Roesti, M., Hendry, A.P., Salzburger, W., Berner, D.: Genome divergence during evolutionary diversification as revealed in replicate lake-stream stickleback population pairs. Mol. Ecol. 21(12), 2852–2862 (2012)

15. Sun, X.H., Gustafson, J.L.: Toward a better parallel performance metric. Parallel Comput. 17(10–11), 1093–1109 (1991). http://dx.doi.org/10.1016/S0167-8191(05)80028-6

16. Wetterstrand, K.: DNA Sequencing Costs: Data from the NHGRI Genome Sequencing Program (GSP). http://www.genome.gov/sequencingcosts

17. Wu, C.E., Bolmarcich, A., Snir, M., Wootton, D., Parpia, F., Chan, A., Lusk, E., Gropp, W.: From trace generation to visualization: a performance framework for distributed parallel systems. In: Proceedings of SC 2000: High Performance Networking and Computing, November 2000

A Data Partitioning Model for Highly Heterogeneous Systems

S. Tabik[1,3(✉)], G. Ortega[2], E.M. Garzón[2], and D. Suárez[3]

[1] Department of Computer Architecture, University of Málaga, 29071 Málaga, Spain
[2] Department of Informatics, Agrifood Campus of International Excellence (ceiA3),
University of Almería, 04120 Almería, Spain
[3] gaZ, University of Zaragoza, 50018 Zaragoza, Spain
siham.tabik@gmail.com

Abstract. Last generation supercomputers running bioinformatics workloads are composed of multiple heterogeneous processing units, requiring intelligent workload distribution. This paper describes an accurate static workload balancing model capable of (i) efficiently balancing the workload with no significant overhead because only a static light offline profiling is required and (ii) deactivating slower devices. The effectiveness of the approach is experimentally validated using several representative bioinformatics workloads on three heterogeneous platforms.

Keywords: Heterogeneous systems · Multi-GPU, multi-CPU systems · Workload distribution · Data-partitioning model

1 Introduction and Motivation

Heterogeneous systems that include multi-core processors, GPUs (Graphics Processing Units) and other accelerators are becoming mainstream to continue improving the performance of parallel applications. However, partition the work among processing units, PUs, is challenging due to their asymmetry, resource contention, low bandwidth of the PCIe bus, etc. This work describes an efficient data-partitioning model tailored for data-parallel applications such as, linear algebra kernels and image processing applications commonly found on the bioinformatics domain.

Finding the optimal workload partitioning among PUs depends on the characteristics of the system, the size of the involved data, and the data-parallel application itself. Previous works make the partitioning decision based on the information obtained from an online or offline profiling of the application. Most strategies target integrated CPU-GPU chips or one discrete GPU based systems and assume that the execution time is a linear function of the problem size $T(v) = av + b$ [8] or even simpler $T(v) = av$ with $b = 0$ [3,5,10,16]. Our main observation is that using a time function per PU provides better results.

In this work, we provide a more accurate workload balancing model that (i) finds the optimal partition on systems with multiple accelerators, (ii) it is able

© Springer International Publishing AG 2017
F. Desprez et al. (Eds.): Euro-Par 2016 Workshops, LNCS 10104, pp. 468–479, 2017.
DOI: 10.1007/978-3-319-58943-5_38

to detect when a device is not worth to be included in the execution time, and (iii) it is simple to use in any hybrid system. The automatic mapping model consists of two stages, *learning stage* and *execution stage*. In the *learning stage*, a light off-line training is carefully crafted to capture the inter-relation between kernel and each one of the dissimilar devices then, the linear approximation of the execution time on each device is calculated and finally the obtained system of equations is solved to find the near-optimal distribution. In the *execution stage* the data-parallel code is executed with the calculated optimal partitioning.

This paper is organized as follows. The description of the proposed mapping model is given in Sect. 2. Its experimental verification on different heterogeneous platforms is shown in Sect. 3 and Sect. 4 concludes.

2 Related Work

Previous work can be divided into two broad categories: on-line and off-line.

On-line training based strategies [1,2]: The partition decision is made at runtime. These techniques are used when (i) the cost per *parallel-for* iteration is very dependent on the characteristics of the input data or/and (ii) the cost of the communications between different devices is either cheap or not needed. Those works are mainly limited by the problem size because they normally store all data in every device and distribute only the computation.

Off-line training based strategies [3,7–10,16]: They partition the data based on the information from previous real runs on different input sizes. These techniques provide optimal results for *parallel-for* with a stable cost per iteration and when data reallocation is avoided. In general, these works assume that the computing power among devices is similar and use an homogeneous model, $T(v) = av$, (where T represents time, a is a constant, and v is the work size), tested on only-CPU or CPUs plus single-GPU systems [3,9,10].

Luk *et al.* build a similar model with $T(v) = av + b$ to calculate the optimal partition as the point where the CPU and GPU fitting curves cross [8]. More complex models use heuristics and tree structures to calculate the optimal partition [7]. The most related paper to our work is [16] which proposes a data-partitioning strategy for multi-GPU multi-core platforms based on the assumption $T(v) = av$; however this approach neither considers the fixed cost of using a non-host processing unit nor can deactivate slow devices when they increase the total execution time. Besides, their simulation framework only includes processing units with similar computing power.

3 Preliminary Considerations

Algorithm 1.1 pseudo-code of a data-parallel application

```
for   t=0, t<N_t;  t++ //serial loop
  for k=0, k<N_k;  k++ //parallel-for
   do_work();
```

Most data-parallel applications can be expressed as a temporal loop that iterates over a spatial *parallel-for* as shown in Algorithm 1.1. The number of operations and memory accesses performed in each individual *parallel-for* iteration are similar and can be considered as the smallest unit of work. The performance model used for these applications, which expresses the execution time T as a function of the problem size v, $T(v) = a_i v + b_i$, was proven to be accurate on individual processing unit i [16], where:

v is the size of the input block of data.
a_i is the coefficient of the independent variable v.
b_i is the fixed initialization computational-cost we have to pay on each PUi.

On multi-GPU multi-core systems the speed of one device may depend on the load of others due to resource contention, therefore they cannot be considered as independent devices, and their execution time can not be measured separately. This work only considers parallel applications allowing flexible distribution of the data and including an optimized kernel for each device architecture.

We model multi-GPU multi-core platforms as a set of abstract PUs. A group of processing elements that execute the same kernel of the application will be represented in the model by an abstract PU. For example if a single-threaded kernel is used, then each CPU core executing this kernel will be represented as one abstract PU. If a multi-threaded kernel is executed in a group of CPU cores, these CPU cores will be grouped into one PU. A GPU is usually controlled by a host process that executes on a dedicated CPU core. Thus, the GPU together with its host CPU core will be considered as one PU.

4   Our Data-Partitioning Model

The main goal of this work is to find the near-optimal partition on a heterogenous system. Hence, given an data-parallel application, a problem size and hardware configuration, we aim at predicting the optimal workload to be assigned to each PU. To ease this discussion we reformulate this mapping problem into finding the optimal chunk sizes, $v(v_1, v_2, ..., v_n)$, to be assigned to each one of a total number of n PUs.

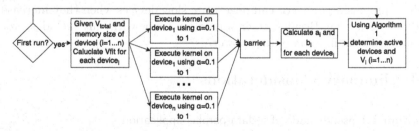

Fig. 1. Flow chart of the automatic data-partitioning.

We carefully design an empirical approach that predicts the execution time, $T(v)$, on each PU in terms of the chunk size v using a linear approximation. Then, we calculate the optimal chunk sizes to be assigned to each PU based on this model. A schematic illustration of the overall approach is depicted in Fig. 1.

4.1 The Learning Stage

It is well-known that *parallel-for* loops with little or no load unbalance are well-suited for both multi-core and accelerators. Therefore, we first need to accurately determine the linear function of the execution time on each asymmetric processing unit. The more accurate the profiling gets, the more precise the partition becomes. We use an off-line profiling measuring the time for multiple input sizes. To guarantee the reliability of these experiments, the measurements are repeated multiple times until the mean values lie in the interval with a confidence level $>= 95\%$.

Let us assume an initial input V_{total} that does not fit in the local memories of some processing units. On each asymmetric PU i we consider a maximum block size $V_{fit}^i = \alpha V_{total}$ that fits the local memory of that PU and we measure the time it takes to process at most 10 block sizes, αV_{fit}^i where $\alpha = 10\%, 20\%, ...100\%$. We start measuring the runtime of the smaller block of size $0,1 \times V_{fit}^i$ and gradually measure the processing time of the rest of chunk sizes. On accelerators, ideal starting block size would be a multiple of the number of cores inside the accelerator. For the applications used in the analysis and verification of the model, we found that three measurements using three problem sizes are enough for an accurate load balancing.

In order to make this stage as short as possible, we profile only the first serial-loop iterations, which represent generally less than 5% of the total serial iterations. The learning process of the first iterations is performed only on dissimilar PUs. The built models of individual PUs can be stored in a kind of database so that they can be reused whenever needed.

4.2 Model for Finding the Optimal Mapping

The time function $T(v) = a_i v + b_i$ for each PU $i = 1, ..., n$ is estimated using a least-squares approximation. The desired balanced scenario occurs when all the involved n devices finish the computation at the same time T. Let the assignment $v_1, \ldots, v_n$ refer to the block sizes that reach execution time $\approx T$ on the PUs. The optimization problem to find the optimal assignment has the following ingredients.

a_i, b_i Parameters of the linear model, computed once per kernel per dissimilar PUs. Calculated internally by the model.

V_{total} Total volume to be mapped. Input of the model.

$v_i \geq 0$ Unknown variable describing the optimal volume to be assigned to PU i. Output of the model

T Execution time on the Heterogeneous System (HS) for the optimal mapping

We intend to minimize the total runtime on the heterogeneous platform, $\min T$, given the assumed relation:

$$\begin{cases} T(v_i) = a_i v_i + b_i & \text{if } v_i > 0 \\ T(v_i) = T(v_j) \equiv T & i, j \in 1, ..., n \\ V_{total} = \sum_i v_i & i \in 1, ..., n \end{cases} \qquad (1)$$

Equation (1) defines a linear system of equations with $n + 1$ unknowns and is the key to determine the optimal execution time T and the corresponding mapping $v_1, ..., v_n$. T represents the optimal execution time on the heterogenous system when the optimal mapping is used and can be estimated from the parameters a_i and b_i as follows:

$$\begin{cases} T \equiv T(V_{total}) = a_H V_{total} + b_H & \text{where} \\ a_H = \sum \frac{1}{a_i}^{-1} \\ b_H = a_H \sum \frac{b_i}{a_i} \\ v_i = \frac{T - b_i}{a_i} \, i \in 1, ..., n \end{cases} \qquad (2)$$

Our aim is to determine the subset Q of $\{1, ..., n\}$ of **active** PUs and the distribution $v_i > 0$ within this set. The parameter b_i is a key parameter in our model to detect too slow PUs. It represents the cost that we must pay for activating PU i. If the computation cost of a PU is lower than the fixed cost b_i, i.e., $T - b_i < 0$, it will be labeled as inactive by setting v_i to zero $v_i = 0$. Besides, if the assigned volume v_i is smaller than the volume needed for one unit-of-work the PU i will be also deactivated. More deactivation criteria can be included in our model according to the objectives of the implementation, like for example criteria for energy optimization.

The optimal mapping will be then computed only for the set of active PUs. The procedure that finds the optimal data-partitioning according to the deactivation criteria is provided below in Algorithm 1.

Algorithm 1. $v(v_1, ..., v_n) = Adaptive\ Mapping(V_{total}, a_i, b_i)$

---

1. *Given* $Q = \{1, ..., n\}$, set of active devices
2. $a_H = \sum \frac{1}{a_i}^{-1}$ and $b_H = a_H \sum \frac{b_i}{a_i}$
3. $T = T(V_{total}) = a_H V_{total} + b_H$
4. **while** $\max_{i \in Q} b_i > T$
5.   remove j with $b_j = \max_{i \in Q} b_i$ from Q
6. $n = n - 1$
7.   Update a_H , b_H
8. $T = T(V_{total}) = a_H V_{total} + b_H$
9. **endwhile**
10. for all $i \in Q$, $v_i = \frac{T - b_i}{a_i}$

---

5   Experiments and Evaluation

This section provides the analysis and validation of our mapping model using multiple data sizes and multiple system configurations. The heterogeneous system used in this study includes the GPUs and multi-core described in Table 1. We consider three platforms based on different combinations of these PUs as follows.

- Platform 1: One CPU core of the Intel Quad Core CPU Q9450 (labeled as cpu0) and two GPUs, GeForce GTX 480 (labeled as GPU0) and Tesla C2070 (labeled as GPU1).
- Platform 2: Three GPUs, GeForce GTX 480 (GPU0), Tesla C2070 (GPU1) and Tesla S2050 (GPU2).
- Platform 3: Two CPU cores of the Intel Quad Core CPU Q9450 (cpu1) and two GPU devices, GeForce GTX 480 (GPU0) and Tesla C2070 (GPU1).

Table 1. Characteristics of the GPUs and multi-core included in the used heterogenous system.

	GeForce GTX 480	Tesla C2070	Tesla S2050	Intel Quad CPU Q9450
Labeled as	GPU0	GPU1	GPU2	cpu0(1 core)/ cpu1(2 cores)
Device memory (GB)	2	6	2	7
Clock rate (GHz)	1.40	1.15	1.15	2.66
Memory bandwidth (GBytes/sec)	177.4	144	148	4.55
Multiprocessors	15	14	14	-
Cores	480	448	448	4
Compute capability	1.5	2	2	-

For testing our approach, we consider the data-parallel applications described in Table 2. Two widely used algebra kernels, the vector vector product, saxpy, and the sparse matrix vector product, SpMV [13,15]. In addition to Anisotropic Nonlinear Diffusion (AND) method which is a complex application for de-noising 3D-images in bio-informatics and structural biology [11,12]. AND iterates over a noisy 3D-image by preserving its edges until it is completely filtered. AND has an iterative structure that allows integrating the learning strategy proposed in this work. For the experiments, we used NVIDIA CUDA (6.5 version) and mpicc compilers with −O2 as optimization option. Our parallel implementation creates one MPI-process per target PUs. Then, each process executes the optimized kernel for the specific PU architecture. We consider the best thread-block configuration [14].

Table 2. Applications used for the validation of our mapping model.

Application	Description	Data type
saxpy	Multiplication of a constant *alpha* by vector x plus vector y, $y := alpha * x + y$	Double and complex numbers
SpMV	Sparse Matrix Vector multiplication $y = Ax$ where A is a sparse matrix and x and y are vectors	Double and complex numbers
AND	Anisotropic Nonlinear Diffusion (AND) method which float efficiently de-noises 3D-tomographic images with the property of conserving the edges of the image	

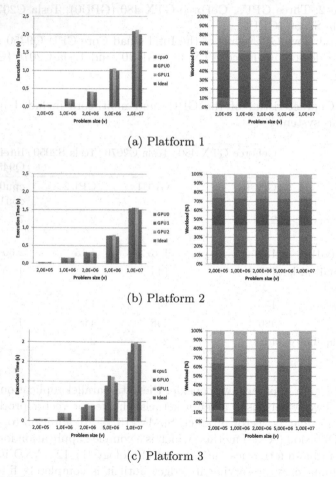

(a) Platform 1

(b) Platform 2

(c) Platform 3

Fig. 2. (left) The execution time of saxpy and (right) workload distribution on each PU of Platforms 1, 2 and 3 using five data volumes.

The proposed methodology balances the workload of the applications under test by following these steps: First, in the learning stage, saxpy, SpMV and AND applications are evaluated using several instances of the problem size on each

PU. For saxpy and SpMV, we used 100.000, 1.000.000 and 5.000.000 problem sizes. Similarly, for AND, we used the execution time for three 3D-image sizes $dimX \times dimY \times 16$, $dimX \times dimY \times 32$ and $dimX \times dimY \times 64$, where $dimX \times dimY$ is the size of one plan of the input 3D-image. These measurements of the execution time were enough to build an accurate performance model for saxpy, SpMV and AND.

Afterwards, in the execution stage, the model defines several hybrid configurations, labeled as Platforms 1, 2 and 3, and takes into account the aforementioned measurements to obtains T for each configuration and calculates the size of the chunk v_i that must be assigned to each PU i. Finally, the applications are launched in platforms 1, 2, and 3 using the calculated v_i for $i = 1, ..., n$.

Figures 2, 3 and 4 show the execution time that each PU takes to carry out the workload assigned by the model for saxpy, SpMV and AND for several

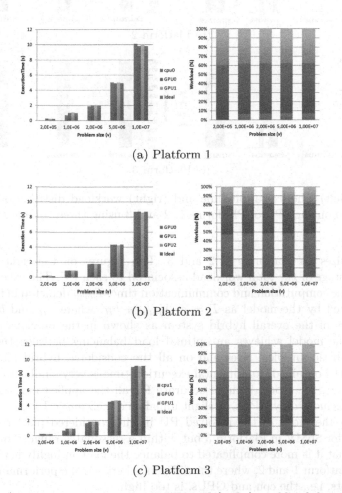

(a) Platform 1

(b) Platform 2

(c) Platform 3

Fig. 3. (left) The execution time of SpMV and (right) workload distribution on each PU of Platforms 1, 2 and 3 using five data volumes.

476   S. Tabik et al.

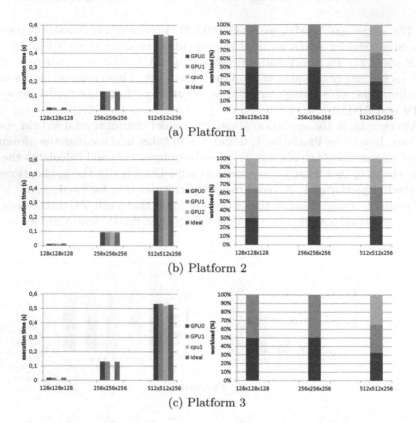

(a) Platform 1

(b) Platform 2

(c) Platform 3

Fig. 4. (left) The execution time and (right) workload distribution of AND-application on each PU of Platforms 1, 2 and 3 using three volume sizes.

problem sizes on Platforms 1, 2 and 3. The Figures on the right side show the percentage of the total workload associated to each PU. The execution time includes the computation and communication time. T_{ideal} depicted in the figures, is calculated by the model as $T = a_H V_{total} + b_H$, where a_H and b_H are the parameters of the overall hybrid system as shown in the previous section. In general, the model achieves an optimal load balancing between the involved PUs for all the problem sizes and on all the considered hybrid platforms. In addition, the obtained experimental execution time is very similar to the T_{ideal}. In particular, the model is more accurate for all the applications on Platform 2, which includes only GPUs. A slight unbalance (i.e., $max(|T_{ideal} - T_i|)/T_{ideal}$, where i is the index of the involved PU in the considered platform <0%) is produced for SpMV in Platform 3 but within a reasonable range. This is due to the fact that it is more complicated to balance the load on highly heterogeneous such as Platform 1 and 2, where the difference between the performance of their components, i.e., the cpu and GPUs, is too high.

The capacity of our model to deactivate too slow PUs can be observed in Fig. 2(a), where cpu0 is deactivated for all problem sizes and Fig. 4(a) and (c) in Platforms 1 and 3, where cpu0 and cpu1 are deactivated for the problem sizes $128 \times 128 \times 128$ and $256 \times 256 \times 256$. In those cases, the model chooses to deactivate cpu0 in Platform 1 or cpu1 in Platform 2 because the assigned volume is either smaller than the volume of one unit of work or because the b parameter of this PUs is larger than the hybrid ideal execution time T_{ideal}.

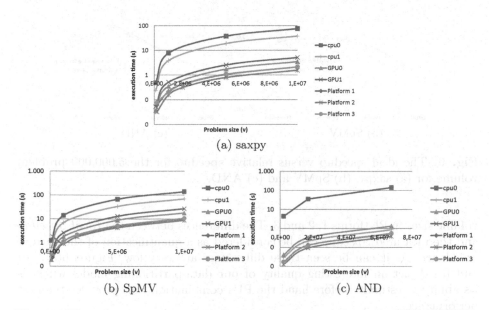

(a) saxpy

(b) SpMV   (c) AND

Fig. 5. The execution time of each platform, i.e., cpu0, cpu1, GPU0, GPU1, Platforms 1, 2 and 3, takes to carry out the overall work for the 5.000.000 problem volume for (a) saxpy, (b) SpMV and (c) AND.

To compare the heterogeneity of the used hybrid platforms and the involved PUs, Figs. 5(a), (b) and (c) show the response time of saxpy, SpMV and AND, using different problem sizes, on cpu0, cpu1, GPU0, GPU1 and Platforms 1, 2 and 3. As it can be observed, it is always worth using hybrid platforms (together with a good load balancing strategy) than individual accelerators such as GPU0 in spite of their heterogeneity and the challenge of load balancing. As we can see the optimal performance is achieved on Platforms 1, 2 and 3 in all tests.

Several metrics have been defined for evaluation and comparison purposes on heterogeneous systems [4,6]. In this analysis, the *Ideal Relative Speedup* is considered. It is calculated as the of ratio between the run-time on the fastest device when the problem of size v is executed and $T_{ideal}(v)$, which represents the estimated run-time on the hybrid platform.

Figures 6(a), (b) and (c) show a comparison between the *Ideal Relative Speedup* and the *Relative Speedup* for saxpy, SpMV and AND, using the largest

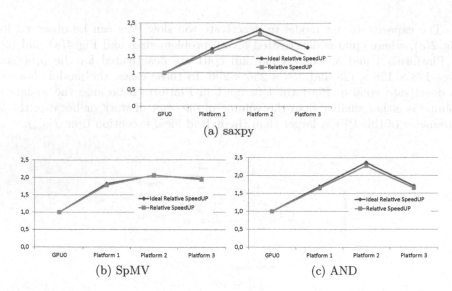

Fig. 6. The ideal speedup versus relative speedup for the 5.000.000 problem volume for (a) saxpy, (b) SpMV and (c) AND.

volume size, on Platforms 1, 2 and 3. The differences between the *Ideal Speedup* and the measured *Speedup* can be considered as a quantification of the current unbalance. As it can be seen these differences are very low. Figures 6(a), (b) and (c) depict an interesting quality of our data-partitioning model which is its ability to estimate before hand the PUs combination that provides the best performance.

6   Conclusions and Future Work

Selecting both the processing units and the amount of work each should perform is a challenging task. This paper proposes a work-balance strategy that helps overcoming these two difficulties. Namely, it builds a global performance model with minimum training enabling to find a close to minimum execution time. Our detailed results show that the model is within less than 3% percent of an ideal unrealistic balancing strategy. As future work, we plan to compare our work to Zhong *et al.* [16] to showcase the advantages of our method.

Acknowledgements. This work was partially supported by the Spanish Ministry of Science throughout projects TIN2010-16144, TIN15-66680 and TIN2012-37483, by J. Andalucía through projects P12-TIC-301, P11-TIC7176 and TIC-8260 and by the European Reg. Dev. Fund (ERDF).

References

1. Augonnet, C., Thibault, S., Namyst, R., Wacrenier, P.A.: StarPU: a unified platform for task scheduling on heterogeneous multicore architectures. Concurr. Comput.-Pract. E **23**(2), 187–198 (2011)
2. Barik, R., Kaleem, R., Majeti, D., Lewis, B.T., Shpeisman, T., Hu, C., Ni, Y., Adl-Tabatabai, A.R.: Efficient mapping of irregular C++ applications to integrated GPUs. In: Proceedings of IEEE/ACM CGO, p. 33. ACM (2014)
3. Belviranli, M.E., Bhuyan, L.N., Gupta, R.: A dynamic self-scheduling scheme for heterogeneous multiprocessor architectures. ACM Trans. Archit. Code Optim. **9**(4), 57 (2013)
4. Chen, Y., Sun, X.H., Wu, M.: Algorithm-system scalability of heterogeneous computing. J. Parallel Distrib. Comput. **68**(11), 1403–1412 (2008)
5. Kaleem, R., Barik, R., Shpeisman, T., Lewis, B.T., Hu, C., Pingali, K.: Adaptive heterogeneous scheduling for integrated GPUs. In: Proceedings of PACT, pp. 151–162. ACM (2014)
6. Kalinov, A.: Scalability of heterogeneous parallel systems. Programm. Comput. Softw. **32**(1), 1–7 (2006)
7. Lee, J., Samadi, M., Park, Y., Mahlke, S.: Transparent CPU-GPU collaboration for data-parallel kernels on heterogeneous systems. In: Proceedings of PACT, pp. 245–256. IEEE Press (2013)
8. Luk, C.K., Hong, S., Kim, H.: Qilin: exploiting parallelism on heterogeneous multiprocessors with adaptive mapping. In: Proceedings of IEEE/ACM MICRO, pp. 45–55. IEEE (2009)
9. Martínez, J., Almeida, F., Garzón, E., Acosta, A., Blanco, V.: Adaptive load balancing of iterative computation on heterogeneous nondedicated systems. J. Supercomput. **58**(3), 385–393 (2011)
10. Martínez, J.A., Garzón, E.M., Plaza, A., García, I.: Automatic tuning of iterative computation on heterogeneous multiprocessors with ADITHE. J. Supercomput. **58**(2), 151–159 (2011)
11. Tabik, S., Garzón, E.M., García, I., Fernández, J.J.: High performance noise reduction for biomedical multidimensional data. Digit. Sig. Process. **17**(4), 724–736 (2007)
12. Tabik, S., Garzón, E., García, I., Fernandez, J.: Implementation of anisotropic nonlinear diffusion for filtering 3D images in structural biology on SMP clusters. In: Proceedings of ParCo, vol. 33, pp. 727–734 (2005)
13. Tabik, S., Ortega, G., Garzón, E.M.: Performance evaluation of kernel fusion BLAS routines on the GPU: iterative solvers as case study. J. Supercomput. **70**(2), 577–587 (2014)
14. Tabik, S., Peemen, M., Guil, N., Corporaal, H.: Demystifying the 16 × 16 threadblock for stencils on the GPU. Concurr. Comput.-Pract. E **27**(18), 5557–5573 (2015)
15. Vázquez, F., Ortega, G., Fernández, J.J., Garzón, E.M.: Improving the performance of the sparse matrix vector product with GPUs. In: 10th IEEE International Conference on Computer and Information Technology, CIT 2010, pp. 1146–1151. IEEE Computer Society (2010)
16. Zhong, Z., Rychkov, V., Lastovetsky, A.: Data partitioning on multicore and multi-GPU platforms using functional performance models. IEEE Trans. Comput. **64**, 2506–2518 (2015)

Seamless HPC Integration of Data-Intensive KNIME Workflows via UNICORE

Richard Grunzke[1]($\boxtimes$), Florian Jug[2]($\boxtimes$), Bernd Schuller[3], René Jäkel[1],
Gene Myers[2], and Wolfgang E. Nagel[1]

[1] Technische Universität Dresden, Dresden, Germany
`richard.grunzke@tu-dresden.de`
[2] Max Planck Institute for Cell Biology and Genetics, Dresden, Germany
`jug@mpi-cbg.de`
[3] Forschungszentrum Jülich, Jülich, Germany

Abstract. Biological research is increasingly dependent on analyzing vast amounts of microscopy datasets. Technologies such as Fiji/ImageJ2 and KNIME support knowledge extraction from biological data by providing a large set of configurable algorithms and an intuitive pipeline creation and execution interface. The increasing complexity of required analysis pipelines and the growing amounts of data to be processed nurture the desire to run existing pipelines on HPC (High Performance Computing) systems. Here, we propose a solution to this challenge by presenting a new HPC integration method for KNIME (Konstanz Information Miner) using the UNICORE middleware (Uniform Interface to Computing Resources) and its automated data processing feature. We designed the integration to be efficient in processing large data workloads on the server side. On the client side it is seamless and lightweight to only minimally increase the complexity for the users. We describe our novel approach and evaluate it using an image processing pipeline that could previously not be executed on an HPC system. The evaluation includes a performance study of the induced overhead of the submission process and of the integrated image processing pipeline based on a large amount of data. This demonstrates how our solution enables scientists to transparently benefit from vast HPC resources without the need to migrate existing algorithms and pipelines.

Keywords: KNIME · UNICORE · High Performance Computing · Integration

1 Introduction

BioImage Computing is central for many biological research projects [3,4,11], and many such projects share two common problems: (*i*) Data is large and analyzing it is time consuming, and (*ii*) both, data as well as the required data

---

R. Grunzke and F. Jug—These authors contributed equally.

F. Desprez et al. (Eds.): Euro-Par 2016 Workshops, LNCS 10104, pp. 480–491, 2017.
DOI: 10.1007/978-3-319-58943-5_39

analysis chain, changes in response to progress in ongoing research projects. Therefore, automated or semi-automated solutions are aiming at minimizing manual user intervention and overall runtime in order to solve these problems.

Dynamic research environments require short execution times of automated analysis pipelines and constant revisions of these pipelines to meet the projects needs. This poses a challenge for smaller research groups or institutes that simply cannot effort to employ dedicated HPC experts. It is desirable therefore to find solutions where the same person who implemented the initial analysis pipeline can also deploy it to available cluster hardware.

As delimitation to previous methods that enable the execution of KNIME workflows on HPC systems, the following methods are mentioned. One solution, the KNIME Cluster Execution module [13], is limited as it is proprietary and only enables access to cluster resources in conjunction with the Oracle Grid Engine. Another solution that is generic in scope converts KNIME workflows to gUSE workflows [5] to execute them on HPC resources. gUSE/WS-PGRADE [12] is a framework to build advanced HPC-enabled science gateways such as MoS-Grid [14]. Due to the technological requirements of such science gateways and that KNIME is our target platform, this second alternative approach is also unsuitable in our use case. KNIME is also capable of executing jobs via Hadoop-like frameworks. Instead of our focus on arbitrary analysis workloads, this approach focuses on sub-workflows with problem structures that needs to fit the framework.

In this article we present a novel HPC access method that allows biological researchers with no HPC infrastructure knowledge to deploy and execute their analysis pipelines to a broad range of existing HPC systems. Users of the proposed setup are not required to learn any new language or HPC concept - they do, in fact, not even have to leave their local every day analysis environment (ImageJ2/KNIME). Regarding the technical realization we base our distribution method on UNICORE, which can be installed on any cluster or HPC resource. We have extended UNICORE's existing Data Oriented Processing [21] module with a parameter sweep feature to be capable of starting multiple parameterized jobs (see Sect. 2.3). This is utilized within the rule we designed that triggers the KNIME workflow execution on the HPC resources (see Sect. 2.3). For KNIME we developed all necessary modules for receiving and interpreting parameters for loading and fractionating the data (see Sect. 2.1). We provide various convenience functions that aim at making the entire process as intuitive and generic as possible. In Sect. 3 we present an evaluation of our approach including a thorough performance analysis.

2   Utilized Methods and Implementation

In this section we first describe the BioImage tools Fiji/ImageJ2 and the KNIME workflow application. Then, the UNICORE HPC middleware is described that greatly facilitates the utilization of HPC systems. We conclude with a description of how we integrated KNIME with HPC resources via UNICORE. This integration enables applying scientists to easily and efficiently utilize vast HPC resources from within their accustomed KNIME workflow application.

2.1 Fiji/ImageJ2 and KNIME

Image analysis tools in biological research are diverse and heterogeneous [3]. Although our proposed method is applicable for most if not for all available tools, here we constrain us to examples using Fiji/ImageJ2 [17] and KNIME (Konstanz Information Miner) [2]. While Fiji/ImageJ2 is the de-facto standard for working with microscopic datasets in biological research [17,18,20], using KNIME for image analysis applications is a more recent trend we believe to become increasingly popular in the near future.

Fiji, by itself, is a distribution of plugins and features for ImageJ [20] and ImageJ2. KNIME, initially a dedicated data mining and workflow management system [2], also developed into a potent image processing tool [3]. The developers of both systems, Fiji/ImageJ2 and KNIME, use a common image processing and analysis library for storing and operating on image data, the ImgLib2 [15]. This enables developers to write plugins that can be used in Fiji as well as in KNIME without additional work or code. Today, a plethora of image analysis methods via plugins are available.

The workflow we use throughout this paper is a data-preprocessing pipeline. It loads microscope images sequences acquired using a microfluidic device called 'Mother Machine' [9,22]. Each image sequence contains multiple experimental setups and the main task of the preprocessing is to enhance image quality and automatically find all regions of interest for extracting each individual experiment for further processing [10].

Parallelization of the overall computation is performed along two axes. Our proposed system submits multiple jobs and assigns equal amounts of data to be processed to each such job. Each image sequence contains multiple experimental setups and the main task of the preprocessing is to enhance image quality and automatically find all regions of interest for extracting each individual experiment for further processing. On top of that, each job can make use of multiple concurrently running threads to further split the data into smaller junks. The latter is implemented directly from within the KNIME workflow by using the 'Parallel Chunk Loop' construction that is freely available in the 'Virtual Nodes' package on the KNIME update site. While a regular loop executes its body for each dataset given, a 'Parallel Chunk Loop' performs for-loop-unrolling using a thread pool of configurable size.

Like many tasks in BioImage Computing, parallelization can be achieved by independently operating on individual images of a given dataset. A system that allows users, without previous exposure to cluster computing, to easily design such a processing pipeline in Fiji/ImageJ2 or KNIME was never done before. Our proposed system achieves this via the HPC middleware UNICORE. This constitutes an important step in unleashing the huge potential of HPC in various use cases in BioImaging and beyond with many potential users.

2.2 HPC Middleware UNICORE

UNICORE (Uniform Interface to Computing Resources) [1] is a middleware for building federated computing solutions. It focuses on providing seamless and secure access to heterogeneous resources such as high-performance computers and compute clusters, remote data storage and file systems. UNICORE is deployed and used in a variety of settings, from small projects to large, multi-site infrastructures involving HPC resources of the highest category. The latter category includes the European PRACE research infrastructure [16], the US XSEDE research infrastructure [23] and the EU flagship Human Brain Project [7].

UNICORE comprises the full middleware software stack from clients to various server components for accessing compute or data resources. Its basic principles are abstraction of resource-specific details, openness, interoperability, operating system independence, security, and autonomy of resource providers. In addition, it is easy to install, configure, administrate and available under a free and open source BSD license.

UNICORE offers services such as job submission and job management, data access and file transfer, metadata management and workflows. It abstracts the details of job submission, batch system commands, heterogeneous cluster properties and much more, allowing for a much simpler user interaction with HPC and data resources. Users typically use one of the UNICORE or custom clients to interact with the system to create and submit jobs. For the present use case, a different, data-driven way of interaction with UNICORE is employed and extended, which is described in detail in the next section.

2.3 Workflow Integration on a Cluster

We performed the integration of KNIME along the workflow that is introduced in Sect. 2.1. We encapsulate the workflow logic for preprocessing the 'Mother Machine' procedure in a meta-Node called 'Workflow Logic'. We have then loaded another Meta-Node called 'Data Setup' (see Fig. 1). This node serves as a generic data loading and filtering module. The only input required from

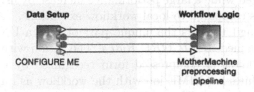

Fig. 1. Submission of a KNIME workflow. After the pipeline is assembled by the user he might choose to hide it in a so called Meta-Node, here called 'Workflow Logic'. After adding the predefined node 'Data Setup', the workflow is cluster ready in two simple steps: (1) the location of the data must be configured, and (2) the workflow must be exported to the submission directory via the standard KNIME export graphical dialog.

the user is the location of the data to be processed. In order to start the workflow on the cluster at hand it suffices to export it to the designated submission folder. This folder is exported from the cluster filesystem and mounted locally on the workstation of the user. The authentication of the user is done transparently by re-using the authentication already done during the local mounting of the network folder. Subsequently, UNICORE executes the user workflows on the cluster under the login of the specific user who submitted the workflow. Below we describe in detail how such a folder is to be configured.

Submitting and running Fiji/ImageJ2 workflows is achieved by very similar means. As mentioned in Sect. 2.1, every ImgeJ2 plugin is also a KNIME node. Therefore one can assemble a sequence of Fiji plugin calls from within KNIME and use the same procedure as described above. This possibility does, of course, not exist for all available tools and functions. Still, as long as the tool of choice is capable of storing a full processing pipeline for later execution our proposed UNICORE method applies.

To enable such easy job submissions and interact with the HPC cluster, the UNICORE feature called "Data Oriented Processing" [21] was used and extended for efficient parameter sweeps to enable the execution of multiple jobs per rule evaluation instead of just one. Here, the UNICORE server is set up to periodically scan a user's specific directory according to a set of user-defined rules. When new files are detected, the UNICORE server executes any matching rules, which lead to the automatic creation and submission of the HPC jobs. The rules are stored in a file in the submission folder. Here, we allow for two possible scenarios. The users themselves provide a rule for the execution of a given workflow. Otherwise, a system administrator provides a rule using specifications how to execute the workflow and how data handling and job creation needs to be performed by UNICORE.

During configuration of the rule, two opposing option have to be balanced. The first is to highly optimize the rule to get the best performance for a specific workflow. Such an optimization might to negatively impact the performance of other workflows and also decreases the usability as one optimized rule for every workflow has to be provided. The second option is find one or a few reasonable rule configurations that fit many workflows at once. This way the complexity for the user is minimized while a large performance increase by using HPC resources can be expected as compared to local workflow executions.

The code Listing 1.1 shows the unique part of such a UNICORE rule that is stored in a file named *.UNICORE_Rules*. The action within the rule is executed when a workflow in compressed form recognized by UNICORE. In our case the action defines a KNIME job with the workflow as import and parameters to steer the execution. The parameter k (line 14) defines that parameter sweep. In this example the job is created ten times (k from 0 to 9). The input dataset (parameter l in line 13) is preprocessed by ten KNIME instances processing independently one of the given chunks. Parameter n (line 15) declares how many instances are executed, whereas w (line 16) denotes the location of the imported input workflow from within the specific UNICORE job. Parameter *tr* (line 18) is the path and name of the workflow that triggered the action. Within the *Resources* (lines 19–22) section the specific job requirements are defined. According to these, UNICORE automatically requests fitting resources from the batch system. For the measurements in Sect. 3.4 up to 100 of such actions (lines 6–23) are activated to trigger KNIME instances.

Listing 1.1. The central section of the UNICORE rule is shown which, among other things, governs how an action is defined and triggered.

```
{                                                                   1
DirectoryScan: { IncludeDirs: ["."], "Interval": "30", },          2
Rules: [ {                                                          3
Name: BioHPCMeasurements_2880_1 ,                                   4
Match: ".*.zip",                                                    5
Action: { Type: BATCH, Job: {                                       6
  Name: knime_headless ,                                            7
  Imports: [{ From: "file://${UC_FILE_PATH}",                       8
              To: workflow.zip },],                                 9
  ApplicationName: knime,                                          10
  ApplicationVersion: 2.11.3_headless ,                            11
  Parameters: {                                                    12
    l: "/lustre/ssd/grunzke/2880_1",                               13
    k: { From: 0, To: 9, Step: 1 },                                14
    n: "10",                                                       15
    w: "../workflow.zip",                                          16
    t: "8",                                                        17
    tr: "${UC_FILE_PATH}",},                                       18
  Resources: {                                                     19
    Memory: 20664M, CPUs: 8,                                       20
    Runtime: 1h, Queue: haswell ,                                  21
    CPUsPerNode: 8,}},},                                           22
}, ... ],}                                                         23
```

As mentioned, the workflow is exported graphically from within KNIME to a given network folder from where it is picked up by the UNICORE submission system. All HPC resources that are attached via UNICORE are available. Depending on the rule, either workflows are submitted to a specific HPC system or UNICORE submits to an arbitrary HPC system that fits the workflow requirements configured in the rule file. In the code Listing 1.1, no specific system is configured otherwise the "Site" option would be defined. All this is transparent to KNIME. Following a specific rule defined in the submission folder, a large number of computing jobs can be seamlessly distributed over the cluster utilizing the batch system transparently.

3   Results

In the following we present the results of our research. First, we discuss how our approach is integrated from a user- and cluster-centric perspective. Second, the number of cores that can be efficiently utilized is identified. Then, the overhead induced be the UNICORE middleware is evaluated. Finally, the number of concurrently processed data is scaled up and evaluated.

3.1   Seamlessness Cluster Integration

A major motivation of our research is to enable the use of large computing infrastructures from within the workflow application KNIME. In the following, we discuss how we have achieved this from two different perspectives.

From a **user-centric perspective**, we achieved mainly two goals: (i) setting up a KNIME workflow submission system, which can be directly used from within KNIME, and (ii) the user does not require deeper knowledge of the HPC system at hand. Users are not obliged to use a specific job scheduling system or have to adopt to a different one used with the HPC infrastructure at hand. Support for various scheduling systems and arbitrary HPC infrastructure is an integral part of UNICORE. When a KNIME user finishes the design of a BioImage pipeline, the workflow can be run on a single workstation, but can now also easily be extended for cluster execution via our generic data handling node (see Fig. 1).

From a **cluster-centric perspective**, the UNICORE middleware monitors a directory for new submissions. The specified rule defines that when a valid KNIME workflows arrives, the submission and execution is automatically triggered. The rule defines the computing task that executes the KNIME workflow on the HPC resources. KNIME is required to be installed on the HPC system and configured in order to be executed in headless mode without graphical user interface. For a specific workflow representation the rule has to be written and tested just once. This enables users to continuously submit workflows for different input data sets to HPC systems and from within their working environment.

3.2   Evaluation of Job Scaling

In order to determine good parameters for the creation of individual jobs on the cluster the number of worker threads for the KNIME workflow is varied. The user can specify the location of the input images to be reconstructed and the number of threads to be used by the KNIME workflow engine.

As discussed in the previous Sect. 2.1, the user can graphically adjust the number of worker threads and therefore the degree of parallelization of individual jobs. The measurements for the runtime estimation use the dataset (2,880 input images and 70,000 output images with a total of 17 GB), a varying the number of worker threads and the overall job runtime was recorded. The HPC nodes used for this estimation are equipped with two Intel Xeon CPUs (E5-2680) with 12 cores each and a local SSD-based filesystem was used during measurements.

From the total run time, the mean processing time per image was calculated and is shown in Fig. 2 on the left side. As can be seen in the figure, the workflow can make use of additional worker threads in the reconstruction and can be reduced to slightly over one second per image (within statistical errors). Starting the given workflow with a larger number of worker threads does not further decrease the mean reconstruction time per image and a value of 8 worker threads seems to be a good trade-off value for minimal runtime per job and efficiency.

Figure 2 on the right side shows the speedup based on the runtime behavior shown on the left side. Also shown is the theoretical linear speedup with respect to the runtime (red line). In general the workload on the system induced by the workflow is rather I/O intense. Therefore, some deviation from the theoretical linear behavior is to be expected. To lower this impact we used local SSD-based storage at the compute node to minimize the I/O effect. As discussed, the increase in the number of threads for computation does not improve the runtime behaviour for values larger than 8 threads, and for the next measurement series we chose this value as default for this particular workflow.

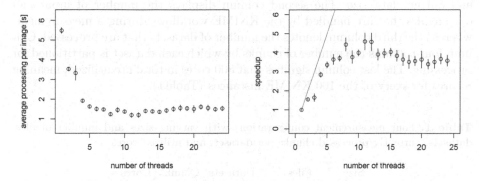

Fig. 2. Evaluation of the number of individual number of threads. The left plot displays the mean processing time per image for a given subset of image data with varying numbers of threads for the Fiji/ImageJ2 KNIME workflow including error bars. The right plot shows the calculated speedup including error bars of the Fiji/ImageJ2 KNIME workflow with a varying number of worker threads per job. The red line displays the theoretical linear speedup. (Color figure online)

3.3 Middleware Induced Overhead

The utilization of UNICORE with its triggering feature induces an overhead in the overall process. We estimate this overhead by measuring the time from which a workflow submission to the corresponding job submission time to the scheduler. One part of the overhead is the time needed for the middleware to register the new workflow in the directory. To reduce unnecessary communication overhead, a time interval for update checks is set to 30 s, which defines the maximum period for the middleware to recognize an new workflow. The second part of the overhead is the time period required by the middleware to execute methods to create compute jobs based on the workflow rule and to send those jobs to the scheduler. The first time measurement was triggered by exporting the workflow to the submission folder. Via the *scontrol* command the relevant submission time was obtained from the SLURM scheduler. The additional middleware overhead was therefore assessed by the difference between these two times. To estimate the variation in the process, the measurement was repeated ten times and in average a time of 27.2 s is the mean additional overhead induced by the UNICORE middleware.

3.4   Runtimes for Increasingly Large Datasets

This measurement series determines how our approach along the previously introduced BioImaging pipeline behaves at a large scale. The number of input and output files is scaled up to 7.488 million files with a total data emergence of up to 1.76 TB. The following table lists the configuration of the individual measurements which were repeated five times each. The size is the combined input and output data size. The second column displays the number of input and output files that are handled by the KNIME workflows during a measurement, whereas the third column denotes the number of datasets that are processed. Column four contains the number of chunks by which each dataset is partitioned for processing. The last column signifies that 800 cores in total are utilized, meaning 8 cores for every of the 100 KNIME instances (Table 1).

Table 1. Four measurement configurations with varying sizes and number of files, datasets, currently processed chunks per dataset, and utilized cores.

Size	Files	Datasets	Chunks	Cores
0.17 TB	0.7488 M	10	10	800
0.35 TB	1.4976 M	20	5	800
0.88 TB	3.744 M	50	2	800
1.76 TB	7.488 M	100	1	800

In our evaluation the number of concurrent KNIME instances is limited to 100. Beyond that, the error rate starts to significantly increase as KNIME is currently not built to handle a high number of parallel instances due to synchronization issues and relying on shared temporary files. A number of issues were solved by switching off OSGI locking and increasing the synchronization interval in knimi.ini[1]. As determined in Sect. 3.2, 8 cores are utilized as this is a sound number for this workflow. In these measurements, HPC nodes (each with two Intel Xeon CPUs (E5-2680) with 12 cores each) were utilized. A local SSD-based filesystem was used for providing the input data and storing the resulting data.

Figure 3 shows that the measurements with up to 1.76 TB of data have a runtime of 1259, 1955, 4318, and 7154 s respectively while utilizing 800 cores in each setting. The error bars show a significant standard deviation. This is due to the fact that the KNIME instances are scheduled as jobs by the HPC

---

[1] "-Dosgi.locking = none", "-Djava.util.prefs.syncInterval = 2000000".

batchsystem at varying points in time due to varying utilization levels of the HPC system. The measurements show that our approach can either process one dataset in parallel with many individual chunks, or it can process many datasets in parallel. Processing the datasets of the largest measurements (1.76 TB) on a local workstation with 4 cores would take about 17 days of continuous processing. With our easy-to-use and HPC-enabled approach the processing time is significantly reduced to just 2 h.

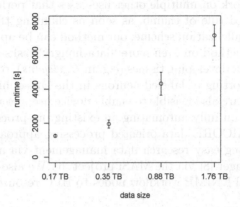

Fig. 3. Measurement results for concurrent processing of increasing number of datasets with an overall data size of up to 1.76 TB in 7.488 M files. The mean runtimes are 1259, 1955, 4318, and 7154 s respectively including error bars. These constitute a significant decrease in runtime compared to local processing on a workstation which would take about 17 days as compared to 2 h on the HPC system.

4   Conclusion

The presented work constitutes a novel approach to easily enable the use of large scale computing resources in the KNIME workflow application suite. Previously, KNIME users were very limited in using large computing infrastructures. Now, every major cluster scheduler is supported via the mature and widely used UNI-CORE HPC middleware. Enabling a high usability, users just need to graphically export a suitable KNIME workflow into a pre-configured directory and gets executed in parallel on the HPC cluster. To enable this, we extended the UNICORE middleware to support parameter sweeps via its data oriented processing feature, developed KNIME methods for interpreting parameters and fractionating input data, described how suitable workflows are created, and implemented it as a complete and generic approach along a concrete BioImaging use case. Performance measurements with up to 1.76 TB in 7.488 million files are presented that show highly favorable characteristics of our method. Trade-offs are required to either configure the method for high efficiency in a specific use case or for reasonable efficiency for multiple use cases. Alternatively, multiple directories can be configured for different use case scenarios offering more flexibility. Our approach can process either individual datasets in many parallel chunks, or many datasets in parallel, or a combination thereof. Now, large datasets in the range of terabytes can be processed in a matter of hours instead of weeks that were needed before.

5 Outlook

The preprocessing pipeline used throughout this work is a first example. We and our collaborators work on multiple other use-cases that perfectly fit our implemented system. As a rule of thumb, as soon as chunking the input in smaller pieces is a valid parallelization scheme, our method can be applied. We are planning to apply our method on even more 'data-hungry' tasks such as automated tracking pipelines for developing tissues (e.g. in *C. elegans*), or the segmentation, classification, and sorting of labeled neurons in the Drosophila fly brain. Other modes of operation are also feasible to enable novice users to use HPC resources. Currently, we work on fully automating an existing pre-processing pipeline [19] by utilizing the UNICORE data oriented processing approach and adding the advantage of enabling easy research data management via an integration with the KIT Data Manager [8] via the MASi project [6]. We also work on a method to offload individual KNIME workflow nodes to HPC resources.

Acknowledgment. The authors would like to thank the German DFG for the opportunity to do research in the MASi (NA711/9-1) project. Financial support by the German BMBF for the competence center for Big Data ScaDS Dresden/Leipzig and the 031A099 project is gratefully acknowledged. Furthermore, the research leading to these results has been supported by the LSDMA project of the German HGF and the Human Brain Project by the European Union.

References

1. Benedyczak, K., Schuller, B., Petrova, M., Rybicki, J., Grunzke, R.: UNICORE 7 - middleware services for distributed and federated computing. In: International Conference on High Performance Computing Simulation (HPCS) (2016, accepted)
2. Berthold, M.R., et al.: KNIME: the Konstanz information miner. In: Preisach, C., Burkhardt, H., Schmidt-Thieme, L., Decker, R. (eds.) Data Analysis, Machine Learning and Applications. Studies in Classification, Data Analysis, and Knowledge Organization, pp. 319–326. Springer, Heidelberg (2008). doi:10.1007/978-3-540-78246-9_38
3. Cardona, A., Tomancak, P.: Current challenges in open-source bioimage informatics. Nat. Methods **9**(7), 661–665 (2012)
4. Eliceiri, K.W., Berthold, M.R., Goldberg, I.G., Ibáñez, L., Manjunath, B.S., Martone, M.E., Murphy, R.F., Peng, H., Plant, A.L., Roysam, B., et al.: Biological imaging software tools. Nat. Methods **9**(7), 697–710 (2012)
5. de la Garza, L., Krüger, J., Schärfe, C., Röttig, M., Aiche, S., Reinert, K., Kohlbacher, O.: From the desktop to the grid: conversion of KNIME workflows to gUSE. In: Proceedings of the International Workshop on Scientific Gateways 2013 (IWSG) (2013)

6. Grunzke, R., Hartmann, V., Jejkal, T., Herres-Pawlis, S., Hoffmann, A., Deicke, A., Schrade, T., Stotzka, R., Nagel, W.E.: Towards a metadata-driven multi-community research data management service. In: 2016 8th International Workshop on Science Gateways (IWSG) (2016, accepted)
7. HBP: The Human Brain Project - High Performance Computing Platform (2015). https://www.humanbrainproject.eu/high-performance-computing-platform1
8. Jejkal, T., Vondrous, A., Kopmann, A., Stotzka, R., Hartmann, V.: KIT data manager: the repository architecture enabling cross-disciplinary research. In: Large-Scale Data Management and Analysis - Big Data in Science, 1st edn (2014). http://digbib.ubka.uni-karlsruhe.de/volltexte/1000043270
9. Jug, F., Pietzsch, T., Kainmüller, D., Funke, J., Kaiser, M., van Nimwegen, E., Rother, C., Myers, G.: Optimal joint segmentation and tracking of *Escherichia Coli* in the mother machine. In: Cardoso, M.J., Simpson, I., Arbel, T., Precup, D., Ribbens, A. (eds.) BAMBI 2014. LNCS, vol. 8677, pp. 25–36. Springer, Cham (2014). doi:10.1007/978-3-319-12289-2_3
10. Jug, F., Pietzsch, T., Kainmüller, D., Myers, G.: Tracking by assignment facilitates data curation. In: IMIC Workshop, MICCAI, vol. 3 (2014)
11. Jug, F., Pietzsch, T., Preibisch, S., Tomancak, P.: Bioimage informatics in the context of Drosophila research. Methods **68**(1), 60–73 (2014)
12. Kacsuk, P., et al.: WS-PGRADE/gUSE generic DCI gateway framework for a large variety of user communities. J. Grid Comput. **10**(4), 601–630 (2012)
13. KNIME: KNIME Cluster Execution (2016). https://www.knime.org/cluster-execution/
14. Krüger, J., Grunzke, R., Gesing, S., Breuers, S., Brinkmann, A., de la Garza, L., Kohlbacher, O., Kruse, M., Nagel, W.E., Packschies, L., Müller-Pfefferkorn, R., Schäfer, P., Schärfe, C., Steinke, T., Schlemmer, T., Warzecha, K.D., Zink, A., Herres-Pawlis, S.: The MoSGrid science gateway - a complete solution for molecular simulations. J. Chem. Theory Comput. **10**, 2232–2245 (2014)
15. Pietzsch, T., Preibisch, S., Tomančák, P., Saalfeld, S.: ImgLib2 - generic image processing in Java. Bioinformatics **28**(22), 3009–3011 (2012)
16. PRACE: PRACE Research Infrastructure (2015). http://www.prace-ri.eu/
17. Schindelin, J., Arganda-Carreras, I., Frise, E., Kaynig, V., Longair, M., Pietzsch, T., Preibisch, S., Rueden, C., Saalfeld, S., Schmid, B., et al.: Fiji: an open-source platform for biological image analysis. Nat. Methods **9**(7), 676–682 (2012)
18. Schindelin, J., Rueden, C.T., Hiner, M.C., Eliceiri, K.W.: The ImageJ ecosystem. an open platform for biomedical image analysis. Mol. Reprod. Dev. **82**(7–8), 518–529 (2015)
19. Schmied, C., Steinbach, P., Pietzsch, T., Preibisch, S., Tomancak, P.: An automated workflow for parallel processing of large multiview SPIM recordings. Bioinformatics **32**, 1112–1114 (2015)
20. Schneider, C.A., Rasband, W.S., Eliceiri, K.W.: NIH image to ImageJ: 25 years of image analysis. Nat. Methods **9**(7), 671–675 (2012)
21. Schuller, B., Grunzke, R., Giesler, A.: Data oriented processing in UNICORE. In: UNICORE Summit 2013 Proceedings, IAS Series, vol. 21, pp. 1–6 (2013)
22. Wang, P., Robert, L., Pelletier, J., Dang, W.L., Taddei, F., Wright, A., Jun, S.: Robust growth of Escherichia coli. Curr. Biol. **20**(12), 1099–1103 (2010)
23. XSEDE: Extreme Science and Engineering Discovery Environment (2015). https://www.xsede.org

Optimized Execution Strategies for Sequence Aligners on NUMA Architectures

Josefina Lenis and Miquel Angel Senar[(✉)]

Universitat Autònoma de Barcelona (UAB), 08193 Bellaterra, Spain
{josefina.lenis,miquelangel.senar}@uab.es

Abstract. Alignment applications are essential for solving genomic variant calling studies. We have analyzed performance problems of four popular aligners from the literature. They constitute representative examples of the two most commonly used algorithmic strategies: hash tables and Burrows-Wheeler Transform. Although they take advantage of multithreading execution, they exhibit significant scalability limitations on systems with a non-uniform memory architecture (NUMA). Data sharing between independent threads and irregular memory access patterns constitute performance limiting factors that affect the studied aligners. We have also evaluated various data distribution strategies that do not require changes to the applications. Significant improvements in speedup were achieved when these techniques were applied to the execution of these aligners on a NUMA system.

Keywords: NUMA · Memory system performance · Genomic aligners · NGS

1 Introduction

New sequencing technologies set the pace of the rapid progress in genomic studies. The steady trend of reducing the sequencing cost and increasing the length of reads force developers to create and maintain more accurate, faster and updated software. Numerous sequence aligning tools have been developed in recent years. They exhibit differences in sensitivity or accuracy [16] and most of them can execute in parallel in modern multicore systems. In general, writing parallel programs that exhibit good scalability on non-uniform memory architectures (NUMA) is far from easy. Achieving good system performance requires that computations are carefully designed in order to harmonize execution of multiple threads and data accesses over multiple memory banks.

This paper is aligned with our previous work where we analyzed the performance of BWA-ALN, (Burrows-Wheeler Aligner) [11], on NUMA architectures. In that study, we detected scalability problems exhibited by BWA-ALN and we proposed simple system-level techniques to alleviate them. We obtained results up to 4-fold speed up over original BWA-ALN multithread implementation. In the present work, we extend the study to BWA-MEM [10] (a newer version of

© Springer International Publishing AG 2017
F. Desprez et al. (Eds.): Euro-Par 2016 Workshops, LNCS 10104, pp. 492–503, 2017.
DOI: 10.1007/978-3-319-58943-5_40

BWA specially suited to deal with longer reads) and to other three well-known mappers, namely, BOWTIE2 [8], GEM [13] and SNAP [18]. These mappers are widely used by the scientific community and real production centers, and frequently updated by its developers. We have applied various data distribution strategies to these mappers, as we did with BWA-ALN, and we obtained promising results on all cases, reducing memory-bound drawbacks and increasing scalability.

The paper is structured as follows. Section 2 presents related work. Section 3 describes basic concepts of NUMA systems and provides concrete details of the system used in our experiments. Section 4 introduces the problem of sequence alignment and a behavioral characterization of mappers used in this study. In Sect. 5, we introduce the methodology and all data distribution scenarios used to improve the performance of the aligners under study. Section 6 shows the results obtained in our experiments. Last section summarizes the main conclusions of our work.

2   Related Work

Genome alignment problems have been considered by Misale [14]. The author implements a framework to work under BOTWIE2 and BWA improving local affinity of the original algorithm. Herzeel *et al.* [4] replaces the pthread-based parallel loop in BWA by a Cilk **for** loop. Rewriting the parallel section using Cilk removes the load imbalance, resulting in a factor 2x performance improvement over the original BWA. On both cases - Misale and Herzeel *et al.* - the source code of the applications -aligners- are modified, which might be a costly action and dependent on the application version. Abuin *et al.* [1] presented a big data approach to solve BWA scalability problems. They introduce a tool name BigData that enables to run BWA in several machines although it does not provide a clear strategy to divide the data or to set the number of instances. In contrast, our approach can be applied to different aligners with minimum effort and, although not tested yet, it can be easily applied to distributed memory systems. Our work is complementary to all the works mentioned above. We present user-level guidelines of execution that help improving memory-bound aligners without modifying their source code, and, in some cases, without increasing the application initial requirements. Our contribution is based on the idea that application performance can be improved taking into account architecture characteristics and application's memory footprint.

3   NUMA Systems

In NUMA systems, main memory is physically distributed in banks among different processors but it looks like one single large memory from a logical perspective, so accesses to different parts is done using global memory addresses [3]. Each processor has its own memory bank and can access to it through its memory controller. A processor and its respective memory bank is called NUMA node. A program running in a particular processor can also access data stored in memory banks associated to other processors in a coherent way but at the cost of increased latency compared to accesses to its own local memory bank. In general, parallel applications that may run using multiple processors are not usually designed taking into account the NUMA architecture. Mainly, because creating a program that uses efficiently NUMA memory subsystems is not a trivial task. Figure 1 shows an example of NUMA architecture that corresponds to the system that we used in this study.

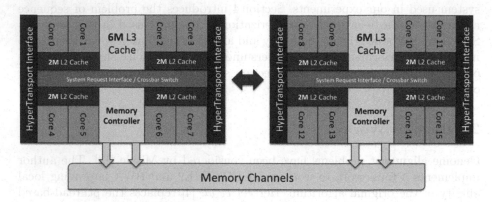

Fig. 1. AMD Bulldozer micro-architecture

It is a four-socket AMD Opteron Processor 6376 (Bulldozer microarchitecture), each socket containing 2 dies packaged onto a common substrate, referred to as a Multi-Chip Module (MCM). Each die (processor) consists of 8 physical cores that share a 6 MB Last Level Cache (LLC) and a memory bank. Only one thread can be assigned to one core and, therefore, up to 64 threads can be executed simultaneously. The system has 128 GB of memory, divided into 8 modules of 16 GB DDR3 1600 MHz each. Nodes are connected by HyperTransport links. Information about the NUMA system configuration can be retrieved on Linux systems by using the *numactl – hardware* command. This command displays the available nodes and access costs to different NUMA nodes. As seen in Table 1, access (or distance) costs within a local NUMA node is 10; this is shown in the diagonal values of the table. According to this information, access to an intermediate distance node costs 1.6x more, and access to the more distant nodes costs more than twice (2.2x). Distance between NUMA nodes is frequently referred to as hops. Where 0 hop is the minimum distance and 2 hops is the maximum.

Table 2 shows the results of a small experiment that we carried out on our system to bear out the accuracy of the information obtained. We modified an available open source benchmark [6], and adapted it to our architecture. The program is written in C and was compiled with GCC version 4.9.1, without optimization flags (−O0). The experiment consisted in reading an array of 100M elements. Each access was performed in such a way that prefetching was skipped

Table 1. Distance map on AMD 6376.   **Table 2.** Bandwidth per thread [MiB/s]

NUMA	0	1	2	3	4	5	6	7
0	10	16	16	22	16	22	16	22
1	16	10	22	16	16	22	22	16
2	16	22	10	16	16	16	16	16
3	22	16	16	10	16	16	22	22
4	16	16	16	16	10	16	16	22
5	22	22	16	16	16	10	22	16
6	16	22	16	22	16	22	10	16
7	22	16	16	22	22	16	16	10

Source	1 Thread	64 Threads
0	3300	700
1	2450	250
2	2200	330
3	1700	220
4	2200	250
5	1700	220
6	2200	330
7	1700	208

and a memory access (and a last level cache miss) was ensured every time. The array was allocated in node 0 and accessed by threads allocated in all cores (64). In the first column, we can see the bandwidth achieved when the array was accessed sequentially by one thread at a time. The "source" indicates to which NUMA node the thread was bound to. Second column shows bandwidth measurements when the same array was accessed by all the available threads at the same time. It is worth mentioning that the displayed values of the bandwidth correspond to the worst case scenarios. According to Table 2 accessing a local node is approximately 3300 MiB/s; bandwidth for medium distance nodes (1 hop) is 2200 MiB/s, the penalty being 1.5x; and accesses from a two-hops node incurs a penalty of 1.9x (bandwidth equals to 1700 MiB/s). Table 2 shows a case that is not revealed in Table 1: accesses from a thread running on the node located at the same socket exhibits a bandwidth of 2450 MiB/s (that might be seen as a node between 0 and 1 hop). Penalty in access latencies between processors and memory is one of the main problems suffered by NUMA-unaware applications. However, another problem arises when applications use a centralized data structure that is located in a single memory bank. When a large number of threads needs to access to this shared data structure, congestion problems might generate a significant degradation in memory accesses, as shown in the second column of Table 2.

4   Sequence Aligners

Sequence aligners - or aligners, for the sake of simplicity - can be classified into two main groups: based on hash tables or based on Burrow Wheeler Transform (BWT) [12]. In hash table based algorithms, given a query P every substring of length s of it is hashed, and can be later easily retrieved. SNAP is an example of hash table based aligner, where given a read to align draws multiple substrings of length s from it and performs an exact look up in the hash index to find locations in the database that contain the same substrings. It then computes the edit distance between the read and each of these candidate locations to find the best alignment. On the other hand, BWT is an efficient data indexing technique that maintains a relatively small memory footprint when searching through a given data block. BWT is used to transform the reference genome into an FM-index, and, as a consequence, the look up performance of the algorithm improves for the cases where a single read matches multiple locations in the genome [12]. Examples of BWT base aligners are BWA, BOWTIE2 and GEM. Hash tables are a straight forward algorithm and are very easy to implement but memory consumption is high; BWT algorithms, on the other hand, are complex to implement but have low memory requirements and are significantly faster [17]. The computational time required by an aligner to map a given set of sequences and the computer memory required are critical characteristics, even for aligners based on BWT. If an aligner is extremely fast but the computer hardware available for performing a given analysis does not have enough memory to run it then the aligner is not very useful. Similarly, an aligner is not useful either if it has low memory requirements but it is very slow. Hence, ideally, an aligner should be able to balance speed and memory usage while reporting the desired mappings [2]. In [14], Misale et al. defines three distinguishing features among the parallelization of sequence aligners:

1. There is a reference data structure indexed (in our study, the human genome reference). Typically this is read-only data.
2. There is a set of reads that can be mapped onto the reference independently.
3. The result consists in populating a shared data structure.

From a high level point of view, this is the behavior of all aligners that we used in this study. Therefore, continuous accesses to the single shared data structure -index- by all threads can increase its memory degradation performance. Additionally, read mapping exhibits poor locality characteristics: when a particular section of the reference index is brought to the local cache of a given core, subsequent reads usually require a completely different section of the reference index and, hence, cache reuse is low.

5   Allocation Strategies and Data Partitioning

In our previous work [9], we presented a series of execution strategies to improve BWA-ALN performance without modifying its source code. In this paper, we have applied our methodology to 4 aligners (GEM3, BOWTIE2, BWA-MEM and SNAP) in order to assess its benefits as a general methodology that can be applied to aligners that exhibit the features mentioned at the end of the previous section. We have developed a series of steps to characterize the behaviour of a memory-bound application and define its best execution strategy (see Fig. 2).

5.1   Analysis and Optimization of Shared Data Distribution (Part A)

Part A of our methodology consists in analyzing whether an aligner is sensitive to different memory allocations. In order to achieve this we carried out 3

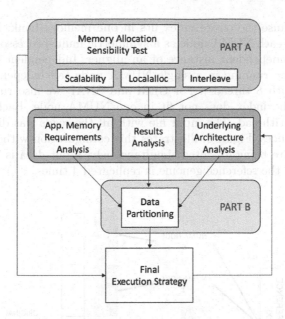

Fig. 2. Proposed methodology to find the best execution strategy

experiments: The first is a traditional scalability study in which we focused on 5 particular cases: using 8, 16, 32, 48 and 64 threads, because each processor has 8 cores and 1 memory bank associated; so 8, 16, 32, 48 and 64 threads implies a minimum usage of 1, 2, 4, 6 and 8 NUMA nodes, respectively. For the other two cases we used the Linux Tool *numactl* to set a memory policy allocation. With the parameter – *localalloc* the data was allocated in the current node where the program is being executed. The idea behind this is to maximize local data affinity, keeping data onto the closest memory to the running processor. Finally, in the third case the – *interleave* parameter is used so that memory is allocated using a round robin fashion between selected nodes. All aligners that we used need two input data files: one that contains all the reads that need to be mapped and a second one that contains the reference genome index.

The objective of this part is, firstly, to gain insight into the level of scalability of the aligner. Additionally, re-running the aligner using different parameters of *numactl* provides us information about the behavior of the application and its data allocation sensitivity by using two extreme cases: when the locality and concurrency increase (*localalloc*) and vice-versa (*interleave*).

5.2 Data Replication and Partitioning Strategies (Part B)

The objective for part B is to reduce the usage of the interconnection bus. This is achieved by data replication and partitioning techniques that imply the execution of simultaneous instances of the application (aligner). For aligners that have a small index as BOWTIE2 and BWA, data partitioning is not that challenging because the entire index fits in one memory bank. In these cases, we can consider each NUMA node as a symmetric multi-processor unit, capable of running an independent instance of an aligner. Independent instances were created, each one running in a single NUMA node (all independent instances were running with 8 threads). For GEM and SNAP we also run independent instances but the index does not fit in one NUMA node. Each one of these instances is multithread. The input file with all the reads was divided into the number of instances. Figure 3, illustrates this configuration with 4 independent instances that are being executed simultaneously. Input data is 1/4 the size of the original and the reference genome is replicated 4 times.

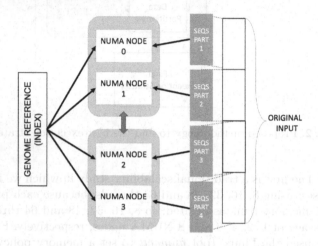

Fig. 3. Data partitioning

For aligners like GEM and SNAP, where the index size is equal or larger than the size of a memory bank, data partitioning becomes more complex because it involves more than one NUMA node. In Table 3, we can see the sizes of the indexes used. This information is crucial for designing how to split the data. Knowing the underlying architecture is also critical. Our system has memory banks of 16 GiB, which is not enough to run SNAP, even if two memory banks are used, the index would barely fit in. This is why we only run 2 simultaneous instances of SNAP (64 GiB each) and 4 instances of GEM (32 GiB each).

6   Experimental Results

In this section, we show the main results obtained during the experimentation. For all the experiments we used the reference human genome GRCh37, maintained by The Genome Reference Consortium, and two data sets were used as input data:

- *Synthetic benchmark* [5]:
  Single end, base length = 100, number of reads = 11M Size = 3.1 GB
- *Segment extracted from NA12878* [19]:
  Single end, base length = 100, number of reads = 22M Size = 5.4 GB

All aligners were compiled using GCC 4.9.1 and we used the latest version available for each, as shown in the second column of Table 3. All results were obtained as an average of five executions.

Table 3. Detailed information about the aligners.

Aligner	Version	Index (GB)	Data partitioning
BOWTIE2	2.2.6	3.9	8x8 threads
BWA-MEM	0.7.12	5.1	8x8 threads
GEM	3.0	15.0	4x16 threads
SNAP	1.0.18	29.0	2x32 threads

In the first part of our experimentation (Part A), we obtained the execution times of the four different aligners shown in Fig. 4. By original we refer to the execution of a given aligner with its default parameters without any particular allocation policy or NUMA control, and letting the operating system handle the allocation. On Linux systems this will normally involve spreading the threads through the system and using first-touch data allocation policy, which means that when a program is started on a CPU, data requested by that program will be stored on a memory bank corresponding to its local CPU [7]. Allocation policy takes effect only when a page is first requested by a process. If we focus on the original execution (shown by a light blue line in Fig. 4), scalability decreases significantly beyond 32 threads in all four aligners. When aligners run on more than 32 cores at least one NUMA node at two-hops distance are used. Therefore, all the speed up gain due to multithreading is mitigated by the latency of remote accesses and traffic saturation of interconnection links. For aligners BWA-MEM Fig. 4b, GEM3 Fig. 4c and SNAP Fig. 4d it can be clearly seen that interleave policy reduces the execution time, specially for the limited scalability scenarios (with 48 and 64 threads).

As explained in Sect. 4, aligners share a common data structure -an index-among all threads. This structure is loaded in memory by the master thread (by default, Linux will place this data on its local memory bank). Therefore, as the number of threads increases, the memory bank that allocates the index becomes a bottleneck. Allocating data in an interleave way does not reduce remote accesses but guarantees a fair share of them between all memory banks and, therefore, prevents access contention, a phenomenon specially prone to happen in this architecture due to reduced memory bandwidth between NUMA nodes [15]. This reason explains why using localalloc policy does not produce any improvement in

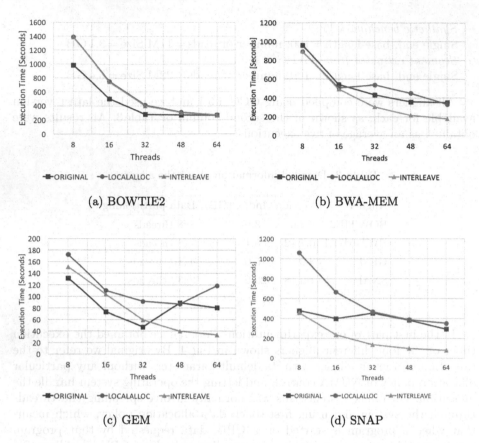

(a) BOWTIE2

(b) BWA-MEM

(c) GEM

(d) SNAP

Fig. 4. Different memory allocation policies. DATASET: synthetic benchmark (Color figure online)

execution times. BOWTIE2 Fig. 4a does not follow this trend; BOWTIE2 running on its defaults configuration performs better than using a explicit memory policy. We could infer some memory optimization might take place at the index load stage but a move precise analysis of the source code would be required to provide more accurate conclusions. In the second part of our experimentation (part B), we use data partitioning and data replication techniques to create multiple instances and run them simultaneously. We found, in our previous work, that this was the best solution for BWA-ALN. Figure 5 shows a complete comparison of all strategies, calculated using the wall time of the original execution with 64 threads (max resources).

Replication of the reference genome index reduces at the same time latency and contention problems while the benefits from multithreading parallelization are maintained: queries are distributed in different groups of threads that share a particular copy of the index stored in a local bank. BOWTIE2 and GEM also increase their performance when creating instances. Although for

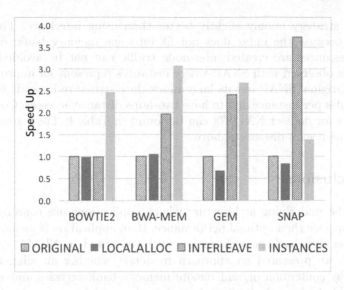

Fig. 5. All strategies. DATASET: synthetic benchmark

Table 4. Complete set of results for dataset NA12878

Aligner	Policy	Execution time [s]					SpeedUp
		Number of threads					Max. threads
		8	16	32	48	64	64
BOWTIE2	Original	679.89	361.20	223.74	279.13	431.11	1.1
	LocalAlloc	826.56	476.09	296.53	305.50	433.93	0.99
	Interleave	834.58	486.59	314.99	290.75	471.62	0.914
	Instances	–	–	–	–	111.11	3.38
BWA-MEM	Original	537.77	340.97	312.95	315.26	307.18	1
	LocalAlloc	618.67	329.11	344.84	354.91	296.83	1.03
	Interleave	482.20	300.89	233.23	193.21	170.23	1.80
	Instances	–	–	–	–	61.93	4.96
GEM3	Original	246.30	132.56	80.82	66.016	60.94	1
	LocalAlloc	405.15	256.65	303.17	202.25	273.75	0.22
	Interleave	327.24	187.32	100.40	64.74	52.58	1.21
	Instances	–	–	–	–	57.46	1.06
SNAP	Original	465.72	237.83	218.67	297.17	297.17	1
	LocalAlloc	705.76	923.40	393.85	343.18	361.02	0.92
	Interleave	199.97	396.54	98.43	79.04	65.27	4.5
	Instances	–	–	–	–	223.39	1.33

GEM this strategy is only slightly better than using interleave. This can be explained because the index does not fit into one memory bank; even when multiple instances are created inter-node traffic can not be avoided. A similar result is observed with SNAP where instances represent an improvement of 40% over Original SNAP but its large index data structure forces it to use four NUMA nodes per instance and to have two-hops distance accesses. Complementary results for dataset NA12878 can be found in Table 4. These results are in line with the results discussed above.

7   Conclusions

Knowing the underlying architecture where applications are running is a key aspect to achieve their optimal performance. If an application is memory-bound, might suffer drawback in performance when executed in NUMA systems. In this paper, we presented an approach to detect whether an aligner is being penalized by contention or/and remote memory bank accesses and whether it is susceptible to improve its execution time, by applying some simple system-level techniques that do not require changes on the original application code. When *interleave* or *instances* based techniques were applied, execution time was reduced in all cases tested. Aligners in which the index size is less than half the size of a single memory bank, data partitioning arises as the best solution because it completely avoids traffic between nodes and ensures only local accesses. In this case, a speedup of 2.5x and 3.1x was obtained for BOWTIE2 and BWA-MEM respectively. It is noteworthy that *instances* based implies an increment on memory requirements. BOWTIE2 and BWA-MEM can easily meet this requirement in modern systems. For other aligners with larger indexes (i.e. SNAP and GEM), *interleave* technique might be a better choice because the index is distributed across the system memory banks, and mitigates the contention produced when all threads try to access the same data structure albeit HyperTransport traffic cannot be reduced. Improvements of 2.5x and for SNAP is 3.6x were obtained for SNAP and GEM, respectively. GEM still achieved and additional slight improvement when the instance based technique was applied because its memory requirements are larger than BWA-MEM and BOWTIE2 but smaller than SNAP. These techniques can be implemented easily and do not require modifying the source code of the applications neither to have privilege permissions. Any user can add these strategies to its current running jobs. As we have seen, very simple configurations at the time of executing an application can generate significant differences in execution times when running on NUMA systems. This adds an extra layer of complexity to the basic techniques of parallelism and performance evaluations. It is an important factor to be taken into account when improving the overall performance of any application.

Acknowledgements. This research was supported by MICINN-Spain under contract TIN2014-53234-C2-1-R.

References

1. Abuín, J.M., Pichel, J.C., Pena, T.F., Amigo, J.: BigBWA: approaching the Burrows-Wheeler aligner to Big Data technologies. Bioinformatics **31**(24), 4003 4005 (2015)
2. Fonseca, N.A., Rung, J., Brazma, A., Marioni, J.C.: Tools for mapping high-throughput sequencing data: supplement. Bioinformatics 1–9 (2012)
3. García-Risueño, P., Ibañez, P.E.: A review of High Performance Computing foundations for scientists. Int. J. Mod. Phys. C **23**(07), 1–33 (2012)
4. Herzeel, C., Ashby, T.J., Costanza, P., Meuter, W.: Resolving load balancing issues in BWA on NUMA multicore architectures. In: Wyrzykowski, R., Dongarra, J., Karczewski, K., Waśniewski, J. (eds.) PPAM 2013. LNCS, vol. 8385, pp. 227–236. Springer, Heidelberg (2014). doi:10.1007/978-3-642-55195-6_21
5. Highnam, G., Wang, J.J., Kusler, D., Zook, J., Vijayan, V., Leibovich, N., Mittelman, D.: An analytical framework for optimizing variant discovery from personal genomes. Nat. Commun. **6**, 6275 (2015)
6. Klöckner, A.: Lec8-Demo (2012). http://github.com/hpc12/lec8-demo
7. Lameter, C., Hsu, B., Sosnick-Pérez, M.: NUMA (Non-Uniform Memory Access): an overview. ACMQueue 1–12 (2013)
8. Langmead, B., Salzberg, S.L.: Fast gapped-read alignment with Bowtie 2. Nat. Methods **9**(4), 357–359 (2012)
9. Lenis, J., Senar, M.A.: On the performance of BWA on NUMA architectures. In: 2015 IEEE Trustcom/BigDataSE/ISPA, pp. 236–241 (2015)
10. Li, H.: Aligning sequence reads, clone sequences and assembly contigs with BWA-MEM, p. 3 (2013). arXiv preprint: arXiv:1303.3997
11. Li, H., Durbin, R.: Fast and accurate short read alignment with Burrows-Wheeler transform. Bioinformatics **25**(14), 1754–1760 (2009)
12. Li, H., Homer, N.: A survey of sequence alignment algorithms for next-generation sequencing. Brief. Bioinform. **11**(5), 473–483 (2010)
13. Marco-Sola, S., Sammeth, M., Guigó, R., Ribeca, P.: The GEM mapper: fast, accurate and versatile alignment by filtration. Nat. Methods **9**, 1185–1188 (2012)
14. Misale, C., Ferrero, G., Torquati, M., Aldinucci, M.: Sequence alignment tools: one parallel pattern to rule them all? BioMed Res. Int. **2014**, 1–12 (2014)
15. Molka, D., Hackenberg, D., Schöne, R.: Main memory and cache performance of intel sandy bridge and amd bulldozer. In: Workshop on Memory Systems Performance and Correctness, MSPC 2014, pp. 4:1–4:10. ACM, New York (2014)
16. Shang, J., Zhu, F., Vongsangnak, W., Tang, Y., Zhang, W., Shen, B.: Evaluation and comparison of multiple aligners for next-generation sequencing data analysis. BioMed Res. Int. **2014**, 1–16 (2014)
17. Trapnell, C., Salzberg, S.L.: How to map billions of short reads onto genomes. Nat. Biotechnol. **27**(5), 455–457 (2009)
18. Zaharia, M., Bolosky, W., Curtis, K.: Faster and more accurate sequence alignment with SNAP, pp. 1–10 (2011). arXiv preprint: arXiv:1111.5572v1
19. Zook, J.M., et al.: Extensive sequencing of seven human genomes to characterize benchmark reference materials, p. 26468 (2015). (bioRxiv)

Architecture for the Execution of Tasks in Apache Spark in Heterogeneous Environments

Estefania Serrano[1]([✉]), Javier Garcia Blas[1], Jesus Carretero[1], and Monica Abella[2,3]

[1] Computer Architecture and Technology Area, Univ. Carlos III, Madrid, Spain
esserran@inf.uc3m.es
[2] Bioengineering and Aerospace Engineering Department,
Univ. Carlos III, Madrid, Spain
[3] Instituto de Investigacion Sanitaria Gregorio Marañon (IiSGM), Madrid, Spain

Abstract. The current disadvantages in computing platforms and the easy migration to the Cloud Computing paradigm have as consequence the migration of scientific applications to different task-based distributed computing frameworks. However, many of them have already been optimized for their execution on specific hardware accelerators like GPUs. In this work, we present an architecture design that aims to facilitate the execution of traditional HPC based applications into Big Data environments. We prove that the bigger memory capacity, the automatic task partitioning, and the higher computational power lead to a convergence to a highly distributed new execution model. Moreover, we present an study of the viability of our proposal through the use of GPUs inside the Apache Spark infrastructure. The architecture presented will be evaluated through a real medical imaging application. The evaluation results demonstrate that our approach obtains competitive execution times compared with the original application.

Keywords: Computed Tomography, CT · GPU scheduling · MapReduce

1 Introduction

The increasing use of distributed computing frameworks that are originally created for Big Data or data analysis problems is triggering the adaptation of these programming paradigms through different methodologies. Examples of these solutions are shown in [5,16]. One of the barriers related to this approximation is the efficiency loss, mainly due to data dependencies.

In the case of scientific applications (e.g. field of medical imaging), developers have traditionally opted for the usage of accelerators, like GPUs (Graphics

E. Serrano—This work has been partially supported by the grant TIN2013-41350-P, *Scalable Data Management Techniques for High-End Computing Systems* from the Spanish Ministry of Economy and Competitiveness, FPU14/03875 from the Spanish Ministry of Education, and by NECRA RTC-2014-3028-1 project. We also want to thank NVidia for providing the device Tesla K40 which with we have been able to perform the experiments.

F. Desprez et al. (Eds.): Euro-Par 2016 Workshops, LNCS 10104, pp. 504–515, 2017.
DOI: 10.1007/978-3-319-58943-5_41

Processing Unit). Because of its SIMD (Single Instruction Multiple Data) architecture, these accelerators allow the fast execution of most of the reconstruction and projection imaging algorithms, since the generation of each of the pixels in the final image is completely independent. The main problem related to the usage of these hardware elements is the lack of memory capacity due to the fact that most of the low-cost graphics cards count only with around 3 GB of GDDR5 memory. Although dedicated devices in the scientific computing field (like NVidia Tesla) can provide more than 10 GB of main memory, this may be insufficient for the future generation of high resolution images, which could require more than 32 GB of data. A possible solution to this problem is the partitioning of the input data into multiple independent tasks on different and coordinated GPUs.

The advantages of distributed computing in terms of memory availability are evident. Memory capacity and computational power are multiplied due to a high number of computing resources. Moreover, heterogeneous clusters with attached GPUs are being a common approach, providing even more computational capabilities. There exist many distributed computing frameworks, mainly aimed at scientific applications and being the most notable example MPI (Message Passing Interface). This approach has already being explored in a previous work [3]. In case of highly parallel scientific problems, the re-implementation of the applications using the MapReduce paradigm can result in larger benefits. This paradigm facilitates the automatic data partitioning, a performance-based tasks model, and locality-aware data placement.

In summary, the contributions of this work are the following. First, we present a solution that provides access to multiple GPUs inside tasks generated by Spark. Second, we detail the methodology followed for the migration of a medical imaging application already implemented for heterogeneous environments. Finally, we present a comparative evaluation of the proposed solution. The contributions of this work are not only applied to the possibility of executing applications from the medical image field, but also to the generalization of the process used here, to any field that can take advantage of GPUs.

The rest of the document is organized as follows. In Sect. 3 a basic explanation of the technologies employed is briefly described. Our architecture proposal is presented in Sect. 4, including a general explanation of how to use GPUs in Apache Spark. In Sect. 5, we introduce the medical imaging application and we evaluate it in Sect. 6. Finally, in Sect. 7 we discuss the obtained results and propose future works to continue with the presented solution.

2 Related Work

The unification of heterogeneous architectures with distributed computing frameworks such as Hadoop has been exploited from different points of view. In Hadoop there exists different examples of this unification focusing on specific GPU programming models such as HadoopCL [8] or trying to generalize accelerator programming supporting both CUDA and OpenCL with a good example in

Hadoop+ [9]. Another example is [14] which combines Hadoop and Aparapi to create MapReduce interfaces for GPU execution (using OpenCL programming model) obtaining an speedup of 80x in an n-Body implementation.

Regarding Spark, it is currently in development a framework improvement called HeteroSpark [11],based in Java RMI, although it is not available at this day. The majority of these frameworks are based, as well as the work presented here, in the independent compilation of kernels programmed in the selected programming model, although the scheduling of the jobs sent to the GPU is not often included. However, other related works have chosen to not modify the framework and add the GPUs at the application level. Examples of this approach are those presented by Zheng and Wu [18] which uses GPUs inside Hadoop to accelerate a kmeans algorithm, or Boubela et al. [4], which makes use of a separated server from Spark for the analysis of MRI images. Our proposal is similar to these approaches since we do not modify Spark, but unlike them, we extend it for a generalized execution of suitable GPU applications.

Beyond the use of GPUs in these distributed environments, some works in the field of medical imaging have focused on their evaluation without the presence of accelerators like in [13]. In this approach, the authors implement the 4-D computed tomography FDK algorithm using the Apache Hadoop MapReduce paradigm. Another solution [6] implements a deconvolution using Apache Spark and compares it to other alternatives such as the use of multicore CPUs or GPUs. A complete framework in this field for real time image analysis that uses as an accelerator Apache Spark is described in [12]. There are also similar alternatives in general image processing applications, being the most popular one HIPI [15], an image processing library that is accelerated through Hadoop MapReduce and it is employed in many other applications.

3   Background

3.1   Apache Spark

Apache Spark [17] is a general purpose distributed computing framework. It is employed in several fields, although it is mainly used in data analysis and Big Data applications. Spark exposes a portable APIs and supports well-known languages such as Scala, Java, Python, R, and specific libraries focused on machine learning. Spark is based on both an extended MapReduce paradigm and a task-based execution model. This solution is compatible with several resource managers and provides connectors for different file systems and distributed databases. One of the main differences with previous frameworks such as Hadoop [1] is the optimization in memory management.

The Spark's architecture has two main actors: the driver and the workers. The driver is in charge of deploying the application and its management inside the cluster, communicating with the chosen resource manager. Workers run inside the different nodes of the cluster and launch the isolated containers in which tasks are executed (executors).

3.2   Python and PyCUDA

The selection of Python as programming language is motivated by the facts that it is used as a prototyping language and the quantity of existing scientific modules. These modules provide several mathematical functions, highly optimized thanks to their inner development in C language. However, the process described in this work could have been done with any other compatible language as long as they have bindings for the GPUs (either CUDA or OpenCL compatible). In Python there are many alternatives for developing accelerators-based applications. We highlight PyCUDA [10] due to its flexible support of NVidia GPUs and its compatibility with existing kernels.

4   GPU Support for Heterogeneous Platforms in Spark

As it can be seen in Figs. 1 and 2, from the application execution point of view, there are three main components: the *driver*, the *executor* allocated in the worker nodes, and the proposed *GPU scheduler*. This architecture is tightly tied with the Apache Spark architecture and execution model previously presented.

The *driver* is in charge of the execution of the main code of the application, stating the required transformations and actions. In case of using a local file system, it will be also responsible of reading and writing the input and output data. However, if we use HDFS file system, each of the worker nodes will be in charge of acquiring the nearest data if it is not already available. The driver is independent from the task execution (except when executing in one node), which makes unnecessary the presence of installed GPUs.

In the *executor*, tasks are finally computed. These tasks can invoke CUDA-based kernels through the PyCUDA interface. As stated in Fig. 1, first we need to check out if the node counts with the required accelerators, in our case NVidia GPUs. This check also includes the presence of the auxiliary tools for GPU programming, either CUDA or OpenCL libraries. After that, it will request a device to the *scheduler*. In case of not counting enough resources the scheduler

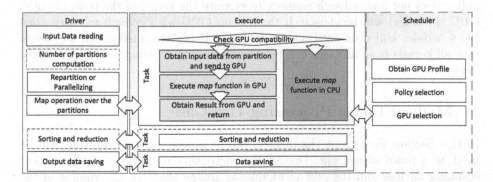

Fig. 1. Architecture of a GPU processing application in Apache Spark.

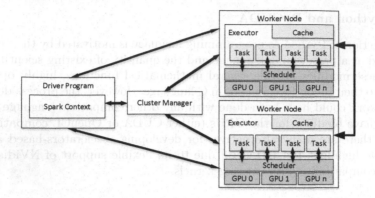

Fig. 2. Spark architecture supporting multiple GPU devices.

will block the assignment process. Then the task will proceed to the online compilation and preparation of the arguments that will be passed to the GPU kernel. Finally, output data from the GPU will be transferred to main memory and returned as the result of the mapping task. An example of a mapping task is presented in Sect. 5.

The *GPU scheduler* consists in an independent service implemented by a Python RPC (RPyC [2]), which is responsible of scheduling and selecting the most suitable GPUs in which the kernels will be deployed. Due to its characteristic of independent service, the *scheduler* is capable of scheduling the GPUs even between independent applications that are executing inside the same node. This component has different policies that can be applied to the scheduling decisions, depending on factors such as available resources in the device, offered performance, number of tasks in execution, etc. There are already three policies implemented: *Round Robin*, in which the GPUs are assigned following their order in the node; *Random*, the GPU is chosen randomly between those available; and *Least processes*, in which the GPU with less executing kernels is chosen. However, and due to the memory limitations of these devices, if the device chosen by the policy does not have enough memory to execute the kernel of the task, the next GPU (in order) will be chosen. If there is no GPU with enough memory, then the scheduler will wait until one is available. Using this mechanism we assure that all kernels from all tasks can be executed without memory problems in the devices.

5   Medical Image Processing Use Case

In this Section we present the medical image processing use case that will be used as a proof of concept. Due to the increasing resolutions of the current scanning devices and the new techniques of image analysis, the volume of the data produced by this type of applications has been also increased notably. The majority of the algorithms have been optimized to be adapted to accelerators such as Intel Xeon Phi or GPUs. However, these devices do not possess the memory capacity necessary to generate images in high resolution 3D, which can occupy more than 10 GB.

An example of this kind of problems is the simulation and reconstruction in the field of medical imaging, which uses more complex algorithms every day to obtain a better quality in the image and a reduction of the doses applied to the patient. They also accept input data of higher sizes, which tests the scalability of the current approaches. This is the case of the simulator Fux-Sim that employs several Computed Tomography (CT) reconstruction methods and simulates several acquisition geometries.

In this work we have taken one part of the simulator (the backprojection phase) and adapted it to the architecture exposed in the previous section. The backprojection is the essential part of the reconstruction, since it is in charge of computing the values of each of the voxels that construct the final 3D image. In our case, the reconstruction algorithm chosen is the analytical backprojection, which is part of the FDK algorithm [7]. Equations 1 and 2 show the mathematical implementation of the algorithm:

$$f(u,v,z) = \sum_{\theta}(Mag \cdot [ucos\theta - usin\theta], vsin\theta + vcos\theta, Mag \cdot z) \quad (1)$$

$$Mag = \frac{DSO + v}{DSO + DDO} \quad (2)$$

where $f(u,v,z)$ is the voxel value in the back-projected image at coordinates (u,v,z), $p(s,z)$ the projection data for angle and position (s,z) in the detector. DSO and DDO are the distance from the center of the FOV to the source and the detector respectively, z is the axial coordinate, common for both detector

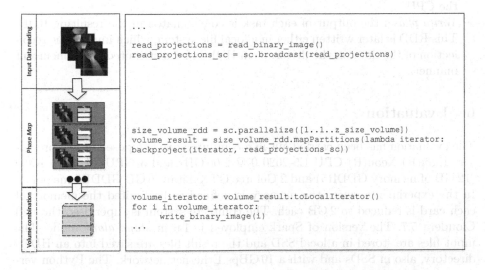

Fig. 3. Pseudocode of the backprojection application in Spark.

and reconstructed volumes reference frames, s is the radial coordinate in the detector, and u, v are the Cartesian coordinates in the reconstructed volume.

Applying the architectures explained, we can reuse the already programmed kernels obtaining automatic distribution over different threads, devices, and nodes thanks to Spark and the GPU scheduler without sacrificing the acceleration provided by the GPU. A general description of the operation of the application on Spark is given in Fig. 3.

Listing 1.1. Pseudocode of non-parallelized backprojection.

```
V = create roi()
for all projections in angles do
    projection = read projection()
    for all u do
        for all v do
            for all z do
                V(u, v, z) = backprojection(projection(s,z))
write roi(V )
```

The flow of the application can be divided in the following phases:

- *Read phase*: the input data are read in the driver from a local file system and broadcasted to each of the executors for their processing. This way, Spark can divide the output data (the 3D volume), which is the most memory consuming data.
- *Map phase*: to convert the projections to the final volume. Each partition is in charge of creating part of the volume which is assigned by Spark. During this phase the GPU kernels are launched. Taking into account the general algorithm shown in Listing 1.1, each of the tasks would divide the fourth loop (the z axis), the kernel would parallelize the second and third loop, and the upper level loop, the projection one, would be taken care inside the task on the CPU.
- *Write phase*: the output of each task is concatenated in the resulting RDD. This RDD is later written either in a local file system, which implies the recollection of the data on the driver, or in HDFS in a distributed and concurrent manner.

6   Evaluation

The evaluation has been carried out in a compute node composed of two processors Intel(R) Xeon(R) CPU E5-2620 0 @ 2.00 GHz and 3 GPUs, 1 Tesla K40c (12 GB of memory GDDR5) and 2 Geforce GTX Titan (6 GB GDDR5 memory). In the experiments where the memory is defined to be limited the memory of each card is reduced to 2 GB each. The complete system is supervised through Cloudera 5.7. The version of Spark employed is 1.6 in *stand-alone* mode. The input files are stored in a local SSD and the result files are saved into an HDFS directory, also in SSDs and with a 10 GBps Ethernet network. The Python version was 2.7 and we used PyCUDA 1.3. The input data for the experiments consisted in 360 projections with 1024×1024 pixels (1.2 GB). The size of the output data was $1024 \times 1024 \times 1024$ voxels (4 GB). In each experiment, we show the average of at least 3 different repetitions as well as the standard error. In the case of the occupancy timelines, data of only one repetition is shown.

6.1 Overall Execution Time

In Fig. 4, we plot the total execution times for the baseline configuration (labeled as simulator) and the Apache Spark version (labeled as Spark) with 3 threads and 3 partitions.

Due to the overload of the execution of an associated runtime (Apache Spark), the execution times for an standard volume of $1024 \times 1024 \times 1024$ voxels of the distributed backprojection application in a node are not as competitive compared with the execution time of the simulator in the case of the same node and number of GPUs. In all cases Spark requires more time to produce the result although, when the number of GPUs is increased, the difference is reduced. This is due to the better exploitation of the resources thanks to the scheduler.

In Fig. 5, we show the execution times of the Apache Spark approach for 3 threads and a variable number of partitions. We evaluate the three policies implemented applying a limited memory scheme on the GPUs. From these results, we can conclude that for the case of a single node, the increase in the number of partitions impacts negatively in the overall execution time due to the increment of the memory usage. With respect to the differences between policies, only *Random* obtains a significantly higher execution time than the other policies, being *RoundRobin* and *LeastProcesses* in the same time range. However, if we look at results from Fig. 6 when we average the execution times for every number of threads and different number of partitions, in general, *Leastprocesses* performs slightly better than Round Robin.

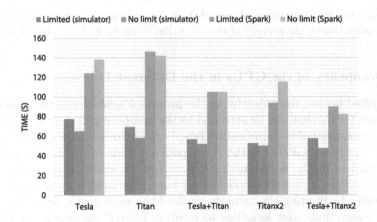

Fig. 4. Execution time for the different combinations of GPUs in a node, with memory limitation, no limitation, in the original setup (simulator) and in its Spark version (Spark).

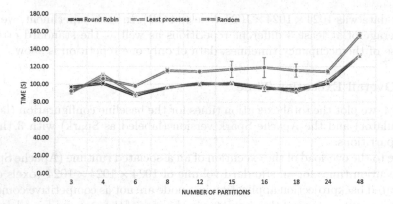

Fig. 5. Results of the evaluation of the application with 3 threads and different number of partitions for each of the policies and their corresponding standard error.

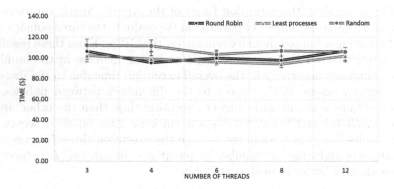

Fig. 6. Results of the evaluation of each of the policies with different number of threads. The execution time is the average of the execution times for each number of partitions.

6.2   Occupancy of the GPUs in the Different Policies

As described before, the objective of the proposed *scheduler* is the exploitation of multiple GPUs that can be attached to the compute nodes. In Fig. 7, we plot the execution time of the application based on 12 threads and 48 partitions, on the three available GPUs for the three policies. This configuration maximizes the parallelism in the node. In this experiment, to evaluate the occupancy of the GPUs with the different policies, we have simulated a more homogeneous environment by limiting the memory available on each device to 2 GB.

The policy that takes less time to finish is *LeastProcesses* as we also concluded in the previous section. *LeastProcesses* exploits the GPUs in a more regular manner. Both *RoundRobin* and *Random* policies possess several spikes in the occupancy meanwhile with the first policy the occupancy is held around 12 tasks assigned to GPUs, which maximizes the maximum number of threads

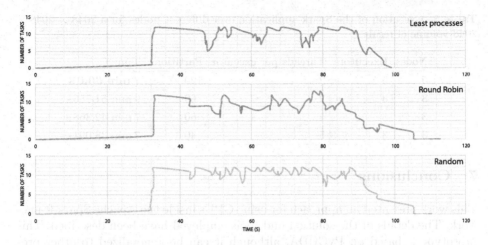

Fig. 7. Timeline of the experiment with 12 threads and 48 partitions for each of the policies. We show the number of tasks assigned to the GPUs in each moment.

running in parallel. The reason is that *LeastProcesses* is capable of balancing the inequalities in the execution of the tasks. In this case, a more exhaustive analysis discovers that the first GPU (Tesla) takes around 50% more time to process tasks than the others solutions. *LeastProcesses* detects that the number of tasks in that GPU is higher and sends the tasks to the other ones which are faster and less overloaded. However in all three policies, we can appreciate regular spikes that are attributed to the finalization of the tasks assigned to the thread. Since we have 48 partitions that equals 48 tasks, each thread will be assigned 4 tasks. In this change of tasks, the GPUs are unused because the mapping functions have not started yet, being the cause of the performance spikes.

6.3 Evaluation with Multiple Nodes

For the evaluation of a bigger volume we chose to execute the application over a set of nodes ranging from three to five, all of similar characteristics to the one employed in the first experiments. The resource manager used was Apache Yarn. All the nodes possessed at least one GPU. The input data for this evaluation was a set of 360 projections of 2048×2048 pixels (5.7 GB) to obtain a resulting volume of $2048 \times 2048 \times 2048$ voxels (32 GB).

Table 1 depicts some of the results for a different number of partitions, nodes, threads, and executors. As a reference, the time needed for a backprojection of that size in a Tesla K40c, a high-end graphics card, is on average 7 min 33 s. If we compare with the best result in Apache Spark (7 min 36 s), we can see that both of them require the same execution time. However, and since Yarn, or any other available resource manager, does not take into account the installed accelerators in the node for the task scheduling and resource allocation, we could still have room for more optimization with a GPU-aware global resource manager.

Table 1. Execution of the Spark application over different nodes for a 2048 × 2048 × 2048 volume of result.

Nodes	Executors	Threads per executor	Partitions	Time
5	5	2	120	**7 min 36.0 s**
3	3	2	60	9 min 51.756 s
3	3	4	60	7 min 42.368 s
3	3	5	40	7 min 38.091 s

7   Conclusions

This work presented an approach for using GPUs inside the Apache Spark framework. The details of the solution and tools employed have been described. This prototype is based on PyCUDA, although it can be generalized to other programming languages that have bindings with the GPUs available, such as Java. Moreover, we provide an additional intranode scheduler to Apache Spark for achieving a better exploitation of the available resources. This scheduler is based on different policies that have been evaluated over multiple configurations.

We have evaluated this approach through the migration of a medical imaging reconstruction application. When the number of employed GPUs increases, our architecture exploits better the available computational resources. This is shown in a better way when a policy uses dynamical parameters of the GPU, such as the number of processes in execution. We also show that for more of one node we can obtain at least the same time as the one obtained with a high-end GPU and, that with a better global scheduler and resource manager the overall results will improve.

The following work steps will be to accomplish a wider evaluation over a distributed heterogeneous cluster, along with the extension of the GPU scheduler to cluster level and the policies implemented. Also, we will test this approach with other applications such as iterative reconstruction algorithms or other medical imaging techniques. At the end, we will incorporate this approach to an analysis phase of the images in terms of different parameters such as quality or radiation dose.

Acknowledgements. This work has been partially supported by the Spanish MINISTERIO DE ECONOMÍA Y COMPETITIVIDAD under the project grant TIN2016-79637-P TOWARDS UNIFICATION OF HPC AND BIG DATA PARADIGMS, and by NECRA RTC-2014-3028-1 project. We also want to thank NVidia for providing the device Tesla K40 which with we have been able to perform the experiments.

References

1. Hadoop. http://hadoop.apache.org/
2. RPyC - Transparent, Symmetric Distributed Computing – RPyC. https://rpyc.readthedocs.io/en/latest/index.html

3. Blas, J.G., Abella, M., Isaila, F., Carretero, J., Desco, M.: Surfing the optimization space of a multiple-GPU parallel implementation of a x-ray tomography reconstruction algorithm. J. Syst. Softw. **95**, 166–175 (2014)
4. Boubela, R.N., Kalcher, K., Huf, W., Našel, C., Moser, E.: Big data approaches for the analysis of large-scale fMRI data using apache spark and GPU processing: a demonstration on resting-state fMRI data from the human connectome project. Front. Neurosci. **9**, Article no. 492 (2015)
5. Caino-Lores, S., Fernandez, A.G., Garcia-Carballeira, F., Perez, J.C.: A cloudification methodology for multidimensional analysis: implementation and application to a railway power simulator. Simul. Model. Pract. Theory **55**, 46–62 (2015)
6. Cao, L., Juan, P., Zhang, Y.: Real-time deconvolution with GPU and spark for big imaging data analysis. In: Wang, G., Zomaya, A., Perez, G.M., Li, K. (eds.) ICA3PP 2015. LNCS, vol. 9530, pp. 240–250. Springer, Cham (2015). doi:10.1007/978-3-319-27137-8_19
7. Feldkamp, L., Davis, L., Kress, J.: Practical cone-beam algorithm. JOSA A **1**(6), 612–619 (1984)
8. Grossman, M., Breternitz, M., Sarkar, V.: HadoopCL: MapReduce on distributed heterogeneous platforms through seamless integration of Hadoop and OpenCL. In: 2013 IEEE 27th International, Parallel and Distributed Processing Symposium Workshops & Ph.D. Forum (IPDPSW), pp. 1918–1927. IEEE (2013)
9. He, W., Cui, H., Lu, B., Zhao, J., Li, S., Ruan, G., Xue, J., Feng, X., Yang, W., Yan, Y.: Hadoop+: modeling and evaluating the heterogeneity for MapReduce applications in heterogeneous clusters. In: Proceedings of 29th ACM on International Conference on Supercomputing, pp. 143–153. ACM (2015)
10. Klöckner, A., Pinto, N., Lee, Y., Catanzaro, B., Ivanov, P., Fasih, A.: PyCUDA and PyOpenCL: a scripting-based approach to GPU run-time code generation. Parallel Comput. **38**(3), 157–174 (2012)
11. Li, P., Luo, Y., Zhang, N., Cao, Y.: HeteroSpark: a heterogeneous CPU/GPU spark platform for machine learning algorithms. In: 2015 IEEE International Conference on Networking, Architecture and Storage (NAS), pp. 347–348. IEEE (2015)
12. Mader, K.: Scaling Up Fast: Real-time Image Processing and Analytics Using Spark. https://spark-summit.org/2014/talk/scaling-up-fast-real-time-image-processing-and-analytics-using-spark
13. Meng, B., Pratx, G., Xing, L.: Ultrafast and scalable cone-beam CT reconstruction using MapReduce in a cloud computing environment. Med. Phys. **38**(12), 6603–6609 (2011)
14. Okur, S., Radoi, C., Lin, Y.: Hadoop+ Aparapi: making heterogeneous MapReduce programming easier
15. Sweeney, C., Liu, L., Arietta, S., Lawrence, J.: HIPI: a hadoop image processing interface for image-based MapReduce tasks. Chris, University of Virginia (2011)
16. Wallskog Pappas, A.: Migration of legacy applications to the cloud - a review on methodology and tools for migration to the cloud. Bachelor thesis, University of Umea (2014)
17. Zaharia, M., Chowdhury, M., Das, T., Dave, A., Ma, J., McCauley, M., Franklin, M.J., Shenker, S., Stoica, I.: Resilient distributed datasets: a fault-tolerant abstraction for in-memory cluster computing. In: Proceedings of 9th USENIX Conference on Networked Systems Design and Implementation, p. 2. USENIX Association (2012)
18. Zheng, H.X., Wu, J.M.: Accelerate K-means algorithm by using GPU in the hadoop framework. In: Chen, Y., Balke, W.-T., Xu, J., Xu, W., Jin, P., Lin, X., Tang, T., Hwang, E. (eds.) WAIM 2014. LNCS, vol. 8597, pp. 177–186. Springer, Cham (2014). doi:10.1007/978-3-319-11538-2_17

PELGA - Performance Engineering for Large-Scale Graph Analytics

Parametric Multi-step Scheme for GPU-Accelerated Graph Decomposition into Strongly Connected Components

Stefano Aldegheri[1], Jiří Barnat[2], Nicola Bombieri[1(✉)], Federico Busato[1], and Milan Češka[3]

[1] Department of Computer Science, University of Verona, Verona, Italy
nicola.bombieri@univr.it
[2] Faculty of Informatics, Masaryk University, Brno, Czech Republic
[3] Faculty of Information Technology, Brno University of Technology, Brno, Czech Republic

Abstract. The problem of decomposing a directed graph into strongly connected components (SCCs) is a fundamental graph problem that is inherently present in many scientific and commercial applications. Clearly, there is a strong need for good high-performance, e.g., GPU-accelerated, algorithms to solve it. Unfortunately, among existing GPU-enabled algorithms to solve the problem, there is none that can be considered the best on every graph, disregarding the graph characteristics. Indeed, the choice of the right and most appropriate algorithm to be used is often left to inexperienced users. In this paper, we introduce a novel parametric multi-step scheme to evaluate existing GPU-accelerated algorithms for SCC decomposition in order to alleviate the burden of the choice and to help the user to identify which combination of existing techniques for SCC decomposition would fit an expected use case the most. We support our scheme with an extensive experimental evaluation that dissects correlations between the internal structure of GPU-based algorithms and their performance on various classes of graphs. The measurements confirm that there is no algorithm that would beat all other algorithms in the decomposition on all of the classes of graphs. Our contribution thus represents an important step towards an ultimate solution of automatically adjusted scheme for the GPU-accelerated SCC decomposition.

1 Introduction

Fundamental graph algorithms such as breadth first search, spanning tree construction, shortest paths, etc., are building blocks to many applications. Sequential implementations of these algorithms become impractical in those application domains where large graphs need to be processed. As a result, parallel algorithms for the processing of large graphs have been devised to efficiently use compute

This work has been supported by the IT4Innovations Excellence in Science project No. LQ1602, the BUT FIT project FIT-S-14-2486, and the Czech Science Foundation grants Nos. GA16-24707Y and GA15-08772S.

© Springer International Publishing AG 2017
F. Desprez et al. (Eds.): Euro-Par 2016 Workshops, LNCS 10104, pp. 519–531, 2017.
DOI: 10.1007/978-3-319-58943-5_42

clusters and multi-core architectures. The transformation of a sequential algorithm into a scalable parallel algorithm, however, is not an easy task. Typically, the best sequential algorithm is not necessarily the best parallel algorithm from the practical point of view. This is especially the case of massively parallel graphics processing units (GPUs). These devices contain several hundreds of arithmetic units and can be harnessed to provide tremendous acceleration for many computation intensive scientific applications. The key to effective utilization of GPUs for scientific computing is the design and implementation of data-parallel algorithms that can scale to hundreds of tightly coupled processing units following a single instruction multiple thread (SIMT) model.

In this paper we focus on the problem of decomposing a directed graph into its strongly connected components (*SCC decomposition*). This problem has many applications leading to very large graphs, including for example web analysis [16], which require high performance processing.

Parallelization of the SCC decomposition is a particularly difficult problem. The reason is that the optimal (i.e., linear) sequential algorithm by Tarjan [21] strongly relies on the depth-first search which is difficult to be computed in parallel. In our previous work [2] we have shown how selected nonlinear parallel SCC decomposition algorithms, namely the FORWARD-BACKWARD (FB) algorithm [9,17], the COLORING algorithm [19] and the OBF algorithm [3], can be modified in order to be accelerated on a vector processing SIMT architecture. In particular, we have decomposed the algorithms into primitive data-parallel graph operations and reformulated the recursion present in the algorithms by means of iterative procedures. This approach has been recently improved by warp-wise and block-wise task allocation for primitive graph operations [8,15]. The authors of [8] have further proposed a SIMT parallelisation of multi-step algorithms by [12,20] extending the FB algorithm and combining it with the COLORING algorithm.

This paper presents a new parametric multi-step scheme that allows us to compactly define a set of algorithms for SCC graph decomposition as well as a type of the parallelisation for individual graph operations. The scheme covers the existing algorithms and techniques mentioned above, but also introduces several new variants of the multistep algorithm. We use the scheme to carry out an extensive experimental evaluation that helps us to dissect the performance of the individual parameterisation on various classes of graphs. Our results indicate that there is no single algorithm that would outperform other algorithms on all type of graphs. Moreover, the results show that there is a nontrivial correlation between the parameterisation and the performance.

Based on the evaluation we identify, for each type of graphs, the key parameters of the scheme that significantly affect the performance and relate such behaviour to the structural properties of the graph. Such analysis is essential for designing an adaptive scheme that would either automatically select an adequate parameterisation based on a priori knowledge of the graph structure or automatically switch to a more viable parameterisation during the decomposition process. The automatic tuning of parameters is part of our current and future work.

2 Parallel Algorithms for SSC Decomposition

In this section we briefly present existing techniques and algorithms for parallel SCC decomposition that form basic building blocks for the parametric scheme.

2.1 Parallel Graph Algorithms for GPUs

In order to design scalable parallel graph algorithms that can effectively utilise modern GPUs, one has to consider key features of the underlying architecture and to employ suitable data structures. Typical GPUs consist of multiple Stream Multiprocessors (SM) with each SM following the SIMT model. This approach establishes a hierarchy of threads arranged into blocks that are assigned for parallel execution on SMs. Threads are hardwired into groups of 32 called warps, which form a basic scheduling unit and execute instructions in a lock-step manner. A sufficient number of threads has to be dispatched to hide the memory access latency and maximise the utilisation. Memory requests exhibiting spatial locality are coalesced to improve the performance. A typical GPU program consists of a CPU host code that calls GPU kernels executing the same scalar sequential program in many independent data-parallel threads.

Data structures encoding the graph have to allow independent thread-local data processing and coalesced access. The adjacency list representation is typically encoded as two one-dimensional arrays [10]. One array keeps the target vertices of all the edges. The second array keeps an index to the first array for every vertex. The index points to the position of the first edge emanating from the corresponding vertex. Other data associated to a vertex are organised in vectors as well. In [2,8,15], techniques for improving memory consumption and access pattern for SCC decomposition algorithms have been proposed.

The core procedure of every graph algorithm is the graph traversal. The SCC decomposition algorithms build on several types of the traversal as explained in the next section. Parallelisation of this procedure fundamentally affects the overall performance of the decomposition. There exist several approaches [5,10,11,18] that differ in the granularity of the task allocation (thread-per-vertex vs. warp-per-vertex vs. block-per-vertex) and in the number of vertices/edges processed during a single kernel (linear vs. quadratic parallelisation). In the context of the SCC decomposition the performance of these approaches significantly depends on the structure of the graphs and the type of the traversal. The parametric scheme presented in Sect. 3 captures various parallelisation strategies.

2.2 Forward-Backward algorithm

The FORWARD-BACKWARD (FB) algorithm [9] represents the fundamental algorithm for parallel SCC decomposition. It is listed as Algorithm 1 and proceeds as follows. A vertex called *pivot* is selected and the strongly connected component the pivot belongs to is computed as the intersection of the forward and backward *closure* of the pivot. Computation of the closures divides the graph into four subgraphs that are all SCC-closed. These subgraphs are (1) the strongly connected component with the pivot, (2) the subgraph given by vertices in the forward closure (3) the subgraph given by vertices in the backward closure, and (4) the subgraph given by the remaining vertices. The later three subgraphs form independent instances of the same problem, and therefore, they are recursively processed in parallel. The time complexity of the FB algorithm is $\mathcal{O}(n \cdot (m+n))$ since it performs $\mathcal{O}(m+n)$ work to detect a single strongly connected component.

Practical performance of the algorithm may be further improved by performing elimination of leading and terminal trivial strongly connected components – the so-called *trimming* [17]. The TRIMMING procedure builds upon a topological sort elimination. A vertex cannot be part of a non-trivial strongly connected component if its in-degree (out-degree) is zero. Therefore, such a vertex can be safely removed from the graph as a trivial SCC, before the pivot vertex is selected. The elimination can be iteratively repeated until no more vertices with zero in-degree (out-degree) exist.

In [2] we designed a GPU-acceleration of the FB algorithm that provides a good performance and scalability on regular graphs. In [15] the acceleration is improved by the linear parallelisation of the graph traversal and by a better pivot selection, which result in a performance gain including also a good performance on less regular graphs. The main limitation of the FB algorithm is that it performs $\mathcal{O}(m+n)$ work to detect a single SCC. This mitigates the benefits of the GPU-acceleration if the graph contains many small but non-trivial components.

Algorithm 1. FB	**Algorithm 2. COLORING**
1 **Procedure** FB(V)	1 **Procedure** COLORING(V)
2 **begin**	2 **begin**
3 pivot ← PIVOTSELECTION(V)	3 (maxColor, V_k) ←
4 F ← FWD-REACH(pivot, V)	FWD-MAXCOLOR(V)
5 B ← BWD-REACH(pivot, V)	4 **for** $k \in$ maxColor **in parallel do**
6 F ∩ B is SCC	5 B_k ← BWD(k, V_k)
7 **in parallel do**	6 B_k is SCC
8 FB(F \ B)	7 **if** $(V_k \setminus B_k \neq \emptyset)$ **then**
9 FB(B \ F)	8 COLORING($V_k \setminus B_k$)
10 FB(V \ (F ∪ B))	

2.3 Coloring Algorithm

The COLORING algorithm [19] is capable of detecting many strongly connected components in a single recursion step, however, for the price of an $\mathcal{O}(n \cdot (m+n))$ procedure. Therefore, the time complexity of the algorithm is $\mathcal{O}((l+1) \cdot n \cdot (m+n))$ where l is the longest path in the component graph.

The pseudo-code of the algorithm is listed as Algorithm 2. It propagates unique and totally ordered identifiers (colors) associated with vertices. Initially, each vertex keeps its own color. The colors are iteratively propagated along edges of the graph (line 3) so that each vertex keeps only the maximum color among the initial color and colors that have been propagated into it (maximal preceding color). After a fixpoint is reached (no color update is possible), the colors associated with vertices partition the graph into multiple SCC-closed subgraphs V_k. All vertices of a subgraph are reachable from the vertex v whose color is associated with the subgraph. Therefore, the backward closure of v restricted to the subgraph forms a SCC component that is removed from the graph before the next recursion step. Propagation procedure is rather expensive if there are multiple large components which limits the overall performance [2].

2.4 Other Algorithms

Both the presented algorithms typically show limited performance and poor scalability when applied to large real-world graph instances with many nontrivial components and a high diameter. Fundamental properties of these graphs have been consider to propose a series of extensions of the FB algorithm [12] and a multistep algorithm [20] that adequately combines the FB and COLORING algorithms. These two, originally multicore, algorithms have been recently redesigned to allow data-parallel processing [8], which led to the fastest GPU-accelerated SCC decomposition.

Barnat and Moravec [3] introduced the OBF algorithm that aims at decomposing the graph in more than three SCC-closed subgraphs within a single recursion step. However, unlike the COLORING algorithm, the price of the OBF procedure is $\mathcal{O}(m + n)$. Despite the better asymptotical complexity, our previous work [2] and also our more recent attempts indicate that effective data-parallelisation of the OBF algorithm is a very hard problem and the approaches based on the multistep algorithm performs generally better on SIMT-based architectures.

Very recently a multi-core version of the Tarjan algorithm based on parallelisation of depth-first search [4] has been proposed. It preserves the liner complexity of SCC decomposition and on a variety of graph instances it outperforms previous multi-core solutions. However, on real-word graphs it considerably lags behind the approaches by [12,20] and the proposed parallelisation is principally not suitable for SIMT architectures.

3 Multi-step Parametric Scheme for SCC Decomposition

This section introduces a new multi-step scheme for SCC decomposition, which consists of two levels of parametrization. The first allows setting the individual steps of the algorithm, while the second allows defining the parallelisation strategy for the graph traversal.

3.1 Parametric Multi-step Algorithm

The multi-step algorithm consists of 3 steps: (1) I_t iterations of the TRIMMING procedure that identifies *trivial components* of the graph (see Sect. 2.2), (2) I_f iterations of the FB algorithm that aims at identifying *big components*, and

(3) the COLORING algorithm that decomposes the rest of the graph. The algorithm parameterisation determines the values of I_t and I_f. Algorithm 3 depicts the host code for the GPU-accelerated version of the algorithm.

In the first step (lines 1–2), the kernel ONESTEPTRIMMING implements a single iteration of the trimming procedure. It identifies and eliminates vertices of G that form trivial SCCs. It stores the eliminated vertices in the array scc. Note that the proposed scheme does not perform the trimming procedure in the later steps of the algorithm, i.e., within every FB iteration as in [2], since the COLORING algorithm handles the remaining trivial components more efficiently.

In the second step (lines 3–7), the algorithm selects a single pivot from the remaining (i.e., not eliminated) part of the graph, it computes the forward and backward closure for such a vertex, and it marks the four subgraphs (see Sect. 2.2) by using the UPDATE kernel. Then, through further iterations of the second step, the algorithm selects multiple pivots and computes multiple

---

Algorithm 3. Parametric Multi-step

Input : $G = (V, E)$, parameters I_t and I_f
Output: SCC decomposition of G
1 **for** $i = 1$; $i \leq I_t \ \wedge \ scc \neq V$; $i = i + 1$ **do**
2 $\quad \lfloor$ ONESTEPTRIMMING(G, scc)
3 **for** $i = 1$; $i \leq I_f \ \wedge \ V \neq scc$; $i = i + 1$ **do**
4 $\quad \vert$ PIVOTSELECTION$(G, pivots, ranges)$
5 $\quad \vert$ FWD-REACH$(G, pivots, ranges, visited.f)$
6 $\quad \vert$ BWD-REACH$(G, pivots, ranges, visited.b)$
7 $\quad \lfloor$ UPDATE$(scc, range, visited)$
8 **while** $terminate = false$ **do**
9 $\quad \vert$ FWD-MAXCOLOR$(G, ranges, colors)$
10 $\quad \vert$ BWD-REACH$(G, ranges, colors, visited.b)$
11 $\quad \lfloor$ UPDATE$(range, visited.b, colors, scc)$

---

closures restricted to the individual subgraphs. The array $ranges$ is used to maintain the identification of the subgraphs, while the arrays $visited$ indicate the vertices visited during the closure computations. The array scc is updated at every iteration to store all vertices that has been already identified in a SCC. For the pivot selection over multiple subgraphs, the algorithm implements the approach proposed in [8] extended to apply the heuristics defined in [20] to favour vertices with a high in-degree and out-degree. The FWD-REACH and BWD-REACH kernels implement parallel BFS visits of the graph, which have been adequately modified for providing reachability results.

The last step implements the coloring algorithm, which is iteratively applied to decompose the remaining subgraphs. The max color is propagated to the successor non-eliminated vertices, and stored in the array $colors$ (line 9). The parametric BWD-REACH kernel implements the backward closure to identify a single component for each subgraph. Finally, the updating kernel partitions each subgraph into multiple subgraphs based on the max colors and updates the ranges accordingly for the next iteration.

Note that in our implementation the data associated to vertices in the form of the aforementioned arrays are merged and stored in two 32-bit arrays.

3.2   Parallelisation Strategy for Graph Traversal

Another dimension of parameterisation relates to the way reachability procedures are implemented within the FB and COLORING parts of the Algorithm 3 (lines 5, 6, and 10 respectively).

Recall that when computing the reachability relation (closure), the longest path along which the algorithm has to traverse is given by the diameter of the graph. Assuming that the closure computation consists of multiple kernel calls, where each kernel call shortens this distance by at least one, we immediately have that the diameter of the graph also gives the bound on the number of kernel calls needed. However, there are multiple strategies how to implement such a single kernel call. If the kernel call is guaranteed to shorten the distance only by one, but its complexity itself is linear (e.g. it inspects all vertices/edges), we obtain an overall procedure that computes the closure in a quadratic amount of work in the worst case with respect to the size of the graph.

Alternatively, we may employ a strategy that mimics the serial graph traversal procedure and uses queue of vertices to be processed as the underlying data structure (the so called frontier queue). In such the case, the complexity of the kernel call is proportional to the amount of vertices processed and the overall complexity of the procedure remains linear. And indeed, when dealing with large graphs, it has been shown that this works the best among various GPU-oriented implementations [5]. On the other hand, the overhead introduced by the maintianance of the frontier queue may render the linear solution inefficient when applied to compute the closure operation on subgraphs with small diameter.

In our parametric scheme we, therefore, allow to specify which strategy should be used to compute the closures in individual phases. In particular, we support the three following options.

1. *Quadratic parallelisation (Q).* The closure computation is based on the quadratic parallel breadth-first search as proposed in [10]. It implements the simplest static workload partitioning and vertex-per-thread mapping, thus involving the smallest runtime computation overhead. This strategy works the best for large graphs with regular structure and small diameter.
2. *Quadratic parallelisation with Virtual Warps (Q_{VW}).* In this strategy we also employ the quadratic parallel breadth-first search, however, the workload partitioning and mapping rely on the *virtual warps* as proposed in [11]. This modification allows for almost even workload assigned to individual threads, which after all results in reduced branching divergence – an aspect very crucial for the performance of GPU algorithm. Virtual warps also allow improved coalescing of memory accesses since more threads of a virtual warp access to adjacent addresses in the global memory. This strategy is supposed to work the best for graphs with uneven edge distribution.
3. *Linear parallelisation (L).* This strategy is our own implementation of the linear closure procedure as proposed in [5]. It provides a highly tunable solution that allows efficient handling of very irregular graphs with the overhead

of queue maintenance and dynamic load balancing at the runtime. This strategy should work the best for graphs with large diameter and nonuniform edge distribution.

Since the TRIMMING step is typically performed only through a couple of iterations, the strategy used in the TRIMMING kernel rely on a very light thread-per-vertex allocation and the quadratic parallelisation. The overhead of the linear or even more complex approach in this step would never pay off. The very same strategy has also been used for the implementation of the maximal color propagation in the COLORING phase (line 9 of Algorithm 3).

4   Experimental Results

The experimental results have been run on a dataset of 17 graphs, which have been collected to represent very different structure of the graphs. The dataset covers both synthetic and real-world graphs from different sources and contexts such as social networks, road networks, and recursive graph models. The real-world graphs have been selected from Stanford Network Analysis Platform (SNAP) [14], Koblenz Network Collection [13], and University of Florida Sparse Matrix Collection [6], while the random and R-MAT graphs have been generated by using the GTGraph tool [1].

Table 1 summarizes the graph features in terms of number of vertices (in million), edges (in million), average degree, the percentage of vertices with out-degree equal to zero ($d(v) = 0$), out-degree standard deviation, average diameter (over 100 BFS from random sources), number of SCCs, percentage of vertices in the largest SCC, and the percentage of vertices in SCCs with size equal to one.

Table 1. Characteristics of the graph dataset.

Graph name	Vertices	Edges	Avg. degree	N. of $d(v) = 0$	Std. deviation	Avg. diameter	N. of SCCs	Largest SCC	Trivial SCCs
amazon-2008 [14]	0.7M	5.2M	7.0	12.0%	3.9	25.7	90,660	85%	12%
LiveJournal [14]	4.8M	69.0M	14.2	11.1%	36.1	12.6	971,232	79%	20%
Flickr [13]	2.3M	33.1M	14.4	32.3%	87.7	8.0	277,277	70%	19%
R-MAT [1]	10.0M	120.0M	12.0	20.2%	22.3	7.8	2,083,372	79%	21%
cit-Patents [14]	3.8M	16.5M	4.4	44.6%	7.8	4.2	3,774,768	0%	100%
Random [1]	10.0M	120.0M	12.0	0.0%	3.5	9.0	125	100%	0%
Pokec [14]	1.6M	30.6M	18.8	12.4%	32.1	9.9	325,892	80%	20%
Language [13]	0.4M	1.2M	3.0	0.0%	20.7	33.6	2,456	99%	1%
Baidu [13]	23.9M	58.3M	8.3	22.7%	23.2	12.8	1,503,003	28%	69%
Pre2 [13]	0.7M	6.0M	9.0	0.0%	22.1	60.7	391	100%	0%
CA-road [14]	23.9M	5.5M	2.8	0.3%	1.0	655.9	2,638	100%	0%
web-Berkstan [13]	0.9M	7.6M	2.8	0.7%	16.4	465.6	109,409	49%	15%
SSCA8 [1]	8.4M	99.0M	11.8	0.2%	4.4	1,535.9	55,900	97%	0%
trec-w10g [13]	1.6M	8.0M	5.0	4.4%	72.0	54.8	531,539	29%	31%
Fullchip [6]	3.0M	26.6M	8.9	0.0%	23.1	37.2	35	100%	0%
USA-road [7]	23.9M	58.3M	2.4	0.0%	0.9	6,277.0	1	100%	0%
Wiki-Talk [14]	18.3M	127.3M	9.4	93.8%	80.0	0.4	14,459,546	21%	79%

The table underlines, for instance, that road networks, such as *CA-road* and *USA-road*, present in general a single SCC, a low average degree, and a low number of vertices with $d(v) = 0$. In contrast, social networks (*LiveJournal* and *Flickr*) and the R-MAT model show small-world network properties, which imply one large SCC and a high number of single-vertex SCCs.

We run the experiments on a Linux system (Ubuntu 14.04) with a NVIDIA Kepler Tesla K40 GPU device with 12 GB of memory, CUDA Toolkit 7.5, AMD Phenom II X6 1055T 3 GHz host processor, and gcc host compiler v. 4.8.4.

We compared three implementations: a sequential version that implements the Tarjan algorithm [21], which is considered the most efficient sequential algorithm. The data-parallel GPU implementation by Devshatwar et al. [8], the fastest GPU solution at the state of the art, and the proposed approach. Table 2 reports the results in terms of runtime (milliseconds) and performance (million of edges per seconds - MTEPS). The results of the proposed implementation are the best we obtained through the parameter configuration, as explained in the following. All the reported values are the average of ten runs. The results show that the application throughput (MTEPS) of the parallel implementations is directly related to the size and the average diameter of graphs. For instance, *cit-Patents* graph shows a high value of MTEPS due to a low average diameter and a regular degree distribution that allow a high GPU utilisation. On the other hand, the performance of the sequential version depends on the number of vertices and edges of the graphs.

Table 3 presents the configuration of the proposed parametric approach that leads to the best performance and compares such performance to those provided by the "static" solution of Devshatwar et al. The configurations are expressed in

Table 2. Runtime (milliseconds) and performance of the three implementations.

Graph name	Sequential SCC		Devshatwar et al. [8]		Proposed implementation	
	Time	MTEPS	Time	MTEPS	Time	MTEPS
amazon-2008	162	32	16	325	17	305
LiveJournal	2,575	26	86	802	87	793
Flickr	821	40	54	611	54	611
R-MAT	9,182	13	193	621	192	625
cit-Patents	536	31	16	1,031	16	1,031
Random	10,619	11	231	519	218	550
Pokec	1,344	23	42	729	33	927
Language	75	16	29	41	22	55
Baidu	582	100	70	832	50	1,166
Pre2	127	47	30	200	19	316
CA-road	223	25	166	33	79	70
web-Berkstan	94	81	1,754	4	717	11
SSCA8	4,237	23.4	1,174	84	465	213
trec-w10g	147	54	12,508	1	2,218	4
Fullchip	547	49	506	53	72	369
USA-road	2,191	27	7,041	8	669	87
Wiki-Talk	5,835	22	18,907	7	731	174

Table 3. Parametrization results and performance comparison.

Graph name	FB alg.	Coloring alg.	Trimming steps	FB steps	Speedup vs. sequential	Speedup vs. Devshatwar et al.[8]
amazon-2008	Q_{VW}/L	Q/L	1	1	9.5x	0.9x
LiveJournal	Q_{VW}	Q/L	1	1	29.6x	1.0x
Flickr	Q_{VW}/L	Q/L	1	1	15.2x	1.0x
R-MAT	Q_{VW}	Q/L	1	1	47.8x	1.0x
cit-Patents	Q/L	Q/L	1	1	33.5x	1.0x
Random	Q_{VW}	Q/L	0	1	48.7x	1.1x
Pokec	Q_{VW}	L	1	1	40.7x	**1.3x**
Language	L	Q	0	2	3.4x	**1.3x**
Baidu	L	L	3	1	11.6x	**1.4x**
Pre2	L	L	0	1	6.7x	**1.6x**
CA-road	L	L	0	1	2.8x	**2.1x**
web-Berkstan	L	L	FULL	17	0.1x	**2.4x**
SSCA8	L	L	0	1	9.1x	**2.5x**
trec-w10g	L	L	2	20	0.1x	**5.6x**
Fullchip	L	L	0	1	7.6x	**7.0x**
USA-road	L	Q	0	1	3.3x	**10.5x**
Wiki-Talk	L	L	5	1	8.0x	**25.9x**

terms of which strategy is used in the FB and in the coloring step, i.e., linear (L), static quadratic (Q), and quadratic with virtual warps (Q_{VW}), and the number of iterations of the trimming and FB steps. Notations Q/L or Q_{VW}/L indicate that the two algorithms provide similar performance.

The proposed implementation provides similar performance compared to Devshatwar et al. for the first six graphs of the dataset, while it reports speedup up to 26 times for the other graphs. This is due to the parametric feature of the proposed approach, which allows properly combining the quadratic and linear algorithms and tuning the algorithm iterations for each step i.e. trimming (I_t parameter), forward-backward (I_f parameter), and coloring. In particular, graphs with low average diameter, such as *Flickr, R-MAT, cit-Patents, Random*, show good performance also with the quadratic traversal algorithms due to less overhead compared to the linear approach that maintains frontier data queues.

The *LiveJournal* graph presents the same average diameter of *Baidu* but shows different SCC characteristics. *LiveJournal* has a very large SCC and a small percentage of trivial components, while *Baidu* the opposite. In this case, a high number of vertices with out-degree equal to zero (22.7%) favours quadratic parallelisation and one iteration of trimming.

The *amazon-2008* graph, even though it has a middle-sized average diameter, shows the best results with the quadratic approach. This is due to its very small size (*amazon-2008* is the second smallest graph in the dataset). The *Language* graph has similar size but it has a high unbalanced out-degree distribution (i.e., standard deviation 20.7 versus 3.9 of *amazon-2008*) and thus the load balancing techniques implemented in the linear BFS outperforms the quadratic parallelisation of the FB algorithm.

The proposed parametric implementation clearly outperforms the static Devshatwar et al. approach on graphs with high average diameter, such as *USA-Road*, and not uniform workload, such as *Wiki-Talk* (std. deviation equal to 80) thanks to the switch to the linear algorithm, which is more efficient in such a kind of graphs. Finally, both parallel implementations provide poor performance in *Web-Berkstan* and *trec-w10g* graphs due to the lack of data parallelism, which results from the small size, high diameter and low average out-degree.

We can also observe that the trimming step in road networks (*CA-Road* and *USA-Road*), *Pre2*, *Random* and *Fullchip* graphs does not significantly improve the overall performance, since the graphs contain small number of trivial SCCs. The *web-Berkstan* and *trec-w10g* require a high number of FB algorithm steps due to a high number of middle-sized SCCs. For instance, *trec-w10g* graph has the sum of the percentages of the largest SCC (29%) and trivial SCCs (31%) equal to 61% which indicates a remaining of 39% of middle-sized SCCs.

Figure 1 illustrates the impact of the parameters I_t and I_f on the overall performance for the selected graphs. The performance is represented using a

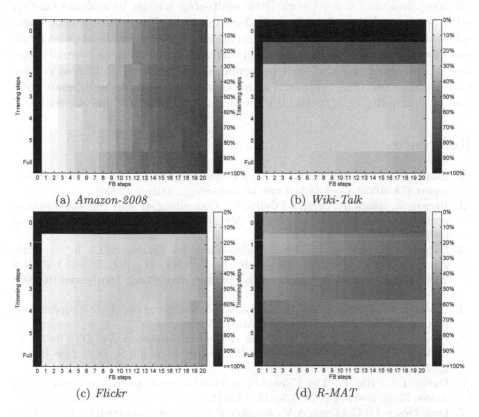

Fig. 1. Performance analysis through parametrization of I_t and I_f. Performance are represented using a color scale where lighter colors denote lower runtime. (Color figure online)

color scale – lighter colors denote lower runtime. The linear parallelisation evaluated on *Amazon-2008* (Fig. 1a) shows that the performance strongly depends on the number of FB iterations (I_f set around 1 gives the best results), while the number of trimming iterations does not affect the execution time. The linear parallelisation applied to *Wiki-Talk* (Fig. 1b) shows the opposite behaviour: I_f has a very low impact on the performance, while setting a wrong I_t (e.g., I_t equal to 1 as in Devshatwar et al.) leads to 60% performance decrease. Such a different behaviour of performance over I_t and I_f relies on the different characteristics of the two graphs. *Amazon-2008* has one large SCC and a very small number of trivial SCCs, while *Wiki-Talk* has a high number of trivial SCCs. The performance of the linear parallelisation over I_t and I_f on graphs *Flickr* and *R-MAT* shows a more uniform behaviour (Fig. 1c and d), since the graphs have one large SCC but also a high number of trivial SCCs.

5   Conclusions

We have presented a novel parametric multi-step scheme to evaluate existing GPU-accelerated algorithms for SCC decomposition. The extensive experimental results clearly indicate that there is no algorithm that would be the best for all classes of the graphs. We have dissected correlations between the internal structure of the algorithms and their performance on structurally different graphs. Our contribution, thus, represents an important step towards an ultimate solution of automatically adjusted GPU-aware algorithm for SCC decomposition.

References

1. Bader, D.A., Madduri, K.: GTgraph: a synthetic graph generator suite. Technical report GA 30332, Georgia Institute of Technology, Atlanta (2006)
2. Barnat, J., Bauch, P., Brim, L., Češka, M.: Computing strongly connected components in parallel on CUDA. In: IPDPS 2011, pp. 541–552. IEEE Computer Society (2011)
3. Barnat, J., Moravec, P.: Parallel algorithms for finding SCCs in implicitly given graphs. In: Brim, L., Haverkort, B., Leucker, M., Pol, J. (eds.) FMICS 2006. LNCS, vol. 4346, pp. 316–330. Springer, Heidelberg (2007). doi:10.1007/978-3-540-70952-7_22
4. Bloemen, V., Laarman, A., van de Pol, J.: Multi-core on-the-fly SCC decomposition. In: PPoPP 2016, pp. 8:1–8:12. ACM (2016)
5. Busato, F., Bombieri, N.: BFS-4K: an efficient implementation of BFS for kepler GPU architectures. IEEE Trans. Parallel Distrib. Syst. **26**(7), 1826–1838 (2015). ISSN 1045-9219
6. Davis, T.A., Hu, Y.: The University of Florida sparse matrix collection. ACM Trans. Math. Softw. (TOMS) **38**(1), 1 (2011)
7. Demetrescu, C., Goldberg, A.V., Johnson, D.S.: The Shortest Path Problem: Ninth DIMACS Implementation Challenge, vol. 74. American Mathematical Society, Providence (2009)

8. Devshatwar, S., Amilkanthwar, M., Nasre, R.: GPU centric extensions for parallel strongly connected components computation. In: GPGPU 2016, pp. 2–11. ACM (2016)
9. Fleischer, L.K., Hendrickson, B., Pınar, A.: On identifying strongly connected components in parallel. In: Rolim, J. (ed.) IPDPS 2000. LNCS, vol. 1800, pp. 505–511. Springer, Heidelberg (2000). doi:10.1007/3-540-45591-4_68
10. Harish, P., Narayanan, P.J.: Accelerating large graph algorithms on the GPU using CUDA. In: Aluru, S., Parashar, M., Badrinath, R., Prasanna, V.K. (eds.) HiPC 2007. LNCS, vol. 4873, pp. 197–208. Springer, Heidelberg (2007). doi:10.1007/978-3-540-77220-0_21
11. Hong, S., Kim, S., Oguntebi, T., Olukotun, K.: Accelerating CUDA graph algorithms at maximum warp. In: PPoPP 2011, pp. 267–276. ACM (2011)
12. Hong, S., Rodia, N.C., Olukotun, K.: On fast parallel detection of strongly connected components (SCC) in small-world graphs. In: SC 2013, pp. 92:1–92:11. ACM (2013)
13. Kunegis, J.: Konect: the koblenz network collection. In: WWW 2013, pp. 1343–1350. ACM (2013)
14. Leskovec, J., Sosič, R.: SNAP: a general purpose network analysis and graph mining library in C++. http://snap.stanford.edu/snap. Accessed May 2016
15. Li, G., Zhu, Z., Cong, Z., Yang, F.: Efficient decomposition of strongly connected components on GPUs. J. Syst. Architect. 60(1), 1–10 (2014)
16. Liu, X., et al.: IMGPU: GPU accelerated influence maximization in large-scale social networks. IEEE Trans. Parallel Distrib. Syst. 25(1), 136–145 (2014)
17. McLendon, W., Hendrickson, B., Plimpton, S.J., Rauchwerger, L.: Finding strongly connected components in distributed graphs. J. Parallel Distrib. Comput. 65(8), 901–910 (2005)
18. Merrill, D., Garland, M., Grimshaw, A.: Scalable GPU graph traversal. In: PPoPP 2012, pp. 117–128. ACM (2012)
19. Orzan, S.: On distributed verification and verified distribution. Ph.D. thesis, Free University of Amsterdam (2004)
20. Slota, G.M., Rajamanickam, S., Madduri, K.: BFS and coloring-based parallel algorithms for strongly connected components and related problems. In: IPDPS 2014, pp. 550–559. IEEE Computer Society (2014)
21. Tarjan, R.: Depth-first search and linear graph algorithms. SIAM J. Comput. 1(2), 140–100 (1972)

Investigations on Path Indexing for Graph Databases

Jonathan M. Sumrall[1], George H.L. Fletcher[2]([✉]), Alexandra Poulovassilis[3],
Johan Svensson[1], Magnus Vejlstrup[1], Chris Vest[1], and Jim Webber[1]

[1] Neo Technology, San Mateo, USA
{max.sumrall,johan,magnus.vejlstrup,chris.vest,
jim.webber}@neotechnology.com
[2] Eindhoven University of Technology, Eindhoven, The Netherlands
g.h.l.fletcher@tue.nl
[3] Birkbeck, University of London, London, UK
ap@dcs.bbk.ac.uk

Abstract. Graph databases have become an increasingly popular choice
for the management of the massive network data sets arising in many contemporary applications. We investigate the effectiveness of path indexing for accelerating query processing in graph database systems, using
as an exemplar the widely used open-source Neo4j graph database. We
present a novel path index design which supports efficient ordered access
to paths in a graph dataset. Our index is fully persistent and designed
for external memory storage and retrieval. We also describe a compression scheme that exploits the limited differences between consecutive
keys in the index, as well as a workload-driven approach to indexing. We
demonstrate empirically the speed-ups achieved by our implementation,
showing that the path index yields query run-times from 2x up to 8000x
faster than Neo4j. Empirical evaluation also shows that our scheme leads
to smaller indexes than using general-purpose LZ4 compression. The
complete stand-alone implementation of our index, as well as supporting
tooling such as a bulk-loader, are provided as open source for further
research and development.

1 Introduction

Massive graph-structured data collections are increasingly common in modern
application scenarios such as social networks and linked open data. Consequently,
there has been a flurry of development of graph database systems to support
scalable analytics on massive graphs. The selection and manipulation of *paths*
forms the core of querying graph datasets. However, the feasibility of a path-
centric approach to indexing massive graphs is an open problem and, to date, no
study has been performed on the benefits of path indexing for processing graph
queries in industry-strength graph databases. To our knowledge, this work is
the first to provide a design and implementation of a path index specifically
for graph databases, as well as an empirical study of the performance of such
indexes.

© Springer International Publishing AG 2017
F. Desprez et al. (Eds.): Euro-Par 2016 Workshops, LNCS 10104, pp. 532–544, 2017.
DOI: 10.1007/978-3-319-58943-5_43

Related Work. The study of path indexing has a long history, with a rich variety of strategies developed in the context of object-oriented [3] and XML [16] databases, and more recently in the indexing of graph data [17]. Related work includes approaches to creating structural summaries of semi-structured data, such as DataGuides [8], T-index [12], AK-index [11] and DK-index [4]. IndexFabric [6] indexes paths in tree-structured data by representing every path in the tree as a string and storing it in a Patricia tree. GraphGrep [14] uses a hash-based method to find occurrences of paths within subgraphs of a graph. For a more detailed review of previous approaches to indexing graph-structured data, we refer the reader to [15]. To our knowledge, the novel approach to path indexing that we present in this paper has not been studied or applied before in the context of any actively supported graph database system.

Contributions. We introduce a path-oriented index for graph-structured data and highlight its benefits for accelerating graph query processing, focusing on the processing of *path queries*. Our index implementation, which is based on the venerable B^+tree data structure, has been custom-built from scratch specifically to be based in external memory and to support and leverage the path structures found in graph datasets. The complete index implementation, as well as supporting tooling such as a bulk-loader, are available open source for further research and development.[1]

We show that use of our index yields, on average, orders of magnitude faster query processing times compared with Neo4j[2], a popular open-source native graph database which offers features such as being fully transactional and supporting a declarative graph query language, Cypher. We stress that our performance studies here compare our standalone index with a fully-fledged graph DBMS. Hence, the performance figures must be interpreted in this light. Nonetheless, the significantly faster query processing times achieved by our index is a clear indication that our solution warrants further investigation towards practical deployment in graph DBMSs. We also highlight the design and benefits of a simple yet highly effective path-centric compression scheme used in our index. We note that, to our knowledge, the proposed approach to path indexing is not found in any current graph database system, and thus the contributions of this paper and their potential for practical impact extend beyond our specific demonstration here by comparison to Neo4j.

Organization. In the next section we define our graph data model and path queries. In Sect. 3 we describe our path index implementation, including index design, initialization and compression. In Sect. 4 we present an empirical evaluation of our implementation. We conclude in Sect. 5 with a summary of our contributions and directions of further work.

---

[1] https://github.com/jsumrall/Path-Index.
[2] http://neo4j.com/docs/stable/.

2   Graphs and Path Queries

Data Model. Although modern graph DBMSs such as Neo4j support a richer property graph data model, we restrict our attention to just the path structure of graphs. In particular, we adopt a basic model of finite, edge-labeled, directed graphs $G = \langle N, E, \mathcal{L} \rangle$ where: N is a finite set of nodes; $\mathcal{L}$ is a finite set of edge labels; and $E \subseteq N \times \mathcal{L} \times N$ is a set of labeled directed edges.

Given a graph G, our interest is in indexing *paths* in G. The simplest paths are edges between adjacent nodes. In particular, for each edge $(s, \ell, t) \in E$, we say there is a path of length one from s to t (resp., from t to s) having label ℓ (resp., ℓ^{-1}).[3]

In general, for $k > 0$, let $paths_k(G)$ denote the set of all vectors of nodes $(n_1, \ldots, n_{j+1}) \in \underbrace{N \times \cdots \times N}_{j+1 \text{ times}}$, for $1 \leqslant j \leqslant k$, such that there is a path of length one from n_i to $n_i + 1$ in G, for each $1 \leqslant i \leqslant j$. The *label-path* of a given path $(n_1, \ell_1, n_2), (n_2, \ell_2, n_3), \ldots, (n_j, \ell_j, n_{j+1})$ is the sequence of edge labels $\ell_1 \ell_2 \cdots \ell_j$ along the path.

As an example, consider a graph G_{ex} with node set $\{sue, tom, zoe, chem101\}$ and edge set

$$\{(sue, takesCourse, chem101), (zoe, teacherOf, chem101),$$
$$(tom, takesCourse, chem101), (sue, knows, tom), (tom, knows, zoe)\}.$$

Then there are two distinct paths in G_{ex} of length two from *sue* to *zoe*, with respective label-paths $knows \cdot knows$ and $takesCourse \cdot teacherOf^{-1}$.

Queries. We focus on the evaluation of *path queries*, which are specified by projections on label-paths over $\mathcal{L}$. Given a label-path $\bar{\ell} = \ell_1 \ell_2 \cdots \ell_k$ and, for some $r \geq 0$, a list of indices $i_1, \ldots, i_r$ each in the range $[1, k+1]$, the semantics of evaluating $\pi_{i_1, \ldots, i_r}(\bar{\ell})$ on G is the set of all vectors of nodes $(m_1, \ldots, m_r) \in \underbrace{N \times \cdots \times N}_{r \text{ times}}$ such that there is a path $(n_1, \ell_1, n_2), (n_2, \ell_2, n_3), \ldots, (n_k, \ell_k, n_{k+1})$ in G with $m_j = n_{i_j}$ for each $1 \leq j \leq r$.

As an example, the following query selects all node pairs (x, z) such that x takes a course taught by z:

$$\pi_{1,3}(takesCourse \cdot teacherOf^{-1}).$$

It evaluates to the result set $\{(sue, zoe), (tom, zoe)\}$ on the graph G_{ex} above.

Here, we consider the execution of path queries of length at most k, for some fixed k. Compilation strategies for arbitrary graph queries targeting our path indexes is outside the scope of this paper and is a topic of ongoing study. In particular, preliminary work along these lines is reported by Fletcher *et al.* [7] which studies the use of path indexing for accelerating *regular path queries* on graphs.

---

[3] ℓ^{-1} denotes the inverse of edge label ℓ, which we just treat as normal edge label.

3   Path Indexing

In this section we describe our path indexing approach, focusing on the requirements, design, initialization and compression of our path indexes. The main
objective is to maintain an index on the set $paths_k(G)$ of a graph G, for some
fixed k, so as to accelerate the execution of path queries. A secondary goal is to
design methods for optimizing the index structure, so as to reduce the overall
size of the index and the cost of building, using and updating it. The size of
$paths_k(G)$ may exceed the amount of internal memory available and hence the
index design must target external memory. For detailed discussion of the design
space considered and the design choices made, we refer the reader to [15].

3.1   Index Design

Path Keys. Given a graph G, our path index maintains an index on the set
$paths_k(G)$, for some fixed k. Members of this set need to be represented in a
standard fashion, using a scheme such that specific elements of a path can be
identified, different paths can be compared to each other, and paths can be
serialized. This indexible form of a path is called a *key*.

To make a transformation from label-paths to keys, we first assign an ordering
to the elements of $\mathcal{L}$. Under this ordering, we convert each label to an integer
value in the range $1, \ldots, |\mathcal{L}|$. As noted above, we also consider the inverse of
labels: for a label identified by integer i, the inverse of the label is assigned
the value $|\mathcal{L}| + i$. A k-label-path can now be uniquely identified by a vector
$(v_1, \ldots, v_k)$ where each v_i is in the range $1, \ldots, 2|\mathcal{L}|$. Based on this vector representation of label-paths, a unique integer is assigned to each label-path: the
label-path's identifier. These identifiers are stored in a mapping dictionary, implemented using a hash map. During query evaluation, the mapping dictionary is
consulted to identify the corresponding identifier for that particular label-path.

To represent specific paths of G, the sequence of *nodes* along a path must also
be considered. Each node is differentiated from all other nodes in the graph by
a unique integer identifier (e.g. as generated by the graph DBMS; in the case of
Neo4j, this corresponds to the physical address of the node). Concatenating the
identifier of a path's label-path with the identifiers of the nodes along the path,
a path can be represented as a vector consisting of first its label-path identifier
followed by its node identifiers. Therefore our data representation of a key is as
a series of integer values, and for a path of length k, the size of the key is $k + 1$
integer values (of 8 bytes each).

Storage and Search. We use a B$^+$tree [5] as the underlying storage mechanism
for keys. This allows keys to be stored and retrieved in sorted order efficiently
for large sets of keys which may exceed the amount of internal memory in the
system. It also allows for searching using any prefix of the keys stored in the
index, e.g. a label-path identifier. Moreover, our path index implementation can
also support alternative sort orderings of the paths, which may be desirable for
join processing as part of a fully-fledged query processor; further discussion of
this is can be found in [15].

Page Design. Our index is designed to be disk-based, and therefore careful attention has been paid to how the bytes of the internal and leaf pages of the index are arranged. All pages contain a header with essential information including sub-tree references and the number of elements in the page. Individual elements are assumed to be of equal size, and therefore delimiter values between elements are not needed.

Figure 1 details the structure of internal pages and leaf pages. The internal pages contain a 25 byte header, followed by references to children pages, followed by the keys which sort the children pages. Leaf pages contain the 25 byte header, followed by the keys. Since the header contains information about the number of keys in the page, it is possible to directly navigate to specific keys by calculating an offset value based on the size of the keys and the ordered position of the desired key.

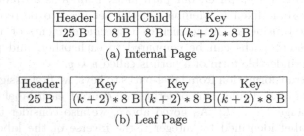

(a) Internal Page

(b) Leaf Page

Fig. 1. Layout of the internal pages and leaf pages of the index.

3.2   Index Compression

We recall that the first value of a key is a label-path id and the subsequent values are node ids, i.e. a key is of the form $pathID, nodeID_1, nodeID_2, nodeID_3, \ldots$. Within the index, keys are sorted lexicographically, first by $pathID$, then by $nodeID_1$, then by $nodeID_2$, and so on. This ordering causes neighbouring keys to be similar. Indeed, many keys will often have the same values of $pathID$ and $nodeID_1$ in particular, since many neighboring keys have the same label-path ids and the same starting node ids along the path. This is similar to the observation of Neumann and Weikum [13] on efficiently storing RDF triples, and allows for a similar compression scheme. The compression method we use involves not storing the full key, but only storing the difference between successive keys. This results in a high compression, as the change between keys is very often quite small.

For each value in a key, the delta (i.e., integer distance) to obtain this value from the value in the same position in the previous key is calculated. Once each delta is obtained, the minimum number of bytes necessary to store the *largest* delta for this key is found. Each delta is then standardized in length to only that minimum number of bytes. A header byte contains a value representing the size of all these deltas. The largest possible delta would require 8 bytes and the minimum delta we consider is 1 byte.

Often, the prefix of a key can be identical to that of the previous key in the page, while the final value in the key can require a large delta. In the compression scheme above, we allocate a number of bytes to store the large delta, but the delta for the first few values would be zero. To compress even further, the first 5 bits in the header can be used to signal when the corresponding value has a delta of zero, essentially forming a gap in the series of deltas stored for this key. We call these "gap bits". By enabling a gap bit, we can avoid writing the delta for that value altogether, and only write the values which have a non-zero delta. An illustration of our compressed key structure can be found in Fig. 2.

Gap	Payload	Delta	Delta	Delta
2 Bits	6 Bits	1-8 Bytes	1-8 Bytes	1-8 Bytes
Header		*Path ID*	*Node ID*	*Node ID*

Fig. 2. Structure of a compressed key with gap bits for a path with $k = 1$.

Compression is applied to individual leaf pages, not across pages. Compressing larger portions of the index would produce a smaller index, but at a cost of greater complexity in maintaining the index under updates. By only compressing individual pages, we can still traverse to any leaf page and immediately begin reading keys. If larger portions of the index were compressed together, then those additional portions would need to be fetched and decompressed before beginning to read keys.

Compression is also not applied to pages representing internal pages in the index. Internal pages account for a much smaller share of the total number of pages in the index, as most pages are leaves. Further, we assume that internal pages will be accessed often during traversals, and the additional decompression time on these pages may not justify the possible space savings.

3.3 Index Initialization: Full vs. Workload-Based Indexing

We have explored two approaches to populating the index. The first is to generate and store all possible paths up to length k. We first perform an external merge sort on the length-1 paths (i.e. the graph's edge set E), and their inverses, and bulk load them into our path index. With the $k = 1$ index constructed, the $k = 2$ index is constructed by performing a merge join on the opposing end nodes of the length-1 paths. In general, the $k = n1$ index is constructed by performing a join on two full length-k_1 and length-k_2 indexes, where $k_1 + k_2 = n + 1$ holds true. For large values of k, this requires an extensive time and space commitment, as we see below. The payoff is that the expected query execution time on any arbitrary k-path query will be very low.

As an alternative to this off-line construction of all paths up to length k, it is possible to index on demand (i.e. as a background process during query execution time) only those paths needed to fulfill a given query workload, i.e. to index a finite set of path queries of arbitrary length. Such an index is first initialized with the length-1 paths, i.e. with the graph's edge set E. Then, as encountered in the query workload, longer paths (of arbitrary length) are dynamically built and added to the index by performing joins on the initial 1-paths and subsequent longer paths which have already been indexed. We refer to the indexes for the first method as *full k indexes* and the latter as *workload-based indexes*.

4   Evaluation

We now describe a set of experiments that investigate our index compression scheme, index sizes, and query execution times using path indexing. All experiments were performed on a 2.0 GHz i7 processor with 8 GB of main memory and a solid state drive, running OSX 10.10. Experiments were run on three different datasets, drawn from different sources and of different sizes. Two datasets, the Lehigh University Benchmark (LUBM) dataset [10] and the Linked Data Benchmark Council (LDBC) dataset [2] are synthetic datasets, while the Advogato dataset [1] is a real-world dataset. All experiments were conducted using the latest version of Neo4j available at the time, Neo4j 2.3.0-M01. We focus here on our experiments with the LUBM and refer the reader to [15] for details of the experiments with the other two datasets.

LUBM graphs model a university scenario (e.g., nodes represent universities, departments, students, teachers, ...). We generated a graph with 50 universities, containing approximately 6.8 million unique edges. We followed the same data preparation steps as taken by Gubichev and Then [9], except our dataset was not enriched with inferred facts derived from ontology rules. For example, nodes of type *Associate Professor* do not also get the more general label *Professor*. LUBM is provided with 14 different queries. Here, we use roughly the same queries as used by Gubichev and Then [9], with substitutions for the length-0 queries. Our queries are listed in the Appendix.

4.1   Index Compression Evaluation

Evaluation of our compression scheme shows that it results in significantly reduced index sizes compared to the uncompressed index size. Further, our compression method outperforms general-purpose LZ4 compression[4] in terms of both speed and scale of compression. A comparison of the size of indexes resulting from each compression technique is shown in Table 1, while a comparison of the speed of the compression techniques is shown in Table 2. The comparison was undertaken by inserting sequentially increasing keys into the index and measuring throughput time and final index size. The evaluation was undertaken for indexes with key sizes of $k = 1, 2, 3$. However, the size of the $k = 3$ index without compression and with the LZ4 algorithm was either too large for our test system or took a significant amount of time. We also include here results for our

---

[4] https://github.com/jpountz/lz4-java.

Table 1. Index size.

Index	Uncompressed	LZ4	Path index
$k = 1$	0.16 GB	0.053 GB	0.02 GB
$k = 2$	15.99 GB	3.67 GB	1.69 GB
$k = 3$	-	-	41.58 GB
Workload-based	-	-	0.1 GB

Table 2. Indexing time, rounded to the nearest minute.

Index	Uncompressed	LZ4	Path Index
$k = 1$	< 1 min	4 min	< 1 min
$k = 2$	28 min	266 min	27 min
$k = 3$	-	-	178 min
Workload-based	-	-	4 min

workload-based index, built using the query workload of the LUBM benchmark, which significantly lowers storage overhead and compression time. Overall, the comparison shows that our scheme outperforms the LZ4 algorithm in terms of both speed and scale of compression.

4.2 Index Size Evaluation

The right-most column of Table 1 shows the index sizes. These results show that the size of the index as k increases becomes a limiting factor to the usability of the index. However, while the index sizes may be large, the evaluation time for path queries using the index remains very low (see below). Moreover, although the full indexes can grow to be quite large, the workload-based index has very low overhead while still supporting efficient query processing, as we see next.

4.3 Query Execution Evaluation

We compare query execution time using our path index with that using Neo4j, subject to the provisos discussed in the Introduction. Only the time needed to retrieve the results is compared for each query: the time needed to open and close the database or index, and to open and close a transaction event is ignored. Six runs were conducted for each query, with each run consisting of 5 executions of the query. Between each run, the system's caches were flushed. The first execution after a cache flush was considered a "cold" run, with empty caches, and the subsequent runs were considered "warm" runs, where caching is likely to result in lower evaluation times. For each query therefore, we obtained 6 "cold run" timings and 24 "warm run" timings. For each set of cold-run and warm-run timings of each query, we excluded 10% of the data from each end of the range of recorded results, eliminating outliers due to nondeterminism in the runtime environment. We report here the mean of the remaining values, focusing on the warm run experiments. A full analysis, including both the warm and the cold runs, can be found in [15].

Full Indexes. We first consider path query performance on a full $k = 3$ index. Results are reported in Table 3, where we give the time to the first result and the time to the last result. For both Neo4j and our path index, the time to the first result is measured as the time from immediately before Neo4j's or the path index's *find* operation is executed, and the time immediately after the first result is found. The time to the last result is measured as the time immediately before Neo4j's or the path index's *find* operation is executed, until the time immediately after the last result is found.

In addition to using the full-length k-paths in the index, queries are also evaluated using the $(k-1)$-paths in the index for Queries 4–10, for comparison purposes. For example, looking at Query 7 in Table 3, we see under the column labeled "Index $k = 2$" the time needed to evaluate Query 7 using the $k = 2$ and $k = 1$ subpaths of the query and joining the results (using a merge join). This

Table 3. Average times (ms) to retrieve the first result and the last result in Neo4j and in the Path Index.

		Neo4j	Index $k = 3$	Index $k = 2$	Index $k = 1$	Speedup
Q1	First Result	480	-	-	0.19	2526x
	Last Result	2080	-	-	37	56x
Q2	First Result	2014	-	-	1	2014x
	Last Result	2014	-	-	1	2014x
Q3	First Result	413	-	-	0.05	8260x
	Last Result	1352	-	-	4	338x
Q4	First Result	774	-	0.8	173	967x
	Last Result	3741	-	112	10932	33x
Q5	First Result	457	-	2	45	228x
	Last Result	13303	-	1439	4645	9x
Q6	First Result	437	-	2	47	218x
	Last Result	2225	-	107	2831	20x
Q7	First Result	8	2	2.4	-	4x
	Last Result	2221	32	179	-	69x
Q8	First Result	1	1	2	-	1x
	Last Result	5319	1992	493	-	2x
Q9	First Result	1	2	2	-	0.5x
	Last Result	1378	8	179	-	172x
Q10	First Result	1	3	2	-	0.3x
	Last Result	1392	4	16	-	348x
Avg	First Result	458	2	1	< 1	1444x
	Last Result	3502	509	552	14	306x

Table 4. Workload experiment with paths constructed from the $k = 1$ index with joined results inserted into the index (average time to last result, in ms).

	Query Plan	Index Const-ruction	Index Query	Neo4j	Speed up
Q4	takesCourse $\bowtie$ teacherOf^{-1}	30289	119	3741	31x
Q5	memberOf $\bowtie$ subOrganizationOf^{-1}	129499	775	13303	17x
Q6	memberOf $\bowtie$ subOrganizationOf	11113	39	2225	57x
Q7A	undergraduateDegreeFrom $\bowtie$ Query 6^{-1}	769	< 1	2221	2221x
Q7B	P_{7B} = subOrganizationOf^{-1} $\bowtie$ memberOf^{-1} undergraduateDegreeFrom $\bowtie$ P_{7B}	15832	< 1	2221	2221x
Q8A	hasAdvisor $\bowtie$ Query4^{-1}	836	2	5319	2659x
Q8B	P_{8B} = teacherOf $\bowtie$ takesCourse^{-1} hasAdvisor $\bowtie$ P_{8B}	2703	2	5319	2659x
Q9	P_9 = worksFor $\bowtie$ subOrganizationOf^{-1} headOf^{-1} $\bowtie$ P_9	8807	2	1378	689x
Q10	P_{10} = worksFor $\bowtie$ subOrganizationOf headOf^{-1} $\bowtie$ P_{10}	822	< 1	1392	1392x
Avg		22296	104	4124	1327x

gives us an indication of query evaluation times if the index only contained the smaller subpaths and not the full $k = 3$ path. The column "Index $k = 1$" for Query 7 is blank, as these experiments only show the times needed to perform a single (merge) join to evaluate a given query. Evaluating Query 7 using only the $k = 1$ paths is possible, but would require joining two subpaths first, and then undertaking a sort merge join with the third subpath or performing a hash join with the third subpath.

Workload-Based Indexes. Experiments were also conducted on workload-based indexes built at runtime, where the necessary $k = 1$ paths are joined to form the paths of length 2 in the queries, or joined a third time to form the paths of length 3. Table 4 shows the cost of building and using the workload-based indexes. The alternatives A/B for Queries 7 and 8 arise from whether or not to reuse paths already constructed in the index from previous query evaluations.

Summary. The above results demonstrate that both full and workload-based path indexes have much lower evaluation times for all path queries compared to Neo4j. Our experiments on the LDBC and Advogato datasets confirm and further strengthen the results reported here, for both warm and cold runs (see [15] for details).

5   Concluding Remarks

This paper has presented a new and simple path indexing approach to improve path query performance for graph database systems. Our empirical study has demonstrated the significant potential of path indexes for graph databases. Keeping in mind that Neo4j is a fully-fledged graph DBMS, our experiments show that, for every query trialled, path indexing provides a non-trivial, often multiple orders of magnitude, improvement in query evaluation time. We have demonstrated the practicality of workload-driven path indexes, where the additional time to first evaluate and store the results of a path query is relatively large, but subsequent query times using the index provide significant speedups, amortizing the index build cost over the lifetime of the query workload. Furthermore, our workload-based indexes are an order of magnitude smaller than the full index. Our implementation includes supporting tools, e.g. for bulk loading the index with paths from the graph in an efficient way. As indicated in the Introduction, the complete codebase is available open-source for further study.

Our empirical results show that workload-based indexing offers the most promise in terms of index size, index construction time, and query performance. Further study of the design, engineering, and deployment in practical graph database systems of these types of indexes is the natural progression of this work. Additional experiments need to be conducted to identify how to best build the index based on encountered queries. Possibilities include examining query logs and building indexes based on frequent queries. Study of index maintenance under mixed transactional workloads is another interesting direction of future study, i.e. policies for updating the path indexes in the face of insertions and deletions of edges in the data graph. Efficient index updates may be achieved by supporting multiple indexes, supporting fast retrieval for multiple dimensions of label-paths. Finally, another important direction for future research is compilation strategies for richer query languages such as Cypher targeting our path indexes as one of the alternative access paths available in the DBMS.

Appendix: LUBM Cypher Queries

```
Q1: MATCH (x)-[:memberOf]->(y) RETURN ID(x),ID(y)

Q2: MATCH (x)-[:memberOf]->(y)
    WHERE x.URI ="http://www.Department0...Student207"
    RETURN ID(x), ID(y)

Q3: MATCH (x)-[:worksFor]->(y) RETURN ID(x),ID(y)

Q4: MATCH (x)-[:takesCourse]->(y)<-[:teacherOf]-(z)
    RETURN ID(x),ID(y),ID(z)

Q5: MATCH (x)-[:memberOf]->(y)<-[:subOrganizationOf]-(z)
    RETURN ID(x),ID(y),ID(z)

Q6: MATCH (x)-[:memberOf]->(y)-[:subOgranizationOf]->(z)
    RETURN ID(x),ID(y),ID(z)

Q7: MATCH (x)-[:undergraduateDegreeFrom]->(y)
```

```
          <-[:subOrganizationOf]-(z)<-[:memberOf]-(x)
     RETURN ID(x),ID(y),ID(z)

Q8:  MATCH (x)-[:hasAdvisor]->(y)-[:teacherOf]->(z)<-[:takesCourse]-(x)
     RETURN ID(x),ID(y),ID(z)

Q9:  MATCH (x)<-[:headOf]-(y)-[:worksFor]->(z)<-[:subOrganisationOf]-(w)
     RETURN ID(x),ID(y),ID(z),ID(w)

Q10:MATCH (x)<-[:headOf]-(y)-[:worksFor]->(z)-[:subOrganisationOf]->(w)
     RETURN ID(x),ID(y),ID(z),ID(w)
```

References

1. Advogato network dataset - KONECT, October 2014. http://konect.uni-koblenz. de/networks/advogato
2. Angles, R., et al.: The linked data benchmark council. ACM SIGMOD Rec. **43**(1), 27–31 (2014). http://dl.acm.org/citation.cfm?id=2627692.2627697
3. Bertino, E., et al.: Object-oriented databases. In: Bertino, E., et al. (eds.) Indexing Techniques for Advanced Database Systems, pp. 1–38. Kluwer, Alphen aan den Rijn (1997)
4. Chen, Q., Lim, A., Ong, K.W.: D(k)-index. In: Proceedings of SIGMOD 2003, p. 134. ACM Press, San Diego, June 2003. http://dl.acm.org/citation.cfm? id=872757.872776
5. Comer, D.: The ubiquitous B-tree. ACM Comput. Surv. **11**(2), 121–137 (1979). http://dl.acm.org/citation.cfm?id=356770.356776
6. Cooper, B., Sample, N., Franklin, M.J., Hjaltason, G.R., Shadmon, M.: A fast index for semistructured data. In: Proceedings VLDB 2001, pp. 341–350. Morgan Kaufmann Publishers Inc., Roma, September 2001. http://dl.acm.org/citation. cfm?id=645927.672202
7. Fletcher, G.H.L., Peters, J., Poulovassilis, A.: Efficient regular path query evaluation using path indexes. In: Proceedings of EDBT 2016, pp. 636–639 (2016)
8. Goldman, R., Widom, J.: DataGuides: enabling query formulation and optimization in semistructured databases. In: Proceedings of VLDB 1997, pp. 436–445. Morgan Kaufmann Publishers Inc., Athens, Greece, August 1997. http://dl.acm. org/citation.cfm?id=645923.671008
9. Gubichev, A., Then, M.: Graph pattern matching - do we have to reinvent the wheel?. In: Proceedings of GRADES 2014, pp. 1–7 (2014)
10. Guo, Y., et al.: LUBM: a benchmark for OWL knowledge base systems. J. Web Seman. **3**(2–3), 158–182 (2005)
11. Kaushik, R., Shenoy, P., Bohannon, P., Gudes, E.: Exploiting local similarity for indexing paths in graph-structured data. In: Proceedings of ICDE 2002, pp. 129–140. IEEE Computer Society, San Jose (2002). http://ieeexplore.ieee.org/lpdocs/ epic03/wrapper.htm?arnumber=994703
12. Milo, T., Suciu, D.: Index structures for path expressions. In: Beeri, C., Buneman, P. (eds.) ICDT 1999. LNCS, vol. 1540, pp. 277–295. Springer, Heidelberg (1999). doi:10.1007/3-540-49257-7_18
13. Neumann, T., Weikum, G.: The RDF-3X engine for scalable management of RDF data. VLDB J. **19**(1), 91–113 (2009). http://dl.acm.org/citation.cfm? id=1731351.1731354

14. Shasha, D., Wang, J.T.L., Giugno, R.: Algorithmics and applications of tree and graph searching. In: Proceedings of PODS 2002, p. 39. ACM Press, Madison, June 2002. http://dl.acm.org/citation.cfm?id=543613.543620
15. Sumrall, J.: Path indexing for efficient path query processing in graph databases. Master's thesis, Eindhoven University of Technology (2015)
16. Wong, K.F., Yu, J.X., Tang, N.: Answering XML queries using path-based indexes: a survey. WWW J. **9**(3), 277–299 (2006)
17. Yan, X., Han, J.: Graph indexing. In: Aggarwal, C.C., Wang, H. (eds.) Managing and Mining Graph Data, pp. 161–180. Springer, Heidelberg (2010)

Improving Performance of Distributed Graph Traversals via Application-Aware Plug-In Work Scheduler

Jesun Sahariar Firoz[✉], Marcin Zalewski, Martina Barnas,
and Andrew Lumsdaine

Center for Research in Extreme Scale Technologies (CREST), Indiana University,
Bloomington, IN, USA
{jsfiroz,zalewski,mbarnas,lums}@indiana.edu

Abstract. Unordered graph algorithms can offer efficient resource utilization that is advantageous for performance in distributed setting. Unordered execution allows for parallel computation without synchronization. In unordered algorithms, work is data-driven and can be performed in any order, refining the result as the algorithm progresses. Unfortunately, a sub-optimal work ordering may lead to more time spent on correcting the results than on useful work. On HPC systems, the issue is compounded by irregular nature of distributed graph algorithms which makes them sensitive to the whole software/hardware stack, collectively referred to as runtime. In this paper, we consider an example of such algorithms: Distributed Control (DC) single-source shortest paths (SSSP). DC relies on performance gains stemming from the inherent asynchrony of unordered algorithms while optimizing work ordering locally. We demonstrate that distributed runtime scheduling policy can prevent effective work ordering optimization. We show that lifting and delegating some scheduling decisions to the algorithm level can result in significantly better performance. We propose that this strategy can be useful for performance engineering.

1 Introduction

Large data sets in application areas such as physical networks, social media, bioinformatics, genomics and marketing, to name a few, are well represented by graphs and studied using graph analytics. Ever increasing size of data forces graph analytics to be performed on distributed systems including supercomputers. It is anticipated that the largest, most complex of such data sets, notably, e.g., in precision medicine, do or will require exascale computing resources. Achieving exascale is a nontrivial undertaking demanding a concerted effort at all levels of software/hardware stack. In order to utilize the modern systems, distributed graph algorithms need to be designed to scale. Scaling in turn requires that the algorithms are designed in a manner that maximizes asychrony. Unfortunately, supercomputing resources are notoriously inefficient for irregular applications.

© Springer International Publishing AG 2017
F. Desprez et al. (Eds.): Euro-Par 2016 Workshops, LNCS 10104, pp. 545–556, 2017.
DOI: 10.1007/978-3-319-58943-5_44

Irregular applications like graph algorithms may exhibit little locality, rarely require any significant computation per memory access, and result in high-rate communication of small messages. In graph applications, work items are generated in an unpredictable pattern. This makes performance of distributed graph algorithms dependent on the whole software/hardware stack, which includes not just the algorithm itself but all levels of the runtime and the hardware. The sensitivity to runtime is correlated with the level of achieved asychrony [7,21]. Moreover, it has been shown that the performance is further dependent on the type of input graph [11], and even a starting point within the same input graph [5].

In this paper, we propose a solution to how these issues can be ameliorated. Our approach is motivated by the recognition that formulating an algorithm to exploit optimistic parallelism [14] is contingent upon adequate assistance from the runtime. Design choices for general-purpose runtime systems are driven by the need to support a wide range of applications at scale. Yet, for many applications, a specific interleaving of execution of algorithm logic and runtime logic is necessary to achieve performance. While dynamic adaptive runtime systems, such as HPX-5 [10], can bookkeep information to assist an algorithm to perform better, a mechanism utilizing the application programmer's insight could improve performance even further. Note that any distributed graph algorithm consists of three parts: work items, data structures, and application-level scheduler. For achieving efficient optimistic parallelism, the application developer can provide *application-aware scheduling policy* to the runtime to be incorporated into the runtime-level scheduler. In this way, the runtime system could utilize programmer's knowledge of the particular algorithm and provide performance benefits due to better scheduling. Here we propose a mechanism to do so.

Specifically, we implement a family of unordered algorithms [20] for SSSP in HPX-5, based on an earlier implementation of distributed control (DC) SSSP [21]. We have chosen SSSP because SSSP and its variation Breadth First Search (BFS) appear as a kernel for many other graph applications. These include, for example, betweenness centrality and connected components. Additionally, they are good representative problems to study system behavior, as proposed by Graph500 benchmark [17]. Previously, we have categorized and demonstrated the relevance of detailed description of a runtime used in the context of executing graph algorithms, and shown that DC is particularly sensitive to lower-level details of the runtime [6,7]. Here we study effects of *runtime-level scheduler* and *network progression*. We propose to incorporate an *application-level plug-in scheduler* in general-purpose asynchronous many-task runtime.

The paper is organized as follows: In Sect. 2, we briefly summarize the DC and Δ-stepping algorithms for SSSP. We use Δ-stepping for comparison. In Sect. 3, we discuss the HPX-5 scheduler and the influence of HPX-5 runtime on graph traversal algorithms, DC in particular. Next, in Sect. 4, we introduce our refinements of the basic DC algorithm based on adaptive network progress frequency and flow control. We present performance comparison of different algorithms with our proposed algorithm in Sect. 5. Finally, we discuss the related work in Sect. 6, and we conclude in Sect. 7.

2   Background

Let us denote an undirected graph with n vertices and m edges by $G(V, E)$. Here $V = \{v_1, v_2, \ldots, v_n\}$ and $E = \{e_1, c_2, \ldots, e_m\}$ represent vertex set and edge set respectively. Each edge e_i is a triple (v_j, v_k, w_{jk}) consisting of two endpoint vertices and the edge weight. We assume that each edge has a nonzero cost (weight) for traversal. In *single source shortest path (SSSP)* problem, given a graph G and a source vertex s, we are interested in finding the shortest distance between s and all other vertices in the graph. In this section we briefly describe the basic Distributed Control based SSSP algorithm [21] and Δ-stepping algorithm [15]. Both of these algorithms approximate the optimal work ordering of Dijkstra's sequential SSSP algorithm [2], but each does that in a different way.

2.1   Basic Distributed Control Algorithm

DC is a work scheduling method that removes overhead of synchronization and global data structures while providing partial ordering of work items according to a priority measure. The algorithm starts by initialization of the distance map and by relaxing the source vertex. The work on the graph is performed by removing a work item (a vertex and a distance pair) from the thread-local priority queue in every iteration and then relaxing the vertex targeted by the work item. Vertex relaxation checks whether the distance sent to a vertex v is better than the distance already in the distance map, and it sends a relax message (work item) to all the neighbors of v with the new distance computed from v's distance d_v and the weight of the edge between v and v's neighbors v_n. A receive handler receives the messages sent from the relax function, and inserts the incoming work items into the thread-local priority queue. When a handler finishes executing, it is counted as finished in *termination detection*. Note that there is no synchronization barrier in the algorithm. All ordering is achieved locally in thread-local priority queues, and all ordering performed on the thread level adds up to an approximation of a perfect global ordering.

2.2 Δ-Stepping

Δ-Stepping approximates the ideal priority ordering by arranging work items into distance ranges (buckets) of size Δ and executing buckets in order. In each epoch i, vertices within the range $i\Delta - (i + 1)\Delta$ contained in a bucket B_i are processed asynchronously by worker threads. Within a bucket, work items are not ordered, and can be executed in parallel. Processing a bucket may produce extra work for the same bucket or for the successive buckets. After processing each bucket, all processes must synchronize before processing the next bucket to maintain work item ordering approximation. The more buckets (the smaller the Δ value), the more time spent on synchronization. Similarly, the fewer buckets (the larger the Δ value), the more sub-optimal work the algorithm generates because larger buckets provide less ordering. With $\Delta = 1$, Δ-stepping produces ordering equivalent to the ordering of the Dijkstra's algorithm (a priority queue ordering of all work items).

3   Interaction of DC with the HPX-5 Scheduler

The HPX-5 runtime system is an initial implementation of the ParalleX model [8]. HPX-5 represents work as *parcels*. The HPX-5 runtime scheduler is responsible for executing actions associated with parcels. It is a multi-threaded, cooperative, work-stealing thread scheduler, where heavy-weight worker threads run scheduler loops that select parcels to be executed. Specifically, each worker thread in HPX-5 maintains a last-in-first-out (LIFO) queue of parcels, with a possibility of stealing the oldest parcels from other threads. The light-weight threads executing parcels can yield, and HPX-5 maintains separate queue for yielded threads. Parcels can be sent to particular heavy-weight scheduler threads using mail queues. Newly generated parcels may be destined for remote locali-ties, and HPX-5 provides transparent network layer with robust implementation based on Photon [13] and an implementation based on the MPI interface.

Algorithm 1. HPX-5 scheduler loop

Input: Plug-In algorithm-level scheduler A_s with a work produce f_p func-tion

1: **while** A task t_i or a work item w_i available **do**
2:     **if** $M_{tid} \neq \emptyset$ **then**   {Mailbox queue (per thread)}
3:         Execute $t_i \leftarrow M_{tid}.pop()$ and **continue**
4:     **else if** $Y_q \neq \emptyset$ **then**   {Yield queue (per process)}
5:         Execute $t_i \leftarrow Y_q.pop()$ and **continue**
6:     **else if** $L_{tid} \neq \emptyset$ **then**   {LIFO queue (per thread)}
7:         Execute $t_i \leftarrow L_{tid}.pop()$ and **continue**
8:     **else if** $w_i \leftarrow f_p$ **not** *NULL* **then**   {Plug-In scheduler}
9:         Execute w_i and **continue**
10:    **else if** $N_r \neq \emptyset$ **then**   {Network receive queue}
11:      $L_{tid}.enqueue(N_r)$ and **continue**
12:    **else**   {Steal from another thread tid'}
13:      Try work stealing from $L_{tid'}$ and **continue**
14:    **end if**
15: **end while**

Every HPX-5 worker thread running the scheduler keeps spinning until it finds a parcel to execute or it has been signaled to stop. The scheduler loop is outlined in Algorithm 1. The mailboxes are given the highest priority, followed by the yield queue, followed by the LIFO queue. Next, a plug-in-scheduler, an extension we discuss in more detail in Sect. 4 gets a chance to execute. Finally, when the scheduler is unable to obtain work from thread-local sources, it first attempts to progress the network and then to steal work from other scheduler threads. It is important to note that executing work in any of the steps causes the loop to start from the beginning. So, for example, all mail tasks will be processed before any LIFO queue tasks, and no network progress will be performed before all work sources that come before it in the scheduler loop are exhausted. While this approach works well for some applications, it turns out that it does not work well for algorithms like DC that depend on continuous feedback for efficient scheduling.

Our DC approach draws concept from optimistic parallelization and self-stabilization [3]. To achieve optimistic parallelism via asynchrony, DC eliminates global synchronization barriers. However, to reduce the amount of sub-optimal work, DC performs local ordering of work items. This necessitates runtime support for quick delivery of messages so that they can be ordered as soon as possible. When we implemented DC based SSSP algorithm in HPX-5 with the default HPX-5 scheduler, we made a couple of observations on the interaction between the default HPX-5 scheduler and the DC algorithm. As the scheduler does not distinguish between runtime tasks and algorithmic work items, it indiscriminately puts both tasks and work item parcels, received over the network, in the current worker's LIFO queue. It then chooses a parcel to execute from the queue, if available, or go through the steps in Algorithm 1 to find and schedule one. This mixing of execution of tasks and work items can hurt algorithm's performance because, in the runtime level, at a particular instance of time, a tradeoff exists between executing tasks vs. work items. For instance, we have encountered situations where most of the work is stuck in the network buffers while the scheduler tries to execute parcels from the application-level priority queue. This left the algorithm to compare and choose from a smaller number of work items. This results dwindling priority queues used for local ordering in DC, even if work items are available in the transport buffers.

Based on these observation, we posit that distinguishing runtime tasks from algorithmic work items by maintaining seperate data structures for them to facilitate scheduling and having a way to provide an algorithm-specific scheduling policy as a plug-in scheduler in the runtime scheduler can benefit unordered algorithms in several ways. First, by separating these sets of works, runtime has better control over when to schedule what type of work. Secondly, runtime can exploit programmer's knowledge about algorithmic work items. For example, application programmer can provide an ordering policy for the work items (priority for parcels containing shorter distances). Third, we note that irregular graph algorithms are communication bound, rather than computation intensive. If, at any particular time instance, the application level does not have enough work items to work on or compare with, it can voluntarily give up control to other scheduling mechanisms like network progress to fetch more work from the underlying transport. Delaying network progression till exhaustion of work items eliminates the chance of propagating better work from other localities. Such interleaving execution of runtime tasks, work items, and network progress can boost the performance of an unordered algorithm.

To alleviate these issues, we extend the default HPX-5 scheduler with a provision for the application-level programmer to incorporate a configurable, plug-in scheduler. The application-level plug-in scheduler consists of 3 parts: work consumer, work producer, and work Stealing. In the next section, we discuss a plug-in scheduler we designed for DC, and in Sect. 5 its performance.

4   Distributed Control with Adaptive Frequency and Flow Control

Algorithm 2 shows the pseudo code for the DC plug-in scheduler algorithm. The algorithm consists of 3 parts: the work produce function f_p that manages extraction of algorithmic work items from the local priority queue, the message handler that receives tasks from other workers, and the relax function that updates distances and generates new work. The basic task of f_p is to remove work items from the thread-level priority queue and to return them to the runtime scheduler for execution and the basic task of the relax function is to send updates to all neighbors of the vertex being relaxed. In this section, we discuss a plug-in-scheduler implementation that goes beyond these basic tasks by employing flow control and adaptive frequency scheduling.

4.1   Flow Control

Local ordering in DC produces more optimal work orderings when more work is available to order in thread-local priority queues. The runtime, however, needs to deliver messages across the network through multiple layers of implementation. This causes a tension between DC and the runtime, where on one hand it is best to deliver majority of work items into DC priority queues, but, on the other hand, minimizing the amount of work items that are in-flight in the runtime comes at a cost of runtime overhead. We implement flow control mechanisms to allow DC to control the flow of network communication through the HPX-5 runtime using customizable parameters.

Work items are moved out from the network layers of HPX-5 when the scheduler loop in Algorithm 1 runs network progress (Line 10). The only way that control reaches Line 10 is when the work produce function returns a null work item (Line 8 in Algorithm 1). Our plug-in scheduler DC maintains an approximate measure of work items that have been sent over the network but not yet delivered. To maintain the approximation, we keep a locality-based global counter $sync\_count$ of work items that have been sent with a request of remote completion notification. When this count grows over some threshold $sync\_threshold$, f_p returns control back to the runtime (Line 3 of Algorithm 2).

In *Relax* function, when the worker thread propagates updated distance to the neighbors (Line 3), it checks how many asynchronous sends has been posted (Line 4). If the count has reached a particular threshold $send\_threshold$, a send with continuation is performed and the $sync\_count$ value is incremented to keep track of how many continuations are expected (Lines 8–9). When calls with continuation are completed remotely, the continuation decrements the $sync\_count$ value on the locality from which the original send call was made. At every send with continuation, the thread-local $send\_count$ is reset to 0. The call with continuation is performed with the hpx_call_with_continuation HPX-5 function:

```
1 hpx_call_with_continuation( addr, action, c_target,
    c_action, ...)
```

Algorithm 2. DC with Adaptive Frequency and Flow Control

Work produce, f_p

1: **if** $sync\_count == sync\_threshold$ **then**
2:                    {Outstanding no. synchronous calls reached the threshold}
3:    **return** NULL
4: **else**
5:    **if not** $q_{tid}.empty()$ **and** $q_{tid}.size() > last\_queue\_size$ **then**
6:       $freq[tid] - -$ {Process work from the priority queue less frequently}
7:    **else**
8:       $freq[tid] + +$ {Process work from the priority queue more frequently}
9:    **end if**
10:    $last\_queue\_size \leftarrow q_{tid}.size()$
11:    **if not** $q.empty()$ **and** $processed\_count[tid] - - > 0$ **then**
12:       $(v, d) \leftarrow q_{tid}.pop()$ {next work item to process}
13:       **return** $w_i \leftarrow (v, d)$
14:    **else**
15:       $processed\_count[tid] = freq[tid]$
16:             {Reset the number of work items to be processed in the next iteration}
17:       **return** NULL
18:    **end if**
19: **end if**

Receive handler

Input: Work item (v, d)
1: $q_{tid}.push(v, d)$ {insert work item into priority queue}

Relax

Input: Work item (v, d), distances D
1: **if** $d < D(v)$ **then**
2:    $D(v) \leftarrow d$
3:    **for** $v_n \in neighbors(G, v)$: **do**
4:       **if** $send\_count[tid] < send\_threshold$ **then**
5:          $send\_count[tid] - -$
6:          $send\_async((v_n, d_v + \text{weight}(v, v_n)))$
7:       **else**
8:          $sync\_count + +$
9:          $send\_async\_with\_cont((v_n, d_v + \text{weight}(v, v_n)), \lambda.sync\_count - -)$
10:          $send\_count[tid] = send\_threshold$
11:       **end if**
12:    **end for**
13: **end if**

---

hpx_call_with_continuation takes an address *addr* (local or remote) and invokes the specified action *action* at that address. Once that action has finished executing, the continuation action *c_action* is invoked at *c_target* address. Implementing flow control is very easy with the semantics provided by the hpx_call_with_continuation interface as the continuation is "fire and forget," and it is automatically handled by the runtime.

4.2 Adapting Frequency of Network Progress

If the current locality keeps receiving messages and the network progress keeps succeeding with adequate amount of work items received over the network, it is an indication that either the algorithm is in the middle of its execution phase or a lot of messages are destined to the current locality. It is thus useful to keep retrieving messages from the network receive buffer and put them in the priority queues in the algorithm level. In this way, when the algorithm gets a chance to progress, it has robust amount of work items in the priority queue to compare and make choices from and minimize the possibility of executing sub-optimal work items.

To get an idea of successful network progression, the algorithm checks the current priority queue size in the f_p function and compares it with the size seen the last time. Growing size of the priority queue is an indication of successful network probing (Line 5). As mentioned earlier, its better to fetch more work items from the network aggressively if the network progression keeps returning a lot of received messages. To achieve this, the algorithm maintains a thread-local counter *freq*. Whenever the queue size grows, the *freq* counter is decremented to indicate that fewer elements will be processed from the priority queue and control will be given to the scheduler to progress the network more frequently (Line 6 in *Work produce*).

It is noteworthy to mention here that progressing the network for every vertex processed is not a viable option. The reason is that network progress incurs much more overhead compared to processing a vertex. Although eager network progress can assist in the reduction of useless work by increasing priority queues' size, it has detrimental effect on algorithm performance due to the associated overhead.

5   Experimental Results

In this section, we evaluate several algorithms based on DC and compare their performance with Δ-stepping algorithm. In the following discussion, algorithms without plug-in scheduler carry np subscript, algorithms which give up control to the runtime schedule at a fixed frequency carry ff subscript, algorithms with flow control carry fc subscript, and algorithms with adaptive frequency for network progress carry af subscript.

5.1   Experimental Setup

We conducted all our experiments on a Cray XC40 system. Each compute node on this system has 32 cores with clockrate of 2.7 GHz, and 64 GB memory. For input, we used Graph500 graphs [9]. For each algorithm, we run 4 problem instances and report the average the execution time with standard deviation of mean as the measurement for uncertainty. We have used $\Delta = 1$ for Δ-Stepping algorithm. We chose the optimal number of threads for each algorithm. The

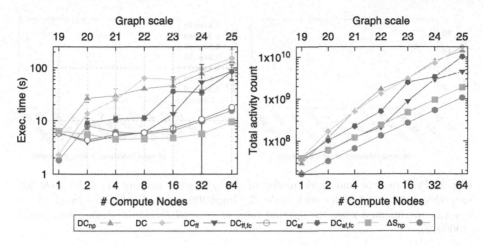

Fig. 1. Performance and work statistics of SSSP algorithms in weak scaling. With full featured plug-in scheduler, DC (green squares) outperforms Δ-stepping (blue circles) (Color figure online)

graph is distributed across different nodes in 1D fashion and represented with a distributed adjacency list data structure. We have compiled our code with gcc 5.1 and with optimization level $-O3$.

5.2   Comparison of Δ-Stepping and Five Versions of DC Algorithms

Figure 1 shows the execution time taken by different SSSP algorithms. DC, which uses the plug-in capability but does not have flow control or adaptive frequency heuristic performs worse than DC_{np}. Adding a fixed frequency heuristic for network progression helped DC_{ff} to perform comparatively up to 8 compute nodes but for larger scale its performance deteriorates. Although for smaller scales fixed frequency heuristic is good enough, to achieve better scaling, the algorithm needs to adjust the network probing according to the work profile, which we do in DC_{af}. Compared to DC_{ff}, this heuristic worked better with scale 24 graph input but did not perform well with scale 25 input. In $DC_{ff,fc}$, we add flow control. Flow control mechanism helps $DC_{ff,fc}$ in achieving almost identical performance as Δ-stepping algorithm. Finally, $DC_{af,fc}$ performs the best. Flow control and adaptive frequency together make $DC_{af,fc}$ achieve better work ordering and balance in executing tasks and work items. Figure 1 also shows the work profiles for different SSSP algorithms. Although Δ-Stepping executes less work items, it takes longer time. On the other hand, $DC_{af,fc}$ algorithm executes more work due to sub-optimal work generation but still runs faster. This is due to the fact that, with proper flow control and adaptive frequency heuristic, $DC_{af,fc}$ can schedule work items efficiently and interleave runtime progress and work item execution in a proper manner.

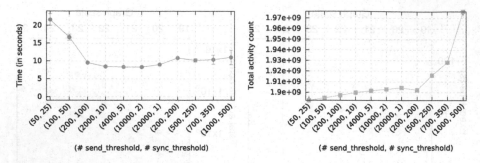

Fig. 2. Performance and work profile of $DC_{af,fc}$ with varying *send_threshold* and *sync_threshold* on 64 nodes with scale 25 Graph500 input. Within the range of values we experimented with, the optimal value of $(\#send\_threshold, \#sync\_threshold)$ is $(10000, 2)$.

5.3 Performance of $DC_{af,fc}$ with various *send_threshold* and *sync_threshold* value

Figure 2 illustrates how the performance of $DC_{af,fc}$ varies with different combinations of values for (*send_threshold*, *sync_threshold*). The results are obtained on 64 nodes and with scale 25 Graph500 input. As can be seen from the figure, a *send_count* value of 10000 and *sync_count* value of 2 gives the best performance for $DC_{af,fc}$. In this case, for every 10000 sent messages, we have issued 2 calls with continuation which gives algorithm $DC_{af,fc}$ better opportunity to progress asynchronously. During our experiments, a cursory search for good values for (*send_threshold*, *sync_threshold*) parameters resulted in the $(200, 100)$ pair. Thus, we have restricted our search space within the vicinity of 20000 messages and experimented with different combinations of (*send_threshold*, *sync_threshold*) for generating 20000 messages. As can be seen from the figure, the execution time reaches a minimum with *send_threshold* of 10000 and *sync_threshold* of 2 and then starts increasing with larger (*send_threshold*, *sync_threshold*) values. Although the total activity count keep increasing, a right combination of (*send_threshold*, *sync_threshold*) value helps to overcome the overhead of executing more work by scheduling work in a timely fashion and gaining better performance in general.

6 Related Work

Nguyen and Pingali [19] have shown that performance of algorithms for various irregular applications can improve significantly by selecting right scheduling policies. They evaluated different synthesized schedulers for shared memory systems.

Distributed runtimes sometimes allow programmers to specify priorities. For example, Charm++ [12] has provision for controlling delivery of messages by allowing users to adjust delivery order of messages by setting the queuing strategy (FIFO, LIFO) as well as two mechanisms for setting priorities (integer and bitvector) [1]. Another recent runtime, Grappa [18], maintains 4 queues: ready worker queue, deadline task queue, private task queue and public task queue for tasks. The deadline task queue manages high priority system tasks. Grappa scheduler allows threads to yield to tolerate communication latency and also has provision for distributed work stealing. Although, in [18], it has been mentioned that programmers can direct scheduling explicitly, its not clear how this can be done from the application level. UPC [4] provides topology-aware hierarchical work stealing [16] based scheduling mechanism.

7 Conclusion

Unordered distributed graph algorithms enable better utilization of resources in HPC systems, but their performance is sensitive to the underlying runtime system. In this paper we have shown on the example of DC SSSP how to improve performance by modifying the algorithm with a plug-in scheduler that bridges the application and the runtime system. The plug-in scheduler then provides an algorithmic specific scheduling policy to the runtime scheduler, thus lifting some functionality of the lower stacks into the algorithm level. A special provision for this feature needs to be made in the runtime system. We have implemented this in HPX-5, and have shown that performance of DC varies with different heuristics. The plug-in scheduler is useful for improving performance.

References

1. Charm++ Documentation (2016). http://charm.cs.illinois.edu/manuals/html/charm++/10.html
2. Dijkstra, E.W.: A note on two problems in connexion with graphs. Numer. Math. 1(1), 269–271 (1959)
3. Dijkstra, E.W.: Self-stabilization in spite of distributed control. In: Dijkstra, E.W. (ed.) Selected Writings on Computing: A Personal Perspective, pp. 41–46. Springer, Heidelberg (1982)
4. El-Ghazawi, T., Carlson, W., Sterling, T., Yelick, K.: UPC: Distributed Shared-Memory Programming. Wiley, Hoboken (2003)
5. Firoz, J.S., Barnas, M., Zalewski, M., Lumsdaine, A.: The value of variance. In: 7th ACM/SPEC International Conference on Performance Engineering (ICPE). ACM (2016)
6. Firoz, J.S., Zalewski, M., Barnas, M., Kanewala, T.A., Lumsdaine, A.: Context matters: distributed graph algorithms and runtime systems. In: Platform for Advanced Scientific Computing (PASC) (2016)
7. Firoz, J.S., Kanewala, T.A., Zalewski, M., Barnas, M., Lumsdaine, A.: Importance of runtime considerations in performance engineering of large-scale distributed graph algorithms. In: Hunold, S., et al. (eds.) Euro-Par 2015. LNCS, vol. 9523, pp. 553–564. Springer, Cham (2015). doi:10.1007/978-3-319-27308-2_45

8. Gao, G., Sterling, T., Stevens, R., Hereld, M., Zhu, W.: ParalleX: a study of a new parallel computation model. In: International Parallel and Distributed Processing Symposium, pp. 1–6, March 2007
9. Graph500: Version 2 Specification (2016). https://github.com/graph500/graph500/tree/v2-spec
10. HPX-5 Runtime (2016). http://hpx.crest.iu.edu/
11. Iosup, A., Hegeman, T., Ngai, W.L., Heldens, S., Pérez, A.P., Manhardt, T., Chafi, H., Capota, M., Sundaram, N., Anderson, M., et al.: LDBC Graphalytics: A Benchmark for Large-scale Graph Analysis on Parallel and Distributed Platforms, a Technical Report (2016)
12. Kale, L.V., Krishnan, S.: Charm++: a portable concurrent object oriented system based on C++. In: Proceedings of the Eighth Annual Conference on Object-Oriented Programming Systems, Languages, and Applications, OOPSLA 1993, pp. 91–108. ACM, New York (1993)
13. Kissel, E., Swany, M.: Photon: remote memory access middleware for high-performance runtime systems. In: First Annual Workshop on Emerging Parallel and Distributed Runtime Systems and Middleware, IPDRM 2016 (2016)
14. Kulkarni, M., Pingali, K.: Scheduling issues in optimistic parallelization. In: IEEE International Parallel and Distributed Processing Symposium, IPDPS 2007, pp. 1–7. IEEE (2007)
15. Meyer, U., Sanders, P.: Δ-stepping: a parallelizable shortest path algorithm. J. Algorithms **49**(1), 114–152 (2003)
16. Min, S.J., Iancu, C., Yelick, K.: Hierarchical work stealing on manycore clusters. In: Fifth Conference on PGAS Programming Models (2011)
17. Murphy, R.C., Wheeler, K.B., Barrett, B.W., Ang, J.A.: Introducing the graph 500 benchmark. Cray User's Group (CUG) (2010)
18. Nelson, J., Holt, B., Myers, B., Briggs, P., Ceze, L., Kahan, S., Oskin, M.: Grappa: a latency-tolerant runtime for large-scale irregular applications. Technical report, Technical Report UW-CSE-14-02-01, University of Washington (2014)
19. Nguyen, D., Pingali, K.: Synthesizing concurrent schedulers for irregular algorithms. In: Proceedings of the Sixteenth International Conference on Architectural Support for Programming Languages and Operating Systems, ASPLOS XVI, pp. 333–344. ACM, New York (2011)
20. Pingali, K., Nguyen, D., Kulkarni, M., Burtscher, M., Hassaan, M.A., Kaleem, R., Lee, T.H., Lenharth, A., Manevich, R., Méndez-Lojo, M., et al.: The tao of parallelism in algorithms. ACM SIGPLAN Not. **46**(6), 12–25 (2011)
21. Zalewski, M., Kanewala, T.A., Firoz, J.S., Lumsdaine, A.: Distributed control: priority scheduling for single source shortest paths without synchronization. In: Proceedings of the Fourth Workshop on Irregular Applications: Architectures and Algorithms, pp. 17–24. IEEE (2014)

Synthetic Graph Generation for Systematic Exploration of Graph Structural Properties

Merijn Verstraaten$^{(\boxtimes)}$, Ana Lucia Varbanescu, and Cees de Laat

University of Amsterdam, Amsterdam, The Netherlands
{m.e.verstraaten,a.l.varbanescu,delaat}@uva.nl

Abstract. High performance graph processing poses significant challenges for both algorithm and platform designers due to the large performance variability it exhibits: performance depends on the algorithm, the dataset, and the (hardware/software) platform. Traditionally, performance variability is tackled by extensive benchmarking, modeling, and, eventually, better or smarter algorithms. Our own research into the impact of datasets on the performance of graph algorithms has convinced us that such extensive benchmarking is very difficult for graph processing simply because we lack input data: the public datasets and graph generation tools currently available are insufficient for a systematic investigation of the impact of different graph properties. In this work we propose to alleviate this problem by using evolutionary computing as a method to generate graphs. Our goal is allow users to request graphs with a given set of properties (e.g., number of vertices, number of edges, degree distribution), and enable the generator to evolve graphs until they satisfy the request. Such a fine-grain, flexible exploration of graphs and their properties will finally enable a statistical take on performance analysis and modeling for graph processing. To this end, our work-in-progress paper presents the design of our generator, discusses the challenges and trade-offs to be encountered, and reveals our preliminary results.

1 Introduction

Graph processing is an important part of data science, due to the flexibility of graphs as a model for highly interrelated data. Combined with the increasing size of datasets, this results in a lot of research being invested in parallel and distributed solutions for graph processing [1,7,8,12–14,16,21,23].

Most such graph processing frameworks simplify working with graphs by hiding the underlying complexity: they maintain a separation between a front-end that lets users specify their algorithm using high-level primitives or domain specific languages, and a back-end that provides high-performance implementations of these primitives for the given software or hardware platform.

In practice, there are often many different ways to implement the same primitive. Different implementations perform best on different hardware: a model that performs well on a CPU might perform horribly on Xeon Phi, GPU, or other accelerators. And to make matters worse, performance is also impacted

© Springer International Publishing AG 2017
F. Desprez et al. (Eds.): Euro-Par 2016 Workshops, LNCS 10104, pp. 557–570, 2017.
DOI: 10.1007/978-3-319-58943-5_45

by the structural properties of the graph being processed. While many studies have already empirically proven this variability for various combinations of algorithms, datasets, and hardware platforms, little progress has been made to quantify or model these sources of performance variation [27,28].

During our efforts to quantify this impact, we ran into an important problem: to conduct any sort of systematic benchmarking to quantify the impact of different structural graph properties, we need control over the input datasets. Specifically, we need datasets with graphs that are similar in all but one property: the property whose impact we try to isolate. No repository of such datasets exists. Instead, most research on graph processing uses (1) input data from several publicly available real world data sets, such as SNAP [18], or (2) synthetically generated graphs using well-known generators/models, such as R-MAT [6], Kronecker graphs [19], and scale-free graphs [15]. These models produce graphs that mimic "real world" networks (such as social networks or various bioinformatics models), and are not flexible enough to generate the fine-grained graph variations we are looking for.

Instead, we propose a generator that allows on-demand graph generation with user-specified parameters—e.g., number of vertices, edges, connected components, and/or degree distribution. Using evolutionary computing, a population of graphs is being evolved in the search of the particular graph configuration the user is looking for. The main challenges for this approach are (discussed further in Sect. 2) (1) selecting a good representation of the graph, which will in turn impact both the design and the output of the evolutionary algorithm, (2) quick convergence, which essentially translates to fast do can the requested graph be found, and (3) scalability, which basically determines whether this method can actually generate large enough graphs without running out of resources (including the user's patience). While genetic algorithms have been used in the past [2] to attempt graph generation, they seem to have failed in at least one of these aspects, as seen in Sect. 3, and thus are not used to generate graphs that are relevant, size-wise, for existing graph processing benchmarking [4]. This is why, we argue, these benchmarks use existing datasets from various sources, like SNAP [18], KONECT [17], or in-house generators [10].

Thus, in this work, we provide *a specific method for using evolutionary algorithms for fine-grain, controlled graph generation*. Moreover, our generator *enables users to specify not only the size of the network, but also its degree distribution*. In this paper, we present the design of our method, we describe our first prototype, and discuss initial results. Our results (see Sect. 4) show that we can, indeed, generate graphs with controlled degree distributions.

2   Design and Implementation

Our end goal is to generate graphs that allow us to explore the impact of different graph properties in a systematic manner. This section introduces the requirements and our proposed design to reach this goal.

2.1 Requirements

Essentially, our generator has to be a "tool" capable of generating graphs that match a set of structural properties of interest. Specifically, this requires the following:

- Fine granularity: vary as little as a single property at a time.
- Possibility to expand: add new structural properties.
- Scalability: generate small *and* large graphs within a reasonable time budget.

In essence, this graph generation problem translates *the search problem of finding a graph or set of graphs conforming to a set of potentially interdependent properties* in the search space potential graphs. Therefore, our design is based on an efficient search method in large spaces: evolutionary computing.

2.2 Evolutionary Computing for Graph Generation

Evolutionary computing is the collective name given to a range of techniques based on principles of natural evolution, such as natural selection and inheritance. A key features of evolutionary computing techniques is their ability to produce good results when dealing with large search spaces large numbers of interdependent parameters; these properties makes evolutionary computing an appealing starting point for our problem.

The basic principle behind most evolutionary computing algorithms is simple:

1. Generate an initial population of candidate solutions.
2. Select a number of solutions for reproduction based on their quality.
3. Perform crossover[1] between selected solutions.
4. With a small probability, randomly change the result.
5. Select survivors for the next generation based on quality.

There are endless variations on how to select parents, the probability of random mutations, how to select survivors, and how many new solutions should be generated in every generation. There are several standard choices that appear to work well for most algorithms, avoiding the need to perform substantial benchmarking to determine the right choices.

However, some of the remaining choices are problem specific and have a large impact on the performance. Since evolutionary algorithms are stochastic, an important point of concern is the time it takes to converge to a set of acceptable graphs. As we want both fine tuning and large scale graphs, we are faced with a large search space and, potentially, a long running algorithm. For example, the larger graphs in SNAP are above 4 million vertices (e.g., soc-Livejournal). This result in an absurdly large search space.

The key to getting obtaining acceptable convergence speeds is to ensure that the primitives used for generating new candidates cover enough of the search

---

[1] With crossover parts of the "genetic code" of different solutions are mixed/recombined to form new solutions.

space quickly. As such, the crossover operation is very important. The key idea behind crossover is that it combines successful or interesting parts of two solutions, resulting in an even better solution.

Another important choice is the rate of mutation: too low and the algorithm takes too long to explore promising related solutions; too high and the algorithm may never converge on any optimal points, continuously hopping over them.

2.3   Solution Representation

For the specific problem of graph generation, an essential choice to be made is that of the solution representation. What a candidate solution looks like strongly impacts the crossover and mutation primitives we can efficiently implement. Several sensible choices exist:

- Individual graphs represented as a connectivity matrix
- Individual graphs represented as an edge list
- Generating functions, i.e. a function that generates one specific graph
- Graph generators, i.e. a generator that generates graphs according to some patterns

Connectivity Matrices. The most straightforward method of implementing mutation in a connectivity matrix-based representation consists of randomly inserting edges and deleting edges. This is done by flipping an index in the matrix from 0 to 1 and vice versa. Now mutation is a matter of, randomly selecting indices to flip.

For crossover there are three simple methods:

Edge-wise, for every index in the connectivity matrix, randomly select a parent and keeps its value.

Vertex-wise, for every vertex in the graph, randomly select a parent and keep it's edge related to that vertex.

Single-point, select a random point and for every edge before that point keep the edges of the first graph, for the remaining edges, keep those of the second graph.

Edge-wise crossover results in a very thorough mixing of two candidate solutions, keeping roughly 50% of the edges from the first and 50% of the second parent. Additionally, it is easy to implement. However, indiscriminately picking edges from either parent will almost certainly destroy any interesting subsections of the graph, the exact thing that crossover is supposed to maintain.

Vertex-wise crossover will preserve significantly more structure from the individual parents, since all vertices from one parent will keep parts of their environment from that parent.

Single-point crossover is even more conservative, since it always preserves sequential sets of vertices. However, since vertices are not necessarily sequentially connected it is unclear if this preserves significantly more structure than vertex-wise crossover. It is also unclear whether this actually produces a net-benefit for convergence.

Edge Lists. The crossover primitives described for connectivity matrices apply equally well to the edge list representation. Mutations that insert or delete are also simple to implement. The biggest difference with connectivity matrices is that certain restrictions are easier to impose on the generation process.

For example, with edge list it is simpler to generate graphs with a fixed number of edges. Instead of inserting and deleting edges, they are only mutated by moving, changing the origin and/or destination of edges to move them.

On the other hand, edge list representations make it more complex to guarantee that the number of vertices in a graph stays constant across crossover and/or mutation. A property that is simple to maintain when performing crossover and/or mutation on connectivity matrices. As such the two representations are complementary depending on the kind of graphs we wish to generate.

Generating Functions. One of the biggest problems with the straightforward solutions proposed above (i.e., directly evolving graphs) is that the entirely random permutation can take a long time to converge on more complicated structures that might be needed to achieve the desired properties. Think of properties such as clustering coefficient.

By evolving a generating function, rather than a graph, such structures are easier to generate, resulting in a faster convergence to desired result graphs. Something similar has been tried in HyperNEAT [11,24], where the authors wanted to scale up the work done on generating neural networks using NEAT [25, 26] (see Sect. 3 for more details) to neural networks of millions of nodes. In HyperNEAT they evolve Compositional Pattern Producing Networks (CPPN); these are, essentially, generating functions for neural networks.

CPPNs were designed to be effective at generating complex structures, such as symmetries, repetition, and repetition with variation. The work on Hyper-NEAT shows that CPPNs can produce complex neural networks. We expect that they will be similarly effective for producing complex graphs. The only open question is whether CPPNs limit the structure of the generated graph in a way that makes it impossible to generate graphs with the desired properties. Our initial expectation is that this should not be a problem.

Generating Generators. A final approach is to generate generators. In this case, instead of evolving a generating function that only produces a single graph, we evolve a generator for a set of graphs.

This approach has been tried before by Bach et al. [2] and Bailey et al. [3]. The main advantage of this approach is that instead of a single graph, the result is a generator for a set of graphs making it easier to produce many similar graphs. However, this comes with the same caveat as the previous section, it is unclear whether the evolved generators can actually produce graphs with the desired properties. It seems unlikely that the type of generators proposed in [2] are sufficiently flexible. Additionally, some initial tests showed that implementation used by Bach et al. has scalability problems, even for very small graphs ($\sim$1,000 vertices). Similarly, in [3] there is no discussion about which types of graphs are ruled out by the design of their generator. Additionally, the authors do not seem to have tried to scale the approach beyond a few 100 vertices (Table 1).

Table 1. Comparison of different generation methods.

	Fine-grain control	Convergence
Connectivity matrix	Very good	Slow
Edge list	Very good	Slow
Generating function	Sufficient	Fast
Generator	Questionable	Fast

2.4 Implementation

We started with a prototype implementation that evolves connectivity matrices directly to test the feasibility of this approach to generating graphs. The reason for using connectivity matrices over edge lists is two fold: *(1)* it was simpler to implement with our existing file format, *(2)* we were more interested in generating graphs with a fixed number of vertices. For our experiments we focused on generating weakly-connected graphs with specific degree distributions.

The first step with any evolutionary algorithm is to define the fitness function. This function maps the candidate solution to a quality metric that indicates the solution's quality.

Matching the distribution of degrees in a graph to a specific distribution is straightforward. The Kolmogorov-Smirnov (KS) test for goodness of fit [22] compares an Empirical Distribution Function (EDF) with a Cumulative Distribution Function (CDF) and gives us the absolute difference between the two. We start with the null-hypothesis that the EDF and CDF come from the same distribution. For tests with N samples[2] we can use the critical values $\frac{1.07}{\sqrt{N}}$ ($p = 0.2$), $\frac{1.14}{\sqrt{N}}$ ($p = 0.15$), and $\frac{1.22}{\sqrt{N}}$ ($p = 0.1$) to verify whether this null-hypothesis should be rejected.

Similarly, we need a metric to judge the weak-connectivity of our graph. We chose to use the percentage of the graph's vertices that were in the same weakly-connected component[3] as our measure, as this was easiest to compute efficiently.

This gives us two independent fitness measures in a range from 0 to 1. For our evolutionary algorithm we need a single fitness metric that can be easily compared. Usual ways to combine multiple fitness criteria are weighted sum of criteria or using a Pareto ranking. For our initial experiments we simply multiplied both values together. Experiments showed that weak-connectivity of the graphs converged to 1 in a few generations. As a result, multiplying the

---

[2] With N larger than 35.

[3] Specifically, the weakly-connected component containing vertex 0.

fitness reduces directly to the result of our Kolmogorov-Smirnov goodness of fit result.

Our algorithm design[4] consisted of:

Population size. 100 candidate solutions.
Parent selection. Weighted random selection.
Number of children. 100 new children every generation.
Crossover. Edge-wise, vertex-wise, single-point.
Mutation rate. $\frac{1}{0.1N^2}$, where N is the number of vertices.
Survivors. Keep best 20% plus weighted random selection.

Our initial populations consists of 100 randomly generated graphs. These graphs we created by computing the approximate number of edges expected for a given number of nodes and a distribution, and then uniform randomly initialising that many edges in our connectivity matrix to 1.

To generate 100 new children we used weighted random selection to pick 100 pairs of graphs from the current population. We generate a new graph by crossing over the two parents and uniform randomly mutating edges in the resulting graph. After the children have been generated the child and parent populations are combined. The top 20% of this population is automatically kept, for the remainder we used weighted random selection to determine survivors. After survivors have been selected all other graphs are removed.

The population size, parent selection, and number of children are all fairly standard values from the evolutionary computing literature. These values seem to work for nearly any problem and adjusting them is unlikely to improve the convergence speed.

The choices for crossover, mutation, and survivor selection *are* are interesting to adjust. Mutations are responsible for both exploring the neighbourhood of existing candidate solutions (by slightly permuting them), and jumping to new areas in the search space by introducing new edges into the gene pool. High mutation rates make it easier to discover new regions of the search space, at the risk of continuously skipping over good solutions. Low mutation rates make exploration around existing solutions easier, but can slow the rate with which new regions are explored.

Crossover combines (successful) sections of different graphs together, exploring the search space between those two graphs. The idea is that by capturing child solutions that contain valuable parts of both parents will produce an even better fitness. However, this requires crossover to preserve "valuable" substructures. Experimenting with different crossover strategies can thus make this operation more effective.

In Sect. 4 we will compare our initial feasibility experiments with the results from related work described in the next section.

---

[4] The actual implementation can be found at https://github.com/merijn/GPU-benchmarks.

3   Related Work

There are two complementary reasons for research into graph generators and graph models: *(1)* real data might be unavailable, because it is proprietary or can't be obtained [20], *(2)* we want to better understand what the essential features of a given type of graph are [5].

Because of the above reasons the focus is on studying and mimicking specific types of real world graphs. The result is that these models are tailored to generating only these types of graphs. This means they are limited in flexibility and the number of parameters that can be tuned. As such they are less suited to our goal of more systematically exploring the different kinds of possible graphs and their impact.

One of the first and most well-known models of graph generation is the Erdös-Rényi model [9]. This model, however did not quite capture the properties of many real world graphs. For example, it does not follow the power law degree distribution found in many real world graphs. The Erdös-Rényi model was later subsumed as a special case of the R-MAT model [6], which can model both power law degree distributions as wel as deviations from it.

Kronecker graphs [19] uses the Kronecker product of a matrix to generate graphs. The authors presented a tool for fitting the graphs generated using this method to the parameters of existing graphs, showing that this makes it possible to approximate real graphs, and use these fitted parameters to study the properties of graphs.

The neural networks community in AI has done research into generating graphs for their neural networks. One of the more promising approach is NeuroEvolution of Augmenting Topologies (NEAT) [25,26]. NEAT uses evolutionary computing starting out with a minimal neural network and incrementally adding vertices and edges to this network. This works well, but has significant scaling issues.

Due to the constructive graph generation approach of adding individual vertices and edges it is very time consuming and memory intensive to produce large neural networks. Additionally, the larger the neural network becomes, the harder it is to produce the complex patterns required to solve their AI problems.

Since the principle of NEAT works well for small neural networks there was follow up research trying to scale NEAT to neural networks of millions of vertices. This resulted in HyperNEAT [11,24].

Instead of evolving a neural network directly HyperNEAT evolves a generating function for the eventual neural network. As described in Sect. 2 these generating functions are designed to more easily produce complex and recurring patterns such as symmetry, anti-symmetry, repetition, repetition with variation, etc. In practice this succeeds in producing neural networks that are orders of magnitude larger than those generated with NEAT. The two main concerns with the HyperNEAT approach is whether the generating functions invented can cover a sufficiently exhaustive subset of possible graphs.

Additionally, one of the steps in HyperNEAT consists of mapping a hypercube pattern (produced by the generating function) to a lower-dimensional space to obtain the actual graph. Depending on mapping method chosen this may result in super-linear complexity, while for scalability reasons it is desirable for the complexity to stay linear in the number of vertices and/or edges.

The work of [2,3] was already mentioned in Sect. 2. Both attempt to evolve generators/models for the generation of graphs. The generators consists of sequences of operations that insert/construct certain motifs or permute the existing graphs.

The nice property of these approaches is that once a graph generator has been evolved it can used to produce an entire set of comparable graphs. The results in both papers show that they can successfully produce very different kinds of graphs. Evolving a generators is also desirable because they can more easily produce more complex patterns and structures, which should lead to faster convergence.

However, there are some downsides to the methods used in both papers. Using an iterative, constructive approach to generation means that generating larger graphs is slow and very memory intensive. In [3] the largest graphs generated are about 1,000 vertices, the generator from [2] already struggles with graphs that size. Given that we are interested in generating graphs that are several orders of magnitude larger this scalability is a serious problem. Additionally, it is unclear whether the motifs and generators proposed in both papers are sufficiently expressive to cover an exhaustive portion of the search space.

4   Initial Results and Analysis

Our initial implementation, as described in Sect. 2, is based on the idea of evolving graphs directly using their representation as a connectivity matrix. The main reason for this design was based on the simplicity of its implementation.

There are three main problems when using evolutionary computing to generate graphs:

Exhaustiveness, if a graph meeting our criteria exists, will we find it?
Convergence, how many generations does it take to find a solution?
Scalability, can we generate sufficiently large graphs?

For evolutionary algorithms that evolve graphs directly, **exhaustiveness** is not a problem. The evolutionary approach is just a probabilistic exhaustive search of the entire search space. Our initial tests generating some small graphs with different degree distributions show that our implementation is able to successfully produce different distributions (e.g. uniform, exponential, normal). Figures 1, 2, and 3 show plots of the EDF for different example graphs generated using this method. We don't see any theoretical reasons this would not generalise to any other distribution.

The next concern is **convergence**, how many generations does it take to *find* the solutions of interest? With tests on small graphs of 100 vertices we saw the solutions converge to good quality results in about 200 generations. Moving on

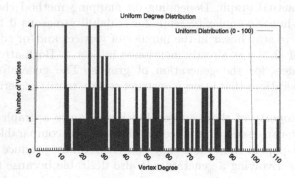

Fig. 1. Empirical degree distribution of graph generated with uniform degree distribution (0–100).

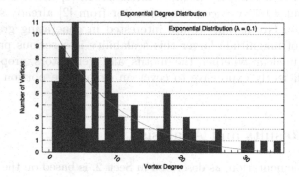

Fig. 2. Empirical degree distribution of graph generated with exponential degree distribution ($\lambda = 0.1$).

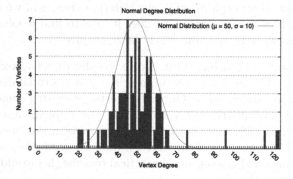

Fig. 3. Empirical degree distribution of graph generated with normal degree distribution ($\mu = 50$, $\sigma = 10$).

to bigger graphs, such as 1,000 or more vertices we see very rapid improvement in the first few tens of generations, but with improvement gradually slows down afterwards.

From experimenting with different combinations of crossover and mutation rates, it is clear that these primitives have an important role. Our initial experiments used edge-wise crossover, which took too long to converge, even on small graphs. With vertex-wise crossover, the number of generations required to converge to a good solution was reduced by 1 to 2 orders of magnitude.

We expect that the convergence plateau hit while generating larger graphs is caused by our crossover method being too simplistic. That is, it does not preserve the structure enough. By randomly keeping vertices from either parent any inherited improvements might be offset by inherited regression, resulting in most children not being a significant improvement over either parents and plateauing before reaching a good solution. Similarly, there are concerns with the simplistic uniform random mutation we are currently using. A completely uniform random mutation rate results in mutations always pressing candidates in the direction of a connectivity matrix that is 50% edges. If the percentage of edges is lower than 50% our randomly selected mutations are more likely to insert edges than delete them. And vice versa if the graph has more than 50% edges. At the time of the submission, we experiment with more complex techniques, but we have not yet found the best one[5].

Our final concern is **scalability**. The rate with which we explore the search space is linearly related to the number of generations, therefore we expect that larger graphs (i.e., larger search spaces) require more generations to produce. Besides fast convergence (i.e., keeping the number of generation as small as possible), there is also the concern of how scalable our primitives are (i.e., how long does one generation take). If evaluating the fitness function, performing crossover, or applying mutations are expensive, each generation will become prohibitively expensive to compute.

Our initial prototype aims to generate graphs as large as the largest graphs in SNAP. We don't think generating much bigger graphs is likely to contribute meaningfully to our investigation into the impact of graph structure on performance, but that remains an open question for future research. Anyway, such graphs have a couple of million vertices and tens of million edges (e.g., soc-LiveJournal has 4M vertices and 68M edges). In an initial test on a graph of 10 thousand vertices and 50 million edges, the entire process of crossover, mutation, and fitness computation takes approximately 20 s (per generation). Based on this number, we foresee no scalability problems: the implementation is linear in the number of edges and the generation of new children is trivially parallelisable.

---

[5] More results to be presented in the final paper. Current code and results are available at https://github.com/merijn/GPU-benchmarks.

5   Summary and Next Steps

Our original goal was to build a tool, in the form of a synthetic graph generator, that uses evolutionary computing to allow a thorough, fine-grain, on-demand exploration of graphs and their properties. How far are we?

Our initial tests indicate that evolutionary computing is suitable for this task: we are able to generate graphs of thousands of vertices within minutes. There are no fundamental challenges for the exhaustiveness, convergence, and scalability of the approach. However, our current prototype is rudimentary. Although our primitives can handle graphs of the sizes we target without a problem, tackling the convergence problem for such large graphs is not yet feasible in a reasonable amount of time. The immediate action needed to speed up this convergence is to experiment with new primitives for crossover and mutation, to ensuring that the improvements in population quality do not plateau.

It is of course possible that more complex primitives for crossover and mutation are too expensive to compute on larger graphs, with a net result of no improvement in the time it takes to generate graphs. If we will reach this dead-end, we will proceed to plan B: use evolution to generate functions, which in turn will generate graphs. A crossover process similar to that found in Hyper-NEAT would be more successful in preserving complex structure and thus result in faster convergence. However, we would still have to explore whether the generating functions produced this way can cover the search space exhaustively enough for our purposes.

To summarize, we believe our results indicate that fine-grain graph generation can be achieved using evolutionary computing. In fact, the graphs we generated are empirical evidence that evolutionary computing is a more flexible approach than the existing graph generators and models. The biggest challenge we are facing now is the trade-off between scalability and dataset scale: convergence speeds slow down as we scale up the size of graphs we wish to generate. Our current experiments with different crossover and mutation methods indicate that convergence can be improved significantly, but we cannot yet claim to have found the right balance.

References

1. Avery, C.: Giraph: large-scale graph processing infrastructure on hadoop. In: Proceedings of the Hadoop Summit, Santa Clara (2011)
2. Bach, B., Spritzer, A., Lutton, E., Fekete, J.-D.: Interactive random graph generation with evolutionary algorithms. In: Didimo, W., Patrignani, M. (eds.) GD 2012. LNCS, vol. 7704, pp. 541–552. Springer, Heidelberg (2013). doi:10.1007/978-3-642-36763-2_48
3. Bailey, A., Ventresca, M., Ombuki-Berman, B.: Automatic generation of graph models for complex networks by genetic programming. In: Proceedings of the 14th Annual Conference on Genetic and Evolutionary Computation, pp. 711–718. ACM (2012)

4. Capotă, M., Hegeman, T., Iosup, A., Prat-Pérez, A., Erling, O., Boncz, P.: Graphalytics: a big data benchmark for graph-processing platforms. In: Proceedings of the GRADES 2015, pp. 7:1–7:6. ACM (2015)
5. Chakrabarti, D., Faloutsos, C.: Graph mining: laws, generators, and algorithms. ACM Comput. Surv. (CSUR) **38**(1), 2 (2006)
6. Chakrabarti, D., Zhan, Y., Faloutsos, C.: R-MAT: a recursive model for graph mining. In: SDM, vol. 4, pp. 442–446. SIAM (2004)
7. T. G. S. Committee: The graph 500 list, 2010–2016
8. Elser, B., Montresor, A.: An evaluation study of bigdata frameworks for graph processing. In: Big Data (2013)
9. Erdös, P., Rényi, A.: On the evolution of random graphs. Publ. Math. Inst. Hung. Acad. Sci **5**, 17–61 (1960)
10. Erling, O., Averbuch, A., Larriba-Pey, J., Chafi, H., Gubichev, A., Prat, A., Pham, M.-D., Boncz, P.: The LDBC social network benchmark: interactive workload. In: Proceedings of the 2015 ACM SIGMOD International Conference on Management of Data, SIGMOD 2015, pp. 619–630. ACM, New York (2015)
11. Gauci, J., Stanley, K.O.: Autonomous evolution of topographic regularities in artificial neural networks. Neural Comput. **22**(7), 1860–1898 (2010)
12. Guo, Y., Biczak, M., Varbanescu, A.L., Iosup, A., Martella, C., Willke, T.L.: How well do graph-processing platforms perform? An empirical performance evaluation and analysis. In: IPDPS (2014)
13. Guo, Y., Varbanescu, A.L., Iosup, A., Epema, D.: An empirical performance evaluation of GPU-enabled graph-processing systems. In: CCGrid 2015 (2015)
14. Han, M., Daudjee, K., Ammar, K., Ozsu, M.T., Wang, X., Jin, T.: An experimental comparison of pregel-like graph processing systems. VLDB **7**, 1047–1058 (2014)
15. Holme, P., Kim, B.J.: Growing scale-free networks with tunable clustering. Phys. Rev. E **65**(2), 026107 (2002)
16. Hong, S., Depner, S., Manhardt, T., Van Der Lugt, J., Verstraaten, M., Chafi, H.: PGX.D: a fast distributed graph processing engine. In: Proceedings of the International Conference for High Performance Computing, Networking, Storage and Analysis, p. 58. ACM (2015)
17. Kunegis, J.: KONECT: the Koblenz network collection. In: Proceedings of the 22nd International Conference on World Wide Web, WWW 2013 Companion, pp. 1343–1350 (2013)
18. Leskovec, J.: Stanford Network Analysis Platform (SNAP). Stanford University, Stanford (2006)
19. Leskovec, J., Chakrabarti, D., Kleinberg, J., Faloutsos, C., Ghahramani, Z.: Kronecker graphs: an approach to modeling networks. J. Mach. Learn. Res. **11**, 985–1042 (2010)
20. Lothian, J., Powers, S., Sullivan, B.D., Baker, M., Schrock, J., Poole, S.W.: Synthetic graph generation for data-intensive HPC benchmarking: background and framework (2013)
21. Lu, Y., Cheng, J., Yan, D., Wu, H.: Large-scale distributed graph computing systems: an experimental evaluation. VLDB **8**, 281–292 (2014)
22. Massey Jr., F.J.: The Kolmogorov-Smirnov test for goodness of fit. J. Am. Stat. Assoc. **46**(253), 68–78 (1951)
23. Satish, N., Sundaram, N., Patwary, M.A., Seo, J., Park, J., Hassaan, M.A., Sengupta, S., Yin, Z., Dubey, P.: Navigating the maze of graph analytics frameworks using massive graph datasets. In: SIGMOD (2014)
24. Stanley, K.O., D'Ambrosio, D.B., Gauci, J.: A hypercube-based encoding for evolving large-scale neural networks. Artif. Life **15**(2), 185–212 (2009)

25. Stanley, K.O., Miikkulainen, R.: Efficient reinforcement learning through evolving neural network topologies. Netw. (Phenotype) **1**(2), 3 (1996)
26. Stanley, K.O., Miikkulainen, R.: Evolving neural networks through augmenting topologies. Evol. Comput. **10**(2), 99–127 (2002)
27. Varbanescu, A.L., Verstraaten, M., Penders, A., Sips, H., de Laat, C.: Can portability improve performance? An empirical study of parallel graph analytics. In: ICPE 2015 (2015)
28. Verstraaten, M., Varbanescu, A.L., de Laat, C.: Quantifying the performance impact of graph structure on neighbour iteration strategies for pagerank. In: Hunold, S., et al. (eds.) Euro-Par 2015. LNCS, vol. 9523, pp. 528–540. Springer, Cham (2015). doi:10.1007/978-3-319-27308-2_43

Towards the Next Generation of Large-Scale Network Archives

Stijn Heldens[1]([✉]), Ana Varbanescu[2], Wing Lung Ngai[1], Tim Hegeman[1], and Alexandru Iosup[1]

[1] Delft University of Technology, Delft, The Netherlands
s.j.heldens@tudelft.nl
[2] University of Amsterdam, Amsterdam, The Netherlands

Abstract. Both data and computer scientists need graph (network) datasets in the design, comparison, and tuning of important scientific results and practical artifacts. Despite the abundance of data in practice, freely available datasets are usually difficult to access, limited in size and diversity, and are collected in small static archives.

This work presents our vision towards a next generation of graph data archives. Therefore, we formulate six key requirements to guide the design of such archives. We further propose GraphPedia, a prototype architecture that addresses these requirements, and provides a large collection of different graphs, in many different storage formats, rich metadata, advanced searching, and on-demand graph generation. Once the open implementation challenges are resolved, GraphPedia will become a dynamic meeting space for exchanging graphs.

1 Introduction

Data and computer scientists are increasingly using graphs (or networks[1]) datasets [9,14,18] in their work. Relevant graph datasets are useful in developing, comparing, and deploying both algorithms [1,16,21], whose results lead to data-driven decisions, and systems [8,10,19,23,25], that can execute these graph processing algorithms.

Despite the existence of large amount of data in practice, researchers have limited access to highly diverse and large-scale graphs. In fact, many research contributions in data and computer science are validated on just a handful of graphs [17,18,22] from a limited set of repositories or, in worse cases, on non-public datasets. This limits the credibility and reproducibility of results, and thus the quality of the scientific and practical processes.

There are many reasons for this sparsity of publicly available graph datasets. Some are technical, as researchers might lack the expertise or budget to set up an infrastructure to allow others to access their datasets. Some are organizational, as researchers from one field of study might not come into contact with other domains. Some are just inconveniences, like the lack of a universal storage format

---

[1] Throughout this paper, the terms *graph* and *network* have the same meaning and are used interchangeably.

© Springer International Publishing AG 2017
F. Desprez et al. (Eds.): Euro-Par 2016 Workshops, LNCS 10104, pp. 571–579, 2017.
DOI: 10.1007/978-3-319-58943-5_46

for graphs which results in different incompatible formats [2,12,15] being used by different researchers.

A small number of archives do offer graph datasets: SNAP [15], KONECT [13], and UFSMC [5]. However, they represent an outdated generation of network archives, lacking the large-scale and diversity of needed to address the quickly changing needs of today's graph producers and consumers.

We believe that this problem is hindering research in graph processing and propose to build the next generation of graph archives. By drawing inspiration from the few existing archives, in this article we propose a new type of graph archive. Our contribution is threefold:

1. We identify a set of six requirements for next-generation network archives (Sect. 3). The requirements focus on a new type of archive: dynamic, with enhanced search and content generation, provenance and impact analysis, and support for user-content.
2. We introduce an archive following this new approach, GraphPedia (Sect. 4). We discuss the key features of our design, and how they match the requirements.
3. We discuss the main research challenges that lay ahead before GraphPedia can be fully implemented in practice (Sect. 5). We discuss in particular here issues of efficiency and convenience (e.g., data formats), community building, and supporting emerging trends in graph processing.

2   State-of-the-Art in Network Datasets

In practice, there are two ways in which researchers obtain graph datasets: download them from public graph repositories or create them using synthetic graph generators. We discuss both options in this section.

2.1   Real-World Network Repositories

We survey five major repositories for real-world graphs which are publicly accessible (Table 1), sorted chronologically by the year of their establishment. All these network archives share (at least) four significant drawbacks that characterize the state-of-the-art. First, the archives are small (less than 300 datasets, except UFSMC), static, and manually managed. They do not encourage their users to add new datasets to expand the collection. WEBSCOPE even requires an account which needs to manually approved before given access to the datasets. Second, the archives only provides datasets in specific storage formats. SNAP and KONECT offer only the edge list format, GTA stores dataset in their custom GTF format, while UFSMC offers three matrix formats. Third, the archives do not perform impact analysis that indicates how the datasets are used in research, with the exception of WEBSCOPE which requests explicitly attribution for usage. Fourth, it is difficult to select specific datasets by filtering and searching. While UFMSMC does offer a stand-alone Java program to browse through the datasets, the datasets are not categorized but rather loosely sorted by source.

Table 1. Five major repositories for real-world graphs datasets.

	Maintainer	Established	#Datasets	#Formats	Domains	Statistics
SNAP [15]	Stanford Univ	2005	Small (~ 100)	1	Various (16)	Basic
UFSMC [5]	Univ. of Florida	2011	Medium (2757)	3	Various	Comprehensive
GTA [9]	TU Delft	2012	Tiny (15)	1	Gaming	Description only
KONECT [13]	Univ. of Koblenz	2014	Small (253)	1	Various (23)	Comprehensive
WEBSCOPE [26]	Yahoo Labs	2016	Tiny (8)	1	Web	None

It is our goal to propose next generation archives that alleviate all these problems by design.

2.2 Synthetic Network Generators

Synthetic network generators are designed to enable graph generation based on users' input. Many graph generators emerged in the past [3], with the explicit goal of testing the correctness and scalability of graph processing algorithms.

For example, random graphs are generated by picking pairs of vertices under some random probability distribution and then connecting them by edges. Using a uniform probability leads to the well-known Erdős-Rényi model [6].

Because random graphs do not reflect the characteristics of real-world networks, more realistic generators have been proposed. For example, LDBC DATAGEN [7] generates large-scale social networks, R-MAT [20] generates scale-free networks, and the Internet Graph Generator [24] produces "World Wide Web"-like graphs.

Although most generators are publicly available, they are usually significantly limited in efficiency and usability: processing time is often prohibitive and deployement is non-trivial. Furthermore, the generated graphs or used parameters (e.g., seed) are rarely archived, making experiments difficult to reproduce and expand. These limitations forced existing archives to ignore synthetic graphs. Our goal is to alleviate these issues and incorporate synthetic graphs into next generation archives.

3   Requirements for Next-Generation Network Archives

Based on the observations listed in Sect. 2, we define a number of essential requirements for a next generation network archive.

(R1) **Variety.** Graphs from different domains have different properties and characteristics, which impacts the performance of graph algorithm and systems. It is important that the archive includes many types of graphs and reflects the variety of datasets in the real-world.

(R2) **Encourage Sharing.** An archive should not just be a static collection of datasets, it should be a meeting space for researchers to exchange both knowledge and data. The archive must provide the means for this collaboration.

(R3) **Different storage formats.** A universal storage format for graphs does
not exist and many different formats are used in practice. Converting
between formats is not always trivial, and this inconvenience can limit
users' choices. An archive should offer as many popular graph formats as
possible.

(R4) **Usability.** The archive should not be an enumeration of available datasets
without any context. Instead, we envision an interactive system that allows
users to browse and search the large collection of available datasets.

(R5) **Synthetic datasets.** The archive should provide access to synthetic
datasets, even created based on users' demands. Although many generators
are publicly available, deploying and using them correctly and efficiently is
not always trivial.

(R6) **Provenance and impact.** An archive should mention where the datasets
originate from (*provenance*) and how they are used in research (*impact*).
This allows users to assess the value of a dataset, and enables the community to report relevant results.

4   Design of GraphPedia

In this section, we present the design of GraphPedia as the first representative
of the new generation of graph archives. We explain how GraphPedia addresses
the requirements listed in Sect. 3, which ultimately define its architecture.

4.1   Data Model of Graphs

To address requirement (R1), GraphPedia uses a generic data model that can be
used to represent many different types of graphs. Each graph consists of a set of
vertices, each uniquely identified by an integer, and a set of edges, each consisting
of the identifiers of its endpoints. Edges can either be *directed* (i.e., edges are
uni-directional) or *undirected* (i.e., edges are bidirectional). Multiple edges are
allowed between two vertices, thus enabling multi-edge graphs. Additionally,
both vertices and edges can have a list of named properties to store data such as
timestamps (temporal graphs), weights (weighted graphs), or labels (bipartite
graphs). A similar data model is used in the Graphalytics benchmark [11].

4.2   Virtual Meeting Space

To address requirements (R1) and (R2), GraphPedia allows its users to add new
datasets to the archive. These datasets are added after (semi-)automated validation by a GraphPedia moderator, to avoid storing incorrect, irrelevant, or simply
duplicate datasets. The possibility to share graphs benefits both the contributors
and the users of the archive. Contributors benefit since it helps them gain recognition of their work and it allows them to share knowledge with peers. Users
benefit because continuously extending the archive increases both the volume
and the variety of the archive over time. Ideally, this dynamic interaction will
also enable interdisciplinary interactions.

4.3   Storage Formats

To tackle requirement (R3), GraphPedia enables access to every dataset in many different storage formats. Datasets are internally stored *once* using a single unified format. Whenever a user requests a different format, the dataset is *either* retrieved from a cache, *or* it is being converted into the appropriate format on-the-fly. This approach keeps the required storage capacity under control, while potentially offering large number of formats.

4.4   Network Metrics

To address requirement (R4), GraphPedia presents many graph metrics for each dataset [4]. Users can therefore quickly gain valuable insight, and decide whether a dataset is useful for their application.

Overall, metrics can be classified into three categories.

- *Basic metrics* describe the basic struture and are light-weight. Examples are number of vertices, density, average degree, and number of components.
- *Complex metrics* describe more complex characteristics. Examples are the average clustering coefficient, spectral norm, diameter, and Lorenz curve.
- *Property metrics* describe the distribution of the vertex/edge properties. Basic statistics can be given for these properties, such as mean, minimum/maximum, and standard deviation.

Clearly, an initial selection of metrics to offer needs to be made, but the design must be flexible enough to add more such metrics on-demand.

4.5   User-Interface

Also addressing requirement (R4), GraphPedia allows users to quickly select the relevant datasets *for their application*. This is an essential feature, since the archive grows over time (e.g., due to user contributions, but not only). Graph-Pedia will include advanced searching to allow users to select, filter, and sort datasets based on their domain, description, and graph characteristics. Note that the graph metrics play a fundamental role here, since they enable characteristics-driven search within the archive.

4.6   Generated Graphs

To cover requirement (R5), GraphPedia does not only offer static real-world datasets, but also provides a service to generate synthetic graphs. Multiple graph generators will be integrated into GraphPedia. Users can obtain a synthetic graph by specifying the type of generator and the corresponding parameters. If this graph is already present in the archive *or* in its cache, it can be downloaded immediately. Otherwise, the graph will be generated and cached. Once a graph is demanded multiple times, a GraphPedia moderator will decide whether it should be made a permanent member of the archive.

In addition to traditional generators, GraphPedia must also offer the ability to "replicate" an existing real-world graph at different scale. Thus, users can "shrink" a graph that is appropriate but too large, or "expand" a small real-world graph to a larger scale, for example to test functionality or study performance at different scales.

4.7 Provenance and Impact

An added value of a centralized archive is the possiblity to study provenance and impact of its items. The archive should contain, as much as possible, datasets with a full "pedigree": source of data, time of collection, extraction procedure, etc. For users providing new data, evidence must be provided (publications, lab reports, raw data, etc.) for the ownership and open nature of the data. This provenance meta-data will be published (annonymized if needed) togehter with the data. In terms of impact, the archive should list, for every dataset, the publications that use it. This information enables researchers to assess how often datasets are used, and which research communities favor the use of particular graphs. It also facilitates a fair comparison and the reproducibility of experimental results.

4.8 Architecture

Figure 1 depicts a high-level overview of the GraphPedia architecture. Users can access the archive via its web-based *frontend* (1). The *backend* of the architecture consists of a number of components: a database for datasets' meta-data (2), separate storage, cached, for the raw datasets themselves (3) (implemented, for example, as a fast (distributed) file system), and a processing platform to handle the processing jobs (4) (e.g., format conversion, synthetic graph generation, or metrics computation).

The web-interface provides four actions: *search* datasets, *download* datasets, *upload* datasets, and *generate* datasets. Searching for datasets is performed using the data from the meta-data storage. When downloading a graph, the *format converter* (5) fetches the raw dataset from the dataset storage, and converts it

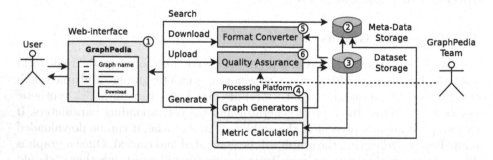

Fig. 1. High-level overview of GraphPedia architecture.

into the appropriate format. We note that for most edge-based formats, this can be done in a streaming fashion, reducing storage requirement and conversion time. When uploading a graph, the graph is submitted to *quality assurance* (6) for approval. Once the submission is successfully checked and approved, it is added to the dataset storage. When generating a graph, a new job is submitted to the processing platform and the resulting graph is added to storage once the job completes. For every new dataset (both uploaded and generated graphs), its meta-data is also added to the meta-data storage. Additionally, jobs are submitted to the processing platform to calculate graph metrics. The results are also saved in the meta-data storage.

5   Open Challenges

There are several challenges in realizing the implementation of GraphPedia.

First challenge is **efficiency**. Since GraphPedia is not just a static collection of datasets, but its provides interactive services that can convert and generate graphs, efficiency is essential to successfully build a large, diverse, dynamic, yet still usable archive. For example, a single user that submits very large conversion and generation jobs, should not prevent other users from submitting smaller jobs. The same job submitted frequently should avoid repeated reprocessing, but its results should be cached and reused More research is required to design and deploy solutions that enable (and measure) the overall efficiency of such a system.

Second, to measure the **impact** of different datasets, GraphPedia must discover all publications that use each dataset. Finding these publications manually is virtually impossible. Thus, automated tools are needed to periodically scan all relevant published work, eventually extracting the ones that use the GraphPedia datasets. Research in information retrieval is required to build this tool.

Third, the topic of **licensing** needs to be thoroughly studied. It cannot be assumed that all datasets are in the Public Domain and users should be able choose a suitable license for their work, which must be respected by the archive and its users.

Finally, although synthetic graph generation is a well-studied research topic, **shrinking** and **expanding** are less known. Research is required to find efficient techniques and tools that can be integrated into GraphPedia while preserving its efficiency. Alternative approaches, such as generating new graphs to mimic existing graphs following non-standard distributions, also require additional research. In particular, capturing and reproducing accurately the characteristics of any type of graph is still an open challenge.

6   Conclusion

Relevant network datasets are increasingly needed, both by data scientists developing and deploying methods to extract meaningful information and by computer scientists developing and tuning systems that enable processing diverse and large-scale network data. Addressing this need, our work proposes Graph-Pedia, a next generation archive for network data.

Key to our design, we do not see GraphPedia as a static collection of datasets, but as a virtual meeting space that allows researchers to meet and share their data. Additionally, GraphPedia offers many novel features such as rich metadata, advanced searching and filtering, different storage formats, and synthetic graphs on-demand. Overall, GraphPedia will benefit many different research communities, including graph algorithm designers, graph system researchers, and performance engineers.

We are currently tackling practical concerns in implementing GraphPedia, including increasing efficiency and providing a variety of graph storage formats. We will further focus on maintaining the community and continuously supporting emerging topics in graphs.

References

1. Bader, D.A., Kintali, S., Madduri, K., Mihail, M.: Approximating betweenness centrality. In: Bonato, A., Chung, F.R.K. (eds.) WAW 2007. LNCS, vol. 4863, pp. 124–137. Springer, Heidelberg (2007). doi:10.1007/978-3-540-77004-6_10
2. Brandes, U., Eiglsperger, M., Lerner, J., Pich, C.: Graph markup language (GraphML). Citeseer (2010)
3. Chakrabarti, D., Faloutsos, C.: Graph mining: laws, generators, and algorithms. ACM Comput. Surv. **38**(1), 2 (2006)
4. Chebotarev, P.: Studying new classes of graph metrics. In: Nielsen, F., Barbaresco, F. (eds.) GSI 2013. LNCS, vol. 8085, pp. 207–214. Springer, Heidelberg (2013). doi:10. 1007/978-3-642-40020-9_21
5. Davis, T.A., Hu, Y.: The University of Florida sparse matrix collection. ACM Trans. Math. Softw. (TOMS) **38**(1), 1 (2011)
6. Erdős, P., Rényi, A.: On random graphs i. Publ. Math. Debrecen **6**, 290–297 (1959)
7. Erling, O., Averbuch, A., Larriba-Pey, J., Chafi, H., Gubichev, A., Prat, A., Pham, M.D., Boncz, P.: The LDBC social network benchmark: interactive workload. In: SIGMOD International Conference on Management of Data. ACM (2015)
8. Gonzalez, J.E., Low, Y., Gu, H., Bickson, D., Guestrin, C.: Powergraph: distributed graph-parallel computation on natural graphs. In: USENIX Symposium on Operating Systems Design and Implementation (2012)
9. Guo, Y., Iosup, A.: The game trace archive. In: 11th Annual Workshop on Network and Systems Support for Games (NetGames) (2012)
10. Hong, S., Depner, S., Manhardt, T., Van Der Lugt, J., Verstraaten, M., Chafi, H.: PGX.D: a fast distributed graph processing engine. In: Proceedings of the International Conference for High Performance Computing, Networking, Storage and Analysis. ACM (2015)
11. Iosup, A., Hegeman, T., Ngai, W., Heldens, S., Prat, A., Manhardt, T., Chafi, H., Capota, M., Sundaram, N., Anderson, M., et al.: LDBC graphalytics: a benchmark for large-scale graph analysis on parallel and distributed platforms. Proc. VLDB Endow. **9**(12), 1317–1328 (2016)
12. Klyne, G., Carroll, J.J.: Resource description framework (RDF): concepts and abstract syntax. Technical report, W3C (2006). http://www.w3.org/TR/rdf-concepts/

13. Kunegis, J.: Konect: the koblenz network collection. In: Proceedings of the 22nd International Conference on World Wide Web Companion, pp. 1343–1350 (2013)
14. Leskovec, J., Kleinberg, J., Faloutsos, C.: Graphs over time: densification laws, shrinking diameters and possible explanations. In: SIGKDD International Conference on Knowledge Discovery and Data Mining, pp. 177–187. ACM (2005)
15. Leskovec, J., Krevl, A.: SNAP Datasets: Stanford large network dataset collection. http://snap.stanford.edu/data
16. Leskovec, J., Lang, K.J., Mahoney, M.: Empirical comparison of algorithms for network community detection. In: Proceedings of the 19th International Conference on World Wide Web, pp. 631–640. ACM (2010)
17. Lu, Y., Cheng, J., Yan, D., Wu, H.: Large-scale distributed graph computing systems: an experimental evaluation. Proc. VLDB Endow. **8**(3), 281–292 (2014)
18. Lumsdaine, A., Gregor, D., Hendrickson, B., Berry, J.: Challenges in parallel graph processing. Parallel Process. Lett. **17**(01), 5–20 (2007)
19. Malewicz, G., Austern, M.H., Bik, A.J., Dehnert, J.C., Horn, I., Leiser, N., Czajkowski, G.: Pregel: a system for large-scale graph processing. In: SIGMOD International Conference on Management of Data, pp. 135–146. ACM (2010)
20. Murphy, R.C., Wheeler, K.B., Barrett, B.W., Ang, J.A.: Introducing the graph 500. Cray Users Group (CUG) (2010)
21. Page, L., Brin, S., Motwani, R., Winograd, T.: The PageRank citation ranking: bringing order to the web. Technical report, Stanford InfoLab, November 1999
22. Satish, N., Sundaram, N., Patwary, M.M.A., Seo, J., Park, J., Hassaan, M.A., Sengupta, S., Yin, Z., Dubey, P.: Navigating the maze of graph analytics frameworks using massive graph datasets. In: SIGMOD International Conference on Management of Data, pp. 979–990. ACM (2014)
23. Sundaram, N., Satish, N., Patwary, M.M.A., Dulloor, S.R., Anderson, M.J., Vadlamudi, S.G., Das, D., Dubey, P.: Graphmat: high performance graph analytics made productive. Proc. VLDB Endow. **8**(11), 1214–1225 (2015)
24. Tauro, S.L., Palmer, C., Siganos, G., Faloutsos, M.: A simple conceptual model for the internet topology. In: GLOBECOM Global Telecommunications Conference, vol. 3, pp. 1667–1671. IEEE (2001)
25. Xin, R.S., Gonzalez, J.E., Franklin, M.J., Stoica, I.: Graphx: A resilient distributed graph system on spark. In: First International Workshop on Graph Data Management Experiences and Systems. ACM (2013)
26. Labs, Y.: Webscope. https://webscope.sandbox.yahoo.com/

REPPAR - International Workshop on Reproducibility in Parallel Computing

Computation-Aware Dynamic Frequency Scaling: Parsimonious Evaluation of the Time-Energy Trade-Off Using Design of Experiments

Luis Felipe Millani[✉] and Lucas Mello Schnorr

Graduate Program in Computer Science (PPGC) Informatics Institute,
Federal University of Rio Grande do Sul (UFRGS),
Caixa Postal 15064, Porto Alegre, RS 91501-970, Brazil
{lfgmillani,schnorr}@inf.ufrgs.br

Abstract. A promising approach to improve the energy-efficiency of HPC applications is to apply energy-saving techniques for different code regions according to their characteristics (blocking communication, load imbalance). Since most applications have many parallel code regions, this strategy requires extensive experimental time to find all the time-energy trade-offs for a given application. In this paper we make use of Design of Experiments (DoE) to (1) reduce the experimental time considering a parsimonious evaluation of execution time and energy; and (2) define the Pareto front with all interesting time-energy trade-offs. We report the use of our methodology for seven benchmarks, each with interesting Pareto fronts with distinct shapes. Among them, out of the 25 parallel regions of the MiniFE benchmark, we detect configurations which reduce energy in 9.27% with a non-significant penalty in runtime when compared with using the high frequency for all regions; and, for the Graph500 benchmark with 17 parallel regions, 7.0% execution time reduction with a increase of 2.4% in energy consumption, when comparing against running all regions in the lowest frequency.

1 Introduction

Performance has historically overshadowed energy efficiency in the HPC field. This scenario is changing and initiatives focusing on energy efficiency, like the Green500 list [24], have gained importance. The current leader of Green500 offers only 7.0GFLOPs per watt. Considering a 20MW exascale supercomputer, the efficiency would have to be of at least 50GFLOPs per watt. Improvements must be made from both the hardware and software sides to make the leap in energy efficiency. Strategies for energy reduction in parallel applications are a step forward to address the problem from the software side.

Software energy reduction strategies can be divided in two groups: inter-node [2], acting in the system level; and intra-node, where code regions are subject to power manipulation. Usually, application idle states trigger these strategies. Opportunities appear during load imbalances [19], blocking communication

© Springer International Publishing AG 2017
F. Desprez et al. (Eds.): Euro-Par 2016 Workshops, LNCS 10104, pp. 583–595, 2017.
DOI: 10.1007/978-3-319-58943-5_47

phases [16,21], inter-node communication [15], MPI operations [26], and wait states [13]. Correlating power consumption to source code is also explored [6]. Dynamic Voltage Frequency Scaling [9] (DVFS) is frequently used, attempting different processor frequencies to execute code regions, targeting energy savings with minimal or no performance loss [5].

HPC applications commonly have many parallel regions subject to frequency scaling. For example, Graph500 [18] has 17 parallel regions; MiniFE [7] has 25. Large HPC codes may have hundreds depending on the application complexity and code size. It is unrealistic to evaluate all time-energy trade-offs considering several processor frequencies. The experimental time would be too large, even more as replications are necessary to account for variability. Others [5,14] have adopted similar per-region strategies but they use simple experimental designs meant to find not all time-energy trade-offs, but a single per-region frequency combination (details in Sect. 2).

The objective of this work is to discover all the time-energy trade-offs when adopting per-region processor frequency scaling. We tackle the explosion in experimental time with a workflow based on Design of Experiments (DoE) techniques [27], such as screening and full factorial designs, ANOVA, and main effect plots [17]. Final results are analyzed with a customized bivariate Pareto front plot demonstrating experimental variability. As far as we know, this is the first time such combined framework is used to evaluate energy savings in HPC.

We report the use of our methodology for seven OpenMP benchmarks with many parallel code regions, each with interesting Pareto fronts with distinct shapes. Among them, out of the 25 parallel regions of the MiniFE benchmark, we detect configurations which reduce energy in 9.27% with a non-significant penalty in runtime when compared with using the high frequency for all regions; and, for the Graph500 benchmark with 17 parallel regions, we obtain a 7% execution time reduction with a 2.4% increase in energy consumption, when comparing against running all regions in the lowest frequency.

Section 2 positions our work against related work. Section 3 presents basic concepts about DoE. Section 4 details our methodology. Section 5 has the evaluation of seven benchmarks. Conclusion and future work appears in Sect. 6. The source code of this paper, including all data that has been used, is publicly available as an org file on https://github.com/lfgmillani/reppar2016/.

2   Related Work

There has been a lot of effort to save energy with minimal performance loss in HPC systems. We focus in application-aware strategies that consider code regions. Freeh and Lowenthal [5] propose per-phase frequency scaling in HPC applications. They define the best processor frequency combination by testing all possible frequencies one by one, sequentially and in order. This is an one-phase at a time design, with a linear experimental time according to the number of phases and processor frequencies. Our approach differs in two main aspects. First, while they verify one factor at a time, our approach combines screening, rapidly discovering regions affecting outcomes, with full factorial designs, detecting all time-energy trade-offs. One factor at a time designs capture only a small subset of such trade-offs. Second, while Freeh et al. evaluate all available frequencies, we are limited to two. Statistical data analysis lacks established tools to analyze measurements with three or more levels per factor (see Sect. 3 for details).

Laurenzano et al. [14] also propose a fine-grained approach to define the best per-loop processor frequency. They generate a series of loops configured with different CPU and memory behavior. In a system characterization step, each loop configuration is evaluated against all possible processor frequencies, ultimately defining which frequency is the best. The real HPC application loops are each one profiled for cache hit rates, flops, and number of memory accesses, forming a loop signature. Frequency determination is obtained by searching the closest point of the loop signature in the system characterization data. Our methodology differs because it works directly with the application code in our screening warm up step. Our methodology also enables the discovery of all time-energy trade-offs that belong to the Pareto front, instead of searching for a single best combination as they do. Laurenzano's approach has been extended by Tiwari et al. [25] with Green Queue, using eight dimensions for frequency selection. Peraza et al. [20] combine power models and performance measurements, using a method that requires only one application run per frequency configuration. Such technique makes it impossible to detect correlations between frequency configurations on different parts of the program, something we address in our method by using a full factorial design.

There are other approaches. Use of runtime systems [21] to detect frequencies for code regions that give a good balance between performance and energy, those that use profile-based information [8] to find the best frequencies, and analytical [13] and prediction models [6]. Preparatory measurements with all available frequencies are also conducted by Dick et al. [3] on a numerical simulation code to deduce the best frequencies in a per-routine basis.

3   Background on Design of Experiments

In Design of Experiments (DoE), factors are variables that can affect the outcome, such as the compiler used, the CPU architecture, the number of cores, etc. They can be quantitative or qualitative. We present a background of DoE concepts, essential for a good understanding of our experimental methodology.

Full Factorial Designs. The full factorial experimental design keeps the effect of factors orthogonal [17], when level distribution is balanced. The orthogonality is important when analyzing experimental results, as it allows the effect of each factor to be estimated independently. With n factors, a two-level full factorial design requires 2^n experiments. Since experimental size grows exponentially with the number of factors, its adoption is unfeasible with many factors. Full factorial designs enable the detection of interactions among factors. Such interaction means that simultaneous changes in multiple factors have combined effects in the measured outcome. This implies that a factor's effect in the outcome depends on another factor. As far as we know, factor interaction is undeveloped (see Sect. 2), being one of the advantages of our approach. Full factorial designs can also be generated for more levels. With l levels and n factors, this kind of design requires l^n experiments. Although possible, the use of $l > 2$ is rare in statistics since there is no rigorous statistical analysis available as of today. For that reason, we limit our methodology to two-level full factorial designs, forcing the analyst to choose two frequencies out of those available. **Main effects plots** can be used to analyze results obtained from factorial designs. They quantify how much each of the factors affects the response. The main effect of each factor is the difference between the mean response for that factor considering its two possible levels [1].

Fractional and Screening Designs. The sparsity of effects principle asserts a system is usually dominated by main effects and low order interactions [17]. As such, identifying factors responsible for the majority of the effect being measured does not require expensive 2^n full factorial designs. This principle does not hold when there are complex interactions between the factors. Fractional factorial and screening designs require less experimental effort than full factorial designs and still give a good exploration of the configuration space. These designs can be used to screen which factors have the most effect. While common in some sciences due to the high cost of each experiment, fractional factorial designs are not often used in parallel computing, where the preference is with one-factor-at-a-time designs or in rare cases full factorial designs. Fractional designs can be extremely useful when the full factorial design requires many experiments, as it can reduce experimental time. Even for a low number of factors the number of experiments can be considerably reduced. These designs have 2^{k-p} runs, where k is the number of factors and p is used to limit the experiment size, at the price of losing complex relations as p grows. **Plackett-Burman (PB)** designs are a kind of fractional design that is mostly used for screening [23]. The number of runs of Plackett-Burman designs is always a multiple of four. A PB design is identical to a fractional design iff its number of runs is a power of two. When it is not, PB designs are non-geometrical. This kind of design has more complex aliasing patterns, making analysis of the interactions between the factors more difficult. When there are only minor interactions, the non-geometric designs can save experimental time. Screening designs with more than two levels are still an open research question in statistics. Three-level screening exists [12], but only for quantitative levels, which can be the case for processor frequency.

4   DoE-Based Methodology to Find Time-Energy Trade-Offs

The objective of our DoE-based methodology is to find all interesting Pareto front cases where the energy-performance correlation balances towards HPC goals, which is minimal performance losses. Figure 1 gives an overview of the methodology, which is detailed in the next subsections. It starts with the screening phase (on the left), where initial parallel code regions (from A to F) have

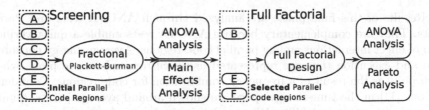

Fig. 1. Our DoE-based methodology to find all time-energy trade-offs.

their impact on the outcome quickly measured. Results are evaluated with a combination of ANOVA and main effects analysis, both provided by most statistical tools. The objective is to detect which code regions significantly affect the outcome. Those which do (B, E, and F in the example) are used in the full factorial phase (right). There, all time-energy trade-offs are discovered using full factorial designs, allowing the detection of interactions among code regions. We employ Pareto and ANOVA to analyze full factorial results.

4.1 Screening Parallel Code Regions, ANOVA and Main Effects Plot

The screening experimental phase uses a two-level Plackett-Burman design, attempting to identify parallel code regions that affect energy consumption and execution time. For simplicity, the parallel code regions comprise OpenMP's parallel code blocks. These code regions are the **factors**, while the **levels** are the possible frequencies. The screening phase uses only two frequencies – low and high – out of those available in current processors. It is up to the performance analyst to define values to be considered as low and high frequencies.

Analysis of variance (ANOVA) and main effects plots [17] are used to analyze measurements. While ANOVA gives a confidence level of which code regions affect the outcome when the frequency changes, it does not tell the magnitude or direction of such change. Main effects plots are complementary because they cover exactly these points, allowing us to rank regions based on how much they affect the outcome when the processor frequency is changed. For the second phase we select only regions that are significant according to ANOVA and whose effect is significant compared to the effect of other code regions.

4.2 Full Factorial Design, ANOVA and Pareto Analysis

This phase considers only regions that truly affect the outcome, according to screening. The objective is to search for parallel code regions for which the processor frequency could be reduced without too much performance penalty; or regions whose execution time is not too negatively affected while offering high energy savings. We also look for parallel code region interactions when scaling frequency. Measurement variability is addressed through experimental replication, obtaining significance levels through ANOVA.

Results of this final phase are analyzed through ANOVA tests and Pareto plots. They are complementary because ANOVA tests enable a quick verification of effect interactions among parallel code regions. Average energy consumption and execution time are represented using customized Pareto plots, where each point is the result of a frequency combination for code regions. Confidence regions [11] in the time-energy space are shown around average points, quantifying experimental variability. We also define the Pareto front [4] by connecting the best time-energy trade-offs (see Figs. 3 and 4).

5 Experimental Evaluation

We evaluate seven OpenMP-based benchmarks using our DoE methodology. Energy consumption is measured for the whole execution time, while we use DVFS [9] to control processor frequency. Parallel code regions (**factors**), identified through letters, are marked manually for evaluation. This process could be automated during compilation, for instance by defining a new region for each parallel task or loop. Our experiments use one node, although the methodology could be extended for use in a heterogeneous cluster. In that case, different regions could be used to differentiate between CPU and accelerator code for the same task. For each code region, we verify how the low and high frequency (**levels**) affect two outcomes: energy consumption and execution time. We present our benchmarks and the experimental platform below; a full analysis of Graph500; and global results of the six remaining benchmarks.

Case studies: Table 1 lists the OpenMP benchmarks with the number of regions, and the low and high processor frequency for each of them. BFS and Delaunay belong to PBBS [22], while the Graph500 [18] is a benchmark on its own. MiniFE, HPCCG, CoMD, and Pathfinder are part of the Mantevo [7] suite.

Table 1. HPC Benchmarks description with low/high frequency parameters in GHz.

Benchmark	Description	Regions	Low	High
BFS [22]	Breadth-first search	7	1.5	2.3
Delaunay [22]	Triangular mesh generation	16	1.5	2.3
Graph500 [18]	Data-intensive load	17	1.8	2.3
MiniFE [7]	Unstructured finite element	25	1.5	2.3
HPCCG [7]	Synthetic linear system	7	1.5	2.3
CoMD [7]	Molecular dynamics	14	1.5	2.3
Pathfinder [7]	Signature search	7	1.2	2.3

Experimental Platform: Experiments are executed on orion, a machine of the GPPD Team of INF/UFRGS. This machine has two Intel Xeon E5-2630 Sandy Bridge processors, with 24 cores (12 physical), with 32 GB of memory.

The processor has twelve clock frequencies, from 1.2 to 2.3 GHz. Benchmarks are compiled with GCC 5.1.1, using the -O3 optimization flag. Energy consumption of the package and memory are measured through Intel's RAPL counters [10].

5.1   Full Analysis of Graph500 Benchmark

Seventeen parallel code regions (from A to Q) of the Graph500 benchmark have been manually instrumented. Table 2 shows the ANOVA results of each factor's impact on energy (left) and time (right). The number of stars on each line's end indicates the significance of each factor's impact. For example, the three stars of region J indicates that a low to high frequency change has a 99.9% chance of impacting both energy and execution time. Therefore, scaling frequency on regions J and L has a 99.9% chance of affecting energy consumption, while on regions E, I and J the impact is on execution time. Figure 2 is the main effect plots for energy (top) and execution time (bottom). It shows the magnitude of the effect when one factor changes its level from low to high. For example, region J increases energy consumption when it goes from low to high, while reducing execution time. We conclude that regions J, L and E have a non-negligible impact on energy when we upscale the processor frequency. Remaining regions could be kept in the highest processor frequency since downscaling has no effect on energy. We observe that regions I, J and E have smaller execution time when upscaling frequency. Remaining regions make no significant difference on execution time, at a 99% confidence level. A promising code region to act upon is I, where we can see in the main effects plot that a significative execution time reduction appears with a minor energy consumption increase when upscaling, compared to the rest. Regions E, I, J and L are the only regions whose scaling affects energy consumption or execution time, with a 99% confidence level (two stars). These regions were selected for the full factorial phase.

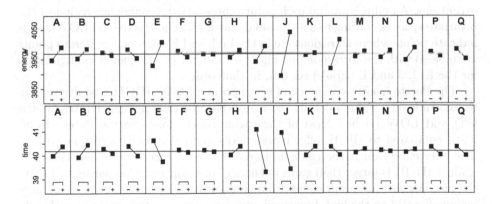

Fig. 2. Main effect plots of energy (top) and exec. time (bottom) of Graph500 screening.

Table 3 shows the ANOVA for the full factorial experiments. Regions E, I, J and L affect execution time and energy consumption at a 99.9% confidence level.

Table 2. ANOVA of energy (left) and execution time (right) of Graph500 screening.

	Sum Sq	F value	Pr(>F)			Sum Sq	F value	Pr(>F)	
A	47202	3.572	0.062298	.	A	3.88	2.297	0.13348	
B	25313	1.916	0.170105		B	6.78	4.009	0.04855	*
C	2197	0.166	0.684514		C	0.82	0.482	0.48947	
D	21324	1.614	0.207569		D	4.04	2.386	0.12626	
E	155973	11.803	0.000931	***	E	19.31	11.418	0.00112	**
F	10309	0.780	0.379685		F	0.26	0.152	0.69771	
G	34	0.003	0.959820		G	0.12	0.071	0.79036	
H	14413	1.091	0.299389		H	3.28	1.943	0.16715	
I	67315	5.094	0.026669	*	I	79.27	46.879	1.27e-09	***
J	543804	41.152	8.52e-09	***	J	58.12	34.373	9.19e-08	***
K	1088	0.082	0.774852		K	3.35	1.980	0.16321	
L	237763	17.992	5.79e-05	***	L	2.94	1.737	0.19115	
M	7698	0.583	0.447497		M	0.52	0.308	0.58020	
N	13177	0.997	0.320938		N	0.05	0.030	0.86216	
O	41888	3.170	0.078716	.	O	0.37	0.219	0.64130	
P	4338	0.328	0.568236		P	2.60	1.535	0.21892	
Q	24679	1.868	0.175494		Q	3.14	1.856	0.17681	

Table 3. ANOVA of energy (left) and time (right) of Graph500 full factorial experiments.

	Sum Sq	F value	Pr(>F)			Sum Sq	Mean Sq	F value	Pr(>F)	
E	1125060	136.64	< 2e-16	***	E	118.9	127.66	< 2e-16	***	
I	254662	30.93	3.76e-08	***	I	692.8	743.71	< 2e-16	***	
J	4067002	493.94	< 2e-16	***	J	350.9	376.63	< 2e-16	***	
L	4265959	518.10	< 2e-16	***	L	31.8	34.15	7.68e-09	***	

Figure 3 presents the Pareto plot showing the correlation between energy savings (in the Y axis) and execution time (in X). The blue line represents the Pareto front, connecting the best time-energy trade-offs. Each point is the average of 50 executions. An ellipse around each point represents the confidence region in the bivariate space according to a 99% confidence level. The HIGH and LOW labels indicate points where all regions are in the high and low frequency. Pareto points are labeled with the corresponding high (+) and low (−) frequency configuration for the E, I, J and L parallel regions, in that order.

The Pareto front is composed of seven points: LOW, HIGH, and five region-based trade-offs. Table 4 details the region-based points against HIGH (at the left) and LOW (right). Most of the region-based points in the Pareto front, when compared to HIGH, offer more energy reduction than performance loss. The only exception is the configuration (+ - - -) whose execution time loss against HIGH is larger than gains in energy consumption. Comparing to LOW, the more interesting result comes from configuration (+ + - -): so setting only regions E and I to the high frequency gives an execution time reduction of 7.0% while increasing energy consumption by 2.4%. Remaining comparison against LOW show that runtime gains are always greater than the increase in energy. Next section shows the Pareto front results of six other benchmarks.

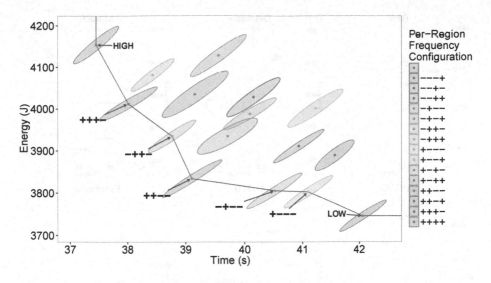

Fig. 3. Time-Energy Pareto plot containing the results for the Graph500 benchmark.

Table 4. Pareto front points and their performance/energy trade-offs for Graph500.

E I J L	Time (%/High)	Energy (%/High)	Time (%/Low)	Energy (%/Low)
- + - -	8.18	−8.39	−3.67	1.60
- + + -	3.51	−5.28	−7.82	5.05
+ - - -	9.74	−8.46	−2.28	1.52
+ + - -	4.42	−7.70	−7.02	2.37
+ + + -	1.50	−3.41	−9.62	7.12

5.2   Global Results Considering Remaining Benchmarks

Figure 4 depicts the detailed Pareto plots for the other benchmarks. Each one shows distinct trade-offs, detailed as follows. **BFS**. The Pareto front is composed of two region-based points: -++ and +--. Remaining region-based points and HIGH and LOW get grouped around these two points, with no significant difference. As we can see, our methodology fails to detect important trade-offs between energy and execution time for this benchmark. It discovers, however, an anomaly with the two points that are above the LOW group but far from the Pareto front. Such anomaly, which should be avoided, provides no performance gains and higher energy cost. **Delaunay**. Only two parallel regions were considered relevant for the full factorial. Results are similar to BFS: the two region-based points are very similar to the LOW and HIGH points, considering experimental variability. There is a significant different in energy consumption when moving from LOW to +-. **MiniFE**. Five parallel regions were considered for MiniFE. As we can see in the Pareto plot, four groups of region-based points are formed: two of them around the LOW and HIGH points, and two that present other energy

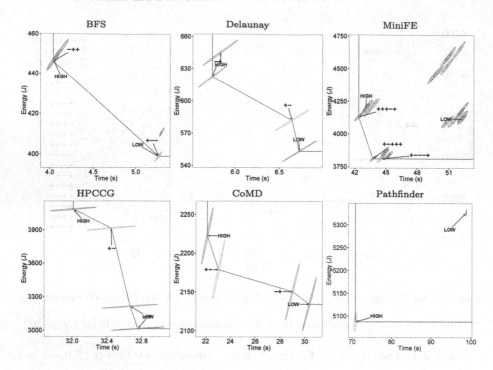

Fig. 4. Detailed Pareto plots for six benchmarks.

performance trade-offs. Combinations below the HIGH group have interesting results. The Pareto point +-+++, for instance, reduces energy by 9.27% with a minor penalty in execution time when compared to HIGH. Another region-based point with combination +++-+ in the HIGH group provides a potential reduction both in time (1.64%) and in energy (1.63%), but results are unclear since there is some overlap with the HIGH point considering the confidence region. For this benchmark, fixing all regions in the lowest frequency would be insufficient to bring enough benefits in energy while causing a large slowdown. In this case, our methodology clearly captures the new trade-off. **HPCCG.** The screening phase has detected only two parallel regions for this benchmark. Results show that the combination -+ offers an energy reduction of 21.35% with a non-significant execution time penalty of only 2.04% when compared to the HIGH point. The other region-based point +- demonstrates energy reduction of 4.21% with a 1.36% penalty in time, also non-significant. These values are based on 50 replications for each combination, indicating a small variability in energy but large in execution time probably due to the small timespan. **CoMD.** Experiments with CoMD with two parallel code regions showed a high variability after 50 replications. The energy scale is very small, indicating that any changes in frequency cause minor energy gains but large performance penalties. The region-based point +- offers 1.97% energy reduction causing 4.1% slowdown, when compared to HIGH. We can conclude that this benchmark is unsuited to energy gains with minor performance losses. **Pathfinder.** Only one region has been selected for the full factorial tests probably indicating that such region is the benchmark's compute-bound. The HIGH point dominates the LOW point, forming a simple Pareto front. We can see that running the parallel code region in LOW frequency causes a 40% slowdown for the application with no significant gains in energy reduction.

6   Conclusion

We propose a workflow based on Design of Experiments to evaluate the time-energy trade-offs when per-region frequency scaling is adopted in HPC applications. Our approach consists of two phases: a screening phase using ANOVA and main effects plots to identify which regions deserve further investigation; and a detailed phase using full factorial designs along with ANOVA and Pareto plots for measurement analysis. We evaluated our strategy with seven OpenMP benchmarks: BFS, Delaunay, Graph500, MiniFE, HPCCG, CoMD and Pathfinder. Our DoE-based methodology enables the discovery of different time-energy trade-offs: for MiniFE, we have found region-based frequency configurations that enable a 9.27% improvement in energy with no significant change in runtime; and for Graph500, a time reduction of 7.0% with an increase of 2.4% in energy consumption, when compared with using the lowest frequency for all regions. In the other benchmarks, per-region frequency scaling resulted in little to no energy improvements when compared against using only one frequency for all regions. Another interesting result is that measurement variability makes the limits of the Pareto front unclear. Distinct Pareto front shape might help better understand the impact of region-based frequency scaling for each HPC application. Planned future work includes a full factorial analysis when all processor frequencies are considered. We also plan to improve the interpretation of the screening by including the time taken to execute each parallel code region.

Acknowledgements. We thank CAPES and CNPq for partially funding this work. In addition, we thank Arnaud Legrand for his ideas on design of experiments that inspired us to develop the work of this paper, and for his series of lectures on Scientific Methodology and Performance Evaluation (SMPE).

References

1. Box, G.E., Hunter, J.S., Hunter, W.G.: Statistics for experimenters: design, innovation, and discovery. AMC **10**, 12 (2005)
2. Cicotti, P., Tiwari, A., Carrington, L.: Efficient speed (ES): Adaptive DVFS and clock modulation for energy efficiency. In: International Conference on Cluster Computing, pp. 158–166 (2014)
3. Dick, B., Vogel, A., Khabi, D., Rupp, M., Küster, U., Wittum, G.: Utilization of empirically determined energy-optimal CPU-frequencies in a numerical simulation code. Comput. Vis. Sci. **17**(2), 89–97 (2015)
4. Ehrgott, M.: Multicriteria Optimization. LNEMS. Springer, Heidelberg (2000)

5. Freeh, V.W., Lowenthal, D.K.: Using multiple energy gears in MPI programs on a power-scalable cluster. In: Symposium on Principles and Practice of Parallel Programming. ACM (2005)
6. Ge, R., Feng, X., Song, S., Chang, H.C., Li, D., Cameron, K.: Powerpack: energy profiling and analysis of high-performance systems and applications. IEEE Trans. Parallel Distrib. Syst. **21**(5), 658–671 (2010)
7. Heroux, M.A., Doerfler, D.W., Crozier, P.S., Willenbring, J.M., Edwards, H.C., Williams, A., Rajan, M., Keiter, E.R., Thornquist, H.K., Numrich, R.W.: Improving performance via mini-applications. Technical report, SAND2009-5574, Sandia (2009)
8. Hotta, Y., Sato, M., Kimura, H., Matsuoka, S., Boku, T., Takahashi, D.: Profile-based Optimization of power performance by using dynamic voltage scaling on a PC cluster. In: IPDPS (2006)
9. Hsu, C.H., Feng, W.: A feasibility analysis of power awareness in commodity-based high-performance clusters. In: Cluster Computing, pp. 1–10. IEEE (2005)
10. Intel: Intel 64 and IA-32 Architectures Software Developer's Manual - Volume 3B. Intel Corporation, September 201
11. Johnson, R.A., Wichern, D.W. (eds.): Applied Multivariate Statistical Analysis. Prentice-Hall Inc., Upper Saddle River (1988)
12. Jones, B., Nachtsheim, C.J.: A class of three-level designs for definitive screening in the presence of second-order effects. Qual. Technol. **43**(1), 1–15 (2011)
13. Kerbyson, D., Vishnu, A., Barker, K.: Energy templates: exploiting application information to save energy. In: IEEE International Conference on Cluster Computing, pp. 25–233 (2011)
14. Laurenzano, M.A., Meswani, M., Carrington, L., Snavely, A., Tikir, M.M., Poole, S.: Reducing energy usage with memory and computation-aware dynamic frequency scaling. In: Jeannot, E., Namyst, R., Roman, J. (eds.) Euro-Par 2011. LNCS, vol. 6852, pp. 79–90. Springer, Heidelberg (2011). doi:10.1007/978-3-642-23400-2_9
15. Lim, M.Y., Freeh, V.W., Lowenthal, D.K.: Adaptive, transparent CPU scaling algorithms leveraging inter-node MPI communication regions. Parallel Comput. **7**(10–11), 667–683 (2011)
16. Lim, M., Freeh, V.W., Lowenthal, D.: Adaptive, transparent frequency and voltage scaling of communication phases in MPI programs. In: Supercomputing, p. 14 (2006)
17. Montgomery, D.C.: Design and Analysis of Experiments. Wiley, Hoboken (2008)
18. Murphy, R.C., Wheeler, K.B., Barrett, B.W., Ang, J.A.: Introducing the graph 500. Cray User's Group (CUG) (2010)
19. Padoin, E., Castro, M., Pilla, L., Navaux, P., Mehaut, J.F.: Saving energy by exploiting residual imbalances on iterative applications. In: International Conference on HPC (2014)
20. Peraza, J., Tiwari, A., Laurenzano, M., Carrington, L., Snavely, A.: PMaC's green queue: a framework for selecting energy optimal DVFS configurations in large scale MPI applications. Concur. Comput.: Pract. Exp. **28**(2), 211–231 (2013)
21. Rountree, B., Lownenthal, D.K., de Supinski, B.R., Schulz, M., Freeh, V.W., Bletsch, T.: Adagio: making DVS practical for complex HPC applications. In: Proceedings of the 23rd International Conference on Supercomputing, pp. 460–469. ACM (2009)

22. Shun, J., Blelloch, G.E., Fineman, J.T., Gibbons, P.B., Kyrola, A., Simhadri, H.V., Tangwongsan, K.: Brief announcement: the problem based benchmark suite. In: 24th Annual ACM Symposium on Parallelism Algorithms and Architectures, pp. 68–70. ACM, New York (2012)
23. Simpson, T., Poplinski, J., Koch, P.N., Allen, J.: Metamodels for computer-based engineering design: survey and recomm. Eng. Comput. **17**(2), 129–150 (2001)
24. Feng, W.C., Cameron, K.: The Green500 list: encouraging sustainable supercomputing. Computer **40**(12), 50–55 (2007). doi:10.1109/MC.2007.445. ISSN 0018-9162
25. Tiwari, A., Laurenzano, M., Peraza, J., Carrington, L., Snavely, A.: Green queue: customized large-scale clock frequency scaling. In: International Conference on Cloud and Green Computing, pp. 260–267, November 2012
26. Venkatesh, A., Vishnu, A., Hamidouche, K., Tallent, N., Panda, D.D., Kerbyson, D., Hoisie, A.: A case for application-oblivious energy-efficient MPI runtime. In: International Conference for High Performance Computing, Networking, Storage and Analysis, NY, USA, pp. 29:1–29:12 (2015)
27. Wu, C., Hamada, M., Wu, C.: Experiments: Planning, Analysis, and Parameter Design Optimization. Wiley, New York (2000)

The Information Needed for Reproducing Shared Memory Experiments

Vincent Gramoli[(✉)]

Data61-CSIRO and University of Sydney, Sydney, Australia
vincent.gramoli@sydney.edu.au

Abstract. Reproducibility of experiments is key to research advances. Unfortunately, experiments involving concurrent programs are rarely reproducible. In this paper, we focus on multi-threaded executions where threads synchronize to access shared memory and present a series of causes for performance variations that illustrate the difficulty of reproducing a concurrent experiment. As one can guess, our experimental results are not intended to be reproducible but are meant to illustrate conditions that affect conclusions one can draw out of concurrent experiments.

Keywords: Reproducibility · Synchrobench · Artifact · NUMA · cTDP · JIT · Pinning

1 Introduction

Science advances faster when researchers do not follow false leads. Interestingly, scientists give the rise of computing tools as a pretext for disclosing information regarding scientific experiments and explains that, with some exceptions, not releasing the source program for results that depend on computation is "intolerable" [1]. The journal *Nature* allows editors to even decide to reject papers if the computer code is unavailable [2]. In computer science research, however, researchers rarely share their source code at the time of publication. Some may not respond to requests asking to share their source code for the sake of reproducibility. And when computer scientists share their code, they sometimes share a different version than what they used in their experiments [3]: "The shoemaker's son always goes barefoot."

That said, remarkable efforts from the programming language community were recently devoted to encourage the reproducibility of computer science experiments [4]. In recent editions of programming language conferences, authors had the opportunity to submit an *artifact* containing their documented source code as well as scripts and required libraries. For example, conferences like OOPSLA and ECOOP accepted artifact submissions since 2013, POPL and PLDI started in 2014 and PPoPP, CGO and CAV started in 2015.[1] After submission,

---

[1] http://evaluate.inf.usi.ch/artifacts.

© Springer International Publishing AG 2017
F. Desprez et al. (Eds.): Euro-Par 2016 Workshops, LNCS 10104, pp. 596–608, 2017.
DOI: 10.1007/978-3-319-58943-5_48

the artifact gets evaluated along four criteria: (i) consistency indicating whether the artifact helps reproducing the results of the paper, (ii) completeness indicating whether the fraction of the reproducible results represent a large fraction of the paper results, (ii) documentation indicating whether the documentation helps applying the method to new inputs, and (iv) simplicity indicating whether the artifact is easy to reuse.

Unfortunately, the replay of shared memory program executions is known to be a difficult problem. One of the reasons is that multi-threaded executions are non-deterministic [5]: the output of the program is not tied to its input. This non-determinism affects the debugging process as it makes it difficult to reproduce an error-prone execution that involves a data race at a particular combinaison of points in the executions of multiple threads [6]. It also affects performance monitoring by leading to different performance based on a precise ordering of memory accesses by concurrent threads [7]. Overall, it makes the reproducibility of an experiment highly dependent on a variety of factors external to the program, like the hardware, the operating system, the programming language and the benchmark.

In this paper we show the importance of documenting these environmental factors for reproducibility. To illustrate our claim we measure the performance variations of Synchrobench, a benchmark suite to evaluate synchronization techniques and shared memory programs [8], when playing with OS, language, hardware and benchmark parameters. In particular, we show that core pinning can improve the benchmark performance up to 24%, just-in-time optimizations can lead to 3.4% performance boost, compilation of bytecode to native code can boost performance by 3.9×, and that configurable Termal Design Power (cTDP) can lead to 34% performance boost. Similar to the measurement bias of natural and social sciences [9] our goal is to outline the measurement bias in the particular context of concurrent programming when varying a parameter rather than capturing precisely all the causes of the performance we obtained in a particular case.

In Sect. 2 we present the problem through a running example. In Sect. 3 we show the impact of the operating system version on the performance of concurrent programs. In Sects. 4 and 5 we show the impact of the hardware configuration and the programming language on the performance, respectively. In Sect. 6 we show the impact of the definition of benchmark parameters on the performance and Sect. 7 concludes.

2   The Problem of Insufficient Description

To illustrate the difficulty of reproducing a concurrent program execution, let us take a simple concurrent list-based set benchmark example. The benchmark consists of a linked list data structure implementing a set, exporting *operations* insert(v) that returns false if v belongs to the set, otherwise it inserts the value v to the set and returns true; delete(v) that returns false if v does not belong to the set, otherwise it removes v from the set and returns true; and a contains(v) that returns true if v is in the set, otherwise it returns false. Indicating that the benchmark written in Java gives the number of operations executed per second with up to k threads on a k-way Intel Xeon machine with 20% updates is insufficient for anyone else to reproduce these experiments. In particular, one must at least indicate details regarding:

- the operating system: the version of the operating system, the memory access policy in use, how threads are pinned to cores;
- the programming language: the version, parameters of the compiler used;
- the hardware: whether overclocking is possible, whether k hardware threads are provided by k independent cores or through hyperthreading;
- the benchmark: how does the benchmark works and what are the parameters.

As we evaluate in the next sections, the impact induced by some changes in each of these environmental settings, meaning the type of operating system, the compiler, the architecture or the benchmark can dramatically affect the performance results. Trying to reproduce such an experiment without such information would likely lead to different results and conclusions.

3   The Operating System Impact

The operating system may or may not be aware of multi-threading within cores to decide on an appropriate strategy to pin threads to cores, a strategy that can dramatically impact performance.

3.1   Core Pinning

Thread placement or *core pinning* is known to greatly impact performance by either minimizing conflicts or maximizing sharing, typically on TLB and caches. In particular, core pinning can have a higher impact on AMD Opteron than

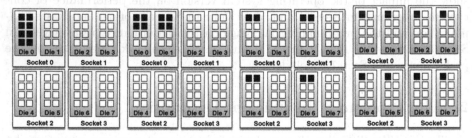

(a) SD config: same socket, same die

(b) SND config: same socket, different dies

(c) NSD config: different sockets - same die

(d) NSND config: different sockets - different dies

Fig. 1. Core pinning strategies as 4 block diagrams of the 4 AMD Opteron 6378 multicore machine

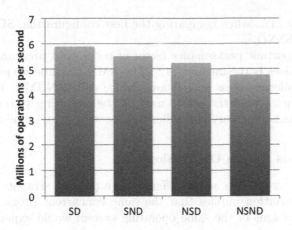

Fig. 2. The impact of the core pinning on a multi-socket NUMA machine: some workloads may benefit from local resource sharing and lead to better performance under a compact core pinning strategy than under a scatter core pinning strategy (error bars represent the sample standard deviation)

on Sun UltraSPARC [8] and in general the strategy differs depending on the programming language and the operating system used.

To illustrate the impact of core pinning on performance of concurrent programs, we implemented different core pinning strategies in Synchrobench C/C++ on an AMD Opteron 6378 featuring four different sockets. Each AMD socket contains multi-chip modules, meaning that two distinct CPU dies are placed in the same processor package [10]. Each socket embeds two different dies connected to an individual memory controllers—memory controllers are omitted in this figure for the sake of clarity. Each die embeds 8 individual cores, leading to a total of 64 cores as indicated in Fig. 1.

Figure 2 depicts the performance of one of the fastest concurrent skip lists to date, the Rotating skip list [11], of the C/C++ version of Synchrobench with four different core pinning strategies. Each experiment ran with C/C++ Synchrobench parameters -i2M-r4M-t8, indicating that 8 threads accessed the skip list initialized with 2M elements randomly chosen among a range of 4M elements [8]. The only difference was the way these threads were pinned to cores, as represented in Fig. 1. We implemented explicit placement strategies in Synchrobench and measured the performance obtained: SD means same socket and same die first, SND means same socket different dies first, NSD means different sockets and same die first, and NSND means different sockets and different dies first.

The best performance is obtained with the SD configuration while the worst performance is obtained with the NSND configuration. In particular the performance degrades as threads get scattered further apart. This indicates that the performance benefits from the sharing of resources of the same die and the same socket. Overall, we observed that the choice of the configuration could boost the performance by 24%, when comparing the best configuration, SD, to the worst configuration, NSND.

Another important performance factor of concurrent programs executed on multicore machines is the memory [12]. The AMD machine we presented above offers a non-uniform access to memory, hence called NUMA. It is especially important to understand the policy used by the operating system of a NUMA machines to select a memory controller to allocate a page in memory [13].

3.2   Variations Across OS Versions

The operating system can adopt different core pinning strategies based on its version. This variation implies that the same concurrent program running on two different versions of the same operating system would experience different performances.

A typical example is the Solaris operating system. On Solaris, threads of the HotSpot JVM are bound to lightweight processes. When a lightweight process for a thread is created, the kernel assigns it to a locality group. In versions 10 and 11 of Solaris, the core pinning strategy differs substantially as Dave Dice pointed out in his blog [14]. More precisely, in the version 10 of Solaris, the core pinning strategy balances threads over dies, then over cores, then over pipelines whereas in the version 11 of Solaris, the strategy groups the threads of a unique process on the same locality group until the workload exhausts half of the resources of this locality group. Our previous experience when using Solaris 10 on an UltraSPARC T2 [8] confirmed that the lightweight processes mapped to the HotSpot JVM were scattered across the physical cores.

4   The Hardware Impact

In this section, we illustrate the impact of the hardware on the performance of the concurrent program. In particular, we discuss the difference between exploiting k hardware threads and k cores and the automatic overclocking that may bias conclusions regarding performance scalability with concurrency.

4.1   Core Multi-threading

Core multi-threading is a technique used by hardware manufacturers to allow multiple threads to share the pipeline, the CPU and caches and to execute multiple instructions per cycle on a single processor. For example, POWER8 supports simultaneous multi-threading allowing up to 8 hardware contexts to run on a single core. Intel supports hyperthreading allowing up to 2 hardware contexts to run on a single core. With simultaneous multi-threading one physical core appears as multiple processors to the operating system.

In Communications of the ACM [15], we quantified the slowdown due to hyperthreading. We indicated the performance obtained when running some benchmarks on two Xeon machines: one using two single-core hyperthreaded

Xeon CPUs and another Xeon with 4 non-hyperthreaded cores. The slow-down was significant at 4 threads as hyperthreading was used in only one of the two machines. Such a difference was explained partially by the fact that in one case, hyperthreading makes two threads share the same processor while in the other case, the processors are not shared. This simple observation led to the conclusion that, in contrast to previous experimental observations, software transactional memories, despite some limitations [16], could scale with the level of concurrency, making it an interesting paradigm rather than a simple "research toy".

4.2 Dynamic Frequency Adjustment

One should be cautious when testing scalability of a concurrent program as its ability to perform better as the level of concurrency increases. The usual scalability graph would plot the performance on the y-axis while the number of threads increases on the x-axis, however, cores may automatically get overclocked if only few threads are active. These higher frequencies at low thread counts can thus result in having fewer threads performing better than more threads. However, this poor scalability is not necessarily due to the contention of the concurrent program, but can be due to an architectural feature as we explain below.

Multicore manufacturers implemented techniques, like dynamic frequency scaling, to reduce the energy consumption [17] when some processes are idle and they also implemented features, like Turbo Boost, that optimizes the performance of one cores when others are inactive. In particular, manufacturers provide *Configurable TDP* (cTDP): Intel explains that the processor may "operate at a power level that is higher than its TDP configuration".[2] The AMD Turbo Core technology increases similarly the core frequency within the thermal and power limits of the accelerated processing unit.[3] This features are enabled depending on the number of cores running. Similar techniques exist on other architectures as well. The On Chip Controller (OCC) is a co-processor embedded directly on the POWER processor die that controls the frequency, power consumption and temperature to maximize performance while minimizing energy usage [18].

Figure 3 compares the Synchrobench performance one can obtain with and without Turbo Boost when running the Versioned List benchmark with a single thread (-t1) on a machine with two Intel Xeon E5-2450 running 8 hyperthreaded cores each, for a total of 32 hardware threads. More precisely, the list of parameters for Synchrobench Java is -W0-t1-d5000-u40-i0-r50-bVersionedListSet. In each of five iterations of the benchmarks, we compare the throughput obtained from the same benchmark with Turbo Boost disabled (w/o Turbo Boost) and with Turbo Boost enabled (w/ Turbo Boost). As its name indicates, Turbo Boost increases performance substantially as we observed a gain in performance between 36% and 38% in each iteration.

[2] http://www.intel.com/content/www/us/en/architecture-and-technology/turbo-boost/turbo-boost-technology.html.
[3] http://www.amd.com/en-us/innovations/software-technologies/turbo-core.

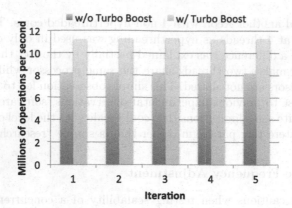

Fig. 3. The impact of the use of dynamic clock frequency adjustment on the performance results: Turbo Boost dynamically increases the clock frequency of a computing core when less cores are active, hence leading potentially to higher single-threaded performance

5 The Programming Language Impact

The choice of programming languages may affect the performance. For example, Java would favor portability rather than low-level optimizations so that in the JDK 9, the package sun.misc.Unsafe would not be usable explicitly. In C/C++, however, one could still pack two data items in one memory word, by exploiting the otherwise unused low-order bit of an x86 aligned memory word. This optimization can speedup the execution by requiring one compare-and-swap to set both data items.

5.1 JVM Optimizations

Another optimization may come from running the JVM for long enough. For example, explaining that the plotted value was measured as the average of 5 runs of the experiments may not be enough information to be able to reproduce the same experiment. In particular in Java, repeating the same experiments as part of the same JVM instance may lead to better performance than running it as part of separate JVM instances.

In Synchrobench, one has the option to run a benchmark, like the Versioned List [19], in five consecutive iterations within the same JVM instances: the user simply has to invoke the benchmark with option -n5 so that the benchmark will run five times in a row, restarting from scratch by cleaning up the data structure between two consecutive runs.

```
java -server -cp bin \
  contention.benchmark.Test -W 0 -t 2 -d 5000 -u 40 -i 0 -r 50 \
  -b linkedlists.lockbased.VersionedListSet -n 5
```

The performance results obtained after running the previous command will be, on average, higher than the performance results obtained after running the following command five times. The only difference is that the user runs the benchmark five times manually, each time specifying that the benchmark should run only once (-n1).

```
java -server -cp bin \
  contention.benchmark.Test -W 0 -t 2 -d 5000 -u 40 -i 0 -r 50 \
  -b linkedlists.lockbased.VersionedListSet -n 1
```

Figure 4 shows steady performance results for the five results when each iteration is run as part of individual JVM instances: the variation is up to 4‰ of the minimum throughput. However, it also shows that the performance varies much more when the five runs are part of the same JVM instance. This variation is up to 3.5% of the minimum throughput. Moreover, the performance obtained in these five consecutive iterations increases with time, which indicates that the performance of the benchmark is optimized during the runtime of the JVM.

Note that in Java, because **synchronized** is built into the JVM it can perform optimizations such as lock elision for thread-confined lock objects and lock-coarsening to eliminate synchronization with intrinsic locks, which indicates that it is better to use **synchronized** locks rather than **ReentrantLock** for performance reasons [20]. There are two Java implementations of the Versioned List [19, 21] in Synchrobench, one uses the `java.util.concurrent.locks.StampedLock` present in the JDK since Java 8, whereas the other uses custom versioned locks. The Versioned list, called **VersionedListSet** used here is the one with the custom versioned locks

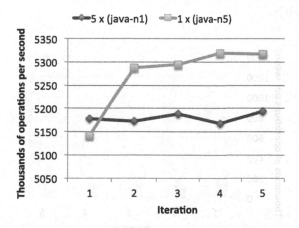

Fig. 4. The impact of the JVM optimizations on performance: the Java code is typically optimized at runtime by the JVM, hence a longer execution within the same JVM instance may lead to better performance than several shorter executions within different instances

as opposed to the VersionedListSetStampLock benchmark that relies on StampedLock.

5.2 Compiler Optimizations

For example, running Synchrobench Java with the following parameters:

```
java -Djava.compiler=NONE -server -cp bin \
   contention.benchmark.Test -W 5 -t 4 -d 5000 -u 40 -i 1024 \
   -r 2048 -b linkedlists.lockbased.VersionedListSet
```

will run the Versioned linked list [19] implementing a list-based set initialized with 2^{10} values (-i1024) taken in a range of 2^{11} elements (-r2048), with only 4 threads (-t4), during 5 s (-d5000) with attempted update ratio of 40% (-u40). The important parameter -Djava.compiler=NONE guarantees that the bytecode will not be compiled to native code during the execution.

Figure 5 depicts the performance results observed with the compiler enabled and with the compiler disabled while running this workload 5 times on an Intel Xeon with 2 sockets of 8 hyperthreaded cores. The compiler offers a 4-fold speedup on average.

Note that other optimizations exist with different compilers. An example is the GNU compiler collection, gcc, that takes an optimization flag as an argument on the command line to optimize the performance of the program. Hence, forgetting to mention the compilation flags may prevent someone else from reproducing the concurrent experiment. Moreover, recent versions of gcc allow for automatic padding of in-memory structures to minimize automatically false-sharing that may trigger unnecessary cache invalidation leading to performance drops. This is in contrast with earlier versions of the same compiler where padding had to be coded explicitly.

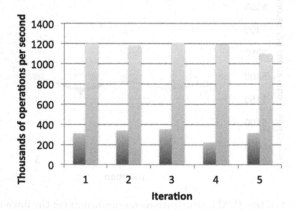

Fig. 5. The impact of the compilation process on the performance: preventing the Java bytecode from being compiled into native code leads to lower performance than when the code gets compiled

6 Benchmarks

Benchmarks are necessary to demonstrate the performance of new concurrent programs. In particular, macro-benchmarks and applications offer realistic workloads while micro-benchmarks typically offer a refined set of tests to nail down the causes of performance variation. These benchmarks are often tuned to test a particular program and are rarely well documented, making it impossible to reproduce experiments.

6.1 Lack of Documentation

Micro-benchmarking is popular to evaluate new concurrent programs. They are invaluable tools that complement macro evaluations and profiling tool boxes. In particular, they are instrumental in confirming how an algorithm can improve the performance of data structures even though the same algorithm negligibly boosts a particular application on a specific hardware or OS [8]. Interestingly, micro-benchmarks are often designed specifically to evaluate a particular concurrent program of synchronization technique [22] and are usually tuned for this purpose. Moreover they are poorly documented, which makes it impossible to reproduce their experiments.

A typical example is the evaluation of contention in concurrent programs. Contention is due to having multiple threads accessing the same shared resources while at least one is trying to modify it. Benchmarks often features a tunable update parameter that allows the programmer to evaluate the performance of a program at different contention levels. In the list-based set example we mention in Sect. 2, one may think that an update is either an `insert` or a `delete` operation and that the `contains` is clearly not an update but rather a read-only operation. This observation, however, is a bit simplistic as one could also consider that an `insert` and a `delete` that returns `false` without modifying the list-based set are rather read-only operations but are not updates.

6.2 Parameter Definitions

To illustrate the importance of precisely defining parameters we compare the performance of two list-based sets using the exact same parameters `-W0-t1-d5000-u40-i0-r50` to compare the performance one would obtain. Update operations in these list algorithms traverse the list until they find the closest node where to insert a node or to delete a node. The Lazy linked list [23] (`linkedlists.lockbased.LazyLinkedListSortedSet`) protects the nodes around this position before the value of the first node is read whereas the Versioned linked list [19] (`linkedlists.lockbased.VersionedListSet`) protects the nodes around this position only if a node is to be inserted or removed.

The problem as indicated on Fig. 6 is that whether the update is effective, meaning that it actually modifies the data structure, matters. In case the update is unsuccessful, then the data structure will not be updated and the resulting attempted update can be viewed as a read-only operation.

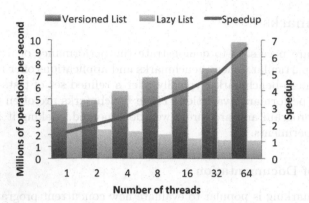

Fig. 6. The impact of attempted vs. effective updates: when update can fail, an algorithm that executes failed updates as read-only operations scales better than an algorithm that acquires locks even during failed updates.

As the Lazy list locks the data structures even if the structure is not updated, it offers significantly lower performance than the Versioned list. In particular, as the list is initially empty, all the removals executed at the beginning of the experiment will probably fail at removing any node, because the node is likely to be absent. Acquiring locks for these attempted updates prevents the Lazy list from scaling with the level of concurrency. By constrast, acquiring locks only when necessary allows the Versioned list to scale with the number of hardware threads without suffering from read-only attempted updates. The speedup of the Versioned list over the Lazy list increases with the level of concurrency as well. To conclude, the notion of "update" in benchmarks has to be carefully documented, like it is documented in Synchrobench for example, to indicate whether updates represent modifications or simply invocations of potentially read-only operations.

7   Conclusion

Synchrobench offers an open-source micro-benchmark suite that was used in multiple institutions for teaching and research. Its C/C++ and Java versions were accepted by the artifact evaluation committee of PPoPP 2015. In this paper we presented the difficulty of reproducing shared memory experiments by illustrating various factors, not restricted to the benchmark, that may affect the performance of concurrent programs. We encourage researchers to document these factors and make use of existing benchmark suites, like Synchrobench, to simplify reproducibility.

Acknowledgments. Some of the observations reported here were presented at the Winter School organized by the ACM SIGOPS France in March 2016. I wish to thank Tim Harris for fruitful discussions on the topic of publishing experimental results of concurrent programs. This research was supported under Australian Research Council's

Discovery Projects funding scheme (project number 160104801) entitled "Data Structures for Multi-Core". Vincent Gramoli is the recipient of the Australian Research Council Discovery International Award.

References

1. Ince, D.C., Hatton, L., Graham-Cumming, J.: The case for open computer programs. Nature **482**, 485–488 (2012)
2. Code share: Papers in nature journals should make computer code accessible where possible. Nature **514**, October 2014
3. Collberg, C., Proebsting, T.A.: Repeatability in computer systems research. Commun. ACM **59**(3), 62–69 (2016)
4. Blackburn, S.M., Diwan, A., Hauswirth, M., Sweeney, P.F., Amaral, J.N., Babka,V., Binder, W., Brecht,T., Bulej, L., Eeckhout, L., Fischmeister, S., Frampton, D., Garner, R., Georges, A., Hendren, L.J., Hind, M., Hosking, A.L., Jones, R., Kalibera, T., Moret, P., Nystrom, N., Pankratius, V., Tuma, P.: Can you trust your experimental results? (2012)
5. Devietti, J., Lucia, B., Ceze, L., Oskin, M.: DMP: deterministic shared memory multiprocessing. In: Proceedings of 14th International Conference on Architectural Support for Programming Languages and Operating Systems, ASPLOS, vol. XIV, pp. 85–96 (2009)
6. Russinovich, M., Cogswell, B.: Replay for concurrent non-deterministic shared-memory applications. In: Proceedings of ACM SIGPLAN 1996 Conference on Programming Language Design and Implementation, PLDI 1996, pp. 258–266 (1996)
7. Choi, J.D., Srinivasan, H.: Deterministic replay of Java multithreaded applications. In: Proceedings of SIGMETRICS Symposium on Parallel and Distributed Tools, SPDT 1998, pp. 48–59 (1998)
8. Gramoli, V.: More than you ever wanted to know about synchronization: synchrobench, measuring the impact of the synchronization on concurrent algorithms. In: Proceedings of 20th ACM SIGPLAN Symposium on Principles and Practice of Parallel Programming, PPoPP 2015, pp. 1–10 (2015)
9. Mytkowicz, T., Diwan, A., Hauswirth, M., Sweeney, P.F.: Producing wrong data without doing anything obviously wrong! In: Proceedings of 14th International Conference on Architectural Support for Programming Languages and Operating Systems, ASPLOS, vol. XIV, pp. 265–276. ACM, New York (2009)
10. Braithwaite, R., McCormick, P., Chun Feng, W.: Empirical memory-access cost models in multicore NUMA architectures. In: Proceedings of International Conference on Parallel Processing (ICPP) (2011)
11. Dick, I., Fekete, A., Gramoli, V.: A skip list for multicore. Pract. Exp. Concurr. Comput. **29**(4) (2016)
12. Drepper, U.: What every programmer should know about memory (2007)
13. Harris, T.: Do not believe everything you read in the papers. Personal Communication at the NICTA SSRG 4th Summer School, February 2016
14. Dice, D.: Thread placement policies on NUMA systems - update (2012)
15. Dragojević, A., Felber, P., Gramoli, V., Guerraoui, R.: Why STM can be more than a research toy. Commun. ACM **54**(4), 70–77 (2011)
16. Gramoli, V., Guerraoui, R.: Democratizing transactional programming. Commun. ACM (CACM) **57**(1), 86–93 (2014)

17. Groen, M., Gramoli, V.: Multicore vs manycore: the energy cost of concurrency. In: Dutot, P.-F., Trystram, D. (eds.) Euro-Par 2016. LNCS, vol. 9833, pp. 545–557. Springer, Cham (2016). doi:10.1007/978-3-319-43659-3_40
18. Rosendahl, T.: On chip controller (OCC). In: 1st Annual OpenPOWER Summit (2015)
19. Gramoli, V., Kuznetsov, P., Ravi, S., Shang, D.: A concurrency-optimal list-based set. Technical report, February 2015. arXiv:1502.01633v1
20. Goetz, B., Peierls, T., Bloch, J., Bowbeer, J., Lea, D., Holmes, D.: Java Concurrency in Practice. Addison-Wesley Professional, Boston (2005)
21. Gramoli, V., Kuznetsov, P., Ravi, S., Shang, D.: Brief announcement: a concurrency-optimal list-based set. In: 29th International Symposium on Distributed Computing (DISC) (2015)
22. Harmanci, D., Felber, P., Gramoli, V., Fetzer, C.: TMunit: testing transactional memories. In: 4th ACM SIGPLAN Workshop on Transactional Computing (TRANSACT) (2009)
23. Heller, S., Herlihy, M., Luchangco, V., Moir, M., Scherer, W.N., Shavit, N.: A lazy concurrent list-based set algorithm. In: Anderson, J.H., Prencipe, G., Wattenhofer, R. (eds.) OPODIS 2005. LNCS, vol. 3974, pp. 3–16. Springer, Heidelberg (2006). doi:10.1007/11795490_3

Reproducible, Accurately Rounded and Efficient BLAS

Chemseddine Chohra[1,2,3]($\boxtimes$), Philippe Langlois[1,2,3], and David Parello[1,2,3]

[1] Univ. Perpignan Via Domitia, Digits, Architectures et Logiciels Informatiques,
66860 Perpignan, France
{Chemseddine.Chohra,Philippe.Langlois,David.Parello}@univ-perp.fr
[2] Univ. Montpellier II, Laboratoire d'Informatique Robotique Et de
Microélectronique de Montpellier, UMR 5506, 34095 Montpellier, France
[3] CNRS, Paris, France

Abstract. Numerical reproducibility failures rise in parallel computation because floating-point summation is non-associative. Massively parallel and optimized executions dynamically modify the floating-point operation order. Hence, numerical results may change from one run to another. We propose to ensure reproducibility by extending as far as possible the IEEE-754 correct rounding property to larger operation sequences. We introduce our RARE-BLAS (Reproducible, Accurately Rounded and Efficient BLAS) that benefits from recent accurate and efficient summation algorithms. Solutions for level 1 (asum, dot and nrm2) and level 2 (gemv) routines are presented. Their performance is studied compared to the Intel MKL library and other existing reproducible algorithms. For both shared and distributed memory parallel systems, we exhibit an extra-cost of 2× in the worst case scenario, which is satisfying for a wide range of applications. For Intel Xeon Phi accelerator a larger extra-cost (4× to 6×) is observed, which is still helpful at least for debugging and validation steps.

1 Introduction and Background

The increasing power of supercomputers leads to a higher amount of floating-point operations to be performed in parallel. The IEEE-754 [8] standard defines the representation of floating-point numbers and requires the addition operation to correctly rounded. However because of errors generated by every addition, the accumulation of more than two floating-point numbers is non-associative. The combination of the non-deterministic behavior in parallel programs and the non-associativity of floating-point accumulation yields non-reproducible numerical results.

Numerical reproducibility is important for debugging and validating programs. Some solutions have been given in parallel programming libraries. Static data scheduling and deterministic reduction ensure the numerical reproducibility of the library OpenMP. Nevertheless the number of threads has to be set for all runs [15]. Intel MKL library (starting with 11.0 release) introduces CNR [15]

© Springer International Publishing AG 2017
F. Desprez et al. (Eds.): Euro-Par 2016 Workshops, LNCS 10104, pp. 609–620, 2017.
DOI: 10.1007/978-3-319-58943-5_49

(Conditional Numerical Reproducibility). This feature limits the use of instruction set extensions to ensure numerical reproducibility between different architectures. Unfortunately this decreases significantly the performance especially on recent architectures, and requires the number of threads to remain the same from run to run to ensure reproducible results.

First algorithmic solutions are proposed in [4]. Algorithms *ReprodSum* and *FastReprodSum* ensure numerical reproducibility independently of the operation order. Therefore numerical results do not depend anymore on hardware configuration. The performance of these latter is improved with the algorithm *OneReduction* [6] by relying on indexed floating-point numbers [5] and requiring a single reduction operation to reduce the communication cost on distributed memory parallel platforms. However, those solutions do not improve accuracy. The computed result even if it is reproducible, it is still exposed to accuracy problems. Especially when we address an ill-conditioned problem.

Another way to guarantee reproducibility is to compute correctly rounded results. Recent works [1,2,11] show that a accurately rounded floating-point summation can be calculated with very little or even no extra-cost. With accurately rounded we mean that the result is either correctly rounded (the nearest floating-point number to the exact result) or faithfully rounded (one of the two floating-point numbers that surround the exact result). We have analyzed in [1] different summation algorithms, and identified those suited for an efficient parallel implementation on recent hardware. Parallel algorithms for correctly rounded *dot* and *asum* and for a faithfully rounded *nrm2* have been designed relying on the most efficient summation algorithms. Their implementation exhibits interesting performance with $2\times$ extra-cost in the worst case scenario on shared memory parallel systems [1].

In this paper we extend our approach to an other type of parallel platforms and to higher BLAS level. We consider the matrix-vector multiplication from the level 2 BLAS. We complete our shared memory parallel implementation with solution for a distributed memory model, and confirm its scalability with tests on the Occigen supercomputer[1]. We also present tests on the Intel Xeon Phi accelerator to illustrate the portability and appreciate the efficiency of our implementation on a many-core accelerator. The efficiency of our correctly rounded dot product scales well on distributed memory parallel systems. Compared to optimized but not reproducible implementations, it has no substantial extra-cost up to about 1600 threads (128 sockets, 12 cores). On Intel Xeon Phi accelerator the extra-cost increases up to $6\times$ mainly because our solution benefits less from the high memory bandwidth of this architecture compared to MKL's implementation. Nevertheless they still could be useful for validation, debugging or for applications that require precision or reproducible results.

This paper is organized as follows. Section 2 presents our sequential algorithms for reproducible and accurate BLAS. Parallel versions are presented in Sect. 3. Section 4 is devoted to implementation and detailed results, and Sect. 5 includes some conclusions and the description of future work.

---

[1] https://www.cines.fr/en/occigen-the-new-supercomputeur/.

2   Sequential RARE BLAS

We present the algorithms for accurately rounded BLAS. This section starts briefly recalling our sequential level 1 BLAS subroutines (*dot*, *asum* and *nrm2*) already introduced in [1]. Then the accurately rounded matrix-vector multiplication is introduced.

2.1   Sequential Algorithms for the Level 1 BLAS

In this section we focus on the sum of absolute values (*asum*), the dot product (*dot*), and the euclidean norm (*nrm2*).

Sum of Absolute Values. The condition number of a sum is defined as $cond(\sum p_i) = \sum |p_i| / \sum p_i$. For the sum of absolute values the condition number is known to equal 1. This justifies the use of algorithm $SumK$ [13].

Picking carefully the value of K ensures that computing $asum(p)$ as $SumK(p)$ is faithfully rounded. Such appropriate value of K only depends on the vector size. We have $K = 2$ for $n \leq 2^{25}$, and $K = 3$ for $n \leq 2^{34}$. For $n \leq 2^{39}$ which represents $4TB$ of data, $K = 4$ is sufficient [1].

Dot Product. Using Dekker's $TwoProd$ [3], the dot product of two n-vectors can be transformed without error to a sum of a $2n$-vector. The sum of the transformed vector is correctly rounded using a mixed solution. For small vectors that fit in high level cache and that can be reused with no memory extra-cost, the algorithm $FastAccSum$ [14] is used, the algorithms $HybridSum$ [17] or $OnlineExact$ [18] are preferred for large vectors (both algorithms exhibit barely the same performance). The idea of these algorithms is to add elements that share the same exponent to a dedicated accumulator —in practice one or two floating-point numbers respectively. Therefore, the $2n$-vector is error-free replaced by a smaller accumulator vector (of size 4096 or 2048 respectively). Here the result and the error calculated with $TwoProd$ are directly accumulated. Finally we apply the distillation algorithm $iFastSum$ [17] to the accumulator vector to compute the correctly rounded dot product.

Euclidean Norm. The euclidean norm of a vector p is defined as $(\sum p_i^2)^{1/2}$. The sum $\sum p_i^2$ can be correctly rounded using the previous dot product. Finally, we apply a square root that returns a faithfully rounded euclidean norm [7]. numbers that enclose the exact result). This does not allow us to compute a correctly rounded norm-2 but this faithful rounding is reproducible.

2.2   Sequential Algorithms for the Level 2 BLAS

Matrix-vector multiplication is defined in the BLAS as $y = \alpha A \cdot x + \beta y$. In the following, we denote $y_i = \alpha a^{(i)} \cdot x + \beta y_i$, where $a^{(i)}$ is the ith row of matrix A.

Algorithm 1 details our proposed reproducible computation: (1) The first step transforms the dot product $a^{(i)} \cdot x$ into a sum of non-overlapping floating-point numbers. This error-free transform uses a minimum extra storage: the transformed result is stored in one array of maximum size 40 (the floating-point number range divided by the mantissa size). This process is done in different ways depending on the vector size. For small vectors we use $TwoProd$ to create a $2n$-vector. The distillation algorithm iFastSum [17] is then used to reduce the vector size. For large ones we do not create the $2n$-vector. The result and the error of $TwoProd$ are directly accumulated in accordance to their exponent as requested by $HybridSum$ or $OnlineExact$. After the dot product has been error-free transformed to a smaller vector, the same distillation process is applied. Let us remark that this step does not compute the dot product $a^{(i)} \cdot x$ but transforms it without error in a small floating point vector. (2) The second step evaluates multiplications by the scalars α and β using $TwoProd$. Again data is transformed with no error. (3) Finally we distillate the results of the previous steps to get a correctly rounded result of $y_i = \alpha a^{(i)} \cdot x + \beta y_i$. The same process is repeated for each row of the matrix A.

3   Parallel RARE BLAS

This section presents our parallel reproducible version of Level 1 and 2 BLAS.

3.1   Parallel Algorithms for the Level 1 BLAS

Sum of Absolute Values. The natural parallel version of algorithm $SumK$ introduced in [16] is used for parallel $asum$. Two stages are required. (1) The first one consists in applying the sequential algorithm $SumK$ on local data without performing the final error compensation. So we end with K floating point numbers per thread. (2) The second stage gathers all these numbers in a single vector. Afterwards the master thread applies a sequential $SumK$ on this vector.

Dot Product and Euclidean Norm. Figure 1 illustrates our correctly rounded dot product. Note that for step 1, the two entry vectors of the dot product are equally split between the threads. We use the same transformation as the one presented in Sect. 2.2 to error-free transform the local dot product. The accumulation of elements with the same exponent is only done for large vectors. As before C' vector size equals 4096 or 2048. For small vectors we create a $2n$-vector using only $TwoProd$. Distillation in step 2 mainly aims at reducing the communication cost of the union that yields the vector C. Since all transformations up to C are error-free, the final call to $iFastSum$ in step 3 returns the correctly rounded result for the dot product.

The euclidean norm is faithfully rounded as explained for the sequential case. Even if we do not calculate a correctly rounded result for euclidean norm, it is guaranteed to be reproducible because it only depends on a reproducible dot product.

Data: $A : m \times n$-matrix; $x : n$-vector; $y : m$-vector; α, β :double precision float;
Result: the input vector y updated as $y = \alpha A \cdot x + \beta y$;
for *row in* $1 : m$ **do**

    currentrow $= A[row, 1 : n]$;
    if *currentrow and x fit in cache* **then**
        declare $2n$-vector C;
        for *column in* $1 : n$ **do**
            $(result, error) = TwoProd(currentrow[column], x[column])$;
            $C[column] = result$; $C[n + column] = error$;
        end
    else
        declare the accumulator vector C;
        for *column in* $1 : n$ **do**
            $(result, error) = TwoProd(currentrow[column], x[column])$;
            accumulate *result* and *error* to corresponding accumulator in C;
        end
    end
    declare a vector *distil*;
    distil $= distillationProcess(C)$;
    declare a vector *finalTransformation*;
    size $= \text{sizeOf(distil)}$;
    /* **Step 2 : multiply by the scalars** α **and** β */
    for i *in* $1 : size$ **do**
        $(result, error) = TwoProd(distil[i], \alpha)$;
        $finalTransformation[i] = result$;
        $finalTransformation[size + i] = error$;
    end
    $(result, error) = TwoProd(y[row], \beta)$;
    $finalTransformation[size \times 2 + 1] = result$;
    $finalTransformation[size \times 2 + 2] = error$;
    /* **Step 3 : use iFastSum to calculate the correctly rounded**
        result   */
    $y[row] = iFastSum(finalTransformation)$;
end

Algorithm 1: Correctly rounded matrix-vector multiplication

3.2 Parallel Algorithms for the Level 2 BLAS

For matrix-vector multiplication, several algorithms are available according to the matrix decomposition. The three possible ones are: row layout, column layout and block decomposition. We opt for row layout decomposition because the algorithms we use are more efficient when working on large vectors. This choice also avoids the additional cost of reduction.

Figure 2 shows how our parallel matrix-vector multiplication is performed. The vector x must be attainable for all threads. On the other side the matrix A and the vector y are split into p parts where p is the number of threads. Each

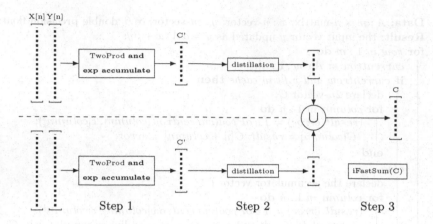

Fig. 1. Parallel algorithm for correctly rounded dot product

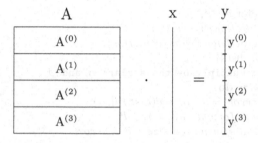

Fig. 2. Parallel algorithm for correctly rounded matrix-vector multiplication

thread handles the panel $A^{(i)}$ of A and the sub-vector $y^{(i)}$ of y. $y^{(i)}$ is updated with $\alpha A^{(i)} \cdot x + \beta y^{(i)}$ as described in Sect. 2.2.

4   Test and Results

In this section, we illustrate the performance and accuracy results of our proposed solution to accurate and reproducible level 1 and level 2 BLAS.

4.1   Experimental Framework

We consider the three frameworks described in Table 1. They are significant of today's practise of floating-point computing.

We test the efficiency of the sequential and the shared memory parallel implementation on platform **A**. Platform **B** illustrates the many core accelerator use. The scalability of our approach on large supercomputers is exhibited on platform **C** (Occigen supercomputer). Only the dot product has been tested on platform **C**. Data for dot product are generated as in [13]. The same idea is used

Table 1. Experimental frameworks

A	Processor	dual Xeon E5-2650 v2 16 cores (8 per socket), No hyper-threading. L1/L2 = 32/256 KB per core. L3 = shared 20 MB per socket.
	Bandwidth	59,7 GB/s
	Compiler	Intel ICC 16.0.0
	Options	-O3 -xHost -fp-model double -fp-model strict -funroll-all-loops
	Libraries	Intel OpenMP 5. Intel MKL 11.3.
B	Processor	Intel Xeon Phi 7120 accelerator, 60 cores, 4 threads per core. L1/L2 = 32/512 KB per core.
	Bandwidth	352 GB/s
	Compiler	Intel ICC 16.0.0
	Options	-O3 -mmic -fp-model double -fp-model strict -funroll-all-loops
	Libraries	Intel OpenMP 5. Intel MKL 11.3.
C	Processor	4212 Xeon E5-2690 v3 (12 cores per socket), No hyper-threading. L1/L2 = 32/256 KB per core. L3 = shared 30 MB per socket.
	Bandwidth	68 GB/s
	Compiler	Intel ICC 15.0.0
	Options	-O3 -xHost -fp-model double -fp-model strict -funroll-all-loops
	Libraries	Intel OpenMP 5. Intel MKL 11.2. OpenMPI 1.8

to generate condition dependent data for matrix-vector multiplication (multiple dot products with a shared vector).

4.2 Implementation and Performance Results

We compare the performance results of our implementation to the highly optimized Intel MKL library, and to implementations based on algorithm OneReduction used on the library ReproBLAS [12]. We have implemented an OpenMP parallel version of this algorithm since ReproBLAS offers only an MPI parallel version. We derive reproducible version of *dot*, *nrm2*, *asum* and *gemv* by replacing all non-associative accumulations by the algorithm OneReduction [6]. These versions are denoted *OneReductionDot*, *OneReductionAsum*, *OneReductionNrm2* and *OneReductionGemv*.

CNR feature [15] is not considered because it does not guarantee reproducibility between sequential and parallel runs. Running time is measured in cycles using the RDTSC instruction. In the parallel case, RDTSC calls have been made out of parallel region before and after function calls. We take the minimum running time over 8 executions for *gemv* and 16 executions for other routines to improve result consistency. We note up to 3% difference in number of cycles between different runs. This difference is due to turbo boost and operating system interruption and it is known that performance results can not be exactly reproduced.

Sequential Performance. Tests are run on platform **A**. Results for *dot*, *asum* and *nrm2* are presented in [1]. These accurately rounded versions exhibit respectively 5×, 2× and 9× extra-cost.

Our *Rgemv* matrix-vector multiplication computes a correctly rounded result using *iFastSum* for small matrices and *HybridSum* for large ones, this latter being slightly more efficient than *OnlineExact* on both platforms **A** and **B**. As shown in Fig. 3a, *Rgemv* costs 8 times more compared to MKL in this sequential case.

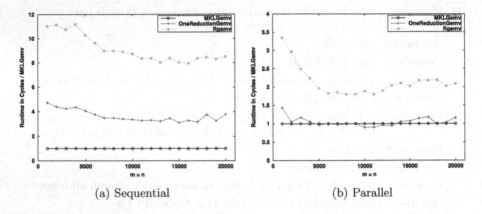

(a) Sequential   (b) Parallel

Fig. 3. Extra-cost of correctly rounded matrix-vector multiplication (cond=10^8)

Shared Memory Parallel Performance. Tests have also been done on platform **A** where 16 cores are used with no hyper-threading. We use OpenMP to implement our parallel algorithms. As for the sequential case, results for *dot*, *asum* and *nrm2* are presented in [1]. The *dot* and *asum* do not exhibit any extra-cost compared to classic versions, and *nrm2* has 2× extra-cost.

For the matrix-vector multiplication, the correctly rounded algorithm costs about twice more compared to MKL as shown in Fig. 3b. As in the sequential case, *MKLGemv* certainly use cache blocking and so benefits from a better memory bandwidth use. Nevertheless our parallel implementation scales well and its extra-cost now reaches the 2× ratio.

Xeon Phi Performance. There is not much difference between implementation for Xeon Phi and previous CPU ones. Thread level parallelism is implemented using OpenMP and intrinsic functions are used to benefit from the available instruction set extensions. A FMA (Fused Multiply and Add) is also available. Therefore *TwoProd* is replaced by *2MultFMA* [10] which only requires two FMAs to compute the product and its error, and so improves performance.

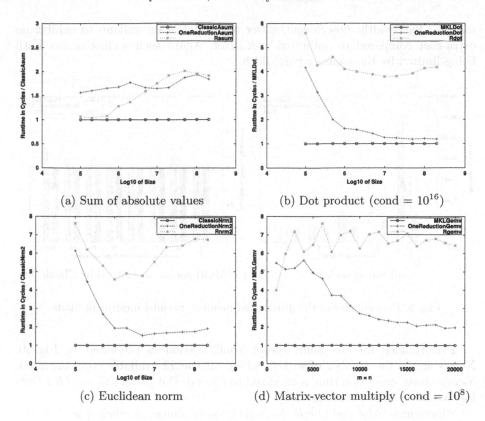

(a) Sum of absolute values

(b) Dot product (cond $= 10^{16}$)

(c) Euclidean norm

(d) Matrix-vector multiply (cond $= 10^8$)

Fig. 4. Extra-cost of Xeon Phi implementation compared to classical algorithms

Figure 4 exhibits respective ratios of $2\times$, $4\times$, $6\times$ and $6\times$ for asum, dot product, euclidean norm and matrix-vector multiplication. So the extra-cost of accurately rounded implementations is larger for this accelerator than for the CPU. Indeed MKL based implementations of these memory bounded routines benefit from both higher memory bandwidth and large vector capabilities (AVX-512) provided by the Xeon Phi more than our accurate ones. Note that on our correctly rounded dot product algorithms there is no efficient way to vectorize the accumulation to the elements of vector C since the access to those elements is not contiguous (see Algorithm 1 and Fig. 1).

Distributed Memory Parallel Performance. Finally we present performance on distributed memory systems. Only dot product tests have been run on the Occigen supercomputer. In this case we have two levels of parallelism: OpenMP is used for thread level parallelism on a single socket, and OpenMPI library for socket communication. The algorithm scalability is tested on a single data set with input vectors of length 10^7 and condition number is 10^{32}.

Figure 5a shows the scalability for a single socket configuration. It is not a surprise that *MKLDot* does not scale so far since it is quickly limited by the memory bandwidth. *OneReductionDot* and *Rdot* scale well up to exhibit no extra-cost compared to optimized *MKLDot*. Again such scaling occurs until being limited by the memory bandwidth.

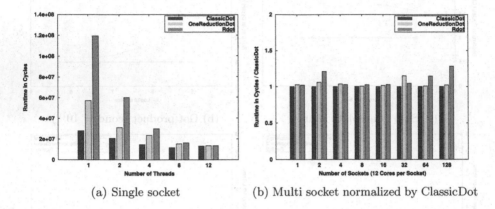

(a) Single socket   (b) Multi socket normalized by ClassicDot

Fig. 5. Performance of the distributed memory parallel implementations.

Performance for the multi socket configuration is presented in Fig. 5b. X-axis shows the number of sockets where all the 12 available cores are used. Y-axis shows execution time normalized to *ClassicDot* (socket local *MKLDots* followed by a MPI sum reduction).

Algorithms *Rdot* and *OneReductionDot* stay almost as efficient as *Classic-Dot*. All algorithms exhibit similar performance because they rely all on a single communication.

4.3   Accuracy Results

We present here accuracy results for *dot* and *gemv* variants. In both Fig. 6a and b, we show the relative error according to the condition number of the problem. Relative errors are calculated according to MPFR library [9] results. The two subroutines *nrm2* and *asum* are excluded from this test because condition number is fixed for both of them. The condition number for the dot product is defined as $cond(\sum X_i \cdot Y_i) = \sum |X_i| \cdot |Y_i| / |\sum X_i \cdot Y_i|$. In almost all cases, solutions based on algorithm *OneReduction* besides being reproducible are more accurate than MKL. However, for ill-conditioned problems both MKL and *OneReduction* derived implementation give worthless results. On the other side RARE-BLAS subroutines ensure that results are always correctly rounded independently from the condition number.

5   Conclusion and Future Work

We have presented algorithms that compute reproducible and accurately rounded results for BLAS. Level 1 and 2 subroutines have been addressed in

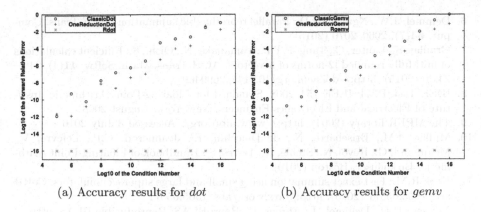

(a) Accuracy results for *dot*   (b) Accuracy results for *gemv*

Fig. 6. Accuracy results for *dot* and *gemv*

this paper. Implementations of these algorithms have been tested on three platforms significant of the floating-point computing practice. While existing solutions tackle only the reproducibility problem, our proposed solutions aim at ensuring both reproducibility and the best precision. We compare them to optimized Intel MKL implementations. We measure interesting performance on CPU based parallel environments. Extra-cost on CPU when all available cores are used is at worst twice. Nevertheless performance on Xeon Phi accelerator is lagging behind: extra-cost is between 4 and 6 times more. Nevertheless, our algorithms remain efficient enough to be used for validation or debugging programs, and also for parallel applications that can sacrifice performance to increase the accuracy and the reproducibility of their results.

Our plan for future development includes achieving reproducibility and precision for other BLAS subroutines. We are currently designing an accurate and reproducible version of triangular solver. Other Level 3 BLAS routines will be addressed even if the performance gap with optimized libraries will enforce the previously identified restriction of the application scope.

References

1. Chohra, C., Langlois, P., Parello, D.: Implementation and Efficiency of Reproducible Level 1 BLAS (2015). http://hal-lirmm.ccsd.cnrs.fr/lirmm-01179986
2. Collange, S., Defour, D., Graillat, S., Iakymchuk, R.: Numerical reproducibility for the parallel reduction on multi- and many-core architectures. Parallel Comput. **49**(C), 83–97 (2015). http://dx.doi.org/10.1016/j.parco.2015.09.001
3. Dekker, T.J.: A floating-point technique for extending the available precision. Numer. Math. **18**, 224–242 (1971)
4. Demmel, J.W., Nguyen, H.D.: Fast reproducible floating-point summation. In: Proceedings of 21th IEEE Symposium on Computer Arithmetic, Austin, Texas, USA (2013)
5. Demmel, J.W., Nguyen, H.D.: Toward Hardware Support for Reproducible Floating-Point Computation. In: SCAN 2014, Würzburg, Germany, September 2014

6. Demmel, J.W., Nguyen, H.D.: Parallel reproducible summation. IEEE Trans. Comput. **64**(7), 2060–2070 (2015)
7. Graillat, S., Lauter, C., Tang, P.T.P., Yamanaka, N., Oishi, S.: Efficient calculations of faithfully rounded l2-norms of n-vectors. ACM Trans. Math. Softw. **41**(4), 24:1–24:20 (2015). http://doi.acm.org/10.1145/2699469
8. IEEE Task P754: IEEE 754–2008, Standard for Floating-Point Arithmetic. Institute of Electrical and Electronics Engineers, New York, August 2008
9. The MPFR library (2004). http://www.mpfr.org/. Accessed 8 July 2016
10. Muller, J.M., Brisebarre, N., de Dinechin, F., Jeannerod, C.P., Lefèvre, V., Melquiond, G., Revol, N., Stehlé, D., Torres, S.: Handbook of Floating-Point Arithmetic. Birkhäuser, Boston (2010)
11. Neal, R.M.: Fast exact summation using small and large superaccumulators. CoRR abs/1505.05571 (2015). http://arxiv.org/abs/1505.05571
12. Nguyen, H.D., Demmel, J., Ahrens, P.: ReproBLAS: Reproducible BLAS. http://bebop.cs.berkeley.edu/reproblas/
13. Ogita, T., Rump, S.M., Oishi, S.: Accurate sum and dot product. SIAM J. Sci. Comput. **26**(6), 1955–1988 (2005)
14. Rump, S.M.: Ultimately fast accurate summation. SIAM J. Sci. Comput. **31**(5), 3466–3502 (2009)
15. Todd, R.: Run-to-Run Numerical Reproducibility with the Intel Math Kernel Library and Intel Composer XE 2013. Intel Corporation, Technical report (2013)
16. Yamanaka, N., Ogita, T., Rump, S., Oishi, S.: A parallel algorithm for accurate dot product. Parallel Comput. **34**(68), 392–410 (2008)
17. Zhu, Y.K., Hayes, W.B.: Correct rounding and hybrid approach to exact floating-point summation. SIAM J. Sci. Comput. **31**(4), 2981–3001 (2009)
18. Zhu, Y.K., Hayes, W.B.: Algorithm 908: online exact summation of floating-point streams. ACM Trans. Math. Softw. **37**(3), 37:1–37:13 (2010)

RESILIENCE - Workshop on Resiliency in High Performance Computing in Clusters, Clouds, and Grids

Horseshoes and Hand Grenades: The Case for Approximate Coordination in Local Checkpointing Protocols

Patrick M. Widener[✉], Kurt B. Ferreira, and Scott Levy

Center for Computing Research, Sandia National Laboratories,
Albuquerque, NM, USA
{pwidene,kbferre,sllevy}@sandia.gov

Abstract. Fault-tolerance poses a major challenge for future large-scale systems. Active research into coordinated, uncoordinated, and hybrid checkpointing systems has explored how the introduction of asynchrony can address anticipated scalability issues. While fully uncoordinated approaches have been shown to have significant delays, the degree of sychronization required to keep overheads low has not yet been significantly addressed. In this paper, we use a simulation-based approach to show the impact of synchronization on local checkpoint activity. Specifically, we show the degree of synchronization needed to keep the impacts of local checkpointing low is attainable with current technology for a number of key production HPC workloads. Our work provides a critical analysis and comparison of synchronization and local checkpointing. This enables users and system administrators to fine-tune the checkpointing scheme to the application and system characteristics available.

1 Introduction

In response to alarming projections of high failure rates due to the increasing scale and complexity of high-performance computing (HPC) systems [5], researchers have devoted significant effort to the development of methods and techniques that will enable the deployment of resilient extreme-scale HPC systems and applications.

The current *de facto* standard for fault tolerance on HPC systems is coordinated checkpoint/restart (cCR). The overhead of cCR increases with the number of application processes. Current projections indicate that on next-generation systems more than half of an application's execution time may be consumed by the overhead of cCR [15]. Much of this overhead results from contention for storage resources: at the end of each checkpoint interval every application process simultaneously attempts to write out its checkpoint data to persistent storage.

Sandia National Laboratories is a multi-program laboratory managed and operated by Sandia Corporation, a wholly-owned subsidiary of Lockheed Martin Corporation, for the U.S. Department of Energy's National Nuclear Security Administration under contract DE-AC04-94AL85000. SAND2016-5027C.

© Springer International Publishing AG 2017
F. Desprez et al. (Eds.): Euro-Par 2016 Workshops, LNCS 10104, pp. 623–634, 2017.
DOI: 10.1007/978-3-319-58943-5_50

Uncoordinated checkpoint/restart (uCR) attempts to reduce contention for storage resources by allowing application processes to checkpoint independently. However, the performance impact of eliminating all inter-process coordination of checkpointing activities has been shown to be prohibitive because of the way that checkpointing-induced delays propagate and aggregate along communication dependencies [17].

In this paper, we examine the space between these two checkpoint protocol extremes, and investigate the impact of approximate checkpoint coordination on application performance. Approximate coordination reduces the contention for persistent storage resources in cCR and impedes the propagation of delays in uCR. Specifically, this paper makes the following contributions:

- a discussion of a new method, *approximate coordination*, for reducing the overhead of uCR;
- a description of a simulation-based approach for studying degrees of checkpoint coordination; and
- an initial examination of the impact of the degree of checkpoint coordination on application performance in an idealized scenario where no contention for persistent storage exists (e.g., node-local burst buffers are available for checkpoint storage).

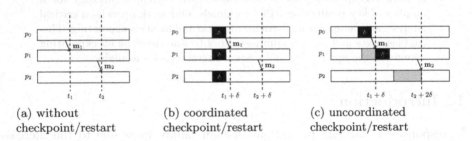

(a) without checkpoint/restart

(b) coordinated checkpoint/restart

(c) uncoordinated checkpoint/restart

Fig. 1. Propagation of uncoordinated checkpointing delay through application communication dependencies. The processes p_1, p_2, and p_3 exchange two messages m_1 and m_2 in each of the three scenarios. The black regions marked with δ represent delays due to the taking of checkpoints. The grey regions represent stalls due to unsatisfied message dependencies.

The remainder of this paper is structured as follows: Sect. 2 provides a discussion of checkpoint/restart and motivates our study of approximate coordination. Section 3 describes our experimental approach and Sect. 4 presents the results of these initial experiments. Section 5 discusses related work. Finally, Sect. 6 discusses potential future work and summarizes our initial study of approximate checkpoint coordination.

2   Background

The most common fault tolerance techniques on today's systems are based on checkpoint/restart. In the fundamental operation of checkpoint/restart, an application's processes periodically record their current state onto stable storage (creating a *checkpoint*). When a failure occurs, the application is *restarted* from a saved checkpoint. To ensure that a set of saved checkpoints represents a consistent state, some checkpoint/restart techniques require additional data to be saved (e.g., all sent messages). Several algorithms have been developed to ensure that a set of processes records a consistent state, deriving from seminal work on distributed system snapshots by Chandy and Lamport [8].

In this paper, we consider the two checkpoint/restart-based techniques introduced in the preceding section: cCR, and uCR. cCR stops the execution of all application processes at the same logical time and records a snapshot of the current state of each process. There are several benefits to cCR. Tight coordination of the timing of checkpoints across application processes ensures that the most recent checkpoint represents a consistent state of the machine [12]. As a result, there is no need to store multiple checkpoints or to record any other execution details (e.g., sent messages). Additionally, inter-process coordination of the timing of checkpoints limits the propagation of checkpointing-induced delays. As shown in Fig. 1b, because every process checkpoints simultaneously, the relative timing of inter-process communication events is preserved. However, because cCR requires that every application process take a checkpoint at the same time, contention for persistent-storage resources may degrade application performance. On next-generation systems, the overheads of coordination and those due to contention for storage resources may be prohibitive. In some cases, an application may spend more of its time on the overhead of cCR than on the computation for which it was designed [15].

To reduce the overhead of contention for storage resources, uCR allows every process to decide when to checkpoint entirely independently from its peers [7,18,22]. However, because of the lack of checkpoint coordination additional information is required in order to guarantee the existence of a set of checkpoints that represent a consistent state of the machine. One common way to resolve this issue is *message logging*. For example, if every process logs every message it sends, then when one process fails it restarts from its last checkpoint. The surviving processes re-send all of the messages that were sent to the failed process in the interval between its failure and its last checkpoint.

If the timing of checkpoints is entirely independent, checkpointing-induced delays can propagate and aggregate, much like OS noise (or *jitter*) [17]. For example, Fig. 1c shows how checkpointing-delays may propagate along communication dependencies. Because process p_0 is delayed because it is taking a checkpoint, process p_1 stalls waiting on the receipt of messages m_1, and the stall of p_1 causes p_2 to stall. Similarly, because process p_1 is subsequently delayed by its own checkpoint, process p_2 continues to stall waiting on the receipt of message m_2.

In this paper, we consider the novel question of whether and to what degree *approximate coordination* of the timing of checkpoints may be able to improve on the performance resulting from the total lack of coordination in uCR without incurring the overheads of resource contention in cCR. In other words, we seek to answer the question of *how uncoordinated* uCR can be while still limiting the propagation of checkpoint-induced delays.

3   Experimental Approach

In this section, we describe the experimental approach used to investigate the influence of approximate checkpoint coordination. First, we describe how we model the impact of checkpoint/restart techniques on application performance. We then discuss how we simulate various degrees of uCR checkpoint coordination.

3.1   Modeling Local Checkpoint/Restart

In general, the communication structure of Message Passing Interface (MPI) programs cannot be determined offline because message matches cannot be established statically [6]. This makes modeling application performance analytically challenging even if all parameters of the application (e.g., the complete communication structure and all relative inter-process timings) are known. We therefore use discrete-event simulation to evaluate the impact of local checkpointing activities on the performance of real applications.

Our simulation-based approach models checkpointing activities as CPU detours: periods of time during which the CPU is taken from the application and used to compute and commit checkpoint data. This approach allows a level of fidelity and control not always possible in implementation-based approaches. It also allows us to examine application performance on systems that are much larger than those that are generally available for systems research.

Our simulation framework is based on LogGOPSim [21] and the tool chain developed by Levy et al. [24]. LogGOPSim uses the LogGOPS model, an extension of the well-known LogP model [9], to account for the temporal cost of communication events. An application's communication events are generated from traces of the application's execution. These traces contain the sequence of MPI operations invoked by each application process. LogGOPSim uses these traces to reproduce all communication dependencies, including indirect dependencies between processes which do not communicate directly.

LogGOPSim can also extrapolate traces from small application runs; a trace collected by running the application with p processes can be extrapolated to simulate performance of the application running with $k \cdot p$ processes. The extrapolation produces exact communication patterns for MPI collective operations and approximates point-to-point communications [21]. The validation of LogGOPSim and its trace extrapolation features have been documented previously [20,21]. Similarly, its ability to accurately predict local checkpointing overheads has also been documented [17,24,25].

3.2   Simulating the Role of Coordination

To simulate the impact of depriving the application of CPU cycles in order to perform local checkpoints, `LogGOPSim` accepts a *checkpointing trace*: an ordered list of checkpoints, expressed as the start time and duration of each checkpointing event. In this paper, we use a checkpoint interval of 120 s and a checkpoint commit time of 1 s. Although the optimal checkpoint interval is not known unless checkpoints are totally coordinated, this checkpoint interval would be optimal for cCR on a platform whose system MTBF is approximately 2 h.

`LogGOPSim` can simulate the degree of checkpointing coordination among application processes by adding an initial offset to the replay of the execution trace. Using an initial offset of zero for application processes will simulate a perfectly coordinated checkpointing scheme. At the other extreme, choosing a uniformly distributed random initial offset for each simulated process will simulate a completely uncoordinated approach. Choosing this offset randomly from a normal distribution will simulate different degrees of coordination depending on the standard deviation of the distribution used. Example probability density functions are shown in Fig. 2. The x-axis in this figure is the time offset from the mean and the y-axis is the probability of a node using that offset value. This figure helps illustrate the range of the degree of approximate coordination that we consider. From the figure, as expected, the greater the standard deviation, the greater the likelihood of a large offset value.

We make two simplifying assumptions in our simulation approach:

- The perfect process synchronization we simulate is not achievable in practice. Even using strong coordination protocols such as those derived from Chandy & Lamport, there will still be some time skew between checkpoint commits in a real-world system. Using a simulation approach allows us to apply a global clock to all simulated process checkpoints.
- Our checkpointing simulation assumes no contention for storage resources even when checkpoints are tightly coordinated. In practice, storage resources are typically shared — even node-local ones such as burst buffers. By disregarding contention for these resources, we can observe directly the impact of coordination in local checkpoint propagation.

As a result of these assumptions, the data we present may be optimistic for highly-coordinated checkpointing cases.

3.3   Application Descriptions

In the remainder of the paper, we present results from simulation experiments based on the behavior of a set of four workloads. These workloads were chosen to be representative of scientific applications that are currently in use and computational kernels thought to be important for future extreme-scale computational science. They include:

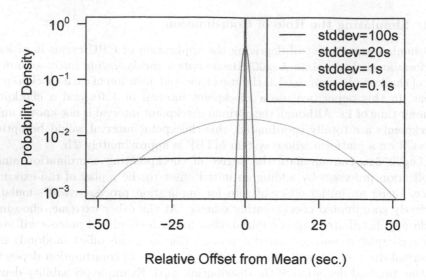

Fig. 2. Normally distributed probability density function of the degree of coordination as a function of standard deviation.

- LAMMPS: A scientific application developed by Sandia National Laboratories to perform molecular dynamics simulations. For our experiments, we used the *Lennard-Jones*(LJ) potential [30].
- CTH: A code developed at Sandia National Laboratories for modeling complex problems that are characterized by large deformations or strong shocks [11].
- HPCCG: A conjugate gradient solver from the Mantevo suite of mini-applications [19,31].
- LULESH: An application that represents the behavior of a typical hydrocode [23].

CTH and LAMMPS are important U.S. Department of Energy (DOE) applications which run for long periods of time on production machines and exhibit a range of different communication structures. HPCCG represents an important computational pattern in key HPC applications. LULESH is an exascale application proxy from the DOE ExMatEx co-design center [14].

4   Results

We conducted a set of experiments to quantify the effects of checkpointing synchronization for uCR in our chosen workloads. As described in the previous section, we staggered the starting offset of simulated checkpointing activity for each simulated process to produce different degrees of synchronization. Completely uncoordinated checkpointing is simulated by choosing a uniformly distributed random starting offset for each process, and completely coordinated checkpointing by using the same offset for each process. Producing offsets representing varying degrees of synchronization is done by drawing values from a normal distribution with mean 0 and a given standard deviation; changing the standard deviation of the distribution changes the degree of synchronization. We chose the following standard deviations for our trials: 1 μs, 100 μs, 75 ms, 100 ms, and 1, 20, 40, 60, 80, and 100 s. In our discussion below we refer to each different distribution of offsets by the value of its associated standard deviation.

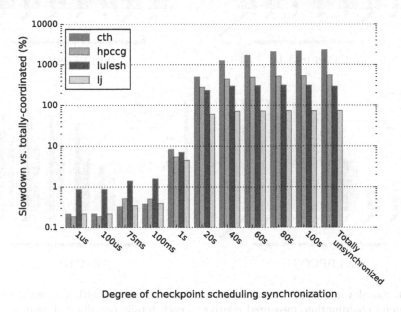

Degree of checkpoint scheduling synchronization

Fig. 3. Application slowdown with varying degrees of synchronization at 32Ki processes, measured relative to each totally coordinated case.

The results of these experiments are presented in Figs. 3 and 4. Figure 3 shows the application slowdown caused by using uCR with varying degrees of synchronization for each of our representative workloads at a fixed application size of 32 Ki processes[1]. We then examined each application in detail for slowdowns at varying process counts (Fig. 4). In each of these figures, we present the slowdown as a percentage of the runtime for a cCR (totally-coordinated checkpointing) execution of the simulation.

For each of the workloads we studied, a significant and increasing performance slowdown occurs as checkpoint synchronization among processes is relaxed beyond 100 ms. Previous work in this area has demonstrated that completely unsynchronized checkpointing will result in severe slowdowns [17]; as this figure also makes clear, some synchronization between checkpointing processes is necessary.

---

[1] Throughout this paper, we use the binary prefixes defined by the International Electrotechnical Commission (IEC). For example, 1 Ki processes is equivalent to 1024 processes.

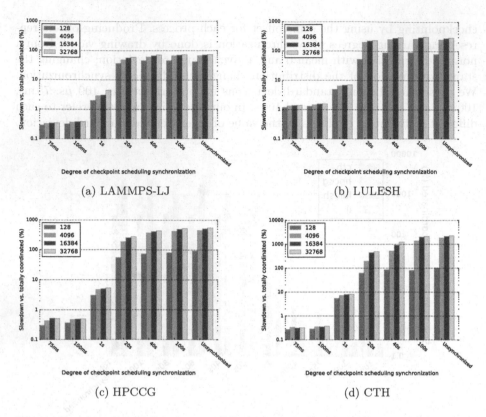

(a) LAMMPS-LJ   (b) LULESH

(c) HPCCG   (d) CTH

Fig. 4. Slowdown in applications at different process counts with varying degrees of checkpoint coordination, measured relative to each totally coordinated case.

Determining the degree of synchronization required in order to maintain performance then becomes the issue, and it is here that our results imply an important insight. Relatively loose synchronization is sufficient to keep the slowdown induced by checkpointing activity to a level much lower than that produced by completely uncoordinated checkpointing. The results presented in Fig. 4 show that if the pattern of checkpoints for all processes follows a normal distribution with standard deviation 100 ms (i.e., on average, 95% of process checkpoints will occur in a 200 ms time window), application runtime is increased by less than 5%. Synchronizing processes to this degree is well within the capabilities of systems with hardware support (such as a dedicated global interconnect or specialized equipment such as a GPS card), which have achieved clock skews on the order of 1μs [1,2]. Even software-based solutions such as NTP are able to achieve synchronization well within the 100 ms case we discuss here [27,29].

Even extremely loose synchronization with standard deviation on the order of 1 s produces approximately 10% application slowdown for our studied workloads. This is a value easily realizable in modern HPC systems and is also possible with acceptable reliability in wide-area or cloud-computing contexts. We also note that much tighter synchronization of uCR checkpointing does not improve performance markedly over that provided at the 100 ms standard-deviation value. Finally, this result is observed for a range of process counts, indicating that this effect is relatively insensitive to scale for this degree of synchronization.

5   Related Work

In this paper, we study the impact of approximate checkpoint coordination on application performance. In this section, we provide an overview of related publications.

The xSim simulator [13] has been used to study the effects of interference amplification and absorption on MPI collectives. Its authors propose its use as a tool for future HPC hardware/software co-design. Pradipta De et al. [10] proposed an emulation approach for studying similar performance impacts. Our simulation framework differs from these approaches in its ability to simulate interference overheads for systems of tens or hundreds of thousands of processes with modest hardware requirements. Our simulation framework also makes a different tradeoff between the level of detail produced and simulation time than these tools do, allowing it to be used for rapid evaluation of different application configurations.

Checkpoint/restart protocols in HPC systems have been extensively studied. There are many descriptions of the foundations of both coordinated and uncoordinated CR protocols available in the literature [4,22,26]. The complete lack of checkpoint coordination in uCR has been frequently relied upon as an important feature [7,18,22].

Beyond uCR and cCR, many other checkpoint/restart protocols have been proposed. Alvisi et al. examined the performance impact of coarse-grained communication patterns on the performance of three communication-induced checkpoint/restart (ciCR) algorithms [3]. ciCR uses the application's communication patterns to avoid checkpoints that cannot be used to recover a consistent global state. Hierarchical checkpointing attempts group application processes into clusters that communicate frequently with each other [18,28]. cCR is used within a cluster and uCR plus message logging is used between clusters. Because the number of processes in a cluster is smaller than the total application, contention for filesystem resources is reduced. Also, because most of the communication is within a cluster, the volume of message log data is also reduced.

Our study has origins in published research that characterizes application behavior in the presence of OS noise [16,20]. Collectively, this research shows that the pattern of OS noise events determines the impact on application performance and the benefits of coordination. Moreover, it shows that perfect coordination of OS noise events can significantly reduce performance impact.

Ferreira et al. [17] used an analogy to OS noise to show that when the timing of checkpoints is completely uncoordinated, checkpoint-induced delays have the potential to propagate and significantly degrade application performance.

In this paper, we extend the results of these studies of OS noise to examine how approximate coordination impacts application performance. Specifically, we show that perfect coordination is unnecessary to mitigate the performance cost of uCR; it may be sufficient to approximately coordinate OS noise events (e.g., local checkpoints).

6   Conclusions and Future Work

Developers of resilient HPC applications face design decisions about how best to implement fault-tolerance measures for extreme-scale computing. As coordinated checkpointing reaches a predicted scalability ceiling, a better understanding of the performance implications of introducing uncoordinated checkpointing is necessary. This paper contributes in several ways. We have: introduced the concept of *approximate coordination* for reducing the overhead of uncoordinated checkpointing; described a validated simulation-based technique for studying the coordination of processes using uncoordinated checkpointing; and presented an examination, carried out using our simulation framework, of the impact that varying degrees of checkpoint coordination has on application performance. Our results show that, while a degree of coordination between processes is necessary in order to avoid severe performance penalties, this degree can be quite modest. Dedicated hardware support for process synchronization is not necessary, and software-based coordination provides a degree of synchronization sufficient to keep checkpointing-related performance slowdowns below 10%.

We are pursuing several directions of future work based on this research. The projections we have presented here do not consider contention between processes for I/O bandwidth; we plan to refine our simulation approach to account for this. We also are working to determine which application and checkpointing features contribute to slowdowns in performance, and to characterize their interactions. Finally, we will use our extended simulation framework to provide more detailed information about how applications can leverage the synchronization of their processes to avoid performance issues.

References

1. Adiga, N., et al.: An overview of the BlueGene/L supercomputer. In: ACM/IEEE 2002 Conference Supercomputing, p. 60, November 2002
2. Almási, G., Heidelberger, P., Archer, C.J., Martorell, X., Erway, C.C., Moreira, J.E., Steinmacher-Burow, B., Zheng, Y.: Optimization of MPI collective communication on BlueGene/L systems. In: Proceedings of the 19th Annual International Conference on Supercomputing, ICS 2005, NY, USA, pp. 253–262 (2005). http://doi.acm.org/10.1145/1088149.1088183
3. Alvisi, L., Elnozahy, E., Rao, S., Husain, S., de Mel, A.: An analysis of communication induced checkpointing. In: Twenty-Ninth Annual International Symposium on Fault-Tolerant Computing, 1999, Digest of Papers, pp. 242–249 (1999)
4. Alvisi, L., Marzullo, K.: Message logging: pessimistic, optimistic, causal, and optimal. IEEE Trans. Softw. Eng. **24**(2), 149–159 (1998)

5. Bergman, K., Borkar, S., Campbell, D., Carlson, W., Dally, W., Denneau, M., Franzon, P., Harrod, W., Hill, K., Hiller, J., Karp, S., Keckler, S., Klein, D., Kogge, P., Lucas, R., Richards, M., Scarpelli, A., Scott, S., Snavely, A., Sterling, T., Williams, R.S., Yelick, K.: Exascale computing study: technology challenges in achieving exascale systems, September 2008. http://www.science.energy.gov/ascr/Research/CS/DARPA/exascale-hardware(2008).pdf

6. Bronevetsky, G.: Communication-sensitive static dataflow for parallel message passing applications. In: Proceedings of the 7th Annual IEEE/ACM International Symposium on Code Generation and Optimization, pp. 1–12. IEEE Computer Society (2009)

7. Cappello, F.: Fault tolerance in petascale/exascale systems: current knowledge, challenges and research opportunities. IJHPCA **23**(3), 212–226 (2009)

8. Chandy, K.M., Lamport, L.: Distributed snapshots: determining global states of distributed systems. ACM Trans. Comp. Syst. **3**(1), 63–75 (1985)

9. Culler, D., Karp, R., Patterson, D., Sahay, A., Schauser, K.E., Santos, E., Subramonian, R., von Eicken, T.: LogP: towards a realistic model of parallel computation. SIGPLAN Not. **28**(7), 1–12 (1993)

10. De, P., Kothari, R., Mann, V.: A trace-driven emulation framework to predict scalability of large clusters in presence of OS jitter. In: 2008 IEEE International Conference on Cluster Computing, pp. 232–241. IEEE (2008)

11. Hertel Jr., E.S., Bell, R.L., Elrick, M.G., Farnsworth, A.V., Kerley, G.I., McGlaun, J.M., Petney, S.V., Silling, S.A., Taylor, P.A., Yarrington, L.: CTH: a software family for multi-dimensional shock physics analysis. In: Proceedings of the 19th International Symposium on Shock Waves, pp. 377–382 July 1993

12. Elnozahy, E.N., Alvisi, L., Wang, Y.M., Johnson, D.B.: A survey of rollback-recovery protocols in message-passing systems. ACM Comput. Surv. **34**(3), 375–408 (2002)

13. Engelmann, C.: Investigating operating system noise in extreme-scale high-performance computing systems using simulation. In: Proceedings of the 11th IASTED International Conference on Parallel and Distributed Computing and Networks (PDCN 2013), pp. 11–13 (2013)

14. Exascale Co-Design Center for Materials in Extreme Environments (ExMatEx). http://exmatex.lanl.gov/. Accessed 10 June 2013

15. Ferreira, K., Riesen, R., Stearley, J., Laros, J.H., Oldfield, R., Pedretti, K., Bridges, P., Arnold, D., Brightwell, R.: Evaluating the viability of process replication reliability for exascale systems. In: Proceedings of the ACM/IEEE International Conference on High Performance Computing, Networking, Storage, and Analysis, (SC 2011), November 2011

16. Ferreira, K.B., Brightwell, R., Bridges, P.G.: Characterizing application sensitivity to OS interference using kernel-level noise injection. In: Proceedings of the 2008 ACM/IEEE Conference on Supercomputing (SC 2008), November 2008

17. Ferreira, K.B., Widener, P., Levy, S., Arnold, D., Hoefler, T.: Understanding the effects of communication and coordination on checkpointing at scale. In: Proceedings of the 2014 International Conference for High Performance Computing, Networking, Storage and Analysis (Supercomputing) (2014)

18. Guermouche, A., Ropars, T., Brunet, E., Snir, M., Cappello, F.: Uncoordinated checkpointing without domino effect for send-deterministic MPI applications. In: International Parallel Distributed Processing Symposium (IPDPS), pp. 989–1000, May 2011

19. Heroux, M.A., Doerfler, D.W., Crozier, P.S., Willenbring, J.M., Edwards, H.C., Williams, A., Rajan, M., Keiter, E.R., Thornquist, H.K., Numrich, R.W.: Improving performance via mini-applications. Technical report, SAND2009-5574, Sandia National Laboratories (2009)
20. Hoefler, T., Schneider, T., Lumsdaine, A.: Characterizing the influence of system noise on large-scale applications by simulation. In: Proceedings of the 2010 ACM/IEEE International Conference for High Performance Computing, Networking, Storage and Analysis, pp. 1–11. IEEE Computer Society (2010)
21. Hoefler, T., Schneider, T., Lumsdaine, A.: LogGOPSim: simulating large-scale applications in the LogGOPS model. In: Proceedings of the 19th ACM International Symposium on High Performance Distributed Computing, pp. 597–604. ACM (2010)
22. Johnson, D.B., Zwaenepoel, W.: Recovery in distributed systems using asynchronous message logging and checkpointing. In: Proceedings of the Seventh Annual ACM Symposium on Principles of Distributed Computing, pp. 171–181 (1988)
23. Karlin, I., Bhatele, A., Chamberlain, B.L., Cohen, J., Devito, Z., Gokhale, M., Haque, R., Hornung, R., Keasler, J., Laney, D., Luke, E., Lloyd, S., McGraw, J., Neely, R., Richards, D., Schulz, M., Still, C.H., Wang, F., Wong, D.: LULESH programming model and performance ports overview. Technical report LLNL-TR-608824, Lawrence Livermore National Laboratory, December 2012
24. Levy, S., Topp, B., Ferreira, K.B., Arnold, D., Hoefler, T., Widener, P.: Using simulation to evaluate the performance of resilience strategies at scale. In: 2013 SC Companion: High Performance Computing, Networking, Storage and Analysis (SCC). IEEE (2013)
25. Levy, S., Topp, B., Ferreira, K.B., Arnold, D., Widener, P., Hoefler, T.: Using simulation to evaluate the performance of resilience strategies and process failures. Technical report SAND2014-0688, Sandia National Laboratories (2014)
26. Maloney, A., Goscinski, A.: A survey and review of the current state of rollback-recovery for cluster systems. Concurr. Comput. Pract. Exp. 21(12), 1632–1666 (2009). doi:10.1002/cpe.1413. ISSN 1532-0634
27. Mills, D.L.: Internet time synchronization: the network time protocol. IEEE Trans. Commun. 39(10), 1482–1493 (1991)
28. Monnet, S., Morin, C., Badrinath, R.: A hierarchical checkpointing protocol for parallel applications in cluster federations. In: 2004 Proceedings of 18th International Parallel and Distributed Processing Symposium, p. 211. IEEE (2004)
29. Murta, C.D., Torres Jr., P.R.T., Mohapatra, P.: Characterizing quality of time and topology in a time synchronization network. In: IEEE Globecom 2006, pp. 1–5, November 2006
30. Plimpton, S.: Fast parallel algorithms for short-range molecular dynamics. J. Comput. Phys. 117(1), 1–19 (1995)
31. Sandia National Laboratory: Mantevo project home page, January 2014. http://mantevo.org

A Massively-Parallel, Fault-Tolerant Solver for High-Dimensional PDEs

Mario Heene[1(✉)], Alfredo Parra Hinojosa[2], Hans-Joachim Bungartz[2], and Dirk Pflüger[1]

[1] University of Stuttgart, Universitätsstraße 38, 70569 Stuttgart, Germany
{mario.heene,dirk.pflueger}@ipvs.uni-stuttgart.de
[2] Technical University of Munich, Boltzmannstraße 3, 85748 Garching, Germany
{hinojosa,bungartz}@in.tum.de

Abstract. We investigate the effect of hard faults on a massively-parallel implementation of the Sparse Grid Combination Technique (SGCT), an efficient numerical approach for the solution of high-dimensional time-dependent PDEs. The SGCT allows us to increase the spatial resolution of a solver to a level that is out of scope with classical discretization schemes due to the curse of dimensionality. We exploit the inherent data redundancy of this algorithm to obtain a scalable and fault-tolerant implementation without the need of checkpointing or process replication. It is a lossy approach that can guarantee convergence for a large number of faults and a wide range of applications. We present first results using our fault simulation framework – and the first convergence and scalability results with simulated faults and algorithm-based fault tolerance for PDEs in more than three dimensions.

Keywords: Fault tolerance · Scalability · High-dimensional PDEs

1 Introduction

For quite some time, the HPC community has acknowledged the central role of hardware faults in large-scale simulations. During 2013, the *Blue Waters* petascale system exhibited a mean time between failures (MTBF) of 4.2 h [7]. The MTBF is becoming so small that it is approaching the checkpointing interval [5]. This makes it clear that alternative approaches to resilience are not only convenient but urgently necessary. This concern has brought together experts from across the scientific spectrum to come up with new solutions [6].

Fault tolerance can be addressed either at the system level (error-correcting code, checkpointing, replication) or at the algorithmic level. There have been promising advances in both areas in the last few years, such as in-memory checkpointing [21] (system-level) or the use of machine learning techniques to identify PDE solvers that are robust against faults [4] (algorithmic level). Sometimes it is possible to use a combination of both approaches in order to get the best of both worlds [16], but in general this is not possible. Although some algorithms are

© Springer International Publishing AG 2017
F. Desprez et al. (Eds.): Euro-Par 2016 Workshops, LNCS 10104, pp. 635–647, 2017.
DOI: 10.1007/978-3-319-58943-5_51

fault tolerant by construction (e.g., iterative, randomized and restarted schemes), most do not have properties that can be used for algorithmic fault tolerance. These algorithms will largely rely on system-level resilience.

We are now approaching the exascale era, which aggravates the problem of resilience. Given how little we know about the hardware- and system-level specifications of future exascale systems, it is crucial to exploit algorithm-based fault tolerance beyond checksum schemes. Algorithm-based resilience, which we interpret broadly as using the properties of numerical schemes to overcome failures, has the advantage of not relying heavily on the specifications of the system. Also, the resource overhead required to implement resilient algorithms is usually much smaller than the more common system-level approaches (most noticeably replication and checkpointing). This is the approach we have adopted for solving high-dimensional PDEs efficiently, using an algorithm that can deal with faults at the algorithmic level: the *Sparse Grid Combination Technique* (SGCT) [8].

The SGCT is an extrapolation method that helps to alleviate the curse of dimensionality for a wide variety of problems. In particular, we are interested in solving PDEs. The idea of the SGCT is the following: since solving a d-dimensional PDE on a finely discretized grid with, say, 2^n discretization points per dimension is usually infeasible (it requires a total of $\mathcal{O}(2^{dn})$ points, leading to the so called *curse of dimensionality*), one solves the PDE *multiple* times, each time on an anisotropic grid of smaller resolution. The different solutions are then combined with appropriate weights in order to approximate the high-definition solution. This algorithm has been shown to scale up to more than 180 000 cores [12] and now has been made fault tolerant (called the *Fault Tolerant Combination Technique*, FTCT) [10]. This makes it a promising candidate for an exascale-ready algorithm, and in this paper we try to support this claim. In particular, we introduce our fault-simulation layer; we present an efficient parallelization strategy for the FTCT and apply it to the well-established PDE toolbox *DUNE* [2]; we show that the overhead to ensure fault tolerance on a full supercomputer is very small, since it requires neither checkpointing nor process replication; and we show the very first results for a fault-tolerant solution of a higher-dimensional PDE in a massively parallel system: the time-dependent advection-diffusion equation in 5 dimensions.

In previous work we have applied the FTCT to the plasma physics code *GENE* [15], which solves the (5+1)D gyrokinetic equations. We carried out tests in serial with simulated faults and gave initial estimates of the computational costs [17]. The authors in [19] carried out tests in parallel in 2 and 3 dimensions, but only with up to about 3000 cores. Our parallelization strategy extends to any dimension and performs well on a full supercomputer, representing a significant improvement of the state of the art.

2   The Sparse Grid Combination Technique

Consider a function $u(\boldsymbol{x}) \in V \subset C([0,1]^d)$, where $\boldsymbol{x} = (x_1, \ldots, x_d) \in \mathbb{R}^d$. This function could represent the solution of a PDE, which we would like to approximate via a discrete function $u_i(x) \in V_i \subset V$. The SGCT (introduced by Griebel et al. in the nineties [8]) mitigates the curse of dimensionality. In its most general form it can be stated as

$$u_n \approx u_n^{(c)} = \sum_{i \in \mathcal{I}} c_i u_i. \tag{1}$$

We call the weights $c_i \in \mathbb{R}$ *combination coefficients*; each u_i is a solution of the PDE on a coarse, anisotropic regular grid $\Omega_i := \Omega_{i_1} \times \cdots \times \Omega_{i_d}$, which has mesh size $h_i := (h_{i_1}, \ldots, h_{i_d}) := 2^{-i}$. Each u_i is called a *component solution*, the corresponding grids Ω_i are called *component grids*, $u_n^{(c)}$ is the *combined solution* and the grid $\Omega_n^{(c)}$, on which the combined solution lives, is the *combined grid*. The set $\mathcal{I}$ is a set of multi-indices, and it defines over which grids the combination is to be performed. Only certain choices of the index set give combinations that properly approximate u_n. For instance, the classical combination technique is given by

$$u_n^{(c)} = \sum_{q=0}^{d-1} (-1)^q \binom{d-1}{q} \sum_{\|i\|_1 = n+(d-1)-q} u_i. \tag{2}$$

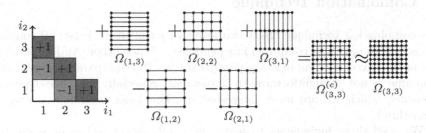

Fig. 1. The classical combination technique in 2D for $n = (3,3)$ $(n = 3)$.

An example in 2D can be seen in Fig. 1 with the choice $n = (3,3)$ $(n = 3)$. The five component solutions u_i are weighted with coefficients $c_i = \pm 1$. The grids depicted have boundary points in both dimensions ($2^{i_j} + 1$ total points per dimension), but one can also leave out the boundary points on a given dimension. Each of these grids has only $\mathcal{O}(h_n^{-1})$ discretization points, and there are $\mathcal{O}(d(\log h_n^{-1})^{d-1})$ such grids [18]. The crucial advantage of the combination technique is that the solutions on the component grids are independent of each other and can therefore be computed in parallel. The results then have to be combined in a reduction step, either once at the end of the computation or, for time-dependent problems, every certain number of time steps.

In general, the combination coefficients in (1) are calculated using the formula

$$c_i = \sum_{i \le j \le i+1} (-1)^{|j-i|} \chi_{\mathcal{I}}(j), \tag{3}$$

with $i \geq 1$, where $\chi_{\mathcal{I}}$ is the indicator function of set $\mathcal{I}$ [9]. This is an application of the inclusion/exclusion principle if the set $\mathcal{I}$ is viewed as a lattice.

Since the most anisotropic grids in the combination technique can introduce some instabilities, one can truncate the combination by defining a minimum level of resolution $i_{\min}$ s.t. $i_{\min} \leq i \leq n$, $\forall i \in \mathcal{I}$. For example, the choice $n = (3,3)$ and $i_{\min} = (2,2)$ results in the combination $u_{(3,3)}^{(c)} = u_{(2,3)} + u_{(3,2)} - u_{(2,2)}$.

The combined solution is usually formulated in the space of the sparse grid. In order to combine the solutions u_i efficiently, they first have to be transformed from their nodal basis representation into the hierarchical basis of the sparse grid by *hierarchization* [12]. In the sparse grid space they can be combined simply by adding up the hierarchical surpluses at all grid points. The inverse operation (going from the hierarchical to the nodal basis) is called *dehierarchization*.

These are all the components required to implement the combination technique in serial. A parallel (and scalable) combination technique presents several challenges, many of which we have addressed in previous work. We have developed a framework to run the combination technique on a massively parallel system, which we now briefly describe.

3   A Software Framework for a Massively Parallel Combination Technique

The combination technique offers two levels of parallelism. First, all combination solutions u_i can be computed independently of each other. And second, each u_i can be solved with an existing parallel solver. But the parallel combination technique is not straightforward to implement, especially for time-dependent problems, which we are most interested in. The basic workflow is given in Algorithm 1.

We need three ingredients to make the combination technique scale: (i) a good parallelization strategy; (ii) a suitable load balancing scheme to distribute

---

Algorithm 1. The Combination Technique in Parallel

---

1 Choose parameters of combination technique (n and $i_{\min}$), generate set $\mathcal{I}$ and compute combination coefficients c_i;
2 **for** $i \in \mathcal{I}$ **do**
3      $u_i \leftarrow u(\mathbf{x}, t = 0)$;   // Set all initial conditions
4 **while** *not converged* **do**
5   **for** $i \in \mathcal{I}$ **do in parallel**
6          $u_i \leftarrow$ solve(u_i, N_t);   // Solve N_t time steps of PDE on grid Ω_i
7          $u_i \leftarrow$ hierarchize(u_i);   // Hierarchize in place
8   **if** *faults detected* **then**
9   recover();   // Recover from faults: use the FTCT
10     $u_n^{(c)} \leftarrow \sum_{i \in \mathcal{I}} c_i u_i$;   // Combine solution (reduce and scatter)
11   **for** $i \in \mathcal{I}$ **do in parallel**
12         $u_i \leftarrow$ dehierarchize($u_n^{(c)}$);   // Transform back to nodal basis

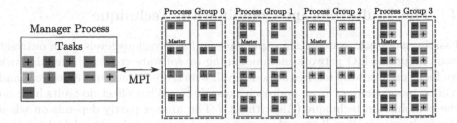

Fig. 2. Manager-worker model. In this example, 11 tasks are distributed among 4 groups of processes, each composed of 2 nodes, with 4 processes per node. A task corresponds to a component grid distributed over all processes of a group.

the workload properly; and (iii) efficient algorithms for distributed systems for the hierarchization/dehierarchization and to combine the component solutions.

(i) Parallelization Strategy: A Manager-Worker Model. To parallelize the combination technique we use the manager-worker model depicted in Fig. 2. First, we create groups of MPI processes, and each group might comprise several compute nodes. A manager process generates a list of tasks – in this case, the list of component solutions u_i to be computed – and distributes them evenly among the groups. Each group in turn has a master process that coordinates the work within its group and communicates with the manager. Each group computes all the component grids it has been assigned to one after the other, asynchronously and independently to the rest of the groups. Almost all of the MPI communication is done within the groups, and only the combination step requires intergroup communication. This framework is implemented within the sparse grid library SG^{++} [1]. A more detailed description can be found in [13].

(ii) Load Balancing. The different combination solutions take different times to be solved. The manager has to take this into consideration when distributing the tasks. We have developed a load balancing scheme that estimates the runtime of each u_i based on the number of grid points and its degree of anisotropy [11].

(iii) Efficient and Scalable Algorithms for Distributed Systems. The combination step and the hierarchization/dehierarchization steps require inter-node communication. Keeping this overhead small is crucial for the parallel combination technique. In previous work we have exploited the hierarchical structure of sparse grids to optimize the combination step [14]. The resulting algorithm outperforms non-hierarchical algorithms by orders of magnitude. We have also adapted the hierarchization algorithm to scale well in distributed systems [12]. Furthermore, we have presented a massively parallel implementation of the combination step, which scales up to more than 180 000 cores in [13].

These three ingredients are sufficient to ensure scalability with the combination technique, but the algorithm would crash in the presence of faults. There is, however, a well-understood version of the combination technique that can tolerate faults. In the following, we describe the principle behind it and the implementation in our framework.

4   The Fault-Tolerant Combination Technique

Existing petascale systems can experience faults at various levels, from outright node failure to I/O network malfunctioning or software errors [5]. In this work we focus on hardware failures at node level, which are already quite frequent and will be more common as we approach exascale [5]. What effect do faults have on the combination technique (Algorithm 1)? The answer partly depends on when the faults occur. Recall that there are four main operations in the algorithm: solve, hierarchize, combine, and dehierarchize. In previous work we have shown that most of the computing time is spent on the actual PDE solver, even in the worst-case scenario where we combine after every time step [13]. Therefore it is reasonable to assume that faults are most likely to occur during the solver call.

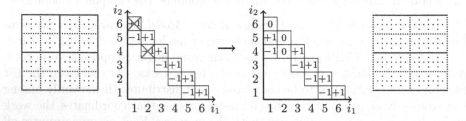

Fig. 3. The fault-tolerant combination technique in 2D with two faults, and the resulting alternative combination.

If we look back at our parallelization scheme (Fig. 2) we can see what would happen if one or multiple nodes fail: the component grids assigned to the corresponding process groups are lost, at least for the number of time steps being simulated at the time of the fault. We avoid the need of checkpointing by applying the *Fault Tolerant Combination Technique* (FTCT) [10], an algorithmic approach to recover the combined solution in the presence of faults. The FTCT is illustrated in Fig. 3. If faults occur, the combination solutions that are lost are given a combination coefficient of zero, and an alternative combination is computed. The new combination avoids using the lost solutions, at the price of having a sparse grid with fewer grid points. It is thus a lossy approach, but as we will show in Sect. 6, the losses are very small. Furthermore, some additional component grids that are not originally needed for the combination (e.g., solution $u_{(1,4)}$ in the figure) have to be computed: They are required for the recovery step. In rare cases, some of the coarsest combination solutions have to be recomputed. Nevertheless, the total overhead is very small. For more details we refer the reader to [10,17].

4.1   Implementation of the FTCT

Our implementation is based on the ULFM specification [3], currently being the most mature specification of a fault-tolerant MPI. It adds further functionality to the MPI Standard which enables to detect crashed processes and to exclude these processes from future communication.

There are two cases how a process group is detected to have *failed*. The master process detects that a process in its own group has failed and notifies the manager. This is implemented by an *MPI_Barrier* on the group, which will return an error code if a process of the group has failed. If a master process crashes, this is detected by the manager. The manager waits for a message from the master process of each group, which signals whether the computation was successful, or whether a process of the group failed. This is implemented with *MPI_Wait*, which will return an error code if the master process has failed. For the case that the application code is not prepared to handle errors in MPI calls (e.g., it does not have a predefined exit strategy), it might block forever after a process failed. We would deal with such cases by using time-outs in the manager process. If a group does not finish its computations within reasonable time (relative to the other groups), it will be marked as having failed. However, we have not yet implemented such a procedure.

After a fault has been detected, the following recovery steps are performed:

1. Create new MPI communicators that exclude the process ranks of the *whole* failed group, using the functions `MPI_Comm_revoke` and `MPI_Comm_shrink`.
2. Compute new combination coefficients to correct the combined solution according to the FTCT algorithm.
3. Redistribute the tasks of the failed group to the living groups. Perform initialization routines if necessary (e.g., set up data structures, etc.).
4. If it is necessary to recompute some of the tasks, initialize these tasks with the last combined solution and compute them (for the required number of time steps). The last combined solution is still available on all alive process groups from the last combination step (basically this is an in-memory checkpoint of the combined solution that we get "for free" at each combination step).

The corrected combined solution will be computed during the next combination step (line 10 in Algorithm 1). The lost tasks that were not recomputed have a combination coefficient of zero and do not contribute to the combined solution. Afterwards, the combination coefficients are reset to the original coefficients (for the next combination step) and Algorithm 1 is resumed normally. We only use the reduced set of component grids to recover the combined solution at the current time step, but we proceed the computation with the full original set of component grids.

Our algorithm can tolerate any number of faults, as long as one healthy group is left to continue the computations. In this work we only detect and correct process failures during the computation phase, but the same procedure could be used for failures during the combination step. To protect the algorithm from the very unlikely event of the manager process failing, one could use a replication strategy, e.g., a second manager process on a different node.

4.2   Fault Simulation Layer

For our experiments we did not use an actual fault-tolerant MPI implementation, because there was none readily available on the HPC systems we had access to. Instead we realized a home-grown fault simulation layer between our framework and the actual MPI system, which can simulate failed processes. This layer extends the MPI system by borrowing some functions of the ULFM interface, emulating the external behaviour of ULFM, e.g., returning appropriate error codes. But our actual internal implementation can differ from ULFM, since we do not consider actual process faults, but only simulated faults. The functions we extended include the most common point-to-point and collective operations, as well as some of the new fault tolerance functions, such as MPI_Comm_shrink and MPI_Comm_revoke. With the fault simulation layer we can let processes crash virtually. When a process calls a function named kill_me() at any point in the code, it stops its normal operation and goes idle. When this happens, it only handles background operations of the fault simulation layer, and it can be detected as *failed* by other processes. If, for example, this process was the destination of an MPI_Send, or if it participated in a collective communication such as MPI_Allreduce, the functions would (according to the specification) return on the other processes with the error message MPI_ERR_PROC_FAILED. Details on the fault simulation layer can be found in [20].

Of course, the fault simulation layer does not provide representative results for the runtime or scalability of the new fault tolerance functions, e.g., MPI_Comm_shrink. However, we do not expect the runtime of these functions to add a significant overhead to our FTCT algorithm, since the contribution to the overall runtime is very low. In contrast, if we used a preliminary FT-MPI implementation (e.g., ULFM, which we expect to be significantly slower than the vendor specific implementation), we would expect a noticeable setback in the performance and scalability of our algorithms, since they all rely heavily on fast communication. The fault simulation layer does come with a certain overhead, but we have the advantage that we can choose, for a given MPI function, between its fault tolerant version or its standard version. By only using the fault tolerant version where it is really necessary (e.g., for detecting faults and shrinking the communicators), but not in the application code or in the performance critical parts, the impact on the performance is negligible.

Assuming that a future FT-MPI implementation provided by the system vendor will be comparably fast to existing implementations, we can get realistic numbers for the overhead of the FTCT on current HPC systems for a large number of cores. This is a major goal of this work. In the future we plan to compare the performance of the FTCT using ULFM and our current approach in order to quantify our arguments. One further advantage of the fault simulation layer is its portability. Since it runs out of the box with any standard MPI implementation, we can easily repeat our experiments on a different HPC system without worrying about installing and running ULFM.

5   Experimental Setup

Our test problem is the d-dimensional advection-diffusion equation

$$\partial_t u - \Delta u + \boldsymbol{a} \cdot \nabla u = f \text{ in } \Omega \times [0, T) \qquad (4)$$
$$u(\cdot, t) = 0 \text{ in } \partial\Omega$$

with $\Omega = [0,1]^d$, $\boldsymbol{a} = (1,1,...,1)^T$ and $u(\cdot, 0) = e^{-100\sum_{i=1}^{d}(x_i - 0.5)^2}$, implemented in the PDE-framework DUNE-pdelab. For the spatial discretization we use the finite volume element (FVE) method on rectangular d-dimensional grids. Here, we use a simple explicit Euler scheme for the time integration. Future work will comprise a geometric multigrid solver that works with regular anisotropic grids. We chose this problem as its numerics are well understood and it allows us to investigate our algorithms in arbitrary dimensionality.

The *solve* function in Algorithm 1 corresponds to computing a component solution u_i with DUNE for one time step Δt in parallel using all processes of the corresponding process group. As DUNE uses its own data structures, after each call to DUNE the data has to be copied and converted to the data structure of the component grid. After the combination step the data is copied back into DUNE in order to set the new initial values for the next time step. For our experiments we use the same time step size for all component grids and combine after each time step. We simulate process failures by calling the kill_me function of our fault simulation layer. The iteration at which the process fails and the rank of the process are defined a priori in a parameters file.

6   Results

6.1   Convergence

The theoretical convergence of the combination technique (and its fault tolerant version) has been studied before [8,10], and our experiments confirm previous results. In all our convergence experiments we vary the number of process groups and let one random group fail, so the percentage of failed tasks varies accordingly. Which exact group fails makes almost no difference, since the tasks are distributed homogeneously among the groups. Thus, we show the results only for one simulation run. Additionally, we did not observe a noticeable difference in the quality of the solution when varying the time step at which the fault occurs. The results shown correspond to a fault simulated during the second iteration (so that all tasks are already assigned to the groups). We compute the relative l_2-error $e = \frac{\|u_n^{(c)} - u_{\text{ref}}\|_2}{\|u_{\text{ref}}\|_2}$ at the end of the simulation ($t = 0.10$ and $\Delta t = 10^{-4}$ in 2D, and $t = 0.05$ and $\Delta t = 10^{-3}$ in 5D), interpolating each combination solution to the resolution of the reference grid. We combine after every time step.

Figure 4 (left) shows the convergence of the combination technique in 2D with $i_{\min} = (3,3)$, and increasing n, compared to a full grid reference solution of level $n = (11,11)$. The recovered combination technique with faults is only minimally worse than without faults (1%–3% worse), even when half of the tasks fail. The difference is more visible in 5D, Fig. 4 (right), where we chose $i_{\min} = (3, 3, 3, 3, 3)$ and a reference solution of size $n = (6, 6, 6, 6, 6)$. To our best knowledge, this is the first, fully fault-tolerant convergence experiment in 5 dimensions with the combination technique. Figure 5 (left) shows a one-dimensional projection of the combined solution at $t = 0.05$ for $n = (5, 5, 5, 5, 5)$ computed on four groups. This shows an excellent match.

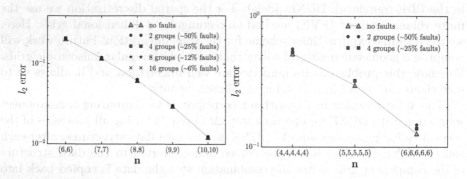

Fig. 4. Convergence of the convection-diffusion equation using the combination technique, with and without faults. A single process fault causes an entire group to fail. **Left:** 2D case. **Right:** 5D case.

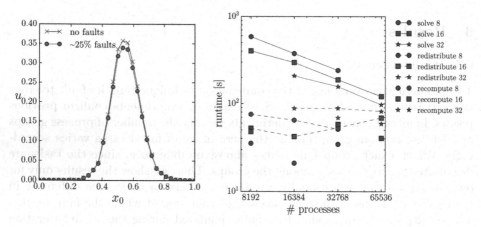

Fig. 5. Left: One-dimensional projection of the 5D solution with and without faults for $i_{\min} = (3, 3, 3, 3, 3)$ and $n = (5, 5, 5, 5, 5)$. **Right:** 5D scaling experiments. The number in the legend indicates the number of process groups.

6.2   Scalability

We performed scaling experiments on the supercomputer *Hazel Hen* to investigate the overhead of the FTCT in a massively parallel setup. We used a 5D combination technique with $n = (8, 8, 7, 7, 7)$ and $i_{min} = (4, 4, 3, 3, 3)$. This resulted in 126 component grids. Note that a computation of the full grid Ω_n would not be feasible anymore – not even on the full machine. For the parallelization we used 8192, 16384, 32768 and 65536 processes distributed on 8, 16 or 32 process groups of size 512, 1024, 2048 or 4096. In all cases one process failed in the second iteration and the entire corresponding group is removed. For the same number of groups, always a process in the super group failed.

Figure 5 shows the time to *solve* all the component grids for one time step (using all groups, before the fault occurs), the time to *redistribute* the component grids of the failed group and the time to *recompute* certain tasks if necessary. Our application code has a rather bad node-level performance, but it scales well when the size of the process group is increased. The time for the combination can be neglected in these experiments since it was below one second in all cases. Two factors cause our curves to look slightly erratic. First, we show results for only one experiment per configuration. This is due to the long time and large computing resources it takes to run each simulation, which makes statistical studies infeasible. Second, there is some degree of randomness in the assignment of the tasks to the process groups, so even when the same group fails, the tasks to be redistributed or recomputed can vary in each run. The time to redistribute a task essentially is the time its initialization routine takes. For 16 and 32 groups the number of tasks to be redistributed is lower than the number of groups, so the time to redistribute is dominated by the slowest task. Furthermore, in our case the initialization function does not scale with the number of processes. This explains why the time to redistribute did not always decrease.

It is not easy to specify the exact overhead of the FTCT, since it depends on various parameters, such as the expected number of time steps between two failures, the number of time steps computed in the solve step and the ratio between the initialization time and the cost of one time step. However, we can easily formulate upper bounds for the two most costly steps of the recovery process. The redistribute step can never take longer than to initialize all tasks. The recompute step can never take longer than the solve step. This means, if the cost of the initialization is small compared to the total amount of work done between two process failures, the overhead of the FTCT will be negligible. This is the main conclusion to be drawn from our experiments.

After the recovery, the time for the solve step increases, since less process groups are available. In the future we plan to mitigate this problem by not removing the whole process group, but instead shrinking it to a smaller size. The optimal case for our algorithm would be an MPI system that allows to request new MPI processes at runtime after a node or process failure happened.

7 Conclusions

Our parallelization strategy for the combination technique can handle hard faults on a large-scale supercomputer on the algorithmic level with only a small overhead. The accuracy of the fault-tolerant combination technique remains very close to the original combination technique after faults occur. In low dimensions, this has been observed before. We were able to show that this holds as well in a higher-dimensional setting. In the future we plan to repeat our experiments with an actual fault tolerant MPI implementation; we will explore ways to exclude single processes instead of whole groups; and we will investigate the effect of silent data corruption additionally to hard faults.

References

1. SG++ library. http://sgpp.sparsegrids.org/
2. Bastian, P., et al.: A generic grid interface for parallel and adaptive scientific computing. Part I: abstract framework. Computing **82**(2–3), 103–119 (2008)
3. Bland, W., et al.: A proposal for user-level failure mitigation in the MPI-3 standard. University of Tennessee (2012)
4. Callenes-Sloan, J., McNamara, H.: Algorithm selection for error resilience in scientific computing. In: Dependable Computing (PRDC), pp. 96–105. IEEE (2014)
5. Cappello, F., et al.: Toward exascale resilience: 2014 update. Supercomput. Front. Innov. **1**(1), 5–28 (2014)
6. Cappello, F., et al.: Toward exascale resilience. Int. J. High Perform. Comput. Appl. **23**(4), 374–388 (2009)
7. Di Martino, C., et al.: Lessons learned from the analysis of system failures at petascale: the case of blue waters. In: Dependable Systems and Networks (DSN), pp. 610–621. IEEE (2014)
8. Griebel, M., Schneider, M., Zenger, C.: A combination technique for the solution of sparse grid problems. In: Iterative Methods in Linear Algebra, pp. 263–281 (1992)
9. Harding, B.: Adaptive sparse grids and extrapolation techniques. In: Garcke, J., Pflüger, D. (eds.) Sparse Grids and Applications - Stuttgart 2014. LNCSE, vol. 109, pp. 79–102. Springer, Cham (2016). doi:10.1007/978-3-319-28262-6_4
10. Harding, B., et al.: Fault tolerant computation with the sparse grid combination technique. SIAM J. Scient. Comput. **37**(3), C331–C353 (2015)
11. Heene, M., Kowitz, C., Pflüger, D.: Load balancing for massively parallel computations with the sparse grid combination technique. In: Parallel Computing: Accelerating Computational Science and Engineering, pp. 574–583 (2014)
12. Heene, M., Pflüger, D.: Efficient and scalable distributed-memory hierarchization algorithms for the sparse grid combination technique. In: Parallel Computing: On the Road to Exascale (2016)
13. Heene, M., Pflüger, D.: Scalable algorithms for the solution of higher-dimensional PDEs. In: Bungartz, H.-J., Neumann, P., Nagel, W.E. (eds.) Software for Exascale Computing - SPPEXA 2013-2015. LNCSE, vol. 113, pp. 165–186. Springer, Cham (2016). doi:10.1007/978-3-319-40528-5_8
14. Hupp, P., Heene, M., Jacob, R., Pflüger, D.: Global communication schemes for the numerical solution of high-dimensional PDEs. Parallel Comput. **52**, 78–105 (2016)

15. Jenko, F., et al.: Electron temperature gradient driven turbulence. Phys. Plasmas (1994-Present) **7**(5), 1904–1910 (2000). http://www.genecode.org/
16. Li, D., Chen, Z., Wu, P., Vetter, J.S.: Rethinking algorithm-based fault tolerance with a cooperative software-hardware approach. In: Proceedings of the International Conference on HPC, Networking, Storage and Analysis, p. 44. ACM (2013)
17. Hinojosa, A.P., Kowitz, C., Heene, M., Pflüger, D., Bungartz, H.-J.: Towards a fault-tolerant, scalable implementation of GENE. In: Mehl, M., Bischoff, M., Schäfer, M. (eds.) Recent Trends in Computational Engineering - CE2014. LNCSE, vol. 105, pp. 47–65. Springer, Cham (2015). doi:10.1007/978-3-319-22997-3_3
18. Pflüger, D.: Spatially Adaptive Sparse Grids for High-Dimensional Problems. Verlag Dr. Hut, München (2010)
19. Strazdins, P.E., Ali, M.M., Harding, B.: Highly scalable algorithms for the sparse grid combination technique. In: 2015 IEEE International Parallel and Distributed Processing Symposium Workshop (IPDPSW), pp. 941–950, May 2015
20. Walter, J.: Design and implementation of a fault simulation layer for the combination technique on HPC systems. Master's thesis, University of Stuttgart (2016)
21. Zheng, G., Ni, X., Kalé, L.V.: A scalable double in-memory checkpoint and restart scheme towards exascale. In: 2012 IEEE/IFIP 42nd International Conference on Dependable Systems and Networks Workshops (DSN-W), pp. 1–6. IEEE (2012)

On the Inherent Resilience of Integer Operations

Laura Monroe[1](✉), William M. Jones[2], Scott R. Lavigne[2],
Claude H. Davis IV[3], Qiang Guan[1], and Nathan DeBardeleben[1]

[1] Los Alamos National Laboratory, Los Alamos, NM, USA
{lmonroe,qguan,ndebard}@lanl.gov
[2] Coastal Carolina University, Conway, SC, USA
{wjones,srlavigne}@coastal.edu
[3] Clemson University, Clemson, SC, USA
clauded@coastal.edu

Abstract. It is of great interest to correctly quantify corruption rates in computing systems. Masking effects of individual operations can complicate this effort by hiding faults. Beyond this, identification of fault-masking operations may be useful in designing resilient algorithms.

We discuss here fault masking that is mathematically inherent to several integer operations. This is not hardware-dependent, so these integer operations will mask faults on any system upon which they are implemented mathematically correctly.

We show the inherent mathematical resilience of multiplication to faults, and discuss the mathematical model of this fault masking. We validate this model through exhaustive and sampled experimentation, and show that model and experiments exactly match, and that both closely match observations on a micro-benchmark under soft-error injection. We also discuss resilience on other integer operators.

Keywords: Resilience · Fault tolerance · Silent data corruption · Soft errors

1   Introduction

Data corruption in high-performance computation (HPC) can be devastating. This is especially true for scientific and national security applications, where computationally complex multi-physics simulations may be the only real way to experiment. Data corruption in this context can cause errors in the calculation that might not even be seen, and thus cause an incorrect result to be accepted.

Thus, it is important to understand the nature and behavior of the physical phenomena that cause faults, and the interactions of these faults with applications. This is usually done by measuring their rates, and then identifying the

N. DeBardeleben—A portion of this work was performed at the Ultrascale Systems Research Center (USRC) at Los Alamos National Laboratory, supported by the U.S. Department of Energy contract DE-FC02-06ER25750. The publication has been assigned the LANL identifier LA-UR-16-26414.

© Springer International Publishing AG 2017
F. Desprez et al. (Eds.): Euro-Par 2016 Workshops, LNCS 10104, pp. 648–659, 2017.
DOI: 10.1007/978-3-319-58943-5_52

impacts they have on running applications. Many studies investigate the impact of silent data corruption (SDC) on application behavior and correctness by using simulation-based fault injection studies to support their conclusions [5, 7].

In contrast to this experimental approach, this paper is based on theory. We develop a first-principles mathematical approach that analyzes the impact of data corruption on low-level operations such as multiplication, within higher-level applications such as matrix multiplication. We then validate these models using experimental results. This theoretical approach strengthens our fault injection work, and provides an exemplar of the development of analytic models of masked errors on general integer operations. This work is complementary to some emerging work done recently on floating point numbers [4].

The genesis of this work was a fault-injection study on fault-tolerant matrix multiplication. Because of the way we injected the faults, all injections should have resulted in observable error. Instead, we were surprised to find that in some of the trials, the output was completely correct. The fault injector was mature and well-validated, and the code we were testing was simple; still, we examined both suites carefully and found no bugs. When we finally turned to the mathematics beneath the code, we found the unexpected theoretical resilience of the multiplication operator that we discuss here. The model we developed matches the error statistics seen in the study, so this mathematical resilience completely explains the unanticipated result.

The contributions of this work are as follows:

- We present an analytical approach to fault analysis and resilience that is theoretically justifiable and explains experimental results. This kind of approach can be used to better estimate resilience and actual error rates.
- We use this approach to develop an analytical model to calculate the resilience inherent to the integer multiplication operation.
- We validate this model through exhaustive and sampled experimentation, and demonstrate that the theoretical model and targeted experimentation exactly match each other, and that together, they closely match the observed behavior in a micro-benchmark under soft-error injection.
  We quantify a "built-in" resilience that may be inherent to many mathematical operations, using integer multiplication as one example. These characteristics are interesting because they provide a measure of resilience that is not coupled with any hardware or software-based fault tolerance mechanisms.
- We present a masking behavior that can influence the process of analysis.

2   Theory of Multiplicative Resilience

In this section, we discuss our theoretical model for resilience of integer multiplication. The concept is quite simple: if a is multiplied by b, and b is a multiple of 2^k, the multiplication essentially invokes a left shift on a by k bits, and any faults in the leftmost k bits of a disappear. Simple as this is, it was unanticipated, and was not our initial approach to analyzing the unexpectedly correct results in our experiment. We have not found this effect mentioned in the literature.

Throughout, we use the term "wordlength" to describe the length of an integer native to the architecture, and the term "bitlength" to describe the minimum number of bits needed to represent a given integer. We do not show the proofs in this short paper, for the sake of brevity.

2.1 Multiplicative Resilience from Overflow Implementation

The implementation of integer multiplicative overflow is truncation at n bits, on every n-bit machine we have tested. If $a \times b$ does not overflow, faults are benign if the least n bits of the result are the same as the least n bits of $a \times b$.

For example, consider the 8-bit multiplication 4×16. The correct result is 64. If there happened to be a single bitflip in the 6th bit of the first factor, the product becomes $(2^6 + 4) \times 16 = 1088$. Truncating this result to the lowest 8 bits gives 64, and the correct answer is returned.

This happens whenever $b = b' \times 2^s$, b' odd, and the bitflips on a take place only within the top s bit positions. Then the entire error will be truncated when the overflow is truncated. If the bitflips occur in the top s bits of a, then the result is correct. This means that benign behavior of multiplicative faults depends only on the power of 2 dividing b and on where the bitflips occur in a.

This is a mathematical property of multiplication. The only machine contingency that affects this result is the treatment of overflow, which is undefined. Every machine we have tested implements overflow by truncating, and this permits the multiplicative resilience we describe in this paper.

Multiplicative behavior upon overflow is undefined in the C/C++ spec [3]. Although there are some non-language compliant compiler-specific options that in some cases can alter the behavior of overflow, these are often ignored. Additionally, there are run-time checks that can be incorporated to detect the possibility of overflow prior to and after instruction execution; however, this functionality is in most cases compiler- and OS-specific, and is almost never enabled by default. Furthermore, this type of protection can be costly as it involves inserting additional instructions after every operation that may result in overflow, which can result in lower run-time performance [3]; an unwanted characteristic in HPC.

This illustrates how the implementation of undefined behavior might be used to affect the resilience of a given operation. For example, one might implement to recover the most significant bits upon overflow. This would not give the resilience to high-bit faults described here, but might give other forms of resilience.

Proposition 1. *Let multiplication overflow be implemented via truncation.*
Let n be the wordlength, let a be an n-bit integer having some number k of bitflips, and let b be an n-bit integer such that 2^j is the largest power of 2 dividing b, so $b = 2^j \times b'$ and b' is odd.
Let h be the bit of smallest index in a (where indices start at 0) that is flipped. Then $a \times b$ gives the same answer pre- and post-bitflip if and only if $h \geq n - j$.

In the next two corollaries, we consider the case where overflow does not occur in the original multiplication $a \times b$. We do this as these corollaries are concerned with correctness, and the calculation will not be correct if there is overflow.

Corollary 1. *Let the conditions on a, b, h and the bitflips be as in Proposition 1, and let a × b give the same answer pre- and post-bitflip. If a × b does not produce overflow, then $a_{bitflipped} \times b$ will be correct.*

Corollary 2. *If b is odd, a × b will always be in error.*
If b is even, a × b may be correct, if the faults in a fall into the right bits and a × b does not produce overflow.

2.2 Probability of Benign Faults on a Uniform Fault Model

We calculate the probability of faults before integer multiply being benign, where an arbitrary k faults following a uniform distribution are injected into n-bit signed integers a or b.

Let $0 \le a < 2^m$ and $0 \le b < 2^m$, for some number of bits m, with $m < n$. We permit faults to fall anywhere in the n available bits. A special case of this calculation is when a and b vary over all n-bit signed integers, so $m = n - 1$.

We note that Proposition 1 may be applied to an arbitrary fault model (including one resulting from a data protection scheme with some SDC). Given the fault rate (protected or not) for a particular hardware or the number of undetected faults possible for a particular ECC scheme, the combinatorial calculation may be performed for that rate or number of faults.

General Probability of Benign Faults. To calculate the overall probability of a benign result after k bitflips, we calculate the number of benign results after k faults, and divide by the total number of (a, b) pairs having k faults. This gives the probability of a benign result.

$$\frac{benign\ (a, b, faults)}{total\ (a, b, faults)}$$

We count the total number of $(a, b \neq 0, faults)$ triples by calculating a sum ranging over the set of $b \neq 0$, so ranging from 1 to $2^m - 1$. For each a corresponding to a b, there are $\binom{n}{k}$ ways of choosing k faults on n bits.

Let *num_benign_a_b* be the number of a corresponding to each $b \neq 0$ having 0 s in the j least significant bits and set of k faults. This number will differ according to the conditions imposed on a and b (i.e., overflow allowed or not in their product). We leave *num_benign_a_b* as a general variable, and obtain

$$\frac{\binom{n}{k}2^m + \sum_{j=k}^{m-1} \binom{j}{k} \sum_{i=0}^{2^{(m-j-1)}-1} num\_benign\_a_b}{\binom{n}{k}2^m + \sum_{b=1}^{2^m-1} \binom{n}{k} num\_a_b} \quad (1)$$

Formula (1) is the general expression of the probability of a benign result upon k bitflips. We now distinguish between the cases where $a \times b$ is permitted to produce overflow, and where $a \times b$ is not.

Probability of Benign Faults When Overflow is Permitted. Since overflow is permitted, the multiply calculation will not get the correct answer if it does overflow. For this case, then, we do not look for correctness per se, but merely ask that the multiply get the same answers in the faulty and fault-free calculations.

num_a_b is the total number of a corresponding to each $b \neq 0$ and set of k faults. We do not care if $a \times b$ overflows, so all a are eligible, and num_a_b is 2^m.

$num\_benign\_a_b$ is the number of a corresponding to each $b \neq 0$ having 0 s in the j least significant bits and set of k faults. Again, there are 2^m of these.

Substituting 2^m for num_a_b and $num\_benign\_a_b$ in Formula (1), we obtain

$$\frac{\binom{n}{k}2^m + \sum_{j=k}^{m-1} \binom{j}{k} \sum_{i=0}^{2^{(m-j-1)}-1} 2^m}{\binom{n}{k}2^m + \sum_{b=1}^{2^m-1} \binom{n}{k}2^m}$$

This reduces to

$$\frac{\binom{n}{k} + \sum_{j=k}^{m-1} \left(\binom{j}{k}2^{(m-j-1)}\right)}{\binom{n}{k}2^m} \tag{2}$$

Proposition 2. *Let integers a and b of word length n and bitlength m be multiplied, with overflow permitted, and let k faults occur in one of the integers. Then the probability of masked-benign results in this integer multiply increases as word length n decreases. In other words, the resilience of integer multiply with overflow permitted increases with shorter word length.*

Probability of Benign Faults When Overflow is Not Permitted. In this case, a and b are chosen so that $a \times b$ does not overflow. This is the meaningful case, since overflow multiply values are incorrect.

This restriction means that $a \times b \leq 2^{n-1} - 1$, or $a \leq \frac{2^{n-1}-1}{b}$. We have the additional restriction that both a and b are less than 2^m. We find values for num_a_b and $num\_benign\_a_b$ and substitute them in to Formula 1, for a probability in the no-overflow case.

We obtain the following values for num_a_b and $num\_benign\_a_b$:

$$num\_a_b = \min(2^m, \lfloor \frac{2^{(n-1)} - 1}{b} \rfloor + 1)$$

$$num\_benign\_a_b = \min(2^m, \lfloor \frac{2^{(n-1)} - 1}{2^j \times (2i+1)} \rfloor + 1)$$

and obtain an overall probability in the case of no overflow of

$$\frac{\binom{n}{k}2^m + \sum_{j=k}^{m-1} \left(\binom{j}{k} \sum_{i=0}^{2^{(m-j-1)}-1} \min(2^m, \lfloor \frac{2^{(n-1)}-1}{2^j \times (2i+1)} \rfloor + 1)\right)}{\binom{n}{k}\left(2^m + \sum_{b=1}^{2^m-1} \min(2^m, \lfloor \frac{2^{(n-1)}-1}{b} \rfloor + 1)\right)} \tag{3}$$

Conjecture 1. Let integers a and b of wordlength n and bitlength m be multiplied, with overflow not permitted, and let k faults occur in one of the integers. Then the probability of masked-benign results in this integer multiply increases as wordlength n decreases. In other words, the resilience of integer multiply with overflow not permitted increases with shorter word length.

All experimental evidence we have generated supports this conjecture. The conjecture is clearly true in the case where $m \leq \lfloor \frac{n}{2} \rfloor$, for word lengths $\geq n$: this reduces to the overflow case described in Proposition 2, since no two m-bitlength integers multiplied together can have more than $2m \leq n$ bits, so cannot overflow.

Special Case: 1 Bitflip with Overflow Permitted. We calculate this case explicitly because it reduces to such a simple form. Setting $m = n-1$, and $k = 1$ gives the following formula directly from Formula 2.

$$\frac{n + \sum_{j=1}^{n-2} j \times 2^{(n-j-2)}}{n \times 2^{(n-1)}} = \frac{1}{n} \tag{4}$$

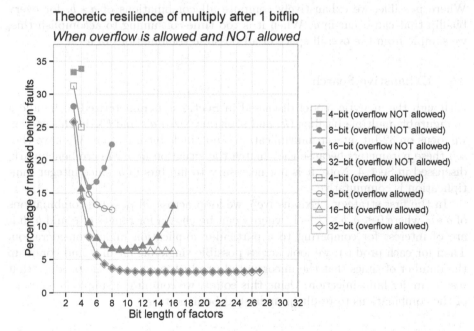

Fig. 1. Results from the analytical model when a and b are chosen such that overflow will not occur in $a * b$ as well as when overflow is allowed to occur (calculated only to bitlength of a and b equal to 27, because of the large amount of time needed to compute the summations for larger bitlength). Note the relatively high percentage of multiplicative resilience when the bitlength of the factors is smaller compared to the architectural width.

2.3 Implications

The theoretical results have three implications: (1) There is non-trivial resilience occurring naturally in multiply, contingent only on overflow handling, (2) Resilience is better when overflow is not permitted on the product of a and b, and (3) Improved resilience is obtained in some cases by using the smallest wordlength possible for a variable (experimental evidence supports this in all cases).

Figure 1 represents the resilience of multiply when a and b have been screened to preclude overflow as well as when overflow is allowed. The results for the two sets of data are the same, up to the point where bitlength of a and b are about half of wordlength. After that, when overflow is allowed, we see continued decreasing convergence to the resilience when a and b are the entire wordlength.

3 Experimental Verification via Exhaustive Multiplication Testing

We verify the theoretical model described in Sect. 2 by simply multiplying integers after bitflips, and calculating the percentage of time the product is correct. Where possible, we exhaustively compute all combinations of $a * b$, for every bit-flip that can occur in a. When it is too time-consuming to accomplish this, we sample from the overall space of all possible combinations of $a * b$.

3.1 Exhaustive Search

Although the analytic model discussed in Sect. 2 is parameterized to handle a configurable multiple bit-flips (k) and arbitrary-sized a's and b's, in this section we focus on 32-bit integer multiplication, and single bit-flips to a. We have chosen these parameters because they match the situation in our micro benchmark, discussed in Sect. 4. Note, it is not necessary to flip bits in b, since integer multiplication is commutative.

In the first strategy, "Exhaustive", we loop across all possible combinations of $a * b$, where $0 \leq a, b \leq 2^i - 1$, where i can be chosen for ranges of a and b that are of interest for comparing to a particular application under consideration. Then for each product, we look across possible single-bit bit-flips and count up the number of times that the uncorrupted product is equal to the product that results under fault injection. Using this count, we compute a simple percentage of the combinations to result in unmasked benign errors.

3.2 Sampled Search

The above "Exhaustive" strategy works well, provided that the ranges of a and b are small enough that the total number of combinations does not become prohibitively expensive to compute. For the machine used in this research, the "cut-off" point for 32-bit integers occurs when i is chosen to be larger than

Table 1. The correspondence between theoretical calculations and experimental results for 32-bit wordlength. Entries represent the percentage of benign bitflips. Experimental and theoretical values are an exact match where we tested exhaustively (bitlength up to 17), and are a close match where we sampled (bitlength greater than 17).

Bitlength	Experiment: no overflow	Theory: no overflow	Experiment: overflow	Theory: overflow
3	25.78%	25.78%	25.78%	25.78%
4	14.06%	14.06%	14.06%	14.06%
5	8.40%	8.40%	8.40%	8.40%
6	5.66%	5.66%	5.66%	5.66%
7	4.35%	4.35%	4.35%	4.35%
8	3.71%	3.71%	3.71%	3.71%
9	3.41%	3.41%	3.41%	3.41%
...	...	...	...	...
25	3.17%	3.18%	3.13%	3.13%
26	3.23%	3.22%	3.13%	3.13%
27	3.23%	3.30%	3.13%	3.13%
28	3.39%	–	3.13%	–
29	3.65%	–	3.13%	–
30	4.15%	–	3.13%	–
31	6.45%	–	3.13%	–
32	6.91%	–	3.13%	–

roughly 17 bits. As such, we were interested in a sampled approach that would allow us to verify the theoretic model for larger values of i. We refer to this strategy as "Sampled". It is similar to the prior strategy in that we look across all possible values of b, but that for each of these values, we randomly choose a, $0 \leq a \leq 2^i - 1$, and then randomly flip one of a's 32 bits. The number of trials across a, a_trials, is chosen to be large enough to give an adequate sampling in a, without the need to iterate across all possible a, as is done in the "Exhaustive" approach.

3.3 Comparison of Experimentation to Theoretical Model

We show in Table 1 a set of experimental results and theoretical calculations for single bitflips on 32-bit integers. When a and b have bitlength greater than 18, we sampled as above, but otherwise we exhaustively tested every $a, b, bitflip$ combination possible. *Note, the results for bits 14 to 22 were identical to those for bits 13 and 23, and were therefore omitted from table in the interest of space.*

As seen in the table, the theoretical model exactly matches the experimental data from the exhaustive testing, and matches very closely the sampled data. In every case we tested, the experimental results matched the theoretic model. When we conducted an exhaustive experiment, the experimental probabilities matched the theoretical calculation exactly. When we sampled, for larger wordlength and bitlength, the sampled results were extremely close.

The theoretical formula is a double summation depending on bitlength and has high time complexity, so can be hard to calculate for large bitlength. Entries in the table represented as "–" denotes these missing calculations. Sampling and multiplying (a,b) pairs is a Monte Carlo method of approximating the theoretical calculations, and in practice converges fast to a useable solution. The experiment columns thus adequately represent the percentage where we did not do the full theoretical calculation.

4   Experimental Verification via Matrix Multiplication Micro-Benchmark

We verify multiplicative resilience in another way by running a common fault-tolerant matrix multiplication algorithm [2,8,9] (ABFT-MM). We injected faults into randomly selected multiplication operands as the inner-products are computed, and observed how often faults were actually caught and corrected. This also allows us to observe the results of multiplicative resilience on more complex code similar to algorithms run in the field.

We provide the results of extensive experimentation under random fault injection and compare these results to those predicted by the theoretical model, as well as those obtained via the sampling multiplicative test discussed in Sects. 2 and 3.

4.1   ABFT-MM Experimentation and Results

We present the results of studying an integer implementation of ABFT MM in the presence of injected faults using the F-SEFI fault injector [6] based on QEMU [1]. In this benchmark, we targeted the fault injection on the traditional triply-nested FOR LOOP structure of the dense matrix multiply. Specifically, we used F-SEFI to corrupt a single randomly-chosen bit in the output of a randomly-chosen IMUL operation in the algorithm's inner-product calculation.

Our benchmark included roughly 60,000 matrix multiplication trials within F-SEFI. In each of these trials, both input matrices A and B were randomly generated where each element, e, ranged from $0 \leq e \leq 2^i - 1$, for $3 \leq i \leq 7$, giving a bitlength of $i + 1$ for signed integers. These ranges were chosen to illustrate the impact of increasing used bitlengths while at the same time, were capped by 127 so as to guarantee that overflow would not occur during the dot-product calculation for matrices of size 45×45 using 32-bit signed integer datatypes.

After each execution, a pre-computed "golden" answer for the matrix product under fault injection, C', was compared to the result of the ABFT MM after error detection and correction to determine whether the algorithm had successfully detected and corrected any errors in C'.

Table 2. Masked Benign error rates

Bit-length	4	5	6	7	8
ABFT-MM	14.1%	8.2%	5.82%	4.32%	3.84%
Theoretical	14.06%	8.4%	5.66%	4.35%	3.71%
Exhaustive	14.06%	8.4%	5.66%	4.35%	3.71%
Sampled	14.06%	8.4%	5.66%	4.35%	3.73%

These results in Table 2 also provide data that allows us to easily compare the empirical results from ABFT-MM under fault injection in F-SEFI with data derived from the theoretical model and other experimental models discussed in Sects. 2 and 3.2. These results show that under fault injection, the percentage of benign errors in ABFT-MM closely matches those predicted by the theoretical model.

5   Preliminary Results on Other Operations

5.1   Experimental Results

We have experimentally demonstrated that this masked benign behavior is not unique to integer multiplication. By making use of the exhaustive search strategy, we explore the resilience of integer division, and modulo, and contrast these with our prior findings for integer multiplication, as shown in Fig. 2. It should be noted that while multiplication is commutative, division and modulo are not, and as such, we provide experimental results for each operation, a **OP** b, both where the bitflip is in a and also where the bitflip is in b, as well as an average across these two results.

These experimental results are provocative, and strongly suggest that this masked benign behavior is present in operations beyond integer multiplication. With this in mind, we intend to explore other integer and floating point arithmetic operations, from both an experimental and theoretical point of view, in our future work.

5.2   Partial Theory of Division Resilience

We present here some preliminary results on the resilience of the integer division operator. We examine the case where only the numerator experiences bitflips, and show experimental verification of the propositions and experimental support for the conjectures. Again, we do not present the proofs of these, in the interest of brevity.

Experimental evidence shows that integer division is much more resilient than integer multiply. Future work will include a complete demonstration as shown earlier for the integer multiplication operator.

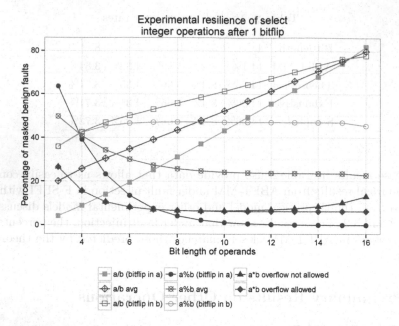

Fig. 2. Results from an exhaustive search for 16-bit a and b space, testing every possible bitflip on a or b as specified, for integer multiplication, division and modulo. Note the relatively high percentage of resilience across each of these operations.

This gives a path forward for the case of the division operator, and demonstrates that a mathematical approach to resilience on arithmetic operators completely shown for multiplication may be extended to other operators.

Division Resilience When Numerator Has an Arbitrary Number of Bitflips. As a proof of concept, we consider the case where only the numerator experiences bitflips.

Proposition 3. *Let b be an n-bit integer equal to 2^k for some k, and let a be an integer such that $0 \le a < 2^n$. Assuming equal probability for any combination of bitflips, the overall percentage of correct answers on $\frac{a}{b}$ when a experiences some number of bitflips is $\frac{2^k}{2^n} = \frac{1}{2^{n-k}}$.*

Conjecture 2. Let b be an n-bit integer, not necessarily a power of 2, and let a be an integer such that $0 \le a < 2^n$. Assuming equal probability for any combination of bitflips, then the overall percentage of correct answers on integer divide when bitflips occur only on a is close to $\frac{b}{2^n}$.

Proposition 4. *Let b be an n-bit integer equal to 2^k for some k, and let a be an integer such that $0 \le a < 2^n$. Then the overall percentage of correct answers on $\frac{a}{b}$ when a experiences m bitflips is $\frac{\binom{k}{m}}{\binom{n}{m}}$.*

Corollary 3. *Let b be an n-bit integer equal to 2^k for some k, and let a be an integer such that $0 \leq a < 2^n$. Let $p(i)$ be the probability that i faults occur in a given fault model. Then the overall probability of correct results using that fault model on integer divide when bitflips occur only on a is $\sum_0^n p(i) \frac{\binom{k}{i}}{\binom{n}{i}}$*

6 Conclusion

Providing an analytic model for the impact that soft errors have on low-level operations forms the basis for establishing confidence in any injection-based empirical study. In this work, we've established this model for integer multiplication and have begun investigation into other integer operations. Furthermore, we have shown a non-trivial multiplicative resilience under the integer multiplication operator and have experimentally shown that the resilience increases as wordlength gets shorter, and that our analytic models are clearly supported through extensive experimentation that also shows promise for other integer operators as well.

References

1. Bellard, F.: QEMU, a fast and portable dynamic translator. In: Proceedings of USENIX Annual Technical Conference (ATEC) (2005)
2. Bosilca, G., Delmas, R., Dongarra, J., Langou, J.: Algorithm-based fault tolerance applied to high performance computing. J. Parallel Distrib. Comput. **69**(4), 410–416 (2009)
3. Dietz, W., Li, P., Regehr, J., Adve, V.: Understanding integer overflow in c/c++. In: Proceedings of the 34th International Conference on Software Engineering, ICSE 2012, pp. 760–770. IEEE Press, Piscataway (2012). http://dl.acm.org/citation.cfm?id=2337223.2337313
4. Elliott, J., Hoemmen, M., Mueller, F.: Exploiting data representation for fault tolerance. J. Comput. Sci. (2016). http://www.sciencedirect.com/science/article/pii/S1877750315300491
5. Guan, Q., DeBardeleben, N., Artkinson, B., Robey, R., Jones, W.M.: Towards building resilient scientific applications: resilience analysis on the impact of soft error and transient error tolerance with the CLAMR hydrodynamics mini-app. In: 2015 IEEE International Conference on Cluster Computing, pp. 176–179, September 2015
6. Guan, Q., Debardeleben, N., Blanchard, S., Fu, S.: F-SEFI: a fine-grained soft error fault injection tool for profiling application vulnerability. In: 2014 IEEE 28th International Parallel and Distributed Processing Symposium, May 2014
7. Guan, Q., DeBardeleben, N., Blanchard, S., Fu, S.: Empirical studies of the soft error susceptibility of sorting algorithms to statistical fault injection. In: Proceedings of the 5th Workshop on Fault Tolerance for HPC at eXtreme Scale, FTXS 2015, NY, USA, pp. 35–40 (2015). http://doi.acm.org/10.1145/2751504.2751512
8. Huang, K.H., Abraham, J.: Algorithm-based fault tolerance for matrix operations. IEEE Trans. Comput. **C–33**(6), 518–528 (1984)
9. Jou, J.Y., Abraham, J.: Fault-tolerant matrix arithmetic and signal processing on highly concurrent computing structures. Proc. IEEE **74**(5), 732–741 (1986)

Pragma-Controlled Source-to-Source Code Transformations for Robust Application Execution

Pedro C. Diniz[1]([✉]), Chunhua Liao[2], Daniel J. Quinlan[2], and Robert F. Lucas[1]

[1] USC Information Sciences Institute,
4676 Admiralty Way, Suite 1001, Marina del Rey, CA 90292, USA
{pedro,rflucas}@isi.edu
[2] Lawrence Livermore National Laboratory,
7000 East Avenue, Livermore, CA 94550, USA
{liao6,dquinlan}@llnl.gov

Abstract. The most widely used resiliency approach today, based on Checkpoint and Restart (C/R) recovery, is not expected to remain viable in the presence of the accelerated fault and error rates in future Exascale-class systems. In this paper, we introduce a series of pragma directives and the corresponding source-to-source transformations that are designed to convey to a compiler, and ultimately a fault-aware run-time system, key information about the tolerance to memory errors in selected sections of an application. These directives, implemented in the ROSE compiler infrastructure, convey information about storage mapping and error tolerance but also amelioration and recovery using externally provided functions and multi-threading. We present preliminary results of the use of a subset of these directives for a simple implementation of the conjugate-gradient numerical solver in the presence of uncorrected memory errors, showing that it is possible to implement simple recovery strategies with very low programmer effort and execution time overhead.

1 Introduction

The resilience of High Performance Computing (HPC) applications in the presence of faults and errors on future extreme scale supercomputing systems is a growing concern. With process technology scaling, future exascale-class systems will be constructed from transistor devices which are less reliable than those used today. Furthermore, the recent trend of aggressive scaling of processor cores and memory chips in order to drive floating-point performance suggests that future exascale class systems will require exponential growth in compute and memory resources [1,13]. However, with increase in the number of system components, the overall reliability of the system will decrease proportionally. The projections on fault rates based on current HPC systems and technology roadmaps predict that exascale class systems will experience several errors per day. This will impact long running scientific applications which will terminate abnormally, or worse, may complete with incorrect results [4].

© Springer International Publishing AG 2017
F. Desprez et al. (Eds.): Euro-Par 2016 Workshops, LNCS 10104, pp. 660–670, 2017.
DOI: 10.1007/978-3-319-58943-5_53

The de-facto approach used today to provide resilient operation is based on Checkpoint and Restart (C/R) which periodically commits the application state to persistent storage. Recovery is initiated only upon failure of a process and entails terminating all the remaining processes and restarting the application from the latest stable global checkpoint. If unchecked by aggressively reducing its frequency and/or the volume of saved data, this approach is inviable. As the applications scale to leverage the capabilities of these large scale machines, the amount of state to be gathered will grow considerably, resulting in proportional increases in the intervals required to create and commit checkpoints as well as recover them from storage. Given that the projected Mean Time to Failure (MTTF) of the exascale systems will be of the order of a few minutes [1], C/R will no longer be effective in scenarios where the C/R interval is greater than the system MTTF.

Still, various HPC applications offer rich possibilities to algorithmically detect and correct the errors in their program state. Algorithm-based fault tolerance (ABFT) [2,9] techniques for linear algebra kernels enable the identification of the error location and correction of bit flip errors using checksum error encoding in the data structures and adapting the algorithms to operate on the encoded data. Similarly, iterative numerical algorithms such as the Adaptive Multi-Grid Solver [5], can tolerate errors at the expense of longer convergence rates or iterations. Even more extreme, algorithms that rely on *random* events, as is the case of algorithm that leverage Monte-Carlo simulation techniques can (in specific contexts) tolerate memory errors provided they do not lead to catastrophic program behavior. Yet, in the face of the wealth of such application acceptability or tolerance characteristics, such algorithmic features are not exposed to the programming environment due to the lack of convenient interfaces.

In this paper, we extend our previous approach that is based on programming model extensions that incorporates simple language-level support that is tightly coupled with the compiler and runtime system to adaptively and dynamically apply redundancy [11,12]. The approach allows users to specify various detections conditions that strongly suggest silent-data corruption in addition to the traditional error detection through abnormal program execution. The programming model extension described here is based on #pragma directives which are then translated as source-to-source code transformations to support application level detection and recovery strategies through retry and multi-threading checking and correction semantics. These detection and recovery mechanisms can be coupled with an introspection runtime system enabling the use of redundant multithreading when too many faults are observed. We have implemented these directives and the corresponding code transformations in the ROSE Compiler Infrastructure [16] and use them to demonstrate their suitability to an illustrative scientific kernel – the conjugate gradient iterative solver. The results, albeit very preliminary, do reveal that with very little programming effort, this pragma-based code transformations approach substantially increases the ability of selected section of codes to survive uncorrected memory errors.

2   Pragma-Based Code Transformation Directives

We next present the various pragma directives and illustrate their use via source-to-source transformations and examples. We begin with the simplest forms where fault-tolerance is indicated to very sophisticated source code transformations where detection and recovery with redundant code execution is used.

2.1   Hardware Error Detection and Correction

In this work we assume that some, but not all the memory faults are corrected via hardware mechanisms such as Error-Correcting-Codes (ECC) and chipKill [14]. As such, the only faults that are signaled via hardware that trigger the execution of the amelioration actions defined by the directives described here, include detected but uncorrected memory errors.[1]

2.2   Tolerant Storage Declaration

This first *tolerant* directive simply indicates that a specific data declaration (to follow the directive) can tolerate a specific maximum number of (uncorrected) errors. Alternatively, when present, the directive also indicates that the corresponding data structure should be placed in a specific data storage as indicated by a secondary integer identifier.[2] The directive has the syntax shown below where exp1 and (the optional) exp2 denote compile-time integer values.

```
#pragma failsafe tolerant ( exp1 : exp2 )
```

A simple example of the use of this directive is shown below where the array A is to be allocated preferentially to the storage labelled with id zero and can only tolerate 1 uncorrected error.

```
#pragma failsafe tolerant (1: 0)
int A[M][N];
```

In the absence of both expression exp1 and exp2 fields, the run-time system assumes that any number of errors are to be tolerated for this specific variable.

This pragma is also applicable to global variables or heap-allocated variables, although the later needs to be explicitly controlled by the use of a tolerant variant

---

[1] As a minor point, we further assume that upon restart (via state restore) data is flush out of cache storages so that erroneous values are not restore as part of the application's state.

[2] We envision a memory system where distinct regions of the storage space have distinct resilience characteristics each of which is identified by a unique numerical or symbolic identifier.

of malloc[3]. The variable to be associated with this behavior can either be a scalar or a statically allocated arrays. In case of a pointer variable, it is the pointer that needs to be labelled as tolerant but not the heap-allocated storage it points to. To that effect we also provide a variant of the `malloc` function labelled as `tolerant_malloc(size, N, K)`. Upon parsing and translation the compiler will produce a simple text file, with the scope of the variables labelled as tolerant and the corresponding statically declared name including the numeric values for `exp1` and `exp2`.

This tolerant data is then parsed by the run-time system and can be incorporated as part of an introspection system. As variables that are deemed less tolerant reach their limit of tolerated errors, they can be migrated to increasingly more robust regions of the address space thus allowing a run-time system to dynamically manage the underlying state of the machine while meeting (or at least attempting to meet) the tolerance requirements of each data structure.

2.3   Sentinel Values for Silent Data Corruption Detection

These constructs, akin to the `#assert` specify a user-defined predicates that must hold at specific execution points of the application. Using these pragmas the user can attempt to correct silent data or uncorrected errors in specific variables and thus proceed with the computation. Still, and even in the event of user amelioration, error variables record the error events and interface with a resilience introspection engine for subsequent application adaptivity.

The syntax of this pragma is shown below and it is the programmers responsibility to ensure that the evaluation scope of the arguments of the handler functions and assertion predicates are appropriately scoped.

```
#pragma failsafe assert ( predicate ) error ( function handler )
```

A simple example of the use of this pragma is shown below:

```
#pragma failsafe assert ( a > 0 ) error ( MyFunction(&b))
```

where it is assumed that `MyFunction` is an integer-returning function and where a non-zero value will indicate the inability to correct an erroneous condition and a zero valued return success in correcting such situation. The translation of the above directive in terms of source C code is as shown below.

---

[3] Automatically, converting the heap-allocated use of a malloc into a tolerant-malloc is rather tricky to do statically as in the general case a compiler would have to track the use of address as function argument and allocation across procedure boundaries to understand when the address of a pointer could have been declared in another scope as tolerant. As a results we restrict the use of this pragma to the storage that is statically allocated either at the file or at the global scope levels.

```
if ( predicate ( ... )  ==  0){
  if ( function_handler  ( ... )  != 0){
    failsafe_error++;
    FAILSAFE_REPORT_ERROR ( 0 , failsafe_error );
    failsafe_error_flag = 0;
  } else {
    FAILSAFE_REPORT_CORRECTION ( 0 , failsafe_error );
  }
}
```

In the absence of the **error** clause, and should the predicate evaluation not hold at runtime, the generated code will terminate the applications execution via the **exit** function as illustrated in the sample code below.

```
if ( predicate ( ... )  ==  0){
  FAILSAFE_REPORT_ERROR_EXIT ( 0 );
}
```

2.4 User-Controlled State Saving and Restoring with Retry

In order to provide users with the capability to control the saving and restoring of program state, we have included a save/restore directive. The directive thus include which program variables constitute relevant program state that needs to be saved and restored and for how many retries the execution of the subsequence control-flow program blocks should be attempted.

This directive can be combined with the assert pragmas described above to detect erroneous execution conditions resulted from silent data corruption.

```
#pragma failsafe save_restore ( var_list ) retry ( exp )
{/* code block */ }
```

This directive is translated into code that saves the state of the set of variables listed in the **var_list** into auxiliary variable via a memory copy construct[4] Upon detection of an uncorrected error in the code block, the control is transferred to the beginning of the block with the state of the saved variable reinstated. The snippet of code below depicts the structure of the generated code as the result of the translation of this directive for a retry value of 2.

```
int fs_num_tries;
volatile int fs_num_errors;
fs_num_tries  = 0;
fs_num_errors = 0;
<code for saving data objects>
do {
  if ( fs_num_tries != 0){
```

---

[4] In the current implementation only supports scalar and statically allocated array variables with known compile-time bounds. The support of dynamically allocated arrays with multiple pointer levels can, however, pose serious implementation challenges in terms of correctness and performance.

```
    <code for restore data objects>
    }
    fs_num_errors = 0;
    <original code block here>
    fs_num_tries++;
} while ((fs_num_errors != 0) && (fs_num_tries < 2));
if (fs_num_errors != 0){
    FAIL_SAFE_EXCEPTION();
}
```

2.5   Redundancy-Based Fault Detection and Recovery

In addition to the pragmas described above, we have also implemented two simple redundancy-based detection and recovery pragmas, namely, using dual and triple computing redundancy that can in some context detect and correct, respectively, errors in the computation by direct comparison of the values in a selected lists of variables. As with the previous pragma directive, a maximum number of retries is attempted before an abnormal execution is reported.

```
#pragma failsafe dual_redundancy save_restore ( var_list1 )
compare ( var_list2 ) retry ( exp )
{ /* code block */ }
```

In addition to the aspects of computation redundancy this directive extends the notion of redundancy by including dual and triple threading (using the OpenMP directives) and detection of errors via the direct comparison of a selected set of variables specified in the compare list var_list2 which is assumed to be disjoint of var_list1 the former list assumed to be the *output* of the code block. In other words all the variables in var_list1 are output variables of the computation so their state need not be saved and restored upon re-execution.

For a simple but generic code, the dual_redundancy directive can be translated into the source code as shown below with a maximum retry of 2 times. The triple_redundancy variant would include three OpenMP threads and three, rather than two, copies of the variable specified in the compare list.

```
int fs_num_tries;
volatile int fs_num_errors;
< declaration of duplicated of variables in var_list2 >
...
fs_num_tries = 0;
fs_num_errors = 0;
<code for saving data in var_list1 >
do
    if (fs_num_tries != 0){
        <code for restore data in var list1 >
    }
    fs_num_errors = 0;
```

```
#omp parallel num_threads(2)
{
    <original code relabeling variables in var_list2>
}

  <compare variables in var_list2 for each thread>

 if(mismatch(var_list2))
    fs_num_errors++;
   fs_num_tries++;
} while ((fs_num_errors != 0) && (fs_num_tries < 2));
if(fs_num_errors != 0){
   FAIL_SAFE_EXCEPTION();
}
```

The code variant for triple redundancy, includes a voting functions rather than a compare function to determine of the three concurrent threads have executed correctly.

3   Experimental Evaluation

We conducted a set of preliminary experiments to evaluate the ability of the proposed program pragmas to lead to applications that survive uncorrected (but detected) memory errors.

For these experiments we focused on a key numerical kernel code, the popular conjugate-gradient iterative linear system solver for the system $Ax = b$. We used an input 40×32 A matrix with a specific structure with a randomly generated b vector as the linear system to be solved. The algorithm requires about 4 MBytes of storage for the system matrix and 0.223 MBytes for the auxiliary intermediate computation vectors. As the system matrix A remains constant throughout the computation, we opted to use checksum column- and row-wise error correction for detected but uncorrected memory errors afflicting the address space regions associated with A.

For these experiments we use the fault-injection infrastructure described in [10] to inject memory errors in the data address space of the application at specific error rates, leading to approximately a single memory error per algorithm iteration to one error per 20 iterations (or a single error per system solve cycle). In these experiments we do not inject errors in the code section of the application address space.

For the errors impinging on data section we opt from two different amelioration strategies. When the error impinging on A we recover by executing the error correction using the column- and row-wise checksums and restart the solver iteration. When the memory error impinges on the auxiliary vectors, we restart the iteration of the algorithm using the previous iterations values of the x vector only as all the other vectors used are temporaries[5]

---

[5] In the parlance of the compiler analysis, there vectors can be privatizable as no data flows across iterations of the loop through them.

The Table 1 below present the numerical results showing the overhead of the use of the `#pragma failsafe save_restore` directive for this example. In the absence of any error of software copy overhead, the specific linear system requires 21 iterations to converge for a preselected numerical convergence tolerance over 10.680 secs for a sequential execution on a desktop computing system.

Table 1. Execution times vs. injected memory rates for CG simple solver.

Error Interval (secs)	Checksum Recovery	Iteration restart Recovery	Algorithm Iterations	Execution Time (secs)	Execution Overhead
2	12	1	34	23.761	122.5%
4	5	1	27	20.537	92.3%
5	4	1	26	18.569	73.9%
10	1	1	23	15.368	4.5%
20	1	0	22	11.310	0.6%

A couple of simple observations are in order. First, in this controlled experiments, all executions are survivable as the error rate is not high enough that the maximum number of retries (set at 2) for the same iteration of the algorithm is ever exceeded. Second, as the storage size of the matrix A dwarfs the storage space of the auxiliary vectors it was thus expected that the number of errors impinging on the matrix A. As such the retries with checksum correctness and copy of previous state are more numerous (and also computationally more expensive) that simple retries where the only the vector x and a couple of integer control variables need to be restated.

4   Implementation Status

We have implemented the parsing and the corresponding source-to-source code transformations of the `#pragma` directives described here in the ROSE compiler infrastructure [16] and tested them for simple C programs. Still, the current implementation has some limitations. First, the code generation for the directives can only support the comparison and voting of the values of either scalar variables or statically declared arrays with compile-time dimension bounds. In other words, we do not yet support the use of dynamically allocated arrays. Second, there is currently no checking of the disjointness of the compare and save/restore list of variables in the redundancy directives. Lastly, there is also no data-flow analysis verification that the variables in the `compare` list are strictly output, *i.e.*, only output variables.

5   Related Work

The most widely HPC programming models do not contain capabilities to offer error resilient application execution. However, various researchers have begun exploring the possibility of incorporating resiliency capabilities into the programming models. The abstraction of transactions has been proposed to capture programmers fault tolerance knowledge. The basic idea is that the application code is divided into blocks of code at the end of which the results of the computation or communication are checked for correctness before proceeding. If the block execution condition is not met, the results are discarded and the block can be re-executed. Such an approach was proposed for HPC applications through the concept of Containment Domains [6] which are based on weak transactional semantics. They enforce the check for correctness of the data value generated within the containment domain before it is communicated to other domains. These domains can be hierarchical and provide means for local error recovery.

Other research has focused on discovery idempotent regions of code that can be freely re-executed without the need to checkpoint and restart program state. Their original proposal however [15] was based on language level support for C/C++ that allowed the application developer to define idempotent regions through specification of relax blocks and recover blocks that perform recovery when a fault occurs. The FaultTM scheme adapts the concept of hardware based transactional memory where atomicity of computation is guaranteed. The approach entails application programmer created vulnerable sections of code for which a backup thread is created. Both the original and the backup thread are executed as atomic transactions and their respective committed result values compared [17].

Complementary to approaches that focus on resiliency of computational blocks, the Global View of Resiliency (GVR) project [8] concentrates on application data and guarantees resilience through multiple snapshot versions of the data whose creation is controlled by the programmer through program annotations. Bridges *et al.* [3] proposed a `malloc_failable` that uses a callback mechanism with the library to handle memory failures on dynamically allocated memory, so that the application programmer can specify recovery actions. In the Global Arrays Partitioned Global Address Space (PGAS) implementation, set of library API for checkpoint and restart with bindings for C/C++/FORTRAN the enable the application programmer to create array checkpoints [7].

6   Conclusion and Future Work

The very limited experiments presented here do confirm the potential benefits of the programming language extension to increase the survivability rate of iterative scientific algorithms such as the case of *conjugate gradient* linear solvers. Here we have only exploited the use of a limited form of computation redundancy for error detection and amelioration.

Clearly, an extension of the practical impact of the use of the proposed `#pragma` directives needs to be carried out, in particular to algorithms other than scientific iterative solvers. In particular, we are actively working on the concurrent threading implementation which require the manipulation of the state of the shared cache storage.

This work also suggests a richer interface that would allow programmer to control the need to restore state of the program based on the progress of the algorithm. This is the case of storage whose life-time includes long periods of inactivity and can thus be considered intermittently dead or simply not contributing to the corruption of further state. Such interface would clearly allow a run-time system to use less expensive recovery strategies than a full-blown computation or iteration restart.

Acknowledgment. Partial support for this work was provided by the US Army Research Office (Award W911NF-13-1-0219) and through the Scientific Discovery through Advanced Computing (SciDAC) program funded by U.S. Department of Energy, Office of Science, Advanced Scientific Computing Research under award number DE-SC0006844. This work was performed under the auspices of the U.S. Department of Energy by Lawrence Livermore National Laboratory under Contract DE-AC52-07NA27344.

References

1. Bergman, K., et. al: ExaScale computing study: technology challenges in achieving exascale systems (2008)
2. Bosilca, G., Delmas, R., Dongarra, J., Langou, J.: Algorithmic Based Fault Tolerance Applied to High Performance Computing. CoRR abs/0806.3121 (2008)
3. Bridges, P.G., Hoemmen, M., Ferreira, K.B., Heroux, M.A., Soltero, P., Brightwell, R.: Cooperative application/OS DRAM fault recovery. In: Alexander, M., et al. (eds.) Euro-Par 2011. LNCS, vol. 7156, pp. 241–250. Springer, Heidelberg (2012). doi:10.1007/978-3-642-29740-3_28
4. Cappello, F., Geist, A., Gropp, W., Kale, L., Kramer, W., Snir, M.: Toward exascale resilience. Int. J. High Perform. Comput. Appl. **23**(4), 374–388 (2009)
5. Casas, M., de Supinski, B.R., Bronevetsky, G., Schulz, M.: Fault resilience of the algebraic multi-grid solver. In: Proceedings of the 26th ACM International Conference on Supercomputing, ICS 2012, pp. 91–100 (2012)
6. Chung, J., Lee, I., Sullivan, M., Ryoo, J.H., Kim, D.W., Yoon, D.H., Kaplan, L., Erez, M.: Containment domains: a scalable, efficient, and flexible resilience scheme for exascale systems. In: Proceedings of the International Conference on High Performance Computing, Networking, Storage and Analysis, SC 2012, CA, USA, pp. 58:1–58:11. IEEE Computer Society Press, Los Alamitos (2012)
7. Dinan, J., Singri, A., Sadayappan, P., Krishnamoorthy, S.: Selective recovery from failures in a task parallel programming model. In: Proceedings of the 2010 10th IEEE/ACM International Conference on Cluster, Cloud and Grid Computing, CCGRID 2010, pp. 709–714. IEEE Computer Society, Washington, DC (2010)
8. Fujita, H., Schreiber, R., Chien, A.: Its time for new programming models for unreliable hardware, provocative ideas session. In: Proceedings of the International Conference on Architectural Support for Programming Languages and Operating Systems (ASPLOS) (2013)
9. Huang, K.H., Abraham, J.A.: Algorithm-based fault tolerance for matrix operations. IEEE Trans. Comput. **33**(6), 518–528 (1984)
10. Hukerikar, S., Diniz, P., Lucas, R.: A programming model for resilience in extreme scale computing. In: Proceedings of the Dependable Systems and Networks Workshops (DSN-W), June 2012

11. Hukerikar, S., Diniz, P., Lucas, R., Teranishi, K.: Opportunistic application-level fault detection through adaptive redundant multithreading. In: Proceedings of the International Conference on High Performance Computing Simulation (HPCS), pp. 243–250, July 2014
12. Hukerikar, S., Teranishi, K., Diniz, P., Lucas, R.: An evaluation of lazy fault detection based on adaptive redundant multithreading. In: Proceedings of the IEEE High Performance Extreme Computing Conference (HPEC), pp. 1–6, September 2014
13. Dongarra, J., et al.: The international exascale software project roadmap. Int. J. High Perform. Comput. Appl. **25**(1), 3–60 (2011)
14. Jian, X., Sartori, J., Duwe, H., Kumar, R.: High performance, energy efficient chipkill correct memory with multidimensional parity. IEEE Comput. Archit. Lett. **12**(2), 39–42 (2013)
15. de Kruijf, M., Nomura, S., Sankaralingam, K.: Relax: an architectural framework for software recovery of hardware faults. In: Proceedings of the 37th Annual International Symposium on Computer Architecture, ISCA 2010, NY, USA, pp. 497–508. ACM, New York (2010)
16. Quinlan, D., et. al: The ROSE Compiler Infrastructure. http://rosecompiler.org
17. Yalcin, G., Unsal, O., Cristal, A.: FaulTM: error detection and recovery using hardware transactional memory. In: Proceedings of the Conference on Design, Automation and Test in Europe (DATE), DATE 2013, San Jose, CA, USA, pp. 220–225 (2013)

A Cooperative Approach to Virtual Machine Based Fault Injection

Thomas Naughton[1](✉), Christian Engelmann[1], Geoffroy Vallée[1],
Ferrol Aderholdt[1], and Stephen L. Scott[1,2]

[1] Oak Ridge National Laboratory Computer Science and Mathematics Division,
Oak Ridge, TN 37831, USA
naughtont@ornl.gov
[2] Computer Science, Tennessee Tech University, Cookville, TN 38505, USA

Abstract. Resilience investigations often employ fault injection (FI)
tools to study the effects of simulated errors on a target system. It is
important to keep the target system under test (SUT) isolated from the
controlling environment in order to maintain control of the experiment.
Virtual machines (VMs) have been used to aid these investigations due
to the strong isolation properties of system-level virtualization. A key
challenge in fault injection tools is to gain proper insight and context
about the SUT. In VM-based FI tools, this challenge of target context is
increased due to the separation between host and guest (VM). We discuss
an approach to VM-based FI that leverages virtual machine introspection (VMI) methods to gain insight into the target's context running
within the VM. The key to this environment is the ability to provide
basic information to the FI system that can be used to create a map of
the target environment. We describe a proof-of-concept implementation
and a demonstration of its use to introduce simulated soft errors into an
iterative solver benchmark running in user-space of a guest VM.

Keywords: Fault injection · Virtualization · Virtual machine introspection · Resilience tools

1 Introduction

Tools for controllably experimenting with synthetic failures are an essential element of resilience investigation. These tools generally employ some form of software implemented fault injection (SWIFI) since it is highly adaptable, in contrast

T. Naughton—This manuscript has been authored by UT-Battelle, LLC under Contract No.DE-AC05-00OR22725 with the U.S. Department of Energy. The United
States Government retains and the publisher, by accepting the article for publication, acknowledges that the United States Government retains a non-exclusive,
paid-up, irrevocable, world-wide license to publish or reproduce the published form
of this manuscript, or allow others to do so, for United States Government purposes.
The Department of Energy will provide public access to these results of federally
sponsored research in accordance with the DOE Public Access Plan (http://energy.
gov/downloads/doe-public-access-plan).

© Springer International Publishing AG 2017
F. Desprez et al. (Eds.): Euro-Par 2016 Workshops, LNCS 10104, pp. 671–682, 2017.
DOI: 10.1007/978-3-319-58943-5_54

to hardware based approaches [11]. However, low-level hardware approaches have some advantages for performing tests that can originate at the lowest layers of the system. System-level virtualization has been explored as a way to combine the advantages of SWIFI with the low-level hardware oriented approaches using virtual machines (VMs) [14,18,21].

There are several advantages to using virtual machines with fault injection. The use of virtualization allows for strong isolation between the system under test (SUT) and control environment. The VMs provide a basis to customize the target environment and setup repeatable testing configurations. The strong isolation provided by the VMs can be beneficial for resilience experiments that might include tests that compromise the overall investigation environment, e.g., data corruption, high crash rates.

A major challenge of virtual machine based fault injection (VMFI) is providing adequate context about the target to inform site selection choices. Additionally, the target's context must be sufficiently understood in order to monitor the target's status and interpret the effects of injected errors. The lack of insight into the target (guest) context is a common issue with virtualization and emerges in many instances where information maintained within the guest's context would be useful outside the guest VM, e.g., process monitoring. The technique of virtual machine introspection (VMI) was developed to overcome just these types of challenges and has been applied to performance monitoring and security.

We have used VMI methods with VM-based fault injection to bridge the gap between the target (in guest) and controller (outside guest). We describe the approach and demonstrate a proof-of-concept experiment where we can perform fault injection on a process in a VM using commands from the host (outside the VM). This approach maintains the strong isolation of VMFI and leverages VMI methods to gain target context.

The primary contributions of this paper are:

- The presentation of tools for HPC Resilience investigations that support experiments at both user and kernel levels, which can be performed with strong separation between control and system under test environments;
- A description of a cooperative VM-based fault-injection (FI) mechanism, which includes a discussion of how VMI can benefit FI;
- The demonstration of proposed FI mechanism to study soft error resilience in iterative solver benchmark running in user-space of guest VM.

2   Background

2.1   Virtualization

The virtualization of physical hardware enables a privileged software layer to multiplex the underlying physical resources. This management layer is called a virtual machine monitor (VMM), or *hypervisor*, and is responsible for providing VMs with efficient, controlled access to the physical resources [20,23]. The VMM runs on a *host* machine, and a VM runs on the VMM. The VM is often termed the *guest* and the operating system (OS) running in the VM is termed the *guest operating system* (or guest OS). There are two categories of VMMs that are distinguished by their position in the software stack with respect to the physical hardware [20]: (i) executes directly on the hardware (*type-I*), (ii) executes atop or within a host OS (*type-II*).

There are several open-source and commercial offerings for virtualization. Palacios [13] is a VMM that has been developed specifically for use in high-performance computing (HPC) environments. It can be embedded within the Kitten light-weight kernel or Linux OS. The implementation uses hardware extensions available in modern x86 processors to provide efficient virtualization. Palacios runs on standard x86 commodity clusters and Cray XT/XK super-computers. Palacios is currently being used as part of the Hobbes OS research project [2].

2.2   Virtual Machine Introspection

Virtual machine introspection allows for a guest's internal state to be exposed to an external viewer, commonly another VM [19], the VMM [1], or a process on the host [8]. Because the VM is executing on a software or hardware abstraction of physical resources, the amount of state exposed by VMI is extensive, ranging from device registers to the memory of the guest. This allows for the external software to both observe and modify the guest's state. However, the view of the guest's state is often difficult to understand because of the "semantic gap" [4]. To overcome this obstacle, researchers often create a bridge across the semantic gap by means of a memory map of a particular process or the guest OS. An example of this bridge with respect to Linux is the System.map file, which holds a significant amount of information including the virtual address of the various functions, data structures, and other data residing within the kernel.

2.3   Fault Injection

Virtualization offers several useful mechanisms for implementing fault injection. Suesskraut et al. [24] used VMs to speed FI campaigns by taking a snapshot of the full execution state before an experiment and then rolling back to the pre-injection state. This also allows for all software dependencies to be fully contained within the guest VM to allow tests to be spread across multiple physical machines. This encapsulation of the experimental environment was noted by Clark et al. [6] as a benefit for reproducing results and performing repeatable research.

DeBardeleben et. al [7,9] have used virtualization to develop a platform for vulnerability assessments. Their approach is based on the widely used QEMU emulator, which supports a dynamic translation layer for evaluating the instructions executed by the guest VM. Their tool, *F-SEFI*, can be used to study the effect of soft errors on applications. They have used the tools to simulate soft errors to affect instruction operands (e.g., corruption of operands to FMUL instruction), which can be done randomly or on a per-function basis for an application. They model soft errors as single or multi-bit corruptions and can inject the errors on a deterministic and probabilistic basis. This work uses a different virtualization environment (QEMU) from our type-II virtualization software (Palacios). Also, they introduce errors at the instruction level via the dynamic translation layer of QEMU, whereas our approach introduces errors via a character device that exposes the guest's memory with VM introspection techniques to identify the full process and memory layout for the target environment.

Le and Tamir [14] highlight advantages and challenges associated with using virtualization for FI based on their experiences developing and using the *Gigan* tool. They studied the fidelity of software implemented fault injection (SWIFI) running injection campaigns in a virtualized context versus running without virtualization (i.e., on bare hardware) and found the environments are comparable with some clear benefits for SWIFI based studies, i.e., isolation, logging, fast boot and crash detection. Their Xen based tool, *Gigan*, employed fault injectors at the (a) VMM level for injecting from outside the guest VM, and (b) kernel level for targeting kernel-space data structures and user-space processes within the VM. Lastly, they used the *Gigan* FI tool to develop a more robust hypervisor (ReHype) [14].

Note, others [5,22] have investigated the fidelity of SWIFI in comparison to other FI approaches, showing that in some instances the software-based approach may be susceptible to an overestimation of errors in contrast to non-SWIFI approaches. The lessons being that single-bit failures introduced via SWIFI at the program level (in contrast to RTL or environment/hardware) may overestimate the effects of bit-flips. This has a bearing on vulnerability analysis that is derived from synthetic injection campaigns. Koopman [12] cited similar concerns for avoiding pitfalls when using fault-injection as a basis for dependability benchmarking. Therefore, the mechanisms employed in our work may not accurately mirror true hardware vulnerabilities, but have use for application testing and controlled experimentation where the user is mindful of the potential overestimations associated with SWIFI.

Li et al. [15] developed a binary instrumentation fault injection tool for studying soft errors in HPC applications. Their tool, *BIFIT*, is based on the PIN instrumentation tool and includes failure characterization based on injections into specific symbols/data-structures in the target HPC application based on profiling information for the applications. This work did not employ virtualization, but did study the effects of simulated "soft errors" on three HPC applications (Nek50000, S3D & GTC) by injecting bit-flips into global, heap and stack data objects. They limited the injections to application specific data, i.e., exclude middle-ware libraries, and observed that global data was significant to the influence of all three application's output and execution state. They also observed time and location of the injection is significant for each application with injections at later stages of application execution seeming to have a greater influence on the application's output & execution state. These soft error injections also affected the execution duration (walltime) of these applications, often with a 2x or greater increase in execution time. In our experiments, we target a different HPC application but focused on application specific data that is algorithmically important.

3   Cooperative Approach to Fault Injection

The placement of the SUT in a virtual machine enables FI campaigns to maintain a separation between the target and controlling system, regardless of whether the victim resides in user or kernel space. The separation of virtual/physical resources allows the resilience tests to operate within a *guest* virtual machine. The FI tests can be run from within the VM or from the *host* level entirely outside of the guest context. This division permits the host to control the guest, and can be an opportunity to modify the state within the guest (e.g., inject virtual device errors, inject data corruption into guest memory). This separation does increase the complexity involved in the experimental environment and requires additional steps to overcome the semantic gap between the host and guest contexts.

3.1   Fault Injection Mechanism

The FI mechanism is implemented using a modification to the Palacios VMM that exports the guest VM's memory as a character device in the host OS. This device file enables host-level access to the memory of the guest OS and user-space tasks. A VM FI utility (VMFI) that runs on the host is configured with details about primary data-structures of the guest OS, e.g., address of the task structure symbol `init_task`. This provides details about the context of the kernel running in the guest VM and is similar to techniques used for VMI [17].

In the guest OS, another utility is used to provide a well-known marker to search for within the list of tasks. This is a small launch utility called *wrapper* that simply starts a command, i.e., `fork()`/`exec()`. This `wrapper` command is used to identify the process to target within the guest context.

On startup the `wrapper` utility prints its process identifier (PID). This PID can be passed as input to the VMFI utility, running outside of the VM, or the VMFI utility can be used to scan for the `wrapper` process in the VM. In the case of scanning for the `wrapper` process, the list of tasks within the guest OS is traversed (from outside the guest OS) to find all instances where the process name matches and the associated PID is displayed. This information (PID) then provides the necessary pointers to obtain the children tasks started by the `wrapper` and details about memory associated with those children. This lookup procedure results in the VMFI utility knowing the location of the memory associated with the `wrapper`'s child process, which is the target (victim) application running in the guest OS.

The startup of the `wrapper` and `vmfi` are currently manual steps. The other critical data that is necessary for the VMFI utility to function correctly is: the symbol names and addresses for the target application (that will run within the guest OS), and the value to write to the victim's target address. These target addresses are limited to symbol names in order to simplify the lookup process. The value to inject is provided as input to the VMFI utility. A brief description with example usage information for the VMFI and `wrapper` utilities is given in Figs. 1 and 2.

```
1   Usage:
2     ./wrapper <executable> [args]
3
4   Description:
5    Wrapper utility to launch application and display useful information.
6    Also, used a sentinel for locating the target process in the guest
7    context, which is the child process of the wrapper utility.
8
9   Example:
10     ./wrapper ./HPCCG 100 200 100
```

Fig. 1. Usage information for wrapper utility that runs within the guest VM context.

```
1   Usage:
2   ./kmem list
3     --or--
4   ./kmem <wrapper_pid> <wrapper_map_file> <victim_map_file>      \
5           <target_symbol> <data_to_inject> <data_num_bytes>      \
6           <offset_from_symbol>
7
8    wrapper_pid            The pid of wrapper process residing in the guest
9    wrapper_map_file       Mapping file for the wrapper process
10   victim_map_file        Mapping file for the victim process
11   target_symbol          The name of the symbol in the victim
12                            process to inject a fault
13   data_to_inject         What to inject into the victim process
14   data_num_bytes         How many bytes to write
15   offset_from_symbol     Any additional bytes (offset) from target symbol
16
17  Description:
18   VMFI utility that can be used to LIST information about the guest context,
19   or used to inject errors into a victim application running in the guest
20   context.
21
22  Example:
23     ./kmem 198 wrapper.map HPCCG.symmap rtrans 6 4 0
```

Fig. 2. Usage information for VMFI utility that runs on the host (outside VM).

4 Evaluation

When performing fault injection experiments the integrity of the target environment can be corrupted and lead to unexpected behavior. The use of virtualization provides a software layer that strengthens the isolation between the guest (target) and host (control). The following tests were performed to demonstrate the cooperative approach to VM-based experiments that use guest system and application context running in the VM to perform fault injection from the host environment (outside the VM). While not tested here, the VM-based FI approach can be used for tests targetting system software in the VM that operates in a privileged mode and could crash or misbehave, without affecting the controller on the host.

4.1 Setup

The experiment used the Palacios VMM running within a Linux v3.5.0 host OS. The guest OS is a Linux v2.6.33.7 kernel using Busybox v1.20 to create a very small system installation. The guest VM configuration included shadow memory paging. The guest used bridged networking, whereby a Linux virtio network interface in the guest was connected to the host's network interface. The HPCCG: Simple Conjugate Gradient Benchmark [16] was used as the target application. All tests were performed on a Linux cluster testbed (*SAL9000*) at ORNL. The machines in the cluster have 1 AMD64 CPU with 24 cores, 64 GB of memory, and dual-bonded 1 Gbps Ethernet. The host operating system was Ubuntu Linux 12.04 LTS.

4.2   Guest Application Errors

To investigate the feasibility of doing host-level injections into a guest-level context, the FI mechanism for Palacios described in Sect. 3 was leveraged. The HPCCG benchmark was used to test this FI functionality. The benchmark performs an iterative refinement until reaching a solution within a given threshold, or until a maximum number of iterations are performed. Previous studies have found iterative algorithms to be resilient to some errors [3], possibly at the cost of taking longer to converge on an appropriate value. The HPCCG benchmark has also been identified as a more representative metric for current scientific applications and was identified by Heroux and Dongarra as an alternate metric for future Top 500 indexes [10]. The HPCCG benchmark was slightly modified to expose the `rtrans` variable in the `HPCCG` function to be a global symbol. This was necessary in order for the `vmfi` utility to locate a target address within the guest OS. The `rtrans` variable was selected through manual code inspection; the variable is used throughout the life of the iterative application. The only other change to HPCCG was to vary the value of `tolerance` to allow the algorithm to adjust the solution threshold. For example, `tolerance=0.0` results in the algorithm always running to the maximum number of iterations [16], in contrast to setting `tolerance=0.0000001` that allows for a slight margin that can satisfy the threshold and (possibly) terminate before the maximum number of iterations. The binary was statically linked and run in serial mode (i.e., no use of MPI or OpenMP).

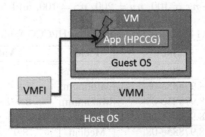

Fig. 3. Diagram showing the VM+FI setup with an application (e.g., HPCCG) target running in the Guest VM.

The overall layout is shown in Fig. 3. The host level vmfi injects a value into a specified memory address within the context of an application running within the VM. The application used in our tests, HPCCG, is reflected by the orange *App (HPCCG)* box that resides in the space of the VM (green box). Figure 3 also illustrates the vmfi utility running outside the VM context and injecting an error into the target running within the VM.

4.3 Discussion and Observations

The guest application error testing confirmed that the host-level injector functioned correctly and caused non-fatal errors in the target application, HPCCG. The intent was to simulate, at a very course-grain, data corruption of a key variable in the HPCCG program. The application was run 30 times both with and without injected errors. The same input parameters were used for all runs, $nx = 100$, $ny = 200$, $nz = 100$, which are the blocks of the matrix in the x/y/z dimensions [16], e.g., wrapper ./test_HPCCG_tol0.0 100 200 100. These values were selected to fit the available memory size and keep the execution time for the benchmark within the VM to a small amount of time to speed testing. The default maximum iterations max_iter=150 was used, and the tolerance was set to tolerance=0.0000001. All non-error cases resulted in identical output for the value of the *Residual* (rtrans) on each iteration, and the *Final residual* printed at the end (normr) as shown in Table 1(a). The same tests were re-run with errors injected into the rtrans variable during the execution. The fault injections took place at 1 second intervals and injected a random value between 1..100. This value was written as 4-bytes into the target variable (rtrans) to emulate multiple bit-flips in a single data value. As expected, there were no fatal errors as the changes were controlled to be only in the specific data value of rtrans, but there were slight perturbations due to the data errors as shown by

Table 1. The effects to the *Final residual* (normr). These statistics show the results for the serial HPCCG test without (a) and with (b) random data errors. In the error case, values between [1..100] at 1 second intervals were injected into the rtrans variable. The statistics are based on the *Final residual* at the end of the benchmark. The parameters for the benchmark were $nx = 100$, $ny = 200$, $nz = 100$, and *tolerance* = 0.0000001.

(a) HPCCG No Errors

Field	Value
Num. runs	30
Minimum	8.97885e-08
Maximum	8.97885e-08
Mean	8.97885e-08
Median	8.97885e-08
Mode	8.97885e-08
Variance	0
Std.Dev.	0

(b) HPCCG With Errors

Field	Value
Num. runs	30
Minimum	8.97878e-08
Maximum	8.97881e-08
Mean	8.97879766666667e-08
Median	8.9788e-08
Mode	8.9788e-08
Variance	8.0500807188788e-27
Std.Dev.	8.97222420522292e-14

Table 1(b) which did not occur in the non-error case of the benchmark. This experiment verified the ability to perform silent data corruption into an application running in a guest OS context from the host OS. All tests (with and without errors) completed in 74 iterations.

5   Conclusion

The use of VMs offers the ability to strongly separate the target from the hosting environment, which is useful when conducting fault injection experiments. The hosting platform has full access to the virtual guest context, but the details within the guest VM are not transparent from outside the guest's context. To overcome this issue a cooperative approach was explored where details about the guest OS were made available to tools in the host context. In the guest context, additional `wrapper` command was added that provides information that host level tools can be leveraged to lookup details within the guest context. Additionally, the symbol maps for the guest kernel and application were made available to the host-level VMFI tools. This cooperative approach helps to reduce the semantic gap between the VM/host contexts.

The VM also provides a reusable execution context to support repeatable test configurations. This is very useful when creating a cooperative testing environment because the guest configuration is well known and customized as appropriate. Therefore assumptions can be made for the purposes of the FI experiments. For example, pre-compiled binaries can be placed in the VM that are also available on the host so symbol information (name/address) can be used for the FI experiments. This holds for the guest OS too, which can be made available at the host level for performing experiments on guest kernel data structures (e.g., via embedded VMM debuggers) or for accessing information about processes within the guest OS. The key insight being that the VM offers a customizable container that can be adapted as needed to simplify and aid FI experiments. The VM also offers full access to the guest context that would otherwise be difficult to achieve from a purely software approach.

A disadvantage of this low level VMFI approach is an increased level of complexity and an increased semantic gap. This gap emerges because the higher level contextual information about the application (target) is divorced from the lower level VM vantage point. To overcome this challenge additional capabilities may need to be put in place, i.e., cooperative services, that provide additional information about the application context. For example, while the memory region for a guest OS is known by the VMM, the guest OS specific data structures within the VM are opaque. Therefore, a cooperative exchange of data is necessary to inform the host about details associated with the guest OS. For example, providing the VMM with a system map with the symbol names and address of functions and data structures of the guest OS running within the VM.

The prototype VMFI approach that we discussed in this paper was greatly influenced by VMI techniques. As demonstrated in the experiment, we were able to use these techniques to inject errors from outside the VM into specific data structures of a real benchmark (HPCCG) running within the guest VM. The iterative solver (HPCCG) reached the correct result, as expected, but the effects of our silent data corruption were detectable in an increased variance in the final residual (`normr`). While this experiment is very simplistic, it does show that the VMFI tool is working correctly and is usable for studies on applications running within a VM.

This work used the strong isolation of VMs to separate the FI controller from the FI target. Another approach that would be interesting to explore is the use of container-based virtualization to provide the isolation between the FI controller and target. The failure isolation properties of VMs and containers are not identical, and the container-based environments are restricted to a single OS kernel. Therefore, if the intent was to pursue FI campaigns against low-level system software (e.g., guest OS targets), the VMFI approach would be a better option than a container-based approach. However, if the target is an entirely user-space application, the isolation between containers may be sufficient for the FI experiments. A container-based approach would not suffer the semantic gap problem associated with VMs because there is a single OS kernel and the FI controller (outside container) could have full visibility of all running processes. In general, further investigation is required to better understand the failure isolation properties of these single and multiple kernel approaches to virtualization.

Acknowledgements. This material is based upon work supported by the U.S. Department of Energy, Office of Science, Advanced Scientific Computing Research program.

References

1. Aderholdt, F., Ghafoor, S., Siraj, A., Scott, S.L.: Integrity based intrusion detection system for enterprise and cloud environments. In: Proceedings of the 4th IEEE/ACM International Conference on Utility and Cloud Computing (2011)
2. Brightwell, R., Oldfield, R., Maccabe, A.B., Bernholdt, D.E.: Hobbes: Composition and virtualization as the foundations of an extreme-scale OS/R. In: Proceedings of the 3rd International Workshop on Runtime and Operating Systems for Supercomputers (ROSS), ROSS 2013, NY, USA, pp. 2:1–2:8 (2013). http://doi.acm.org/10.1145/2491661.2481427
3. Bronevetsky, G., de Supinski, B.: Soft error vulnerability of iterative linear algebra methods. In: Proceedings of the 22nd Annual International Conference on Supercomputing, ICS 2008, NY, USA, pp. 155–164 (2008). http://doi.acm.org/10.1145/1375527.1375552
4. Chen, P.M., Noble, B.D.: When virtual is better than real. In: Proceedings of the Eighth Workshop on Hot Topics in Operating Systems, HOTOS 2001, pp. 133–138 (2001) http://dl.acm.org/citation.cfm?id=874075.876409
5. Cho, H., Mirkhani, S., Cher, C.Y., Abraham, J.A., Mitra, S.: Quantitative evaluation of soft error injection techniques for robust system design. In: 2013 50th ACM/EDAC/IEEE Design Automation Conference (DAC), pp. 1–10, May 2013

6. Clark, B., Deshane, T., Dow, E., Evanchik, S., Finlayson, M., Herne, J., Matthews, J.N.: Xen and the art of repeated research. In: Proceedings of the Annual Conference on USENIX Annual Technical Conference, ATEC 2004, pp. 47–47. USENIX Association, Berkeley (2004). http://dl.acm.org/citation.cfm?id=1247415.1247462

7. DeBardeleben, N., Blanchard, S., Guan, Q., Zhang, Z., Fu, S.: Experimental framework for injecting logic errors in a virtual machine to profile applications for soft error resilience. In: Alexander, M., et al. (eds.) Euro-Par 2011. LNCS, vol. 7156, pp. 282–291. Springer, Heidelberg (2012). doi:10.1007/978-3-642-29740-3_32

8. Garfinkel, T., Rosenblum, M.: A virtual machine introspection based architecture for intrusion detection. In: Proceedings of Network and Distributed Systems Security Symposium, February 2003

9. Guan, Q., Debardeleben, N., Blanchard, S., Fu, S.: F-SEFI: a fine-grained soft error fault injection tool for profiling application vulnerability. In: 2014 IEEE 28th International Parallel and Distributed Processing Symposium, pp. 1245–1254, May 2014

10. Heroux, M.A., Dongarra, J.: Toward a new metric for ranking high performance computing systems. Technical Report SAND2013-4744, Sandia National Laboratories. http://www.sandia.gov/~maherou/docs/~HPCG-Benchmark.pdf. Accessed 26 April 2014

11. Hsueh, M.C., Tsai, T.K., Iyer, R.K.: Fault injection techniques and tools. Computer 30(4), 75–82 (1997)

12. Koopman, P.: What's wrong with fault injection as a benchmarking tool? In: Proceedings of the Workshop on Dependability Benchmarking (WDB 2002), 25 June 2002. (In Conjunction with IEEE Conference on Dependable Systems and Networks (DSN-2002)) http://homepages.laas.fr/kanoun/ifip_wg_10_4_sigdeb/external/02-06-25/index.html

13. Lange, J., Pedretti, K., Hudson, T., Dinda, P., Cui, Z., Xia, L., Bridges, P., Gocke, A., Jaconette, S., Levenhagen, M., Brightwell, R.: Palacios and Kitten: new high performance operating systems for scalable virtualized and native supercomputing. In: IEEE International Symposium on Parallel Distributed Processing (IPDPS), pp. 1–12, April 2010

14. Le, M., Tamir, Y.: Fault injection in virtualized systems - challenges and applications. Trans. Dependable Secure Comput. 12(3), 284–297 (2015). http://www.cs.ucla.edu/~tamir/papers/tdsc15.pdf

15. Li, D., Vetter, J.S., Yu, W.: Classifying soft error vulnerabilities in extreme-scale scientific applications using a binary instrumentation tool. In: International Conference for High Performance Computing, Networking, Storage and Analysis (SC). ACM, November 2012

16. Mantevo mini-application downloads, http://www.mantevo.org/packages.php, project URL: http://www.mantevo.org/packages.php. Accessed 6 April 2014

17. Nance, K., Bishop, M., Hay, B.: Virtual machine introspection: observation or interference? IEEE Secur. Priv. 6(5), 32–37 (2008)

18. Naughton, T., Vallée, G., Engelmann, C., Scott, S.L.: A case for virtual machine based fault injection in a high-performance computing environment. Euro-Par 2011. LNCS, vol. 7155, pp. 234–243. Springer, Heidelberg (2012). doi:10.1007/978-3-642-29737-3_27

19. Payne, B.D., Carbone, M., Sharif, M., Lee, W.: Lares: an architecture for secure active monitoring using virtualization. In: Proceedings of the IEEE Symposium on Security and Privacy, May 2008

20. Popek, G.J., Goldberg, R.P.: Formal requirements for virtualizable third generation architectures. Commun. ACM 17(7), 412–421 (1974)

682   T. Naughton et al.

21. Potyra, S., Sieh, V., Cin, M.D.: Evaluating fault-tolerant system designs using FAUmachine. In: Proceedings of the 2007 Workshop on Engineering Fault Tolerant Systems (EFTS 2007), NY, USA, p. 9. ACM, New York (2007)
22. Schirmeier, H., Borchert, C., Spinczyk, O.: Avoiding pitfalls in fault-injection based comparison of program susceptibility to soft errors. In: 2015 45th Annual IEEE/IFIP International Conference on Dependable Systems and Networks, pp. 319–330, June 2015
23. Smith, J.E., Nair, R.: Virtual Machines: Versatile Platforms for Systems and Processes. Morgan Kaufmann, Burlington (2005)
24. Süßkraut, M., Creutz, S., Fetzer, C.: Fast fault injection with virtual machines (Fast Abstract). In: Supplement of the 37th Annual IEEE/IFIP International Conference on Dependable Systems and Networks (DSN2007). http://wwwse.inf.tu-dresden.de/papers/preprint-suesskraut2007DSNb.pdf

ROME - Workshop on Runtime and Operating Systems for the Many-Core Era

Dealing with Layers of Obfuscation in Pseudo-Uniform Memory Architectures

Randolf Rotta$^{(\boxtimes)}$, Robert Kuban, Mark Simon Schöps, and Jörg Nolte$^{(\boxtimes)}$

Brandenburg University of Technology Cottbus-Senftenberg, Cottbus, Germany
{rottaran,kubanrob,schoema3,joerg.nolte}@b-tu.de

Abstract. Pseudo-Uniform Memory Architectures hide the memory's throughput bottlenecks and the network's latency differences in order to provide near-peak average throughput for computations on large datasets. This obviates the need for application-level partitioning and load balancing between NUMA domains but the performance of cross-core communication still depends on the actual placement of the involved variables and cores, which can result in significant variation within applications and between application runs.

This paper analyses the pseudo-uniform memory latency on the Intel Xeon Phi Knights Corner processor, derives strategies for the optimised placement of important variables, and discusses the role of localised coordination in pUMA systems. For example, a basic cache line ping-pong benchmark showed a 3x speedup between adjacent cores. Therefore, pUMA systems combined with support for controlled placement of small datasets are an interesting option when processor-wide load balancing is difficult while localised coordination is feasible.

1 Introduction

Large-scale multi- and many-core processors have to compromise between the scalability of the memory architecture, its space and power consumption, and the usability for application developers. Efficient memory interconnects are usually inherently non-uniform and their latency varies with the distance between core and memory while the peak throughput diminishes with growing distance. Therefore, tasks and their data should be placed close together in order to reduce latency and increase throughput but, at the same time, should be distributed in order to increase parallelism and balance the load over multiple bottlenecks [1].

Coherent caching layers further complicate the situation. Directory-based coherency protocols [2] as well as distributed shared caches [3, 4] employ global directory components that route requests to recent copies and coordinate global invalidation and updating. In order to resolve throughput bottlenecks at these components, multiple of them are distributed across the network and the request load should be distributed uniformly across them.

Non-Uniform Memory Architectures group memory channels, directories, and compute cores such that an almost uniform low latency and high throughput is provided within each group—also known as NUMA domain or node. In order

© Springer International Publishing AG 2017
F. Desprez et al. (Eds.): Euro-Par 2016 Workshops, LNCS 10104, pp. 685–696, 2017.
DOI: 10.1007/978-3-319-58943-5_55

to utilise the system's peak throughput, it is the application's responsibility to balance data and compute tasks across these domains. This requires basically the same strategies as in distributed systems, for example a domain decomposition with bin-packing for load balancing. As a positive side effect, this also results in a more localised coordination, which enables synchronisation with low latency and low congestion. However, while successful on medium-sized NUMA systems, the effort and load balancing challenge increases with the ratio between a growing number of domains and the size of the shared memory.

A more convenient alternative are *pseudo-Uniform Memory Architectures* that use hardware-based address interleaving, for example with cache line granularity, in order to uniformly distribute the load over many memory channels and coherence directories. Provided that the network can cope with the aggregated peak throughput, applications do not need to worry neither about throughput bottlenecks nor the co-located placement of data and tasks.

Unfortunately, this is true only for throughput-bound computations on large-enough datasets: any synchronisation between cores is still dominated by the cache coherence latency, which depends on the distance between the involved cores and coherence directory. While the hardware's interleaving has no mitigating effect on the usually small synchronisation variables, their seemingly random spatial placement leads to difficult-to-predict overheads and performance variations. For synchronisation, the convenient pseudo-uniformity becomes a layer of obfuscation [5]. A few badly positioned synchronisation variables can slow down the whole application. Analysing such performance bottlenecks is further impaired by placement-dependent variation between repeated runs of the same application outside of the developer's control.

This paper studies the pseudo-uniform architecture of the Intel Xeon Phi Knights Corner (KNC) many-core processor [6] and derives strategies for the optimised placement of synchronisation variables and similar latency-bound objects. The KNC provides 59–61 cores with four hardware threads each, four memory controllers, and 64 cache coherence directories—all connected via a shared point-to-point ring network. Compared to previous Xeon processors, the path between a core, the responsible directory, and the destination cache or memory controller can be very long, which results in considerable placement-dependent latency variation.

To this end, we reconstruct a mapping from cache line addresses to neighbouring cores based on latency measurements and use this mapping to initialise a pUMA-aware cache line allocator. For a basic cache line ping-pong pattern, this pUMA-aware placement enabled a 3x speedup between adjacent cores.

The next section reviews related work with respect to memory architectures and locality awareness. Section 3 devises generic experiments to study the effects of interleaving across directories and memory channels. Then, Sect. 4 discusses the experiment results obtained on the Intel Xeon Phi KNC. Finally, Sect. 5 discusses the broader implications on placement and coordination on the KNC and similar pUMA architectures.

2 Related Work

This section surveys performance studies related to the Intel XeonPhi KNC processor and uniform memory architectures. The last part reviews coordination strategies from NUMA systems with relevance to uniform memory architectures.

Studies Related to the Intel Xeon Phi KNC. The Larrabee architecture for visual computing [7] is the ancestor of the Knights Corner processors. The article proposes a many-core architecture based on simple x86 cores with SIMD short vector units, private L2 caches, and an on-chip ring network for cache coherency. In order to keep the ring latency small compared to the latency of the DRAM memory channels, multiple "short linked" rings are proposed without discussing implications for the cache coherency. The authors point out that synchronisation between threads within a core is fast because of the shared L1 cache and cross-core synchronisation is inherently much slower. Hence, computations that access the same data should be placed onto the same core.

Based on the available technical documentation and micro-benchmarks on the KNC 5110P, Ramos and Hoefler [8] provide a detailed overview of the KNC's directory-based cache coherence and present a quantitative performance model for cross-core communication. Likewise, Fang et al. [9,10] published extensive studies of the KNC. Both groups consider the *average latency over a large number of cache lines* and report similar results. Reading from any other cache takes 243 cycles in average and reading from the memory takes 318–346 cycles in average. The latency of reading a single cache line from another core's cache is examined in [10]. There, a latency variation from 160–340 cycles depending on the partner core is visible. The authors note, that the latency does not relate to the distance of both cores because of the distributed coherence directories.

Gerofi et al. [5] studied the "hidden non-uniformity" of the KNC processor with respect to reading from main memory. They show a 60% variation in latency when reading different cache lines from the main memory and propose a respective memory allocator that reduces this cache miss latency. The authors argue, that such placement could speed up algorithms that exhibit difficult to predict access patterns, for example, because of recursive data structures like linked lists, trees, and graphs. Their evaluation demonstrates a 17–28% throughput improvement for an A* shortest path algorithm with optimised allocation of the graph nodes. In contrast to [5], the present paper focuses on cross-core communication, that is the latency of accessing another core's cache.

Other UMA and pUMA Systems. The IBM Cyclops processor [11] has 16 embedded memory banks and the contiguous address space can be interleaved over caches and memory banks in order to balance the congestion. A crossbar switch is used to provide uniform latency between all cores, caches, and memory banks. Similarly, the Oracle Sparc T5 processors [12] use a crossbar for uniform latency.

Multi-socket Intel Xeon processors are operated as NUMA systems usually with one (pseudo-)uniform domain per socket. However, the address interleaving is configurable and can span multiple sockets [13] by combining bits of the physical address into a 3 bit target index. The "low-order" interleave uses bits 6–8 as target, which distributes consecutive lines over adjacent targets, and the "low/mid-hash" interleave uses bits 6–8 exclusive-or bits 16–18. In addition, the "hemisphere" variant replaces the first target bit with an exclusive-or of the bits 6, 10, 13, and 19 in order to better distribute accesses with a fixed stride.

To a limited degree, interleaving can be implemented by software. The processor's virtual address spaces can be used for interleaving on page granularity [1,14] and applications can distribute the placement of their data structures [15].

The Tilera Tile processors use a distributed shared L2 cache with a local cache at each core [4]. Requests are routed to the line's home cache, which is configured on page-size granularity. While interleaving over multiple L2 components is possible, synchronisation variables can simply be allocated in dedicated pages with known placement.

Coordination in NUMA Systems. Alongside the ratio of parallel to sequential computations, the scalability depends considerably on the overhead associated with distributing tasks across threads and synchronising the actions of concurrently active tasks. This overhead depends on the communication latency and the congestion on memory channels and network [1] and, thus, also on the *contention* as number of threads competing for a shared resource [16].

Some NUMA strategies reduce the latency by moving shared variables closer to their threads. One example is frequent polling on locally cached flags and rare signalling to remote flags as done by queue locks [17,18] and work stealing [19]. Tightly related are strategies that reduce contention by distributing the load over multiple peers. Examples are the replication of services [20] and hierarchically distributed locks [21]. *Software Combining* generalises both aspects by combining multiple local accesses into fewer remote messages [16,17,22].

Finally, some strategies reduce the data migration between NUMA domains, for example, by keeping related tasks in the same domain as in hierarchical work stealing [19], preferring threads of the same domain as in cohort locking [23], or moving tasks to specific domains as in delegation locks [24].

3   Measuring Latency: Reading from Caches vs. Memory

Latency-bound phases can be accelerated by reducing the stall time when reading from main memory with unpredictable access patterns (like [5]) and by reducing the latency when synchronising nearby threads via shared variables. Both aspects cannot be mitigated by hardware or software prefetching. The objective therefore is to reduce the latency by placing the data into cache lines that are locally managed and stored. Unfortunately, the pUMA address interleaving, while balancing the congestion for improved throughput, obfuscates the actual placement. In lack of documentation about the interleaving, latency measurements can uncover sufficient information for a pUMA-aware allocator, for example by assigning lines to the cores with lowest latency. This section devises latency measurements that provide such information.

Assuming a processor with cache coherence based on a shared distributed directory and private caches per core, the latency depends on the distances between the client core (C), the responsible directory component (D), and the remote cache that currently owns the line (O) or respectively the responsible memory channel (M). The responsible directory and memory channel are selected by the hardware's interleaving scheme. The directory tracks the sharing state of previously accessed lines and routes read requests accordingly to the current owner cache or to a memory channel. Similar to Ramos and Hoefler [8] two cases can be distinguished as illustrated in Fig. 1: *Cache Read* is routed to the current owner cache (O) and *Memory Read* is routed to the off-chip memory (M) because the line is invalid (not present) in all caches.

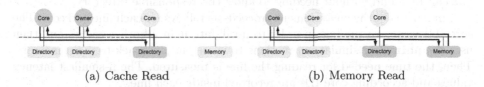

(a) Cache Read   (b) Memory Read

Fig. 1. Communication path for reading a line from another cache or the memory.

The read latency for both cases is $d_{C,D} + d_{D,O/M} + d_{O/M,C} + o$, where $d_{x,y}$ is the latency introduced by the network between x and y, and o is the processing overhead for cache, directory, and memory lookups. The network latency grows with the distance and the link congestion, whereas the processing overhead grows with the contention. The unwanted influence of the congestion and contention can be circumvented by recording the minimum latency over multiple measurements and putting all unneeded cores into sleep.

Cache Read Benchmark. Given the address of a cache line, the directory D is fixed while C and O can be chosen. Intuitively, any two cores C, O that minimise the latency for a fixed line must be neighbours in the network. For such pairs, the latency is approximately $2d_{C,D} + o$ and can be used to study the placement of the directories relative to cores. Basically, each line can be assigned to the core that has the lowest read latency with one of its neighbours.

Similar to [8], the measurement proceeds as follows for each line and client core: An arbitrary neighbour core writes to the line in order to become the owner (O) and invalidate the line in all other caches. Then, it sets a helper flag in an unrelated line to notify the client core (C). This core (C) then measures the time needed for reading from the cache line. The n-smallest latency values and according core IDs are recorded inside each line.

The basic benchmark can be accelerated by considering two lines and two adjacent cores: Each line contains one flag for notification and measurement and the line is initially owned by the respective core. One core (C) measures the time needed for accessing the other core's flag by using the atomic fetch-and-add instruction while the other core (O) reads the same flag using the atomic fetch-and-add instruction with zero increment. Thus, the line's ownership is transferred just once for the measurement and immediately back to the other core (O) due to the polling. The other core (O) is notified about the finished measurement by seeing the incremented value. Then, both cores change their role (C, O) and operate on the other cache line.

Memory Read Benchmark. Given the address of a cache line, both D and M are fixed while the core C can be chosen freely. When selecting a core with minimal distance to the directory, the latency is approximately $2d_{C,M} + o$ and can be used to study the placement of the memory channels relative to directories. By taking the smallest memory read latency over all cores, the best core for each line can be found without needing to know the responsible directory.

Similar to [5], the measurement proceeds as follows for each line and core: The core (C) writes to the line in order to invalidate it in all other caches and then uses the `wbinvd` or similar instructions to write the line back to main memory. Then, the time needed for reading the line is measured. The n-smallest latency values and according core IDs are recorded inside each line.

4   Two Layers of Interleaving on the Xeon Phi KNC

This section discusses results of the *Cache Read* and *Memory Read* benchmarks obtained on the KNC processor. Subsequently, a ping-pong micro-benchmark like in [8] is examined as prototype of many synchronisation protocols.

The processor (B1PRQ-5110P) used in this study has 60 in-order cores with fair time multiplexing among 4 hardware threads per core and a frequency of 1.05 GHz. In order to reduce fluctuations caused by the other threads, they are put into sleep with the `delay` instruction. The measurements use the core's *time stamp counter* via the `rdtsc` instruction, which has quite low fluctuations because of the simple cores and sleeping threads.

The cores, directories, and memory channels are spread across a ring network and, thus, each core has two adjacent neighbours. Actually, multiple rings in both directions are used and these rings do not necessarily take the same path across the chip area. An exact assignment of cache lines to directories will be difficult because each directory has multiple nearby cores that should observe similarly low latency in the benchmark's described above. Messages on the ring can "bounce" [6] at their destination due to contention. This causes the message to traverse the whole ring until reaching the destination again. Hence, unrelated memory traffic should be avoided in order to reduce contention at the directories.

Each core has a hardware prefetcher that discovers access patterns [9] and reads the next lines speculatively. In order to protect the Memory Read benchmark we considered power-of-two large address ranges and selected the next line by reversing the bit order in the cache line's index.

In order to reduce interference as much as possible, we implemented the benchmarks as kernel extension of the MyThOS operating system prototype.

During the boot sequence, the studied address range is reserved to keep other data structures away. The timer interrupts were disabled on all hardware threads.

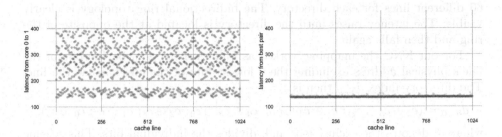

Fig. 2. Cache Read latency (in cycles) from one core pair versus the best pair.

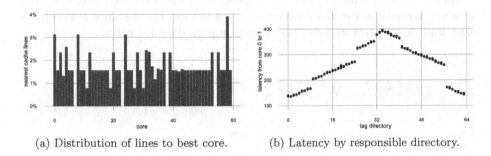

(a) Distribution of lines to best core.   (b) Latency by responsible directory.

Fig. 3. Distribution of the directories across the ring and distance to core 0.

Cache Read Results. Figure 2 shows the Cache Read latency measured from core 0 to 1 as well as the best latency over all pairs. For a fixed pair of cores, the latency ranges from 136 to 396 cycles with an average latency of 262 cycles (248,9 ns). This is comparable to the 243 cycles [10], respectively 235.8 ns [8], found in the literature. Considering the best pair, the latency ranges from 135 to just 152 cycles with 95% of the lines below 140 cycles.

In conclusion, the responsible directory of each line is near to at least one core and its neighbours. Thus, synchronisation between nearby cores has a good potential for acceleration by placing the synchronisation variables in lines managed by nearby directories. The average latency for a single access can be reduced from 260 to 140 cycles and, more importantly, the worst case latency of 400 cycles can be avoided systematically.

Figure 3(a) shows the distribution of lines over cores based on the minimal latency. Most cores have the lowest latency for around 1.7% of the lines as can be expected for 60 cores. However, distributing 64 directories over 60 cores cannot be completely fair. While some cores get less or no lines, their neighbours seem to be nearer to these directories. Fortunately, the excess amount can be balanced over neighbours without increasing the latency much. For example, we assigned lines greedily to one of the three-best cores with fewest assigned lines.

After careful examination, we were able to partially recover the mapping from cache line address to directory for the 256 KiB range starting at 4 GiB in the physical address space. Figure 3(b) shows the latency from core 0 to 1 for 60 different lines for each directory. The bidirectional ring topology is clearly visible: The latency raises until the directory is located at the opposite of the ring and then falls again.

For our KNC the mapping worked as follows: Let $c_{17...0}$ be the bits of the line's physical address excluding the 6 lowest bits of the offset inside the line. The directory index $d_{5...0}$ then is

$$d_{5...0} = (c_2 \oplus c_5 \oplus c_{11}; c_1 \oplus c_4 \oplus c_{10}; c_0 \oplus c_3 \oplus c_9; c_2 \oplus c_8; c_1 \oplus c_7; c_0 \oplus c_6),$$

where $\oplus$ denotes the exclusive-or and; divides the individual bits. This scheme is reasonably close to the interleaving documented for multisocket Intel Xeon processors [13] as described in Sect. 2. Please note, that bits from outside the examined 256 KiB address range are missing above and the mapping may vary between variants of the KNC processor. In addition, the distance between the cores and these directories can vary depending on disabled cores.

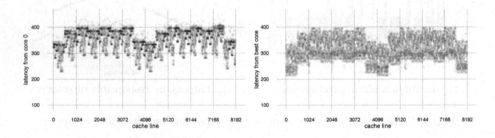

Fig. 4. Memory Read latency (in cycles) from one core versus the best core.

Memory Read Results. Figure 4 shows the Memory Read latency measured from core 0 as well as the best latency across all cores. For a fixed core, the latency varies from 211 to 441 cycles with an average of 350 cycles (332.5 ns). When accessing the lines from the respective best core, the latency still varies from 195 to 400 cycles with an average of 314 cycles. The latencies for memory read latencies found in the literature are 302 cycles [9] for reads with a stride of 64 byte when the dataset is larger than 512 KiB. Ramos and Hoefler [8] report an even lower mean memory read latency of 278.8 ns. The repeating pattern in Fig. 4 suggest that there are address ranges where such low average latency can be observed.

In conclusion, reading from memory can be accelerated only by selecting a subset of lines with sufficiently low latency. Following Sect. 3, the best core's latency corresponds to the distance between directory and memory channel. If the lines would be interleaved across the memory channels near the responsible directory, the worst latency would be much better than the worst ring distance of 200 cycles. Therefore we can assume, that the lines are interleaved across the memory channels independently of the interleaving across directories.

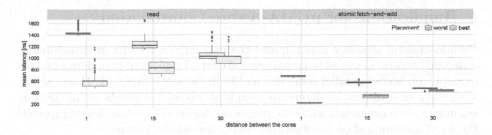

Fig. 5. Ping-pong round-trip time depending on distance between the cores.

Ping-Pong Benchmark Results. In practise, the latency of reading from a shared variable is just half the story because actual synchronisation protocols have write to the variable. The time needed to acquire exclusive write access from the directory and the time until other cores observe the new value has to be taken into account. Furthermore, protocols may consist of multiple write/read steps which can amplify the impact of the placement-dependent overhead.

As first micro-benchmark for synchronisation scenarios, we implemented a single-line ping-pong similar to [8]. The average ping-pong latency over 1000 runs was measured for multiple cache lines with optimal and worst placement as well as for different distances between the participating cores. A *read* and an *atomic* variant have been examined. The *read* variant implements the polling by repeatedly reading from the flag until the value changes. This temporarily brings the line into a shared state between both cores. The *atomic fetch-and-add* variant polls by adding zero. Here, the line is never shared and just the ownership travels between cores [25].

Figure 5 shows the distribution of the round-trip time as boxplots for cache lines placed near to one of the two cores ("best") and farthest away from both cores ("worst"). For the *read* variant and adjacent cores, the average round-trip time is 577 ns for the best placement and 1434 ns for the worst placement. With growing distance, the placement's impact diminished, reaching an average of 990 ns. For the *atomic* variant and adjacent cores, the average round-trip time is 222 ns for the best placement and just 685 ns for the worst placement. Again, the placement's impact diminished with growing distance and reaches an average of 433 ns. In comparison, Ramos et al. reported 497 ns for this situation [8]. The *atomic* variant also shows much smaller fluctuations.

The results show that the placement information obtained by the Cache Read benchmark can be used to improve the average latency of actual communication schemes provided that the communicating cores are near to each other. Without pUMA-aware placement the round-trip time would fluctuate up to 3x over the best-case time depending on the distance between cores and directory. For communication patterns that involve shared cache lines, the invalidation broadcasts caused by the request for ownership add considerable overhead and fluctuation. Polling by non-mutating writes or write-hint prefetches [25] can reduce the round-trip time up to 2.5x over read-based polling.

5   Implications for pUMA-Aware Coordination

Pseudo-uniform memory may improve the usability of NUMA architectures as data and tasks do not need to be partitioned over a large number of domains. One example are nested parallel computation like in OpenMP and Cilk. However, the scalability of coordination-intensive computations still depends on minimising communication overheads while the pseudo-uniform address interleaving spreads the local communication involuntarily across the whole system.

This paper analysed the address interleaving across memory channels and cache coherence directories on the Intel Xeon Phi KNC processor. The micro-benchmarks show that both layers of interleaving are independent and, hence, different placement strategies are needed for optimised reading from memory versus optimised communication between cores. Just a subset of the available cache lines is useful for large linked data structures like linked lists, trees, and graphs as studied in [5]. In contrast, a significant latency reduction is achievable for access to shared variables provided that the communicating cores are in proximity to the responsible coherence directory.

As [8,10] pointed out, the impact of contention at the coherence directories is considerable with 60 ns extra latency per concurrent thread in the ping-pong example. This situation arises naturally when a large number of threads accesses the same synchronisation variables, for example global semaphores and barriers. Hierarchical strategies and software combining strategies as reviewed in Sect. 2 can mitigate this contention bottleneck. These approaches lead naturally to a spatial partitioning of the cores in order to keep the majority of the communication localised. In such settings, the pUMA-aware placement of the local synchronisation variables should provide noticeable additional acceleration while reducing placement-dependent latency and throughput variations.

Ideal candidates for such improvements are scalable services of parallel run-time environments and of the operating system, for example the distributed memory and thread management, cross-core thread synchronisation, basic messaging and notification primitives, and application-level task schedulers.

On the practical side, improved system support is needed: For a pure user-land implementation, pinning of mapped pages in the virtual memory management, the translation from virtual to physical addresses, and the assignment from cache lines to nearby cores is needed. The KNC's Linux supports the first two aspects but leaves the assignment to the application. Without control over the used physical address ranges, applications would need on-line measurements or a large database like in [5]. Instead, a pUMA kernel module could provide a mmap service that returns pages pre-initialised with the assignment to nearby cores.

Acknowledgments. This work was financed by the German Federal Ministry of Education and Research (BMBF) in the MyThOS project, grant no. 01IH13003C.

References

1. Dashti, M., Fedorova, A., Funston, J., Gaud, F., Lachaize, R., Lepers, B., Quema, V., Roth, M.: Traffic management: a holistic approach to memory placement on NUMA systems. In: Proceedings of the Eighteenth International Conference on Architectural Support for Programming Languages and Operating Systems, ASPLOS 2013, pp. 381–394. ACM, New York (2013)
2. Agarwal, A., Simoni, R., Hennessy, J., Horowitz, M.: An evaluation of directory schemes for cache coherence. SIGARCH Comput. Archit. News **16**(2), 280–298 (1988)
3. Hackenberg, D., Molka, D., Nagel, W.E.: Comparing cache architectures and coherency protocols on x86–64 multicore SMP systems. In: Proceedings of the 42nd Annual IEEE/ACM International Symposium on Microarchitecture, MICRO 42, pp. 413–422. ACM, New York (2009)
4. Choi, I., Zhao, M., Yang, X., Yeung, D.: Experience with improving distributed shared cache performance on tilera's tile processor. Comput. Archit. Lett. **10**(2), 45–48 (2011)
5. Gerofi, B., Takagi, M., Ishikawa, Y.: Exploiting hidden non-uniformity of uniform memory access on manycore CPUs. In: Lopes, L., et al. (eds.) Euro-Par 2014. LNCS, vol. 8806, pp. 242–253. Springer, Cham (2014). doi:10.1007/978-3-319-14313-2_21
6. Intel Corporation: Intel Xeon Phi Coprocessor System Software Developers Guide. https://software.intel.com/en-us/articles/intel-xeon-phi-coprocessor-system-software-developers-guide
7. Seiler, L., Carmean, D., Sprangle, E., Forsyth, T., Abrash, M., Dubey, P., Junkins, S., Lake, A., Sugerman, J., Cavin, R., et al.: Larrabee: a many-core x86 architecture for visual computing. In: ACM Transactions on Graphics (TOG), vol. 27, p. 18. ACM (2008)
8. Ramos, S., Hoefler, T.: Modeling communication in cache-coherent SMP systems: a case-study with Xeon Phi. In: Proceedings of the 22nd International Symposium on High-Performance Parallel and Distributed Computing, HPDC 2013, pp. 97–108. ACM, New York (2013)
9. Fang, J., Sips, H., Zhang, L., Xu, C., Che, Y., Varbanescu, A.L.: Test-driving Intel Xeon Phi. In: Proceedings of the 5th ACM/SPEC International Conference on Performance Engineering, ICPE 2014, pp. 137–148. ACM, New York (2014)
10. Fang, Z., Mehta, S., Yew, P.C., Zhai, A., Greensky, J., Beeraka, G., Zang, B.: Measuring microarchitectural details of multi- and many-core memory systems through microbenchmarking. ACM Trans. Archit. Code Optim. **11**(4) 55:1–55:26 (2015)
11. Cascaval, C., Castanos, J.G., Ceze, L., Denneau, M., Gupta, M., Lieber, D., Moreira, J.E., Strauss, K., Warren, H.S.: Evaluation of a multithreaded architecture for cellular computing. In: 2002 Proceedings of Eighth International Symposium on High-Performance Computer Architecture, pp. 311–321, February 2002
12. Feehrer, J., Jairath, S., Loewenstein, P., Sivaramakrishnan, R., Smentek, D., Turullols, S., Vahidsafa, A.: The Oracle Sparc T5 16-core processor scales to eight sockets. IEEE Micro **33**(2), 48–57 (2013)
13. Intel Corporation: Intel Xeon Processor 7500 Series Datasheet, vol. 2, March 2010. http://www.intel.com/content/www/us/en/processors/xeon/xeon-processor-7500-7500-series-vol-2-datasheet.html
14. Lameter, C.: NUMA (non-uniform memory access): an overview. Queue, **11**(7) 40:40–40:51 (2013)

15. Bianchini, R., Crovella, M.E., Kontothanassis, L., LeBlanc, T.J.: Software inter-leaving. In: 1994 Proceedings of Sixth IEEE Symposium on Parallel and Distributed Processing, pp. 56–65, October 1994
16. Tang, P., Yew, P.C.: Software combining algorithms for distributing hot-spot addressing. J. Parallel Distrib. Comput. **10**(2), 130–139 (1990)
17. Mellor-Crummey, J.M., Scott, M.L.: Algorithms for scalable synchronization on shared-memory multiprocessors. ACM Trans. Comput. Syst. **9**(1), 21–65 (1991)
18. Magnusson, P., Landin, A., Hagersten, E.: Queue locks on cache coherent multiprocessors. In: 1994 Proceedings of Eighth International Parallel Processing Symposium, pp. 165–171, April 1994
19. Min, S.J., Iancu, C., Yelick, K.: Hierarchical work stealing on manycore clusters. In: 5th Conference on Partitioned Global Address Space Programming Models (2011)
20. Gamsa, B., Krieger, O., Appavoo, J., Stumm, M.: Tornado: maximizing locality and concurrency in a shared memory multiprocessor operating system. In: Proceedings of the Third Symposium on Operating Systems Design and Implementation, OSDI 1999, Berkeley, CA, USA, pp. 87–100. USENIX Association (1999)
21. Radovic, Z., Hagersten, E.: Hierarchical backoff locks for nonuniform communication architectures. In: Proceedings of the Ninth International Symposium on High-Performance Computer Architecture, HPCA-9 2003, pp. 241–252, February 2003
22. Yew, P.C., Tzeng, N.F., Lawrie, D.H.: Distributing hot-spot addressing in large-scale multiprocessors. IEEE Trans. Comput. **C-36**(4) 388–395 (1987)
23. Dice, D., Marathe, V.J., Shavit, N.: Lock cohorting: a general technique for designing NUMA locks. SIGPLAN Not. **47**(8), 247–256 (2012)
24. Fatourou, P., Kallimanis, N.D.: Revisiting the combining synchronization technique. SIGPLAN Not. **47**(8), 257–266 (2012)
25. David, T., Guerraoui, R., Trigonakis, V.: Everything you always wanted to know about synchronization but were afraid to ask. In: Proceedings of the Twenty-Fourth ACM Symposium on Operating Systems Principles SOSP 2013, pp. 33–48. ACM, New York (2013)

Exploring Task Parallelism for Heterogeneous Systems Using Multicore Task Management API

Suyang Zhu[1], Sunita Chandrasekaran[2(✉)], Peng Sun[1], Barbara Chapman[1], Marcus Winter[3], and Tobias Schuele[3]

[1] Department of Computer Science, University of Houston, Houston, USA
zsuyang@uh.edu, {psun5,chapman}@cs.uh.edu
[2] Department of Computer and Information Sciences, University of Delaware, Newark, USA
schandra@udel.edu
[3] Siemens Corporate Technology, Princeton, USA
{marcus.winter.ext,tobias.schuele}@siemens.com

Abstract. Current trends in multicore platform design indicate that heterogeneous systems are here to stay. Such systems include processors with specialized accelerators supporting different instruction sets and different types of memory spaces among several other features. These features increase the programming effort to port applications to target platforms. We need effective programming strategies that can exploit the rich feature set of such heterogeneous multicore architectures and yet not require increased learning curve to apply these strategies.

To distribute workload effectively across such systems that have different cores running at different speed, we have explored task-based programming models in this paper. This model allows decomposition of a problem into a set of tasks for simultaneous execution. We present a task-based approach that employs the Multicore Association's (MCA) Task Management API (MTAPI), a robust, cross-platform, scalable API that avoids unnecessary synchronization thus offering a tiered and flexible approach and distributing workload efficiently across processors of varying types. For evaluation purposes, we use an NVIDIA Jetson TK1 board (ARM + GPU) as our test bed. As applications, we employ codes from benchmark suites such as *Rodinia* and *BOTS*.

Keywords: Multicore systems · Runtime · Heterogeneity · Accelerators · MTAPI

1 Introduction

Embedded multicore systems are widely used in areas such as networking, automobiles, and robotics. Some of these systems even compete with HPC platforms [1] and are promising to deliver high GFLOPS/Watt. Since parallelism has become a major driving force in computing, microprocessor vendors concentrate on integrating accelerators together with the central processing unit

© Springer International Publishing AG 2017
F. Desprez et al. (Eds.): Euro-Par 2016 Workshops, LNCS 10104, pp. 697–708, 2017.
DOI: 10.1007/978-3-319-58943-5_56

(CPU) on the same platform. The current trend of such platforms is that they are heterogeneous in nature, i.e., their operating systems and memory spaces are usually different [2] from traditional platforms. For example, Qualcomm's heterogeneous processor Snapdragon 810 integrates an ARM Cortex CPU and an Adreno 430 GPU on the same chip. Such an integration produces hardware platforms that satisfy the requirements regarding performance, flexibility, and energy consumption of embedded systems. Unfortunately the software to port applications to such systems is often still immature and typically fine tuned for a specific platform. As a result, maintaining a single code base across multiple platforms is not feasible; this is a major concern.

Programming models designed for high performance computing (HPC) platforms are not necessarily the best for handling embedded multicore systems, especially when these systems have limited resources, such as a small number of cores, or limited memory. Among the models, a high-level directive-based model is OpenMP [3] that has been recently extended to support accelerators. However embedded systems are still unique unlike traditional accelerators such as GPUs, so OpenMP in its current status will still not be suitable for embedded devices. An alternate language is OpenCL [4] that is known for its portability but OpenCL involves steep learning curve making it a challenge to adopt the language on hardware.

To address these challenges, the Multicore Association (MCA)[1] was formed by a group of leading-edge companies addresses the programming challenges of heterogeneous embedded multicore platforms. MCA's primary objective is the definition of a set of open specifications and application program interfaces (API) to facilitate multicore product development. MCA offers industry standard APIs for data sharing among different types of cores namely the Multicore Resource Management API (MRAPI), inter-core communication namely the Multicore Communication API (MCAPI), and for task management namely the Multicore Task Management API (MTAPI). Since the APIs are system agnostic, they facilitate development of portable code, thus improving the feasibility of running the same application on more than just one hardware platform.

This paper makes the following contributions:

- Creates a light-weight, task-based portable software stack to target resource-constrained heterogeneous embedded multicore systems using MTAPI
- Assesses the software stack by evaluation case studies on an embedded platform equipped with ARM processors and GPUs
- Showcases two open source MTAPI implementations for programmers to use[2]

Note: This paper does not aim to compare and contrast between the two implementations. Instead, the goal is to discuss how they can be used by software developers to port applications to heterogeneous multicore systems.

---

[1] https://www.multicore-association.org.

[2] UH-MTAPI and Siemens MTAPI: Software created by researchers at the University of Houston and Siemens.

The rest of the paper is organized as follows: Sect. 2 discusses the state-of-the-art and Sect. 3 gives an overview of MTAPI. The design and implementation strategies of our runtime library (RTL) implementation is given in Sect. 4. Section 5 discusses the experimental results and Sect. 6 presents conclusions along with some ideas for future work.

2 Related Work

In this section, we discuss some state-of-the-art parallel programming models for heterogeneous multicore systems from the task parallelism perspective.

OpenMP has been widely used in HPC for exploring shared memory parallelism [5] until recent advancements in the standard to support heterogeneous systems. OpenMP 3.1 ratified tasks, and task parallelism for multicore SoCs was implemented by several frameworks [6–8] deployed on shared memory systems. OpenMP 4.0 extended tasks to support task dependencies evaluated in [9] again using traditional shared memory-based architectures.

Other task-based efforts include Intel's TBB [10] that treats operations as tasks and assigns them to multiple cores through a runtime library. As most frameworks, however, TBB targets desktop or server applications and is not designed for low-footprint embedded and heterogeneous systems.

Cilk [11] is a C language extensions developed by MIT for multithreaded parallel computing. While Cilk simplifies task parallel applications, it only supports shared memory environment which limits its application to homogeneous systems.

OpenCL [4] is a standard designed for data parallel processing used to program CPUs, GPUs, DSPs, FPGAs, etc. Although the standard can target multiple platforms, there is a steep learning curve making it a challenge to be adaptable.

OmpSs (OpenMP SuperScalar) [12] is a task-based programming model which exploits parallelism based on annotations using pragmas. OmpSs has been extended to many-core processors with accelerators such as multiple GPU systems. However, OmpSs needs special compiler support which limits its usability for embedded, heterogeneous systems.

StarPU [13] is a tasking API that allows developers to design applications in heterogeneous environments. StarPU's runtime schedules the tasks and corresponding data transfers among the CPU and GPU accelerators. However, the necessary extension plug-in for GCC puts constraints on the deployment of StarPU to embedded systems with limited resources or bare-metal devices.

As discussed above, there are many approaches that explore task parallelism. However, they may not be best suited for embedded platforms which, unlike traditional platforms, lack plenty of resources and sometimes do not even have an OS. Additionally, many embedded systems are subject to real-time constraints and forbid dynamic memory allocation during operation which is completely ignored by the discussed approaches.

Our prior work in [14] uses MCAPI to establish communication through well-pipelined DMA protocols between Freescale P4080's Power Architecture and the specialized RegEx Pattern Matching Engine (PME) accelerator. We also created an abstraction layer for easy programmability by translating OpenMP to MRAPI [15,16]. Designed and implemented in ANSI C, MCAPI and MRAPI do not require specific compiler support or user-defined language extensions.

3   MTAPI Overview

Figure 1 gives an overview of MTAPI. Applications can be developed by directly calling the MTAPI interface or via further abstraction layers such as OpenMP (a translation from OpenMP to MTAPI is described in [17]). MTAPI can be implemented on most operating systems or even bare metal thanks to its simple design and minimal dependencies.

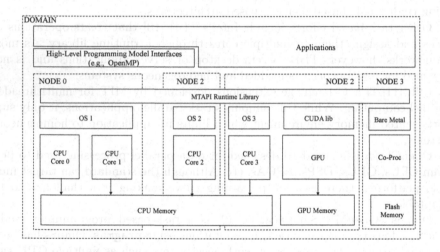

Fig. 1. MTAPI framework

In the following, we describe the main concepts of MTAPI.

Node: An MTAPI node is an independent unit of execution. A node can be a process, a thread, a thread pool, a general purpose processor or an accelerator.

Job and Action: A job is an abstraction representing the work and is implemented by one or more actions. For example, a job can be implemented by one action on the CPU and another action on the GPU. The MTAPI system binds tasks to the most suitable actions during runtime.

Task: An MTAPI task is an instance of a job together with its data environment. Tasks are very light-weight with fine granularity which allows creating, scheduling, and executing numerous tasks in parallel. A task can be offloaded to a neighboring node other than its origin node depending on the dynamic action binding. Therefore, optimized and efficient scheduling algorithms are desired for task management on heterogeneous multicore platforms.

Queue: A queue is defined by the MTAPI specification to guarantee sequential execution of tasks.

Group: MTAPI groups are defined for synchronization purposes. A group is similar to a `barrier` in other task models. Tasks attached to the same group must be completed before the next step by calling `mtapi_group_wait`.

Related work on MTAPI includes the European Space Agency (ESA) creating an MTAPI implementation [18] for a LEON4 processor, which is a synthesizable VHDL model of a 32-bit processor compliant with the SPARC V8 architectures. Wallentowitz et al. [19] developed a baseline implementation and plans for deploying MCAPI and MTAPI on tiled many-core SoCs.

This project is in collaboration with Siemens who created an own industry-grade MTAPI implementation as part of a larger open source project called Embedded Multicore Building Blocks (EMB^2) [20]. EMB^2 has been specifically designed for embedded systems and the typical requirements that accompany them, such as predictable memory consumption, which is essential for safety-critical applications, and real-time capability. For the latter, the library supports task priorities and affinities, and the scheduling strategy can be optimized for non-functional requirements such as minimal latency and fairness.

Besides the task scheduler, EMB^2 provides parallel algorithms like loops and reductions, concurrent data structures, and high-level patterns for implementing stream processing applications. These building blocks are largely implemented in a non-blocking (lock-free) fashion, thus preventing frequently encountered pitfalls like lock contention, deadlocks, and priority inversion. As another advantage in real-time systems, the algorithms and data structures give certain progress guarantees [21].

We evaluate both the implementations and demonstrate the usability and applicability of MTAPI for heterogeneous embedded multicore platforms.

4   MTAPI Design and Usage

4.1   Job Scheduling and Actions

As mentioned earlier, MTAPI decomposes computations into multiple tasks, schedules them among the available processing units, and combines the results after synchronization. Here a task is defined as a light-weight operation that describes the job to be done. However, during the task-creation cycle, the task does not know with which action it will be associated. MTAPI provides a dynamic binding policy between tasks and actions. This is to facilitate jobs to be scheduled on more than one hardware type. The scheduler handles the load-balancing issues. Depending on the where the task is located, it is marked either a local task or a remote task. If the task is assigned to an action residing on the same node, the task is marked as a local task; otherwise the task is marked as a remote task. Figure 2 gives an example the relationship between task and action. In the example, tasks a, b and d are assigned actions a, b, and, d, respectively, on remote nodes other than node 1, thus becoming remote tasks. On the other hand, task c is associated with action c on node 1, making it a local task. Each node consists of different processors.

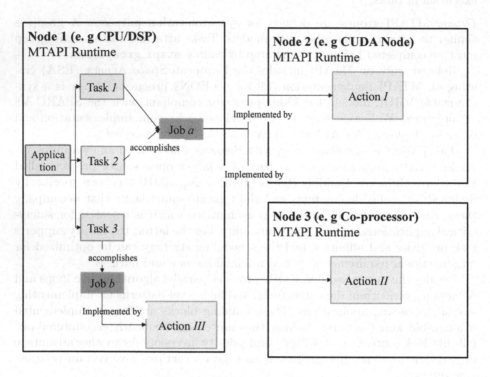

Fig. 2. MTAPI Job and Action

The MTAPI RTL defines an abstract interface for thread control including thread creation, termination, and synchronization using mutexes or semaphores. MTAPI kernel developers may implement this interface with particular thread libraries for the target platform, thus making MTAPI portable across a wide range of architectures. This portable and flexible approach is one of the appealing factors of MTAPI.

Listing 1.1 demonstrates the matrix multiplication program using MTAPI. In this code, we see there are two action functions that implements the matrix multiplication job. ActionFunction_GPU is implemented with CUDA kernel while ActionFunction_CPU is implemented with sequential CPU kernel. After defining the two action functions, we initialize the MTAPI environment by attaching these two actions to the same matrix multiplication job. Then we create three tasks respectively. arg_GPU and arg_CPU are pointers to the matrix data. These tasks are then assigned to different actions to execute. Thus, the GPU and CPU are utilized to do the computation in parallel.

```
void ActionFunction_GPU (
            const void* arguments,
            const mtapi_size_t arguments_size,
            void* result,
            const mtapi_size_t result_size,
            const void* node_local_data,
            const mtapi_size_t node_local_data_size,
            mtapi_task_context_t* const context
        )
{
        Argument_t* arg = (Argument_t*)arguments;
        kernel(arg->A, arg->B, arg->C, arg->n);
}

void ActionFunction_CPU (
            const void* arguments,
            const mtapi_size_t arguments_size,
            void* result,
            const mtapi_size_t result_size,
            const void* node_local_data,
            const mtapi_size_t node_local_data_size,
            mtapi_task_context_t* const context
        )
{
        Argument_t* arg = (Argument_t*)arguments;
        iter_matmul(arg->A, arg->B, arg->C, arg->n);
}


mtapi_action_create(JOBID, ActionFunction_CPU, NULL, 0,
    NULL, &status);
mtapi_action_create(JOBID, ActionFunction_GPU, NULL, 0,
    NULL, &status);
mtapi_task_hndl_t task[3];
task[0] = mtapi_task_start (0, job, arg_CPU, sizeof(
    Argument_t), NULL, 0, NULL, group, &status);
task[1] = mtapi_task_start (0, job, arg_GPU, sizeof(
    Argument_t), NULL, 0, NULL, group, &status);
task[2] = mtapi_task_start (0, job, arg_GPU2, sizeof(
    Argument_t), NULL, 0, NULL, group, &status);
mtapi_task_wait(task[0], MTAPI_INFINITE, &status);
mtapi_task_wait(task[1], MTAPI_INFINITE, &status);
mtapi_task_wait(task[2], MTAPI_INFINITE, &status);
```

Listing 1.1. MTAPI Matrix Multiplication Kernel

4.2 Inter-Node Communication

Essentially, each node has one receiver thread and a sender thread. These threads initialize the MCAPI environment and create MCAPI endpoints for message passing through MCAPI function calls. They together compose the MCAPI communication layer between nodes within the domain. Technically, the data and information transported between MTAPI nodes are packed as an MCAPI message. MCAPI then transports these messages across the nodes for load balancing of tasks, information update, and synchronization. The message contains the domain ID, node ID, and port ID. Once a message is created, it is inserted into a central message queue on the node waiting for the sender to initiate the communication. Every message is assigned a priority. The high priority messages such as action updates are inserted at the head of the message queue while the low priority messages, like load balancing, are inserted at the tail of the queue. The sender wraps the MTAPI message into an MCAPI message, according to its type, and sends it to its destination node. The receiver thread keeps listening to its neighboring nodes to check if there is an MCAPI message sent to this node. Upon receipt of an MCAPI message, the receiver decodes the MCAPI message and creates an MTAPI message carrying the necessary information. Then, the receiver pushes the newly created MTAPI message into the message queue, waiting for the next cycle of message processing by the sender thread. Finally, the receiver thread continues listening to its neighbor nodes. In the UH-MTAPI design, a priority scheduler manages the message queue. The priority scheduler uses a centralized message queue, where the messages are sorted.

5 Performance Evaluation

In this section, we evaluate the Siemens MTAPI implementation[3] and UH-MTAPI[4]. We select applications from BOTS [7] and Rodinia Benchmarks [22] to demonstrate their performance. The benchmarks are executed on NVIDIA's Jetson TK1 embedded development platform [23] with a Tegra K1 processor which integrates a 4-Plus-1 quad-core ARM Cortex-A15 processor and a Kepler GPU with 192 cores. We use the GCC OpenMP implementation shipped with the board by NVIDIA as reference for comparison purposes.

SparseLU Benchmark: The SparseLU factorization benchmark from *BOTS* computes an LU matrix factorization for sparse matrices. A sparse matrix contains submatrix blocks that may not be allocated. The vacancy of certain unallocated submatrix blocks leads to imbalance. Thus, task parallelism has better performance over other work sharing directives such as OpenMP's `parallel for`. In the SparseLU factorization, tasks are created only for the allocated submatrix blocks to reduce the overhead caused by imbalance.

The sparse matrix contains 50×50 submatrices, where each submatrix has size 100×100 on both hardware platforms. We collect multiple metrics such

---

[3] https://github.com/siemens/embb.
[4] https://github.com/MCAPro2015/OpenMP_MCA_Project.

as execution time, matrix size, and number of threads. The execution time for calculating the speed-up is measured on the CPU for the core part of the computation, excluding I/O and initial setup.

Figure 3(a) shows the speed-up using different implementations. The UH-MTAPI implementation demonstrates comparable performance with the Siemens MTAPI implementation as well as GCC's OpenMP version. Both Siemens and UH-MTAPI implementations achieve a roughly linear speed-up which indicates their scalability on multicore processors.

Heartwall Benchmark: The Heartwall tracking benchmark is an application from *Rodinia* [22] which tracks the changing shapes of a mouse heart wall. We reorganized it by splitting loop parallelism into tasks, where each task handles a chunk of the image data. The image procedures are encapsulated in an action function that processes the data associated with the corresponding tasks. Figure 3(b) shows the speed-up over a single thread. We observe that task parallelism conducted by UH-MTAPI matches the performance of data parallelism offered by OpenMP **parallel for** and the Siemens MTAPI implementation. However, none of the three versions meets the expectation of linear speedup as the number of threads increases.

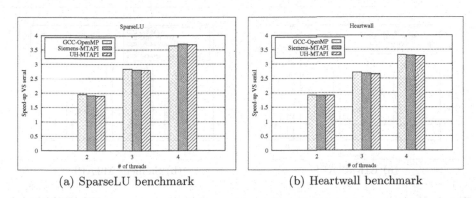

(a) SparseLU benchmark   (b) Heartwall benchmark

Fig. 3. Speed-up for SparseLU and Heartwall benchmarks with OpenMP, Siemens MTAPI and UH-MTAPI on NVIDIA Tegra TK1 board

Matrix-Matrix Multiplication: This benchmark (multiplication for dense matrices) is relatively compute-intensive. The complexity of a traditional multiplication of two square matrices is $\mathcal{O}(n^3)$. Although matrix multiplication can be implemented using the parallel working directives such as OpenMP's *parallel for*, the computation takes a lot of time due to the limited number of CPU threads and poor data locality. In contrast, heterogeneous systems with accelerators such as GPUs are a good fit for such algorithms, specifically as their architecture with a large amount of processing units allow to run many threads concurrently. Additionally, GPU matrix-matrix multiplication algorithms are potentially more cache friendly than CPU algorithms [24]. We implemented different types of action functions targeting the different processing units. The CPU action is implemented in C++ while the GPU action relies on CUDA [25]. Moreover, we designed four different approaches to execute the benchmark and an additional approach was used by Siemens to achieve maximum performance using both CPU and GPU:

ARM-Seq. Sequential implementation on ARM CPU.
MTAPI-CPU. MTAPI implementation with a single action for ARM CPU.
MTAPI-CPU-GPU. MTAPI implementation with actions for CPU and GPU.
MTAPI-GPU. MTAPI implementation with a single action for GPU.
MTAPI-CPU-GPU-Opt. Same as MTAPI-CPU-GPU, but with work item sizes tailored to the particular needs of the respective computation units and copying of data to the GPU overlapped with computation.

Figure 4(a) shows the normalized execution times for matrix sizes 128, 256, 512, and 1024 for UH-MTAPI. Figure 4(a) shows the results for Siemens MTAPI. We observe that the ARM action has comparable performance with the GPU action for matrices with sizes less than 128.

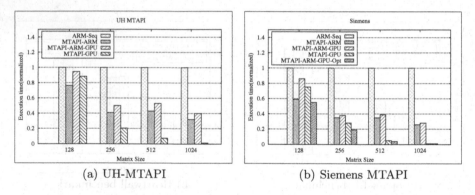

(a) UH-MTAPI   (b) Siemens MTAPI

Fig. 4. Normalized execution time for matrix multiplication with UH-MTAPI and Siemens MTAPI on NVIDIA Tegra TK1 board

The data being copied between the CPU and the GPU pose a major communication overhead. However, as the matrix size increases, the data copying time can be largely ignored for which reason the GPU action outperforms the CPU action. A simple distribution of the work to both processing units did not yield a speedup. In fact, the CPU action is far slower than the GPU action, and equally sized work items let the GPU finish while the CPU is still calculating. For this reason, the optimized version uses bigger work items for the GPU and smaller ones for the CPU. Moreover, data is transferred asynchronously, thus hiding the transfer time in computations. This technique results in a speedup in all tested cases, but the contribution of the CPU shrinks with increasing matrix size as expected.

6   Conclusion and Future Work

Programming models for heterogeneous multicore systems are important yet challenging. In this paper, we described the design and implementation of a parallel programming standard, the Multicore Task Management API (MTAPI). MTAPI enables application-level task parallelism on embedded devices with symmetric or asymmetric multicore processors. We showed that MTAPI provides a convenient way to develop portable and scalable applications targeting heterogeneous systems in a straight-forward manner. Our experimental results of MTAPI using different benchmarks show competitive performance compared to OpenMP while being more flexible. In the future, we will target further platforms such as DSPs.

Our sincere gratitude to the anonymous reviewers and many thanks to Markus Levy, President of the Multicore Association for his continued support.

References

1. Stotzer, E., Jayaraj, A., Ali, M., Friedmann, A., Mitra, G., Rendell, A.P., Lintault, I.: OpenMP on the low-power TI keystone II ARM/DSP system-on-chip. In: Rendell, A.P., Chapman, B.M., Müller, M.S. (eds.) IWOMP 2013. LNCS, vol. 8122, pp. 114–127. Springer, Heidelberg (2013). doi:10.1007/978-3-642-40698-0_9
2. Li, T., Brett, P., Knauerhase, R., Koufaty, D., Reddy, D., Hahn, S.: Operating system support for overlapping-ISA heterogeneous multi-core architectures. In: IEEE 16th International Symposium on High Performance Computer Architecture (HPCA), pp. 1–12. IEEE (2010)
3. Dagum, L., Enon, R.: OpenMP: an industry standard API for shared-memory programming. IEEE Comput. Sci. Eng. 5(1), 46–55 (1998)
4. Stone, J.E., Gohara, D., Shi, G.: OpenCL: a parallel programming standard for heterogeneous computing systems. Comput. Sci. Eng. 12(1–3), 66–73 (2010)
5. Chapman, B., Jost, G., Van Der Pas, R.: Using OpenMP: Portable Shared Memory Parallel Programming, vol. 10. MIT Press, Cambridge (2008)
6. Chapman, B., Huang, L., Biscondi, E., Stotzer, E., Shrivastava, A., Gatherer, A.: Implementing OpenMP on a high performance embedded multicore MPSoC. In: Parallel and Distributed Processing, pp. 1–8. IEEE (2009)
7. Duran, A., Corbalán, J., Ayguadé, E.: Evaluation of OpenMP task scheduling strategies. In: Eigenmann, R., Supinski, B.R. (eds.) IWOMP 2008. LNCS, vol. 5004, pp. 100–110. Springer, Heidelberg (2008). doi:10.1007/978-3-540-79561-2_9
8. Liao, C., Hernandez, O., Chapman, B., et al.: OpenUH: an optimizing, portable OpenMP compiler. Concurrency Comput.: Practice Exp. 19(18), 2317–2332 (2007)
9. Ghosh, P., Yan, Y., Eachempati, D., Chapman, B.: A prototype implementation of OpenMP task dependency support. In: Rendell, A.P., Chapman, B.M., Müller, M.S. (eds.) IWOMP 2013. LNCS, vol. 8122, pp. 128–140. Springer, Heidelberg (2013). doi:10.1007/978-3-642-40698-0_10
10. Reinders, J.: Intel Threading Building Blocks: Outfitting C++ for Multi-core Processor Parallelism. O'Reilly Media Inc., Sebastopol (2007)
11. Blumofe, R.D., Joerg, C.F., Kuszmaul, B.C., Leiserson, C.E., Randall, K.H. Zhou, Y.: Cilk: an efficient multithreaded runtime system, vol. 30. ACM (1995)

12. Duran, A., Ayguadé, E., Badia, R.M., Labarta, J., Martinell, L., Martorell, X., Planas, J.: OmpSS: a proposal for programming heterogeneous multi-core architectures. Parallel Process. Lett. **21**(02), 173–193 (2011)
13. Augonnet, C., Thibault, S., Namyst, R., Wacrenier, P.-A.: StarPU: a unified platform for task scheduling on heterogeneous multicore architectures. Concurrency Comput.: Practice Exp. **23**(2), 187–198 (2011)
14. Sun, P., Chandrasekaran, S., Chapman, B.: Targeting Heterogeneous SoCs using MCAPI. In: SRC TECHCON 2014, in the GRC Research Category Section 29.1 (2014)
15. Wang, C., Chandrasekaran, S., Sun, P., et al.: Portable mapping of openMP to multicore embedded systems using MCA APIs. In: Proceedings of LCTES 2013, pp. 153–162 (2013)
16. Wang, C., Chandrasekaran, S., Chapman, B., Holt, J.: libEOMP: a portable OpenMP runtime library based on MCA APIs for embedded systems. In: Proceedings of PMAM, pp. 83–92 (2013)
17. Sun, P., Chandrasekaran, S., Zhu, S., Chapman, B.: Deploying OpenMP task parallelism on multicore embedded systems with MCA task APIs. In: Proceedings of IEEE HPCC (2015, to appear)
18. Cederman, D., Hellstrom, D., Sherrill, J., Bloom, G., Patte, M., Zulianello, M.: RTEMS SMP for LEON3/LEON4 multi-processor devices. In: Data Systems in Aerospace (2014)
19. Wallentowitz, S., Wagner, P., Tempelmeier, M., et al.: Open tiled manycore system-on-chip. arXiv preprint arXiv:1304.5081 (2013)
20. Siemens. Embedded Multicore Building Blocks. https://github.com/siemens/embb
21. Herlihy, M., Shavit, N.: On the nature of progress. In: Fernàndez Anta, A., Lipari, G., Roy, M. (eds.) OPODIS 2011. LNCS, vol. 7109, pp. 313–328. Springer, Heidelberg (2011). doi:10.1007/978-3-642-25873-2_22
22. Che, S., Boyer, M., Meng, J., et al.: Rodinia: a benchmark suite for heterogeneous computing. In: Proceedings of IISWC, pp. 44–54. IEEE (2009)
23. NVIDIA Jetson TK1 Development Kit. http://developer.download.nvidia.com/embedded/jetson/TK1/docs/Jetson_platform_brief_May2014.pdf
24. Fatahalian, K., Sugerman, J., Hanrahan, P.: Understanding the efficiency of GPU algorithms for matrix-matrix multiplication. In: Proceedings of Conference on Graphics Hardware, pp. 133–137. ACM (2004)
25. NVIDIA. CUDA programming guide (2008)

Reducing Response Time with Preheated Caches

Mathias Gottschlag[(✉)] and Frank Bellosa[(✉)]

Karlsruhe Institute of Technology, Karlsruhe, Germany
os@itec.kit.edu

Abstract. CPU performance is increasingly limited by thermal dissipation, and soon aggressive power management will be beneficial for performance. Especially, temporarily idle parts of the chip (including the caches) should be power-gated in order to reduce leakage power. Current CPUs already lose their cache state whenever the CPU is idle for extended periods of time, which causes a performance loss when execution is resumed, due to the high number of cache misses when the working set is fetched from external memory. In a server system, the first network request during this period suffers from increased response time. We present a technique to reduce this overhead by preheating the caches in advance before the network request arrives at the server: Our design predicts the working set of the server application by analyzing the cache contents after similar requests have been processed. As soon as an estimate of the working set is available, a predictable network architecture starts to announce future incoming network packets to the server, which then loads the predicted working set into the cache. Our experiments show that, if this preheating step is complete when the network packet arrives, the response time overhead is reduced by an average of 80%.

Keywords: Leakage power · Caches · Preheating · Response time · Working set estimation

1 Introduction

CPU performance is increasingly limited by thermal dissipation. While smaller feature sizes provide us with additional transistors which could be used to implement more and more cores on one chip, the increased power density will soon create a situation where a significant portion of the available chip area has to be powered off (*dark silicon* [5]). Several techniques have been developed to make use of additional chip area even if continuous usage of the whole chip would violate thermal limits. One such technique is *Computational Sprinting*, which lets a CPU temporarily utilize all of the chip area to reduce the response time of the system. At other points in time, the chip is operating with significantly reduced power dissipation to keep the average power below the thermal limit [12].

We envision computational sprinting to be useful in a data center environment, because many web services have critical response time requirements. In such a setting, a server system would process several requests at full performance

© Springer International Publishing AG 2017
F. Desprez et al. (Eds.): Euro-Par 2016 Workshops, LNCS 10104, pp. 709–720, 2017.
DOI: 10.1007/978-3-319-58943-5_57

and therefore with low response times, and then would enter a low-power state in order to reduce the chip temperature. As leakage power is responsible for a significant part of the overall power consumption in modern CPUs [8], deep CPU sleep states (e.g., the ACPI PC7 state of modern Intel CPUs) shut down as much of the chip area as possible, including the caches [13]. As a result, the caches lose their state during idle periods. When the CPU resumes execution, the server application therefore incurs a performance loss because the working set has to be fetched from external memory. For the nginx web server serving a static web site, we have measured the response time overhead caused by cold caches to be as high as 35%.

The high response time from the initially cold caches would affect the tail latency of the system, even if, as described above, we expect servers to process requests in bursts between low-power periods. In modern large-scale web services, however, the tail latency of single systems is critical: Because operations are often parallelized on hundreds of machines (e.g., database shards), the final result will be delayed even if a single sub-operation experiences increased latency [2]. It is therefore important to reduce the impact of power management on the tail latency of server systems.

Zhu et al. propose anticipatory wakeups as a technique to hide the exit latency of CPU sleep states by waking the CPU up in advance before an event occurs [17]. Our experiments, however, have shown that the exit latency is low compared to the latency overhead caused by cold caches. Additionally, anticipatory wakeups can only function when the wakeup source is well predictable, whereas incoming network packets are hardly predictable. In this paper, we build upon the theory of anticipatory wakeups and extend it to solve these two problems. The key contributions of this paper, which are elaborated in Sect. 3, are as follows:

– We describe a technique to construct a fine-grained estimate of the working set of a server application. Such an estimate is required for efficient cache preheating. We generate the estimate by analyzing the tag bits of the last-level cache.
– We present a technique to predict future incoming network packets, in order to enable the system to wake up early and preheat the cache in anticipation of the network packets. Our design uses a network architecture which implements congestion control in a central arbiter. Having an overview over all packets sent in the near future, this arbiter is able to announce future packets to the receiver system.
– We discuss a mechanism to preheat the cache in anticipation of an event, so that the response time to that event is reduced significantly because the working set is already present in the caches.

These contributions are evaluated with measurements of a prototype implementation (see Sects. 4 and 5). We outline further improvements and future work in Sect. 6.

2   Background and Related Work

Leakage-Power Reduction: Leakage power dominates the power consumption of modern CPUs with small feature sizes [8], and as caches constitute a significant portion of the chip area, many approaches have been developed to reduce their leakage power. These approaches can be categorized into destructive and nondestructive techniques, depending on whether the cache contents are destroyed by the power management technique. Nondestructive techniques usually have lower impact on performance, but also provide lower power-saving advantages. For example, drowsy caches [3] can temporarily reduce the supply voltage of the cache to a point where the memory cells retain their content, but no access is possible. Significantly better leakage power reduction can be achieved by completely disconnecting memory cells from the power supply. Gated-V_{dd} [11] is a technique which performs such destructive power gating and combines it with a dynamically resizable cache. The decision to shrink or grow the cache is based on the number of cache misses during a time interval, and the inactive parts of the cache are disabled to conserve power.

This policy is completely reactive and uses very simple heuristics. Some dynamic situations however require a more flexible predictive approach for maximum performance: For example, the cache should be completely disabled during idle periods, but the content should be restored before the system is reactivated again. Such predictive tasks require information which is commonly only known to the operating system.

In a similar scenario, Zhu et al. therefore propose strong software engagement of the OS with the power management mechanisms of the hardware [17]. Especially, they show that the operating system can hide the wakeup latency of current CPUs by predicting future events and waking the CPU up in advance, so that it is fully awake by the arrival time of the events [17]. We extend these anticipatory wakeups with a technique to predict future incoming network packets and with a mechanism to preheat the caches when they have been flushed by the low-power state.

Centrally Arbitrated Networks: To be able to preheat the cache contents for an incoming network packet, our system needs to know the arrival time of that packet in advance. We use a network architecture with a central arbiter to predict future packets. Such networks have been studied in-depth [4,10,14], albeit with a different goal: Central arbiters are frequently used to implement connection switching, which has been proposed for low-latency traffic in data center networks.

Packet switching requires queues in all switches in order to deal with temporary congestion in some network segments, and these queues can significantly delay the queued packets. Connection switching, however, can provide superior network latencies compared to networks with traditional packet switching and congestion control [10]. In networks based on connection switching, a network arbiter temporarily allocates a connection with a fixed guaranteed bandwidth to a pair of systems. As the arbiter has a global view of the network, it can prevent any congestion by exclusively allocating network links to a single connection [4]. Despite the differences between such a network architecture and current network stacks, connection switching can be implemented on top of off-the-shelf ethernet hardware [14] and can even coexist with traditional packet switching by assigning different types of packets to different priority classes [10].

Adaptive Pre-paging: Whenever a network packet has been predicted, our design loads the predicted working set of the server application into the cache. Similar techniques have been developed to reduce the overhead caused by the migration of virtual machines [6]:

Post-copy migration of virtual machines achieves low downtimes by immediately resuming the virtual machine at the target system and then using on-demand paging to move the working set from the source system to the target. The problem of this technique is that initially, right after execution has been resumed on the target system, the whole working set is still placed on the source system. Therefore, many expensive page faults are generated. One approach to reduce the number of page faults is to already move the predicted working set of the virtual machine to the target system before execution is resumed (*adaptive pre-paging*) [6]. We use a similar approach to improve performance right after a system has resumed from a deep sleep state. However, instead of preventing page faults, we try to prevent cache misses by loading the estimated working set into the cache before execution is resumed. Our design therefore predicts the working set with cache line granularity instead of page granularity.

Adaptive pre-paging is further extended by Zhang et al. in their Picocenter virtualization system [16], which uses adaptive pre-paging to quickly restore virtual machines from checkpoints. The Picocenter system differentiates between different types of events which can reactivate a virtual machine (e.g., network packets which target different server applications) and creates a separate working set prediction for each type, by logging which pages have been accessed in the past after similar events. We employ a similar technique to maintain separate predicted working sets, and we select one of them to be loaded into the cache depending on the target port of the incoming network packet. In contrast to the Picocenter virtualization system, though, our design can already predict the type of future incoming network packets before they arrive.

3   Design

We present a system which loads the working set into the cache right before a network packet arrives. As shown in Fig. 1, our design consists of two phases: Initially, in the working set estimation phase, the system estimates the working set of the active server application. Once an estimate is available, the system enters the cache preheating phase. It resumes regular operation, with one exception: Whenever the system is woken up from a deep sleep state, the predicted working set is fetched into the CPU caches in order to reduce the response time

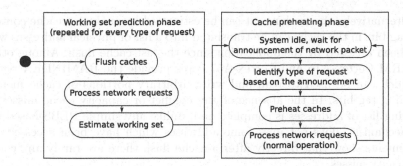

Fig. 1. The two phases of our cache preheating solution: first, the working set of the server application is estimated, then the estimate is used to preheat the caches for all following network requests. Incoming network packets are announced by an external component (described in Sect. 3.2).

of the system. For most server applications, the principle of locality is valid even over long timeframes, so the working set does not significantly change over time. Therefore, working set estimation is only performed once, but the predicted working set is reused to preheat the caches many times.

Working set estimation and cache preheating are implemented as part of the OS and are designed to work with arbitrary unmodified server applications. Similarly, the extensions to the network architecture as described in Sect. 3.2 are completely transparent to both the server application and its clients.

3.1 Working Set Estimation

In current systems, working set estimation is usually performed with page granularity, for example to provide efficient virtual memory. Often, the application only requires parts of a page, though. A cache preheating system should not load more data into the cache than necessary, so the working set must be predicted with cache line granularity. On current hardware, we have identified two hardware mechanisms which can be used to provide fine-grained information about the current working set.

First, some CPU architectures are able to trace and record all cache misses. The list of the cache misses and the accessed memory locations can be analyzed to create an estimate of the application's working set. For example, current Intel processors provide processor event-based sampling (PEBS) as a tracing facility for various types of events [7]. PEBS monitors an event counter and stores a copy of the most important CPU registers (along with the accessed memory address in case of memory events) to a buffer whenever the counter reaches a user-defined value. In theory, this facility can be used to trace all cache misses. In practice, however, whenever an event is logged, PEBS frequently misses other events which occur at approximately the same time [9]. It is therefore neither an effective working set estimation mechanism, nor is it efficient, as it also causes significant overhead when every event is recorded.

Alternatively, the working set can be estimated by analyzing cache contents. The tag bits in the cache can be translated into a list of physical addresses which have been accessed by the application since the last cache flush. Among others, the ARM Cortex-A15 and Cortex-A57 cores provide the RAMINDEX register [1] which can be used to read and write arbitrary portions of cache memory, including tag bits. In the absence of any conflict or capacity cache misses, the resulting list of addresses is complete and, unlike any simple PEBS-based tracing mechanism, does not miss some addresses which have been accessed. Our experiments show that directly after a cache flush there are rarely any conflict or capacity misses.

As cache tag bit analysis is a viable technique for working set estimation, we use a ARM Cortex-A15 system as the basis of our design: First, the caches are flushed to remove any unwanted data from the cache, and hardware prefetching is temporarily disabled to ensure that only accessed data is loaded into the cache. Afterwards, the server resumes normal operation and processes incoming network requests. After one or more requests have been processed, the last-level cache tag memory is read and analyzed. The result is a list of all memory locations which have been accessed since the cache flush. Future invocations of the server application might access slightly different memory locations, though. For example, network buffers are likely placed at different locations. To remove such dynamic regions from the working set, all these steps are repeated several times (8 times in our prototype). The final working set estimate then only contains those memory locations which have been repeatedly accessed.

3.2   Network Packet Prediction

Once a good working set estimate is available, the system switches back to regular operation, but activates cache preheating. The cache preheating mechanism however not only requires a prediction of the working set, but the system also needs to know when to preheat the caches. Because the arrival time of network packets is usually highly nondeterministic, anticipatory cache preheating is not possible with traditional network architectures. Our solution makes use of a centrally arbitrated network architecture such as Fastpass [10] to predict future incoming network packets.

Figure 2 shows how a central arbiter can announce future packets: First, the sender requests a time slot to send the packet. The network arbiter receives all

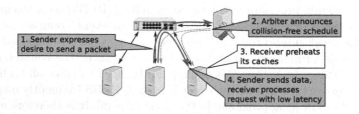

Fig. 2. Future network packets are announced by the network arbiter in advance, so that the receiver can preheat the caches in anticipation of the packets.

such requests from all systems in the network, and creates a schedule for the packets. Normally, this schedule only needs to be sent to the sender systems so that they know when to send their packets. In our system, however, the schedule is also sent to all affected receiver systems as an announcement of future network packets. When a system receives such an announcement while it is in a low-power state with flushed caches, it wakes up a CPU core which then starts to preheat the caches so that the network packet can be efficiently processed.

Ideally, the receiver system not only knows in advance when packets arrive, but also which type of request they carry. When different types of requests are processed, the server applications can have significantly different working sets. While the network is mostly oblivious to the type of request carried by a network packet, some indicators are transferred along with the data (e.g., the target TCP port). We modify the network arbitration scheme so that the sender system not only announces the target address to the arbiter, but also includes the target port. The arbiter forwards this information to the receiver system, which can, depending on the port, preheat the predicted working set of the corresponding server application.

3.3   Preheating

When an incoming packet has been announced by the network arbiter, the receiving system wakes the CPU and loads the estimated working set into the last-level cache. The main problem here is the short time span between the announcement and the arrival of the packet. For example, Fastpass calculates schedules only $65\,\mu s$ in advance [10]. Waking up the CPU requires half of that time already [13], so only approximately $30\,\mu s$ are left to preheat the cache. Preheating is therefore highly time-critical. However, the nginx web server only requires 235.8 KiB to serve a static website from RAM, and even a TPC-C-like MariaDB workload only requires 621.8 KiB to serve most requests. The required memory bandwidth to load these working sets into RAM in the available time (7.5 GiB/s and 19.8 GiB/s respectively) is well within the capabilities of current server hardware.

To preheat the last-level cache, the preheating code loops over all memory locations in the working set and loads them into the cache. To effectively utilize all the available memory bandwidth, the memory locations are sorted by increasing physical address. A linear access order minimizes the number of DRAM row activations and therefore improves memory throughput. As sorting is costly, the data is sorted as a preprocessing step during the working set estimation phase.

Additionally, the working set description is run-length encoded. Compression of the working set description increases the preheating memory throughput, as less additional data needs to be fetched from RAM. Run-length encoding provides significantly lower computational complexity compared to more complex cache state compression methods found in literature (e.g., dictionary-based compression [15]). The decoding overhead is low enough that it can be mostly hidden behind memory operations. Also, the regular structure of the addresses enables sufficient compression factors: Applications frequently access long consecutive memory regions, so many consecutive cache lines can be described in one "run".

As an example, the working set description of the nginx web server can be reduced by 68%, from 14528 bytes (one 32-bit address per 64-byte cache line in the working set) down to 4596 bytes, thereby increasing preheating performance by 5.7%.

These optimizations produce a fairly optimized memory access pattern which utilizes most of the available memory bandwidth. However, on modern systems, a single core often cannot saturate the memory bandwidth anymore. On our prototype platform, parallelizing the preheating code on two cores results in a 10% performance gain.

4   Evaluation

We have conducted a prototypical evaluation of our design, in order to answer the following questions: Can cache preheating be used to reduce the response time to network requests when the caches have been flushed? Is such preheating efficient enough so that it is a viable technique when combined with existing network architectures?

In this paper, we present a proof of concept based on a limited prototype which, while not being functionally complete, is able to show that cache preheating is a viable technique. Our prototype is designed to run on a system with ARM Cortex-A15 cores, and all benchmarks are executed on a Hardkernel Odroid-XU3 single board computer. This system provides a Samsung Exynos 5422 SoC with four Cortex-A15 cores and four Cortex-A7 cores.

The system's network support is limited to an USB ethernet adapter, which prevents any meaningful network latency benchmarks. Therefore, our prototype is not yet integrated with a real predictable network architecture, but instead simulates the network architecture in the benchmark client. The benchmarked server application is executed on a Cortex-A15 along with the cache preheating software, whereas the benchmark client is executed on a Cortex-A7 core on the same system, connected by a local TCP connection. As the SoC provides separate last-level caches for the different types of cores, this setup mostly isolates the cache footprints of the two processes. For the response time comparisons below, the benchmark client optionally flushes the caches of the Cortex-A15 cores to simulate CPU sleep states and optionally triggers cache preheating before issuing any request. The Cortex-A15 cores have private 64 KiB L1 caches as well as a shared 2 MiB L2 cache. The latter has shown to be large enough to accomodate the working sets of our benchmarks. Applications with a larger working set require a more complex approach to working set estimation.

4.1   Response Time Reduction

We measure the response time of several benchmark applications to show that preheating effectively mitigates the performance penalty of cold caches. We compare the response time with warm caches, flushed caches, and after caches have been first flushed and then preheated. Our three main benchmark applications are the nginx web server and the memcached key-value store, both serving static data, and a more complex dynamic TPC-C-like workload (DBT-2) executed on the MariaDB database.

Figure 3 shows the cumulative histogram of the response time of 100000 requests to the three applications. In all three cases, the average response time of requests is significantly reduced by cache preheating compared to when the requests hit cold caches as shown in Table 1. On average, the response time over-head (difference between response times for cold and warm caches) is reduced by 79.8%. To show that this improvement can be attributed to cache preheating, we also measure the average number of cycles per instruction (CPI). The CPI are a good indicator for the effectiveness of cache preheating, because a reduced number of cache misses is only beneficial for performance if it in turn reduces the number of CPU stall cycles. Our experiments show that the response time improvement is accompanied by 66% less cache misses (on average) as well as significantly improved CPI.

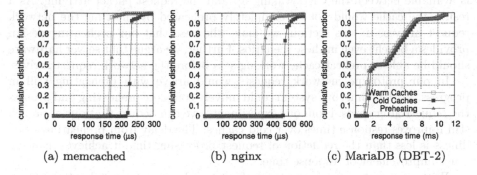

(a) memcached   (b) nginx   (c) MariaDB (DBT-2)

Fig. 3. Cumulative histogram of the response time with and without cache preheating.

Table 1. Averaged benchmark results with cold, warm and preheated caches as well as the corresponding cycles per instruction, predicted working set size and preheating costs.

	Response time (µs)			CPI			Working set	Preheating
	Warm	Cold	Preheated	Warm	Cold	Preheated		
nginx	367.6	498.0	388.5	3.63	5.78	4.12	235.8 KiB	77.4 µs
memcached	178.8	238.8	188.5	3.81	5.66	4.30	142.3 KiB	53.0 µs
MariaDB	3970	4320	4069	2.20	2.44	2.29	621.8 KiB	146.4 µs

4.2 Preheating Cost

Packets are only announced several dozens of microseconds in advance, thereby limiting the time available for loading the working set into the caches. Along with the response time, we have also measured the time required for preheating (in the "preheating" column of Table 1). The cost of preheating is approximately linear to the size of the predicted working set.

We have stated in Sect. 3.3 that preheating must not take more than $30\,\mu s$. Our prototype clearly violates this limit for all selected benchmarks, with preheating taking between 53.0 and $146.4\,\mu s$. The achieved average memory throughput is 3.17 GiB/s, which is close to the maximum throughput which can be achieved with well optimized code.

5   Discussion

Our evaluation shows that cache preheating improves response time significantly over cold caches. The potential response time reduction is large enough that the resulting energy savings should compensate the energy cost of preheating. In our prototype, however, cache preheating requires up to four times more time than is available between the CPU waking up and the request packet arriving. As a result, the cache would not be completely preheated by the time the network request arrives. In this section, we make the case that our preheating design provides a benefit even in these scenarios. Further, we argue that server hardware should be able to preheat cache working sets before the network request arrives.

In our prototype, network requests would arrive with preheating still in progress. At that time, our system could naively complete preheating and process the request afterwards. From our experiments, we can deduct that our approach still improves response times over cold caches: The delay from preheating's tardiness is less than the reduction of request processing time it achieves, causing a net improvement of response time.

With memcached for example, we found preheating to overshoot the $30\,\mu s$ available (see Sect. 3.3) by $23\,\mu s$. However, preheating reduced the request processing time by $50\,\mu s$ (see Table 1), thereby lowering the response time by $27\,\mu s$ (11%) overall. Similarly, even for the MariaDB benchmark which overshoots the preheating deadline by almost $120\,\mu s$, our preheating approach would still provide a $130\,\mu s$ response time reduction.

In practice, server hardware will require significantly less time, though, and can preheat the caches in time for the arriving network packets. Current server systems provide significantly higher memory bandwidth than the hardware platform of our prototype. The memory throughput of the Hardkernel Odroid-XU3 system is merely 3.17 GiB/s in our benchmarks, and even the *pmbw* parallel memory bandwidth benchmark only achieves slightly better results for a completely sequential access pattern. According to the pmbw benchmark, a recent Intel Skylake system with dual-channel memory in contrast provides almost 8 times more bandwidth. This performance increase should allow preheating to be completed in time before the corresponding network packet arrives, even for complex workloads such as the presented MariaDB benchmark.

6 Conclusion and Outlook

Deep CPU sleep states have negative effects on server response times, yet such power management methods are required in order to improve overall performance in a world with significant amounts of dark silicon. We have identified frequent cache flushes as the most problematic side effect of aggressive power management. Previous work usually suggested different power management methods which keep the cache state intact, but waste significant amounts of energy instead or which reduce performance. We argue that a more efficient system can be built if the operating system is in charge of cache content management.

We propose a system which preheats the caches in anticipation of events which cause the system to resume from a deep sleep state, in order to mitigate the effect of cold caches. When the arrival time of the next wakeup event is known, the estimated working set can be loaded into the cache in order to reduce the cache miss rate shortly after the event. We also describe a method to predict future incoming network packets with the help of a centrally arbitrated network architecture. Benchmarks show that such cache preheating can mitigate most of the overhead caused by cold caches. The time required to preheat the caches is too long in our current prototype though, due to the low memory bandwidth of our prototype platform. We show that cache preheating still results in a net response time reduction, and we argue that current server hardware provides enough memory bandwidth that cache preheating is completed quickly enough.

Our working set estimation code is currently limited to certain ARM CPU cores. On Intel CPUs, we are therefore evaluating whether PEBS—despite its limitations—can be used to trace all cache misses and to derive the working set from them. Additionally, we are currently integrating our cache preheating system with the Fastpass [10] network architecture, in order to be able to use cache preheating in a representative server system and to evaluate its effect on power usage in such a system.

References

1. Cortex-A15 Technical Reference Manual: 4.3.57. RAM Index Register. http://infocenter.arm.com/help/index.jsp?topic=/com.arm.doc.ddi0438c/BABEJEAJ.html. Accessed 05 May 2015
2. Dean, J., Barroso, L.A.: The tail at scale. Commun. ACM **56**(2), 74–80 (2013)
3. Flautner, K., Kim, N.S., Martin, S., Blaauw, D., Mudge, T.: Drowsy caches: simple techniques for reducing leakage power. In: Proceedings of the 29th Annual International Symposium on Computer Architecture (ISCA 2002), pp. 148–157. IEEE (2002)
4. Grosvenor, M.P., Schwarzkopf, M., Moore, A.W.: R2D2: bufferless, switchless data center networks using commodity Ethernet hardware. In: ACM SIGCOMM Computer Communication Review, vol. 43, pp. 507–508. ACM (2013)
5. Hardavellas, N., Ferdman, M., Falsafi, B., Ailamaki, A.: Toward dark silicon in servers. IEEE Micro **31**, 6–15 (2011)

6. Hines, M.R., Gopalan, K.: Post-copy based live virtual machine migration using adaptive pre-paging and dynamic self-ballooning. In: Proceedings of the 2009 ACM SIGPLAN/SIGOPS International Conference on Virtual Execution Environments (VEE 2009), pp. 51–60. ACM (2009)
7. Intel Corporation: Intel® 64 and IA-32 Architectures Software Developer's Manual - vol. 3: System Programming Guide. No. 325384-058US, April 2016
8. Kim, N.S., Austin, T., Baauw, D., Mudge, T., Flautner, K., Hu, J.S., Irwin, M.J., Kandemir, M., Narayanan, V.: Leakage current: Moore's law meets static power. Computer **36**(12), 68–75 (2003). IEEE
9. Larysch, F.: Fine-grained estimation of memory bandwidth utilization. Master thesis, Operating Systems Group, Karlsruhe Institute of Technology (KIT), Germany, March 2016
10. Perry, J., Ousterhout, A., Balakrishnan, H., Shah, D., Fugal, H.: Fastpass: a centralized "zero-queue" datacenter network. ACM SIGCOMM Comput. Commun. Rev. **44**(4), 307–318 (2015)
11. Powell, M., Yang, S.H., Falsafi, B., Roy, K., Vijaykumar, T.: Gated-V$_{dd}$: a circuit technique to reduce leakage in deep-submicron cache memories. In: Proceedings of the 2000 International Symposium on Low Power Electronics and Design (ISPLED), pp. 90–95. ACM (2000)
12. Raghavan, A., Luo, Y., Chandawalla, A., Papaefthymiou, M., Pipe, K.P., Wenisch, T.F., Martin, M.M.K.: Computational sprinting. In: Proceedings of the 18th International Symposium on High Performance Computer Architecture (HPCA), pp. 1–12. IEEE (2012)
13. Schöne, R., Molka, D., Werner, M.: Wake-up latencies for processor idle states on current x86 processors. Comput. Sci. Res. Dev. **30**(2), 219–227 (2015). Springer
14. Vattikonda, B.C., Porter, G., Vahdat, A., Snoeren, A.C.: Practical TDMA for datacenter Ethernet. In: Proceedings of the 7th ACM European Conference on Computer Systems (EuroSys 2012), pp. 225–238. ACM (2012)
15. Vishnoi, A., Panda, P.R., Balakrishnan, M.: Cache aware compression for processor debug support. In: Proceedings of the Conference on Design, Automation and Test in Europe (DATE 2009), pp. 208–213. European Design and Automation Association (2009)
16. Zhang, L., Litton, J., Cangialosi, F., Benson, T., Levin, D., Mislove, A.: Picocenter: supporting long-lived, mostly-idle applications in cloud environments. In: Proceedings of the 11th European Conference on Computer Systems (EuroSys 2016), p. 37. ACM (2016)
17. Zhu, Q., Zhu, M., Wu, B., Shen, X., Shen, K., Wang, Z.: Software engagement with sleeping CPUs. In: 15th Workshop on Hot Topics in Operating Systems (HotOS XV). USENIX Association, May 2015

Viability of Virtual Machines in HPC
A State of the Art Analysis

Jens Breitbart[1]([⊠]), Simon Pickartz[2], Josef Weidendorfer[1],
and Antonello Monti[2]

[1] Chair for Computer Architecture, Department of Informatics,
Technical University Munich, Munich, Germany
{j.breitbart,josef.weidendorfer}@tum.de
[2] Institute for Automation of Complex Power Systems, E.ON ERC,
RWTH Aachen University, Aachen, Germany
{spickartz,amonti}@eonerc.rwth-aachen.de

Abstract. Virtualization is common in various areas ranging from mobiles to large data centers operated by cloud providers. Theoretically, virtualization provides various benefits that could be useful to HPC as well, e.g., suspend a large application before system maintenance or migrate a process before a node fails due to hardware malfunctioning.

In this paper, we analyze the current state of the art of virtual machines for HPC with respect to their performance and energy consumption. Furthermore, we report on our findings on the compatibility of the current HPC software stack with virtual machines and how they complicate application analysis and application tuning, as well as how current HPC hardware limits some benefits of VMs.

1 Introduction

Due to numerous advantages, virtualization is omnipresent in seemingly all areas of computing nowadays. Mobiles use virtualized instruction sets for a simplified application develop- and deployment. Embedded systems rely on virtualization to run multiple specialized operating systems for resource partitioning within one device. Desktop users employ Virtual Machines (VMs) to run different operating systems for an isolation of applications running on the same hardware, and even large commercial data centers rely on VMs for a flexible assignment of resources to their customers. As a result, most of today's processors have all kinds of hardware support for effective virtualization built-in, there is a large choice of hypervisors which can use these hardware features, and all major operating systems run well both as guests or hosts in virtualization scenarios.

Despite this pervasive support and various use cases, this technology is currently not employed in High-Performance Computing (HPC). In this paper we investigate some use cases and benefits of virtualization and perform an analysis

J. Breitbart and S. Pickartz—Supported by the Federal Ministry of Education and Research (BMBF) under Grant 01IH13004 (Project FAST).

F. Desprez et al. (Eds.): Euro-Par 2016 Workshops, LNCS 10104, pp. 721–733, 2017.
DOI: 10.1007/978-3-319-58943-5_58

of the state-of-the-art with respect to the HPC software stack, the performance, the energy consumption, and the support for current hardware. We also examine its impact on the exploitation of today's many-core architectures. The additional degree of freedom with respect to the mapping of the applications onto the hardware topology provides new facilities for performance fine-tuning. Our findings reveal that using VMs hardly results in any overhead. Furthermore, VM migration may facilitate an increased overall system throughput, but requires special support within the communication stack when using HPC interconnects. However, VMs complicate application analysis and tuning, as the new virtualization layer is not well supported in tools and various benefits of VMs like stopping and migrating are not possible with the default HPC software stack. Overall, we conclude that VMs are still not ready for large scale deployment in HPC.

The paper is organized as follows. First, Sect. 2 describes VMs and their implementation, followed by Sects. 3 and 4 which introduce the hardware and applications/benchmarks used for the rest of the paper. Section 5 shows our measurements with memory bandwidth limited and compute bound applications. Section 6 introduces possible benefits of using VMs in HPC, whereas Sect. 7 discusses if these benefits can currently be achieved. The paper finishes with an overview of related work and conclusions, in Sects. 8 and 9, respectively.

2   Virtual Machines

In this paper, we focus on system VMs, which virtualize the target hardware, i.e., a process is started on the native host hardware that itself provides a complete substitute for a system and boots a new Operating System (OS). The *hypervisor* is a software used for the management of multiple guest VMs. Modern x86 hypervisors implementations rely on hardware support such as Intel's VT-x extension [20] or AMD-V. The former was introduced with the Pentium 4 processor in 2005 and is almost identical to AMD-V, which was introduced only half a year later.

As applications running within VMs have their own virtual address space within the address space of the process representing the VM, an additional dimension of virtual memory/address translation is introduced including additional page tables (so called guest page tables). The address space of the VM is typically accessed by means of guest physical addresses and the address space of the application running within the VM by guest virtual addresses; host physical/virtual addresses refer to the native equivalents. Memory accesses from within the VM require a translation from guest virtual addresses to host physical addresses. This is performed in two steps: the guest's page tables translate guest virtual addresses to guest physical/host virtual addresses, which are again translated to host physical addresses. This so-called two level page walk is supported via VT-x in hardware by *nested paging* [2]. With VT-x the Translation Lookaside Buffer (TLB) caches mappings involve both translation levels.

VMs introduce a further degree of freedom with respect to the mapping of virtual CPUs (VCPUs) onto Hardware Thread Contexts (HTCs). Although any VM configuration is feasible, the following three are of main interest when scheduling parallel applications on NUMA systems:

Outside pinning. Fill up the threads/processes VCPUs by VCPUs and pin theses to the physical cores in accordance to the pinning strategy suitable for the particular application. This configuration only uses as many VCPUs as needed by the application.

Outside pinning (all VCPUs). In contrast to the previous one, in this configuration all VCPUs are passed to the VM regardless of the amount of threads/processes being executed.

Host-topology. Map the host's topology onto that of the VM, i.e., perform an identity mapping of VCPUs to CPUs, and pin the threads/processes within the VM with the respective strategy from above.

3   Hardware Overview

All measurements were performed on two-socket NUMA nodes equipped with two Intel Xeon E5-2670 CPUs based on Intel's Sandy Bridge architecture. Each CPU has 8 cores resulting in a total of 16 CPU cores in the entire system whereby each core has support for two HTCs resulting in a total of 32 HTCs for the whole system. The L3 cache is shared among all cores of a CPU, both L1 and L2 cache as well as the instruction pipeline are shared among HTCs of the same core. Our systems are equipped with a total of 128 GiB of RAM (64 GiB per CPU) each. Furthermore, there are both a QDR InfiniBand Host Channel Adapter and a 1 Gbit/s Ethernet network card in the systems.

The so-called thermal design power (TDP) of each CPU in our system is 115 W, i.e., the CPU consumes about 115 W on average when all 8 cores are active and measured for a reasonably long time frame. Energy measurements were carried out by using two mechanisms: (1) the so-called Running Average Power Limit (RAPL) CPU counters which measure CPU cores, DRAM and CPU package energy consumption and (2) a MEGWARE Clustsafe, which measures the energy consumption of a whole system on the primary side.

4   Applications/Benchmarks

We used two example applications in this paper: a slightly modified version of mpiBLAST 1.6.0 and the CG solver from the numerical library LAMA [5,10]. Furthermore, we used the well known STREAM benchmark for an assessment of the impact of virtualization on memory-bound applications [14].

4.1   mpiBLAST

mpiBLAST is an application from computational biology. Using MPI-only, it is a parallel version of the original BLAST algorithm for a heuristic comparison of local similarities between genome or protein sequences from different organisms.

Due to its embarrassingly parallel nature, mpiBLAST allows for perfect scaling across tens of thousands of compute cores [11]. mpiBLAST uses a two-level master-slave approach and requires therefore at least 3 processes. The data structures used in the different steps of the BLAST search typically fit into the L1 cache resulting in a low number of cache misses. The search mostly consists of a series of indirections resolved from L1 cache hits allowing for good overlapping of different searches on the two HTCs of one core. Our modified version of mpiBLAST is available on GitHub[1]. In contrast to the original mpiBLAST we removed all sleep() function calls which were supposed to prevent busy waiting.

4.2 LAMA

LAMA is an open-source C++ library for numerical linear algebra. We use LAMA's standard implementation of a Conjugate Gradient (CG) solver, a hybrid OpenMP/MPI application. The library is compiled with Intel's MKL library to use basic BLAS operations within a step of the CG solver. Each solver iteration contains various global reduction operations resulting in frequent synchronization of threads as well as MPI tasks. As the involved data structures do not fit into CPU caches, the performance is fundamentally limited by main memory bandwidth and inter-core/node bandwidth for reduction operations. Thus, the CG solver obtains the best performance with just using a few cores. Consequently, it benefits from the so-called scatter pinning, i.e., threads are equally distributed among the NUMA domains and main memory bandwidth of all CPUs can be saturated with fewer threads. We use scatter pinning for all measurements involving LAMA.

5 Performance and Energy Consumption

Figure 1 presents the results of our scalability analysis of mpiBLAST and LAMA's CG solver. Figure 2 shows the average power consumption during the measurements and energy consumption of one application run. Each meter point was captured by the execution of the respective application in a loop for 30 min and averaging the individual results afterwards.

5.1 Memory Bandwidth Applications

The available memory bandwidth is slightly lower within a VM resulting an overhead of less than 5% (cf. Table 1). For the "Small" measurements[2] the TLBs can store all required translations generating hardly any page walks. Although running STREAM on the "Large" array size should result in more page walks, we notice a small overhead decrease. Hence, the effect of the additional page walk is in the order of measurement noise. As a result, memory bandwidth bound

---

[1] https://github.com/jbreitbart/mpifast.
[2] An array of 153 MiB (458 MiB STREAM memory consumption in total).

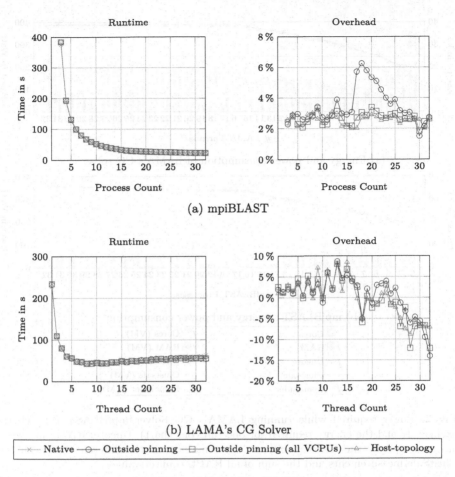

Fig. 1. Runtime of mpiBLAST and LAMA's CG Solver with varying number of processes/threads for all three VM configurations. The overhead is computed based on the native execution.

applications may suffer from a small constant performance loss, when running inside a VM. We use all 32 HTCs, compact pinning, and the host-topology configuration for the shown STREAM measurements.

As the CG solver is memory-bound, it scales up to only 11 threads with an average runtime of 41.45 s in native execution. At this meter point using a VM results in a performance penalty of around 6%. In accordance with our previous findings the CG solver only scales up to 8 threads within a VM (cf. Fig. 1) due to the lower memory bandwidth. Considering its best performance at 8 threads with 42.44 s (outside pinning) and 42.97 s (host-topology), we get an effective performance degradation of less than 4%. For thread counts exceeding 25 the VM outperforms native execution which is due less remote memory accesses within the VM. There is hardly any difference in energy consumption between native execution and using a VM (cf. Fig. 2). We expect this to be a result from different first-touch runtime behavior.

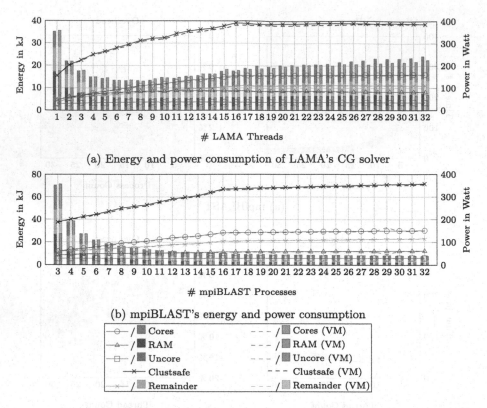

(a) Energy and power consumption of LAMA's CG solver

(b) mpiBLAST's energy and power consumption

Fig. 2. Power required while running LAMA's CG Solver/mpiBLAST (line chart) exclusively and the energy required for one run (bar chart). Uncore, RAM, and cores are measured by the RAPL counters. The remainder is the difference between the ClustSafe measurements and the sum of all RAPL counter values.

Table 1. STREAM benchmark results on array sizes of 152.6 MiB (Small) and 1.22 GiB (Large). The throughput is given in GiB/s and the Overhead (OHD) in %.

Kernel	Small			Large		
	Native	VM	OHD	Native	VM	OHD
Copy	53.23	50.76	4.64	65.22	63.69	2.34
Scale	64.27	62.79	2.30	65.99	64.73	1.91
Add	67.18	65.18	2.97	67.06	65.27	2.66
Triad	67.18	64.94	3.33	67.17	65.26	2.84

5.2 Compute Bound Applications

We do not expect compute bound applications to suffer a major performance loss when running in VM and Fig. 1 mostly confirms our expectations. The trend is the same for both, native execution and the virtualized environment showing the best performance with 32 processes. The VM only generates little overhead of up to 3% in runtime and even less for energy consumption. However, there is one notable effect: when we start to use two HTCs per core for computation, outside pinning with a VCPU count equal to the number of processes has significant impacts on the generated overhead, e.g., about 6% for 18 processes. As mpiBLAST almost entirely works on data residing within the first-level cache, a higher number of cache miss is the most probable reason which may stem from additional system noise. However, further research is required to identify the exact cause.

6   Benefits of Virtualization

So far we have only shown that VMs have a small impact on performance and energy consumption. However, we have not discussed any of their potential benefits for HPC.

6.1   Isolation

In cloud computing VMs are often used for provisioning of isolated environments between different customers. In HPC, computing centers achieve the required isolation by a dedication of complete compute nodes to users. This strategy decreases the overall system utilization if the application is not capabable of a full system exploitation. To our knowledge, only few HPC computing centers schedule jobs at a finer granularity purely relying on Linux for a prevention of resources conflicts. Furthermore, this strategy cannot be applied if users explicitly specify thread affinities.

Nonetheless, co-scheduling jobs with diverse resource demands is known to increase overall system throughput [4]. For an evaluation of the performance penalties caused by VMs in such a scenario, we co-scheduled mpiBLAST and LAMA each within their own VM on the same host. As mpiBLAST performance is insensitive regarding the pinning, we derive its pinning from the requirements of LAMA, i.e., scatter pinning is used.

Figures 3 and 4 show the results of our measurements for both runtime and energy consumption. The efficiency is computed based on the fastest native execution, i.e., with 16 processes in co-scheduling mpiBLAST achieves about 45% of the performance of its native execution with 32 processes and LAMA achieves about 80% of the performance of its native execution with 11 threads. In general, we observe an increase of the overall application throughput similar to the results presented in [4]. The power consumption (cf. Fig. 4) is slightly increased compared to the exclusive application runs. This, however, is expected behavior as the system is doing more work while achieving a higher energy efficiency when taking the application throughput into account.

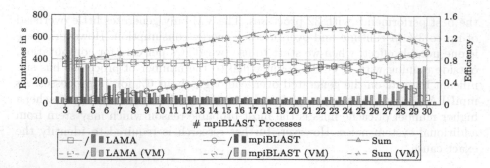

Fig. 3. Application runtime (bar chart, left y-axis) and efficiency (line chart, right y-axis) when running both LAMA and mpiBLAST concurrently. The efficiency is computed based on the most efficient exclusive application run. The x-axis shows the number of mpiBLAST processes running, the HTCs used by LAMA can be computed via 31 minus the number of mpiBLAST processes. We used 31 HTCs in total to allow for comparisons with [4].

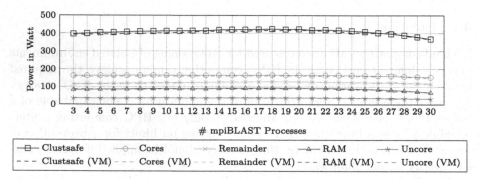

Fig. 4. Power Consumption when Co-scheduling LAMA and mpiBLAST. Uncore, RAM, and cores are measured by the RAPL counters. The remainder is the difference between the ClustSafe measurements and the sum of all RAPL counter values.

6.2 Transparent Start, Stop, and Migrate

VMs can be stopped and restarted at any time transparently from within the VM. Such a feature may ease hardware maintenances during applications runs without losing the current progress. Furthermore, VMs can also be restarted on another host or migrated from one host to another. Cloud providers leverage this feature exactly for these reasons: VMs are moved to nodes with little or no load for hardware/software maintenances or load balancing without generating application downtimes.

HPC centers typically take their system off-line for maintenance and do not apply any automatic load balancing. Resources are dedicated to jobs regardless of their actual usage. However, based on the results of our co-scheduling measurements (cf. Sect. 5), we can also show that VM migration can contribute to an increased overall system throughput. Figure 5 presents an example schedule

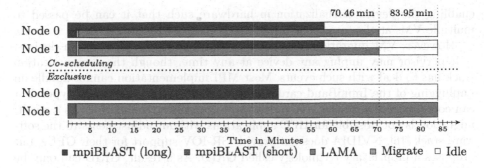

Fig. 5. Co-scheduling vs. Exclusive scheduling.

and the resulting runtime of three jobs. We expect the jobs mpiBLAST (long) and mpiBLAST (short) to be in the job queue at the beginning and LAMA to be added shortly after the start of mpiBLAST (short). The exclusive case runs natively on the hardware, whereas the co-scheduling case employs VMs in conjunction with migration reducing the runtime by about 16%. This performance increase stems from the fact that LAMA memory-bound and profits from the execution on two nodes. Executing LAMA on two nodes is only possible via migration, as Node 1 is already fully utilized by the job mpiBLAST (long). The migration time (27 s) is very short compared to the total runtime of the jobs. The energy consumption is almost identical for both scenarios with the co-scheduling case consuming 3.1 MJ and the exclusive scheduling requiring 3.2 MJ. We used Ethernet to communicate between the two nodes, as Infiniband cannot be used in conjunction with migration without changes to the software stack [16,17].

7   State of the Art

Despite the benefits of virtualization for HPC, there are certain limitations that come with this technology. This section summarizes implications thereof to the HPC software stack.

7.1   HPC Hardware/Software Support

As noted before, common hard- and software come with support for virtualization. However, major challenges are OS-bypass techniques, i.e., hardware that is directly controlled in user space such as InfiniBand or GPUs. Their employment requires support of the HPC software stack whereas two approaches for their virtualization are common: (1) the device is entirely emulated in software which typically results in unacceptable performance penalties, or (2) the guest is granted direct access to the hardware device via PCIe pass-through [1]. This is usually done in conjunction with Single Root I/O Virtualization (SR-IOV) enabling the device virtualization in hardware such that it can be passed to multiple VMs at the same time at nearly native performance [18].

However, VM migration is impossible with attached pass-through devices. A hypervisor may unplug any device at any time, though the communication stack has to deal with such events. Most MPI implementation cannot handle an unplugging of the InfiniBand card during runtime and seemingly no hypervisor can communicate with the MPI processes to coordinate the unplug. As a result, migration is not possible for HPC applications without adjustments to the software stack [16]. NVIDIA does not provide SR-IOV support for their GPUs, but proposes a propriatary technology called GRID. As a result, GRID can only be used with a small subset of the available hypervisors (VMWare, Xen) that are directly supported by NVIDIA. AMD announced SR-IOV support at the end of 2015[3]. However, neither AMD nor NVIDIA solve the issues that come with VM migration.

Initially Kernel-based Virtual Machine (KVM) restricted VMs to run within a single NUMA domain [9] only. However, this limitation has been resolved with Version 2.0 released in 2014 allowing for the provision of virtual NUMA topologies to VMs comprising multiple VCPUs. This has implications to both GNU OpenMP and Intel OpenMP as the pinning strategies may not behave correctly, depending on the CPU/VCPU mappings.

Inter-VM intra-host communication is usually rather slow, unless a locality aware MPI implementation is deployed. Support for this feature, however, requires an experimental feature (ivshmem) that was added with the latest KVM version released in December 2015. Usually, a virtual Ethernet device (or an IB device passed through to the VM) is used for this communication path, even though shared memory would be possible [15]. Running multiple VMs with the same application on the same host is important, as the size of a VM is also the granularity at which processes may be migrated between nodes. Overall, migration is an interesting feature, however currently no HPC system scheduler leverages this mechanism for automatic load balancing. Besides being a non-trivial task by itself, VM migration limits the usable hardware.

7.2 Increased Complexity

The additional software layer that comes with virtualization adds to the complexity of the system. This layer complicates various tasks that are common in HPC. For example, we were unable to pinpoint the exact reason for the performance difference of running LAMA with a high number of threads within a VM compared to native execution. We observe a reduction of remote memory accesses when running within a VM. Further investigations with a currently unreleased NUMA simulator indicate an unstable first touch behavior, i.e., the exact distribution between NUMA nodes depends on the runtime characteristics, although it is identical in native execution among various runs. We would not

---

[3] http://www.amd.com/en-us/press-releases/Pages/amd-unveils-worlds-2015aug31.a spx.

be surprised if other applications reveal similar subtle (performance) bugs when running within a VM that could result in a notable performance degradation.

The virtualization layer adds a degree of freedom with respect to the affinity, i.e., the VCPUs have to be mapped to the real cores in addition to the threads/processes that map onto the VCPUs. As current OpenMP and MPI implementations lack support for this two-level pinning, we had to implement it manually for all measurements. Depending on the exact pinning strategy, we could observe efficiency variations of up to 10%.

8 Related Work

Virtualization is regularly evaluated for HPC in the recent years [12,19,21]. However, the focus is usually put on the comparison of different hypervisors on the overhead for common HPC workloads and not on the overall HPC stack. Furthermore, the migration of VMs—one of the main arguments for virtualization—is a topic of major interest [7]. Huang et al. present Nomad, a thin virtualization layer between the user processes and the InfiniBand hardware for a transparent VM migration with attached pass-through devices [8].

For effective co-scheduling, an understanding of the resource utilization and the mutual influence of applications is beneficial. Different proposals exist to come up with good predictions, often based on empirical slow-down measurements [3,6,13].

9 Conclusion

In this paper we studied the current state of the art of VMs for HPC. When looking at raw performance and energy efficiency number, VMs arguably have almost no drawback. VMs can offer various benefits for computing centers like stopping and restarting jobs or automatic load balancing, but the HPC software and hardware stack prevents the deployment of such features. The increased complexity when using VMs also adds to the burden of HPC specialists analyzing and optimizing applications. The additional indirection complicates finding the source of potential performance degradation, as we found no tool that can correlate host measurements to guest processes.

There are still various areas of research to be explored. We have preliminary OS noise/jitter measurements that indicate higher noise when using VMs, which can limit scalability of some applications. Further work is required to exactly quantify the impact. Furthermore, we plan to investigate the benefits of migration at a larger scale.

References

1. Intel Virtualization Technology for Directed I/O. Technical report, Intel Corporation (2014)
2. Bhargava, R., Serebrin, B., et al.: Accelerating two-dimensional page walks for virtualized systems. In: ASPLOS XIII: Proceedings of the 13th International Conference Architectural Support for Programming Languages and Operating System ACM (2008)
3. de Blanche, A., Lundqvist, T.: Addressing characterization methods for memory contention aware co-scheduling. J. Supercomput. **71**(4), 1451–1483 (2015)
4. Breitbart, J., Trinitis, C., et al.: Case study on co-scheduling for HPC applications. In: Proceedings of International Workshop Scheduling and Resource Management for Parallel and Distributed Systems, September 2015
5. Darling, A., Carey, L., et al.: The Design, Implementation, and Evaluation of mpiBLAST. In: Proceedings of ClusterWorld, June 2003
6. Eklov, D., Nikoleris, N., et al.: Bandwidth bandit: quantitative characterization of memory contention. In: IEEE/ACM International Symposium on Code Generation and Optimization (CGO) 2013, February 2013
7. Huang, W., Gao, Q., et al.: High performance virtual machine migration with RDMA over modern interconnects. In: 2007 IEEE International Conference on Cluster Computing (CLUSTER). IEEE (2007)
8. Huang, W., Liu, J., et al.: Nomad: migrating OS-bypass networks in virtual machines. In: VEE 2007: Proceedings of the 3rd International Conference on Virtual Execution Environments. ACM (2007)
9. Ibrahim, K.Z., Hofmeyr, S.A., et al.: Characterizing the performance of parallel applications on multi-socket virtual machines. In: CCGRID (2011)
10. Kraus, J., Förster, M., et al.: Using LAMA for efficient AMG on hybrid clusters. Comput. Sci. Res. Dev. **28**(2), 211–220 (2013)
11. Lin, H., Balaji, P., et al.: Massively parallel genomic sequence search on the Blue Gene/P architecture. In: International Conference for High Performance Computing, Networking, Storage and Analysis (SC 2008). IEEE (2008)
12. Luszczek, P., Meek, E., Moore, S., Terpstra, D., Weaver, V.M., Dongarra, J.: Evaluation of the HPC challenge benchmarks in virtualized environments. In: Alexander, M., et al. (eds.) Euro-Par 2011. LNCS, vol. 7156, pp. 436–445. Springer, Heidelberg (2012). doi:10.1007/978-3-642-29740-3_49
13. Mars, J., Vachharajani, N., et al.: Contention aware execution: online contention detection and response. In: Proceedings of the 8th Annual IEEE/ACM International Symposium on Code Generation and Optimization (CGO) (2010)
14. McCalpin, J.D.: Memory bandwidth and machine balance in current high performance computers. IEEE Computer Society Technical Committee on Computer Architecture (TCCA) Newsletter, December 1995. https://www.cs.virginia.edu/stream/ref.html#citing
15. Pickartz, S., Breitbart, J., et al.: Implications of process-migration in virtualized environments. In: Proceedings of 1th Workshop Co-Scheduling of HPC Applications, January 2016
16. Pickartz, S., Clauss, C., et al.: Application migration in HPC–a driver of the exascale era? In: International Conference High Performance Computing and Simulation (HPCS), July 2016
17. Pickartz, S., Clauss, C., et al.: Non-intrusive migration of MPI processes in OS-bypass networks. In: Parallel and Distributed Processing Symposium Workshops (IPDPSW) (2016)

18. Pickartz, S., Gad, R., Lankes, S., Nagel, L., Süß, T., Brinkmann, A., Krempel, S.: Migration techniques in HPC environments. In: Lopes, L., et al. (eds.) Euro-Par 2014. LNCS, vol. 8806, pp. 486–497. Springer, Cham (2014). doi:10.1007/978-3-319-14313-2_41

19. Regola, N., Ducom, J.C.: Recommendations for virtualization technologies in high performance computing. In: CloudCom (2010)

20. Uhlig, R., Neiger, G., et al.: Intel virtualization technology. Computer **38**(5), 48–56 (2005)

21. Younge, A.J., Henschel, R., et al.: Analysis of virtualization technologies for high performance computing environments. In: IEEE International Conference on Cloud Computing (CLOUD). IEEE (2011)

UCHPC - UnConventional High-Performance Computing

The ICARUS White Paper: A Scalable, Energy-Efficient, Solar-Powered HPC Center Based on Low Power GPUs

Markus Geveler[✉], Dirk Ribbrock, Daniel Donner, Hannes Ruelmann,
Christoph Höppke, David Schneider, Daniel Tomaschewski, and Stefan Turek

Institute for Applied Mathematics, TU Dortmund, Vogelpothsweg 87, 44227
Dortmund, Germany
markus.geveler@math.tu-dortmund.de,
http://www.icarus-green-hpc.org

Abstract. We present a unique approach for integrating research in
High Performance Computing (HPC) as well as photovoltaic (PV) solar
farming and battery technologies into a container-based compute center
designed for a maximum of energy efficiency, performance and extensi-
bility/scalability. We use NVIDIA Jetson TK1 boards to build a considerably dimensioned cluster of 60 low-power GPUs, attach a 7.5 kWp
solar farm and a 8 kWh Lithium-Ion battery power supply and integrate
everything into a single-container, standalone housing. We demonstrate
the success of our system by evaluating the performance and energy efficiency for common versatile dense and sparse linear algebra kernels as
well as a full CFD code. By this work we can show, that with current
technology, energy consumption-induced follow-up cost of HPC can be
reduced to zero.

Keywords: Energy-efficient HPC · ARM cluster · GPGPU · Solar
power · Battery power supply

1 Introduction

In the age of transitioning from nuclear- and fossil-driven energy supplies to
renewables, besides energy harvesting and energy grids adapting to this decentralized energy production, *energy consumers* (such as computer hardware) have
to be adapted, which in principle means a necessary increase in *energy efficiency*.
Today's HPC centers mostly rely on massively parallel distributed memory clusters whose compute nodes are also multi-level parallel and heterogeneous. The
nodes usually comprise one or more high-end server CPUs based on the x86,
Power, or SPARC architectures optionally accelerated by GPUs or other (accelerator) hardware. Large HPC sites of this type have substantial energy requirements so that the associated expenses over the lifetime of the system may reach
the same order of magnitude as the initial acquisition costs. In addition, the
energy supply for supercomputers is not always an integral part of its overall

© Springer International Publishing AG 2017
F. Desprez et al. (Eds.): Euro-Par 2016 Workshops, LNCS 10104, pp. 737–749, 2017.
DOI: 10.1007/978-3-319-58943-5_59

design - consumers (such as the compute-cluster, cooling, networking, management hardware) are often developed independently from the key technologies of the energy revolution, e.g. renewable energy sources, battery- and power-grid techniques. The Power Wall has been accepted to be one of the major challenges in high scale computing. However, as a consequence of decades of performance-centric hardware development, there is a huge gap between pure performance and energy efficiency in these designs: The Top500 list's best performing HPC system (dissipating power in the 20 MW range making a power supply by local solar farming for instance an impossible-to-achieve aim) is only ranked 84th on the corresponding Green500 list, whereas the most energy-efficient system in place only performs 160th in the metric of raw floating point performance [4,17]. The most obvious feature all Green500 top ten systems share is, that they rely on accelerators - mostly GPUs, but the top three even on an unconventional micro architecture. From an HPC center's point of view, there are two possible ways to tune the energy efficiency: For a given HPC installation, an optimal reduced processor voltage and frequency can be found [23,24], or – at the hardware-design stage – more energy efficient hardware components can be selected. Recently, power and energy metrics started being included into performance models for numerical software [1,2,12,15]. However, developers of scientific software can (if at all) only control the energy efficiency of their 'production'-code, while hardware of the targeted HPC centers is out of their influence. The most impacting reason for this is the fact, that the cluster design is prone to principles of mass markets or in other words, HPC users do not determine the properties of available compute hardware. The users are literally trapped between very 'traditional' chip vendor- and HPC center construction markets concentrating on raw performance and being as much versatile as possible on the one hand and relatively application-oblivious acquisition processes on the HPC-site level (i.e. university-level- or even regional resources) on the other. Hence, there is a huge potential in energy savings in HPC. Recently, a game-changing impulse in this regard for HPC may come from mobile/embedded computing with devices featuring a long history of being developed under one major aspect: they have had to be operated with a (limited) battery power supply. Hence, as opposed to x86 and other commodity designs (with a focus on chipset compatibility and performance), the resulting energy efficiency advantage can be made accessible to the HPC community. In our earlier work [10] we demonstrated reductions in the energy-to-solution of simulations by using ARM-based processors. Those findings were obtained on a cluster prototype built with NVIDIA Tegra 2 and continued later with Tegra 3 microarchitecture [21]. Both chips are based on the Cortex-A9 processor; our current work employs NVIDIA Tegra K1 with Cortex-A15 CPUs [6] and – focused in this paper – the embedded GPU. In the meantime, using low-power (ARM) hardware in the HPC context, especially as a 'low energy-to-solution' alternative to commodity CPUs, has become an active research topic [3]. With the NVIDIA Tegra K1, even a programmable embedded low power Kepler GPU becomes accessible alongside the ARM cores on one System-on-Chip (SoC), making a huge jump in theoretical peak performance whilst preserving minimum power requirements.

This may hence offer a way to change hosting of simulations, making them accessible to more universities/enterprises/data centers. Also, we believe that in order to make a change it is necessary to take a look at the problem of too much overall energy consumption (and therefore carbon dioxide pollution) from a greater angle than any scientific field alone can provide. Our idea is to bring to life a lighthouse project, that overcomes the limits regarding (energy) efficiency of scientific software development on the one hand side and standard HPC center construction on the other. Our system combines the high ends in energy-efficient floating point hardware, renewable energies and battery storage with a self-made housing and cooling. Normally, we are concerned with hardware-oriented simulation software. In this paper, we deliberately switch angles designing a versatile, extensible and scalable HPC resource *at zero follow-up cost after installation*. Our approach comprises 60 NVIDIA Tegra K1 SoC that is 240 ARM CPU cores and 60 GPUs offering a theoretical peak performance of more than 21 TFlop/s at a total power dissipation of less than 1 kW with no additional energy costs due to an insular solar power supply and battery system. We show for a range of very versatile numerical kernels, that compared to commodity CPUs and -accelerators, energy efficiency is enhanced to a great extend. Also, we demonstrate, that such a system can be built by means of mass-market components and that it works properly with a 7.5 kWp solar power supply and a 8 kWh battery. The remainder of this paper is organised as follows: In Sect. 2 we provide a deep-as possible insight into all components of the project. We then dedicate Sect. 3 to evaluating the system, putting a clear focus on the HPC aspects but also presenting first results concerning the whole system. Finally, we conclude in Sect. 4.

2 System Design

ICARUS is short hand for **I**nsular **C**ompute center for **A**pplied Mathematics, powered by **R**enewables, built upon **U**nconventional hardware combined with high-end **S**imulation Software. It is intended to be a system integration pilot project covering two pillars of the energy revolution, namely renewable energies and energy-efficient consumers [9].

2.1 System Overview

There are several basic design principles for ICARUS: All energy consumers have to fulfill the latest standards regarding energy efficiency. For the digital components such as switches for instance, the IEEE 802.3az [13] standard has to be applicable. The system has to be independent, which means in particular, independence from the public energy grid and any architectural constraints. The reason for this choice is to free it from any infrastructural necessities in order to maintain versatility of operation. For instance with its holistic design, ICARUS can be used standalone in areas with little or no power grid development. The supercomputer component as well as its housing, cooling, management hardware, solar power supply and battery storage must be able to be used in parallel, without inducing super linear cost in any regard (such as space, monetary- and energy cost) in order to be scalable. With respect to these paradigms, ICARUS is aggregated by the following key components: (1) A prototype of a compute-cluster built solely from compute nodes with mobile SoCs featuring programmable floating point accelerators. This is our main focus and is described in Sect. 2.2. (2) A state-of-the-art photovoltaic solar farm that is sufficiently dimensioned to provide power for operating the cluster under full load whole day plus charging the battery both *in summer* that is, with sufficient sun harvesting at weather in Dortmund, Germany. (3) For operation at night, a sufficiently sized battery rack is employed that is capable to power the cluster under full load after full charge for 8 h without sunlight. (4) A simple housing that contains everything (except the solar modules of the PV farm). We achieve the goal of scalability by the design of a housing implemented by a modified oversees cargo container see Sect. 2.3. Images of the fully assembled system can be found in Fig. 1. Years after the ICARUS project started in 2013, there are several comparable approaches nowadays. Recently, NASA published a data center in a container, in order to be movable and scalable [18]. Another container-based data center is commercially available as a standalone, fuel- and battery-power supply driven resource [14]. Using mobile SoCs in the context of HPC and building small clusters of unconventional hardware [5,11] as well as exploring Jetson TK1 for this purpose has also been performed [20] or at least considered [16] by others. However, to the best of our knowledge there is currently no group or enterprise that has driven this kind of system integration this far and ICARUS is the only container-based system combined with customised renewable energies power supply.

(a) primary PV modules (b) secondary PV modules (c) assembled helix (d) full cluster

Fig. 1. ICARUS system construction site in March 2016 and cluster assembly.

2.2 The Tegra K1 Cluster

The system's core component is the NVIDIA Jetson TK1 development board released in late 2014. The Tegra K1 chip is a SoC hosting a quad-core 32 Bit ARM Cortex-A15 CPU and a programmable Low-Power Kepler GPU sharing the DRAM. The chip is of special interest because of the CUDA-capable GPU promising a theoretical (single precision) performance of around 300 GFlops/s at a power dissipation of ca. 10 W. The Jetson is a carrier board intended as development environment for the Tegra K1 SoC. It includes everything to be used as a standalone, 'single-circuit' computer, featuring (inter alia) a GigaBit Ethernet adapter, a small fan for cooling the SoC, an SD-card slot (which we use for secondary storage) and a Ubuntu-based Linux OS [19]. In the course of this paper, we denote a single Jetson board to be one compute node in ICARUS. For comparison in Sect. 3, we employ two workstations representing different hardware generations, featuring (1) a Haswell CPU and a GeForce 980 Ti, representing the high-end in commodity (desktop) computer hardware. (2) An older IvyBride CPU alongside GeForce GTX660 and Tesla K20x GPUs, representing an average workstation with desktop- and compute GPUs. Hardware details can be obtained from Tables 1 and 2. It must be noted, that the Jetson TK1 is not exactly intended to serve as a cluster node. A slightly over sized fan and (for the purpose of HPC) unwanted board components such as I/O pins stemming from the intention to be used in embedded systems both induce a power dissipation malus. The greatest drawback of the board is its comparatively small RAM (2 GB). However, recently, the Tegra K1 has also been released as a card-sized compute module [22]. In addition, the 64 Bit follow up to the Tegra K1, called Tegra X1 has become available in 2016, featuring the augmented 1.9 GHz ARM Cortex-A57 CPU, a 1 GHz Maxwell GPU, almost doubling the theoretical peak performance via its much better LPDDR4 memory interface.

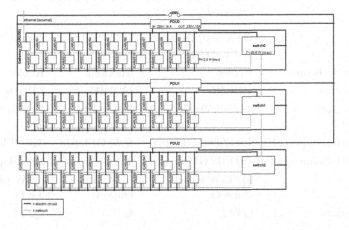

Fig. 2. Power- (blue) and network (red) topology of the cluster. (Color figure online)

The network in ICARUS is composed of three 28 port GiB Ethernet switches (Cisco SG300-28) with a switching capacity of 56 GB/s and a power dissipation of 19–20 W peak only due to fanless cooling. We depict the network topology in Fig. 2. Note that for technical reasons, we provide access to the cluster via a dedicated gateway node. The additional Ethernet port on that board is provided by a compatible Mini-PCI-e-to-Ethernet adapter. The on-board eMMC memory (16 GB) is used for the operating system and primary data. In addition, we provide each with a 128 GB Ultra SDXC 128 GB 40 MB/s Class 1 SD-card.

Table 1. CPU Hardware details and measured base (idle-) power of carrier environments.

	i5-3470	i5-4690K	Jetson TK1
Micro-architecture	Ivy Bridge	Haswell	Cortex-A15 (Tegra K1)
N_{cores}	4	4	4
Clock speed	3.20 GHz (turbo 3.60 GHz)	3.50 GHz (turbo 3.9 GHz)	2.3 GHz
L1-cache	4×32 KB + 4×32 KB	4×32 KB + 4×32 KB	32 KB + 32 KB
L2-/L3-cache	4×256 KB/6 MB	4×256 KB/6 MB	2 MB/–
Memory type	DDR3	DDR3	LPDDR3
Peak memory bandwidth	25.6 GByte/s	25.6 GByte/s	14.9 GByte/s
P_{base}	51 W (Intel chipset)	41 W (Intel chipset)	3.9 W (Jetson TK1)
Release date	Q2'12	Q2'14	Q2'14

Table 2. GPU Hardware details and measured base (idle-) power of carrier environments.

	GTX 660/Tesla K20x systems	GTX 980 system	Jetson TK1
Micro-architecture	Kepler	Maxwell	Kepler
Memory type	GDDR5	GDDR5	LPDDR3
Peak memory bandwidth	144.2/250 GByte/s	336.5 GByte/s	14.9 GByte/s
Peak performance (SP)	1881/3935 GFlop/s	6054 GFlop/s	326 GFlop/s
Peak performance (DP)	78/1312 GFlop/s	189 GFlop/s	13 GFlop/s
P_{base}	41/45 W (Intel chipset)	51 W (Intel chipset)	3.9 W (Jetson TK1)
Release date	Q3'12	Q2'15	Q2'14

For mass storage, the Max-Planck Institute for the Dynamics of Complex Systems has developed an energy-efficient RAID system intended to be used within ICARUS. This system is based on the BananaPi board and with its mere 50 W of peak power dissipation, it is a perfect device for ICARUS. All compute hardware and switches together (plus management hardware and power loss in the converters) ICARUS is calculated to be a less-than 1 kWp system. The boards (and PDUs, see below) are built into a single, modified rack unit whose side-panels have been removed for a maximum of passive cooling. The boards have been aligned in a 'double-helix' layout, which has proved itself to be very effective for avoiding heat-nests. This unique construction can be assembled using commercially available metal or plastics standoffs of different lengths. Full cluster images are depicted in Fig. 5. Due to its new and unique design, some compounds had to be constructed from scratch, such as a mount for the Jetson TK1 power adapter which we constructed using 3D-printing.

2.3 Power Supply, Housing, Cooling

The photovoltaic farming is implemented by 30 solar modules (Heckert Nemo 60 P) with a single peak power generation of 255 W each, resulting in a 7.65 kWp solar farm. The high output is needed due to the need of charging the battery whilst providing an additional 1 kW of power for the (peaked-out) cluster. DC/AC conversion is done by 2 converters (SMA Sunny Boy) and the energy-buffering (i.e. control of battery charge/discharge in conjunction with providing solar power to the consumers) is performed by an island converter (SMA Sunny Island). As power distribution units (PDU), we employ 3 rack PDUs for vertical installation (APC Rack PDU 2 G AP8959, see Fig. 2) with 24 outlets each. To one of these, we attach a sensor for temperature and humidity. These PDUs can be remotely used for monitoring and control the different banks/outlets. In addition, for the purpose of double checking, to each AC-inlet, we attach a high-sampling-rate energy meter that connects via Bluetooth to a central management unit (SMA Sunny HomeManager). This way, we can monitor power dissipation levels even 'in front of' the PDUs. Both, climate and power data is collected by a dashboard-system that runs on a RaspberryPi, adding only negligible power consumption. For energy storage, we use a lithium ion battery rack (HOPPECKE sun powerpack premium), scaled for providing close to 8 kWh of energy for the night (and day times with weather providing too low power levels from the solar system). In order to be independent from any architectural infrastructure, we designed all subsystems for being able to be packed into a heavily modified overseas cargo container a so called Steel Dry Cargo Container (High Cube) with dimensions 20 × 8 × 10 feet. Here, the main task is to provide a climate-proof isolation in order to keep the hardware cool in summer and warm in winter times. For this purpose, we lined the walls, roof and floor with a 120 mm commodity heat-isolation. In addition, we provide it with fans (three inlets, three outlets), powered by secondary PV units in order to induce a proper airflow within the container for ventilation and cooling, see Fig. 1(b). In winter, these fans can also be used to heat up the airflow at the inlet.

3   Exploring the System's Limits

3.1   Hardware- and Energy Efficiency, Scalability

In the following, we will provide energy- as well as performance measurements. Energy measurements are provided via taking the power P at the AC inlet of the carrier system, multiplied by execution time T. In the case of cluster benchmarks, we include total power consumption that is, including dissipation induced by all electric consumers of the system such as switches, converters, etc. For energy measurement, in this study, we consider an ideal race-to-idle situation, where a core is either 'on' (i.e., operating at a preset peak frequency) or 'off' (i.e., cut off from the system clock) and neglect frequent adjustments of voltage and clock speed as well as any dynamic power dissipation due to heat.

Results for the single node measurements for the general matrix multiply kernel are depicted in Fig. 3. In the (two leftmost) plots denoted CPU, we show the results (log scale) for different numbers of cores: with increasing core count, performance increases (data point 'moves' to the right), and E decreases (data point 'moves' downwards) since power behaves like $P = P_{base} + kP_{core}, k = 1 \ldots N_{cores}$. We employ kernels based on the newest versions of OpenBLAS on the CPUs and cuBLAS, respectively, on the GPUs. What we can find first is, that the Cortex-A15 cannot compete with its x86 counterparts for computationally intense tasks (as expected). Note that this is not the case for memory-bound codes, that is less computationally intense kernels with lower flop per byte ratio. All three CPU architectures behave as expected for this type of task, when increasing the number of threads used (i.e. good scaling) with the exception of the Cortex-A15 on 4 threads suffering due to its comparatively thin memory interface. However, the primary design paradigm of ICARUS was the exploitation of the GPUs. Hence, in the remainder of the single node benchmarks in this paper, we concentrate on the GPGPU architectures. Here, for S/DGEMM we can find that the Tegra K1 can beat the GTX660 GPU easily in terms of energy to solution (as a metric for energy efficiency). This is due to the mobile chip achieving 210 GFlop/s in single and 12 GFlop/s in double precision respectively, both at approximately only 14 W power dissipation in its host system. The GTX660 on the other side can offer 1000 GFlop/s in single at around 171 W and – with slightly more power – 1.6 GFlop/s using 64 Bit precision. In the plots, speedup as well as power-down values between the Tegra K1 and the respective other systems, that ultimately lead to this higher energy efficiency. Note that concerning energy-to-solution, the low-power Kepler GPU can even outperform a compute card of that time, the Tesla K20x in single precision. Taking the high-end GTX980 Ti into account, the Tegra has to surrender to its tremendous more than 6000 GFlop/s in single precision sustainable performance at an average overall power dissipation of 271 W. Surprisingly, with DGEMM, the relation between performance and power favors the Tegra K1, which can be addressed to the 980 Ti being almost 30 times slower with double precision than with 32 Bit data. This phenomenon however is not present in the comparison with the Tesla model. However, the fact, that the Tegra can even compete with (slightly outdated) commodity floating point specialists on this 'far end' of the range of computational intensities is promising when taking the advances on this segment of the chip market into account, even already with the Tegra X1, that virtually doubles performance at constant power.

As a common member of the class of memory-bound operations (i.e. low flop per byte ratio) we examine the sparse matrix vector multiply (SpMV).

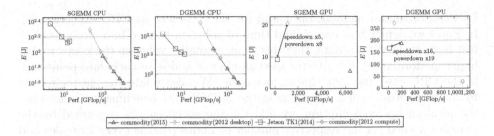

Fig. 3. Total energy consumption (E) and performance (Perf) of the dense matrix matrix product in single (SGEMM) and double (DGEMM) precision for all covered hardware architectures.

This kernel is versatile (especially in the context of PDE-based simulations) and very well understood regarding optimisation for GPUs. In previous work we have demonstrated how very sophisticated multigrid solvers can be constructed out of combinations from calls to SpMV based on ELLPACK-type storage and kernels [7]. Benchmark results are given in Fig. 4 analogously to those in the GPU part of the S/DGEMM results. Modelling the relative performance of this type of kernel on different architectures boils down to the comparison of the respective memory interfaces. Here, only more on-chip memory bandwidth can generate speedup. As one can see in the results, the speedups perfectly align with the factor that lies between the values for memory bandwidth: The LPDDR3 memory of the Tegra SoC can only a tenth of that of the GTX660. With its 12 times lower power dissipation however, the Jetson board remains more energy-efficient than its desktop counterpart as well as the Tesla card, regardless if computing in single or double precision. However now, the Tegra system stands no chance against the advanced 340 GByte/s interface of the GTX980 Ti.

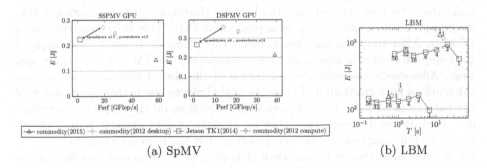

Fig. 4. SpMV and CFD benchmarks. Left: SpMV performance and energy to solution. Right: LBM solver time- and energy to solution (upper data series: CPU, lower series: GPU).

As a final benchmark, we demonstrate the effectiveness of the full ICARUS Tegra K1 cluster with a sophisticated CFD solver based on the

Lattice-Boltzmann method, optimised for GPU as well as CPU execution [8]. In Fig. 4 we depict how energy and time to solution behave in a strong scaling test in single precision (note, that this time, a smaller value on the x-axis means higher performance). We give the used number of nodes for each data-point and, in the CPU case, use four threads per node. We also relate the cluster results to the competitor workstations as in the S/DGEMM benchmark. Concerning the total energy consumption, we add the measured energy consumed by the switches needed for the respective number of nodes (that is every 20 nodes add the energy value of the switch). This can be seen for instance in the rise of the energy level when going from 16 to 32 nodes. In both CPU and GPU configurations, the ICARUS systems scales well and provides higher energy efficiency then the respective architecture with the host-workstations. Note, that the increase in power when using additional nodes is very small and is dominated by the necessity to use an additional switch. The potential for scaling up the cluster is therefore quite high. We can also determine the number of ICARUS nodes needed for beating the reference workstations in terms of time to solution: For the Cortex-A15, we can see, that with 4 or more ICARUS nodes, lower execution time is needed than with the commodity hardware, at a considerably lower energy consumption. This state is reached with 16 ICARUS GPUs, where the combined GK20a beat even the most augmented floating point accelerator at the time of writing this paper in both, performance and energy efficiency.

3.2   Energy Supply, Temperature and Humidity

For solar systems, the solar cycle is of major importance and it is elemental to know the time-spread of the hours of sunshine, which additionally includes charging breaks effected by cloudy conditions. Figure 5(a, left) shows power P over time T in April, with sunrise at 6 am and sunset at 9 pm. The complete charging power of the solar system can be used, because the energy spent over night needs to be recovered, and the battery charging status is entering a hot-loading-phase in which it reaches a peak at 2.6 kW (this value can rise up to 7.5 kW). After fully charging the battery, the power decreases to the usage of the compute cluster in idle mode at approximately 0.36 kW between 11 am and 1 pm. Afterwards, the energy consumption of the cluster increases due to some calculations performed on it. Figure 5(a, right) shows the percentaged charge of the battery in May for two different load intensities on the respective previous day. Here it can be seen, that even on slightly cloudy days, it is possible to reach the full charge of the battery, proofing that the dimensioning of the power supply system is correct for the current cluster size. Concerning cooling of the system, currently we observe that the climate in the server room is very stable and beneficial for the cluster: on the warmest day in July (with 31 °C external temperature and around 50% relative humidity) we measure an average ambient temperature of 33 °C and an ambient relative humidity of around 35% within the conmtainer. The Tegra boards are usually as cool as 39–43 ° in idle mode and up to 53–68 ° under load, which prooves our custom made cooling system to be sufficiently dimensioned.

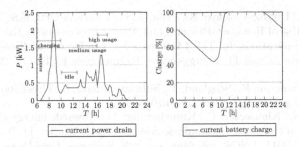

Fig. 5. Typical daytime solar power provision and nighttime battery discharge cycles.

4 Conclusion, Discussion, and Future Work

Since starting operation in March 2016, ICARUS has passed all our expectations. Even almost three years after starting its design, we were able to show, that the Tegra K1 can compete with state-of-the art commodity hardware. In this paper, we are the first to publish a system-integration success that combines a technology-mixture from these very different fields. However, we have only just begun to explore the limits of the cluster and its power supply systems. Also, the dynamics of the mobile compute hardware market is so fast, that hardware from a current generation, i.e. Tegra X1 must be added. All together, we find our approach for energy-efficient HPC based on unconventional embedded hardware to be well worth the effort.

Acknowledgements. ICARUS hardware is financed by MIWF NRW under the lead of MERCUR. This work has been supported in part by the German Research Foundation (DFG) through the Priority Program 1648 'Software for Exascale Computing' (grant TU 102/48). We thank the participants of student project Modeling and Simulation 2015/16 at TU Dortmund for initial support. We also want to thank Markus Borowski at Borowski GmbH for advice regarding the solar farming and battery supply as well as Björn Henkel at Bloedorn Containers for his advice in designing the container unit.

References

1. Anzt, H., Quintana-Ortí, E.S.: Improving the energy efficiency of sparse linear system solvers on multicore and manycore systems. Phil. Trans. R. Soc. A **372**(2018) (2014)
2. Benner, P., Ezzatti, P., Quintana-Ortí, E., Remón, A.: On the impact of optimization on the time-power-energy balance of dense linear algebra factorizations. In: Aversa, R., Kołodziej, J., Zhang, J., Amato, F., Fortino, G. (eds.) ICA3PP 2013. LNCS, vol. 8286, pp. 3–10. Springer, Cham (2013). doi:10.1007/978-3-319-03889-6_1

3. Castelló, A., Duato, J., Mayo, R., Peña, A.S., Quintana-Ortí, E.S., Roca, V., Silla, F.: On the Use of Remote GPUs and Low-Power Processors for the Acceleration of Scientific Applications. In: The 4 International Conference on Smart Grids, Green Communications and IT Energy-aware Technologies ENERGY 2014, pp. 57–62 (2014)
4. Feng, W., Cameron, K., Scogland, T., Subraumaniam, B.: Green500 list, July 2015. http://www.green500.org/lists/green201506
5. Fürlinger, K., Klausecker, C., Kranzlmüller, D.: Towards energy efficient parallel computing on consumer electronic devices. In: Kranzlmüller, D., Toja, A.M. (eds.) ICT-GLOW 2011. LNCS, vol. 6868, pp. 1–9. Springer, Heidelberg (2011). doi:10. 1007/978-3-642-23447-7_1
6. Geveler, M., Reuter, B., Aizinger, V., Göddeke, D., Turek, S.: Energy efficiency of the simulation of three-dimensional coastal ocean circulation on modern commodity and mobile processors - a case study based on the Haswell and Cortex-A15 microarchitectures. Comput. Sci. Res. Dev. **31**, 225–234 (2016). doi:10.1007/s00450-016-0324-5
7. Geveler, M., Ribbrock, D., Göddeke, D., Zajac, P., Turek, S.: Towards a complete FEM-based simulation toolkit on GPUs: unstructured grid finite element geometric multigrid solvers with strong smoothers based on sparse approximate inverses. Comput. Fluids **80**, 327–332 (2013). doi:10.1016/j.compfluid.2012.01.025
8. Geveler, M., Ribbrock, D., Mallach, S., Göddeke, D., Turek, S.: A simulation suite for Lattice-Boltzmann based real-time-CFD applications exploiting multi-level parallelism on modern multi- and many-core architectures. J. Comput. Sci. **2**, 113–123 (2011). doi:10.1016/j.jocs.2011.01.008
9. Geveler, M., Turek, S.: ICARUS project homepage (2016). http://www.icarus-green-hpc.org
10. Göddeke, D., Komatitsch, D., Geveler, M., Ribbrock, D., Rajovic, N., Puzovic, N., Ramirez, A.: Energy efficiency vs. performance of the numerical solution of PDEs: an application study on a low-power arm-based cluster. J. Comput. Phys. **237**, 132–150 (2013)
11. Grasso, I., Radojkovic, P., Rajovic, N., Gelado, I., Ramirez, A.: Energy efficient HPC on embedded SoCs: optimization techniques for mali GPU. In: Proceedings of the 2014 IEEE 28th International Parallel and Distributed Processing Symposium, IPDPS 2014, pp. 123–132. IEEE Computer Society, Washington, D.C. (2014). http://dx.doi.org/10.1109/IPDPS.2014.24
12. Hager, G., Treibig, J., Habich, J., Wellein, G.: Exploring performance and power properties of modern multi-core chips via simple machine models. Concurr. Comput.: Pract. Exp. **28**(2), 189–210 (2016)
13. IEEE: IEEE 802.3 standard (2015). http://standards.ieee.org/getieee802/download/802.3bm-2015.pdf
14. InfoTech: Mobile Data Center MDC40 (2015). https://www.infotech.de/2_MDC40/2015_Oktober/Data%20sheet.pdf
15. Malas, T.M., Hager, G., Ltaief, H., Keyes, D.E.: Towards energy efficiency and maximum computational intensity for stencil algorithms using wavefront diamond temporal blocking. CoRR abs/1410.5561 (2014). http://arxiv.org/abs/1410.5561
16. Mantovani, F.: High performance computing based on mobile embedded processors. In: International conferences, Mont-Blanc Project (2015). https://www.montblanc-project.eu/sites/default/files/publications/Mont-Blanc-EMiT15-lq-public.pdf
17. Meuer, H., Strohmeier, E., Dongarra, J., Simon, H., Meuer, M.: Top500 list, July 2015. http://top500.org/lists/2015/06/

18. NASA: High End Computing Capability, Project Status Report (2015). https://www.nas.nasa.gov/hecc/assets/monthlies/pdf/HECC_10-15.pdf. Modular Supercomputing Facility
19. NVIDIA Corp: NVIDIA Jetson TK1 Development Kit - Bringing GPU-Accelerated Computing to Embedded Systems (2014). http://developer.download.nvidia.com/embedded/jetson/TK1/docs/Jetson_platform_brief_May2014.pdf
20. Paolucci, P.S., Ammendola, R., Biagioni, A., Frezza, O., Cicero, F.L., Lonardo, A., Martinelli, M., Pastorelli, E., Simula, F., Vicini, P.: Power, energy and speed of embedded and server multi-cores applied to distributed simulation of spiking neural networks: ARM in NVIDIA tegra vs intel xeon quad-cores. CoRR abs/1505.03015 (2015). http://arxiv.org/abs/1505.03015
21. Rajovic, N., Rico, A., Vipond, J., Gelado, I., Puzovic, N., Ramirez, A.: Experiences with mobile processors for energy efficient HPC. In: Design, Automation Test in Europe Conference Exhibition (DATE) 2013, pp. 464–468, March 2013
22. Toradex: Tegra K1 System on Module - Pressemitteilung (2016). https://www.toradex.com/de/news/toradex-embedded-computer-nvidia-tegra-k1
23. Treibig, J., Dolz, M.F., Guillen, C., Navarrete, C., Knobloch, M., Rountree, B.: Tools and methods for measuring and tuning the energy efficiency of HPC systems. Sci. Program. **22**, 273–283 (2014)
24. Wittmann, M., Hager, G., Zeiser, T., Wellein, G.: An analysis of energy-optimized lattice-Boltzmann CFD simulations from the chip to the highly parallel level. CoRR abs/1304.7664 (2013). http://arxiv.org/abs/1304.7664

Exploiting In-Memory Processing Capabilities for Density Functional Theory Applications

Paul F. Baumeister[1]($\boxtimes$), Thorsten Hater[1], Dirk Pleiter[1], Hans Boettiger[2], Thilo Maurer[2], and José R. Brunheroto[3]

[1] Jülich Supercomputing Centre, Forschungszentrum Jülich, 52425 Jülich, Germany
p.baumeister@fz-juelich.de
[2] IBM Deutschland Research & Development GmbH, 71032 Böblingen, Germany
[3] IBM T.J. Watson Research Center, Yorktown Heights, NY 10598, USA

Abstract. Processing-in-memory (PIM) is an approach to address the data transport challenge in future HPC architectures and various designs have been explored in the past. Despite, it remains unclear how scientific applications could efficiently exploit massively-parallel HPC architectures integrating PIM modules. In this paper we address this question for material science applications for which we ported relevant kernels to the Active Memory Cube architecture developed by IBM Research.

1 Introduction

Over at least two decades exponential growth of arithmetic performance of HPC architectures could be sustained. Exploiting this performance becomes more challenging as with growing complexity massively-parallel architectures will become limited by data transport. One approach to mitigate this problem is to move processing pipelines closer to the locations where data is stored, as it is done in processing-in-memory (PIM) architectures. Such architectures could be particularly attractive for future, power-constrained supercomputers, because potentially energy consuming data movements may be avoided. A recent example of PIM architectures is IBM Research's Active Memory Cube (AMC) [18].

While there are architectural arguments in favour of PIM-based HPC architectures, it remains unclear how efficiently such architectures could be exploited by relevant scientific applications. The goal of this paper is to explore this question for two materials science applications on the basis of the AMC architecture.

As of today, materials science applications consume a significant fraction of the available HPC resources. It is one of the areas in science and engineering that will significantly benefit from further growth of computational resources and is expected to require exascale computing capabilities in the future.

A key technique in materials sciences is Density Functional Theory (DFT). DFT simulations give access to an accurate prediction of the electronic ground state structure, equilibrium geometries and thermodynamic properties of most classes of materials, see [5] for an overview. The approach has grown from fundamental research to wide application in the field of materials research and design.

© Springer International Publishing AG 2017
F. Desprez et al. (Eds.): Euro-Par 2016 Workshops, LNCS 10104, pp. 750–762, 2017.
DOI: 10.1007/978-3-319-58943-5_60

In this paper we consider two selected DFT-based applications, which differ significantly in terms of application performance characteristics. Both have in common that they are highly scalable on current supercomputers. We have ported performance relevant parts of these codes to the AMC architecture to evaluate the performance in cycle-accurate simulations and assess the overall benefits from performance profiles obtained on existing systems.

This paper makes the following contributions:

- We show results from implementations of relevant kernels of selected DFT applications on a future processing-in-memory architecture and provide a performance analysis based on cycle accurate simulations.
- To better understand the opportunities of such future technology, we provide an assessment of future requirements of DFT applications.
- Based on results from implementation and performance analysis we explore the features of the AMC architecture as well as its hardware parameters.

In the next section we provide background information on DFT-based methods and future developments in this application area, which is followed by details of the AMC architecture in Sect. 3. After discussing details and performance characteristics of the specific DFT applications considered in this paper (Sect. 4) we discuss their implementation on AMC (Sect. 5). Based on an analysis of the obtained performance, which is presented in Sect. 6, we discuss the suitability of the AMC architecture in Sect. 7. Before concluding we provide a short overview on related work in Sect. 8.

2   Application Background

In this investigation, we analyse kernels of two different implementations of Density Functional Theory (DFT), juRS [4] and KKRnano [23]. Both applications are optimised for high scalability and to address problems with a large number of atoms, $N_{atom} \gg 1,000$, on massively-parallel machines. Their approach to the problem differs as juRS solves for eigenstates of the DFT Hamiltonian whereas KKRnano finds the electronic structure by operator inversion. KKRnano even allows a truncation of very long-ranged interactions and, thus, transits into an $\mathcal{O}(N_{atom})$ scaling behaviour. The linear scaling mode makes a million atoms feasible as computer systems grow. So far, more than 200,000 atomic sites could already be processed during a pioneering run on an IBM Blue Gene/Q^{TM} system providing a peak performance of 5.9 PFlop/s [25].

Future application requirements. While we will use today's applications to evaluate a future technology, i.e. the Active Memory Cube, we also analyse future requirements of these applications. Based on a questionnaire we analysed together with domain experts on how, e.g., the application domain, the used methods and algorithms, problem size and the resource requirements are expected to evolve.

According to [6] the development of methods for ab initio studies exhibits various trends, one being the development towards a more precise methodology overcoming the drawbacks of approximations made in current applications [17]. More computing resources will be required to either facilitate high throughput for medium-sized problems as well as to address large-scale challenges. The former will, e.g., be required to scan parameter spaces and evaluate high-dimensional phase diagrams. The latter involves problems where a large number of atoms, N_{atom}, are required. Challenging problems are related to broken symmetries, i.e. crystals with impurities, random alloys or amorphous materials. To address these questions $N_{atom} \gg 10^5$ atoms are often necessary.

The aforementioned applications, juRS and KKRnano, target such large problem sizes. With the $\mathcal{O}(N_{atom})$-mode of KKRnano exascale compute resources allow to determine the electronic structure of a million atoms within less than an hour and structural relaxation within a single day.

3   Active Memory Cubes

Recently, several new high-bandwidth memory technologies have been introduced. Both, Hybrid Memory Cube (HMC) [14] as well as High Bandwidth Memory (HBM) [15] have in common that they foresee a stack of DRAM dies on top of a logical die. This logic die is currently mainly foreseen to facilitate data transport, e.g. in the HMC architecture the logic die implements the memory controller and a network interface via which the processor can access the memory. But in principle also processing of data could be supported at this level. This approach is explored in a recent architectural proposal by IBM Research: the Active Memory Cube (AMC) [18]. In this architecture 32 computational lanes are added to the logic die, which also have access to the memory, i.e. the memory becomes dual-ported as it continues to be accessible from the CPU.

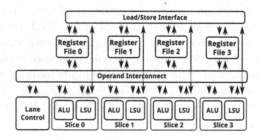

Fig. 1. Sketch of the AMC lane architecture. For more details see [18].

Each lane is composed of four computation slices, which comprise a load-store unit (LSU) as well as an arithmetic-logic unit (ALU), plus a control unit. Each slice has a register file, which includes 32 scalar plus 16 vector computation registers. All registers are 64-bit wide and each vector register has 32 elements. See Fig. 1 for a sketch of the AMC lane architecture.

The computational lanes are micro-coded. In each clock cycle a lane can process one Very Long Instruction Word (VLIW) composed of nine sub-instructions. The instructions are read from a buffer which can hold 512 VLIW instructions. Due to the length of a VLIW instructions it is important to reduce the required number of these instructions. In this architecture this is facilitated through a temporal single-instruction-multiple-data (SIMD) paradigm. Instructions can be repeated up to 32 times, matching the length of the vector registers.

The arithmetic pipelines take 64-bit input operands and can complete in each clock cycle one double-precision Fused Multiply-Add (FMA) or a two-way SIMD single-precision FMA. Thus, up to 8 double-precision floating-point (FP) operations can be completed per clock cycle in one lane. The peak performance of one AMC running at a clock speed of 1.25 GHz is thus 320 GFlop/s in double-precision. A slice can read the vector registers of the other slices, which allows to distribute data over multiple register files. Furthermore, double-precision complex arithmetic with real and imaginary part distributed over different slices can be implemented without the need for data re-ordering instructions.

Load/store requests are buffered in a load-store queue with 192 entries. A lane can load or store 8 Byte/cycle from or to the internal interconnect, i.e. the ratio of memory bandwidth vs. FP performance is 1 Byte/Flop and thus significantly larger than in typical processor architectures. Additional non-exposed arithmetic units are given inside the memory controllers allowing to issue atomic update operations onto memory locations. Here, the instruction set architecture foresees integer and also 64-bit FP addition operations.

Each AMC features a network interface with a bandwidth of 32 GByte/s. It can be used to connect to a processor or to chain multiple AMC devices in a similar way as HMC devices.

The execution model foresees main programs to be executed on a general-purpose CPU with computational lanes being used for off-loading small kernels. It is planned to have VLIW instructions for the off-loaded kernels being generated by a compiler controlled through directives, e.g. OpenMP-4.0, see [18] for details. Such a compiler is not yet available and therefore all sequences of VLIW instructions have been implemented manually.

The maximum power envelope for dies within a 3D stack is small, since layers cannot be cooled individually, yet. Assuming a design based on 14 nm technology, the power consumption for an AMC device is expected to be around 10 W.

4   Applications and Performance Characteristics

Real-space grid DFT: juRS represent the DFT Hamiltonian on a uniform Cartesian real-space grid and follows the approach of iterative diagonalisation, see [4] for details. The application of the grid Hamiltonian to wave functions reads

$$\hat{H}\,|\Psi_k\rangle = \left[-\frac{\hbar^2}{2m}\left(\partial_{xx} + \partial_{yy} + \partial_{zz}\right) + V_{\mathrm{loc}}(x,y,z) \right] |\Psi_k\rangle. \tag{1}$$

The 3D Laplacian represents the kinetic energy operator in real-space representation. In juRS, it is approximated by an 8th-order finite-differences (FD) scheme which leads to a 3D stencil operation on a uniform lattice of grid points. This allows for a controllable accuracy and avoids FFTs and the related parallel scalability issues completely. The selected FD approximation is symmetric around the central coefficient, c_0, with legs of 4 constant coefficients reaching into both directions of each of the three spatial dimensions, see left side of Fig. 2. On most architectures, the decomposition into three 1D FD stencils is benefitial. Then, only one stencil (x, kernel fdd-Vx) carries the central coefficients and the local potential $V_{\text{loc}}(x, y, z)$, see right side of Fig. 2, and the kernel fdd-yz with its eight non-zero coefficients is called twice with different array strides. The grid Hamiltonian may be applied to several wave functions Ψ with index k at once in order to bundle communication of grid-halos. Details about the requirements of the juRS finite-difference kernel are summarized in Table 1.

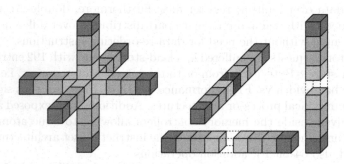

Fig. 2. Decomposition of a 3D finite-difference stencil (left) into three 1D stencils (right). The central coefficient of the y and z-direction (horizontal and vertical) are merged into that of x (red) leaving gaps.(Color figure online)

Table 1. Requirements for the relevant DFT kernels. The arithmetic intensity (AI), given in the limit of $n_{x|y|z} \to \infty$, represents the ratio between compute and data movement in Flop/Byte.

Kernel	Flops	Loads (8 Byte)	Stores	AI
fdd-Vx	$32 \cdot 17\,n_x$	$32 \cdot (8 + n_x) + n_x$	$32\,n_x$	1.1
fdd-yz	$32 \cdot 16\,n_{y|z}$	$32 \cdot (8 + 2\,n_{y|z})$	$32\,n_{y|z}$	0.7
zgemm-16	32768	1536	512	2.0

Green function DFT: KKRnano directly inverts the the DFT Hamiltonian matrix, H. Instead of finding eigenstates, we search for columns of the Green function, x, i.e. a linear equation with multiple right-hand sides is solved. The so-called tight-binding or screened formulation of the Green function formalism allows for representing the Hamiltonian as short-ranged in real-space [26], i.e. its application to a trial vector only couples elements that are associated to basis functions localised on neighbouring atomic sites.

The parallelisation strategy foresees one atom per MPI process and we typically deal with 16 basis functions per atom and energy, resolving states with different angular momentum. The solutions are found using the transpose-free quasi-minimal residual technique [8] for 16 right hand sides at a time. Here, the performance of the application depends almost exclusively on that of applying the matrix H to vector x as

$$y_i = \sum_j H_{ij} x_j, \qquad y_i, H_{ij}, x_j \in \mathbb{C}^{16 \times 16}. \tag{2}$$

All elements of this equation are complex matrices of dimension 16, which thus leads to a large number of multiplications of (double-precision) complex matrices of dimension 16. These are implemented in a kernel called zgemm-16.

For this kernel we have an arithmetic intensity AI $= 2$ (see Table 1). As each AMC lane features a compute performance versus memory bandwidth ratio of 1 Flop/Byte we expect the performance of this kernel to be limited by the compute capability.

5   Implementation on AMC

KKRnano. The most important kernel of KKRnano, zgemm-16, can be considered as a specialised version of the BLAS routine zgemm which implements the operation

$$C \leftarrow C + A \cdot B, \qquad A, B, C \in \mathbb{C}^{16 \times 16}. \tag{3}$$

Equation (2) is evaluated many times to solve the linear set of equations iteratively and the kernel zgemm-16 is invoked even more often. Within each application of the Hamiltonian to a vector, zgemm-16 is executed about 16000 times per atom in KKRnano's $\mathcal{O}(N_{\text{atom}})$-mode and even more times without truncation for linear scaling.

Our implementation in microcode makes use of the fact that the AMC's vector registers of each lane can hold up to 6 kbyte of data. Therefore, all elements of A can be kept in the vector registers once they are loaded. Register spills can be avoided completely. The elements of B are loaded successively into scalar registers. The loops can be fully unrolled resulting in a kernel comprising 16384 multiply-add operations. Exploiting the temporal (SIMD) paradigm of pipelining we only need 384 VLIW instructions for implementing this kernel (neglecting some entry and exit code). Due to the organisation of the vector register hardware, random access is to vector register elements not possible. This necessitates the reorganisation of the matrix-matrix product algorithm to accumulate multiple results simultaneously, in our case 16 real and 16 imaginary values. In other words, we compute one column of the solution matrix leveraging the SIMD-in-time model

$$C_{0...15,j} \leftarrow C_{0...15,j} + \sum_k A_{0...15,k} \cdot B_{k,j} \tag{4}$$

juRS finite-differences. As the Hamiltonian is always applied to a larger set of independent states at a time, we tile the set with index k into coherent subsets of length 32 to match to AMC's vector length.

A single-pass implementation of the finite-difference Laplacian stencil on a 3D array with $n_x \times n_y \times n_z$ lattice sites can only exploit data re-use in the direction of the traversal of the 3D stencil. This corresponds to an arithmetic intensity of 49 Flop/144Byte = 0.34Flop/Byte. On AMC such an implementation would be memory-bandwidth-bound. As no caches are present on the AMC, it is advantageous to decompose the 3D stencil and perform three passes of a 1D FD stencil with index strides 1, n_x and $n_x n_y$ for the x-, y-, and z-direction, respectively, as described in Sect. 4 and Fig. 2. An overview of the characteristic numbers of the FD kernels `fdd-Vx` and `fdd-yz` is given in Table 1.

Figure 3 explains the slice-parallelisation strategy of the 1D FD derivative for the implementation on AMC. Elements of the source array `A` holding the set of wave functions to be derived are distributed in a cyclic fashion over the four slices. All slices process the same sequence of instructions except for a phase shift by one VLIW (32 cycles due to the vectorisation) between adjacent slices. Therefore, all slices access the same lattice element at the same time exploiting that the read access to a vector register is shared across the slices of a lane. We schedule the load instruction on elements of `A` seven VLIWs (although Fig. 3 shows only a distance of four VLIWs) before all four slices access the shared vector register holding elements of `A` for reading. This is equivalent to 7×32 cycles between the issuing of the load and the usage of the element if no stalls are encountered. This hides the typical memory access latencies of the AMC. Furthermore, a four-fold loop unrolling allows for an efficient register allocation for this microcode so that 4×4 elements on 32 independent grids are processed per iteration.

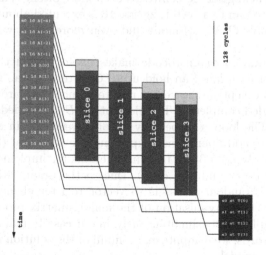

Fig. 3. Slice parallelisation scheme for finite-differences. Data flows from left to right while time propagates from top to bottom in the diagram.

The kernel fdd-Vx utilises the memory bandwidth mostly for loading elements of A and for storing the target array T. All arithmetic instructions are double-precision FMAs except for the first element. Therefore, 8 Byte are loaded, 8 Byte stored and 17 Flop performed per lattice site. Hence, the AI is about 1 Flop/Byte. The kernel fdd-yz for the other two derivatives ∂_{yy} and ∂_{zz} consists of update operations, i.e. we need to load the source array A and the target array T before updating T, which increases the amount of data to be loaded by 50 % compared to fdd-Vx. Due to the missing central FD coefficient, we perform 8 FMAs per 24 Byte, i.e. an AI of 0.7. This is below the specifications of the AMC with a ratio of at least 1 Flop/Byte, therefore, we expect this kernel to be memory-bound. As an alternative to this load-update-store scheme, *atomic* update operations can reduce the pressure on the memory interface.

6 Performance Analysis

The relevant performance metric for the investigate compute kernels is GFlop/s. During the analysis, we define the floating-point efficiency ϵ_{FP} as the ratio of achieved FP performance over the maximum of the AMC of 256 Flop/cycle or 320 GFlop/s when using all 32 lanes.

KKRnano. The fully unrolled implementation of the double-precision $\mathbb{C}^{16 \times 16}$-matrix-matrix multiplication requires only 4886 AMC cycles to finish on a single lane. This is equivalent to a floating-point efficiency $\epsilon_{FP} = 84\%$. As this kernel has a high theoretical arithmetic intensity (AI) (see Table 1), we expect it to be compute bound. There are two potential causes for a lower effective performance. First, the time required to setup the registers and read the corresponding values from the stack memory. Second, the time overhead for offloading and returning control to the CPU.

The data layout for the complex arrays was tuned to allow for load combines, i.e. bundled memory requests of 16 or 32 Byte of data with adjacent memory addresses. This reduces the total number of memory requests which is important to sustain the performance also in multi-lane execution.

The resulting implementation is highly efficient, the instructions issued to the four ALUs are almost exclusively FMAs (98%) and only very few slots remain empty (2%). About 600 cycles are spent to setup the kernel and preload the initial values of the first matrix, A, which is then kept in the vector registers during kernel execution. Values of B are streamed through the scalar registers individually. Accordingly, the kernel utilises the memory interface efficiently (LSU instruction mix: 8% load, 5% store, 88% nop).

Most rows of H in KKRnano contain around 14 non-zero matrices. By introducing an index list into the kernel that contains the start addresses of the next pair of small matrices we can pipeline zgemm-16 and, hence, distribute the start-up latency over the execution time for all elements in a row. Furthermore, we could save the storing and loading of C increasing the AI to 3.5. Asymptotically, we expect $\epsilon_{FP} \simeq 98\%$ for a fully pipelined implementation of the block sparse matrix product, with a single kernel per row of 14 blocks.

We investigate the behaviour of the kernel when scaling to multiple processing elements. Each is issuing a separate instance of the problem, simulating the final implementation, where each lane concurrently computes one block of y and traverses a row of block in H. Results of multi-lane experiments can be found in Table 2. Here, excellent scaling is observed when increasing the number of active lanes. The sustained performance on all 32 lanes of an AMC is 262 GFlop/s which corresponds to $\epsilon_{FP} = 82\%$. With more lanes working in parallel the number of stall cycles relative to those spent on executing instructions grows significantly. We suspect congestion on the memory system to be the cause. The effect was larger for allocation strategies controlling the placement in memory vaults other than the one used for these measurements. This indicates that the balancing of the memory requests to the different vault controllers is a crucial compontent to multi-lane efficiency. As each lane processes a disjoint problem set, the amount of memory requests in flight increases proportionally puts more load on the internal interconnect. We presented the optimal result from high level tuning of the memory locality. While more fine grained control on the actual location of memory allocations could alleviate the issue for elements of H, the access into y is hard to optimise.

juRS. The AI of the FD kernel `fdd-Vx` ranges in a field where small changes in terms of requested memory traffic lead to a transition from being FP performance limited to memory-bandwidth-bound, compare Table 1. Both `fdd`-kernels process the grid in rows of the length of one of the domain dimensions. Each row starts and ends with a halo region of four grid elements that need to be loaded but do not exhibit an 8 or 9-fold data re-use as it is in the bulk of the row. Therefore, shorter rows have a reduced average AI and, consequently, larger domain sizes lead to larger ϵ_{FP}. In addition to the halo-related overhead, the loads experience congestion effects when executed on multiple lanes as shown in Table 2 for `fdd-Vx`. Here, the number of lattice sites in one domain was 16×16^2 or 32×32^2 where the row length n_x is 16 and 32, respectively. The number of rows that are processed independently, 16^2 and 32^2, were distributed evenly among the number of lanes. Taking the halo-related overhead into account, the corresponding AIs are 0.84 and 0.93 Flop/Byte, respectively, compare Table 1. These translate into a maximum efficiency that is achieved only on a single lane in the smaller case. All multi-lane runs exhibit memory congestion effects that infer additional stall cycles and, hence, lower the total FP efficiency. Nevertheless, a sustained efficiency $\epsilon_{FP} = 43\%$ can be measured.

For the `fdd-yz` kernel, the amount of memory accesses can be reduced by one third using the `AtomicAdd` instruction rather than a usual `LoadStore` scheme. Then, the *atomic* store operation only sends the numerical difference to be added to the content of the (64-bit) memory location. This allows to improve the single-lane efficiency from $\epsilon_{FP} = 60\%$ to 80% for a domain of 32×32 grid points.

Application performance. It is difficult to make predictions of the overall speed-up of the juRS Hamiltonian action as the balance between the FD operations and other kernels depends on the input. This includes the species of atoms, their

Table 2. Results for the execution of the juRS finite-difference derivative `fdd-Vx` and KKRnano `zgemm-16` kernels on **L** AMC lanes.

	fdd-Vx 16^3			fdd-Vx 32^3			zgemm-16			
L	Cycles	Stalls	ϵ_{FP}	Cycles	Stalls	ϵ_{FP}	Cycles	Stalls	ϵ_{FP}	GFlop/s
1	324 k	45 k	0.86	2.6 M	366 k	0.85	4886	682	0.83	8.4
2	186 k	47 k	0.74	1.4 M	293 k	0.79	4807	603	0.85	17.0
4	126 k	56 k	0.55	904 k	347 k	0.61	4893	689	0.83	33.5
8	63 k	28 k	0.55	454 k	176 k	0.61	4955	751	0.82	66.1
16	29 k	11 k	0.60	216 k	77 k	0.64	5007	803	0.81	130.9
32	20 k	11 k	0.43	160 k	90 k	0.43	4991	787	0.82	262.6

density, the grid spacing, and the required accuracy of the projector representation. All these can change significantly for different types of runs. Typically, the application spends between 30 to 60 % in FD operations. However, on standard CPU architectures we found the FP efficiency for these kernels to be typically $\epsilon_{FP} \lesssim 10\%$. For instance, on BG/Q [4] ϵ_{FP} could be as low as 2%. For all kernels, which we have ported to AMC, we observe an efficiency $\epsilon_{FP} \geq 43\%$. We thus expect the execution for the juRS Hamiltonian to be at least 7× faster on a single AMC device compared to a BG/Q processor, that features a peak performance of 204.8 GFlop/s.

As the fraction of the work executed within the kernels considered in this paper reduces for larger N_{atom}, we refrain from make predictions on the overall application performance of juRS in the presence of AMC devices.

7   Discussion of AMC Architecture

For all kernels investigated here, the arithmetic intensities are high which results in a good usage of the ALU pipeline. The implementations exhibit a constant flow of arithmetic instructions inside the bulk of a kernel execution. Merely during startup and finalisation some VLIWs are found that carry only LSU instructions. Table 3 shows a measure of the NOP instructions. For example the `zgemm-16` kernel that runs 4886 cycles is implemented with only 1.6% pure LSU instructions for all slices. Also for the juRS-kernels the number of ALU-NOP instructions is independent of the problem size. In contrast, the number of LSU-NOP instructions is large and scales with the problem size, therefore, the fraction of LSU-NOP instructions over possible LSU instruction slots is given here. The largest usage of LSU instructions is 25% found at `fdd-yz` in the `LoadStore` scheme. Using the `AtomicAdd` scheme, this fraction is halfed.

The AMC architecture exhibits also other useful features for processing linear algebra tasks within DFT applications. Of particular interest are variants of real and complex double-precision matrix-matrix multiplications where a complete set of variants of multiply-add instructions, strong vectorisation and the

Table 3. Usage of AMC hardware resources and NOP-metric for the microcode.

Kernel	ALU-NOP	LSU-NOP	VLIW	VectorReg.
fdd-Vx	163	89%	216 (42%)	6
fdd-yz	194	75%	206 (40%)	8
zgemm-16	78	88%	398 (78%)	16

overlap of load latencies with computations allows to achieve high efficiencies for sparse operator arithmetics. For the investigated kernels, 32 elements in each vector and four slices per lane can be employed to a full extent. In all kernels, load latencies are hidden by unrolling loops and the possibility to issue load or store instructions in the same cycle with arithmetic operations allows to run at floating-point efficiencies close to 100% given that the AI is sufficiently high. The manually assembled micro-code implementations of the kernels make use of most of the 32 scalar registers per slice. The number of used vector registers per slice and the filling of the instruction buffer are listed in the right columns of Table 3 for the different kernels. Only for the zgemm-16 kernel all 16 vector registers have been used. The latter indicates that the size of the register file is suitable for these application kernels. Despite completely unrolled loops in zgemm-16 the instruction buffer with up to 512 VLIWs is large enough to host the instructions for the investigated operations without reloading.

All kernels make extensive use of overlapping load latencies with computations. When scheduling the loads in the sequence of VLIWs we have to balance between too early which would stall the lane due to overfilling of the load queue and too late which leads to stall cycles waiting for data to arrive. A shorter load queue than 192 items is expected to increase the pressure on this trade-off and the dependence of the total runtime on memory congestion effects.

8   Related Work

Over the last years numerous DFT simulation codes have been developed for high-end HPC systems. For some of these codes performance analysis results for different architectures have been published. The authors of [2, 4] focus on the performance of the CP2K and juRS codes on the Blue Gene architecture. An overview of performance evaluations for Quantum Espresso on different high-end HPC systems is given in [10]. Recently, there has been increased interest in exploiting massively-parallel compute devices like GPUs for this type of applications [9, 11, 12, 20, 21, 24].

Extensive research on PIM architectures has been performed in the 90s resulting in various architectures being proposed and explored, including Computational RAM [7], Intelligent RAM [19], DIVA [13], Gilgamesh [22], and FlexRAM [16]. Recently, a reviving interest can be observed (see, e.g., [1, 18]). Different application kernels have been mapped to these architectures to explore their performance, with focus on kernels that feature irregular memory access patterns.

Similar to the approach taken for this work, we analysed the relevant kernels of a fluid dynamics code using the Lattice Boltzmann method and the Dirac operator from a Lattice Quantum Chromodynamics application and implemented these for the AMC architecture [3].

9   Conclusions

By porting relevant kernels of high-scalable density functional theory applications to the Active Memory Cube (AMC) we could demonstrate the potential of this architecture to be efficiently used for such scientific applications, where regular linear algebra and stencil operations dominate.

In particular, matrix-matrix multiplications can be executed efficiently even if it involves many tasks with small matrix dimensions. Using a suitable data layout for complex numbers a floating-point efficiency $\epsilon_{FP} \gtrsim 80\%$ could be achieved, which is significantly above the efficiency of about 15% observed on Blue Gene/Q^{TM} for the same kernel. When using KKRnano in its linear scaling mode with 2229 atoms in the interaction region on BG/Q, about 91% of the time is spent in this kernel. Therefore, a single AMC has the potential to speed-up the overall application by a factor 5, while a single AMC is expected to consume about 5 times less power compared to a BG/Q processor. For this energy efficiency assessment the power consumed by the CPU is, however, not taken into account.

In addition to variants of matrix-matrix operations, we investigated a stencil operation that arises from 3D finite-difference derivatives and can be mapped to 1D stencils. Here, a floating-point efficiency $\epsilon_{FP} = 43\%$ could be measured. A speed-up of the juRS Hamiltonian depends on the balance between finite-difference kernel and other tasks, which in return depend on several input quantities. Thus a typical overall speed-up of the application is difficult to assess.

For any of the relevant kernels we observed a floating-point efficiency $\epsilon_{FP} > 40\%$, which corresponds to a double-precision floating-point performance of at least 128 GFlop/s within an estimated power-envelope of 10 W. In particular the implementation of matrix-matrix multiplications with $\epsilon_{FP} \simeq 80\%$ translates into 25 GFlop/s per Watt. This significantly exceeds power efficiencies on current architectures, it takes, however, only the power consumed by the AMC into account.

In regard of the hand-written microcode implementations generated for this investigation it remains unclear if compilers (once fully functional) will achieve similar performance numbers.

Acknowledgments. We thank the AMC team at IBM Research, in particular Jaime Moreno, for sharing their knowledge on the AMC, continued help and many fruitful discussions. We also acknowledge the collaboration of Stefan Blügel and his group.

References

1. Ahn, J., et al.: PIM-enabled instructions. In: Proceedings of the ISCA 2015, p. 336 (2015)

 2. Alam, S., Bekas, C., Boettiger, H., et al.: IBM J. Res. Dev. **57**(1), 161–169 (2013)
 3. Baumeister, P.F., Boettiger, H., Brunheroto, J.R., Hater, T., Maurer, T., Nobile, A., Pleiter, D.: Accelerating LBM and LQCD application Kernels by in-memory processing. In: Kunkel, J.M., Ludwig, T. (eds.) ISC High Performance 2015. LNCS, vol. 9137, pp. 96–112. Springer, Cham (2015). doi:10.1007/978-3-319-20119-1_8
 4. Baumeister, P.F.: Ph.D. thesis, RWTH Aachen University (2012)
 5. Becke, A.D.: J. Chem. Phys. **140**(18), 18A301 (2014) and references therein
 6. Blügel, S., Wortmann, D., et al.: EIC Co-design Questionnaire for DFT. (Unpublished)
 7. Elliott, D.G., et al.: Computational RAM. In: Proceedings IEEE, p. 30.6.1 (1992)
 8. Freund, R.W., Nachtigal, N.: QMR. Numer. Math. **60**(1), 315 (1991)
 9. Genovese, L., Ospici, M., Deutsch, T., et al.: J. Chem. Phys. **131**(3), 034103 (2009)
10. Girotto, I., et al.: Enabling of Quantum ESPRESSO. PRACE (2012)
11. Hacene, M., et al.: Accelerating VASP. J. Comput. Chem. **33**(32), 2581–2589 (2012)
12. Hakala, S., Havu, V., Enkovaara, J., Nieminen, R.: Parallel electronic structure calculations using multiple graphics processing units (GPUs). In: Manninen, P., Öster, P. (eds.) PARA 2012. LNCS, vol. 7782, pp. 63–76. Springer, Heidelberg (2013). doi:10.1007/978-3-642-36803-5_4
13. Hall, M., et al.: Mapping irregular applications to DIVA. In: SC 1999 Conference, p. 57 (1999)
14. Hybrid Memory Cube Consortium: Hybrid Memory Cube specification (2013)
15. JEDEC: JEDEC Standard High Bandwidth Memory (HBM) DRAM Spec. (2013)
16. Kang, Y., Huang, W., et al.: FlexRAM. In: ICCD 1999 Conference, pp. 192–201 (1999)
17. Kümmel, S., Kronik, L.: Rev. Mod. Phys. **80**, 3–60 (2008)
18. Nair, R., Antao, S.F., et al.: IBM J. Res. Dev. **59**(2/3), 17:1–17:14 (2015)
19. Patterson, D., et al.: A case for intelligent RAM. IEEE Micro **17**(2), 34–44 (1997)
20. Solcà, R., Kozhevnikov, A., Haidar, A., Tomov, S., Dongarra, J., Schulthess, T.C.: Efficient implementation of quantum materials simulations on distributed CPU-GPU systems. In: Proceedings of the International Conference for High Performance Computing, Networking, Storage and Analysis, pp. 10:1–10:12. ACM, New York (2015). doi:10.1145/2807591.2807654, ISBN 978-1-4503-3723-6
21. Spiga, F., Girotto, I.: phiGEMM. In: Euromicro 2012 Proceedings, p. 368 (2012)
22. Sterling, T.L., Zima, H.P.: Gilgamesh. In: SC 2002 Proceedings, p. 48 (2002)
23. Thiess, A., Zeller, R., et al.: KKRnano. Phys. Rev. B **85**, 235103 (2012)
24. Wang, L., Wu, Y., Jia, W., Gao, W., Chi, X., Wang, L.-W.: Large scale plane wave pseudopotential density functional theory calculations on GPU clusters. In: Proceedings of 2011 International Conference for High Performance Computing, Networking, Storage and Analysis, pp. 71:1–71:10. ACM, New York (2011). doi:10.1145/2063384.2063479, ISBN 978-1-4503-0771-0
25. Zeller, R.: KKRnano. VSR Seminar, October 2014, JSC, FZ Jülich, Germany (2014)
26. Zeller, R., et al.: Phys. Rev. B **52**, 8807–8812 (1995)

Are Low-Power SoCs Feasible for Heterogenous HPC Workloads?

Max Plauth[(⊠)] and Andreas Polze

Operating Systems and Middleware Group, Hasso Plattner Institute for Software
Systems Engineering, University of Potsdam, Potsdam, Germany
{max.plauth,andreas.polze}@hpi.uni-potsdam.de

Abstract. Energy efficiency has become a crucial aspect in the domain
of High Performance Computing since running costs for electricity often
exceed the initial acquisition costs. In consequence, low-power System-
on-a-Chip designs are drawing much attention from the HPC community. Driven by the demand for high performance and long battery life in
mobile consumer devices, all building blocks of SoCs are undergoing drastic improvements. In addition to the end-user availability of SoCs based
on the ARMv8-A instruction set architecture, heterogenous aspects ranging from the big.LITTLE paradigm to compute-capable GPUs are gaining popularity. Focusing on the heterogenous nature of SoCs, we investigate both performance and energy consumption of todays state-of-the-art
SoCs for heterogenous workloads using the Rodinia benchmark suite.
Based on the results, we anticipate the potential of forthcoming SoC
designs in the HPC domain.

1   Introduction

In the domain of High Performance Computing (HPC), energy consumption has
always been an important factor in the design of new HPC setups. Recently
however, the aspect of energy efficiency has acquired an additional facet for the
HPC sector, as increasing energy costs have reached a level where the running
costs exceed the initial acquisition costs. This issue is reflected by the emergence
of numerous conferences[1], workshops[2] and projects[3] that are solely dedicated
to the goal of increasing energy efficiency in the HPC domain. Animated by
the motive of energy efficiency, the search for new approaches has engaged the
interest of the HPC community in low-power System-on-a-Chip (SoC) designs
[1,5,19–21].

Originating from the embedded and mobile sectors, the prime design goals of
SoC designs are energy efficiency and reduced manufacturing costs [8]. However,
the tremendous demand for compute intensive applications such as multimedia
capabilities of high-end smartphones has driven major advances in the compute

---

[1] Energy-Aware High Performance Computing, http://www.ena-hpc.org.
[2] UnConventional High Performance Computing, http://uchpc.lrr.in.tum.de.
[3] Green500 List, http://www.green500.org.

© Springer International Publishing AG 2017
F. Desprez et al. (Eds.): Euro-Par 2016 Workshops, LNCS 10104, pp. 763–774, 2017.
DOI: 10.1007/978-3-319-58943-5_61

performance of modern SoCs as well. In addition to steady improvements of the chip design, SoCs have a history of employing special purpose hardware accelerators to meet high computational demands at a minimum level of energy consumption [23].

Focusing on the heterogenous property of SoCs, this paper evaluates the feasibility of state-of-the-art SoCs for heterogenous HPC workloads using the Rodinia benchmark suite [6]. Furthermore, the memory subsystem of all test platforms is evaluated using the STREAM [16,17] benchmark and TinyMemBench [22]. In addition to mere *Time-to-Computation* (TtC) performance measurements, we also provide energy readings and the corresponding *Energy-to-Computation* (EtC) ratings. This evaluation targets recent trends such as heterogenous multiprocessing introduced by the *big.LITTLE* CPU paradigm as well as general purpose compute capabilities of SoC-grade GPUs. Furthermore, this work extends the scope of the evaluation to include SoCs based on the 64 bit *ARMv8-A* architecture, since previous evaluations of SoC hardware for HPC use cases have mostly dealt with hardware based on the 32 bit *ARMv7-A* architecture. For the measurements, we employed a variety of Single Board Computers (SBCs) to cover the range of the aforementioned characteristics.

To provide a representative for the current state of the art in x86_64 based systems, all tests were also performed on a rack-scale HPE Moonshot system. Even though technically the employed cartridges do not comprise SoC hardware, the growing density of rack-scale server systems indicates increasing opportunities for the use of SoCs in future rack-scale systems.

We provide the following contributions:

- We investigate the heterogenous properties of state-of-the-art SoCs, elaborating on both the compute capabilities of SoC-grade GPUs and the heterogenous multiprocessing feature of *big.LITTLE* CPUs.
- We analyze improvements of *ARMv8-A* compared to *ARMV7-A* SoCs.
- Based on the narrowing gap between ARM and x86_64 based SoCs, we anticipate the potential of forthcoming ARM designs in the HPC domain.

This work is structured as follows: In Sect. 2, we are going to present an overview of related publications that deal with the evaluation of low-power hardware for HPC workloads. Based on the research gaps, the Sect. 3 presents the choice of target platforms that will be evaluated in the further course of this work. In Sect. 4, all details of our benchmarking procedure are explicated. Subsequently, Sect. 5 presents the detailed results retrieved from our benchmark procedure and provides a thorough discussion. Finally, Sect. 6 concludes this work with final thoughts.

2   Related Work

In 2002, one of the first attempts at using low-power hardware in HPC scenarios was GreenDestiny, which accommodates a cluster of 240 Transmeta TM5600 667-MHz CPUs in a single rack and achieved 13.5 MFLOPS/Watt roughly an improvement of a factor two compared to competing systems built from COTS hardware at the time [24]. In a similar approach presented in 2005, MegaProto is built from 512 Transmeta TM8820 CPUs and achieved roughly 100 MFLOP-S/Watt [18]. Unfortunately, even though the specifications of both approaches looked promising, neither one found its way into larger installations.

In an economic study conducted by HP Labs in 2011, the authors prognosticated that with further improvements of the production node, employing SoCs in server and HPC systems would yield major economic benefits in the future [15]. In 2013, the Mont-Blanc project [19] demonstrated the practical feasibility of employing ARM-based SoCs for HPC workloads using the Tibidabo cluster [20]. Tibidabo was the first ARM-based HPC cluster and was built from 128 NVIDIA Tegra 2 dual-core ARM Cortex-A9 processors. The setup achieved roughly 120 MFLOPS/Watt, which was competitive with CPUs from Intel (Xeon X5660) and AMD (Opteron 6128) at the time. The biggest issue of the hardware was the lack of Gigabit Ethernet and the unstable implementation of PCI Express. On the software side, linux distributions lacked the support for hardware floating point units and there was no software support for employing GPU-based accelerators for general purpose computations using CUDA or OpenCL. However, the authors reached a positive verdict and stated that the Cortex-A15 might reach competitive performance levels and that switching to the *ARMv8-A* architecture would yield drastic performance improvements.

In 2015, two publications have surfaced that investigate the performance characteristics of *ARMv8-A*-based SoCs. The publication by Rusitoru [21] takes on a very abstract approach, as the architectural properties of the *ARMv8-A* architecture are evaluated for HPC workloads using simulated hardware. This work explores the sensitivities of HPC workloads for in-order and out-of-order cpu configurations. A more practical approach has been applied in the work of Abdurachmanov et al. [1], which evaluates the performance of the Applied Micro X-Gene SoC for high throughput scientific computing tasks and compares the performance to an Intel Xeon CPU and a Xeon Phi accelerator card. While the X-Gene fails to keep up with the performance of the Intel-based platforms, it yields a much better performance per joule ratio. The authors conclude that ARM-based SoCs like the X-Gene are very promising and that with improving maturity of compilers and further hardware iterations, ARM-based SoCs might become valid competitors to x86-64-based CPUs.

Focusing on energy consumption versus performance tradeoffs, a very recent publication by Calore et al. [5] investigated the interactions between HPC workloads and energy consumption using Tegra K1 SoCs, which are based on the ARM Cortex-A15. Using a time-accurate measurement setup, the authors observed both compute performance and energy consumption for a benchmark that has been implemented for both the CPU and the GPU portion of the SoC. As the measurements were performed at different clock speeds and energy states, the evaluation yielded *Time-to-Computation* (TtC) as well as *Energy-to-Computation* (EtC) figures for many configurations. The authors came to the conclusion that due to significant background energy dissipation, the best overall energy efficiency can be reached when all resources are driven at the fastest clock-speed in order to complete computations faster and then cut power.

Finally, the performance behavior of the heterogenous multiprocessing feature of *big.LITTLE* CPUs has been investigated by Butko et al. [4]. In their work, the authors used the OpenMP-based CPU implementations from the Rodinia benchmark suite [6] to evaluate the performance of the Samsung Exynos 5422 SoC, which comprises four ARM Cortex-A7 cores and four ARM Cortex-A15 cores. Contrary to the naïve assumption that running all cores simultaneously would yield certain performance improvements, the authors demonstrated that the best performance could be achieved using the Cortex-A15 cores only. In most benchmarks, using the Cortex-A7 cores as well resulted in severely decreased performance, which suggests that current parallel programming paradigms are unable to deal with the heterogenous CPUs where cores come with varying performance characteristics.

3   Hardware Targets

In this work, we are using the latest generation of Single Board Computers (SBCs) in order to cover three major points of interest:

– Heterogeneous multiprocessing in *big.LITTLE* CPUs.
– Performance and compute capabilities of SoC-grade GPUs.
– Architectural improvements of *ARMv8-A* compared to *ARMV7-A*.

We decided to use SBCs due to their wide availability even though high-end ARMv8-A SoCs are available in server-scale hardware like the HPE ProLiant m400 Server Cartridge [12], which is based on the Applied Micro X-Gene SoC. The large demand from the hobbyist community has created a large spectrum ranging from low-cost, low-power hardware to more performant products. From the upper range of the performance spectrum, we are employing the Odroid-XU4 [3,10] to cover both the aspects of heterogenous multiprocessing in *big.LITTLE* CPUs as well as the compute capabilities of SoC-grade GPUs. However, the XU4 still uses *ARMv7-A*-based CPU designs (ARM Cortex-A7 and A15) and thus does not represent recent advances in ARM processor design. For the investigation of advances introduced by *ARMv8-A*, we are using the Odroid-C2 [11] and the Raspberry Pi 3 [7], which are both based on the ARM Cortex-A53. It should be noted that the A53 is a low-power design, which is intended to be used as the energy efficient counterpart to the more powerful A57 in *ARMv8-A*-based *big.LITTLE* CPUs. The detailed specifications of all SBCs utilized in this work are denoted in Table 1.

To evaluate whether energy efficient SoCs might become a serious threat to the predominance of x86-64 in the field of High Performance Computing and to the server market in general, we extended our measurements to include the HPE ProLiant m710p Server Cartridge (detailed specifications denoted in Table 2). Systems belonging to the class of so-called Rack-Scale Computers [14] are particularly interesting, as energy-efficient but performant SoCs are the prime target for a system architecture that aims at highly increased levels of hardware

Table 1. Detailed specifications of the employed Single Board Computers (SBCs).

	Raspberry Pi 3 [7]	Odroid C-2 [11]	Odroid XU-4 [3,10]
SoC	Broadcom BCM2837	Amlogic S905	Samsung Exynos 5422
CPU	4×ARM Cortex-A53	4×ARM Cortex-A53	ARM big.LITTLE octa core
	1.2 GHz, in-order	2.0 GHz, in-order	4×A7, 1.5 GHz, in-order
			4×A15, 2.0 GHz, out-of-order
Arch	ARMv8-A (64 bit)	ARMv8-A (64 bit)	ARMv7-A (32 bit)
L1$ (I/D)	32 KB/32 KB	32 KB/32 KB	32 KB/32 KB
L2$	512 KB	512 KB	512 KB (A7), 2 MB (A15)
Memory	1 GB LPDDR2	2 GB DDR3	2 GB LPDDR3
	900 MHz	32 bit/912 Mhz	32 bit/933 MHz, PoP
GPU	BCM VideoCore IV	ARM Mali-450	ARM Mali-T628 MP6
Compute	no	no	OpenCL 1.1
OS	Ubuntu MATE 15.10	Ubuntu MATE 16.04	Ubuntu MATE 15.10
Kernel	4.1.18-v7+ (armv7l)	3.14.29-29 (aarch64)	3.10.96-78 (armv7l, HMP)
Compiler	GCC v5.2.1	GCC v5.3.1	GCC v5.2.1

Table 2. Detailed specifications of the x86_64 based reference system.

	HPE ProLiant m710p Server Cartridge [13]
CPU	Intel Xeon E3-1284L v4, 4C/8T, 2.90 GHz, out-of-order
Arch	x86_64
L1$ (I/D)	32 KB/32 KB (per core)
L2$	256 KB (per core)
L3$	6 MB (shared)
L4$	128 MB eDRAM
Memory	32 GB, 4×8 GB PC3L-12800 (DDR3-1600) SODIMM
GPU	Iris Pro Graphics P6300 BroadWell GT3
Compute	OpenCL 1.2
OS	Ubuntu 16.04 LTS
Kernel	Linux 4.4.0-21 (x86_64)
Compiler	GCC v5.3.1

density. Even though the Intel Xeon E3-1284L v4 employed in the m710p is no SoC, it represents the latest advances of performance-optimized x86_64 hardware targeting compact and energy efficient form factors.

4   Benchmark Procedure

Corresponding to the focus on heterogenous hardware, we used a selection of tests from the Rodinia benchmark suite [6], which is specialized on heterogenous computing environments. The Rodinia suite comprises more than 20 benchmarks from various application domains, each implemented in OpenMP, OpenCL and CUDA. To provide an additional level of categorization, each benchmark is classified according to the *Berkley Dwarves* [2].

With the goal of prohibiting any bias, we ignored the specific hardware characteristics of each target platform and did not apply any modifications to the benchmark implementations, except for minor adaptations of the makefiles. While the OpenMP-based implementations for CPUs worked flawlessly on all platforms, the OpenCL-based implementations had certain issues on the ARM Mali-T628 MP6 GPU of the Odroid-XU4. Implemented with high-end workstation and server-grade GPUs in mind, several benchmarks failed to run properly on the XU4 without profound alterations of the implementation. As this forced us to narrow down the choice of benchmarks, we decided to pick one benchmark per *Berkley Dwarf* covered by the Rodinia benchmark suite:

- *Structured Grid*: Leukocyte tracking
- *Unstructured Grid*: Computational Fluid Dynamics
- *Dense Linear Algebra*: k-Nearest Neighbors
- *Graph Traversal*: Breadth-First Search

Except for the leukocyte tracking benchmark, all workloads are memory-bound [6] and thus sensitive to memory performance. Hence, memory bandwidth was measured using the STREAM benchmark [16,17], whereas TinyMemBench [22] was used to obtain memory latency measurements.

All performance measurements were performed on a clean, freshly rebooted system with no other active users or background tasks running. In order to retrieve a sufficiently meaningful dataset, each benchmark was executed 10 times. Furthermore, each benchmark was preceded by a warm-up run in order to eliminate any confounding factors. The power consumption values denoted in Table 3

Table 3. Power consumption in watts for the states *Off, Idle* and *Load*.

	RPI 3	C2	XU4 (A7)	XU4 (A15)	XU4 (GPU)	m710p (CPU)	m710p (GPU)
Off	0.50	1.00	0.70	0.70	0.70	9.85	9.85
Idle	1.70	2.30	3.80	3.80	3.80	20.65	20.65
Load	2.70	4.10	5.10	11.70	6.60	79.45	67.93

were measured using a power consumption meter switched in between the SBC power supply and the wall socket. For the m710p cartridge, the readings were retrieved from the management interface of the cartridge chassis.

5   Results and Discussion

In this section, we provide *Time-to-Computation* (TtC) and *Energy-to-Computation* (EtC) results for application domains representing four major *Berkley Dwarves*: *Structured Grid* (see Fig. 1), *Unstructured Grid* (see Fig. 2), *Dense Linear Algebra* (see Fig. 3) and *Graph Traversal* (see Fig. 4). Except for the *Structured Grid* benchmark, all presented benchmarks are memory-bound [6].

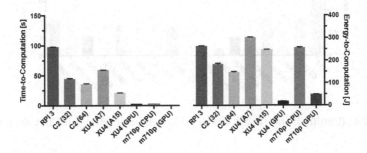

Fig. 1. Results of the *Structured Grid* benchmark (Leukocyte Tracking).

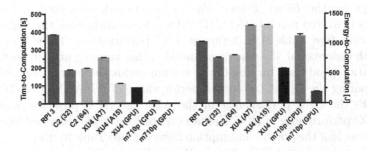

Fig. 2. Results of the *Unstructured Grid* benchmark (Computational Fluid Dynamics).

5.1   Heterogenous Properties

Analyzing the heterogeneous multiprocessing properties of the Odroid-XU4 (XU4), we were able to reproduce the findings of Butko et al. [4], that using both the A7 and A15 cores simultaneously results in decreased performance levels (data not shown). As this result has been expected, we were more interested

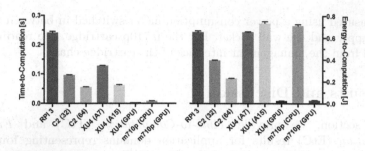

Fig. 3. Results of the *Dense Linear Algebra* benchmark (k-Nearest Neighbors).

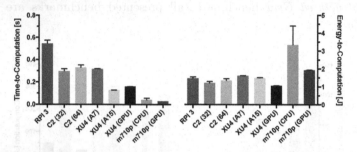

Fig. 4. Results of the *Graph Traversal* benchmark (Breadth-First Search).

in conditions where only the A7 or the A15 cores are used exclusively in order to evaluate whether the decreased compute performance of A7 cores might yield better *EtC* performance.

Except for the *Dense Linear Algebra* benchmark presented in Fig. 3, the A15 cores delivered much better *TtC* values, even mitigating the higher power consumption (see Table 3) in terms of *EtC* performance. These observations agree with Calore et al. [5], who recommended that running at high performance configurations and then turning of the system yields the best energy efficiency.

Comparing the OpenCL compute performance of the ARM Mali-T628 MP6 GPU with the CPU performance of the A15, the GPU provides significantly faster *TtC* performance in all disciplines except for *Graph Traversal* (see Fig. 4). With almost half the power consumption however (see Table 3), the GPU exceeds CPU performance in the *EtC* category. While these results are already impressive enough, it should be noted that without further modifications to the benchmark code, only four out of six shader cores can be utilized and various optimization schemes remain untapped, including the use of vector types and zero-copy memory transfers. As a result thereof, the GPU employed in the XU4 offers a lot of potential for further performance improvements.

5.2   Improvements of ARMv8-A

The Raspberry Pi 3 (RPI 3) and the Odroid-C2 (C2) represent two different SoC designs that are based on the A53 CPU. Both in terms of *TtC* and *EtC* performance, the RPI 3 represents a low-key configuration, whereas the C2 demonstrates the strengths of the A53 design. In addition, the availability of a Linux kernel supporting the *aarch64* state makes the C2 the prime target for analyzing the improvements introduced by the *ARMv8-A* architecture.

Foremost, all benchmarks demonstrate that regardless of running in 32 or 64 bit mode, the A53 provides decent improvements compared to the A7 both with respect to *TtC* and *EtC* performance. Providing decent performance improvements at reduced energy uptake levels, the A53 delivers *EtC* performance improvements of 105% (*Structured Grid*, Fig. 1), 71% (*Unstructured Grid*, Fig. 2) and 186% (*Dense Linear Algebra*, Fig. 3).

Focusing on the 64 bit mode of operation, both the *Structured Grid* benchmark (see Fig. 1) and the *Dense Linear Algebra* benchmark (see Fig. 3) demonstrate performance improvements of 24% and 73% compared to the 32 bit mode of operation, respectively. In contrast to that, the 64 bit mode causes a mild slowdown for the *Unstructured Grid* benchmark (see Fig. 2) and the *Graph Traversal* benchmark (see Fig. 4) with 5% and 10% respectively. While the beneficial benchmarks seem to profit from the increased register count and width of the *aarch64* mode, the slight performance drop in the remaining disciplines might be caused by the amenable state of platform specific optimizations of current *aarch64* compilers [1]. Both with improvements on the compiler side and manual optimizations on the benchmark side, it seems probable that decent performance improvements could be achieved for all conditions.

5.3   Competitiveness with x86_64

In terms of *TtC* performance, the x86_64 CPU evaluated in our benchmarks is far ahead of the ARM-based CPUs. However, this outcome should not come as a surprise, as comparing SBCs to high end server cartridges is close to a comparison between apples and oranges. Most notably, SBCs employ a much more basic configuration level of the memory subsystem, which is demonstrated by the memory subsystem performance discussed in Sect. 3. While the investigated SBCs employ single channel memory controllers and lower clock frequencies of the memory chips, the x86_64 system features a multi-channel memory controller and much higher memory frequencies. While this limitation is inherent to the class of SBCs, ARM-based SoCs targeted at server applications such as the Applied Micro X-Gene have demonstrated that memory subsystems with competitive performance can be implemented [9].

Taking on the position of *EtC* performance, the overall picture changes drastically as most ARM-based SoCs delivered better results in this discipline. With todays available technology, this win comes at the price of much higher computation times. However, if we consider the heterogenous aspects of SoCs and compare SoC-grade GPUs with x86_64 CPUs, the XU4 SBC manages to get close to the CPU performance of the m710p cartridge in the *Structured Grid* and *Dense Linear Algebra* benchmarks (see Figs. 1 and 3, respectively). Of course, the Iris Pro GPU on the x86_64 side also manages to provide performance boosts both in terms of *TtC* and *EtC*, but the SoC-grade GPU of the XU4 still manages to keep up in the latter discipline (Fig. 5).

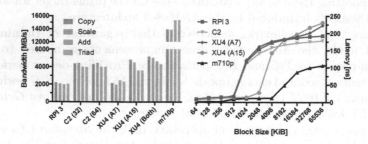

Fig. 5. Memory bandwidth as reported by the STREAM benchmark [16,17] (left). Dual read memory latency relative to L1$ as retrieved by TinyMemBench [22] (right).

6   Conclusion

Focusing on the heterogenous capabilities and architectural improvements of SoCs, this paper evaluated the feasibility of state-of-the-art SoCs for heterogenous HPC workloads using the Rodinia benchmark suite [6]. Furthermore, the memory subsystem of all test platforms was evaluated using the STREAM [16,17] benchmark and TinyMemBench [22]. Next to *Time-to-Computation* measurements, we also provided *Energy-to-Computation* figures to address the pressing subject of energy efficiency.

In our evaluation, we incorporated recent trends such as heterogenous multiprocessing introduced by the *big.LITTLE* CPU paradigm as well as general purpose compute capabilities of SoC-grade GPUs. Furthermore, this work investigated the improvements introduced by the *ARMv8-A* architecture, since previous evaluations of SoC hardware for HPC use cases have mostly dealt with hardware based on the 32 bit *ARMv7-A* architecture.

Considering that already lower-end in-order execution SoCs based on the Cortex-A53 indicated decent performance improvements compared to previous generations, promising improvements in the field of ARM-based CPUs are on their way. Similarly, surprising performance levels both in terms of *Time-to-Computation* and *Energy-to-Computation* were observed for SoC-grade GPUs. In an attempt to anticipate the near future based on our findings, the trend towards heterogeneous designs will be the key to superior performance. Hence, the potential of utilizing energy efficient hardware in compute intensive scenarios seems to be growing steadily.

Disclaimer

This paper reflects only the authors' views and the European Commission is not responsible for any use that may be made of the information it contains.

Acknowledgement. This paper has received funding from the European Union's Horizon 2020 research and innovation programme 2014–2018 under grant agreement No. 644866.

References

1. Abdurachmanov, D., Bockelman, B., Elmer, P., Eulisse, G., Knight, R., Muzaffar, S.: Heterogeneous high throughput scientific computing with APM X-Gene and Intel Xeon Phi. J. Phys.: Conf. Ser. **608**(1), 012033 (2015)
2. Asanovic, K., Bodik, R., Catanzaro, B.C., Gebis, J.J., Husbands, P., Keutzer, K., Patterson, D.A., Plishker, W.L., Shalf, J., Williams, S.W., Yelick, K.A.: The landscape of parallel computing research: a view from berkeley. Technical report UCB/EECS-2006-183, EECS Department, University of California, Berkeley, December 2006
3. Aufranc, J.L.: ARM Cortex A15/A17 SoCs Comparison. http://www.cnx-software.com/2014/05/21/comparison-nvidia-tegra-k1-samsung-exynos-5422-rock chip-rk3288-allwinner-a80/
4. Butko, A., Bessad, L., Novo, D., Bruguier, F., Gamatié, A., Sassatelli, G., Torres, L., Robert, M.: OpenMP scheduling on ARM big.LITTLE architecture. In: Proceedings of the Ninth International Workshop on Programmability and Architectures for Heterogeneous Multicores (MULTIPROG), Prague, Czech Republic, January 2016
5. Calore, E., Schifano, S.F., Tripiccione, R.: Energy-performance tradeoffs for HPC applications on low power processors. In: Hunold, S., et al. (eds.) Euro-Par 2015. LNCS, vol. 9523, pp. 737–748. Springer, Cham (2015). doi:10.1007/978-3-319-27308-2_59
6. Che, S., Boyer, M., Meng, J., Tarjan, D., Sheaffer, J.W., Lee, S.H., Skadron, K.: Rodinia: a benchmark suite for heterogeneous computing. In: Proceedings of the 2009 IEEE International Symposium on Workload Characterization (IISWC), pp. 44–54. IEEE, October 2009
7. element14 Community: Raspberry Pi 3 Specifications (2016). https://www.element14.com/community/community/raspberry-pi?ICID=rpimain-pi3doc-techs pecs
8. Flautner, K., Flynn, D., Roberts, D., Patel, D.I.: IEM926: an energy efficient SoC with dynamic voltage scaling, p. 30324, February 2004
9. Gelas, J.D.: X-Gene 1, Atom C2000 and Xeon E3: Exploring the Scale-Out Server World. http://www.anandtech.com/show/8357/exploring-the-low-end-and-micro-server-platforms
10. Hardkernel Co., Ltd: ODROID-XU4 Hardware Information (2015). http://odroid.com/dokuwiki/doku.php?id=en:xu4_hardware
11. Hardkernel Co., Ltd: ODROID-C2 Hardware Information (2016). http://odroid.com/dokuwiki/doku.php?id=en:c2_hardware
12. Hewlett Packard Enterprise: HPE ProLiant m400 Server Cartridge Quick Specs. (2015) https://www.hpe.com/h20195/v2/GetDocument.aspx?docname=c0 4384048

13. Hewlett Packard Enterprise: HPE ProLiant m710p Server Cartridge Quick-Specs (2015). https://www.hpe.com/h20195/v2/GetDocument.aspx?docname= c04760473

14. Intel Corporation: Intel Rack Scale Architecture Overview, September, 2013. http://presentations.interop.com/events/las-vegas/2013/free-sessions---keynote-p resentations/download/463

15. Li, S., Lim, K., Faraboschi, P., Chang, J., Ranganathan, P., Jouppi, N.P.: System-level integrated server architectures for scale-out datacenters. In: Proceedings of the 44th Annual IEEE/ACM International Symposium on Microarchitecture - MICRO-44 2011, p. 260. ACM, New York, December 2011

16. McCalpin, J.D.: Stream: sustainable memory bandwidth in high performance computers. Technical report, University of Virginia, Charlottesville, Virginia (1991–2007). A continually updated Technical report. http://www.cs.virginia.edu/ stream/

17. McCalpin, J.D.: Memory bandwidth and machine balance in current high performance computers. In: IEEE Computer Society Technical Committee on Computer Architecture (TCCA) Newsletter, pp. 19–25, December 1995

18. Nakashima, H., Nakamura, H., Sato, M., Boku, T., Matsuoka, S., Takahashi, D., Hotta, Y.: MegaProto: 1 TFlops/10kW rack is feasible even with only commodity technology. In: ACM/IEEE SC 2005 Conference (SC 2005), pp. 28–28. IEEE (2005)

19. Rajovic, N., Carpenter, P.M., Gelado, I., Puzovic, N., Ramirez, A., Valero, M.: Supercomputing with commodity CPUs: are mobile SoCs ready for HPC? In: Proceedings of the 2013 International Conference for High Performance Computing, Networking, Storage and Analysis (SC), pp. 1–12. ACM Press, New York, November 2013

20. Rajovic, N., Rico, A., Puzovic, N., Adeniyi-Jones, C., Ramirez, A.: Tibidabo: making the case for an ARM-based HPC system. Future Gener. Comput. Syst. **36**, 322–334 (2014)

21. Rusitoru, R.: ARMv8 micro-architectural design space exploration for high performance computing using fractional factorial. In: Proceedings of the 6th International Workshop on Performance Modeling, Benchmarking, and Simulation of High Performance Computing Systems, pp. 8:1–8:10, PMBS 2015. ACM, New York, November 2015

22. Siamashka, S.: TinyMemBench. https://github.com/ssvb/tinymembench

23. Silven, O., Jyrkkä, K.: Observations on power-efficiency trends in mobile communication devices. EURASIP J. Embed. Syst. **2007**, 1–10 (2007)

24. Warren, M., Weigle, E.: High-density computing: a 240-processor Beowulf in one cubic meter. In: ACM/IEEE SC 2002 Conference (SC 2002), pp. 61–61. IEEE (2002)

In-Cache Streaming: Morphable Infrastructure for Many-Core Processing Systems

Nuno Neves[(⊠)], Adrien Mussio, Fabien Gonçalves, Pedro Tomás,
and Nuno Roma

INESC-ID, Instituto Superior Técnico, Universidade de Lisboa,
Rua Alves Redol, 9, 1000-029 Lisboa, Portugal
nuno.neves@inesc-id.pt

Abstract. Although conventional cache structures often reduce or mitigate the memory wall problem, they often struggle when dealing with memory-bound applications or with arbitrarily complex memory access patterns that are hard (or even impossible) to capture with dynamic prefetching mechanisms. Stream-based communication infrastructures have proved to efficiently tackle such issues in certain application domains, by allowing the programmer to explicitly describe the memory access pattern to achieve increased system throughputs. However, most conventional computing architectures only adopt a single interfacing paradigm, making it difficult to efficiently handle both communication approaches. To circumvent this problem, an efficient unification is herein proposed by means of a seamless adaptation of the communication infrastructure, capable of simultaneously providing both address-based and stream-based models. This newly proposed in-cache streaming infrastructure is able to dynamically adapt memory resources according to runtime application requirements, while mitigating the hardware requirements related to the co-existence of both cache and stream buffers. The presented experimental evaluation considered arithmetic, bioinformatics and image processing applications and it showed that the proposed structure is capable of increasing their performance up to 14x, 5x and 12x, respectively, with a limited amount of additional hardware resources.

1 Introduction

The ever increasing demand for computational processing power at a significantly low-energy consumption has pushed the research for alternative heterogeneous and often specialized many-core processing architectures. However, the design of such architectures is usually mainly focused on the processing blocks, often neglecting the power/performance impact of the inherent data transfers and general data indexing. In fact, a common approach is to rely on conventional cache structures to avoid the usually high memory access latencies. However, although they are well suited for compute-bound applications, they struggle when the application dataset is very large and does not fit in the cache, or

© Springer International Publishing AG 2017
F. Desprez et al. (Eds.): Euro-Par 2016 Workshops, LNCS 10104, pp. 775–787, 2017.
DOI: 10.1007/978-3-319-58943-5_62

when dealing with memory-bound applications, or even with arbitrarily complex memory access patterns, where data locality cannot be efficiently exploited.

Several solutions have been proposed to handle those applications and access patterns, usually relying on efficient prefetching techniques [5,7] and/or stream-based communication systems capable of handling complex data-patterns [6,11]. However, although viable, these techniques can hardly deal with certain application domains (e.g. those based on graphs, on dynamically indexed procedures or on non-deterministic/runtime generated data access patterns), whose implementation is usually more efficient with conventional cache-based approaches.

This duality presents an interesting opportunity to combine both approaches in a single and adaptable communication infrastructure that is capable of in-time switching its paradigm to better suit a running application. Moreover, by combining the advantages of such approaches in a single structure, highly efficient and adaptable communication systems can be deployed, providing the means for exploiting both data-locality and complex data access patterns.

Accordingly, a novel in-cache streaming architecture is herein proposed based on a dynamic adaptation of cache memories at the processing nodes, in order to exploit both stream-based and address-based communication paradigms with the same hardware infrastructure. The proposed architecture is based on a hybrid in-cache stream controller that takes advantage of a conventional n-way set-associative cache organization, by making each way individually usable as a stream buffer, capable of accommodating multiple streams. At the main memory side, the proposed infrastructure relies on a specially devised shared memory controller that combines a conventional address-based memory access controller with an efficient stream generation controller (that deploys the stream-based communication paradigm previously proposed in [11]). The communication between all the system's Processing Elements (PEs) and the main (shared) memory is assured by a high-performance and low-footprint ring-type Network on Chip (NoC), supported by a dedicated message-based protocol.

The envisaged approach contrasts to (and complements) other established strategies based on the sole exploitation of adaptable data-processing structures. Several examples use dynamic reconfiguration capabilities of nowadays Field-Programmable Gate Array (FPGA) devices, where the processing infrastructures can adapt to the target application by reconfiguring its PEs in runtime [1,10,12]. However, such adaptation is usually only applied to the processing architecture, since the reconfiguration process still results in non-negligible time overheads and power dissipation that can greatly impact the performance and energy consumption of the communication infrastructure. Nonetheless, energy-efficiency has been targeted with the adaptation of the communication subsystem, such as cache architectures with dynamically reconfigurable parameters [13] (such as size and associativity); power-gated hybrid designs built with combinations of different memory technologies [2]; or partial reconfiguration of local scratchpad memories into second level caches, to support implicit and explicit communication [8]. However, although widely adaptable, all these approaches still incur in inevitable delays in the reconfiguration process and struggle when dealing with complex memory access patterns. On the contrary, the efficient and adaptable communication structure that is now proposed is deployed by exploiting a coarser-grained adaptation, that is capable of efficiently and seamlessly switching between address-based and stream-based communication paradigms.

The proposed in-cache streaming architecture capabilities for prefetching and data reutilization through stream-based communication were demonstrated through an experimental evaluation using three benchmark applications. When compared to a baseline conventional cache setup, the obtained result, with a system configuration with 16 PEs, show performance increases of up to 14x for a block matrix multiplication application, 5x for a biological sequence alignment algorithm and 12x for an histogram equalization kernel.

2 Data Streaming with Compiler-Assisted Prefetching

In many common applications (including memory-bound), the PEs are able to perform elementary operations much faster than the main memory accesses, leading to considerable performance losses when off-chip memory modules are accessed. Although a multi-level cache hierarchy can considerably mitigate such overheads, it still presents several drawbacks, namely those resulting from the common utilization of shared communication infrastructures, allied with the inherent main memory access concurrency and bus contention; and also those resulting from the intrinsic characteristics of the executed applications (e.g. memory-bound kernels or complex memory access patterns), which in turn result in reduced data-locality exploitation.

2.1 Dynamic and Static Prefetching

Advanced *static* and *dynamic* prefetching techniques are often considered to hide data transfer overheads behind the PEs computation, by fetching data from memory in advance and storing it in local buffers or caches.

Dynamic prefetching usually relies on complex dedicated modules aggregated to the PEs (or caches), which analyze the recent memory access pattern and try to predict future accesses based on prediction heuristics. The most commonly used techniques are based on stride prefetching, where the prefetcher calculates the difference (or stride) between the most recent requested addresses and issues requests to memory for subsequent addresses based on that difference. However, although such an approach allows a complete abstraction of the prefetching procedure from the application perspective, it can fall short in arbitrarily complex access patterns. Moreover, this technique imposes an increased amount of resources, often related to the adopted level of prefetching aggressiveness [5].

In contrast, static prefetching is usually performed with the aid of compile-time procedures, where the code is pre-analyzed to extract/model the application memory access pattern. Such information is then fed to on-chip prefetching modules, which autonomously generate the required memory address sequence. Such an approach requires far simpler hardware structures, since no on-time analysis is performed, thus resulting in lower-footprint and more energy efficient controllers, at the cost of an increased pre-processing effort. Furthermore, static prefetching also promotes the exploitation of highly efficient stream-based communication means, allied to several other approaches to further improve the communication efficiency, such as data reutilization and reorganization, complemented with implicit stream manipulation operations [11].

2.2 Stream-Based Communication and Data Reutilization

Instead of relying on prefetching structures, stream-based communication systems rely on dedicated address generation units to pre-fetch the data, according to pre-determined memory access sequences, and on generating the requested data stream. Such units are commonly devised based on the fact that, independently of their application domain, many algorithms are characterized by memory access patterns represented by an n-dimensional affine function [4], where the memory address (y) is calculated based on an initial *offset*, increment variables x_k and *stride* multiplication factors, as follows:

$$y(x_1,\cdots,x_n) = \text{offset} + \sum_{k=1}^{n} x_k \times \text{stride}_k, \ x_k \in \{0,\cdots,\text{size}_k\}$$

Since such representation allows indexing many regular access patterns, it is commonly used by Direct Memory Access (DMA) controllers and other similar data-fetch controllers, although typically restricted to 2D patterns ($n = 2$).

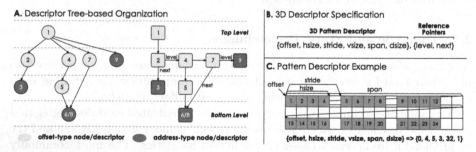

Fig. 1. 3D data-pattern descriptor specification, illustrating its (A) tree-based hierarchical organization, (B) the descriptor parameter encoding, and (C) a pattern description example. The numbers in (A) indicate the order in which the descriptors are solved and in (C) the order in which data blocks are accessed.

Naturally, to describe other arbitrarily complex memory access patterns, affine functions with higher dimensionality can be used, and even allied with hierarchical combinations of several functions, where the affine functions in the higher levels of the hierarchy are used to calculate either the *offset* or the *stride* of the functions in the lower levels. Hence, each complex data stream can be defined by a set of *descriptors*, each encapsulating the set of parameters required to generate the sequence of addresses at a given hierarchy level.

Accordingly, the herein proposed stream-based infrastructure adopts the 3D tree-based descriptor specification, previously proposed in [11] (depicted in Fig. 1). Such memory access pattern is represented by the tuple {OFFSET, HSIZE, STRIDE, VSIZE, SPAN, DSIZE, LEVEL, NEXT}, specifying the starting address of the first memory block (OFFSET), the size of each contiguous block (HSIZE), the starting position of the next contiguous block with relation to the previous (STRIDE), the number of repetitions of the two previous parameters (VSIZE), the starting of the next 2D pattern in relation to the previous (SPAN), and the number of repetitions of the four previous parameters (DSIZE). Also, several descriptors can be combined in a tree-based hierarchical scheme (depicted in Fig. 1.A), in which multiple parent-child relations are established between descriptors, representing dependencies between different descriptor levels. Hence, each descriptor has a reference to a child descriptor (NEXT) and a reference to a descriptor that shares the same parent descriptor (LEVEL).

To allow detaching the PEs computational effort from the memory address generation, and to promote the re-utilization of data streams among multiple PEs, multiple address-generation units can co-exist within a single many-core system. Hence, to maximize the utilization efficiency of the available memory bandwidth, a *stream management* unit, included in the memory controller (see Fig. 2.A), is used to broadcast multiple streams (from the main memory) to one or more PEs, or to organize the writting of data from multiple streams (generated by the PEs) to the main memory. On the other hand, special-purpose stream controllers are located next to the PEs, to manage the flow of data into/out of each PE, effectively allowing data to be directly streamed from one PE to another, or to be broadcasted to multiple PEs or to the main memory.

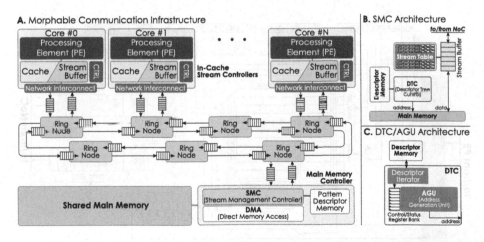

Fig. 2. Morphable communication infrastructure overview (A), comprising the proposed in-cache stream controllers at the PEs interface, the main memory controller and a ring-based NoC. The main memory controller is composed of a SMC (B), responsible for generating/storing data stream to/from the main memory, to which the address generation is performed by a dedicated DTC (C).

3   In-Cache Streaming Architecture

The herein proposed in-cache streaming architecture allows each individual PE to seamlessly switch its local communication infrastructure between two distinct paradigms: (*i*) conventional *memory-addressed* data access; and (*ii*) *packed-stream* data access. However, to avoid a complete switching of the two paradigms, which could result in potential performance penalties in non-pure streaming applications, the proposed approach allows morphing a PE n-way set-associative cache memory into a set of n_1 cache ways plus $n-n_1$ stream buffers, each capable of holding multiple streams. Accordingly, not only does the proposed approach support both *memory-addressed* and *packed-stream* data accesses, but it also supports mixed scenarios composed of compile-time predictable and non-predictable/runtime generated memory access patterns. To attain such a morphable infrastructure, the proposed approach relies on an in-cache stream controller to seamless adapt (in runtime) the cache memory according to the instantaneous requirements of the running application (see Fig. 2.A).

3.1   Hybrid Cache/Stream Infrastructure

The proposed in-cache streaming controller, supported by a specially devised main memory controller, comprises two independent modules: a *hybrid cache controller* and a *stream controller* (depicted in Fig. 3), together with an internal n-way set-associative memory that is managed by one of these modules at a time. The adoption of such a switched control structure (instead of relying on dynamic reconfiguration) ensures an immediate switch of the communication paradigm, since no reconfiguration time is imposed.

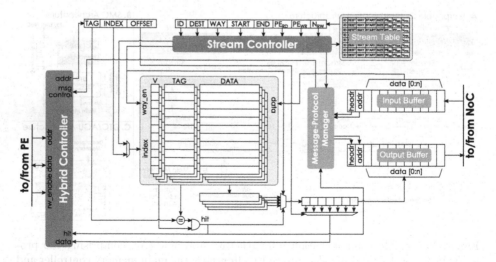

Fig. 3. Hybrid Controller architecture. The *cache controller* and the *stream controller* (supported by the information stored in the stream table) perform an exclusive access to an n-way set-associative cache memory depending on the requests received from the PE and from the communication infrastructure.

In-Cache Stream Controller: The default *memory-addressed* communication paradigm can be assured by a conventional *cache controller* (see Fig. 3), using any arbitrarily replacement and write policies. Notwithstanding, the used controller is implemented by means of a simple and efficient hardware structure that deploys a write-through-invalidate, write no-allocate snooping protocol on the local memory, managed by a binary-tree-based Pseudo-Least Recently Used (LRU) replacement policy.

The cache access time is limited to two clock cycles (disregarding cache miss penalties) and hit/miss-related action is taken according to the coherence and consistency protocols in place. PE requests are only answered with a *wait* state when there is a read miss, until the required data is fetched. Upon a write miss scenario, the written data block is immediately sent to the main memory and is followed by an invalidation broadcast, thus minimizing the waiting times and the number of on-the-fly messages in the communication infrastructure.

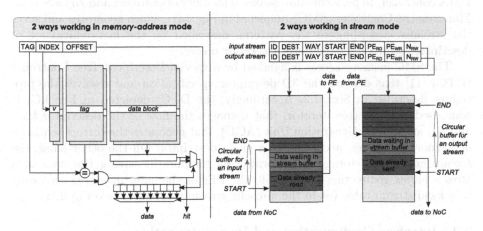

Fig. 4. Configuration example, where a 4-way cache is configured to use 2 ways for conventional memory-address mode and 2 ways for stream mode.

On the other hand, in order to reuse the resources of the n-way set-associative cache memory for a stream-based communication, its access mechanism has to be conveniently adapted. Hence, each cache way is viewed as an independent buffering structure and it is accessed with a dedicated set of read and write pointers to the memory region where a stream is stored. This transforms the n-way set-associative memory in m independent stream buffers, each capable of storing multiple streams, while allowing the remaining $n-m$ ways to be accessed using traditional *memory-address* load/store operations (see Fig. 4).

Accordingly, the stream-based paradigm requires a set of auxiliary data structures (stored in a programmable *stream table*), including the information and the state of every stream currently stored and handled by the controller. Each table entry (depicted in Fig. 3) comprises: *(i)* a unique stream identifier; *(ii)* the way used for buffering the stream; *(iii)* pointers to the start and end of the buffering region within the way; *(iv)* pointers for identifying the PE local read/write positions in the inbound/outbound stream; *(v)* the stream destination (own identification, if it is an incoming stream); and *(vi)* a read/write pointer for identifying the current read/write position for a *Message-Protocol Manager*, which transparently handles the communication of the data into/out of the PE.

Hence, whenever a read/write request is performed for a given stream identifier (see Fig. 4), the local memory is accessed according to the information depicted in the stream table, with the consequent update of its read/write pointers. Outgoing streams are automatically sent as soon as they become available and its transmission is granted by the scheduling manager of the processor aggregate. However, the output transmission does not immediately erase the stream data from the local memory, allowing the data to be reused by the PE.

Main Memory Controller: The in-cache stream controllers are served by a remote main memory controller (see Fig. 2.A), composed of: *(i)* a low-profile DMA controller, to perform address-based memory operations; and *(ii)* a Stream Management Controller (SMC) (depicted in Fig. 2.B), which generates and saves the streams, according to the patterns described by the hierarchical set of descriptors stored in the *pattern descriptor memory*.

The SMC memory access is handled by a special Descriptor Tree Controller (DTC) [11] that deploys the 3D descriptor specification and resolves the procedure described in Sect. 2.2. Accordingly, the DTC (depicted in Fig. 2.C) is composed of: *(i)* a tree iterator, that manages the flow of the descriptor tree; and *(ii)* an Address Generation Unit (AGU), that generates the correct sequence of memory addresses, according to a given descriptor. On the other hand, the stream generation/storage is performed by temporarily saving the data in a *stream buffer*, redirecting it (either to the PEs or the main memory) according to a local stream table (as in the in-cache stream controller) (see Fig. 2.B).

3.2   Interface Configuration and Parameterization

To handle both memory-address and stream-based read/write requests at each PE, a generic and parameterizable interface is provided. In particular, each PE request to the cache addressing space is handled by the *cache controller*, whereas requests to the stream addressing space are handled by the *steam controller*, where the stream identifier is encoded in the interface's address and the local memory is accessed according to the stream table.

The hybrid controller interfaces with the communication infrastructure by means of two input/output register-based buffers. Such an approach not only allows contention mitigation through intermediate buffering, but it also provides isolation between the PEs and the interconnection operating frequencies, allowing them to operate with different clock frequencies. Each buffer accommodates a complete message to/from the NoC. Hence, depending on the assigned message type (see protocol definition in Sect. 3.3), incoming messages are handled either by the *cache controller* or the *stream controller*. Outgoing messages are generated by one of the controllers, depending on which is activated at the time.

3.3   Unified Message-Passing Protocol

To abstract the underlying ring-based NoC infrastructure from the PEs morphable interface perspective, and to keep the impact on the performance of the inter-communication between the system components as low as possible, a simple message-passing protocol was adopted, which consists on a 32-bit *header*, an optional memory *address* and a number of *data* words that, at most, add up to the size of a cache line. The *header* is composed of: *(i)* a message identification; *(ii)* flags for invalidate, read/write and data access mode (*memory-addressed* or *packed-stream*); *(iii)* message size; and *(iv)* identification of the message sender.

The bidirectional ring-based NoC infrastructure itself was devised to deploy a very efficient and low-profile interconnection. Hence, each node routes the incoming messages to/from its two adjacent nodes (right and left) and to/from its connected component. To overcome the contention caused by simultaneously arriving packets, a simple round-robin priority function was devised that rotates the priority between channels upon the completion of a message transmission.

4   Experimental Evaluation

To validate the proposed infrastructure, a complete prototype was implemented in a Xilinx VC707 board, equipped with a XC7VX485T Virtex-7 FPGA and a 1 GB DDR3 SODIMM 800 MHz/1600 Mbps memory module. The proposed infrastructure was evaluated against a conventional cache-based system, using three representative benchmarks from the computational algebra, image processing and bioinformatics domains. For such purpose, both computing infrastructures are composed of multiple PEs, each one comprising an adapted MB-LITE [9] processor, a private scratchpad for program data, and a memory-mapped interface to the proposed in-cache stream controller.

To guarantee a fair and realistic comparison, the cache configuration of the baseline system was made identical to a typical ARM Cortex A7 configuration. Hence, each PE is associated with a 8KB 4-way set-associative cache memory with 64-Byte cache lines. According to the considered cache line size, each message of the proposed communication protocol is composed of (at most) 16 32-bit data words plus the header and the address fields, totaling an 18-word message.

4.1   Hardware Resource Overhead

The FPGA implementation results are presented in Table 1. Despite the added versatility of the offered streaming capabilities, the results obtained for the devised in-cache stream controller represent a very low increase of the hardware resources, with an impact as small as 28 MHz in the maximum operating frequency. In fact, each of the devised components requires less than 2% of the FPGA resources. Moreover, due to the inherent scalability of the adopted ring-based NoC interconnection, it can be efficiently used to support a very large number of processing elements, being the only limiting factor the increased communication latency between nodes. The presented BRAM utilization refers to the buffering structures that are present at each component, except for the in-cache stream controller where they are implemented with registers.

4.2 Performance Evaluation

To evaluate and demonstrate the data-transfer and communication capabilities of the proposed infrastructure, three different benchmarks were considered.

Table 1. Resource usage of the morphable communication infrastructure

	Available resources	Baseline cache ctrl.	In-cache stream ctrl.	Main memory stream ctrl.	Ring node
Slices	75,900	1896	2370	852	155
LUTs	303,600	3602	4367	1666	297
Registers	607,200	365	1176	991	164
BRAM	3,090	0	0	2	2
Max. freq. [MHz]	-	238	210	232	278

- A Block-based Matrix Multiplication kernel that performs the $C = C + AB$ operation, where A, B and C are 128×128 matrices, divided in 8×8 sub-blocks, in order to maximize the cache usage. Since the matrices do not entirely fit in the cache memory, each row of matrix A is fetched once from memory (and maintained in the cache memory for as long as it is required), while matrix B is fetched once for each sub-block of matrix C.
- A Biological Sequence Alignment application that performs the computation of the alignment score between a reference and several query sequences (all randomly generated with a size of 1024 symbols). Two steps are considered, namely: (i) a pre-processing stage, where sequence data is reorganized to generate a query profile; and (ii) the computation of the alignment score matrix, by using the algorithm proposed in [3].
- A Histogram Equalization application to enhance the contrast by adjusting the intensities of a 256×256 pixels image. Two steps are required: (i) computation of the 8-bit image intensity histogram and corresponding cumulative distribution function (CDF), and (ii) scaling of the image intensities according to the obtained CDF. The first step is applied by evenly distributing the original image to the different PEs, such that multiple partial histograms are firstly obtained and then reduced and accumulated in a single PE, in order to generate the CDF. In the second step, each PE reads the CDF and applies the image intensity scaling to an individual block of the original image.

The first benchmark highlights the prefetching and broadcasting capabilities of the proposed system, the second one illustrates the proposed system capabilities when dealing with complex memory access patterns and data reorganization and the third demonstrates the advantages of deploying a morphable communication infrastructure that can adapt itself to the requirements of a running application. The obtained results for the three evaluation benchmarks are depicted in the graphs of Fig. 5, by considering a variable number of PEs.

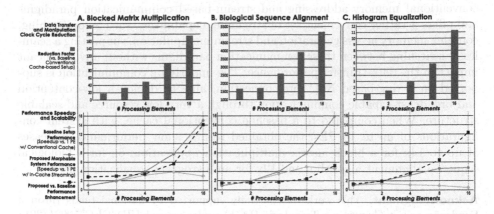

Fig. 5. Comparison of the proposed morphable infrastructure with the considered baseline conventional cache-based system, in what concerns data transfer and manipulation latency (top graphs) and performance scalability (bottom graphs). (Color figure online)

In particular, the bar plots present the data transfer clock cycle reduction attained by the proposed framework due to the offered streaming and broadcasting capabilities. As it can be observed, the proposed infrastructure provides a significant reduction of the data transfer overheads in all benchmarks, which results from an efficient data prefetching and reutilization, allowing not only a mitigation of the shared memory latency, but also a reduction of the total number of memory accesses, therefore decreasing the contention in the shared interconnections. Naturally, these offered advantages are directly reflected in the resulting performance, as presented in the line plots, representing: the system performance scalability (n-PEs vs 1-PE) when relying on traditional pure cache-based approaches (orange); the system performance scalability (n-PEs vs 1-PE) when relying on the proposed morphable infrastructure (blue); and the speedup offered by an n-PE processing system using the proposed morphable infrastructure, regarding a traditional n-PE based system (black).

A careful analysis of the presented results evidences a poor scalability of the conventional cache-based system (orange), which even leads to a performance degradation when a higher number of PEs is used. On the other hand, the proposed morphable infrastructure is characterized by data transfer overheads that are mostly mitigated by its prefetching capabilities, partially aided by the broadcast capabilities of the supporting ring interconnection. As a result, a performance speedup of up to 15.03x, 15.9x and 4.7x is observed in the block matrix multiplication (Fig. 5.A), biological sequence alignment (Fig. 5.B) and histogram equalization (Fig. 5.C) benchmarks, respectively, with a 16-PE configuration.

5   Conclusion

A novel in-cache streaming architecture for many-core systems was proposed. Depending of the PE data request, the devised controller is able to deploy both conventional memory-addressing and stream-based communication paradigms and offers a rather convenient set of streaming capabilities, such as prefetching, complex memory access generation and stream manipulation, supporting a seamlessly switching between these communication paradigms without any significant impact in the data-transfer performance. The underlying communication is supported on a ring-based NoC interconnection, able to deploy a low-contention and broadcast-capable communication through a very low resource and scalable structure. When compared to a baseline conventional cache, with system configurations of up to 16 PEs, the obtained results show performance increases of up to 14x for a block matrix multiplication application, 5x for a biological sequence alignment algorithm and 12x for an histogram equalization kernel.

Acknowledgment. This work was partially supported by national funds through Fundação para a Ciência e a Tecnologia (FCT) under project UID/CEC/50021/2013 and research grant SFRH/BD/100697/2014.

References

1. Chau, T.C.P., Niu, X., Eele, A., Luk, W., Cheung, P.Y.K., Maciejowski, J.: Heterogeneous reconfigurable system for adaptive particle filters in real-time applications. In: Brisk, P., Figueiredo Coutinho, J.G., Diniz, P.C. (eds.) ARC 2013. LNCS, vol. 7806, pp. 1–12. Springer, Heidelberg (2013). doi:10.1007/978-3-642-36812-7_1
2. Chen, Y.T., Cong, J., Huang, H., Liu, B., Liu, C., Potkonjak, M., Reinman, G.: Dynamically reconfigurable hybrid cache: an energy-efficient last-level cache design. In: Design, Automation & Test in Europe Conference & Exhibition (DATE), 2012, pp. 45–50. IEEE (2012)
3. Farrar, M.: Striped Smith-Waterman speeds database searches six times over other SIMD implementations. Bioinformatics 23(2), 156 (2007)
4. Ghosh, S., Martonosi, M., et al.: Cache miss equations: an analytical representation of cache misses. In: ACM International Conference on Supercomputing, pp. 317–324. ACM Press (1997)
5. Guo, Y., Narayanan, P., Bennaser, M.A., Chheda, S., Moritz, C.A.: Energy-efficient hardware data prefetching. IEEE Trans. Very Large Scale Integr. Syst. 19(2), 250–263 (2011)
6. Hussain, T., Shafiq, M., Pericàs, M., Navarro, N., Ayguadé, E.: PPMC: a programmable pattern based memory controller. In: Choy, O.C.S., Cheung, R.C.C., Athanas, P., Sano, K. (eds.) ARC 2012. LNCS, vol. 7199, pp. 89–101. Springer, Heidelberg (2012). doi:10.1007/978-3-642-28365-9_8
7. Jain, A., Lin, C.: Linearizing irregular memory accesses for improved correlated prefetching. In: IEEE/ACM International Symposium on Microarchitecture (MICRO-46), pp. 247–259. ACM (2013)

8. Kalokerinos, G., Papaefstathiou, V., Nikiforos, G., Kavadias, S., Katevenis, M., Pnevmatikatos, D., Yang, X.: FPGA implementation of a configurable cache/scratchpad memory with virtualized user-level RDMA capability. In: International Symposium on Systems, Architectures, Modeling, and Simulation, 2009 (SAMOS 2009), pp. 149–156. IEEE (2009)

9. Kranenburg, T., van Leuken, R.: MB-LITE: a robust, light-weight soft-core implementation of the MicroBlaze architecture. In: Design, Automation and Test in Europe Conference and Exhibition (DATE), pp. 997–1000, March 2010

10. Modarressi, M., Tavakkol, A., Sarbazi-Azad, H.: Application-aware topology reconfiguration for on-chip networks. IEEE Trans. Very Large Scale Integr. Syst. **19**(11), 2010–2022 (2011)

11. Neves, N., Tomás, P., Roma, N.: Efficient data-stream management for shared-memory many-core systems. In: 2015 25th International Conference on Field Programmable Logic and Applications (FPL), pp. 508–515. IEEE (2015)

12. Pal, R., Paul, K., Prasad, S.: ReKonf: a reconfigurable adaptive manycore architecture. In: IEEE International Symposium on Parallel and Distributed Processing with Applications (ISPA), pp. 182–191 (2012)

13. Sundararajan, K.T., Jones, T.M., Topham, N.P.: The smart cache: an energy-efficient cache architecture through dynamic adaptation. Int. J. Parallel Program. **41**(2), 305–330 (2013)

A Low-Cost Energy-Efficient Raspberry Pi Cluster for Data Mining Algorithms

João Saffran[1], Gabriel Garcia[1], Matheus A. Souza[1(✉)], Pedro H. Penna[2],
Márcio Castro[2], Luís F.W. Góes[1], and Henrique C. Freitas[1]

[1] Computer Architecture and Parallel Processor Team (CArT),
Pontifícia Universidade Católica de Minas Gerais (PUC Minas),
Belo Horizonte, Brazil
{joao.saffran,gabriel.garcia,matheus.alcantara}@sga.pucminas.br,
{lfwgoes,cota}@pucminas.br
[2] Laboratório de Pesquisa em Sistemas Distribuídos (LAPeSD),
Universidade Federal de Santa Catarina (UFSC), Florianópolis, Brazil
pedro.penna@posgrad.ufsc.br, marcio.castro@ufsc.br

Abstract. Data mining algorithms are essential tools to extract information from the increasing number of large datasets, also called Big
Data. However, these algorithms demand huge amounts of computing
power to achieve reliable results. Although conventional High Performance Computing (HPC) platforms can deliver such performance, they
are commonly expensive and power-hungry. This paper presents a study
of an unconventional low-cost energy-efficient HPC cluster composed
of Raspberry Pi nodes. The performance, power and energy efficiency
obtained from this unconventional platform is compared with a well-
known coprocessor used in HPC (Intel Xeon Phi) for two data mining
algorithms: Apriori and K-Means. The experimental results showed that
the Raspberry Pi cluster can consume up to 88.35% and 85.17% less
power than Intel Xeon Phi when running Apriori and K-Means, respectively, and up to 45.51% less energy when running Apriori.

Keywords: Raspberry Pi cluster · Intel Xeon Phi · Apriori · K-Means

1 Introduction

Petaflop computing relied on the advent of massively parallel architectures,
such as vector processing units and manycore processors. For instance, Graphics
Processing Units (GPUs) and the Intel Xeon Phi have been used extensively in
current High Performance Computing (HPC) platforms, since they have proven
to significantly increase the overall processing power of these platforms. However,
several challenges still have to be overcome to reach the exascale computing era
[11,15]. First, current cutting-edge parallel machines are power-hungry. This characteristic has motivated the community to seek for strategies to reduce energy
consumption while delivering high performance [3,16]. Second, HPC platforms
are expensive to obtain, which may be unaffordable for small- and medium-size

© Springer International Publishing AG 2017
F. Desprez et al. (Eds.): Euro-Par 2016 Workshops, LNCS 10104, pp. 788–799, 2017.
DOI: 10.1007/978-3-319-58943-5_63

institutes. In this context, the use of such architectures might be unworkable, but the demand for performance must not be disregarded.

One of the research domains that are gaining attention in the HPC community is Big Data, which is a term applied to data sets whose size or type is beyond the ability of relational databases to capture, manage, and process the data with low-latency. Big Data comes from sensors, devices, video/audio, networks, log files, transactional applications, web, and social media (much of it generated in real time and in a very large scale). To extract insights from unstructured data in a feasible time, Big Data applications usually exploit HPC platforms.

The already mentioned massively parallel architectures (*e.g.*, GPUs and the Intel Xeon Phi) have been used to process Big Data applications with high performance. However, their expensive financial cost and recent issues related to energy consumption leads the scientific community to consider the use of low-cost and low-power architectures to build scalable machines. This way, high performance may be achieved with lower financial cost [4,13].

In this paper, we study the use of an unconventional low-cost energy-efficient HPC cluster composed of eight Raspberry Pi boards, interconnected by a network switch, to verify whether it can be used as an alternative for HPC. Although these boards are not optimized for high performance, they can be considered as a good candidate to scalable systems with very low energy consumption.

Our main goal is to evaluate the performance, power and energy consumption of the Raspberry Pi cluster for two well-known data mining algorithms commonly used in Big Data applications: Apriori and K-Means. The results obtained with the Raspberry Pi cluster are compared with a well-known coprocessor used extensively in HPC (Intel Xeon Phi). Our results show that the Raspberry Pi cluster can achieve better energy efficiency than Intel Xeon Phi, consuming up to 45.51% less energy than Intel Xeon Phi when running Apriori and K-Means kernels.

The remainder of this paper is organized as follows. Section 2 presents an overview of the related work. In Sect. 3 we briefly present the architectures used in this work. In Sect. 4 we describe the applications we have chosen and explain their implementations. Section 5 presents our experimental methodology and the evaluation of the observed results. Finally, in Sect. 6, we present our conclusions and suggestions for future research.

2 Motivation and Related Work

As aforementioned, the energy efficiency of parallel computers is an obstacle to be overcome on the way to the exascale era. Future HPC computers will be limited to about 20 MW of power consumption in the coming decade [3,18]. Thus, energy efficiency is a relevant aspect to be addressed.

Recently, many high performance architectures have been designed driven by low-power consumption constraints. Kruger [9] proposed a cluster of low-cost Parallella boards, each one featuring a 16-core Epiphany RISC System-on-Chip (SoC) and a dual-core ARM Cortex-A9. They concluded that the cluster achieved better performance than an Intel i5-3570. However, Parallella lacks hardware for complex arithmetic operations, which can degrade the performance of few specific applications. Although they mention the importance of energy efficiency, the work did not present a rigorous power consumption analysis.

Similarly to our work, d'Amore et al. [5] proposed the use of Raspberry Pi boards. They built a cluster of six Raspberry Pi boards to evaluate the performance of Big Data applications. The authors concluded that the cluster is an affordable solution to their problem, but the work only focused on how the data can be retrieved and used. However, the authors did not conduct any power/energy or quantitative performance evaluation.

In order to analyze the power efficiency of different processors, Aroca and Gonçalves [2] compared Intel, AMD and ARM processors. They used five different processors in their analysis, running web servers, database servers and serial applications from the Linpack benchmark. They concluded that devices with low-power characteristics (e.g., the Intel Atom and ARM ones) are good candidates to compose the infrastructure of data centers. On the other hand, aspects of HPC systems were not considered, such as parallel applications that are mainly CPU-bound.

Other initiatives are also worried about these issues related to energy consumption. ARM processors attempt to be a suitable alternative for low-power consumption in HPC. This is the proposal of the *Mont-Blanc and Mont-Blanc2* projects [14], which intend to design a new computer architecture to establish HPC standards based on energy-efficient platforms. Similarly, the *Glasgow Raspberry Pi Cloud (PiCloud)* [17] is a cluster of Raspberry Pi devices designed to be a scale model of a cloud computing platform, in order to address cloud simulations and applications.

Both projects proved to be energy efficient in their proposals, which reinforces the applicability of our work, that evaluates the behavior of Big Data application kernels in parallel architectures, as well as in [5]. We compare the use of a cluster of low-cost and low-power platforms with a coprocessor designed specifically for HPC (Intel Xeon Phi). Furthermore, we measure the power and energy consumption of both architectures when running two data mining algorithms used in the Big Data research domain.

3   Experimental Platforms

In this section we detail the platforms that we considered in this work, highlighting their main features.

3.1   Intel Xeon Phi

The Intel Xeon Phi is a 64-bit coprocessor that primarily targets HPC workloads. This coprocessor features Intel's Many Integrated Core (MIC) architecture and provides full compatibility with the x86-64 Instruction Set Architecture (ISA)[1].

---

[1] Intel markets this coprocessor with several different specifications. In this work we refer as Intel Xeon Phi to the one codenamed Knight's Corner.

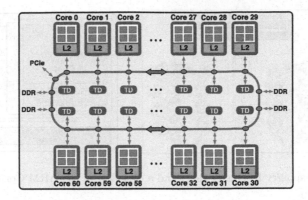

Fig. 1. Overview of the Intel Xeon Phi coprocessor.

An overview of the Intel Xeon Phi is presented in Fig. 1. It features 61 dual-issue, out-of-order processing cores with 4-way simultaneous multithreading, enabling up to 244 working threads. Cores are interconnected by a bidirectional ring topology. Each core has 32 kB instruction and 32 kB data L1 caches and 256 kB of L2 cache, which is the last level of cache in the architecture. All caches are private and coherent. With regard to power consumption, this coprocessor has a Thermal Design Power (TDP) of 300 W. The Intel Xeon Phi coprocessor is usually connected to a host machine through a Peripheral Component Interconnect Express (PCIe) bus. A single Intel Xeon Phi board may have up to 16 GB of memory.

3.2 Raspberry Pi Cluster

The Raspberry Pi is a low-cost general purpose SoC. It has a quad-core 64-bit processor based on the ARMv7 architecture. In our work, we used a Raspberry Pi 2, which features a quad-core Cortex-A7 CPU running at 900 MHz. Each of the four cores has 64 kB instruction and 64 kB data L1 caches and 512 kB of L2 cache shared among all cores. The L2 is the last level cache in Raspberry Pi 2. The total amount of memory is 1 GB.

This type of SoC is not usually used in HPC due to its low performance. However, some characteristics make it much more energy efficient, e.g., the absence of peripheral controllers and hardware support for complex arithmetic operations. Hence, given the possibility of scaling this type of architectures, the overall energy efficiency of a larger system could be improved while achieving decent performance. The Raspberry has all components that conventional computers have, thus, it can be connected to a local area network using an Ethernet interface. Many Raspberry units can be clustered, conceiving a low-power and low-cost system with high potential to achieve high performance [4,13].

A schematic diagram of our Raspberry Pi cluster is depicted in Fig. 2. In our work, we opted to group eight Raspberry Pi 2 devices in order to conceive

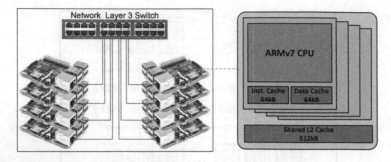

Fig. 2. The Raspberry Pi cluster (left) and a overview of the ARM Cortex-A7 (right).

the cluster. The devices were interconnected by the means of a layer 3 switch, constituting a local network.

4   Data Mining Algorithms

To conduct our work, we chose two data mining algorithms used in the Big Data domain. These algorithms play an important role in different fields, including pattern recognition, image analysis and bioinformatics [19]. In this section, we detail these algorithms and their parallel versions.

4.1   Association Rule Learning

Association rule learning is a very common method used to discover relations between variables in large databases. Apriori is a state-of-the-art association rule machine-learning technique used for frequent itemset mining [1]. Given a list of itemsets, it identifies association rules between those items based on their frequency. These rules reveal subsets of items that frequently occur together in the same itemsets. The algorithm is driven by the following rule: all non-empty frequent itemsets must be also frequent. This rule allows the algorithm to eliminate all itemsets that are not composed of frequent item subsets, reducing significantly the search space. The Apriori algorithm works as follows. For each association rule $A \to B$, where A and B are subsets of items of a frequent itemset, the Apriori algorithm calculates its *confidence*, presented in Eq. 1. High confidence levels mean that most of the time an itemset A is present in a frequent itemset, the itemset B is also there.

$$\text{Conf}(A, B) = \frac{support(A \wedge B)}{support(A)} \tag{1}$$

In this paper, the multi-threaded version of the algorithm follows a Map-Reduce parallel pattern. After identifying the itemsets of size $K = 1$, items from S are distributed among the threads (Map stage). Each thread then counts the occurrences of its subset of items $e_i \in S$. With all frequencies calculated, the subsets are regrouped (Reduce stage). Thus, the itemsets that do not meet the minimum support (i.e. a threshold used to eliminate infrequent itemsets) are removed, and then the confidence is calculated to form the association rules. This steps are repeated incrementing K until the subsets of size K are empty.

In the distributed version, the itemsets are assigned first to the nodes instead of threads. Each node then runs a multi-threaded version of the algorithm, exactly as described before.

4.2 K-Means Clustering

The K-Means clustering is a clustering approach widely used and studied [12]. Formally, the K-Means clustering problem can be defined as follows. Given a set of n points in a real d-dimensional space, the problem is to partition these n points into k partitions, so as to minimize the mean squared distance from each point to the center of the partition it belongs to. Several heuristics have been proposed to address the K-Means clustering problem [6,8]. We opted to use the Lloyd's algorithm [7], which is based on an iterative strategy that finds a locally minimum solution for the problem. The minimum Euclidean distance between partitions and centroids is used to cluster the data points. The algorithm takes as input the set of *data points*, the number of partitions k, and the minimum accepted distance between each point and the centroids.

The K-Means algorithm works as follows. First, data points are evenly and randomly distributed among the k partitions, and the initial centroids are computed. Then, data points are re-clustered into partitions taking into account the minimum Euclidean distance between them and the centroids. The centroid of each partition is recalculated taking the mean of all points in the partition. The whole procedure is repeated until no centroid is changed and every point is farther than the minimum accepted distance.

The multi-threaded version of this algorithm takes an additional parameter t, that is the total number of threads. An unique range of points and partitions is assigned to each thread, with two processing phases, A and B. In phase A, each thread re-clusters its own range of points into the k partitions. In phase B, each thread works in its own range of partitions, in order to recalculate centroids.

The distributed K-Means algorithm takes the number of available nodes that, by themselves, spawn working threads. The strategy employed in this algorithm is to first distribute the data points and replicate the data centroids among the available nodes, and then to loop over a two-phase iteration. In the first phase, partitions are populated, as in the multi-threaded algorithm, and in the second phase, data centroids are recalculated. For this recalculation, first each node uses its local data points to compute partial centroids, *i.e.*, a partial sum of data points and population within a partition. Next, nodes exchange partial centroids so that each peer ends up with the partial centroids of the same partitions. Finally, nodes compute their local centroids and broadcast them.

5 Experimental Results

In this section, we first describe the experimental setup and discuss important implementation details for each platform. Then, we present the results obtained with the data mining algorithms on both platforms.

5.1 Setup and Implementation Details

We used the multi-threaded implementations of both algorithms to carry out the experiments on the Intel Xeon Phi, since the memory is shared among all cores in this processor. More precisely, we parallelized the algorithms using the OpenMP programming model and we compiled them with Intel C/C++ Compiler (icc) version 16.0.1.

The Intel's MIC System Management and Configuration (MICSMC) tool was used to monitor the processor's power consumption. Power measurements obtained from MICSMC are very accurate as shown in [10]. Intel Xeon Phi can be either used in *offload* or *native* modes. In the former mode, the main application code is executed on the host and performance-critical sections of the application are offloaded to the coprocessor. In the latter mode, the entire application is executed on the coprocessor. In this paper, we chose the latter since we intend to compare the performance and energy consumption of the coprocessor only.

For the Raspberry Pi cluster, on the other hand, we adopted a hybrid programming model: we used the OpenMPI library to implement the distributed version of the applications (*i.e.*, to make use of all nodes available in the Raspberry Pi cluster) and OpenMP inside each node to exploit four cores available in it. We compiled both applications with mpicc version 1.4.5 with GNU C Compiler (GCC) version 4.6.3. To measure the energy consumption of this cluster, we used a watt-meter instrument connected before the power supply of the devices, except the network switch, taking the total consumption in kilowatts-hour (kWh) of the whole system. The Eq. 2 was used to convert our results to Joules (J).

$$E_{(J)} = 1000 \times 3600 \times E_{(kWh)} \tag{2}$$

The power consumption was calculated for the Raspberry Pi cluster, as well as the energy consumption, for the Intel Xeon Phi. To calculate these values, we used Eq. 3.

$$E_{(J)} = P_{(W)} \times t_{(s)} \tag{3}$$

We ran each application varying the number of available nodes or threads, depending on the target platform. For the Raspberry Pi cluster, we used four threads per cluster and varied the number of nodes in 4 (12.5% of the total number of cores), 8 (25% of the total number of cores), 16 (50% of the total number of cores) and 32 (all available cores). Similarly, we varied the number of threads proportionally to the number of cores available in the Intel Xeon Phi, *i.e.*, 30, 60, 120 and 240 threads. This allows us to compare both platforms when the same percentages of the overall resources available in each platform are used.

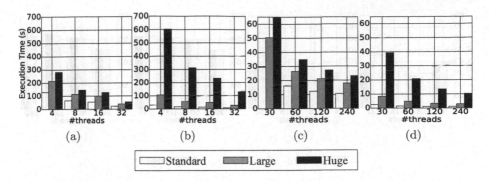

Fig. 3. Execution time: (a) Raspberry Pi cluster - Apriori, (b) Raspberry Pi cluster - K-Means, (c) Intel Xeon Phi - Apriori (d), Intel Xeon Phi - K-Means.

Three workload sizes were defined for each algorithm, to evaluate the behavior of both systems when the workload increases. For the Apriori algorithm, the increase on the workload size can be achieved by reducing the minimum support. We used the following minimum support values: 70 for the standard workload, 60 for large and 50 for huge. For K-Means, we increased the number of data points to be clustered. We used the following number of data points: 2^{14} for the standard workload, 2^{15} for large and 2^{16} for the huge one.

Finally, we performed 10 runs for each configuration (number of threads/nodes and workload sizes) and computed the average execution time and power. The maximum standard deviation observed in Raspberry Pi cluster executions was 11.04%, while the Intel Xeon Phi presented at most 7.07%.

5.2 Evaluation

We used three metrics to compare the platforms: execution time, power consumption, and energy consumption. Figure 3 presents the execution time of the algorithms when executed on both architectures. As it can be observed, Apriori proved to be more scalable than K-Means. It was possible to reduce the execution time by 82.05% with the Apriori when changing from 1 node to 8 nodes in the Raspberry Pi cluster, while in K-Means with same configurations the reduction was about 74.97%. This is due to the fact that the Apriori algorithm has more independent work units than the K-Means, which leads to less synchronization when parallel work finishes.

Comparing the Raspberry Pi cluster and Intel Xeon Phi execution time, the Intel Xeon Phi presented better results. It is an architecture with more processing power, featuring a larger thread support (up to 240), thus it was an expected behavior. However, the Intel Xeon Phi presented poorer scalability than the Raspberry Pi cluster for both algorithms. For instance, the maximum execution time reduction, starting from 30 threads, was 73.85% when running K-Means with the full architecture (240 threads). The communication in the Raspberry Pi cluster, although done by the means of a local area network, is

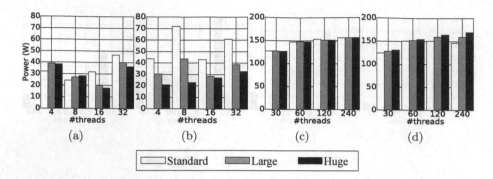

Fig. 4. Power consumption: (a) Raspberry Pi cluster - Apriori, (b) Raspberry Pi cluster - K-Means, (c) Intel Xeon Phi - Apriori (d), Intel Xeon Phi - K-Means.

not surpassed by the synchronization time spent by the 240 threads on the Intel Xeon Phi, in the case of Apriori. Considering K-Means, it presents a similar behavior when increasing the resources of the architectures. On the other hand, with this application, the increase in the workload has run better in the Intel Xeon Phi. It is worth noting that the multi-threaded version of the codes are the same for both architectures, without specific optimizations. Thus, despite the Intel Xeon Phi code could be improved, the Raspberry Pi cluster presents better efficiency with a lower number of threads (32 at full use).

Figure 4 presents the observed power consumption in our experiment. The applications are naturally unbalanced, thus, the power consumption varies depending on the execution time spent by each work unit, which are irregular (the cores and nodes present different times to solve their own work unit). With the Apriori algorithm, changing the workload size results in less variation in power consumption than when running the K-Means algorithm. Usually, with Apriori, the power consumption reduces when increasing the workload size. With respect to K-Means running in the Raspberry Pi cluster, the power consumption reduces when the workload size is increased, but with the Intel Xeon Phi the opposite occurs. In the Raspberry Pi cluster, each node has its own slave process and, when it finishes its computation, the power consumption of the entire node is drastically reduced while other nodes are still active.

We noticed a much more significant variation in power consumption on the Raspberry Pi cluster than on the Intel Xeon Phi. This is due to the fact that when less cores are used on the Intel Xeon Phi, the coprocessor idle cores keep consuming a portion of the energy, since they are in the same device. On the Raspberry Pi cluster, there is less impact from this fact, since the devices are completely independent. Overall, the Raspberry Pi cluster is superior when compared to Intel Xeon Phi. It was possible to obtain up to 88.35% of reduction in power consumption with Apriori when using the Raspberry Pi cluster over the Intel Xeon Phi. In the same way, for K-Means, the biggest reduction was 85.17%.

Figure 5 presents the energy consumption results, which were obtained by multiplying the average power by the execution time. As it can be observed, the

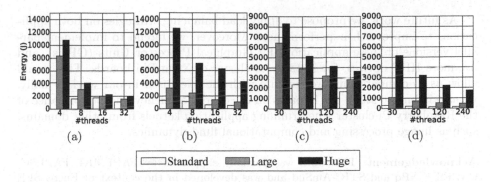

Fig. 5. Energy consumption: (a) Raspberry Pi cluster - Apriori, (b) Raspberry Pi cluster - K-Means, (c) Intel Xeon Phi - Apriori (d), Intel Xeon Phi - K-Means

energy consumption increases as we increase the workload size. This is due the increase in the execution time that the algorithms spent to reach a solution.

Another observation concerns the energy consumed when varying the number of threads/nodes. We observed a significant reduction in energy consumption when more threads are used. This can be explained by the fact that if more resources are used, the power consumption increases, but the time to solution tends to decrease, due to the increase in the computational power. Thus, since the power consumption is less determinant than the execution time in our experiment, the energy consumption decreases when more resources are used.

In summary, the Raspberry Pi cluster proved to be more energy efficient than the Intel Xeon Phi for Apriori, although the opposite occurs with K-Means. This is due to the higher execution time difference for K-Means, since as more time is spent running an application more energy is consumed during this time. The Apriori algorithm was less energy-efficient in the Raspberry Pi cluster when using more than a single node, however, when more nodes are employed, the Raspberry Pi cluster starts to be more energy-efficient, consuming up to 45.51% less energy than the Intel Xeon Phi. With respect to the financial costs, as mentioned before, the Raspberry Pi cluster is about ten times cheaper than the Intel Xeon Phi, thus presenting better price-performance ratio (*i.e.*, cost-benefit).

6   Concluding Remarks

In this paper we evaluated the performance, power and energy consumption of an unconventional low-cost energy-efficient HPC cluster composed of Raspberry Pi nodes when running two well-known data mining algorithms used in Big Data (Apriori and K-Means). The results obtained on this cluster were compared to a coprocessor widely adopted in the HPC domain (Intel Xeon Phi). Our results showed that the Raspberry Pi cluster achieved a better tradeoff between execution time and power consumption for the Apriori kernel. On the other hand, the Intel Xeon Phi presented better performance on K-Means.

As future work, we propose to apply load balancing strategies on both applications to improve their performances. Moreover, we intend to implement parallel versions of these applications for Graphical Processor Units (GPUs), and use more HPC devices, for instance, a cluster of Xeon Phi boards. This would allow us to compare this architecture with the ones used in our work. Finally, we also intend to study the impacts on the energy efficiency and performance of the Raspberry Pi cluster when running application kernels from other domains, such as image processing and computational fluid dynamics.

Acknowledgement. This work was partially supported by FAPEMIG, FAPESC, CAPES, CNPq and STIC-AmSud and was developed in the context of EnergySFE and ExaSE cooperation projects.

References

1. Agrawal, R., Srikant, R.: Fast algorithms for mining association rules in large databases. In: Proceedings of the 20th International Conference on Very Large Data Bases, pp. 487–499, VLDB 1994. Morgan Kaufmann Publishers Inc., San Francisco, CA, USA (1994)
2. Aroca, R.V., Gonçalves, L.M.G.: Towards green data centers: a comparison of x86 and ARM architectures power efficiency. J. Parallel Distrib. Comput. **72**(12), 1770–1780 (2012)
3. Ashby, S., Beckman, P., Chen, J., Colella, P., et al.: The opportunities and challenges of exascale computing. Technical report, Summary report of the advanced scientific computing advisory committee (ASCAC) subcommittee - Office of Science, U.S. Department of Energy Fall (2010)
4. Cox, S.J., Cox, J.T., Boardman, R.P., et al.: Iridis-Pi: a low-cost, compact demonstration cluster. Cluster Comput. **17**(2), 349–358 (2013)
5. d'Amore, M., Baggio, R., Valdani, E.: A practical approach to big data in tourism: a low cost Raspberry Pi cluster. In: Tussyadiah, I., Inversini, A. (eds.) Information and Communication Technologies in Tourism 2015, pp. 169–181. Springer, Cham (2015). doi:10.1007/978-3-319-14343-9_13
6. Jain, A.K., Dubes, R.C.: Algorithms for Clustering Data. Prentice-Hall Inc., Upper Saddle River (1988)
7. Kanungo, T., Mount, D., Netanyahu, N., et al.: An efficient k-means clustering algorithm: analysis and implementation. IEEE Trans. Pattern Anal. Mach. Intell. **24**(7), 881–892 (2002)
8. Kaufman, L., Rousseeuw, P.J.: Finding Groups in Data: An Introduction to Cluster Analysis. Wiley, New York (1990)
9. Kruger, M.J.: Building a Parallella board cluster. Bachelor of science honours thesis, Rhodes University, Grahamstown, South Africa (2015)
10. Lawson, G., Sosonkina, M., Shen, Y.: Energy evaluation for applications with different thread affinities on the Intel Xeon Phi. In: Workshop on Applications for Multi-Core Architectures (WAMCA), pp. 54–59. IEEE Computer Society (2014)
11. Lim, D.J., Anderson, T.R., Shott, T.: Technological forecasting of supercomputer development: the march to exascale computing. Omega **51**, 128–135 (2015)
12. MacQueen, J.: Some methods for classification and analysis of multivariate observations. In: Proceedings of the Fifth Berkeley Symposium on Mathematical Statistics

and Probability, volume 1: Statistics, pp. 281–297. University of California Press, Berkeley (1967)

13. Pfalzgraf, A.M., Driscoll, J.A.: A low-cost computer cluster for high-performance computing education. In: IEEE International Conference on Electro/Information Technology, pp. 362–366, June 2014

14. Rajovic, N., Carpenter, P.M., Gelado, I., Puzovic, N., Ramirez, A., Valero, M.: Supercomputing with commodity CPUS: are mobile SoCs ready for HPC? In: Proceedings of the International Conference on High Performance Computing, Networking, Storage and Analysis, SC 2013, NY, USA, pp. 40:1–40:12 (2013). http://doi.acm.org/10.1145/2503210.2503281

15. Simon, H.D.: Barriers to exascale computing. In: Daydé, M., Marques, O., Nakajima, K. (eds.) VECPAR 2012. LNCS, vol. 7851, pp. 1–3. Springer, Heidelberg (2013). doi:10.1007/978-3-642-38718-0_1

16. Trefethen, A.E., Thiyagalingam, J.: Energy-aware software: challenges, opportunities and strategies. J. Comput. Sci. 4(6), 444–449 (2013). Scalable Algorithms for Large-Scale Systems Workshop (ScalA2011), Supercomputing 2011

17. Tso, F.P., White, D.R., Jouet, S., Singer, J., Pezaros, D.P.: The glasgow Raspberry Pi cloud: a scale model for cloud computing infrastructures. In: 33rd International Conference on Distributed Computing Systems Workshops, pp. 108–112. IEEE, July 2013

18. Villa, O., Johnson, D.R., O'Connor, M., et al.: Scaling the power wall: a path to exascale. In: Proceedings of the International Conference for High Performance Computing, Networking, Storage and Analysis, pp. 830–841. IEEE Press (2014)

19. Xu, R., Wunsch, D.: Survey of clustering algorithms. IEEE Trans. Neural Netw. 16(3), 645–678 (2005)

Theano-MPI: A Theano-Based Distributed Training Framework

He Ma[1(✉)], Fei Mao[2], and Graham W. Taylor[1]

[1] School of Engineering, University of Guelph, Guelph, Canada
{hma02,gwtaylor}@uoguelph.ca
[2] SHARCNET, Compute Canada, London, Canada
feimao@sharcnet.ca

Abstract. We develop a scalable and extendable training framework that can utilize GPUs across nodes in a cluster and accelerate the training of deep learning models based on data parallelism. Both synchronous and asynchronous training are implemented in our framework, where parameter exchange among GPUs is based on CUDA-aware MPI. In this report, we analyze the convergence and capability of the framework to reduce training time when scaling the synchronous training of AlexNet and GoogLeNet from 2 GPUs to 8 GPUs. In addition, we explore novel ways to reduce the communication overhead caused by exchanging parameters. Finally, we release the framework as open-source for further research on distributed deep learning (https://github.com/uoguelph-mlrg/Theano-MPI).

1 Introduction

With the constant improvement of hardware and discovery of new architectures, algorithms, and applications, deep learning is gaining popularity in both academia and industry. Object recognition [20], is now dominated by deep learning methods, which in many cases, rival human performance. Recent success in areas such as activity recognition from video [13] and statistical machine translation [14] is an example of deep learning's ascent both in performance and at scale.

With the new generations of GPU cards and increased device memory, researchers are able to design and train models with more than 140 million parameters (c.f. VGGNet [21]) and models that are as deep as 150 layers (c.f. ResNet [9]).

The emergence of larger datasets, e.g. ImageNet [20] and MS-COCO [18], challenges artificial intelligence research and leads us to design deeper and more expressive models so that the complexity of models is sufficient for the task.

Despite of the increased computing power of GPUs, it usually takes weeks to train such large models to desired accuracy on a single GPU. This is due to the increased time associated with training deeper models and iterating over the examples in larger datasets. This is where distributed training of deep learning models becomes crucial, especially for activities such as model search which may involve training and evaluating models thousands of times.

© Springer International Publishing AG 2017
F. Desprez et al. (Eds.): Euro-Par 2016 Workshops, LNCS 10104, pp. 800–813, 2017.
DOI: 10.1007/978-3-319-58943-5_64

A naïve approach to scaling up is running several copies of the same model in parallel on multiple computing resources (e.g. GPUs), each computing its share of the dataset and averaging their parameters at every iteration. This approach is summarized as data parallelism, and its efficient implementation is the focus of our work. More sophisticated forms of distributed training, including model parallelism are important but outside the current scope of our framework.

Theano [23] is an open-source Python library for developing complex algorithms via mathematical expressions. It is often used for facilitating machine learning research. Its support for automatic symbolic differentiation and GPU-accelerated computing has made it popular within the deep learning community. Like other deep learning platforms, including Caffe [12], Torch [3], TensorFlow [1] and MXNet [2], Theano uses CUDA as one of its main backends for GPU accelerated computation. Since a single GPU is limited by its device memory and available threads when solving compute-intensive problems, very recently researchers have started to build multi-GPU support into the most popular frameworks. This includes the multi-GPU version of Caffe (FireCaffe [11]), Torch and Theano (Platoon).

Because the Theano environment usually compiles models for one GPU per process, we need to drive multiple GPUs using multiple processes. So finding a way to communicate between processes becomes a fundamental problem within a multi-GPU framework. There are several existing approaches of implementing inter-process communication besides manually programming on sockets, such as Signals, Message Queues, Message Passing, Pipes, Shared Memory, Memory Mapped Files, etc. However, among those approaches, Message Passing is most suitable for collective communication between multiple programs across a cluster because of its well-developed point-to-point and collective protocols. Message Passing Interface (MPI) is a language-independent communication protocol that can undertake the task of inter-process communication across machines. It is a standardized message-passing system designed for programming on large-scale parallel applications.

Parameter transfer is a basic operation in the distributed training of deep learning models. Therefore, the transfer speed between processes severely impacts the overall data throughput speedup[1]. Since the parameters to be transferred are computed on GPUs, a GPU-to-GPU transfer is required. Compared to the basic `transfer()` function in Theano, NVIDIA GPUDirect P2P technology makes this possible by transferring data between GPUs without passing through host memory. Specifically, it enables CUDA devices to perform direct read and write operations on other CUDA host and device memory. In the context of MPI, GPUDirect P2P technology allows a `GPUArray` memory buffer to be transferred in basic point-to-point and collective operations, making MPI "CUDA-Aware".

Leveraging CUDA-aware MPI, we have developed a scalable training framework that provides multi-node and multi-GPU support to Theano and efficient inter-GPU parameter transfer at the same time. To the best of our knowledge,

---

[1] We define data throughput speedup as the change in total time taken to process a certain amount of examples. It includes both training and communication time.

this is to-date the most convenient way to deploy Theano processes on a multi-node multi-GPU cluster.

2 Related Work

The idea of exploiting data parallelism in machine learning has been widely explored in recent years in both asynchronous and synchronous ways. To accelerate the training of a speech recognition model on distributed CPU cores, Down-Pour, an asynchronous parameter exchanging method [6], was proposed. It was the largest-scale method to-date for distributed training of neural networks. It was later found that controlling the maximum staleness of parameter updates received by the server leads to faster training convergence [10] on problems like topic modeling, matrix factorization and lasso regression compared to a purely asynchronous approach. For accelerating image classification on the CIFAR and ImageNet datasets, an elastic averaging strategy between asynchronous workers and the server was later proposed [25]. This algorithm allows more exploration of local optima than DownPour and alleviates the need for frequent communication between workers and the server.

Krizhevsky proposed his trick on parallelizing the training of AlexNet [16] on multiple GPUs in a synchronous way [15]. This work showed that eight GPU workers training on the same batch size of 128 can give up to 6.25× data throughput speedup and nearly the same convergence as trained on a single GPU when exploiting both model and data parallelism. Notably, the increase in effective batch size[2] leads to very small changes in the final convergence of AlexNet when the learning rate is scaled properly. Following his work, a Theano-based two-GPU synchronous framework [7] for accelerating the training of AlexNet was proposed, where both weights and momentum are averaged between two GPUs after each iteration. The model converges to the same level as using a single GPU but in less time.

There has been more development on the acceleration of vision-based deep learning in recent years. NVIDIA developed a multi-GPU deep learning framework, DIGITS, which shows 3.5× data throughput speedup when training AlexNet on 4 GPUs. Purine [17] pipelines the propagation of gradients between iterations and overlaps the communication of large weights in fully connected layers with the rest of back-propagation, giving near 12× data throughput speedup when training GoogLeNet [22] on 12 GPUs. Similarly, MXNet [2] also shows a super-linear data throughput speedup on training GoogLeNet under a distributed training setting.

The Platoon project is a multi-GPU extension for Theano, created and maintained by the official Theano team. It currently supports only asynchronous data parallelism *inside one compute node* based on posix_ipc shared memory. In comparison, our framework, Theano-MPI, is designed to support GPUs that are distributed over multiple nodes in a cluster, providing convenient process management and faster inter-GPU memory exchanging based on CUDA-aware MPI.

---

[2] Effective batch size = batch size × number of workers.

3   Implementation

Our goal is to make the field of distributed deep learning more accessible by developing a scalable training framework with two key components. First is Theano as a means of constructing an architecture and optimizing it by Stochastic Gradient Descent (SGD). Second is Massage Passing Interface (MPI) as an inter-process parameter exchanger. We also aim to explore various ways to reduce communication overhead in parallel SGD and expose some phenomena that affect convergence and speedup when training deep learning models in a distributed framework.

3.1   Hardware and Software Environment

The software was developed and tested on a PI-contributed SHARCNET cluster, named *copper*. As shown in Fig. 1, each node in the cluster is a dual socket system with two NVIDIA Tesla K80 GPUs on each socket. The whole cluster is interconnected with Mellonox Infiniband FDR. We also tested on another cluster, *mosaic*, which features distributed GPUs across nodes connected by Infiniband QDR. Each node has one NVIDIA K20m GPU.

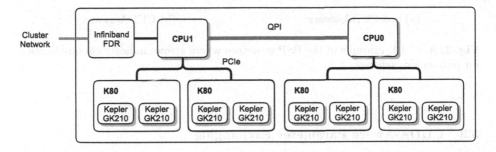

Fig. 1. Hardware connection layout of a copper node

For high-level access to MPI functionality, we use its Python binding mpi4py, compiled against OpenMPI 1.8.7. All models mentioned in this report are constructed in Theano 0.8 and their implementation is available in our Github project. Convolution and pooling operations in the computational graph depend on CUDA 7.0 and the cuDNN v4 library. We also support cudaconvnet as an alternative backend.

3.2   The BSP Structure

Bulk Synchronous Parallel (BSP) [24] is an intuitive way to implement parallel computing. In the BSP paradigm, workers proceed with training in a synchronous way. Figure 2a shows a 4 GPU example of the proposed BSP structure where the same model is built and run within four processes, P_0, P_1, P_2, P_3. Each process uses one CPU and one GPU. After the model's training graph is compiled on the GPU, those parameters in the graph become arrays in GPU memory whose values can be retrieved from device to host and set from host to device. When training starts, the training dataset is split into four parts. In every iteration, each worker process takes a mini-batch of examples from its share and performs SGD on it. After that, all workers are synchronized and model parameters are exchanged between worker processes in a collective way.

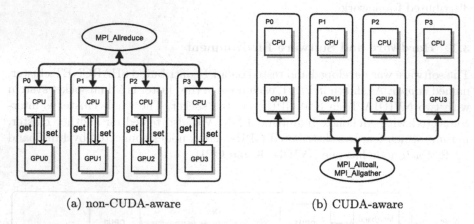

(a) non–CUDA-aware   (b) CUDA-aware

Fig. 2. A 4-GPU example of the BSP structure where arrows indicate communication for parameter exchange.

3.3 CUDA-Aware Parameter Exchanging

Synchronous parameter exchange is an array reduction problem which consists of both data transfer and calculation. The GPUDirect P2P technology allows exchanging parameters between GPUs without passing through host memory, making MPI functions "CUDA-aware". Based on this, we explored various strategies trying to minimize the data transfer and calculation time, and make more efficient use of QPI, PCIe and network card bandwidth during data transfer. The basic strategy is to use the MPI `Allreduce()` function. However, the CUDA-aware version of it in OpenMPI 1.8.7 does not give much improvement since any collective MPI function with arithmetic operations still needs to copy data to host memory. Functions like `Alltoall()` and `Allgather()` do not involve any arithmetic and therefore the CUDA-aware version of them (Fig. 2b) can avoid passing through host memory unless data transfer crossing the QPI bus is needed. We therefore implemented a CUDA-aware `Alltoall-sum-Allgather` strategy which separates the data transfer and computation. An example of this strategy is demonstrated in Fig. 3. Here, the summation kernels required for

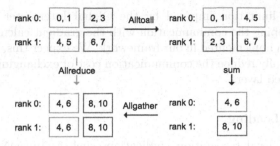

Fig. 3. An example demonstrating the reduction of arrays on rank 0 and rank 1 with the proposed Alltoall-sum-Allgather strategy compared to MPI Allreduce. Sub-arrays of data items (indicated by same-coloured boxes) need to be summed and the results exchanged with the other ranks. (Color figure online)

parameter exchange are executed in parallel on GPUs. Our test shows the GPU summation kernel takes only 1.6% of the total communication time.

Using low precision data types for weights or activations (or both) in the forward pass during training of deep neural networks has received much recent interest [4,5]. It was shown that training Maxout networks [8] at 10 bits fixed point precision can still yield near state-of-art test accuracy [5]. In light of this, we also implemented the transfer of parameters at half-precision while summing them at full precision, in order to further reduce communication overhead.

Figure 4 shows the improvement of the combination of strategies over MPI `Allreduce`. The "ASA" strategy shows three times faster communication relative to MPI `Allreduce` and the half precision version of it gives nearly 6 times faster performance. Those results are obtained on cluster *mosaic* with distributed GPUs. Each node hosts one GPU.

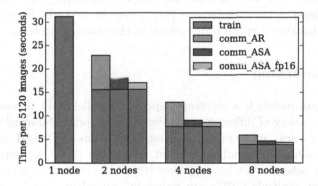

Fig. 4. Computation (train) vs. relative communication overhead of different parameter exchanging strategies during training AlexNet-128b (AR: Allreduce, ASA: CUDA-aware Alltoall-sum-Allgather).

Due to the limitation imposed by the Global Interpreter Lock (GIL) in Python, overlapping the communication with the gradient calculation as in [17] has not yet been implemented in our framework. We expect this, if implemented, would substantially reduce the communication cost of exchanging large matrices in fully-connected layers.

3.4   Parallel Loading

For large-scale visual recognition applications such as ImageNet LSVRC, the data required for training is on the order of hundreds of Gigabytes. Therefore, it is difficult to load all image data completely into memory after training starts. Instead, images are stored as batch files on local or remote disks and loaded one file at a time by each process. Loading image batches x from disk can be time consuming[3]. It is affected by various factors, including file size, file format, disk I/O capability and network bandwidth if reading from remote disks. If in every iteration, the training process waits for all data to load in order to proceed, one can imagine the time cost by loading data will be critical to the overall performance. One way to circumvent this, given the independence of loading and training, is to load those files in parallel with the forward and backward propagations on the last loaded batch. This assumes loading one batch of images takes shorter than one iteration of training the model. This auxiliary loading process should follow the procedure outlined in Algorithm 1 to collaborate efficiently with its corresponding training process:

Different from the `multiprocessing` and `Queue` messaging method in [7], we used the MPI `Spawn` function to start a child process from each training process and used the resulting MPI intra-communicator to pass messages between the training process and its child process. As shown in Algorithm 1, the parallel loading process can read image files, subtract the mean image, crop sub-images and finally load preprocessed data onto GPUs. By doing this, we are able to overlap the most compute-intensive part (Step 10 to 13 in Algorithm 1) with forward and backward graph propagation in the training process.

4   Benchmarking

Exchanging parameters is a necessary aspect of parallel SGD, however, it can be achieved in a variety of different ways. Parameters updated during SGD include weights (and biases), momentum (if using momentum SGD) and raw gradients. Averaging *weights* after gradient descent (AWAGD) [7,15] is a straightforward parallel SGD scheme. We have proven [19] that training a perceptron using this scheme on multiple GPUs can either be equivalent to or a close approximate of sequential SGD training on a single GPU depending on whether or not effective batch size is kept constant. In this scheme, the learning rate is scaled

---

[3] Loading labels y, on the other hand, is much faster, therefore labels can be loaded completely into memory.

Algorithm 1. The parallel loading process

Require:

    Host memory allocated for loading image batch $hostdata_x$.

    GPU memory allocated for preprocessed image batch $gpudata_x$

    GPU memory allocated for the actual model graph input $input_x$,

    $mode$=None, $recv$=None, $filename$=None.

    Mean image $image\_mean$

Ensure:

1: **while** True **do**

2:     Receive the $mode$ (train, validate or stop) from training process

3:     **if** $recv$="stop" **then**

4:         **break**

5:     **else**

6:         $mode \leftarrow recv$

7:     Receive the first filename to be loaded from training process $filename \leftarrow recv$

8:     **while** True **do**

9:         Load file "filename" from disk into host memory $hostdata_x$.

10:         $hostdata_x = hostdata_x - image\_mean$

11:         Crop and mirror $hostdata_x$ according to $mode$.

12:         Transfer $hostdata_x$ from host to GPU device memory $gpudata_x$.

13:         Wait for training on the last $input_x$ to finish by receiving the next filename
            to be loaded.

14:         **if** $recv$ in ["stop", "train", "val"] **then**

15:             **break**

16:         **else**

17:             $filename \leftarrow recv$

18:         Transfer $gpudata_x$ to $input_x$.

19:         Synchronize GPU context.

20:         Notify training process to precede with the newly loaded $input_x$

---

with the number of GPUs used [15], namely k. It can also be shown that this scheme is equivalent to summing up the *parameter updates* from all GPUs before performing gradient descent (SUBGD), which does not require scaling up the learning rate. However, our experiments show that tuning the learning rate is still dependent on k to ensure initial convergence of the model. Table 1 lists the learning rates we used and the convergence we achieved in training AlexNet[4] and GoogLeNet[5] at different scales (number of workers).

Recent work has applied low precision to weights and activations during training [5]. In the extreme, binary data types have been considered [4]. This enables efficient operation of the low-precision network both at deployment (test time) and during the forward propagation stage during training. However, gradients

---

[4] Top-5 error at epoch 62. The implementation is based on theano_alexnet from uoguelph-mlrg. https://github.com/uoguelph-mlrg/theano_alexnet.

[5] Top-5 error at epoch 70. BVLC GoogLeNet implementation in Caffe is referenced in building the model. https://github.com/BVLC/caffe/tree/master/models/bvlc_googlenet. The top-5 error is taken from [22].

used for parameter updates must still be stored at high-precision or learning will fail. Our training results of AlexNet and GoogLeNet, however, show that the reduced-precision parameter exchange does not affect much final convergence. This can be seen from Table 1, where the validation top-5 error from the "fp16" training is almost the same as its full precision counterpart.

Table 1. Trade-off between accuracy and speedup under different hyper parameter settings in training AlexNet and GoogLeNet based on the ASA strategy. The learning rate reported was the best one found empirically for the particular setting (HP: hyper-parameters, LR: learning rate, BS: batch size).

# of workers	AlexNet				GoogLeNet			
	HP		Result		HP		Result	
	LR	BS	Accuracy	Speedup	LR	BS	Accuracy	Speedup
1 GPU	0.01	128	19.75%	1×	0.01	32	10.51%	1×
2 GPU	0.01	128	20.00%	1.7×	0.007	32	10.20%	1.9×
4 GPU	0.01	128	20.38%	3.4×	0.005	32	10.48%	3.7×
8 GPU	0.005	128	20.73%	6.7×	0.005	32	10.87%	7.2×
8 GPU-fp16	0.005	128	20.67%	7.1×	0.005	32	10.86%	7.3×
8 GPU	0.005	32	20.10%	4.9×	-			
8 GPU-fp16	0.005	32	20.17%	5.7×	-			

Figures 5 and 6 show the convergence of two models trained with SUBGD and the `Alltoall-sum-Allgather` strategy, in which AlexNet is trained on 1, 2, 4 and 8 GPUs with momentum SGD and 128 batch size on each GPU[6]. Similarly, GoogLeNet is trained on 2, 4 and 8 GPUs with a batch size of 32. We see that as more workers are used, the effective batch size becomes too large and the approximation from parallel SGD to sequential SGD becomes worse. As shown in Table 1, one way to preserve convergence at such a large-scale is to reduce the batch size (from 128 to 32) on each worker so that the effective batch size stays small. This gives the model more potential to explore further at low learning rates, though the accuracy improvement at the beginning is slow. However, using smaller batch sizes means more frequent parameter exchanges between workers, which demands attention toward further reducing the communication overhead.

The speedup of training AlexNet and GoogLeNet are evaluated on 8 distributed GPU nodes (1 GPU per node). To show the performance of accelerating larger models, we build VGGNet and test its scaling performance on 8 GPUs in a single node (in *copper*). This setup meets the memory requirements of VGGNet. Table 2 gives an overview of the structural difference between those three models. Table 3 reports the training and communication time taken to process 5,120 images across different models. We see that these three models scale differently

---

[6] Tested on the ILSVRC14 dataset [20].

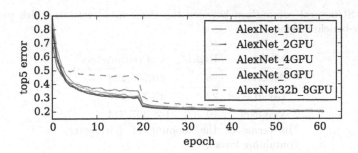

Fig. 5. Validation top-5 error of AlexNet trained at different scales (and batch sizes). Best viewed in colour.

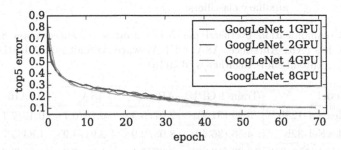

Fig. 6. Validation top-5 error of GoogLeNet trained at different scales. Best viewed in colour.

in the framework due to differences in the complexity of their operations as well as the number of free parameters. CUDA-aware parameter exchanging helps boost the speedup of the framework, especially when the number of parameters is relatively large.

Observing the GoogLeNet benchmark result in Fig. 6, we would expect that the framework provides a convergence speedup close to the throughput speedup reported in Table 3, if the convergence of parallel SGD closely approximates that of sequential SGD. However, it is difficult to give the exact convergence speedup provided by the framework, since different settings of the hyper-parameters (learning rate tuning policy, weight decay, batch size, cropping randomness) leads to a different convergence path and complicates comparison.

Besides the synchronous framework, we also explored reducing the communication overhead in the asynchronous setting. Referencing the implementation of EASGD in *Platoon*, a Theano-based multi-GPU framework that exploits data parallelism, we re-implemented the framework based on the CUDA-aware MPI SendRecv() function without the Round-Robin scheme [25]. Our test shows, when training AlexNet on 8 GPUs, the asynchronous communication overhead in our framework is 42% lower than that in Platoon when worker processes communicate with the server in the most frequent way ($\tau = 1$). We also performed a grid search on the hyper-parameters α and τ to achieve better convergence

Table 2. Structural comparison between the three architectures which were implemented for benchmarking.

Model	Depth[a]	# of parameters[b]
AlexNet	8	60,965,224
GoogLeNet	22	13,378,280[c]
VGGNet	19	138,357,544

[a]In terms of the amount of parameter-containing layers.
[b]In terms of the amount of float32 parameters.
[c]This includes the parameters of the two auxiliary classifiers.

Table 3. Communication overhead per 5,120 images (s)/speedup on 8 GPUs for different models (AR: Allreduce, ASA: CUDA-aware Alltoall-sum-Allgather, ASA16: CUDA-aware Alltoall-sum-Allgather w/float16).

Model	Train(1 GPU)	AR	ASA	ASA16
AlexNet-128b	3.90 (31.2)	2.01/5.3×	0.75/6.7×	0.47/7.1×
AlexNet-32b	4.56 (36.40)	8.03/2.9×	2.94/4.9×	1.83/5.7×
GoogLeNet-32b	16.82 (134.9)	2.07/7.1×	1.96/7.2×	1.76/7.3×
VGGNet-32b	51.79 (405.2)	41.41/4.3×	8.60/6.7×	4.84/7.2×

when training AlexNet on eight distributed GPUs, each processing a batch size of 128. The best top-5 error we achieved from this framework was 21.12% at a global epoch of 49 when the moving rate was $\alpha = 0.5$ and averaging period was $\tau = 1$ with a data throughput speedup of 6.7×.

5   Discussion

We have attempted to scale up the training of deep learning models in an accessible way by developing a scalable training framework built around Theano. Key technical features of our framework are more efficient interprocess communication strategies and parallel data loading techniques. Factors affecting the speedup of the framework can be associated with the model to be trained (i.e. architectural), the training data loading strategy, synchronization in the computational graph, implementation of GPU kernels, system memory and network bandwidth.

Importantly, we try not to compromise the convergence of models trained under our framework since measured speedup is based on the time taken to reach a certain error rate. However, the convergence achieved by a parallel framework also depends on the tuning of that framework's hyper-parameters. The convergence results in Table 1 can therefore be improved if better hyper-parameters are found. Factors affecting model convergence include the number of worker processes, effective batch size and corresponding learning rate, parameter averaging frequency τ^7, moving rate α in EASGD and the initialization of model parameters.

The main contributions of our work include: providing multi-node and improved multi-GPU support to the Theano library based on MPI, eliminating substantial communication overhead, exposing convergence and speedup phenomena in parallel SGD, and an implementation of a more efficient parallel loading method.

Our effort towards eliminating the communication overhead involves several aspects: leveraging CUDA-aware MPI for direct data transfer, separating data transfer and summation for more efficient summation on GPUs, and exploring half precision data transfer for faster communication. Our benchmarking results show that our effort on eliminating communication overhead works well on both the 1-GPU-per-node cluster, *mosaic*, and the 8-GPU-per-node cluster, *copper*.

Note that the multi-node testing results in this report are obtained *without* GPUDirect RDMA support due to a limitation in the cluster configuration. Also, the QPI bus topology of a *copper* node limits the usage of GPUDirect P2P technology. This is because the GPUDirect P2P requires all GPUs to be under the same PCIe switch. If a path traversing the QPI is needed, the data transfer would go through CPU RAM first. As a result, further improvement of communication performance based on the current hardware setting would involve consideration of overlapping data transfer with the summation kernel, overlapping parameter exchange with gradient calculation, and designing better inter-node and intra-node strategies that could balance the bandwidth usage among QPI, PCIe and Infiniband networking.

Acknowledgements. We thank the developers of Theano, and specifically *Platoon*, which demonstrates a way to build asynchronous training structures. We are also grateful for funding and support from Compute Canada, CFI, SRI, and DARPA.

References

1. Abadi, M., Agarwal, A., Barham, P., Brevdo, E., Chen, Z., Citro, C., Corrado, G.S., Davis, A., Dean, J., Devin, M., et al.: Tensorflow: large-scale machine learning on heterogeneous distributed systems. arXiv preprint arXiv:1603.04467 (2016)
2. Chen, T., Li, M., Li, Y., Lin, M., Wang, N., Wang, M., Xiao, T., Xu, B., Zhang, C., Zhang, Z.: MXNet: a flexible and efficient machine learning library for heterogeneous distributed systems. arXiv preprint arXiv:1512.01274 (2015)
3. Collobert, R., Kavukcuoglu, K., Farabet, C.: Torch7: a matlab-like environment for machine learning. In: BigLearn, NIPS Workshop (2011)
4. Courbariaux, M., Bengio, Y.: Binarynet: training deep neural networks with weights and activations constrained to +1 or −1. arXiv preprint arXiv:1602.02830 (2016)

---

^{7} In BSP, we use $\tau = 1$ since larger τ tends to affect convergence in the same way as increasing batch size.

5. Courbariaux, M., Bengio, Y., David, J.P.: Low precision arithmetic for deep learning. arXiv preprint arXiv:1412.7024 (2014)
6. Dean, J., Corrado, G., Monga, R., Chen, K., Devin, M., et al.: Large scale distributed deep networks. In: Advances in Neural Information Processing Systems, vol. 25, pp. 1232–1240 (2012)
7. Ding, W., Wang, R., Mao, F., Taylor, G.: Theano-based large-scale visual recognition with multiple GPUs. arXiv preprint arXiv:1412.2302 (2014)
8. Goodfellow, I.J., Warde-Farley, D., Mirza, M., Courville, A.C., Bengio, Y.: Maxout networks. ICML 3(28), 1319–1327 (2013)
9. He, K., Zhang, X., Ren, S., Sun, J.: Deep residual learning for image recognition. arXiv preprint arXiv:1512.03385 (2015)
10. Ho, Q., Cipar, J., Cui, H., Lee, S., Kim, J., et al.: More effective distributed ML via a stale synchronous parallel parameter server. In: Advances in Neural Information Processing Systems, vol. 26, pp. 1223–1231. Curran Associates, Inc. (2013)
11. Iandola, F.N., Ashraf, K., Moskewicz, M.W., Keutzer, K.: Firecaffe: near-linear acceleration of deep neural network training on compute clusters. arXiv preprint arXiv:1511.00175 (2015)
12. Jia, Y., Shelhamer, E., Donahue, J., Karayev, S., Long, J., Girshick, R., Guadarrama, S., Darrell, T.: Caffe: Convolutional architecture for fast feature embedding. In: Proceedings of the 22nd ACM International Conference on Multimedia, pp. 675–678. ACM (2014)
13. Karpathy, A., Toderici, G., Shetty, S., Leung, T., Sukthankar, R., Fei-Fei, L.: Large-scale video classification with convolutional neural networks. In: Proceedings of the IEEE Conference on Computer Vision and Pattern Recognition, pp. 1725–1732 (2014)
14. Koehn, P., Haddow, B.: Towards effective use of training data in statistical machine translation. In: Proceedings of the Seventh Workshop on Statistical Machine Translation, WMT 2012, pp. 317–321. Association for Computational Linguistics, Stroudsburg (2012)
15. Krizhevsky, A.: One weird trick for parallelizing convolutional neural networks. arXiv preprint arXiv:1404.5997 (2014)
16. Krizhevsky, A., Sutskever, I., Hinton, G.E.: ImageNet classification with deep convolutional neural networks. In: Advances in Neural Information Processing Systems, pp. 1097–1105 (2012)
17. Lin, M., Li, S., Luo, X., Yan, S.: Purine: a bi-graph based deep learning framework. arXiv preprint arXiv:1412.6249 (2014)
18. Lin, T.-Y., Maire, M., Belongie, S., Hays, J., Perona, P., Ramanan, D., Dollár, P., Zitnick, C.L.: Microsoft COCO: common objects in context. In: Fleet, D., Pajdla, T., Schiele, B., Tuytelaars, T. (eds.) ECCV 2014. LNCS, vol. 8693, pp. 740–755. Springer, Cham (2014). doi:10.1007/978-3-319-10602-1_48
19. Ma, H.: Developing a scalable deep learning framework based on MPI. Master's thesis, University of Guelph, Guelph, ON, CA (2015)
20. Russakovsky, O., Deng, J., Su, H., Krause, J., Satheesh, S., et al.: Imagenet large scale visual recognition challenge. Int. J. Comput. Vis. 115(3), 211–252 (2015)
21. Simonyan, K., Zisserman, A.: Very deep convolutional networks for large-scale image recognition. arXiv preprint arXiv:1409.1556 (2014)
22. Szegedy, C., Liu, W., Jia, Y., Sermanet, P., Reed, S., Anguelov, D., Erhan, D., Vanhoucke, V., Rabinovich, A.: Going deeper with convolutions. In: Proceedings of the IEEE Conference on Computer Vision and Pattern Recognition, pp. 1–9 (2015)

23. Theano Development Team: Theano: A Python framework for fast computation of mathematical expressions. arXiv preprint arXiv:1605.02688 (2016)
24. Valiant, L.G.: A bridging model for parallel computation. Commun. ACM **33**(8), 103 (1990)
25. Zhang, S., Choromanska, A.E., LeCun, Y.: Deep learning with elastic averaging sgd. In: Advances in Neural Information Processing Systems, vol. 28, pp. 685–693. Curran Associates, Inc. (2015)

Acceleration of Turbomachinery Steady Simulations on GPU

Mohamed Hassanine Aissa[1]([✉]), Lasse Müller[1],
Tom Verstraete[1], and Cornelis Vuik[2]

[1] Von Karman Institute for Fluid Dynamics,
Waterloosesteenweg 72, 1640 Sint-Genesius-Rode, Belgium
aissa@vki.ac.be
[2] Delft University of Technology, 2628 CD Delft, The Netherlands
http://www.vki.ac.be

Abstract. Steady state simulations in Computational Fluid Dynamics (CFD), which rely on implicit time integration, are not experiencing great accelerations on GPUs. Moreover, most of the reported acceleration effort concerns solving the linear system of equations while neglecting the acceleration potential of running the entire simulation on the GPU. In this paper, we present the software implementation of an implicit RANS CFD solver, which is fully running on GPU. We use the GMRES linear solver of the Paralution package combined with the incomplete LU factorization for the preconditioning. We propose also a control mechanism - *on-demand* factorization - capable of reducing the number of times an incomplete LU factorization is performed. The *on-demand* factorization accelerates the linear solver without altering the flow convergence. The GPU implementation achieved a speedups of 9.2x compared to a single-core CPU and 3.5x compared to a 4-cores CPU for 3-D flow predictions in turbine applications.

Keywords: Steady CFD · Linear systems · GPU · ILU · Krylov subspace · GMRES

1 Introduction

1.1 Sparse Linear Systems in Turbomachinery

Turbomachinery components are nowadays designed by using optimization algorithms, which scan the design space guided by CFD simulations [1]. These algorithms require therefore a large number of simulations making any time gain on the CFD level very beneficial for the overall optimization procedure. These steady CFD simulations advance an initial flow solution based on an explicit or implicit numerical time integration scheme. Implicit schemes are more stable and faster to converge due to a larger allowed time step. This property comes however at a high cost of assembling and solving a linear system of equations

© Springer International Publishing AG 2017
F. Desprez et al. (Eds.): Euro-Par 2016 Workshops, LNCS 10104, pp. 814–825, 2017.
DOI: 10.1007/978-3-319-58943-5_65

$Ax = b$ at every flow iteration. The system assembly comprises the computation of the system matrix A and the right-hand side b. The linear solver, due to the sparsity character, uses an iterative solver such as the Generalized Minimal Residual Algorithm for Solving Non-symmetric Linear Systems (GMRES) [6].

For CFD problems in turbomachinery, this system of equations is large but sparse. With the growth of the problem size and complexity, the use of High Performance Computing (HPC) becomes inevitable. In this field, Graphics Processing Units (GPUs) are gaining in importance through the reported speedups of many CFD applications [2,4]. While dense matrix vector operations are very efficient on GPUs [5], solving a sparse linear system of equations is more challenging, since there are less independent operations for the large GPU computational power. Moreover, most linear systems require a factorization-based preconditioner to converge, which enhances the serial aspect of the algorithm and thus reduces drastically the GPU performance gain.

1.2 Related Work

In some GPU-accelerated applications [9,20] with a major part of the execution time for the linear solver, the CPU is used for the system assembly, for which the high porting effort is not worth the performance gain. A linear solver is in general implemented on a GPU using a low-level programming language. The flexibility of the low-level approach makes it possible to adapt the data storage and the algorithm to the sparsity pattern (non-zero elements distribution) of the system matrix in order to enhance the performance. In this context, the effort is concentrated on accelerating the sparse matrix-vector product (SpMV), which constitutes the core of many linear solvers. Bell and Garland [20] examined the optimization possibilities for SpMV on GPU without reordering the system matrix. He identified the diagonal format (DIA) as suitable for structured meshes and the Hybrid matrix format (HYB) for unstructured ones. The optimization is part of the CUSP library. Cecka et al. [10] did similar work for problems based on Finite Element Methods (FEM). He examined the effect of the memory optimization on the overall performance comparing local, global and shared memory. Istvan and Giles [11] reviewed relevant research for SpMV on GPU and concentrated on GPU tuning of SpMV operations for the Compressed Sparse Row (CSR) matrix format making use of the L1-cache locality, shared memory, and thread cooperation. The author presented a speedup of 1.4x over cuSparse and suggested that cache hit maximization was the key method behind the observed performance gain.

GPU iterative solver performance has been gradually increasing but the bottleneck remains the serial preconditioners such as the Incomplete LU factorization (ILU). These functions have been the subject of extended research [15]. In order improve the performance, the system matrix has to be reordered. This expose more fine-grained parallelism and thus provide the GPU with more independent instructions. Level-scheduling is one established alternative to elevate the parallelism of the factorization, where independent rows of the system matrix are implicitly grouped in the same level. Graph-coloring is another method where an explicit reordering is performed giving independent matrix elements the same color, then every color is thread-safe for a massively parallel linear solver. Naumov et al. [12] showed a parallel graph coloring method reaching a higher parallelism than in level scheduling. His work is included in the cuSparse Nvidia library. Another method to extract more parallelism, introduced by Chow and Patel [19], is to transform the ILU factorization in a minimization problem of a set of equations that could be computed in groups independently. Groups can be so small to contain only one equation making it possible for every non-zero element of the incomplete L and U matrices to be computed asynchronously and in parallel. This ILU version can be found in ViennaCL[1].

1.3   Contributions

In this work, the reference CFD simulation is performed on CPU using PETSc [8] and 70% of the execution time is spend on the system assembly, while the rest is for the system linear solver. The same balance is also found in some FEM applications, e.g. Darve et al. [13] ported a CPU application based on PETSc with 80% of execution time for the system assembly. This observation motivated us to port the assembly part to the GPU to avoid any data transfer to the CPU during the simulation. The linear solver is the preconditioned GMRES solver of the Paralution library[2], which uses building blocks of the efficient cuSparse library. This library has been reported [18] to allow a speedup of factor 5x for a neutron diffusion problem. Paralution performs, however, the assembly of the system matrix on the host, which implies a data transfer from GPU to the host CPU. To address this issue we developed an interface to connect the system of equations, which is assembled on the GPU, to the linear solver. We propose an algorithm - *on-demand* LU factorization- to optimize the frequent use of linear solvers in steady simulations. The algorithm is capable of reducing the number of times an ILU preconditioner matrix is built for the linear solver without altering the flow accuracy. This new technique enables the linear solver to use previously computed LU matrix as preconditioner instead of computing a new one in every iteration. We combine this technique with standard ILU to deliver the best speedups for coarse and fine meshes.

Our contributions are:

- A GPU solver based on implicit time stepping with no CPU-GPU data transfer.
- An *on-demand* ILU preconditioner build to reduce the computational time.
- Analysis of the advantages and drawbacks of the GPU for implicit solvers.
- An interface to Paralution and ViennaCL linear solvers.
- A sorting algorithm to transform unordered matrix entries to COO then CSR.

The rest of the paper is structured as follow: Sect. 2 introduces the numerical scheme used by the CFD solver while Sect. 3 describes the implementation of

---

[1] Rupp, K. "ViennaCL." http://viennacl.sourceforge.net.
[2] PARALUTION Labs "PARALUTION v1.0.0", 2015, http://www.paralution.com.

the solver on the GPU. Results are shown in Sect. 4 and main findings are summarized in Sect. 5.

2 Numerical Scheme

The flow solver uses a cell-centered finite volume discretization on multiblock structured grids. It solves the Reynolds-Averaged Navier Stokes (RANS) equations in time-dependent integral form [16]:

$$\frac{\partial}{\partial t} \int_\Omega W \, d\Omega + \oint_{\partial\Omega} (F_c - F_v) dS = \int_\Omega Q \, d\Omega, \tag{1}$$

with $W = \{\rho, \rho V_x, \rho V_y, \rho V_z, \rho E\}$ the vector of conservative variables, Ω the cell volume and S the cell surface. The convective fluxes F_c are computed using a Roe upwind approximation of a Riemann Solver while second order accuracy is achieved through the MUSCL approach (Monotone Upstream-Centered Schemes for Conservation Law). The viscous fluxes F_v are approximated using a central discretization scheme. The source term Q contains contributions from the Spalart-Allmaras (SA) one-equation turbulence model.

The implicit time integration on steady simulations follows the equation below:

$$\left[\frac{(\Omega I)}{\Delta t} + \left(\frac{\delta R}{\delta W}\right)\right] \Delta W^n = -R^n. \tag{2}$$

with R the residual containing the fluxes and the source term, $\Delta W = W^{n+1} - W^n$ the solution change, I the identity matrix and $\frac{\delta R}{\delta W}$ an approximate *Jacobian* matrix. When Eq. 2 is applied to the entire mesh a large linear system is build with the form $Ax = b$. Residuals and Jacobian are first evaluated on cell surfaces and then summed in a local assembly procedure (see Eq. 1). The global assembly concatenates the local items to a large global matrix and right-hand side containing all the problem unknowns. A multistage time stepping method such as implicit Runge-Kutta [17] solves multiple successive linear systems for every flow iteration, in which only the right-hand side is updated then multiplied by a different stage coefficient α. The nature of the flow solved in this work and the mesh complexity leads to a stiff system matrix that requires further treatment, e.g. preconditioning, to enhance the linear system convergence. A preconditioner is any form of modification to the original linear system, which accelerates the convergence of an iterative method [7]. The linear system of equations is modified as follow:

$$M^{-1}Ax = M^{-1}b, \tag{3}$$

with M the preconditioning matrix. M can be filled by an incomplete factorization of the original system matrix: $A = LU - R$, where L and U are upper and lower matrices respectively while R is the residual of the factorization. The general algorithm of the incomplete LU factorization can be found in [7]. This factorization - involving a Gaussian elimination process - is inherently serial with recursive computations, in which every value of the L and U matrices depends on the computation of several values of previous rows and columns. This dependency makes any parallelization difficult.

3   Flow Solver Implementation

The reference CPU-based implicit solver, written in C++, solves the linear system of equations using the PETSc package. The residual and flux Jacobians are computed serially in a loop over all mesh faces. Profiling has revealed that the ILU preconditioner is not the bottleneck in the CPU implementation taking a small portion of the execution time. Three libraries have been considered for solving the linear system of equations on GPU: PETSc (GPU version), viennaCL and Paralution. While PETSc requires only a small change on the data type of the system matrix and right-hand side to run the linear solver on GPU, the library does not provide a GPU implementation of incomplete LU factorization. Moreover, it does not accept external data computed on GPU, which reduces the scope of the parallelization to the linear solver minimizing the expected global speedup. A second alternative is to use ViennaCL. While this OpenCL-based library can process data residing on the GPU, it performs a costly data copy from CUDA type of data to OpenCL. The third alternative is Paralution, which can process data residing on the GPU and is at the same time based on CUDA cuSparse library. The latter library has been chosen for the linear solver. To describe the flow solver implementation, we first introduce briefly some GPU computing techniques used in this work before we present the two main parts of the GPU flow solver (see Fig. 1) namely the system assembly and the linear solver.

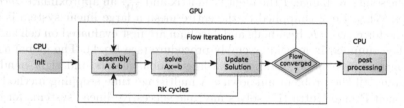

Fig. 1. Flow solver algorithm with an outer loop for the flow iteration: $W^{n+1} = W^n + \Delta W$, and an inner loop of Runge-Kutta cycles for the computation of ΔW

3.1   GPU Computing

The GPU is a co-processor featuring a large number of cores organized in streaming multiprocessors, which access directly a global memory. Every multiprocessor is a set of scalar processors with access to a shared memory local to the multiprocessor. Each of these processors has its own local and register memory. Programs running on GPU are called kernels. When calling a kernel the GPU starts a large number of threads (unit of execution) grouped in blocks of threads. Threads among the same block are grouped in warps of 32 threads with consecutive thread ID that execute the same instructions. When threads of the same warp execute different operations, they are executed serially and this performance decreasing situation is called *thread divergence*. The GPU acceleration is based on overlapping the memory access time (latency) with computations. When a warp is blocked waiting for data the GPU schedules another warp to take over with no overhead for the scheduling. This technique is more effective, if a kernel with a large number of blocks is executed, as more warps are likely to be available for the scheduler. An accurate measure of code performance on GPU is the throughput as floating operations per second which combines arithmetical and memory performance. A first hint to optimize a GPU code then is through increasing the number of active warps, which can run simultaneously (occupancy). At the same time occupancy should not be the only key of performance assessment, as it can be misleading for some cases [3]. In the second place, the algorithm should ensure that neighboring threads, which run together in one warp, access neighbor memory positions in order to avoid long wait times for variables load. This access is called a *coalesced* access.

The number of active warps defining the occupancy is proportional to the number of started threads and the memory consumption per thread in terms of registers and shared-memory. The variables declared in a kernel are locally saved in fast access registers until there are no registers anymore and the rest of the data is stored in global memory. Since all threads share a certain amount of registers the kernel consumption on registers limits the number of blocks of threads that could run simultaneously. In case the kernel needs to start few threads, a technique called multi-streaming can be used to increase the number of active warps by starting multiple independent kernels at the same time. Every kernel contributes to the occupancy by providing active warps. This is different from the standard one-stream approach, in which kernels are executed one after the other. As this section is intended to provide a short overview of techniques used in this work, further details to the GPU architecture and the programming model along with some applications can be found in: [20,24].

3.2 System Assembly

The global system matrix is a concatenation of local block matrices, which are divided in diagonal and off-diagonal blocks. The dominance of the diagonal blocks, which contain the inverse of the time step, improves the convergence of the linear solver. Therefore, when small time steps are used (see Eq. 2) GMRES converges with fast Jacobi preconditioner without the need for factorization. However, large time steps decrease the diagonal dominance and with it the condition number requiring thus the incomplete LU factorization to accelerate the linear solver convergence. The off-diagonal blocks contain mainly the flux Jacobians defining the bandwidth of the matrix.

Within the finite volume scheme, the global assembly of the linear system is made by looping over the cell faces in the mesh. On every cell face a contribution to the cell local system matrix is computed along with a residual. Since every cell receives the contributions of six faces, a risk of *race condition* is eminent, in which up to six threads simultaneously update the system matrix of the same cell. To avoid race conditions *atomic add* or *graph-coloring* are generally used. These techniques are known for deteriorating the coalesced access.

In this work another alternative that conserves the data coalescence has been chosen, in which the contributions are stored along with their positions in the system matrix (row, column). The face contribution belonging to two neighbor-cells is stored twice with the belonging cell index and sign. Computing and storing all face contributions leads to three large arrays: two for indices (column array, row array) and a third array for the contribution's value. Contributions belonging to the same cell are identified over identical index in column and row arrays then summed up using *sort* and *reduce* functions of the THRUST library [14]. This library generates 3 arrays free of repetition hosting the positions and values of all non-zero elements (nnz) of the system matrix. This data arrangement is known under Coordinate format (COO). The COO format stores nnz values in double precision and $2 * nnz$ integers. To reduce the storage size while keeping the same information content, the row array can be transformed in row offset array, in which the column offset of the first non-zero element in every row is stored. This operation is performed by the CUSP library, which provides the CSR arrays that constitute the input for the iterative solver of Paralution. A similar but less complicated algorithm allows to sort and scan the right-hand side for duplicated entries. Finally, all Kernels in this work are based on the same global memory access pattern and the coalesced access is assured by using the thread index as an offset for the array index.

3.3   Linear Solver with *on-demand* Factorization

The flow solver has a modular design with an interface to PETSc, Paralution and ViennaCL libraries. We use the GMRES linear solver of Paralution library along with the incomplete LU preconditioner (ILU). To accelerate the linear solver while preserving the accuracy of the solution, the LU matrix should be provided for a lower cost. As reported by many authors [7,19], the accuracy of the Lower Upper matrices affects the conditioning of the system leading to a larger number of linear system iterations to convergence. Since iterations of the linear solver are faster on the GPU than the incomplete LU factorization, the additional inner iterations cost generally less time than performing the incomplete LU factorization. The accuracy of the factorization is here traded against performance.

To decrease the time spent in the factorization, the linear solver uses the LU matrix of previous flow iteration. As a result, the linear solver skips the factorization for some flow iterations. The factorization is performed only *on-demand*, when the LU quality is so decreased that the linear solver needs more iterations to converge than a user defined threshold:

Pseudo-code of the on-demand LU factorization

```
if (itr> MAX_ITR ) M <-LU_Factorization (A)
(x, itr) <- GMRES (A,M,b)
```

where A, M and b are defined in Eq. 3. The maximum number of iterations MAX_ITR depends on the condition number and thus on the time step. As the time step depends on the CFL and the mesh cell size a relation between MAX_ITR and CFL number can be found for a given mesh:

$$MAX\_ITR = a + b * CFL, \qquad (4)$$

with a and b two tuning parameters. Parameter a plays an important role for applications with a low CFL number and b increases with the mesh refinement. The *on-demand* factorization changes only the entries of L and U matrices not the ordering of the non-zero elements, therefore it does not affect the flow solver convergence and accuracy.

4   Results

The numerical results were obtained using a Tesla K40 GPU with a theoretical peak performance of 1,682 Gflops in double precision and 12 GB of global memory. The GPU implementation is realized with CUDA 7.0. The host CPU (double quad-core) is an Intel(R) Xeon(R) CPU E5-2640 with a clock rate of 2.50 GHz and a 15 MB cache size. The CPU parallelization is performed on mesh block level, as blocks are distributed to processors (1 to 4) assuring a good load balancing. For the benchmark case with seven mesh blocks of different sizes, using more than 4 processors deteriorates the load balancing which damage the CPU performance. Therefore a maximum of 4 CPU cores is used.

The test case is a transonic flow over the LS89 inlet guide vane cascade [21], which experiences a turning of 74° through the NGV geometry and a passage shock with a peak Mach number of 1.15. The validation of the flow solver against experimental data can be found in [23]. The stopping criterion for the linear solver is a 10^{-6} reduction of the relative Residual and the flow solver stops when the minimization of the L_2 norm of the residual reaches 10^{-6}. The 2-stages Runge-Kutta (RK) time stepping method has been chosen for the benchmark, since the RK methods with more stages presented no flow convergence acceleration in the treated CFD case while costing extra execution-time. Two types of meshes are treated (coarse and fine) to explore the GPU potential (see Table 1).

Table 1. Characteristics of used meshes and underlying linear systems

Mesh	N_{Cells}	N_{Rows}	nnz	nnz/row
Coarse	40k	200k	5.7M	[20 ... 30]
Fine	300k	1500k	52.6M	[20 ... 35]

4.1   Assembly Acceleration

The assembly phase on the GPU experiences a 7x acceleration for the coarse mesh compared to a single-core CPU and 12x acceleration for the fine one (see Figs. 2 and 3). The multi-streaming contributed to the speedup by 10% improve

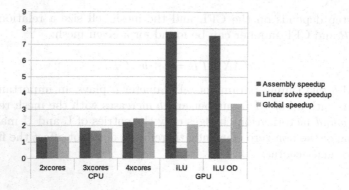

Fig. 2. Speedups of the flow solver on the coarse mesh with GPU ILU and *on-demand* ILU compared to a single-core to 4-cores CPU

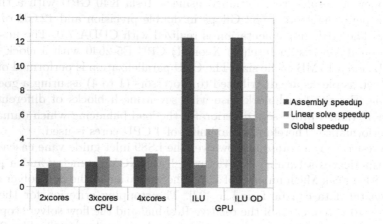

Fig. 3. Speedups of the flow solver on the fine mesh with GPU ILU and *on-demand* ILU compared to a single-core to 4-cores CPU

of the performance compared to the one-stream GPU version for the coarse mesh. The coalesced memory access has more impact on the performance with an improve of 23% compared to a striped access for the same coarse mesh. A multiblock mesh layout originates, in general, from the mesh generator designed to improve the mesh quality towards accurate CFD results. For complicated geometries it leads to multi-block meshes presenting blocks of different sizes and many interfaces between the mesh blocks.

An analysis of the achieved acceleration is proposed by addressing possibilities for further improvements considering: first large, then small mesh blocks and finally the interface update between all kind of blocks. Large blocks provide the GPU kernels with a high amount of independent operations for processing at the same time, which maximizes the number of active threads. The limiting factor in this case is the register usage. Since the kernels are starting large number of threads and computing long algorithms, the total number of used registers is very high. The register consumption limits the achieved occupancy (see Sect. 3.1). A way to improve the occupancy for these kernels is to divide them when possible into small, less memory demanding, sub-kernels. Blocks with few cells on the other hand, are in fact not limited by register usage but by the small number of started threads. The GPU is not provided with enough active threads to hide the memory latency. In this case, the multi-streams technique (see Sect. 3.1) can improve the occupancy by starting more than one kernel at the same time. The mesh block interfaces require a cell update between blocks and this procedure involves few cells proportional to the *surface to volume* ratio ($r_{StoV} * N_{Cells}$). A solution is to use a mesh generator that takes into account the reduction of the number of blocks and neighboring blocks along with the increase of block size in terms of cells (e.g. hMETIS [22]). The higher speedup of the assembly phase on the GPU for the fine mesh is then due to the larger blocks and lower *surface to volume* ratio.

4.2 Linear Solver Acceleration

The linear solver on the coarse mesh is 40% slower than on the single-core CPU. This is mainly caused by: (1) the ILU preconditioner, (2) the total number of linear solver calls and (3) the size of the system matrix. The ILU preconditioner contains low fine-grained parallelism and is more efficient on CPU. Moreover, the CPU implementation of ILU factorization has a set of techniques to improve the linear solver convergence, which decreases dramatically the GPU performance once ported to the GPU. This results on the flow solver using GPU ILU to perform 32% more linear solver iterations. The flow convergence is on the other hand exactly the same for CPU and GPU implementation in terms of number of flow iterations, this for the sake of a fair comparison.

For 2-stages RK, the flow requires 827 flow iterations to converge. The standard ILU performs one factorization per flow iteration, while the *on-demand* ILU (ILU-OD) reduces the total number of factorization to only 113. This corresponds to a decrease of 86%, which explains the improved speedup for the linear solver when ILU-OD is used. The *on demand* ILU is only as fast as a 2-cores CPU, because the size of the system matrix is not enough to observe the advantage of GPUs for sparse matrix-vector products (SpMV). The fine mesh presents, on the other hand, a larger system matrix with more non-zero elements. While the standard ILU implementation is 1.8x faster than the single-core ILU, the ILU-OD is 5.5x faster than single-core ILU and 2.05x faster than a 4-cores CPU. The *on-demand* mechanism decreased here also the number of factorization by 86%. In addition to that the size of the matrix showed the advantage of GPU for SpMV.

4.3 Global Acceleration of the Flow Solver

The global speedup depends heavily on the mesh size. For the fine mesh the GPU performance reaches a speedup of 4.8 and 9.43 for the flow solver using ILU and ILU-OD respectively compared to a single-core CPU. ILU and ILU-OD are 1.8x and 3.4x faster than 4-cores CPU. On the coarse mesh, the acceleration is 2.07x and 3.35x for ILU and ILU-OD respectively compared to a single-core CPU. This correspond to a speedup of 1.15x and 1.5x compared to a 4-cores CPU. The larger contribution of the speedup is done in the assembly phase.

GPUs are rather adapted for system assembly as a stencil-based operation and for solving very large sparse linear systems not exceeding the storage capacity of GPUs. Small linear systems are solved more efficiently on cache-based machines. Moreover GPUs are inherently co-processor and cannot replace a CPU for the entire simulation including pre- and post-processing. Therefore, the cooperation between the two architectures is more of interest rather than the competition for speedups as the latter can be misleading [25].

5   Conclusion

In this paper, we presented a flow solver with one order of magnitude acceleration on GPU compared to an optimized serial CPU version. We demonstrated that implicit time stepping in CFD applications can profit from the GPU computational power, provided an appropriate GPU occupancy is reached and a good mesh in terms of surface to volume ratio is used. As the bottleneck of the GPU flow solver is the incomplete LU factorization, the *on-demand* ILU factorization presented in this work improved the overall speedup by 60% to 80%. The *on-demand* ILU can be applied as well on cache-based processors (x86) but it is expected to have a very limited effect since factorization is not a bottleneck for serial execution. On the other hand it is expected to improve the performance of other SIMD machines (e.g. Xeon Phi). This once again shows that acceleration techniques can be very different on various architectures.

Acknowledgments. The research leading to these results has received funding from the European Union Seventh Framework Programme (FP7/2007-2013), Marie Curie Initial Training Networks (ITN) action, under grant agreement no. 316394, AMEDEO. We are also grateful to NVIDIA for the hardware donation.

References

1. Shahpar, S., Caloni, S.: Aerodynamic optimization of high-pressure turbines for lean-burn combustion system. J. Eng. Gas Turbines Power **135**(5), 055001 (2013)
2. Brandvik, T., Pullan, G.: Acceleration of a two-dimensional Euler flow solver using commodity graphics hardware. Proc. Inst. Mech. Eng. Part C: J. Mech. Eng. Sci. **221**(12), 1745–1748 (2007)
3. Volkov, V.: Better performance at lower occupancy. In: Proceedings of the GPU Technology Conference, GTC, vol. 10 (2010)
4. Lin, F., et al.: A multi-block viscous flow solver based on GPU parallel methodology. Comput. Fluids **95**, 19–39 (2014)
5. Barrachina, S., Castillo, M., Igual, F.D., Mayo, R., Quintana-Ortí, E.S.: Solving dense linear systems on graphics processors. In: Luque, E., Margalef, T., Benítez, D. (eds.) Euro-Par 2008. LNCS, vol. 5168, pp. 739–748. Springer, Heidelberg (2008). doi:10.1007/978-3-540-85451-7_79

6. Saad, Y., Schultz, M.H.: GMRES: a generalized minimal residual algorithm for solving nonsymmetric linear systems. SIAM J. Sci. Stat. Comput. **7**(3), 856–869 (1986)
7. Saad, Y.: Iterative Methods for Sparse Linear Systems. Siam, New Delhi (2003)
8. Balay, S., et al.: PETSc Users Manual Revision 3.5. No. ANL-95/11 Rev. 3.5. Argonne National Laboratory (ANL) (2014)
9. Serban, G., et al.: GPU acceleration for FEM-based structural analysis. Arch. Comput. Methods Eng. **20**(2), 111–121 (2013)
10. Cecka, C., et al.: Assembly of finite element methods on graphics processors. Int. J. Numer. Methods Eng. **85**(5), 640–669 (2011)
11. Istvan, R., Giles, M.: Efficient sparse matrix-vector multiplication on cache-based GPUs. In: Innovative Parallel Computing (InPar). IEEE (2012)
12. Naumov, M., et al.: Parallel Graph Coloring with Applications to the Incomplete-LU Factorization on the GPU. NVIDIA TR NVR-2015-001, May 2015
13. Wong, J., Kuhl, E., Darve, E.: A new sparse matrix vector multiplication graphics processing unit algorithm designed for finite element problems. Int. J. Numer. Methods Eng. **102**(12), 1784–1814 (2015)
14. Bell, N., Hoberock, J.: Thrust: a productivity-oriented library for CUDA. In: GPU Computing Gems: Jade Edition (2012)
15. Saad, Y.V., der Vorst, H.A.: Iterative solution of linear systems in the 20th century. J. Comput. Appl. Math. **123**, 1–33 (2000)
16. Blazek, J.: Computational Fluid Dynamics: Principles and Applications. Elsevier, Amsterdam (2005)
17. Xu, S., et al.: Stabilisation of discrete steady adjoint solvers. J. Comput. Phys. **299**, 175–195 (2015)
18. Trost, N., et al.: Accelerating COBAYA3 on multi-core CPU and GPU systems using PARALUTION. Ann. Nucl. Energy **82**, 252–259 (2014)
19. Chow, E., Patel, A.: Fine-grained parallel incomplete LU factorization. SIAM J. Sci. Comput. **37**(2), C169–C193 (2015)
20. Bell, N., Garland, M.: Implementing sparse matrix-vector multiplication on throughput-oriented processors. In: Proceedings of the Conference on High Performance Computing Networking, Storage and Analysis. ACM (2009)
21. Arts, T., et al.: Aero-thermal Investigation of a highly loaded transonic linear Turbine Guide Vane Cascade von Karman Institute for Fluid Dynamics TN-174 (1990)
22. Karypis, G., Kumar, V.: hMETIS 1.5: a hypergraph partitioning package. Technical report, Department of Computer Science, University of Minnesota (1998)
23. Aissa, M.H., Verstraete, T., Vuik, C.: Aerodynamic optimization of supersonic compressor cascade using differential evolution on GPU. In: 13th International Conference of Numerical Analysis and Applied Mathematics (ICNAAM 2015) September 23–29 2015, Rhodes, Greece (2015)
24. Garland, M., et al.: Parallel computing experiences with CUDA. IEEE Micro **4**, 13–27 (2008)
25. Lee, V.W., et al.: Debunking the 100X GPU vs. CPU myth: an evaluation of throughput computing on CPU and GPU. In: ACM SIGARCH Computer Architecture News, vol. 38, no. 3. ACM (2010)

Author Index

Printed in the United States
By Bookmasters